TransnationalManagement

TEXT, CASES, AND READINGS IN CROSS-BORDER MANAGEMENT

FIFTH EDITION

Christopher A. Bartlett
Harvard Business School

Sumantra Ghoshal
London Business School

Paul W. Beamish
Ivey Business School
The University of Western Ontario

McGraw Hill

Boston   Burr Ridge, IL   Dubuque, IA   Madison, WI   New York   San Francisco   St. Louis
Bangkok   Bogotá   Caracas   Kuala Lumpur   Lisbon   London   Madrid   Mexico City
Milan   Montreal   New Delhi   Santiago   Seoul   Singapore   Sydney   Taipei   Toronto

About the Authors

Christopher Bartlett is the Thomas D. Casserly, Jr., Professor Emeritus of Business Administration at Harvard Graduate School of Business Administration. He received an economics degree from the University of Queensland, Australia, and both masters and doctorate degrees in business administration from Harvard University. Prior to joining the faculty of Harvard Business School, he was a marketing manager with Alcoa in Australia, a management consultant in McKinsey and Company's London office, and general manager at Baxter Laboratories' subsidiary company in France.

Since joining the faculty of Harvard Business School in 1979, his interests have focused on strategic and organizational challenges confronting managers in multinational corporations and on the organizational and managerial impact of transformational change. He served as faculty chair of the International Senior Management Program, area head of the School's General Management Unit, faculty chairman of the Program for Global Leadership, and as chair of the Humanitarian Leadership Program.

He has published eight books, including (coauthored with Sumantra Ghoshal) *Managing Across Borders: The Transnational Solution,* named by *Financial Times* as one of the 50 most influential business books of the century; and *The Individualized Corporation,* winner of the Igor Ansoff Award for the best new work in strategic management and named one of the Best Business Books for the Millennium by *Strategy 1 Business* magazine. Both books have been translated into over 10 foreign languages. His articles have appeared in journals such as *Harvard Business Review, Sloan Management Review, Strategic Management Journal, Academy of Management Review,* and *Journal of International Business Studies.* He has also researched and written over 100 case studies and teaching notes. He has been elected by his colleagues as a fellow of the Academy of Management, the Academy of International Business, the Strategic Management Society, and the World Economic Forum.

The late Sumantra Ghoshal was Professor of Strategic and International Management at the London Business School. He also served as the Founding Dean of the Indian School of Business in Hyderabad and was a member of The Committee of Overseers of the Harvard Business School. *Managing Across Borders: The Transnational Solution,* a book he coauthored with Christopher Bartlett, has been listed in the *Financial Times* as one of the 50 most influential management books and has been translated into 11 languages. *The Differentiated Network: Organizing the Multinational Corporation for Value Creation,* a book he coauthored with Nitin Nohria, won the George Terry Book Award in 1997. *The Individualized Corporation,* coauthored with Christopher Bartlett, won the Igor Ansoff Award in 1997 and has been translated into multiple foreign languages. His last book, *Managing Radical Change* (with Christopher Bartlett and Gita Piramel), won the Management Book of the Year award in India. With doctoral degrees from both the MIT School of Management and Harvard Business School, Sumantra served on the editorial boards of several academic journals and was a fellow of the Academy of Management, the Academy of International Business, and the World Economic Forum.

Paul Beamish   holds the Canada Research Chair in International Business at the Ivey Business School, University of Western Ontario. He is the author or coauthor of numerous books, articles, contributed chapters, and teaching cases. His articles have appeared in *Academy of Management Review, Academy of Management Journal, Strategic Management Journal, Journal of International Business Studies* (*JIBS*), and elsewhere. He has received best research awards from the Academy of Management and the Academy of International Business (AIB). In 1997 and 2003, he was recognized in the *Journal of International Management* as one of the top three contributors worldwide to the international strategic management literature in the previous decade. He served as Editor-in-Chief of *JIBS* from 1993–97 and is a Fellow of the AIB. He worked for Procter & Gamble and Wilfrid Laurier University before joining Ivey's faculty in 1987.

Paul has supervised 18 doctoral dissertations, many involving international joint ventures and alliances. His consulting, management training, and joint venture facilitation activities have been in both the public and private sector.

At Ivey, he has taught in a variety of school programs, including the Executive MBA offered at its campus in Hong Kong. From 1999–2004, he served as Associate Dean of Research. He currently serves as Director of Ivey Publishing, the distributor of Ivey's collection of over 2,400 current cases; Ivey's Asian Management Institute (AMI); and the newly established cross-enterprise center, Engaging Emerging Markets.

Preface

This fifth edition of *Transnational Management* is dedicated to Sumantra Ghoshal, a longtime friend, colleague, and coauthor whose name has been on the cover of this book since it was first published more than 15 years ago. During our 20-year research and writing partnership, Sumantra was always concerned about how to bring knowledge into the classroom. In our field research, he wanted to ensure that we could create powerful teaching material out of the data and stories we were uncovering and the conclusions we were reaching. Indeed, he believed that it was impossible to unravel the twin strands of teaching and learning, claiming that together they created a much stronger cord of knowledge. To Sumantra, discussion in the classroom raised questions that drove him into the field, and the findings from the field created teaching materials that did much more than provide insight for students; they provoked more questions for research.

To the outside world, the numerous awards Sumantra won as an outstanding teacher and case material developer were a testimony to his lifelong commitment to the classroom. But for those of us fortunate enough to have worked with him personally, whether as a student, a colleague, or a consulting client, Sumantra was much more than a gifted teacher. His brilliant questioning and insightful challenges pushed us to think harder and deeper but were complemented by his bold imagination and supportive encouragement that gave us the courage to take risks. Although he passed away in 2004, we list him as a coauthor in this new edition not only to honor his memory but also to reflect the significant and lasting contribution he made to the concepts, perspectives, and materials that are at the core of this book.

To ensure that this and future editions of *Transnational Management* keep alive the spirit of challenge and excitement that Sumantra brought to it, I am delighted to be joined by Paul Beamish as a new coauthor of this fifth edition. Paul is an old friend whose reputation as a researcher, course developer, and teacher in the field of International Business and International Management is so widely known that he hardly needs an introduction in these pages. His extensive work on international joint ventures and alliances has led the field, as has his expertise in managing in the Asian region. At the University of Western Ontario's Ivey Business School, Paul has served as Associate Dean for Research, as well as the founding director of Ivey's Asian Management Institute. In the broader academy, he has gained widespread respect not only for his own research, but also as the editor *Journal of International Business Studies* (*JIBS*) for five years. To this book, he brings an even more valuable skill however: the commitment to translate his extensive knowledge and experience into first-rate classroom materials. He is a welcome edition to *Transnational Management*. His contribution to this edition will be evident in the following pages and undoubtedly will continue through many future editions of this text.

Distinguishing Characteristics of the MNE

What makes the study of the multinational enterprise (MNE) unique? The most fundamental distinction between a domestic company and an MNE derives from the social, political, and economic context in which each exists. The former operates in a single national environment where social and cultural norms, government regulations, customer tastes and preferences, and the economic and competitive context of a business tend to be fairly consistent. Although within-country local variations do exist for most of these factors, they are nowhere near as diverse or as conflicting as the differences in demands and pressures the MNE faces in its multiple host countries.

The one feature that categorically distinguishes these intercountry differences from the intracountry ones, however, is *sovereignty*.[1] Unlike the local or regional bodies, the nation-state generally represents the ultimate rule-making authority against whom no appeal is feasible. Consequently, the MNE faces an additional and unique element of risk: the political risk of operating in countries with different political philosophies, legal systems, and social attitudes toward private property, corporate responsibility, and free enterprise.

A second major difference relates to competitive strategy. The purely domestic company can respond to competitive challenges only within the context of its single market; the MNE can, and often must, play a much more complex competitive game. Global-scale or low-cost sourcing may be necessary to achieve a competitive position, implying the need for complex cross-border logistical coordination. Furthermore, on the global chessboard, effective competitive strategy might require that the response to an attack in one country be directed to a different country—perhaps the competitor's home market. These are options and complexities a purely domestic company does not face.

Third, a purely domestic company can measure its performance in a single comparable unit—the local currency. Because currency values fluctuate against each other, however, the MNE is required to measure results with a flexible measuring stick. In addition, it is exposed to the economic risks associated with shifts in both nominal and real exchange rates.

Finally, the purely domestic company must manage an organizational structure and management systems that reflect its product and functional variety; the MNE organization is intrinsically more complex because it must provide for management control over its product, functional, *and* geographic diversity. Furthermore, the resolution of this three-way tension must be accomplished in an organization that is divided by barriers of distance and time and impeded by differences in language and culture.

The Management Challenge

Historically, the study of international business focused on the environmental forces, structures, and institutions that provided the context within which MNE managers had to operate. In such a macro approach, countries or industries rather than companies were the primary units of analysis. Reflecting the environment of its time, this traditional

---

[1]This difference is elaborated in J. N. Behrman and R. E. Grosse, *International Business and Governments: Issues and Institutions* (Columbia: University of South Carolina Press, 1990). See also J. J. Boddewyn, "Political Aspects of MNE Theory," *Journal of International Business Studies* 19, no. 3 (1988), pp. 341–63.

approach directed most attention to trade flows and the capital flows that defined the foreign investment patterns.

During the 1970s and 1980s, a new perspective on the study of international management began to emerge, with a far greater emphasis on the MNE and management behavior rather than on global economic forces and international institutions. With the firms as the primary unit of analysis and management decisions as the key variables, these studies both highlighted and provided new insights into the management challenges associated with international operations.

This book builds on the company- and management-level perspective. More specifically, we adopt what is often called the *administrative point of view*. In other words, in order to make sense of the practice of managing the MNE, it is necessary to see the world through the eyes of the executive who is in the thick of it—whether that is the CEO of the corporation, the global account manager, the country subsidiary manager, or the frontline business manager. The most powerful way to do this is to employ cases that require decisions to be made, and most provide the reader not only with data on the business context but also with detailed information about the characters involved, their roles, responsibilities, and personal motivations. In many instances, videos and follow-up cases lead to further insight.

We have also chosen to focus on *managerial processes* such as the entrepreneurial process (identifying and acting on new opportunities), the integrative learning process (linking and leveraging those pockets of entrepreneurial initiative), or the leadership process (articulating a vision and inspiring others to follow). It would be easy to build our structure around the traditional functions of the company—R&D, manufacturing, marketing, etc.—and many texts have done so. But we find such an approach limiting because almost all real-world problems cut across these functional boundaries. They require executives to understand all the disparate parts of the organization, and they demand integrative solutions that bring together, rather than divide, the people working in their traditional functional silos. (This is a reality reflected in the multidimensional organizations most MNEs have developed.) A process perspective is more difficult to grasp than a functional one, but ultimately it provides a more fulfilling and realistic approach to the management of today's MNE.

By adopting the perspective of the MNE manager, however, we do not ignore the important and legitimate perspectives, interests, and influences of other key actors in the international operating environment. However, we do view the effects of these other key actors from the perspective of the company and focus on understanding how the various forces they influence shape the strategic, organizational, and operational tasks of MNE managers.

The Structure of the Book

The book is divided into three parts (see figure on page xi). **Part 1** consists of three chapters that examine the development of strategy in the MNE. In Chapter 1, we focus on the motivations that draw—or drive—companies abroad, the means by which they expand across borders, and the mind-sets of those who built the worldwide operations. Understanding what we call a company's "administrative heritage" is important because it shapes both the current configuration of assets and capabilities and the cognitive orientations of managers toward future growth—attitudes that can either enable or constrain future growth.

In Chapter 2, we examine the political, economic, and social forces that shape the business environment in which the MNE operates. In particular, the chapter explores the tension created by the political demands to be responsive to national differences, the economic pressures to be globally integrated, and the growing competitive need to develop and diffuse worldwide innovation and learning.

In Chapter 3, the focus shifts from the global business environment to MNEs' competitive responses to those external pressures. Building on the themes developed in Chapter 2, we examine the various approaches an MNE can use to generate competitive advantage in its international context. We identify three traditional strategic approaches—global, international, and multinational—each of which focuses on a different source of competitive advantage. We then go on to describe the transnational strategy, which combines the benefits of the other three models.

Part 2 changes the focus from the MNE's strategic imperatives to the organizational capabilities required to deliver them. Chapter 4 examines the organizational structures and systems that need to be put in place to be effective in a complex and dynamic world. Mirroring the three traditional strategic approaches, we explore three organizational models that all appear to be evolving toward the integrated network form required to manage transnational strategies.

Chapter 5 focuses on one of the most important processes to be developed in a transnational organization. The need to manage effective cross-border knowledge transfer and worldwide learning is creating new organizational demands, and in this chapter, we explore how such processes are built and managed.

Then, in Chapter 6, we lift our organizational analysis up a level to examine the boundary-spanning structures and processes needed to create joint ventures, alliances, and interfirm networks in a global context. In this chapter, we explore how such partnerships can be built and managed to develop strategic capabilities that may not be available inside any single MNE.

Part 3 focuses on the management challenges of operating a successful MNE. In Chapter 7, the focus is on those who must implement the transnational strategies, operate within the integrated network organizations, and above all, deliver the results. This chapter allows us to look at the world through the eyes of frontline country subsidiary managers, and shows how their actions can have important implications for the competitiveness of the entire corporation.

Finally in Chapter 8, we ask some broad questions about the present and future role of the multinational enterprise in the global economy. The powerful forces unleashed by globalization have had a largely positive impact on economic and social development worldwide. But like all revolutions, the forces of changes have acted unevenly, and there have been casualties. As the divide between the "haves" and "have nots" expands, the challenge facing MNEs is to determine what role they can and should play in mitigating some of the unintended consequences of the globalization revolution. It is a challenge that should confront every current executive and be central to the task of the next generation of leadership in transnational companies.

In our continual commitment to keep this book current, more than half of the case studies and half of the readings are new to this edition. In addition, we have enriched the overall conceptual framework of the book by adding a new final chapter that addresses some important challenges for the MNE of the future. We hope these changes show our commitment to keep this book current and relevant while recognizing the need for continuity in the broad concepts and frameworks within which the material is presented.

Acknowledgments

First, we would like to acknowledge the many enduring contributions Julian Birkinshaw made to the fourth edition of this book. *Transnational Management* has also benefited from the comments, suggestions, and insights provided by colleagues at the hundreds of institutions around the world that have adopted this book. In particular, we would like to acknowledge the role played by the Editorial Advisory Board (listed on page x) who committed significant effort to providing a detailed critique of the last edition. We have also had extraordinary support from our colleagues in other institutions who have provided valuable feedback and suggestions for improvement. In particular, we would like to acknowledge Michael Mulford, *Buena Vista University;* Michael Wakefield, *Colorado State University;* Ernst Verwaal, *Eramus University;* Phillip Bryans, *Napier University;* Laura Whitcomb, *California State University-Los Angeles;* Carol Howard, *Oklahoma City University;* George Redmond, *Franklin University;* Nikos Bozionelos, *University of Durham;* and Cinzia DalZotto, *Jonkoping University—Sweden.*

Next, we are extraordinarily grateful to the researchers and colleagues who have contributed new materials to this edition. In addition to our own case materials, new case studies were provided by Pankaj Ghemawat, Linda Hill, Tarun Khanna, and Allan Morrison. Articles new to this edition and focused on important research have been contributed by Julian Birkinshaw and Cristina Gibson, Diana Farrell, Pankaj Ghemawat, Larry Huston, Walter Kuemmerle, and C. K. Prahalad.

We must also acknowledge the coordination task undertaken by our respective administrative assistants who worked over many months to coordinate the flow of manuscript documents back and forth among Boston, Sydney, and London, Ontario. To Jan Simmons and Mary Roberts, we give our heartfelt thanks for helping us through the long and arduous revision process. To Ryan Blankenship, our sponsoring editor, and Allison Belda, our editorial coordinator, at McGraw-Hill, as well as Beth Baugh, our developmental editor at Carlisle Publishing, we thank you for your patience and tolerance through this long process and look forward to a long and productive working relationship.

Despite the best efforts of all the contributors, however, we must accept responsibility for the shortcomings of the book that remain. Our only hope is that they are outweighed by the value you find in these pages and the exciting challenges they represent in the constantly changing field of transnational management.

Christopher A. Bartlett
Paul W. Beamish

■ Editorial Advisory Board

Our sincere thanks to the following faculty who provided detailed feedback and suggestions on the materials for this edition.

Name	School
Joe Cheng	University of Illinois at Urbana-Champaign
John Epps	University of Maryland
Nabarun Ghose	Tiffin University
Sumit Kundu	Florida International University
Lilach Nachum	Baruch College
Jaimie Ortiz	Texas A&M International University
Davina Vora	University of Texas at Dallas

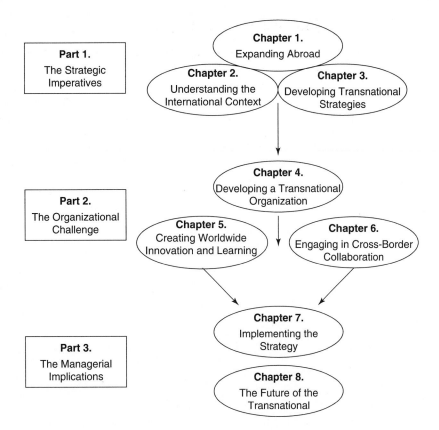

Part 1.
The Strategic Imperatives

Chapter 1.
Expanding Abroad

Chapter 2.
Understanding the International Context

Chapter 3.
Developing Transnational Strategies

Chapter 4.
Developing a Transnational Organization

Part 2.
The Organizational Challenge

Chapter 5.
Creating Worldwide Innovation and Learning

Chapter 6.
Engaging in Cross-Border Collaboration

Chapter 7.
Implementing the Strategy

Part 3.
The Managerial Implications

Chapter 8.
The Future of the Transnational

Table of Contents

Chapter 5

*Creating Worldwide Innovation and
Learning: Exploiting Cross-Border
Knowledge Management*   455

Cases

Readings

Chapter 6

*Engaging in Cross-Border
Collaboration: Managing across
Corporate Boundaries*   559

Cases

Readings

Part 3   The Managerial Implications

Chapter 7

*Implementing the Strategy: Building
Multidimensional Capabilities*   648

Cases

Readings

Chapter 8

*The Future of the Transnational:
An Evolving Global Role*

Cases

Readings

Index

Transnational Management

CHAPTER 1

Expanding Abroad:

Motivations, Means, and Mentalities

> In this chapter, we look at a number of important questions that companies must resolve before taking the huge leap to operate outside their home environment. What market opportunities, sourcing advantages, or strategic imperatives drive their international expansion? By what means will they expand their overseas presence—through exports, licensing, joint ventures, wholly owned subsidiaries, or some other means? And how will the attitudes, assumptions, and beliefs that they bring to their international ventures affect their chances of success? Before exploring these important questions, however, we first need to develop a definition of this entity—the multinational enterprise (MNE)—that we plan to study and develop some sense of its size and importance in the global economy.

This book focuses on the management challenges associated with developing the strategies, building the organizations, and managing the operations of companies whose activities stretch across national boundaries. Clearly, operating in an international rather than a domestic arena presents managers with many new opportunities. Having worldwide operations not only gives a company access to new markets and low-cost resources, it also opens up new sources of information and knowledge and broadens the options for strategic moves the company might make in competing with its domestic and international rivals. However, with all these new opportunities come the challenges of managing strategy, organization, and operations that are innately more complex, diverse, and uncertain.

Our starting point is to focus on the dominant vehicle of internationalization, the multinational enterprise (MNE), and briefly review its role and influence in the global economy.[1] Only after understanding the origins, interests, and objectives of this key actor will we be in a position to explore the strategies it pursues and the organization it develops to achieve them.

---

[1]Such entities are referred to variously—and often interchangeably—as *multinational, international,* and *global enterprises.* (Note that we use the term "enterprise" rather than "corporation" because some of the cross-border entities we will examine are nonprofit organizations whose strategies and operations are every bit as complex as their corporate brethren's.) At the end of this chapter, we assign each of those terms—*multinational, international,* and *global*—specific meanings, but throughout the book, we adopt the widely used MNE abbreviation in a broader, more general sense to refer to all enterprises whose operations extend across national borders.

The MNE: Definition, Scope, and Influence

An economic historian could trace the origins of international business back to the sea-faring traders of Greece and Egypt, through the merchant traders of medieval Venice and the great British and Dutch trading companies of the 17th and 18th centuries. By the 19th century, the newly emerged capitalists in industrialized Europe began investing in the less-developed areas of the world (including the United States) but particularly within the vast empires held by Britain, France, Holland, and Germany.

Definition

In terms of the working definition we use, few if any of these entities through history could be called true MNEs. Most early traders would be excluded by our first qualification, which requires that an MNE have *substantial direct investment* in foreign countries, not just the trading relationships of an import–export business. And even most of the companies that had established international operations in the 19th century would be excluded by our second criterion, which requires that they be engaged in the *active management* of these offshore assets rather than simply holding them in a passive investment portfolio.

Thus, though companies that source their raw materials offshore, license their technologies abroad, export their products into foreign markets, or even hold minority equity positions in overseas ventures without any management involvement may regard themselves as "international," by our definition, they are not true MNEs unless they have substantial, direct investment in foreign countries *and* actively manage and regard those operations as integral parts of the company, both strategically and organizationally.

Scope

According to our definition, the MNE is a very recent phenomenon, with the vast majority developing only in the post–World War II years. However, the motivations for international expansion and the nature of MNEs' offshore activities have evolved significantly over this relatively short period, and we will explore some of these changes later in this chapter.

It is interesting to observe how the United Nations has changed its definition of the MNE as these companies have grown in size and importance.[2] In 1973, it defined such an enterprise as one "which controls assets, factories, mines, sales offices, and the like in two or more countries." By 1984, it had changed the definition to an enterprise (a) comprising entities in two or more countries, regardless of the legal form and fields of activity of those entities; (b) which operates under a system of decision making permitting coherent policies and a common strategy through one or more decision-making centers; and (c) in which the entities are so linked, by ownership or otherwise, that one or more of them may be able to exercise a significant influence over the activities of the others, in particular to share knowledge, resources, and responsibilities.

---

[2] The generic term for companies operating across national borders in most U.N. studies is *transnational corporation* (TNC). Because we use that term very specifically, we continue to define the general form of organizations with international operations as MNEs.

Table 1-1   Comparison of Top MNEs and Selected Countries: 2003

Company[†]	Value-Added (millions)	Rank	Country[*]	Value-Added (millions)	Rank
ExxonMobil	$72,468	1	United States	$10,881,609	1
Royal Dutch/Shell	48,692	2	Japan	4,326,444	2
BP	47,123	3	Germany	2,400,655	3
Toyota Motor	45,143	4	Poland	209,563	24
Ford Motor	42,483	5	Chile	72,416	46
DaimlerChrysler	42,426	6	Syria	21,517	64
General Electric	40,302	7	Tanzania	9,872	82
Wal-Mart	40,192	8	Nepal	5,835	99
General Motors	38,184	9	Haiti	2,745	117
ChevronTexaco	30,008	10	Burundi	669	133

Notes: "Value-added" refers to gross domestic product (GDP) for countries and to the sum of salaries, pretax profits, and depreciation and amortization for companies.

[†] Calculated from data from *World Investment Report 2005,* assuming the same value-added to sales ratios as in *World Investment Report 2000.* For ChevronTexaco, the value-added is estimated by the authors.

[*] Data are from *World Development Report 2005*, published by the World Bank.

In essence, the changing definition highlights the importance of both strategic and organizational integration, and thereby, the *active, coordinated management* of operations located in different countries, as the key differentiating characteristic of an MNE. The resources committed to those units can take the form of skilled people or research equipment just as easily as plants and machinery or computer hardware. What really differentiates the MNE is that it creates an internal organization to carry out key cross-border tasks and transactions internally rather than depending on trade through the external markets, just as the companies in Table 1-1 do. This more recent U.N. definition also expands earlier assumptions of traditional ownership patterns to encompass a more varied set of financial, legal, and contractual relationships with different foreign affiliates. With this understanding, our definition of MNEs includes Intel, Unilever, and Samsung but also Singapore Airlines, McKinsey & Company, and Starbucks.

MNE Influence in the Global Economy

Most frequent international business travelers have had an experience like the following: She arrives on her British Airways flight, rents a Toyota at Hertz, and drives to the downtown Hilton hotel. In her room, she flips on the Sony TV and absent-mindedly gazes out at neon signs flashing "Coca-Cola," "Canon," and "BMW." The latest episode of *Desperate Housewives* is flickering on the screen when room service delivers dinner along with the bottle of Perrier she ordered. All of a sudden, a feeling of disorientation engulfs her. Is she in Sydney, Singapore, Stockholm, or Seattle? Her surroundings and points of reference over the past few hours have provided few clues.

Such experiences, more than any data, provide the best indication of the enormous influence of MNEs in the global economy. As the cases and articles in this book show, few sectors of the economy and few firms—not even those that are purely domestic in their operations—are free from this pervasive influence. According to U.N. estimates, by 2004, the number of MNEs had risen to approximately 70,000, collectively managing at least 690,000 foreign affiliates and with total revenues in excess of $18.7 trillion. The top 500 MNEs account for nearly 70 percent of world trade. About 85 percent of the world's automobiles, 70 percent of computers, 35 percent of toothpaste, and 65 percent of soft drinks are produced and marketed by MNEs.

Not all MNEs are large, but most large companies in the world are MNEs. Indeed, the largest 100 MNEs, excluding those in banking and finance, accounted for $8.0 trillion of total worldwide assets in 2003, of which $4.0 trillion was located outside their respective home countries.

A different perspective on their size and potential impact is provided in Table 1-1, which compares the overall value-added of several of the largest MNEs with the gross domestic products (GDPs) of selected countries. According to the 2002 *World Investment Report,* the measure of company value added (the sum of salaries, pretax profits, amortization, and depreciation) provides a more meaningful comparison with country GDP than simply looking at a company's gross revenues. By using this measure, it is clear that the world's largest MNEs are equivalent in their economic importance to medium-sized economies such as Chile, Hungary, or Pakistan and considerably more economically important than smaller or less developed economies such as Tanzania, Estonia, or Sri Lanka. They have considerable influence on the global economy, employ a high percentage of business graduates, and pose the most complex strategic and organizational challenges for their managers. For the same reasons, they provide the focus for much of our attention in this book.

The Motivations: Pushes and Pulls to Internationalize

What motivates companies to expand their operations internationally? Although occasionally the motives may be entirely idiosyncratic, such as the desire of the CEO to spend time in Mexico or link to old family ties in Europe, an extensive body of research suggests some more systematic patterns.

Traditional Motivations

Among the earliest motivations that drove companies to invest abroad was the need to *secure key supplies*. Aluminum producers needed to ensure their supply of bauxite, tire companies went abroad to develop rubber plantations, and oil companies wanted to open new fields in Canada, the Middle East, and Venezuela. By the early part of this century, Standard Oil, Alcoa, Goodyear, Anaconda Copper, and International Nickel were among the largest of the emerging MNEs.

Another strong trigger for internationalization could be described as *market-seeking* behavior. This motivation was particularly strong for companies that had some intrinsic advantage, typically related to their technology or brand recognition, that gave them a competitive advantage in offshore markets. Although their initial moves were often opportunistic, many companies eventually realized that additional sales enabled them to exploit economies of scale and scope, thereby providing a source of competitive advantage over their domestic rivals. This market seeking was a particularly strong motive for some European multinationals whose small home markets were insufficient to support the volume-intensive manufacturing processes that were sweeping through industries from food and tobacco to chemicals and automobiles. Companies like Nestlé, Bayer, and Ford expanded internationally primarily in search of new markets.

Another traditional and important trigger of internationalization was the desire to *access low-cost factors* of production. Particularly as tariff barriers declined in the 1960s, the United States and many European countries, for which labor represented a major cost, found that their products were at a competitive disadvantage compared with imports. In response, a number of companies in clothing, electronics, household appliances, watch-making, and other such industries established offshore sourcing locations to produce components or even complete product lines. Soon it became clear that labor was not the only productive factor that could be sourced more economically overseas. For example, the availability of lower-cost capital (perhaps through a government investment subsidy) also became a strong force for internationalization.

These three motives (or two, if we ignore their historical differences and combine securing supplies and accessing low-cost factors into a single resource-seeking motive) were the main traditional driving force behind the overseas expansion of MNEs. The ways in which these motives interacted to push companies—particularly those from the United States—to become MNEs are captured in the well-known product cycle theory developed by Professor Raymond Vernon.[3]

This theory suggests that the starting point for an internationalization process is typically an innovation that a company creates in its home country. In the first phase of exploiting the development, the company—let's assume it is in the United States—builds production facilities in its home market not only because this is where its main customer base is located but also because of the need to maintain close linkages between research and production in this phase of its development cycle. In this early stage, some demand also may be created in other developed countries—in European countries, for example—where consumer needs and market developments are similar to those of the United States. These requirements normally would be met with home production, thereby generating exports for the United States.

As the product matures and production processes become standardized, the company enters a new stage. By this time, demand in the European countries may have become quite sizable, and export sales, originally a marginal side benefit, have become an important part of the revenues from the new business. Furthermore, competitors probably begin to see the growing demand for the new product as a potential opportunity to establish themselves in the markets served by exports. To prevent or counteract such competition and to meet the foreign demand more effectively, the innovating company typically sets up production facilities in the importing countries, thereby making the transition from being an exporter to becoming a true MNE.

Finally, in the third stage, the product becomes highly standardized, and many competitors enter the business. Competition focuses on price and, therefore, on cost. This trend activates the resource-seeking motive, and the company moves production to low-wage, developing countries to meet the demands of its customers in the

---

[3]Raymond Vernon, "International Investment and International Trade in the Product Cycle," *Quarterly Journal of Economics,* May 1966, pp. 190–207.

developed markets at a lower cost. In this final phase, the developing countries may become net exporters of the product while the developed countries become net importers.

Although the product cycle theory provided a useful way to describe much of the internationalization of the postwar decades,[4] by the 1980s, its explanatory power was beginning to wane, as Professor Vernon himself was quick to point out. As the international business environment became increasingly complex and sophisticated, companies developed a much richer rationale for their worldwide operations.

Emerging Motivations

Once MNEs had established international sales and production operations, their perceptions and strategic motivations gradually changed. Initially, the typical attitude was that the foreign operations were strategic and organizational appendages to the domestic business and should be managed opportunistically. Gradually, however, managers began to think about their strategy in a more integrated, worldwide sense. In this process, the forces that originally triggered their expansion overseas often became secondary to a new set of motivations that underlay their emerging global strategies.

The first such set of forces was the increasing *scale economies, ballooning R&D investments,* and *shortening product life cycles* that transformed many industries into global rather than national structures and made a worldwide scope of activities not a matter of choice but an essential prerequisite for companies to survive in those businesses. These forces are described in detail in the next chapter.

A second factor that often became critical to a company's international strategy—though it was rarely the original motivating trigger—was its global *scanning and learning* capability.[5] A company drawn offshore to secure supplies of raw materials was more likely to become aware of alternative, low-cost production sources around the globe; a company tempted abroad by market opportunities was often exposed to new technologies or market needs that stimulated innovative product development. The very nature of an MNE's worldwide presence gave it a huge informational advantage that could result in it locating more efficient sources or more advanced product and process technologies. Thus, a company whose international strategy was triggered by a technological or marketing advantage could enhance that advantage through the scanning and learning potential inherent in its worldwide network of operations.

A third benefit that soon became evident was that being a multinational rather than a national company brought important advantages of *competitive positioning*. Certainly, the most controversial of the many global competitive strategic actions taken by MNEs in recent years have been those based on cross-subsidization of markets. For example,

---

[4]The record of international expansion of countries in the post–World War II era is quite consistent with the pattern suggested by the product cycle theory. For example, between 1950 and 1980, U.S. firms' direct foreign investment (DFI) increased from $11.8 billion to $200 billion. In the 1950s, much of this investment focused on neighboring countries in Latin America and Canada. By the early 1960s, attention had shifted to Europe, and the European Economic Community's share of U.S. firms' DFI increased from 16 percent in 1957 to 32 percent by 1966. Finally, in the 1970s, attention shifted to developing countries, whose share of U.S. firms' DFI grew from 18 percent in 1974 to 25 percent in 1980.

[5]This motivation is highlighted by Raymond Vernon in "Gone Are the Cash Cows of Yesteryear," *Harvard Business Review,* November–December 1980, pp. 150–55.

a Korean mobile phone producer could challenge a national company in Europe by subsidizing its European losses with funds from its profitable Asian or South American operations.

If the European company did not have strong positions in the Korean company's key Asian and South American markets, its competitive response could only be to defend its home market positions—typically by seeking government intervention or matching or offsetting the Korean challenger's competitive price reductions. Recognition of these competitive implications of multicountry operations led some companies to change the criteria for their international investment decisions to reflect not only market attractiveness or cost-efficiency choices but also the leverage such investments provided over competitors.[6]

Although for the purposes of analysis—and to reflect some sense of historical development—the motives behind the expansion of MNEs have been reduced to a few distinct categories, it should be clear that companies were rarely driven by a single motivating force. More adaptable companies soon learned how to capitalize on the potential advantages available from their international operations—ensuring critical supplies, entering new markets, tapping low-cost factors of production, leveraging their global information access, and capitalizing on the competitive advantage of their multiple market positions—and began to use these strengths to play a new strategic game that we will describe in later chapters as *global chess*.

The Means of Internationalization: Prerequisites and Processes

Having explored *why* an aspiring MNE wants to expand abroad (i.e., its motivation), we must now understand *how* it does so by exploring the means of internationalization. Beyond the desire to expand offshore, a company must posses certain competencies—attributes that we describe as prerequisites—if it is to succeed in overseas markets. It must then be able to implement its desire to expand abroad through a series of decisions and commitments that define the internationalization process.

Prerequisites for Internationalization

In each national market, a foreign company suffers from some disadvantages in comparison with local competitors, at least initially. Being more familiar with the national culture, industry structure, government requirements, and other aspects of doing business in that country, domestic companies have a huge natural advantage. Their existing relationships with relevant customers, suppliers, regulators, and so on provide additional advantages that the foreign company must either match or counteract with some unique strategic capability. Most often, this countervailing strategic advantage comes from the MNE's superior knowledge or skills, which typically take the form of advanced technological expertise or specific marketing competencies. At other times, scale economies in R&D, production, or some other part of the value chain become the main source of the MNE's advantage over domestic firms. It is important to note, however, that the MNE

---

[6]These competitive aspects of global operations are discussed in detail in Chapter 3.

cannot expect to succeed in the international environment unless it has some distinctive competency to overcome the liability of its foreignness.[7]

But even such knowledge or scale-based strategic advantages are, by themselves, insufficient to justify the internationalization of operations. Often with much less effort, a company could sell or license its technology to foreign producers, franchise its brand name internationally, or sell its products abroad through general trading companies or local distributors, without having to set up its own offshore operations. This approach was explicitly adopted by General Sarnoff, the postwar CEO of RCA who decided that his company should aggressively license its extensive television and other patents to European and Japanese companies rather than set up its own international operations. He argued that the safe return generated by license fees was preferable to the uncertainties and complexities of multinational management.

The other precondition for a company to become an MNE therefore is that it must have the organizational capability to leverage its strategic assets more effectively through its own subsidiaries than through contractual relations with outside parties. If superior knowledge is the main source of an MNE's competitive advantage, for example, it must have an organizational system that provides better returns from extending and exploiting its knowledge through direct foreign operations than the return it could get by selling or licensing that knowledge.[8]

To summarize, three conditions must be met for the existence of an MNE. First, some foreign countries must offer certain location-specific advantages to provide the requisite *motivation* for the company to invest there. Second, the company must have some *strategic competencies* or ownership-specific advantages to counteract the disadvantages of its relative unfamiliarity with foreign markets. Third, it must possess some *organizational capabilities* to achieve better returns from leveraging its strategic strengths internally rather than through external market mechanisms such as contracts or licenses.[9] Understanding these prerequisites is important not only because they explain why MNEs exist but also, as we show in Chapter 3, because they help define the strategic options for competing in worldwide businesses.

The Process of Internationalization

The process of developing these strategic and organizational attributes lies at the heart of the internationalization process through which a company builds its position in world markets. This process is rarely well thought out in advance, and it typically builds on a combination of rational analysis, opportunism, and pure luck. Nonetheless, it is still possible to discern some general patterns of behavior that firms typically follow.

---

[7]The need for such strategic advantages for a company to become an MNE is highlighted by the *market imperfections theory of MNEs*. For a comprehensive review of this theory, see Richard E. Caves, *Multinational Enterprise and Economic Analysis*, 2nd ed. (Cambridge: Cambridge University Press, 1996).

[8]The issue of organizational capability is the focus of what has come to be known as the *internalization theory of MNEs*. See Alan M. Rugman, "A New Theory of the Multinational Enterprise: Internationalization versus Internalization," *Columbia Journal of World Business,* Spring 1982, pp. 54–61. For a more detailed exposition, see Peter J. Buckley and Mark Casson, *The Future of Multinational Enterprise* (London: MacMillan, 1976).

[9]These three conditions are highlighted in John Dunning's eclectic theory. See John H. Dunning, *International Production and the Multinational Enterprise* (Winchester, MA: Allen & Unwin, 1981).

Figure 1-1   A Learning Model of Internationalization

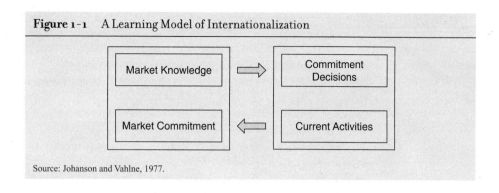

Source: Johanson and Vahlne, 1977.

The most well-known model for internationalization was developed during the 1970s by two Swedish academics based in Uppsala, who described foreign-market entry as a learning process.[10] The company makes an initial commitment of resources to the foreign market, and through this investment, it gains local market knowledge about customers, competitors, and regulatory conditions. On the basis of this market knowledge, the company is able to evaluate its current activities, the extent of its commitment to the market, and thus the opportunities for additional investment. It then makes a subsequent resource commitment, perhaps buying out its local distributor or investing in a local manufacturing plant, which allows it to develop additional market knowledge. Gradually, and through several cycles of investment, the company develops the necessary levels of local capability and market knowledge to become an effective competitor in the foreign country (see Figure 1-1).

Whereas many companies internationalize in the manner depicted by the so-called Uppsala model, a great many do not. Some companies invest in or acquire local partners to shortcut the process of building up local market knowledge. For example, Wal-Mart entered the United Kingdom by buying the supermarket chain ASDA rather than developing its own stores. Others prefer to minimize their local presence by subcontracting to local partners. Amazon.com has a business in Canada without a single Canadian employee—it manages its Web site from the United States, and it fulfills orders through the Canadian postal service. Cases such as these highlight the complexity of the decisions MNEs face in entering a foreign market. One important set of factors is the assimilation of local market knowledge by the subsidiary unit, as suggested by the Uppsala model. But other, equally important factors to the MNE include its overall level of commitment to the foreign market in question, the required level of control of foreign operations, and the timing of its entry. To help make sense of these different factors, it is useful to think of the different modes of operating overseas in terms of two factors: the level of market commitment made and the level of control needed (see Figure 1-2).

Some companies internationalize by gradually moving up the scale, from exporting through joint venturing to direct foreign investment. Others, like Wal-Mart, prefer to

[10]Jan Johanson and Jan-Erik Vahlne, "The Internationalization Process of the Firm—a Model of Knowledge Development and Increasing Foreign Market Commitments," *Journal of International Business Studies* 88 (1977), pp. 23–32.

Figure 1-2   Approaches to Foreign Market Entry

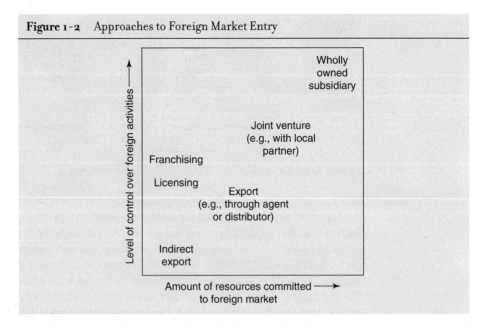

move straight to the high-commitment–high-control mode of operating, in part because they are entering mature markets in which it would be very difficult to build a business from nothing. Still others choose to adopt a low-commitment–low-control mode, such as exporting or subcontracting. For example, Amazon.com is able to make this approach work in Canada because it retains control of its Web site from the United States and has secured a reliable local partner for order fulfillment. To be clear, none of these approaches is necessarily right or wrong, but they should be consistent with the overall strategic intentions and motivations of the MNE.

The Evolving Mentality: International to Transnational

Even from this brief description of the changing motivations for and means of internationalization, it should be clear that a gradual evolution has occurred in the strategic role that foreign operations play in emerging MNEs. We can categorize this evolutionary pattern into four stages that reflect the way in which management thinking has developed over time as changes have occurred in both the international business environment and the MNE as a unique corporate form.

Although such a classification is necessarily generalized and somewhat arbitrary, it enables us to achieve two objectives. First, it highlights that for most MNEs, the objectives that initially induced management to go overseas evolve into a very different set of motivations over time, thereby progressively changing management attitudes and actions. Second, such a classification provides a specific language system that we use throughout this book to describe the very different strategic approaches adopted by various MNEs.[11]

[11]It should be noted that the terms *international, multinational, global,* and *transnational* have been used very differently—and sometimes interchangeably—by various writers. We want to give each term a specific and different meaning and ask that readers put aside their previous usage of the terms—at least for the duration of our exposition.

International Mentality

In the earliest stages of internationalization, many company's overseas operations as distant outposts mestic parent company in different ways, such as c domestic manufacturing operations. We label this a mentality.

The *international* terminology derives directly fro theory, which reflects many of the assumptions implic developed for the domestic market and only subsequen   ...y and other knowledge are transferred from the parent compan   ...s operators; and offshore manufacturing represents a means to protect ... company's home market. Companies with this mentality regard themselves fundamentally as domestic with some foreign appendages. Managers assigned to overseas operations are often domestic misfits who happen to know a foreign language or have previously lived abroad. Decisions related to the foreign operations tend to be made in an opportunistic or ad hoc manner.

Multinational Mentality

The exposure of the organization to foreign environments and the growing importance of sales and profits from these sources gradually convince managers that international activities can provide opportunities of more than marginal significance. Increasingly, they also realize that to leverage those opportunities, they must do more than ship out old equipment, technology, or product lines that had been developed for the home market. The success of local competitors in the foreign markets and the demands of host governments often accelerate the learning of companies that retain an unresponsive, international mentality for too long.

A *multinational* strategic mentality develops as managers begin to recognize and emphasize the differences among national markets and operating environments. Companies with this mentality adopt a more flexible approach to their international operations by modifying their products, strategies, and even management practices country by country. As they develop national companies that are increasingly sensitive and responsive to their local environments, these companies undertake a strategic approach that is literally multinational: Their worldwide strategy is built on the foundation of the multiple, nationally responsive strategies of the company's worldwide subsidiaries. In companies operating with such a multinational mentality, managers of foreign operations tend to be highly independent entrepreneurs, often nationals of the host country.

Using their local market knowledge and the parent company's willingness to invest in these growing opportunities, these entrepreneurial country managers often can build significant local growth and considerable independence from headquarters.

Global Mentality

Although the multinational mentality typically results in very responsive ma approaches in the different national markets, it also gives rise to an manufacturing infrastructure within the company. Plants are built more to marketing advantages or improve political relations than to maximize production efficiency. Similarly, the proliferation of products designed to meet local needs contributes to a general loss of efficiency in design, production, logistics, distribution, and other functional tasks.

In an operating environment of improving transportation and communication facilities and falling trade barriers, some companies adopt a very different strategic approach in their international operations. These companies think in terms of creating products for a world market and manufacturing them on a global scale in a few highly efficient plants, often at the corporate center.

We define this approach as a classic *global* strategic mentality, because it views the world, not individual national markets, as its unit of analysis. The underlying assumption is that national tastes and preferences are more similar than different or that they can be made similar by providing customers with standardized products at adequate cost and with quality advantages over those national varieties they know. Managers with this global strategic approach subscribe to Professor Levitt's provocative argument in the mid-1980s that the future belongs to companies that make and sell "the same thing, the same way, everywhere."[12]

This strategic approach requires considerably more central coordination and control than the others and is typically associated with an organizational structure in which various product or business managers have worldwide responsibility. In such companies, research and development and manufacturing activities are typically managed from the headquarters, and most strategic decisions also take place at the center.

Transnational Mentality

In the closing decades of the twentieth century, many of these global companies seemed invincible, chalking up overwhelming victories over not only local companies but international and multinational competitors as well. Their success, however, created and strengthened a set of countervailing forces of localization.

To many host governments, for example, these global companies appeared to be a more powerful and thus more threatening version of earlier unresponsive companies with their unsophisticated international strategic mentality. Many host governments increased both the restrictions and the demands they placed on global companies, requiring them to invest in, transfer technology to, and meet local content requirements of the host countries.

Customers also contributed to this strengthening of localizing forces by rejecting homogenized global products and reasserting their national preferences—albeit without relaxing their expectations of high quality levels and low costs that global products had offered. Finally, the increasing volatility in the international economic and political environments, especially rapid changes in currency exchange rates, undermined the efficiency of such a centralized global approach.

---

[12]See Theodore Levitt, "The Globalization of Markets," *Harvard Business Review,* May–June 1983, pp. 92–102.

As a result of these developments, many worldwide companies recognized that demands to be responsive to local market and political needs *and* pressures to develop global-scale competitive efficiency were simultaneous, if sometimes conflicting, imperatives.

In these conditions, the either/or attitude reflected in both the multinational and the global strategic mentalities became increasingly inappropriate. The emerging requirement was for companies to become more responsive to local needs while capturing the benefits of global efficiency—an approach to worldwide management that we call the *transnational* strategic mentality.

In such companies, key activities and resources are neither centralized in the parent company nor so decentralized that each subsidiary can carry out its own tasks on a local-for-local basis. Instead, the resources and activities are dispersed but specialized, to achieve efficiency and flexibility at the same time. Furthermore, these dispersed resources are integrated into an interdependent network of worldwide operations.

In contrast to the global model, the transnational mentality recognizes the importance of flexible and responsive country-level operations—hence the return of *national* into the terminology. And compared with the multinational approach, it provides for means to link and coordinate those operations to retain competitive effectiveness and economic efficiency, as is indicated by the prefix *trans*. The resulting need for intensive, organization-wide coordination and shared decision making implies that this is a much more sophisticated and subtle approach to MNE management. In subsequent chapters, we will explore its strategic, organizational, and managerial implications.

It should be clear, however, that there is no inevitability in either the direction or the endpoint of this evolving strategic mentality in worldwide companies. Depending on the industry, the company's strategic position, the host countries' diverse needs, and a variety of other factors, a company might reasonably operate with any one of these strategic mentalities. More likely, bearing in mind that ours is an arbitrary classification, most companies probably exhibit some attributes of each of these different strategic approaches.[13]

Summary and Concluding Comments

This chapter provides the historical context of the nature of the MNE and introduces a number of important concepts on which subsequent chapters will build. In particular, we have described the evolving set of *motivations* that led companies to expand abroad in the first place; the *means* of expansion, as shaped by the processes of internationalization they followed; and the typical *mentalities* that they developed. Collectively, these motivations, means, and mentalities are the prime drivers of what we call a company's *administrative heritage,* the unique and deeply embedded structural, process, and cultural biases that play an important part in shaping every company's strategic and organizational capabilities.

---

[13]Professor Howard Perlmutter was perhaps the first to highlight the different strategic mentalities. See his article, "The Tortuous Evolution of the Multinational Corporation," *Columbia Journal of World Business,* January–February 1969, pp. 9–18, reproduced in the readings section of this chapter.

Case 1-1   Cameron Auto Parts (A)–Revised

Alex Cameron's first years in business were unusually harsh and turbulent. He graduated from a leading Michigan business school in 2001 when the American economy was just falling into a recession caused by the combination of the bursting of the telecom and dot.com bubble and the terrorist attacks of September 11. It was not that Alex had difficulty finding a job, however; it was that he took over the reins of the family business. His father timed his retirement to coincide with Alex's graduation and left him with the unenviable task of cutting back the workforce to match the severe sales declines the company was experiencing.

History

Cameron Auto Parts was founded in 1965 by Alex's father to seize opportunities created by the signing of the Auto Pact between Canada and the United States. The Auto Pact permitted the Big Three automotive manufacturers to ship cars, trucks and original equipment (OEM) parts between Canada and the United States tariff free, as long as they maintained auto assembly facilities on both sides of the

Richard Ivey School of Business
The University of Western Ontario

Professor Paul Beamish revised this case (originally prepared by Professor Harold Crookell) solely to provide material for class discussion. The authors do not intend to illustrate either effective or ineffective handling of a managerial situation. The authors may have disguised certain names and other identifying information to protect confidentiality. Ivey Management Services prohibits any form of reproduction, storage or transmittal without its written permission. This material is not covered under authorization from CanCopy or any reproduction rights organization. To order copies or request permission to reproduce materials, contact Ivey Publishing, Ivey Management Services, c/o Richard Ivey School of Business, The University of Western Ontario, London, Ontario, Canada, N6A 3K7; phone (519) 661-3208; fax (519) 661-3882; e-mail cases@ivey.uwo.ca.

border. The Pact had been very successful with the result that a lot of auto parts firms sprang up in Canada to supply the Big Three. Cameron Auto Parts prospered in this environment until, by 1999, sales had reached $60 million with profits of $1.75 million. The product focus was largely on small engine parts and auto accessories, such as oil and air filters, fan belts and wiper blades, all sold as original equipment under the Auto Pact.

When Alex took over in 2001, the company's financial position was precarious. Sales in 2000 dropped to $48 million and for the first six months of 2001 to $18 million. Not only were car sales declining in North America, but the Japanese were taking an increasing share of the market. As a result, the major North American auto producers were frantically trying to advance their technology and to lower their prices at the same time. It was not a good year to be one of their suppliers. In 2000, Cameron Auto Parts lost $2.5 million, and had lost the same amount again in the first six months of 2001. Pressure for modernization and cost reduction had required close to $4 million in new investment in equipment and computer-assisted design and manufacturing systems. As a result, the company had taken up over $10 million of its $12 million line of bank credit at an interest rate which stood at 7.0 percent in 2001.

Alex's first six months in the business were spent in what he later referred to as "operation survival." There was not much he could do about working capital management, as both inventory and receivables were kept relatively low via contract arrangements with the Big Three. Marketing costs were negligible. Where costs had to be cut were in production and, specifically, in people, many of whom had been with the company for over 15 years and were personal friends of Alex's father. Nevertheless, by the end of 2001, the workforce had been cut from 720 to 470, the losses had been stemmed and the company saved from almost certain bankruptcy. Having to be the hatchet man, however, left an indelible impression on Alex. As things began to pick up during 2002 and 2003, he added as few permanent workers as possible, relying instead on overtime, part-timers or subcontracting.

Recovery and Diversification

For Cameron Auto Parts, the year 2001 ended with sales of $38 million and losses of $3.5 million (see Exhibit 1). Sales began to pick up in 2002, reaching $45 million by year-end with a small profit. By mid-2003, it was clear that the recovery was well underway. Alex, however, while welcoming the turnaround, was suspicious of basis for it. Cameron's own sales hit $27 million in the first six months of 2003 and company profits were over $2 million. The Canadian dollar had dropped as low as 77 cents in terms of U.S. currency and Cameron was faced with more aggressive competition from Canadian parts manufacturers. The short-term future for Cameron, however, seemed distinctly positive, but the popularity of Japanese cars left Alex feeling vulnerable to continued total dependence on the volatile automotive industry. Diversification was on his mind as early as 2001.

He had an ambition to take the company public by 2007 and diversification was an important part of that ambition.

Unfortunately, working as an OEM parts supplier to the automotive industry did little to prepare Cameron to become more innovative. The auto industry tended to standardize its parts requirements to the point that Cameron's products were made to precise industry specifications and consequently, did not find a ready market outside the industry. Without a major product innovation it appeared that Cameron's dependence on the Big Three was likely to continue. Furthermore, the company had developed no "in-house" design and engineering strength from which to launch an attempt at new product development. Because product specifications had always come down in detail from the Big Three, Cameron had never needed to design and develop its own products and had never hired any design engineers.

In the midst of "operation survival" in 2001, Alex boldly decided to do something about diversification. He personally brought in a team of

Exhibit 1   Income Statements (for years ended December 31, 2001, 2002, 2003 ($000s))

	2001	2002	2003
Net Sales	$38,150	$45,200	$67,875
Cost of goods sold:			
Direct materials	6,750	8,050	12,400
Direct labor	12,900	10,550	12,875
Overheads (including depreciation)	16,450	19,650	27,600
Total	36,100	38,250	52,875
Gross Profit	2,050	6,950	15,000
Expenses:			
Selling and administration (includes design team)	3,150	3,800	6,200
Other (includes interest)	2,400	2,900	3,000
Total	5,500	6,700	9,200
Net Profit before Tax	(3,500)	250	5,800
Income Tax	(500)	—	200
Net Profit after Tax	$(3,000)	$ 250	$ 5,600

Note: Alex expected total sales to reach $85 million in 2004 with profits before tax of $10 million. Flexible couplings were expected to contribute sales of $30 million and profits of $5 million on assets of $12 million.

four design engineers and instructed them to concentrate on developing products related to the existing line but with a wider "non-automotive" market appeal. Their first year together showed little positive progress, and the question of whether to fund the team for another year (estimated budget $425,000) came to the management group:

Alex: Maybe we just expected too much in the first year. They did come up with the flexible coupling idea, but you didn't seem to encourage them, Andy (production manager).

Andy McIntyre: That's right! They had no idea at all how to produce such a thing in our facilities. Just a lot of ideas about how it could be used. When I told them a Canadian outfit was already producing them, the team sort of lost interest.

John Ellis (Finance): We might as well face the fact that we made a mistake, and cut it off before we sink any more money into it. This is hardly the time for unnecessary risks.

Alex: Why don't we shorten the whole process by getting a production licence from the Canadian firm? We could start out that way and then build up our own technology over time.

Andy: The team looked into that, but it turned out the Canadians already have a subsidiary operating in United States—not too well from what I can gather—and they are not anxious to licence anyone to compete with it.

Alex: Is the product patented?

Andy: Yes, but apparently it doesn't have long to run.

At this point a set of ideas began to form in Alex's mind, and in a matter of months he had lured away a key engineer from the Canadian firm with an $110,000 salary offer and put him in charge of the product development team. By mid-2003, the company had developed its own line of flexible couplings with an advanced design and an efficient production process using the latest in production equipment. Looking back, in retrospect, Alex commented:

We were very fortunate in the speed with which we got things done. Even then the project as a whole had cost us close to $1 million in salaries and related costs.

Marketing the New Product

Alex continued:

We then faced a very difficult set of problems, because of uncertainties in the market place. We knew there was a good market for the flexible type of coupling because of its wide application across so many different industries. But, we didn't know how big the market was nor how much of it we could secure. This meant we weren't sure what volume to tool up for, what kind or size of equipment to purchase, or how to go about the marketing job. We were tempted to start small and grow as our share of market grew, but this could be costly too and could allow too much time for competitive response. Our Canadian engineer was very helpful here. He had a lot of confidence in our product and had seen it marketed in both Canada and the United States. At his suggestion, we tooled up for a sales estimate of $30 million which was pretty daring. In addition, we hired eight field sales representatives to back up the nationwide distributor and soon afterwards hired several Canadian-based sales representatives to cover major markets. We found that our key Canadian competitor was pricing rather high and had not cultivated very friendly customer relations. We were surprised how quickly we were able to secure significant penetration into the Canadian market. It just wasn't being well-serviced.

During 2003, the company actually spent a total of $2.5 million on equipment for flexible coupling production. In addition, a fixed commitment of $1.5 million a year in marketing expenditures on flexible couplings arose from the hiring of sales representatives. A small amount of trade advertising was included in this sum. The total commitment represented a significant part of the company's resources and threatened serious damage to the company's financial position if the sales failed to materialize.

"It was quite a gamble at the time," Alex added. "By the end of 2003, it was clear that the gamble was going to pay off."

Cameron's approach to competition in flexible couplings was to stress product quality, service and speed of delivery, but not price. Certain sizes of

		Sales by Market Sector ($ millions)		
	OEM Parts Sales	**Flexible Couplings Sales**	**Total Sales**	**After Tax Profits**
1999	60	Nil	60	1.75
2000	48	Nil	48	(2.50)
2001	38	Nil	38	(3.50)
2002	45	Nil	45	0.25
2003	58	10 (six months)	68	5.80

couplings were priced slightly below the competition but others were not. In the words of one Cameron sales representative:

Our job is really a technical function. Certainly, we help predispose the customer to buy and we'll even take orders, but we put them through our distributors. Flexible couplings can be used in almost all areas of secondary industry, by both large and small firms. This is why we need a large distributor with wide reach in the market. What we do is give our product the kind of emphasis a distributor can't give. We develop relationships with key buyers in most major industries, and we work with them to keep abreast of new potential uses for our product, or of changes in size requirements or other performance characteristics. Then we feed this kind of information back to our design group. We meet with the design group quite often to find out what new types of couplings are being developed and what the intended uses are, etc. Sometimes they help us solve a customer's problem. Of course, these 'solutions' are usually built around the use of one of our products.

Financing Plant Capacity

When Alex first set his diversification plans in motion in 2001, the company's plant in suburban Detroit was operating at 50 per cent capacity. However, by early 2004, sales of auto parts had recovered almost to 1999 levels and the flexible coupling line was squeezed for space. Andy McIntyre put the problem this way:

I don't see how we can get sales of more than $85 million out of this plant without going to a permanent two-shift system, which Alex doesn't want to do. With two full shifts we could probably reach sales of $125

million. The problem is that both our product lines are growing very quickly. Auto parts could easily hit $80 million on their own this year, and flexible couplings! Well, who would have thought we'd sell $10 million in the first six months? Our salespeople are looking for $35 million to $40 million during 2004. It's wild! We just have to have more capacity.

There are two problems pressing us to consider putting flexible couplings under a different roof. The first is internal: we are making more and more types and sizes, and sales are growing to such a point that we may be able to produce more efficiently in a separate facility. The second is external: The Big Three like to tour our plant regularly and tell us how to make auto parts cheaper. Having these flexible couplings all over the place seems to upset them, because they have trouble determining how much of our costs belong to Auto Parts. If it were left to me I'd just let them be upset, but Alex feels differently. He's afraid of losing orders. Sometimes I wonder if he's right. Maybe we should lose a few orders to the Big Three and fill up the plant with our own product instead of expanding.

Flexible couplings were produced on a batch basis and there were considerable savings involved as batches got larger. Thus as sales grew, and inventory requirements made large batches possible, unit production costs decreased, sometimes substantially. Mr. McIntyre estimated that unit production costs would decline by some 20 percent as annual sales climbed from $20 million to $100 million and by a further 10 percent at $250 million. Scale economies beyond sales of $250 million were not expected to be significant.

John Ellis, the company's financial manager, expressed his own reservations about new plant

Exhibit 2   Balance Sheets (for years ended December 31, 2001, 2002, 2003 ($000s))

	2001	2002	2003
Assets			
Cash	$ 615	$ 430	$ 400
Accounts Receivable	5,850	6,850	10,400
Inventories	4,995	4,920	7,500
Total Current Assets	11,460	12,200	18,300
Property, plant and equipment (net)	10,790	11,800	13,000
Total Assets	22,250	24,000	31,300
Liabilities			
Accounts Payable	4,850	5,900	9,500
Bank loan	11,500	12,000	10,000
Accrued Items (including taxes)	450	400	500
Total Current Liabilities	16,800	18,300	20,000
Common Stock (Held by Cameron family)	500	500	500
Retained Earnings	4,950	5,200	10,800
Total Equity	5,450	5,700	11,300
Total Liabilities	$22,250	$24,000	$31,300

expansion from a cash flow perspective:

We really don't have the balance sheet (Exhibit 2) ready for major plant expansion yet. I think we should grow more slowly and safely for two more years and pay off our debts. If we could hold sales at $75 million for 2004 and $85 million for 2005, we would be able to put ourselves in a much stronger financial position. The problem is that people only look at the profits. They don't realize that every dollar of flexible coupling sales requires an investment in inventory and receivables of about 30 cents. It's not like selling to the Big Three. You have to manufacture to inventory and then wait for payment from a variety of sources.

As it is, Alex wants to invest $10 million in new plant and equipment right away to allow flexible coupling sales to grow as fast as the market will allow. We have the space on our existing site to add a separate plant for flexible couplings. It's the money I worry about.

Foreign Markets

As the company's market position in North America began to improve, Alex began to wonder about foreign markets. The company had always been a major exporter to Canada, but it had never had to market there. The Big Three placed their orders often a year or two in advance, and Cameron just supplied them. As Alex put it:

It was different with the flexible coupling. We had to find our own way into the market. We did, however, start getting orders from Europe and South America, at first from the subsidiaries of our U.S. customers and then from a few other firms as word got around. We got $40,000 in orders during 2003 and the same amount during the first four months of 2004. This was a time when we were frantically busy and hopelessly understaffed in the management area, so all we did was fill the orders on an FOB, Detroit basis. The customers had to pay import duties of approximately three percent into most European countries, and a value added tax of about 20 percent (20 to 50 percent into South America), on top of the freight and insurance, and still orders came in.

Seeing the potential in Europe, Alex promptly took a European Patent from the European Patent Office in the United Kingdom. The cost of the whole process was under $10,000.

A Licensing Opportunity

In the spring of 2004, Alex made a vacation trip to Scotland and decided while he was there to drop in on one of the company's new foreign customers, McTaggart Supplies Ltd. Cameron Auto Parts had received unsolicited orders from overseas amounting to $40,000 in the first four months of 2004, and over 10 percent of these had come from McTaggart. Alex was pleasantly surprised at the reception given to him by Sandy McTaggart, the 60-year-old head of the company.

Sandy: Come in! Talk of the devil. We were just saying what a shame it is you don't make those flexible couplings in this part of the world. There's a very good market for them. Why, my men can even sell them to the English!

Alex: Well, we're delighted to supply your needs. I think we've always shipped your orders promptly, and I don't see why we can't continue . . . .

Sandy: That's not the point! Those orders are already sold before we place them. The point is we can't really build the market here on the basis of shipments from America. There's a three percent tariff coming in, freight and insurance cost us another 10 percent on top of your price, then there's the matter of currency values. I get my orders in pounds (£),[1] but I have to pay you in dollars. And on top of all that, I never know how long the goods will take to get here, especially with all the dock strikes we have to put up with. Listen, why don't you license us to produce flexible couplings here?

After a lengthy bargaining session, during which Alex secured the information shown in Exhibit 3, he came round to the view that a license agreement with McTaggart might be a good way of achieving swift penetration of the U.K. market via McTaggart's sales force. McTaggart's production skills were not as up-to-date as Cameron's, but his plant showed evidence of a lot of original ideas to keep manufacturing costs down. Furthermore, the firm seemed committed enough to invest in some new equipment and to put a major effort into developing the U.K. market. At this point the two

[1] In 2004, one pound was equivalent to US$1.83.

executives began to discuss specific terms of the license arrangements:

Alex: Let's talk about price. I think a figure around three percent of your sales of flexible couplings would be about right.

Sandy: That's a bit high for an industrial license of this kind. I think one and a half percent is more normal.

Alex: That may be, but we're going to be providing more than just blueprints. We'll have to help you choose equipment and train your operators as well.

Sandy: Aye, so you will. But we'll pay you for that separately. It's going to cost us £500,000 in special equipment as it is, plus, let's say, a $100,000 fee to you to help set things up. Now you have to give us a chance to price competitively in the market, or neither of us will benefit. With a royalty of one and a half percent, I reckon we could reach sales of £500,000 in our first year and £1 million in our second.

Alex: The equipment will let you produce up to £4 million of annual output. Surely you can sell more than a million. We're getting unsolicited orders without even trying.

Sandy: With the right kind of incentive, we might do a lot better. Why don't we agree to a royalty of two and a half percent on the first million in sales and one and a half percent after that. Now mind you, we're to become exclusive agents for the U.K. market. We'll supply your present customers from our own plant.

Alex: But just in the United Kingdom! Now two percent is as low as I'm prepared to go. You make those figures three percent and two per cent and you have a deal. But it has to include a free technology flow-back clause in the event you make any improvements or adaptations to our manufacturing process.

Sandy: You drive a hard bargain! But it's your product, and we do want it. I'll have our lawyers draw up a contract accordingly. What do you say to a five-year deal, renewable for another five if we are both happy?

Alex: Sounds good. Let's do it.

Alex signed the contract the same week and then headed back to America to break the news. He travelled with mixed feelings, however. On the

Exhibit 3   Data on McTaggart Supplies Ltd.

2003 Sales	£35 million (down from £44 million in 2001).
Total Assets	£11 million: Equity £6.5 million
Net profit after tax	±£1.5 million
Control	McTaggart Family
Market coverage	15 sales representatives in United Kingdom, two in Europe, one in Australia, one in New Zealand, one in India.
Average factory wage rate	£8.00 per hour (which is below the U.K. mean of £12.00 due to the factory being located in a depressed area) (versus $18.00 in America).
Factory	Old and larger than necessary. Some very imaginative manufacturing know-how in evidence.
Reputation	Excellent credit record, business now 130 years old, good market contacts (high calibre sales force).
Other	Company sales took a beating during 2001–2002 as one of the company's staple products was badly hurt by a U.S. product of superior technology. Company filled out its line by distributing products obtained from other manufacturers. Currently about one-half of company sales are purchased from others. Company has capacity to increase production substantially.

Pricing	*Index*
Cameron's price to McTaggart	100
(same as net price to distributor in America)	
+ Import duty	3
+ Freight and insurance	10
Importer's Cost	113
+ Distributor's (McTaggart's) Margin (30%)	34
+ Value Added Tax (17.5% on cost plus margin)	26
= Price charged by McTaggart	173
vs. Price charged by American distributor in U.S.	120

Note: Under the European Union agreement, all imports from non-EU countries were subject to common customs tariffs. In 2004, the common customs tariff for the flexible coupling had an import duty of 2.7 percent. In addition to the import duty, all imported items were subjected to the value added tax (VAT) which was applied on all manufactured goods—both imported as well as locally made. The VAT was going through a harmonization process but was expected to take some years before a common VAT system was in place. As of 2004, the VAT for United Kingdom was 17.5 percent, and France 19.6 percent. Denmark, Hungary, and Sweden had the highest VAT at 25 percent.

one hand, he felt he had got the better of Sandy McTaggart in the bargaining, while on the other, he felt he had no objective yardstick against which to evaluate the royalty rate he had agreed on. This was pretty much the way he presented the situation to his executive group when he got home.

Alex: . . . so I think it's a good contract, and I have a cheque here for $100,000 to cover our costs in helping McTaggart get set up.

John: We can certainly use the cash right now. And there doesn't seem to be any risk involved. I like the idea, Alex.

Andy (production): Well, I don't. And Chuck (head of the Cameron design team) won't either when (production) he hears about it. I think you've sold out the whole U.K. market for a pittance. I thought you wanted to capture foreign markets directly.

Alex: But Andy, we just don't have the resources to capture foreign markets ourselves. We might as well get what we can through licensing, now that we've patented our process.

Andy: Well, maybe. But I don't like it. It's the thin edge of the wedge if you ask me. Our know-how on the production of this product is pretty special, and it's getting better all the time. I hate to hand it over to old McTaggart on a silver platter. I reckon we're going to sell over $20 million in flexible couplings in the United States alone during 2004.

Case 1-2   Jollibee Foods Corporation (A): International Expansion

Protected by his office air conditioner from Manila's humid August air, in mid-1997, Manolo P. ("Noli") Tingzon pondered an analysis of demographic trends in California. As the new head of Jollibee's International Division, he wondered if a Philippine hamburger chain could appeal to mainstream American consumers or whether the chain's proposed U.S. operations could succeed by focusing on recent immigrants and Philippine expatriates. On the other side of the Pacific, a possible store opening in the Kowloon district of Hong Kong raised other issues for Tingzon. While Jollibee was established in the region, local managers were urging the company to adjust its menu, change its operations, and refocus its marketing on ethnic Chinese customers. Finally, he wondered whether entering the nearly virgin fast food territory of Papua New Guinea would position Jollibee to dominate an emerging market—or simply stretch his recently-slimmed division's resources too far.

With only a few weeks of experience in his new company, Noli Tingzon knew that he would have to weigh these decisions carefully. Not only would they shape the direction of Jollibee's future internalization strategy, they would also help him establish his own authority and credibility within the organization.

▌ Professor Christopher A. Bartlett and Research Associate Jamie O'Connell prepared this case. HBS cases are developed solely as the basis for class discussion. Cases are not intended to serve as endorsements, sources of primary data, or illustrations of effective or ineffective management.
▌ Copyright © 1998 President and Fellows of Harvard College. All rights reserved. Harvard Business School case 399-007.

▌ Company History

Started in 1975 as an ice cream parlor owned and run by the Chinese-Filipino Tan family, Jollibee had diversified into sandwiches after company President Tony Tan Caktiong (better known as TTC) realized that events triggered by the 1977 oil crisis would double the price of ice cream. The Tans' hamburger, made to a home-style Philippine recipe developed by Tony's chef father, quickly became a customer favorite. A year later, with five stores in metropolitan Manila, the family incorporated as Jollibee Foods Corporation.

The company's name came from TTC's vision of employees working happily and efficiently, like bees in a hive. Reflecting a pervasive courtesy in the company, everyone addressed each other by first names, prefaced by the honorific "Sir" or "Ma'am," whether addressing a superior or subordinate. Friendliness pervaded the organization and become one of the "Five Fs" that summed up Jollibee's philosophy. The others were flavorful food, a fun atmosphere, flexibility in catering to customer needs, and a focus on families (children flocked to the company's bee mascot whenever it appeared in public). Key to Jollibee's ability to offer all of these to customers at an affordable price was a well developed operations management capability. A senior manager explained:

It is not easy to deliver quality food and service consistently and efficiently. Behind all that fun and friendly environment that the customer experiences is

Exhibit 1   Jollibee Philippines Growth, 1975–1997

Year	Total Sales (millions of pesos)	Total Stores at End of Year	Company-Owned Stores	Franchises
1975	NA	2	2	0
1980	NA	7	4	3
1985	174	28	10	18
1990	1,229	65	12	54
1991	1,744	99	21	80
1992	2,644	112	25	89
1993	3,386	124	30	96
1994	4,044	148	44	106
1995	5,118	166	55	113
1996	6,588	205	84	124
1997 (projected)	7,778	223	96	134

NA = Not available.

a well-oiled machine that keeps close tabs on our day-to-day operations. It's one of our key success factors.

Jollibee expanded quickly throughout the Philippines, financing all growth internally until 1993. (**Exhibit 1** shows growth in sales and outlets.) Tan family members occupied several key positions, particularly in the vital operations functions, but brought in professional managers to supplement their expertise. "The heads of marketing and finance have always been outsiders," TTC noted. (**Exhibit 2** shows a 1997 organization chart.) Many franchisees were also members or friends of the Tan family.

In 1993, Jollibee went public and in an initial public offering raised 216 million pesos (approximately US$8 million). The Tan family, however, retained the majority ownership and clearly controlled Jollibee. Although the acquisition of Greenwich Pizza Corporation in 1994 and the formation of a joint venture with Deli France in 1995 diversified the company's fast food offerings, in 1996 the chain of Jollibee stores still generated about 85% of the parent company's revenues. (**Exhibits 3** and **4** present Jollibee's consolidated financial statements from 1992 through 1996.)

McDonald's: Going Burger to Burger   The company's first serious challenge arose in 1981, when McDonald's entered the Philippines. Although Jollibee already had 11 stores, many saw McDonald's as a juggernaut and urged TTC to concentrate on building a strong second-place position in the market. A special meeting of senior management concluded that although McDonald's had more money and highly developed operating systems, Jollibee had one major asset: Philippine consumers preferred the taste of Jollibee's hamburger by a wide margin. The group decided to go head to head with McDonald's. "Maybe we were very young, but we felt we could do anything," TTC recalled. "We felt no fear."

McDonald's moved briskly at first, opening six restaurants within two years and spending large sums on advertising. Per store sales quickly surpassed Jollibee's and, by 1983, McDonald's had grabbed a 27% share of the fast food market, within striking range of Jollibee's 32%. The impressive performance of the Big Mac, McDonald's largest and best-known sandwich, led Jollibee to respond with a large hamburger of its own, called the Champ. Jollibee executives bet that the Champ's one wide hamburger patty, rather than the Big Mac's smaller two, would appeal more to Filipinos' large appetites. Market research indicated that Filipinos still preferred Jollibee burgers' spicy taste to McDonald's plain beef patty, so the Champ's promotions focused on its taste, as well as its size.

Exhibit 2 Jollibee Corporation Organization Chart, 1997 (members of Tan family shaded)

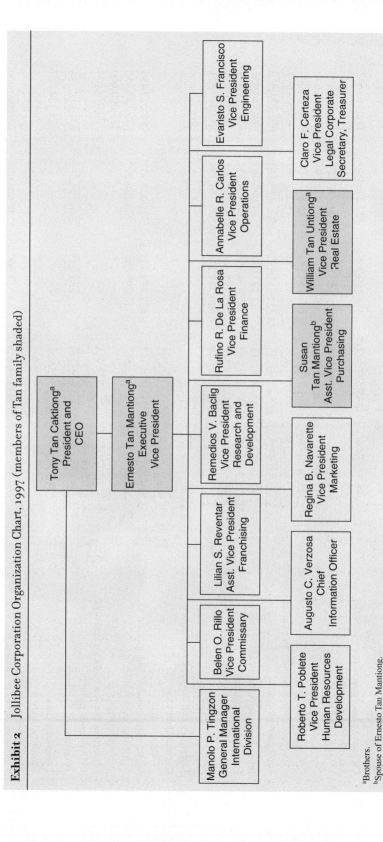

[a]Brothers.
[b]Spouse of Ernesto Tan Mantiong.

23

Exhibit 3 Jollibee Foods Corporation Consolidated Balance Sheets (in Philippine pesos)

	Years Ended December 31				
	1996	1995	1994	1993	1992
Assets					
Current assets					
Cash and cash equivalents	480,822,919	355,577,847	474,480,298	327,298,749	116,716,643
Accounts receivable:					
Trade	579,089,680	206,045,303	135,663,597	107,680,327	86,885,668
Advances and others	105,836,646	70,731,546	66,224,534	35,838,295	15,091,648
Inventories	323,019,198	201,239,667	183,154,582	135,263,988	116,828,086
Prepaid expenses and other current assets	223,680,221	132,077,935	88,995,824	41,462,780	66,028,987
Total current assets	1,712,448,664	965,672,298	948,518,835	647,544,139	401,551,032
Investments and advances	283,758,590	274,878,713	132,277,028	67,000,362	60,780,936
Property and equipment	2,177,944,193	1,181,184,783	753,876,765	568,904,831	478,857,474
Refundable deposits and other assets—net	363,648,234	224,052,247	91,575,543	92,035,464	72,310,079
Total assets	4,537,799,681	2,645,788,041	1,926,248,171	1,375,484,796	1,013,499,521
Liabilities and Stockholders' Equity					
Current liabilities:					
Bank loans	771,690,724	—	—	—	—
Accounts payable and accrued expenses	1,274,801,219	715,474,384	497,238,433	323,029,967	297,029,436
Income tax payable	58,803,916	28,103,867	17,205,603	23,206,109	19,851,315
Notes payable	—	—	—	—	133,000,000
Current portion of long-term debt	6,707,027	7,524,098	—	—	22,034,635
Dividends payable	16,810,812	—	—	—	—
Total current liabilities	2,128,813,698	751,102,349	514,444,036	346,236,076	471,915,386
Long-term debt	28,936,769	33,725,902	—	—	21,127,827
Minority interest	45,204,131	1,479,723	1,331,529	—	—
Stockholders' equity					
Capital stock—par value	880,781,250	704,625,000	563,315,000	372,000,000	66,000,000
Additional paid-in capital	190,503,244	190,503,244	190,503,244	190,503,244	—
Retained earnings	1,263,560,589	964,351,823	656,654,362	466,745,476	454,456,308
Total stockholders' equity	2,334,845,083	1,859,480,067	1,410,472,606	1,029,248,720	520,456,308
Total liabilities	4,537,799,681	2,645,788,041	1,926,248,171	1,375,484,796	1,013,499,521
Average exchange rate during year: pesos per US$	26.22	25.71	26.42	27.12	25.51

Exhibit 4 Jollibee Foods Corporation Consolidated Statements of Income and Retained Earnings (in Philippine pesos)

	Years Ended December 31				
	1996	**1995**	**1994**	**1993**	**1992**
Systemwide Sales (incl. franchisees)	8,577,067,000	6,894,670,000	5,277,640,000	4,102,270,000	NA
Company sales	6,393,092,135	4,403,272,755	3,277,383,084	2,446,866,690	2,074,153,386
Royalties and franchise fees	511,510,191	448,200,271	328,824,566	255,325,825	221,884,104
	6,904,602,326	4,851,473,026	3,606,207,650	2,702,192,515	2,296,037,490
Cost and Expenses					
Cost of sales	4,180,809,230	2,858,056,701	2,133,240,206	1,663,600,632	1,469,449,458
Operating expenses	1,943,536,384	1,403,151,840	1,013,999,640	674,288,268	545,749,275
Operating income	780,256,712	590,264,485	458,967,804	364,303,615	280,838,757
Interest and other income—net	44,670,811	102,134,296	83,342,805	32,716,223	(13,599,219)
Minority share in net earnings of a subsidiary	—	—	499,770	—	—
Provision for income tax	219,900,353	168,589,520	138,001,953	104,230,670	66,172,056
Income before minority interest and cumulative effect of accounting change	605,027,170	523,809,261	403,808,886	292,789,168	201,067,482
Minority interest	2,829,654	137,694	—	—	—
Cumulative effect of accounting change		13,733,644			
Net income	602,197,516	537,405,211	403,808,886	292,789,168	201,067,482
Earnings per share	0.68	0.61	0.81	0.59	0.58
Average exchange rate (pesos per $US)	26.22	25.71	26.42	27.12	25.51

But the Champ's intended knockout punch was eclipsed by larger events. In August 1983, political opposition leader Benigno Aquino was assassinated as he returned from exile. The economic and political crisis that followed led most foreign investors, including McDonald's, to slow their investment in the Philippines. Riding a wave of national pride, Jollibee pressed ahead, broadening its core menu with taste-tested offerings of chicken, spaghetti and a unique peach-mango dessert pie, all developed to local consumer tastes. By 1984, McDonald's foreign brand appeal was fading.

In 1986, dictator Ferdinand Marcos fled the Philippines in the face of mass demonstrations of "people power" led by Aquino's widow, Corazon. After she took office as president, optimism returned to the country, encouraging foreign companies to reinvest. As the local McDonald's franchisee once again moved to expand, however, its management found that Jollibee now had 31 stores and was clearly the dominant presence in the market.

Industry Background

In the 1960s, fast food industry pioneers, such as Ray Kroc of McDonald's and Colonel Sanders of Kentucky Fried Chicken, had developed a value proposition that became the standard for the industry in the United States and abroad. Major fast food outlets in the United States, which provided a model for the rest of the world, aimed to serve time-constrained customers by providing good-quality food in a clean dining environment and at a low price.

Managing a Store   At the store level, profitability in the fast food business depended on high customer traffic and tight operations management. Opening an outlet required large investments in equipment and store fittings, and keeping it open imposed high fixed costs for rent, utilities, and labor. This meant attracting large numbers of customers ("traffic") and, when possible, increasing the size of the average order (or "ticket"). The need for high volume put a premium on convenience and made store location critical. In choosing a site, attention had to be paid not only to the potential of a city or

neighborhood but also to the traffic patterns and competition on particular streets or even blocks.

Yet even an excellent location could not make a store viable in the absence of good operations management, the critical ingredient in reducing waste, ensuring quality service and increasing staff productivity. Store managers were the key to motivating and controlling crew members responsible for taking orders, preparing food, and keeping the restaurant clean. Efficient use of their time—preparing raw materials and ingredients in advance, for example—not only enabled faster service, but could also reduce the number of crew members needed.

Managing a Chain   The high capital investment required to open new stores led to the growth of franchising, which enabled chains to stake out new territory by rapidly acquiring market share and building brand recognition in an area. Such expansion created the critical mass needed to achieve economies of scale in both advertising and purchasing.

Fast food executives generally believed that chain-wide consistency and reliability was a key driver of success. Customers patronized chains because they knew, after eating at one restaurant in a chain, what they could expect at any other restaurant. This not only required standardization of the menu, raw material quality, and food preparation, but also the assurance of uniform standards of cleanliness and service. Particularly among the U.S. chains that dominated the industry, there also was agreement that uniformity of image also differentiated the chain from competitors: beyond selling hamburger or chicken, they believed they were selling an image of American pop culture. Consequently, most major fast food chains pushed their international subsidiaries to maintain or impose standardized menus, recipes, advertising themes, and store designs.

Moving Offshore: 1986–1997

Jollibee's success in the Philippines brought opportunities in other Asian countries. Foreign businesspeople, some of them friends of the Tan family, heard about the chain's success against McDonald's and began approaching TTC for franchise rights in their countries. While most of his family and other executives were caught up in the thriving Philippine business, TTC was curious to see how Jollibee would fare abroad.

Early Forays: Early Lessons

Singapore   Jollibee's first venture abroad began in 1985, when a friend of a Philippine franchisee persuaded TTC to let him open and manage Jollibee stores in Singapore. The franchise was owned by a partnership consisting of Jollibee, the local manager, and five Philippine-Chinese investors, each with a one-seventh stake. Soon after the first store opened, however, relations between Jollibee and the local manager began to deteriorate. When corporate inspectors visited to check quality, cleanliness, and efficiency in operations, the franchisee would not let them into his offices to verify the local records. In 1986, Jollibee revoked the franchise agreement and shut down the Singapore store. "When we were closing down the store, we found that all the local company funds were gone, but some suppliers had not been paid," said TTC. "We had no hard evidence that something was wrong, but we had lost each other's trust."

Taiwan   Soon after the closure in Singapore, Jollibee formed a 50/50 joint venture with a Tan family friend in Taiwan. Although sales boomed immediately after opening, low pedestrian traffic by the site eventually led to disappointing revenues. Over time, conflict arose over day-to-day management issues between the Jollibee operations staff assigned to maintain local oversight and the Taiwanese partner. "Because the business demands excellent operations, we felt we had to back our experienced Jollibee operations guy, but the partner was saying, 'I'm your partner, I've put in equity. Who do you trust?'" When the property market in Taiwan took off and store rent increased dramatically, Jollibee decided to dissolve the joint venture and pulled out of Taiwan in 1988.

Brunei   Meanwhile, another joint venture opened in August 1987 in the small sultanate of Brunei,

located on the northern side of the island of Borneo. (Exhibit 5 shows the locations of Jollibee International stores as of mid-1997.) The CEO of Shoemart, one of the Philippines' largest department stores, proposed that Jollibee form a joint-venture with a Shoemart partner in Brunei. By the end of 1993, with four successful stores in Brunei, TTC identified a key difference in the Brunei entry strategy: "In Singapore and Taiwan, the local partners ran the operation, and resented our operating control. In Brunei, the local investor was a silent partner. We sent managers from the Philippines to run the operations, and the local partner supported us."

Indonesia   An opportunity to enter southeast Asia's largest market came through a family friend. In 1989, Jollibee opened its first store, in Jakarta. Initially, the operation struggled, facing competition from street vendors and cheap local fast food chains. When conflict between the local partners and the manager they had hired paralyzed the operation, in late 1994, Jollibee dissolved the partnership and sold the operation to a new franchisee. Nevertheless, the company viewed the market as promising.

TTC summed up the lessons Jollibee had learned from its first international ventures:

> McDonald's succeeded everywhere because they were very good at selecting the right partners. They can get 100 candidates and choose the best—we don't have the name to generate that choice yet.
>
> Another key factor in this business is location. If you're an unknown brand entering a new country or city, you have trouble getting access to prime locations. McDonald's name gets it the best sites. People were telling us not to go international until we had solved these two issues: location and partner.

Building an Organization   In 1993, TTC decided that Jollibee's international operations required greater structure and more resources. Because most of his management team was more interested in the fast-growing domestic side of the business, in January 1994, he decided to hire an experienced outsider as Vice President for International Operations. He selected Tony Kitchner, a native of Australia, who had spent 14 years in Pizza Hut's

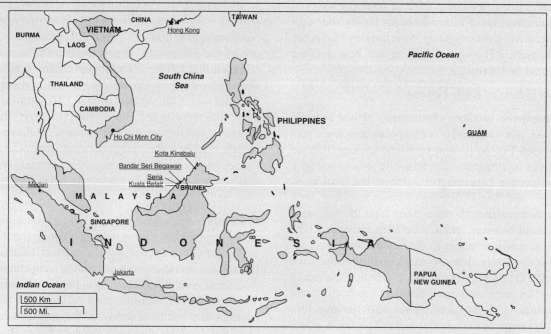

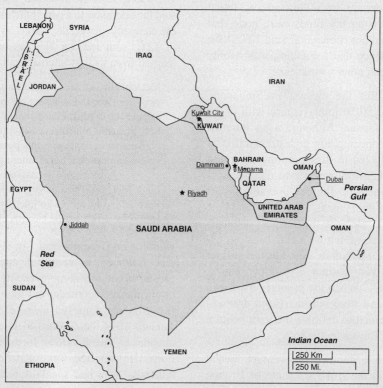

Asia-Pacific regional office in Hong Kong. Reporting directly to TTC, Kitchner asked for the resources and autonomy to create an International Division.

Kitchner felt that his new division needed to be separate from Jollibee's Philippine side, with a different identity and capabilities. He agreed with TTC that attracting partners with good connections in their markets should be a priority, but worried that Jollibee's simple image and basic management approach would hamper these efforts. To project an image of a world-class company, he remodeled his division's offices on the seventh floor of Jollibee's Manila headquarters and instituted the company's first dress code, requiring his managers to wear ties. As one manager explained, "We had to look and act like a multinational, not like a local chain. You can't have someone in a short-sleeved open-neck shirt asking a wealthy businessman to invest millions."

Within weeks of his arrival, Kitchner began recruiting experienced internationalists from inside and outside Jollibee. To his inherited three-person staff, he quickly added seven more professionals, including new managers of marketing, finance, and quality control and product development that he brought in from outside Jollibee. The addition of two secretaries rounded out his staff. He claimed that greater internal recruiting had been constrained by two factors—Philippine management's resistance to having their staff "poached," and employees' lack of interest in joining this upstart division.

Strategic Thrust   While endeavoring to improve the performance of existing stores in Indonesia and Brunei, Kitchner decided to increase the pace of international expansion with the objective of making Jollibee one of the world's top ten fast food brands by 2000. Kitchner's strategy rested on two main themes formulated during a planning session in the fall of 1994—"targeting expats" and "planting the flag."

The Division's new chief saw the hundreds of thousands of expatriate Filipinos working in the Middle East, Hong Kong, Guam, and other Asian territories as a latent market for Jollibee and as a good initial base to support entry. Looking for a new market to test this concept, he focused on the concentrations of Filipino guest-workers in the Middle East. After opening stores in Dubai, Kuwait, and Dammam, however, he found that this market was limited on the lower end by restrictions on poorer workers' freedom of movement, and on the upper end by wealthier expatriates' preference for hotel dining, where they could consume alcohol. Not all overseas Filipinos were potential customers, it seemed.

The other strategic criterion for choosing markets rested on Kitchner's belief in first-mover advantages in the fast food industry. Jay Visco, International's Marketing manager, explained:

> We saw that in Brunei, where we were the pioneers in fast food, we were able to set the pace and standards. Now, we have six stores there, while McDonald's has only one and KFC has three. . . . That was a key learning: even if your foreign counterparts come in later, you already have set the pace and are at top of the heap.

The International Division therefore began to "plant the Jollibee flag" in countries where competitors had little or no presence. The expectation was that by expanding the number of stores, the franchise could build brand awareness which in turn would positively impact sales. One problem with this approach proved to be its circularity: only after achieving a certain level of sales could most franchisees afford the advertising and promotion needed to build brand awareness. The other challenge was that rapid expansion led to resource constraints—especially in the availability of International Division staff to support multiple simultaneous startups.

Nonetheless, Kitchner expanded rapidly. Due to Jollibee's success in the Philippines and the Tan family's network of contacts, he found he could choose from many franchising inquiries from various countries. Some were far from Jollibee's home base—like the subsequently abandoned plan to enter Romania ("our gateway to Europe" according to one manager). In an enormous burst of energy,

Exhibit 6   Jollibee International Store Openings

Location	Date Opened	
Bandar Seri Begawan, *Brunei*	August 1987	
Bandar Seri Begawan, Brunei (second store)	June 1989	
Seria, Brunei	August 1992	
Jakarta, *Indonesia*	August 1992	
Jakarta, Indonesia (second store)	March 1993	
Bandar Seri Begawan, Brunei (third store)	November 1993	International Division created
Kuala Belait, Brunei	November 1994	
Dubai, *United Arab Emirates*	April 1995	
Kuwait City, *Kuwait*	December 1995	
Dammam, *Saudi Arabia*	December 1995	
Guam	December 1995	
Jiddah, Saudi Arabia	January 1996	
Bahrain	January 1996	
Kota Kinabalu, *Malaysia*	February 1996	
Dubai (second store)	June 1996	
Riyadh, Saudi Arabia	July 1996	
Kuwait City, Kuwait (second store)	August 1996	
Kuwait City, Kuwait (third store)	August 1996	
Jiddah, Saudi Arabia (second store)	August 1996	
Hong Kong	September 1996	
Bandar Seri Begawan, Brunei (fourth store)	October 1996	
Ho Chi Minh City, *Vietnam*	October 1996	
Medan, Indonesia	December 1996	
Hong Kong (second store)	December 1996	
Dammam, Saudi Arabia	April 1997	
Hong Kong (third store)	June 1997	
Jakarta, Indonesia (third store)	July 1997	
Jakarta, Indonesia (fourth store)	September 1997	

Italics represent new market entry.

between November 1994 and December 1996, the company entered 8 new national markets and opened 18 new stores. The flag was being planted. (See **Exhibit 6**.)

Operational Management

Market Entry   Once Jollibee had decided to enter a new market, Tony Kitchner negotiated the franchise agreement, often with an investment by the parent company, to create a partnership with the franchisee. At that point he handed responsibility for the opening to one of the division's Franchise

Services Managers (FSMs). These were the key contacts between the company and its franchisees, and Kitchner was rapidly building a substantial support group in Manila to provide them with the resources and expertise they needed to start up and manage an offshore franchise. (See Exhibit 7.)

About a month before the opening, the FSM hired a project manager, typically a native of the new market who normally would go on to manage the first store. The FSM and project manager made most of the important decisions during the startup process, with the franchisees' level of involvement

Exhibit 7 International Division Organization Chart, Late 1996 (pre-restructuring)

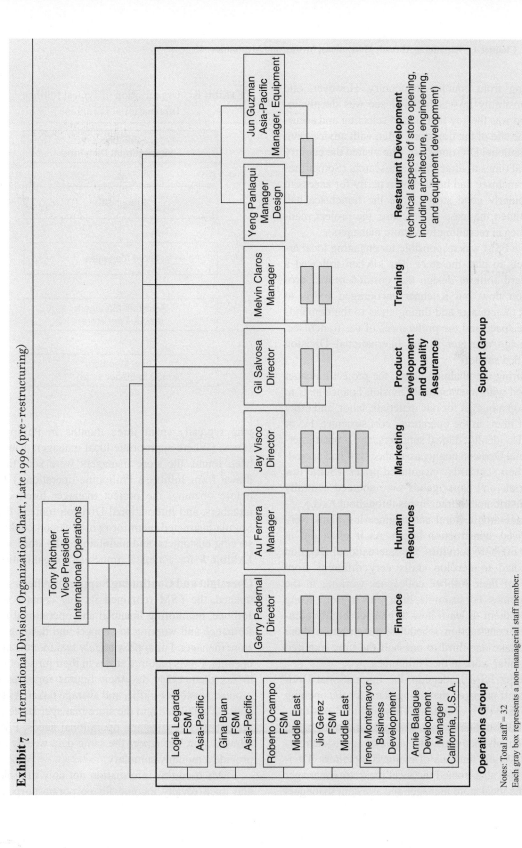

Notes: Total staff = 32
Each gray box represents a non-managerial staff member.

31

varying from country to country. However, one responsibility in which franchisee was deeply involved was the key first step of selecting and securing the site of the first store, often with advice from International Division staff, who visited the country several times to direct market research. (Sometimes the franchisee had been chosen partly for access to particularly good sites.) Once the franchisee had negotiated the lease or purchase, the project manager began recruiting local store managers.

The FSM was responsible for engaging local architects to plan the store. The kitchen followed a standard Jollibee design that ensured proper production flow, but Kitchner encouraged FSMs to adapt the counter and dining areas to the demands of the space and the preferences of the franchisee. A design manager in the International Division provided support.

During the planning phase, the project manager worked with International Division finance staff to develop a budget for raw materials, labor, and other major items in the operation's cost structure. He or she also identified local suppliers, and—once International Division quality assurance staff had accredited their standards—negotiated prices. (Some raw materials and paper goods were sourced centrally and distributed to franchisees throughout Asia.)

Once architectural and engineering plans were approved, construction began. As it often did in other offshore activities, the International Division staff had to develop skills very different from those of their Jollibee colleagues working in the Philippines. For example, high rents in Hong Kong forced them to learn how to manage highly compacted construction schedules: construction there could take one-third to one-half the time required for similar work in the Philippines.

Under FSM leadership, the International Division staff prepared marketing plans for the opening and first year's operation. They included positioning and communications strategies and were based on their advance consumer surveys, aggregate market data, and analysis of major competitors. Division staff also trained the local marketing manager and the local store manager and assistant managers

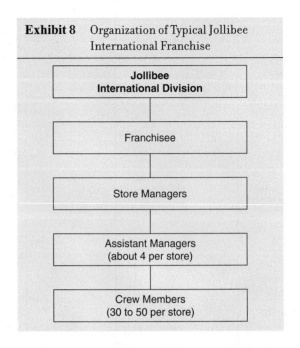

Exhibit 8   Organization of Typical Jollibee International Franchise

who typically spent three months in Philippine stores. (Where appropriate local managers had not been found, the store managers were sometimes drawn from Jollibee's Philippine operations.) Just before opening, the project manager hired crew members, and International Division trainers from Manila instructed them for two weeks on cooking, serving customers, and maintaining the store. (See **Exhibit 8** for a typical franchise's organization.)

Oversight and Continuing Support   After a store opened, the FSM remained its key contact with Jollibee, monitoring financial and operational performance and working to support and develop the store manager. For approximately two months after opening, FSMs required stores in their jurisdictions to fax them every day their figures for sales by product, customer traffic, and average ticket. As operations stabilized and the store manager started to see patterns in sales and operational needs, FSMs allowed stores to report the same data weekly and provide a monthly summary.

FSMs used this information not only to project and track royalty income for corporate purposes, but also to identify ways they could support the local franchisee. When the data suggested problems, the FSM would contact the store manager, highlight the issue, and ask for an appropriate plan of action. For example, if FSM Gina Buan saw a decline in sales for two consecutive weeks, she demanded specific plans within 24 hours of her call. If managers could not come up with solutions themselves, she would coach them to help them generate answers. "My aim," she remarked with a smile, "is to turn them into clones of me—or at least teach them my expertise."

In addition to the required sales reports, many stores voluntarily reported on their costs, because they found their FSM's analysis so helpful. This open partnership fit with TTC's view of franchise relations. "We get data from franchisees more to help us provide consulting assistance than for control," he said. Ernesto Tan, TTC's brother, explained that although Jollibee's royalty was a percentage of franchisees' sales, and local operations were focused more on profits, both interests were similar: "We want sales to grow, so that our royalty grows. But this will not happen if stores are not profitable, because our franchisees will not push to expand."

As well as support, however, the International Division was also concerned with control—especially in quality. Unannounced on-site inspections every quarter were Jollibee's primary tool. Over two days, the FSM evaluated every aspect of operations in detail, including product quality and preparation (taste, temperature, freshness, availability, and appearance), cleanliness, restaurant appearance, service speed, and friendliness. The manual for intensive checks was several inches thick. All international staff had been trained in Jollibee's quality standards and conducted less detailed "quick checks" whenever they traveled. Based on a 15-page questionnaire, a quick check took roughly two hours to complete and covered all of the areas that intensive ones did, although with less rigor and detail. Each store received an average of two quick checks per quarter.

In addition to FSMs' own rich industry experiences—Gina Buan, for example, had managed stores, districts, and countries for Jollibee and

another chain—these field managers engaged the expertise of International Division functional staff. While they tried to shift responsibility gradually to the franchisee, division support staff often bore much of the responsibility long after startup. For example, the marketing staff tried to limit their franchise support role to creating initial marketing plans for new openings and reviewing new store plans. However, often they were drawn into the planning of more routine campaigns for particular stores, work they felt should be handled by the franchisee and store managers.

International vs. Domestic Practice As operations grew, Kitchner and his staff discovered that international expansion was not quite as simple as the metaphor of "planting flags" might suggest. It sometimes felt more like struggling up an unconquered, hostile mountain. After numerous market entry battles, the international team decided that a number of elements of Jollibee's Philippine business model needed to be modified overseas. For example, the company's experience in Indonesia led Visco to criticize the transplantation of Jollibee's "mass-based positioning":

> When Jollibee arrived in Indonesia, they assumed that the market would be similar to the Philippines. But the Indonesian masses are not willing to spend as much on fast food as the Philippine working and lower-middle class consumers, and there were lots of cheap alternatives available. We decided that we needed to reposition ourselves to target a more up-market clientele.

Kitchner and Visco also felt that Jollibee needed to present itself as "world class," not "local" or "regional." In particular, they disliked the Philippine store design,—a "trellis" theme with a garden motif—which had been transferred unchanged as Jollibee exported internationally. Working with an outside architect, a five-person panel from the International Division developed three new store decors, with better lighting and higher quality furniture. After Kitchner got TTC's approval, the Division remodeled the Indonesian stores and used the designs for all subsequent openings.

International also redesigned the Jollibee logo. While retaining the bee mascot, it changed the red background to orange and added the slogan, "great burgers, great chicken." Visco pointed out that the orange background differentiated the chain's logo from those of other major brands, such as KFC, Coca-Cola, and Marlboro, which all had red-and-white logos. The slogan was added to link the Jollibee name and logo with its products in people's minds. Visco also noted that, unlike Wendy's Old Fashioned Hamburgers, Kentucky Fried Chicken, and Pizza Hut, Jollibee did not incorporate its product in its name and market tests had found that consumers outside the Philippines guessed the logo signified a toy chain or candy store.

Kitchner and his staff made numerous other changes to Jollibee's Philippine business operating model. For example, rather than preparing new advertising materials for each new promotion as they did in the Philippines, the international marketing group created a library of promotional photographs of each food product that could be assembled, in-house, into collages illustrating new promotions (e.g., a discounted price for buying a burger, fries, and soda). And purchasing changed from styrofoam to paper packaging to appeal to foreign consumers' greater environmental consciousness.

Customizing for Local Tastes   While such changes provoked grumbling from many in the large domestic business who saw the upstart international group as newcomers fiddling with proven concepts, nothing triggered more controversy than the experiments with menu items. Arguing that the "flexibility" aspect of Jollibee's "Five Fs" corporate creed stood for a willingness to accommodate differences in customer tastes, managers in the International Division believed that menus should be adjusted to local preferences.

The practice had started in 1992 when a manager was dispatched from the Philippines to respond to the Indonesian franchisee's request to create a fast food version of the local favorite *nasi lema,* a mixture of rice and coconut milk. Building on this precedent, Kitchner's team created an international menu item they called the Jollimeal. This was typically a rice-based meal with a topping that could vary by country—in Hong Kong, for example, the rice was covered with hot and sour chicken, while in Vietnam it was chicken curry. Although it accounted for only 5% of international sales, Kitchner saw Jollimeals as an important way to "localize" the Jollibee image.

But the International Division expanded beyond the Jollimeal concept. On a trip to Dubai, in response to the local franchisee's request to create a salad for the menu, product development manager Gil Salvosa spent a night chopping vegetables in his hotel room to create a standard recipe. That same trip, he acquired a recipe for chicken masala from the franchisee's cook, later adapting it to fast food production methods for the Dubai store. The International Division also added idio-syncratic items to menus, such as dried fish, a Malaysian favorite. Since other menu items were seldom removed, these additions generally increased the size of menus abroad.

Although increased menu diversity almost always came at the cost of some operating efficiency (and, by implication, complicated the task of store level operating control), Kitchner was convinced that such concessions to local tastes were necessary. In Guam, for example, to accommodate extra-large local appetites, division staff added a fried egg and two strips of bacon to the Champ's standard large beef patty. And franchisees in the Middle East asked the Division's R&D staff to come up with a spicier version of Jollibee's fried chicken. Although Kentucky Fried Chicken (KFC) was captivating customers with their spicy recipe, R&D staff on the Philippine side objected strenuously. As a compromise, International developed a spicy sauce that customers could add to the standard Jollibee chicken.

Overall, the International Division's modification of menus and products caused considerable tension with the Philippine side of Jollibee. While there was no controversy about reformulating hamburgers for Muslim countries to eliminate traces of pork, for example, adding new products or changing existing ones led to major arguments. As a result, International received little cooperation from the larger Philippine research and development staff and customization remained a source of disagreement and friction.

Strained International-Domestic Relations
As the International Division expanded, its relations with the Philippine-based operations seemed to deteriorate. Tensions over menu modifications reflected more serious issues that had surfaced soon after Kitchner began building his international group. Philippine staff saw International as newcomers who, despite their lack of experience in Jollibee, "discarded practices built over 16 years." On the other side, International Division staff reported that they found the Philippine organization bureaucratic and slow-moving. They felt stymied by requirements to follow certain procedures and go through proper channels to obtain assistance.

The two parts of Jollibee continued to operate largely independently, but strained relations gradually eroded any sense of cooperation and reduced already limited exchanges to a minimum. Some International Division staff felt that the Philippine side, which controlled most of Jollibee's resources, should do more to help their efforts to improve and adapt existing products and practices. Visco recalled that when he wanted assistance designing new packaging, the Philippine marketing manager took the attitude that international could fend for itself. Similarly, Salvosa wanted more cooperation on product development from Philippine R&D, but was frustrated by the lengthy discussions and approvals that seemed to be required.

However, the domestic side viewed things differently. Executive Vice President Ernesto Tan, who was in charge of Jollibee in the Philippines, recalled:

> The strains came from several things. It started when International tried to recruit people directly from the Philippine side, without consulting with their superiors. There also was some jealousy on a personal level because the people recruited were immediately promoted to the next level, with better pay and benefits.
>
> The international people also seemed to develop a superiority complex. They wanted to do everything differently, so that if their stores did well, they could take all the credit. At one point, they proposed running a store in the Philippines as a training facility,

but we thought they also wanted to show us that they could do it better than us. We saw them as lavish spenders while we paid very close attention to costs. Our people were saying, "We are earning the money, and they are spending it!" There was essentially no communication to work out these problems. So we spoke to TTC, because Kitchner reported to him.

Matters grew worse throughout 1996. One of the first signs of serious trouble came during a project to redesign the Jollibee logo, which TTC initiated in mid-1995. Triggered by International's modification of the old logo, the redesign project committee had representatives from across the company. Having overseen International's redesign, Kitchner was included. During the committee's deliberations, some domestic managers felt that the International vice-president's strong opinions were obstructive, and early in 1996 Kitchner stopped attending the meetings.

During this time, TTC was growing increasingly concerned about the International Division's continuing struggles. Around November 1996, he decided that he could no longer support Kitchner's strategy of rapid expansion due to the financial problems it was creating. Many of the International stores were losing money, but the cost of supporting these widespread unprofitable activities was increasing. Despite the fact that even unprofitable stores generated franchise fees calculated as a percentage of sales, TTC was uncomfortable:

> Kitchner wanted to put up lots of stores, maximizing revenue for Jollibee. Initially, I had supported this approach, thinking we could learn from an experienced outsider, but I came to believe that was not viable in the long term. We preferred to go slower, making sure that each store was profitable so that it would generate money for the franchisee, as well as for us. In general, we believe that whoever we do business with— suppliers and especially franchisees—should make money. This creates a good, long-term relationship.

In February 1997, Kitchner left Jollibee to return to Australia. A restructuring supervised directly by TTC shrank the International Division's staff from 32 to 14, merging the finance, MIS and human resources functions with their bigger Philippine counterparts. (See **Exhibit 9.**) Jay Visco became

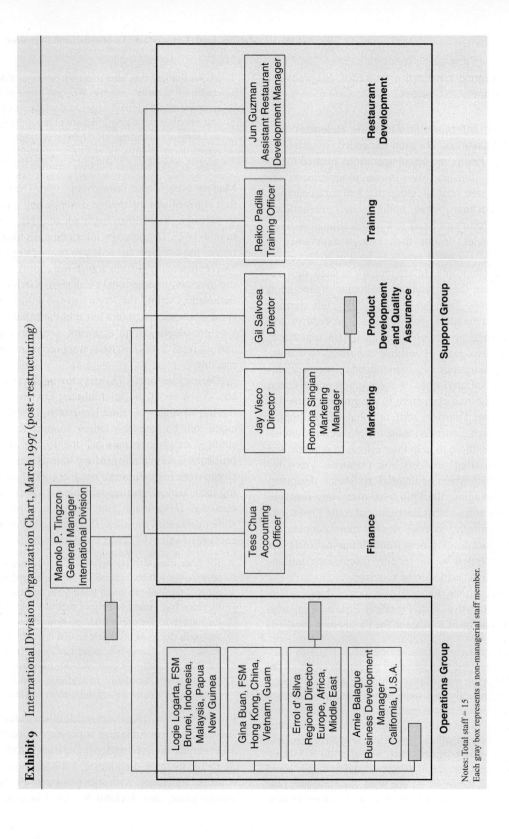

Exhibit 9   International Division Organization Chart, March 1997 (post-restructuring)

Manolo P. Tingzon
General Manager
International Division

Operations Group

Logie Logarta, FSM
Brunei, Indonesia,
Malaysia, Papua
New Guinea

Gina Buan, FSM
Hong Kong, China,
Vietnam, Guam

Errol d' Silva
Regional Director
Europe, Africa,
Middle East

Arnie Balague
Business Development
Manager
California, U.S.A.

Support Group

Tess Chua
Accounting
Officer

Finance

Jay Visco
Director

Romona Singian
Marketing
Manager

Marketing

Gil Salvosa
Director

**Product
Development
and Quality
Assurance**

Reiko Padilla
Training Officer

Training

Jun Guzman
Assistant Restaurant
Development Manager

**Restaurant
Development**

Notes: Total staff = 15
Each gray box represents a non-managerial staff member.

interim head of International while TTC searched for a new Division leader.

A New International Era: 1997

In the wake of Kitchner's departure, TTC consulted intensively with Jollibee's suppliers and other contacts in fast food in the Philippines regarding a replacement. The name that kept recurring was Manolo P. ("Noli") Tingzon, one of the industry's most experienced managers. Although based in the Philippines his entire career, Tingzon had spent much of this time helping foreign chains crack the Philippine market. In 1981 he joined McDonald's as a management trainee and spent the next 10 years in frustrating combat with Jollibee. After a brief experience with a food packaging company, in 1994 he took on the challenge to launch Texas Chicken, another U.S. fast food chain, in its Philippines entry. When TTC contacted him in late 1996, he was intrigued by the opportunity offered by his old nemesis and joined the company in July 1997 as general manager, International Division.

A Fresh Look at Strategy   Upon his arrival, Tingzon reviewed International's current and historical performance. (See **Exhibit 10.**) He concluded that because of the scale economies of fast food franchising, an "acceptable" return on investment in international operations would require 60 Jollibee restaurants abroad with annual sales of US$800,000 each, the approximate store level sales at McDonald's smaller Asian outlets. Feeling that Jollibee's international expansion had sometimes been driven less by business considerations than by a pride in developing overseas operations, Tingzon thought that a fresh examination of existing international strategies might reveal opportunities for improvement. As he consulted colleagues at Jollibee, however, he heard differing opinions.

Many of his own staff felt that the rapid expansion of the "plant-the-flag" approach had served Jollibee well and should be continued. For example, Visco argued that establishing a presence in each market before competitors conferred important first-mover advantages in setting customer expectations, influencing tastes and building brand. He and others felt that Jollibee's success in the Philippines and Brunei illustrated this point especially well.

Others, particularly on Jollibee's domestic side, felt the flag-planting strategy was ill-conceived, leading the company into what they saw as rash market choices such as the Middle East, where

Exhibit 10   International Store Sales by Country: 1996 (in U.S. dollars at contemporary exchange rates)

		1996	
		Sales	**Number of Stores**
Bahrain		262,361	1
Brunei		2,439,538	6
Guam		1,771,202	1
Hong Kong		1,142,240	2
Indonesia		854,259	3
Kuwait		864,531	3
Malaysia		391,328	1
Saudi Arabia		976,748	4
United Arab Emirates		487,438	2
Vietnam		112,578	1
Total	US$	9,302,223	24

outlets continued to have difficulty attracting either expatriates or locals. For example, Ernesto Tan advised Tingzon to "focus on expanding share in a few countries while making sure each store does well." He urged Tingzon to consolidate and build on existing Jollibee markets that had either high profit potential, such as Hong Kong, or relatively mild competition, such as Malaysia and Indonesia.

With respect to the strategy of initially focusing on Filipino expatriates in new markets, Tingzon appreciated that this approach had eased Jollibee's entry into Guam and Hong Kong, but wondered whether it might trap the chain. "Might we risk boxing ourselves into a Filipino niche that prevents us from growing enough to support operations in each country?" he asked. Again opinion was divided between those favoring the expatriate-led strategy and those who felt it was time for Jollibee to shake its Philippine identity and target the mainstream market wherever it went.

Strategy in Action: Three Decisions   Although he eventually wanted to resolve these issues at the level of policy, Tingzon faced three immediate growth opportunities that he knew would shape the emergence of the future strategy.

Papua New Guinea: Raising the Standard   In early 1996, at the recommendation of Quality Assurance Manager Gil Salvosa, a local New Guinea entrepreneur in the poultry business approached Tony Kitchner about a Jollibee franchise. He described a country of five million people served by only one poorly managed, 3-store fast-food chain, that had recently broken ties with its Australian chicken restaurant franchise. "Port Moresby does not have a single decent place to eat," he told Kitchner. He believed Jollibee could raise the quality of service and food enough to take much of the Australian chain's market share while discouraging further entrants.

Although the original plan had been to open just one store in the foreseeable future—in the capital, Port Moresby—Tingzon was certain that the franchisee could only cover the costs of developing the market if he put in at least three or four stores soon after. But he was uncertain whether Papua New Guinea could support the 20 stores that he saw as the target critical mass for new markets. (For comparison, in the Philippines, approximately 1,200 fast food outlets competed for the business of 75 million people. GNP per capita in both countries was almost at US$2,500.)

When Tingzon explained his concerns, the would-be franchisee's response was that he would negotiate with a major petroleum retailer and try to open stores in five of their service stations around the country. Furthermore, he emphasized that he was willing to build more stores if necessary and would put up all the capital so that Jollibee would risk no equity in the venture.

Hong Kong: Expanding the Base   Also on Tingzon's plate was a proposal to expand to a fourth store in Hong Kong. The franchise, owned by Jollibee in partnership with local businessmen and managed by Tommy King, TTC's brother-in-law, opened its first store in September 1996 to instant, overwhelming success. Located near a major transit hub in the Central district, it became a gathering place for Filipino expatriates, primarily domestic workers. However, appealing to the locals had proven more difficult. While volume was high on weekends, when the Filipinos came to Central to socialize, it fell off during the week, when business was primarily from local office workers.

Although two more stores in Central had attracted many Filipinos, they both relied extensively on Chinese customers and generated sales of only about one-third of the first outlet. One problem was that, despite strenuous efforts, Jollibee had been unable to hire many local Chinese as crew members. According to one manager, Chinese customers who did not speak English well were worried that they would be embarrassed if they were not understood by the predominantly Philippine and Nepalese counter staff. Another problem was that in a city dominated by McDonald's, Jollibee's brand recognition among locals was weak. Working with Henry Shih, the sub-franchisee who owned the second store, Jollibee staff were trying to help launch a thematic advertising campaign, but due to the Hong Kong operation's small size, the franchise could not inject sufficient funds.

Shih also blamed rigidity over menu offerings for Jollibee's difficulties appealing to Chinese customers. In early 1997, his Chinese managers had suggested serving tea the Hong Kong way—using tea dust (powdered tea leaves) rather than tea bags and adding evaporated milk. More than six months later, he had still not received a go-ahead. His proposal to develop a less-fatty recipe for Chicken Joy, one of Jollibee's core menu items, had met more direct resistance. "The Chinese say that if you eat lots of deep-fried food you become hot inside and will develop health problems," said Shih who believed that the domestic side had pressured the International Division to reject any experimentation with this "core" menu item.

Meanwhile, staffing problems were worsening. The four locally recruited Chinese managers clashed with the five Filipinos imported from Tommy King's Philippine franchise, with the Chinese calling the Filipinos' discipline lax and their style arrogant, while the Filipinos saw the Chinese managers as uncommitted. By August 1997, all of the Chinese managers had resigned, leaving Jollibee with only Filipinos in store-level management positions. Shih was afraid this would further undermine Jollibee's ability to hire local crews, as Chinese preferred to work for Chinese.

Partly due to staff turnover, store managers were focused on dealing with day-to-day operations issues such as uneven product quality and had little time to design even short-term marketing strategies. King's focus on his Philippine stores slowed decision-making. And while Gina Buan, the FSM, had visited Hong Kong more often than any other markets she supervised (including for an extraordinary month-long stay), she had been unable to resolve the management problems. In June, King appointed Shih General Manager to oversee the entire Hong Kong venture.

In this context, Shih and King proposed to open a fourth store. The site in the Kowloon district was one of the busiest in Hong Kong, located at one of just two intersections of the subway and the rail line

that was the only public transport from the New Territories, where much of the city's workforce resided. However, the area saw far fewer Filipinos than Central and the store would have to depend on locals. Acknowledging that the fourth store would test Jollibee's ability to appeal to Hong Kong people, Shih argued that the menu would have to be customized more radically. However, Tingzon wondered whether expansion was even viable at this time, given the Hong Kong venture's managerial problems. Even if he were to approve the store, he wondered if he should support the menu variations that might complicate quality control. On the other hand, expansion into such a busy site might enhance Jollibee's visibility and brand recognition among locals, helping increase business even without changing the menu. It was another tough call.

California: Supporting the Settlers   Soon after signing his contract, Tingzon had learned of a year-old plan to open one Jollibee store per quarter in California starting in the first quarter of 1998. Supporting TTC's long-held belief that Jollibee could win enormous prestige and publicity by gaining a foothold in the birthplace of fast food, Kitchner had drawn up plans with a group of Manila-based businessmen as 40% partners in the venture. Once the company stores were established, they hoped to franchise in California and beyond in 1999.

Much of the confidence for this bold expansion plan came from Jollibee's success in Guam, a territory of the US. Although they initially targeted the 25% of the population of Filipino extraction, management discovered that their menu appealed to other groups of Americans based there. They also found they could adapt the labor-intensive Philippine operating methods by developing different equipment and cooking processes more in keeping with a high labor cost environment. In the words of one International Division veteran, "In Guam, we learned how to do business in the United States. After succeeding there, we felt we were ready for the mainland."

The plan called for the first store to be located in Daly City, a community with a large Filipino population but relatively low concentration of fast-food competitors in the San Francisco area. (With more than a million immigrants from the Philippines living in California, most relatively affluent, this state had one of the highest concentrations of Filipino expatriates in the world.) The menu would be transplanted from the Philippines without changes. After initially targeting Filipinos, the plan was to branch out geographically to the San Francisco and San Diego regions, and demographically to appeal to other Asian-American and, eventually, Hispanic-American consumers. The hope was that Jollibee would then expand to all consumers throughout the U.S.

Like the expansion strategies in PNG and Hong Kong, this project had momentum behind it, including visible support from Filipino-Americans, strong interest of local investors, and, not least, TTC's great interest in succeeding in McDonald's back-yard. Yet Tingzon realized that he would be the one held accountable for its final success and wanted to bring an objective outsider's perspective to this plan before it became accepted wisdom. Could Jollibee hope to succeed in the world's most competitive fast-food market? Could they provide the necessary support and control to operations located 12 hours by plane and eight time zones away? And was the Filipino-to-Asian-to-Hispanic-to-mainstream entry strategy viable or did it risk boxing them into an economically unviable niche?

Looking Forward   Noli Tingzon had only been in his job a few weeks, but already it was clear that his predecessor's plan to open 1000 Jollibee stores abroad before the turn of the century was a pipe dream. "It took McDonald's 20 years for its international operations to count for more than 50% of total sales," he said. "I'll be happy if I can do it in 10." But even this was an ambitious goal. And the decisions he made on the three entry options would have a significant impact on the strategic direction his international division took and on the organizational capabilities it needed to get there.

Case 1-3   Acer, Inc.: Taiwan's Rampaging Dragon

With a sense of real excitement, Stan Shih, CEO of Acer, Inc., boarded a plane for San Francisco in early February 1995. The founder of the Taiwanese personal computer (PC) company was on his way to see the Aspire, a new home PC being developed by Acer America Corporation (AAC) Acer's North American subsidiary. Although Shih had heard that a young American team was working on a truly innovative product, featuring a unique design, voice

Professor Christopher A. Bartlett and Research Associate Anthony St. George prepared this case as the basis for class discussion rather than to illustrate either effective or ineffective handling of an administrative situation. Some historical information was drawn from Robert H. Chen, "Made in Taiwan: The Story of Acer Computers," Linking Publishing Co., Taiwan, 1996, and Stan Shih, "Me-too is Not My Style," Acer Foundation, Taiwan, 1996. We would like to thank Eugene Hwang and Professor Robert H. Hayes for their help and advice.

recognition, ease-of-use, and cutting-edge multimedia capabilities, he knew little of the project until Ronald Chwang, President of AAC had invited him to the upcoming product presentation. From Chwang's description, Shih thought that Aspire could have the potential to become a blockbuster product worldwide. But he was equally excited that this was the first Acer product conceived, designed, and championed by a sales-and-marketing oriented regional business unit (RBU) rather than one of Acer's production-and-engineering focused strategic business units (SBUs) in Taiwan.

Somewhere in mid-flight, however, Shih's characteristic enthusiasm was tempered by his equally well-known pragmatism. Recently, AAC had been one of the company's more problematic overseas units, and had been losing money for five years. Was this the group on whom he should pin his hopes for Acer's next important growth initiative? Could such a radical new product succeed in the highly competitive American PC market? And if so, did this unit—one of the company's sales-and-marketing-oriented RBUs—have the resources and capabilities to lead the development of this important new product, and, perhaps, even its global rollout?

Birth of the Company

Originally known as Multitech, the company was founded in Taiwan in 1976 by Shih, his wife, and three friends. From the beginning, Shih served as CEO and Chairman, his wife as company accountant. With $25,000 of capital and 11 employees, Multitech's grand mission was "to promote the application of the emerging microprocessor technology." It grew by grasping every opportunity available—providing engineering and product design advice to local companies, importing electronic components, offering technological training courses, and publishing trade journals. "We will sell anything except our wives," joked Shih. Little did the founders realize that they were laying the foundations for one of Taiwan's great entrepreneurial success stories. (See **Exhibit 1.**)

Laying the Foundations   Because Multitech was capital constrained, the new CEO instituted a strong norm of frugality. Acting on what he described as "a poor man's philosophy," he leased just enough space for current needs (leading to 28 office relocations over the next 20 years) and, in the early years, encouraged employees to supplement their income by "moonlighting" at second jobs. Yet while Multitech paid modest salaries, it offered key employees equity, often giving them substantial ownership positions in subsidiary companies.

Frugality was one of many business principles Shih had learned while growing up in his mother's tiny store. He told employees that high-tech products, like his mother's duck eggs, had to be priced with a low margin to ensure turnover. He preached the importance of receiving cash payment quickly and avoiding the use of debt. But above all, he told

them that customers came first, employees second, and shareholders third, a principle later referred to as "Acer 1-2-3."

Shih's early experience biased him against the patriarch-dominated, family-run company model that was common in Taiwan. "It tends to generate opinions which are neither balanced nor objective," he said. He delegated substantial decision-making responsibility to his employees to harness "the natural entrepreneurial spirit of the Taiwanese." With his informal manner, bias for delegation, and "hands-off" style, Shih trusted employees to act in the best interests of the firm. "We don't believe in control in the normal sense. . . . We rely on people and build our business around them," he said. It was an approach many saw as the polar opposite of the classic Chinese entrepreneur's tight personal control. As a result, the young company soon developed a reputation as a very attractive place for bright young engineers.

Shih's philosophy was reflected in his commitment to employee education and his belief that he could create a company where employees would constantly be challenged to "think and learn." In the early years, superiors were referred to as "shifu," a title usually reserved for teachers and masters of the martial arts. The development of strong teaching relationships between manager and subordinate was encouraged by making the cultivation and grooming of one's staff a primary criterion for promotion. The slogan, "Tutors conceal nothing from their pupils" emphasized the open nature of the relationship and reminded managers of their responsibility.

This created a close-knit culture, where coworkers treated each other like family, and the norm was to do whatever was necessary for the greater good of the company. But is was a very demanding "family," and as the patriarch, Stan Shih worked hard to combat complacency—what he called "the big rice bowl" sense of entitlement—by creating a constant sense of crisis and showering subordinates with ideas and challenges for their examination and follow-up. As long as the managers took responsibility for their actions—acted as responsible older sons or daughters—they had the freedom to make

Exhibit 1   Selected Financials: Sales, Net Income, and Headcount, 1976–1994

	1976	1977	1978	1979	1980	1981	1982	1983	1984
Sales ($M)	0.003	0.311	0.80	0.77	3.83	7.08	18.1	28.3	51.6
Net income ($M)	N/A	N/A	N/A	N/A	N/A	N/A	N/A	1.4	0.4
Employees	11	12	18	46	104	175	306	592	1,130

decisions in the intense, chaotic, yet laissez-faire organization. Besides his constant flow of new ideas, Shih's guidance came mainly in the form of the slogans, stories, and concepts he constantly communicated.

This philosophy of delegation extended to organizational units, which, to the extent possible, Shih forced to operate as independent entities and to compete with outside companies. Extending the model externally, Shih began experimenting with joint ventures as a way of expanding sales. The first such arrangement was struck with a couple of entrepreneurs in central and southern Taiwan. While capturing the partners' knowledge of those regional markets, this approach allowed Multitech to expand its sales without the risk of hiring more people or raising more capital.

Early successes through employee ownership, delegated accountability, management frugality, and joint ventures led to what Shih called a "commoner's culture." This reflected his belief that the way to succeed against wealthy multinationals— "the nobility"—was to join forces with other "commoners"—mass-market customers, local distributors, owner-employees, small investors and supplier-partners, for example. The "poor man's" values supported this culture and guided early expansion. As early as 1978, Shih targeted smaller neighboring markets that were of lesser interest to the global giants. At first, response to Multitech's promotional letters was poor since few foreign distributors believed that a Taiwanese company could supply quality hi-tech products. Through persistence, however, Multitech established partnerships with dealers and distributors in Indonesia, Malaysia, Singapore, and Thailand. Shih described this early expansion strategy:

It is like the strategy in the Japanese game Go—one plays from the corner, because you need fewer resources to occupy the corner. Without the kind of resources that Japanese and American companies had, we started in smaller markets. That gives us the advantage because these smaller markets are becoming bigger and bigger and the combination of many small markets is not small.

Expansion abroad—primarily through Asia, Middle East and Latin America—was greatly helped by a growing number of new products. In 1981, Multitech introduced its first mainstream commercial product, the "Microprofessor" computer. Following the success of this inexpensive, simple computer (little more than an elaborate scientific calculator), Shih and his colleagues began to recognize the enormous potential of the developing PC market. In 1983, Multitech began to manufacture IBM-compatible PCs—primarily as an original equipment manufacturer (OEM) for major brands but also under its own Multitech brand. In 1984 sales reached $51 million, representing a sevenfold increase on revenues three years earlier.

By 1986, the company felt it was ready to stake a claim in Europe, establishing a marketing office in Dusseldorf and a warehouse in Amsterdam. Multitech also supplemented the commission-based purchasing unit it had previously opened in the United States with a fully-fledged sales office.

Birth of the Dragon Dream   By the mid-1980s, Multitech's sales were doubling each year and confidence was high. As the company approached its tenth anniversary, Shih announced a plan for the next ten years that he described as "Dragon Dreams." With expected 1986 revenues of $150 million, employees and outsiders alike gasped at his projected sales of $5 billion by 1996. Critics soon began quoting the old Chinese aphorism, "To allay

1985	1986	1987	1988	1989	1990	1991	1992	1993	1994
94.8	165.3	331.2	530.9	688.9	949.5	985.2	1,259.8	1,883	3,220
5.1	3.9	15.3	26.5	5.8	(0.7)	(26.0)	(2.8)	85.6	205
1,632	2,188	3,639	5,072	5,540	5,711	5,216	5,352	7,200	5,825

your hunger, draw a picture of a big cake." But Shih saw huge potential in overseas expansion. After only a few years of international experience, the company's overseas sales already accounted for half the total. In several Asian countries Multitech was already a major player: in Singapore, for example, it had a 25% market share by 1986. To build on this Asian base and the new offices in Europe and the United States, Shih created the slogan, "The Rampaging Dragon Goes International." To implement the initiative, he emphasized the need to identify potential overseas acquisitions, set up offshore companies, and seek foreign partners and distributors.

When the number of Acer employees exceeded 2000 during the tenth year anniversary, Shih held a "Renewal of Company Culture Seminar" at which he invited his board and vice presidents to identify and evaluate the philosophies that had guided Multitech in its first ten years. Middle-level managers were then asked to participate in the process, reviewing, debating, and eventually voting on the key principles that would carry the company forward. The outcome was a statement of four values that captured the essence of their shared beliefs: an assumption that human nature is essentially good; a commitment to maintaining a fundamental pragmatism and accountability in all business affairs; a belief in placing the customer first; and a norm of pooling effort and sharing knowledge. (A decade later, these principles could still be found on office walls worldwide.)

Finally, the anniversary year was capped by another major achievement: Acer became the second company in the world to develop and launch a 32-bit PC, even beating IBM to market. Not only did the product win Taiwan's Outstanding Product Design Award—Acer's fifth such award in seven years—it also attracted the attention of such major

overseas high-tech companies as Unisys, ICL and ITT, who began negotiations for OEM supply, and even technology licensing agreements.

Rebirth as Acer: Going Public Unfortunately, Multitech's growing visibility also led to a major problem. A U.S. company with the registered name "Multitech" informed its Taiwanese namesake that they were infringing its trademark. After ten years of building a corporate reputation and brand identity, Shih conceded he had to start over. He chose the name "Acer" because its Latin root meant "sharp" or "clever", because "Ace" implied first or highest value in cards—but mostly because it would be first in alphabetical listings. Despite advice to focus on the profitable OEM business and avoid the huge costs of creating a new global brand, Shih was determined to make Acer a globally recognized name.

Beyond branding, the success of the 32-bit PC convinced Shih that Acer would also have to maintain its rapid design, development and manufacturing capability as a continuing source of competitive advantage. Together with the planned aggressive international expansion, these new strategic imperatives—to build a brand and maintain its technological edge—created investment needs that exceeded Acer's internal financing capability. When officials from Taiwan's Securities and Exchange Commission approached Shih about a public offering, he agreed to study the possibility although he knew that many Taiwanese were suspicious of private companies that went public.

A program that allowed any employee with one year of company service to purchase shares had already diluted the Shihs' original 50% equity to about 35%, but in 1987 they felt it may be time to go further. (Shih had long preached that it was "better to lose control but make money" and that "real control came through ensuring common interest.") An internal committee asked to study the issue of going public concluded that the company would not only raise needed funds for expansion but also would provide a market for employee-owned shares. In 1988, Acer negotiated a complex multi-tiered financing involving investments by companies (such as Prudential, Chase Manhattan, China Development Corporation, and Sumitomo), additional sales to employees and, finally, a public offering. In total, Acer raised NT $2.2 billion (US $88 million). Issued at NT $27.5, the stock opened trading at NT $47 and soon rose to well over NT $100. After the IPO, Acer employees held about 65% of the equity including the Shihs' share, which had fallen to less than 25%.

The Professionalization of Acer

While the public offering had taken care of Acer's capital shortage, Shih worried about the company's acute shortage of management caused by its rapid growth. In early 1985, when the number of employees first exceeded 1,000, he began to look outside for new recruits "to take charge and stir things up with new ideas." Over the next few years, he brought in about a dozen top-level executives and 100 middle managers. To many of the self-styled "ground troops" (the old-timers), these "paratroopers" were intruders who didn't understand Acer's culture or values but were attracted by the soaring stock. For the first time, Acer experienced significant turnover.

Paratroopers and Price Pressures Because internally-grown managers lacked international experience, one of the key tasks assigned to the "paratroopers" was to implement the company's ambitious offshore expansion plans. In late 1987, Acer acquired Counterpoint, the U.S.-based manufacturer of low-end minicomputers—a business with significantly higher margins than PCs. To support this new business entry, Acer then acquired and expanded the operations of Service Intelligence, a computer service and support organization.

Subsequently, a dramatic decline in the market for minicomputers led to Acer's first new product for this segment, the Concer, being a dismal disappointment. Worse still, the substantial infrastructure installed to support it began generating huge losses.

Meanwhile, the competitive dynamics in the PC market were changing. In the closing years of the 1980s, Packard Bell made department and discount stores into major computer retailers, while Dell established its direct sales model. Both moves led to dramatic PC price reductions, and Acer's historic gross margin of about 35% began eroding rapidly, eventually dropping ten percentage points. Yet despite these problems, spirits were high in Acer, and in mid-1989 the company shipped its one millionth PC. Flush with new capital, the company purchased properties and companies within Taiwan worth $150 million. However, Acer's drift from its "commoner's culture" worried Shih, who felt he needed help to restore discipline to the "rampaging dragon." The ambition to grow had to be reconciled with the reality of Acer's financial situation.

Enter Leonard Liu   Projected 1989 results indicated that the overextended company was in a tailspin. Earnings per share were expected to fall from NT $ 5 to NT $ 1.42. The share price, which had been as high as NT $150, fell to under NT $20. (See **Exhibit 2.**) Concerned by the growing problems, Shih decided to bring in an experienced top-level executive. After more than a year of courting, in late 1989, he signed Leonard Liu, Taiwan-born, U.S.-based, senior IBM executive with a reputation for a no-nonsense professional management style. In an announcement that caught many by surprise, Shih stepped down as president of the Acer Group, handing over that day-to-day management role to Liu. In addition, Liu was named CEO and Chairman of AAC, the company's North American subsidiary.

Given Shih's desire to generate $5 billion in sales by 1996, Liu began to focus on opportunities in the networking market in the United States. Despite the continuing problems at Counterpoint

Exhibit 2   Acer Share Price History, November 1988-January 1995

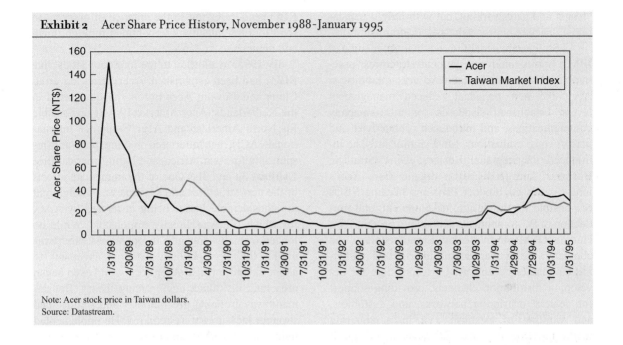

Note: Acer stock price in Taiwan dollars.
Source: Datastream.

and Service Intelligence, he agreed with those who argued that Acer could exploit this market by building on its position in high-end products, particularly in the advanced markets of the United States and Europe. In particular, Liu became interested in the highly regarded multi-user minicomputer specialist, Altos. Founded in 1977, this Silicon Valley networking company had 700 employees, worldwide distribution in 60 countries, and projected sales of $170 million for 1990. Although it had generated losses of $3 million and $5 million in the previous two years, Liu felt that Altos's $30 million in cash reserves and $20 million in real estate made it an attractive acquisition. In August 1990, Acer paid $94 million to acquire the respected Altos brand, its technology and its distribution network.[1] Almost immediately, how-

ever, powerful new PCs began to offer an alternative means of multi-user networking, and, as if to remind management of the eclipse of Counterpoint's minicomputers, within a year of its purchase, Altos was losing $20 million. Through the 1990s, AAC's losses increased.

In addition to this strategic thrust, Liu also began working on Acer's established organization and management approaches. For example, under Shih's leadership, while managers had been given considerable independence to oversee their business units, they had not been given profit and loss responsibility. Furthermore, because of the family-style relationship that existed among long-time company members, inter-company transfers were often priced to do friends a favor and ensure that a buyer did not "lose face" on a transaction. Even outsourced products were often bought at prices negotiated to make long-term suppliers look good. With no accountability for the profits of their business units, managers had little incentive to ensure quality or price, and would let the group absorb the loss. As one Acer observer noted, the company was

[1]Because this was a much larger deal than either Counterpoint (acquired for $1 million plus a stock swap) or Service Intelligence (a $500,000 transaction), Shih suggested the deal be structured as a joint venture to maintain the Altos managers' stake in the business. However, Liu insisted on an outright acquisition to ensure control, and Shih deferred to his new president's judgment.

"frugal and hard-working, but with little organizational structure or procedure-based administration."

As Shih had hoped, Liu brought to Acer some of IBM's professional management structures, practices and systems. To increase accountability at Acer, the new president reduced management layers, established standards for intra-company communications, and introduced productivity and performance evaluations. Most significantly, he introduced the Regional Business Unit/ Strategic Business Unit (RBU/SBU) organization. Acer's long-established product divisions became SBUs responsible for the design, development, and production of PC components and system products, including OEM product sales. Simultaneously, the company's major overseas subsidiaries and marketing companies became RBUs responsible for developing distribution channels, providing support for dealers, distributor networks, and customers, and working to establish JVs in neighboring markets. All SBUs and RBUs had full profit responsibility. "The pressure definitely increased. I was eating fourteen rice boxes a week," said one

RBU head, referring to the practice of ordering in food to allow meetings to continue through lunch and dinner.

By 1992, in addition to the four core SBUs, five RBUs had been established: Acer Sertek covering China and Taiwan; Acer Europe headquartered in the Netherlands; Acer America (AAC) responsible for North America; and Acer Computer International (ACI), headquartered in Singapore and responsible for Asia, Africa, and Latin America. (See **Exhibits 3a** and **3b.**) One of the immediate effects of the new structures and systems was to highlight the considerable losses being generated by AAC, for which Liu was directly responsible. While no longer formally engaged in operations, Shih was urging the free-spending Altos management to adopt the more frugal Acer norms, and even began preaching his "duck egg" pricing theory. But demand was dropping precipitously and Liu decided stronger measures were required. He implemented tight controls and began layoffs.

Meanwhile, the company's overall profitability was plummeting. (See **Exhibits 4** and **5.**) A year

Exhibit 3a   The Acer Group in 1994

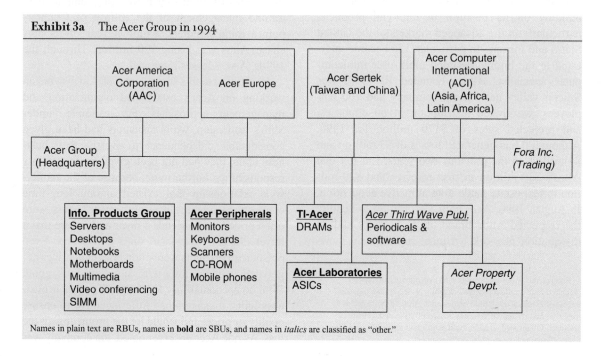

Names in plain text are RBUs, names in **bold** are SBUs, and names in *italics* are classified as "other."

Exhibit 3b   Acer's Geographical Distribution in 1994

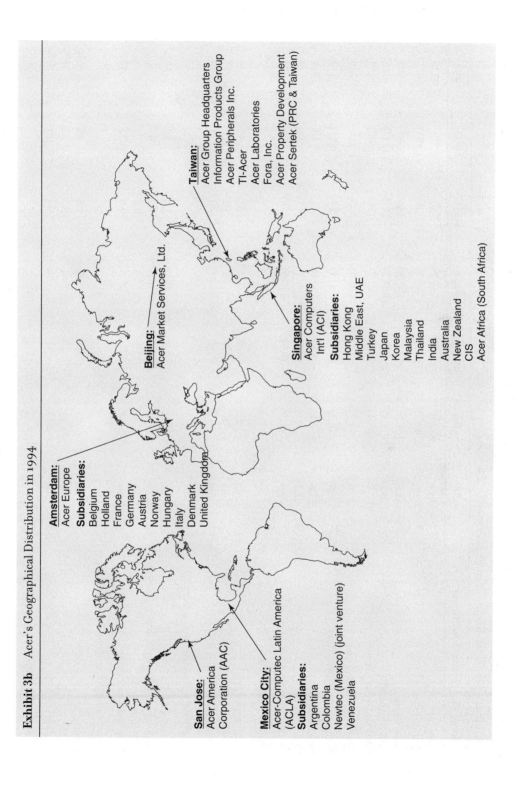

Amsterdam:
Acer Europe
Subsidiaries:
Belgium
Holland
France
Germany
Austria
Norway
Hungary
Italy
Denmark
United Kingdom

Beijing:
Acer Market Services, Ltd.

Taiwan:
Acer Group Headquarters
Information Products Group
Acer Peripherals Inc.
TI-Acer
Acer Laboratories
Fora, Inc.
Acer Property Development
Acer Sertek (PRC & Taiwan)

Singapore:
Acer Computers
Int'l (ACI)
Subsidiaries:
Hong Kong
Middle East, UAE
Turkey
Japan
Korea
Malaysia
Thailand
India
Australia
New Zealand
CIS
Acer Africa (South Africa)

San Jose:
Acer America
Corporation (AAC)

Mexico City:
Acer-Computec Latin America
(ACLA)
Subsidiaries:
Argentina
Colombia
Newtec (Mexico) (joint venture)
Venezuela

Exhibit 4 Acer Combination Income Statement, 1988–1994

Income Statement ($ millions)	1988	1989	1990	1991	1992	1993	1994
Turnover	530.9	688.9	949.5	985.2	1,260	1,883	3,220
Cost of sales	(389.4)	(532.7)	(716.7)	(737.7)	(1,000)	(1,498)	(2,615)
Gross Profit	141.6	156.3	232.8	247.5	260	385	605
SG&A expenses	(88.2)	(118.2)	(192.2)	(217.2)	(217)	(237)	(316)
R&D and other expenses	(17.9)	(25.4)	(47.7)	(42.3)	(38)	(48)	(59)
Operating Profit/(Loss)	35.6	12.7	(7.1)	(12.0)	5	100	230
Non-operating profit/(loss)	(8)	(6.3)	(1.5)	(15)	(4)	(11)	(19)
Profit Before Tax	27.6	6.4	(8.6)	(27.0)	1	89	212
Tax	(1.2)	(1)	(1.2)	1	(3)	(3)	(7)
Profit (Loss) After Tax	26.4	5.4	(9.8)	(26.0)	(3)	86	205
Sales by Region (%)							
North America	na	31	31	31	38	44	39
Europe	na	32	28	28	22	23	17
Rest of world	na	37	41	41	40	33	44
Combination Revenue by Product (%)							
Portables	na	na	3.2	2.9	7.9	18	60%
Desktops and motherboards	na	na	60.9	56.3	54.9	47	
Minicomputers	na	na	13.9	11.3	6.6		
Peripherals and other	na	na	22	29.5	30.6	35	40%
Combination Revenue by Business (%)							
Brand	na	53	47	na	58	68	56%
OEM	na	34	22	na	18	32	36%
Trading	na	13	31	na	24	na	7%

Source: Company Annual Reports, year ending December 31

Exhibit 5   Consolidated Balance Sheet, 1988–1994

Acer Group Balance Sheet ($ millions)	1988	1989	1990	1991	1992	1993	1994
Current Assets	277.30	448.80	579.50	600.90	700.20	925.00	1355.00
Fixed Assets							
Land, plant, and equipment (after depreciation)	53.10	126.90	191.10	161.50	179.60	590.00	645.00
Deferred charges and other assets	11.50	22.90	60.90	239.50	212.30	69.00	82.00
Total Assets	341.90	598.60	831.50	1001.90	1092.10	1584.00	2082.00
Total current liabilities	189.40	248.60	464.60	505.80	504.20	752.00	1067.00
Long-term liabilities	11.20	16.60	43.70	168.50	214.30	342.00	312.00
Total Liabilities	200.60	265.20	508.40	674.30	718.50	1094.00	1379.00
Stockholders Equity and Minority Interest (including new capital infusions)	141.30	333.40	323.10	327.60	373.60	490.00	703.00

Source: Company documents.

earlier, Shih had introduced an austerity campaign that had focused on turning lights off, using both sides of paper, and traveling economy class. By 1990, however, Liu felt sterner measures were called for, particularly to deal with a payroll that had ballooned to 5,700 employees. Under an initiative dubbed Metamorphosis, managers were asked to rank employee performance, identifying the top 15% and lowest 30%. In January 1991, 300 of the Taiwan-based "thirty percenters" were terminated— Acer's first major layoffs.

The cumulative effect of declining profits, layoffs, more "paratroopers," and particularly the new iron-fisted management style challenged Acer's traditional culture. In contrast to Shih's supportive, family-oriented approach, Liu's "by-the-numbers" management model proved grating. There was also growing resentment of his tendency to spend lavishly on top accounting and law firms and hire people who stayed at first-class hotels, all of which seemed out of step with Acer's "commoner's culture." Soon, his credibility as a highly respected world-class executive was eroding and Acer man-

agers began questioning his judgement and implementing his directives half-heartedly.

In January 1992, when Shih realized that Acer's 1991 results would be disastrous, he offered his resignation. The board unanimously rejected the offer, suggesting instead that he resume his old role as CEO. In May 1992, Leonard Liu resigned.

Rebuilding the Base

Shih had long regarded mistakes and their resulting losses as "tuition" for Acer employees' growth—the price paid for a system based on delegation. He saw the losses generated in the early 1990s as part of his personal learning, considering it an investment rather than a waste. ("To make Acer an organization that can think and learn," he said, "we must continue to pay tuition as long as mistakes are unintentional and long-term profits exceed the cost of the education.") As he reclaimed the CEO role, Shih saw the need to fundamentally rethink Acer's management philosophy, the organizational model that reflected it, and even the underlying basic business concept.

"Global Brand, Local Touch" Philosophy   At Acer's 1992 International Distributors Meeting in Cancun, Mexico, Shih articulated a commitment to linking the company more closely to its national markets, describing his vision as "Global Brand, Local Touch." Under this vision, he wanted Acer to evolve from a Taiwanese company with offshore sales to a truly global organization with deeply-planted local roots.

Building on the company's long tradition of taking minority positions in expansionary ventures, Shih began to offer established Acer distributors equity partnerships in the RBU they served. Four months after the Cancun meeting, Acer acquired a 19% interest in Computec, its Mexican distributor. Because of its role in building Acer into Mexico's leading PC brand, Shih invited Computec to form a joint venture company responsible for all Latin America. The result was Acer Computec Latin America (ACLA), a company subsequently floated on the Mexican stock exchange. Similarly, Acer Computers International (ACI), the company responsible for sales in Southeast Asia planned an initial public offering in Singapore in mid-1995. And in Taiwan, Shih was even considering taking some of Acer's core SBUs public.

As these events unfolded, Shih began to articulate an objective of "21 in 21," a vision of the Acer Group as a federation of 21 public companies, each with significant local ownership, by the 21st century. It was what he described as "the fourth way," a strategy of globalization radically different from the control-based European, American or Japanese models, relying instead on mutual interest and voluntary cooperation of a network of interdependent companies.

Client Server Organization Model   To reinforce the more networked approach of this new management philosophy, in 1993, Shih unveiled his client-server organization model. Using the metaphor of the network computer, he described the role of the Taiwan headquarters as a "server" that used its resources (finance, people, intellectual property) to support "client" business units, which controlled key operating activities. Under this concept of a company as a network, business units could leverage their own ideas or initiatives directly through other RBUs or SBUs without having to go through the corporate center which was there to help and mediate, not dictate or control. Shih believed that this model would allow Acer to develop speed and flexibility as competitive weapons.

While the concept was intriguing, it was a long way from Acer's operating reality. Despite the long-established philosophy of decentralization and the introduction of independent profit-responsible business units in 1992, even the largest RBUs were still viewed as little more than the sales and distribution arms of the Taiwan-based SBUs. To operationalize the client server concept, Shih began to emphasize several key principles. "Every man is lord of his castle," became his battle cry to confirm the independence of SBU and RBU heads. Thus, when two SBUs—Acer Peripherals (API) and Information Products (IPG)—both decided to produce CD-ROM drives, Shih did not intervene to provide a top-down decision, opting instead to let the market decide. The result was that both units succeeded, eventually supplying CD-ROMs to almost 70% of PCs made in Taiwan, by far the world's leading source of OEM and branded PCs.

In another initiative, Shih began urging that at least half of all Acer products and components be sold outside the Group, hoping to ensure internal sources were competitive. Then, introducing the principle, "If it doesn't hurt, help," he spread a doctrine that favored internal suppliers. However, under the "lord of the castle" principle, if an RBU decided to improve its bottom line by sourcing externally, it could do so. But it was equally clear that the affected SBU could then find an alternative distributor for its output in that RBU's region. In practice, this mutual deterrence—referred to as the "nuclear option"—was recognized as a strategy of last resort that was rarely exercised. Despite Shih's communication of these new operating principles, the roles and relationships between SBU and RBUs remained in flux over several years as managers worked to understand the full implications of the client server model on their day-to-day responsibilities.

The Fast Food Business Concept   But the biggest challenges Shih faced on his return were strategic. Even during the two and a half years he had stepped back to allow Liu to lead Acer, competition in the PC business had escalated significantly, with the product cycle shortening to 6 to 9 months and prices dropping. As if to highlight this new reality, in May 1992, the month Liu left, Compaq announced a 30% across-the-board price reduction on its PCs. Industry expectations were for a major shakeout of marginal players. Given Acer's financial plight, some insiders urged the chairman to focus on OEM sales only, while others suggested a retreat from the difficult U.S. market. But Shih believed that crisis was a normal condition in business and that persistence usually paid off. His immediate priority was to halve Acer's five months of inventory—two months being inventory "in transit."

Under Shih's stimulus, various parts of the organization began to create new back-to-basics initiatives. For example, the System PC unit developed the "ChipUp" concept. This patented technology allowed a motherboard to accept different types of CPU chips—various versions of Intel's 386 and 486 chips, for example—drastically reducing inventory of both chips and motherboards. Another unit, Home Office Automation, developed the "2-3-1 System" to reduce the new product introduction process to two months for development, three months for selling and one month for phase-out. And about the same time, a cross-unit initiative to support the launch of Acer's home PC, Acros, developed a screwless assembly process, allowing an entire computer to be assembled by snapping together components, motherboard, power source, etc.[2] Integrating all these initiatives and several

others, a team of engineers developed Uniload, a production concept that configured components in a standard parts palette for easy unpacking, assembly, and testing, facilitating the transfer of final assembly to RBU operations abroad. The underlying objective was to increase flexibility and responsiveness by moving more assembly offshore.

Uniload's ability to assemble products close to the customer led the CEO to articulate what he termed his "fast-food" business model. Under this approach, small, expensive components with fast-changing technology that represented 50%–80% of total cost (e.g., motherboards, CPUs, hard disc drives) were airshipped "hot and fresh" from SBU sources in Taiwan to RBUs in key markets, while less-volatile items (e.g., casings, monitors, power supplies) were shipped by sea. Savings in logistics, inventories and import duties on assembled products easily offset higher local labor assembly cost, which typically represented less than 1% of product cost.

As Shih began promoting his fast-food business concept, he met with some internal opposition, particularly from SBUs concerned that giving up systems assembly would mean losing power and control. To convince them that they could increase competitiveness more by focusing on component development, he created a presentation on the value added elements in the PC industry. "Assembly means you are making money from manual labor," he said. "In components and marketing you add value with your brains." To illustrate the point, Shih developed a disintegrated value added chart that was soon dubbed "Stan's Smiling Curve." (See **Exhibit 6**.)

The Turnaround   Describing his role as "to provide innovative stimulus, to recognize the new strategy which first emerges in vague ideas, then to communicate it, form consensus, and agree on action," Shih traveled constantly for two years, taking his message to the organization. Through 1993, the impact of the changes began to appear. Most dramatically, the fast-food business concept

---

[2]To promote the innovative idea, Shih sponsored internal contests to see who could assemble a computer the fastest. Whereas his personal best time was more than a minute, experts accomplished the task in 30 seconds.

Exhibit 6   Stan Shih's PC Industry Conceptualization

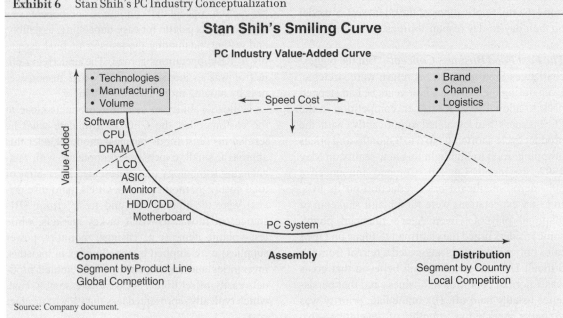

Source: Company document.

(supported by Liu's systems) caused inventory turnover to double by late 1993, reducing carrying costs while lowering the obsolescence risk. In early 1994, the Group reported a return to profit after three years of losses.

Acer America and the Aspire

After Liu's resignation in April 1992, Shih named Ronald Chwang to head AAC. With a Ph.D. in Electrical Engineering, Chwang joined Acer in 1986 in technical development. After overseeing the start-up of Acer's peripherals business, in 1991 he was given the responsibility for integrating the newly acquired Altos into AAC as president of the Acer/Altos Business Unit.

Because AAC had been losing money since 1987, Chwang's first actions as CEO focused on stemming further losses. As part of that effort, he embraced the dramatic changes being initiated in Taiwan, making AAC's Palo Alto plant the first test

assembly site of the Uniload system. Under the new system, manufacture and delivery time was cut from 80 days to 45 days, reducing inventory levels by almost 45%. To support its Uniload site, AAC established a department of approximately 20 engineers, primarily to manage component testing, but also to adapt software design to local market needs. By 1994, AAC was breaking even. (See **Exhibit 7.**)

Birth of Aspire   Despite these improvements, AAC and other RBUs still felt that Acer's Taiwan-based SBUs were too distant to develop product configurations that would appeal to diverse consumer and competitive situations around the globe. What might sell well in Southeast Asia could be a year out of date in the United States, for example. However, the emerging "global brand, local touch" philosophy and the client server organization model supporting it gave them hope that they could change the situation.

Exhibit 7   AAC Selected Financials (1990–1994)

AAC Results ($millions)	1990	1991	1992	1993	1994
Revenue	161	235	304	434	858
Cost of sales	133	190	283	399	764
Selling and marketing	27	61	25	23	55
General administration	20	16	17	19	20
Research and development	5	8	6	4	4
Operating profit/(loss)	(24)	(40)	(26)	(11)	15
Non-operating profit/(loss)	(1)	(7)	(3)	(5)	(3)
Profit/(loss) before tax	(25)	(47)	(29)	(16)	12
Tax	1	(2)	0	0	1
Net income/(loss)	(26)	(45)	(29)	(16)	11
Current assets	155	153	123	144	242
Fixed assets (net)	39	43	28	25	25
Other assets (net)	37	37	31	19	11
Total Assets	231	233	182	188	278
Current liabilities	155	169	154	136	218
Long-term debt	17	15	18	58	47
Stockholder equity (including additional capita)	58	50	10	(6)	12
Total Liabilities	231	233	182	188	278

Source: Company documents.
Note: Totals may not add due to rounding.

In January 1994, Mike Culver was promoted to become AAC's Director of Product Management, a role that gave him responsibility for the product development mandate he felt RBUs could assume under the new client-server model. The 29-year-old engineer and recent MBA graduate had joined Acer America just 2½ years earlier as AAC's product manager for notebook computers. Recently, however, he had become aware of new opportunities in home computing.

Several factors caught Culver's attention. First, data showed an increasing trend to working at home—from 26 million people in 1993 to a projected 29 million in 1994. In addition, there was a rapidly growing interest in the Internet. And finally, developments in audio, telecom, video, and computing technologies were leading to industry rumblings of a new kind of multimedia home PC. Indeed, rumor

had it that competitors like Hewlett Packard were already racing to develop new multimedia systems. Sharing this vision, Culver believed the time was right to create "the first Wintel-based PC that could compete with Apple in design, ease-of-use, and multimedia capabilities."

In October of 1994, Culver commissioned a series of focus groups to explore the emerging opportunity. In one of the groups, a consumer made a comment that had a profound impact on him. She said she wanted a computer that wouldn't remind her of work. At that moment, Culver decided that Acer's new home PC would incorporate radically new design aesthetics to differentiate it from the standard putty-colored, boxy PCs that sat in offices throughout the world.

By November, Culver was convinced of the potential for an innovative multimedia consumer PC, and began assembling a project team to develop the concept. While the team believed the Acer Group probably had the engineering capability to develop the product's new technical features, they were equally sure they would have to go outside to get the kind of innovative design they envisioned. After an exhaustive review, the team selected Frog Design, a leading Silicon Valley design firm that had a reputation for "thinking outside of the box." Up to this point, Culver had been using internal resources and operating within his normal budget. The selection of Frog Design, however, meant that he had to go to Chwang for additional support. "The approval was incredibly informal," related Culver, "it literally took place in one 20 minute discussion in the hallway in late November. I told Ronald we would need $200,000 for outside consulting to create the cosmetic prototype." Chwang agreed on the spot, and the design process began.

In 1994, Acer was in ninth place in the U.S. market, with 2.4% market share, largely from sales of the Acros, Acer's initial PC product, which was an adaptation of its commercial product, the Acer Power. (See **Exhibit 8** for 1994 market shares.) Culver and Chwang were convinced they could not only substantially improve Acer's U.S. share, but also create a product with potential to take a larger share of the global multimedia desktop market estimated at 10.4 million units and growing at more than 20% annually, primarily in Europe and Asia.

Working jointly with designers from Frog Design, the project team talked to consumers, visited computer retail stores and held discussions to brainstorm the new product's form. After almost two months, Frog Design developed six foam models of possible designs. In January 1995, the Acer team chose a striking and sleek profile that bore little resemblance to the traditional PC. Market research also indicated that customers wanted a choice of colors, so the team decided that the newly named Aspire PC would be offered in charcoal grey and emerald green. (See **Exhibit 9.**)

Meanwhile, the team had been working with AAC software engineers and a development group in Taiwan to incorporate the new multimedia capabilities into the computer. One significant introduction was voice-recognition software that

Exhibit 8   Top Ten PC Manufacturers in the United States and Worldwide in 1994

Company	U.S. Market Share	Worldwide Market Share
Compaq	12.6%	9.8%
Apple	11.5%	8.1%
Packard Bell	11.4%	5.1%
IBM	9.0%	8.5%
Gateway 2000	5.2%	2.3%
Dell	4.2%	2.6%
AST	3.9%	2.7%
Toshiba	3.6%	2.4%
Acer	2.4%	2.6%
Hewlett-Packard	2.4%	2.5%

Source: *Los Angeles Times,* January 31, 1996.

Exhibit 9   First-Generation Aspire Prototype Design

enabled users to open, close, and save documents by voice commands. However, such enhancements also required new hardware design: to accommodate the voice-recognition feature, for example, a microphone had to be built in, and to properly exploit the machine's enhanced audio capabilities, speakers had to be integrated into the monitor. The multimedia concept also required the integration of CD-ROM capabilities, and a built-in modem and answering machine incorporating fax and telephone capabilities. This type of configuration was a radical innovation for Acer, requiring significant design and tooling changes.

In early 1995 the price differential between upper-tier PCs (IBM, for example) and lower-end products (represented by Packard Bell) was about 20%. Culver's team felt the Aspire could be positioned between these two segments offering a high quality innovative product at a less-than-premium price. They felt they could gain a strong foothold by offering a product range priced from $1,199 for the basic product to $2,999 for the highest-end system with monitor. With a September launch, they budgeted US sales of $570 million and profits of $17 million for 1995. A global rollout would be even more attractive with an expectation of breakeven within the first few months.

Stan Shih's Decisions

On his way to San Jose in February 1995, Stan Shih pondered the significance of the Aspire project. Clearly, it represented the client-server system at work: this could become the first product designed and developed by an RBU, in response to a locally sensed market opportunity. Beyond that, he had the feeling it might have the potential to become Acer's first global blockbuster product.

Despite its promise, however, Shih wanted to listen to the views of the project's critics. Some pointed out that AAC had just begun to generate profits in the first quarter of 1994, largely on the basis of its solid OEM sales, which accounted for almost 50% of revenues. Given its delicate profit position, they argued that AAC should not be staking its future on the extremely expensive and highly competitive branded consumer products business. Established competitors were likely to launch their own multimedia home PCs—perhaps even before Acer. Building a new brand in this crowded, competitive market was extremely difficult as proven by many failed attempts, including the costly failure of Taiwan-based Mitac, launched as a branded PC in the early 1990s.

Even among those who saw potential in the product, there were several who expressed concern about the project's implementation. With all the company's engineering and production expertise located in Taiwan, these critics argued that the task of coordinating the development and delivery of such an innovative new product was just too risky to leave to an inexperienced group in an RBU with limited development resources. If the project were to be approved, they suggested it be transferred back to the SBUs in Taiwan for implementation.

Finally, some wondered whether Acer's client-server organization model and "local touch" management would support Aspire becoming a viable global product. With the growing independence of the RBUs worldwide, they were concerned that each one would want to redesign the product and marketing strategy for its local market, thereby negating any potential scale economies.

As his plane touched down in San Francisco, Shih tried to resolve his feelings of excitement and concern. Should he support the Aspire project, change it, or put it on hold? And what implications would his decisions have for the new corporate model he had been building?

Reading 1-1   The Tortuous Evolution of the Multinational Corporation

Howard V. Perlmutter

Four senior executives of the world's largest firms with extensive holdings outside the home country speak:

Company A: "We are a multinational firm. We distribute our products in about 100 countries. We manufacture in over 17 countries and do research and development in three countries. We look at all new investment projects—both domestic and overseas—using exactly the same criteria."

Company B: "We are a multinational firm. Only 1% of the personnel in our affiliate companies are non-nationals. Most of these are U.S. executives on temporary assignments. In all major markets, the affiliate's managing director is of the local nationality."

Company C: "We are a multinational firm. Our product division executives have worldwide profit responsibility. As our organizational chart shows, the United States is just one region on a par with Europe, Latin America, Africa, etc., in each product division."

Company D (non-American): "We are a multinational firm. We have at least 18 nationalities represented at our headquarters. Most senior executives speak at least two languages. About 30% of our staff at headquarters are foreigners."

While a claim to multinationality based on their years of experience and the significant proportion of sales generated overseas is justified in each of

these four companies, a more penetrating analysis changes the image.

The executive from Company A tells us that most of the key posts in Company A's subsidiaries are held by home-country nationals. Whenever replacements for these men are sought, it is the practice, if not the policy, to "look next to you at the head office" and "pick someone (usually a home-country national) you know and trust."

The executive from Company B does not hide the fact that there are very few non-Americans in the key posts at headquarters. The few who are there are "so Americanized" that their foreign nationality literally has no meaning. His explanation for this paucity of non-Americans seems reasonable enough: "You can't find good foreigners who are willing to live in the United States, where our headquarters is located. American executives are more mobile. In addition, Americans have the drive and initiative we like. In fact, the European nationals would prefer to report to an American rather than to some other European."

The executive from Company C goes on to explain that the worldwide product division concept is rather difficult to implement. The senior executives in charge of these divisions have little overseas experience. They have been promoted from domestic posts and tend to view foreign consumer needs "as really basically the same as ours." Also, product division executives tend to focus on the domestic market because the domestic market is larger and generates more revenue than the fragmented European markets. The rewards are for global performance, but the strategy is to focus on domestic. His colleagues say "one pays attention to what one understands—and our senior executives simply do not understand what happens overseas and really do not trust foreign executives in key positions here or overseas."

▌ Trained as an engineer and a psychologist, Howard V. Perlmutter spent eight years at M.I.T.'s Center for International Studies and five years at the Institut pour l'Etude des Methodes de Direction de l'Enterprise (IMEDE) in Lausanne, Switzerland. His main interests are in the theory and practice of institution building, particularly the international corporation. He has recently been appointed Director for Research and Development of Worldwide Institutions in association with the Management Science Center at the University of Pennsylvania, as well as a member of the faculty at the Wharton School.
▌ Used with permission of Howard V. Perlmutter.

The executive from the European Company D begins by explaining that since the voting shareholders must by law come from the home country, the home country's interest must be given careful consideration. In the final analysis he insists: "We are proud of our nationality; we shouldn't be ashamed of it." He cites examples of the previous reluctance of headquarters to use home-country ideas overseas, to their detriment, especially in their U.S. subsidiary. "Our country produces good executives, who tend to stay with us a long time. It is harder to keep executives from the United States."

A Rose by Any Other Name . . .

Why quibble about how multinational a firm is? To these executives, apparently being multinational is prestigious. They know that multinational firms tend to be regarded as more progressive, dynamic, geared to the future than provincial companies which avoid foreign frontiers and their attendant risks and opportunities.

It is natural that these senior executives would want to justify the multinationality of their enterprise, even if they use different yardsticks: ownership criteria, organizational structure, nationality of senior executives, percent of investment overseas, etc.

Two hypotheses seem to be forming in the minds of executives from international firms that make the extent of their firm's multinationality of real interest. The first hypothesis is that the degree of multinationality of an enterprise is positively related to the firm's long-term viability. The "multinational" category makes sense for executives if it means a quality of decision making which leads to survival, growth and profitability in our evolving world economy.

The second hypothesis stems from the proposition that the multinational corporation is a new kind of institution—a new type of industrial social architecture particularly suitable for the latter third of the twentieth century. This type of institution could make a valuable contribution to world order and conceivably exercise a constructive impact on the nation-state. Some executives want to understand how to create an institution whose presence is considered legitimate and valuable in each nation-state. They want to prove that the greater the degree of multinationality of a firm, the greater its total constructive impact will be on host and home nation-states as well as other institutions. Since multinational firms may produce a significant proportion of the world's GNP, both hypotheses justify a more precise analysis of the varieties and degrees of multinationality.[1] However, the confirming evidence is limited.

State of Mind

Part of the difficulty in defining the degree of multinationality comes from the variety of parameters along which a firm doing business overseas can be described. The examples from the four companies argue that (1) no single criterion of multinationality such as ownership or the number of nationals overseas is sufficient, and that (2) external and quantifiable measures such as the percentage of investment overseas or the distribution of equity by nationality are useful but not enough. The more one penetrates into the living reality of an international firm, the more one finds it is necessary to give serious weight to the way executives think about doing business around the world. The orientation toward "foreign people, ideas, resources," in headquarters and subsidiaries, and in host and home environments, becomes crucial in estimating the multinationality of a firm. To be sure, such external indices as the proportion of nationals in different countries holding equity and the number of foreign nationals who have reached top positions, including president, are good indices of multinationality. But one can still behave with a home-country orientation despite foreign shareholders, and one can have a few home-country nationals overseas but still pick those local executives who are home-country oriented or who are provincial and chauvinistic. The attitudes men hold are clearly more relevant than their passports.

Three primary attitudes among international executives toward building a multinational enterprise

---

[1] H. V. Perlmutter, "Super-Giant Firms in the Future," *Wharton Quarterly,* Winter 1968.

Table 1   Three Types of Headquarters Orientation toward Subsidiaries in an International Enterprise

Organization Design	Ethnocentric	Polycentric	Geocentric
Complexity of organization	Complex in home country, simple in subsidiaries	Varied and independent	Increasingly complex and interdependent
Authority; decision making	High in headquarters	Relatively low in headquarters	Aim for a collaborative approach between headquarters and subsidiaries
Evaluation and control	Home standards applied for persons and performance	Determined locally	Find standards which are universal and local
Rewards and punishments; incentives	High in headquarters, low in subsidiaries	Wide variation; can be high or low rewards for subsidiary performance	International and local executives rewarded for reaching local and worldwide objectives
Communication; information flow	High volume to subsidiaries; orders, commands, advice	Little to and from headquarters; little between subsidiaries	Both ways and between subsidiaries; heads of subsidiaries part of management team
Identification	Nationality of owner	Nationality of host country	Truly international company but identifying with national interests
Perpetuation (recruiting, staffing, development)	Recruit and develop people of home country for key positions everywhere in the world	Develop people of local nationality for key positions in their own country	Develop best men everywhere in the world for key positions everywhere in the world

are identifiable. These attitudes can be inferred from the assumptions upon which key product, functional and geographical decisions were made.

These states of mind or attitudes may be described as ethnocentric (or home-country oriented), polycentric (or host-country oriented) and geocentric (or world-oriented).[2] While they never appear in pure form, they are clearly distinguishable. There is some degree of ethnocentricity, polycentricity or geocentricity in all firms, but management's analysis does not usually correlate with public pronouncements about the firm's multinationality.

[2]H. V. Perlmutter, "Three Conceptions of a World Enterprise," *Revue Economique et Sociale,* May 1965.

Home-Country Attitudes

The ethnocentric attitude can be found in companies of any nationality with extensive overseas holdings. The attitude, revealed in executive actions and experienced by foreign subsidiary managers, is: "We, the home nationals of X company, are superior to, more trustworthy and more reliable than any foreigners in headquarters or subsidiaries. We will be willing to build facilities in your country if you acknowledge our inherent superiority and accept our methods and conditions for doing the job."

Of course, such attitudes are never so crudely expressed, but they often determine how a certain type of "multinational" firm is designed. Table 1 illustrates how ethnocentric attitudes are expressed in determining the managerial process at home and overseas. For example, the ethnocentric executive is more apt to say: "Let us manufacture the simple products overseas. Those foreign nationals are not yet ready or reliable. We should manufacture the complex products in our country and keep the secrets among our trusted home-country nationals."

In a firm where ethnocentric attitudes prevailed, the performance criteria for men and products are "home-made." "We have found that a salesman should make 12 calls per day in Hoboken, New Jersey (the headquarters location), and therefore we apply these criteria everywhere in the world. The salesman in Brazzaville is naturally lazy, unmotivated. He shows little drive because he makes only two calls per day (despite the Congolese salesman's explanation that it takes time to reach customers by boat)."

Ethnocentric attitudes are revealed in the communication process where "advice," "counsel," and directives flow from headquarters to the subsidiary in a steady stream, bearing this message: "This works at home; therefore, it must work in your country."

Executives in both headquarters and affiliates express the national identity of the firm by associating the company with the nationality of the headquarters: this is "a Swedish company," "a Swiss company," "an American company," depending on the location of headquarters. "You have to accept the fact that the only way to reach a senior post in our firm," an English executive in a U.S. firm said, "is to take out an American passport."

Crucial to the ethnocentric concept is the current policy that men of the home nationality are recruited and trained for key positions everywhere in the world. Foreigners feel like "second-class" citizens.

There is no international firm today whose executives will say that ethnocentrism is absent in their company. In the firms whose multinational investment began a decade ago, one is more likely to hear, "We are still in a transitional stage from our ethnocentric era. The traces are still around! But we are making progress."

Host-Country Orientation

Polycentric firms are those which, by experience or by the inclination of a top executive (usually one of the founders), begin with the assumption that host-country cultures are different and that foreigners are difficult to understand. Local people know what is best for them, and the part of the firm which is located in the host country should be as "local in identity" as possible. The senior executives at headquarters believe that their multinational enterprise can be held together by good financial controls. A polycentric firm, literally, is a loosely connected group with quasi-independent subsidiaries as centers—more akin to a confederation.

European multinational firms tend to follow this pattern, using a top local executive who is strong and trustworthy, of the "right" family and who has an intimate understanding of the workings of the host government. This policy seems to have worked until the advent of the Common Market.

Executives in the headquarters of such a company are apt to say: "Let the Romans do it their way. We really don't understand what is going on there, but we have to have confidence in them. As long as they earn a profit, we want to remain in the background." They assume that since people are different in each country, standards for performance, incentives and training methods must be different. Local environmental factors are given greater weight (see Table 1).

Many executives mistakenly equate polycentrism with multinationalism. This is evidenced in the legalistic definition of a multinational enterprise as a cluster of corporations of diverse nationality joined together by ties of common ownership. It is no accident that many senior executives in headquarters take pride in the absence of non-nationals in their subsidiaries, especially people from the head office. The implication is clearly that each subsidiary is a distinct national entity, since it is incorporated in a different sovereign state. Lonely senior executives in the subsidiaries of polycentric companies complain that: "The home office never tells us anything."

Polycentrism is not the ultimate form of multinationalism. It is a landmark on a highway. Polycentrism is encouraged by local marketing managers who contend that: "Headquarters will never understand us, our people, our consumer needs, our laws, our distribution, etc. . . ."

Headquarters takes pride in the fact that few outsiders know that the firm is foreign-owned. "We want to be a good local company. How many Americans know that Shell and Lever Brothers are foreign-owned?"

But the polycentric personnel policy is also revealed in the fact that no local manager can seriously aspire to a senior position at headquarters. "You know the French are so provincial; it is better to keep them in France. Uproot them and you are in trouble," a senior executive says to justify the paucity of non-Americans at headquarters.

One consequence (and perhaps cause) of polycentrism is a virulent ethnocentrism among the country managers.

A World-Oriented Concept

The third attitude which is beginning to emerge at an accelerating rate is geocentrism. Senior executives with this orientation do not equate superiority with nationality. Within legal and political limits, they seek the best men, regardless of nationality, to solve the company's problems anywhere in the world. The senior executives attempt to build an organization in which the subsidiary is not only a good citizen of the host nation but is a leading exporter from this nation in the international community and contributes such benefits as (1) an increasing supply of hard currency, (2) new skills and (3) a knowledge of advanced technology. Geocentrism is summed up in a Unilever board chairman's statement of objectives: "We want to Unileverize our Indians and Indianize our Unileverans."

The ultimate goal of geocentrism is a worldwide approach in both headquarters and subsidiaries. The firm's subsidiaries are thus neither satellites nor independent city states, but parts of a whole whose focus is on worldwide objectives as well as local objectives, each part making its unique contribution with its unique competence. Geocentrism is expressed by function, product and geography. The question asked in headquarters and the subsidiaries is: "Where in the world shall we raise money, build our plant, conduct R&D, get and launch new ideas to serve our present and future customers?"

This conception of geocentrism involves a collaborative effort between subsidiaries and headquarters to establish universal standards and permissible local variations, to make key allocational decisions on new products, new plants, new laboratories. The international management team includes the affiliate heads.

Subsidiary managers must ask: "Where in the world can I get the help to serve my customers best in this country?" "Where in the world can I export products developed in this country—products which meet worldwide standards as opposed to purely local standards?"

Geocentrism, furthermore, requires a reward system for subsidiary managers which motivates them to work for worldwide objectives, not just to defend country objectives. In firms where geocentrism prevails, it is not uncommon to hear a subsidiary manager say, "While I am paid to defend our interests in this country and to get the best resources for this affiliate, I must still ask myself the question 'Where in the world (instead of where in my country) should we build this plant?'" This approach is still rare today.

In contrast to the ethnocentric and polycentric patterns, communication is encouraged among subsidiaries in geocentric-oriented firms. "It is your duty to help us solve problems anywhere in the world," one chief executive continually reminds the heads of his company's affiliates. (See Table 1.)

The geocentric firm identifies with local company needs. "We aim not to be just a good local company but the best local company in terms of the quality of management and the worldwide (not local) standards we establish in domestic and export production." "If we were only as good as local companies, we would deserve to be nationalized."

The geocentric personnel policy is based on the belief that we should bring in the best man in the world regardless of his nationality. His passport should not be the criterion for promotion.

The EPG Profile

Executives can draw their firm's profile in ethnocentric (E), polycentric (P) and geocentric (G) dimensions. They are called EPG profiles. The degree of ethnocentrism, polycentrism and geocentrism by product, function and geography can be established. Typically R&D often turns out to be more geocentric (truth is universal, perhaps) and less ethnocentric than finance. Financial managers are likely to see their decisions as ethnocentric. The marketing function is more polycentric, particularly in the advanced economies and in the larger affiliate markets.

The tendency toward ethnocentrism in relations with subsidiaries in the developing countries is marked. Polycentric attitudes develop in consumer goods divisions, and ethnocentrism appears to be greater in industrial product divisions. The agreement is almost unanimous in both U.S.- and European-based international firms that their companies are at various stages on a route toward geocentrism but none has reached this state of affairs. Their executives would agree, however, that:

1. A description of their firms as multinational obscures more than it illuminates the state of affairs;
2. The EPG mix, once defined, is a more precise way to describe the point they have reached;
3. The present profile is not static but a landmark along a difficult road to genuine geocentrism;
4. There are forces both to change and to maintain the present attitudinal "mix," some of which are under their control.

Forces Toward and Against

What are the forces that determine the EPG mix of a firm? "You must think of the struggle toward functioning as a worldwide firm as just a beginning—a few steps forward and a step backward," a chief executive puts it. "It is a painful process, and every firm is different."

Executives of some of the world's largest multinational firms have been able to identify a series of external and internal factors that contribute to or hinder the growth of geocentric attitudes and decisions. Table 2 summarizes the factors most frequently mentioned by over 500 executives from at least 17 countries and 20 firms.

From the external environmental side, the growing world markets, the increase in availability of managerial and technological know-how in different countries, global competition and international customers' advances in telecommunications, regional political and economic communities are positive factors, as is the host country's desire to increase its balance-of-payments surplus through the location of export-oriented subsidiaries of international firms within its borders.

In different firms, senior executives see in various degrees these positive factors toward geocentrism: top management's increasing desire to use human and material resources optimally, the observed lowering of morale after decades of ethnocentric practices, the evidence of waste and duplication under polycentric thinking, the increased awareness and respect for good men of other than the home nationality, and, most importantly, top management's own commitment to building a geocentric firm as evidenced in policies, practices and procedures.

The obstacles toward geocentrism from the environment stem largely from the rising political and economic nationalism in the world today, the suspicions of political leaders of the aims and increasing power of the multinational firm. On the internal side, the obstacles cited most frequently in U.S.-based multinational firms were management's inexperience in overseas markets, mutual distrust between home-country people and foreign executives, the resistance to participation by foreigners in the power structure at headquarters, the increasing difficulty of getting good men overseas to move, nationalistic tendencies in staff, and linguistic and other communication difficulties of a cultural nature.

Any given firm is seen as moving toward geocentrism at a rate determined by its capacities to build on the positive internal factors over which it has control and to change the negative internal factors which are controllable. In some firms the geocentric goal is openly discussed among executives of different nationalities and from different subsidiaries as well as headquarters. There is a consequent improvement in the climate of trust and acceptance of each other's views.

Programs are instituted to assure greater experience in foreign markets, task forces of executives

Table 2   International Executives' View of Forces and Obstacles toward Geocentrism in Their Firms

Forces toward Geocentrism		Obstacles toward Geocentrism	
Environmental	Intra-Organizational	Environmental	Intra-Organizational
1. Technological and managerial know-how increasing in availability in different countries	1. Desire to use human versus material resources optimally	1. Economic nationalism in host and home countries	1. Management inexperience in overseas markets
2. International customers	2. Observed lowering of morale in affiliates of an ethnocentric company	2. Political nationalism in host and home countries	2. Nation-centered reward and punishment structure
3. Local customers' demand for best product at fair price	3. Evidence of waste and duplication in polycentrism	3. Military secrecy associated with research in home country	3. Mutual distrust between home-country people and foreign executives
4. Host country's desire to increase balance of payments	4. Increasing awareness and respect for good people of other than home nationality	4. Distrust of big international firms by host-country political leaders	4. Resistance to letting foreigners into the power structure
5. Growing world markets	5. Risk diversification in having a worldwide production and distribution system	5. Lack of international monetary system	5. Anticipated costs and risks of geocentrism
6. Global competition among international firms for scarce human and material resources	6. Need for recruitment of good people on a worldwide basis	6. Growing differences between the rich and poor countries	6. Nationalistic tendencies in staff
7. Major advances in integration of international transport and telecommunications	7. Need for worldwide information system	7. Host-country belief that home countries get disproportionate benefits of international firms' profits	7. Increasing immobility of staff
8. Regional supranational economic and political communities	8. Worldwide appeal products	8. Home-country political leaders' attempts to control firm's policy	8. Linguistic problems and different cultural backgrounds
	9. Senior management's long-term commitment to geocentrism as related to survival and growth		9. Centralization tendencies in headquarters

are upgraded, and international careers for executives of all nationalities are being designed.

But the seriousness of the obstacles cannot be underestimated. A world of rising nationalism is hardly a precondition for geocentrism; and overcoming distrust of foreigners even within one's own firm is not accomplished in a short span of time. The route to pervasive geocentric thinking is long and tortuous.

Costs, Risks, Payoffs

What conclusions will executives from multinational firms draw from the balance sheet of advantages and disadvantages of maintaining one's present state of ethnocentrism, polycentrism or geocentrism? Not too surprisingly, the costs and risks of ethnocentrism are seen to out-balance the payoffs in the long run. The costs of ethnocentrism are ineffective planning because of a lack of good feedback, the departure of the best men in the subsidiaries, fewer innovations, and an inability to build a high calibre local organization. The risks are political and social repercussions and a less flexible response to local changes.

The payoffs of ethnocentrism are real enough in the short term, they say. Organization is simpler. There is a higher rate of communication of know-how from headquarters to new markets. There is more control over appointments to senior posts in subsidiaries.

Polycentrism's costs are waste due to duplication, to decisions to make products for local use but which could be universal, and to inefficient use of home-country experience. The risks include an excessive regard for local traditions and local growth at the expense of global growth. The main advantages are an intense exploitation of local markets, better sales since local management is often better informed, more local initiative for new products, more host-government support, and good local managers with high morale.

Geocentrism's costs are largely related to communication and travel expenses, educational costs at all levels, time spent in decision making because consensus seeking among more people is required, and an international headquarters bureaucracy. Risks include those due to too wide a distribution of power, personnel problems and those of reentry of international executives. The payoffs are a more powerful total company throughout, a better quality of products and service, worldwide utilization of best resources, improvement of local company management, a greater sense of commitment to worldwide objectives, and last, but not least, more profit.

Jacques Maisonrouge, the French-born president of IBM World Trade, understands the geocentric concept and its benefits. He wrote recently:

> "The first step to a geocentric organization is when a corporation, faced with the choice of whether to grow and expand or decline, realizes the need to mobilize its resources on a world scale. It will sooner or later have to face the issue that the home country does not have a monopoly of either men or ideas. . . .
>
> "I strongly believe that the future belongs to geocentric companies. . . . What is of fundamental importance is the attitude of the company's top management. If it is dedicated to 'geocentrism,' good international management will be possible. If not, the best men of different nations will soon understand that they do not belong to the 'race des seigneurs' and will leave the business."[3]

Geocentrism is not inevitable in any given firm. Some companies have experienced a "regression" to ethnocentrism after trying a long period of polycentrism, of letting subsidiaries do it "their way." The local directors built little empires and did not train successors from their own country. Headquarters had to send home-country nationals to take over. A period of home-country thinking took over.

There appears to be evidence of a need for evolutionary movement from ethnocentrism to polycentrism to geocentrism. The polycentric stage is likened to an adolescent protest period during which subsidiary managers gain their confidence as equals by fighting headquarters and proving "their manhood," after a long period of being under headquarters' ethnocentric thumb.

---

[3]Jacques Maisonrouge, "The Education of International Managers," *Quarterly Journal of AIESEC International,* February 1967.

"It is hard to move from a period of headquarters domination to a worldwide management team quickly. A period of letting affiliates make mistakes may be necessary," said one executive.

Window Dressing

In the rush toward appearing geocentric, many U.S. firms have found it necessary to emphasize progress by appointing one or two non-nationals to senior posts—even on occasion to headquarters. The foreigner is often effectively counteracted by the number of nationals around him, and his influence is really small. Tokenism does have some positive effects, but it does not mean geocentrism has arrived.

Window dressing is also a temptation. Here an attempt is made to demonstrate influence by appointing a number of incompetent "foreigners" to key positions. The results are not impressive for either the individuals or the company.

Too often what is called "the multinational view" is really a screen for ethnocentrism. Foreign affiliate managers must, in order to succeed, take on the traits and behavior of the ruling nationality. In short, in a U.S.-owned firm the foreigner must "Americanize"—not only in attitude but in dress and speech—in order to be accepted.

Tokenism and window dressing are transitional episodes where aspirations toward multinationalism outstrip present attitudes and resources. The fault does not lie only with the enterprise. The human demands of ethnocentrism are great.

A Geocentric Man—?

The geocentric enterprise depends on having an adequate supply of men who are geocentrically oriented. It would be a mistake to underestimate the human stresses which a geocentric career creates. Moving where the company needs an executive involves major adjustments for families, wives and children. The sacrifices are often great and, for some families, outweigh the rewards forthcoming—at least in personal terms. Many executives find it difficult to learn new languages and overcome their cultural superiority complexes, national pride and discomfort with foreigners. Furthermore, international careers can be hazardous when ethnocentrism prevails at headquarters. "It is easy to get lost in the world of the subsidiaries and to be 'out of sight, out of mind' when promotions come up at headquarters," as one executive expressed it following a visit to headquarters after five years overseas. To his disappointment, he knew few senior executives. And fewer knew him!

The economic rewards, the challenge of new countries, the personal and professional development that comes from working in a variety of countries and cultures are surely incentives, but companies have not solved by any means the human costs of international mobility to executives and their families.

A firm's multinationality may be judged by the pervasiveness with which executives think geocentrically—by function, marketing, finance, production, R&D, etc., by product division and by country. The takeoff to geocentrism may begin with executives in one function, say marketing, seeking to find a truly worldwide product line. Only when this worldwide attitude extends throughout the firm, in headquarters and subsidiaries, can executives feel that it is becoming genuinely geocentric.

But no single yardstick, such as the number of foreign nationals in key positions, is sufficient to establish a firm's multinationality. The multinational firm's route to geocentrism is still long because political and economic nationalism is on the rise, and, more importantly, since within the firm ethnocentrism and polycentrism are not easy to overcome. Building trust between persons of different nationality is a central obstacle. Indeed, if we are to judge men, as Paul Weiss put it, "by the kind of world they are trying to build," the senior executives engaged in building the geocentric enterprise could well be the most important social architects of the last third of the twentieth century. For the institution they are trying to erect promises a greater universal sharing of wealth and a consequent control of the explosive centrifugal tendencies of our evolving world community.

The geocentric enterprise offers an institutional and supranational framework which could conceivably make war less likely, on the assumption that bombing customers, suppliers and employees is in nobody's interest. The difficulty of the task is thus matched by its worthwhileness. A clearer image of the features of genuine geocentricity is thus indispensable both as a guideline and as an inviting prospect.

Reading 1-2   Distance Still Matters: The Hard Reality of Global Expansion

Pankaj Ghemawat

When it was launched in 1991, Star TV looked like a surefire winner. The plan was straightforward: The company would deliver television programming to a media-starved Asian audience. It would target the top 5% of Asia's socioeconomic pyramid, a newly rich elite who could not only afford the services but who also represented an attractive advertising market. Since English was the second language for most of the target consumers, Star would be able to use readily available and fairly cheap English-language programming rather than having to invest heavily in creating new local programs. And by using satellites to beam programs into people's homes, it would sidestep the constraints of geographic distance that had hitherto kept traditional broadcasters out of Asia. Media mogul Rupert Murdoch was so taken with this plan—especially with the appeal of leveraging his Twentieth Century Fox film library across the Asian market—that his company, News Corporation, bought out Star's founders for $825 million between 1993 and 1995.

The results have not been quite what Murdoch expected. In its fiscal year ending June 30, 1999,

Pankaj Ghemawat is the Jaime and Josefina Chua Tiampo Professor of Business Administration at Harvard Business School in Boston. His article "The Dubious Logic of Global Megamergers," coauthored by Fariborz Ghadar, was published in the July/August 2000 issue of *HBR*. Reprinted by permission of *Harvard Business Review*. From "Distance Still Matters: The Hard Reality of Global Expansion," by Pankaj Ghemawat, September 2001. Copyright © 2001 by the President and Fellows of Harvard College. All rights reserved.

Star reportedly lost $141 million, pretax, on revenues of $111 million. Losses in fiscal years 1996 through 1999 came to about $500 million all told, not including losses on joint ventures such as Phoenix TV in China. Star is not expected to turn in a positive operating profit until 2002.

Star has been a high-profile disaster, but similar stories are played out all the time as companies pursue global expansion. Why? Because, like Star, they routinely overestimate the attractiveness of foreign markets. They become so dazzled by the sheer size of untapped markets that they lose sight of the vast difficulties of pioneering new, often very different territories. The problem is rooted in the very analytic tools that managers rely on in making judgments about international investments, tools that consistently underestimate the costs of doing business internationally. The most prominent of these is country portfolio analysis (CPA), the hoary but still widely used technique for deciding where a company should compete. By focusing on national GDP, levels of consumer wealth, and people's propensity to consume, CPA places all the emphasis on potential sales. It ignores the costs and risks of doing business in a new market.

Most of those costs and risks result from barriers created by distance. By distance, I don't mean only geographic separation, though that is important. Distance also has cultural, administrative or political, and economic dimensions that can make foreign markets considerably more or less attractive. Just how much difference does distance make? A recent study by economists Jeffrey Frankel and Andrew

Rose estimates the impact of various factors on a country's trade flows. Traditional economic factors, such as the country's wealth and size (GDP), still matter; a 1% increase in either of those measures creates, on average, a .7% to .8% increase in trade. But other factors related to distance, it turns out, matter even more. The amount of trade that takes place between countries 5,000 miles apart is only 20% of the amount that would be predicted to take place if the same countries were 1,000 miles apart. Cultural and administrative distance produces even larger effects. A company is likely to trade ten times as much with a country that is a former colony, for instance, than with a country to which it has no such ties. A common currency increases trade by 340%. Common membership in a regional trading bloc increases trade by 330%. And so on. (For a summary of Frankel and Rose's findings, see the exhibit "Measuring the Impact of Distance.")

Much has been made of the death of distance in recent years. It's been argued that information technologies and, in particular, global communications are shrinking the world, turning it into a small and relatively homogeneous place. But when it comes to business, that's not only an incorrect assumption, it's a dangerous one. Distance still matters, and companies must explicitly and thoroughly account for it when they make decisions about global expansion. Traditional country portfolio analysis needs to be tempered by a clear-eyed evaluation of the many dimensions of distance and their probable impact on opportunities in foreign markets.

The Four Dimensions of Distance

Distance between two countries can manifest itself along four basic dimensions: cultural, administrative, geographic, and economic. The types of distance influence different businesses in different ways. Geographic distance, for instance, affects the costs of transportation and communications, so it is of particular importance to companies that deal with heavy or bulky products, or whose operations

---

Measuring the Impact of Distance

Economists often rely on the so-called gravity theory of trade flows, which says there is a positive relationship between economic size and trade and a negative relationship between distance and trade.

Models based on this theory explain up to two-thirds of the observed variations in trade flows between pairs of countries. Using such a model, economists Jeffrey Frankel and Andrew Rosel have predicted how much certain distance variables will affect trade.

Distance Attribute	Change in International Trade (%)
Income level: GDP per capita (1% increase)	+0.7
Economic size: GDP (1% increase)	+0.8
Physical distance (1% increase)	−1.1
Physical size (1% increase)*	−0.2
Access to ocean*	+50
Common border	+80
Common language	+200
Common regional trading bloc	+330
Colony–colonizer relationship	+900
Common colonizer	+190
Common polity	+300
Common currency	+340

Jeffrey Frankel and Andrew Rose, "An Estimate of the Effects of Currency Unions on Growth," unpublished working paper, May 2000.
*Estimated effects exclude the last four variables in the table.

require a high degree of coordination among highly dispersed people or activities. Cultural distance, by contrast, affects consumers' product preferences. It is a crucial consideration for any consumer goods or media company, but it is much less important for a cement or steel business.

Each of these dimensions of distance encompasses many different factors, some of which are readily apparent; others are quite subtle. (See the exhibit "The CAGE Distance Framework" for an overview of the factors and the ways in which they affect particular industries.) In this article, I will review the four principal dimensions of distance, starting with the two overlooked the most—cultural distance and administrative distance.

Cultural Distance   A country's cultural attributes determine how people interact with one another and with companies and institutions. Differences in religious beliefs, race, social norms, and language are all capable of creating distance between two countries. Indeed, they can have a huge impact on trade: All other things being equal, trade between countries that share a language, for example, will be three times greater than between countries without a common language.

Some cultural attributes, like language, are easily perceived and understood. Others are much more subtle. Social norms, the deeply rooted system of unspoken principles that guide individuals in their everyday choices and interactions, are often nearly invisible, even to the people who abide by them. Take, for instance, the long-standing tolerance of the Chinese for copyright infringement. As William Alford points out in his book *To Steal a Book Is an Elegant Offense* (Stanford University Press, 1995), many people ascribe this social norm to China's recent communist past. More likely, Alford argues, it flows from a precept of Confucius that encourages replication of the results of past intellectual endeavors: "I transmit rather than create; I believe in and love the Ancients." Indeed, copyright infringement was a problem for Western publishers well before communism. Back in the 1920s, for example, Merriam Webster, about to introduce a bilingual dictionary in China, found that the Commercial Press in

Shanghai had already begun to distribute its own version of the new dictionary. The U.S. publisher took the press to a Chinese court, which imposed a small fine for using the Merriam Webster seal but did nothing to halt publication. As the film and music industries well know, little has changed. Yet this social norm still confounds many Westerners.

Most often, cultural attributes create distance by influencing the choices that consumers make between substitute products because of their preferences for specific features. Color tastes, for example, are closely linked to cultural prejudices. The word "red" in Russian also means beautiful. Consumer durable industries are particularly sensitive to differences in consumer taste at this level. The Japanese, for example, prefer automobiles and household appliances to be small, reflecting a social norm common in countries where space is highly valued.

Sometimes products can touch a deeper nerve, triggering associations related to the consumer's identity as a member of a particular community. In these cases, cultural distance affects entire categories of products. The food industry is particularly sensitive to religious attributes. Hindus, for example, do not eat beef because it is expressly forbidden by their religion. Products that elicit a strong response of this kind are usually quite easy to identify, though some countries will provide a few surprises. In Japan, rice, which Americans treat as a commodity, carries an enormous amount of cultural baggage.

Ignoring cultural distance was one of Star TV's biggest mistakes. By supposing that Asian viewers would be happy with English-language programming, the company assumed that the TV business was insensitive to culture. Managers either dismissed or were unaware of evidence from Europe that mass audiences in countries large enough to support the development of local content generally prefer local TV programming. If they had taken cultural distance into account, China and India could have been predicted to require significant investments in localization. TV is hardly cement.

Administrative or Political Distance   Historical and political associations shared by countries

The CAGE Distance Framework

The cultural, administrative, geographic, and economic (CAGE) distance framework helps managers identify and assess the impact of distance on various industries. The upper portion of the table lists the key attributes underlying the four dimensions of distance. The lower portion shows how they affect different products and industries.

Cultural Distance	Administrative Distance	Geographic Distance	Economic Distance
Attributes Creating Distance			
Different languages Different ethnicities; lack of connective ethnic or social networks Different religions Different social norms	Absence of colonial ties Absence of shared monetary or political association Political hostility Government policies Institutional weakness	Physical remoteness Lack of a common border Lack of sea or river access Size of country Weak transportation or communication links Differences in climates	Differences in consumer incomes Differences in costs and quality of: • natural resources • financial resources • human resources • infrastructure • intermediate inputs • information or knowledge
Industries or Products Affected by Distance			
Products have high linguistic content (TV) Products affect cultural or national identity of consumers (foods) Product features vary in terms of: • size (cars) • standards (electrical appliances) • packaging Products carry country-specific quality associations (wines)	Government involvement is high in industries that are: • producers of staple goods (electricity) • producers of other "entitlements" (drugs) • large employers (farming) • large suppliers to government (mass transportation) • national champions (aerospace) • vital to national security (telecommunications) • exploiters of natural resources (oil, mining) • subject to high sunken costs (infrastructure)	Products have a low value-to-weight or bulk ratio (cement) Products are fragile or perishable (glass, fruit) Communications and connectivity are important (financial services) Local supervision and operational requirements are high (many services)	Nature of demand varies with income level (cars) Economies of standardization or scale are important (mobile phones) Labor and other factor cost differences are salient (garments) Distribution or business systems are different (insurance) Companies need to be responsive and agile (home appliances)

greatly affect trade between them. Colony-colonizer links between countries, for example, boost trade by 900%, which is perhaps not too surprising given Britain's continuing ties with its former colonies in the commonwealth, France's with the franc zone of West Africa, and Spain's with Latin America. Preferential trading arrangements, common currency, and political union can also increase trade by more than 300% each. The integration of the European Union is probably the leading example of deliberate efforts to diminish administrative and political distance among trading partners. (Needless to say, ties must be friendly to have a positive influence on trade. Although India and Pakistan share a colonial history—not to mention a border and linguistic ties—their mutual hostility means that trade between them is virtually nil.)

Countries can also create administrative and political distance through unilateral measures. Indeed, policies of individual governments pose the most common barriers to cross-border competition. In some cases, the difficulties arise in a company's home country. For companies from the United States, for instance, domestic prohibitions on bribery and the prescription of health, safety, and environmental policies have a dampening effect on their international businesses.

More commonly, though, it is the target country's government that raises barriers to foreign competition: tariffs, trade quotas, restrictions on foreign direct investment, and preferences for domestic competitors in the form of subsidies and favoritism in regulation and procurement. Such measures are expressly intended to protect domestic industries, and they are most likely to be implemented if a domestic industry meets one or more of the following criteria:

- *It is a large employer*. Industries that represent large voting blocs often receive state support in the form of subsidies and import protection. Europe's farmers are a case in point.
- *It is seen as a national champion*. Reflecting a kind of patriotism, some industries or companies serve as symbols of a country's modernity and competitiveness. Thus the showdown between Boeing and Airbus in capturing the large passenger-jet market has caused feelings on both sides of the Atlantic to run high and could even spark a broader trade war. Also, the more that a government has invested in the industry, the more protective it is likely to be, and the harder it will be for an outsider to gain a beachhead.
- *It is vital to national security*. Governments will intervene to protect industries that are deemed vital to national security—especially in high-tech sectors such as telecommunications and aerospace. The FBI, for instance, delayed Deutsche Telekom's acquisition of Voicestream for reasons of national security.
- *It produces staples*. Governments will also take measures to prevent foreign companies from dominating markets for goods essential to their citizens' everyday lives. Food staples, fuel, and electricity are obvious examples.
- *It produces an "entitlement" good or service*. Some industries, notably the health care sector, produce goods or services that people believe they are entitled to as a basic human right. In these industries, governments are prone to intervene to set quality standards and control pricing.
- *It exploits natural resources*. A country's physical assets are often seen as part of a national heritage. Foreign companies can easily be considered robbers. Nationalization, therefore, is a constant threat to international oil and mining multinationals.
- *It involves high sunk-cost commitments*. Industries that require large, geography-specific sunk investments—in the shape, say, of oil refineries or aluminum smelting plants or railway lines—are highly vulnerable to interference from local governments. Irreversibility expands the scope for holdups once the investment has been made.

Finally, a target country's weak institutional infrastructure can serve to dampen cross-border economic activity. Companies typically shy away from doing business in countries known for corruption or social conflict. Indeed, some research

How Far Away Is China, Really?

As Star TV discovered, China is a particularly tough nut to crack. In a recent survey of nearly 100 multinationals, 54 % admitted that their total business performance in China had been "worse than planned," compared with just 25% reporting "better than planned." Why was the failure rate so high? The survey provides the predictable answer: 62% of respondents reported that they had overestimated market potential for their products or services.

A quick analysis of the country along the dimensions of distance might have spared those companies much disappointment. Culturally, China is a long way away from nearly everywhere. First, the many dialects of the Chinese language are notoriously difficult for foreigners to learn, and the local population's foreign-language skills are limited. Second, the well-developed Chinese business culture based on personal connections, often summarized in the term *guanxi,* creates barriers to economic interchange with Westerners who focus on transactions rather than relationships. It can even be argued that Chinese consumers are "home-biased"; market research indicates much less preference for foreign brands over domestic ones than seems to be true in India, for example. In fact, greater China plays a disproportionate role in China's economic relations with the rest of the world.

Administrative barriers are probably even more important. A survey of members of the American Chamber of Commerce in China flagged market-access restrictions, high taxes, and customs duties as the biggest barriers to profitability in China. The level of state involvement in the economy continues to be high, with severe economic strains imposed by loss-making state-owned enterprises and technically insolvent state-owned banks. Corruption, too, is a fairly significant problem. In 2000, Transparency International ranked the country 63rd out of 90, with a rating of one indicating the least perceived corruption. Considerations such as these led Standard & Poor's to assign China a political-risk ranking of five in 2000, with six being the worst possible score.

So, yes, China is a big market, but that is far from the whole story. Distance matters, too, and along many dimensions.

suggests that these conditions depress trade and investment far more than any explicit administrative policy or restriction. But when a country's institutional infrastructure is strong—for instance, if it has a well-functioning legal system—it is much more attractive to outsiders.

Ignoring administrative and political sensitivities was Star TV's other big mistake. Foreign ownership of broadcasting businesses—even in an open society like the United States—is always politically loaded because of television's power to influence people. Yet shortly after acquiring the company, Rupert Murdoch declared on record that satellite television was "an unambiguous threat to totalitarian regimes everywhere" because it permitted people to bypass government-controlled news sources. Not surprisingly, the Chinese government enacted a ban on the reception of foreign satellite TV services soon thereafter. News Corporation has begun to mend fences with the Chinese authorities, but it has yet to score any major breakthroughs in a country that accounts for nearly 60 percent of Star TV's potential customers. Murdoch of all people should have foreseen this outcome, given his experience in the United States, where he was required to become a citizen in order to buy the television companies that now form the core of the Fox network.

Geographic Distance   In general, the farther you are from a country, the harder it will be to conduct business in that country. But geographic distance is not simply a matter of how far away the country is in miles or kilometers. Other attributes that must be considered include the physical size of the country, average within-country distances to borders, access to waterways and the ocean, and topography. Man-made geographic attributes also must be taken into account—most notably, a country's transportation and communications infrastructures.

Obviously, geographic attributes influence the costs of transportation. Products with low value-to-weight or bulk ratios, such as steel and cement, incur particularly high costs as geographic distance increases. Likewise, costs for transporting fragile or perishable products become significant across large distances.

Beyond physical products, intangible goods and services are affected by geographic distance as well. One recent study indicates that cross-border equity flows between two countries fall off significantly as the geographic distance between them rises. This phenomenon clearly cannot be explained by transportation costs—capital, after all, is not a physical good. Instead, the level of information infrastructure (crudely measured by telephone traffic and the number of branches of multinational banks) accounts for much of the effect of physical distance on cross-border equity flows.

Interestingly, companies that find geography a barrier to trade are often expected to switch to direct investment in local plant and equipment as an alternative way to access target markets. But current research suggests that this approach may be flawed: Geographic distance has a dampening effect, overall, on investment flows as well as on trade flows. In short, it is important to keep both information networks and transportation infrastructures in mind when assessing the geographic influences on cross-border economic activity.

Economic Distance   The wealth or income of consumers is the most important economic attribute that creates distance between countries, and it has a marked effect on the levels of trade and the types of partners a country trades with. Rich countries, research suggests, engage in relatively more cross-border economic activity relative to their economic size than do their poorer cousins. Most of this activity is with other rich countries, as the positive correlation between per capita GDP and trade flows implies. But poor countries also trade more with rich countries than with other poor ones.

Of course, these patterns mask variations in the effects of economic disparities—in the cost and quality of financial, human, and other resources. Companies that rely on economies of experience, scale, and standardization should focus more on countries that have similar economic profiles. That's because they have to replicate their existing business model to exploit their competitive advantage, which is hard to pull off in a country where customer incomes—not to mention the cost and quality of resources—are very different. Wal-Mart in India, for instance, would be a very different business from Wal-Mart in the United States. But Wal-Mart in Canada is virtually a carbon copy.

In other industries, however, competitive advantage comes from economic arbitrage—the exploitation of cost and price differentials between markets. Companies in industries whose major cost components vary widely across countries—like the garment and footwear industries, where labor costs are important—are particularly likely to target countries with different economic profiles for investment or trade.

Whether they expand abroad for purposes of replication or arbitrage, all companies find that major disparities in supply chains and distribution channels are a significant barrier to business. A recent study concluded that margins on distribution within the United States—the costs of domestic transportation, wholesaling, and retailing—play a bigger role, on average, in erecting barriers to imports into the United States than do international transportation costs and tariffs combined.

More broadly, cross-country complexity and change place a premium on responsiveness and agility, making it hard for cross-border competitors,

Industry Sensitivity to Distance

The various types of distance affect different industries in different ways. To estimate industry sensitivity to distance, Rajiv Mallick, a research associate at Harvard Business School, and I regressed trade between every possible pair of countries in the world in each of 70 industries (according to their SIC designations) on each dimension of distance. The results confirm the importance of distinguishing between the various components of distance in assessing foreign market opportunities. Electricity, for instance, is highly sensitive to administrative and geographic factors but not at all to cultural factors. The following table lists some of the industries that are more and less sensitive to distance.

CULTURAL DISTANCE Linguistic Ties	ADMINISTRATIVE DISTANCE Preferential Trading Agreements	GEOGRAPHIC DISTANCE Physical Remoteness	ECONOMIC DISTANCE Wealth Differences
More Sensitive			
Meat and meat preparations	Gold, nonmonetary	Electricity current	(Economic distance decreases trade)
Cereals and cereal preparations	Electricity current	Gas, natural and manufactured	Nonferrous metals
Miscellaneous edible products and preparations	Coffee, tea, cocoa, spices	Paper, paperboard	Manufactured fertilizers
Tobacco and tobacco products	Textile fibers	Live animals	Meat and meat preparations
Office machines and automatic data-processing equipment	Sugar, sugar preparations, and honey	Sugar, sugar preparations, and honey	Iron and steel
			Pulp and waste paper
Less Sensitive			
Photographic apparatuses, optical goods, watches	Gas, natural and manufactured	Pulp and waste paper	(Economic distance increases trade)
Road vehicles	Travel goods, handbags	Photographic apparatuses, optical goods, watches	Coffee, tea, cocoa, spices
Cork and wood	Footwear	Telecommunications and sound-recording apparatuses	Animal oils and fats
Metalworking machinery	Sanitary, plumbing, heating, and lighting fixtures	Coffee, tea, cocoa, spices	Office machines and automatic data-processing equipment
Electricity current	Furniture and furniture parts	Gold, nonmonetary	Power-generating machinery and equipment
			Photographic apparatuses, optical goods, watches

More Sensitive ◀━━━━━━━━━━━━━━━━━━━━━━━━━━━▶ Less Sensitive

particularly replicators, to match the performance of locally focused ones because of the added operational complexity. In the home appliance business, for instance, companies like Maytag that concentrate on a limited number of geographies produce far better returns for investors than companies like Electrolux and Whirlpool, whose geographic spread has come at the expense of simplicity and profitability.

A Case Study in Distance

Taking the four dimensions of distance into account can dramatically change a company's assessment of the relative attractiveness of foreign markets. One company that has wrestled with global expansion is Tricon Restaurants International (TRI), the international operating arm of Tricon, which manages the Pizza Hut, Taco Bell, and KFC fast-food chains and which was spun off from Pepsico in 1997.

When Tricon became an independent company, TRI's operations were far flung, with restaurants in 27 countries. But the profitability of its markets varied greatly: Two-thirds of revenues and an even higher proportion of profits came from just seven markets. Furthermore, TRI's limited operating cash flow and Tricon's debt service obligations left TRI with less than one-tenth as much money as archrival McDonald's International to invest outside the United States. As a result, in 1998, TRI's president Pete Bassi decided to rationalize its global operations by focusing its equity investments in a limited number of markets.

But which markets? Exhibit 1a, "Country Portfolio Analysis: A Flawed Approach," provides a portfolio analysis of international markets for the fast-food restaurant business, based on data used by TRI for its strategy discussions. The analysis

Exhibit 1a   Country Portfolio Analysis (a flawed approach)

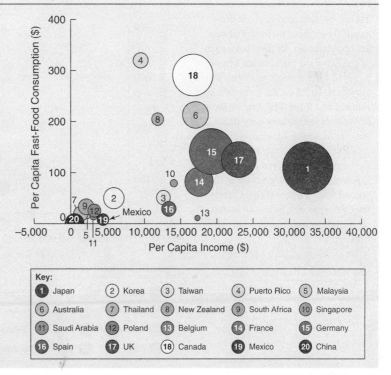

Here's how country portfolio analysis (CPA) works. A company's actual and potential markets are plotted on a simple grid, with a measure of per capita income on one axis and some measure of product performance, often penetration rates, on the other. The location of the market on the grid reflects the attractiveness of the market in terms of individual consumer wealth and propensity to consume. The size of the bubble represents the total size of the market in terms of GDP or the absolute consumption of the product or service in question. The bubbles provide a rough estimate of how large the relative revenue opportunities are. This CPA map compares a number of non–U.S. markets for fast-food restaurants.

Key:
1. Japan   2. Korea   3. Taiwan   4. Puerto Rico   5. Malaysia
6. Australia   7. Thailand   8. New Zealand   9. South Africa   10. Singapore
11. Saudi Arabia   12. Poland   13. Belgium   14. France   15. Germany
16. Spain   17. UK   18. Canada   19. Mexico   20. China

suggests that the company's top markets in terms of size of opportunity would be the larger bubbles to the center and right of the chart.

Applying the effects of distance, however, changes the map dramatically. Consider the Mexican market. Using the CPA method, Mexico, with a total fast-food consumption of $700 million, is a relatively small market, ranking 16th of 20. When combined with estimates of individual consumer wealth and per capita consumption, this ranking would imply that TRI should dispose of its investments there. But Exhibit 1b, "Country Portfolio Analysis: Adjusted for Distance," tells a different story. When the fast-food consumption numbers for each country are adjusted for their geographic distance from Dallas, TRI's home base, Mexico's consumption decreases less than any other coun-

try's, as you might expect, given Mexico's proximity to Dallas. Based on just this readjustment, Mexico leaps to sixth place in terms of market opportunity.

Further adjusting the numbers for a common land border and for membership in a trade agreement with the United States pushes Mexico's ranking all the way up to second, after Canada. Not all the adjustments are positive: adjusting for a common language—not a characteristic of Mexico—pushes Mexico into a tie for second place with the United Kingdom. Additional adjustments could also be made, but the overall message is plain. Once distance is taken into account, the size of the market opportunity in Mexico looks very different. If TRI had used the CPA approach and neglected distance, the company's planners might well have

---

Exhibit 1b   Country Portfolio Analysis (adjusted for distance)

Taking distance into account dramatically changes estimates of market opportunities. In this chart, each of the fast-food markets has been adjusted for a number of distance attributes, based on the estimates by Frankel and Rose. The relative sizes of the bubbles are now very different. For example, Mexico, which was less than one-tenth the size of the largest international markets, Japan and Germany, ends up as the second largest opportunity. Clearly, the CPA approach paints an incomplete picture, unless it is adjusted for distance.

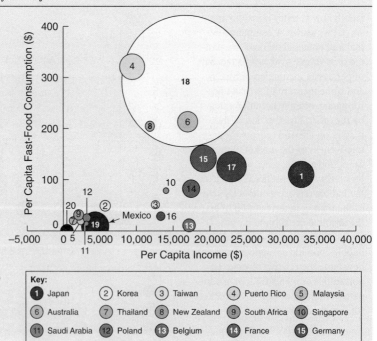

ended up abandoning a core market. Instead, they concluded, in Bassi's words, that "Mexico is one of TRI's top two or three priorities."

Factoring in the industry effects of distance is only a first step. A full analysis should consider how a company's own characteristics operate to increase or reduce distance from foreign markets. Companies with a large cadre of cosmopolitan managers, for instance, will be less affected by cultural differences than companies whose managers are all from the home country. In TRI's case, consideration of company-specific features made Mexico even more attractive. The company already owned more than four-fifths of its Mexican outlets and had a 38% share of the local market, well ahead of McDonald's.

Consideration of the interaction of company-specific features and distance is beyond the scope of this article. But whether the analysis is at the industry or company level, the message is the same: Managers must always be conscious of distance—in all its dimensions. The CAGE distance framework is intended to help managers meet that challenge. While it is necessarily subjective, it represents an important complement to the tools used by most companies seeking to build or rationalize their country market portfolios. Technology may indeed be making the world a smaller place, but it is not eliminating the very real—and often very high—costs of distance.

Reading 1-3   Going Global: Lessons from Late Movers

Christopher A. Bartlett and Sumantra Ghoshal

In his autobiography, former South African president Nelson Mandela recalls his dismay when he boarded an airplane and found that the pilot was African. With shock, he realized his reaction was exactly what he had been fighting against all his life. Mandela was discussing racism, but the same involuntary reactions surface in commerce. Consider labels such as "Made in Brazil" and "Made in Thailand." Someday they may be symbols of high quality and value, but today many consumers expect products from those countries to be inferior. Unfortunately, that perception is often

▌ **Christopher A. Bartlett** is the Daewoo Professor of Business Administration at Harvard Business School in Boston.
▌ **Sumantra Ghoshal** is the Robert P. Bauman Professor of Strategic Leadership at London Business School.
▌ Reprinted by permission of Harvard Business Review. "Going Global: Lessons from Late Movers" by Christopher A. Bartlett and Sumantra Ghoshal Harvard Business Review (March–April 2000). pp. 132–142.
▌ Copyright © 2000 by the President and Fellows of Harvard College. All rights reserved.

shared by managers of the local companies that are striving to become global players.

That's just one reason why companies from peripheral countries find it so difficult to compete against established global giants from Europe, Japan, and the United States—the triad that dominates global commerce. And when they do compete, the experience of emerging multinationals often reinforces their self-doubt. Consider Arvind Mills, an Indian garment manufacturer that in the mid-1990s found a niche supplying denim to leading Western apparel companies. As Arvind's overseas sales grew, its stock soared on the Bombay Stock Exchange, and the company's CEO confidently declared that the company was well on its way to becoming a powerful global player. But within a couple of years, Arvind had become a victim of the fickle demands of the fashion business and the cutthroat competition among offshore apparel makers battling for the shrinking U.S. jeans market.

Stories such as Arvind's are told and retold in management circles. The moral is consistently negative. Companies from developing countries have entered the game too late. They don't have the resources. They can't hope to compete against giants. Yet despite the plausibility of such stories, we believe they are condescending and represent the counsel of despair. Indeed, there is plenty of evidence of an altogether different story. After all, companies like Sony, Toyota, and NEC transformed the cheap, low-quality image of Japanese products in little more than a decade. Is that type of turnaround still possible? To find out, we looked at companies that, unlike Arvind, have successfully built a lasting and profitable international business from home countries far from the heart of the global economy.

We studied 12 emerging multinationals in depth. They operate in a wide range of businesses, but they are all based in countries that have not produced many successful multinationals—from large emerging markets like Brazil to relatively more prosperous yet still peripheral nations such as Australia to small developing countries like the Philippines. And while these companies are distinguished by strategic, organizational, and management diversity, they share some common traits. Most notably, each used foreign ventures in order to build capabilities to compete in more-profitable segments of their industry.

The evolution into more-profitable product segments can be clearly tracked on what we call the value curve. All industries can be seen as a collection of product market segments; the value curve is a tool used to differentiate the various segments. (For an example, see Figure 1 "The Pharmaceutical Industry's Value Curve.") The more profitable a segment, the more sophisticated are the capabilities needed to compete in it—in R&D, distribution, or marketing. The problem for most aspiring multinationals from peripheral countries is that they typically enter the global marketplace at the bottom of

Figure 1   The Pharmaceutical Industry's Value Curve

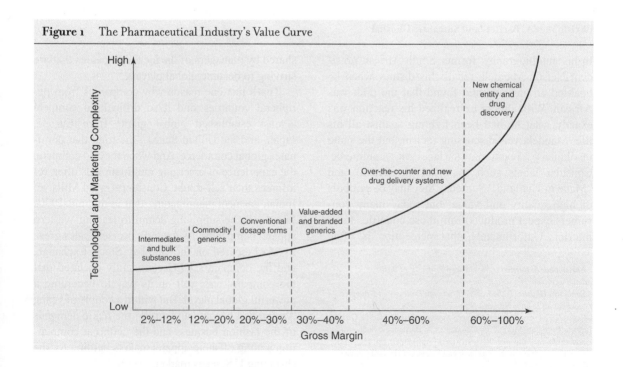

Navigating the PC Industry's Value Curve

The drive up the value curve sometimes requires a company not just to shift product market segments but also to migrate to different points in the supply chain. Consider Acer, the Taiwanese company that started in 1976 as an electronic components importer and became the world's number three manufacturer of personal computers in just two decades.

As the PC market matured, Acer used its growing global presence to build capabilities at both ends of the supply chain, where the margins are higher than in the assembly business, which was its early focus. Acer learned from its exposure to global technology and best manufacturing practices, which helped the company move upstream into manufacturing motherboards, peripherals, and central processing units. In 1989, Acer partnered with Texas Instruments to produce semiconductors. Nine years later, it bought out TI's share.

Downstream, Acer's regional business units took over local assembly, started sourcing locally, opened new channels, and invested in the global brand that the company felt was key to freeing it from the low-margin OEM business. CEO Stan Shih calls this reorientation his "smiling curve." "Assembly means you are making money from manual labor. In components and marketing, you add value with your brains."

Shih's commitment to push his company to add value through the "smiling curve" saved Acer from the fate of dozens of other Taiwanese electronics suppliers that became captive suppliers of OEM goods to major computer companies. More than that, it has led Acer's continuing evolution in the global market. The company is now developing software and Internet businesses, which it believes will be the high-end value-added segments that will drive the next stage of Acer's global expansion.

Figure 2 Stan Shih's Smiling Curve

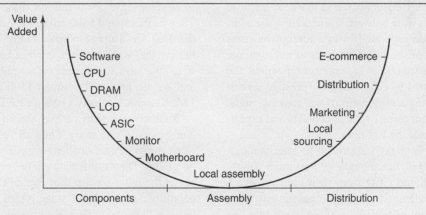

Recognizing that Acer's focus on assembling PCs was keeping the company in the least profitable segment of the market, CEO Stan Shih decided to move up the value curve by developing capabilities in components and distribution. Succeeding in components required strong technology and enough manufacturing skill to produce economies of scale. Succeeding in distribution required a solid brand, established channels, and effective logistics. Acer has built both.

the value curve—and they stay there. This is true even when a company's internal capabilities exceed the demands of a particular segment. Arvind Mills, for example, expanded abroad with commodity-like products even though it competed successfully in higher-value segments at home. And it's not that companies don't see the profitability of value-added products; the performance of companies above them on the value curve is usually quite evident. Basically, their failure is due to a paralysis of will. Managers either lack confidence in their organization's ability to climb the value curve or they lack the courage to commit resources to mounting that challenge. Often, as Nelson Mandela's memoir illustrates, they are crippled by a vision of themselves as second-class citizens.

A Model of Success

The Indian pharmaceutical company Ranbaxy is one of the success stories. For 18 years after it launched its export business in 1975, Ranbaxy was trapped at the bottom of the pharmaceutical value curve. Even though it had developed advanced product and process capabilities in its home market, when Ranbaxy decided to go overseas it opted to produce and sell bulk substances and intermediates in relatively unsophisticated markets. Because gross margins were between 5% and 10%, the additional revenue generated by the foreign business did not even offset the added costs of international sales and distribution. Management justified the negative returns by celebrating the prestige associated with being a multinational and making vague promises about using overseas contacts and experience to upgrade the business.

In 1993, Ranbaxy's approach to internationalization changed fundamentally. Parvinder Singh, the chairman and CEO from then until his death in 1999, challenged the top management team with his dream of transforming Ranbaxy into "an international, research-based pharmaceutical company." When his colleagues questioned how a small Indian company could compete with the rich giants from the West, he responded, "Ranbaxy cannot change India. What it can do is to create a pocket of excellence. Ranbaxy must be an island within India."

Once there was a shift in mind-set, the strategy was straightforward. The company moved into the higher-margin business of selling branded generics in large markets like Russia and China—a change that required building new customer relationships, a strong brand image, and different distribution channels. Ranbaxy then entered the U.S. and European markets, in which the company needed to meet much more stringent regulatory requirements. But by using its growing international knowledge and experience to develop new resources and capabilities, Ranbaxy established a profitable international business that accounted for more than half of its $250 million in revenue in 1996.

Not content with that, Ranbaxy has already begun the long, slow climb to the upper regions of the pharmaceutical value curve. Thanks to consistently investing 4% to 6% of its revenue in R&D, the company has built a world-class laboratory staffed by 250 scientists. Pushed by Singh's persistent question—Why do we say that new drug discovery is the exclusive preserve of the United States and Europe?—these scientists are committed to developing a $500 million drug before 2003. They cannot spend $300 million in R&D to develop the drug, the average expense in the West, but they believe they can cut that figure by a factor of four or five. "We have significant cost advantages in R&D, and we are prepared to invest $100 million," says J.M. Khanna, Ranbaxy's head of R&D.

Ranbaxy's growth path is shared by the other companies in our study. They all faced and overcame the same core challenges as they attempted to go global. Their immediate challenge was to break out of the mind-set that they couldn't compete successfully on the global stage. Once freed of that burden, they had to find strategies in which being a late mover was a source of competitive advantage rather than a disadvantage. Finally, they had to develop a culture of continual cross-border learning.

a lock on over
bilities. Being
establish VHS
videocassette
There are,
turning up late
multinationals
late-mover ad
started by be
players and the
exploiting nic
overlooked. O
tive, though ri
comer status
capitalizing o
players' busine

Benchmark
companies wit
that they will
global compe
ments. Yet in t
to go abroad
tion. Sooner o
result, emergi
compete again
ply by adaptin
they enter the
Philippines-ba
When the U.S
stores in Ma
Jollibee's tiny
CEO Tony Tan
decided to use
ground to brin
Going hea
global compa
hand view of
that allowed
costs, and ser
came at an ide
ment, when th
was the major
what better m
whose refined

Winning companies enjoyed global success because they learned how to learn from the constant
flow of new demands, opportunities, and challenges that international competition brings. This is
quite a leap for most emerging multinationals; the
ability to see globalization as more than a path to
new markets or resources is rare in all but the most
sophisticated global companies.

Breaking Out of the Marginal Mind-Set

Let's take a closer look at the psychological factors
that hold back most companies and the ways our
emerging multinationals dealt with them. Companies from peripheral countries can fall into several
traps, which we call liabilities of origin. First, some
companies feel as though they are locked in a prison
of local standards because of the gap between technical requirements and design norms at home and
world-class standards abroad. If demand at home is
strong, managers then can reasonably postpone the
investments needed to comply with international
standards. This insidious situation causes potential
multinationals to duck the challenge of going abroad.

Some companies fall into a second trap. Even
though their products and services are already up to
snuff, because of the peripheral location, management is either unaware of the company's global
potential or too debilitated by self-doubt to capitalize on it.

Finally, there are a few companies for which the
liability of origin derives from a limited exposure to
global competition, leaving them overconfident in
their abilities or blind to potential dangers. Unfortunately, there are no quick solutions to any of these
psychological barriers. But our emerging multinationals started to overcome them by creating a push
from home and a pull from abroad.

Push from Home   There are basically two ways
for a company to create a push from home. In the
first, a moment of truth stimulates the initial steps
down the long path toward internationalization.
This is particularly the case for companies that are
so blinded by their domestic success that they fail

to see that their origins present a liability. Therefore, management's greatest challenge is to shock
or challenge the company to push it from its nest. It
was just such a moment of truth that enabled the
Korean giant Samsung to turn around its international sales of consumer electronics. Less than a
decade ago, Samsung was struggling to expand into
overseas markets, even though its products were
technologically equal to its competitors' offerings.
The problem was that most of Samsung's managers
were unaware of or denied the existence of negative
consumer perceptions abroad, largely because
Samsung's products were so well regarded at home.

To force the company to deal with the problem,
chairman Kun-Hee Lee flew 100 senior managers
to the United States to show them how Samsung's
products were treated. The visit was traumatic.
Prominently displayed in storefronts were Sony,
Bang & Olufsen, and the products of other prestigious companies. Lined up behind them were
brands such as Philips, Panasonic, Toshiba, and
Hitachi. In the back of the stores, frequently with
big "bargain sale" stickers on them, were the
Samsung TVs and VCRs, often with a layer of dust
dulling the high-quality finish that the company had
invested trillions of *won* to achieve. As the dis-
traught executives joined their chairman in dusting
their products with their handkerchiefs, he spelled
out what all of them could clearly see: they had a lot
of work to do to change overseas consumers'
expectations. That moment of truth had an enduring
impact. The executives initiated a series of actions
that eventually led to a major turnaround of
Samsung's global consumer electronics business.

The second way to create a push from home requires a leap of faith more than a shock of recognition. These leaps can be dramatic, and they are
always risky, like performing on a trapeze without a
net. Some CEOs, for example, demonstrate their
commitment to globalization by investing far ahead
of demand, even if doing so reduces the company's
responsiveness to its successful home market.

Consider Thermax, a domestic Indian manufacturer of small boilers. Thermax had developed a

radically diffe
duced their si
could be a wi
mand for such
this new boile
it virtually un
the company
national techr
a fundamenta
markets dema
sive, integrate
installation, v
lowed domes
installation ta
market accou
and 100% o
Nalwade non
for internatio
tion gave the
into the Europ
was right. To
ducer of smal

Pull from A
pensable, but
expansion to
need to inves
their oversea
Simply sendir
charge to exp
rarely achieve
engaged trad
post. Compa
senior execut
provide the y
ibility and c
nally. Strong
greatly increa
nationals w
organizationa
side their hor

Natura, a
has been na
for three con
hard way. Al

had established 24 overseas stores in ten countries, mostly in Southeast Asia and the Middle East. Though hardly on the scale of McDonald's network of more than 3,000 overseas outlets in almost 100 countries, Jollibee's operations nonetheless formed a sound basis for building a global franchise. In 1998, the company felt ready to take on the most demanding fast-food market in the world. Today, its first San Francisco store is performing at almost 50% above forecast levels, and two new stores have just opened. And Jollibee plans to roll out new stores in 17 other locations in California over the next 18 months.

Confront and Challenge   Jollibee's success illustrates how a late entrant can benchmark and adapt the business models of its competitors. A more radical strategy is to introduce new business models that challenge the industry's established rules of competition. Though risky, this approach can be very effective in industries deeply embedded with tradition or comfortably divided among an established oligopoly. The typical business model in these industries has become inflexible. Among the companies we studied, the one that took advantage of others' inflexibilities the best was BRL Hardy, an Australian wine company that defied many of the well-entrenched traditions of international wine production, trading, and distribution—despite the fact that its home country produces only 2% of the world's wine.

From a 1991 base of $31 million in export sales—much of it bulk for private labels and the rest a potpourri of bottled products sold through distributors—Hardy built its foreign sales to $178 million in 1998, almost all of it directly marketed as branded products. Managing director Steve Millar describes the insight that triggered this turnaround: "We began to realize that for a lot of historical reasons, the wine business—unlike the soft-drinks or packaged-foods industries—had very few true multinational companies and therefore very few true global brands. There was a great opportunity, and we were as well placed as anyone to grab it."

Millar was alluding to the inflexibility of the European practice of labeling wines by region, subregion, and even village—the French *appellation* or the Italian *dominazione* systems are classic examples. A vineyard could be further categorized according to its historical quality classification such as the French premier grand cru, the grand cru, and so on. The resulting complexity not only confuses consumers but also fragments producers, whose small scale prevents them from building brand strength or distribution capability. This created an opportunity for major retailers, such as Sainsbury's in the United Kingdom, to overcome consumers' confusion—and capture more value themselves—by buying in bulk and selling under the store's own label.

For decades, BRL Hardy's international business was caught in this trap. It distributed its Hardy label wines to retailers through local agents and sold bulk wine directly for private labels. But Millar's insight gave the company a way out, if it was willing to change the rules of the game on both the demand and supply sides. First, new staff was appointed and new resources allocated to upgrade overseas sales offices. Instead of simply supporting the sales activities of distributing agents, they took direct control of the full sales, distribution, and marketing. Their primary objective was to establish Hardy as a viable global brand. The company's supply-side decision was even more significant. In order to exploit the growing marketing expertise of these overseas units, Hardy encouraged them to supplement their Australian product line by sourcing wine from around the world. Not only did Hardy offset the vintage uncertainties and currency risks of sourcing from a single country, it also gained clout in its dealings with retailers. By breaking the tradition of selling only its own wine, Hardy was able to build the scale necessary for creating strong brands and negotiating with retail stores.

The advantages have been clear and powerful. The company's range of wines—from Australia as well as France, Italy, and Chile—responds to supermarkets' needs to deal with a few broad line suppliers. At the same time, the scale of operation has supported the brand development so vital to pulling products out of the commodity range. Results have been outstanding. In Europe, the volume of Hardy's brands has increased 12-fold in seven years, making it the leading Australian wine brand in the huge UK market, and number two overall to Gallo in the United Kingdom. And branded products from other countries have grown to represent about a quarter of its European volume. Hardy has evolved from an Australian wine exporter to a truly global wine company.

The company's new strategy and capabilities are visible in its recent introduction of a branded wine from Sicily called D'istinto. Under a supply agreement and marketing program initiated by BRL Hardy Europe, in its first year this product has sold 200,000 cases in the United Kingdom alone—an exceptional performance. As the brand is introduced to the rest of Europe, North America, and Australia, Hardy expects sales to top a million cases by 2003.

Learning How to Learn

Ask most managers why they are steering their companies into international expansion and they will talk about increasing sales or securing low-cost labor and raw materials. Important as those objectives are, they do not ensure a company's success abroad. The global marketplace is information based and knowledge intensive. To survive in this environment, you must know how to learn: it is the central skill that allows a company to move up the value curve. Yet all learning requires tuition, and every company faces the risk that the effort involved in acquiring new capabilities may draw off too many vital resources and threaten the domestic business. The trick is to protect the past while building the future.

Protect the Past   The first rule of companies that want to learn is to fully exploit the resources and

capabilities that have provided competitive advantage to date. This is a simple notion, yet in the quest for global position, too many companies become so focused on where they are going that they forget where they are coming from. In the early stages of Jollibee's expansion, for example, an aggressive international division manager fell into the trap of trying to reinvent the company's business. By constantly emphasizing the differences of overseas markets, he deliberately isolated his overseas managers from the highly successful Philippines fast-food organization. Then he systematically differentiated his operating systems, store design, menus, advertising themes, and even the company's logo and slogan. Despite his enthusiasm and energy, Jollibee's international sales struggled and losses mounted. Eventually that manager was replaced with someone more willing to build on existing expertise.

The new manager took a few simple steps that were crucial to the company's subsequent international growth. First, he broke down the barriers between the international and domestic organizations and began building relationships that acknowledged his respect for their success and dependence on the home country's expertise. For example, international managers now train in the Philippines operations, learning from that organization's experience and making useful support contacts as they do. They also have given up trying to manage all their own financial and operations reporting systems, relying instead on the efficient home market staff. And when major overseas appointments come up—as one did to manage the key China and Hong Kong operations—the international group now feels comfortable drawing on the best and brightest from the Philippines—in this case the domestic VP of operations—rather than trying to staff from international ranks.

This sort of close cooperation between the parent company and its overseas subsidiaries establishes a dynamic of mutual learning. In Jollibee's case, the domestic organization's openness and exposure to international developments has allowed it to benefit from some of the adaptations and adjustments made to accommodate different situations abroad. For example, even through it is only a year old, the U.S. operations have already located chicken and beef suppliers for its restaurants in Southeast Asia, and the Philippines stores have just launched a cheesy bacon-mushroom sandwich originally developed for the U.S. market. So the operation that started by teaching its international managers has ended up learning from them. Such cross-pollination of ideas is key if emerging multinationals are to compete successfully with the giants they take on.

Build the Future   Entering a new market successfully usually requires considerably more than simply tweaking the home-market formula. Often companies lack the expertise needed to tailor the product or strategy to the new environment. So many emerging multinationals try to take a shortcut to learning by entering into a partnership with a foreign company. But while some of these international partnerships become successful long-term ventures, more fall apart due to an asymmetry of interests or a shift in the partners' power balance. When that happens, the emergent multinational as a new and small player is often left at a serious disadvantage.

Consider the situation faced by VIP Industries, India's largest luggage company and the world's second-largest producer after Samsonite of molded luggage. When it entered the UK market, VIP formed a marketing partnership with a local distributor that promised access to the country's largest retailers. A breakthrough came when the distributor, with VIP's help, won the franchise to establish a specialty luggage department in each of Debenham's 75 stores nationwide. VIP invested heavily in staff training for the specialty departments, and it was rewarded with a 60% share of Debenham's hard luggage sales. Yet when Samsonite offered VIP's distributor exclusive rights to its revolutionary Oyster II model, the local agent switched allegiances with hardly a thought. With no direct investment in its own local sales and

marketing capabilities, VIP was powerless to respond.

In theory, companies can sidestep the disadvantages of partnering by buying the necessary capabilities. But that can create problems of its own. That was the mistake that Hardy made when it committed to international expansion. In the course of just two business trips to Europe, the company's management had snapped up two established London wine merchants, a large French winery and estate, and a historic Italian vineyard. Hardy believed the acquisitions would provide an asset base and knowledge pool to broaden its product sources and increase its marketing clout. But the challenge of simultaneously developing expertise in Italian and French wine making as well as English marketing proved overwhelming and soon placed huge financial and management strains on the company.

After that false start, Hardy realized that in international business new capabilities cannot simply be installed; they must be developed and internalized. That's why, despite acute financial pressures, the company rejected a tempting opportunity to rapidly expand its UK market volume by supplying wine for a leading grocery chain's private label. Instead, it opted for the more difficult task of building Hardy's own brand image and the marketing and distribution capabilities to support it. That has required considerable investment in new personnel and training, as well as a major reorientation of internal culture.

In 1991, Christopher Carson, an experienced international wine marketer, was appointed managing director of the company's UK operations. Over the next 18 months, Carson pruned three-quarters of the items in the fragmented product line, replaced half his management team, and began building a culture around creativity and disciplined execution. Within three years, he had not only quadrupled sales of Hardy brands but also developed one of his imported wines from Chile into the biggest-selling Chilean brand in the United Kingdom. Hardy's revenues and profits have amply rewarded this investment, and the organization has developed a worldwide pool of knowledge and expertise that benefits the entire company. Carson, for example, has become the company's acknowledged expert in structuring sourcing partnerships and marketing outsourced wine brands. After building experience negotiating the Chilean partnership, he led the company's efforts on the Italian joint venture that sourced and marketed the successful D'istinto brand. Leveraging this expertise, he is now leading a new Spanish project.

Having the Right Stuff

As we examined the activities of this handful of companies that overcame their liabilities of origin, exploited their late-mover advantages, and captured and leveraged learning in global markets, we were struck by one commonality. From fast food to pharmaceuticals, from Brazil to Thailand, moving from the periphery into the mainstream of global competition is such a big leap that it was always led from the top. In each and every case, the emerging multinationals had leaders who drove them relentlessly up the value curve. These leaders shared two characteristics. First, their commitment to global entrepreneurialism was rooted in an unshakable belief that their company would succeed internationally. Second, as their operations expanded, they all exhibited a remarkable openness to new ideas that would facilitate internationalism—even when those ideas challenged established practice and core capabilities.

With a PhD in pharmacology from the University of Michigan, Ranbaxy's Parvinder Singh was always a scientist-entrepreneur at heart. It was Singh who envisioned Ranbaxy as an international, research-based pharmaceutical company. Every time urgent domestic needs appeared to overwhelm R&D priorities, he protected the programs that would support foreign markets and those that searched for either new drugs or new drug-delivery systems. Whenever the well-established intermediates business appeared to monopolize international managers's time and energy, he reminded them that their ultimate purpose was to move up the value curve and that the intermediates business was a means, not the end. Beyond specific actions, Singh protected the faith. Just like the ancient priests in rural India who seldom intervene in the community but who nonetheless exert a constant influence over the lives and behaviors of the villagers, Singh was always there, standing up for internationalization. Respecting him meant respecting his dream, and that perhaps more than anything else pushed senior managers to persist with international initiatives, even when the costs appeared too high.

The second quality of global leadership—openness to new ideas—was most clearly and forcibly displayed by Dr. Peter Farrell, CEO of ResMed. ResMed is an Australia based medical equipment company that specializes in the treatment of a breathing disorder known as obstructive sleep apnea (OSA). Spun off in 1989 by U.S. giant Baxter International, ResMed was a struggling start-up with a crude early product generating just $1 million in annual revenue. By 1999, it was the world's number two competitor in the fast-growing market for OSA treatment devices, and its products were generating sales of some $90 million a year.

Farrell's receptivity to new ideas was responsible for this dramatic change in fortune. Although the company's cofounder, Dr. Colin Sullivan, the inventor of ResMed's product, was acknowledged as one of the industry's most knowledgeable experts, Farrell pushed ResMed's researchers to build strong networks with other leaders in the international medical community. He led a team on a worldwide fact-finding tour of leading researchers and physicians, for example, and he put together a medical advisory board to help ResMed develop its products to be the industry standard. To help shape the medical debate, the company also organized annual global medical conferences on OSA, distributing the proceedings in ResMed-sponsored CD-ROMs. More recently, Farrell launched a campaign to have the medical profession recognize the strong links between sleep-disordered breathing and the incidence of strokes and congestive heart failure. It is a bold initiative and requires substantial investment, but it has the potential to raise the medical profile of OSA dramatically, and in doing so, multiply ResMed's target market substantially. Farrell has also moved the company's center of operations in order to be closer to his largest and most sophisticated markets. In these and other ways, Farrell pushed the company to act like a leading global player long before that was an operating reality.

Strong leaders changed the fates of ResMed and Ranbaxy, Hardy and Jollibee, and the other companies discussed here. These leaders are models for the heads of thousands of marginal companies in peripheral economies that have the potential to become legitimate global players. Like Nelson Mandela, they can lead their followers out of the isolationism and parochialism that constrains them. They can do so by climbing up the value curve into the mainstream of the global economy.

CHAPTER 2

Understanding the International Context:
Responding to Conflicting Environmental Forces

In this chapter, we shift our focus from the internal forces that drive companies to expand to the larger, external, international environment in which they must operate. In particular, we focus on three sets of macro forces that drive, constrain, and shape the industries in which entities compete globally. First, we examine the pressures—mostly economic—that drive companies in many industries to integrate and coordinate their activities across national boundaries to capture scale economies or other sources of competitive advantage. Second, we explore the forces—often social and political—that shape other industries and examine how they can drive MNEs to disaggregate their operations and activities to respond to national, regional, and local needs and demands. And third, we examine how, in an information-based, knowledge-intensive economy, players in a growing number of industries must adapt to opportunities or threats wherever they occur in the world by developing innovative responses and initiatives that they diffuse rapidly and globally to capture a knowledge-based competitive advantage.

Recent changes in the international business environment have revolutionized the task facing MNE managers. Important shifts in political, social, economic, and technological forces have combined to create management challenges for today's MNEs that differ fundamentally from those facing companies just a couple of decades ago. Yet despite intense study by academics, consultants, and practicing managers, both the nature of the various external forces and their strategic and organizational implications are still widely disputed.

Twenty-five years ago, when Professor Theodore Levitt's classic *Harvard Business Review* article, "The Globalization of Markets," was published, his ideas provoked widespread debate. In Levitt's view, technological, social, and economic trends were combining to create a unified world marketplace that was driving companies to develop globally standardized products that would enable them to capture global economies. His critics, however, claimed that Levitt presented only one side of the story. They suggested that, like many managers, he had become so focused on the forces for globalization that he was blind to their limitations and equally powerful countervailing forces.

The ensuing debate helped better define the diverse, changeable, and often contradictory forces that were reshaping so many industries in the closing years of the 20th century. In this chapter, we summarize a few of the most powerful of these environmental forces and suggest how they have collectively led to a new and complex set of challenges that require managers of MNEs to respond to three simultaneous yet often conflicting sets of external demands: cross-market integration, national responsiveness, and worldwide learning.

Forces for Global Integration and Coordination

The phenomenon of globalization in certain industries, as described by Levitt, was not a sudden or discontinuous development. It was simply the latest round of change brought about by economic, technological, and competitive factors that, 100 years earlier, had transformed the structures of many industries from regional to national in scope. Economies of scale, economies of scope, and national differences in the availability and cost of productive resources were the three principal economic forces that drove this process of structural transformation of businesses, of which globalization was the latest stage.[1] And the impact of these forces on MNE strategy had been facilitated by the increasingly liberal trading environment of the 1980s and 1990s. We now examine these forces of change in more detail.

Forces of Change: Scale, Scope, Factor Costs, and Free Trade

The Industrial Revolution created pressures for much larger plants that could capture the benefits of the *economies of scale* offered by the new technologies it spawned. Cheap and abundant energy combined with good transportation networks and new production technologies and began to restructure capital-intensive industries. For the first time, companies combined intermediate processes into single plants and developed large-batch or continuous-process technologies to achieve low-cost volume production.

However, in many industries, such as fine chemicals, automobiles, airframes, electronics, and oil refining, production at scale-economy volumes often exceeded the sales levels that individual companies could achieve in all but the largest nations, which pushed them to seek markets abroad. Even in industries in which the largest companies could retain a large enough share of their domestic markets to achieve scale economies without exports, those on the next rung were forced to seek markets outside their home countries if they were to remain competitive. In less capital-intensive industries, even companies that were largely unaffected by scale economies were transformed by the opportunities for *economies of scope* that were opened by more efficient, worldwide communication and transportation networks.

One classic example of how such economies could be exploited internationally was provided by trading companies that handle consumer goods. By exporting the products of many companies, they achieved a greater volume and lower per unit cost than any narrow-line manufacturer could in marketing and distributing its own products abroad.

In many industries, there were opportunities for economies of both scale and scope. Consumer electronics companies such as Matsushita, for example, derived scale

---

[1]For a more detailed analysis of these environmental forces, see Alfred D. Chandler Jr., "The Evolution of the Modern Global Corporation," in *Competition in Global Industries,* ed. Michael Porter (Boston: Harvard Business School Press, 1986), pp. 405–48. For those interested in an even more detailed exposition, Chandler's book, *Scale and Scope* (Cambridge, MA: Harvard University Press, 1990) will prove compelling reading.

advantages from their standardized TV, VCR, and DVD plants and scope advantages through their marketing and sales networks that offered service, repair, and credit for a broad range of consumer electronics.

With changes in technology and markets came the requirement for access to new resources at the best possible prices, making differences in *factor costs* a powerful driver of globalization. Often no home-country sources could supply companies wishing to expand into new industry segments. European petroleum companies, for example, explored the Middle East because they had limited domestic crude oil sources. Others went overseas in search of bauxite from which to produce aluminum, rubber to produce tires for a growing automobile industry, or tea to be consumed by an expanding middle class.

Less capital-intensive industries such as textiles, apparel, and shoes turned to international markets as a source of cheap labor. The increased costs of transportation and logistics management were more than offset by much lower production costs. However, many companies found that, once educated, the cheap labor rapidly became expensive. Indeed, the typical life cycle of a country as a source of cheap labor for an industry is now only about five years. Therefore, companies chased cheap labor from southern Europe to Central America to the Far East and later to Eastern Europe.

Whereas the economics of scale and scope and the differences in factor costs between countries provided the underlying motivation for global coordination, the *liberalization of world trade* agreements facilitated much of the broad transition that has occurred in the past half-century. Beginning with the formation of the General Agreement on Tariffs and Trade (GATT) in 1945 and moving through various rounds of trade talks, the creation of regional free trade agreements such as the European Union (EU) and North American Free Trade Agreement (NAFTA), and the formation of the World Treaty Organization (WTO), the dominant trend has been toward the reduction of barriers to international trade. The result is that the international trading environment of the 21st century is probably less restricted than ever before, which has enabled MNEs to realize most of the potential economic benefits that arise from global coordination.

The Expanding Spiral of Globalization

During the 1970s and 1980s, these forces began to globalize the structure and competitive characteristics of a variety of industries. In some, the change was driven by a major technological innovation that forced a fundamental realignment of industry economics. The impact of transistors and integrated circuits on the design and production of radios, televisions, and other consumer electronics represents a classic example of how new technologies drive the minimum efficient scale of production beyond the demand of most single markets. More recently, advances in semiconductor technology led to the boom in the PC industry, and innovations in wireless technology have led to the creation of the mobile phone industry.

Many other industries lack strong external forces for change but transformed themselves through internal restructuring efforts, such as rationalizing their product lines, standardizing parts design, and specializing manufacturing operations. This trend led to a further wave of globalization, with companies in industries as diverse as automobiles, office equipment, industrial bearings, construction equipment, and machine tools all seeking to gain competitive advantages by capturing scale economies that extended beyond national markets.

Even some companies in classically local rather than global businesses have begun to examine the opportunities for capturing economies beyond their national borders. Rather than responding to the enduring differences in consumer tastes and market structures across European countries, many large, branded packaged goods companies such as Procter & Gamble and Unilever have transformed traditionally national businesses like soap and detergent manufacturing. By standardizing product formulations, rationalizing package sizes, and printing multilingual labels, they have been able to restructure and specialize their nationally dominated plant configurations and achieve substantial scale economies, which gives them significant advantages over purely local competitors.

Even labor-intensive local industries, such as office cleaning and catering, are not immune to the forces of globalization. For example, ISS, the Danish cleaning services company, has built a successful international business by transferring practices and know-how across countries and offering consistent, high-quality service to its international customers. Sodexho, a French company, has adopted a similar approach in the catering and food services industry and become highly successful on an international basis.

In market terms also, the spread of global forces expanded from businesses in which the global standardization of products was relatively easy (e.g., watches, cameras) to others in which consumers' preferences and habits only slowly converged (e.g., automobiles, appliances). Again, major external discontinuities often facilitate the change process, as in the case of the 2005 global oil price increases, which triggered a worldwide demand for smaller, more fuel-efficient or alternative-energy cars.

Even in markets in which national tastes or behaviors vary widely, globalizing forces can be activated if one or more competitors in a business chooses to initiate and influence changes in consumer preference. Food tastes and eating habits were long thought to be the most culture-bound of all consumer behaviors. Yet, as companies like McDonald's, Coca-Cola, and Starbucks have shown, in Eastern and Western countries alike, even these culturally linked preferences can be changed.

Global Competitors as Change Agents

As the forces driving companies to coordinate their worldwide operations spread from industries in which such changes were triggered by some external structural discontinuity to those in which managers had to create the opportunity themselves, there emerged a new globalization force that spread rapidly across many businesses. It was a competitive strategy that some called *global chess* and that could be played only by companies that managed their worldwide operations as interdependent units that implemented a coordinated global strategy. Unlike the traditional multinational strategic approach, which was based on the assumption that each national market was unique and independent of the others, these global competitive games assumed that a company's competitive position in all markets was linked by financial and strategic interdependence.

Regardless of consumer tastes or manufacturing scale economies, it was suggested that corporations with worldwide operations had great advantages over national companies, in that they could use funds generated in one market to subsidize their position in another.

Whereas the classic exponents of this strategy were the Japanese companies that used the profit sanctuary of a protected home market to subsidize their loss-making expansions abroad in the 1980s, many others soon learned to play "global chess." For example, British Airways rose to become one of the most profitable airlines in the world because its dominant position at Heathrow Airport enabled it to make large profits on its long-haul routes (particularly the trans-Atlantic route) and essentially subsidize its lower margin U.K. and European business. In turn, it could fend off new entrants in Europe by pushing its prices down there while not putting its most profitable routes at risk. And existing competitors such as British Midland suffered because they lacked access to the lucrative Heathrow–U.S. routes.

Although few challenged the existence or growing influence of these diverse globalizing forces that were transforming the nature of competition worldwide, some questioned the unidimensionality of their influence and the universality of their strategic implications. They took issue, for example, with Levitt's suggestions that "the world's needs and desires have been irrevocably homogenized," that "no one is exempt and nothing can stop the process," and that "the commonality of preference leads inescapably to the standardization of products, manufacturing, and the institution of trade and commerce." Critics argued that, though these might indeed be long-term trends in many industries, there were important short- and medium-term impediments and countertrends that had to be taken into account if companies were to operate successfully in an international economy that jolts along—*perhaps* eventually toward Levitt's "global village."

Forces for Local Differentiation and Responsiveness

There are many different stories of multinational companies making major blunders in transferring their successful products or ideas from their home countries to foreign markets. General Motors is reported to have faced difficulties in selling the popular Chevrolet Nova in Mexico, where the product name sounded like "no va," meaning "does not go" in Spanish.[2] Similarly, when managers began investigating why the advertising campaign built around the highly successful "come alive with Pepsi" theme was not having the expected impact in Thailand, they discovered that the Thai copy translation read more like "come out of the grave with Pepsi." Although these and other such cases have been widely cited, they represent the most extreme and often simple-minded examples of an important strategic task facing managers of all MNEs: how to sense, respond to, and even exploit the differences in the environments of the many different countries in which their company operates.

National environments differ on many dimensions. For example, there are clear differences in the per capita gross national product or the industry-specific technological

---

[2]For this and many other such examples of international marketing problems, see David A. Ricks, *Blunders in International Business,* 3d ed. (Cornwall: Blackwell Publishing, 1999).

capabilities of Japan, Australia, Brazil, and Poland. They also differ in terms of political systems, government regulations, social norms, and the cultural values of their people. It is these differences that force managers to be sensitive and responsive to national, social, economic, and political characteristics of the host countries in which they operate.

Far from being overshadowed by the forces of globalization, the impact of these localizing forces have been felt with increasing intensity and urgency throughout recent decades. First, in the early 1990s, many Japanese companies that had so successfully ridden the wave of globalization began to feel the strong need to become much more sensitive to host-country economic and political forces. This shift led to a wave of investment abroad, as Japanese companies sought to become closer to their export markets and more responsive to host governments.

Second, as the 1990s progressed, many North American and European companies also realized that they had pushed the logic of globalization too far and that a reconnection with the local environments in which they were doing business was necessary. For example, in March 2000, Coca-Cola's incoming CEO, Douglas Daft, explained his company's shift in policy in the *Financial Times*: "As the 1990s were drawing to a close, the world had changed course, and Coca-Cola had not." Said Daft, "We were operating as a big, slow, insulated, sometimes even insensitive 'global' company; and we were doing it in an era when nimbleness, speed, transparency and local sensitivity had become absolutely essential."

Cultural Differences

A large body of academic research provides strong evidence that nationality plays an important and enduring role in shaping the assumptions, beliefs, and values of individuals. Perhaps the most celebrated work describing and categorizing these differences in the orientations and values of people in different countries is Geert Hofstede's study that describes national cultural differences along four key dimensions: power distance, uncertainty avoidance, individualism, and "masculinity."[3] The study demonstrates how distinct cultural differences across countries result in wide variations in social norms and individual behavior (e.g., the Japanese respect for elders, the culturally embedded American response to time pressure) and is reflected in the effectiveness of different organizational forms (e.g., the widespread French difficulty with the dual-reporting relationships of a matrix organization) and management systems (e.g., the Swedes' egalitarian culture leads them to prefer flatter organizations and smaller wage differentials).

However, cultural differences are also reflected in nationally differentiated consumption patterns, including the way people dress or the foods they prefer. Take the example of tea as a beverage consumed around the globe. The British drink their tea as a light

---

[3]For a more detailed exposition, see Hofstede's book *Culture's Consequences,* 2/e (Beverly Hills, CA: Sage Publications, 2001). A brief overview of the four different aspects of national culture are presented in the reading "Culture and Organization" at the end of this chapter. For managerial implications of such differences in national culture, see also Nancy J. Alder, *International Dimensions of Organizational Behavior,* 4th ed. (Boston: Kent Publishing, 2000), and Fons Trompenaars and Charles Hampden-Turner, *Riding the Waves of Culture* (London: Nicholas Brealey Publishing, 1997).

Issue Receipt

14-10-2008

Issued at:
16:30

Item: Transnational management : text,
cases, and readings in cross-border
management / Christopher A. Bartlett,
Sumantra Ghoshal, Paul W. Beamish
Due Date: 21/10/2008 21.45

brew further diluted with milk, whereas Americans consume it primarily as a summer drink served over ice, and Saudi Arabians drink theirs as a thick, hot, heavily sweetened brew. To succeed in a world of such diversity, companies often must modify their quest for global efficiency through standardization and find ways to respond to the needs and opportunities created by cultural differences.

Government Demands

Inasmuch as cultural differences among countries have been an important localizing force, the diverse demands and expectations of home and host governments have perhaps been the most severe constraint to the global strategies of many MNEs. Traditionally, the interactions between companies and host governments have had many attributes of classic love–hate relationships.

The "love" of the equation was built on the benefits each could bring to the other. To the host government, the MNE represented an important source of funds, technology, and expertise that could help further national priorities, such as regional development, employment, import substitution, and export promotion. To the MNE, the host government represented the key to local market or resource access, which provided new opportunities for profit, growth, and improvement of its competitive position.

The "hate" side of the relationship—though more often it emerges as frustration rather than outright antagonism—arose from the differences in the motivations and objectives of the two partners.

To be effective global competitors, MNEs sought three important operating objectives: unrestricted access to resources and markets throughout the world; the freedom to integrate manufacturing and other operations across national boundaries; and the unimpeded right to coordinate and control all aspects of the company on a worldwide basis. The host government, in contrast, sought to develop an economy that could survive and prosper in a competitive international environment. At times, this objective led to the designation of another company—perhaps a "national champion"—as its standard bearer in the specific industry, bringing it into direct conflict with the MNE. This conflict is particularly visible in the international airline business, in which flag-carrying companies such as Air France or Malaysia Airlines compete only after receiving substantial government subsidies. But it also has been a thorny issue among their biggest suppliers, with Boeing complaining to the WTO that Airbus is violating free trade agreements through the support it receives from various European governments.

Even when the host government does not have such a national champion and is willing to permit and even support an MNE's operations within its boundaries, it usually does so only at a price. Although both parties might be partners in the search for global competitiveness, the MNE typically tried to achieve that objective within its global system, whereas the host government strove to capture it within its national boundaries, thereby leading to conflict and mutual resentment.

The potential for conflict between the host government and the MNE arose not only from economic but also from social, political, and cultural issues. MNE operations often cause social disruption in the host country through rural exodus, rising consumerism, rejection of indigenous values, or a breakdown of traditional community structures.

Similarly, even without the maliciousness of MNEs that, in previous decades, blatantly tried to manipulate host government structures or policies (e.g., ITT's attempt to overthrow the Allende government in Chile), MNEs can still represent a political threat because of their size, power, and influence, particularly in developing economies.

Because of these differences in objectives and motivations, MNE–host government relationships are often seen as a zero-sum game in which the outcome depends on the balance between the government's power (arising from its control over local market access and competition among different MNEs for that access) and the MNE's power (arising from its financial, technological, and managerial resources and the competition among national governments for those resources).

If, in the 1960s, the multinational companies had been able to hold "sovereignty at bay," as one respected international researcher concluded,[4] by the 1980s, the balance had tipped in the other direction. In an effort to stem the flood of imports, many countries began bending or sidestepping trade agreements signed in previous years. By the early 1980s, even the U.S. government, traditionally one of the strongest advocates of free trade, began to negotiate a series of orderly marketing agreements and voluntary restraints on Japanese exports, while threats of sanctions were debated with increasing emotion in legislative chambers around the globe. And countries became more sophisticated in the demands they placed on inward-investing MNEs. Rather than allowing superficial investment in so-called "screwdriver plants" that provided only limited, low-skill employment, governments began to specify the levels of local content, technology transfer, and a variety of other conditions, from reexport commitment to plant location requirements.

In the 1990s, however, the power of national governments was once again on the wane. The success of countries such as Ireland and Singapore in driving their economic development through foreign investment led many other countries—both developed and developing—to launch aggressive inward investment policies of their own.

This increased demand for investment allowed MNEs to play countries off one another and, in many cases, to extract a high price from the host country. For example, according to *The Economist,* the incentives paid by Alabama to Mercedes for its 1993 auto plant cost the state $167,000 per direct employee.

In the first years of the new millennium, the once-troublesome issue of MNE–country bargaining power evolved into a relatively efficient market system for inward investment, at least in the developed world. However, the developing world was a rather different story, with MNEs continuing to be embroiled in political disputes, such as the 1995 hanging of environmental activist Ken Saro-Wiwa by the Nigerian government because of his opposition to Shell's exploitation of his people's land. In addition, MNEs have attracted the brunt of criticism from so-called antiglobalization protestors during WTO meetings in Seattle, Genoa, and elsewhere. The antiglobalization movement includes a diverse mix of groups with different agendas but that are united in their concern that the increasing liberalization of trade through the WTO is being pursued for the benefit of MNEs and at the expense of people and companies in less developed parts of the world.

[4]Raymond Vernon, *Sovereignty at Bay* (New York: Basic Books, 1971).

Although this movement does not have a coherent set of policy proposals of its own, it provides a salutary reminder to policymakers and the executives managing MNEs that the globalization of business remains a contentious issue. The rewards are not spread evenly, and for many people in many parts of the world, the process of globalization makes things worse before it makes them better. The movement has forced MNEs to rethink their more contentious policies and encouraged them to articulate the benefits they bring to less developed countries. For example, the oil majors Shell and BP now actively promote polices for sustainable development—including research into renewable sources of energy and investments in the local communities in which they operate around the world.

Growing Pressures for Localization

Although there is no doubt that the increasing frequency of world travel and the ease with which communication linkages occur across the globe have done a great deal to reduce the effects of national consumer differences, it would be naïve to believe that worldwide tastes, habits, and preferences have become anywhere near homogenous. Furthermore, even though many companies have succeeded in appealing to—and accelerating—such convergence worldwide, even the trend toward standardized products that are designed to appeal to a lowest common denominator of consumer demand has a flip side. In industry after industry, a large group of consumers has emerged to reject the homogenized product design and performance of standardized global products.

By reasserting traditional preferences for more differentiated products, they have created openings—often very profitable ones—for companies willing to respond to, and even expand, the need for products and services that are more responsive to those needs.

Other consumer and market trends are emerging to counterbalance the forces of global standardization of products. In an increasing number of markets, from telecommunications to office equipment to consumer electronics, consumers are not so much buying individual products as selecting systems. With advances in wireless and Internet technology, for example, the television set is becoming part of a home entertainment and information system, connected to a DVD player, music system, home computer, gaming system, and online databank and information network. This transformation is forcing companies to adapt their standard hardware-oriented products to more flexible and locally differentiated systems that consist of hardware plus software services. In such an environment, the competitive edge lies less with the company that has the most scale-efficient global production capability and more with the one that is sensitive and responsive to local requirements and able to develop the software and services to meet those demands.

In addition to such barriers, other important impediments exist. Although the benefits of scale economies obviously must outweigh the additional costs of supplying markets from a central point, companies often ignore that those costs consist of more than just freight charges. In particular, the administrative costs of coordination and scheduling worldwide demand through global-scale plants usually is quite significant and must be taken into account. For some products, lead times are so short or market service requirements so high that these scale economies may well be offset by other costs.

More significantly, developments in computer-aided design and manufacturing, robotics, and other advanced production technologies have made the concept of flexible manufacturing a viable reality. Companies that previously had to produce tens or hundreds of thousands of standardized printed circuit boards (PCBs) in a central, global-scale plant now can achieve the minimum efficient scale in smaller, distributed, national plants closer to their customers. Flexible manufacturing technologies mean there is little difference in unit costs between making 1,000 or 100,000 PCBs. When linked to the consumer's growing disenchantment with homogenized global products, this technology appears to offer multinational companies an important tool that will enable them to respond to localized consumer preferences and national political constraints without compromising their economic efficiency.

Forces for Worldwide Innovation and Learning

The trends we have described have created an extremely difficult competitive environment in many industries, and only those firms that have been able to adapt to the often conflicting forces for global coordination and national differentiation have been able to survive and prosper. But on top of these forces, another set of competitive demands has been growing rapidly around the need for fast, globally coordinated innovation. Indeed, in the emerging competitive game, victory often goes to the company that can most effectively harness its access to worldwide information and expertise to develop and diffuse innovative products and processes on a worldwide basis.

The trends driving this shift in the competitive game in many ways derive from the globalizing and localizing forces we described previously. The increasing cost of R&D, coupled with shortening life cycles of new technologies and the products they spawn, have combined to reinforce the need for companies to seek global volume to amortize their heavy investments as quickly as possible. At the same time, even the most advanced technology has diffused rapidly around the globe, particularly during the past few decades. In part, this trend has been a response to the demands, pressures, and coaxing of host governments as they bargain for increasing levels of national production and high levels of local content in the leading-edge products being sold in their markets. But the high cost of product and process development has also encouraged companies to transfer new technologies voluntarily, with licensing becoming an important source of funding, cross-licensing a means to fill technology gaps for many MNEs, and joint development programs and strategic alliances a strategy for rapidly building global competitive advantage.

When coupled with converging consumer preferences worldwide, this diffusion of technology has had an important effect on both the pace and locus of innovation. No longer can U.S.-based companies assume, as they often did in the immediate postwar decades, that their domestic environment provided them with the most sophisticated consumer needs and the most advanced technological capabilities, and thus the most innovative environment in the world. Today, the newest consumer trend or market need might emerge in Australia or Italy, and the latest technologies to respond to these new needs may be located in Japan or Sweden. Innovations are springing up worldwide, and companies are recognizing that they can gain competitive advantage by sensing needs in one country, responding with capabilities located in a second, and diffusing the resulting innovation to markets around the globe.

A related trend is the increasing importance of global standards in such industries as computer software, telecommunications, consumer electronics, and even consumer goods. The winners in the battle for a new standard—from software platforms to razor blade cartridges—can build and defend dominant competitive positions that can endure worldwide for decades. First-mover advantages have increased substantially and provided strong incentives for companies to focus attention not only on the internal task of rapidly creating and diffusing innovations within their own worldwide operations but also on the external task of establishing the new product as an industry standard. This issue is so vital for MNEs today that we will return to examine it in greater detail in Chapter 5.

Responding to the Diverse Forces Simultaneously

Trying to distill key environmental demands in large and complex industries is a hazardous venture but, at the risk of oversimplification, we can make the case that until the late 1980s, most worldwide industries presented relatively unidimensional environmental requirements. But, though it led to the development of industries with very different characteristics—those we distinguish as global, multinational, and international industries—more recently, this differentiation has been eroding with important consequences for companies' strategies.

Global, Multinational, and International Industries

In some businesses, the economic forces of globalization were historically strong and dominated other environmental demands. For example, in the consumer electronics industry, the invention of the transistor led to decades of inexorable expansion in the benefits of scale economics: Successive rounds of technological change, such as the introduction of integrated circuits and microprocessors, led to an increase of the minimum efficient scale of operations from about 50,000 television sets per annum to more than 3 million per annum. In an environment of falling transportation costs, relatively low tariffs, and increasing homogenization of national markets, these huge-scale economics dominated the strategic tasks for managers of consumer electronics companies in the closing decades of the last century.

Such industries, in which the economic forces of globalization are dominant, we designate as *global industries*. In these businesses, success typically belongs to companies that adopt the classic *global strategies* of capitalizing on highly centralized, scale-intensive manufacturing and R&D operations and leveraging them through worldwide exports of standardized global products.

In other businesses, the localizing forces of national, cultural, social, and political differences dominate the development of industry characteristics. In laundry detergents, for example, R&D and manufacturing costs were relatively small parts of a company's total expenses, and all but the smallest markets could justify an investment in a detergent tower and benefit from its scale economies. At the same time, sharp differences in laundry practices, perfume preferences, phosphate legislation, distribution channels, and other such attributes of different national markets led to significant benefits from differentiating products and strategies on a country-by-country basis.

This differentiation is typical of what we call *multinational industries*—worldwide businesses in which the dominance of national differences in cultural, social, and political environments allow multiple national industry structures to flourish. Success in such businesses typically belongs to companies that follow *multinational strategies* of building strong and resourceful national subsidiaries that are sensitive to local market needs and opportunities and allow them to manage their local businesses by developing or adapting products and strategies to respond to the powerful localizing forces.

Finally, in some other industries, technological forces are central, and the need for companies to develop and diffuse innovations is the dominant source of competitive advantage. For example, the most critical task for manufacturers of telecommunications switching equipment has been the ability to develop and harness new technologies and exploit them worldwide. In these *international industries,* it is the ability to innovate and appropriate the benefits of those innovations in multiple national markets that differentiates the winners from the losers.

In such industries, the key to success lies in a company's ability to exploit technological forces by creating new products and to leverage the international life cycles of the product by effectively transferring technologies to overseas units. We describe this as an *international strategy*—the ability to effectively manage the creation of new products and processes in one's home market and sequentially diffuse those innovations to foreign affiliates.

Transition to Transnationality

Our portrayal of the traditional demands in some major worldwide industries is clearly oversimplified. Different tasks in the value-added chains of different businesses are subject to different levels of economic, political, cultural, and technological forces. We have described what can be called the *center of gravity* of these activities—the environmental forces that have the most significant impact on industry's strategic task demands.

By the closing years of the 20th century however, these external demands were undergoing some important changes. In many industries, the earlier dominance of a single set of environmental forces was replaced by much more complex environmental demand, in which each of the different sets of forces was becoming strong simultaneously. For example, new economies of scale and scope and intensifying competition among a few competitors were enhancing the economic forces toward increased global integration in many multinational and international industries. In the detergent business, product standardization has become more feasible because the growing penetration and standardization of washing machines has narrowed the differences in washing practices across countries. Particularly in regional markets such as Europe or South America, companies have leveraged this potential for product standardization by developing regional brands, uniform multilingual packaging, and common advertising themes, all of which have led to additional economies.

Similarly, localizing forces are growing in strength in global industries such as consumer electronics. Although the strengths of the economic forces of scale and scope have continued to increase, host government pressures and renewed customer demand for differentiated products are forcing companies with global strategies to reverse their earlier strategies, which were based on exporting standard products. To protect their competitive positions, they have begun to emphasize the local design and production of differentiated product ranges in different countries and for different international segments.

Finally, in the emerging competitive battle among a few large firms with comparable capabilities in global-scale efficiency and nationally responsive strategies, the ability to innovate and exploit the resulting developments globally is becoming more and more important for building durable comparative advantage, even in industries in which global economic forces or local political and cultural influences had previously been dominant. In the highly competitive mobile phone business, for example, all surviving major competitors must have captured the minimum scale efficiency to play on the global field, as well as the requisite government relationships and consumer understanding to respond to market differences. Today, competition in this industry consists primarily of a company's ability to develop innovative new products—perhaps in response to a consumer trend in Japan, a government requirement in Germany, or a technological development in the United States—and then diffuse it rapidly around the world.

In the emerging international environment, therefore, there are fewer and fewer examples of pure global, textbook multinational, or classic international industries. Instead, more and more businesses are driven by *simultaneous* demands for global efficiency, national responsiveness, and worldwide innovation. These are the characteristics of what we call a *transnational industry*. In such industries, companies find it increasingly difficult to defend a competitive position on the basis of only one dominant capability. They need to develop their ability to respond effectively to all the diverse and conflicting forces at one and the same time to manage efficiency, responsiveness, and innovation without trading off any one for the other.

The emergence of the transnational industry has not only made the needs for efficiency, responsiveness, and innovation simultaneous, it has also made the tasks required to achieve each of these capabilities more demanding and complex. Rather than achieve world-scale economies through centralized and standardized production, companies must instead build global efficiency through a worldwide infrastructure of distributed but specialized assets and capabilities that exploit comparative advantages, scale economies, and scope economies simultaneously. In most industries, a few global competitors now compete head-to-head in almost all major markets.

To succeed in such an environment, companies must understand the logic of global chess: Build and defend profit sanctuaries that are impenetrable to competitors; leverage existing strengths to build new advantages through cross-subsidizing weaker products and market positions; make high-risk, preemptive investments that raise the stakes and force out rivals with weaker stomachs and purse strings; and form alliances and coalitions to isolate and outflank competitors. These and other similar maneuvers must now be combined with world-scale economies to develop and maintain global competitive efficiency.

Similarly, responsiveness through differentiated and tailor-made local-for-local products and strategies in each host environment is neither necessary nor feasible anymore. National customers no longer demand differentiation; they demand sensitivity to their needs, along with the level of cost and quality standards for global products to which they have become accustomed. At the same time, host governments' desire to build their national competitiveness dominates economic policy in many countries, and MNEs are frequently viewed as key instruments in the implementation of national competitive strategies. Changes in regulations, tastes, exchange rates, and related factors have become less predictable and more frequent. In such an environment, more responsiveness has become inadequate. The flexibility to change product designs, sourcing patterns, and pricing policies continuously to remain responsive to continually changing national environments has become essential for survival.

And finally, exploiting centrally developed products and technologies is no longer enough. MNEs must build the capability to learn from the many environments to which they are exposed and to appropriate the benefits of such learning throughout their global operations. Although some products and processes must still be developed centrally for worldwide use and others must be created locally in each environment to meet purely local demands, MNEs must increasingly use their access to multiple centers of technologies and familiarity with diverse customer preferences in different countries to create truly transnational innovations. Similarly, environmental and competitive information acquired in different parts of the world must be collated and interpreted to become a part of the company's shared knowledge base and provide input to future strategies.

Concluding Comments: The Strategic and Organizational Challenge

The increasing complexity of forces in the global environment and the need to respond simultaneously to their diverse and often conflicting demands have created some major challenges for many multinational companies. The classic global companies, such as many highly successful Japanese and Korean companies whose competitive advantage is rooted in a highly efficient and centralized system, have been forced to respond more effectively to the demands for national responsiveness and worldwide innovation. The traditional multinational companies—many of them European—have the advantage of national responsiveness but face the challenge of exploiting global-scale economic and technological forces more effectively. And U.S. companies, with their more international approach to leveraging home country innovations abroad, struggle to build more understanding of the cultural and political forces and respond to national differences more effectively while simultaneously enhancing global-scale efficiency through improved scale economies.

For most MNEs, the challenge of the 2000s is both strategic and organizational. On the one hand, they are forced to develop a more complex array of strategic capabilities that enable them to capture the competitive advantages that accrue to efficiency, responsiveness, and learning. On the other hand, the traditional organizational approaches of these companies, developed to support their earlier global, multinational, or international approaches, have become inadequate for the more complex strategic tasks they now must accomplish. In Chapters 3 and 4, we discuss some of the ways in which companies can respond to these new strategic and organizational challenges.

Case 2-1   Hitting the Wall: Nike and International Labor Practices

Moore: Twelve year olds working in [Indonesian] factories? That's O.K. with you?
Knight: They're not 12-year-olds working in factories . . . the minimum age is 14.
Moore: How about 14 then? Does that bother you?
Knight: No.

—Phil Knight, Nike CEO, talking to Director Michael Moore in a scene from documentary film *The Big One*, 1997.

Nike is raising the minimum age of footwear factory workers to 18. . . . Nike has zero tolerance for underage workers.[1]

—Phil Knight, 1998

In 1997, Nguyen Thi Thu Phuong died while making sneakers. As she was trimming synthetic soles in a Nike contracting factory, a co-worker's machine broke, spraying metal parts across the factory floor and into Phuong's heart. The 23-year-old Vietnamese woman died instantly.[2]

Although it may have been the most dramatic, Phuong's death was hardly the first misfortune to hit Nike's far-flung manufacturing empire. Indeed, in the 1980s and 1990s, the corporation had been plagued by a series of labor incidents and public relations nightmares: underage workers in Indonesian plants, allegations of coerced overtime in China, dangerous working conditions in Vietnam. For a while, the stories had been largely confined to labor circles and activist publications. By the time of Phuong's death, however, labor conditions at Nike had hit the mainstream. Stories of reported abuse at Nike plants had been carried in publications such as *Time* and *BusinessWeek* and students

from major universities such as Duke and Brown had organized boycotts of Nike products. Even Doonesbury had joined the fray, with a series of cartoons that linked the company to underage and exploited Asian workers. Before these attacks, Nike had been widely regarded as one of the world's coolest and most successful companies. Now Nike, the company of Michael Jordan and Tiger Woods; Nike, the sign of the swoosh and athletic prowess, was increasingly becoming known as the company of labor abuse. And its initial response—"We don't make shoes"—was becoming harder and harder to sustain.[3]

Nike, Inc.

Based in Beaverton, Oregon, Nike had been a corporate success story for more than three decades. It was a sneaker company, but one armed with an inimitable attitude, phenomenal growth, and the apparent ability to dictate fashion trends to some of the world's most influential consumers. In the 1970s, Nike had first begun to capture the attention of both trend-setting teenagers and financial observers. Selling a combination of basic footwear and street-smart athleticism, Nike pushed its revenues from a 1972 level of $60,000 to a startling $49 million in just ten years.[4] It went public in 1980

Research Associate Jennifer L. Burns prepared this case under the supervision of Professor Debora L. Spar. This case was developed from published sources. HBS cases are developed solely as the basis for class discussion. Cases are not intended to serve as endorsements, sources of primary data, or illustrations of effective or ineffective management.

[1]"Nike CEO Phil Knight Announces New Labor Initiatives," *PR Newswire*, May 12, 1998.

[2]Tim Larimer, "Sneaker Gulag: Are Asian Workers Really Exploited?" *Time International*, May 11, 1998, p. 30.

[3]The quote is from Martha Benson, Nike's regional spokeswoman in Asia. See Larimer, p. 30.

[4]David B. Yoffie, *Nike: A (Condensed)*, HBS Case 391-238 (Boston: HBS Press, 1991), p. 1.

and then astounded Wall Street in the mid-1990s as annual growth stayed resolutely in the double digits and revenues soared to over $9 billion. By 1998, Nike controlled over 40% of the $14.7 billion U.S. athletic footwear market. It was also a growing force in the $64 billion sports apparel market, selling a wide range of sport-inspired gear to consumers around the globe.[5]

What differentiated Nike from its competitors was not so much its shoes as its strategy. Like Reebok and adidas and New Balance, Nike sold a fairly wide range of athletic footwear to a fairly wide range of consumers: men and women, athletes and non-athletes, in markets around the world. Its strategy, though, was path breaking, the product of a relatively simple idea that CEO Phil Knight had first concocted in 1962 while still a student at Stanford Business School. The formula had two main prongs. First, the company would shave costs by outsourcing *all* manufacturing. There would be no in-house production, no dedicated manufacturing lines. Rather all product would be made by independent contracting factories, creating one of the world's first "virtual" corporations—a manufacturing firm with no physical assets. Then, the money saved through outsourcing would be poured into marketing. In particular, Knight focussed from the start on celebrity endorsements, using high-profile athletes to establish an invincible brand identity around the Nike name. While other firms had used celebrity endorsements in the past, Nike took the practice to new heights, emblazoning the Nike logo across athletes such as Michael Jordan and Tiger Woods, and letting their very celebrity represent the Nike image. "To see name athletes wearing Nike shoes," Knight insisted, "was more convincing than anything we could say about them."[6] With the help of the "swoosh," a distinctive and instantly recognizable logo, Nike became by the 1990s one of the world's

best known brands, as well as a global symbol of athleticism and urban cool.

But within this success story lay a central irony that would only become apparent in the late 1990s. While the *marketing* of Nike's products was based on selling a high profile fashion item to affluent Americans who only wished they could "Just Do It" as well as Woods or Jordan, the *manufacture* of these sneakers was based on an arm's-length and often uneasy relationship with low-paid, non-American workers. For according to Knight's original plan, not only would Nike outsource, but it would outsource specifically to low cost parts of the world.

Nike signed its first contracts with Japanese manufacturers but eventually shifted its supply base to firms in South Korea and Taiwan, where costs were lower and production reliable. In 1982, 86% of Nike sneakers came from one of these two countries and Nike had established a large network of suppliers in both nations. But as South Korea and Taiwan grew richer, costs rose and Nike began to urge its suppliers to move their operations to new, lower cost regions. Eager to remain in the company's good graces, most manufacturers rapidly complied, moving their relatively inexpensive plants to China or Indonesia. By 1990, these countries had largely replaced South Korea and Taiwan as the core of Nike's global network. Indonesia, in particular, had become a critical location, with six factories that supplied Nike and a booming, enthusiastic footwear industry.[7]

Taking Care of Business

At first, Indonesia seemed an ideal location for Nike. Wages were low, the workforce was docile, and an authoritarian government was yearning for foreign direct investment. There were unions in the country and occasional hints of activism, but the Suharto government clearly was more interested in wooing investors than in acceding to any union demands. So wages stayed low and labor demands were minimal. In 1991, the daily minimum wage in

---

[5]Both figures are for retail sales. *Footwear 1999* (North Palm Beach: Athletic Footwear Association, 1999), introduction; Dana Eisman Cohen and Sabina McBride, *Athletic Footwear Outlook 1999* (New York: Donaldson, Lufkin & Jenrette, 1998), p. 3.

[6]Yoffie, p. 6.

[7]Philip M. Rosenzweig and Pam Woo, *International Sourcing in Footwear: Nike and Reebok,* HBS Case 394-189 (Boston: HBS Press, 1994), pp. 2–5.

Indonesia's capital city was barely $1, compared to a typical daily wage of $24.40 in South Korea[8] and a U.S. hourly wage in athletic shoe manufacturing of about $8.[9] For firms like Nike, this differential was key: according to a reporter for the *Far Eastern Economic Review,* shoes coming out of China and Indonesia cost roughly 50% less than those sourced from Taiwan and South Korea.[10]

Just as Nike was settling into its Indonesian operations, though, a rare wave of labor unrest swept across the country. Strikes, which had been virtually nonexistent in the 1980s, began to occur with increasing frequency; according to government figures, there were 112 strikes in 1991,[11] a sharp increase from the 19 reported in 1989.[12] A series of polemical articles about foreign companies' labor abuses also appeared in Indonesian newspapers, triggering unprecedented demands from factory workers and empowering a small but potent band of labor organizers.

The source of these strikes and articles was mysterious. Some claimed that the Indonesian government was itself behind the movement, trying to convince an increasingly suspicious international community of the country's commitment to freedom of speech and labor rights. Others saw the hand of outside organizers, who had come to Indonesia solely to unionize its work force and embarrass its foreign investors. And still others saw the outbursts as random eruptions, cracks in the authoritarian veneer which quickly took on a life of their own. In any case, though, the unrest occurred just around the time of Nike's expansion into Indonesia. In 1991 the Asian-American Free Labor Association (AAFLI, a branch of the AFL-CIO) published a highly critical report on foreign companies in Indonesia. Later that

year, a group of Indonesian labor economists at the Institut Teknology Bandung (ITB), issued a similar report, documenting abusive practices in Indonesian factories and tracing them to foreign owners. In the midst of this stream of criticism was a labor organizer with a deep-seated dislike for Nike and a determination to shape its global practices. His name was Jeff Ballinger.

The Role of Jeff Ballinger A labor activist since high school, Ballinger felt passionately that any company had a significant obligation towards even its lowliest workers. He was particularly concerned about the stubborn gap between wage rates in developed and developing worlds, and about the opportunities this gap created for rich Western companies to exploit low-wage, politically repressed labor pools. In 1988, Ballinger was assigned to run the AAFLI office in Indonesia, and was charged with investigating labor conditions in Indonesian plants and studying minimum wage compliance by overseas American companies. In the course of his research Ballinger interviewed workers at hundreds of factories and documented widespread worker dissatisfaction with labor conditions.

Before long, Nike emerged as a key target. Ballinger believed that Nike's policy of competing on the basis of cost fostered and even encouraged contractors to mistreat their workers in pursuit of unrealistic production quotas. Although Indonesia had worker protection legislation in place, widespread corruption made the laws essentially useless. While the government employed 700 labor inspectors, Ballinger found that out of 17,000 violations reported in 1988, only 12 prosecutions were ever made. Bribery took care of the rest.[13] Nike contractors, in particular, he believed, were regularly flouting Indonesian labor laws and paying below-subsistence wages that did not enable workers to meet their daily requirements for food and other necessities. And to top matters off, he found Nike's attitude in the face of these labor practices galling: "It was right around the time that the swoosh started appearing on everything and

[8]Elliot B. Smith, "K-Swiss in Korea," *California Business,* October 1991, p. 77.

[9]Rosenzweig and Woo, p. 3.

[10]Mark Clifford, "Pain in Pusan," *Far Eastern Economic Review,* November 5, 1992, p. 59.

[11]Suhaini Aznam, "The Toll of Low Wages," *Far Eastern Economic Review,* April 2, 1992, p. 50.

[12]Margot Cohen, "Union of Problems: Government Faces Growing Criticism on Labour Relations," *Far Eastern Economic Review,* August 26, 1993, p. 23.

[13]Interview with casewriter, Cambridge, MA, July 6, 1999.

everyone," Ballinger remembered. "Maybe it was the swagger that did it."[14]

What also "did it," though, was Ballinger's own strategic calculation—a carefully crafted policy of "one country–one company." Ballinger knew that his work would be effective only if it was carefully focused. And if his goal was to draw worldwide attention to the exploitation of third-world factory workers by rich U.S. companies, then Nike made a nearly ideal target. The arithmetic was simple. The same marketing and branding power that drove Nike's bottom line could also be used to drive moral outrage against the exploitation of Asian workers. After the publication of his AAFLI report, Ballinger set out to transform Nike's competitive strength into a strategic vulnerability.

For several years he worked at the fringes of the activist world, operating out of his in-laws' basement and publishing his own newsletter on Nike's practices. For the most part, no one really noticed. But then, in the early 1990s Ballinger's arguments coincided with the strikes that swept across Indonesia and the newfound interest of media groups. Suddenly his stories were big news and both the Indonesian government and U.S. firms had begun to pay attention.

Early Changes   The first party to respond to criticism from Ballinger and other activists was the government itself. In January 1992 Indonesia raised the official minimum daily wage from 2100 rupiah to 2500 rupiah (US\$1.24). According to outside observers, the new wage still was not nearly enough: it only provided 70% of a worker's required minimal physical need (as determined by the Indonesian government) and was further diluted by the way in which many factories distributed wages and benefits.[15] The increased wage also had no impact on "training wages," which were lower than the minimum wage and often paid long after the training period had expired. Many

factories, moreover, either ignored the new wage regulations or successfully petitioned the government for exemption. Still, the government's actions at least demonstrated some willingness to respond. The critics took note of this movement and continued their strikes and media attacks.

Despite the criticism, Nike insisted that labor conditions in its contractors' factories were not—could not—be Nike's concern or its responsibility. And even if labor violations did exist in Nike's contracting factories, stated the company's general manager in Jakarta, "I don't know that I need to know."[16] Nike's company line on the issue was clear and stubborn: without an inhouse manufacturing facility, the company simply could not be held responsible for the actions of independent contractors.

Realizing the severity of the labor issue, though, Nike did ask Dusty Kidd, a newly-hired member of its public relations department, to draft a series of regulations for its contractors. In 1992, these regulations were composed into a Code of Conduct and Memorandum of Understanding and attached to the new contracts sent to Nike contractors. In the Memorandum, Nike addressed seven different aspects of working conditions, including safety standards, environmental regulation and worker insurance. It required its suppliers to certify they were following all applicable rules and regulations and outlined general principles of honesty, respect, and nondiscrimination.

Meanwhile, other shoe companies had been facing similar problems. Reebok, a chief competitor of Nike, also sourced heavily from Indonesia and South Korea. Like Nike, it too had been the subject of activist pressure and unflattering media. But unlike Nike, Reebok had moved aggressively into the human rights arena. In 1988, it created the Reebok Human Rights Award, bestowed each year on youthful contributors to the cause of human rights, and in 1990 it adopted a formal human rights policy.[17] When activists accused the company of

---

[14]Ibid.

[15]A factory, for example, could pay a base wage lower than 2500 rupiah, but bring total compensation up to legal levels by the addition of a food allowance and incentive payments (see Aznam, p. 50).

[16]Adam Schwarz, "Running a Business," *Far Eastern Economic Review,* June 20, 1991, p. 16.

[17]Rosenzweig and Woo, p. 7.

violating workers' rights in Indonesia, Reebok responded with a far-reaching set of guidelines, one that spoke the explicit language of human rights, set forth specific standards for the company's contractors and promised to audit these contractors to ensure their compliance.[18] It was a big step for an American manufacturer and considerably farther than Nike had been willing to go.

Into the Spotlight

By 1992, criticism of Nike's labor practices had begun to seep outside of Indonesia. In the August issue of *Harper's Magazine,* Ballinger published an annotated pay-stub from an Indonesian factory, making the soon-to-be famous comparison between workers' wages and Michael Jordan's endorsement contract. He noted that at the wage rates shown on the pay stub, it would take an Indonesian worker 44,492 years to make the equivalent of Jordan's endorsement contract.[19] Then the Portland *Oregonian,* Nike's hometown newspaper, ran a series of critical articles during the course of the 1992 Barcelona Olympics. Also at the Olympics, a small band of protestors materialized and handed out leaflets that charged Nike with exploitation of factory workers. The first mainstream coverage of the issue came in July 1993, when CBS interviewed Indonesian workers who revealed that they were paid just 19¢ an hour. Women workers could only leave the company barracks on Sunday, and needed a special letter of permission from management to do so. Nike responded somewhat more forcefully to this next round of allegations, hiring accounting firm Ernst & Young to conduct formal audits of its overseas factories. However, because Ernst & Young was paid by Nike to perform these audits, activists questioned their objectivity from the start. Public criticism of Nike's labor practices continued to mount.

Then suddenly, in 1996, the issue of foreign labor abuse acquired a name and a face: it was Kathie Lee Gifford, a popular daytime talk show host. In April human rights activists revealed that a line of clothing endorsed by Gifford had been manufactured by child labor in Honduras. Rather than denying the connection Gifford instantly rallied to the cause. When she appeared on television, crying and apologetic, a wave of media coverage erupted. Or as Ballinger recalls, "That's when my phone really started ringing."[20] Although Nike was not directly involved in the Gifford scandal, it quickly emerged as a symbol of worker exploitation and a high-profile media scapegoat.

Child labor was the first area of concern. In July, *Life Magazine* ran a story about child labor in Pakistan, and published a photo of a 12 year old boy stitching a Nike soccer ball.[21] Then Gifford herself publicly called upon fellow celebrities such as Michael Jordan to investigate the conditions under which their endorsed products were made and to take action if need be. Jordan brushed away suggestions that he was personally responsible for conditions in Nike factories, leaving responsibility to the company itself. When Nike refused to let Reverend Jesse Jackson tour one of its Indonesian factories the media jumped all over the story, noting by contrast that Reebok had recently flown an executive to Indonesia just to give Jackson a tour.

At this point, even some pro-business observers began to jump on the bandwagon. As an editorial in *BusinessWeek* cautioned: "Too few executives understand that the clamor for ethical sourcing isn't going to disappear with the wave of a magic press release. They have protested, disingenuously, that conditions at factories run by subcontractors are beyond their control. . . . Such attitudes won't wash anymore. As the industry gropes for solutions," the editorial concluded, "Nike will be a key company to watch."[22]

---

[18]Ibid., pp. 16–17.

[19]Jeff Ballinger, "The New Free-Trade Heel," *Harper's Magazine,* August 1992, p. 64.

[20]Casewriter interview.

[21]Nike's vigorous protests stopped the magazine from running the photo on its cover. Nike convincingly argued that the photo was staged, because the ball was inflated so that the Nike "swoosh" was clearly visible. In fact, soccer balls are stitched while deflated. However, the company did admit it had inadvertently relied on child labor during its first months of production in Pakistan.

[22]Mark L. Clifford, "Commentary: Keep the Heat on Sweatshops," *BusinessWeek,* December 23, 1996, p. 90.

The View From Washington   Before long, the spotlight on the labor issue extended all the way to Washington. Sensing a hot issue, several senators and representatives jumped into the action and began to suggest legislative solutions to the issue of overseas labor abuse. Representative George Miller (D-CA) launched a campaign aimed at retailers that would mandate the use of "No Sweat" labels to guarantee that no exploited or child labor had been employed in the production of a garment. "Parents," he proclaimed, "have a right to know that the toys and clothes they buy for their children are not made by exploited children." To enforce such guarantees, Miller added, "I think Congress is going to have to step in."[23]

On the heels of this public outcry, President Clinton convened a Presidential task force to study the issue, calling on leaders in the apparel and footwear industries to join and help develop acceptable labor standards for foreign factories. Known as the Apparel Industry Partnership (AIP), the coalition, which also included members of the activist, labor, and religious communities, was meant to be a model collaboration between industry and its most outspoken critics, brokered by the U.S. government. Nike was the first company to join.

In order to supplement its hiring of Ernst & Young, in October 1996 Nike also established a Labor Practices Department, headed by former public relations executive Dusty Kidd. In a press release, Knight announced the formation of the new department and praised Nike's recent initiatives regarding fair labor practices, such as participation in Clinton's AIP, membership in the organization Business for Social Responsibility, and an ongoing dialogue with concerned non-governmental organizations (NGOs). "Every year we continue to raise the bar," said Knight. "First by having Ernst & Young audits, and now with a group of Nike employees whose sole focus will be to help make things better for workers who make Nike products. In labor practices as in sport, we at Nike believe

'There is No Finish Line.'"[24] And indeed he was right, for the anti-Nike campaign was just getting started.

The Hotseat   As far as public relations were concerned, 1997 was even worse for Nike than 1996. Much as Ballinger had anticipated, Nike's giant marketing machine was easily turned against itself and in a climate awash with anti-Nike sentiment, any of Nike's attempts at self promotion became easy targets. In 1997 the company began expanding its chain of giant retail stores, only to find that each newly opened Niketown came with an instant protest rally, complete with shouting spectators, sign waving picketers, and police barricades. Knowing a good story when they saw it, reporters eagerly dragged Nike's celebrity endorsers into the fracas. Michael Jordan was pelted with questions about Nike at press conferences intended to celebrate his athletic performance, and football great Jerry Rice was hounded to the point of visible agitation when he arrived at the grand opening of a new Niketown in San Francisco.[25]

Perhaps one of the clearest indicators that Nike was in trouble came in May 1997, when Doonesbury, the popular comic strip, devoted a full week to Nike's labor issues. In 1,500 newspapers, millions of readers watched as Kim, Mike Doonesbury's wife, returned to Vietnam and found a long-lost cousin laboring in dismal conditions at a Nike factory. The strips traced Kim's growing involvement in the activist movement and the corrupt factory manager's attempts to deceive her about true working conditions in Nike contracting factories. In Doonesbury, Nike had reached an unfortunate cultural milestone. As one media critic noted: "It's sort of like getting in Jay Leno's monologue. It means your perceived flaws have reached a critical mass, and everyone feels free to pick on you."[26] The

[23]"Honduran Child Labor Described," *The Boston Globe*, May 30, 1996, p. 13.

[24]"Nike Establishes Labor Practices Department," *PR Newswire*, October 2, 1996.
[25]"Protestors Swipe at the Swoosh, Catch Nike's Jerry Rice Off Guard," *The Portland Oregonian*, February 21, 1997, p. C1.
[26]Jeff Manning, "Doonesbury Could Put Legs on Nike Controversy," *The Portland Oregonian*, May 25, 1997, p. D01.

appearance of the Doonesbury strips also marked the movement of anti-Nike sentiment from the fringes of American life to the mainstream. Once the pet cause of leftist activists, Nike bashing had become America's newest spectator sport.

Even some of the company's natural friends took a dim view of its actions. *The Wall Street Journal* ran an opinion piece alleging that "Nike Lets Critics Kick it Around." The writer argued that Nike had been "its own worst enemy" and that its public relations efforts had only made the problem worse. According to the writer, had Nike acknowledged its wrongdoing early on and then presented economic facts that showed the true situation of the workers, the crisis would have fizzled.[27] Instead it had simply gathered steam. Even more trouble loomed ahead with the anticipated release of *The Big One,* a documentary film by Michael Moore that was widely expected to be highly critical of Nike's labor practices.

Damage Control

Late in 1996 the company decided to turn to outside sources, hiring Andrew Young, the respected civil rights leader and former mayor of Atlanta, to conduct an independent evaluation of its Code of Conduct. In January 1997, Knight granted Young's newly-formed GoodWorks International firm "blanket authority . . . to go anywhere, see anything, and talk with anybody in the Nike family about this issue."[28]

Shortly thereafter Young went to Asia, visited Nike suppliers and returned to issue a formal report. On the day the report was released, Nike took out full-page advertisements in major newspapers that highlighted one of Young's main conclusions: "It is my sincere belief that Nike is doing a good job. . . . But Nike can and should do better."[29] Young did not give Nike carte blanche with regard to labor practices. Indeed, he made a number of recommendations, urging Nike to improve their systems for reporting

workers' grievances, to publicize their Code more widely and explain it more clearly, and to implement cultural awareness and language training programs for expatriate managers. Young also stated that third party monitoring of factories was necessary, but agreed that it was not appropriate for Nike's NGO critics to fulfill that function.

Rather than calming Nike's critics, though, Young's report had precisely the opposite effect. Critics were outraged by the report's research methodology and conclusions, and unimpressed by Young's participation. They argued that Young had failed to address the issue of factory wages, which was for many observers the crux of the issue, and had spent only 10 days interviewing workers. During these interviews, moreover, Young had relied on translators provided by Nike, a major lapse in accepted human rights research technique. Finally, critics also noted that the report was filled with photos and used a large, showy typeface, an unusual format for a research report.

From the start, Nike executives had argued in vain that they were the target of an uninformed media campaign, pointing out that although Nike was being vigorously monitored by activists and the media, no one was monitoring the monitors. This point was forcefully made by the publication of a five page *New Republic* article in which writer Stephen Glass blasted the Young report for factual inaccuracies and deception, and summed up: "This was a public relations problem, and the world's largest sneaker company did what it does best: it purchased a celebrity endorsement."[30] Glass's claims were echoed by several other media outlets that also decried Nike's disingenuousness and Young's ineptitude. However, within months a major scandal erupted at the *New Republic* when it was discovered that most of Glass's articles were nearly fictional. Apparently, Glass routinely quoted individuals with whom he had never spoken or who did not even exist, and relied upon statistics and information from organizations he invented himself.

[27]Greg Rushford, "Nike Lets Critics Kick it Around," *The Wall Street Journal,* May 12, 1997, p. A14.
[28]Andrew Young, *Report: The Nike Code of Conduct* (GoodWorks International, LLC, 1997), p. 27.
[29]Young, p. 59.

[30]Stephen Glass, "The Young and the Feckless," *The New Republic,* September 8, 1997, p. 22.

The Issue of Wages

In the public debate, the question of labor conditions was largely couched in the language of human rights. It was about child labor, or slave labor, or workers who toiled in unsafe or inhumane environments. Buried beneath these already contentious issues, though, was an even more contentious one: wages. According to many labor activists, workers in the developing world were simply being paid too little–too little to compensate for their efforts, too little compared to the final price of the good they produced, too little, even, to live on. To many business economists, though, such arguments were moot at best and veiled protectionism at worst. Wages, they maintained, were simply set by market forces: by definition, wages could not be too low, and there was nothing firms could or should do to affect wage rates. As the debate over labor conditions evolved, the argument over wages had become progressively more heated.

Initially, Nike sought to defuse the wage issue simply by ignoring it, or by reiterating the argument that this piece of the labor situation was too far beyond their control. In the Young Report, therefore, the issue of wages was explicitly set aside. As Young explained in his introduction: "I was not asked by Nike to address compensation and 'cost of living' issues which some in the human rights and NGO community had hoped would be a part of this report." Then he went on: "Are workers in developing countries paid far less than U.S. workers? Of course they are. Are their standards of living painfully low by U.S. standards? Of course they are. This is a blanket criticism that can be leveled at almost every U.S. company that manufactures abroad. . . . But it is not reasonable to argue that any one particular U.S. company should be forced to pay U.S. wages abroad while its direct competitors do not."[31] It was a standard argument, and one that found strong support even among many pro-labor economists. In the heat of public debate, however, it registered only as self-serving.

The issue of wages emerged again in the spring of 1997, when Nike arranged for students at Dartmouth's Amos Tuck School of Business to conduct a detailed survey on "the suitability of wages and benefits paid to its Vietnamese and Indonesian contract factory workers."[32] Completed in November 1997, the students' *Survey of Vietnamese and Indonesian Domestic Expenditure Levels* was a 45 page written study with approximately 50 pages of attached data. The authors surveyed both workers and residents of the areas in which the factories were located to determine typical spending patterns and the cost of basic necessities.

In Vietnam, the students found that "The factory workers, after incurring essential expenditures, can generate a significant amount of discretionary income."[33] This discretionary income was often used by workers to purchase special items such as bicycles or wedding gifts for family members. In Indonesia, results varied with worker demographics. While 91% of workers reported being able to support themselves individually, only 49% reported being able to also support their dependents. Regardless of demographic status, 82% of workers surveyed in Indonesia either saved wages or contributed each month to their families.[34]

Additionally, the survey found that most workers were not the primary wage earners in their households. Rather, in Vietnam at least, factory wages were generally earned by young men or women and served "to *augment* aggregate household income, with the primary occupation of the household parents being farming or shopkeeping."[35] The same was often true in Indonesia. For instance, in one Indonesian household the students visited, a family of six had used one daughter's minimum wage from a Nike factory to purchase luxury items such as leather couches and a king sized bed.[36]

---

[31]Young, pp. 9–11.

[32]Derek Calzini, Shawna Huffman, Jake Odden, Steve Tran, and Jean Tsai, *Nike, Inc: Survey of Vietnamese and Indonesian Domestic Expenditure Levels,* November 3, 1997, Field Study in International Business (Dartmouth, NH: The Amos Tuck School, 1997), p. 5.

[33]Ibid., p. 8.

[34]Ibid., p. 9.

[35]Ibid., p. 31.

[36]Ibid., p. 44.

While workers in both countries managed to save wages for future expenditure, the authors found that Indonesians typically put their wages in a bank, while Vietnamese workers were more likely to hold their savings in the form of rice or cows.

Economically, data such as these supported the view that companies such as Nike were actually furthering progress in the developing countries, providing jobs and wages to people who formerly had neither. In the public view, however, the social comparison was unavoidable. According to the Tuck study, the average worker in a Vietnamese Nike factory made about $1.67 per day. A pair of Penny Hardaway basketball sneakers retailed at $150. The criticism continued to mount.

In November there was even more bad news. A disgruntled Nike employee leaked excerpts of an internal Ernst & Young report that uncovered serious health and safety issues in a factory outside of Ho Chi Minh City. According to the Ernst & Young report, a majority of workers suffered from a respiratory ailment caused by poor ventilation and exposure to toxic chemicals. The plant did not have proper safety equipment and training, and workers were forced to work 15 more hours than allowed by law. But according to spokesman Vada Manager the problems no longer existed: "This shows our system of monitoring works. We have uncovered these issues clearly before anyone else, and we have moved fairly expeditiously to correct them."[37] Once again, the denial only made the criticism worse.

Hitting the Wall

Fiscal Year 1998   Until the spring of 1997, Nike sneakers were still selling like hotcakes. The company's stock price had hit $76 and futures orders reached a record high. Despite the storm of criticism lobbied against it, Nike seemed invincible.

Just a year later, however, the situation was drastically different. As Knight admitted to stockholders, Nike's fiscal year 1998 "produced considerable pain." In the third quarter 1998, the company was beset by weak demand and retail oversupply, triggered in part by the Asian currency crisis. Earnings fell 69%, the company's first loss in 13 years. In response, Knight announced significant restructuring charges and the layoff of 1,600 workers.[38]

Much the same dynamic that drove labor criticism drove the 1998 downturn: Nike became a victim of its own popularity. Remarked one analyst: "When I was growing up, we used to say that rooting for the Yankees is like rooting for U.S. Steel. Today, rooting for Nike is like rooting for Microsoft."[39] The company asserted that criticism of Nike's labor practices had nothing to do with the downturn. But it was clear that Nike was suffering from a serious image problem. For whatever reasons, Americans were sick of the swoosh. Although Nike billed its shoes as high performance athletic gear, it was well known that 80% of its shoes were sold for fashion purposes. And fashion was a notoriously fickle patron. Competing sneaker manufacturers, particularly adidas, were quick to take advantage of the giant's woes. Adidas' three-stripe logo fast replaced Nike's swoosh among the teen trendsetter crowd; rival brands New Balance and Airwalk tripled their advertising budgets and saw sales surge.

To make matters worse, the anti-Nike headlines had trickled down to the nation's campuses, where a newly invigorated activist movement cast Nike as a symbol of corporate greed and exploitation. With its roots deep in the University of Oregon track team (Knight had been a long distance runner for the school), Nike had long treasured its position as supplier to the top athletic universities. Now, just as young consumers were choosing adidas over Nike at the cash register, campus activists rejected Nike's contracts with their schools and demanded all contracts cease until labor practices were rectified. In late 1997, Nike's $7.2 million endorsement deal

[37]Tunku Varadarajan, "Nike Audit Uncovers Health Hazards at Factory," *The Times of London*, November 10, 1997, p. 52.

[38]Nike Corporation, *Annual Report 1998* (Nike, Inc.: Beaverton, OR), pp. 1, 17–30.

[39]Quoted in Patricia Sellers, "Four Reasons Nike's Not Cool," *Fortune*, March 30, 1998, p. 26.

Exhibit 1 Nike, Inc. Financial History, 1989–1999 (in millions of dollars)

Year Ended May 31	1999	1998	1997	1996	1995	1994	1993	1992	1991	1990	1989
Revenues	$8,776.9	$9,553.1	$9,186.5	$6,470.6	$4,760.8	$3,789.7	$3,931.0	$3,405.2	$3,003.6	$2,235.2	$1,710.8
Gross margin	3,283.4	3,487.6	3,683.5	2,563.9	1,895.6	1,488.2	1,544.0	1,316.1	1,153.1	851.1	636.0
Gross margin %	37.4	36.5	40.1	39.6	39.8	39.3	39.3	38.7	38.4	38.1	37.2
Restructuring charge, net	45.1	129.9	—	—	—	—	—	—	—	—	—
Net income	451.4	399.6	795.8	553.2	399.7	298.8	365.0	329.2	287.0	243.0	167.0
Cash flow from operations	961.0	517.5	323.1	339.7	254.9	576.5	265.3	435.8	11.1	127.1	169.4
Price range of common stock											
High	65.500	64.125	76.375	52.063	20.156	18.688	22.563	19.344	13.625	10.375	4.969
Low	31.750	37.750	47.875	19.531	14.063	10.781	13.750	8.781	6.500	4.750	2.891
Cash and equivalents	$198.1	$108.6	$445.4	$262.1	$216.1	$518.8	$291.3	$260.1	$119.8	$90.4	$85.7
Inventories	1,199.3	1,396.6	1,338.6	931.2	629.7	470.0	593.0	471.2	586.6	309.5	222.9
Working capital	1,818.0	1,828.8	1,964.0	1,259.9	938.4	1,208.4	1,165.2	964.3	662.6	561.6	419.6
Total assets	5,247.7	5,397.4	5,361.2	3,951.6	3,142.7	2,373.8	2,186.3	1,871.7	1,707.2	1,093.4	824.2
Long-term debt	386.1	379.4	296.0	9.6	10.6	12.4	15.0	69.5	30.0	25.9	34.1
Shareholders' equity	3,334.6	3,261.6	3,155.9	2,431.4	1,964.7	1,740.9	1,642.8	1,328.5	1,029.6	781.0	558.6
Year-end stock price	60.938	46.000	57.500	50.188	19.719	14.750	18.125	14.500	9.938	9.813	4.750
Market capitalization	17,202.2	13,201.1	16,633.0	14,416.8	5,635.2	4,318.8	5,499.3	4,379.6	2,993.0	2,942.7	1,417.4
Geographic Revenues:											
United States	$5,042.6	$5,460.0	$5,538.2	$3,964.7	$2,997.9	$2,432.7	$2,528.8	$2,270.9	$2,141.5	$1,755.5	$1,362.2
Europe	2,255.8	2,096.1	1,789.8	1,334.3	980.4	927.3	1,085.7	919.8	664.7	334.3	241.4
Asia/Pacific	844.5	1,253.9	1,241.9	735.1	515.6	283.4	178.2	75.7	56.2	29.3	32.0
Americas (exclusive of U.S.)	634.0	743.1	616.6	436.5	266.9	146.3	138.3	138.8	141.2	116.1	75.2
Total revenues	$8,776.9	$9,553.1	$9,186.5	$6,470.6	$4,760.8	$3,789.7	$3,931.0	$3,405.2	$3,003.6	$2,235.2	$1,710.8

All per common share data has been adjusted to reflect the 2-for-1 stock splits paid October 23, 1996, October 30, 1995 and October 5, 1990. The Company's Class B Common Stock is listed on the New York and Pacific Exchanges and traded under the symbol NKE. At May 31, 1999, there were approximately 170,000 shareholders.
Source: Nike, Inc., *Annual Report 1999.*

Exhibit 2	Estimated Cost Breakdown of an Average Nike Shoe, 1999
$3.37	Labor costs
$3.41	Manufacturer's overhead
$14.60	Materials
$1.12	Profit to factory
$22.50	Factory price to Nike
$45	Wholesale price
$90	Retail price

Source: Jennifer Lin, "Vietnam Gives Nike a Run for Its Money," *The Philadelphia Enquirer,* March 23, 1998, p. 1.

with the University of North Carolina sparked protests and controversy on campus; in early 1998 an assistant soccer coach at St. John's University, James Keady, publicly quit his job rather than wear the swoosh. "I don't want to be a billboard for a company that would do these things," said Keady.[40]

Before long, the student protests spread to campuses where Nike had no merchandising contracts. Organized and trained by unions such as UNITE! and the AFL-CIO, previously apathetic college students stormed university buildings to protest sweatshop labor and the exploitation of foreign workers. In 1999, activists took over buildings at Duke, Georgetown, the University of Michigan and the University of Wisconsin, and staged sit-ins at countless other colleges and universities. The protests focused mostly on the conditions under which collegiate logo gear was manufactured. Declared Tom Wheatley, a Wisconsin student and national movement leader: "It really is quite sick. Fourteen-year-old girls are working 100-hour weeks and earning poverty-level wages to make my college T-shirts. That's unconscionable."[41] University administrators heeded the student protests, and many began to consider codes of conduct for contract manufacturers.

[40]William McCall, "Nike's Image Under Attack: Sweatshop Charges Begin to Take a Toll on the Brand's Cachet," *The Buffalo News,* October 23, 1998, p. 5E.
[41]Nancy Cleeland, "Students Give Sweatshop Fight the College Try," *Los Angeles Times,* April 22, 1999, p. C1.

Saving the Swoosh   Nike's fiscal woes did what hundreds of harsh articles had failed to do: they took some of the bravado out of Phil Knight. In a May 1998 speech to the National Press Club, a humbled Knight admitted that "the Nike product has become synonymous with slave wages, forced overtime, and arbitrary abuse."[42] Knight announced a series of sweeping reforms, including raising the minimum age of all sneaker workers to 18 and apparel workers to 16; adopting U.S. OSHA clean air standards in all its factories; expanding its monitoring program; expanding educational programs for workers; and making micro loans available to workers. Although Nike had been formally addressing labor issues since 1992, Knight's confession marked a turning point in Nike's stance towards its critics. For the first time, he and his company appeared ready to shed their defensive stance, admit labor violations did occur in Nike factories, and refashion themselves as leaders in the effort to reform third world working conditions.

Nike's second step was to get more involved with Washington-based reform efforts. In the summer of 1998, President Clinton's initial task force on labor, the Apparel Industry Partnership (AIP), lay deadlocked over the ever-delicate issues of factory monitoring and wages. Although the AIP had a tentative proposal, discussion ground to a halt when the task force's union, religious, and corporate members clashed.

While the AIP proclaimed itself as an exemplar of cooperative solution making, it soon became apparent that its members had very different views. One key concept—"independent monitoring"—was highly contentious. To Nike, the hiring of a separate and unrelated multinational firm like Ernst & Young fulfilled any call for independent monitoring. But activists and other critics alleged that if an independent monitor, such as an accounting firm, was hired by a corporation, it thereby automatically lost autonomy and independence. According to such critics, independent monitoring could only

[42]John H. Cushman Jr., "Nike to Step Forward on Plant Conditions," *The San-Diego Union-Tribune,* May 13, 1998, p. A1.

Exhibit 3   Prices of Some Popular Running Shoe Styles in New York City, 1996

	Nike Air Max		New Balance 999		Saucony Grid Shadow	
	Men's	Women's	Men's	Women's	Men's	Women's
Foot Locker	$140	$135	$124	$105	$85	$85
Paragon Sports	140	135	135	109	70	70
Sports Authority	140	140	101	101	78	78
Super Runners Shop	140	130	125	110	85	85

Source: "Feet Don't Fail . . . ," *The New York Times,* November 3, 1996, Section 13, p. 12.

Exhibit 4   Summary Revenue and Expense Profile of Minimum Wage Workers by Demographic Type
(in Indonesian Rupiah)

	SH	SO	Dorm	MH	MO	Total (weighted)
Number of respondents	67	161	33	21	32	314
Base wages	172,812	172,071	172,197	173,905	172,650	172,424
Total wages	**225,378**	**238,656**	**239,071**	**248,794**	**244,458**	**236,893**
Rent	14,677	40,955	12,121[a]	24,775	56,050	32,838
Food	84,774	95,744	90,455	103,421	128,793	103,020
Transportation	48,984	24,189	7,219	17,471	38,200	28,560
Savings	38,369	41,783	70,303	29,412	49,185	44,154
Contribution to home	22,175	37,594	57,644	25,222	25,089	34,441
Total uses	**208,980**	**240,266**	**237,741**	**200,301**	**297,318**	**243,013**

[a]17 of the 33 respondents were provided free housing by the factory. The remaining 16 paid a subsidized monthly rent of Rp 25,000.
Note: Monthly Wages and Total Uses of wages may not match due to averaging.

Key to demographic type:

SH—Single workers living at home.
SO—Single workers living away from home and paying rent.
Dorm—Single workers living away from home and living in factory subsidized housing.
MH—Married workers living at home.
MO—Married workers living away from home.

Source: Derek Calzini, Shawna Huffman, Jake Odden, Steve Tran, and Jean Tsai, *Nike, Inc: Survey of Vietnamese and Indonesian Domestic Expenditure Levels,* November 3, 1997, Field Study in International Business (Dartmouth, NH: The Amos Tuck School, 1997), pp. 9–10.

be done by an organization that was not on a corporate payroll, such as an NGO or a religious group. The corporations, by contrast, insisted that a combination of internal monitoring and audits by accounting firms was sufficient. Upset at what they saw as corporate intransigence, the task force's union and religious membership abruptly exited the coalition.

The remaining corporate members of the AIP were soon able to cobble together a more definitive

Exhibit 5   Typical "Basket" of Basic Food Expenditures for Indonesian Workers (in rupiah)

Rice	800–1,300	per 5 servings
Instant Noodles	300–500	per serving
Eggs	2,800–3,000	per 18 eggs
Tofu	1,500	per 15 servings
Tempe	1,500	per 15 servings
Kancang Pangung	1,500	per 15 servings
Peanuts	2,600	per kilogram
Oil	2,300	per liter
Other "luxury" foods		
Fish	6,000	per kilogram
Chicken	4,500–5,000	per chicken

Source: Derek Calzini, Shawna Huffman, Jake Odden, Steve Tran, and Jean Tsai, *Nike, Inc: Survey of Vietnamese and Indonesian Domestic Expenditure Levels,* November 3, 1997, Field Study in International Business (Dartmouth, NH: The Amos Tuck School, 1997), p. 45.

Exhibit 6   Strikes and Lockouts in Indonesia, 1988–1997

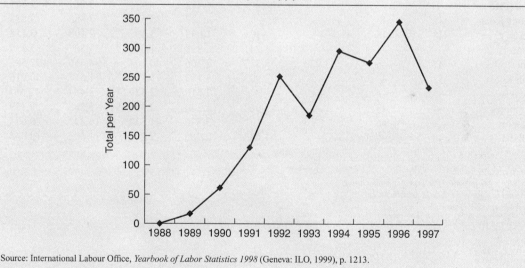

Source: International Labour Office, *Yearbook of Labor Statistics 1998* (Geneva: ILO, 1999), p. 1213.

agreement, complete with an oversight organization known as the Fair Labor Association (FLA). The FLA was to be a private entity controlled evenly by corporate members and human rights or labor representatives (if they chose to rejoin the coalition). It would support a code of conduct that required its members to pay workers the legal minimum wage or the prevailing local standard, whichever was higher. The minimum age of workers was set at 15, and employees could not be required to work more than 60 hours per week. Companies that joined the Association would be required to comply with these

Exhibit 7   Wages and Productivity in Industrialized and Developing Nations (figures in $ per year)

	Average Hours Worked Per Week		Yearly Minimum Wage		Labor Cost Per Worker in Manufacturing		Value Added Per Worker in Manufacturing	
	1980–84	1990–94	1980–84	1990–94	1980–84	1990–94	1980–84	1990–94
North America								
United States	35	34	6,006	8,056[b]	19,103	32,013[b]	47,276	81,353
Canada	32	33	4,974	7,897[b]	17,710	28,346[b]	36,903	60,712
Mexico	—	34	1,002	843	3,772	6,138	17,448	25,991
Europe								
Denmark	—	37	9,170	19,933[b]	16,169	35,615[b]	27,919	49,273
France	39	39	10,815	22,955[b]	16,060	38,900[b]	26,751	61,019[e]
Germany	41	40	[a]	[a]	21,846[d]	63,956[b,d]	—	—
Greece	—	41	—	5,246	6,461	15,899[b]	14,561	30,429
Ireland	41[c]	41[c]	—	—	10,190	25,414[b]	26,510	86,036
Netherlands	40	39	9,074	15,170[b]	18,891	39,865[b]	27,491	56,801
Asia								
China (PRC)	—	—	—	—	472	434[d]	3,061	2,885
Hong Kong	48	46	—	—	4,127	13,539[b]	7,886	19,533
India	48	48	—	408	1,035	1,192	2,108	3,118
Indonesia	—	—	—	241	898	1,008	3,807	5,139
Japan	47	46	3,920	8,327[b]	12,306	40,104[b]	34,456	92,582
South Korea	52	48	—	3,903[b]	3,153	15,819[b]	11,617	40,916
Malaysia	—	—	—	[a]	2,519	3,429	8,454	12,661
Philippines	—	43	—	1,067	1,240	2,459	5,266	9,339
Singapore	—	46	—	—	5,576	21,534[b]	16,442	40,674
Thailand	48	—	—	1,083	2,305	2,705	11,072	19,946

[a] Country has sectoral minimum wage but no minimum wage policy.
[b] Data refer to 1995–1999.
[c] Data refer to hours worked per week in manufacturing.
[d] Data refer to wage per worker in manufacturing.
[e] International Labor Organisation data.

Source: World Bank, *World Development Indicators 1999* (Washington, D.C.; World Bank, 1999), pp. 62–64.

guidelines and to establish internal monitoring systems to enforce them; they would then be audited by certified independent inspectors, such as accounting firms. In the first three years after a company joined, auditors would inspect 30% of a company's factories; later they would inspect 10%. All audits would be confidential.

Nike worked tirelessly to bring other manufacturers into the FLA, but the going was tough. As of August 1999, the only other corporate members were adidas, Liz Claiborne, Reebok, Levi's, L.L.Bean, and Phillips Van Heusen. However, Nike's efforts to foster the FLA hit pay dirt with U.S. colleges and universities. The vocal

Exhibit 8   Indonesia: Wages and Inflation, 1993–97

	1993		1994		1995		1996		1997	
	Mini-mum	Maxi-mum	Mini-mum	Maxi-mum	Mini-mum	Maxi-mum	Mini-mum	Maxi-mum	Mini-mum	Maxi-mum
Monthly wages in manufacturing industry (thousands of rupiah)	196	2,920	207	3,112	238	3,453	241	3,453	439	6,050
Minimum wage regional average[a] (thousands of rupiah)	72		94		112		118		130	
Annual percent change	17.7		30.8		19.5		5.4		10.2	
Consumer price inflation	8.5		9.4		8.0		6.7		57.6	
Exchange rates (average Rp:$)	2,161		2,249		2,342		2,909		10,014	

Source: International Monetary Fund, Economist Intelligence Unit.
Figures are based on periodic surveys of primarily urban-based business establishments and include transportation, meal, and attendance allowances.
[a] Calculated from minimum daily figure for 30 days per month. Increased by 9% to Rp122,000 in 1996 and by 10% to Rp135,000 in 1997.

student anti-sweatshop movement had many administrators scrambling to find a solution, and over 100 colleges and universities eventually signed on. Participants ranged from the large state universities that held Nike contracts to the eight Ivy League schools. The FLA was scheduled to be fully operational by the fall of 2000.

Meanwhile, by 1999 Nike was running extensive training programs for its contractors' factory managers. All managers and supervisors were required to learn the native language of their workers, and received training in cultural differences and acceptable management styles. In addition to 25 employees who would focus solely on corporate responsibility, Nike's 1,000 production employees were explicitly required to devote part of their job to maintaining labor standards. In Vietnam, the company partnered with the National University of Vietnam in a program designed to identify and meet worker needs. It also helped found the Global Alliance, a partnership between the International Youth Foundation, the MacArthur Foundation, the World Bank, and Mattel, that was dedicated to improving the lives of workers in the developing world.

Although Nike's various concessions and new programs were welcomed as a victory by several human rights groups, other observers argued that Nike still failed to deal with the biggest problem, namely wages.[43] Wrote *New York Times* columnist Bob Herbert: "Mr. Knight is like a three-card monte player. You have to keep a close eye on him at all times. The biggest problem with Nike is that its overseas workers make wretched, below-subsistence wages. It's not the minimum age that needs raising, it's the minimum wage."[44] Similarly, while some labor leaders accepted the FLA as the best compromise possible, others decried it as sham agreement that simply provided cover for U.S. corporations. A main objection of these critics was that the FLA standards included notification of factories that were to be inspected, a move criticized by some as equivalent to notifying a restaurant when a critic

[43] John H. Cushman, Jr., "Nike Pledges to End Child Labor and Apply U.S. Rules Abroad," *The New York Times,* May 13, 1998, p. D1.
[44] Bob Herbert, "Nike Blinks," *The New York Times,* May 21, 1998, p. A33.

Exhibit 9   *Life Magazine* Photo of Pakistani Child Worker

Source: *Life Magazine,* June 1996, p. 39.

Exhibit 10   Doonesbury Cartoons About Nike

Doonesbury
BY GARRY TRUDEAU

Doonesbury
BY GARRY TRUDEAU

Doonesbury
BY GARRY TRUDEAU

Exhibit 11   Anti-Nike Activist Materials

Nike, Inc. in Indonesia I

JUST DO IT!

"You know when you need a break. And you know when it's time to take care of yourself, for yourself. Because you know it's never too late to have a life." (Nike advertisement)

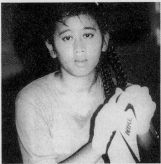

Twelve thousand Indonesian woman work 60 hours a week making Nike shoes. Many earn less than their government's minimum wage of $1.80 a day. Numerous strikes and protests have been broken up by security forces eager to placate foreign capital; labor activists have even been murdered. Factories producing Nike shoes have been cited in the State Department's Human Rights Report to Congress. Asked about local labor practices, Nike VP David Taylor said: "I don't feel bad about it. I don't think we are doing anything wrong."

One percent of Nike's advertising budget would double the wages of the women making the company's shoes and raise them above the poverty line.

Nike, Inc. in Indonesia newsletter: $20 for six months, teachers free Press for Change, Inc. PO Box 230, Bayonne, New Jersey, 07002-9998

Source: Jeff Ballinger; http://www.nikeworkers.org [10/29/99]; http://www.corpwatch.org/nike/ [10/29/99].

was coming to dine. According to Jeff Ballinger, Nike's original critic, the company's reform record was mixed. Ballinger was confident that Nike had at least removed dangerous chemicals from factories, but otherwise he remained skeptical: "If you present yourself as a fitness company you can't very well go around the globe poisoning people. But on wages, they're still lying through their teeth."[45]

[45]Casewriter interview.

Case 2-2   Global Wine Wars: New World Challenges Old (A)

It's an art, not a science. We're creating products that are crafted, just as an artist or a chef would create.

—Jean-Claude Boisset, CEO of a French wine company

We bring a total commitment to innovation . . . from vine to palate.

—Mission Statement, Australia Wine Foundation

In early 2002, these two views reflected an honest difference of wine-making practice that had grown into a fierce competitive battle between traditional wine makers and some new industry players for the $90 billion global wine market. Many companies from the Old World wine producers—France, Italy, Germany, and Spain, for example—found themselves constrained by embedded traditions and practices, restrictive industry regulations, and complex national and European Community legislation. This provided opportunities for New World wine companies—from Australia, the United States, Chile, and South Africa, for instance—to challenge the more established Old World producers by introducing innovations at every stage of the value chain.

After decades of being dismissed and even ridiculed for their attempts to compete with exports from traditional wine countries, in the 1980s and 1990s the New World companies began winning international respect, and with it global market share. At the November 2000 annual charity wine auction in Beaune, Louis Trébuchet, head of the Burgundy Growers Association, told his French colleagues that they needed to be on guard against

increasing challenges from Australian, South African, and South American wines.[1] The warning was underscored by a market forecast that in 2002 Australia would overtake France as the leading wine exporter to the United Kingdom, the world's highest-value import market and a bellwether for trends in other importing countries.

In the Beginning[2]

Grape growing and wine making have been human preoccupations for many thousands of years. Early archeological evidence of wine making has been found in Mesopotamia, and ancient Egyptians and Greeks offered wine as tributes to dead pharaohs and tempestuous gods. Under the Roman Empire, viticulture spread throughout the Mediterranean region, where almost every town had its local vineyards and wine maker.

In the Christian era, wine became part of liturgical services, and monasteries planted vines and built wineries. While today wine is often considered a sophisticated drink, during most of European history it was a peasant's beverage to accompany everyday meals. Eventually, the Benedictine monks raised viticulture to a new level, making wine not

Professor Christopher A. Bartlett prepared this case with the research assistance of Janet Cornebise and Andrew N. McLean. This case was developed from published sources. HBS cases are developed solely as the basis for class discussion. Cases are not intended to serve as endorsements, sources of primary data, or illustrations of effective or ineffective management.

[1]"Le success des vins du nouveau monde inquite la filiere viticole [Burgundy Winegrowers Worried about Success of New World Wines]," *La Tribune,* October 24, 2000, p. 25.

[2]Historical discussions are indebted to Harry W. Paul, *Science, Vine and Wine in Modern France* (Cambridge University Press, 1996), pp. 2-15; to Jancis Robinson, ed., *The Oxford Companion to Wine, 2nd Ed.* (Oxford University Press, 1999); and to James Wilson, *Terroir* (Berkeley: University of California Press, 1998), pp. 10–45.

only for religious use but also to show hospitality to travelers requiring lodging. By the Middle Ages, the European nobility began planting vineyards as a mark of prestige, competing with one another in the quality of wine served at their tables. A niche market for premium wine was born.

Wine Production   Tending and harvesting grapes has always been labor intensive, and one worker could typically look after only a three-hectare lot (one hectare equals approximately 2.5 acres)—less for hillside vineyards. The introduction of vineyard horses in the early 19th century led to vines being planted in rows and to more efficient tending and harvesting. One person could now work a seven-hectare plot.

Yet despite these efficiencies, vineyards became smaller, not larger, over time. Over many centuries, small agricultural holdings were continually fragmented as land was parceled out by kings and emperors, taken through war, or broken up through inheritance. During the French Revolution, for example, many large estates were seized, divided, and sold at auction. After 1815, the Napoleonic inheritance code prescribed how land had to be passed on to all rightful heirs. By the mid-19th century, the average holding in France was 5.5 hectares and was still being subdivided. (In Italy, similar historical events left the average vineyard holding at 0.8 hectares.)

While the largest estates made their own wine, most small farmers sold their grapes to the local wine maker or *vintner*. Because payment was often based on weight, they had little incentive to adopt practices that reduced yield but intensified grapes' flavor. Eventually, some small growers formed cooperatives, hoping to gain more control and to participate in wine making's downstream profit.

Distribution and Marketing   Traditionally, wine was sold in bulk to merchant traders—*négociants* in France—who often blended and bottled the product before distributing it. As *négociants* began shipping the product abroad, they soon found that poor roads and complex toll and tax systems made transportation extremely expensive. For example,

in the early 19th century, shipments of wine from Strasbourg to the Dutch border had to pass through 31 toll stations.[3] Furthermore, wine often did not travel well, and much of it spoiled on long journeys. As a result, only the most sophisticated *négociants* could handle exports, and only the rich could afford the imported luxury.

In the late 18th and early 19th centuries, innovations such as the mass production of glass bottles, the introduction of the cork stopper, and the development of pasteurization revolutionized the industry. With greater wine stability and longevity, distribution to more distant markets and bottle aging of the best vintages became normal practice. Together, these factors led to increased vine plantings, expanded production, and the expansion of the market for fine wines.

Regulation and Classification   As the industry developed, it became increasingly important to the cultural and economic life of the producing countries. In France, wine was a staple item on every table, and in the mid-18th century it supported 1.5 million grower families and an equal number in related businesses. At one-sixth of France's total trading revenue, it became the country's second-largest export.

The industry's growing cultural and economic importance soon attracted a great deal of political attention. Over the years laws, regulations, and policies increasingly controlled almost every aspect of wine making. For example, Germany's 1644 wine classification scheme eventually expanded to encompass 65 classes of quality, with legislation prescribing ripeness required for harvesting, definitions of minimum sugar content, and penalties for those who added sugar. (Even as late as 1971, laws were passed in Germany requiring the registration of each vineyard and the appointment of a government panel to taste each vineyard's annual vintage and assign it a quality level.)[4] Similar laws and regulations prescribing wine-making practices also developed in France and Italy.

[3]Robinson, p. 308.
[4]Ibid., p. 312.

Rather than resisting, producers often supported and even augmented the classification schemes and regulatory controls as a way of differentiating their products and raising entry barriers. The venerable French classification system was created by a Bordeaux committee in preparation for the 1855 Exposition in Paris. To help consumers recognize their finest wines, they classified about 500 vineyards on one of five levels, from *premier cru* (first growth) to *cinquième cru* (fifth growth).

Because it helped consumers sort through the complexity of a highly fragmented market, this marketing tool immediately gained wide recognition, leading the government to codify much of it in the *Appellation d'Origin Controllée* (AOC) laws. These laws also defined the boundaries and set the standards for vineyards and wine makers in France's major wine-growing regions.[5] Eventually, almost 400 AOC designations were authorized, from the well known (St. Emilion or Beaujolais) to the obscure (Fitou or St. Péray). A similar classification scheme was later introduced in Italy defining 213 *denominazione di origne controllate* (or DOC) regions, each with regulations prescribing area, grape varieties permitted, yields, and so on. These laws also prescribed almost all aspects of production, from permissible types of grape, to required growing practices, to acceptable alcohol content.[6]

Later, other wine regions of France were given official recognition with the classification of *Vins Delimités de Qualite Superieure* (VDQS), but these were usually regarded as of lower rank than AOC wines. Below VDQS were *Vins de Pays,* or country wine, primarily producing *vins ordinaries*. For example, the Languedoc, France's oldest wine region located in southern France, produced more than a third of the country's wine, yet remained largely unconstrained by AOC or VDQS regulation. It produced inexpensive but very drinkable wine for French tables—and increasingly, for export. There was almost no movement across the categories or

within the hierarchies created by these classifications, since the French nurtured the concept of *terroir*, the almost mystical combination of soil, aspect, microclimate, rainfall, and cultivation they passionately believed was at the heart of the unique taste of each region's—and indeed, each vineyard's—grapes and wine.

But *terroir* could not always guarantee quality. As an agricultural product, wine was always subject to the vagaries of weather and disease. In the last quarter of the 19th century, a deadly New World insect, phylloxera, devastated the French vine stock. From a production level of over 5 million hectoliters in 1876, output dropped to just 2 million hectoliters by 1885. (A hectoliter is 100 liters, or about 25 gallons.) But a solution was found in an unexpected quarter: French vines were successfully grafted onto phylloxera-resistant vine roots native to the eastern United States and imported from the upstart Californian wine industry. It was the first time many in the Old World acknowledged the existence of a wine industry outside Europe. It would not be the last.

Stirrings in the New World

Although insignificant in both size and reputation compared with the well-established industry in traditional wine-producing countries, vineyards and wine makers had been set up in many New World countries since the 18th century. In the United States, for example, Thomas Jefferson, an enthusiastic oenologist, became a leading voice for establishing vineyards in Virginia. And in Australia, vines were brought over along with the first fleet carrying convicts and settlers in 1788. At the same time, nascent wine industries were developing in Argentina, Chile, and South Africa, usually under the influence of immigrants from the Old World wine countries.

Opening New Markets   While climate and soil allowed grape growing to flourish in each of these new environments, the consumption of wine in local markets varied widely. Wine quickly became a central part of the national cultures of Argentina

---

[5]Dewey Markham, *1855: A History of the Bordeaux Classification* (New York: Wiley, 1998), p. 177.

[6]Robinson, p. 235.

and Chile, and by the mid 1960s, per capita consumption was about 80 liters per annum in Argentina and 50 liters in Chile. While such rates were comparable with the 60 liter annual level in Spain, they were behind those of France and Italy, which boasted rates of 110–120 liters per person annually. (See **Exhibit 1** for wine consumption figures over time.)

Other New World cultures were not so quick to embrace the new industry. In Australia, the hot climate and a dominant British heritage made beer the alcoholic beverage of preference, with wine being consumed mostly by Old World immigrants. The U.S. market developed in a more complex, schizophrenic way. Born of the country's role as a key player in the rum trade, one segment of the population followed a tradition of distilling and

drinking hard liquor. But another large group, perhaps reflecting the country's Puritan heritage, espoused temperance. (As recently as 1994, a Gallup survey found that 45% of U.S. respondents did not drink at all, and 21% favored a renewal of the prohibition of the sale of alcohol.) As a result, until the post–World War II era, wine was largely made by and sold to European immigrant communities.

In the postwar era, however, demand for wine began to increase dramatically in the United States and Australia, as well as in other New World producers such as South Africa and New Zealand. In the United States, for example, consumption grew from a post-Prohibition per capita level of 1 liter per annum to 8 liters by 1976. In Australia the increase was even more dramatic: from less than 2 liters in 1960 to 22 liters by 1986. Equally

Exhibit 1   Wine Consumption Per Capita, Selected Countries, 1966–1998

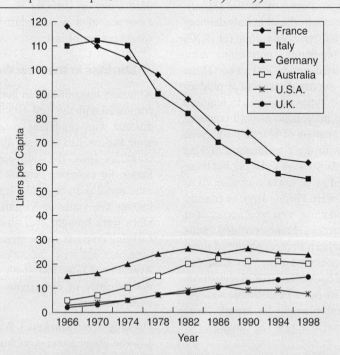

Source: Figures for 1966 through 1994 adapted by casewriters from Annemiek Geene, Arend Heijbroek, Anne Lagerwerf, and Rafi Wazir, "The World Wine Business," Market Study, May 1999, available from Rabobank International. Figures for 1998 from Wine Institute, "Wine Institute, the Voice for California Wine" Web site, http://www.wineinstitute.org/communications/statistics/index.htm, accessed September 10, 2002.

important, this growth in total consumption was coupled with a growing demand for higher-quality wines. It was this boom in domestic demand for both quality and quantity that established the young wine industry in these New World countries.

Challenging Production Norms   Expanding on the back of the postwar economic boom, New World wine producers developed in a very different industry environment than most of their European counterparts. First, suitable land was widely available and less expensive, allowing the growth of much more extensive vineyards. In the early 1990s, the average holding for a vineyard among New World producers was 158 hectares, compared with less than one hectare in the Old World countries.[7]

Unconstrained by either small size or tradition, New World producers began to experiment with new technology in both grape growing and wine making. In Australia, controlled drip irrigation reduced vintage variability and allowed expansion into new growing regions. (Predictably, irrigation was strictly forbidden in France under AOC regulations.) Larger New World vineyards also favored the use of specialized equipment. Mechanical harvesters, then mechanical pruners, became the industry standard. And night harvesting became the norm to maximize grape sugars. Trellis systems, developed in Australia, permitted vineyard planting at twice the traditional density, while other experiments with fertilizers and pruning methods increased yield and improved grape flavor. These bold experiments, when coupled with sunny climates, allowed the New World producers to make remarkably consistent wines year to year. In contrast, the rainy maritime climate in Bordeaux made late autumn harvests risky and held producers hostage to year-to-year vintage variations.

Experimentation also extended to wine making, where again the New World companies were more willing to break with industry traditions. Large estates usually had on-site labs to run tests and provide data helpful in making growing and harvest decisions. More controversially, by the 1990s many employed some form of a reverse osmosis technology to concentrate the juice (or *must*), thus ensuring a deeper-colored, richer-tasting wine. (Ironically, the technique was developed by a French desalination equipment maker, but most French producers publicly deplored the practice as "removing the poetry of wine.") The newer wine makers also developed processes that allowed much of the fermentation and even the aging to occur in huge, computer-controlled, stainless steel tanks rather than in the traditional small oak barrels. To provide oak flavor, some added oak chips—another practice strictly forbidden in most traditional-producing countries.

Reinventing the Marketing Model   Beyond their experiments in growing and wine making, New World producers also innovated in packaging and marketing. While following the European example of targeting the huge bulk wine market, the Americans and Australians did so in their own way. In the United States, the Old World standard liter bottle of *vin de table* was replaced by the half-gallon flagon, while the Australians developed the innovative "wine-in-a-box" package. Employing a collapsible plastic bag in a compact cardboard box with a dispensing spigot, the box's shape and weight not only saved shipping costs, it also made storage in the consumer's refrigerator more convenient. More recently, Australian producers had begun to use screw caps on premium wines—particularly the delicate whites susceptible to spoiling if corks are deficient.

In both countries, producers also began differentiating their products and making them more appealing to palates unaccustomed to wine. Several new products developed for unsophisticated palates were wildly successful—Ripple in the United States and Barossa Pearl in Australia, for example—but were held in great disdain by wine connoisseurs. These experiments led to forays into branding and marketing, skills that were rare in this industry prior to the 1970s.

[7]Ibid., p. 391.

Exhibit 2   Wine Industry Value Chain

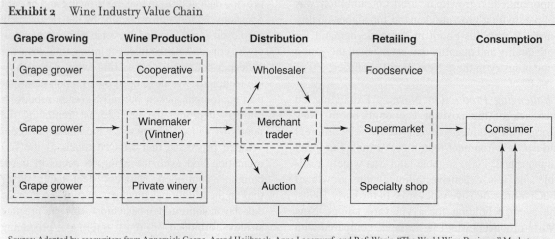

Source: Adapted by casewriters from Annemiek Geene, Arend Heijbroek, Anne Lagerwerf, and Rafi Wazir, "The World Wine Business," Market Study, May 1999, available from Rabobank International.

When Coca-Cola acquired Taylor California Cellars in 1977—soon followed by other experienced consumer marketers such as Nestlé, Pillsbury, and Seagram—the conventional wisdom was that the application of sophisticated marketing techniques would finally crack the last major consumer product still largely unbranded. But forecasts of 25% annual demand growth proved wildly optimistic and within a decade almost all the outsiders had sold out. Yet their influence endured, and experiments with branding, labeling, and other market innovations continued.

The other major change driven by New World companies occurred in distribution. Historically, fragmented producers and tight government regulations had created a long, multilevel value chain. (See **Exhibit 2** for a representation.) In the Old World, the tasks of grape growing, wine making, distribution, and marketing were typically handled by different entities, with many of them lacking either the scale or the expertise to operate efficiently.[8]

[8]To overcome the competitive disadvantage of this long, compartmentalized chain, in the 1930s some small grape growers had formed cooperatives. The co-ops allowed them to integrate into wine making, or at least increase their bargaining power with *négociants* who had moved upstream into wine making and downstream into branding and marketing. But because they usually paid members based on weight rather than quality, growers' cooperatives rarely produced premium wines.

In contrast, the large wine companies from the New World typically controlled the full value chain, extracting margins at every level and retaining bargaining power with increasingly concentrated retailers. Because they retained responsibility for the final product, quality was ensured at every step.

To traditionalists, the New World's breaks with established grape-growing and wine-making ways were sacrilege. They argued that in the drive for efficiency and consistency, and in the desire to cater to less sophisticated palates, New World producers had lost the character and unpredictable differences that came with more variable vintages made in traditional ways. What piqued the critics even more was that, as part of their marketing approach, these upstart wineries were selling their more engineered products using appellation names—Chablis, Burgundy, Champagne, and so on. In the 1960s, the European Economic Community passed regulations making it illegal to use such names on wines other than those produced in the region.

While some New World producers continued their unauthorized labeling for decades, most New World wine makers responded to the EEC challenge by labeling their wines with the grape variety being used. Eventually consumers recognized and developed preferences defined by varietal type—

cabernet sauvignon versus merlot, or chardonnay versus sauvignon blanc, for example. Indeed, many seemed to find this easier to understand than trying to penetrate the different regional designations that each of the traditional wine-producing countries had promoted.

The Judgment of Paris: 1976   On May 24, 1976, in a publicity-seeking activity linked to America's Bicentenary, a British wine merchant set up a blind-tasting panel to rate top wines from France and California. In an event held in Paris with a judging panel of nine French wine critics, the French had an enormous "home field advantage." Against all odds, the American entries took top honors in both the red and white competitions. When French producers complained that the test that became known as "The Judgment of Paris" was rigged, a new judging was held two years later. Again, Californian wines triumphed.[9]

The event was a watershed in the industry for several reasons. The surrounding publicity raised public awareness of quality wines from New World sources and undermined the views of those who dismissed innovative approaches to wine making. It was a wake-up call to traditional producers, many of whom began taking their new challengers seriously for the first time. And finally, it gave confidence to New World producers that they had the quality to compete against the best in global markets. In short, it was the bell for the opening round in a fight for export sales.

Maturing Markets, Changing Demand

"The Judgment of Paris" was only one element of a series of disruptive changes the wine industry faced in the last quarter of the 20th century. More immediately alarming for most traditional producers was a pattern of declining demand that saw a 25% drop in worldwide consumption from 1976 to 1990. When coupled with some radical changes in consumer tastes and preferences, these trends presented industry participants with an important new set of opportunities and threats.

Country Demand Patterns   The most dramatic decline in demand occurred in the highest-consumption countries, France and Italy. In the mid-1960s, per capita consumption in both countries was around 120 liters annually; by the late 1980s it had fallen to half that level. Key causes of the decline were a younger generation's different drinking preferences, an older generation's concern about health issues, and stricter drunk-driving penalties. Similar steep declines occurred in other countries during the same two decades—Spain dropped from 60 liters to 30, Argentina from 80 to 40, and Chile from 50 to 15.

Although not fast enough to offset the losses in the traditional-producing countries, demand was growing in most wine-importing countries during the last two decades of the century, a change that served to escalate competition for export sales. (See **Exhibit 3.**) From 1966 to 1998, per capita annual consumption in the United Kingdom rose from 3 liters to 14 liters, in Belgium from 10 liters to 25 liters, in Sweden from 5 liters to 15 liters, and in Canada from 3 liters to 8 liters. Even more promising was the more recent growth of new markets, particularly in Asia. Starting from a per capita consumption base of less than 1 liter per annum, Asia's largest wine-importing countries—China, Japan, Taiwan, Singapore, South Korea, and Thailand—grew imports at an average of 12% annually through the 1990s. In Japan, where wine emerged as the fashionable drink of the late 1990s, per capita consumption doubled in just three years—from 1.5 liters in 1996 to 3 liters in 1999.[10]

Shift to Quality   Another trend partly offsetting the overall volume decline was a growing demand for higher-quality wines. In terms of the five consumer segments defined by industry analyst

---

[9]Gideon Rachman, "The Globe in a Glass," *The Economist,* December 18, 1999, p. 91.

[10]All statistics from Wine Institute, "Wine Institute, the Voice for California Wine" Web site, http://www.wineinstitute.org/communications/statistics/index.htm, accessed September 10, 2002.

Exhibit 3   Consumption, Production, Export, and Import Figures for Selected Old World and New World Wine Producing and Consuming Countries, 2001

Country	Consumption		Production	Exports		Imports	
	Liters Per Capita	Total hls (000s)	Total hls (000s)	Total hls (000s)	Value ($Millions)	Total hls (000s)	Value ($Millions)
France	59.5	35,217	58,243	17,484	5,800.6	6,030	470.7
Italy	52.3	30,197	51,300	17,983	2,439.7	811	199.2
Argentina	34.0	12,743	15,796	1,041	155.5	134	13.2
Spain	38.5	15,199	31,127	11,662	1,346.1	309	82.6
Germany	24.1	19,825	9,662	2,488	368.1	13,453	1,975.3
Australia	20.6	3,990	9,080	3,750	901.0	140	54.7
United Kingdom	15.9	9,497	15	263	127.0	12,312	2,695.2
United States	7.9	22,401	23,800	2,839	511.2	5,657	2,155.2

Source: K. Anderson and D. Norman, *Global Wine Production, Consumption and Trade, 1961–2001: A Statistical Compendium* (Adelaide: Centre for International Economic Studies, 2003).
Note: In several European countries, production does not equal consumption (plus exports minus imports) due to excess production being subject to government purchase.

Exhibit 4   Quality Segments in the Wine Industry

	Icon	Ultra-Premium	Super-Premium	Premium	Basic
Price range (approx)	More than $50	$20–$50	$10–$20	$5–$10	Less than $5
Consumer profile	Connoisseur	Wine lover	Experimenting consumer	Experimenting consumer	Price-focused consumer
Purchase driver	Image, style	Quality, image	Brand, quality	Price, brand	Price
Retail outlets	Winery, boutique, food service	Specialty shop, food service	Better supermarket, specialty shop	Supermarket	Supermarket, discounter
Market trend	Little growth	Little growth	Growing	Growing	Decreasing
Competition	Limited, "closed" segment	Gradually increasing	Increasing, based on brand and quality/price ratio	Fierce, based on brand, price	Based on price
Volume market share	1%	5%	10%	34%	50%
Availability	Scarce	Scarce	Sufficient, year round	Large quantities, year round	Surplus

Source: Adapted by casewriters from Annemiek Geene, Arend Heijbroek, Anne Lagerwerf, and Rafi Wazir, "The World Wine Business," Market Study, May 1999, available from Rabobank International.

Rabobank (see **Exhibit 4**), the major shift was from the basic segment to premium and super-premium wines. While the basic segment (less than $5 a bottle) still accounted for half the world market in volume, the premium ($5 to $7) and the super-premium ($7 to $14) now represented 40% of the total—and closer to 50% in younger markets such as the United States and Australia.

The trend was worldwide. Even in the 12 European Union (EU) countries, where overall demand was declining, consumption of premium wine kept rising. Despite government subsidies, per capita consumption of basic wine in the EU fell from 31 liters in 1985 to 20 liters in 1997, even as demand for quality wine increased from 10 liters to 14 liters. In the same 12-year period, jug wine sales in the United States declined from 800 million to 650 million liters, while consumption of premium wines increased from 150 million to 550 million liters.

Fluctuations in Fashion With the declining importance of working families consuming locally produced table wine, the market was increasingly driven by upscale urban consumers. The whole buying process changed dramatically, as educated consumers chose bottles on the basis of grape variety, vintage, and source. With the shift to quality came a greater fashion element that caused wider fluctuations in demand.

In the 1980s, an emphasis on light foods resulted in an increase in demand for white wines. In the U.S. market, the trend led to white-wine spritzers (wine with soda water and a lime) becoming a fashionable drink. By the late 1980s, white wine represented over 75% of U.S. sales. In the 1990s, however, the trend was reversed following the 1991 publication of a medical report identifying red-wine consumption as the major reason for the "French paradox"—the curious fact that the French enjoyed very low rates of heart disease, despite their well-known love for rich food. The report, widely covered in the press and featured on the television program *60 Minutes*, gave a huge boost to red-wine sales. In the United States, market share for red wine went from 27% in 1991 to 43% five years later, while in fashion-conscious Japan, red's share jumped from 25% to 65% in just two years.[11]

Even within this broad trend of red versus white preference, wine made from different grape varieties also moved with the fashions. The white-wine boom made chardonnay the grape of choice, with other white varietals falling in relative popularity.

In red wine, a love affair with cabernet sauvignon was followed by a boom in demand for merlot, particularly in the United States.

Such swings in fashion posed a problem for growers. Although vines had a productive life of 60 to 70 years, they typically took 3 to 4 years to produce their first harvest, 5 to 7 years to reach full productive capacity, and up to 35 years to produce the best-quality grapes for wine. It was a cycle that did not respond well to rapid changes in demand. Nonetheless, New World wine regions still had capacity to plant new vineyards. For example, the California acreage planted with chardonnay grapes increased 36% in the 1990s, and merlot plantings increased 31%.

As these trends continued, the rankings of the world's top wine companies underwent radical change. Despite their relative newness and the comparative smallness of their home markets, U.S. and Australian wine companies took nine slots on the list of the world's top 20, which until recently had been dominated by French, German, and other Old World companies (see **Exhibit 5**).

The Government Solution For producers in many Old World regions, however, the shifts in demand were more challenging. First, there was often no new land available to plant, particularly in controlled AOC regions. Equally restrictive were the numerous regulations prescribing grape varieties for a region's wines, affording no flexibility when consumer preferences shifted. One of the biggest victims of the fashion switch from sweeter white wines to drier reds was the German wine industry. Constrained by tight regulations on sugar content, German wine makers watched their exports drop from over 3 million hectoliters in 1992 to under 2 million just five years later.

Unable to respond as New World producers had, European growers sought government help. In France, growers regularly staged demonstrations and traffic blockages to pressure the government for higher price guarantees. EU agriculture supports and national agricultural subsidies were approved to support the overproduction of primarily

[11]Rachman, p. 100.

Exhibit 5   World's 20 Largest Wine Companies, 1998

Company	Country	Wine Sales ($000s)	Major Brands
LVMH[a]	France	$1,462,000	Moet & Chandon, Krug, Dom Perignon, Veuve Cliquot, Pommery, Green Point (Australia), Domaine Chandon (Napa and Argentina); stakes in Chateau d'Yquem and Cloudy Bay (New Zealand)
E&J Gallo[b]	U.S.	1,428,000	Livingston Cellars, Carlo Rossi, Turning Leaf, Garnet Point, Ecco Domani (Italy), E&J Gallo
Seagram[c]	Canada	800,000	Wineries in 12 countries, including Sterling, Monterey, and Mumm Cuvee (United States)
Castel Frères[d]	France	700,000	Castelvins, Nicolas, Vieux Papes
Canandaigua[e]	U.S.	614,000	Inglenook, Almaden, Paul Masson, Arbor Mist, Franciscan Estate
Hengell & Sohnein Group[f]	Germany	521,000	Henkell Trocken (sparkling wine), Dienhard, Schloss Johannisberg
Reh Gruppe[f]	Germany	500,000	Kenderman, Black Tower
Diageo	U.K.	500,000	Le Piat d'Or (France), Blossom Hill, Glen Ellen, Beaulieu (United States), Croft Port, Navarro (Argentina)
Wein International Verw.[f]	Germany	480,000	Mainly generic wines for supermarkets
The Wine Group	U.S.	426,000	Franzia
Val d'Orbieu[g]	France	400,000	
Grands Chais de France[d]	France	390,000	Supermarket label wines in France
Southcorp[c]	Australia	376,000	Penfolds, Lindemans, Seppelt, Coldstream Hills, Rouge Homme (Australia), Lames Herrick (France), Seven Peaks (United States)
R. Mondavi[h]	U.S.	325,000	Woodbridge, Mondavi Coastal, Opus One (with Rothschild), Vichon (France), ventures in Chile and Italy
Freixenet[i]	Spain	318,000	Own-label sparkling wine
BRL Hardy Ltd.	Australia	292,000	Nottage Hill, Hardy's Stamp, D'Istinto (Italy)
Beringer Wine Estates	U.S.	279,000	Own-label varieties, Stag's Leap, Meridian
Mildara Blass	Australia	260,000	Wolf Blass, Rothbury, Mildara
Brown-Foreman Beverage	U.S.	260,000	Fetzer
Pernod Ricard[e]	France	250,000	Jacob's Creek (Australia), Long Mountain (South Africa), Terra Andina (Chile), Alexis Lichine (France), Etechart (Argentina), Dragon Seal (China)

Source: Adapted by casewriters from Gideon Rachman, "The Globe in a Glass," *The Economist*, December 18, 1999, p. 102; and from Annemiek Geene, Arend Heijbroek, Anne Lagerwerf, and Rafi Wazir, "The World Wine Business," Market Study, May 1999, available from Rabobank International.

[a] Mainly champagne.
[b] Largest wine company in volume.
[c] Diversified company.
[d] Négociant.
[e] Beverage company.
[f] Includes *sekt*, a sparkling wine.
[g] Cooperative in Corbiéres and Minervois.
[h] All wine.
[i] World's largest sparkling wine producer.

low-quality, cheap wines. Most EU and national state aid was directed at the purchase of surplus wine—to be distilled into industrial alcohol—as well as for payments to reduce vineyard acreage.

By 2002, however, doubts were being voiced about this strategy in Brussels. After authorizing the purchase of 4 million hectoliters of excess European production, EU Agriculture Commissioner Franz Fischler challenged France on its frequent return to the EU commission for aid. "They are operating aids which do not bring about structural improvements in the sector," he said.[12] The EU commission was also attempting to reduce overproduction in Italy and Spain, with mixed results.[13] But the structural problem was not limited to low-quality, inexpensive wines. In 2002, over 13 million bottles of Beaujolais—10% of the region's production—went unsold. Beaujolais producers were compensated at 70 euros (€) per hectoliter, for a total payout of €7 million.[14]

The Battle for Britain

In the turmoil occurring in markets worldwide, nowhere were the stakes more important than in the bellwether U.K. wine market. It became the front line in the battle between Old World and New World producers, with France acting as the standard bearer of the traditional producers and Australia as the leader among the challengers.

The Prize: The Huge U.K. Market   Long before Napoleon derided the English as a nation of shopkeepers, England was a nation of importers. The preferences of the traditional upper crust were satisfied with French, German, and Italian wines, while the tastes of the rest of the nation ran to beer and pub fare. But by 2000, the burnished image of the upper class importing claret by the case was a thing of the past, as the British middle classes

increasingly turned to wine as a mealtime beverage of choice. As the world's largest and most competitive import market, the United Kingdom represented not only a major market opportunity but also crucial territory in any quest for world wine domination (see **Exhibit 6**).

As their domestic markets shrank, many traditional European wine producers began looking at the U.K. market as more than a source of opportunistic or incremental sales. At the same time, however, newly confident companies from the emerging wine countries began expanding their export ambitions. The United Kingdom became a prime target, particularly for countries with old British Commonwealth ties. The battle lines were drawn for a serious engagement to which the contestants would bring different weapons—and an entirely different understanding of the rules.

Ascendancy of Brand Power   The extreme fragmentation of European producers gave few of them the volume to support a branding strategy. As a result, only the handful of producers whose wines achieved icon status—Lafite, Margaux, Veuve Cliquot, and Chateau d'Yquem, for example—became recognized brands. But these appealed to the elite, who represented only a tiny fraction of an exploding U.K. market.

Government efforts to compensate for lack of branding through classification schemes such as France's AOC had been only partially successful in ensuring consumer confidence. Their value had been eroded by their complexity and consumers' recognition that most classifications had been compromised.[15] For example, Burgundy's most famous vineyard, Chambertin, had its 32 acres divided among 23 different proprietors. While many produced the high-quality wine that had earned *grand cru* status, others rode on that reputation to sell—at

[12]"Farm Council–Agriculture ministers approve wine aid, fail to agree to tobacco aid," *European Report,* February 20, 2002.

[13]William F. Doering, "Production up, trade down in 2000," *Wines & Vines,* July 1, 2002, p. 36.

[14]Carl Mortishead, "Beaujolais swallows hard and turns wine into vinegar," *The Times of London,* June 25, 2002.

[15]The same problem plagued wines from Italy, where DOC regulations were so often violated that the government introduced a DOCG classification in 1980 (the G stood for *guarantita*) to restore consumer confidence in notable wine regions. And in Germany, government standards were so diluted that, even in mediocre years, over 75% of wine produced was labeled *Qualitatswein,* while less than 5% earned the more modest *Tatelwein* (table wine) designation.

Exhibit 6   World Wine Imports and Exports: Share by Country

Imports as % of World Wine Imports by Value, 1989–2001

	1989	1992	1995	1998	2001
France	5%	5%	5%	4%	3%
Belgium-Luxembourg	6	8	7	6	6
Germany	16	19	17	16	14
Netherlands	5	6	6	6	5
United Kingdom	19	19	17	18	19
United States	14	13	10	12	15
Japan	4	4	4	8	6
Rest of World	30	27	34	30	31
Total (Millions of 1999 $US)	$8,765	$10,133	$11,606	$14,283	$13,345

Exports as % of World Wine Exports by Value, 1989–2001

	1989	1992	1995	1998	2001
France	51%	48%	42%	42%	41%
Italy	17	18	20	18	17
Spain	8	9	9	10	10
Germany	6	5	5	3	3
Australia	1	2	3	4	6
United States	1	2	2	4	4
Chile	1	1	2	4	5
South Africa	0	0	2	1	2
Rest of World	14	13	15	14	12
Total (Millions of 1999 $US)	$8,765	$10,133	$11,606	$14,283	$13,345

Source: Adapted by casewriters from K. Anderson and D. Norman, *Global Wine Production, Consumption and Trade, 1961–2001: A Statistical Compendium* (Adelaide: Centre for International Economic Studies, 2003).

$150 a bottle—legitimately labeled Chambertin that wine critic Robert Parker described as "thin, watery, and a complete rip-off."[16]

As wine consumption broadened well beyond educated connoisseurs, new consumers in the fast-growing premium wine segment were faced with hundreds of options on the shelf and insufficient knowledge to make an informed—or even a comfortable—choice. To make a good choice, they felt they had to learn the intricacies of region, vintage, and vineyard reputation. And even when they found a wine they liked, chances were that by their next purchase, the same producer was not stocked or the new vintage was much less appealing. Unsurprisingly, survey data showed 65% of shoppers had no idea what they would choose when they entered a wine store.

For years, the wine industry appeared ripe for branding. Compared to soft drinks, beer, and liquor, where global brands are dominant, in 1990 no wine brand had even 1% of the global wine market. Although European producers and their importing agents had succeeded in promoting a handful of brands on the basic segment in the 1960s and 1970s (e.g., Blue Nun, Mateus, Liebfraumilch, Hirondelle), it was the New World producers that made branding and labeling a routine part of wine

[16]Robert M. Parker, Jr., *Parker Wine Buyer's Guide*, 5th Edition (New York: Fireside Press, 1999), p. 276.

Exhibit 7   Southcorp's Penfolds Red Wine U.S. Brand Structure, 2002

Label	Varietal Type	Years Before Release	Price Segment	Suggested U.S. Retail Price per Bottle ($US)
Rawson's Retreat	Varietal range[a]	1	Premium	$8.99
Koonunga Hill	Varietal range[a]	1–2	Premium	$10.99
Thomas Hyland	Varietal range[a]	1–2	Premium	$14.99
Bin 138	Shiraz Mourvedre Grenache	2	Super Premium	$19.00
Bin 128	Shiraz	3	Super Premium	$24.00
Bin 28	Shiraz	3	Super Premium	$24.00
Bin 389	Cabernet Shiraz	3	Super Premium	$26.00
Bin 407	Cabernet Sauvignon	3	Super Premium	$26.00
St. Henri	Shiraz	5	Ultra Premium	$39.00
Magill Estate	Shiraz	4	Ultra Premium	$50.00
RWT	Shiraz	4	Ultra Premium	$69.00
Bin 707	Cabernet Sauvignon	4	Ultra Premium	$80.00
Grange	Shiraz	6	Icon	$185.00

Source: Southcorp Wines, the Americas.

[a] Typical red varietal range included of these brands Merlot, Shiraz Cabernet, and Cabernet Sauvignon. (These brands also offer a range of white wines.)

marketing. A typical example was the red-wine offerings of Australian wine maker Penfolds. Over the years, it had built a hierarchy of brands with informative labels to help consumers move up each step from $9 to $185 wines as their tastes matured. (See **Exhibit 7.**) By sourcing grapes from various vineyards in multiple regions—even for its icon Grange brand—Penfolds ensured the vintage-to-vintage consistency that branding demanded.

After developing their marketing expertise in the 1960s and 1970s, producers in both the United States and Australia dominated their home markets with strong brands by the 1980s. By the mid-1990s, for example, 75% of sales on the Australian market were accounted for by 6% of the brands. It was also in their highly competitive home market that producers learned to respond to consumer preferences for the simpler, more fruit-driven wines that were easy to appreciate. With these lessons from their home market, particularly through the 1990s these producers took those wines and the marketing and branding skills that backed them into the export

markets. In a bold statement of strategic intent, in 1996 Wine Australia announced Strategy 2025, by which it committed to a 300% increase in sales to $4.5 billion by 2025, with exports providing most of the growth. The 2025 target was achieved over the next five years, and by 2001, the Australians claimed 6 of the top 10 wine brands sold in the United Kingdom (see **Exhibit 8** for top U.K. brands).

Apart from the high-value champagnes, the French had only one wine brand—LePiat, a *négociant's* label—among the top 10 brands in the United Kingdom. No other traditional-producing country made the list. Due to the fragmentation of Old World vineyards (Bordeaux alone had 20,000 producers), most had become accustomed to competing at the low end on price, the middle level on the umbrella reassurance of the AOC's reputation, and at the top end on the image of the icon brands. As a result, they lacked the skills, the resources, and even the interest to enter the battle developing for the increasingly branded middle market. "We are bottling history," said Paul Pontellier, chief

Exhibit 8   Ten Largest Wine Brands in the United Kingdom, 1998

Brand	Company and Country of Origin	Sales ($000s)
E&J Gallo	Gallo (U.S.)	$55,600
Hardy's	BRL Hardy (Australia)	38,500
Jacob's Creek	Orlando (Australia)	38,400
Moet et Chandon	LVMH (France)	28,500
Le Piat[a]	Le Piat (France)	27,200
Sowells of Chelsea	Matthew Clark (U.K.)	26,400
Penfolds	Southcorp (Australia)	19,200
Lindemans	Southcorp (Australia)	15,200
Rosemount	Rosemount Estate (Australia)	13,000
Lanson	Lanson (France)	12,300

Source: Adapted by casewriters from Annemiek Geene, Arend Heijbroek, Anne Lagerwerf, and Rafi Wazir, "The World Wine Business," Market Study, May 1999, available from Rabobank International.
[a] Négociant.

winemaker at Chateau Margaux. "We must concentrate on our field of excellence and not spread ourselves too thin."

There were a few exceptions, however. As early as the 1930s, Baron Philipe de Rothschild had created a second label for "output deemed unworthy" of the icon level Mouton-Rothschild brand. Mouton Cadet grew to be a significant midprice brand. More recently, Baron Philipe's daughter, Baroness Philippine, had begun sourcing wines from the south of France and marketing them as Cadet Chardonnay, Cadet Merlot, and so on.

Lacking a response by growers, some intermediaries started filling the need for consistent quality and supply that branding ensured. Indeed, the names of *négociants* such as Georges Deboeuf and Louis Jardot became better known than the vast majority of Beaujolais and Burgundy producers they represented. And U.K. wine merchants such as Sowells of Chelsea and Oddbins developed their own brands to minimize buyer confusion while also capturing some of the value that branding provided in the fast-growing premium market segment.

A different approach was being followed by other traditional producers that felt they were too small and unskilled to mount their own marketing plans.

They saw their best hope in linking up with the established marketing and distribution powerhouses such as the Australians and the Americans. For example, in 1997, Vinicola Caltrasi, a family-owned Sicilian company linked to local growers' cooperatives, entered into a joint venture with Australian producer BRL Hardy, a company that had already used its experience in branding and marketing to make a wine it imported from Chile the leading brand in its segment. Hardy developed the brand, label design, and marketing strategy for a line of Italian wines it called *D'Istinto* ("Instinctively"), which it launched on the U.K. market at prices from £3.49 to £6.99 per bottle (roughly $5.76 to $11.53).[17]

Increasing Distribution Power   Because branding and marketing had typically been handled by their *négociants,* most European producers were still very isolated from increasingly fast-changing consumer tastes and preferences—particularly in export markets like the United Kingdom. Equally problematic was their lack of bargaining power

---

[17]For a full account of BRL Hardy's global strategy, including its Italian sourcing and branding decisions, see Christopher A. Bartlett, "BRL Hardy: Globalizing an Australian Wine Company," HBS Case No. 300-018 (Boston: Harvard Business School Publishing, 1999).

Exhibit 9   U.K. Off-License Wine Sales by Outlet, 1989–1995

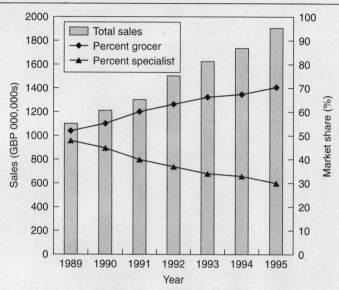

Source: Adapted by casewriters from Annemiek Geene, Arend Heijbroek, Anne Lagerwerf, and Rafi Wazir, "The World Wine Business," Market Study, May 1999, available from Rabobank International.

when dealing with retailers, particularly the rapidly concentrating supermarket chains such as Tesco and Sainsbury (see **Exhibit 9**). In contrast, New World wine companies tended to control operations from the vineyard to the retailer. They used their scale and integration to achieve market power in their domestic markets—in Australia, the largest five wine companies accounted for 85% of market share—thereby generating the resources and expertise to attack export markets. In contrast, the largest five French wine companies (excluding champagne specialists) accounted for only 8% of their market. The comparable number in Italy was 4%.

The large New World producers also developed significant distribution advantages from their scale and scope. By controlling the distribution chain, they added even more cost advantages to their lower production costs by avoiding more handling stages, holding less inventory, and capturing the intermediaries' markup. Even the transport and trade

economics that once favored European suppliers selling into the United Kingdom had changed in the last decades of the century. Tariff barriers dropped under successive World Trade Organization negotiations, and transportation differentials shifted as trucking costs rose while container-ship costs fell. As a result, the cost of shipping wine from Australia to the United Kingdom was now about the same as trucking it from the south of France.

Size had also given the New World companies bargaining power in their dealings with the concentrating retail sector. For example, Australian giant Southcorp had 50 sales reps in Britain; CVBG, one of France's largest producers with sales of $150 million, could support only two. Because they could respond to retailers' need for consistent supplies of branded products, the Australians captured the high-volume sales.[18] As consumers became even more sensitive to

[18]Rachman, p. 99.

Exhibit 10   U.K. Retail Wine Sales: Market Share by Source, 1988–2002E

	1988	1994	2000	2002E
France	43%	39%	26%	22%
Germany	30	19	11	9
Italy	10	10	13	12
Other (including Chile and South Africa)	15	23	27	25
United States	1	2	7	10
Australia	2	8	17	22
	100%	100%	100%	100%

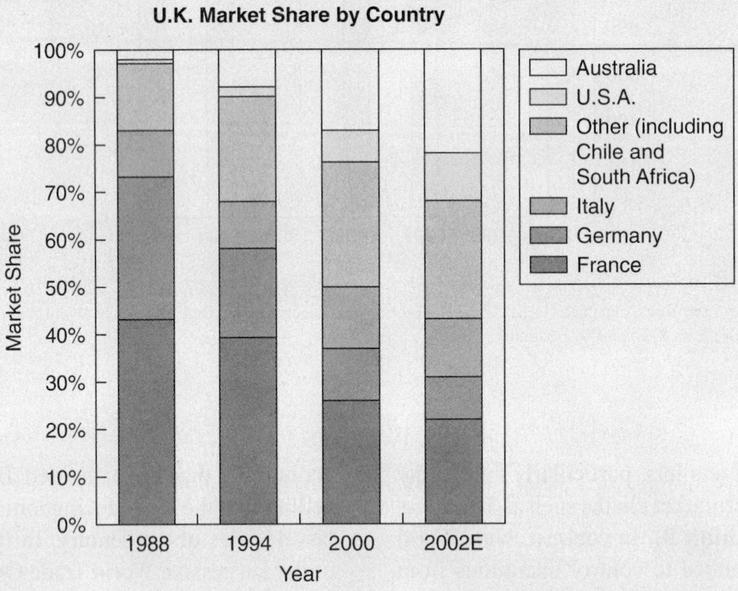

U.K. Market Share by Country

Source: Adapted by casewriters from Sheryle Bagwell, "The French Correction," *Business Review Weekly*, August 29, 2002, p. 34; and Paul Tranter and Christian van Tienhoven, "Why the New World is Winning in the Wine Industry," unpublished manuscript, May 3, 2002.

pricing than brand, retailers reported that their sales trends followed whatever product offered the highest perceived quality-to-value ratio. With their cost advantage, Australian producers responded with aggressive pricing. In the face of this distribution-based, pricing-driven growth, French market share was maintained only with the aid of frequent promotions.[19] Even so, its share continued to slip.

[19]Annemiek Geene, Arend Heijbroek, Anne Lagerwerf, and Rafi Wazir, "The World Wine Business," Market Study, May 1999, available from Rabobank International.

Reports from the Front: Victories, Defeats, and Responses   Results in the wine companies' Battle for Britain—and particularly in the contest between Australia and France for dominance in the U.K. market—were dramatic. During the 1990s French wine exports to the United Kingdom increased approximately 5% annually, while Australian imports grew seven times faster. So while French market share eroded from 39% in 1994 to 26% in 2000, the Australians' share increased from 8% to 17%. But of greater concern to the French was the forecast

Exhibit 11   Price Point Breakdown of Volume of U.K. Imports by Country of Origin, 2001

Price range (£)	Australia	United States	France	Germany
>£4.51	41%	31%	18%	2%
£4.01–£4.50	16	22	7	2
£3.01–£4.00	41	44	43	28
£2.06–£3.00	2	3	29	47
<£2.05	—	—	3	21
	100%	100%	100%	100%

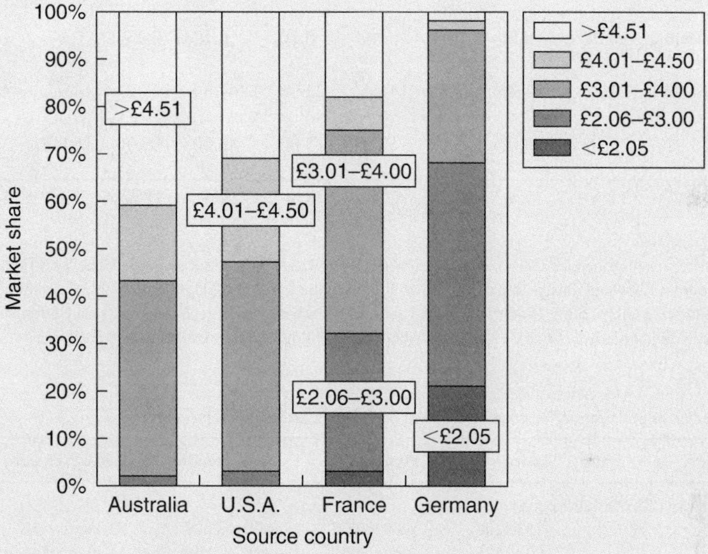

Source: Adapted by casewriters from Mike Gibbs, Steve Branley-Jackson, Claire Ross, Mark Lynch, Stephen Potter, Lisa Heffernan, and Girish Pamnani, "Beverages: Wines," Europe, February 11, 2002, available from Goldman Sachs Global Equity Research.

that the Australians would overtake them as market leaders some time during 2002. (See **Exhibit 10** for source country market share in the United Kingdom.)

The Australian claim for dominance was even stronger than simple market share indicated. The bulk of French wine sales were in the less expensive (and less profitable) categories, which also were the market segments that expected little or no growth. Australian wines were largely positioned in the premium and super-premium seg-

ments, where trends indicated the greatest potential for growth. (See **Exhibit 11** for distributions of price points of U.K. imports.) Moreover, for many historic and structural reasons discussed earlier, French producers faced greater production costs in these segments than their New World rivals (see **Exhibit 12**).

In early 2002, many in the French wine industry were becoming concerned. Twelve months earlier, the French minister of agriculture had appointed his general controller, Jacques Berthomeau, as

Exhibit 12   Estimates of Nationally Variable Production Costs and Revenue by Market Segment for Selected Producer Countries[1]

($US per 9 L case)	Australia				France				US			
	Basic	Premium	Super	Ultra	Basic	Premium	Super	Ultra	Basic	Premium	Super	Ultra
Grape costs[2]	$1.03	$6.43	$22.58	$45.45	$1.32	$6.43	$28.23	$104.55	$1.32	$5.71	$25.00	$63.64
Crush and capital costs	12.94	15.71	17.74	20.00	13.53	16.43	18.55	20.91	13.53	16.43	18.55	20.91
Barrel costs (corks, labels, etc.)[3]	0.00	0.00	0.94	2.25	0.00	0.00	0.94	2.25	0.00	0.00	0.94	2.25
Dry goods costs per case	0.06	0.08	0.09	0.10	0.08	0.10	0.12	0.13	0.07	0.09	0.10	0.11
Total winery costs	14.03	22.22	41.35	67.80	14.94	22.96	47.84	127.83	14.92	22.23	44.59	86.90
Ex-winery revenue[4]	16.00	25.00	50.00	155.00	16.00	25.00	50.00	155.00	16.00	25.00	50.00	155.00
winery margin	12%	11%	17%	56%	7%	8%	4%	18%	7%	11%	12%	44%

Source: Adapted by casewriters from Annemiek Geene, Arend Heijbroek, Anne Lagerwerf, and Rafi Wazir, "The World Wine Business," Market Study, May 1999, available from Rabobank International; "The Global Wine Industry," April 23, 2001, available from Morgan Stanley Dean Witter Global Equity Research; and Mike Gibbs, Steve Branley-Jackson, Claire Ross, Mark Lynch, Stephen Potter, Lisa Heffernan, and Girish Pamnani, "Beverages: Wines Europe," Market Study, February 11, 2002, available from Goldman Sachs Global Equity Research.

Notes:

[1] All costs are best estimates from a wide range of available sources. Wide variations occur.

[2] Grape cost per case is median of price spread for grapes purchased on the open market in each country:

	Basic	Premium	Super Premium	Ultra Premium
Price for Grapes (US$ per metric ton)				
Australia	$75 to 100	$200 to 600	$800 to 2000	$2,000 to 3000
France	100 to 125	200 to 700	1,100 to 2500	3,000 to 7000
US	75 to 150	200 to 600	1,100 to 2000	2,500 to 4500
Metric tons per acre	8 to 20	5 to 7	3 to 5	2 to 3
Cases per metric ton	85	70	62	55
Cases per acre	680 to 1700	350 to 490	200 to 310	110 to 165
Grape prices reflect differences in mechanization, and particularly differences in land prices ($US per acre):				
Australia	$8,000	$15,000	$22,000	$30,000
France [a]	10,000	22,000	55,000	100,000
US	12,000	20,000	50,000	75,000

[3] Cost per vintage of barrel use assuming 7-year life of 300L American new oak barrel at $375. Ultra premium is 20% of barrel cost ("new oak"). Super premium is 8% of barrel cost (not "new oak").

[4] Note that shipping and marketing costs as well as distribution and retailer margins of approx. 30% and 40% respectively must be added to bring price up to retail level.

wine-crisis manager and asked him to prepare a report on the French industry. Released in July 2001, the report was frank in its evaluation and strong in its recommendations. "[The French wine industry] has lived too long on its past good name," it concluded. "It needs to come out of its haughty elitism and take the threat of the New World challenge seriously."[20]

[20]Jacques Berthomeau, "Comment mieux positionner les vins français sur les marchés d'exportation?" Report to Jean Glavany, French minister of agriculture, July 31, 2001.

One of the report's main recommendations was that the French industry had to adopt some of the technical and marketing advances that had allowed the Australians and Americans to succeed. In particular, it proposed developing a much stronger commitment to branding. Said Berthomeau: "The French . . . have marketed wine based on heritage of growing regions, down to the fields of the chateaus where the vines are planted. France's rivals, by contrast, address the consumer the way you would with beer. . . . The question for us French is, can we do the same thing? The answer is yes."[21]

In the months that followed, the response to the report was as diverse as it was emotional. Jean-Luc Darien, director of *Onivins,* the French wine industry association, worried that a brand-driven approach was too radical and risked simplifying the product to such a degree it would "toss the baby out with the bathwater." After all, even though its share had declined from 50% in 1990, French wine still had 40% of the global market and was still the standard by which most consumers gauged other countries' wines. Rather than seeing the great fragmentation and diversity of French wine markets as a liability, he felt the industry should work to make them an asset.[22]

The *Federation des Exportateurs des Vins et Spiritueux,* which represented 2,000 companies that traded 80% of French exports, proposed a different solution. In its view, French AOC and VDQS wines should be produced and marketed as they had been historically. But wines for the lower half of the market should be grouped as "the country wines of France," sourced from multiple regions, and labeled based on grape variety, not region. In this way, France could produce more consistent wines with the fruit-driven taste that New World producers had made so popular.[23]

But Rene Renou, president of the *Institut National des Appelations D'Origine,* the body that administered the AOC rules, called this approach foolhardy. He proposed a renewed emphasis on *terroir* as the means to distinguish French wines from the worldwide glut. "We must claim the right to be unique, to be specific," he said. "There are thousands of Chardonnays, but there is only one wine from Bonnezeaux."[24]

As the debate raged, a new forecast from the Australian Bureau of Agricultural and Resource Economics saw Australia's wine exports growing 75% over the next five years. With exports eclipsing domestic sales for the first time in 2002—and expected to account for 67% of production by 2008—growers were aggressively expanding their vineyards. By 2007 180,000 hectares would be planted—almost three times the area planted in 1996.[25] Even M. Berthomeau took time out from his role as French critic to grumble that "[The Australians'] heads are getting a little too big."[26]

As French domestic consumption continued to fall and its share of the world market continued to decline by about 1% a year, there was little agreement within the industry on what strategy would reverse the trends. Equally concerning was the growing French realization that the biggest challenge would lie not so much in what strategic direction to take, but how to align the diverse industry and government interests to act on it.

---

[21]John Tagliabue, "For French Vintners, Lessons in Mass Marketing," *The New York Times,* April 14, 2002, Section 3, p. 4.
[22]Ibid.
[23]John Lichfield, "Our man in Paris," *The Independent,* October 12, 2002, p. 23.
[24]Larry Walker, "Worldbeat," *Wines & Vines,* May 1, 2002, p. 86.
[25]Daniel Lewis, "Fine time for wine as growers try to sate world thirst," *Sydney Morning Herald,* March 8, 2003, p. 3
[26]John Carreyrou, "Australians Give French a Lesson in Winemaking," *The Wall Street Journal,* May 30, 2003, p. A1.

Case 2-3   HSBC Holdings

Today we are a contender and not yet the champion. We aim to change that.

—Sir John Bond, HSBC Holdings Group Chairman[1]

On March 28, 2003, HSBC Holdings PLC completed the $14 billion acquisition of U.S.-based consumer finance company Household International.[2] Though dwarfed by HSBC's assets of $840 billion, the bank's presence in 79 countries, and market capitalization of $97.5 billion, Household's $98 billion in assets and 53 million accounts gave HSBC access to a broad U.S. retail demographic that its earlier acquisitions of Marine Midland and Republic Bank of New York had not. With Household, the group could now book 30% of pretax earnings in North America, 32% in Europe, and 37% in Asia (see **Exhibits 1** and **2**).[3] While Household exemplified group chairman John Bond's goal of making HSBC "the world's local bank," many felt that the distressed firm also embodied HSBC's primary challenge: creating from its patchwork of acquisitions a seamless enterprise that followed a common design, a whole that exceeded the sum of its parts.[4]

The 1.27 billion shares paid in consideration of Household began trading April 1 on the Hong Kong, London, New York, and Paris stock exchanges.[5] Skeptical analysts rated the new shares a sell, however: "It's because of the Household deal. The risks outweigh the rewards."[6] Household raised challenges both broad and specific. Forty percent of its loans were "subprime"—made to customers with blemished credit records. Few could picture these customers alongside HSBC USA's private banking and wealth management clients. Others worried how well Household Chairman and CEO Bill Aldinger would fit into HSBC's culture of collegial conservatism. The $37.5 million that HSBC had promised to Aldinger for three years outstripped Bond's annual $3 million and overshadowed Youssef Nasr (HBS MBA '79), who ran HSBC USA operations at the time of the Household acquisition after rising through the ranks at HSBC USA and HSBC Canada.

International Banks

The first banks to internationalize financed emerging market governments and international trade or supported direct and portfolio investments from their own countries in mining and manufacturing ventures abroad. In 2003 only a handful of banks—Citigroup, Standard Chartered, and HSBC—could claim to operate in multiple foreign markets for multiple client segments. The Japanese banks that led the world in assets during the 1980s

▌ Professor Tarun Khanna and Global Research Group Senior Researcher David Lane wrote the original version of this case, "HSBC Holdings," HBS No. 704-434, with assistance from the Asia-Pacific, Europe, and Latin American Research Centers. It is being replaced by this version, prepared by Tarun Khanna and David Lane. HBS cases are developed solely as the basis for class discussion. Cases are not intended to serve as endorsements, sources of primary data, or illustrations of effective or ineffective management.
▌[1]Kerry Capell and Mark Clifford, "John Bond's HSBC," *BusinessWeek,* September 20, 1999, www.businessweek.com:/1999/99_38/b3647011.htm?script Framed, accessed October 17, 2003.
▌[2]Jane Croft, "HSBC to Expand Consumer Finance Business," *The Financial Times,* September 19, 2003.
▌[3]In asset terms, the percentages differed somewhat: 30% were in North America, 29% in Asia, and 40% in Europe. "HSBC Completes Household International Purchase," *AFX News,* available from Factiva, www.factiva.com, accessed October 27, 2003.
▌[4]Kerry Capell and Mark Clifford, "John Bond's HSBC," *BusinessWeek,* September 20, 1999, www.businessweek.com/1999/99_38/b3647011.htm?scriptFramed, accessed October 17, 2003.

▌[5]"HSBC Completes Household Purchase," *South China Morning Post,* April 1, 2003, available from Factiva, www.factiva.com, accessed October 16, 2003.
▌[6]"HSBC and Household—The Doubts Remain," *Citywire,* March 30, 2003, available from Factiva, www.factiva.com, accessed October 16, 2003.

Exhibit 1   Summary HSBC Financial, Company, and Share Data, 1993–2003

(in £ mil, FY ending March)	2003	2002	2001	2000	1999	1998	1997	1996	1995	1994	1993
Revenue	35,261	27,530	33,469	33,183	24,317	26,147	22,876	18,481	16,904	13,975	14,575
Earnings before Income Taxes	7,725	6,323	5,506	6,447	4,857	3,880	4,902	4,436	3,596	3,080	2,489
Net Profit Excl. Extraordinary Items	5,332	4,134	3,755	4,382	3,342	2,604	3,355	3,112	2,462	2,053	1,806
Return on Equity (%)	12.8%	12.8%	12.0%	14.5%	16.2%	15.8%	20.4%	20.5%	18.4%	19.0%	19.3%
Net Property Plant & Equip	8,819	8,806	9,289	9,394	7,965	7,301	7,914	6,238	5,790	4,917	4,781
Total Assets	577,522	470,504	477,185	450,850	352,108	291,208	286,333	236,501	226,746	201,484	206,007
Net Worth (Shareholder Equity)	41,705	32,225	31,206	30,154	20,676	16,523	16,442	15,187	13,387	10,790	9,334
Wages, Salaries & Benefits	7,360	5,704	5,941	5,327	4,136	3,812	3,660	3,069	2,834	2,646	2,502
Number of Employees	222,719	184,405	171,049	161,624	145,847	144,521	132,969	109,298	109,093	106,861	104,027
Fiscal Year End Stock Price (per share)	8.79	6.87	8.05	9.80	8.59	5.46	5.24	4.35	3.35	2.36	3.25
Million Common Shares Outstanding	10,960	9,481	9,355	9,268	8,458	8,097	8,027	7,984	7,905	7,817	7,584
Market Value of all Stock Issues	96,339	65,086	75,305	90,828	72,655	44,186	42,039	34,752	26,496	18,410	24,626
Book Value of Common Stock	41,705	32,225	31,206	30,154	20,676	16,523	16,442	15,187	13,387	10,790	9,334

Source: Worldscope, a Thomson Financial product.

had dropped out of sight, weighed down in the 1990s by bad domestic loans. European firms that in the 1990s sought a foothold in the booming U.S. investment and wealth management markets—Deutsche Bank (which bought Bankers Trust), Credit Suisse (Donaldson Lufkin Jenrette), UBS (Paine Webber), and Dresdner Kleinwort Benson (Wasserstein Perella)—suffered with U.S. securities after 2000. Thus, while other banks tried to break into this league, none had staying power. But with half of the growth in world demand to 2030 expected to come from developing economies, prospects looked good for those that did.

Citigroup   Citigroup in 2003 (Citicorp before 1998) was the world's largest and most profitable financial institution, with assets exceeding $1 trillion, a market capitalization of $177 billion, and a return on average equity of 17.7% (see **Exhibit 2**). Despite offices in 100 countries, over 60% of Citigroup's income came from North America, where it was the largest credit card issuer and cross-sold financial services from a stable of brands that included Travelers Insurance, Smith Barney, and Citibank.

In its primary markets, line of business rather than local market concerns drove Citigroup's

Exhibit 2   Summary 2002 Financial Data: HSBC, Citibank, and Standard Chartered

Balance Sheet (standardized, year-end 2002, in US$ mil)	HSBC	Citigroup	Standard Chartered
Assets:			
Other Earning Assets, Total	265,522	481,049	25,430
Net Loans	447,840	436,704	73,010
Other Assets	53,796	127,041	10,230
Total Assets	759,246	1,097,590	112,953
Liabilities:			
Total Deposits	548,371	430,895	82,476
Total Debt	18,371	320,199	5,455
Other Liabilities	92,925	233,768	11,930
Total Liabilities	706,840	1,010,872	105,683

Income Statement (standardized, year-end 2002, in US$ mil)	HSBC	Citigroup	Standard Chartered
Net Interest Income	15,460	37,691	3,063
Net Interest Income after Loan Loss Provision	14,139	27,696	2,358
Non-Interest Income	12,691	33,617	1,476
Net total revenues	26,830	61,313	3,834
Income before Tax	9,650	20,537	1,262
Net Income	6,239	15,276	844

Source: Data provided by OneSource® Business Browser[SM], an online business information product of OneSource Information Services, Inc. ("OneSource"), accessed March 13, 2004.

management and business decisions. In Europe, for example, Citigroup moved in the early 1990s to a regional rather than country-based posture. This suited the cross-border needs of its multinational corporation (MNC) clients but deemphasized local operations. Outside Europe and North America, country managers oversaw customer, product, and administrative staff who generated revenues primarily through the lending of local deposits and the sale of financial products that were similar everywhere. Local support for foreign multinationals was a small but significant part of the business. Support for the overseas operations of local firms was less developed.

Outside the United States, Citigroup shunned joint ventures, operating as a branch of the parent, not as a subsidiary.[7] Citigroup operated as a single bank with a single balance sheet and was classified legally in its overseas markets as a foreign person. Local regulators therefore treated Citigroup differently from locally domiciled capital, a category that included the local subsidiaries of other foreign banks. In general, Citigroup was less constrained in its financial bets than local banks, which were subject to restrictions on capital ratios or the cross-border lending of deposits, to take two examples.

Until the 1973 oil shock, international operations generated half of Citicorp's earnings. Thereafter,

[7]Larry Li, Adrienne Young, and David W. Conklin, "Citibank, N.A., in China," Ivey School of Business (University of Western Ontario, Canada) Case No. 9A97G016, December 22, 1997, pp. 8–9.

Revenues by Location (%) (year-end 2002, in US$ mil)	HSBC		Citigroup	Standard Chartered
	2002	1995[a]		
Asia:	32.8%	56.6%	18.0%	68.4%
of which Japan			8.0%	
of which Hong Kong	22.5%	42.4%		31.2%
of which India				8.7%
Europe	46.9%	33.7%	7.0%	
North America (incl. Mexico)	15.7%	9.8%	69.0%	13.3%
South America	4.6%			
Central Europe				
Middle East [b]			6.0%	11.0%
Africa				7.3%
Total	100.0%	100.0%	100.0%	100.0%

Revenues by Business (%) (year-end 2002, in US$ mil)	HSBC	Citigroup	Standard Chartered
Personal finance	42.0%	60.0%	35.0%
Wealth management		13.0%	18.0%
Private banking	5.0%	5.0%	
Corporate & Investment banking	29.0%	22.0%	22.0%
Trade finance/commercial lending	24.0%		17.0%
Other			8.0%
Total	100.0%	100.0%	100.0%

Source: Company annual reports.

Note: Boxed information represents cumulative share for all of the headings that the boxes enclose.

[a] 1995 data are pretax profit rather than revenue.

[b] For Standard Chartered, Middle East includes South Asia except India.

led by Citicorp, the seven largest U.S. banks in 1976 collectively held $11.3 billion in OPEC deposits;[8] lending those deposits to Latin America increased Citicorp's international earnings to 72% of its total income that year. Citicorp was hit hard when those loans soured in the 1980s and remained burdened by heavy loan loss provisions into the early 1990s. In 1998, Travelers Group bought Citicorp and renamed the combined entity Citigroup, thereby creating the first true one-stop shop for financial services in the United States.

[8]Richard B. Miller, *Citicorp: The Story of a Bank in Crisis* (New York: McGraw-Hill, 1993), p. 106.

Citigroup continued to grow by acquisition thereafter, in 2000 buying European investment bank Schroders plc, credit card portfolios in Canada and Britain, a Polish retail bank, and Associates First Capital, a Texas-based consumer finance company. With Associates, Citigroup paid $31 billion to double the size of its consumer finance division, which it renamed CitiFinancial. In turn, the organization received much greater oversight, ended predatory lending, and became a strong performer. In May 2001, Citigroup bought Mexico's largest independent bank and brokerage, Banamex, with an eye on the estimated annual $8 billion of remittances from Mexicans working in the United States. Banamex helped boost

Citigroup's income from emerging markets to 25% of its total earnings, up from 17% in 1999.[9] Institutional investors owned two-thirds of Citigroup's shares. Apart from the Banamex CEO and the chairman of Banco Nacional de Mexico, Citigroup's 12-member board consisted entirely of U.S.-based executives.

Standard Chartered Bank[10] Headquartered in London, Standard Chartered specialized in emerging market banking, employing 28,000 in 500 offices in over 50 countries. With over $113 billion in assets and a market capitalization of $12.5 billion in March 2003 (**Exhibit 2**), the bank targeted consumers and smaller firms with a wide variety of retail and wholesale products. The bank emerged from the 1969 merger of two banks originally created to finance Britain's colonial trade, the Standard Bank of British South Africa (established 1862) and the Chartered Bank of India, Australia, and China (established 1853). Although Standard Chartered was larger than HSBC in the early 1970s, it failed to grow as quickly thereafter, hobbled by Third World debt exposure in the 1980s that resulted in the divestiture of U.S., U.K., and European assets. Electing to serve local consumers and western companies in emerging markets rather than become all things to all people, Standard Chartered retained particular strength in Hong Kong, Singapore, India, and Africa. However, occasional lapses and bad bets continued to hold Standard Chartered back in the 1990s, especially in Argentina, where losses in 2001 led the bank to curtail sharply its Latin American operations. In response, Standard Chartered restructured and restaffed in an attempt to lift return on equity (ROE) from 11% to 20% by increasing its penetration of consumer banking markets, focusing wholesale business on higher-margin products, controlling risk, and reducing costs. In 2003, 15%

of Standard Chartered was owned by a Malaysian investor, Khoo Teck Puat. U.K. insurer Prudential plc owned 5%. British executives comprised two-thirds of the 18-member board of directors in 2002.

HSBC: Origins and Expansion

Scotsman Thomas Sutherland launched the Hongkong and Shanghai Banking Corporation (Hongkong Bank) in 1865 to finance the China trade, thereby serving the expatriate British merchant houses that clustered in Hong Kong.[11] The bank also issued bank notes and held government funds in Hong Kong, a privilege it retained more than a century later. By 1900, the bank also issued bank notes and managed British government accounts in China, Hong Kong, Japan, Malaysia, and Singapore; issued public loans for governments in China, Japan, Siam, and the Philippines; and advised the Japanese government on banking and currency. Through the late nineteenth and early twentieth centuries, Hongkong Bank operated primarily in Asia including India, opening branches in Europe and the Americas as trade dictated. The bank drew managerial staff primarily from British banks, training them in London for postings throughout Asia.

In the postwar years, Hongkong Bank expanded dramatically through acquisition, beginning with The British Bank of the Middle East (Persia and the Gulf states) and the Mercantile Bank (India and Malaya) in 1959, followed by a majority interest in Hong Kong's Hang Seng Bank in 1965. The bank bought into the United Kingdom and Europe (from 1973), North America (starting in 1980), Latin America (from 1997), as well as selected Asian

---

[9]Amey Stone and Michael Brewster, *King of Capital: Sandy Weill and the Making of Citigroup* (New York: Wiley, 2002), pp. 266–269.

[10]See "Standard Chartered plc," Hoover's Online, http://premium. hoovers.com/subscribe/co/overview. Xhtml?COID=90401, accessed October 15, 2003.

[11]For a longer account, see Frank H. H. King, *The History of the Hong Kong and Shanghai Banking Corporation,* four volumes (Cambridge: Cambridge University Press, 1987–1991). This section also draws heavily upon "The HSBC Group: A Brief History," available at www.hsbc.com (accessed September 15, 2003). For a thorough history of British merchants abroad, see Geoffrey Jones, *Merchants to Multinationals: British Trading Companies in the Nineteenth and Twentieth Centuries* (Oxford: Oxford University Press, 2000).

markets. (**Exhibit 3** summarizes HSBC's major acquisitions.) Having reorganized as HSBC Holdings in 1991, the group moved headquarters in 1993 from Hong Kong to London, where HSBC presided a decade later over an international network of 220,000 employees in 9,500 offices from a newly built tower in Canary Wharf. Of a total of about 190,000 shareholders at year-end 2002,[12] the top 50 held just under half of shares outstanding. The 21-member HSBC Board included seven nationalities (**Exhibit 4**).

Selected   Acquisitions   Although   many   of Hongkong Bank's acquisitions expanded its geographic footprint, one of the most successful did not: for £4.4 million ($12.3 million), Hongkong Bank bought a 51% stake in Hang Seng Bank during a local banking crisis in 1965. Hongkong Bank's interest eventually grew to 62%, a stake worth over $13 billion at the end of 2002.[13] Hang Seng retained its own brand and managerial autonomy, turning in consistently strong performances thereafter.

To access the world's reserve currency and diversify away from its Hong Kong stronghold, Chairman Michael Sandberg in 1980 paid $314 million for 51% of Marine Midland, a regional bank in upstate New York. The purchase of the remaining 49% in 1987 doubled Hongkong Bank's total assets and created a meaningful U.S. presence. However, the retention of Marine Midland's senior management—a condition of the acquisition— significantly delayed the turnaround Hongkong Bank had planned.

William Purves, Sandberg's successor, oversaw the purchase of the U.K.'s Midland Bank in 1992 (having taken an initial 14.9% stake in 1987) and promptly inserted HSBC managers at the top. One of the largest banking acquisitions then on record,

Midland dramatically enhanced HSBC's presence in Europe and again doubled HSBC's assets, as Marine Midland Bank had done in 1987.[14] HSBC managers uniformly saw the deal as a transformative acquisition, in part because it dramatically broadened HSBC's geographic scope. A subtler but perhaps deeper shift lay in the impetus the Midland acquisition gave to HSBC's gradual emergence as a global financial services company in the minds of its senior managers.

Acquisitions continued in the 1990s. Republic Bank and Safra Holdings in the United States doubled the size of HSBC's private banking business. In Latin America, HSBC built on minor stakes to acquire Brazilian and Argentine banks in 1997, plus Mexico's Bital in 2002. In France, HSBC acquired CCF in 2000, creating a significant presence in the euro zone. CCF Chairman Charles de Croisset applauded HSBC's approach and commitment: "HSBC is uniquely multinational. It is profoundly ingrained in HSBC that the Chinese are not English and the French are French."[15]

Managing HSBC

Organization and Control   As a holding company, HSBC after 1991 set group policy for what one senior manager dubbed "11 independent banks," each a subsidiary with its own balance sheet. To promote rapid decision making and local accountability, the head office provided only essential functions, including strategic planning, human resource management, and legal, administrative, and financial planning and control.[16] As part of this effort, London maintained the HSBC Universal Banking system (HUB), the platform on which most IT applications were run, as well as a multifaceted risk and credit control system. The center

---

[12]These figures understate the number of interested parties with a direct interest in HSBC's shares due to the ADR program. The Depository (The Bank of New York) is one registered holder on the actual register, but this hides some 75,000 holders of the ADSs—either directly or indirectly via brokers.

[13]Caroline Merrell, "Banking Giant with a Reputation for Thrift," *The Times,* December 30, 2002, p. 4.

[14]Despite their similar names, no relationship existed between Marine Midland and Midland Bank.

[15]Joe Leahy, James Mackintosh, Charles Pretzlik, and Gary Silverman, "How Bond Laid Foundations for the World's 'Local Bank,'" *The Financial Times,* August 10, 2002, p. 12.

[16]"The HSBC Group: A Brief History," available at www.hsbc.com, accessed September 15, 2003, p. 29.

Exhibit 3   Selected HSBC Acquisitions, 1959–2003

Date	Acquisition	Terms	Times Book Value	Benefits	Subsequent Performance	Comments
1959	Mercantile Bank (India and Southeast Asia)	—	~1.0×	Local branches and deposits		
1960	British Bank of the Middle East (Gulf region)	—	—	Local branches and deposits		
1965	Hang Seng Bank, 62% (Hong Kong)	HK$ 100 mn for 51%	—	Local branches and deposits	Paid $12.3 mn for 51%; 62% stake worth $13 bn in 2002	
1980	Marine Midland (US)	$314 mn for 51%	~0.8×	Local branches and deposits; doubled total HSBC assets		Retention of senior management as a purchase condition slows turnaround
1992	Midland Bank (UK)	£3.6 bn for 85%	1.8×	Local branches and deposits; doubled total HSBC assets	Contributed half of HSBC 1994 earnings; grew pretax profits to $1.9 bn for H1 1999 for an ROE of 27.7%	Also brought HSBC controlling interests in German and Swiss private banks and smaller stakes in Latin American banks
1997	Banco Bamerindus (Brazil)	$940 mn	—	2,200 branches; $5.7 bn government credits as part of deal	From 1996 collapse to 21.5% ROE and $8.7 bn in assets in 2000	Citigroup's first South American office opened in Rio de Janeiro in 1915.
	Banco Roberts (Argentina)	$600–$688 mn	—	Local branches and deposits		Amount paid for the 70.1% HSBC did not already own

Year	Company	Amount	Multiple	Description		Notes
1999	Republic New York/Safra Holdings (US, Switzerland)	$9.85 bn	3.2×	Doubled private banking clientele in U.S., Luxembourg, Switzerland; synergies with HSBC USA		Reports of top staff departures and integration issues
2000	Credit Commercial de France (France)	$10.4 bn	~3.6×	Euro zone presence; private banking clientele; 650 branches in France	2000 gross operating profit of $506.4 mm	France's most profitable bank but sixth largest by assets
2002	Grupo Financiero Bital (Mexico)	$1.1 bn	1.4×	12.5% of Mexico's deposit market; 1,400 branches		Citigroup bought Banamex, Mexico's largest independent bank and brokerage, in 2001.
2003	Ping An Insurance (China)	$60 mm for 10%		China's third-largest life insurer		
	Household International (US, UK, France)	$14 bn	1.7×	53 mm retail finance accounts; U.S. distribution		Citigroup bought Associated, a consumer finance firm, in 2000.

Source: Casewriter compilation from published sources and from Mark Collins, "HSBC's Global Expansion," December 6, 2002. **Exhibit 6.**

Exhibit 4   HSBC Holdings Board of Directors, March 2003

Executive Directors

Sir John Bond, Chairman, HSBC Holdings

Sir Keith Whitson, Chief Executive, HSBC Holdings

David G. Eldon, Chief Executive, Hongkong and Shanghai Banking Corporation

Charles F. W. de Croisset, Chairman and Chief Executive, CCF

Stephen K. Green, Executive Director, HSBC Holdings, Corporate, Investment Banking, and Markets

Douglas J. Flint, Finance Director, HSBC Holdings

Alan W. Jebson, Group IT Director, HSBC Holdings

William R. P. Dalton, Chief Financial Officer, HSBC Bank

Nonexecutive Directors

The Baroness Dunn, Deputy Chairman and Senior Nonexecutive Director. Director, John Swire Ltd. Formerly Hong Kong Legislative Council and Executive Council member.

Sir Brian Moffat, Deputy Chairman and Senior Nonexecutive Director. Formerly Chairman, Corus and CEO, British Steel.

William K. L. Fung, Group Managing Director and CEO, Li & Fung Ltd.

The Lord Butler, Master, University College, Oxford and Nonexecutive Director of Imperial Chemical Industries plc. Formerly U.K. Secretary of the Cabinet and Head of the Home Civil Service.

R. K. F. Ch'ien, Chairman, HSBC Private Equity (Asia) Ltd. Executive Chairman, chinadotcom Corporation, and Director, MTR Corporation, Ltd., Inchcape plc, and The Wharf (Holdings) Ltd.

S. Hintze. Formerly COO, Barilla S.P.A.; SVP, Nestle, S.A.; and EVP, M&M/Mars.

Sir John Kemp-Welch. Formerly Joint Senior Partner of Cazenove & Co. and Chairman, London Stock Exchange.

The Lord Marshall, Chairman, British Airways plc and Invensys plc.

Sir Mark-Moody-Stuart, Chairman, Anglo American. Formerly Chairman, Shell Transport and Trading Company and Royal Dutch/Shell Committee of Managing Directors.

S. W. Newton, Retired founder of Newton Investment Management.

Helmut Sohmen, Chairman, World-Wide Shipping Agency and World-Wide Shipping Group Ltd.

C. S. Taylor, Chairman, Canadian Broadcasting Corporation.

Sir Brian Williamson, Chairman, London International Financial Futures and Options Exchange.

Source: HSBC 2003 Annual Report.

delegated operational authority to subsidiary heads, each of whom worked to meet annual operating plan targets in conjunction with a five-year group strategic plan. CFO Douglas Flint updated capital and capital expansion plans every six months. An executive committee, comprising Chairman Bond, CEO Stephen Green, CFO Douglas Flint, and COO Alan Jebson as well as regional and line-of-business managers, met monthly to adjust targets and renegotiate plans as necessary.

HSBC subsidiaries were locally incorporated banks and their capital was locally domiciled. Each had lengthy local history and expertise, extending over more than a century in several cases. A manager elaborated: "Our traditional *modus operandi* really was as the world's local bank. We had a local customer base, local management, local deposit base, and local lending. We acknowledged that the world is not a homogenous place that could be micromanaged from several thousand miles away." According to Russell Picot, group chief accounting officer, the holding company provided equity capital to the subsidiaries but expected them to raise debt independently. Moreover, he noted, "We fund very little on a wholesale basis; almost everything is funded from local deposits." At the same time,

Year	Company (location)	Amount		Description	Notes
1999	Republic New York/Safra Holdings (US, Switzerland)	$9.85 bn	3.2×	Doubled private banking clientele in U.S., Luxembourg, Switzerland; synergies with HSBC USA	Reports of top staff departures and integration issues
2000	Credit Commercial de France (France)	$10.4 bn	~3.6×	Euro zone presence; private banking clientele; 650 branches in France	2000 gross operating profit of $506.4 mn / France's most profitable bank but sixth largest by assets
2002	Grupo Financiero Bital (Mexico)	$1.1 bn	1.4×	12.5% of Mexico's deposit market; 1,400 branches	Citigroup bought Banamex, Mexico's largest independent bank and brokerage, in 2001.
2003	Ping An Insurance (China)	$60 mn for 10%		China's third-largest life insurer	
	Household International (US, UK, France)	$14 bn	1.7×	53 mn retail finance accounts; U.S. distribution	Citigroup bought Associated, a consumer finance firm, in 2000.

Source: Casewriter compilation from published sources and from Mark Collins, "HSBC's Global Expansion," December 6, 2002. **Exhibit 6.**

Exhibit 4   HSBC Holdings Board of Directors, March 2003

Executive Directors

Sir John Bond, Chairman, HSBC Holdings

Sir Keith Whitson, Chief Executive, HSBC Holdings

David G. Eldon, Chief Executive, Hongkong and Shanghai Banking Corporation

Charles F. W. de Croisset, Chairman and Chief Executive, CCF

Stephen K. Green, Executive Director, HSBC Holdings, Corporate, Investment Banking, and Markets

Douglas J. Flint, Finance Director, HSBC Holdings

Alan W. Jebson, Group IT Director, HSBC Holdings

William R. P. Dalton, Chief Financial Officer, HSBC Bank

Nonexecutive Directors

The Baroness Dunn, Deputy Chairman and Senior Nonexecutive Director. Director, John Swire Ltd. Formerly Hong Kong Legislative Council and Executive Council member.

Sir Brian Moffat, Deputy Chairman and Senior Nonexecutive Director. Formerly Chairman, Corus and CEO, British Steel.

William K. L. Fung, Group Managing Director and CEO, Li & Fung Ltd.

The Lord Butler, Master, University College, Oxford and Nonexecutive Director of Imperial Chemical Industries plc. Formerly U.K. Secretary of the Cabinet and Head of the Home Civil Service.

R. K. F. Ch'ien, Chairman, HSBC Private Equity (Asia) Ltd. Executive Chairman, chinadotcom Corporation, and Director, MTR Corporation, Ltd., Inchcape plc, and The Wharf (Holdings) Ltd.

S. Hintze. Formerly COO, Barilla S.P.A.; SVP, Nestle, S.A.; and EVP, M&M/Mars.

Sir John Kemp-Welch. Formerly Joint Senior Partner of Cazenove & Co. and Chairman, London Stock Exchange.

The Lord Marshall, Chairman, British Airways plc and Invensys plc.

Sir Mark-Moody-Stuart, Chairman, Anglo American. Formerly Chairman, Shell Transport and Trading Company and Royal Dutch/Shell Committee of Managing Directors.

S. W. Newton, Retired founder of Newton Investment Management.

Helmut Sohmen, Chairman, World-Wide Shipping Agency and World-Wide Shipping Group Ltd.

C. S. Taylor, Chairman, Canadian Broadcasting Corporation.

Sir Brian Williamson, Chairman, London International Financial Futures and Options Exchange.

Source: HSBC 2003 Annual Report.

---

delegated operational authority to subsidiary heads, each of whom worked to meet annual operating plan targets in conjunction with a five-year group strategic plan. CFO Douglas Flint updated capital and capital expansion plans every six months. An executive committee, comprising Chairman Bond, CEO Stephen Green, CFO Douglas Flint, and COO Alan Jebson as well as regional and line-of-business managers, met monthly to adjust targets and renegotiate plans as necessary.

HSBC subsidiaries were locally incorporated banks and their capital was locally domiciled. Each had lengthy local history and expertise, extending over more than a century in several cases. A manager elaborated: "Our traditional *modus operandi* really was as the world's local bank. We had a local customer base, local management, local deposit base, and local lending. We acknowledged that the world is not a homogenous place that could be micromanaged from several thousand miles away." According to Russell Picot, group chief accounting officer, the holding company provided equity capital to the subsidiaries but expected them to raise debt independently. Moreover, he noted, "We fund very little on a wholesale basis; almost everything is funded from local deposits." At the same time, the holding company required subsidiaries to remit surplus profits to the center. Surplus profit was what remained after accounting for HSBC's 12.5% cost of capital, Tier 1 ratio requirements,[17] and a negotiated cushion.

HSBC's traditional strategy was to invest surplus profits from its dominant position in Hong Kong elsewhere, commonly by acquiring distressed assets and improving their performance. Marine Midland Bank had suffered from loan problems in Latin America; Midland Bank was hurt by bad debts in California. HSBC was said to examine one acquisition candidate and place $100 billion to $115 billion on the overnight market every day.

Beginning in 1998, HSBC overlaid "customer groups," or lines of business, upon its existing geographic organization. This both exploited the group's global reach and centralized and shared best practices in product development, management, and marketing. The customer groups included Corporate and Investment Banking and Markets, Personal Financial Services, Private Banking, Commercial Mid-Market, and—following the Household acquisition—Consumer Finance. (In addition to global management of HSBC's top 1,400 corporate customers, Corporate and Investment Banking and Markets consolidated three of the group's poorer performers. Corporate finance and equities accounted for 2% of group revenues but 4% of costs; the investment banking group made just $7 million between 2000 and August 2002.)

Several customer group heads also served as geographic region heads. Reporting to the regional and customer group heads, respectively, were country heads and regional customer group managers. As CEO Green emphasized, "We think it's extremely important to keep that nexus of a geographic perspective and a customer group perspective as closely linked as possible. It helps us to think about customer groups globally as well as locally.

You could not possibly ignore geography and prosper. But it does mean that you start to think about what kind of customers we have and where the commonalities lie between, say, financial services clients in Mexico, Hong Kong, Brazil, or France." Michael Broadbent, director of group corporate affairs, concurred: "If you develop a Sharia-based Islamic finance product because you have a major presence in the Middle East, would it not make sense to roll out that service to Muslim communities in Britain, or Indonesia, or wherever there is customer demand?"

HSBC's risk and credit function developed and monitored the implementation of group lending guidelines on a global basis according to country, sector, line of business, financial instrument, and counterparty bank ratings. All transactions exceeding $50 million were submitted to London for same-day approval, which required conformance with sectoral and company risk and regulatory parameters.[18] In this, HSBC differed from competitors that allocated risk limits geographically and left it to local managers to decide what instruments to use to generate revenue locally. Transactions submitted to London were categorized by type of risk and approved for that purpose alone. London would not allow local managers to buy bonds if it had approved corporate lending, for example.

Culture and Character: "Boring Is Good" A cautious deliberation pervaded HSBC. Outsiders characterized the company as thrifty, cautious, disciplined, and risk averse. HSBC managers generally agreed and emphasized the benefits of caution. "Boring is good," one senior executive muttered at a results presentation.[19] "We could be criticized for being a little bit cautious when everything is going

---

[17]Financial institutions had to abide by various requirements designed to stabilize financial markets. Tier 1 capital described the capital adequacy of a bank and comprised core capital, including equity capital and disclosed reserves.

[18]Many regulators would not permit banks to lend over 25% of their capital to a single group, and HSBC's internal limits were much tighter, limiting global lending to related firms—which it grouped at 25% rather than the more common 50% interdependent ownership level—to 5% of bank capital.

[19]Joe Leahy, James Mackintosh, Charles Pretzlik, and Gary Silverman, "How Bond Laid Foundations for the World's 'Local Bank,'" *The Financial Times,* August 10, 2002, p. 12.

gung-ho," said another. But, noted Bond: "Our experience over generations has been to avoid excesses in the final stages of bull markets wherever possible and make sure that we are better prepared for bear markets than our competitors."[20] Survival was the bank's highest objective, and Bond stressed that the bank took a 50-year view of markets. As Broadbent noted: "We invest in countries for the very long term. I recall us being asked to leave countries in extreme circumstances. I don't recall us ever packing up and going voluntarily. We have been invited to leave Indonesia and then invited back later. We had to leave Vietnam at the end of the war for a while, but we returned. We're usually the last out and the first back in again."

Indeed, despite its conservatism, HSBC executives believed that volatility, including political crises, tended to benefit HSBC. According to Hongkong Bank Chairman David Eldon, "We have always kept the bank open. I have worked in Saudi Arabia during the 1991 Gulf War. I have worked through civil war in Beirut. Every single time there is a crisis in the world, we see a surge in deposits." Outsiders were less sanguine. Some reported that HSBC's profit performance varied sharply from market to market. Moreover, the 1997–1998 Asian financial crisis hit HSBC hard. HSBC was believed to be one of the biggest lenders to Korea's Daewoo Group, which came dangerously close to defaulting on its $10 billion in foreign debt. Loose risk controls in Malaysia led to half of the $425 million in bad debts in HSBC's Asia portfolio outside Hong Kong.[21]

Compensation was low relative to other international banks. In 1998, Bond earned $1.1 million, far less than Sanford Weill's $167 million in his first year at Citigroup.[22] In 2002, HSBC surprised many by deciding not to pay bonuses for the 2001 performance of its equity research arm. The research

director and 150 analysts quit shortly thereafter. Green, who headed the division at the time, stated, "Cheque-book diplomacy with masses of mid-career recruitment is not the way forward. We're not in the business simply to have a profit in a league table in a way that destroys value."[23] Frugality was a virtue at HSBC, where all staff flew economy class on flights of under three hours, including Chairman Bond.[24] Bond's predecessor, Purves, reviewed expense reports personally, occasionally phoning up employees for clarification. Bond took the subway to work and encouraged staff to switch off the office lights at night. Vincent Cheng elaborated: "We pay ourselves so little compared with U.S. banking executives. We recruit better-than-average people rather than paying millions and millions of dollars to get one or two star-quality people who cannot lead a team."

International Managers From the cadre of London-trained bankers sent to Hongkong Bank's Asian outposts emerged HSBC's International Manager (IM) program for bright young recruits, who committed themselves to an expatriate HSBC career of three-year assignments, often in challenging markets. IMs were obligated to go where HSBC assigned them and until recently could not marry and remain IMs without a superior's approval. As they gained experience in varied functions and economies, IMs became HSBC's elite bankers—troubleshooters, a source of institutional memory, a mechanism to apply best practices throughout the organization, and a source of senior executive talent. Shared initial training and common exposure to a wide variety of challenging contexts gave IMs an *espirit de corps* that bred trust and collegiality. Shared backgrounds, said Eldon, allowed HSBC to manage crisis "by osmosis. If you face a problem in Jakarta or Beirut, there will be three folks on the

[20]Ibid.

[21]Kerry Capell and Mark Clifford, "John Bond's HSBC," *BusinessWeek,* September 20, 1999, www.businessweek.com:/1999/99_38/b3647011.htm?script Framed, accessed October 17, 2003.

[22]Ibid.

[23]Karina Robinson, "HSBC's Killer Move," *The Banker,* October 2003, p. 24.

[24]Kerry Capell and Mark Clifford, "John Bond's HSBC," *BusinessWeek,* September 20, 1999, www.businessweek.com:/1999/99_38/b3647011.htm?script Framed, accessed October 17, 2003.

executive committee who have worked there."
Broadbent noted the value placed on such experience: "One of the great strengths in this place is
continuity of management. The top 35 executive directors and general managers between them have
800 years of experience at HSBC." The talent pool
gave HSBC the depth to claim three qualified internal candidates for each of its top 50 managerial
positions. Moreover, none of the contenders left the
bank after Green was made chief executive.

For many years, few substitutes for IMs existed.
HSBC did not recruit MBAs. By 2003, however,
HSBC's headcount had swelled to 220,000, dual-
career families were common, and few parents
were happy to send children to boarding school
while on assignment abroad. IMs no longer dominated the upper ranks of HSBC management
(**Exhibit 5**). They instead were part of a high-
potential talent pool comprising about 1,000 leading young executives from around the world who
had been identified as deserving of development
opportunities in the form of secondment or cross-
posting.

The Bond Era

John Bond joined Hongkong Bank in 1961 and
spent much of his early career in Asia and the
United States. In the late 1980s he was credited
with turning around Marine Midland Bank. Bond
then moved on to Britain's Midland Bank before
becoming HSBC's first chief executive under
Purves in 1993 and then succeeding him as chairman in 1998.[25] Colleagues characterized Bond as
both entrepreneurial, like Sandberg, and hands-on,
like Purves. To him fell the fundamental task of articulating and executing HSBC's global strategy.
Bond's goals were ambitious: to make HSBC the
most profitable of nine competing banks, from
Citigroup to ABN Amro; to overtake Citigroup by
the time HSBC moved in 2002 to new London
headquarters; to double total shareholder return by

2003;[26] and to balance earnings equally between
developed and developing countries.[27]

Bond brought new vigor to HSBC's acquisitions, pushing beyond the constraints of its traditional commercial banking approach in a bid to
gain traction in new and high-growth financial
segments, including wealth management, investment banking, online retail financing, and consumer
finance. He looked specifically at shareholder value
measures and economic profit to decide when acquisition premiums were in order.[28] In this, Bond over-
turned the strictures of his predecessor Purves, for
whom acquisitions priced at three times book value
or more were unthinkable. But as Bond noted, "You
can't have a wealth management strategy and buy
distressed banks, because wealthy people tend not
to be banking with banks that are in difficulty."[29]

In April 2000, Bond announced an ambitious
joint venture with Merrill Lynch & Co. to offer
online banking and brokerage services to affluent
customers around the world. The business was
shuttered after poor customer response.[30] By 2001
Bond had spent more than $21 billion on acquisi-
tions and new ventures,[31] including $9.85 billion
for Republic Bank of New York and Safra Holdings. HSBC was soon accused of overpaying. Flint
admitted that CCF did not cover its 8.5% cost of
capital in its first year under HSBC control, although he argued that it was too soon to demand
payback. One analyst believed both CCF and
Republic missed their return on investment (ROI)
targets: the two acquisitions occurred at the top of

[26]Kerry Capell and Mark Clifford, "John Bond's HSBC,"
BusinessWeek, September 20, 1999, www.businessweek.com:/
1999/99_38/b3647011.htm?script Framed, accessed October 17, 2003.
Capell and Clifford write that these goals included doubling HSBC's
stock price every five years. However, HSBC's group manager of
corporate communications stated on April 1, 2004 that the goal was in
fact to double total shareholder return in the period 1998 to 2003.
[27]Ibid.
[28]Kevin Hamlin, "The Quiet Revolution at HSBC," *Institutional
Investor,* January 2001, p. 54.
[29]Ibid.
[30]Caroline Merrell, "Banking Giant with a Reputation for Thrift," *The
Times,* December 30, 2002, p. 4.
[31]Kevin Hamlin, "The Quiet Revolution at HSBC," *Institutional
Investor,* January 2001, p. 54.

[25]Ibid.

Exhibit 5   Summary Biographies of Selected HSBC Executives, March 2003

Sir John Bond, Chairman, HSBC Holdings   International Manager. Sir John joined The Hongkong and Shanghai Banking Corporation Limited in 1961 and worked in Asia for 25 years and the USA for four years, before coming to London in 1993. He became an Executive Director of The Hongkong and Shanghai Banking Corporation in 1988. In 1990, he moved to Hong Kong and assumed responsibility for the whole Group's commercial banking operations. He returned to the USA in 1991 as President and Chief Executive Officer of HSBC USA Inc., a wholly owned subsidiary of HSBC Holdings. He became Group Chief Executive of HSBC Holdings on 1 January 1993 and became Group Chairman on 29 May 1998. He became a nonexecutive director of Ford Motor Company in July 2000 and of the Bank of England in June 2001.

Stephen Green, Chief Executive, HSBC Holdings   Lateral hire. Stephen Green was educated at Oxford University and received a master's degree from Massachusetts Institute of Technology. He began his career with the British government's Ministry of Overseas Development. In 1977 he joined McKinsey & Co. Inc., management consultants, with which he undertook assignments in Europe, North America and the Middle East. Mr. Green joined The Hongkong and Shanghai Banking Corporation Limited in 1982 with responsibility for corporate planning activities. Since 1985 he has been in charge of the development of the bank's global treasury operations. In 1992 he became Group Treasurer of HSBC Holdings plc, with responsibility for the HSBC Group's treasury and capital markets businesses globally. He was made a Director of HSBC Bank plc (formerly Midland Bank) in 1995. In March 1998 Stephen Green was appointed to the Board of HSBC Holdings plc as Executive Director, Investment Banking and Markets responsible for the Investment Banking, Private Banking and Asset Management activities of the Group. He assumed additional responsibility for the Group's corporate banking business in May 2002, and became Chief Executive of HSBC Holdings plc in 2003.

M. Bert McPhee, General Manager Risk and Credit, HSBC Holdings   Lateral hire. Bert McPhee joined HSBC Bank Canada in 1984 as Senior Vice President, Credit, following a successful career with another major Canadian financial institution. In 1992, he was transferred to The Hongkong and Shanghai Banking Corporation Limited in Hong Kong, where he held the position of Group Risk Controller. With the acquisition in 1992 of Midland Bank (now HSBC Bank plc) by HSBC Holdings plc, Mr. McPhee was transferred to London and, following a brief period assisting in the establishment of the Group holding company, was appointed to the position of Head of Credit and Risk, HSBC Bank. He held this position for the three years prior to his current position as Group General Manager, Credit and Risk, HSBC Holdings plc.

Michael Geoghegan, Group General Manager, South America & Chairman, HSBC Brazil   International Manager from age 20. His career includes seven years in the Middle East in Bahrain, Abu Dhabi, and Yemen; nine years in Asia in Hong Kong and Singapore, specializing in workouts of corporate debt; and 2.5 years in Chile before taking responsibility for HSBC Latin America and for Brazil in 1997.

Youssef Nasr, Chief Executive Officer, HSBC USA   Local hire. Youssef Nasr was appointed President and Chief Executive Officer of HSBC USA Inc. and its principal subsidiary, HSBC Bank USA in December 1999. He also serves as an HSBC Group General Manager, and oversees Group business activities in North America. Mr. Nasr previously served as President and Chief Executive Officer of HSBC Bank Canada. Since joining the HSBC Group in 1976 and receiving an MBA from Harvard Business School in 1979, Mr. Nasr has held a succession of executive positions in New York, London, Toronto and Vancouver.

Source: HSBC.

the market. "They could have spent this money more wisely elsewhere," he asserted. Bond retorted that had Republic not been available, HSBC's lack of scale in New York state could have forced the sale of the Marine Midland assets. And with CCF,

access to the euro zone immediately generated new business from existing clients.[32]

[32]Joe Leahy, James Mackintosh, Charles Pretzlik, and Gary Silverman, "How Bond Laid Foundations for the World's 'Local Bank,'" *The Financial Times,* August 10, 2002, p. 12.

Branding Coincident with Bond's appointment as chairman, HSBC's senior managers had realized that the group was meeting the limits of decentralization. As Broadbent recounted: "To some extent this was reflected in our market value. Customers were confused about our identity, and the financial community felt that we were punching somewhat below our weight. In 1998 we formulated a new strategic plan. Since then we have pulled the whole group more tightly together to ensure that the whole really is greater than the sum of the parts."

Bond in 1998 adopted the HSBC brand, retaining The Hongkong & Shanghai Banking Corp. name only for its Hong Kong-based bank. The acronym was then applied to HSBC's subsidiary banks around the world, local institutions whose customers were until then sometimes wholly unaware of their corporate parent. This would change, asserted one senior manager: "Very few people know what the initials in IBM stand for. They only know IBM has something to do with computers. HSBC will be the same for banking." It was not until late 2000, however, that HSBC began to consider the substance and meaning of the brand behind the name. HSBC created the role of group head of marketing to spearhead the effort. Until then, according to one manager, "We didn't have a group message. Each operating company had its own marketing budget." Discussions with retail customers in the 35- to 50-year demographic started in early 2001—the corporate world already knew HSBC.

In March 2002, HSBC rolled out the tagline "the world's local bank," which it supported with an initial outlay of between $100 million and $200 million, of which $50 million went for advertising. According to one manager, "The global piece differentiated us, and the local piece made us relevant to local consumers." Air travelers around the world were greeted by HSBC placards depicting the peculiarly local meanings of apparently ordinary actions and things, or the varied ways in which different peoples expressed the same sentiment (see **Exhibit 6** for examples). Just five years after the 1998 launch of HSBC's first group marketing campaign, Interbrand ranked HSBC as the world's 37th most recognizable global brand, with an associated value of about $8 billion.

Performance In 2000, about half of HSBC's assets were in the developing world, making the bank particularly vulnerable to periodic emerging market crises.[33] Most HSBC earnings came from Hong Kong and Britain, which were mature markets; 95% of group profits came from five economies. India and Latin America each accounted for 1% of group profit.[34]

Bond wanted HSBC's different divisions and main countries to work together to cultivate its most profitable customers. Retail banking operations had begun to pass their richest customers on to the private bank, and the investment bank was being integrated into the corporate banking division.[35] "We want to do 100% of our clients' business," Bond declared.[36] Bond pushed cross-selling hard, and in two years HSBC went from $75 billion of funds under management to around $270 billion. Insurance sales rose at a 33% compound annual rate between 1997 and 2000. During 1999 the bank increased its insurance sales staff by 19% and its bank staff licensed to sell insurance products by 26%.[37] Bond also pushed HSBC toward Hong Kong's new Mandatory Provident Fund, a compulsory pension scheme for local workers that began taking contributions in December 2000. HSBC signed up more than 40% of the employees who joined the plan, which was expected to generate first-year contributions of up to $1.9 billion and assets of some $130 billion by 2030.[38] Organic growth accounted for relatively little of

[33]John Barham, "The Thinking Banker's Thinking Banker," *LatinFinance,* September 2001, p. 10.

[34]Karina Robinson, "HSBC's Killer Move," The Banker, October 2003, p. 24.

[35]Joe Leahy, James Mackintosh, Charles Pretzlik, and Gary Silverman, "How Bond Laid Foundations for the World's 'Local Bank,'" *The Financial Times,* August 10, 2002, p. 12.

[36]Kerry Capell and Mark Clifford, "John Bond's HSBC," *BusinessWeek,* September 20, 1999, www.businessweek. com:/1999/99_38/b3647011.htm?script Framed, accessed October 17, 2003.

[37]Kevin Hamlin, "The Quiet Revolution at HSBC," *Institutional Investor,* January 2001, p. 54.

[38]Ibid.

Exhibit 6   Sample Advertisements for "HSBC—The World's Local Bank"

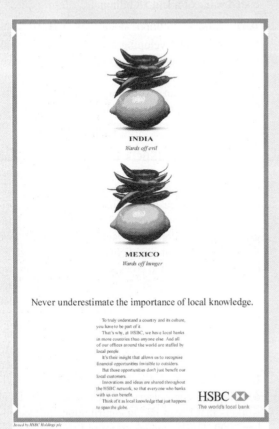

Source: HSBC.

HSBC's results, however; stripped of currency fluctuations and the contributions from acquisitions, pretax profits grew on a cash basis by 4.5% in the first half of 2003.

Household International

Household International became the basis of HSBC's Consumer Finance customer group after its acquisition in March 2003. Previously, Household had been the second-largest U.S. consumer finance firm, behind Citigroup's CitiFinancial and ahead of GE Consumer Finance, AIG, and Wells Fargo. According to Chairman and CEO Bill Aldinger, Household was "a category killer in five or six products in middle-class America." Through subsidiaries and their branch networks, Household provided cobranded credit cards (as with General Motors), private-label credit cards (as with Best Buy and Saks store cards), personal non-credit cards, mortgage financing, and auto loans. Mortgages generated 46% of Household revenues as of mid-2002. Cards generated another 47%. Auto loans accounted for the remaining 7% (**Exhibit 7**).[39] The typical Household customer was a homeowner between 40 and 50 years old, with household income between $45,000 and $60,000.[40]

To accurately forecast the likelihood that customers would repay debt, Household—unlike banks—used a 13-year database of consumer behavior to generate risk profiles for every adult citizen of the United States. The data underlying the modeling came in part from the transactions recorded by users of Household credit cards, as well as from credit bureaus and other sources. With these data, Household ran neural networks—computer programs that could assimilate, adapt, and learn from past patterns of consumer behavior—in order to isolate the personality traits and patterns shared by both safe and unsafe credit risks. Thus, Household loaned not against assets but against the

propensity to repay. The process fascinated Bond: "It is safer to lend to build a deck on a house than it is to lend to people going on holiday. You shouldn't lend to someone my age the money to buy a Jet-Ski, but apparently I'm actually not a bad credit risk for a Harley-Davidson." To maintain and improve the system, Household employed about 150 Ph.D.s on an analytical staff of 250. The complexity of Household's process was illustrated by the fact that its system evaluated 300 variables to underwrite a first mortgage. Most banks evaluated just 15 variables.

Household processed 2 billion transactions each year, at a rate of up to 1,000 per second. For the 70 retail chains that relied on Household credit services, Household managed not just creditworthiness but pricing, mailing, and collections, even answering phones and providing technical support. The associated purchase data helped refine Household's modeling and analytic systems. As for results, said Bobby Mehta, head of retail services, "We have $17 billion in credit card receivables, of which $12 billion comes from prime customers. The subprime business is fee driven; 70% of earnings from subprime lending come from fees. The prime business is the opposite: 60% of earnings come from spread income." Aldinger said that Household was the low-cost provider among consumer finance companies, having improved its cost/income ratio from 53%—the level of most large U.S. banks—to 33%.

To finance its loans, Household by 2001 became one of the five top global issuers of corporate bonds, alongside Ford, General Electric, Enron, and WorldCom. Household raised 35% of its debt funding from international sources. However, spreads between the Treasury bond yield curve and Household's debt widened to over 350 basis points during summer 2002. One source attributed that to concerns in the marketplace over a spate of lawsuits filed against Household by consumer groups concerned with its high interest rates, fees, and penalties.[41] Others felt that the widening spread

---

[39]HSBC, "A Transforming Transaction Combining Two Successful Business Models," investor presentation available from www.hsbc.com, November 14, 2002, accessed December 9, 2003.

[40]Jane Croft, "HSBC to Expand Consumer Finance Business," *The Financial Times,* September 19, 2003.

[41]Erick Bergquist, "At Sign-off Deadline, Household Restates," *American Banker,* August 15, 2002, p. 1.

Exhibit 7   Household International, Summary Financials, 1998–2002

	2002	2001	2000	1999	1998
Income Statement					
Revenue	11,178.5	9,606.5	7,905.4	6,616.4	6,294.7
Provision for losses on owned receivables	3,732.0	2,912.9	2,116.9	1,716.4	1,516.8
Tax	695.0	970.8	868.9	700.6	404.4
Net income	1,557.8	1,847.6	1,630.6	1,428.3	481.8
Balance Sheet					
Total assets	97,860.6	88,910.9	76,309.2	60,451.8	52,647.7
Total owned receivables:					
Real estate secured	45,818.5	43,856.8	35,179.7	24,661.9	18,692.7
Auto finance	2,023.8	2,368.9	1,850.6	1,233.5	805.0
Mastercard/Visa	8,946.5	8,141.2	8,053.6	6,314.4	7,180.2
Private label cards	11,339.6	11,663.9	10,347.3	10,119.7	9,566.0
Personal loans	13,970.9	13,337.0	11,328.1	9,151.6	7,108.6
Commercial & other	463.0	506.9	598.6	808.3	853.4
Total owned receivables	82,562.3	79,874.7	67,357.9	52,289.4	44,205.9
Deposits	821.2	6,562.3	8,676.9	4,980.0	2,105.0
Commercial paper, bank & other borrowings	6,128.3	12,024.3	10,787.9	10,777.8	9,917.9
Senior and senior subordinated debt	74,776.2	56,823.6	45,053.0	34,887.3	30,438.6
Preferred securities of subsidiary trusts	975.0	975.0	675.0	375.0	375.0
Common shareholders' equity	9,222.9	7,842.9	7,667.2	6,237.0	6,065.6
Ratios					
Return on average assets	1.62%	2.26%	2.35%	2.55%	0.96%
Return on average equity	17.3%	24.1%	23.2%	23.2%	7.6%
Net interest margin	7.57%	7.85%	7.68%	7.74%	7.22%
Efficiency ratio	42.6%	38.4%	39.6%	39.5%	60.3%
Consumer net charge-off ratio	3.81%	3.32%	3.18%	3.67%	3.76%
Reserves as a percentage of net charge-offs	106.5%	110.5%	109.9%	101.1%	112.6%

Source: Household International, December 31, 2002 10-K (Prospect Heights, Illinois: Household International, 2002), p. 19, http://www.household.com/HI200210K.pdf, accessed March 27, 2004.

reflected investor caution about the prospects for the consumer finance business in a market environment reeling from the collapse of Enron and other major debt issuers.

Hobson's Choice?

Household tripled HSBC's provisions for bad or doubtful debts to $2.4 billion in June 2003 from $715 million a year earlier. Nonperforming loans equaled 3.76% of Household's total loans, whereas bad and doubtful loans were 0.45% of HSBC's total loans.[42] Household had also settled a court case to do with excessively high interest rates for over $484 million in October 2002. HSBC hoped to avoid further controversy by keeping Household and its subsidiary brands separate from the main bank brand and by spending $150 million in 2003 on extra compliance, training, and monitoring.[43]

[42]This figure excludes HSBC's exposure in Argentina and a purchase in Mexico. Karina Robinson, "HSBC's Killer Move," *The Banker,* October 2003, p. 21.
[43]Ibid.

One outstanding topic was how integration would proceed. As bankers who lent against assets, HSBC and its IMs had no experience in consumer finance using the empirically generated analytics on which Household depended. Yet HSBC expected to move quickly to launch the Household model in Brazil, China, India, and Mexico. This created both external and internal obstacles. External challenges boiled down to how best to access and evaluate data on repayment risk in emerging markets. Few economies, let alone emerging markets, aggregated the quantity and quality of credit and demographic data that Household relied upon in the United States. Even extant credit data varied substantially. One country might lack credit bureaus. Another might compile only negative credit data. Popular scoring of individual creditworthiness worked in very select geographies. For example, the much-used Fair Isaac measures did not yet work with data outside the U.S., the U.K., and South Africa. Absent useful third-party data, HSBC would have to develop local consumer data in these markets itself. Citigroup typically did so by blitzing target consumers with cards, initially set with low spending limits to limit losses. HSBC hoped to do so by partnering with the local subsidiaries of existing corporate clients and by cross-selling financial products to its remittance customers and their cross-border counterparts.

Internally, HSBC's reliance on Household's skills required smooth cultural integration and training across the two organizations. Of course, this depended upon how the relationships between new colleagues developed. As one analyst concluded, "This can be an expensive mistake in North America. Either you get stuck and replace the management, but then you have no knowledge of the market, or else you let the management have free rein. It's Hobson's choice."[44]

[44]Martin Cross, quoted in "HSBC and Household—The Doubts Remain," *Citywire,* March 30, 2003, available from Factiva, www.factiva.com, accessed October 16, 2003.

Reading 2-1   Culture and Organization

Susan Schneider and Jean-Louis Barsoux

Intuitively, people have always assumed that bureaucratic structures and patterns of action differ in the different countries of the Western world and even more markedly between East and West. Practitioners know it and never fail to take it into account. But contemporary social scientists . . . have not been concerned with such comparisons.

—Michel Crozier[1]

Just how does culture influence organization structure and process? To what extent do organizational structures and processes have an inherent logic which overrides cultural considerations? Given the nature of today's business demands, do we find convergence in the ways of organizing? To what extent will popular techniques such as team management and empowerment be adopted across cultures? With what speed and with what possible (re) interpretation? What cultural dimensions need to be recognized which may facilitate or hinder organizational change efforts?

In this chapter, we present the evidence for national differences and consider the cultural reasons for these differences. Examining the degree to which organizations have centralized power,

SCHNEIDER, SUSAN C.; BARSOUX, JEAN-LOUIS, *MANAGING ACROSS CULTURES,* 2nd Edition, © 2002. Adapted by permission of Pearson Education, Inc., Upper Saddle River, NJ.
[1]Crozier, M. (1964) *The Bureaucratic Phenomenon,* Chicago: University of Chicago Press, p. 210.

specialized jobs and roles, and formalized rules and procedures, we find distinct patterns of organizing which prevail despite pressures for convergence. This raises concerns regarding the transferability of organizational forms across borders and questions the logic of universal "best practices."

Different Schools, Different Cultures

While many managers are ready to accept that national culture may influence the way people relate to each other, or the "soft stuff," they are less convinced that it can really affect the nuts and bolts of organization: structure, systems, and processes. The culture-free argument is that structure is determined by *organizational* features such as size and technology. For example, the famous Aston studies,[2] conducted in the late 1960s in the United Kingdom and widely replicated, point to size as the most important factor influencing structure: larger firms tend to have greater division of labor (specialized) and more formal policies and procedures (formalized) although not necessarily more centralized. Furthermore, the nature of technology, such as mass production, is considered to favor a more centralized and formal (mechanistic) rather than decentralized and informal (organic) approach.[3]

Other management scholars argue that the *societal* context, for example culture, creates differences in structure in different countries.[4] In effect, the "structuralists" argue that structure creates

culture, while the "culturalists" argue that culture creates structure. The debate continues, with each side arming up with more sophisticated weapons: measurements and methodologies.

Taking an historical perspective, theories about how best to organize—Max Weber's (German) bureaucracy, Henri Fayol's (French) administrative model, and Frederick Taylor's (American) scientific management—all reflect societal concerns of the times as well as the cultural backgrounds of the individuals.[5] Today, their legacies can be seen in the German emphasis on structure and competence, the French emphasis on social systems, roles and relationships (unity of command), and the American emphasis on the task system or machine model of organization, most recently popularized in the form of reengineering.

Indeed, many of the techniques of modern management—performance management, participative management, team approach, and job enrichment all have their roots firmly embedded in a particular historical and societal context. Furthermore, these approaches reflect different cultural assumptions regarding, for example, human nature and the importance of task and relationships. While the scientific management approach focused on how best to accomplish the task, the human relations approach focused on how best to establish relationships with employees. The human resources approach assumed that workers were self-motivated, while earlier schools assumed that workers needed to be motivated by more or less benevolent management.

These models of management have diffused across countries at different rates and in different ways. For example, mass-production techniques promoted by scientific management were quickly adopted in Germany, while practices associated with the human relations school transferred more

[2]Pugh, D.S., Hickson, D.J., Hinings, C.R., and Turner, C. (1969) "The context of organization structure," *Administrative Science Quarterly,* 14, 91–114; Miller, G.A. (1987) "Meta-analysis and the culture-free hypothesis," *Organization Studies,* 8(4), 309–25; Hickson, D.J. and McMillan, I. (eds) (1981) *Organization and Nation:The Aston Programme IV,* Farnborough: Gower.

[3]Burns, T. and Stalker, G.M. (1961) *The Management of Innovation,* London: Tavistock.

[4]Child, J. (1981) "Culture, contingency and capitalism in the crossnational study of organizations" in L.L. Cummings and B.M. Staw (eds) *Research in Organizational Behavior,* Vol 3, 303–56, Greenwich, CT: JAI Press; Scott, W.R. (1987) "The adolescence of institutional theory," *Administrative Science Quarterly,* 32, 493–511; Lincoln, J. R., Hanada, M. and McBride, K. (1986) "Organizational structures in Japanese and US manufacturing," *Administrative Science Quarterly,* 31, 338–64.

[5]Weber, M. (1947) *The Theory of Social and Economic Organization,* New York: Free Press; Fayol, H. (1949) *General Industrial Management,* London: Pitman; Taylor, F. (1947, first published 1912) *Scientific Management,* New York: Harper & Row.

readily to Spain.[6] For this reason the historical and societal context needs to be considered to understand the adoption and diffusion of different forms of organization across countries. While some theorists focus on the *institutional arrangements,*[7] such as the nature of markets, the educational system, or the relationships between business and government, to explain these differences, we focus here, more specifically, on the cultural reasons.

This does not mean that institutional factors are irrelevant. In effect, it is quite difficult to separate out the influence of institutions from culture as they have both evolved together over time and are thus intricately linked. For example, the strong role of the state and the cultural emphasis on power and hierarchy often go hand in hand, as in the case of France. Or in the words of the French *roi soleil* Louis XIV, *L'état, c'est moi* ("The state is me"). Our argument (the culturalist perspective) is that different forms of organization emerge which reflect underlying cultural dimensions.

Hofstede's Findings   One of the most important studies which attempted to establish the impact of culture differences on management was conducted by Geert Hofstede, first in the late 1960s, and continuing through the next three decades.[8] The original study, now considered a classic, was based on an employee opinion survey involving 116,000 IBM employees in 40 different countries. From the results of this survey, which asked people for their preferences in terms of management style and work environment, Hofstede identified four "value"

dimensions on which countries differed: power distance, uncertainty avoidance, individualism/collectivism, and masculinity/femininity.

Power distance indicates the extent to which a society accepts the unequal distribution of power in institutions and organizations. Uncertainty avoidance refers to a society's discomfort with uncertainty, preferring predictability and stability. Individualism/collectivism reflects the extent to which people prefer to take care of themselves and their immediate families, remaining emotionally independent from groups, organizations, and other collectivities. And the masculinity/femininity dimension reveals the bias towards either "masculine" values of assertiveness, competitiveness, and materialism, or towards "feminine" values of nurturing, and the quality of life and relationships. Country rankings on each dimension are provided in Table 1.

Although some concern has been voiced that the country differences found by Hofstede were not representative due to the single company sample and that the data he originally collected is over thirty years old, further research supports these dimensions and the preferences for different profiles of organization. Efforts to replicate the factors found in 1994 version of Hofstede's survey proved difficult, however significant differences were found among countries and in most cases similar rankings.[9]

Given the differences in value orientations, Hofstede questioned whether American theories could be applied abroad and discussed the consequences of cultural differences in terms of motivation, leadership, and organization.[10] He argued, for example, that organizations in countries with high power distance would tend to have more levels of

---

[6]Kogut, B. (1991) "Country capabilities and the permeability of borders," *Strategic Management Journal*, 12, 33–47; Kogut, B. and Parkinson, D. (1993) "The diffusion of American organizing principles to Europe" in B. Kogut (ed.) *Country Competitiveness: Technology and the Organizing of Work*, Ch. 10, New York: Oxford University Press, 179–202; Guillen, M. (1994) "The age of eclecticism: Current organizational trends and the evolution of managerial models," *Sloan Management Review*, Fall, 75–86.

[7]Westney, D.E. (1987) *Imitation and Innovation*, Cambridge, MA: Harvard University Press.

[8]Hofstede, G. (1980) *Cultures Consequences*, Beverly Hills, CA: Sage; Hofstede, G. (1991) *Cultures and Organizations: Software of the Mind*, London: McGraw-Hill.

[9]Spector, P.E., Cooper, C.L., and Sparks, K. (2001) "An international study of the psychometric properties of the Hofstede values survey module 1994: A comparison of individual and country/province level results," *Applied Psychology: An International Review*, 30 (2), 269–81.

[10]Hofstede, G. (1980) "Motivation, leadership, and organization: Do American theories apply abroad?" *Organizational Dynamics*, Summer, 42–63.

Table 1   Hofstede's Rankings

Country	Power Distance		Individualism		Masculinity		Uncertainty Avoidance	
	Index	Rank	Index	Rank	Index	Rank	Index	Rank
Argentina	49	35–6	46	22–3	56	20–1	86	10–15
Australia	36	41	90	2	61	16	51	37
Austria	11	53	55	18	79	2	70	24–5
Belgium	65	20	75	8	54	22	94	5–6
Brazil	69	14	38	26–7	49	27	76	21–2
Canada	39	39	80	4–5	52	24	48	41–2
Chile	63	24–5	23	38	28	46	86	10–15
Colombia	67	17	13	49	64	11–12	80	20
Costa Rica	35	42–4	15	46	21	48–9	86	10–15
Denmark	18	51	74	9	16	50	23	51
Equador	78	8–9	8	52	63	13–14	67	28
Finland	33	46	63	17	26	47	59	31–2
France	68	15–16	71	10–11	43	35–6	86	10–15
Germany (F.R.)	35	42–4	67	15	66	9–10	65	29
Great Britain	35	42–4	89	3	66	9–10	35	47–8
Greece	60	27–8	35	30	57	18–19	112	1
Guatemala	95	2–3	6	53	37	43	101	3
Hong Kong	68	15–16	25	37	57	18–19	29	49–50
Indonesia	78	8–9	14	47–8	46	30–1	48	41–2
India	77	10–11	48	21	56	20–1	40	45
Iran	58	19–20	41	24	43	35–6	59	31–2
Ireland	28	49	70	12	68	7–8	35	47–8
Israel	13	52	54	19	47	29	81	19
Italy	50	34	76	7	70	4–5	75	23
Jamaica	45	37	39	25	68	7–8	13	52
Japan	54	33	46	22–3	95	1	92	7
Korea (S)	60	27–8	187	43	39	41	85	16–17
Malaysia	104	1	26	36	50	25–6	36	46
Mexico	81	5–6	30	32	69	6	82	18
Netherlands	38	40	80	4–5	14	51	53	35
Norway	31	47–8	69	13	8	52	50	38
New Zealand	22	50	79	6	58	17	49	39–40
Pakistan	55	32	14	47–8	50	25–6	70	24–5
Panama	95	2–3	11	51	44	34	86	10–15
Peru	64	21–3	16	45	42	37–8	87	9
Philippines	94	4	32	31	64	11–12	44	44
Portugal	63	24–5	27	33–5	31	45	104	2
South Africa	49	36–7	65	16	63	13–14	49	39–40
Salvador	66	18–19	19	42	40	40	94	5–6
Singapore	74	13	20	39–41	48	28	8	53
Spain	57	31	51	20	42	37–8	86	10–15
Sweden	31	47–8	71	10–11	5	52	29	49–50

(continued)

Country	Power Distance		Individualism		Masculinity		Uncertainty Avoidance	
	Index	Rank	Index	Rank	Index	Rank	Index	Rank
Switzerland	34	45	68	14	70	4–5	58	33
Taiwan	58	29–30	17	44	45	32–3	69	26
Thailand	64	21–3	20	39–41	34	44	64	30
Turkey	66	18–19	37	28	45	31–3	85	16–17
Uruguay	61	26	36	29	38	42	100	4
United States	40	38	91	1	62	15	46	43
Venezuela	81	5–6	12	50	73	3	76	21–2
Yugoslavia	76	12	27	33–5	21	48–9	88	8
Regions:								
East Africa	64	21–3	27	33–5	41	39	52	36
West Africa	77	10–11	20	39–41	46	30–1	54	34
Arab countries	80	7	38	26–7	53	23	68	27

Rank numbers: 1—Highest, 53—Lowest.

Source: Geert Hofstede, *Cultures and Organizations* (New York: McGraw-Hill, 1991).

hierarchy (vertical differentiation), a higher proportion of supervisory personnel (narrow span of control), and more centralized decision-making. Status and power would serve as motivators, and leaders would be revered or obeyed as authorities.

In countries with high uncertainty avoidance, organizations would tend to have more formalization evident in greater amount of written rules and procedures. Also there would be greater specialization evident in the importance attached to technical competence in the role of staff and in defining jobs and functions. Managers would avoid taking risks and would be motivated by stability and security. The role of leadership would be more one of planning, organizing, coordinating, and controlling.

In countries with a high collectivist orientation, there would be a preference for group as opposed to individual decision-making. Consensus and cooperation would be more valued than individual initiative and effort. Motivation derives from a sense of belonging, and rewards are based on being part of the group (loyalty and tenure). The role of leadership in such cultures is to facilitate team effort and integration, to foster a supportive atmosphere, and to create the necessary context or group culture.

In countries ranked high on masculinity, the management style is likely to be more concerned with task accomplishment than nurturing social relationships. Motivation will be based on the acquisition of money and things rather than quality of life. In such cultures, the role of leadership is to ensure bottom-line profits in order to satisfy shareholders, and to set demanding targets. In more feminine cultures, the role of the leader would be to safeguard employee well-being, and to demonstrate concern for social responsibility.

Having ranked countries on each dimension, Hofstede then positioned them along two dimensions at a time, creating a series of cultural maps. He found country clusters—Anglo, Nordic, Latin, and Asian—similar to those found in prior research.[11]

One such cultural map, as shown in Figure 1 (see also Table 2), is particularly relevant to structure in that it simultaneously considers power distance (acceptance of hierarchy) and uncertainty avoidance (the desire for formalized rules and

[11]Ronen, S. and Shenekar, O. (1985) "Clustering countries on attitudinal dimensions: A review and synthesis," *Academy of Management Review*, 10(3), 435–54.

Figure 1   Hofstede's Maps

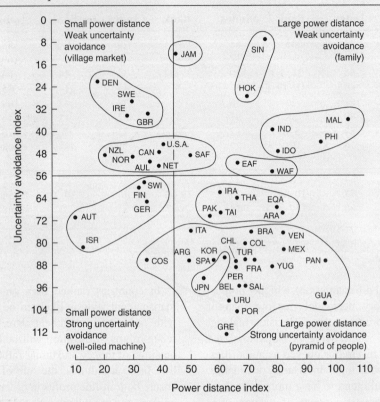

Source: G. Hofstede (1991) *Cultures and Organizations,* McGraw-Hill, Maidenhead.

procedures). Countries which ranked high both on power distance and uncertainty avoidance would be expected to be more "mechanistic"[12] or what is commonly known as bureaucratic. In this corner we find the Latin countries.

In the opposite quadrant, countries which rank low both on power distance and uncertainty avoidance are expected to be more "organic"[13]—less hierarchic, more decentralized, having less formalized rules and procedures. Here we find the Nordic countries clustered and to a lesser extent, the Anglo countries.

In societies where power distance is low but uncertainty avoidance is high, we expect to find

organizations where hierarchy is downplayed, decisions are decentralized, but where rules and regulations are more formal, and task roles and responsibilities are more clearly defined. Thus there is no need for a boss, as the organization runs by routines. This is characteristic of the Germanic cluster.

In societies where power distance is high but uncertainty avoidance is low, organizations resemble families or tribes. Here, "the boss is the boss", and the organization may be described as paternalistic. Subordinates do not have clearly defined task roles and responsibilities (formalization), but instead social roles. Here we find the Asian countries where business enterprise is often characterized by centralized power and personalized relationships.

[12]Burns and Stalker, *Op. cit.*
[13]*Ibid.*

Table 2 Abbreviations for the Countries and Regions Studied

Abbreviation	Country or Region	Abbreviation	Country or Region
ARA	Arabic-speaking countries (Egypt, Iraq, Kuwait, Lebanon, Libya, Saudi Arabia, United Arab Emirates)	ITA	Italy
		JAM	Jamaica
		JPN	Japan
		KOR	South Korea
ARG	Argentina	MAL	Malaysia
AUL	Australia	MEX	Mexico
AUT	Austria	NET	Netherlands
BEL	Belgium	NOR	Norway
BRA	Brazil	NZL	New Zealand
CAN	Canada	PAK	Pakistan
CHL	Chile	PAN	Panama
COL	Colombia	PER	Peru
COS	Costa Rica	PHI	Philippines
DEN	Denmark	POR	Portugal
EAF	East Africa (Ethiopia, Kenya, Tanzania, Zambia)	SAF	South Africa
		SAL	Salvador
EQA	Equador	SIN	Singapore
FIN	Finland	SPA	Spain
FRA	France	SWE	Sweden
GBR	Great Britain	SWI	Switzerland
GER	Germany F.R.	TAI	Taiwan
GRE	Greece	THA	Thailand
GUA	Guatemala	TUR	Turkey
HOK	Hong Kong	URU	Uruguay
IDO	Indonesia	USA	United States
IND	India	VEN	Venezuela
IRA	Iran	WAF	West Africa (Ghana, Nigeria, Sierra Leone)
IRE	Ireland (Republic of)		
ISR	Israel	YUG	Yugoslavia

Source: G. Hofstede (1991) *Cultures and Organizations,* McGraw-Hill, Maidenhead.

Emerging Cultural Profiles: Converging Evidence
These differences in structural preferences also emerged in a study conducted by Stevens[14] at INSEAD. When presented with an organizational problem, a conflict between two department heads within a company, MBA students from Britain, France, and Germany proposed markedly different solutions. The majority of French students referred

[14]Stevens, O.J., cited in Hofstede, G. (1991) *Cultures and Organizations,* London: McGraw-Hill, 140–2.

the problem to the next level up, the president. The Germans argued that the major problem was a lack of structure; the expertise, roles, and responsibilities of the two conflicting department heads had never been clearly defined. Their suggested solution involved establishing procedures for better coordination. The British saw it as an interpersonal communication problem between the two department heads which could be solved by sending them for interpersonal skills training, preferably together.

Figure 2   Emerging Cultural Profiles

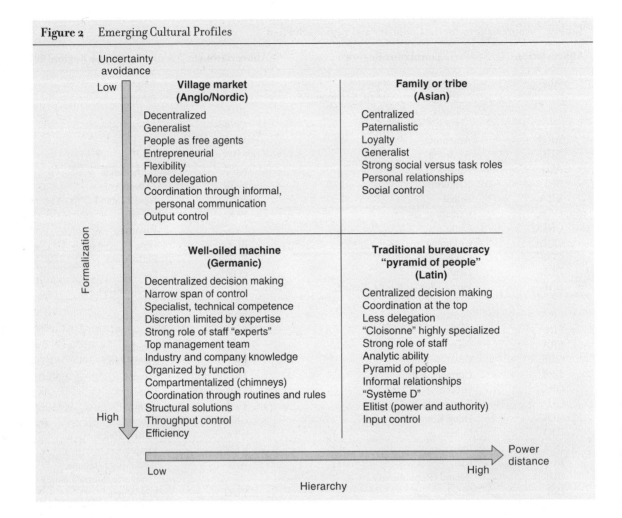

On the basis of these findings, Stevens described the "implicit model" of the organization held by each culture. For the French, the organization represents a "pyramid of people" (formalized and centralized). For the Germans, the organization is like a "well-oiled machine" (formalized but not centralized), in which management intervention is limited to exceptional cases because the rules resolve problems. And for the British, it was more like a "village market" (neither formalized nor centralized) in which neither the hierarchy nor the rules, but rather the demands of the situation determine structure.

Going beyond questionnaires by observing the actual behavior of managers and company practices, further research reveals such cultural profiles as shown in Figure 2. Indeed, in studies comparing firms in France, Germany, and the United Kingdom,[15] French firms were found to be more

[15]Brossard, A. and Maurice, M. (1976) "Is there a universal model of organization structure?" *International Studies of Management and Organizations*, 6, 11–45; Horovitz, J. (1980) *Top Management Control in Europe*, London: Macmillan; Stewart, R., Barsoux, J.-L., Kieser, A., Ganter, D. and Walgenbach, P. (1994) *Managing in Britain and Germany*, London: Macmillan.

centralized and formalized with less delegation when compared with either German or British firms. The role of the PDG (French CEO) was to provide coordination at the top and to make key decisions, which demands a high level of analytical and conceptual ability that need not be industry or company specific. The staff function plays an important role in providing analytic expertise. These capabilities are developed in the elite *grandes écoles* of engineering and administration.

The research findings confirmed the image of German firms as "well-oiled machines" as they were more likely to be decentralized, specialized, and formalized. In fact, German managers were more likely to cite structure as a key success factor, having a logic of its own, apart from people. German firms were more likely to be organized by function (sometimes to the extent that they are referred to as "chimney" organizations) with coordination achieved through routines and procedures. Although German organizations tended to be flatter and to have a broader span of control when compared with the French, middle managers had less discretion than their British counterparts as they were limited to their specific technical competence. The premium placed on competence was expressed in the concern to find competent people to perform specialized tasks, the strong role of staff to provide technical expertise, and expectations that top management not only has specific technical competence, but also in-depth company knowledge. Furthermore, top management typically consists of a managing board, *Vorstand,* which integrates the specialized knowledge of the various top managers (rather than in the head of a lone individual as in the case of France, Britain, or the United States).

In contrast to the well-oiled machine model with its greater concern for efficiency, the "village market" model reflects a greater concern for flexibility. Indeed, structure in British firms was found to be far more flexible, more decentralized and less formalized, when compared with the French and German firms. Organized by divisions, there is greater decentralization and delegation in the company and the role of central staff is far less important. Here, the burden of coordinating functions was placed on individual managers requiring a constant need for persuasion and negotiation to achieve cooperation.[16]

British managers, compared with Germans, were more ready to adapt the structure to the people working in it. Changes in personnel were often used as opportunities to reshuffle the jobs and responsibilities in order to accommodate available talent, and to create opportunities for personal development (free agents). Top management's role was to identify market opportunities and convince others to pursue them, underlining the importance of taking a more strategic view and of being able to communicate it persuasively.[17]

Studies in Asia have also found companies to fit the "family model," being more hierarchic and less formalized, with the exception of Japan. When compared with the Japanese, Hong Kong Chinese firms were less likely to have written manuals and Hong Kong Chinese bosses were also found to be more autocratic and paternalistic.[18] Another study of thirty-nine multinational commercial banks from fourteen different countries operating in Hong Kong found the Hong Kong banks to have the greatest number of hierarchical levels (eleven); the banks from Singapore, the Philippines, and India were also among those most centralized.[19]

A recent study of Chinese entrepreneurs found the Confucian tradition of patriarchal authority to be remarkably persistent. Being part of the family is seen as a way of achieving security. Social roles

---

[16]Stewart et al., Op. cit.

[17]Ibid.

[18]Redding, S.G. and Pugh, D.S. (1986) "The formal and the informal: Japanese and Chinese organization structures" in S. Clegg, D. Dunphy, and S.G. Redding (eds) *The Enterprise and Management in East Asia,* Hong Kong: Center of Asian Studies, University of Hong Kong, 153–68; Vertinsky, I., Tse, D.K.,Wehrung, D.A. and Lee, K. (1990) "Organization design and management norms: A comparative study of managers' perceptions in the People's Republic of China, Hong Kong and Canada," *Journal of Management,* 16(4), 853–67.

[19]Wong, G.Y.Y. and Birnbaum-More, P.H. (1994) "Culture, context and structure: A test on Hong Kong banks," *Organization Studies,* 15(l), 99–23.

are clearly spelled out in line with Confucian precepts, which designate the responsibilities for the roles of father, son, brothers, and so on. Control is exerted through authority, which is not questioned. In 70 percent of the entrepreneurial firms studied, even large ones, the structure of Chinese organizations was found to resemble a hub with spokes around a powerful founder, or a management structure with only two layers.[20]

Recent studies of Russian managers using Hofstede's framework found them to be autocratic and political (reflecting high power distance), while expected to take care of their subordinates (low masculinity). Managers tend to seek security and to be risk averse (high uncertainty avoidance). While performance appraisal is still seen to be highly political, motivation is however becoming more calculative based on growing individualism.[21]

What begins to emerge from these various research studies is a converging and coherent picture of different management structures when comparing countries within Europe, as well as when comparing countries in Europe, the United States, and Asia.

The primary cultural determinants appear to be those related to relationships between people in terms of power and status and relationship with nature, for example how uncertainty is managed and how control is exercised.

These underlying cultural assumptions are expressed in beliefs (and their subsequent importance, or value) regarding the need for hierarchy, for formal rules and procedures, specialized jobs and functions. These beliefs and values, in turn, are observable in behavior and artifacts, such as deference to the boss, the presence of executive parking and dining facilities ("perks"), and the existence of written policies and procedures, specific job descriptions, or manuals outlining standard operating procedures.

The research findings in the above-mentioned studies were based on observations as well as questionnaires and interviews of managers and companies in different countries. The same, of course, can be done comparing companies in different industries or within the same industry, and managers in different functions providing corresponding models of industry, corporate and/or functional cultures. From these findings, management scholars interpret underlying meaning.

The Meaning of Organizations: Task versus Social System

André Laurent argues that the country differences in structure described above reflect different conceptions (or understandings) of what is an organization.[22] These different conceptions were discovered in surveys which asked managers to agree or disagree with statements regarding beliefs about organization and management. A sample of the questions is shown in Table 3.

The results of this survey are very much in line with the discussion above in that they show similar cultural differences regarding power and uncertainty in views of organizations as systems of hierarchy, authority, politics, and role formalization. What would these different views of organization actually look like, were we to observe managers at work and even to question them? What arguments would managers from different countries put forth to support their responses?

Having a view of organizations as **hierarchical systems** would make it difficult, for example, to tolerate having to report to two bosses, as required in a matrix organization, and it would make it difficult to accept bypassing or going over or around the boss. The boss would also be expected to have precise answers to most of the questions that subordinates have about their work. Asian and Latin managers argue that this is necessary in order

---

[20]Kao, J. (1993) "The world wide web of Chinese business," *Harvard Business Review,* March–April, 24–35.

[21]Elenkov, D.S. (1998) "Can American management concepts work in Russia?" *Academy of Management Review,* 40(4), 133–56.

[22]Laurent, A. (1983) "The cultural diversity of western conception of management," *International Studies of Management and Organization,* 13(1-2), 75–96.

Table 3   Management Questionnaire

A = Strongly agree
B = Tend to agree
C = Neither agree, nor disagree
D = Tend to disagree
E = Strongly disagree

1.	When the respective roles of the members of a department become complex, detailed job descriptions are a useful way of clarifying.	A	B	C	D	E
2.	In order to have efficient work relationships, it is often necessary to bypass the hierarchical line.	A	B	C	D	E
8.	An organizational structure in which certain subordinates have two direct bosses should be avoided at all costs.	A	B	C	D	E
13.	The more complex a department's activities, the more important it is for each individual's functions to be well-defined.	A	B	C	D	E
14.	The main reason for having a hierarchical structure is so that everyone knows who has authority over whom.	A	B	C	D	E
19.	Most organizations would be better off if conflict could be eliminated forever.	A	B	C	D	E
24.	It is important for a manager to have at hand precise answers to most of the questions that his/her subordinates may raise about their work.	A	B	C	D	E
33.	Most managers have a clear notion of what we call an organizational structure.	A	B	C	D	E
38.	Most managers would achieve better results if their roles were less precisely defined.	A	B	C	D	E
40.	Through their professional activity, managers play an important role in society.	A	B	C	D	E
43.	The manager of tomorrow will be, primarily, a negotiator.	A	B	C	D	E
49.	Most managers seem to be more motivated by obtaining power than by achieving objectives.	A	B	C	D	E
52.	Today there seems to be an authority crisis in organizations.	A	B	C	D	E

Source: André Laurent. Reproduced by permission.

for bosses to be respected, or to have power and authority. And if the most efficient way to get things done is to bypass the hierarchical line they would consider that there was something wrong with the hierarchy.

Scandinavian and Anglo managers, on the other hand, argue that it is perfectly normal to go directly to anyone in the organization in order to accomplish the task. It would seem intolerable, for example, to have to go through one's own boss, who would contact his or her counterpart in a neighboring department before making contact with someone in that other department.

Furthermore, they argue that it is impossible to have precise answers, since the world is far too complex and ambiguous, and even if you could provide precise answers, this would not develop the capability of your subordinates to solve problems. Thus a Swedish boss with a French subordinate can anticipate some problems: the French subordinate is likely to think that the boss, not knowing the answers, is incompetent, while the Swedish boss may think that the French subordinate does not know what to do and is therefore incompetent.

Those who view the organization as a **political system** consider managers to play an important political role in society, and to negotiate within the organization. Thus obtaining power is seen as more important than achieving specific objectives. Here again, Latin European managers are more likely to adhere to this view than their Nordic and Anglo counterparts.

In France, for example, executives have often played important roles in the French administration before assuming top positions in companies. Furthermore, Latin managers are acutely aware that it is necessary to have power in order to get things done in the organization. Nordic and Anglo managers, however, tend to downplay the importance of power and therefore reject the need for political maneuvering.

When organizations are viewed as systems of **role formalization,** managers prefer detailed job descriptions, and well-defined roles and functions. These serve to clarify complex situations and tasks. Otherwise it is difficult to know who is responsible for what and to hold people accountable. In addition they argue that lack of clear job descriptions or role definitions creates overlap and inefficiency. Nordic and Anglo managers, on the other hand, argue that the world is too complex to be able to clearly define roles and functions. Furthermore they say that detailed descriptions interfere with maintaining flexibility and achieving coordination.

From his research, Laurent concluded that underlying these arguments managers had different conceptions of organization: one which focused on the task, called **instrumental,** and one which focused on relationships, called **social.** For Latin European managers, organizations are considered as **social systems,** or systems of relationships, where personal networks and social positioning are important. The organization achieves its goals through relationships and how they are managed (as prescribed by Fayol). Roles and relationships are defined formally (by the hierarchy) and informally, based on authority, power, and status which are attributes of

the person, not the task or function. Personal loyalty and deference to the boss are expected.

However, getting things done means working around the system—using informal, personal networks to circumvent the hierarchy as well as the rules and regulations—what the French call, *Système D*. According to sociologist Michel Crozier, it is this informal system that gives the French "bureaucratic model" its flexibility.[23] Organizations are thus considered to be necessarily political in nature. When asked to diagnose organizational problems, French social scientists and consultants typically start by analyzing the power relationships and power games (*les enjeux*).[24]

In contrast, for Anglo-Saxon, and northern European managers, the organization is a system of tasks where it is important to know what has to be done, rather than who has power and authority to do so (as in the socio/political view). This instrumental or functionalist view of organizations (very much in keeping with Taylor's scientific management) focuses on what is to be achieved and whether objectives are met (achievement orientation). Structure is defined by activities—what has to be done—and the hierarchy exists only to assign responsibility. It follows that authority is defined by function and is limited, specific to the job not the person.

Here, coordination and control are impersonal, decentralized, and reside in the structure and systems. Rules and regulations are applied universally. If the rules and regulations are dysfunctional, then they are changed rather than circumvented or broken. Management consultants are called in to figure out the best way to devise strategy, design structure, classify jobs and set salary scales, and develop concrete programs such as "total quality" or "performance management."

These findings can be further corroborated by asking managers to describe the approach to

[23]Crozier, M. (1964) *The Bureaucratic Phenomenon,* Chicago: University of Chicago Press.
[24]Crozier, M. and Friedberg, E. (1977) *L'Acteur et le système: Les contraintes de l'action collective,* Paris: Seuil.

management in their countries, or "how we see us." For example, many of the research results discussed above place Scandinavian managers at one end of a continuum, with Latin and Asian managers at the other. Jan Selmer,[25] a Swedish management professor, proposed the following profile of "Viking Management." Compare this with the self-descriptions of Brazilian[26] and Indonesian managers in Table 4.

According to self-reports, clear differences and similarities emerge in terms of the nature of relationships (hierarchy) and the relationship with nature (uncertainty and control). For example, in keeping with the findings discussed above, Viking Management is characterized as decentralized (less hierarchy) when compared with the Brazilian and Indonesian views, which emphasize status and power or respect for elders.

On the other hand, in each case there is a strong emphasis on the importance of relationships: family and friends, avoiding conflict, being tolerant, seeking consensus, and "keeping everyone happy." For the Swedes, this corresponds to their "mother–daughter" relationships between headquarters and subsidiaries, and their keen concern for social well-being and quality of relationships, reflected in their number one ranking on Hofstede's femininity dimension.

In all three self descriptions there is less emphasis placed on formalization. In Swedish companies, organization structures and decision processes are often experienced as vague and ambiguous. Uncertainty is managed though "values and not rules", and communication is informal. For the Indonesians, higher order principles (The Five Principles) provide guidance not organizational ones. Furthermore, as the perceived control over nature is low, they are more likely to "go with the flow". Brazilian managers, faced with great uncertainty in the day-to-day business environment over which they feel

Table 4 As We See Us . . .

Viking Management

Decentralized decision making
Organization structure is often ambiguous
Perceived by others to be indecisive
Goal formulation, long-range objectives, and performance evaluation criteria are vague and implicit
Informal channels of communication
Coordinate by values not rules (normative versus coercive)
Case-by-case approach versus standard procedures
Consensus-oriented
Avoid conflict
Informal relationships between foreign subsidiaries and headquarters (mother–daughter relationships)

Brazilian Management

Hierarchy and authority; status and power are important
Centralized decision making
Personal relationships are more important than the task
Rules and regulations are for enemies
Flexible and adaptable (too much?) *Jeitiñho*
Anything is possible
Short-term oriented—immediatism
Avoid conflict—seen as win/lose
Rely on magic—low control over environment
Decisions based on intuition and feeling

Indonesian Management

Respect for hierarchy and elders
Family-oriented
Group- versus individual-oriented
Friendly and helpful, hospitable
Tolerant
Decisions based on compromise—"keep everyone happy"
Importance of religion—Islam
Five principles
Bhinneka Tunggal Ika (unity through diversity)

[25]Selmer, J. (1988) Presentation, International Conference on Personnel and Human Resource Management Conference, Singapore.
[26]Amado, G. and Brasil, H.V. (1991) "Organizational behaviors and cultural context: The Brazilian 'Jeitiñho,'" *International Studies of Management and Organization*, 21(3), 38–61.

they have little control, say that they have developed a finely tuned sense of intuition, having learned to trust their "gut" feel. For the Brazilians, the notion of *Jeitiñho* is similar to that of the French

Système D, going around the system in order to get things done. This assures flexibility and adaptability such that anything is possible (although perhaps too much so as Brazilian managers themselves acknowledge).

Now imagine a Brazil–Sweden–Indonesia joint venture. This raises the possibility that three firms would have to resolve their differences on several fronts while using their similarities to create a shared sense of purpose. In particular, there would probably be a clash between the cultural assumptions underlying Swedish management—little concern with power and status and high perceived control over the environment—with those of Brazilian and Indonesian management—more emphasis on power and authority and less perceived control.

This would probably cause the biggest headaches for the Swedes when it came to efforts to delegate decision-making and to encourage individual responsibility and accountability. For the Indonesian and Brazilian managers, the frustration would come from confusion as to "who is the boss?" and "why isn't he/she making decisions?" and "how can I be held responsible when I have no control over what happens?" In decision-making, the Brazilians would find the Indonesians and Swedes interminably slow, seeking consensus or democratic compromise, while they in turn would see the Brazilians as impetuous, and too individualistic. On the other hand, the similarity in importance placed on relationships, on informal communication, and on avoiding conflict can help to work through these difficulties together, on a personal basis.

Although there are variations within countries, due to industry and corporate culture, as well as individual styles of key managers, the above research findings and self-descriptions point to different cultural profiles of organization. The underlying assumptions can be interpreted to reveal the nature of relationships, as seen in the importance of hierarchy, and control over nature, as seen in the need for formal or social rules and procedures. The underlying cultural meaning of the organization can then be interpreted as systems of tasks versus systems of relationships. These cultural profiles provide a starting point to explore different structural preferences and to begin to anticipate potential problems when transferring practices from one country to another or in forming joint ventures and strategic alliances.

On a less serious note, these differences have been caricatured in the organizational charts shown in Figure 3. Using these caricatures can provoke discussion of structural differences across countries in a humorous mode while allowing us to discover the grain of truth within and to imagine how our own organization chart might seem to others. Constructing cultural profiles enables us to appreciate the impact of culture on management as multidimensional. It would therefore be a mistake to base a prediction regarding structure or process on a single cultural dimension.

In addition, managers need to recognize that the relationships between cultural dimensions and structure are not simple cause–effect links, but instead, are multi-determined. Similar approaches may exist for different cultural reasons, and different approaches may exist for the same reason. Thus formalized rules and procedures or participative management approaches may have a different *raison d'être* on different sides of the national border.

Transferability of Best Practice? Alternative Approaches

By pulling together the various experiences of managers and more systematic research studies, we have demonstrated how culture affects organization structure and process. We have proposed different profiles or models of organizing which evolve from different underlying cultural assumptions. This raises questions about what is considered to be "universal wisdom" and the transferability of "best practice." For the most part, arguments for transferability are in line with convergence notions which claim universality; "Management is management and best practice can be transferred anywhere." This was the rationale behind the 1980s rush to copy Japanese management practice and more recent rash of American-style restructuring and re-engineering.

Figure 3   The Organization Chart

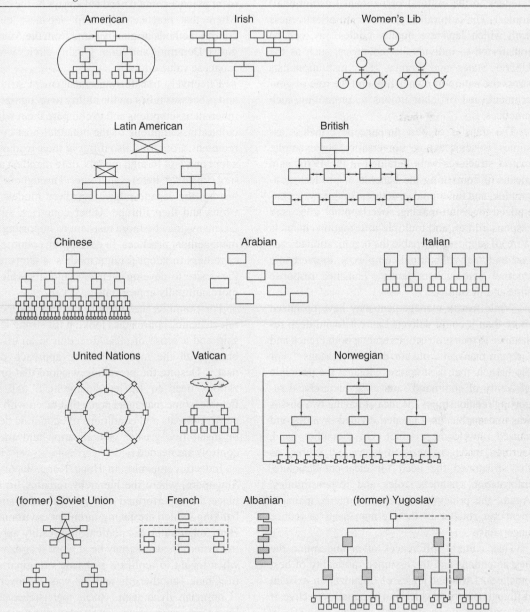

Those that question transferability point to differences in the cultural or national (institutional) context. The culturalists question the effectiveness with which Japanese quality circles, say, can be transferred to individualist countries, such as the United States and France. The institutionalists stress the nature of ownership, and the role of government, and of labor unions in promoting such practices.

The transfer of best practice nevertheless assumes, to some extent, universality. For example, matrix structures were heralded in the 1970s as a means of combining the benefits of product, geographic, and functional structures. In theory, decentralized decision-making, overlapping roles and responsibilities, and multiple information channels were all supposed to enable the organization to capture and analyze external complexity, to overcome internal parochialism, and to enhance response time and flexibility.[27]

While matrix management may have promised more than it could deliver, Laurent found deep resistance to matrix structures among both French and German managers, but for different reasons.[28] For the French, matrix structures violated the principle of "unity of command" and clear hierarchical reporting relationships. The idea of having two bosses was undesirable, as it created divided loyalties and caused unwelcome conflict. On the other hand, German managers resisted matrix structures, as they frustrated the need for clear-cut structure, information channels, roles and responsibilities. Again, the principles underlying matrix management ran counter to the German need to reduce uncertainty.

Thus cultural differences often undermine the best intentions and the assumed rationality of best practices. Different logics of organization exist in different countries, which can be equally effective, if not more so, given different societal contexts. In fact, there seems to be little doubt that some contexts

are more favorable to the success of certain management practices, and it need not always be the country where that practice originated. Japanese quality-control methods originally came from the American gurus, Demming and Juran. Quality circles were the Japanese value-added.

Effectively transferring management structures and processes relies on the ability to recognize their inherent assumptions and to compare them with the cultural assumptions of the potential host country recipient. Countries also differ in their readiness to adopt or adapt foreign models, or to manifest a NIH (not invented here) syndrome. Throughout their history, the Japanese have borrowed models from China and then Europe. Other countries, such as Germany, may be more resistant to importing alien management practices. In developing countries, the eagerness to adopt foreign models is tempered by the desire to develop their own models which are more culturally appropriate.

For example, managers in Eastern Europe may reject "team" approaches looking for strong leadership and a sense of clear direction in an effort to break with the more collective approach of the past.[29] Despite the prevailing wisdom that organizations need to be less hierarchical and more flexible, some managers argue that faced with competitive threats and conditions of economic decline or instability, greater centralization and stronger controls are needed.

Indeed, companies in Hong Kong, Japan, and Singapore, where the hierarchy remains firmly in place, have performed well in industries, such as banking, which are facing turbulent environments. Here, other value orientations, not readily apparent in Western business, may be at work. For example, when trying to replicate Hofstede's original study in China, another dimension was discovered— "Confucian dynamism," thrift, persistence and a long-term perspective. This added dimension was considered to account for the competitiveness of

[27]Davis, S. and Lawrence, P.R. (1977) *Matrix,* Reading, MA: Addison-Wesley.
[28]Laurent, A. (1981) "Matrix organization and Latin cultures," *International Studies of Management and Organization,* 10(4), 101–14.

[29]Cyr, D.J. and Schneider, S.C. (1996) "Implications for learning: human resources management in east-west joint ventures," *Organization Studies,* 17(2), 207–226.

the "Five Asian Dragons": China, Hong Kong, Taiwan, Japan, and South Korea.[30]

Consider this testimony regarding the entrepreneurial, family model characteristic of the overseas Chinese business community which has been quite successful whether transplanted to Malaysia or Canada.

> The Confucian tradition of hard work, thrift and respect for one's social network may provide continuity with the right twist for today's fast-changing markets. And the central strategic question for all current multinationals—be they Chinese, Japanese or Western—is how to gather and integrate power through many small units. The evolution of a worldwide web of relatively small Chinese businesses, bound by undeniable strong cultural links, offers a working model for the future.[31]

Whatever the model of the future, be it team management or network organizations, we need to consider how culture may facilitate or hinder their diffusion. Will the more collective culture of Russia facilitate the team approach, while the greater relationship orientation of Chinese culture facilitate creating networks? Could it be that the greater emphasis on the task and the individual, which prevails in the performance management approach, will actually hinder American firms in their attempts to become more team- and network-oriented?

Given recent trends in the United States and Europe towards participative management and empowerment, the role of the leadership is changing. Rather than the more authoritarian notion of being the "boss," the role model is that of the "coach." Rather than directing and controlling, the new role calls for facilitating and developing. Notions of empowerment and the leader as coach, however, may not readily transfer.

Take, for example, two items from the Management Questionnaire designed by Laurent regarding

the role of the boss (hierarchy) and of power as shown in Figure 4. Comparing the responses of managers attending training seminars from 1990 to 1994 with the results reported in 1980, we find some signs of convergence. According to self-reports, managers are becoming less authoritarian and more concerned with achieving objectives than obtaining power. Nevertheless, while country differences may have eroded, the different country rankings remain in place.

Even in countries which supposedly do not put much stock in hierarchy, such as The Netherlands and the United Kingdom, this new leadership behavior may be difficult to achieve. Therefore, what will that mean for countries in Asia where the hierarchy is still revered? What would the Asian version of empowerment look like? Perhaps there are different means of achieving this end. In the case of Japanese firms, the hierarchy is clearly, albeit implicitly, present. Nevertheless, there are apparently high levels of participation.

And as hierarchies collapse and as cooperation between units becomes more of a necessity, there is a greater need for negotiation and persuasion. Managers will increasingly have to elicit the cooperation of people over whom they have no formal authority. In fact this may demand a more political view of organizations to which Latin firms may be more attuned.

These are the challenges facing many companies as they remodel their corporate structures. They must not lose sight of the impact of national culture in their search for a model of organization that can respond best to the demands of the rapidly changing business context, and the pressures for internationalization. They must also recognize that the "best models" are not necessarily "home grown," but that other ways of organizing may be equally, if not more, effective. And as local managers in these regions gain experience and knowledge, they become less willing to adopt models imposed by head offices from other countries. Thus searching for 'best practices' wherever they may be located becomes an increasing strategic imperative.

[30]Hofstede, G. and Bond, M.H. (1988) "The Confucius connection: From cultural roots to economic growth," *Organizational Dynamics*, 16, 4–21; see also Hofstede, G. (1991) *Cultures and Organizations: Software of the Mind*, London: McGraw-Hill.

[31]Kao, *Op. cit.*, p. 36.

Figure 4   Convergence?

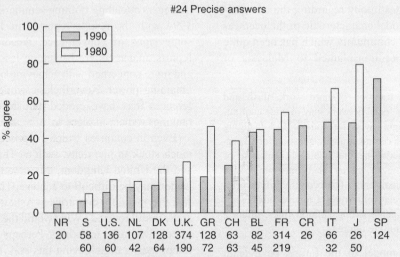

#24 Precise answers

It is important for a manager to have at hand precise answers to most of the questions his/her subordinates may raise about their work.

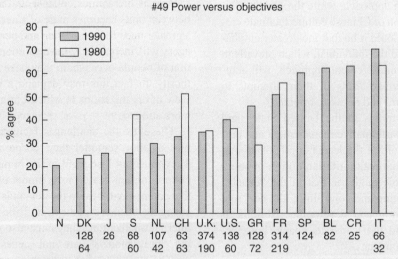

#49 Power versus objectives

Most managers seem to be more motivated by obtaining power than by achieving objectives.

Source: Reproduced by permission of A. Laurent.

Reading 2-2   Clusters and the New Economics of Competition

Michael E. Porter

Now that companies can source capital, goods, information, and technology from around the world, often with the click of a mouse, much of the conventional wisdom about how companies and nations compete needs to be overhauled. In theory, more open global markets and faster transportation and communication should diminish the role of location in competition. After all, anything that can be efficiently sourced from a distance through global markets and corporate networks is available to any company and therefore is essentially nullified as a source of competitive advantage.

But if location matters less, why, then, is it true that the odds of finding a world-class mutual-fund company in Boston are much higher than in most any other place? Why could the same be said of textile-related companies in North Carolina and South Carolina, of high-performance auto companies in southern Germany, or of fashion shoe companies in northern Italy?

Today's economic map of the world is dominated by what I call *clusters:* critical masses—in one place—of unusual competitive success in particular fields. Clusters are a striking feature of virtually every national, regional, state, and even metropolitan economy, especially in more economically advanced nations. Silicon Valley and Hollywood may be the world's best-known clusters.

Michael E. Porter is the C. Roland Christensen Professor of Business Administration at the Harvard Business School in Boston, Massachusetts. Further discussion of clusters can be found in two new essays—"Clusters and Competition" and "Competing Across Locations"—in his new collection titled *On Competition* (Boston: Harvard Business School Press, 1998).

Reprinted by permission of *Harvard Business Review*. "Clusters and the New Economics of Competition" by Michael E. Porter (November–December 1998).

Clusters are not unique, however; they are highly typical—and therein lies a paradox: the enduring competitive advantages in a global economy lie increasingly in local things—knowledge, relationships, motivation—that distant rivals cannot match.

Although location remains fundamental to competition, its role today differs vastly from a generation ago. In an era when competition was driven heavily by input costs, locations with some important endowment—a natural harbor, for example, or a supply of cheap labor—often enjoyed a *comparative advantage* that was both competitively decisive and persistent over time.

Competition in today's economy is far more dynamic. Companies can mitigate many input-cost disadvantages through global sourcing, rendering the old notion of comparative advantage less relevant. Instead, competitive advantage rests on making more productive use of inputs, which requires continual innovation.

Untangling the paradox of location in a global economy reveals a number of key insights about how companies continually create competitive advantage. What happens *inside* companies is important, but clusters reveal that the immediate business environment *outside* companies plays a vital role as well. This role of locations has been long overlooked, despite striking evidence that innovation and competitive success in so many fields are geographically concentrated—whether it's entertainment in Hollywood, finance on Wall Street, or consumer electronics in Japan.

Clusters affect competitiveness within countries as well as across national borders. Therefore, they lead to new agendas for all business executives—not just those who compete globally. More broadly, clusters represent a new way of thinking about location, challenging much of the conventional wisdom about how companies should be configured, how institutions such as universities can contribute to competitive success, and how governments can promote economic development and prosperity.

What Is a Cluster?

Clusters are geographic concentrations of interconnected companies and institutions in a particular field. Clusters encompass an array of linked industries and other entities important to competition. They include, for example, suppliers of specialized inputs such as components, machinery, and services, and providers of specialized infrastructure. Clusters also often extend downstream to channels and customers and laterally to manufacturers of complementary products and to companies in industries related by skills, technologies, or common inputs. Finally, many clusters include governmental and other institutions—such as universities, standards-setting agencies, think tanks, vocational training providers, and trade associations—that provide specialized training, education, information, research, and technical support.

The California wine cluster is a good example. It includes 680 commercial wineries as well as several thousand independent wine grape growers. (See the Figure 1 "Anatomy of the California Wine Cluster.") An extensive complement of industries supporting both wine making and grape growing exists, including suppliers of grape stock, irrigation and harvesting equipment, barrels, and labels; specialized public relations and advertising firms; and numerous wine publications aimed at consumer and trade audiences. A host of local institutions is

Figure 1   Anatomy of the California Wine Cluster

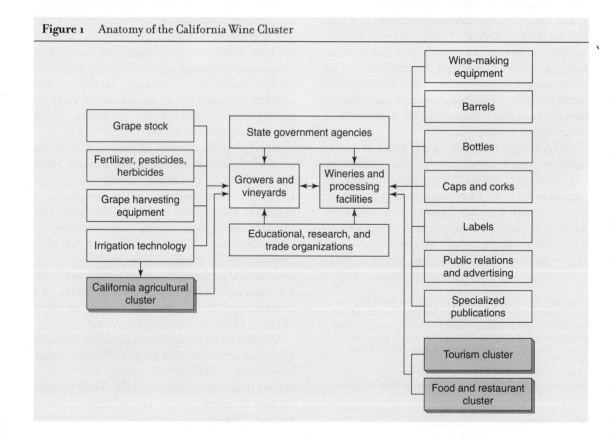

involved with wine, such as the world-renowned viticulture and enology program at the University of California at Davis, the Wine Institute, and special committees of the California senate and assembly. The cluster also enjoys weaker linkages to other California clusters in agriculture, food and restaurants, and wine-country tourism.

Consider also the Italian leather fashion cluster, which contains well-known shoe companies such as Ferragamo and Gucci as well as a host of specialized suppliers of footwear components, machinery, molds, design services, and tanned leather. (See the Figure 2 "Mapping the Italian Leather Fashion Cluster.") It also consists of several chains of related industries, including those producing different types of leather goods (linked by common inputs and technologies) and different types of footwear (linked by overlapping channels and technologies). These industries employ common marketing media and compete with similar images in similar customer segments. A related Italian cluster in textile fashion, including clothing, scarves, and accessories, produces complementary products that often employ common channels. The extraordinary strength of the Italian leather fashion cluster can be attributed, at least in part, to the multiple linkages and synergies that participating Italian businesses enjoy.

A cluster's boundaries are defined by the linkages and complementarities across industries and institutions that are most important to competition. Although clusters often fit within political boundaries, they may cross state or even national borders. In the United States, for example, a pharmaceuticals cluster straddles New Jersey and Pennsylvania near Philadelphia. Similarly, a chemicals cluster in Germany crosses over into German-speaking Switzerland.

Clusters rarely conform to standard industrial classification systems, which fail to capture many

Figure 2   Mapping the Italian Leather Fashion Cluster

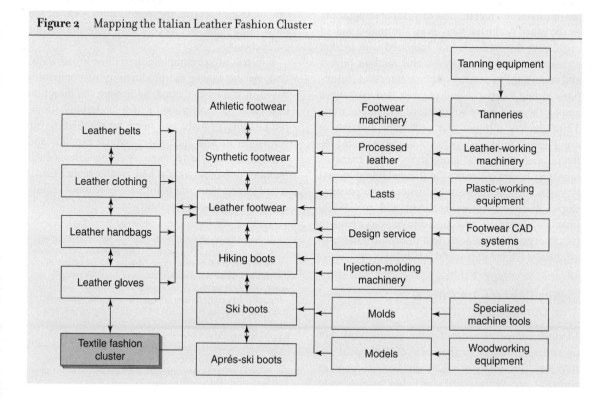

important actors and relationships in competition. Thus significant clusters may be obscured or even go unrecognized. In Massachusetts, for example, more than 400 companies, representing at least 39,000 high-paying jobs, are involved in medical devices in some way. The cluster long remained all but invisible, however, buried within larger and overlapping industry categories such as electronic equipment and plastic products. Executives in the medical devices cluster have only recently come together to work on issues that will benefit them all.

Clusters promote both competition and cooperation. Rivals compete intensely to win and retain customers. Without vigorous competition, a cluster will fail. Yet there is also cooperation, much of it vertical, involving companies in related industries and local institutions. Competition can coexist with cooperation because they occur on different dimensions and among different players.

Clusters represent a kind of new spatial organizational form in between arm's-length markets on the one hand and hierarchies, or vertical integration, on the other. A cluster, then, is an alternative way of organizing the value chain. Compared with market transactions among dispersed and random buyers and sellers, the proximity of companies and institutions in one location—and the repeated exchanges among them—fosters better coordination and trust. Thus clusters mitigate the problems inherent in arm's-length relationships without imposing the inflexibilities of vertical integration or the management challenges of creating and maintaining formal linkages such as networks, alliances, and partnerships. A cluster of independent and informally linked companies and institutions represents a robust organizational form that offers advantages in efficiency, effectiveness, and flexibility.

▌ Why Clusters Are Critical to Competition

Modern competition depends on productivity, not on access to inputs or the scale of individual enterprises. Productivity rests on *how* companies compete, not on the particular fields they compete in. Companies can be highly productive in any industry—shoes, agriculture, or semiconductors—if they employ sophisticated methods, use advanced technology, and offer unique products and services. All industries can employ advanced technology; all industries can be knowledge intensive.

The sophistication with which companies compete in a particular location, however, is strongly influenced by the quality of the local business environment.[1] Companies cannot employ advanced logistical techniques, for example, without a high-quality transportation infrastructure. Nor can companies effectively compete on sophisticated service without well-educated employees. Businesses cannot operate efficiently under onerous regulatory red tape or under a court system that fails to resolve disputes quickly and fairly. Some aspects of the business environment, such as the legal system, for example, or corporate tax rates, affect all industries. In advanced economies, however, the more decisive aspects of the business environment are often cluster specific; these constitute some of the most important microeconomic foundations for competition.

Clusters affect competition in three broad ways: first, by increasing the productivity of companies based in the area; second, by driving the direction and pace of innovation, which underpins future productivity growth; and third, by stimulating the formation of new businesses, which expands and strengthens the cluster itself. A cluster allows each member to benefit *as if* it had greater scale or *as if* it had joined with others formally—without requiring it to sacrifice its flexibility.

▌[1]I first made this argument in *The Competitive Advantage of Nations* (New York: Free Press, 1990). I modeled the effect of the local business environment on competition in terms of four interrelated influences, graphically depicted in a diamond: factor conditions (the cost and quality of inputs); demand conditions (the sophistication of local customers); the context for firm strategy and rivalry (the nature and intensity of local competition); and related and supporting industries (the local extent and sophistication of suppliers and related industries). Diamond theory stresses how these elements combine to produce a dynamic, stimulating, and intensely competitive business environment.

A cluster is the manifestation of the diamond at work. Proximity—the colocation of companies, customers, and suppliers—amplifies all of the pressures to innovate and upgrade.

Clusters and Productivity   Being part of a cluster allows companies to operate more productively in sourcing inputs; accessing information, technology, and needed institutions; coordinating with related companies; and measuring and motivating improvement.

Better Access to Employees and Suppliers
Companies in vibrant clusters can tap into an existing pool of specialized and experienced employees, thereby lowering their search and transaction costs in recruiting. Because a cluster signals opportunity and reduces the risk of relocation for employees, it can also be easier to attract talented people from other locations, a decisive advantage in some industries.

A well-developed cluster also provides an efficient means of obtaining other important inputs. Such a cluster offers a deep and specialized supplier base. Sourcing locally instead of from distant suppliers lowers transaction costs. It minimizes the need for inventory, eliminates importing costs and delays, and—because local reputation is important—lowers the risk that suppliers will overprice or renege on commitments. Proximity improves communications and makes it easier for suppliers to provide ancillary or support services such as installation and debugging. Other things being equal, then, local outsourcing is a better solution than distant outsourcing, especially for advanced and specialized inputs involving embedded technology, information, and service content.

Formal alliances with distant suppliers can mitigate some of the disadvantages of distant outsourcing. But all formal alliances involve their own complex bargaining and governance problems and can inhibit a company's flexibility. The close, informal relationships possible among companies in a cluster are often a superior arrangement.

In many cases, clusters are also a better alternative to vertical integration. Compared with in-house units, outside specialists are often more cost effective and responsive, not only in component production but also in services such as training. Although extensive vertical integration may have once been the norm, a fast-changing environment can render vertical integration inefficient, ineffective, and inflexible.

Even when some inputs are best sourced from a distance, clusters offer advantages. Suppliers trying to penetrate a large, concentrated market will price more aggressively, knowing that as they do so they can realize efficiencies in marketing and in service.

Working against a cluster's advantages in assembling resources is the possibility that competition will render them more expensive and scarce. But companies do have the alternative of outsourcing many inputs from other locations, which tends to limit potential cost penalties. More important, clusters increase not only the demand for specialized inputs but also their supply.

Access to Specialized Information   Extensive market, technical, and competitive information accumulates within a cluster, and members have preferred access to it. In addition, personal relationships and community ties foster trust and facilitate the flow of information. These conditions make information more transferable.

Complementarities   A host of linkages among cluster members results in a whole greater than the sum of its parts. In a typical tourism cluster, for example, the quality of a visitor's experience depends not only on the appeal of the primary attraction but also on the quality and efficiency of complementary businesses such as hotels, restaurants, shopping outlets, and transportation facilities. Because members of the cluster are mutually dependent, good performance by one can boost the success of the others.

Complementarities come in many forms. The most obvious is when products complement one another in meeting customers' needs, as the tourism example illustrates. Another form is the coordination of activities across companies to optimize their collective productivity. In wood products, for instance, the efficiency of sawmills depends on a reliable supply of high-quality timber and the ability to put all the timber to use—in furniture (highest quality), pallets and boxes (lower quality), or wood chips (lowest quality). In the early 1990s, Portuguese sawmills suffered from poor timber quality because local landowners did not invest in timber management. Hence most timber was processed for use in pallets and boxes, a lower-value use that limited the price paid to landowners. Substantial improvement in productivity was possible, but only if several parts of the cluster changed simultaneously. Logging operations, for example, had to modify cutting and sorting procedures, while sawmills had to develop the capacity to process wood in more sophisticated ways. Coordination to develop standard wood classifications and measures was an important enabling step. Geographically dispersed companies are less likely to recognize and capture such linkages.

Other complementarities arise in marketing. A cluster frequently enhances the reputation of a location in a particular field, making it more likely that buyers will turn to a vendor based there. Italy's strong reputation for fashion and design, for example, benefits companies involved in leather goods, footwear, apparel, and accessories. Beyond reputation, cluster members often profit from a variety of joint marketing mechanisms, such as company referrals, trade fairs, trade magazines, and marketing delegations.

Finally, complementarities can make buying from a cluster more attractive for customers. Visiting buyers can see many vendors in a single trip. They also may perceive their buying risk to be lower because one location provides alternative suppliers. That allows them to multisource or to switch vendors if the need arises. Hong Kong thrives as a source of fashion apparel in part for this reason.

Access to Institutions and Public Goods   Investments made by government or other public institutions—such as public spending for specialized infrastructure or educational programs—can enhance a company's productivity. The ability to recruit employees trained at local programs, for example, lowers the cost of internal training. Other quasi-public goods, such as the cluster's information and technology pools and its reputation, arise as natural by-products of competition.

It is not just governments that create public goods that enhance productivity in the private sector. Investments by companies—in training programs, infrastructure, quality centers, testing laboratories, and so on—also contribute to increased productivity. Such private investments are often made collectively because cluster participants recognize the potential for collective benefits.

Better Motivation and Measurement   Local rivalry is highly motivating. Peer pressure amplifies competitive pressure within a cluster, even among noncompeting or indirectly competing companies. Pride and the desire to look good in the local community spur executives to attempt to outdo one another.

Clusters also often make it easier to measure and compare performances because local rivals share general circumstances—for example, labor costs and local market access—and they perform similar activities. Companies within clusters typically have intimate knowledge of their suppliers' costs. Managers are able to compare costs and employees' performance with other local companies. Additionally, financial institutions can accumulate knowledge about the cluster that can be used to monitor performance.

Clusters and Innovation   In addition to enhancing productivity, clusters play a vital role in a company's ongoing ability to innovate. Some of the same characteristics that enhance current productivity have an even more dramatic effect on innovation and productivity growth.

Because sophisticated buyers are often part of a cluster, companies inside clusters usually have a better window on the market than isolated competitors do. Computer companies based in Silicon Valley and Austin, Texas, for example, plug into customer needs and trends with a speed difficult to match by companies located elsewhere. The ongoing relationships with other entities within the cluster also help companies to learn early about evolving technology, component and machinery availability, service and marketing concepts, and so on. Such learning is facilitated by the ease of making site visits and frequent face-to-face contact.

Figure 3   Mapping Selected U.S. Clusters

Here are just some of the clusters in the United States. A few—Hollywood's entertainment cluster and High Point, North Carolina's household-furniture cluster—are well known. Others are less familiar, such as golf equipment in Carlsbad, California, and optics in Phoenix, Arizona. A relatively small number of clusters usually account for a major share of the economy within a geographic area as well as for an overwhelming share of its economic activity that is "exported" to other locations. *Exporting clusters*—those that export products or make investments to compete outside the local area—are the primary source of an area's economic growth and prosperity over the long run. The demand for local industries is inherently limited by the size of the local market, but exporting clusters can grow far beyond that limit.

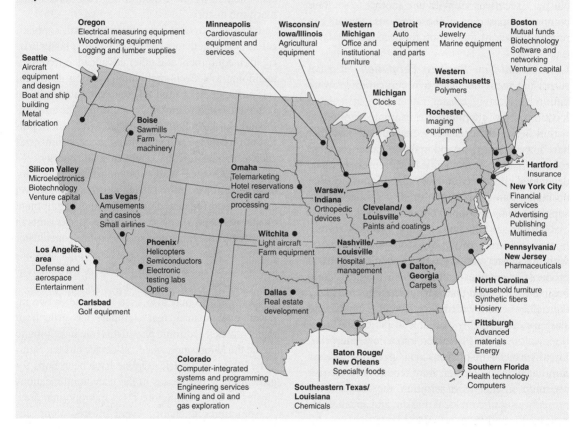

Clusters do more than make opportunities for innovation more visible. They also provide the capacity and the flexibility to act rapidly. A company within a cluster often can source what it needs to implement innovations more quickly. Local suppliers and partners can and do get closely involved in the innovation process, thus ensuring a better match with customers' requirements.

Companies within a cluster can experiment at lower cost and can delay large commitments until they are more assured that a given innovation will pan out. In contrast, a company relying on distant suppliers faces greater challenges in every activity it coordinates with other organizations—in contracting, for example, or securing delivery or obtaining associated technical and service support.

Innovation can be even harder in vertically integrated companies, especially in those that face difficult trade-offs if the innovation erodes the value of in-house assets or if current products or processes must be maintained while new ones are developed.

Reinforcing the other advantages for innovation is the sheer pressure—competitive pressure, peer pressure, constant comparison—that occurs in a cluster. Executives vie with one another to set their companies apart. For all these reasons, clusters can remain centers of innovation for decades.

Clusters and New Business Formation   It is not surprising, then, that many new companies grow up within an existing cluster rather than at isolated locations. New suppliers, for example, proliferate within a cluster because a concentrated customer base lowers their risks and makes it easier for them to spot market opportunities. Moreover, because developed clusters comprise related industries that normally draw on common or very similar inputs, suppliers enjoy expanded opportunities.

Clusters are conducive to new business formation for a variety of reasons. Individuals working within a cluster can more easily perceive gaps in products or services around which they can build businesses. Beyond that, barriers to entry are lower than elsewhere. Needed assets, skills, inputs, and staff are often readily available at the cluster location, waiting to be assembled into a new enterprise. Local financial institutions and investors, already familiar with the cluster, may require a lower risk premium on capital. In addition, the cluster often presents a significant local market, and an entrepreneur may benefit from established relationships. All of these factors reduce the perceived risks of entry—and of exit, should the enterprise fail.

The formation of new businesses within a cluster is part of a positive feedback loop. An expanded cluster amplifies all the benefits I have described—it increases the collective pool of competitive resources, which benefits all the cluster's members. The net result is that companies in the cluster advance relative to rivals at other locations.

Birth, Evolution, and Decline

A cluster's roots can often be traced to historical circumstances. In Massachusetts, for example, several clusters had their beginnings in research done at MIT or Harvard. The Dutch transportation cluster owes much to Holland's central location within Europe, an extensive network of waterways, the efficiency of the port of Rotterdam, and the skills accumulated by the Dutch through Holland's long maritime history.

Clusters may also arise from unusual, sophisticated, or stringent local demand. Israel's cluster in irrigation equipment and other advanced agricultural technologies reflects that nation's strong desire for self-sufficiency in food together with a scarcity of water and hot, arid growing conditions. The environmental cluster in Finland emerged as a result of pollution problems created by local process industries such as metals, forestry, chemicals, and energy.

Prior existence of supplier industries, related industries, or even entire related clusters provides yet another seed for new clusters. The golf equipment cluster near San Diego, for example, has its roots in southern California's aerospace cluster. That cluster created a pool of suppliers for castings and advanced materials as well as engineers with the requisite experience in those technologies.

New clusters may also arise from one or two innovative companies that stimulate the growth of many others. Medtronic played this role in helping to create the Minneapolis medical-device cluster. Similarly, MCI and America Online have been hubs for growing new businesses in the telecommunications cluster in the Washington, D.C., metropolitan area.

Sometimes a chance event creates some advantageous factor that, in turn, fosters cluster development—although chance rarely provides the sole explanation for a cluster's success in a location. The telemarketing cluster in Omaha, Nebraska, for example, owes much to the decision by the United States Air Force to locate the Strategic Air Command (SAC) there. Charged with a key role in the country's nuclear deterrence strategy, SAC was the site of the first installation of fiber-optic telecommunications cables in the United States. The local Bell operating company (now U.S. West) developed unusual capabilities through its dealings with such a demanding customer. The extraordinary telecommunications capability and infrastructure that consequently developed in Omaha, coupled with less unique attributes such as its central-time-zone location and easily understandable local accent, provided the underpinnings of the area's telemarketing cluster.

Once a cluster begins to form, a self-reinforcing cycle promotes its growth, especially when local institutions are supportive and local competition is vigorous. As the cluster expands, so does its influence with government and with public and private institutions.

A growing cluster signals opportunity, and its success stories help attract the best talent. Entrepreneurs take notice, and individuals with ideas or relevant skills migrate in from other locations. Specialized suppliers emerge; information accumulates; local institutions develop specialized training, research, and infrastructure; and the cluster's strength and visibility grow. Eventually, the cluster broadens to encompass related industries. Numerous case studies suggest that clusters require a decade or more to develop depth and real competitive advantage.[2]

Cluster development is often particularly vibrant at the intersection of clusters, where insights, skills, and technologies from various fields merge, sparking innovation and new businesses. An example from Germany illustrates this point. The country has distinct clusters in both home appliances and household furniture, each based on different technologies and inputs. At the intersection of the two, though, is a cluster of built-in kitchens and appliances, an area in which Germany commands a higher share of world exports than in either appliances or furniture.

Clusters continually evolve as new companies and industries emerge or decline and as local institutions develop and change. They can maintain vibrancy as competitive locations for centuries; most successful clusters prosper for decades at least. However, they can and do lose their competitive edge due to both external and internal forces. Technological discontinuities are perhaps the most significant of the external threats because they can neutralize many advantages simultaneously. A cluster's assets—market information, employees' skills, scientific and technical expertise, and supplier bases—may all become irrelevant. New England's loss of market share in golf equipment is a good example. The New England cluster was based on steel shafts, steel irons, and wooden-headed woods. When companies in California began making golf clubs with advanced materials, East Coast producers had difficulty competing. A number of them were acquired or went out of business.

A shift in buyers' needs, creating a divergence between local needs and needs elsewhere, constitutes another external threat. U.S. companies in a variety of clusters, for example, suffered when energy efficiency grew in importance in most parts of the world while the United States maintained low energy prices. Lacking both pressure to improve and insight into customer needs, U.S. companies were slow to innovate, and they lost ground to European and Japanese competitors.

Clusters are at least as vulnerable to internal rigidities as they are to external threats. Overconsolidation, mutual understandings, cartels, and other restraints to competition undermine local rivalry. Regulatory inflexibility or the introduction of restrictive union rules slows productivity improvement. The quality of institutions such as schools and universities can stagnate.

Groupthink among cluster participants—Detroit's attachment to gas-guzzling autos in the 1970s is one example—can be another powerful form of rigidity. If companies in a cluster are too inward looking, the whole cluster suffers from a collective inertia, making it harder for individual companies to embrace new ideas, much less perceive the need for radical innovation.

[2]Selected case studies are described in "Clusters and Competition" in my book *On Competition* (Boston: Harvard Business School Press, 1998), which also includes citations of the published output of a number of cluster initiatives. Readers can also find a full treatment of the intellectual roots of cluster thinking, along with an extensive bibliography.

Such rigidities tend to arise when government suspends or intervenes in competition or when companies persist in old behaviors and relationships that no longer contribute to competitive advantage. Increases in the cost of doing business begin to outrun the ability to upgrade. Rigidities of this nature currently work against a variety of clusters in Switzerland and Germany.

As long as rivalry remains sufficiently vigorous, companies can partially compensate for some decline in the cluster's competitiveness by outsourcing to distant suppliers or moving part or all of production elsewhere to offset local wages that rise ahead of productivity. German companies in the 1990s, for example, have been doing just that. Technology can be licensed or sourced from other locations, and product development can be moved. Over time, however, a location will decline if it fails to build capabilities in major new technologies or needed supporting firms and institutions.

Implications for Companies

In the new economics of competition, what matters most is not inputs and scale, but productivity—and that is true in all industries. The term *high tech,* normally used to refer to fields such as information technology and biotechnology, has distorted thinking about competition, creating the misconception that only a handful of businesses compete in sophisticated ways.

In fact, there is no such thing as a low-tech industry. There are only low-tech companies—that is, companies that fail to use world-class technology and practices to enhance productivity and innovation. A vibrant cluster can help any company in any industry compete in the most sophisticated ways, using the most advanced, relevant skills and technologies.

Thus executives must extend their thinking beyond what goes on inside their own organizations and within their own industries. Strategy must also address what goes on outside. Extensive vertical integration may once have been appropriate, but companies today must forge close linkages with buyers, suppliers, and other institutions.

Specifically, understanding clusters adds the following four issues to the strategic agenda.

1. Choosing locations. Globalization and the ease of transportation and communication have led many companies to move some or all of their operations to locations with low wages, taxes, and utility costs. What we know about clusters suggests, first, that some of those cost advantages may well turn out to be illusory. Locations with those advantages often lack efficient infrastructure, sophisticated suppliers, and other cluster benefits that can more than offset any savings from lower input costs. Savings in wages, utilities, and taxes may be highly visible and easy to measure up front, but productivity penalties remain hidden and unanticipated.

More important to ongoing competitiveness is the role of location in innovation. Yes, companies have to spread activities globally to source inputs and gain access to markets. Failure to do so will lead to a competitive *disadvantage.* And for stable, labor-intensive activities such as assembly and software translation, low factor costs are often decisive in driving locational choices.

For a company's "home base" for each product line, however, clusters are critical. Home base activities—strategy development, core product and process R&D, a critical mass of the most sophisticated production or service provision—create and renew the company's product, processes, and services. Therefore locational decisions must be based on both total systems costs and innovation potential, not on input costs alone. Cluster thinking suggests that every product line needs a home base, and the most vibrant cluster will offer the best location. Within the United States, for example, Hewlett-Packard has chosen cluster locations for the home bases of its major product lines: California, where almost all of the world's leading personal computer and workstation businesses are located, is home to personal computers and workstations; Massachusetts, which has an extraordinary concentration of world-renowned research hospitals and leading medical instrument companies, is home to medical instruments.

Clusters, Geography, and Economic Development

Poor countries lack well-developed clusters; they compete in the world market with cheap labor and natural resources. To move beyond this stage, the development of well-functioning clusters is essential. Clusters become an especially controlling factor for countries moving from a middle-income to an advanced economy. Even in high-wage economies, however, the need for cluster upgrading is constant. The wealthier the economy, the more it will require innovation to support rising wages and to replace jobs eliminated by improvements in efficiency and the migration of standard production to low-cost areas.

Promoting cluster formation in developing economies means starting at the most basic level. Policymakers must first address the foundations: improving education and skill levels, building capacity in technology, opening access to capital markets, and improving institutions. Over time, additional investment in more cluster-specific assets is necessary.

Government policies in developing economies often unwittingly work against cluster formation. Restrictions on industrial location and subsidies to invest in distressed areas, for example, can disperse companies artificially. Protecting local companies from competition leads to excessive vertical integration and blunted pressure for innovation, retarding cluster development.

In the early stages of economic development, countries should expand internal trade among cities and states and trade with neighboring countries as important stepping stones to building the skills to compete globally. Such trade greatly enhances cluster development. Instead, attention is typically riveted on the large, advanced markets, an orientation that has often been reinforced by protectionist policies restricting trade with nearby markets. However, the kinds of goods developing countries can trade with advanced economies are limited to commodities and to activities sensitive to labor costs.

While it is essential that clusters form, *where* they form also matters. In developing economies, a large proportion of economic activity tends to concentrate around capital cities such as Bangkok and Bogotá. That is usually because outlying areas lack infrastructure, institutions, and suppliers. It may also reflect an intrusive role by the central government in controlling competition, leading companies to locate near the seat of power and the agencies whose approval they require to do business.

This pattern of economic geography inflicts high costs on productivity. Congestion, bottlenecks, and inflexibility lead to high administrative costs and major inefficiencies, not to mention a diminished quality of life. Companies cannot easily move out from the center, however, because neither infrastructure nor rudimentary clusters exist in the smaller cities and towns. (The building of a tourism cluster in developing economies can be a positive force in improving the outlying infrastructure and in dispersing economic activity.)

Even in advanced economies, however, economic activity may be geographically concentrated. Japan offers a particularly striking case, with nearly 50% of total manufacturing shipments located around Tokyo and Osaka. This is due less to inadequacies in infrastructure in outlying areas than to a powerful and intrusive central government, with its centralizing bias in policies and institutions. The Japanese case vividly illustrates the major inefficiencies and productivity costs resulting from such a pattern of economic geography, even for advanced nations. It is a major policy issue facing Japan.

An economic geography characterized by specialization and dispersion—that is, a number of metropolitan areas, each specializing in an array of clusters—appears to be a far more productive industrial organization than one based on one or two huge, diversified cities. In nations such as Germany, Italy, Switzerland, and the United States, this kind of internal specialization and trade—and internal competition among locations—fuels productivity growth and hones the ability of companies to compete effectively in the global arena.

Figure 4 Mapping Portugal's Clusters

In a middle-income economy like Portugal, exporting clusters tend to be more natural-resource labor intensive.

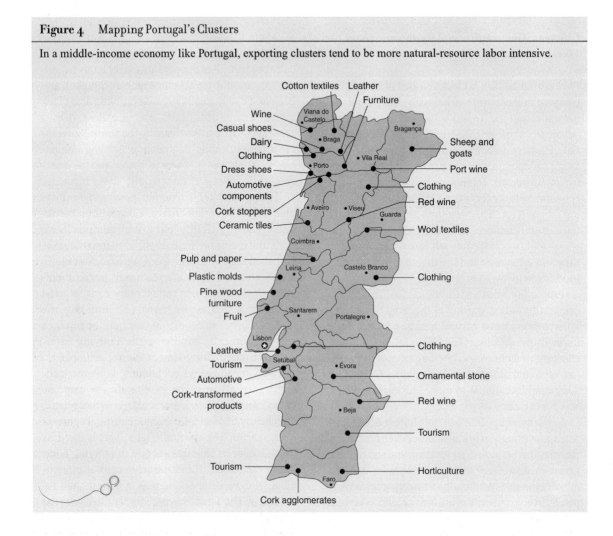

As global competition nullifies traditional comparative advantages and exposes companies to the best rivals from around the world, a growing number of multinationals are shifting their home bases to more vibrant clusters—often using acquisitions as a means of establishing themselves as insiders in a new location. Nestlé for example, after acquiring Rowntree Mackintosh, relocated its confectionary business to York, England, where Rowntree was originally based, because a vibrant food cluster thrives there. England, with its sweet-toothed consumers, sophisticated retailers, advanced advertising agencies, and highly competitive media companies, constitutes a more dynamic environment for competing in mass-market candy than Switzerland did. Similarly, Nestlé has moved its headquarters for bottled water to France, the most competitive location in that industry. Northern Telecom has relocated its home base for central office switching from Canada to the United States—drawn by the vibrancy of the U.S. telecommunications-equipment cluster.

Cluster thinking also suggests that it is better to move groups of linked activities to the same place than to spread them across numerous locations. Colocating R&D, component fabrication, assembly, marketing, customer support, and even related businesses can facilitate internal efficiencies in sourcing and in sharing technology and information. Grouping activities into campuses also allows companies to extend deeper roots into local clusters, improving their ability to capture potential benefits.

2. Engaging locally. The social glue that binds clusters together also facilitates access to important resources and information. Tapping into the competitively valuable assets within a cluster requires personal relationships, face-to-face contact, a sense of common interest, and "insider" status. The mere colocation of companies, suppliers, and institutions creates the *potential* for economic value; it does not necessarily ensure its realization.

To maximize the benefits of cluster involvement, companies must participate actively and establish a significant local presence. They must have a substantial local investment even if the parent company is headquartered elsewhere. And they must foster ongoing relationships with government bodies and local institutions such as utilities, schools, and research groups.

Companies have much to gain by engaging beyond their narrow confines as single entities. Yet managers tend to be wary, at least initially. They fear that a growing cluster will attract competition, drive up costs, or cause them to lose valued employees to rivals or spin-offs. As their understanding of the cluster concept grows, however, managers realize that many participants in the cluster do not compete directly and that the offsetting benefits, such as a greater supply of better trained people, for example, can outweigh any increase in competition.

3. Upgrading the cluster. Because the health of the local business environment is important to the health of the company, upgrading the cluster should be part of management's agenda. Companies upgrade their clusters in a variety of ways.

Consider Genzyme. Massachusetts is home to a vibrant biotechnology cluster, which draws on the region's strong universities, medical centers, and venture capital firms. Once Genzyme reached the stage in its development when it needed a manufacturing facility, CEO Henri Termeer initially considered the pharmaceuticals cluster in the New Jersey and Philadelphia area because it had what Massachusetts lacked: established expertise in drug manufacturing. Upon further reflection, however, Termeer decided to influence the process of creating a manufacturing capability in Genzyme's home base, reasoning that if his plans were successful, the company could become more competitive.

Thus Genzyme deliberately chose to work with contractors committed to the Boston area, bypassing the many specialized engineering firms located near Philadelphia. In addition, it undertook a number of initiatives, with the help of city and state government, to improve the labor force, such as offering scholarships and internships to local youth. More broadly, Genzyme has worked to build critical mass for its cluster. Termeer believes that Genzyme's success is linked to the cluster's—and that all members will benefit from a strong base of supporting functions and institutions.

4. Working collectively. The way clusters operate suggests a new agenda of collective action in the private sector. Investing in public goods is normally seen as a function of government, yet cluster thinking clearly demonstrates how companies benefit from local assets and institutions.

In the past, collective action in the private sector has focused on seeking government subsidies and special favors that often distort competition. But executives' long-term interests would be better served by working to promote a higher plane of competition. They can begin by rethinking the role of trade associations, which often do little more than lobby government, compile some statistics, and host social functions. The associations are missing an important opportunity.

Trade associations can provide a forum for the exchange of ideas and a focal point for collective action in overcoming obstacles to productivity and growth. Associations can take the lead in such activities as establishing university-based testing facilities and training or research programs;

collecting cluster-related information; offering forums on common managerial problems; investigating solutions to environmental issues; organizing trade fairs and delegations; and managing purchasing consortia.

For clusters consisting of many small and midsize companies—such as tourism, apparel, and agriculture—the need is particularly great for collective bodies to assume scale-sensitive functions. In the Netherlands, for instance, grower cooperatives built the specialized auction and handling facilities that constitute one of the Dutch flower cluster's greatest competitive advantages. The Dutch Flower Council and the Association of Dutch Flower Growers Research Groups, in which most growers participate, have taken on other functions as well, such as applied research and marketing.

Most existing trade associations are too narrow; they represent industries, not clusters. In addition, because their role is defined as lobbying the federal government, their scope is national rather than local. National associations, however, are rarely sufficient to address the local issues that are most important to cluster productivity.

By revealing how business and government together create the conditions that promote growth, clusters offer a constructive way to change the nature of the dialogue between the public and private sectors. With a better understanding of what fosters true competitiveness, executives can start asking government for the right things. The example of MassMEDIC, an association formed in 1996 by the Massachusetts medical-devices cluster, illustrates this point. It recently worked successfully with the U.S. Food and Drug Administration to streamline the approval process for medical devices. Such a step clearly benefits cluster members and enhances competition at the same time.

What's Wrong with Industrial Policy

Productivity, not exports or natural resources, determines the prosperity of any state or nation. Recognizing this, governments should strive to create an environment that supports rising productivity. Sound macroeconomic policy is necessary but not sufficient. The microeconomic foundations for competition will ultimately determine productivity and competitiveness.

Governments—both national and local—have new roles to play. They must ensure the supply of high-quality inputs such as educated citizens and physical infrastructure. They must set the rules of competition—by protecting intellectual property and enforcing antitrust laws, for example—so that productivity and innovation will govern success in the economy. Finally, governments should promote cluster formation and upgrading and the buildup of public or quasi-public goods that have a significant impact on many linked businesses.

This sort of role for government is a far cry from industrial policy. In industrial policy, governments target "desirable" industries and intervene—through subsidies or restrictions on investments by foreign companies, for example—to favor local companies. In contrast, the aim of cluster policy is to reinforce the development of *all* clusters. This means that a traditional cluster such as agriculture should not be abandoned; it should be upgraded. Governments should not choose among clusters, because each one offers opportunities to improve productivity and support rising wages. Every cluster not only contributes directly to national productivity but also affects the productivity of *other* clusters. Not all clusters will succeed, of course, but market forces—not government decisions—should determine the outcomes.

Government, working with the private sector, should reinforce and build on existing and emerging clusters rather than attempt to create entirely new ones. Successful new industries and clusters often grow out of established ones. Businesses involving advanced technology succeed not in a vacuum but where there is already a base of related activities in the field. In fact, most clusters form independently of government action—and sometimes in spite of it. They form where a foundation of locational advantages exists. To justify cluster development efforts, some seeds of a cluster should have already passed a market test.

Cluster development initiatives should embrace the pursuit of competitive advantage and specialization rather than simply imitate successful clusters in other locations. This requires building on local sources of uniqueness. Finding areas of specialization normally proves more effective than head-on competition with well-established rival locations.

New Public-Private Responsibilities

Economic geography in an era of global competition, then, poses a paradox. In a global economy—which boasts rapid transportation, high-speed communication, and accessible markets—one would expect location to diminish in importance. But the opposite is true. The enduring competitive advantages in a global economy are often heavily local, arising from concentrations of highly specialized skills and knowledge, institutions, rivals, related businesses, and sophisticated customers. Geographic, cultural, and institutional proximity leads to special access, closer relationships, better

information, powerful incentives, and other advantages in productivity and innovation that are difficult to tap from a distance. The more the world economy becomes complex, knowledge based, and dynamic, the more this is true.

Leaders of businesses, government, and institutions all have a stake—and a role to play—in the new economics of competition. Clusters reveal the mutual dependence and collective responsibility of all these entities for creating the conditions for productive competition. This task will require fresh thinking on the part of leaders and the willingness to abandon the traditional categories that drive our thinking about who does what in the economy. The lines between public and private investment blur. Companies, no less than governments and universities, have a stake in education. Universities have a stake in the competitiveness of local businesses. By revealing the process by which wealth is actually created in an economy, clusters open new public–private avenues for constructive action.

Reading 2-3   Beyond Offshoring: Assess Your Company's Global Potential

Diana Farrell

In the past few years, most companies have become aware that they can reduce their costs significantly through offshoring—moving jobs to lower-wage locations. But this practice is just the tip of the iceberg in terms of how globalization can transform industries, according to a recent comprehensive study by the McKinsey Global Institute. By streamlining their production processes and supply chains globally, rather than just nationally or regionally, companies

Diana Farrell is the director of the McKinsey Global Institute, McKinsey & Company's economics think tank, in San Francisco.
Reprinted by permission of *Harvard Business Review*. From "Beyond Offshoring: Assess Your Company's Global Potential," by Diana Farrell, December 2004.

can dramatically lower their costs and drop their prices to increase demand for their products, attract new customers, and even enter new markets.

To date, however, few businesses have recognized the full scope of performance improvements that globalization makes possible, much less developed proactive strategies for capturing these opportunities. Indeed, organizations' narrow focus on offshoring is obscuring the bigger picture—that this trend is just the latest in the evolution toward a truly global economy.

More than 100 years ago, the prospect of reaching huge pools of new customers in foreign markets lured large trading companies out of their home territories. In the 1980s, manufacturers based in

North America, Europe, and Japan built plants and hired workers in low-wage countries, then exported the finished goods back home. In the 1990s, companies in a handful of industries, such as consumer electronics, pushed globalization even further by relocating their component production and final assembly to countries with the strongest cost advantages. Now, globalization is beginning to transform the service industries.

Thanks to plummeting telecommunications costs and the digitization of some paper-based business processes, many service jobs and back-office functions are now being performed remotely. Data entry, transaction processing, and call-center customer support have been the obvious candidates, but even high-skill jobs in software development, manufacturing design, and pharmaceutical research are being migrated to low-wage countries.

Service businesses currently employ 83% of all U.S. workers and represent a similar share of the GDP. By contrast, manufacturing now accounts for less than 11% of all U.S. jobs. The situation is similar in other developed countries. The IT research firm Forrester projects that by 2015, U.S. companies will move 3.3 million service jobs to low-cost countries, including 8% of IT jobs. This all sounds ominous—until you consider that in the U.S. services sector, more than a million people change jobs *every month*.

Although most managers are focused on globalization (particularly the offshoring opportunity) as a lever to reduce costs, they should be viewing it as a means to generate new revenues, as well. Organizations that can capture the full potential of globalization will see dramatic revenue growth, while those that can't will lose market share.

How Global Are You?

To realize the full potential of globalization, you first need to assess where your industry falls along the globalization spectrum; not all sectors of the economy face the same challenges or opportunities at the same time. To measure how global your industry is, calculate the ratio of the annual value of global trade (which includes trade in product components as well as final goods) to the annual value of industry sales. Ratios over 100% indicate industries that are very global. Consumer electronics, for instance, boasts a trade-to-sales ratio of 118%, which means the industry generates 18% more value from the trade of components and finished goods among global business partners than from the sales of final goods to consumers. (For an overview of where the five industries we studied fall along the globalization spectrum, see the exhibit "How Global Is Your Industry?")

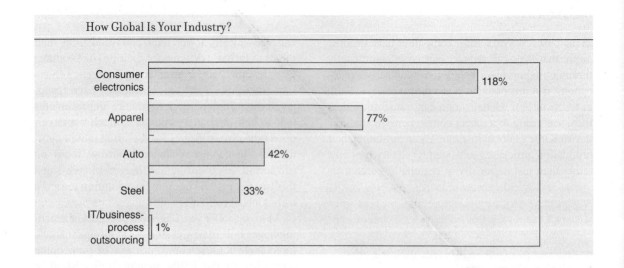

How Global Is Your Industry?

Industry	Ratio
Consumer electronics	118%
Apparel	77%
Auto	42%
Steel	33%
IT/business-process outsourcing	1%

In the past decade, consumer electronics companies have been under competitive pressure to innovate quickly and cut costs aggressively. The end result? A globally disaggregated, specialized, low-cost value chain. For example, the PC on a U.S. worker's desk today might have been designed in Taiwan, assembled in Mexico (using components from South Korea, China, and Thailand), and marketed and sold in the United States by a company that focuses most of its attention on marketing and selling the computer under its brand name, rather than on designing, sourcing, and manufacturing the machine.

The consumer electronics industry was ripe for globalization. It uses small, lightweight, high-value components that are cheap and relatively easy to ship. It can exploit large economies of scale, particularly when producing the standardized components used in multiple electronics products. Equally important, in most countries there are few governmental or organizational barriers—protectionist restrictions, tariffs, or union opposition—to prevent consumer electronics companies from shifting various production processes from one nation to another.

But not every industry is ready for such high levels of globalization. On the globalization spectrum, the apparel, automotive, and steel industries fall somewhere in the middle: They all have much to gain but face some daunting obstacles.

The apparel industry has a relatively high trade-to-sales ratio (77%)—and is therefore fairly global—for two reasons. First, labor accounts for the bulk of the industry's production costs, which makes it attractive for manufacturers to move parts of their production processes to low-wage locations. Second, clothing is lightweight, which makes it cost-effective for companies to transport finished goods to consumers, no matter the distance. But the industry has been constrained by the Multifiber Arrangement (MFA), an international system of quotas and import restrictions that protects textile and clothing producers in more than 30 developed countries and handicaps the world's lowest-cost apparel makers. The result has been inflated prices and distorted trade patterns across the industry.

All this will change when the MFA quotas expire January 1, 2005. There will be a complete upheaval in garment manufacturing, an industry that employs 40 million people worldwide. Large buyers in the United States and Europe will begin to consolidate their purchases with just a few countries. Among those countries, China is expected to be the biggest winner, while smaller garment-producing nations are in for a struggle. In the United States, where employment in apparel manufacturing fell from about 929,000 in 1990 to about 293,000 in 2004, as many as 70% of the remaining jobs could disappear over time after the MFA is lifted.

However, some segments of the apparel industry will be easier to globalize than others. Fast-fashion retailers like H&M, Old Navy, and Zara, which focus on selling trendy clothes that go out of style quickly, need to locate their production processes close to the regional markets they sell in. Indeed, those companies are willing to pay slightly higher labor costs in exchange for greater speed and flexibility. Meanwhile, retailers that deal in basic apparel—where speed to market isn't as critical—can optimize their cost savings by locating their sourcing and sewing operations in low-wage countries.

In the automotive industry, which has a trade-to-sales ratio of 42%, globalization has been slow because component parts aren't standardized. Many of the parts are bulky and, therefore, expensive to ship. These factors make it difficult for auto manufacturers to disaggregate their supply chains the way PC companies have done. The industry also faces some regulatory and organizational barriers to globalization. These include import restrictions and tariffs on auto parts in many developing countries, aggressive government incentives for manufacturers to locate their production processes where the cars will be sold, and strong unions in developed nations.

Globalization of the steel industry, which has a trade-to-sales ratio of 33%, has been hampered by the capital intensity of steel mills, high tariffs and government-mandated cleanup costs, the industry's relatively low share of labor costs compared with its total costs, and the expense of transporting the

An In-Depth Look at Globalization

The McKinsey Global Institute recently completed a comprehensive, yearlong study of globalization in which my colleagues and I looked closely at four major developing economies (China, India, Brazil, and Mexico) and five important and diverse industries (automotive, consumer electronics, food retailing, retail banking, and IT/business-process offshoring). Complementing this work were studies we have conducted over the past ten years examining the apparel and steel industries in multiple countries. We analyzed macroeconomic and company- and industry-specific data, and we conducted more than 150 interviews with executives and industry and country experts.

finished products. While regulatory change alone wouldn't eliminate all those constraints, it could significantly reduce the cost of steel and accelerate global trade. For example, if the state of California had not been required to use domestic steel only, construction costs for the earthquake-damaged Bay Bridge in San Francisco could have been reduced by an estimated $400 million.

Compared with the above examples, the service industries are still in the early stages of structural change from globalization. Even in business-service functions such as payroll processing, IT, and transaction processing, the trade-to-sales ratio is a mere 1%. Many customer-service industries such as banking and retail, because of their very nature, often need their production processes to be close to where consumption is. This requirement has left globalization of the service industries in the hands of multinational companies such as Wal-Mart and Carrefour, which export their home-country retail business models to new markets. Some service organizations are expanding their markets by developing new business lines, such as 24/7 technical support or customer service, that are managed remotely. And some companies are sourcing their goods globally.

How Global Can You Be?

Once you understand how global your industry is, you need to define globalization's full potential for your company. Although every company is different, most are affected by the same types of internal and external forces. The challenge is to figure out how these forces will strengthen or weaken over time—and how to capitalize on that evolution. Three types of factors determine the course of globalization in an industry or a company: production, regulatory, and organizational.

Production   In this category, there are two factors that, in combination, determine an industry's potential for disaggregating its value chain: *relocation sensitivity* (how feasible and attractive it is for an industry to relocate parts of its production processes) and *location-specific advantages.*

To figure out your relocation sensitivity, consider metrics such as your typical bulk-to-value ratios (the currency value per pound of production material), the ease with which your company can ensure quality standards remotely, how quickly your products or components become obsolete, the volatility of the demand for your service, and any sunk costs. Industries that make bulky items that are hard to transport, such as steel or timber, may have little incentive to move their production processes. Companies that have already made huge capital investments in developed countries may not be able to justify shutting down existing factories even if the variable costs of production in developing countries are much lower.

To determine your location-specific advantages, look at variables including labor intensity, skill requirements, natural-resources intensity, and economies of scale and scope. Labor-intensive industries, such as apparel, have a greater incentive to move production to lower-wage countries. The exception would be a business whose workforce must possess specific skills that are not available outside a few countries. Industries that rely heavily on natural resources, such as the furniture sector, may find it advantageous to locate their production processes in countries where those resources are plentiful and therefore less expensive. Industries in which components are standardized, like consumer electronics, can take advantage of economies of scale in the production of individual components such as microprocessors and memory chips.

Regulatory Host countries' regulations can inhibit globalization in several ways. A country can impose tariffs, set quotas for imports and exports, require foreign companies to enter into joint ventures with local companies, specify minimum content from local production, ban foreign investment outright, or fail to invest in regulatory and legal infrastructures. Indeed, regulatory factors—particularly countries' efforts to restrict imports or foreign investment—are among the biggest constraints to globalization in many industries today.

Organizational Three organizational factors can limit globalization for a company or an industry: internal management structures, incentive systems, and unionization. For example, offshoring in many U.S. companies has been slowed by midlevel managers' reluctance to give up some responsibility for the migrated positions. Companies must realign management incentives with global, not local, performance metrics, while still allowing for local innovation and risk taking. If companies lean too far toward either extreme, they are likely to miss some important opportunities to restructure and improve.

Production, regulatory, and organizational forces evolve over time, and the full potential of globalization for companies and industries changes with the geopolitical and macroeconomic environment. The development of the General Agreement on Tariffs and Trade and the World Trade Organization, for instance, has enabled rapid growth in global trade for most manufacturing products and, more recently, for services. The decline in cargo costs due to standardization of containers and more efficient transport service has encouraged more companies to ship bulky products globally. GPS technology has allowed some companies to closely monitor their road freight and achieve better logistics control, enabling them to disaggregate their value chains. And the improved quality and radically reduced costs of international telecommunications have created the offshoring opportunities we cited earlier.

Escalating competition, steady trade liberalization, and the continual introduction of new technologies will increase the pressure on companies to globalize. Businesses that view the status quo as fixed and neglect to capitalize on emerging global opportunities will be blindsided; those that find ways around the obstacles and prepare for the next stages in their industries will win out. IKEA has pushed the envelope by creating a new business model around low transportation costs. The modular design of its furniture (customer assembly is required for nearly all items) means IKEA can transport its goods worldwide much more cost-effectively than traditional furniture manufacturers can. Companies like IKEA shape and accelerate their industry's global evolution by identifying which of the barriers to globalization can be changed.

Standardization is a critical part of globalization in many industries, but it has been resisted by some. Standards can penetrate an industry in two ways— companies can voluntarily adopt them, or governments can impose them. Consumer electronics was transformed when a critical mass of companies, driven by competition in the industry, voluntarily embraced standards. By contrast, it's been hard for manufacturers in the wireless handset business to achieve global economies of scale: Europe mandated the GSM standard, while Japan chose the PDC standard. And in the auto industry, there's been neither regulatory nor competitive pressure to increase standardization, despite the potential scale opportunities in components like windshield wipers and headlights.

How Do You Get to Global?

After you've considered which constraints to globalization can be changed, you need to identify your options for capturing value in the new global environment. Our research demonstrates that industries and companies both tend to globalize in stages, and at each stage, there are different opportunities for creating value. Most multinational companies have invested abroad either to seek new markets and customers or to achieve greater production efficiencies. But the full profit opportunities go well beyond these objectives. Let's consider each stage of globalization.

Stage One: Market Entry   Companies enter new countries using production models that are very similar to the ones they deploy in their home markets. To gain access to local customers, these companies typically need to establish a production presence, either because of the nature of their businesses (as in service industries like food retail or banking) or because of local countries' tariffs and import restrictions (as in the auto industry).

Stage Two: Product Specialization   Companies transfer the full production process of a particular product to a single low-cost location and export the goods to various consumer markets. Different locations begin to specialize in different products or components and trade in finished goods. The North American auto industry entered this stage with the passage of NAFTA in 1994. GM now manufactures all Pontiac Azteks in Mexico and all Chevrolet TrailBlazers in the United States.

Stage Three: Value Chain Disaggregation   Companies start to disaggregate the production process and focus each activity in the most advantageous location. Individual components of a single product might be manufactured in several different locations and assembled into final products elsewhere—think PCs, for instance. Another example is the recent trend by U.S. companies to offshore some of their business processes and IT services.

Stage Four: Value Chain Reengineering   Companies don't just replicate their production processes abroad; they increase their cost savings by reengineering their processes to suit local market conditions—notably by substituting lower-cost labor for capital. Carmakers in India, for example, have tailored their manufacturing processes to take advantage of low labor costs. Not only do they use a more labor-intensive production process, but they also design and build the capital equipment for their plants locally.

Stage Five: Creation of New Markets   This final stage represents the expansion of the market. Stages three and four together have the potential to reduce costs by more than 50% in many industries, which gives companies the opportunity to substantially lower their sticker prices in both old and new markets and to expand demand. (See the exhibit "Expanding Your Market.") The McKinsey Global Institute estimates that if a carmaker dropped the unit price of a vehicle by 30%—from $10,000 to $7,000—demand would nearly double over time, from 22 million to 41 million units sold (factoring in typical price elasticities). The value of new revenues generated in this stage is often greater than the value of cost savings in the other stages.

The five stages aren't necessarily a rigid sequence that all industries follow; companies can skip or combine steps. In consumer electronics, product specialization and value chain disaggregation (stages two and three) occurred together as different locations started to specialize in producing different components (Taiwan focused on semiconductors and China on computer mouses and keyboards). And many consumer-electronics multinationals that were initially attracted by China's huge customer base have started to take advantage of the country's low costs to produce goods for export as well (stages one and two). (For an overview of this section, see the exhibit "The Five Stages of Global Restructuring.")

◼ What's It Worth to You?

If you want to shape rather than react to your industry's evolution, you'll need to size up the opportunities that emerge for your business at each stage of globalization. This means determining the potential cost savings you could capture from global industry restructuring and identifying the new market opportunities this restructuring can create.

The first, and most obvious, cost-saving opportunity is in labor. The wage differentials between

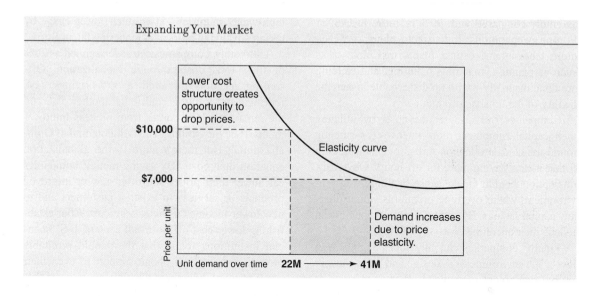

Expanding Your Market

The Five Stages of Global Restructuring

Industries and companies tend to globalize in phases; at each stage, there are different value-creating opportunities. In the first three stages, value comes from basic improvements to typical business practices. In the last two stages, it comes from true process innovations and market expansion. The stages are not necessarily sequential.

LESS GLOBAL				HIGHLY GLOBAL
1 Enter New Markets	**2 Move Production Abroad**	**3 Disaggregate the Value Chain**	**4 Reengineer the Value Chain**	**5 Create New Markets**
Companies use production models similar to the ones they deploy at home to enter new countries and expand their customer bases.	Companies relocate their entire production processes to take advantage of cost differentials; they export finished goods globally.	Companies' individual product components are manufactured in different locations or regions; countries may specialize in component manufacturing, assembly, or both.	Companies redesign their production processes, taking local factors into account, to maximize efficiencies and cost savings.	Given lower costs due to globalization, companies can offer new products at lower prices and can penetrate new market segments or geographies, or both.

developed and developing nations are so large that they invariably offset any extra capital investments or management costs required to relocate jobs. For every data-entry worker who is paid $20 an hour in the United States, there is an equally qualified competitor in India who's paid $2 an hour. U.S. companies can typically cut their total costs by 45% to 55% by outsourcing their business processes to India.

Companies can also reduce their costs by reengineering their production processes to substitute low-cost labor for high-cost capital. An offshore payments processor, for example, might hire people to input checks manually into a computer system rather than purchase an expensive license for imaging software. Certain auto manufacturers in China use robots for only 30% of the welding done in car assembly compared with 90% or more in U.S. or European operations. Indian auto plants are even more labor-intensive than plants in China; tasks such as painting, materials handling, and welding are done manually—with no discernable loss in the quality of the finished product.

Companies can also reduce costs by utilizing their capital equipment more intensively—running round-the-clock production shifts, for example, even if that means paying more for off-hours. Obviously, this option wouldn't make sense in a high-wage environment, where overtime premiums would offset any capital savings. By adding shifts, companies can reduce their operating costs 30% to 40%.

Finally, companies can hire local engineers in low-wage environments to design and build cheaper capital equipment or manage other fixed costs of doing business. Some business-process service providers in India are developing their own software instead of purchasing expensive licenses from branded global software companies. Maruti Udyog, an Indian carmaker, designed its own robots for its assembly lines, which cost the company a fraction of what Suzuki, its Japanese partner, paid a third-party vendor for similar machines. Companies can maintain the same level of automation as they do in high-wage countries—at a much lower cost—by taking advantage of local engineering talent.

Ultimately, companies can save as much as 70% of their total costs through globalization. Off-shoring accounts for about a 50% savings, task redesign and training contribute another 5%, and the remaining 15% comes from process improvements. (See the exhibit "The Full Potential of Globalization.") But there's more to the globalization equation than costs. By saving money, companies can lower their prices and offer new or improved products or services to existing customers and to new lower-income customer segments. After establishing lower-cost offshore call centers, U.S. financial institutions found that they could profitably provide personalized phone support to even their small-account customers. One airline relocated its accounts-receivable and collections functions to India—and reaped an additional $75 million in previously lost payments. Because the airline's collection costs are lower, it can now track down and handle delinquent accounts more profitably. A leading U.S. PC manufacturer has established a customer service center in India—and has significantly increased the number of customer problems resolved on the first call (both by phone and via e-mail).

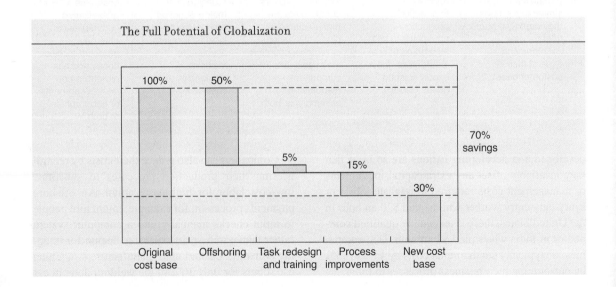

The Full Potential of Globalization

In developing countries, new market opportunities abound in the burgeoning middle classes. In China, local consumer-electronics companies have designed more affordable air conditioners aimed at very low-end market segments. In the Indian auto industry, Tata Motors is targeting the domestic market with the Indica, produced for a fraction of the cost of similar compact cars in the developed world.

Revenues from these kinds of opportunities will often exceed the cost savings from globalization. By our estimates, the global auto industry could lower its costs by $150 billion annually and earn $170 billion in additional revenue ($100 billion in developing markets and $70 billion in developed markets) by introducing lower-cost cars.

What Are the Risks?

No one company—whether it's seeking new revenues or lower costs—has a template for operating successfully in all developing markets. Indeed, the landscape is littered with companies that attempted to expand abroad and failed. Growth through global expansion can be risky. In the consumer electronics industry, shareholder returns are driven by a company's degree of globalization. But in the retail and auto industries, there is little correlation between the percentage of revenue that companies generate outside their home markets and the companies' total returns to shareholders.

The experiences of French retailer Carrefour and U.S. retailer Wal-Mart in Brazil and Mexico illustrate the need for both optimism and caution in the pursuit of globalization. Carrefour succeeded in Brazil but not Mexico, while Wal-Mart's experience was the reverse. Success in food retailing requires a balance of strong local knowledge and global capabilities. The former can be achieved through partnerships or acquisitions or over time. The latter can be built through the transfer of talent, technology, and best practices.

Carrefour successfully introduced the hypermarket store format—large stores that carry groceries as well as department store merchandise—in Brazil in 1975. Because of the variety of products they carried, Carrefour's stores had a particularly strong value proposition during Brazil's hyperinflation of the 1980s and early 1990s. Consumers could make all their purchases in one place immediately after receiving their paychecks. Because Carrefour was an early mover in Brazil, it was able to acquire local knowledge before competitors arrived. Recently, however, the company has intentionally been less aggressive in global acquisitions and greenfield growth than other players. In Carrefour's joint venture with multiformat Mexican retailer Gigante, there were disagreements about what mix of formats the stores would use. The JV failed, and since then Carrefour has chosen to grow slowly through organic expansion.

As the first international retailer in Mexico, Wal-Mart was very successful. It acquired Cifra, a leading Mexican retailer, and spent a great deal of time coaching the acquired management team. Wal-Mart shared its U.S. business processes, technologies, and best practices with the team. Few executives from the United States were transferred, however; Wal-Mart's senior management in Mexico today is made up almost exclusively of former Cifra managers, with a few additions hired to fill skills gaps, such as in global operations. But Wal-Mart couldn't repeat this experience when it entered Brazil, which offered no suitable acquisition target among leading domestic retailers. Wal-Mart's initial, smaller-scale joint venture there failed. And slow, organic expansion has not yet given Wal-Mart the scale necessary to offer lower prices than its competitors.

These examples illustrate that while there is huge potential in globalization, not every company that globalizes is able to successfully capitalize on this strategy. A few companies will lead the charge; for others, change will become a matter of survival.

How to Win

To ensure success as your industry restructures along global lines, you'll need a sound strategy, consistent execution, and new ways of viewing your business and managing your people. Here are some lessons drawn from the experiences of companies that have done so successfully.

Abandon Incremental Thinking   Globalization creates opportunities for steep changes in performance. A company's goals need to reflect this. The leading companies in an industry will replace their traditional, incremental targets for performance improvement with much higher expectations; the laggards will fall further behind. So adopt bold performance targets sooner rather than later.

Use Global Assets Effectively and Efficiently
The right mix of capital and labor will be very different in developing countries than in developed countries. Companies can get the best mix by doing three things: increasing labor resources to better use expensive capital, improving shift utilization, and developing cheaper capital equipment where appropriate. Doing just one of these things won't be enough.

Tailor Best Practices to Local Conditions   Successful global companies must leverage the best practices they learn globally in ways that fit conditions in the host country. In Mexico, Wal-Mart uses the same trademark "everyday low price" strategy it uses in the United States—focusing on low, non-promotional prices and comparing its prices to those of the leading nearby competitors. But the retailer has also done extensive local market research, and, as a result, Wal-Mart prices only the "most notable products" below those of its key competitors. Bear in mind that one size does not fit all.

Aim for Higher Quality   By moving production to lower-wage countries, companies can upgrade workers' and managers' skills and still save money. They can interview more job candidates for each job and conduct more extensive training. Philippines call-center provider eTelecare puts applicants through a seven-step screening process; by contrast, U.S. call centers review résumés and conduct just a single interview. ETelecare extends offers to just 2% of its applicants, but it enjoys a 90% acceptance rate and very low turnover. With low labor costs, offshore operations can also increase the ratio of supervisors to line workers, thereby improving quality while still saving money. Don't settle for the same level of quality; aim for more.

CHAPTER 3

Developing Transnational Strategies:

Building Layers of Competitive Advantage

In this chapter, we discuss how the numerous conflicting demands and pressures described in the first two chapters shape the strategic choices that MNEs must make. In this complex situation, an MNE determines strategy by balancing the motivations for its own international expansion with the economic imperatives of its industry structure and competitive dynamics, the social and cultural forces of the markets it has entered worldwide, and the political demands of its home- and host-country governments. To frame this complex analysis, in this chapter, we examine how MNEs balance strategic means and ends to build the three required dimensional capabilities: global-scale efficiency and competitiveness, multinational flexibility and responsiveness, and worldwide innovation and learning. After defining each of the dominant historic strategic approaches—what we term classic multinational, international, and global strategies—we explore the emerging transnational strategic model that most MNEs must adopt today. Finally, we describe not only how companies can develop this approach themselves but also how they can defend against transnational competitors.

The strategies of MNEs at the start of the 21st century were shaped by the turbulent international environment that redefined global competition in the closing decades of the 20th century. It was during that turmoil that a number of different perspectives and prescriptions emerged about how companies could create strategic advantage in their worldwide businesses.

Consider, for example, three of the most influential articles on global strategy published during the 1980s—the decade in which many new trends first emerged.[1] Each is reasonable and intuitively appealing. What soon becomes clear, however, is that their prescriptions are very different and often contradictory, a reality that highlights not only the complexity of the strategic challenge that faced managers in large, worldwide companies but also the confusion of advice being offered to them.

- In one of the most provocative articles of that era, Theodore Levitt argued that effective global strategy was not a bag of many tricks but the successful practice of just

[1]See Theodeore Levitt, "The Globalization of Markets" *Harvard Business Review* 61, no. 3 (1983), pp. 92–102; T. Hout, M. E. Porter, and E. Rudden, "How Global Companies Win Out," *Harvard Business Review* 60, no. 5 (1982), pp. 98–109; G. Hamel and C. K. Prahalad, "Do You Really Have a Global Strategy?" *Harvard Business Review* 63, no. 4 (1985), pp. 139–49.

one: product standardization. According to him, the core of a global strategy lay in developing a standardized product to be produced and sold the same way throughout the world.

• In contrast, an article by Michael Porter and his colleagues suggested that effective global strategy required the approach not of a hedgehog, who knows only one trick, but that of a fox, who knows many. These "tricks" include exploiting economies of scale through global volume, taking preemptive positions through quick and large investments, and managing interdependently to achieve synergies across different activities.

• Gary Hamel and C. K. Prahalad's prescription for a global strategy contradicted Levitt's even more sharply. Instead of a single standardized product, they recommended a broad product portfolio, with many product varieties, so that investments in technologies and distribution channels could be shared. Cross-subsidization across products and markets and the development of a strong worldwide distribution system were at the center of these authors' view of how to succeed in the game of global chess.

As we described in the preceding chapter, what was becoming increasingly clear during the next two decades was that to achieve sustainable competitive advantage, MNEs needed to develop layers of competitive advantage—global-scale efficiency, multinational flexibility, and the ability to develop innovations and leverage knowledge on a worldwide basis. And though each of the different prescriptions focuses on one or another of these different strategic objectives, the challenge for most companies today is to achieve all of them simultaneously.

Worldwide Competitive Advantage: Goals and Means

To develop worldwide advantage, a company must achieve three strategic objectives: It must build global-scale efficiency in its existing activities, it must develop multinational flexibility to manage diverse country-specific risks and opportunities, and it must create the ability to learn from its international exposure and opportunities and exploit that learning on a worldwide basis. Competitive advantage is developed by taking strategic actions that optimize a company's achievement of these different and, at times, conflicting goals.

In developing each of these capabilities, the MNE can utilize three very different tools and approaches, which we described briefly in Chapter 1 as the main forces motivating companies to internationalize. It can leverage the scale economies that are potentially available in its different worldwide activities, it can exploit the differences in sourcing and market opportunities among the many countries in which it operates, and it can capitalize on the diversity of its activities and operations to create synergies or develop economies of scope.

The MNE's strategic challenge therefore is to exploit all three sources of global competitive advantage—scale economies, national differences, and scope economies—to optimize global efficiencies, multinational flexibility, and worldwide learning. And thus, the key to worldwide competitive advantage lies in managing the interactions between the different goals and the different means.

The Goals: Efficiency, Flexibility, and Learning

Let us now consider each of these strategic goals in a little more detail.

Global Efficiency

Viewing an MNE as an input–output system, we can think of its overall efficiency as the ratio of the value of its outputs to the value of its inputs. In this simplified view of the firm, its efficiency could be enhanced by increasing the value of outputs (i.e., securing higher revenues), lowering the value of its inputs (i.e., lowering costs), or doing both. This is a simple point but one that is often overlooked:

- Efficiency improvement is not just cost reduction but also revenue enhancement.

To help understand the concept of global efficiency, we use the global integration–national responsiveness framework first developed by C. K. Prahalad (see Figure 3–1).[2] The vertical axis represents the potential benefits from the global integration of activities—benefits that largely translate into lower costs through scale and scope economies. The horizontal axis represents the benefits of national responsiveness—those that result from the country-by-country differentiation of product, strategies, and activities. These benefits essentially translate into better revenues from more effective differentiation in response to national differences in tastes, industry structures, distribution systems, and government regulations.

As Figure 3–1 illustrates, the framework can be used to understand differences in the benefits of integration and responsiveness at the aggregate level of industries, as well as to identify and describe differences in the strategic approaches of companies competing in the same industry. Also as the figure indicates, industry characteristics alone do not determine company strategies. In automobiles, for example, Fiat has long pursued a classical multinational strategy, helping establish national auto industries through its joint venture partnerships and host government support in Spain, Yugoslavia, Poland, and

Figure 3-1   The Integration–Responsiveness Framework

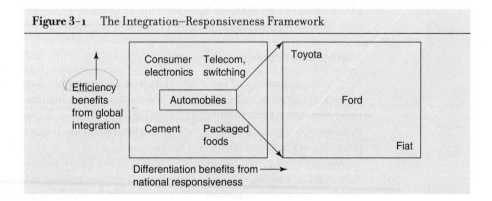

[2]For a detailed exposition of this framework, see C. K. Prahalad and Yves Doz, *The Multinational Mission* (New York: The Free Press, 1987).

many other countries with state-sponsored auto industries. Toyota, by contrast, succeeded by developing products and manufacturing them in centralized, globally scaled facilities in Japan. While Toyota appears on the basis of current evidence to have produced the more sustainable position, it is important to clarify that it made a strategic choice to focus on the objective of global efficiency (rather than local responsiveness) and that this chosen objective creates vulnerabilities and challenges as well as clear benefits.

Multinational Flexibility

A worldwide company faces an operating environment characterized by diversity and volatility. Some opportunities and risks generated by this environment are endemic to all firms; others, however, are unique to companies operating across national borders. A key element of worldwide competitiveness, therefore, is multinational flexibility—the ability of a company to manage the risks and exploit the opportunities that arise from the diversity and volatility of the global environment.[3]

Although there are many sources of diversity and volatility, it is worth highlighting four that we regard as particularly important. First, there are *macroeconomic risks* that are completely outside the control of the MNE, such as changes in prices, wages, or exchange rates caused by wars or natural calamities. Second, there are *political risks* that arise from policy actions of national governments, such as managed changes in exchange rates or interest rate adjustments. Third, there are *competitive risks* arising from the uncertainties of competitors' responses to the MNE's own strategies. And fourth, there are *resource risks,* such as the availability of raw materials, capital, or managerial talent. In all four categories, the common characteristic of the various types of risks is that they vary across countries and change over time. This variance makes flexibility the key strategic management requirement, because diversity and volatility create attendant opportunities that must be considered jointly.

In general, multinational flexibility requires management to scan its broad environment to detect changes and discontinuities and then respond to the new situation in the context of the worldwide business. MNEs following this approach exploit their exposure to diverse and dynamic environments to develop strategies in more general and more flexible terms so as to be robust to different international environmental scenarios.

Worldwide Learning

Most existing theories of the MNE view it as an instrument to extract additional revenues from internalized capabilities. The assumption is that the firm goes abroad to make more profits by exploiting its technology, brand name, or management capabilities in different countries around the world. And most traditional theory assumes that the key competencies reside at the MNE's center.

Although the search for additional profits or the desire to protect existing revenues may explain why MNEs come to exist, it does not provide a complete explanation of why some of them continue to grow and flourish. As we suggested in Chapter 1, an

---

[3]This issue of multinational flexibility is discussed more fully in Bruce Kogut, "Designing Global Strategies: Profiting from Operating Flexibility," *Sloan Management Review,* Fall 1985, pp. 27–38.

alternative view may well be that a key asset of the multinational is the diversity of environments in which it operates. This diversity exposes the MNE to multiple stimuli, allows it to develop diverse capabilities, and provides it with broader learning opportunities than are available to a purely domestic firm. Furthermore, its initial stock of knowledge provides the MNE with strength that allows it to create organizational diversity in the first place. In Chapter 5, we engage in a detailed discussion of the approaches that MNEs use to deliver on the objective of worldwide learning.

The Means: National Differences, Scale, and Scope Economies

There are three fundamental tools for building worldwide competitive advantage: exploiting differences in sourcing and market potential across countries, exploiting economies of scope, and exploiting economies of scale. In this section, we explore each of them in more depth.

National Differences

In the absence of efficient markets, the fact that different nations have different factor endowments (e.g., an abundance of labor, land, materials) leads to intercountry differences in factor costs. Because different activities of the firm, such as R&D, production, or marketing, use various factors to different degrees, a firm can gain cost advantages by configuring its value chain so that each activity is located in the country that has the least cost for its most intensively used factor. For example, R&D facilities may be placed in the United Kingdom because of the available supply of high-quality, yet modestly paid, scientists; manufacturing of labor-intensive components may be undertaken in Taiwan to capitalize on the low-cost, efficient labor force; and software development could concentrate in India, where skilled software engineers are paid a fraction of Western salaries.

National differences may also exist in output markets. As we have discussed, customer tastes and preferences may differ in different countries, as may distribution systems, government regulations applicable to the pertinent product markets, or the effectiveness of different promotion strategies. A firm can obtain higher prices for its output by tailoring its offerings to fit the unique requirements in each national market.

Scale Economies

Microeconomic theory provides a strong basis for evaluating the effect of scale on cost reduction, and the use of scale as a competitive tool is common in industries ranging from roller bearings to semiconductors. Whereas scale, by itself, is a static concept, there may be dynamic benefits of scale through what has been variously described as the experience or learning effect. The higher volume that helps a firm exploit scale benefits also allows it to accumulate learning, which leads to progressive cost reduction as the firm moves down its learning curve. So though emerging Korean electronics firms were able to match the scale of experienced Japanese competitors, they were unable to compensate for the innumerable process-related efficiencies the Japanese had learned after decades of operating their global-scale plants.

Table 3-1   Scope Economies in Product and Market Diversification

	Sources of Scope Economies	
	Product Diversification	**Market Diversification**
Shared physical assets	Factory automation with flexibility to produce multiple products (Ford)	Global brand name (Nokia)
Shared external relations	Using common distribution channels for multiple products (Samsung)	Servicing multinational customers worldwide (Citibank)
Shared learning	Shared R&D in computer and communications business (NEC)	Pooling knowledge developed in different markets (Procter & Gamble)

Scope Economies

The concept of scope economies is based on the notion that certain economies arise from the fact that the cost of the joint production (or development or distribution) of two or more products can be less than the cost of producing them separately.[4] Such cost reductions may take place for many reasons—for example, resources such as information or technologies, once acquired for use in producing one item, are available without cost for production of other items.

The strategic importance of scope economies arises from a diversified firm's ability to share investments and costs across the same or different value chains—a source of economies that competitors without such internal and external diversity cannot match. Such sharing can take place across segments, products, or markets and may involve the joint use of different kinds of assets (see Table 3–1).

Mapping Ends and Means: Building Blocks for Worldwide Advantage

Table 3–2 shows a mapping of the different goals and means for achieving worldwide competitiveness. Each goals–means intersection suggests some of the factors that may enhance a company's strategic position. Although the factors are only illustrative, it may be useful to study them carefully and compare them against the proposals of the different articles mentioned at the beginning of the chapter. It will become apparent that each author focuses on a specific subset of factors—essentially, some different goals–means combinations—and the differences among their prescriptions can be understood in terms of the differences in the particular aspect of worldwide competitive advantage on which they focus.

---

[4]For a detailed exposition of scope economies, see W. J. Baumol, J. C. Panzer, and R. D. Willig, *Contestable Markets and the Theory of Industry Structure* (New York: Harcourt Brace Jovanovich, 1982).

Table 3-2   Worldwide Advantage: Goals and Means

Strategic Objectives	Sources of Competitive Advantage		
	National Differences	Scale Economies	Scope Economies
Achieving efficiency in current operations	Benefiting from differences in factor costs—wages and cost of capital	Expanding and exploiting potential scale economies in each activity	Sharing of investments and costs across markets and businesses
Managing risks through multinational flexibility	Managing different kinds of risks arising from market- or policy-induced changes in comparative advantages of different countries	Balancing scale with strategic and operational flexibility	Portfolio diversification of risks and creation of options and side bets
Innovation, learning, and adaptation	Learning from societal differences in organizational and managerial processes and systems	Benefiting from experience—cost reduction and innovation	Shared learning across organizational components in different products, markets, or businesses

Multinational, International, Global, and Transnational Strategies

In Chapter 2, we described how environmental forces in different industries shaped alternative approaches to managing worldwide operations that we described as multinational, international, global, and transnational. We now elaborate on the distinctions among these different approaches, as well as their respective strengths and vulnerabilities in terms of the different goals–means combinations we have just described.

Multinational Strategy

The multinational strategic approach focuses primarily on one means (national differences) to achieve most of its strategic objectives. Companies adopting this approach tend to focus on the revenue side, usually by differentiating their products and services in response to national differences in customer preferences, industry characteristics, and government regulations. This approach leads most multinational companies to depend on local-for-local innovations, a process requiring the subsidiary to not only identify local needs but also use its own local resources to respond to those needs. Carrying out most activities within each country on a local-for-local basis also allows those adopting a multinational strategy to match costs and revenues on a currency-by-currency basis.

Historically, many European companies such as Unilever, ICI, Philips, and Nestlé followed this strategic model. In these companies, assets and resources historically were widely dispersed, allowing overseas subsidiaries to carry out a wide range of activities from development and production to sales and services. Their self-sufficiency was typically accompanied by considerable local autonomy. But, though such independent national units were unusually flexible and responsive to their local environments, they inevitably suffered problems of inefficiencies and an inability to exploit the knowledge and competencies of other national units.

International Strategy

Companies adopting this broad approach focus on creating and exploiting innovations on a worldwide basis, using all the different means to achieve this end. MNEs headquartered in large and technologically advanced countries often adopted this strategic approach but limited it primarily to exploiting home-country innovations to develop their competitive positions abroad. The international product cycle theory we described in Chapter 1 encompasses both the strategic motivation and competitive posture of these companies: At least initially, their internationalization process relied heavily on transferring new products, processes, or strategies developed in the home country to less advanced overseas markets.

This approach was common among U.S.-based MNEs such as Kraft, Pfizer, Procter & Gamble, and General Electric. Although these companies built considerable strengths out of their ability to create and leverage innovations, many suffered from deficiencies of both efficiency and flexibility because they did not develop either the centralized and high-scale operations of companies adopting global strategies or the very high degree of local responsiveness that multinational companies could muster through their autonomous, self-sufficient, and entrepreneurial local operations.

Global Strategy

Companies adopting the classic global strategic approach, as we have defined it, depend primarily on developing global efficiency. They use all the different means to achieve the best cost and quality positions for their products.

This means has been the classic approach of many Japanese companies such as Toyota, Canon, Komatsu, and Matsushita. As these and other similar companies have found, however, such efficiency comes with some compromises of both flexibility and learning. For example, concentrating manufacturing to capture global scale may also result in a high level of intercountry product shipments that can raise risks of policy intervention, particularly by host governments in major importer countries. Similarly, companies that centralize R&D for efficiency reasons often find they are constrained in their ability to capture new developments in countries outside their home markets or to leverage innovations created by foreign subsidiaries in the rest of their worldwide operations. And finally, the concentration (most often through centralization) of activities like R&D and manufacturing to achieve a global scale exposes such companies to high sourcing risks, particularly in exchange rate exposure.

Transnational Strategy

Beneath each of these three traditional strategic approaches lie some implicit assumptions about how best to build worldwide competitive advantage. The global company assumes that the best-cost position is the key source of competitiveness; the multinational company sees differentiation as the primary way to enhance performance; and the international company expects to use innovations to reduce costs, enhance revenues, or both. Companies adopting the transnational strategy recognize that each of these traditional approaches is partial, that each has its own merits but none represents the whole truth.

To achieve worldwide competitive advantage, costs and revenues have to be managed simultaneously, both efficiency and innovation are important, and innovations can arise in many different parts of the organization. Therefore, instead of focusing on any subpart of the set of issues shown in Table 3–2, the transnational company focuses on exploiting each and every goals–means combination to develop layers of competitive advantage by exploiting efficiency, flexibility, and learning simultaneously.

To achieve this ambitious strategic approach, however, the transnational company must develop a very different configuration of assets and capabilities than is typical of traditional multinational, international, and global company structures. The global company tends to concentrate all its resources—either in its home country or in low-cost overseas locations—to exploit the scale economies available in each activity. The multinational company typically disperses its resources among its different national operations to be able to respond to local needs. And the international company tends to centralize those resources that are key to developing innovations but decentralize others to allow its innovations to be adapted worldwide.

The transnational, however, must develop a more sophisticated and differentiated configuration of assets and capabilities. It first decides which key resources and capabilities are best centralized within the home-country operation, not only to realize scale economies but also to protect certain core competencies and provide the necessary supervision of corporate management. Basic research, for example, is often viewed as such a capability, with core technologies kept at home for reasons of strategic security as well as competence concentration. For different reasons, the global account team or international management development responsibility may be located centrally to facilitate top-management control over these key corporate resources.

Certain other resources may be concentrated but not necessarily at home—a configuration that might be termed "excentralization" rather then decentralization. World-scale production plants for labor-intensive products may be built in a low-wage country such as Mexico or Malaysia. The advanced state of a particular technology may demand concentration of relevant R&D resources and activities in Japan, Germany, or the United States. Such flexible specialization—or excentralization—complements the benefits of scale economies with the flexibility of accessing low input costs or scarce resources and the responsiveness of accommodating national political interests. This approach can also apply to specific functional activities. For example, Sony relocated its treasury operations to London to improve its access to financial markets.

Some other resources may best be decentralized on a regional or local basis, because either potential economies of scale are small or there is a need to create flexibility by avoiding exclusive dependence on a single facility. Local or regional facilities may not only afford protection against exchange rate shifts, strikes, natural disasters, and other disruptions but also reduce logistical and coordination costs. An important side benefit provided by such facilities is the impact they can have in building the motivation and

Table 3-3   Strategic Orientation and Configuration of Assets and Capabilities in Multinational, International, Global, and Transnational Companies

	Multinational	International	Global	Transnational
Strategic orientation	Building flexibility to respond to national differences through strong, resourceful, and entrepreneurial national operations	Exploiting parent-company knowledge and capabilities through worldwide diffusion and adaptation	Building cost advantages through centralized, global-scale operations	Developing global efficiency, flexibility, and worldwide learning capability simultaneously
Configuration of assets and capabilities	Decentralized and nationally self-sufficient	Sources of core competencies centralized, others decentralized	Centralized and globally scaled	Dispersed, interdependent, and specialized

capability of national subsidiaries, an impact that can easily make small efficiency sacrifices worthwhile.

Table 3–3 summarizes the differences in the asset configurations that support the different strategic approaches of the various MNE models. We explore these strategy–organizational linkages in more detail in Chapter 4.

Worldwide Competitive Advantage: The Strategic Tasks

In the final part of this chapter, we look at how a company can respond to the strategic challenges we have described. The task will clearly be very different depending on the company's international posture and history. Companies that are among the major worldwide players in their businesses must focus on defending their dominance while also building new sources of advantage. For companies that are smaller but aspire to worldwide competitiveness, the task is one of building the resources and capabilities needed to challenge the entrenched leaders. And, for companies that are focused on their national markets and lack either the resources or the motivation for international expansion, the challenge is to protect their domestic positions from others that have the advantage of being MNEs.

Defending Worldwide Dominance

Over the past decade or so, the shifting external forces we have described have resulted in severe difficulties—even for those MNEs that had enjoyed strong historical positions in their businesses worldwide.

Typically, most of these companies pursued traditional multinational, international, or global strategies, and their past successes were built on the fit between their specific strategic capability and the dominant environmental force in their industries. In multinational industries such as branded packaged products in which forces for national responsiveness were dominant, companies such as Unilever developed strong worldwide positions by adopting multinational strategies. In contrast, in global industries like consumer electronics or semiconductor chips, companies such as Matsushita or Hitachi built leadership positions by adopting global strategies.

In the emerging competitive environment, however, these companies could no longer rely on their historic ability to exploit global efficiency, multinational flexibility, or worldwide learning. As an increasing number of industries developed what we have termed transnational characteristics, companies faced the need to master all three strategic capabilities simultaneously. The challenge for the leading companies was to protect and enhance the particular strength they had while simultaneously building the other capabilities.

For many MNEs, the initial response to this new strategic challenge was to try to restructure the configuration of their assets and activities to develop the capabilities they lacked. For example, global companies with highly centralized resources sought to develop flexibility by dispersing resources among their national subsidiaries; multinational companies, in contrast, tried to emulate their global competitors by centralizing R&D, manufacturing, and other scale-intensive activities. In essence, these companies tried to find a new "fit" configuration through drastic restructuring of their existing configuration.

Such a zero-based search for the ideal configuration not only led to external problems, such as conflict with host governments over issues like plant closures, but also resulted in a great deal of trauma inside the company's own organization. The greatest problem with such an approach, however, was that it tended to erode the particular competency the company already had without effectively adding the new strengths it sought.

The complex balancing act of protecting existing advantages while building new ones required companies to follow two fairly simple principles. First, they had to concentrate at least as much on defending and reinforcing their existing assets and capabilities as on developing new ones. Their approach tended to be one of building on—and eventually modifying—their existing infrastructure instead of radical restructuring. To the extent possible, they relied on modernizing existing facilities rather than dismantling the old and creating new ones.

Second, most successful adaptors looked for ways to compensate for their deficiency or approximate a competitor's source of advantage, rather than trying to imitate its asset structure or task configuration. In searching for efficiency, multinational companies with a decentralized and dispersed resource structure found it easier to develop efficiency by adopting new flexible manufacturing technologies in some of their existing plants and upgrading others to become global sources rather than to close those plants and shift production to lower-cost countries to match the structure of competitive global companies.

Similarly, successful global companies found it more effective to develop responsiveness and flexibility by creating internal linkages between their national sales subsidiaries and their centralized development or manufacturing units rather than trying to mimic multinational companies by dispersing their resources to each country operation and, in the process, undermining their core strength of efficiency.

Challenging the Global Leader

Over the past two decades, a number of companies have managed to evolve from relatively small national players to major worldwide competitors, challenging the dominance of traditional leaders in their businesses. Dell in the computer industry, Magna in auto parts, Electrolux in the domestic appliances business, and CEMEX in the cement industry are some examples of companies that have evolved from relative obscurity to global visibility within relatively short periods of time.

The actual processes adopted to manage such dramatic transformations vary widely from company to company. Electrolux, for example, grew almost exclusively through acquisitions, whereas Dell built capabilities largely through internal development, and Magna and CEMEX used a mix of greenfield investments and acquisitions. Similarly, whereas Dell built its growth on the basis of cost advantages and logistics capabilities, it expanded internationally because of its direct-sales business model and its ability to react quickly to changes in customer demand. Despite wide differences in their specific approaches, however, most of these new champions appear to have followed a similar step-by-step approach to building their competitive positions.

Each developed an initial toehold in the market by focusing on a narrow niche—often one specific product within one specific market—and developing a strong competitive position within that niche. That competitive position was built on multiple sources of competitive advantage rather than on a single strategic capability.

Next, they expanded their toehold to a foothold by limited and carefully selected expansion along both product and geographic dimensions and by extending the step-by-step improvement of both cost and quality to this expanded portfolio. Such expansion was typically focused on products and markets that were not of central importance to the established leaders in the business. By staying outside the range of the leaders' peripheral vision, the challenger could remain relatively invisible, thereby building up its strength and infrastructure without incurring direct retaliation from competitors with far greater resources. For example, emerging companies often focused initially on relatively low-margin products such as small-screen TV sets or subcompact cars.

While developing their own product portfolio, technological capabilities, geographic scope, and marketing expertise, challengers were often able to build up manufacturing volume and its resulting cost efficiencies by becoming original equipment manufacturer suppliers to their larger competitors. Although this supply allowed the larger competitor to benefit from the challenger's cost advantages, it also developed the supplying company's understanding of customer needs and marketing strategies in the advanced markets served by the leading companies.

Once these building blocks for worldwide advantage were in place, the challenger typically moved rapidly to convert its low-profile foothold into a strong permanent position in the worldwide business. Dramatic scaling up of production facilities—increasing VCR capacity 30-fold in eight years as Matsushita did, or expanding computer production 20-fold in seven years as Acer did a decade later—typically preceded a wave of new product introductions and expansion into the key markets through multiple channels and their own brand names.

Protecting Domestic Niches

For reasons of resources or other constraints, some national companies may not be able to aspire to such worldwide expansion, though they are not insulated from the impact of global competition. Their major challenge is to protect their domestic niches from worldwide players with superior resources and multiple sources of competitive advantage.[5] This concern is particularly an issue in developing markets such as India and China, where local companies face much larger, more aggressive, and deeper-pocketed competitors.

There are three broad alternative courses of action that can be pursued by such national competitors. The first approach is to defend against the competitor's global advantage. Just as MNE managers can act to facilitate the globalization of industry structure, so their counterparts in national companies can use their influence in the opposite direction. An astute manager of a national company might be able to foil the attempts of a global competitor by taking action to influence industry structure or market conditions to the national company's advantage. These actions might involve influencing consumer preference to demand a more locally adapted or service-intensive product; it could imply tying up key distribution channels; or it might mean preempting local sources of critical supplies. Many companies trying to enter the Japanese market claim to have faced this type of defensive strategy by local firms.

A second strategic option would be to offset the competitor's global advantage. The simplest way to do this is to lobby for government assistance in the form of tariff protections. A more ambitious approach is to gain government sponsorship to develop equivalent global capabilities through funding of R&D, subsidizing exports, and financing capital investments. As a "national champion," the company would theoretically be able to compete globally. However, in reality, it is very unusual for such a company to prosper. Airbus Industrie, which now shares the global market for large commercial airplanes with Boeing, is one of the few exceptions—rising from the ashes of other attempts by European governments to sponsor a viable computer company in the 1970s and then to promote a European electronics industry a decade later.

The third alternative is to approximate the competitors' global advantages by linking up in some form of alliance or coalition with a viable global company. Numerous such linkages have been formed with the purpose of sharing the risks and costs of operating in a high-risk global environment. By pooling or exchanging market access, technology, and production capability, smaller competitors can gain some measure of defense against global giants. One example of such an approach is the way in which Siemens, ICL, and other small computer companies entered into agreements and joint projects with Fujitsu to enable them to maintain viability against the dominant transnational competitor, IBM.

Concluding Comments

Although these three strategic responses obviously do not cover every possible scenario, they highlight two important points from this chapter. First, the MNE faces a complex set of options in terms of the strategic levers it can pull to achieve competitive advantage, and the framework in Table 3–2 helps make sense of those options by separating out means and ends. Second, the competitive intensity in most industries is such that a company cannot just afford to plough its own furrow. Rather, it is necessary to gain competitive parity on all relevant dimensions (efficiency, flexibility, learning) while also achieving differentiation on one. To be sure, the ability to achieve multiple competitive

[5]For a detailed discussion of such strategies, see N. Dhawar and T. Frost, "Competing with Giants: Survival Strategies for Local Companies Competing in Emerging Markets," *Harvard Business Review* 77, no. 2 (1999), pp. 119–30.

objectives at the same time is far from straightforward, and as a result, we see many MNEs experimenting with new ways of organizing their worldwide activities. And this organization will be the core issue we will address in the next chapter.

Case 3-1   TCL Multimedia

Multimedia is like a car: there are different ways to go to the same place. If you confront an obstacle, go around it. We are very flexible and suited to change. This is characteristically Chinese.

TCL Thomson Enterprise is a milestone for China. If it succeeds, all the Chinese companies will follow. If we have trouble, they will not.

—Charls Zhao, President, TCL Thomson Enterprise

In spring 2005, TCL Group Chairman Li Dongsheng considered what TCL's most recent results said about its strategic and competitive position in the television market. Net profits for 2004 were HK$317 million ($40.5 million), down 51% from the previous year despite a 69% annual increase in turnover to HK$26 billion ($3.3 billion). He wondered if the company was on the right track. Already a leading consumer electronics manufacturer within China, Shenzhen-based TCL had begun to internationalize its television production in the late 1990s through majority-owned joint ventures in emerging markets around the world. The purchase in 2004 of the television assets of France's Thomson S.A. then made TCL—after just 12 years in the business—the world's largest television manufacturer. The Thomson assets, which recast TCL's Multimedia division as TCL Thomson Enterprise (TTE), a 67%–33% joint venture, gave TCL access to European and North American markets in ways its previous overseas forays had not. The deal also

forced TCL to consider how to strengthen its technical and competitive position. Though TTE President Charls Zhao had targeted break-even in the United States and Europe in 2005, that achievement might have to wait until 2006.

World Television Production

In the 1960s, U.S. companies including CBS, RCA, and Zenith dominated world production of television sets. Color television, which used the same cathode-ray-tube (CRT) technology employed in earlier black-and-white models, became ubiquitous in the 1970s, several years after Japanese players Sony and Matsushita entered the fray. Japanese production efficiencies in the 1980s initiated a permanent shift in the locus of manufacture from the United States to Asia. High local labor costs in Japan and Europe led their TV makers to source components in South Korea and Taiwan throughout the 1970s and 1980s, and soon firms there were producing complete sets on an original equipment manufacturer (OEM) basis for markets in both the United States and Japan.

All of these manufacturers were quick to take advantage of the advent of China's opening in 1979, relocating both television assembly and manufacturing to benefit from China's lower labor costs. Consumer electronics manufacturing moved to China steadily through the 1990s to the point that one journalist concluded, "Nearly every chemical, component, plastic,

Professors Tarun Khanna and Felix Oberholzer-Gee and Global Research Group Senior Researcher David Lane prepared the original version of this case, "TCL Multimedia," HBS No. 705-404, which is being replaced by this version prepared by Professors Tarun Khanna and Felix Oberholzer-Gee and Global Research Group Senior Researcher David Lane. HBS cases are developed solely as the basis for class discussion. Cases are not intended to serve as endorsements, sources of primary data, or illustrations of effective or ineffective management.

Exhibit 1   Chinese Provinces and Major Cities, 2004

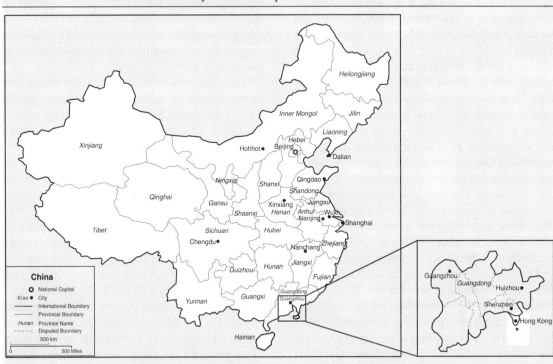

Source: Adapted by casewriter from http://www.lib.utexas.edu/maps/cia04/china_sm04.gif, accessed February 25, 2005.

machine tool, and packing material required in the manufacture of electronics components is now available within the Pearl River Delta area, making most components 20% cheaper in China than in the United States."[1] China's television manufacturers, which were said to number as many as 1,000 during the 1990s, consolidated into a handful of highly competitive electronics manufacturers, including Changhong (based in Chengdu, Sichuan Province), Hisense (Qingdao, Shandong), Konka (Shenzhen, abutting Hong Kong), and TCL. See **Exhibit 1** for a map of China indicating these sites.

Companies manufacturing televisions typically produced a portfolio of consumer electronics, balancing older, low-margin "cash cow" products with newer, high-margin, yet capital-intensive devices. As products matured, their manufacturers either consolidated or otherwise left the market. Over time, product life cycles had shortened as product penetration quickened: while VCR shipments did not reach 30 million units for 13 years, CD players and DVD players reached 30 million shipments in just eight and five years, respectively.[2]

Along with radio cassette players, portable audio devices, and VCRs, CRT televisions were the mainstay of consumer electronics firms into the 1990s, when digital technologies began to emerge. As the twenty-first century dawned, flat-panel display technology in the form of liquid crystal

[1]Pete Engardio and Dexter Roberts, "The China Price," *BusinessWeek*, no. 3911, December 6, 2004, p. 102.

[2]Eric Elalouf, Nicolas Gaudois, and Yuki Sugi, "Thomson: From Black Box to Box Office," Deutsche Bank Equity Research, July 9, 2003, pp. 123–126.

displays (LCDs) and plasma display panels (PDPs) had begun to displace CRT television sets and computer monitors in the United States, Europe, and Japan.[3] Analysts predicted global demand for displays would rise at over 13% annually to $113.5 billion in 2008,[4] meaning that 2003 sales of 160 million units would rise to over 200 million units by 2008.[5] Flat-panel technology was expected to account for nearly all of that growth. Similarly, the largest television sets used a variety of rear-projection technologies, all of which were displacing CRT technology. One such technology, the microdisplay, was slimmer, lighter, and brighter than its predecessor and usually cost half of a similar-sized PDP.[6] Shipments of microdisplay-based rear-projection televisions were expected to exceed 1.5 million units in 2004, up from 400,000 in 2003, and were predicted to surpass CRT television sales in 2006.[7]

The increasing availability of standardized flat-panel and video-integrated circuits (ICs) in the 1990s opened the market beyond the vertically integrated firms that previously dominated video-processing technology. Many of the newer players at first relied on original design manufacturing (ODM) orders for others. The shift from bulky, heavy CRTs to flat panels also lowered shipping costs, thereby making ODMs in low-cost regions competitive.[8]

Japanese consumer electronics companies—typically vertically integrated—increasingly pulled back on their production of CRTs and CRT-based televisions, while Chinese television manufacturers stepped in, producing both for export and to supply the growing domestic market.[9]

Television sets dominated the $60.5 billion consumer electronics market in 2003, accounting for 35% of the market by volume and 62% by value.[10] In 2003, China accounted for 29% of the world's television production by value[11] and 40% of production by volume.[12] Prior to the Thomson acquisition, TCL ranked third in the world by number of sets sold, at 10.7 million units. Among domestic manufacturers, TCL competed intensely with Changhong, Konka, and Skyworth (Shenzhen) for Chinese sales. None had a significant market-share advantage. In 2002, Changhong had led domestic sales with a 17.2% market share. In 2003, Konka edged out the others with an 18.7% domestic share on sales of 7.91 million units to TCL's 7.83 million units.[13] For the third quarter of 2004, Konka was followed closely by TCL, each with an 18% share. Skyworth and Changhong held 13% shares.[14] CRT sets made up about 94% of China's 2004 television production,[15] though TCL was China's leading producer of LCD displays.[16]

[3]In May 2004, analysts projected production numbers for PDP TVs to double in 2004 and to grow at compound annual rates of 57% from 2003 to 2007. Paul Semenza, "Television Fuels TFT-LCD Growth," *EE Times,* May 28, 2004, available at www.eet.com/article/showArticle.jhtml?articleId=21400220, accessed January 12, 2005.

[4]"World Electronic Displays," *Freedonia,* no. 1867, November 2004, www.freedonia.com, accessed January 11, 2005.

[5]The current ramp-up in production began at the end of 2003, when Samsung, Chi Mei Optoelectronics, and Quanta Display began production at their new fifth-generation fabs. At the end of 2003, these companies were operating a total of seven such plants. Another eight fabs were set to open in 2004, at an estimated cost of up to $2 billion each. See Paul Semenza, "Television fuels TFT-LCD growth," *EE Times,* May 28, 2004, available at www.eet.com/article/showArticle.jhtml?articleId=21400220, accessed January 12, 2005.

[6]Wilson Rothman, "Projection TVs Slim Down with an All-Chip Diet," *The New York Times,* June 10, 2004, p. G7, www.lexis-nexis.com, accessed January 11, 2005.

[7]Paul Semenza, "Television fuels TFT-LCD growth," *EE Times,* May 28, 2004, available at www.eet.com/article/showArticle.jhtml?articleId=21400220, accessed January 12, 2005.

[8]Ibid.

[9]In 2003, 42.3 million television sets sold in China. "China's Konka Top TV Seller in 2003 with 18.7 Pct Domestic Market Share," *AFX Asia,* March 23, 2004, available from Factiva, www.factiva.com, accessed January 13, 2005.

[10]At the high end, these included LCD and PDP TVs. CRT TVs, VCRs, DVDs, stereos, and portable audio equipment rounded out the category. "World Electronic Displays," *Freedonia,* no. 1867, November 2004, available from www.freedonia.com, accessed January 11, 2005.

[11]Deutsche Bank report, July 9, 2003, p. 126.

[12]"E-Information Industry China's No. 1 Industry," IPR Strategic Information Database, March 10, 2004, available from Factiva, www.factiva.com, accessed January 13, 2005.

[13]"China's Konka Top TV Seller in 2003 with 18.7% Pct Domestic Market Share—MII," AFX Asia, March 23, 2004, available from Factiva, www.factiva.com, accessed January 13, 2005.

[14]"New Display Search Report Provides TV Shipments for All Regions and Technologies by Brand," *Business Wire,* January 3, 2005, available from Factiva, www.factiva.com, accessed January 13, 2005.

[15]Ibid.

[16]Ibid.

TCL Origins and Growth

TCL was founded in 1982 as an audiotape manufacturer. One of the founders, Li Dongsheng, remained TCL Group chairman in 2005 and had led the firm into a series of consumer electronics product lines. Throughout the 1980s, it was TCL's production of handsets for fixed-line telephones that gave the company a reputation for quality. By the early 1990s, TCL also sold under the Tongli brand audio equipment made in a joint venture with a Hong Kong firm. An audio research and development (R&D) department was launched in 1992, focusing on product development and production efficiencies. Around the same time, TCL began to develop a national distribution system, after attempts to sell its audio equipment foundered when large distributors, primarily state owned, proved unwilling or unable to support the company's products. The distributors' primary interest was in turnover and cash in hand, and they did little if any product promotion. Distributors did not tell manufacturers how well their products were selling to retailers and paid no attention to subsequent retail sales. "Distributors lost interest in the product as soon as retailers purchased the inventory," one TCL manager recalled. TCL also launched its first advertising and marketing efforts in 1993–1994.

Under the Wangpai ("King") brand, TCL in 1992 began to sell color televisions that were produced by Hong Kong–based joint-venture partner Changcheng. TCL continued to purchase TVs from Changcheng on an OEM basis for domestic sale through 1996. According to one insider, TCL's shift into the manufacture of television sets came by happenstance:

Starting TV sales was not due to any strategic foresight. The hi-fi business went into a slump. Chairman Li knew the head of Changcheng and had a good relationship with him. Changcheng lacked a license to produce televisions in China, but Mr. Li secured one, and TCL got an order from Changcheng to sell them. The hi-fi business had established a sales network that enabled us to sell our TVs. We also began TV production by chance,

when the head of Changcheng died in a 1996 car accident. His wife decided to sell the business, but we did not have the resources to buy it. Our OEM relationship with Changcheng ended, and we had to build production facilities of our own. But we didn't pursue every opportunity that came along. We decided not to go into making VCD players in 1996. We also turned down real estate development, though both were booming at the time.

Instead, TCL in 1996 paid HK$150 million ($19 million) to form a joint venture with a Hong Kong manufacturer, Luk's Industrial, to produce televisions in Shenzhen. Luk's contributed its existing Shenzhen television factory, and TCL maintained a controlling interest in the venture, eventually building a new Shenzhen factory and moving its R&D operations into the old one. The deal also included Luk's television factory in Vietnam.

Though TCL was among the few major Chinese firms to establish distribution before manufacturing, it was not without teething pains. Terry Yi, who in 2004 was president of TCL's Overseas Business unit, recalled what he faced when sent in 1996 to overhaul the company's sales and marketing in one key market:

Nanjing was a challenge. Jiangsu province was one of the first places where TCL had sold its products, and we were in competition there and in Anhui, the two provinces I was responsible for, with Panda [a local manufacturer]. At the time, TCL had one distributor per province, but that didn't mean the distributors understood us. In fact, we ended up sending senior people to convey our strategy to our sales outlets. For Jiangsu and Anhui, I did extensive research at the county level and significantly improved the sales network, which remained TCL owned. In every county, TCL chose two promising distributors whose culture and mission were close to ours, and we worked closely with them to craft a marketing and sales plan. Distributors were both state owned and private. We planned together with them for three years. There was no change to the basic distribution system, we just worked with them more collaboratively.

After a year that included closing TCL's sales organization in Anhui province, Yi increased sales from RMB 30 million in 1996 to RMB 190 million in 1997.[17] Through these and other efforts, TCL's TV sales exceeded RMB 100 million in 1995 and grew quickly in 1996 to RMB 1.3 billion once TCL did its own manufacturing. TV sales exceeded RMB 3 billion in 1997 and RMB 6 billion in 1998. As they did, TCL grew through acquisition, first buying a factory in Xinxiang, Henan province in 1997, another in Hohhot, Inner Mongolia in 1999, a third in Wuxi, Jiangsu in 2000, and a fourth in Nanchang, Jiangxi. The five centers also functioned as logistics and distribution centers. Unlike foreign multinationals that targeted customers in China's wealthier coastal provinces, TCL built national coverage: "north, south, east, west, and center." Even so, the company expanded only into locations where local government policy made it advantageous to do so.

From 1999, TCL began to integrate what had previously been isolated capabilities in production, R&D, and marketing. According to Shi Wanwen, TCL Multimedia president, "In early 2000, our TVs ranked third in China, but we were way behind [market leader] Changhong. We rose to number one by the end of 2003, partly through integration, partly by increased R&D spending, and partly improved production efficiencies. We did better than our competitors in these dimensions." The benefits of integrating sales with production and R&D were clear, Shi added:

In 2001, price competition broke out among TV makers. However, we had forecast that some of our competitors were going to lower their prices. Based on this, we made adjustments to our procurement and sold off our old inventory. Therefore, the sets in the market on which we lowered our prices were brand new, while our competitors were left trying to dump their old inventory. We could sell at a cheaper price and faster than they did. That helped us survive. Our competitors were not as responsive to the market.

Shi elaborated on TCL's success factors. First, Li Dongsheng had anticipated major changes in the

industry, as illustrated by his decision in 2000 to move TCL into big-screen TV production. Second, TCL's structure allowed and promoted innovative learning: "From TVs we went into PCs, mobile phones, white goods, and electronics components. TCL was the most comprehensive Chinese manufacturer." Third was a strong sales network, TCL's "biggest advantage," according to Zhao. The company had begun to monitor sales and inventory in certain parts of China via the Internet as early as 1997.[18] In 2003, TCL organized sales into 27 provincial-level companies that oversaw 167 sales offices in leading cities—each with its own profit and loss (P&L) responsibility—that in turn put TCL products on the shelves of some 20,000 domestic outlets. Two-thirds of TCL's senior executives active in 2004 had come up through the sales organization, one manager estimated.

Managers said that company culture also contributed to growth. Zhao explained that TCL differed from most Chinese enterprises, which tended to be either family owned or run as a strict, "militaristic" hierarchy: "TCL has an immigrant culture. That means independent ideas can flourish here. Chairman Li makes the rules of the game but leaves each manager with the autonomy to deliver results." He added that a personality test had revealed 35 of 40 TCL managers as "tigers": "TCL is full of tigers, each powerful within its own territory. Plus we move fast on our own initiative. We say, first have the son, then have a father."

As handicaps, TCL managers listed the company's limited scale and technological capabilities relative to global competitors, a higher liabilities-to-assets ratio than its peers, and a relative dearth of employees with international expertise.[19]

Organization and Ownership

The TCL corporate structure was complex (see **Exhibit 2**). At the start of 2004, TCL operated eight business units: Multimedia, Overseas Business, Telecommunications, Home Appliances, Personal

---

[17]The RMB:$1 exchange rate was 8.27:1.

[18]TCL IPO Prospectus, p. 100.
[19]Ibid., p. 101.

Exhibit 2 TCL Group Structure, Year-End 2003

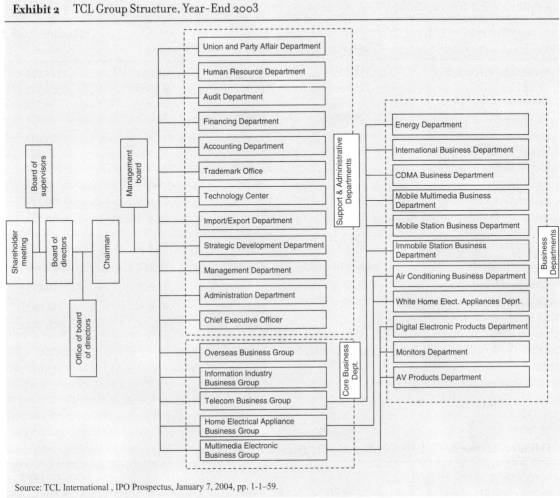

Source: TCL International , IPO Prospectus, January 7, 2004, pp. 1-1–59.

Computers, Consumer Electronics, Electronics Components, and CD/DVD distribution. Of these, Multimedia was the largest, encompassing 41 of TCL's 103 subsidiaries and generating RMB 10 billion in sales. Telecommunications, for which mobile handsets generated another RMB 8 billion to RMB 10 billion, came second, followed by Overseas Business (including most of the Philips TV and DVD products sold by Wal-Mart, for example), PCs at RMB 3 billion, Home Appliances at RMB 2 billion, and Consumer Electronics for about RMB 1 billion.

Total 2003 sales reached RMB 39.3 billion (see **Exhibits 3** and **4** for additional data). Multimedia produced monitors, home theater, and audio equipment in addition to color televisions, but TVs accounted for 94% of 2003 division sales. All TCL business units were growing except mobile handsets, which had peaked in 2002, according to one manager. Another described the organization more broadly, as six functions—manufacturing, R&D, sourcing, supply, product planning, and finance—and four operating platforms—information

Exhibit 3   TCL Sales by Product Category, 2000–H1 2003 (in RMB 10,000)

	2000	2001	2002	January–June 2003
Multimedia Electronics:	753,025	753,228	1,040,655	545,784
Color TVs	728,933	712,667	982,969	516,772
Monitors	66	13,191	20,907	14,539
AV products	24,026	27,370	36,778	16,473
Communications	88,499	275,930	877,213	538,634
Fixed line phones	55,756	53,655	37,991	16,375
Mobile phones	27,142	215,917	832,750	515,734
Batteries	5,631	6,358	6,472	6,525
Household Electronics	90,927	100,110	75,679	70,553
Refrigerators	10,783	25,547	8,648	16,907
Washing machines	38,938	27,556	11,599	8,243
Air conditioners	41,206	47,007	55,432	45,403
Personal Computers	117,248	92,030	153,262	73,440
Components and Fixtures	26,094	30,590	39,689	20,993
Other	93,361	84,991	69,616	42,065
Total	1,107,797	1,276,866	2,211,651	1,270,568

Source: TCL International IPO Prospectus, January 7, 2004, pp. 1-1–97/98.

Exhibit 4   Summary TCL Financials, 2000–H1 2003 (in RMB 10,000)

	2000	2001	2002	January–June 2003
Total assets	91,513	186,391	491,497	555,908
Total liabilities	58,987	132,534	334,120	381,052
Shareholders' equity	26,883	28,098	44,299	57,666
Assets/liabilities	64.5%	71.1%	68.0%	68.5%
Main operating revenues	92,294	276,901	872,259	525,775
Annual increase in revenues	n/a	200.0%	215.0%	51.2%
Operating income	−11,561	20,613	115,489	47,449
Net income	−8,356	2,154	27,639	14,518
Annual increase in net income	n/a	488%	1183%	28%
EPS (RMB)	−0.444	0.115	1.469	0.7718
Net assets per share (RMB)	1.429	1.494	2.355	3.0656
EPS/Net assets per share	−31.08%	7.67%	62.39%	25.2%

Source: TCL IPO Prospectus, January 7, 2004, pp. 1-1–90.

Exhibit 5   TCL Group Ownership, 2004

Rank	December 30, 2003	%	June 30, 2004	%
1	Huizhou Investment Holding Co., Ltd.	40.97	Huizhou Investment Holding Co., Ltd.	25.22
2	TCL Corp. Trade Union Committee	14.79	TCL Corp. Trade Union Committee	9.10
3	Nam Tai Electronics Inc.	6.00	Li Dongsheng	5.59
4	Philips Electronics China BV	4.00	Nam Tai Electronics Inc.	3.69
5	Lucky Concept Ltd.	3.00	Philips Electronics China BV	2.46
6	Regal Trinity Ltd.	3.00	Lucky Concept Ltd.	1.85
7	Toshiba Corp.	2.00	Regal Trinity Ltd.	1.85
8	Sumitomo Trading Corp.	0.38	Toshiba Corp.	1.23
9	Li Dongsheng	9.08	Yuan Xincheng	0.96
10	Yuan Xincheng	1.56	Zhen Quanlie	0.91
11–50	Other TCL managers	15.22		

Source: TCL Group IPO Prospectus, January 7, 2004, pp. 1-1-45-46, and http://finance.sina.com.cn/stock/company/sz/ 000100/4.html, accessed January 13, 2005.

technology, human resources, strategic planning, and six sigma.

As of mid-2004, the Huizhou government was TCL's largest single owner, with 25.22%. Managers and staff cumulatively held another 25.01%, strategic partners held 11.32%, and the public held 38.45% through listings of the TV business in Hong Kong in November 1999 and of the parent company, TCL Corporation, in Shenzhen in January 2004 (see **Exhibit 5**). TCL was unusual for a government-invested local firm in that the Huizhou government had acted only as a guarantor rather than as the source of funds for the initial RMB 5,000 investment made by the TCL founders. "The Huizhou government owns shares but keeps its hands off management because it's in their interest to do so," explained Zeng Nianliang, Multimedia finance vice president. Indeed, TCL in 1997 was "privatized." Prior to that time, according to one manager, TCL had been more concerned about survival than growth. In 2000, TCL reorganized into two stock companies. TCL took on foreign corporate strategic investors, including Sumitomo Trading and Toshiba in 2002 and Philips in early 2003. By 2004, managers asserted, TCL's government relations amounted to lobbying for favorable tax policies and for policy exceptions such as access to electricity in times of forced outages.

Operations

Financial Management   Zhao described TCL's centralized financial management as "conservative and stable." Centralized borrowing gave TCL access to better rates. Bank loans for the group amounted to over RMB 4 billion and came mostly from Huizhou, Shenzhen, and Hong Kong banks. Multimedia carried just RMB 200 million in loans on RMB 4 billion in assets.

All revenues were forwarded to the center, though a negotiated percentage of local sales was retained to finance local sales operations. In 1998, TCL reached an agreement with the Bank of China and the Commercial and Industrial Bank of China to provide real-time settlement and transmission of funds from local offices to headquarters. This arrangement allowed for the repatriation of locally gathered revenues in six hours.

Speed was also of the essence for receivables. Given the narrow profit margins on consumer electronics, TCL maximized profits through high sales volume and tight receivables management, which averaged 9.7 days in 2002, ahead of many peers.[20] Group receivables collection declined from 22 days in 2003 to 14 days in the first half of 2004. Business

[20]Ibid.

unit receivables collection declined to nine days in the first half of 2004. Outstanding receivables amounted to RMB 10 million on RMB 10 billion of sales. This was the best in China, managers asserted, topping even Sony and Samsung, TCL's two primary benchmarks. In the first half of 2004, Multimedia paid RMB 60,000 in financial fees on RMB 4.6 billion in revenues.

Supply-Chain and Production Management   In 2003, Multimedia employed some 80 people in sourcing, including 34 incoming quality-control managers in Huizhou. The division bought about RMB 8 billion in products that year, including about RMB 2.5 billion in commodity items and RMB 1 billion of imported products, primarily integrated circuits and display panels. All picture tubes were made in China. China's electronic components supply was abundant; even TCL's Turkish plant imported 90% of its components fr om China. Japanese and Korean competitors also sourced from China, but TCL managers felt that their local knowledge gave TCL an edge. "After all," asked Li Yuguo, worldwide general manager for sourcing:

> If all the products have common components, why did TCL make RMB 500 million while the others all lost money? The answer is supply-chain management [SCM]. Factory competition is basically SCM competition. Sourcing is not just about buying things; it also includes supplier development, plant inspection, and the confirmation of contract terms and conditions. Also, the center optimizes production volumes among our five manufacturing centers.

TCL inventory turns exceeded those at its Chinese peers, reaching 4.5 times in 2002 (see **Exhibit 6**) and 5.4 times in 2003. TCL managers estimated inventory turns at their leading competitor, Changhong, as between one and two times. Better forecasting also allowed TCL to carry proportionately less inventory than Changhong. Li Yuguo detailed how TCL stayed in front:

> In our business, I can confidently say that we are the fastest, at 15 days between purchasing and production. Losses from materials in 2003 were less than RMB 2 million, and 60% of this was caused by

Exhibit 6   Inventory Management Statistics, TCL Group and Listed Competitors, 2002

	Inventory Book Value (RMB mn)	Planned Reductions (RMB mn)	Expected Savings (%)	Inventory Turnover (x)
Color TVs				
Changhong	9,675	277	2.9%	0.9
Konka	3,167	122	3.8%	3.3
Xoceco (Prima)	802	41	5.1%	2.7
Hisense	1,323	30	2.2%	3.3
Average	*3,742*	*117*	*3.1%*	*1.7*
Mobile phones				
Bird	2,030	333	16.4%	4.7
Kejian	390	7	1.8%	6.0
Amoi Electronics	1,089	95	8.7%	4.3
Average	*3,509*	*434*	*12.4%*	*4.8*
TCL Group	4,517	159	3.5%	4.5
Color TVs	2,032	38	1.9%	4.2
Mobile phones	1,477	74	5.0%	5.6

Source: TCL Group IPO Prospectus, pp. 1-1–229.

changing product specifications and features after parts were already bought. In 2003 we eliminated about 24 procedures to maximize efficiency and simplicity. For example, last year purchasing managers were responsible for planning but not actual purchase orders or supplier delivery status. Yet people placing the orders weren't following up on delivery status either. So we gave all procurement responsibility to the purchasing management function. Now the whole chain knows what suppliers are doing.

R&D and Product Innovation   TCL prided itself on rapid product and process innovation, said Forest Luo, head of Multimedia R&D. Each business unit had an R&D department; Multimedia's was largest with 550 staff, followed by Telecommunications, which employed 350 to develop handsets. Multimedia's R&D spending historically ranged between 1% and 3% of sales but never exceeded 3% and was below that of most TCL competitors. For 2005, TCL had a global target of 5% of sales for R&D expenditures. Luo justified this level by arguing that TCL's cost structure was lower than those of its benchmarks, Sony and Samsung:

Sony is a technology leader, requiring higher R&D investments. We make profitable use of older technology. We don't do collaborative research. While there is a need for this, there's no suitable means to achieve it. We might get involved with a manufacturer to get what we need made. For example, Samsung may not have a tube on the market yet, so I'll give them our specifications so that it biases them towards filling our needs and away from others.

Different players competed against TCL along each element of the TV value chain: chassis (which involved the integration of IC, software, and parts), display (CRT and flat-panel expertise), and cabinet (tooling). TCL excelled at making cabinets and non–flat-panel displays, and R&D goals included increasing production throughput and matching designs to consumer taste. "We value speed," explained Luo. "Control of intellectual property is not important to us. We work with outside research labs opportunistically, and though we are weak in patents, we are good in manufacturing." Industrial

design was a key TCL competence and the focus of dozens of designers. Thus, while certain testing instruments might cost $40,000 if bought from Hewlett-Packard, TCL made its own at considerable savings.

"Ideas for new products come in from the marketing side," said Shi:

Those that are deemed worthy are passed to R&D, which evaluates the concept, technology, and resources and creates product development road maps for those that pass muster. Prototype evaluation is followed by quality and market evaluation. The process normally takes six months or so for a new product. Changes to existing products can be done in a month or two. Obviously we can reject ideas much more quickly.

New features and product extensions were developed continuously, Shi added: "We were the first to produce Web TV, surge-protected TV, and energy-saving TVs. There are so many examples where we were first with a feature. In Southeast Asia, the cabinets on our TVs can be changed with the seasons. Those are quite popular." Another example came from a sales executive's suggestion to integrate hi-fi audio with a TV set so that the audio remained functional when the TV was turned off. The product played TV programs in higher-than-normal fidelity and appealed to customers who did not want to purchase separate TV and audio systems. "We did feasibility, sourcing, design, R&D, and production all in one month. It was very profitable," Shi said.

Marketing   TCL came late to marketing, according to Shi, who built up that function after 2000: "At TCL, the distinction between sales and marketing was not clear." However, by 2004, TCL marketers had developed a strong database on consumer purchasing behavior. They divided China into four income categories. The large affluent cities—Beijing, Shanghai, Guangzhou, Shenzhen—came first. In the next segment were cities such as Chengdu (Sichuan province), Nanjing (Jiangsu), and Xian (Shaanxi). After them were the less developed cities and counties. Most product-marketing initiatives were local, appealing to local tastes, Shi said: "Rural consumers like big things cheap. Urban buyers want flat screens and vivid color. In Beijing you will sell more plasma, LCD, and high-definition products. But the farmers out west are buying 21-inch or 25-inch CRT sets."

Despite increasing product segmentation, Shi said that TCL managers devoted little time to the development and use of a corporate brand. Instead, they acted opportunistically to capitalize on market trends. Nonetheless, a 2003 assessment by a Beijing agency valued the TCL name at RMB 26.7 billion, sixth among domestic brands.[21]

International Expansion

TCL's international experience began in 1998, when it took over a Luk's factory in Vietnam that had been operating for two years. After a few weeks in Vietnam evaluating the operation's potential, Yi realized that there was a local market for televisions that most of the Japanese and Taiwanese manufacturers in Vietnam producing for export had ignored. After informing Li that the business was worth pursuing, Yi built up market share in Vietnam before branching out into sales and then production in the Philippines, Indonesia, and Thailand. By 2004, TCL held 18% of Vietnam's television market. TCL also had 40% shares of the Pakistan, South Africa, and Sri Lanka TV markets. Yi explained how pivotal his Vietnam experience was as a springboard to Southeast Asia:

> There were lots of foreign firms there. The distribution system was still weak, so it made sense to develop our own marketing and sales channels. We did a market survey to get a sense of how Vietnam was different from China. Success in Vietnam gave us practice and the confidence to go on to Southeast Asia. We were so busy with these markets that none of us were worrying about entering the U.S. or Europe.

According to Yuan Xincheng, part of the rationale for international expansion was that "being number one in China is not enough, even if we have

half of the domestic market. The run-up to China's WTO [World Trade Organization] entry meant that TCL had to be ready for international competition." Zhao offered more idealistic goals: "The country can't be strong without top-level firms, but China has no brands besides Lenovo or Haier." Yi suggested some practical bases for internationalization:

> First, we are a Guangdong company: we are aware of the international opportunity. Second, domestic competition was strong. We were top five, but that was not enough to ensure strength. Third, we already had a certain domestic foundation to build upon. Finally, the July 1998 foreign exchange crisis in Southeast Asia reduced our exports through Hong Kong. That led us to want to go direct to understand local demand and reduce volatility.

TCL took a consistent approach when entering emerging markets, especially in the first years, emphasizing each market's characteristics and holding focused trials to see what worked. TCL also chose for international sales products with the most homogenous consumer purchasing characteristics across countries: mobile phones and televisions. White goods and consumer electronics sales, segments in which international tastes were more varied, were left for sale within China only. Usually TCL took a majority stake in local joint ventures. TCL also preferred niche and local markets to national coverage.

In doing so, TCL managers were clear that they were learning from the failed internationalization strategies of other Chinese firms, which in their view had been too aggressive. Changhong and Konka used local trading partners to enter the Russian market, for example, but did not work with them to ensure that the trading companies understood and promoted the Chinese brands. In contrast, TCL took its time to understand the local culture before entering the market. It also moved more deliberately. In Russia, for example, TCL initially worked with partners in Moscow and the Russian Far East to be sure that TCL product features would suit local tastes. Half of TCL's Russia sales were made under its own brand, and half were sold on an OEM basis.

---

[21]Ibid., p. 100.

Beyond Southeast Asia   In 2001, TCL managers began talking to potential partners in Korea, the United States, and Japan about ways to mount a major push into western markets. "We hired some retired managers from Toshiba, Matsushita, and LG to advise us, to help plan our globalization," Yuan recalled. In 2002, using primarily its Vietnam factory, TCL produced and sold 195,000 color TVs to emerging markets outside China, accounting for 15% of the group's total sales. The picture in the United States and Europe was very different, however. In the United States, distribution channels were more sophisticated. Margin pressures were strong, and expectations about product preparation and delivery date were demanding. "We can be docked 50% for missing delivery dates in Europe or the United States," Yi noted. At the same time, TCL managers were aware that Konka had "failed miserably" in its attempts to sell direct in the United States. Selling as an OEM was both a way to enter the U.S. market and a way to upgrade TCL skills through forced compliance with legal and consumer protection measures. "Through OEM we tested our products and learned about the U.S. market," Yi explained.

In Europe, low-cost manufacturers such as TCL ran up against antidumping laws, Shi recalled:

> We tried to enter the European market in 1989, but antidumping policies basically kept us out. Even in 2002, Chinese manufacturers were restricted to selling 400,000 units in the EU, a market with annual TV sales of 22 million units. We did try to sell through agents there, but we had no brand name or price advantage. In North America also, our sales through distributors were disappointing. We chose to go around these barriers through mergers and acquisitions.

In September 2002, TCL acquired Schneider, Germany's seventh-largest TV producer, for €8.2 million.[22] Based in Turkheim, Schneider had a 113-year history but had halted TV manufacture in May 2002. At the time, Schneider had 650 employees[23] and three TV production lines with total capacity of 1 million units.[24] Both sides saw the virtues of co-operation. TCL managers had correctly perceived that the EU TV sector would consolidate: older manufacturers were looking to escape the constraints of high operating costs, and partnering with Chinese manufacturers looked attractive. To Schneider, TCL underlined its uniqueness—customer focus, careful expansion, and no competing direct-sales presence in the EU. According to Yuan:

> Schneider's main problem was high costs. Given their assets and brands, the purchase price could have been very high. But because the local government didn't want the plants to close and create unemployment, our cost was very low. We thought we might integrate some of our low-cost technology, such as circuit boards, and let Schneider do the assembly in Spain or Portugal and sell the sets in Germany. A Schneider TV has German design and a recognizably German history. But the insides are not visible. We ship unassembled TVs designed to German taste to Schneider to -assemble locally. It preserves jobs, gives us a brand, and avoids antitariff barriers.

TCL planned to rehire 100 Schneider employees to operate two of the firm's three production lines.[25] In October 2003, however, Li Dongsheng conceded that the plans faced challenges. "Production in Germany is too expensive," he said. End-of-September sales within Europe reached €20 million, but at the time Li was still hoping for €100 million for 2003 on the basis of upcoming contracts despite Schneider's declining market share. Growth was to come from flat-screen as well as LCD or plasma TVs.[26] As of mid-2004, though Yuan said that unit sales doubled in its first year of ownership, TCL had not yet turned around Schneider's loss-making operations.[27] In late

[22]Ibid.

[23]Rico Ngai, "Update 2: TCL To Buy German TV Maker for 8.2 Million Euros," *Reuters News,* September 19, 2002, available from Factiva, www.factiva.com, accessed February 10, 2005.

[24]"China's Electronics Giant TCL Said To Acquire Germany's Schneider Electric Appliance Co.," *Interfax China Business News,* September 17, 2002, available from Factiva, www.factiva.com, accessed February 10, 2005.

[25]Rico Ngai, "Update 2: TCL To Buy German TV Maker for 8.2 Million Euros," *Reuters News,* September 19, 2002, available from Factiva, www.factiva.com, accessed February 10, 2005.

[26]Gerhard Hegmann, "Chinesen haben für Schneider ehrgeizige Pläne," *Financial Times Deutschland* (Hamburg), October 13, 2003, available from Factiva, www.factiva.com, accessed May 3, 2005.

[27]Jeannie Cheung, "TCL International: EPS Drag for Two Years," Credit Suisse First Boston Equity Research, August 12, 2004, p. 10.

September 2004, TCL did not renew the lease on Schneider's production facilities. German media reported that TV production would stop in 2005 in Turkheim and that 70 of the 120 employees would be laid off. The rest would continue to run marketing, distribution, and R&D in Bavaria.[28]

In 2003, TCL spent $5 million to buy Go Video in the United States, a 100-person, $200 million company that sold audio and portable audio equipment to retailers such as RadioShack. Previously, TCL sold CD players to Go Video on an OEM basis. "Mainly they have a good knowledge of sales channels," Yuan said.

The Dragon Tiger Plan

Televisions became TCL's biggest business in 1999, and from 2000 TCL executives targeted annual growth of 5% to 2010. "Regardless of sales numbers," Yuan qualified, "it became more important to become a top three global producer in all our product lines." To this end, TCL in 2003 embarked on a conscious policy of internationalization encapsulated by the Dragon Tiger plan. The plan stipulated that, by 2010, TCL would be among the world's top three TV and handset makers and, within China, among the top three producers of information technology (PCs and laptops), white goods (washers and dryers, refrigerators, and air conditioners), light switches and fixtures, electronic components, and the distribution of CD and DVD disks. In 2003 TCL was already China's largest distributor of CDs and DVDs, including Sony and Warner Music products.

The Thomson Venture To reach the global prominence set out in the Dragon Tiger plan required much more, however: a strong TCL presence in Europe and North America. Yuan elaborated:

> Our emerging market strategy is not appropriate for the U.S. and European markets, where distribution networks are well established and consumer behavior is relatively uniform. The Chinese model just won't work. So we decided to cooperate with Thomson to utilize the strengths of each company. Thomson has good R&D and knows the North American market well, so we gain sales channels, brands, and technology.

In January 2004, TCL and Thomson signed an agreement creating TTE (TCL Thomson Enterprise), a joint venture (JV) that combined the television assets of each. TTE would sell Thomson-branded sets in Europe, RCA sets in North America, and TCL and Thomson TVs everywhere else. TTE officially started operations in August 2004, and Li Dongsheng was made an Officer de La Legion D'Honneur in September, the highest honor France had yet bestowed upon a Chinese entrepreneur.[29] TCL owned 67% of TTE through TCL International, the Hong Kong-listed subsidiary of TCL Group. In addition to its television manufacturing and R&D assets, Thomson contributed €70 million, the option to either acquire Thomson's global DVD business for no additional consideration before December 2004 or receive another €20 million in Thomson assets up to €33 million in reimbursed restructuring costs, as well as other production and current assets, for a total of approximately €218 million. TCL in turn contributed its entire television business, including all fixed assets in China, Germany, and Southeast Asia, for a total of about €210 million. Said Yuan, "We acquired Thomson's plants in Poland, with a 3 million unit capacity, in Mexico (4 million units), and in Thailand. Together with this Thomson JV, we are producing about 22 million units of the 120 million sold each year, the most in the world."

The resulting entity would generate 34% of its revenue from China where the TCL brand dominated, another 34% from Thomson's 12% market share for its RCA brand in the Americas, and 28% from Thomson's 8% market share in Europe.[30] Separately, Thomson would receive commissions from TTE for the use of its sales and distribution

[28]Gerhard Hegmann, "Anzeichen für Produktionsstopp bei Schneider," *Financial Times Deutschland* (Hamburg), September 25, 2004, available from Factiva, www.factiva.com, accessed May 3, 2005.

[29]"News in Brief," *South China Morning Post,* September 4, 2004, available from Factiva, www.factiva.com, accessed May 4, 2005.
[30]Ibid., p. 9.

networks in Europe and the Americas. TCL would also pay Thomson royalties for its use of Thomson-patented technology.

Yuan explained the background of the deal:

In 1991–1992, we were procuring a lot of parts and technology from Thomson, so they understood our company and our growth very well. After Thomson privatized and restructured in 1998, their Asia regional head talked to chairman Li and I in 1999 about a joint venture. There was some divisiveness, as they wanted 51% of a new JV that would include our sales channels. We didn't accept this. We proposed two firms: one selling high-end products—LCD and high-definition TVs—that Thomson would hold 51% of, and one low-end company making CRT sets that TCL would own 51% of. But Thomson wanted 51% of each of those businesses as well.

After suspending talks with Thomson, our CEO devoted his attention to finding another global partner. We hoped for Japanese or Korean partners, but they were not as willing to share their knowledge as the Europeans. So we spent a lot of effort on this, starting in 2000. Philips at one point offered RMB 2 billion for our sales network. Though we rejected the offer, Philips still wanted us to ODM for them because their manufacturing costs in China were too high. Philips' ODM requirements were very stringent. We learned a lot from them about planning, communication, production, quality management, and operations. They felt that the faster we learned, the better their products would get. In globalization, you cannot skip this step of helping others produce. You can accelerate it, but you cannot skip it.

While TCL was working with Philips, Thomson managers held talks with Changhong and Konka that gave them a more realistic view of their own bargaining position with respect to the Chinese firms. In France, Thomson was privatized in 1998, and in 2003 its consumer electronics division lost €124 million on revenue of €3.2 billion. In China, Thomson therefore returned to TCL and agreed to its terms. **Exhibit 7** shows Thomson and TCL income statement data for 2002–2004; **Exhibit 8** shows quarterly change in TCL revenues.

TCL's deal with Thomson in some ways resembled Lenovo's $1.25 billion purchase of IBM's PC

division in December 2004.[31] Lenovo PCs would be marketed through IBM's worldwide distribution and sales network. (Eighty percent of PCs worldwide sold through retailers and other resellers.)[32] Lenovo also received the right to use the IBM name on its PCs for five years—it would retain the ThinkPad and ThinkCentre names permanently—and became IBM's preferred PC supplier. In turn, IBM became Lenovo's preferred supplier of services and financing. The deal made Lenovo the world's third-largest PC maker behind Dell and HP, with revenues of about $13 billion on 14 million units. By share, this amounted to about a third of the China PC market and 7% of the global PC market. The goal was to double profits in three years and to displace Dell or HP as number two by 2010. More immediately, a Gartner research note asserted that Lenovo would have to increase profits by 2% by the second half of 2006 to fund growth and an anticipated market downturn.[33] It was clear that both sides had room to learn: IBM learned to meet Chinese expectations after failing to send a car to the airport for arriving Lenovo executives, while Lenovo came to understand the symbolic value of retaining New York over Beijing as world headquarters for its newly global operations.[34]

---

[31]Lenovo announced the purchase of IBM's PC unit for $1.25 billion, split roughly evenly between cash and stock, and shouldered $500 million in IBM corporate debt. IBM retained an 18.9% stake in the company that in 2005 was reduced to 13.4% with a $350 million investment in Lenovo by a group of three private equity investment firms that each received a seat on the Lenovo Board. IBM's final consideration for the deal was therefore expected to amount to about $800 million in cash and $450 million in Lenovo shares. See "Lenovo Completes Acquisition of IBM's Personal Computer Division," *The Asian Banker*, May 15, 2005, available from Factiva, www.factiva.com, accessed May 17, 2005.

[32]Dexter Roberts and Louise Lee, "East Meets West," *BusinessWeek*, May 9, 2005, available from Factiva, www.factiva.com, accessed May 17, 2005.

[33]Andy McCue, "IBM PC Unit Sale Should Be Exploited, Says Gartner," Silicon.com, May 10, 2005, available from Factiva, www.factiva.com, accessed May 17, 2005.

[34]Dexter Roberts and Louise Lee, "East Meets West," *BusinessWeek*, May 9, 2005, available from Factiva, www.factiva.com, accessed May 17, 2005.

Exhibit 7   Thomson and TCL Income Statements, Year-End 2002–2004 (in $ million)

	2002	2003	2004
Thomson			
Sales	$9,630.8	$9,572.8	$9,925.5
Cost of sales	6,920.3	7,010.7	7,699.3
Gross profit	2,710.5	2,562.1	2,226.2
SG&A	1,261.2	1,267.5	1,290.0
R&D	353.6	333.8	397.3
Operating income	605.1	488.9	538.9
Restructuring charge			921.3
EBITDA	1,053.2	960.8	−419.7
Pretax income	393.3	109.8	−680.4
Net income	352.6	29.4	−789.7
TCL			
Sales	$1,562.6	$1,944.9	$3,165.6
Cost of sales	1,257.0	1,601.5	2,725.3
Gross profit	305.6	343.4	561.8
SG&A	238.5	250.4	474.1
R&D	7.9	7.3	30.9
Operating income	34.0	63.6	81.5
EBITDA	58.8	89.0	44.9
Pretax income	83.8	94.2	56.4
Net income	73.1	82.4	40.7

Source: Standard & Poor's, Global Vantage; company reports.
Note: Figures may not match those in **Exhibits 3, 4,** and **8** due to differences in data sources.

Exhibit 8   TCL Multimedia Quarterly Revenues, 2003–2004 (in HK$ million)

	Q1 2003	Q2 2003	Q3 2003	Q4 2003	Q1 2004	Q2 2004	Q3 2004	Q4 2004	2003	2004
TVs	2,961	2,219	3,095	4,148	3,307	2,810	5,963	9,715	12,422	21,795
Total	3,477	2,771	3,731	5,170	4,026	3,819	6,983	10,772	15,149	25,600
QoQ	−5%	−20%	35%	39%		−22%	−5%	83%	54%	
YoY	16%	16%	19%	41%	16%	38%	87%	108%	24%	69%

Source: Company data, cited in Jack Tse, "TCL Multimedia," Bear Stearns Equity Research, April 26, 2005, p. 4.
Note: HK$7.8 = US$1.

Just as Lenovo anticipated with IBM PCs, for the short term at least, TTE would focus on sales of the predominant product, the CRT set, said Shi:

We understand that Thomson's U.S. losses are significant, so we must keep their cash flow steady. For this

to happen, our CRT business must predominate. LCD and plasma are definitely the trend of the future, but right now volumes are small but investment is big. We are a follower in this area because we lack the core technologies, so we'll try to produce more cheaply and efficiently. We don't make our own panels, so it's not very practical for us to invest heavily in this area. However, we will invest heavily in a projection-TV technology that Thomson has already done a lot of research on and has some advantage.

"Our strategy is clear," Yuan explained. "We want to create value in consumer products, sell high-margin products at the high end, reduce costs by increasing unit sales volume, and run an efficient supply chain."

Looking Forward   TCL managers distinguished both competitive and integration challenges ahead of them. Universally, they perceived their strongest competitors as LG and Samsung, not firms from Taiwan or Japan. The Korean firms had advantages similar to TCL: efficiency, low costs, and aggressiveness. Li Yuguo summarized: "Japan lacks efficiency and is not aggressive, though it has advanced technology. Although they are very persistent, Japanese companies react very slowly. Taiwan only does supply-chain work. It has no other advantages—neither brand nor sales and marketing. But the Koreans are very fast; Samsung has already surpassed Sony."

Integration also posed challenges. Li Yuguo summarized his perceptions:

> Chinese companies are still behind in technology, but our biggest advantage is our flexibility and finesse. We find Thomson a bit slow in reacting. So now we have to see whether we can infuse TCL's flexibility into TTE to make it a strong organization. We already contribute our low-cost structure to Thomson, but can we bring TCL supply-chain efficiency to Thomson? We are targeting €50 million savings in North American sales.

Yi pointed to immediate problems in India, Russia, Singapore, Mexico, and Latin America, where TCL operations overlapped with Thomson's. In all locations, TCL aimed to eliminate unnecessary costs, become more aggressive and pragmatic, and improve supply-chain efficiency. To this end, TCL hired K. S. Cho, a South Korean executive, to head up the integration effort. Cho had previously overseen the integration of Samsung's

purchase of the assets of AST Computer, a U.S. firm. By mid-2004, international integration had already occupied 200 people at headquarters and was taking place elsewhere in the company as well: "We've seconded 1,000 R&D engineers at each other's companies so far, half here and half at Thomson." TCL's cost advantages were clear: Chinese hourly manufacturing wages averaged $1.01 in 2003 compared with $8.79 in France[35]— but this gap created thorny problems for TTE executives: top Chinese managers who headed the venture's only profitable operations there earned less than foreign subordinates in the unsteady U.S. and European segments.[36]

"We are large but not strong," conceded TCL managers, particularly compared to the scope, product diversity, and advertising budgets of LG and Samsung. To support TCL's overseas operations, China's Export-Import Bank made the company two loans, including one of RMB 6 billion.[37] But after three months of integration, senior TTE executives reported that "the challenges and difficulties are deeper than we thought"[38] and in spring 2005 pushed TTE's expected break-even date into 2006. In addition to the compensation gap, problems reportedly included linguistic barriers and unexpectedly high costs in European operations.[39] But the alternatives were worse, argued TTE finance chief Vincent Yan: "It would take five or 10 years to reach the level of recognition that Thomson and RCA have in their markets. And in that time, anything can happen. So instead of taking that risk, we took this risk."[40]

---

[35]Economist Intelligence Unit, *China Country Forecast,* January 2005; Economist Intelligence Unit, *Country Commerce (France),* 2004.

[36]Ibid.

[37]"Ex-Im Bank Grants TCL US$722 Million Loan," *Business Daily Update,* March 16, 2005, available from Factiva, www.factiva.com, accessed March 20, 2005.

[38]Evan Ramstad, "East Meets West in TV Sets: Huge Sino-French Venture Is Still Tuning the Relationship," *The Wall Street Journal,* November 26, 2004, p. A7.

[39]Ibid.

[40]Ibid.

Case 3-2   The Global Branding of Stella Artois

In April 2000, Paul Cooke, chief marketing officer of Interbrew, the world's fourth largest brewer, contemplated the further development of their premium product, Stella Artois, as the company's flagship brand in key markets around the world. Although the long-range plan for 2000–2002 had been approved, there still remained some important strategic issues to resolve.

A Brief History of Interbrew

Interbrew traced its origins back to 1366 to a brewery called Den Hoorn, located in Leuven, a town just outside of Brussels. In 1717, when it was purchased by its master brewer, Sebastiaan Artois, the brewery changed its name to Artois.

The firm's expansion began when Artois acquired a major interest in the Leffe Brewery in Belgium in 1954, the Dommelsch Brewery in the Netherlands in 1968, and the Brassiere du Nord in France in 1970. In 1987, when Artois and another Belgian brewery called Piedboeuf came together, the merged company was named Interbrew. The new company soon acquired other Belgian specialty beer brewers, building up the Interbrew brand portfolio

IVEY

Richard Ivey School of Business
The University of Western Ontario

with the purchase of the Hoegaarden brewery in 1989 and the Belle-Vue Brewery in 1990.

Interbrew then entered into a phase of rapid growth. The company acquired breweries in Hungary in 1991, in Croatia and Romania in 1994, and in three plants in Bulgaria in 1995. Again in 1995, Interbrew completed an unexpected major acquisition by purchasing Labatt, a large Canadian brewer also with international interests. Labatt had operations in the United States, for example, with the Latrobe brewery, home of the Rolling Rock brand. Labatt also held a substantial minority stake in the second largest Mexican brewer, Femsa Cervesa, which produced Dos Equis, Sol, and Tecate brands. Following this major acquisition, Interbrew went on, in 1996, to buy a brewery in the Ukraine and engaged in a joint venture in the Dominican Republic. Subsequently, breweries were added in China in 1997, Montenegro and Russia in 1998, and another brewery in Bulgaria and one in Korea in 1999.

Thus, through acquisition expenditures of US$2.5 billion in the previous four years, Interbrew had transformed itself from a simple Belgian brewery into one of the largest beer companies in the world. By 1999, the company had become a brewer on a truly global scale that now derived more than 90 per cent of its volume from markets outside Belgium. It remained a privately held company, headquartered in Belgium, with subsidiaries and joint ventures in 23 countries across four continents.

The International Market for Beer

In the 1990s, the world beer market was growing at an annual rate of one to two per cent. In 1998, beer consumption reached a total of 1.3 billion hectolitres (hls). There were, however, great regional differences in both market size and growth rates. Most industry analysts split the world market for beer between growth and mature markets. The mature markets were generally considered to be North America, Western Europe and Australasia.

Exhibit 1   The World Beer Market in 1998

Region	% of Global Consumption	Growth Index ('98 Vs 92)	Per Capita Consumption
Americas	35.1%	112.6	57
Europe	32.8%	97.7	54
Asia Pacific	27.2%	146.2	11
Africa	4.6%	107.7	8
Middle East/Central Asia	0.4%	116.0	2

Source: Canadean Ltd.

The growth markets included Latin America, Asia, Central and Eastern Europe including Russia. Although some felt that Africa had considerable potential, despite its low per capita beer consumption, the continent was not considered a viable market by many brewers because of its political and economic instability (see Exhibit 1).

Mature Markets   The North American beer market was virtually stagnant, although annual beer consumption per person was already at a sizeable 83 litres per capita (lpc). The Western European market had also reached maturity with consumption of 79 lpc. Some analysts believed that this consumption level was under considerable pressure, forecasting a decline to near 75 lpc over the medium term. Australia and New Zealand were also considered mature markets, with consumption at 93 lpc and 84 lpc, respectively. In fact, volumes in both markets, New Zealand in particular, had declined through the 1990s following tight social policies on alcohol consumption and the emergence of a wine culture.

Growth Markets   Given that average consumption in Eastern Europe was only 29 lpc, the region appeared to offer great potential. This consumption figure, however, was heavily influenced by Russia's very low level, and the future for the large Russian market was unclear. Further, some markets, such as the Czech Republic that consumed the most beer per person in the world at 163 lpc, appeared to have already reached maturity. Central and South America, on the other hand, were showing healthy growth and, with consumption at an average of 43 lpc, there was

believed to be considerable upside. The most exciting growth rates, however, were in Asia. Despite the fact that the market in this region had grown by more than 30 per cent since 1995, consumption levels were still comparatively low. In China, the region's largest market, consumption was only 16 lpc and 20 to 25 lpc in Hong Kong and Taiwan. Although the 1997 Asian financial crisis did not immediately affect beer consumption (although company profits from the region were hit by currency translation), demand in some key markets, such as Indonesia, was reduced and in others growth slowed. The situation, however, was expected to improve upon economic recovery in the medium term.

Beer Industry Structure

The world beer industry was relatively fragmented with the top four players accounting for only 22 per cent of global volume—a relatively low figure as compared to 78 per cent in the soft drinks industry, 60 per cent in tobacco and 44 per cent in spirits. This suggested great opportunities for consolidation, a process that had already begun two decades prior. Many analysts, including those at Interbrew, expected that this process would probably accelerate in the future. The driver behind industry rationalization was the need to achieve economies of scale in production, advertising and distribution. It was widely recognized that the best profit margins were attained either by those with a commanding position in the market or those with a niche position. However, there were several factors that mitigated the trend towards rapid concentration of the brewing industry.

One factor that slowed the process of consolidation was that the ratio of fixed versus variable costs of beer production was relatively high. Essentially, this meant that there was a limited cost savings potential that could be achieved by bringing more operations under a common administration. Real cost savings could be generated by purchasing and then rationalizing operations through shifting production to more efficient (usually more modern) facilities. This approach, however, required large initial capital outlays. As a result, in some markets with "unstable" economies, it was desirable to spread out capital expenditures over a longer period of time to ensure appropriate profitability in the early stages. A second factor that may have had a dampening effect on the trend towards industry consolidation was that local tastes differed. In some cases, beer brands had hundreds of years of heritage behind them and had become such an integral part of everyday life that consumers were often fiercely loyal to their local brew. This appeared to be a fact in many markets around the world.

Interbrew's Global Position

Through Interbrew's acquisitions in the 1990s, the company had expanded rapidly. During this period, the company's total volumes had increased more than fourfold. These figures translated to total beer production of 57.5 million hls in 1998 (when including the volume of all affiliates), as compared to just 14.7 million hls in 1992. Volume growth had propelled the company into the number four position among the world's brewers.

Faced with a mature and dominant position in the declining Belgian domestic market, the company decided to focus on consolidating and developing key markets, namely Belgium, the Netherlands, France and North America, and expansion through acquisition in Central Europe, Asia and South America. Subsequently, Interbrew reduced its dependence on the Belgian market from 44 per cent in 1992 to less

than 10 per cent by 1998 (total volumes including Mexico). Concurrently, a significant milestone for the company was achieved by 1999 when more than 50 per cent of its total volume was produced in growth markets (including Mexico). Interbrew had shifted its volume so that the Americas accounted for 61 per cent of its total volume, Europe added 35 per cent, and Asia Pacific the remaining four per cent.

Taken together, the top 10 markets for beer accounted for 86 per cent of Interbrew's total volume in 1998 (see Exhibit 2). The Mexican beer market alone accounted for 37 per cent of total volume in 1998. Canada, Belgium, the United States and the United Kingdom were the next most important markets. However, smaller, growing markets such as Hungary, Croatia, Bulgaria, and Romania had begun to increase in importance.

Adding to its existing breweries in Belgium, France and the Netherlands, Interbrew's expansion strategy in the 1990s had resulted in acquisitions in Bosnia-Herzegovina, Bulgaria, Canada, China, Croatia, Hungary, Korea, Montenegro, Romania, Russia, the Ukraine, the United States, in a joint venture in South Korea, and in minority equity positions in Mexico and Luxembourg. Through these breweries, in addition to those that were

Exhibit 2   Interbrew's 1998 Share of the World's Top 10 Markets

Rank	Country	Volume (000 HL)	Market Share
1	USA	3,768	1.6%
2	China	526	0.3%
3	Germany	—	—
4	Brazil	—	—
5	Japan	—	—
6	UK	3,335	5.5%
7	Mexico	21,269	45.0%
8	Spain	—	—
9	South Africa	—	—
10	France	1,915	8.4%
Total		30,813	3.6%

Source: Canadean Ltd.

covered by licensing agreements in Australia, Italy, Sweden and the United Kingdom, Interbrew sold its beers in over 80 countries.

Interbrew's Corporate Structure

Following the acquisition of Labatt in 1995, Interbrew's corporate structure was divided into two geographic zones: the Americas and Europe/Asia/Africa. This structure was in place until September 1999 when Interbrew shifted to a fully integrated structure to consolidate its holdings in the face of industry globalization. Hugo Powell, formerly head of the Americas division, was appointed to the position of chief executive officer (CEO). The former head of the Europe/Africa/Asia division assumed the role of chief operating officer, but subsequently resigned and was not replaced, leaving Interbrew with a more conventional structure, with the five regional heads and the various corporate functional managers reporting directly to the CEO.

Recent Performance

1998 had been a good year for Interbrew in terms of volume in both mature and growth markets. Overall, sales volumes increased by 11.1 per cent as most of the company's international and local brands maintained or gained market share. In terms of the compounded annual growth rate, Interbrew outperformed all of its major competitors by a wide margin. While Interbrew's 1998 net sales were up 29 per cent, the best performing competitor achieved an increase of only 16 per cent. Of Interbrew's increased sales, 67 per cent was related to the new affiliates in China, Montenegro and Korea. The balance was the result of organic growth. Considerable volume increases were achieved also in Romania (72 per cent), Bulgaria (28 per cent), Croatia (13 per cent), and the United States (14 per cent). While volumes in Western Europe were flat, duty-free sales grew strongly. In the U.S. market, strong progress was made by Interbrew's Canadian and Mexican brands, and Latrobe's Rolling Rock was successfully relaunched. In Canada, performance was strong, fuelled by a two per cent increase in domestic consumption. Labatt's sales of Budweiser (produced under license from Anheuser-Busch) also continued to grow rapidly.

Given that the premium and specialty beer markets were growing quickly, particularly those within the large, mature markets, Interbrew began to shift its product mix to take advantage of this trend and the superior margins it offered. A notable brand success was Stella Artois, for which total global sales volumes were up by 19.7 per cent. That growth came from sales generated by Whitbread in the United Kingdom, from exports, and from sales in Central Europe where Stella Artois volumes took off. The strong growth of Stella Artois was also notable in that it was sold in the premium lager segment. In Europe, Asia Pacific and Africa, Interbrew's premium and specialty beers, which generated a bigger margin, increased as a proportion of total sales from 31 per cent in 1997 to 33 per cent in 1998. This product mix shift was particularly important since intense competition in most markets inhibited real price increases.

Success was also achieved in the United States specialty beer segment where total volume had been growing at nine per cent annually in the 1990s. In 1998, Interbrew's share of this growing market segment had risen even faster as Labatt USA realized increased sales of 16 per cent. The other continuing development was the growth of the light beer segment, which had become over 40 per cent of the total sales. Sales of Labatt's Blue Light, for example, had increased and Labatt Blue had become the number three imported beer in the United States, with volumes up 18 per cent. Latrobe's Rolling Rock brand grew by four per cent, the first increase in four years. Interbrew's Mexican brands, Dos Equis, Tecate and Sol, were also up by 19 per cent.

Following solid volume growth in profitable market segments, good global results were realized in key financial areas. Net profit, having grown for each of the previous six consecutive years, was 7.7 billion Belgian francs (BEF) in 1998, up 43.7 per cent from the previous year. Operating profit also rose 7.9 per cent over 1997, from 14.3 to 15.4 BEF; in both the Europe/Asia/Africa region and the Americas, operating profit was up by 8.5 per cent and 4.9 per cent respectively. Further, Interbrew's EBIT margin was up 58.1 per cent as compared to the best performing competitor's figure of 17.0 per cent. However, having made several large investments in Korea and Russia, and exercising an option to increase its share of Femsa Cerveza in Mexico from 22 per cent to 30 per cent, Interbrew's debt-equity ratio increased from 1.04 to 1.35. As a result, interest payments rose accordingly.

Interbrew also enjoyed good results in volume sales in many of its markets in 1999. Although Canadian sales remained largely unchanged over 1998, Labatt USA experienced strong growth in 1999, with volumes up by 10 per cent. There was a positive evolution in Western European volumes as well, as overall sales were up by 6.5 per cent overall in Belgium, France and the Netherlands. Central European markets also grew with Hungary showing an increase of 9.6 per cent, Croatia up by 5.5 per cent, Romania by 18.9 per cent, Montenegro by 29 per cent, and Bulgaria with a rise of 3.6 per cent in terms of volume. Sales positions were also satisfactory in the Russian and Ukrainian markets. Further, while South Korean sales volume remained unchanged, volumes in China were 10 per cent higher, although this figure was still short of expectations.

Interbrew Corporate Strategy

The three facets of Interbrew's corporate strategy, i.e., brands, markets and operations, were considered the "sides of the Interbrew triangle." Each of these aspects of corporate strategy was considered to be equally important in order to achieve the fundamental objective of increasing shareholder value. With a corporate focus entirely on beer, the underlying objectives of the company were to consolidate its positions in mature markets and improve margins through higher volumes of premium and specialty brands. Further, the company's emphasis on growth was driven by the belief that beer industry

rationalization still had some way to go and that the majority of the world's major markets would each end up with just two or three major players.

Operations Strategy Cross fertilization of best practices between sites was a central component of Interbrew's operations strategy. In the company's two main markets, Belgium and Canada, each brewery monitored its performance on 10 different dimensions against its peers. As a result, the gap between the best and the worst of Interbrew's operations had narrowed decisively since 1995. Employees continuously put forward propositions to improve processes. The program had resulted in significantly lower production costs, suggesting to Interbrew management that most improvements had more to do with employee motivation than with pure technical performance. In addition, capacity utilization and strategic sourcing had been identified as two areas of major opportunity.

Capacity Utilization   Given that brewing was a capital-intensive business, capacity utilization had a major influence on profitability. Since declining consumption in mature markets had generated excess capacity, several of Interbrew's old breweries and processing facilities were scheduled to be shut down. In contrast, in several growth markets such as Romania, Bulgaria, Croatia and Montenegro, the opposite problem existed, so facilities in other locations were used more fully until local capacities were increased.

Strategic Sourcing   Interbrew had begun to rationalize its supply base as well. By selecting a smaller number of its best suppliers and working more closely with them, Interbrew believed that innovative changes resulted, saving both parties considerable sums every year. For most of the major commodities, the company had gone to single suppliers and was planning to extend this approach to all operations worldwide.

Market Strategy The underlying objectives of Interbrew's market strategy were to increase volume and to lessen its dependence on Belgium and Canada, its two traditional markets. Interbrew dichotomized its market strategy into the mature and growth market segments, although investments were considered wherever opportunities to generate sustainable profits existed. One of the key elements of Interbrew's market strategy was to establish and manage strong market platforms. It was believed that brand strength was directly related to a competitive and dedicated market platform (i.e., sales and distribution, wholesaler networks, etc.) to support the brand. Further, Interbrew allowed individual country teams to manage their own affairs and many felt that the speed of success in many markets was related to this decentralized approach.

Mature Markets   Interbrew's goals in its mature markets were to continue to build market share and to improve margins through greater efficiencies in production, distribution and marketing. At the same time, the company intended to exploit the growing trend in these markets towards premium and specialty products of which Interbrew already possessed an unrivalled portfolio. The key markets in which this strategy was being actively pursued were the United States, Canada, the United Kingdom, France, the Netherlands and Belgium.

Growth Markets   Based on the belief that the world's beer markets would undergo further consolidation, Interbrew's market strategy was to build significant positions in markets that had long-term volume growth potential. This goal led to a clear focus on Central and Eastern Europe and Asia, South Korea and China in particular. In China, for example, Interbrew had just completed an acquisition of a second brewery in Nanjing. The Yali brand was thereby added to the corporate portfolio and, together with its Jingling brand, Interbrew became the market leader in Nanjing, a city of six million people.

In Korea, Interbrew entered into a 50:50 joint venture with the Doosan Chaebol to operate the Oriental Brewery, producing the OB Lager and Cafri pilsener brands. With this move, Interbrew took the number two position in the Korean beer market with a 36 per cent share and sales of 5.1 million hls. The venture with Doosan was followed in December 1999 by the purchase of the Jinro Coors brewery. This added 2.5 million hls and increased Interbrew's market share to 50 per cent of total Korean volume. Thus, the Interbrew portfolio in Korea consisted of two mainstream pilsener brands, OB Lager and Cass, the two local premium brands, Cafri and Red Rock, and Budweiser, an international premium brand.

In Russia, Interbrew expanded its presence by taking a majority stake in the Rosar Brewery in Omsk, adding the BAG Bier and Sibirskaya Korona brands. Rosar was the leading brewer in Siberia with a 25 per cent regional market share, and held the number four position in Russia. New initiatives were also undertaken in Central Europe with acquisitions of a brewery in Montenegro and the Pleven brewery in Bulgaria, as well as the introduction of Interbrew products into the Yugoslavian market. Finally, although Interbrew had just increased its already significant investment in Mexico's second largest brewer from 22 per cent to 30 per cent, Latin America remained a region of great interest.

Brand Strategy   A central piece of Interbrew's traditional brand strategy had been to add to its portfolio of brands through acquisition of existing brewers, principally in growth markets. Since its goal was to have the number one or two brand in every market segment in which it operated, Interbrew concentrated on purchasing and developing strong local brands. As it moved into new territories, the company's first priority was to upgrade product quality and to improve the positioning of the acquired local core lager brands. In mature markets, it drew on the strength of the established brands such as Jupiler, Belgium's leading lager brand, Labatt Blue, the famous Canadian brand, and Dommelsch, an important brand in the Netherlands. In growth markets, Interbrew supported brands like Borsodi Sor in Hungary, Kamenitza in Bulgaria, Ozujsko in Croatia, Bergenbier in Romania,

Jingling in China, and OB Lager in Korea. In addition, new products were launched such as Taller, a premium brand in the Ukraine, and Boomerang, an alternative malt-based drink in Canada.

A second facet of the company's brand strategy was to identify certain brands, typically specialty products, and to develop them on a regional basis across a group of markets. At the forefront of this strategy were the Abbaye de Leffe and Hoegaarden brands and, to a lesser extent, Belle-Vue. In fact, both Hoegaarden and Leffe achieved a leading position as the number one white beer and abbey beer in France and Holland. The Loburg premium pilsener brand also strengthened its position when it was relaunched in France. Further, in Canada, Interbrew created a dedicated organization for specialty beers called the Oland Specialty Beer Company. In its first year of operation, the brands marketed by Oland increased its volumes by over 40 per cent. More specifically, sales of the Alexander Keith's brand doubled and the negative volume trend of the John Labatt Classic brand was reversed. The underlying message promoted by Oland was the richness, mystique and heritage of beer.

To support the regional growth of specialty beers, Interbrew established a new type of café. The Belgian Beer Café, owned and run by independent operators, created an authentic Belgian atmosphere where customers sampled Interbrew's Belgian specialty beers. By 1999, Belgian Beer Cafés were open in the many of Interbrew's key markets, including top selling outlets in New York, Auckland, Zagreb and Budapest, to name a few. The business concept was that these cafés were to serve as an ambassador of the Belgian beer culture in foreign countries. They were intended to serve as vehicles to showcase Interbrew's specialty brands, benefiting from the international appeal of European styles and fashions. Although these cafés represented strong marketing tools for brand positioning, the key factors that led to the success of this concept were tied very closely to the individual establishments and the personnel running them. The bar staff, for example, had to be trained to serve the beer in the right branded glass, at the right temperature, and

with a nice foamy head. It was anticipated that the concept of the specialty café would be used to support the brand development efforts of Interbrew's Belgian beers in all of its important markets.

The third facet of Interbrew's brand strategy was to identify a key corporate brand and to develop it as a global product. While the market segment for a global brand was currently relatively small, with the bulk of the beer demand still in local brands, the demand for international brands was expected to grow, as many consumers became increasingly attracted to the sophistication of premium and super-premium beers.

The Evolution of Interbrew's Global Brand Strategy

Until 1997, Interbrew's brand development strategy for international markets was largely *laissez faire*. Brands were introduced to new markets through licensing, export and local production when opportunities were uncovered. Stella Artois, Interbrew's most broadly available and oldest brand, received an important new thrust when it was launched through local production in three of the company's subsidiaries in Central Europe in 1997. This approach was consistent with the company's overall goals of building a complete portfolio in high growth potential markets.

By 1998, however, the executive management committee perceived the need to identify a brand from its wide portfolio to systematically develop into the company's global brand. Although the market for global brands was still small, there were some growing successes (e.g., Heineken, Corona, Foster's and Budweiser) and Interbrew believed that there were several basic global trends that would improve the viability of this class of product over the next couple of decades. First, while many consumers were seeking more variety, others were seeking lower prices. It appeared that the number of affluent and poor consumer segments would increase at the expense of the middle income segments. The upshot of this socioeconomic trend was that eventually all markets would likely evolve in such a way that demand for both premium and economy-priced beers would increase, squeezing the mainstream beers in the middle. A second trend was the internationalization of the beer business. As consumers travelled around the world, consuming global media (e.g., CNN, Eurosport, MTV, international magazines, etc.), global media were expected to become more effective for building brands. A global strategy could, therefore, lead to synergies in global advertising and sponsoring. In addition, the needs of consumers in many markets were expected to converge. As a result of these various factors, Interbrew believed that there would be an increasing interest in authentic, international brands in a growing number of countries. Interbrew had a wide portfolio of national brands that it could set on the international stage. The two most obvious candidates were Labatt Blue and Stella Artois.

The Labatt range of brands included Labatt Blue, Labatt Blue Light and Labatt Ice. To date, however, the exposure of these brands outside of North America had been extremely limited and they were not yet budding global brands. Of the total Labatt Blue volume in 1998, 85 per cent was derived from the Canadian domestic and U.S. markets, with the balance sold in the United Kingdom. The Labatt brands had been introduced to both France and Belgium, and production had been licensed in Italy, but these volumes were minimal. The only real export growth market for Labatt Blue appeared to be the United States, where the brand's volume in 1998 was some 23 per cent higher than in 1995, behind only Corona and Heineken in the imported brand segment. The Labatt Ice brand was also sold in a limited number of markets and, after the appeal of this Labatt innovation had peaked, its total volume had declined by more than 25 per cent since 1996. Total Labatt Ice volume worldwide was just 450,000 hls in 1998, of which 43 per cent was sold in Canada, 33 per cent in the United States, and 21 per cent in the United Kingdom.

Stella Artois as Interbrew's International Flagship Brand

The other potential brand that Interbrew could develop on a global scale was Stella Artois, a brand that could trace its roots back to 1366. The modern version of Stella Artois was launched in 1920 as a Christmas beer and had become a strong market leader in its home market of Belgium through the 1970s. By the 1990s, however, Stella's market position began to suffer from an image as a somewhat old-fashioned beer, and the brand began to experience persistent volume decline. Problems in the domestic market, however, appeared to be shared by a number of other prominent international brands. In fact, seven of the top 10 international brands had experienced declining sales in their home markets between 1995 and 1999 (see Exhibit 3).

Exhibit 3   Domestic Sales History of Major International Brands (million hectolitre)

	1995	1996	1997	1998
Budweiser (incl. Bud Light until '98)	69.48	71.10	72.43	40.00
Bud Light	n/a	n/a	n/a	30.00
Heineken	3.87	3.78	3.85	3.78
Beck's	1.68	1.71	1.72	1.78
Carlsberg	1.47	1.39	1.31	1.22
Stella Artois	1.08	1.00	0.96	0.92
Foster's	1.48	1.11	1.40	1.43
Kronenbourg	5.65	5.53	5.35	5.60
Amstel	2.30	2.23	2.21	2.18
Corona	12.89	14.09	14.80	15.18

Stella Artois had achieved great success in the United Kingdom through its licensee, Whitbread, where Stella Artois became the leading premium lager beer. Indeed, the United Kingdom was the largest market for Stella Artois, accounting for 49 per cent of total brand volume in 1998. Stella Artois volume in the U.K. market reached 2.8 million hls in 1998, a 7.6 per cent share of the lager market, and came close to 3.5 million hls in 1999, a 25 per cent increase over the previous year. By this time, over 32,000 outlets sold Stella Artois on draught.

Apart from the United Kingdom, the key markets for Stella Artois were France and Belgium, which together accounted for a further 31 per cent of total brand volume (see Exhibit 4). With these three markets accounting for 81 per cent of total Stella Artois volume in 1999, few other areas represented a significant volume base (see Exhibit 5). Beyond the top three markets, the largest market for Stella Artois was Italy, where the brand was produced under license by Heineken. Stella Artois volume in Italy had, however, declined slightly to 166,000 hls in 1998. Licensing agreements were also in place in Sweden and Australia, but volume was small.

Stella Artois was also produced in Interbrew's own breweries in Hungary, Croatia and Romania, with very pleasing 1998 volumes of 84,000 hls,

120,000 hls, and 60,000 hls, respectively. After only three years, the market share of Stella Artois in Croatia, for example, had reached four per cent—a significant result, given that the brand was a premium-priced product. In all Central European markets, Stella Artois was priced at a premium; in Hungary, however, that premium was lower than in Croatia and Romania where, on an index comparing Stella's price to that of core lagers, the indices by country were 140, 260 and 175 respectively.

Promising first results were also attained in Australia and New Zealand. Particularly in New Zealand, through a "seeding" approach, Interbrew and their local partner, Lion Nathan, had realized great success in the Belgian Beer Café in Auckland where the brands were showcased. After only two years of support, Stella Artois volume was up to 20,000 hls, and growing at 70 per cent annually, out of a total premium segment of 400,000 hls. Interbrew's market development plan limited distribution to top outlets in key metropolitan centres and priced Stella Artois significantly above competitors (e.g., 10 per cent over Heineken and 20 per cent over Steinlager, the leading domestic premium lager brand).

The evolution of the brand looked very positive as world volumes for Stella Artois continued to grow. In fact, Stella Artois volume had increased

Exhibit 4   1999 World Sales Profile of Stella Artois

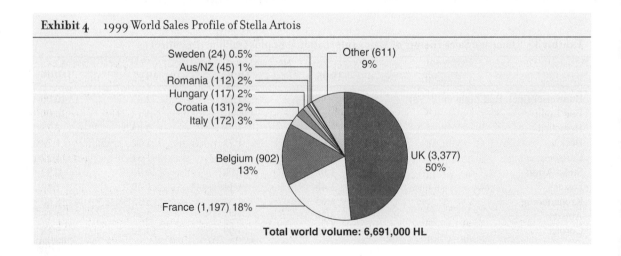

Sweden (24) 0.5%
Aus/NZ (45) 1%
Romania (112) 2%
Hungary (117) 2%
Croatia (131) 2%
Italy (172) 3%
Other (611) 9%
Belgium (902) 13%
UK (3,377) 50%
France (1,197) 18%

Total world volume: 6,691,000 HL

Exhibit 5   Stella Artois Sales Volume Summary (ooo hectolitre)

	1997	1998	1999
Production			
Belgium	965	921	902
France	1,028	1,110	1,074
Hungary	59	84	117
Croatia	54	120	133
Romania	17	60	112
Bulgaria	—	—	3
Bosnia-Herzegovina	—	—	2
Montenegro	—	—	0
Total Production	**2,123**	**2,295**	**2,343**
License Brewing			
Italy	162	166	172
Australia	6	11	22
New Zealand	7	11	22
Sweden	29	27	24
Greece	7	7	10
UK	2,139	2,815	3,377
Total Licensed	**2,350**	**3,037**	**3,627**
Export			
USA	—	—	7
Canada	—	—	5
Other Countries	92	49	202
Duty Free	245	389	507
Total Export	**337**	**438**	**721**
Overall Total	**4,810**	**5,770**	**6,691**

from 3.4 million hls in 1992 to a total of 6.7 million hls in 1999, a rise of 97 per cent. Ironically, the only market where the brand continued its steady decline was in its home base of Belgium. Analysts suggested a variety of reasons to explain this anomaly, including inconsistent sales and marketing support, particularly as the organization began to favor the rising Jupiler brand.

Overall, given Interbrew's large number of local brands, especially those in Mexico with very high volumes, total Stella Artois volume accounted for only 10 per cent of total Interbrew volume in 1999 (14 per cent if Femsa volumes are excluded).

Interbrew's strategy of nurturing a wide portfolio of strong brands was very different as compared to some of its major competitors. For example, Anheuser-Busch, the world's largest brewer, focused its international strategy almost exclusively on the development of the Budweiser brand. Similarly, Heineken sought to centre its international business on the Heineken brand and, to a lesser extent, on Amstel. While the strategies of Anheuser-Busch and Heineken focused primarily on one brand, there were also great differences in the way these two brands were being managed. For example, Budweiser, the world's largest brand by volume, had the overwhelming bulk of its volume in its home U.S. market (see Exhibit 6). Sales of the Heineken brand, on the other hand, were widely distributed across markets around the world (see Exhibit 7). In this sense, Heineken's strategy was much more comparable to that of Interbrew's plans for Stella Artois. Other brands that were directly comparable to Stella Artois, in terms of total volume and importance of the brand to the overall sales of the company, were Carlsberg and Foster's with annual sales volumes in 1998 of 9.4 million hls and 7.1 million hls, respectively. While Foster's was successful in many international markets, there was a heavy focus on sales in the United Kingdom and the United States (see Exhibit 8). Carlsberg sales volume profile was different in that sales were more widely distributed across international markets (see Exhibit 9).

Stella's Global Launch

In 1998, Interbrew's executive management committee settled on Stella Artois, positioned as the premium European lager, as the company's global flagship brand. In fact, the Interbrew management felt that stock analysts would be favorably disposed to Interbrew having an acknowledged global brand with the potential for a higher corporate valuation and price earnings (P/E) multiple.

As the global campaign got under way, it became clear that the organization needed time to adapt to centralized co-ordination and control of Stella Artois brand marketing. This was, perhaps,

Exhibit 6   Top 10 Brewers by International Sales

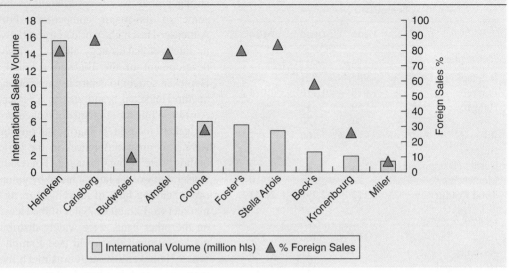

Exhibit 7   1998 Heineken World Sales Profile

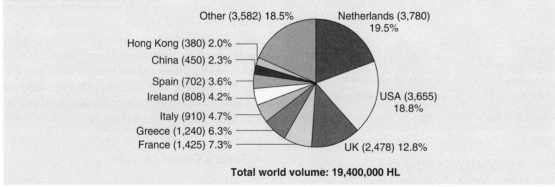

Total world volume: 19,400,000 HL

not unexpected given that Interbrew had until recently operated on a regional basis; the new centralized Stella brand management approach had been in place only since September 1998. In addition, there were often difficulties in convincing all parties to become part of a new global approach, particularly the international advertising campaign that was the backbone of the global plan for Stella Artois. Belgium, for example, continued with a specific local advertising program that positioned Stella as a mainstream lager in its home market, and in the United Kingdom, Whitbread maintained its "reassuringly expensive" advertising slogan that had already proved to be so successful. For other less-established markets, a global advertising framework was created that included a television concept and a series of print and outdoor executions. This base advertising plan was rolled out in

Exhibit 8   1998 Foster's World Sales Profile

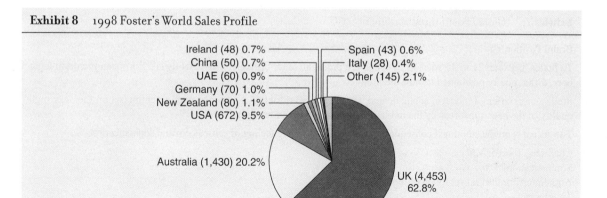

Ireland (48) 0.7%
China (50) 0.7%
UAE (60) 0.9%
Germany (70) 1.0%
New Zealand (80) 1.1%
USA (672) 9.5%

Spain (43) 0.6%
Italy (28) 0.4%
Other (145) 2.1%

Australia (1,430) 20.2%

UK (4,453)
62.8%

Total world volume: 7,079,000 HL

Exhibit 9   1998 Carlsberg World Sales Profile

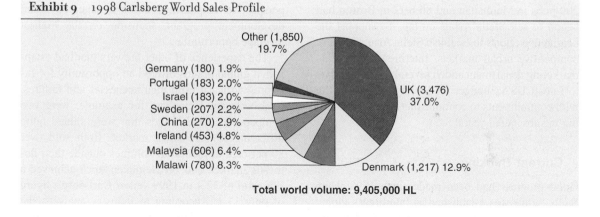

Other (1,850)
19.7%

Germany (180) 1.9%
Portugal (183) 2.0%
Israel (183) 2.0%
Sweden (207) 2.2%
China (270) 2.9%
Ireland (453) 4.8%
Malaysia (606) 6.4%
Malawi (780) 8.3%

UK (3,476)
37.0%

Denmark (1,217) 12.9%

Total world volume: 9,405,000 HL

1999 in 15 markets, including the United States, Canada, Italy, Hungary, Croatia, Bulgaria, Romania, New Zealand and France (with a slightly changed format) after research suggested that the campaign had the ability to cross borders. The objective of this campaign was to position Stella Artois as a sophisticated European lager. It was intended that Stella Artois should be perceived as a beer with an important brewing tradition and heritage but, at the same time, also as a contemporary beer (see Exhibit 10).

In 1998, an accelerated plan was devised to introduce Stella Artois to two key markets within the United States, utilizing both local and corporate funding. The U.S. market was believed to be key for the future development of the brand since it was the most developed specialty market in the world (12 per cent specialty market share, growing 10 per cent plus annually through the 1990s), and because of the strong influence on international trends. Thus, Stella Artois was launched in New York City and Boston and was well received by the demanding

Exhibit 10   Global Positioning Statement

Brand Positioning

To males, between 21 to 45 years of age, that are premium lager drinkers, Stella Artois is a European premium lager beer, differentially positioned toward the product.

Stella Artois offers a modern, sophisticated, yet accessible drinking experience with an emphasis on the very high quality of the beer supported by the noble tradition of European brewing.

The accent is on the emotional consequence of benefit: a positive feeling of self-esteem and sophistication.

Character, Tone of Voice
Sophistication
Authenticity, tradition, yet touch of modernity
Timelessness
Premium quality
Special, yet accessible
Mysticism
European

U.S. consumer and pub owner. Within 1999, over 200 pubs in Manhattan and 80 bars in Boston had begun to sell Stella Artois on tap. To support the heightened efforts to establish Stella Artois in these competitive urban markets, Interbrew's corporate marketing department added several million dollars to Labatt USA's budget for Stella Artois in 2000, with commitments to continue this additional funding in subsequent years.

Current Thinking

Good progress had been made since 1998 when Stella Artois was established as Interbrew's global brand. However, management had revised its expectations for P/E leverage from having a global brand. The reality was that Interbrew would be rewarded only through cash benefits from operational leverage of a global brand. There would be no "free lunch" simply for being perceived as having a global brand. In addition, in an era of tight fiscal management, it was an ongoing challenge to maintain the funding levels required by the ambitious development plans for Stella Artois. As a result, in early 2000 the prevailing view at Interbrew began to shift, converging on a different long-range

approach towards global branding. The emerging perspective emphasized a more balanced brand development program, focusing on the highest leverage opportunities.

The experience of other brewers that had established global brands offered an opportunity for Interbrew to learn from their successes and failures. Carlsberg and Heineken, for example, were two comparable global brands that were valued quite differently by the stock market. Both sold over 80 per cent of their total volumes outside their domestic market, and yet Heineken stock achieved a P/E ratio of 32.4 in 1999 versus Carlsberg's figure of only 17.1. According to industry analysts, the driving force behind this difference was that Heineken maintained a superior market distribution in terms of growth and margin (see Exhibit 11). The key lesson from examining these global brands appeared to be that great discipline must be applied to focus resources in the right places.

In line with this thinking, a long range marketing plan began to take shape that made use of a series of strategic filters to yield a focused set of attractive opportunities. The first filter that any potential market had to pass through was its long-term volume potential for Stella Artois. This volume

Exhibit 11   A Comparison of Carlsberg and Heineken

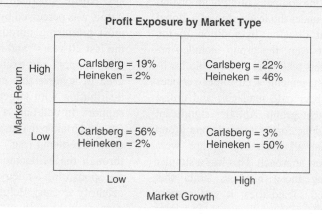

Profit Exposure by Market Type

		Low Market Growth	High Market Growth
Market Return	High	Carlsberg = 19% Heineken = 2%	Carlsberg = 22% Heineken = 46%
	Low	Carlsberg = 56% Heineken = 2%	Carlsberg = 3% Heineken = 50%

had to trace back to a large and/or growing market, the current or potential sizeable premium lager segment (at least five per cent of the total market), and the possibility for Stella Artois to penetrate the top three brands. The second screen was the potential to achieve attractive margins after an initial starting period of approximately three years. The third filter was whether or not a committed local partner was available to provide the right quality of distribution and to co-invest in the brand. The final screen was the determination that success in the chosen focus markets should increase leverage in other local and regional markets. For example, the size and stature of Stella Artois in the United Kingdom was a significant factor in the easy sell-in of Stella Artois into New York in 1999.

Once filtered through these strategic market development screens, the global branding plans for Stella Artois began to take a different shape. Rather than focus on national markets, plans emerged with an emphasis on about 20 cities, some of which Interbrew was already present in (e.g., London, Brussels, New York, etc.). This approach suggested that the next moves should be in such potential markets as Moscow, Los Angeles and Hong Kong. Some existing cities would receive

focused efforts only when distribution partner issues had been successfully resolved to solidify the bases for sustained long term growth. The major cities that fit these criteria provided the right concentration of affluent consumers, who would be attracted to Stella's positioning, thus providing scale for marketing and sales, investment leverage, as well as getting the attention and support of motivated wholesalers and initial retail customers. These venues would thereby become highly visible success stories that would be leverageable in the company's ongoing market development plans.

Thus, the evolving global branding development plan required careful planning on a city-by-city basis. Among the demands of this new approach were that marketing efforts and the funding to support them would have to be both centrally stewarded and locally tailored to reflect the unique local environments. A corporate marketing group was, therefore, established and was charged with the responsibility to identify top priority markets, develop core positioning and guidelines for local execution, assemble broadly based marketing programs (e.g., TV, print advertising, global sponsorships, beer.com content, etc.), and allocate resources to achieve the accelerated growth objectives in these targeted cities. To ensure an integrated development effort the company brought all pivotal resources together, under the leadership of a global brand development director. In addition to the brand management team, the group included regional sales managers who were responsible for licensed partner management, a customer services group, a Belgian beer café manager, and cruise business management group. Another significant challenge that faced the corporate marketing group was to ensure that all necessary groups were supportive of the new approach. This was a simpler undertaking among those business units that were wholly owned subsidiaries; it was a more delicate issue in the case of licensees and joint ventures. A key element of managing brands through a global organizational structure was that the head office team had to effectively build partnerships with local managers to ensure their commitment.

Fortunately, much of the initial effort to establish Stella Artois as a global brand had been done on a city-by-city basis and, as such, there was ample opportunity for Interbrew to learn from these experiences as the new global plan evolved. In the late 1990s, for example, Stella Artois was introduced to various Central European cities (e.g., Budapest, Zagreb, Bucharest and Sofia). In each of these cities, Interbrew's marketing efforts were launched when the targeted premium market was at an early stage of development. Further, distribution and promotion was strictly controlled (e.g., product quality, glassware, etc.) and the development initiatives were delivered in a concentrated manner (e.g., a media "blitz" in Budapest). In addition, results indicated that the presence of a Belgian Beer Café accelerated Interbrew's market development plans in these new areas. These early successes suggested that brand success could be derived from the careful and concentrated targeting of young adults living in urban centres, with subsequent pull from outlying areas following key city success.

The key lessons of these efforts in Central Europe proved to be very valuable in guiding the market development plan in New York City. In this key North American city, the rollout of Stella Artois was perceived by the analysts as "one of the most promising introductions in New York over the last 20 years" and had generated great wholesaler support and excitement. Among the tactics used to achieve this early success was selective distribution with targeted point of sale materials support. In addition, a selective media campaign was undertaken that included only prestigious outdoor advertising (e.g., a Times Square poster run through the Millennium celebrations). Similarly, the sponsoring strategy focused only on high-end celebrity events, Belgian food events, exclusive parties, fashion shows, etc. Finally, the price of Stella Artois was targeted at levels above Heineken, to reinforce its gold standard positioning. This concerted and consistent market push created an impact that resulted in the "easiest new brand sell" in years, according to wholesalers. The success of this launch also built brand and corporate credibility, paving the way to introductions in other U.S. cities as well as "opening the eyes" of other customers and distribution partners around the world.

To pursue this new global development plan over the next three years, a revised marketing budget was required. Given that the corporate marketing department was responsible for both the development of core programs as well as the selective support of local markets, the budget had to cover both of these key elements. To achieve these ends, total spending was expected to more than double over the next three years.

While great progress had been made on the global branding of Stella Artois, Cooke still ruminated on a variety of important interrelated issues. Among these issues was the situation of Stella Artois in Belgium—would it be possible to win in the "global game" without renewed growth in the home market? What specific aspirations should Interbrew set for Belgium over the next three years? Further, what expectations should Interbrew have of its global brand market development (e.g., volumes, profit levels, number of markets and cities, etc.)?

How should global success be measured? With respect to Interbrew's promotional efforts, how likely would it be that a single global ad campaign could be successful for Stella Artois? Was there a particular sponsorship or promotion idea that could be singled out for global leverage? And what role should the Internet play in developing Stella Artois as a true global brand?

Case 3-3   The Globalization of CEMEX

Geographic diversification enables us to operate in multiple regions with different business cycles. For the long term, we are trying to ensure that no one market accounts for more than one third of our business. Yet we do not diversify simply to balance cyclic downturns and upswings. We do not see volatility as an occasional, random element added to the cost of doing business in an interconnected global marketplace. We plan for volatility. We prepare for it. We have learned how to profit from it.

—Lorenzo Zambrano, CEO of CEMEX.[1]

In 1990, Cementos Mexicanos was a Mexican cement company that faced trade sanctions in its major export market, the United States. By the end of 1999, CEMEX operated cement plants in 15 countries, owned production or distribution facilities in a total of 30, and traded cement in more than 60. Non-Mexican operations accounted for nearly 60% of assets, slightly over 50% of revenues and 40% of EBITDA (earnings before interest, taxes, depreciation, and amortization) that year. CEMEX's sales revenues had increased from less than $1 billion in 1989 to nearly $5 billion in 1999, and it had become the third largest cement company in the world in terms of capacity, as well as the largest international trader. Growth had been achieved without compromising profitability: in the late 1990s, its ratio of EBITDA to sales ranged between 30% and 40%—ten to fifteen percentage points higher than its leading global competitors. In addition, the company was celebrated as one of the few multinationals from Latin America, and as a model user of information technology in an otherwise low-tech setting.

CEMEX executives sometimes characterized the company's international operations as a "ring of grey gold," comprising commitments to high-growth markets, mostly developing and mostly falling in a band that circled the globe north of the Equator. By the end of 1990s, the addition of countries such as Indonesia and Egypt to the ring had prompted discussions about the scope and speed of CEMEX's international expansion. So had the hostile bid, in early 2000, by Lafarge, the second-largest cement competitor worldwide in cement for Blue Circle, the sixth largest. Hector Medina, CEMEX's Executive Vice President of Planning and Finance, likened the takeover struggle to "ripples in an agitated environment" that could have significant implications for the other cement majors.

This case begins with a brief overview of the cement industry and international competition within it. It then describes the globalization of CEMEX and how it was managed.

Professor Pankaj Ghemawat and Research Associate Jamie L. Matthews prepared this case drawing, in part, on a course paper by Pau Cortes, Heriberto Diarte and Enrique A. Garcia. HBS cases are developed solely as the basis for class discussion. Cases are not intended to serve as endorsements, sources of primary data, or illustrations of effective or ineffective management.

[1]CEMEX 1998 annual report, p. 4.

Exhibit 1   How CEMEX Makes Cement

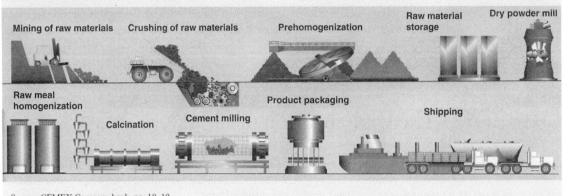

Source: CEMEX Company book, pp. 18–19.

The Cement Industry

Cement had been used since antiquity as a binding agent that hardened when mixed with water. It was first made in its modern form in England during the early part of the 19th century. The production process, which remained broadly unchanged, involved burning a blend of limestone (or other calcareous rocks) and smaller quantities of materials containing aluminum, silicon, and iron in a kiln at high temperatures to yield marble-sized pellets of "clinker." Clinker was then ground with gypsum and other minerals to yield cement, a fine gray powder. The mixture of cement, aggregates, and water that hardened into a rocklike mass after hydration was known as concrete. Concrete could be mixed "on site" where it was to be used, or it could be obtained in "ready-mix" form from a central drum at the plant or a ready-mix truck.

Supply   Since limestone, clay and the other raw materials required were abundant in many regions of the world, cement could usually be produced locally. Cement companies often owned raw material quarries and located their production facilities close by to minimize materials handling. The production technology was continuous process, consisted of a number of stages (see **Exhibit 1**) and

was marked by high capital- and energy-intensity. It was also considered relatively mature: no major innovations had been recorded in the last 20 years. The minimum efficient scale (MES) for a cement plant approximated 1 million tons of capacity per year. New capacity cost about $120–$180 per ton, depending on local factors such as the cost of land, environmental legislation, and the need for ancillary equipment and infrastructure, including investment in quarries and kilns. A cement plant's assets were largely dedicated to the production of cement and might last for decades. Operating costs typically ranged from $20–$50 per ton, with labor accounting for well under $10 per ton.[2] Transportation costs, in contrast, could account for as much as one-third of total delivered costs.

High transportation costs in relation to production costs meant that there was only a limited distance within which a plant could deliver cement at competitive prices. Road transportation was the most expensive, and limited the effective distribution radius to 150–300 miles.[3] Waterborne transportation was the most economical and, as a

[2]Merrill Lynch, "Ownership Changes in Asian Cement," December 3, 1999, p. 117.
[3]"ING Barings," *European Cement Review*, February 2000, p. 24.

Exhibit 2   Cost Structure of Asian Exports to the United States

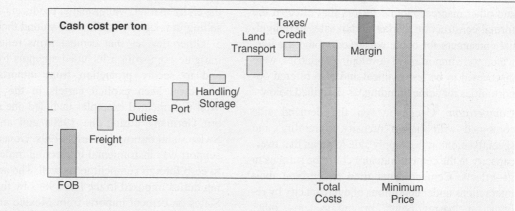

Source: Holderbank, as quoted in "The Global Cement, Aggregates and Plasterboard Analyser," Warburg Dillon Read, September 1999, p. 229.

result of innovations since the mid-1950s, had led to a substantial expansion of MES.[4] New systems of loading and unloading barges were introduced and specialized ships for carrying cement were developed. As a result, cement producers began to establish much larger plants that shipped cement to distribution terminals in distant markets as well as serving local ones. Still, a host of other costs had to be layered on top of the costs of ocean freight for long-distance trade to take place (see **Exhibit 2**). In the late 1990s, international seaborne traffic in cement and clinker averaged about 50 million tons per year. It was believed that about 10 million tons of this traffic was carried by small vessels on short coastal or estuarial voyages, and about 40 million tons by oceangoing vessels.[5]

Demand   Cross-country comparisons indicated that the long-run demand for cement was directly related to GDP, with per capita consumption increasing up to the $20,000-plus per capita income

[4]Hervé Dumez and Alain Jeunemaître, *Understanding and Regulating the Market at a Time of Globalization: The Case of the Cement Industry,* p. 113.

[5]Drewry Shipping Consultants, *Cement Shipping: Opportunities in a Complex and Volatile Market,* January 1998.

mark and then declining very gradually. Numerous other local attributes affected cement demand as well. Rainfall had a negative effect since it made cement-based construction more difficult and increased the likelihood of using substitutes such as wood or steel instead. Population density had a positive effect, as higher density led to taller buildings and more complex infrastructure. Demand also tended to be higher in areas with a warm climate and lower under extremes of heat or cold. Demand generally decreased with a long coastline, since more sea transport meant fewer roads, and increased with the share of governmental expenditures in GDP. CEMEX forecast total world demand to grow at slightly under 4% per annum through 2010. Demand growth was expected to be highest in the developing Asian economies, Central America, the Caribbean, and sub-Saharan Africa, where it would approach or exceed 5%, and lowest in Western Europe and North America, where it would be closer to 1%.

In the short run, cement demand varied directly with GDP and, even more reliably, with construction expenditure/investment. As a result, construction plans could be used to develop short-run forecasts for cement demand. However, the cyclicality of the construction sector made medium-run forecasts somewhat dicey. Bulk sales were very sensitive to GDP growth, interest rates, and other macroeconomic factors that affected the formal construction market. Retail sales to individual consumers for home construction and the like, which were important in developing countries, were discovered to be less cyclical and also offered opportunities for some branding, as described below.

Competition Cyclicality on the demand side combined with capital-intensity, durability, and specialization on the supply side to mean that overcapacity in the cement industry could be ruinous in its effects. Cement firms tried to cushion their interactions under conditions of overcapacity by relying on "basing point" pricing systems, other leadership strategies, and even direct restraints on competition.

The basing point system had been common in the United States until the end of World War II, and in Europe until much more recently. Under this system, the leading firm set a base price, and the other firms calculated their prices by taking the base price and increasing it by the cost of transportation from the leading firm's plant to the delivery point. This offered

a transparent price structure in the absence of hidden discounts, and let the biggest players sell throughout the entire market, while smaller producers ended up selling in relatively small areas around their plants.

Other devices that cement firms relied on to mitigate competition included attempts to collude and to secure protection from imports. There had even been explicit cartels in the industry. Well-documented examples included one in southern Germany during the 1980s and another in Switzerland during the early 1990s. Governmental support was instrumental in erecting trade barriers to curb foreign competitors as well. The antidumping duties imposed in the late 1980s by the United States on cement imports from Mexico are an example that will be discussed in some detail later on.

International Competitors By 1999, six major international competitors had emerged in cement: Holderbank, Lafarge, CEMEX, Heidelberger, Italcementi, and Blue Circle. Given their geographic diversification, these competitors tended to be outperformed in any given year by competitors focused on local markets that happened to be "booming" (see **Exhibit 3**), but they had achieved

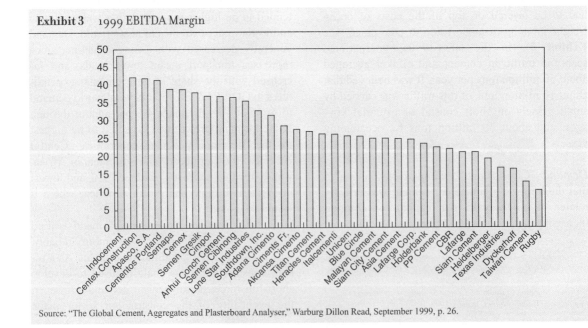

Exhibit 3   1999 EBITDA Margin

Source: "The Global Cement, Aggregates and Plasterboard Analyser," Warburg Dillon Read, September 1999, p. 26.

Exhibit 4 Selected Data on Global Competitors (December 1999)

Company	Holderbank	Lafarge	CEMEX	Heidelberger	Italcementi	Blue Circle
Accounting Data						
Sales (US$ m)	7,618	10,552	4,828	6,404	3,414	3,604
Cement volume (m tons)	74.6	64.3	39.1	46.0	37.8	NA
EBIT (US$ m)	1,066	1,766	1,436	645	511	466
EBITDA (US$ m)	1,785	2,446	1,791	1,195	838	684
CAPEX (US$ m)	784	1,144	262	540	310	295
Free Cash Flow (US$ m)	144	511	862	487	200	(294)
Net debt (US$ m)	4,767	5,422	4,794	2,957	1,731	538
Net debt/EBITDA	.7	2.2	2.7	2.5	2.1	0.8
Total debt to capitalization	54.1%	46.5%	44.1%	51.3%	43.0%	31.0%
Interest coverage	4.6	6.6	3.6	4.8	6.8	5.7
Stock Market Data[a] (to Dec. '99)						
Market value (US$ m)	11,122	12,132	7,203	4,209	2,488	4,707
Profitability of stock US$b (12 mth)	16%	22%	114%	3%	9%	12%
TEV[c] (US$ m)	17,015	19,157	12,500	7,373	5,050	5,593
TEV adjusted/ton (US$)[d]	160	130	172	86	90	93
Capacity Data						
Footprint[e] (m tons)	140	107	85	71	55	45
Degree of control of footprint	72%	79%	77%	75%	98%	97%
Controlled capacity (m tons)	101	85	65	53	54	44
Number of Countries	53	38	15	33	14	14

Sources: Annual Reports; Datastream; JP Morgan; CEMEX.
[a] End-of-period exchange rate used for calculations.
[b] For Holderbank, class B stock; for CEMEX, New CPO.
[c] TEV defined as total enterprise value (debt plus equity).
[d] Excluding non-cement assets for Lafarge (35%), Heidelberger (10%) and Blue Circle (25%).
[e] Footprint defined as total capacity in which a given company has a significant stake.

significantly greater stability in their returns. In aggregate, the six majors controlled 500 million tons of capacity, representing slightly over one-quarter of the world total, or over one-third of the total excluding China. The six-firm concentration ratio had been only 12% in 1988, with Votorantim of Brazil edging out CEMEX for the sixth spot.[6]

[6]Podolny, Joel, John Roberts, Joon Han, and Andrea Hodge, 1999, "CEMEX, S.A. de C.V.: Global Competition in a Local Business," Stanford, CA: Stanford University. ECCH #IB17.

In 1999, each of the six major international competitors still had clearly identifiable national origins and controlled a significant share of its home market. But each had also come to operate production facilities in anywhere between a dozen and several dozen countries around the world. **Exhibit 4** supplies financial data on the six majors, and **Exhibit 5** summarizes their capacity shares in a number of major markets.

Although some of the majors, such as Holderbank, had operated in several countries for decades,

Exhibit 5   Capacity Shares of the Big 6 in Selected Markets

Country	Holderbank	Lafarge	CEMEX	Heidelberger	Italcementi	Blue Circle
Japan	0.0%	0.0%	0.0%	0.0%	0.0%	0.0%
Korea	0.0%	12.0%	0.0%	0.0%	0.0%	0.0%
Taiwan	0.0%	0.0%	0.0%	0.0%	0.0%	0.0%
Indonesia	0.0%	2.6%	43.7%	0.0%	0.0%	0.0%
Malaysia	0.0%	6.6%	0.0%	3.9%	0.0%	46.4%
Philippines	37.5%	20.5%	22.0%	0.0%	0.0%	16.7%
Thailand	25.3%	0.0%	0.0%	0.0%	13.2%	0.0%
India	1.4%	0.3%	0.0%	0.0%	0.0%	0.0%
South Africa	36.3%	25.8%	0.0%	0.0%	0.0%	0.0%
Egypt	5.4%	5.0%	16.9%	0.0%	0.0%	3.3%
Greece	0.0%	0.0%	0.0%	0.0%	5.5%	58.9%
Poland	0.0%	21.2%	0.0%	22.4%	0.0%	0.0%
Turkey	0.0%	8.3%	0.0%	17.3%	9.2%	0.0%
France	12.6%	33.9%	0.0%	26.8%	26.4%	0.0%
Germany	6.6%	7.0%	0.0%	25.3%	0.0%	0.0%
Italy	6.2%	5.0%	0.0%	0.0%	36.9%	0.0%
Portugal	0.0%	0.0%	0.0%	0.0%	0.0%	0.0%
Spain	9.9%	19.3%	26.5%	0.0%	6.6%	0.0%
UK	0.0%	0.0%	0.0%	23.8%	0.0%	50.3%
Canada	19.1%	32.9%	0.0%	20.4%	11.2%	13.8%
US	13.5%	8.3%	1.8%	11.2%	4.6%	6.2%
Argentina	37.6%	11.2%	0.0%	0.0%	0.0%	0.0%
Brazil	10.0%	13.4%	0.0%	0.0%	0.0%	0.0%
Mexico	19.2%	4.3%	64.6%	0.0%	0.0%	0.0%
Venezuela	24.5%	23.6%	40.6%	0.0%	0.0%	0.0%

Source: CEMEX

internationalization, particularly in an interregional sense, did not begin until the 1970s. This was when European players began to penetrate the United States. During the 1960s and 1970s, the U.S. cement industry had fallen into a crisis as profitability dropped with the collapse in prices, and domestic firms responded by lowering investment in cement and diversifying into other lines of business. This resulted in shortages in some regional markets and provided an opening for European cement firms that had remained strong and were looking to expand. By 2000, European groups controlled 65% of the U.S. market.

Cross-border investment in the United States had been concentrated in certain periods—most recently, 1985–1988 and 1991–1993—instead of trickling in more continuously. Such waves were characteristic of cross-border investment in other regions as well, given the cement majors' emphasis on buying existing capacity rather than adding new capacity to enter new markets (see **Exhibit 6**). Obviously, acquisitions were most attractive to them when the market values of target companies were less than their underlying values—a condition more likely to be fulfilled at the bottom of the local economic cycle rather than the top. The underlying values of acquired franchises could be assessed by estimating their average profitability, capacity utilization, weighted average cost of capital and, probably most problematically, expected long-run

Exhibit 6   Waves of Acquisitions

Period	Region
1985–1988	U.S./Canada
1987–1990	Latin America
1989–1991	Mediterranean
1991–1993	U.S.
1990–1994	E. Europe
1995–1997	Latin America
1996–1998	E. Europe
1998 onwards	SE. Asia
1999 onwards	W. Europe

Source: Adapted by casewriters from ING Barings, European
Cement Review, February 2000.

growth rates. See **Exhibit 7** for an attempt by an investment bank to perform such calculations at the country level. In practice, of course, such country-level analyses had to be supplemented with target-specific considerations such as the target's cost position and market share, and the kind of base it afforded for further cost-reduction and expansion.

Starting in 1997 and particularly after the summer of 1998, the largest and most concentrated wave of cross-border investment ever began in South East Asia. The international players had their eye on the market for many years, but had been unable to justify the entry premium—some companies in the region had been valued at up to $300 per ton of capacity on an enterprise value basis! The Asian crisis that began in 1997 changed the situation dramatically and gave the majors the opportunity they were waiting for. The six majors' Asian cement deals through fall 1999 are summarized in **Exhibit 8.** They quickly increased their share of capacity in Asia, excluding China, from less than 20% to about 60%.

Of the leading international competitors in cement, two, Holderbank and Lafarge, were larger than CEMEX. Holderbank had cement operations on five continents and in more than 50 countries, making it the most global as well as the largest international competitor. Its globalization strategy could be traced back to the early 1920s when the company (formed in 1912) first moved out of

Switzerland and into neighboring France, Belgium, and the Netherlands. The company's 1999 sales were $7,618 million and its EBIT was $1,066 million. Cement accounted for 68% of 1999 sales and concrete and aggregates for 24%.

Lafarge was ranked second in the global cement market and also had strong positions in other building such as plaster, aggregates, concrete, and gypsum. Its 1999 sales were $10,552 million and EBIT was $1,766 million. Cement accounted for 35% of 1999 sales and concrete and aggregates for another 30%. Lafarge was not as focused on emerging markets as some of the other global players. In February 2000, it mounted a hostile bid, valued at nearly $5.5 billion, for Britain's Blue Circle, the sixth-largest cement competitor. Motives for the deal included achieving a certain size in order to remain visible and attractive to investors, expanding cash-flow and, relatedly, geographic presence and, probably, dislodging Holderbank from the top spot in the global cement industry. However, by May, Lafarge had managed to attract only 44% of Blue Circle's shares with its aggressively priced offer.

CEMEX

By the year 2000, CEMEX had become the third largest cement company in the world with approximately 65 million tons of capacity (see **Exhibit 9** for historical financial data). CEMEX traced its origins back to 1906 when the Cementos Hidalgo cement plant was opened, with a capacity of less than 5,000 tons per year, in northern Mexico, near Monterrey. In 1931, it was merged with Cementos Portland Monterrey, founded by Lorenzo Zambrano, to form Cementos Mexicanos, later renamed CEMEX. Over the next half-century, the company expanded its capacity to about 15 million tons, and was well on its way to becoming Mexico's market leader by the early 1980s.

In 1985, Lorenzo Zambrano, scion of the Zambrano family that still controlled CEMEX and a grandson as well as namesake of the company's founder, took over as CEO. In his first few years at the helm, CEMEX continued to grow by constructing

Exhibit 7 Market Statistics and Valuations for Selected Countries[a]

Country	Ex-plant Price per Ton (US$)	Cash Cost per Ton (US$)	EBITDA per Ton (US$)	Risk Free Rate (%)	Equity Risk Premium (%)	Market Gearing (%)	WACC (%)	Value/Ton of Demand (US$)	Domestic Demand (m tons)	Domestic Capacity (m tons)	Value/Ton of Capacity (no growth) (US$)	Trend Growth (%)	Value/Ton of Capacity (trended) (US$)
Japan	48	38	10	1.8	5.0	50.0	4.8	208	72.8	97.0	156	0.1	160
Korea	50	33	17	8.5	8.0	20.0	15.1	113	47.6	62.1	86	5.0	129
Taiwan	58	37	21	5.7	8.0	25.0	12.0	176	20.5	24.5	147	3.0	196
Indonesia	41	23	18	12.0	8.0	50.0	16.5	109	18.1	45.3	44	7.5	80
Malaysia	41	28	13	8.0	8.0	25.0	14.3	90	8.2	17.5	42	7.8	93
Philippines	49	34	15	14.0	8.0	50.0	18.5	81	12.5	20.4	50	8.0	88
Thailand	48	26	22	10.0	8.0	40.0	15.2	145	25.6	58.0	64	8.0	135
India	52	38	14	9.5	8.0	40.0	19.0	74	80.8	85.0	70	7.5	116
S. Africa	55	37	18	15.0	6.0	15.0	20.3	89	8.8	12.0	65	0.9	68
Egypt	53	33	20	10.0	8.0	0.0	18.0	111	24.7	23.0	119	5.9	178
Greece	58	30	28	6.4	6.0	20.0	11.4	246	8.5	15.0	139	1.5	161
Poland	38	28	10	9.5	6.0	20.0	14.5	69	13.8	16.3	58	5.0	89
Turkey	40	26	14	10.3	8.0	0.0	18.3	77	36.4	61.0	46	6.5	71
France	78	49	29	4.7	4.0	30.0	7.8	372	19.1	28.1	253	-1.5	211
Germany	72	51	21	4.6	4.0	25.0	7.9	268	37.0	51.0	194	1.0	221
Italy	55	38	17	4.8	4.0	25.0	8.1	211	35.0	52.5	141	-0.3	136
Portugal	66	40	26	4.8	5.0	10.0	9.4	277	10.0	9.6	289	0.0	289
Spain	64	40	24	4.8	5.0	10.0	9.4	255	31.0	39.3	201	2.7	283
UK	74	51	23	5.4	4.0	10.0	9.1	253	12.8	14.4	225	-0.2	219
Argentina	62	40	22	12.0	8.0	40.0	17.2	128	8.2	9.5	110	3.0	134
Brazil	59	39	20	13.0	8.0	40.0	18.2	110	40.1	45.8	96	5.0	133
Mexico	96	40	56	12.0	8.0	50.0	16.5	339	25.7	44.0	198	2.5	233
Venezuela	95	35	60	15.0	8.0	20.0	21.6	278	4.5	8.6	145	-0.5	142
Canada	67	42	25	5.5	4.0	0.0	9.5	263	8.6	15.2	148	0.5	157
US	69	48	21	5.7	4.0	0.0	9.7	216	107.1	97.3	238	1.0	266

Source: Adapted by casewriters from ING Barings, European Cement Review, February 2000, p. 29.

[a] Franchise value represents the theoretical value of one ton of capacity (assuming all sales are made domestically). The first step in its derivation is to obtain the capital value of cash flow generated in perpetuity by one ton of production. This value is calculated by taking EBITDA per ton ($) and dividing by the weighted average cost of capital. The second step is to find the ratio of domestic demand to domestic supply. Dividing the value of one ton of production by the ratio calculated in the second step gives the value of one ton of capacity. (The idea is that if domestic demand exceeds available supply, the value of owning capacity is greater than the value suggested by current EBITDA alone.) The final step is to adjust franchise value for growth in domestic demand, trend growth, which is defined as the average of rolling averages for the previous 5, 10, and 20 years and is therefore less vulnerable to short-run fluctuations in growth rates.

Exhibit 8 Cement Majors' Asian Deals after the Asian Crisis

	Country	Date	Stake %	Price (US$ m)	Capacity (m tons)	Value/Ton (US$)	Source
Holderbank							
Union Cement	Philippines	Jul-98	40%	210	5.8	146	A
Alsons Cement	Philippines	Jan-99	25%	22	2.5	130	B
Tengara Cement	Malaysia	Jun-98	70%	28	1.1	42	A
Siam City Cement	Thailand	Aug-98	25%	153	12.3	95	A
Huaxin Cement	China	Jan-99	23%	20	1.4	61	A
Total				433	23.1	107	
Lafarge							
Republic Cement	Philippines	Feb-98	14%	25	1.6	119	A
Continental Cement and South East Asia			100%				
Cement	Philippines	Oct-98	64%	460	4.6	132	C
Haifa Cement	Korea	Jul-99	33%	100	7.4	68	A
Andalas	Indonesia	n/a	16%	10	1.2		D
Tisco	India	1999	100%	127	0.3	107	A
Total[20]				712	13.9	109	
CEMEX							
Rizal and Solid Cement	Philippines	Dec 97, Nov 98	70%	219	2.8	166	C
Apo Cement	Philippines	Jan-99	100%	400	3.0	164	A
Semen Gresik	Indonesia	mid-98	14%	115	20.1	55	A
Semen Gresik	Indonesia	Nov-98	8%	49	20.1	56	A
Semen Gresik	Indonesia	1999	4%	28	20.1	58	A
Total				811	25.9	109	
Italcementi							
Jalaprathan Cement	Thailand	Oct-98	55%	26	1.6	58	A
Asia Cement	Thailand	Jul-99	53%	180	4.8	131	A
Total				206	6.4	112	
Blue Circle							
Iligan Cement Corp	Philippines	Jul-99	95%	53	0.5	109	C
Kedah Cement	Malaysia	Oct-98	65%	185	3.5	164	A
APMC	Malaysia	Dec-98	50%	309	4.7	157	A
Inflow from Minorities in Malaysian rights	Malaysia	Dec-98	65%	−118			D
Republic Cement	Philippines	1998	54%	90	1.6	138	C
Fortune Cement	Philippines	Jul-98	20%	35	1.9	114	A
Fortune Cement	Philippines	Jan-99	31%	86	1.9	147	A
Zeus Holdings	Philippines	Jul-98	73%	31	0.4	204	A
Total[b]				671	12.6	153	

Sources: Adapted by casewriters from (A) CEMEX; (B) SDC database, Cembureau, *World Cement Directory 1996*, p. 322; (C) Warburg Dillon Read, Global Equity Research, *The Global Cement, Aggregates and Plasterboard Analyser*, September 1999, p. 230; (D) Merrill Lynch, *Asian Cement*, December 1999, p. 5.

[a] Excludes Andalas. Also, value/ton includes a weighting of 94 percent for Continental/SEACem to reflect the breakdown of capacity between the companies.
[b] Includes inflow from minorities in Malaysian rights in total price.
[20] Excludes Andalas. Also, value/ton includes a weighting of 94% for Continental/SEACem to reflect breakdown of capacity between the companies.

Exhibit 9 CEMEX Financials (millions of US dollars, except share and per share amounts)

Income Statement	1988	1989	1990	1991	1992	1993	1994	1995	1996	1997	1998	1999
Net Sales	612	988	1,305	1,706	2,194	2,897	2,101	2,564	3,365	3,788	4,315	4,828
Cost of Sales	428	772	928	1,064	1,371	1,747	1,212	1,564	2,041	2,322	2,495	2,690
Gross Profit	184	215	377	642	823	1,150	889	1,000	1,325	1,467	1,820	2,138
Operating Expenses	61	120	178	221	286	444	325	388	522	572	642	702
Operating Income	123	95	199	420	537	706	564	612	802	895	1,178	1,436
Comprehensive Financing (Cost)	2	52	(5)	124	179	25	(16)	567	529	159	(132)	(29)
Other Income (Expenses) Net	70	4	(42)	(47)	(89)	(101)	(133)	(162)	(171)	(138)	(152)	(296)
Income Before Taxes & Others	195	151	152	498	628	630	415	1,017	1,160	916	893	1,111
Minority Interest	26	25	30	60	70	97	45	109	119	107	39	56
Majority Net Income	167	121	148	442	545	522	376	759	977	761	803	973
Earnings per Share	0.15	0.11	0.13	0.40	0.52	0.49	0.35	0.59	0.75	0.59	0.64	0.77
Dividends per Share	0.01	0.01	0.02	0.06	0.07	0.09	0.06	0.07	0.0	0.12	0.14	0.17
Shares Outstanding (millions)	1,114	1,114	1,114	1,114	1,056	1,056	1,077	1,286	1,303	1,268	1,258	1,366
ROE	14.2	9.5	10.6	24.1	18.7	16.2	13.3	26.4	29.3	21.7	20.7	18.8
Balance Sheet												
Cash and Temporary Investments	189	186	145	202	384	326	484	355	409	380	407	326
Net Working Capital	140	226	236	286	562	595	528	567	611	588	638	699
Property, Plant, & Equipment, Net	1,117	2,037	2,357	2,614	4,124	4,407	4,093	4,939	5,743	6,006	6,142	6,922
Total Assets	1,710	2,940	3,438	3,848	7,457	8,018	7,894	8,370	9,942	10,231	10,460	11,864
Short-Term Debt	69	360	261	144	884	684	648	870	815	657	1,106	1,030
Long-Term Debt	142	792	1,043	1,267	2,436	2,866	3,116	3,034	3,954	3,961	3,136	3,341
Total Liabilities	355	1,354	1,566	1,607	3,897	4,022	4,291	4,603	5,605	5,535	5,321	5,430
Minority Interest	182	306	474	408	649	771	771	889	1,000	1,181	1,251	1,253
Stockholders' Equity, excluding Minority Interest	1,173	1,280	1,398	1,833	2,911	3,225	2,832	2878	3,337	3,515	3,887	5,182
Total Stockholders' Equity	1,355	1,586	1,872	2,242	3,560	3,996	3,603	3767	4,337	4,696	5,138	6,435
Book Value per Share	1.05	1.15	1.25	1.65	2.76	3.05	2.63	2.24	2.57	2.74	3.08	3.79
Other Financial Data												
Operating Margin (%)	20.2	9.6	15.3	24.6	24.5	24.4	26.9	23.9	23.8	23.6	27.3	29.8
EBITDA Margin (%)	28.6	17.9	24.8	33.2	31.9	31.6	34.2	31.8	32.3	31.5	34.4	37.1
EBITDA	175	177	324	567	700	914	719	815	1,087	1,193	1,485	1,791

Source: CEMEX.

additional cement capacity. It also began to diversify horizontally into areas such as petrochemicals, mining, and tourism in order to reduce the risks related to its dependence on a highly cyclical core business. However, it wasn't long before Zambrano decided to refocus the company on cement and cement-related businesses. Based partly on the work of the Boston Consulting Group, he had concluded that geographic diversification within the cement business was preferable to horizontal diversification outside it. All the non-core assets were eventually divested and CEMEX switched to a strategy of growth through acquisitions.

This strategy focused, in the first instance, on Mexico. As Mexico began to open up in the late 1980s, large firms such as Holderbank and Lafarge viewed it as a possible market to expand their operations. Faced with this threat, CEMEX decided to unify its Mexican operations. In 1987, CEMEX acquired Cementos Anahuac, giving the company access to Mexico's central market and bolstering its export capabilities with the addition of two plants and four million tons of capacity. Two years later, the acquisition of Cementos Tolteca, Mexico's second-largest cement producer with seven new plants and 6.6 million tons of capacity, made CEMEX Mexico's largest producer. These mergers, which cost CEMEX nearly $1 billion, secured its position in Mexico and gave it the size and financial resources to begin the process of geographic expansion.

When the 1994/1995 peso crisis struck, CEMEX had just finished a plan for revamping its Mexican operations. In December 1994, after a year of political instability that included the assassination of a presidential candidate, Mexico's foreign reserves dropped to about $5 billion, down from nearly $30 billion in March. Incoming President Ernesto Zedillo warned his citizens to prepare for tough times. CEMEX quickly reworked its planned Mexican revamp and compressed it from 18 months to 3 months. Despite the recession that followed, it managed to maintain margins at reasonable levels. One reason was that many Mexicans did not have credit, so the self-construction part of the market was affected to only a limited extent, even though

demand from the formal sector went down by 50%.[7] Another was that the company had already begun to expand into foreign markets. At the start of the year 2000, CEMEX was the leader in the Mexican market, with an installed capacity of 28 million tons, or about 60% of the country's total. Apasco, which Holderbank had acquired and invested heavily in expanding in the early 1990s, was the second largest player, with another 9 million tons of capacity. Analysts did not expect further increases in CEMEX's share of the Mexican market.

International Expansion   After having secured its leadership in Mexico, CEMEX began to look for opportunities beyond Mexico's borders. Internationalization began with exports, principally to the United States. By 2000, CEMEX was the largest international cement trader in the world, with projected trading volumes of 13 million tons of cement and clinker that year, 60% of which was expected to be third-party product.[8] International trade offered opportunities to arbitrage price differentials across national boundaries and to divert low-priced imports away from one's own markets. It also expanded the range of options available to deal with threats from particular competitors and let CEMEX study local markets and their structure at minimal cost before deciding whether to make more of a commitment to them by acquiring capacity locally.

After the imposition of trade sanctions by the United States, foreign direct investment had become a much more important component of CEMEX's internationalization strategy than pure trade. CEMEX's foreign investments focused on acquiring existing capacity rather than building "greenfield" plants. Its major international moves are summarized in **Exhibit 10** and described in more detail in the rest of this section.

The United States   CEMEX had begun to export to the U.S. market in the early 1970s. In the late 1980s, it established distribution facilities in the

[7]Interview with Hector Medina, Executive Vice President Planning and Finance.
[8]Interview with Jose L. Saenz de Miera, President of Europe-Asia Region.

Exhibit 10   Timeline of CEMEX's International Expansion

Year	Event
1985	GATT signed; CEMEX began to concentrate on cement and divests other business lines
1987	Acquired Cementos Anáhuac in Mexico
1989	Acquired Cementos Tolteca; became Mexico's largest producer and one of ten largest worldwide
1992	Acquired Valenciana and Sanson in Spain; became world's fifth largest cement producer
1993–1994	Acquired 0.7 mt of capacity in Jamaica, 0.4 mt in Barbados, and 0.7 mt in Trinidad & Tobago
1994	Acquired Vencemos in Venezuela, Cemento Bayano in Panama, and the Balcones plant in Texas
1995	Acquired Cementos Nacionales in the Dominican Republic
1996	Acquired a majority stake in Colombia's Cementos Diamante and Industrias e Inversiones Samper; became world's third largest cement company
1997	Acquired 30% stake in Rizal Cement Company in the Philippines
1998–1999	Acquired a 20% interest in PT Semen Gresik in Indonesia; acquired an additional 40% of Rizal, and 99.9% of APO Cement Corp, also in the Philippines
1999	Acquired Assiut in Egypt, a 12% stake in Bio Bio in Chile, and Cemento del Pacifico in Costa Rica
2000	Announced availability of $1.175 billion for global acquisitions during the course of the year (36% more than 1999 spending)

Source: CEMEX.

southern United States in order to expand this effort. However, the U.S. economy and the construction industry in particular were experiencing a downturn. As a result, eight U.S. producers banded together to file an antidumping petition claiming that they were being harmed by low-cost Mexican imports and demanding protection. After finding that cement prices were higher in Mexico than in the southern United States and inferring that Mexican producers were dumping cement in the U.S. market at artificially low prices, the U.S. International Trade Commission (ITC) imposed a 58% countervailing duty on CEMEX's exports from Mexico to the United States. The duty was reduced to 31% after CEMEX started limiting exports to U.S. states where prices were relatively high.[9] The company tried to fight these actions before the relevant U.S. bodies, but this proved very difficult. Medina recalled that at one point, CEMEX was simultaneously being investigated by the ITC for artificially lowering prices and by the U.S. Federal

[9]David P. Baron, "Integrated Strategy: Market and Nonmarket Components," *California Management Review*, vol. 37, no. 2 (Winter 1995), pp. 51–52.

Trade Commission for purchasing a distribution terminal with the intent of artificially raising them! A ruling by the General Agreement on Tariffs and Trade (GATT) in 1992 sided with Mexico in this dispute, but the United States refused to give way. As of early 2000, the countervailing duty was still in place, although there were also reports that the United States was finally moving closer to repealing it.

After the countervailing duty was imposed, CEMEX had acquired a 1 million ton cement plant in Texas to reinforce its ready-mix and distribution facilities in the southern United States. Zambrano sometimes referred to this constellation of facilities as a firewall protecting the Mexican market from incursions from the United States. In addition, CEMEX's coastal terminals in the United States continued to import cement into the United States, from third parties as well as from the company's other plants. Thus, CEMEX credited imports of Chinese cement to the west coast of the United States for doubling the profits of its activities in the United States during 1999, to the point where they accounted for 12% of CEMEX's total sales and 7% of its EBITDA.

Spain   In 1991, CEMEX built distribution terminals in Spain to trade cement that was produced in Mexico, and also to study the European market. In July 1992, it spent about $1.8 billion to acquire what ended up being 68% of the stock and 94% of the voting rights in two large Spanish cement companies, Valenciana and Sanson, with a total of nearly 12 million tons of capacity. These acquisitions yielded a market-leading 28% share in one of Europe's largest cement markets, which then happened to be in the throes of a major boom. The acquisitions also lowered dependence on the Mexican market, gave CEMEX significant capacity in a major market for Holderbank and Lafarge, and raised its international profile. But shareholders generally took a dim view of the deals: CEMEX's American Depositary Receipts, issued just a year earlier (another first for a Latin American company), tumbled by about one-third around the dates at which the acquisitions were announced. And immediately afterwards, the Spanish economy plunged into its deepest recession in 30 years, with the Spanish *peseta* having to be devalued three times during late 1992 and 1993. These developments added to the urgency of orchestrating major turnarounds at the two Spanish companies.

It was in this context that CEMEX began to develop and codify its post-merger integration process. Every aspect of the Spanish acquisitions was reviewed, from procurement policies to the location of the mines to the use of automation. Processes were streamlined, as was the workforce (by 25%) and investments in information technology were stepped up. Simultaneously, CEMEX moved quickly to harmonize and integrate the systems for its Spanish operations with its Mexican ones. The post-merger integration process reportedly took a little more than a year, or less than one-half the amount of time originally budgeted, and was followed by major improvements in operating margins, from 7% at the time of the acquisitions to about 20% by 1994 and an average of 25% for the second half of the 1990s. The Spanish operations turned out to be critical in helping CEMEX weather the Mexican peso crisis of 1994/1995.

In 1998, CEMEX sold its cement plant in Sevilla for $260 million. The Sevilla plant, which had accounted for about 10% of CEMEX's capacity in Spain, was relatively old, and had high production costs. CEMEX remained the largest competitor in the Spanish market after the sale. It used the proceeds to invest in capacity in South East Asia, particularly Indonesia. According to its annual report for 1998, "We effectively exchanged one million metric tons of production capacity in Spain for the equivalent of approximately 4 million metric tons in Southeast Asia, a higher long-term growth market." In 1999, Spain accounted for 16% of CEMEX's revenues and 15% of EBITDA.

Latin America   CEMEX's next major international move was entry into Venezuela, which initiated a broader series of engagements in Latin America, mostly around the Caribbean Basin. Venezuela had been wracked by macroeconomic instability since the late 1980s, depressing demand for cement and forcing large losses on the industry. In April 1994, CEMEX paid $360 million for a 61% stake in industry leader Vencemos, which operated about 4 million tons of capacity, or about 40% of the Venezuelan total. Virtually all remaining Venezuelan capacity ended up in the hands of Holderbank and Lafarge. As in Spain, CEMEX moved quickly to integrate and improve the efficiency of its Venezuelan operations. Vencemos' operating margin improved from 9% in the third quarter of 1994 to 41% a year later,[10] and stood at 34% in 1998.[11] Although the Venezuelan economy had continued to disappoint, Vencemos was able to keep capacity utilization high even when domestic demand was low because it was located near a major port facility. This permitted it to export surplus production to places such as the Caribbean islands and the southern United States. In 1998, Venezuela accounted for 12% of CEMEX's revenues and 13% of EBITDA. Earnings were down in 1999, however.

---

[10]"Global Invasion," *International Cement Review,* Jan. 2000, p. 35.
[11]Company fact book.

In mid-1996, CEMEX acquired a 54% interest—subsequently increased—in Cementos Diamante, Colombia's second-largest cement producer, for $400 million, and a 94% interest in Inversiones Samper, the third-largest producer, for $300 million. The acquisitions gave CEMEX 3.5 million tons of capacity, or a bit less than one-third of the - Colombian total, behind industry leader Sindicato Antioqueño—a loose confederation of small cement producers—with a share of about 50%. Weak demand topped off by a price war caused CEMEX's operating margins in Colombia to decline from more than 20% at the beginning of 1998 to 3% by late in the year. Margins began to recover, however, during 1999.[12] That year, Colombia accounted for 3–4% of CEMEX's revenues and EBITDA.

Next, CEMEX entered Chile, paying $34 million for a 12% stake in Cementos Bio-Bio, Chile's third-largest competitor. The largest producer in Chile was Cement Polpaico, a subsidiary of Holderbank, and the second-largest was one of Blue Circle's subsidiaries. Compared to them, Bio-Bio was relatively focused on the northern and southern parts of Chile rather than on its populous middle. Elsewhere in Latin America, CEMEX acquired controlling stakes in the largest producers in Panama, the Dominican Republic, and Costa Rica.[13]

Other Regions Between late 1997 and early 1999, CEMEX invested in Filipino cement producers Rizal (a 70% interest in 2.3 million tons of capacity for $218 million) and APO (a 100% interest in 2.0 million tons of capacity for $400 million). Both Rizal and APO were close to ports and therefore had export as well as domestic potential. The Philippines itself had been a Spanish colony in the 19th century, and was one of the first East Asian economies to experience macroeconomic pressures in the second half of the 1990s. Less than 20% of Filipino cement capacity had been controlled by foreign firms in early 1997, when there had been nearly 20 producers and a supply shortage as the result of a decade in which demand had grown at about 10% per year.[14] But the Filipino market expanded just as large capacity additions by domestic competitors were coming on line. This gave international competitors their opening. CEMEX ended up controlling about 22% of Filipino cement capacity, well behind Holderbank but slightly ahead of Lafarge and Blue Circle. In 1999, the Philippines accounted for 2.5% of CEMEX's revenues and approximately one-half that percentage of its EBITDA.

Indonesia was the other Southeast Asian market in which CEMEX had established a presence: in September 1998, it paid $115 million for a 14% stake in Semen Gresik, Indonesia's largest cement company with 17 million tons of capacity, and considered by many to be its most efficient. Originally, 35% of the company was supposed to have been sold (out of a total of 65% held by the Indonesian government), but public protests reduced the number of shares offered. By 2000, CEMEX had increased its stake to 25% by spending another $77 million, but continued to have the Indonesian state as a major partner. The political and economic environment in Indonesia remained fluid, and further negotiations to buy out more of the government's stake were complicated by weakened institutions and the turnover of officials, as well as by continued public opposition. In addition, excess capacity of almost 20 million tons—the largest such amount in the region—needed to be restructured. Still, the Indonesian market had significant long-run potential, not least because its population numbered 220 million (three times that of the Philippines). As the dollar value of the Indonesian *rupiah* collapsed, the dollar price of cement in the local market had decreased from about $65 per ton in early 1997 to less than $20 per ton in 1998, before starting to recover in 1999. As part of its investment in Semen Gresik, CEMEX had also entered into export commitments, which it intended to fulfill in part by setting up a grinding mill in Bangladesh to receive and process shipments of clinker from Indonesia.

---

[12]*International Cement Review,* January 2000, pp. 35–36.

[13]Ibid, p. 36.

[14]*International Cement Review,* January 2000, p. 37.

Exhibit 11   Capacity Consolidation Potential (millions of tons)

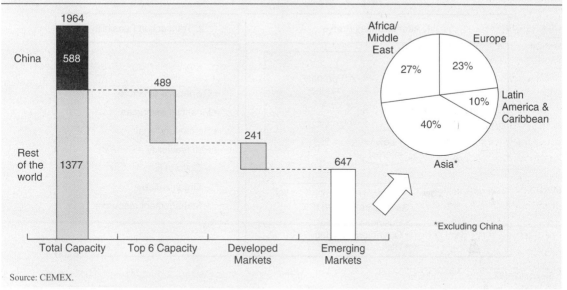

Source: CEMEX.

In November 1999, CEMEX acquired a 77% stake in Assiut Cement Company, the largest cement producer in Egypt with about 4 million tons in capacity, for a total of about $370 million. In May 2000, CEMEX announced plans to invest in expanding Assiut's capacity to 5 million tons, and to add 1.5 million tons of capacity in a new Egyptian facility. These plans catered to the Egyptian government's interest in increasing domestic production of cement to help meet demand that had been growing at an average annual rate of 11% since 1995. But the Egyptian market remained fragmented—Assiut accounted for only 17% of it—and the Egyptian regulatory context cumbersome.

The Future   In May 2000, CEMEX announced that it had accumulated $1.175 billion to spend on global acquisitions. China was an obvious target because of the size of its market, variously pegged at about half a billion tons by official estimates and closer to half that according to independent analysts.[15] However, approximately 75% of Chinese production took place in small, technologically

obsolete kilns owned by local authorities and not run on a commercial basis. Even after discounting opportunities in China, the bulk of the capacity that might be consolidated by the six major international competitors was located in emerging markets, particularly in Asia and Africa/the Middle East (see **Exhibit 11**). CEMEX was thought likely to enter India, where it thought the restructuring process was farther advanced, before China. Indian demand amounted to about 100 million tons, or more than three times Mexico's, and was served by 28 competitors, the eight largest of which combined to account for two-thirds of total demand. Holderbank and Lafarge already had a degree of presence there. In Latin America, CEMEX had its eye on Brazil, although it was unwilling to pay prices for acquisitions that, at $250 or more per ton, exceeded its capacity valuations. In May 2000, the company announced that it was negotiating with the Portuguese government over a 10% stake in Cimentos de Portugal (Cimpor), that country's largest cement maker. Such a deal might permit consolidation of operations around the Mediterranean as well as giving CEMEX access to Brazil

[15]"ING Barings," *European Cement Review,* February 2000, p. 40.

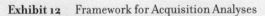

Exhibit 12   Framework for Acquisition Analyses

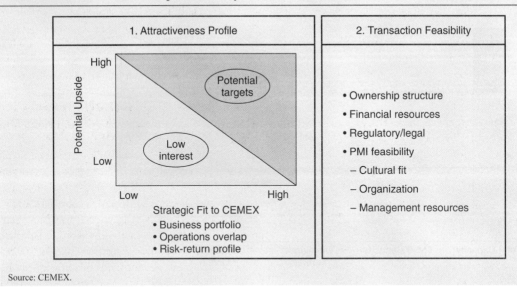

Source: CEMEX.

and some African markets. Holderbank and Lafarge were reportedly also interested.

The Expansion Process   As CEMEX moved to more distant markets, the various stages in the expansion process—opportunity identification, due diligence, and post-merger integration—became more formalized and greater attempts were made to standardize them, reflecting past experiences.

Opportunity Identification   While the logic of expanding to the U.S., Spain, and, in particular, Latin America, had been relatively obvious, CEMEX had had to develop better tools for screening opportunities as it ventured farther afield. CEMEX looked at several factors in deciding whether to invest in other countries. A country had to have a large population and high population growth as well as a relatively low level of current consumption. In addition, CEMEX wanted to lead the market or at least control 25% of it. These considerations tended to favor opportunities in emerging countries. Quantitative factors were assigned a 65% weight in country analysis, and qualitative

factors, such as political risk, a weight of 35%. The analysis was complicated by the fact that CEMEX looked at countries in a regional context rather than as independent markets and was particularly interested in the Caribbean Basin, South East Asia, and the Mediterranean. According to CFO Rodrigo Treviño, "We now have a very balanced and well-diversified portfolio and we can afford to be more selective."[16]

If detailed market analysis was the top-down component of the process for identifying opportunities, the process of identifying target companies constituted its bottom-up component. CEMEX's conceptual framework for looking at targets is summarized in **Exhibit 12.** CEMEX pursued controlling stakes—often as close to 100% as possible—in the companies that it bought into, in order to maximize flexibility. When identifying a possible acquisition target, CEMEX also examined the potential for restructuring both the target company and the market as a whole. Restructuring the target

---

[16]Tim Duffy, "CEMEX's CFO: Still Eying International Markets for Diversification," *Dow Jones International News,* March 7, 2000.

company meant increasing its efficiency and opti-mizing capacity utilization. Restructuring the market might involve reductions in the number of players or volume of imports, moves toward rational pricing, fragmentation of distribution channels, product differentiation and other attempts to get closer to the customer. Speed in both respects was very important to improving target valuations.

Due Diligence   After a target was identified, a process of due diligence was performed whereby it was assessed in depth by a team of people. In 1999, about 20 processes of due diligence were undertaken, resulting in three acquisitions. The due diligence process typically lasted one to two weeks and involved about ten people per team, half of whom usually had prior experience with the process. Once a team was formed, it was briefed on the target company and given a standardized methodology to follow in assessing it. Negotiations with the government usually continued through the due diligence process, and meetings with local competitors and industry associations were often held as well to allay any concerns about the acquisition. The final output from the due diligence process was a standardized report, to be presented to the Executive Vice President of Planning and Finance, Hector Medina, that was critical in pricing deals. Only rarely, however, would CEMEX bid prices that exceeded top-down estimates of the value of capacity in particular markets (as illustrated in **Exhibit 7**).

Especially in Southeast Asia, CEMEX had recently found itself looking at the same targets as other international cement companies. CEMEX believed that its due diligence process was more specific and systematic. To cite just one example, the human resources component of its process looked at the age, education, and average years of service of the target's employees, and at labor union affiliations, government involvement, and relationship to the community in order to estimate the optimal number of employees and recommend strategies for moving towards those targets. Other issues related to human resources, such as training

programs and organizational restructuring, were also covered. Such thoroughness was thought to reduce the possibility of unpleasant surprises down the road, and to speed up the post-merger integration process if an acquisition was, in fact, undertaken. The process methodology was revised every six months to reflect recent experiences.

Post-Merger Integration (PMI) Process   Once the decision to proceed with an acquisition was made, CEMEX formed a PMI team. The purpose was to improve the efficiency of the newly obtained operation and adapt it to CEMEX's standards and culture. PMI teams had become more diverse and multinational over time. The PMI process took anywhere from six months to a year, during which team members kept their original positions and salaries, returning home one week in every six. At the beginning of the process, the team was briefed on the country and methodology, and attended cultural awareness and teambuilding workshops. The process itself had a monthly cadence: the regional director visited every month, the country president of the new operation reported to headquarters in Monterrey every month in the same format as the other CEMEX country presidents, and CEO Zambrano, the regional directors and all the country presidents met every month in Monterrey or, occasionally, New York or Madrid.

The PMI process involved integration at three levels: the improvement of the situation at the plant acquired, sharing or replication of basic management principles, and the harmonization of cultural beliefs. CEMEX tried to send in a PMI team as soon after an acquisition as possible and, while there were differences in terms of how quickly and to what extent the team tried to take charge, regarded itself as moving much more quickly in this respect than its leading international competitors. Integration almost always involved substantial manpower reductions, most of which were concentrated within the first six months. But the PMI team also tried to discover whom to retain or promote to managerial positions. It was possible for as many as half the members of a PMI team to stay on as expatriates after the process was over. CEMEX also viewed the PMI process as a vehicle for continuous improvement in existing operations. Thus, every two or three years, a PMI process was performed on CEMEX's Mexican operations, which were looked at as if they had just been acquired.

Management   As CEMEX expanded internationally, other broad aspects of its management changed as well. Geographic diversification had reduced earnings volatility: thus, over 1994–1997, the standard deviation of quarterly cash flow margins averaged 7.1% for CEMEX as a whole, compared to 9.5% for Mexico, 12% for Spain, 22% for the U.S., and 30% for Venezuela. Financing, nevertheless loomed large as an issue because of the asset-intensity of the international acquisition strategy, which included not only paying for equity but also the assumption of significant debt and incurral of large investments in modernization—up to 50% of purchase prices in some cases. While high costs of capital had always been a major issue for Mexican companies, the situation was exacerbated by the peso crisis, which simultaneously raised domestic interest rates and restricted the extent to which Mexican cashflows could be used to finance foreign direct investment (because of the 70% devaluation of the peso against the U.S. dollar). CEMEX responded by folding the ownership of its non-Mexican assets into its Spanish operations and financing new acquisitions through the latter. This was several hundred basis points cheaper for CEMEX, partly because Spain had an investment-grade sovereign rating, and partly because all interest expenses were tax-deductible in Spain (compared to just real interest expenses in Mexico). Consolidating its bank debt through the Spanish operations in 1996 was estimated to have saved CEMEX about $100 million per year in interest costs, and to have better matched dollar-linked assets and its principally dollar-denominated debt.[17]

CEMEX's net debt amounted to $4.8 billion at the end of 1999, leaving it relatively close to the 55% limit on debt-to-total-capital that was specified in bank covenants. The company had managed, however, to satisfy the cap on leverage and the floor on interest coverage that it had set for itself more than one year ahead of schedule, and further strengthening of capital structure had been promised. CEMEX had also tried to broaden its sources of capital. In 1998, it sold its plant in Sevilla, as described above. In early 1999, it partnered with AIG, the insurance company, and the private equity arm of the Government of Singapore Investment Corporation, among others, to set up a fund of up to $1.2 billion to invest in some of the cement assets it was acquiring in Asia. In September 1999, CEMEX listed and started to trade on the New York Stock Exchange. And while no new shares were offered in conjunction with that listing, the company issued $500 million of warrants later on in the year.

CEMEX also continued to distinguish itself by the intent of its emphasis on emerging markets, even though some of its competitors had moved in the same direction. The company calculated that the weighted average growth rate in cement demand in the countries in which it was present was close to 4%, compared to 3% for Holderbank and Lafarge and 2% for the three other international majors. CEMEX also thought that its emerging market business should command higher price–earnings ratios in cement than business in advanced markets—the reverse of the situation that prevailed. According to CEO Lorenzo Zambrano, "They assign us the ratios of developing-country companies, even though we have very little volatility and our risk is limited due to our geographical diversification."[18]

Despite the increasing number of countries in which CEMEX participated, Mexico continued to play a critical role in its strategy as a lab for developing, testing, and refining new ideas about how to

---

[17]CEMEX 1997 Annual Report, and *International Cement Review,* December 1999, p. 40.

[18]James F. Smith, "Making Cement a Household Word," *Los Angeles Times,* January 16, 2000, p. C1.

compete in emerging markets. Thus, in addition to reinforcing CEMEX's skills at handling macroeconomic fluctuations, the peso crisis had led to the discovery of a distinct customer segment involving informal construction that demanded bagged cement through retail channels, exhibited less cyclicality than the formal construction sector, and was apparently ubiquitous in emerging markets. Such demand lent itself to branding and promotion, which CEMEX first worked out in Mexico, before rolling out marketing campaigns to other countries. Another example was provided by the idea of using global positioning satellites to link dispatchers, truckers, and customers in a system that could track deliveries and guarantee them to within 20 minutes, rather than the usual three-hours-plus. This idea originated with visits to Federal Express in Memphis and an emergency call center in Houston and required the assistance of consultants from the U.S. in using complexity theory to model cement delivery logistics. The innovation was, once again, first implemented in Mexico, aided by imaginative advertising comparing the speeds of cement and pizza delivery. Customer willingness-to-pay went up while fuel, maintenance, and payroll costs came down.

CEMEX's organizational arrangements also differed in important ways from its competitors'. One key difference was that country-level managers at CEMEX reported directly to regional directors whereas competitors often had an extra layer of area managers between regional and country managers. CEMEX plants were organized into 7–9 departments, each with its own vice president. Every month, the vice presidents reported to the country president and the regional manager during the latter's visit. The reports covered all aspects of the plants and used a standardized format. In addition, the country presidents, regional directors, CEO Zambrano, and his executive committee all met every month as well. Other global competitors might hold such meetings as infrequently as once a quarter and tended to be more decentralized in their decisionmaking. CEMEX had recently reorganized from a structure with a Mexican division

and an international one to a structure with three regional divisions: North America, South America and the Caribbean, and Europe and Asia. Also, while it resisted setting up full-fledged regional offices, it had made some recent attempts to coordinate more formally across different countries within a region. For example, it had consolidated the administrative and financial functions for six countries in the South American and Caribbean region in Venezuela.

At the apex of this structure sat CEMEX's CEO, Lorenzo Zambrano. Zambrano had begun working at CEMEX during the summers in the early 1960s while he was a teenager attending nearby ITESM (Monterrey Tech), and had returned to the company after earning his MBA from Stanford University in 1968. Lorenzo Zambrano favored a very hands-on approach to running CEMEX, often checking kiln statistics and sales data on a daily basis. He was a bachelor who devoted the vast majority of his time to the company, and encouraged his subordinates to do the same. He also got personally involved in sending and receiving e-mail and using Lotus Notes, which was still unusual among local CEOs.

Zambrano's personal commitment to information technology mirrored CEMEX's early and consistent use of IT. When Zambrano took over as CEO in the mid-1980s, heavy investments in IT in Mexico seemed to be overruled by the country's weak telecom infrastructure. Zambrano was convinced, however, that the importance of using IT to increase productivity would become more apparent as the Mexican economy opened up, and that the optimal private response to the disabilities of Mexico's public infrastructure was to invest more rather than less in this area. In 1987, CEMEX created a satellite system to link the Mexican plants it had begun to acquire. In 1988, the company transferred internal voice and data communications to its own private network. The Spanish acquisitions were also connected immediately to each other as well as to the Mexican operations. In 1992, the company founded Cemtec, which was supposed to complement the company's IT department by performing the functions of software development and hardware installation, and which was eventually spun off. In 1987, CEMEX spent about 0.25% of its sales on IT; by 1999, this figure had increased to about 1%. CEMEX's competitors were considered slower at capitalizing on the possibilities afforded by IT, although they were moving in the same direction.

CEMEX's use of IT had transformed the way the company worked in numerous ways. The 20-minute site delivery guarantee, already described, was a very visible example that led to the company's being canonized as a master of "digital business design."[19] The company was also connected via the Internet to distributors and suppliers. More recently, it had announced plans to launch a Latin American e-business development accelerator and, in alliance with B2B specialist Ariba and three large Latin American companies (Alfa of Mexico, and Bradespar and Votorantim of Brazil), a neutral business-to-business integrated supplier exchange, Latinexus, that was supposed to become the leading e-procurement marketplace in Latin America. Within CEMEX, IT made an enormous amount of information became available to Zambrano and his top management. Sales figures were reported daily, broken out by product and geography. On the production side, various operating metrics were available kiln by kiln. Even emissions data were included. And information flowed sideways as well as upwards: country managers could view data from other countries, and kiln managers were able to look at other kilns.

CEMEX provided its employees with a number of IT training programs and had also been aggressive in using new technology to overhaul its training function. A private satellite TV channel was acquired for this purpose, and CEMEX developed a virtual MBA program in collaboration with Monterrey Tech that combined satellite TV, the Internet, and the university's network of campuses to deliver courses to executive (part-time) MBA students. Recruitment was greatly aided by the company's public profile and included not only the graduates of Mexico's top educational institutions, but also Mexican graduates of top foreign business schools and alumni of other leading firms. Thus, while the Boston Consulting Group had long been CEMEX's principal strategy consultant, more than one of the professionals in the company's strategic planning function was a McKinsey alumnus. Overall, many regarded CEMEX as having shifted over time from an engineering-driven approach to one more dependent on economics.

Outlook

While CEMEX faced a number of issues in 2000, perhaps the most important one concerned how far its competitive advantage could travel. CEMEX's entry into Indonesia and Egypt, in particular, stirred some concerns about the difficulties of working across language barriers and the challenges of adapting to different cultures—such as incorporating prayer-breaks into continuous process operations in Muslim countries. Others, however, were more optimistic, pointing out that the CEMEX already used English as its semiofficial language, arguing that cement itself was a language of sorts, and noting that the company had its own strong culture that could serve as a binder. And everybody recognized that while Lafarge's hostile bid for Blue Circle appeared to have failed, consolidation at a new level—of international competitors rather than by them—might be the next big dynamic in the cement industry.

[19]Adrian J. Slywotzky and David J. Morrison, with Ted Moser, Kevin A. Mundt, and James A. Quella, *Profit Patterns: 30 Ways to Anticipate and Profit from Strategic Forces Reshaping Your Business,* New York: Times Business/Random House, April 1999.

Case 3-4 General Electric Medical Systems, 2002

In early 2002, Joe Hogan, president and CEO of Milwaukee-based General Electric Medical Systems Division (GEMS), the world's leading manufacturer of diagnostic imaging equipment, faced a difficult challenge. Hogan had been tapped to lead GEMS in November 2000 when his former boss, Jeff Immelt, was named to replace the legendary Jack Welch in the top position at GEMS' celebrated corporate parent, General Electric (GE). By 2002, GE had the world's largest market capitalization ($400 billion), built on its much-admired six-sigma and globalization initiatives, and its competitive culture (**Exhibits 1** and **2**). GE was *Fortune*'s Global Most Admired Company in 1998, 1999, and 2000.

Meanwhile, GEMS, as the leader in global practices within GE, had built a formidable global presence, especially on the backs of the Global Product Company (GPC) concept, implemented during Immelt's time. GPC's philosophy was to concentrate manufacturing—and ultimately other activities—wherever in the world it could be carried out to GE's exacting standards most cost-effectively. Yet opportunities in China were stressing the GPC model. Hogan wondered whether he should modify GPC by adopting an "In China for China" policy so as to focus squarely on the Chinese market.

In parallel, technological changes—represented by advances in genomics and healthcare information technology—were making personalized medicine and personalized diagnostics possible. These could radically alter GEMS' business model, by demanding that the organization embrace a move away from its engineering heritage toward biochemistry and learn to compete intensely with entrepreneurial software companies. Demographic changes complicated matters further. Populations were aging in advanced nations, and global information flows made healthcare disparities between developed and developing nations more stark—and unacceptable. Ultimately, GE demanded that GEMS grow annually at 20% and return on capital rise from its current 26% to 35%. The spotlight was on GEMS as Immelt moved toward a technology-focused twenty-first century GE.

Healthcare Systems Around the World

There were wide variations in the world's healthcare systems at the beginning of the 21st century, even as medical expertise, drugs, and technologies spread across national boundaries at varying rates (**Exhibit 3**). Healthcare spending as a percentage of GDP had increased worldwide over the previous three decades. The worldwide aging of populations implied fewer working-age people to pay for more intense care. The emerging middle-classes of Asia, Eastern Europe and Latin America were increasingly aware of, and interested in receiving, better healthcare.

The United States The United States spent more than any other country on healthcare, overall and on a per capita basis. Roughly 45% of total expenditures came from government programs primarily for the elderly, poor, and disabled, 33% came from private insurance, 17% were out-of-pocket expenses paid by patients, and the remainder came from other private sources.[1] Employers paid the majority of private insurance premiums with a significant minority portion paid by the covered employees. The U.S. was the only wealthy, industrialized country to fund the majority of its healthcare from private sources. Because there was no government-funded universal healthcare coverage and because coverage through employer plans was not mandated, over 15% of the population had no health insurance.[2] Nearly all individuals with insurance

[1]Walter W. Wieners, editor, *Global Healthcare Markets: A Comprehensive Guide to Regions, Trends, and Opportunities Shaping the International Healthcare Arena* (San Francisco: Jossey-Bass, 2001), p. 386.

[2]Ibid., p. 382.

Exhibit 1   GE Corporate Financial Data

	For Years Ended December 31 ($ millions)					
	1996	1997	1998	1999	2000	2001
Revenues						
Sales of goods	$36,106	$40,675	$ 43,749	$47,785	$54,828	$52,677
Sales of services	11,791	12,729	14,938	16,283	18,126	18,722
Other income	638	2,300	649	798	436	234
Earnings of GECS	—	—	—	—	—	—
GECS revenues from service	30,544	35,136	41,133	46,764	56,463	54,280
Total revenues	79,179	90,840	100,469	111,630	129,853	125,913
Costs and expenses						
Cost of goods sold	26,298	30,889	31,772	34,554	39,312	35,678
Cost of services sold	8,293	9,199	10,508	11,404	12,511	12,419
Interest and other financial charges	7,904	8,384	9,753	10,013	11,720	11,062
Insurance losses and policyholder and annuity benefits	6,678	8,278	9,608	11,028	14,399	15,062
Provision for losses on financing receivables	1,033	1,421	1,603	1,671	2,045	2,481
Other costs and expenses	17,898	21,250	23,483	27,018	30,993	28,162
Minority interest in net earnings of consolidated affiliates	269	240	265	365	427	348
Total costs and expenses	68,373	79,661	86,992	96,053	111,407	106,212
Earnings before income taxes	10,806	11,179	13,477	15,577	18,446	19,701
Provision for income taxes	(3,526)	(2,976)	(4,181)	(4,860)	(5,711)	(5,573)
Net earnings	$7,280	$8,203	$9,296	$10,717	$12,735	$13,684
Total assets	$272,402	$304,012	$355,935	$405,200	$437,006	$495,023

General Electric Co. Balance Sheet	December 31					
	1996	1997	1998	1999	2000	2001
Total assets	$272,402	$304,012	$355,935	$405,200	$437,006	$495,023
Total debt	129,446	144,678	175,041	201,773	201,312	232,882
Total equity	31,125	34,438	38,880	42,557	50,492	54,824
Fiscal year-end stock price	16.479	24.458	34	51.583	47.938	40.08

Source: General Electric 2001 Annual Report.

were covered for diagnostic testing. Both the new equipment and replacement markets were growing slowly.

Through for-profit managed care organizations (MCOs), government and employer payers had demanded cost cutting over the past decade.

Increasingly, coverage was provided primarily through MCOs, with less use for indemnity plans—fee-for-service plans where doctors could order any medically necessary procedure and insurers were obligated to pay. MCOs were consolidating and demanding price reductions from providers and

Exhibit 2   Summary of Operating Segments

	For Years Ended December 31 ($ millions)							
	1994	1995	1996	1997	1998	1999	2000	2001
Revenues								
GE								
Aircraft engines	$5,830	$6,098	$6,302	$7,799	$10,294	$10,730	$10,779	$11,389
Appliances	5,204	5,137	5,586	5,801	5,619	5,671	5,887	5,810
Industrial Products and Systems	9,375	10,209	10,401	10,984	11,222	11,555	11,848	11,647
NBC	3,361	3,919	5,232	5,153	5,269	5,790	6,797	7,069
Plastics	5,681	6,647	6,509	6,695	6,633	6,941	7,776	5,769
Power Systems	5,357	6,962	7,704	7,986	8,500	10,089	14,861	20,211
Technical Products and Services[a]	4,285	4,430	4,700	4,861	5,323	6,863	7,915	9,011
All others	253	292	—	—	—	—	—	—
Eliminations	(1,068)	(1,082)	(1,093)	(1,247)	(1,401)	(1,767)	(2,075)	(2,900)
Total GE segment revenues	39,278	42,612	45,341	48,032	51,459	55,882	63,788	68,006
Corporate items	1,135	1,154	1,407	3,227	771	619	517	445
GECS[b] earnings	2,085	2,415	2,817	3,256	3,796	4,443	5,192	5,586
Total GE revenues	42,498	46,181	49,565	54,515	56,026	60,944	69,497	74,037
GECS segment revenues	19,875	26,492	32,713	39,931	48,694	55,749	66,177	58,353
Eliminations	(2,264)	(2,645)	(3,099)	(3,606)	(4,251)	(5,063)	(5,821)	(6,477)
Consolidated revenues	$60,109	$70,028	$79,179	$90,840	$100,469	$111,630	$129,853	$125,913
Segment profit								
GE								
Aircraft engines	$987	$1,135	$1,214	$1,366	$1,769	$2,104	$2,464	$2,609
Appliances	704	682	748	771	755	655	684	643
Industrial Products and Systems	1,305	1,488	1,587	1,789	1,880	2,095	2,187	1,843
NBC	540	797	1,020	1,216	1,349	1,576	1,797	1,596
Plastics	981	1,435	1,443	1,500	1,584	1,651	1,923	1,602
Power Systems	1,354	782	1,189	1,275	1,338	1,753	2,809	5,182
Technical Products and Services	805	810	855	988	1,109	1,359	1,718	1,970
All others	245	285	—	—	—	—	—	—
Total GE operating profit	5,922	7,414	8,056	8,905	9,784	11,193	13,582	15,445
GECS net earnings	2,085	2,415	2,817	3,256	3,796	4,443	5,192	5,586
Total segment profit	9,007	9,829	10,873	12,161	13,580	15,636	18,774	21,031
Corporate items and eliminations	(800)	(548)	(703)	(1,351)	(584)	(902)	(1,429)	(1,893)
GE interest and other financial charges	(410)	(649)	(595)	(797)	(883)	(810)	(811)	(817)
GE provision for income taxes	(1,882)	(2,059)	(2,295)	(1,810)	(2,817)	(3,207)	(3,799)	(4,193)
Consolidated net earnings	$5,915	$6,573	$7,280	$8,203	$9,296	$10,717	$12,735	$13,684

Source: General Electric 2001 Annual Report.

[a] Technical Products and Services is primarily GEMS but also includes some other GE businesses.

[b] GECS means General Electric Capital Services, Inc., and all of its affiliates and associated companies. The segment profit measure for GE's industrial business is operating profit (earnings before interest and other financial charges, and income taxes). The segment profit measure for GECS is net earnings, reflecting the importance of financing and tax considerations to its operating activities.

Exhibit 3   Country Healthcare Statistics

Country	% GDP Spent on Healthcare (1997)[a]	Healthcare Expenditures per Capita (1997, $)[a]	Number of Hospitals[b]	Hospital Beds per 1000 Capita[b]	% of Population Over Age 65[a]	Medical Device Exp. per Capita ($)[b]
United States	13.9	4,095	6,100	3.5	12.7	174
Japan	7.2	1,760	8,400	10.1	14.6	109
Germany	10.7	2,364	2,300	7.3	15.6	86
France	9.6	2,047	3,300	8.8	15.4	68
United Kingdom	6.8	1,391	1,600	4.9	15.6	50
Canada	9.2	2,175	1,200	5.7	12.0	75
Mexico	4.7	363	3,700	1.2	4.1	6
China	4.0[b]	27[b]	68,000	2.3	7.1[c]	1
India	5.6	69	15,000	1.0	4.7[c]	1

Sources: [a] Walter W. Wieners, editor, *Global Healthcare Markets: A Comprehensive Guide to Regions, Trends, and Opportunities Shaping the International Healthcare Arena* (San Francisco: Jossey-Bass, 2001), pp. 26 and 36.
[b] Company documents.
[c] *The World Factbook*, Central Intelligence Agency, online edition, November 19, 2001, www.odci.gov/cia/publications/factbook.

equipment manufacturers. But there was mounting dissatisfaction about MCOs occasionally using this power to inappropriately supersede physician authority in determining appropriate treatment.

Approximately 70% of hospitals were private, not-for-profit institutions; much of the remainder were private for-profit and a small percentage were government owned.[3] An increasing portion of care was provided by outpatient clinics, nearly all of which were privately owned and many for-profit. Some clinics specialized in providing diagnostic imaging services and were often owned by the doctors who referred patients to them. Many hospitals faced difficult economic times. Increased outpatient and in-home care and shorter hospital stays had created excess capacity in the hospital sector. In 1999, the Balanced Budget Act reduced reimbursement rates for Medicare payments, further eroding hospital profits and tightening capital budgets.

Japan   Japan provided universal health coverage. However, the majority of individuals received coverage through workplace-based insurance societies. Workers had payroll deductions that paid for their

own insurance and contributed to insurance pools that covered retirees and other segments of the population. Additionally, those seeking care made significant copayments. Hospitals were owned by doctors and were mostly for-profit, although Japanese law prohibited distributing profits to outside shareholders. Hospitals also tended not to specialize in particular medical disciplines. Finally, they were reimbursed through a regulated fee-for-service system which stifled price competition, and encouraged competition through the acquisition of advanced medical technologies. The system's historical success had made it well-liked. But it was also increasingly unsuited to the ongoing demographic changes. By 2025, Japan was projected to have 27% of its population older than age 65 compared with 20% in the United States.[4]

France   The government-sponsored universal healthcare insurance system was funded largely through payroll contributions by employers and covered approximately 75% of the nation's total healthcare costs.[5] Additionally, many people

[3]Ibid., p. 391.

[4]Ibid., p. 360.
[5]Ibid., p. 166.

purchased supplemental insurance. Roughly 20% of overall costs were paid out-of-pocket by patients. This helped check healthcare costs in a system that allowed patients to choose doctors and specialists on their own and where doctors were paid on a fee-for-service basis. Most hospitals were government-owned and funded with a global budget, while most ambulatory care services were privately provided. In the mid- to late-1990s, a number of modest reforms were introduced in an effort to slow the growth of healthcare costs. Ultimately, these reforms, modeled on U.S. cost control efforts, were expected to introduce restrictions on patient choice, employ primary care providers to serve as gatekeepers, adopt capitation funding, and slow the introduction of expensive new technologies.

India   Very few people had private health insurance coverage in India. There was considerable variation in the public health amenities across India's various states. Overall, the poor quality of such amenities as they existed led those who could afford it to choose private healthcare providers and pay out-of-pocket. Individuals paid 75% as out-of-pocket expenses.[6] The vacuum of poor healthcare was partly filled by a few academic hospitals, some hospitals run by charities, and several for-profit hospital chains that had emerged in the 1990s to serve the economically well-off. In the late 1990s, India instituted a number of market reforms that would allow the development of a private healthcare insurance market and encourage foreign investment. The healthcare industry was expected to grow at 13% annually.[7] As in other major developing nations, this growth included a transformation in focus from the major communicable diseases, maternity and infant illnesses, to chronic conditions generally faced by an older population. The treatment of such medical conditions required enhanced use of sophisticated diagnostic equipment.

China   Before the early 1980s, the Chinese government both paid for and delivered the majority of healthcare services in China. In the years since, many health programs had been discontinued. By the end of the 1990s, individuals largely paid for their own healthcare as out-of-pocket expenses. Roughly half the urban population and 10% of the rural population had some level of health insurance.[8] The health services that were still provided by the government were largely done at the provincial and other local levels with very little funding by the central government. The government continued to run some 70,000 hospitals, a large fraction of the total number, where patients paid out-of-pocket.[9] A miniscule 1% of these were large and well-funded.[10] Private hospitals had been established recently, sometimes financed by Taiwanese investors. The central government set the prices that providers could charge patients at one-quarter to one-half of the actual costs of the service. To make up the shortfall, providers took cash under the table, or prescribed drugs and diagnostic testing since these were not subject to price controls. The same lack of price regulations on testing led investor groups, some of which were foreign, to form diagnostic testing centers that purchased or leased high-tech diagnostic testing equipment. Hospitals' reputations came to be based on the ownership of such equipment. Demand for diagnostic equipment was high in proportion to the overall amount spent on healthcare, even though the installed base was still low. In countries like China and India, some opined that it made more sense to focus on expanding basic coverage rather than on emphasizing high-technology medicine.

Key Technological Trends in Healthcare

Two emerging ideas in healthcare had the potential to revolutionize the practice of medicine in coming decades: personalized medicine and a move from a focus on cures to a focus on prevention. Personalized medicine involved developing drugs for a specific individual, or small group, based on the

[6]Ibid., p. 340.
[7]Ibid., p. 348.

[8]Ibid., p. 324.
[9]Ibid., p. 321.
[10]Ibid., p. 321.

individual's genetic code, rather than drugs aimed at entire populations. In the future, it would be possible to look for genetic indicators of disease preemptively, and treat preventively. Both trends required advances in diagnostic imaging.

Genomics   Genomics and proteomics were broad terms used to describe the study of hereditary traits and potential abnormalities of cells and cell function. Genes, which were found in the cell's DNA, determined cell function by controlling various proteins. Gene therapy involved replacing faulty DNA in diseased cells with healthy DNA. The basic steps included identifying the defective portion of the DNA, growing the corrected genes, and inserting the new genes into the appropriate cells using "vectors," which were typically viruses made harmless. Each step in the process had high failure rates—the vector might not survive long enough, the new gene might not arrive at the correct cells, might not get inside the cell nucleus to access the DNA, and might not function if it did get inside. Because of this failure rate, and because the technology of genetic diagnosing had advanced further than genetic therapies, physicians were debating whether it was ethical to tell patients they would contract diseases for which there was no treatment.

For these embryonic techniques to progress, significant advances in diagnostic imaging capabilities were required. Traditional imaging techniques, such as X-ray and MRI, did not have an image resolution high enough to see whether the gene therapy was performing correctly or which step in the process might be breaking down (see **Appendix**). Newer techniques, such as PET scanning, held promise. Researchers had created reporter genes that tracked the movement and activity of the corrective gene and were visible to the PET machines.

Developing these new imaging techniques would challenge medical equipment manufacturers. Manufacturers' expertise typically lay in the areas of engineering and physics; however, the newer techniques called for expertise in biomedical sciences. Further, companies would be required to collaborate with the pharmaceutical companies

that developed the viruses and chemical reagents that the imaging equipment had to detect. Joint technological development could also complicate the regulatory approval process for equipment makers. Imaging companies working jointly with pharmaceutical companies would likely be subject to the latter's longer regulatory approval cycles.

Such factors were expected to force changes in the business model for imaging equipment companies. Traditional revenue streams consisted of a sizeable up-front payment, at the time of initial equipment sale, and an ongoing and very profitable servicing revenue stream. Overall operating margins, with three-to-five year development cycles, could be as high as 20%. In contrast, in some chemical-intensive businesses, equipment was sold "at cost" and most profits were made from ongoing sale of chemical reagents. In pharmaceutical companies, operating margins were closer to 30%, product development times were about 10 years, and the "hit rate" of successful products was very low compared with 90% for imaging equipment makers. One GEMS senior manager cautioned that, while regulatory factors were country-specific, ultimately "the great thing is that we are all, country and race notwithstanding, genetically much more similar than we are not. It is a global opportunity."

Healthcare IT   The generation of massive amounts of data, and the associated need for managing it appropriately, had created an information technology (IT) market that was approximately $3 billion in size in the U.S. and growing at 20% per year, with the worldwide market estimated to be twice as big.[11] The major competitors—GEMS, Siemens, and Philips—had focused attention on this new market and, by 2002, controlled 80% of what in the mid-1990s had been a fragmented market.

Digital Imaging   Digital imaging—at the simplest level, viewing images on computer screens instead of X-ray films—was responsible for a flood

---

[11]This refers to the market for information technology for clinicians. It is distinct from administrative IT systems used in the healthcare sector, which are no different from systems used in other industries. The latter was a $20 billion market in the U.S.

of new data. Observing the actual functioning of an organ, often in three dimensions, required the generation of thousands of images. Digital imaging could also be combined with computer-aided detection software, so that clinicians could manipulate images, combine them with images from other detection equipment, and integrate them with other patient health data to achieve a far more detailed and meaningful picture of the disease state. Promising applications were already in various stages of development. For example, it was hoped that digital X-rays of particular organs could automatically be computer-searched for signs of other abnormalities. Newer imaging technologies were expected to be able to "light up" contrast agents, injected into the patient, which attached themselves to particular diseased cell receptors, thus facilitating more precise diagnoses than currently feasible. It might also be possible to verify whether or not specific drugs were reaching the targeted areas, as had begun to be the case in treatments of brain lesions that characterized Alzheimer's disease.

Electronic Patient Records   Electronic patient records (EPRs) allowed patient data to be easily stored and accessed remotely. They held out the prospect of addressing the frustrating fact that patient records often were not in one central place, either physically or online. To illustrate this problem, an industry executive described a hypothetical situation often faced by diabetics:

> Diabetes requires constant monitoring. Often a patient who is not in a location near his or her regular physician or endocrinologist is in trouble because patient records are hard to locate. The physician has to make decisions based on inadequate data. When the patient goes on vacation, changes in dietary habits or exercise levels cause fluctuations in blood sugar levels. The patient decides to wait to see a doctor since it is unlikely that adequate treatment will be provided by someone unfamiliar with the case. Such a patient could go into potentially fatal insulin shock. EPRs partly address such problems by centralizing records and enabling remote access, though they create concerns about patient privacy and data ownership.

Because electronic records would enable clinicians to get maximum medical value from diagnostic images, creating unified, compatible database technologies had become a focus of imaging technology companies. By developing healthcare IT systems, imaging companies could ensure that the images from their own diagnostic equipment would be compatible with hospital IT systems.

Disease Management Systems   Healthcare IT systems were also expected to play a key role in developing disease management systems, which helped payers and providers assist patients who had chronic conditions follow prescribed treatment plans. Industry experts noted that IT systems impacted disease management programs at several stages including patient selection, data acquisition and transmission, data evaluation and storage, and education and intervention.[12] Further, the creation of EPRs meant that patients could be tracked over several years and, with accumulation of sufficient data across potentially millions of individuals, clinical pathways leading to particular diseases could be identified.

Competitors

Each of GEMS' principal competitors—divisions of Siemens, Philips and Toshiba—had broad product lines and each accounted for under 10% of its parent company's revenues. These firms were just four of 10 prominent full-line diagnostics players in the early 1980s.[13] By 1995, GEMS' market share had reached 21%, and GEMS, Siemens, and Philips collectively had a 52% share.[14] By 2002, GEMS' share was just shy of 50%, and the three leaders accounted for over 80% of worldwide sales.

Siemens Medical Solutions   Siemens Medical Solutions, based in Germany, held the number-two market share position worldwide and led in several

[12]Alin Adomeit, Axel Baur, and Rainer Salfeld, "A New Model for Disease Management," *The McKinsey Quarterly,* Number 4, 2001.

[13]"Diagnostic Imaging Industry-Update," Joseph Eichinger, The Investext Group Boston, MA, November 16, 1983, p. 5.

[14]Electrical Equipment report, Ann M. Schwetje and Heve Francois, Smith Barney, April 24, 1995, p. 20.

Exhibit 4   Global Market Share Leaders by Modality

Modality	No. 1 Market Share	No. 2 Market Share	No. 3 Market Share
X-ray	GEMS	Philips	Siemens
Computed Tomography	GEMS	Philips	Siemens
Magnetic Resonance	GEMS	Siemens	
Nuclear Medicine	Siemens	GEMS	Philips
PET	GEMS	Siemens	
Ultrasound	GEMS	Philips	Siemens
Healthcare IT	Siemens	GEMS	
Patient Monitoring	Philips	GEMS	
Cardiology	GEMS		

Source: Company documents.

product segments (**Exhibit 4**). It had revenues of $4 billion with parent company revenues at $78 billion. Siemens obtained roughly half of its medical sales in the U.S. market and located the headquarters of three of its 10 divisions in the country. One-third of sales were from the European market with nearly 20% in Germany. Siemens had close relations with German regulators and was well-positioned in the future growth markets of the developing world, with special access to Eastern Europe. In 1996, Siemens formed a health services division to provide consulting and other services. Siemens made two major acquisitions of U.S.-based companies in 2000—Shared Medical Systems (SMS) for $2 billion to help its healthcare IT effort, and Acuson for $700 million to bolster its ultrasound offering. GEMS executives estimated that Siemens' 10% margins in 2000 (up from a loss in 1997) were driven by a 5% margin in equipment sales, 15% in services, and 3% in information technology–related services, and generated a return on total capital of 9%. Part of Siemens strategy was to "win business at any cost" by offering low price.

Philips Medical Systems   Philips Medical Systems, based in the Netherlands, held a strong overall third place market share, led in nuclear medicine and ultrasound, and was particularly strong in vascular and cardiologic X-ray. Philips' sales by region pattern nearly matched that of Siemens: roughly half were from the U.S., one-third from Europe, and 15% from Asia. In recent years, Philips had aggressively expanded through acquisition, including the 2001 acquisitions of Marconi Medical Systems and Agilent. Once these acquisitions were completed later in 2001, Philips would have doubled in size over the past couple of years, surpassing Siemens and taking the number-two market share position with nearly $5 billion in sales. Over the coming year, Philips planned to focus on restructuring and integrating its recent acquisitions which had underperformed in the recent past. The company was also pushing into the healthcare IT segment, but was not a major competitor in this segment in 2001. Margins at Philips had fluctuated in recent years between 2% to 3% losses to gains of nearly 9%—driven by 3% margins in equipment sales and 10% margins in services—and return on total capital was 6%. Philips spent approximately 8% of sales on R&D.

Toshiba Medical Systems   Toshiba Medical Systems, headquartered in Japan, had the fourth-largest market share position with sales estimated at $2.3 billion. Toshiba was particularly strong in the ultrasound and CT modalities, was known for producing cost-effective and reliable products, and had the second-largest market share in Asia. It recently began developing its own imaging equipment service business whereas previously it had contracted with an outside vendor. Toshiba was also growing its healthcare IT business and had recently formed a joint venture with an applications service provider. Its margins were estimated to be in the range of 5%, and it was considered an acquisition target.

Separately, there was competition in providing after-sales services. In the U.S., each of the four principal rivals serviced equipment from any OEM, and were labeled "multi-vendors." Other OEMs serviced their own equipment only. There were also independent service organizations (ISOs) who were typically multi-vendors, and who often received contracts from insurance companies who specialized in insuring the diagnostic equipment of their hospital customers. In 2002 OEMs' share in the U.S. had increased to 77%, while that of ISOs and in-house staff had fallen to 10% and 13% respectively, with insurers falling by the wayside.[15] The services sector was organized quite differently outside the U.S. Since many nations' authorities insisted that OEMs serviced their own products, there was little scope for multi-vendors to exist.

General Electric Medical Systems

GEMS' strong performance under Jeff Immelt from 1997 to 2000 had been a factor in his promotion to chairman of GE. GEMS' roots began in the 1940s with the purchase of an X-ray business in Chicago. Long an industry innovator, GEMS developed CT technology in the 1970s and MR (magnetic resonance) in the 1980s, and competed in all medical imaging modalities in over 100 countries by 2002. It boasted the number-one position in MR and CT imaging worldwide, and had the leading market share in all regions (Americas, Europe/Africa, and Asia).

Most revenues were earned in high-cost, industrialized countries while manufacturing was increasingly carried out in low-cost, developing nations. Profits tended to be highest in developed nations where reimbursement rates were higher and where demand for higher-end products was greater.

GEMS executives expected each of its main modalities to reach $1 billion in worldwide sales. By 2001, both the CT and MR businesses had exceeded this mark, and nuclear medicine and the PET business were growing rapidly. (See **Exhibit 5** for GEMS financial data.)

Global Evolution of GEMS   The evolution of GEMS from a U.S. company to one whose non-U.S. revenues exceeded 50% in 2002 was a multi-stage process. GEMS' first major step outside the U.S. was a joint venture in the early 1980s with Yokogawa Medical Systems to build and sell MRI products in Japan. In 1988, GEMS gained a foothold in the European market, by exchanging GE's consumer electronic business (televisions) with the medical devices business unit of the French company Thomson.

In 1987, John Trani, newly named GEMS head, set out more formally to create a global company. Trani emphasized the training and development of business leaders in global management and brought in a number of leading academics to develop a program. This consisted partly of forming small teams of American, Asian, and European managers and having them train together in each of the three regions. By 1992, nearly 300 of GEMS' top managers had been through the program. Initially, the majority of GEMS' international managers were American nationals working outside the U.S. The development program, however, sought to identify and develop local managers, of whom some were brought to the U.S. to hold management positions. In the 1990s, Trani also invested in developing the Asian market organization outside of Japan. This consisted primarily of the India and China markets which, although small, had enormous growth potential. GEMS became a leader within GE in terms of developing a global business.[16] Trani responded to reductions in healthcare reimbursement in the late 1980s to mid 1990s by emphasizing cost reductions.

---

[15]Some information in this paragraph comes from "Total Medical Imaging Equipment Services Market," a report by Frost and Sullivan, 2002.

[16]In June 2001, Yoshiaki Fujimori, an early participant in GEMS global training and development program and a GEMS manager throughout the 1990s, become the first non-American to run a major GE business when he was named president and CEO of GE's plastics division.

Exhibit 5   GEMS Financial Data ($ millions)

	1995	1996	1997	1998	1999	2000	2001
Sales	3,665	3,960	4,100	4,620	6,170	7,240	8,400
Operating Margin	500	570	690	825	1,055	1,280	1,485
Net Income	305	345	400	480	615	760	890
Funds Flow	245	290	310	(845)	—	15	170
Cash from Operating Activities	340	545	470	565	820	915	965
P&E Reinvestment Ratio	2.1	2.0	1.7	1.6	1.0	1.0	1.0
Working Capital—5-pt average	601	577	489	485	780	830	930
Product Line Sales							
Ultrasound		190			550	750	900
CT		615			825	1,000	1,150
MR		735			1,010	1,140	1,200
X-ray		620			650	1,005	1,240
Functional Imaging (NM/PET)		55			200	235	390
IT		—	50	130	850	1,000	1,300
Service		1,520			1,950	2,020	2,220
Other		225			135	90	—
Total Sales		3,960			6,170	7,240	8,400
Regional Sales							
Americas		2,200		2,850	3,945	4,640	5,230
Europe		850		885	1,075	1,200	1,510
Asia		910		885	1,150	1,400	1,660
Total Sales		3,960		4,620	6,170	7,240	8,400

Source: Company documents.

Immelt inherited a $4 billion company. His first major effort was to step up acquisitions. Size, Immelt believed, would be critical to obtaining sufficient capital to invest in emerging businesses. In 2000, one of the acquired companies formed the basis for GEMS-IT, a new subsidiary focused on healthcare IT. Second, Immelt spearheaded an initiative called the Global Products Company (GPC) that was geared toward cutting costs by shifting manufacturing activities, and eventually design and engineering activities, out of high-cost countries and moving them into low-cost countries. (For details, see the next section.) Third, Immelt invested in developing marketing and sales organizations within key markets. Activities such as hosting

symposia deepened GEMS' relationships with local opinion leaders and made GEMS more than just an equipment company in the eyes of its customers. Greg Lucier (HBS MBA '90), CEO of GEMS-IT, referred to this as being "more German than the Germans."

Consistent with this emphasis on local sales and marketing was GEMS' new organizational structure. GEMS was organized around three groups: the poles, the businesses, and the functions. The poles were three geographically based sales, marketing, and service organizations: the Americas— North and South America; Europe—including Eastern Europe and Africa; and Asia—including Australia. Each pole was headed by a regional vice president reporting to Joe Hogan. GEMS also had eight business heads, such as the MR and CT businesses, reporting to Hogan. The head of GEMS-IT also reported to Hogan. Finally, functional heads—running manufacturing, engineering, R&D, global supply chain, customer advocacy, legal, finance, and HR—reported to Hogan.

Current Strategy   Salient features of key activities are described below.

Manufacturing   Since the launch of GPC in 1997, manufacturing was shifted from high-cost to low-cost countries. Each product was to be built in one or two "Centers of Excellence (COE)" that could then be shipped anywhere in the world (**Exhibit 6**). Between 60% and 96% of product made in a COE ended up being sold elsewhere.

GEMS, with its extensive sales and marketing organizations around the world, was ideally positioned among GE divisions to pioneer GPC. By 2001, manufacturing had moved from Paris to Budapest, from Milwaukee to Mexico City, and from Tokyo to Shanghai and Bangalore.

A high portion of GEMS' production activities consisted of the assembly of parts and sub-assemblies manufactured by outside suppliers. Marc Onetto, the vice president of GEMS' global supply chain, stated, "Because we buy so many things, the game for us is very much a supply-chain game and not a manufacturing game" (**Exhibit 7**). These assembly "inputs" were not simple parts like bolts, resistors, or metal frames, but rather complex, high-value-added assemblies such as computer boards, precision-machined assemblies, and

Exhibit 6   Global Product Company

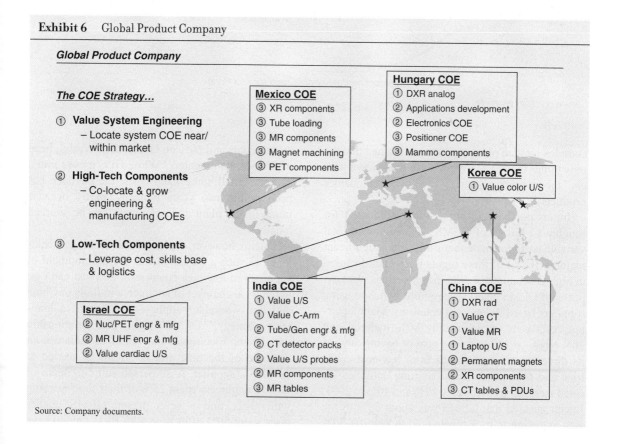

Source: Company documents.

Exhibit 7   Global Supply Chain

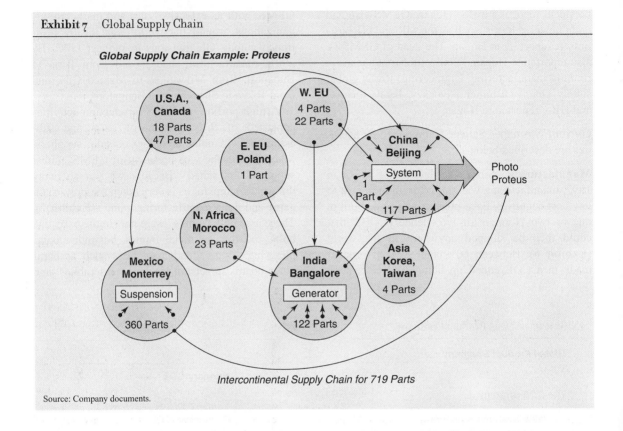

Global Supply Chain Example: Proteus

Intercontinental Supply Chain for 719 Parts

Source: Company documents.

complex molded plastics. Onetto explained that the only things that GEMS made were the "crown jewels," the proprietary heart of each of the company's products.

Inputs purchased from vendors accounted for roughly $2 billion of GEMS' $2.3 billion in total variable costs for manufacturing, and a significant majority (85%) of these inputs were manufactured in high-cost countries. Significant savings were expected if GEMS could successfully switch to using suppliers based in low-cost countries. Manufacturing costs were approximately 80% material and 20% labor. GEMS had set a goal of having 50% of its direct material purchases from low-cost countries and 60% of its manufacturing activities located there, up from roughly 15% and 40% in 2001. Lucier guessed that GEMS was about 60% of the way to getting to its ultimate goal to save 10–30%

on materials and 50% on labor. Brian Worrel, head of finance, commented, "While GPC moves into a country entail some fixed costs, the payback has been within two years typically, partly because much of the plant and equipment can be sourced locally."

Onetto, however, explained that the biggest challenge in such a transition was the development of suppliers in low-cost countries: "You just can't go to the local chamber of commerce in India or China and find workable suppliers—it must be a long-term strategy." GEMS' eight year relationship with Bharat Electronics Ltd. (BEL) of India was an example of the time and commitment needed to develop a supplier. A 20-person sourcing team of GEMS engineers spent 25% of their time working with BEL, and a seven-person GEMS quality team spent 50% of its time with BEL. Onetto gave a six-sigma class to BEL's CEO and senior management team. GEMS initially purchased simpler, less critical parts from BEL and over time bought more complex parts. By 2001, BEL was supplying parts to all of GEMS that used to be made only in the U.S. and Japan. Onetto further explained that because GEMS wanted truly independent suppliers and not quasi-GE plants, GEMS had not provided financing to its developing suppliers, but noted that the existence of a GEMS contract enabled suppliers to obtain their own financing. First-year cost savings of moving to a low-cost country were about 30%, with expectations of further ongoing cost reductions of 10% annually.

Offsetting these gains were GPC-specific costs. These included inventory, logistics, documentation, and import-duty costs relating to moving materials and products around the world. It was costly to rely on a less experienced workforce in the new location. Each time an operation shifted to a low-cost country, employees from both the old location and headquarters endured long trips from home. For example, when one printed circuit-board plant was moved to Budapest, 6–8 employees had to practically move there for six months. Those left behind often lost their jobs, creating a human toll on the workforce. Despite this, total GEMS employment in the U.S. was higher due to the company's growth and increased need for knowledge workers. Reinaldo Garcia, head of GEMS Europe, commented that managing reduced investment in countries like France, Spain and Italy, had involved extensive, and often difficult, communications with various public entities. Moving away from developed countries also meant losing the concessions these countries often provided to encourage export-generating investment. On the other hand, Lucier emphasized one of the broad offsetting benefits: "GPC has been a great way to attract talent from new regions as it is our first major step in many countries. It tends to make us insiders in countries that have considerable nationalistic pride."

Aware of the difficulties inherent in moving production from one location to another, GEMS used a "pitcher–catcher" concept to facilitate the moves. For each move, a pitching team at the site of the existing plant worked with a catching team at the new site. Managers were measured on the effectiveness of the move and a move was not considered complete until the performance of the catching team met or exceeded that of the pitching team. The pitcher–catcher concept had been developed elsewhere within GE and had subsequently diffused throughout the company. Indeed, Lucier believed there were other opportunities to learn from GE. For example, the Industrial Products division had developed a measurement called "span" that looked at whether a shipment was sent before or after the targeted ship date as a means of controlling factory throughputs. "Design for reliability" techniques, advanced in the Aircraft Engines division, were also relevant.

John Chiminski observed that this infrastructure was supported by an efficient parts organization:

> We use 90 warehouses across five continents to ship two million parts annually. There are half a million different types of parts, of which 80,000 will ship in any given year, with half of these repeating the following year. In general, demand is spiky. No use for several years will be followed by demand surges of uncertain duration. We measure our performance by the "span," or the time it takes to fulfill a certain percentage of the demand for our services. Seventy-five percent of our demand is met in four hours, and 95% is met within 75 hours. Stated differently, it takes no more than 24 hours to ship intra-region, and no more than 48 hours to ship from outside the region.

Mark Ship, global logistics manager, observed that the supply chain worked well enough that, in the wake of the 9/11 tragedy, despite air freight to major manufacturing sites stopping for five days, there were no plant shutdowns and no missed customer commitments. This required several GE business units working with U.S. customs, chartered planes and van lines, and local police and the FBI, with 24/7 communication within and outside GEMS, as the world cleared air- and other freight backlogs over the following 10 days.

R&D and Product Design GEMS typically spent 7% to 9% of sales on R&D projects and held the philosophy that the best technology would always win in the marketplace. New products within existing platforms might take a year or two to develop and cost $5 million to $10 million. New platforms might take three years to develop while significant breakthroughs might take 10 years. Often longer-term projects focused on more basic research were done at the GE corporate R&D level. The corporate R&D group had invented CT technology in the 1970s, for example. More recently, it had invested over $100 million to develop digital detectors for X-ray machines that would replace the need for X-ray film. Corporate R&D had also been involved in the development of remote monitoring and diagnostic technologies that GEMS used in their equipment service activities. This technology linked the diagnostic imaging equipment installed at customer sites with GEMS servicing centers, which made it possible for GEMS to observe the operating performance of the equipment and diagnose problems before sending out a service technician. In some cases, equipment problems could be solved remotely. The technology had since diffused throughout GE to be used wherever GE had assets in the field, as in aircraft engines and power systems.

The GPC philosophy had begun to seep through to the R&D function, causing product design responsibility to gravitate toward countries with talented but underutilized human capital. Steve Patscot, the human resources manager for GEMS-IT, recalled: "I took a trip through Eastern Europe a couple of years ago and found highly capable engineers with masters degrees making $1.50 per hour. There was nothing for them to do after the Cold War and the collapse of the aerospace and military industries. We had to learn to harness this talent pool." The ability to absorb new talent pools would be fundamental going forward as Patscot opined that "GEMS is not likely to be beaten by existing competitors, but more by some unforeseeable coalition."

Shifting knowledge bases of relevance certainly created the potential for being blindsided. Gene Saragnese, vice president of technology, described the changes:

> Five years ago we built boxes (MR, CT, X-ray) and R&D was comprised largely of electrical engineers, mechanical engineers, and physicists. Then we added integrated solutions and we brought in a lot of software engineers. Tomorrow we will move into the biochemical world and we will need different skills. Each evolution brings broader market development and, in theory, broader revenues.

Lucier envisioned a possible two-step transition to make GEMS relevant in this biochemical world of diagnostics. Step one involved collaborating with pharmaceutical companies to develop equipment capable of detecting the reagents developed by the pharmaceutical companies. Step two entailed, in some sense, a return to the business of selling and servicing equipment, albeit of a different kind. There were two ways to make this two-step transition. Organic growth over the five-to-ten year period would likely entail capital outlays on the order of $100 million per year. Alternatively, a multibillion dollar acquisition of an appropriate company could get GEMS started down this road.

Sales GEMS treated sales as a local operation. Local expertise and relationships were needed to deal with governmental regulatory bodies, healthcare infrastructures, and customers in each country.

Given the high price of GEMS products, often in excess of $1 million, the sales process was long and typically involved managers at multiple levels within the hospital, clinic, or other healthcare organization. Depending on the cost of the equipment and the size of the hospital budget, approval decisions might be made anywhere from the department head level to the board of directors. Members of the sales team met with financial managers to discuss costs, reimbursements, and financing; with heads of radiology departments to discuss and demonstrate image quality and throughput (number of procedures per time period); and with technicians to discuss how the equipment was operated. Increasingly, sales team members also met with physicians, such as cardiologists, to discuss ways in which the images could be used. Often, the radiology department head wrote a business plan indicating the need for the equipment, the types and numbers of patients to be served, and the reimbursement values from insurance providers. The level of reimbursement, typically set by a government health agency, and the equipment throughput, were big factors in determining the price the purchaser could afford. The sales process typically took 6 to 12 months. The imaging equipment had a life cycle of approximately seven years in most western countries and a bit longer in poorer nations. While the equipment itself, with proper maintenance, could last much longer, it became technically obsolete.

Garcia explained that GEMS usually relied on a wholly-owned direct sales organization, especially if the market was large enough to support such an infrastructure. As an example, GEMS had arm's-length dealings with distributors in Egypt a decade ago, but, as demand rose and the installed base of GEMS products increased, GEMS bought out the major distributors and accelerated its investments in developing the Egyptian market. African countries, with the exception of South Africa and Egypt, continued to primarily be served through arm's-length dealings. Overall, GEMS earned roughly 60% of its revenues through equipment sales, with the remainder from services such as equipment repair, healthcare IT systems, and productivity improvement consulting with customers. Service contracts earned significantly higher margins than did equipment sales. With the larger installed base of equipment, service contract sales were proportionally higher in the mature markets. Paul Mirabella, head of the worldwide healthcare solutions group, pointed out two recent changes in the way GEMS viewed services. First, they had tried to move away from a purely price-based discussion about a maintenance contract to one that focused on value-added services. Second, they had moved toward thinking of in-house service providers as a different kind of customer, rather than as competitors.

Marketing   There were at least three different marketing challenges—customizing products to suit country needs, marketing used products, and marketing newer generation products and services (Healthcare IT).

GEMS believed that customers and patients were basically the same around the world, but at the same time realized that some customization of products was required for each country. The desire to follow GPC to drive down costs had to be reconciled with the need to recognize differences between countries. Beyond the obvious differences in languages that might appear on a machine, richer countries tended to buy more sophisticated equipment. Some advanced-country buyers also chose lower-priced and used equipment. There were differences in cultural feelings as well. France, for example, tended to do proportionally more MR exams than CT scans because of concerns about the amount of X-ray exposure. Other countries used less nuclear medicine due to health concerns. Complicating things further were nationalist beliefs that caused purchasers from some countries to avoid buying equipment made in certain other countries. Though GEMS designed products to be easily adaptable to the different markets, engineers in one country did not always understand the needs of others. Mike Jones, GEMS' global business and market development manager, stated: "People in the U.S. can't design a low-end product for China. They will add needless bells and whistles and they just won't get it right. Similarly, China can't design a product for the Mayo Clinic."

Another form of customization was necessary to cater to the needs of developing nations, lacking the "soft" infrastructure needed for diagnostic healthcare delivery. Garcia explained:

> GEMS held a round-table for Eastern European customers in Budapest last year. The Croatian contingent made clear that their radiologists needed to be trained to use advanced equipment. It became apparent to us that a real differentiation opportunity exists here. We plan to hold seminars for users, regardless of whether or not they are using our products currently. We also spend a lot of time marketing to the regulators, explaining to them that it is not cost effective to save on capital investment in, say, MR machines.

GEMS had put in place a "Gold Seal" program to market used equipment. Bob Cancalosi, Global General Manager for Gold Seal, described the pre-owned market as having two parts. The "as-is-where-is" business entailed GEMS acquiring used equipment from one location and relocating it. The refurbishing business acquired used equipment satisfying stringent criteria—using state-of-the-art digitized databases—brought it back to OEM specs, and resold it. Traditionally GEMS refurbished only its own products, although it was in the midst of acquiring a large refurbisher of non-GEMS products. Cancalosi commented:

> This is a $1 billion global market, growing at 15% per year. We have a 30% share of it already, and are moving in the direction of doing more refurbishing rather than as-is-where-is work. I can't get my hands on enough pre-owned assets to satisfy the demand we know exists. We run facilities in Milwaukee, Paris, and Tokyo, and are so far out of capacity that we are considering another facility in Bangalore. Ten percent of used sales that we complete crosses national borders, though my guess is that cross-border potential business as a fraction of the total used business is more in the range of 30%. The one thing that scares me most about this business is the 800-odd broker/dealers with whom we compete, who have no passion for six-sigma type quality and very low overheads.

Different challenges presented themselves in marketing healthcare IT products to clinicians. Vik Khetarpal described a spectrum of possible products. At one extreme were the "if we build it they will come" type of products, with a clear value proposition for the adopters. This included products that replaced illegible white-board handwriting with products to help with emergency room patient-tracking, and products that replaced manual monitoring with centralized, simultaneous, automated surveillance of dozens of patients in an obstetrics environment. Image-archiving products that helped fulfill the legal requirements of maintaining extremely data-intensive records for long time-periods were also eagerly adopted. Most of these products involved gathering and processing existing data more efficiently. At the other extreme were products

that required physicians to change behavior. Physician order-entry provided the classic example. Systemwide costs would be greatly reduced if computer entry occurred, but most doctors continued to prefer to hand-write their orders, often illegibly. GEMS estimated that it would take 3–5 years to get hospitals to move from the former to the latter kind of product. Even in 2002, only a handful of U.S. hospitals had automated order-entry, and these only because they had mandated the change for medical students. Khetarpal commented:

> Our ideal customer is one operating multiple facilities that are geographically dispersed, with a mobile patient population. It turns out that these are found globally. Germany, Malaysia, and U.K. have all been hot markets for us. It was a pleasant surprise to find that interacting with doctors was quite similar worldwide, in the sense that they had similar needs. Vital signs, meds, and disease markers are the same; the ICU feels the same worldwide. But understanding doctors' incentives to embrace products is important. Hospitals act differently around the world. For example, ER medicine is more advanced in the U.S. than anywhere else. In Germany, you have ER hospitals, rather than ER rooms in each hospital.

Managing the Regulatory Interface Keith Morgan, senior legal counsel, explained:

> The key to healthcare is understanding that it is halfway between a utility and a free market enterprise. Government involvement is ubiquitous and spans the spectrum from provider to payor to regulator. Government tends to get more involved as society develops. Look at the U.S. The Food and Drug Administration regulates equipment for efficacy and safety, the manner in which we promote our products, and our business practices. Health and Human Services administers Medicare and has a huge impact on our economics.

Morgan described his role as combining "defense and offense." Defense involved ensuring across-the-board compliance, complicated by variations in rules across countries. It also included ensuring a level playing field against domestic competitors in other countries. Offense included trying to influence evolving rules and regulations, especially in the "wild west show" that tended to characterize newer regulatory systems in some countries.

Human Resources   Under Welch, GE had emphasized developing highly competent technical and managerial talent. The company was known for having a very deep bench. Executives in one division regularly selected their own managers from other parts of GE. Naren Gursahaney, GEMS' current Asia head, was a typical example. His six years in several GE businesses were followed by a two-year stint at GE corporate in Connecticut. Within GEMS, he first ran service operations in Asia, moved back to Milwaukee to a staff position for a short while, and returned to Tokyo to his current position. Hogan said, "For senior GEMS management positions, I always ask whether the individual can run a GE company—not just GEMS—and whether the GEMS position in question develops the person. Who runs GEMS is ultimately Jeff Immelt's call."

Within GEMS, extensive emphasis had been placed on developing managers capable to succeed in a global environment. This included both moving managers around from one country to another, and also developing local managers within each country. Steve Patscot, GEMS' HR director who had been at GEMS since the late 1980s, noted, "To be a truly global company you must surrender national identity." Indeed, GEMS headcount had increased tenfold in China since 1995, fivefold in India, and three times over in Mexico and Eastern Europe, while remaining roughly stable elsewhere. The average cost of a GE engineer had fallen steadily in the late 1990s because of international sourcing of talent, especially from India, by several GE business units including GEMS.

Lucier acknowledged that reallocating human resources away from mature segments toward newer ones was a perennial human resources challenge. GEMS addressed this partly by creating new units, such as GEMS-IT, to separate the businesses. Lucier highlighted two challenges that GEMS-IT had faced in recent times. Both converting the talent that GEMS-IT acquired as part of its acquisitions, and

converting them into "leaders" in the GE sense, required considerable ongoing effort. Yet, as Lucier put it, "Working with cutting-edge technology at a leading company to help save people's lives is a compelling value proposition for talent, and has allowed us to maintain lower than usual attrition rates."

Managing Acquisitions   Although several key acquisitions had been made in the 1980s to launch globalization at GEMS, there were very few major acquisitions before Immelt's arrival at GEMS in 1997. Under Immelt, GEMS then purchased nearly 100 businesses ranging in value from $1 million to nearly $1 billion. This was several times over similar activity at any of the major competitors. Many of these acquisitions were outside of the U.S. Because of this acquisition strategy and successful post-acquisition integration, GEMS had been growing at over 25% in some markets that were growing at less than 10%. While GE Capital was the one GE division that had made more acquisitions than GEMS, its acquisitions did not have to be as fully integrated into the rest of the division as did acquisitions at GEMS.

Often, an acquisition, particularly of foreign distributors, occurred after some period of a growing relationship. Such a relationship might evolve from a joint venture to partial ownership before a full acquisition was completed. Aside from growth, GEMS acquired companies to obtain new product lines and associated technical expertise to fill gaps in its own product offerings, to gain access to new markets, and to achieve efficiency gains to keep up with the ever-present pressures from equipment purchasers to reduce prices. Mike Jones stated, "Many times, the companies we buy are not global, but a big part of the value that we bring is to be able to leverage our existing infrastructure, our distribution and service capabilities around the world, and take those products and services global." Thus, Lunar Corporation, which made equipment to measure bone density to detect osteoporosis, had little international presence. GEMS planned to grow it by 20% annually and expand its presence in the women's healthcare segment. GEMS acquired Marquette—a leader in diagnostic cardiology, patient monitoring devices, and clinical information systems—and made it a key piece in the newly formed GEMS-IT division. GEMS-IT planned to spend anywhere from $0.5–$1 billion annually on acquisitions for several years to continue to build its businesses.

Pulling the Activities Together   GEMS' introduction of Signa, its open MR system, served as an example of how all the functions came together to develop and launch a new product line. Traditional MR systems involved patients having to slide on a table into a cylindrical scanning tunnel. Claustrophobic or very large patients often found this uncomfortable. In the mid-1990s, a competitor developed a MR system with magnets above and below, but not surrounding, the exam table. The magnetic field strength of the competitor's product was low and the resulting image quality was far below traditional MR systems. GEMS then invested some $50 million over two and a half years to develop what it believed was a far better system, which put them a couple years ahead of the competition. Lucier noted that GEMS was only able to do this because it had already spent some $1 billion in the MR business.

GEMS launched the Signa simultaneously all over the world. Previous products were launched in the U.S. first, then in Europe and Japan, and eventually elsewhere. The product was sold by convincing radiologists that they would attract more patients because it was a more comfortable system, and it produced great images. GEMS helped hospitals and clinics target specific markets with promotional advertisements aimed at medical consumers, using words such as "no more fears." GEMS spent between $10 million and $15 million on the product rollout and marketing campaigns.

GEMS sold 300 units in 18 months at approximately $1.5 million each. Actual selling prices varied widely in different countries depending on reimbursement rates for the various procedures that the Signa could perform. Americans, Lucier explained, seemed willing to pay more to live longer and had the highest reimbursement rates. Japan and Europe paid less well. For markets such as China,

and other sites with restricted funding opportunities, GEMS had designed a less powerful Signa machine that sold for half as much. Hospitals and clinics increased profits by increasing the numbers of patients they imaged. Service contracts were particularly profitable as GEMS could receive $100,000 per year for what usually amounted to minor adjustments to the machines. The service was provided largely by GEMS' 7,000 worldwide field service engineers who were supplemented by a few contractors in some markets. GEMS then expected to acquire used units at about $300–$400K each, to spend $100K in refurbishing, and to resell these for $800K with a year's warranty included. [17]

GEMS in China

GEMS sold its first CT unit in China in 1979 in response to an order placed directly with its Milwaukee headquarters. Subsequent developments included a Hong Kong office, followed by a "rep office" in China in 1986, and a 1991 manufacturing joint venture to get around import quotas. In 1995, following the elimination of quotas, the China team competed aggressively with other GE teams for the rights to become the "Center of Excellence" for low-end CT manufacturing within GE. Chih Chen, head of GEMS' China effort for the past five years, commented: "Korea and India, and a newly acquired unit in Japan, all wanted the same position. Within GE, there is extensive market competition. We won after a year and a half of inspections of competing GE factories worldwide."

Separate joint ventures were established for CT, X-ray, and ultrasound involving partnerships with multiple regulatory authorities (Ministry of Health, and the State Drug Administration—SDA) and their subsidiary manufacturing units. Chen described the challenges of these ventures. "In one joint venture, the partner firm would receive orders for equipment, and then service the orders from its separately and wholly owned factory, thus cutting us out. We couldn't stop this practice. So we had to

---

[17]GEMS would also sell five-year contracts to customers at $125K per year, plus accessories sales as needed.

renegotiate." By 2002, GE had acquired 100% ownership of two of the ventures and 90% of the third.

There were three categories of products at GEMS China—locally made products for local use, locally made products for sale by GEMS around the world, and products imported from other GEMS plants worldwide. In 2002, 70% of GEMS China's production was for export, up from 60% three years ago. In contrast, the Siemens JV in China, which predated GEMS' arrival, was set up solely to manufacture for the local market. GEMS had a 40% market share, greater than the sum of Siemens' and Philips' shares. The remaining market was populated with hundreds of assemblers and trading companies, many of which had tried to set up manufacturing facilities but with limited success. Chen—a native of Taiwan, U.S.-educated including Ph.D., and a veteran of GE postings in Silicon Valley, Singapore, Taiwan and Beijing—attributed the leadership position to knowing how to "work in the jungle." Keith Morgan also pointed out that GEMS tried to constructively influence the evolution of business practices in China:

> Some years ago, brokers purchased used medical equipment from the West and dumped it in China. The Chinese government deemed this insulting and banned the sale of used equipment. We spent a lot of time suggesting that the problem was not with the equipment but with the lack of rules governing its use. Without such equipment, rural hospitals would be denied functionality. Even the U.S. allows a regulated used-equipment market.

Chen explained that the importance of the China market to GEMS was a function of its size and composition:

> China is already the third-largest market for medical diagnostics worldwide, behind the U.S. and Japan, and growing the fastest of these three. It also has the largest demand for low-end medical diagnostic products. For example, we sell a CT Economy scanner for $300,000 in China, whereas the U.S. model costs $1 million. These low-end products can be used all over the world ultimately, even in some parts of rich countries. The low end probably accounts for 20% of worldwide industry revenues, with the high end and

Exhibit 8   Economics of Patient Monitoring Device Made in Mexico for the Chinese Market

	$ Millions	$/Unit
Sales	$2.6	$3,300
Total variable cost	2.1	2,570
Variable margin	0.6	730
Incremental fixed cost	0.0	
Profit	0.6	
Number of units	800	

Source: Company documents.

middle-tier accounting for 45% and 35%, respectively. To succeed in the high end and middle tier, you have to be in the U.S. and Japan respectively; to succeed in the low end, you will have to own the Chinese market.

Chen's team advocated an "In China for China" policy, which would involve bending the tenets of the GPC policies that had propelled GEMS through its recent successes. It would entail moving plants already in low-cost countries to China, partly duplicating existing infrastructure, under the logic that domestic production would have greater demand. As an example, **Exhibit 8** shows the per unit and total economics of the part of a patient monitoring product made in Mexico for the Chinese market. The product was sold in developing countries around the world and to individual clinics in advanced economies, and was a simpler version of a networked monitoring device sold worldwide. Demand in China was such that a drop in price of 10% could probably raise sales by 50%. Moving the production to China would not require incremental fixed costs of more than $1 million, since physical space was already available. Incrementally smaller variable costs could be expected—of the order of 2%—by avoiding duties and tariffs and by local sourcing, limited in the immediate term.

Looking Ahead

The challenges facing GEMS, under the new stewardship of Hogan, varied extensively around the world. For example, the strategic issues could not be more different from Japan to Hungary. The former, trapped in decade-long economic stasis, was unlikely to support high growth rates; the latter was on the cusp of becoming a major market for medical diagnostics, where GEMS and other major diagnostic imaging firms had the opportunity to shape usage patterns. In Europe's lead market, Germany, GEMS had eaten away gradually at Siemens' lead, and had seen its share rise from 5% to 25% over the previous decade. Becoming an "insider" in Germany had been a slow process and involved creating relationships with universities, acquiring German companies, and understanding the needs of German doctors. But Siemens' continued dominance rankled. Yet perhaps the greatest challenge had to do with China. China demanded attention. Hogan realized that the "In China For China" policy represented a continuous allocation of resources away from other parts of Asia—especially Japan—toward China. Further, he had to consider the excitement of continued technological ferment in the core markets and the prospect of scrutiny from the omniscient corporate parent, GE.

Appendix: Major Modalities of Diagnostic Imaging Competitors

X-Ray   X-rays were the original imaging technology and represented over half of all diagnostic images taken. The equipment consisted of a radiation generator and a detector. Various body tissues absorbed or transmitted X-rays sent by the generator to various degrees. A two-dimensional contrasting image showing internal body structures thus formed on the detector. X-ray systems were useful for viewing structural abnormalities, such as broken bones or tumors, but were less adept at viewing soft tissues. Images were still pictures and often contained structures above and below the area of interest. The introduction of digital X-rays in the 1990s enabled images to be stored and shared electronically rather than on film, and constituted a major advance.

Computed Tomography (CT)   CT imaging systems, which included computer-axial tomography (CAT) systems, were an advanced form of X-ray imaging. In a CT system, an X-ray generator was located in one side of a donut shaped (toroidal) cabinet and an X-ray detector was located in the opposite side. The patient lay on a table that slid through the donut hole. As the patient moved through the hole, the X-ray generator and X-ray detector rotated inside the cabinet and around the patient to take multiple images from many different angles. The image data was computer processed into two-dimensional views of the body. As with X-ray systems, CT images were based on differences in tissue density. CT was used in facial reconstruction, tumor detection, and the treatment of various traumas and blood vessel blockages.

Magnetic Resonance (MR) Imaging   MR imaging involved a patient lying on a table inside a cylindrical tunnel. The tunnel walls contained high-powered magnets, radio wave generators, and radio wave detectors. The magnetic field and radio waves generated by the MR system caused the hydrogen atoms in the patient's water molecules to line up in a single direction. When the MR radio waves were turned off, the hydrogen atoms return to their original positions and in the process they emitted their own radio waves. These waves were detected by the MR system and used to create detailed two-dimensional and three-dimensional images. The 1990s development of open MR systems increased patient comfort by placing magnets above and below the patient table rather than surrounding the table. Higher-strength MR systems formed higher-quality images more quickly than lower-strength systems. MR systems were used to view soft tissues, particularly heart and circulatory systems, and muscular/skeletal abnormalities. Increasingly, MR systems were used in functional imaging where organs could be viewed in action.

Nuclear Medicine (NM) Imaging   Radioactive isotopes were injected, ingested, or inhaled into the patient. Various tissues absorbed varying amounts of the isotopes that emitted gamma radiations. Gamma cameras detected the emissions which were then computer processed and displayed on a monitor. NM imagers were used in functional imaging of organs, body systems, and disease condition, and not in snapshot structural imaging. The images provided exceptional detail to the cellular level and could be used to detect diseases much earlier than other modalities. The radio isotopes could be purchased or in some cases manufactured on-site. Positron emission tomography (PET) systems, a recent advancement in the NM field, produced images with significantly higher resolutions. However, PET systems were more expensive (approaching $2 million compared with less than $1 million for NM) and additionally required short-lived isotopes that had to be produced on-site using $2 million cyclotrons.

Ultrasound   Ultrasound systems used a transducer to transmit ultrasound waves into the body. Internal organs and structures reflected the sound back to the transducer, were computer processed, and then displayed on a video monitor. While ultrasound systems were continually being improved and could produce detailed structural images, system costs remained low compared with other modalities.

Typical applications included viewing heart function, blood flow, various organs, and pregnancy conditions.

Non-Imaging Diagnostic Segments

Patient Monitoring   Patient monitoring was a broad field of products used to monitor various patient conditions within a variety of hospital settings. Patient monitoring devices included neonatal monitoring, fetal monitoring, anesthesiology and other products.

Cardiology   Cardiology diagnostic equipment also covered a broad range and was often divided into invasive and non-invasive segments. Invasive cardiology products included equipment for catheter procedures that tested various aspects of a heart's electrical systems. Non-invasive cardiology covered electrocardiograph (ECG) equipment and ambulatory devices that recorded heart electrical function through wires attached to the body, and also stress test equipment and heart defibrillators.

Reading 3-1   The Forgotten Strategy

Pankaj Ghemawat

Pankaj Ghemawat is the Jaime and Josefina Chua Tiampo Professor of Business Administration at Harvard Business School in Boston.

Ten years ago, globalization seemed unstoppable. Today, the picture looks very different. Even Coca-Cola, widely seen as a standard-bearer of global business, has had its doubts about an idea it once took for granted. It was a Coke CEO, the late Roberto Goizueta, who declared in 1996: "The labels 'international' and 'domestic' . . . no longer apply." His globalization program, often summarized under the tagline "think global, act global," had included an unprecedented amount of

standardization. By the time he passed away in 1997, Coca-Cola derived 67% of its revenues and 77% of its profits from outside North America.

But Goizueta's strategy soon ran into trouble, due in large part to the Asian currency crisis. By the end of 1999, when Douglas Daft took the reins, earnings had slumped, and Coke's stock had lost nearly one-third of its peak market value—a loss of about $70 billion. Daft's solution was an aggressive shift in the opposite direction. On taking over, he avowed, "The world in which we operate has changed dramatically, and we must change to succeed. . . . No one drinks globally. Local people get thirsty and . . . buy a locally made Coke."

Unfortunately, "local" didn't seem to be any better a description of Coke's market space than "global." On March 7, 2002, the *Asian Wall Street Journal* announced: "After two years of lackluster sales . . . the 'think local, act local' mantra is gone. Oversight over marketing is returning to Atlanta."

If the business climate can force Coke, which historically was (and is) more profitable internationally than domestically, to seesaw back and forth on globalization in this way, think of the pressures on the typical large company, for which international business is usually much less profitable than domestic business, as the sidebar "A Poor Global Showing" reveals.

Why is globalization proving so hard to get right? The answer is related in part to how companies frame their globalization strategies. In many if not most cases, companies see globalization as a matter of taking a superior (by assumption) business model and extending it geographically, with necessary modifications, to maximize the firm's economies of scale. From this perspective, the key strategic challenge is simply to determine how much to adapt the business model—how much to standardize from country to country versus how much to localize to respond to local differences. Recently, as at Coke, many companies have moved toward more localization and less standardization. But no matter how they balance localization and standardization, all companies that view global strategy in this way focus on similarities across countries, and the potential for the scale economies that such commonalities unlock, as their primary source of added value. Differences from country to country, in contrast, are viewed as obstacles that need to be overcome.

Correctly choosing how much to adapt a business model is certainly important for extracting value from international operations. But to focus exclusively on the tension between global scale economies and local considerations is a mistake, for it blinds companies to the very real opportunities they could gain from exploiting differences. Indeed, in their rush to exploit the similarities across borders, multinationals have discounted the original global strategy: arbitrage, the strategy of difference.

Of course, we're all familiar with arbitrage in its traditional, and least-sustainable, form—the pure exploitation of price differentials. But the world is not so homogeneous as to have removed arbitrage from a company's strategic tool kit. In fact, many forms of arbitrage offer relatively sustainable sources of competitive advantage, and as some opportunities for arbitrage disappear, others spring up to take their place. I do not claim that arbitrage to exploit differences is any more a complete strategic solution than the optimal exploitation of scale economies. To the contrary: If they are to get their global strategies right in the long term, many companies will have to find ways to combine the two approaches, despite the very real tensions between them.

The Strategy of Differences

Arbitrage gets little respect these days as a global strategy. This partly reflects the tendency of companies to equate size with a global presence, which naturally focuses the mind on scale economies rather than on the absolute economies that underlie arbitrage. But it also reflects the fact that arbitrage has been around for so long. Many of the industries in which arbitrage has historically been applied—farming, mining, and textiles—are regarded as low-tech and mature. There is also the sense that well-run global enterprises have already reaped what competitive advantage they can from arbitraging such generic factors of production as capital or labor, which, as one leading management guru has put it, can now be sourced efficiently with the click of a mouse.

But arbitrage is about much more than cheap capital or labor (although these, as we will see, continue to be very important). Indeed, the scope for arbitrage is as wide as the differences that remain among countries, which continue to be broad and deep. Some of the empirical evidence for this can be found in my last *HBR* article, "Distance Still Matters: The Hard Reality of Global Expansion" (September 2001) [see Reading 1–2], where I presented a four-dimensional framework for measuring distance between countries. I argued that distance could be measured not only by geography but also by the extent of differences in culture, differences in the administrative and institutional context, and differences in economic attributes (which all together I call the CAGE framework).[1] Let us consider each type of arbitrage in turn to examine both the traditional and less obvious ways companies can apply arbitrage strategies to exploit differences.

Cultural Arbitrage   Arbitrage strategies have in fact long exploited differences in culture. For example, French culture (or, more specifically, its cachet abroad) has long underpinned the international success of French haute couture, cuisine, wines, and perfumes. But cultural arbitrage can also be applied to newer products and services. Consider, for example, the extraordinary international dominance of U.S.-based fast-food chains, which at the end of the 1990s accounted for 27 of the world's top 30 fast-food chains and for over 60% of worldwide fast-food sales. In their international operations, these chains exploit to varying extents the general global surge of American popular culture by serving up slices of Americana (at least as it's perceived locally) along with their food. Nor, certainly, is this advantage reserved for rich nations; many poor countries are important platforms for cultural arbitrage. Think of Haitian *compas* music and dance music from the Congo, which enjoy image advantages in their respective regions.

Claims that the scope for cultural arbitrage is decreasing over time are clearly not true for all countries and product categories. The persistent association of Brazil with football, carnival, beaches, and sex—which all resonate powerfully in the marketing of youth-oriented products and services—illustrates the unexploited potential of some countries in this regard, though in this case the potential is starting to be recognized. Witness Molson's

recent launch in the Canadian market of A Marca Bavaria, a superpremium beer imported from its Brazilian subsidiary, which uses its association with Brazil's high-energy and sensual image to target primarily 19- to 24-year-old men. In fact, new opportunities for reinforcing cultural arbitrage are appearing all the time. For instance, the push by the European Union to restrict labels such as Parma ham and Cognac brandy to only those products that actually come from those places is a move to reinforce the natural advantages of particular geographic areas. What's more, as Finland's recently developed reputation for excellence in wireless technology shows, in certain product categories, such advantages can now be created much faster than before, in years rather than decades or centuries. Reduction in other dimensions of difference—tariffs or transport costs, for instance—can also increase the viability of cultural arbitrage.

Administrative Arbitrage   Legal, institutional, and political differences from country to country open up a host of strategic arbitrage opportunities. Tax differentials are an obvious example. Through the 1990s, to take one case, Rupert Murdoch's News Corporation paid income taxes at an average rate of less than 10%, rather than the statutory 30% to 36% of the three main countries in which it operated: Britain, the United States, and Australia. By comparison, major competitors such as Disney were paying close to the official rates. These tax savings were critical to News Corporation's expansion into the United States, given the profit pressures on the company: net margins consistently less than 10% of sales in the second half of the 1990s and an asset-to-sales ratio that had ballooned to three to one. By placing its U.S. acquisitions into holding companies in the Cayman Islands, News Corporation could deduct interest payments on the debt used to finance the deals against the profits generated from its newspaper operations in Britain. Overall, the company has incorporated approximately 100 subsidiaries in havens with no or low corporate taxes and limited financial disclosure laws. The intangibility of its informational assets has helped in this

---

[1]For an even more extensive, market-based review of the evidence, see my article, "Semiglobalization and International Business Strategy," *Journal of International Business Studies,* June 2003.

A Poor Global Showing

Since 1990, the foreign operations of large companies have consistently posted lower average returns on sales than their domestic operations. Nor do foreign revenues work as a hedge against slumping domestic results. As the graph below clearly shows, foreign and domestic margins generally move in the same direction. Based on data supplied by Michael Gestrin of the OECD, the graph compares the foreign and domestic operating margins for 147 of the companies in the *Fortune* Global 500 for which such data were available for at least six years.

Of course, an international presence could theoretically add value even if international operations were persistently less profitable, in accounting terms, than domestic operations. Say,

for instance, that significant fixed costs incurred at home can be avoided by entering foreign markets. But other recent studies, based on market values rather than accounting data, also tend to indicate that, on average, an international presence impairs performance instead of improving it.

Such studies are certainly subject to many caveats (about data, inferences of causality, and so on). And in any case, they reflect average tendencies around which there is substantial—and predictable—variation. So one should not conclude from them that individual companies ought never expand beyond their home countries. A more sensible lesson to draw is that companies need to think harder about how globalization can add value instead of assuming that if they are profitable at home, they will surely be profitable abroad.

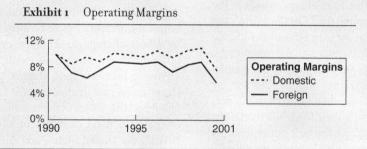

Exhibit 1   Operating Margins

regard. As one accounting authority puts it: "There's absolutely no reason why a piece of paper, which is the right to show something, couldn't sit anywhere. So it could be sitting in the Cayman Islands."

Few managers ever explicitly treat tax or other administrative arbitrages as a strategic tool, despite their potential. That's partly because executives are reluctant to draw attention to such arrangements for fear that they might be outlawed. For instance, many Chinese businesspeople channel investment funds through foreign third parties and then back into China to secure better legal protection, tax concessions, or otherwise favorable treatment. In fact,

about half the foreign direct investment flowing into China is estimated to have originated in China. Similar considerations explain why Mauritius is one of the top two sources of FDI flowing into India.

In some cases, administrative arbitrageurs are actually breaking the law. By some estimates, more than half the regular filter cigarettes smoked in India are smuggled in. Given the taxes and tariffs evaded, they can be sold for 30% to 50% less than cigarettes legally produced and sold there. Major international tobacco companies have been widely accused in the press of conniving in such activities to boost profits and market penetration. And if India has high tariffs, "there is," as the CEO of a candy

Complex Aggregation Strategies

A number of strategists have proposed that rather than adapt its business model country by country, a company should organize its operating units along regional lines, business lines, or some combination of both. The idea is to avoid thinking in terms of a country-level trade-off between localization and standardization and instead build global networks that can share knowledge, find and train global managers, and create a truly global corporate culture.

The most famous practitioner of this approach was ABB's Percy Barnevik, who broke up the bureaucracy and geographic fiefdoms he had inherited in the power and automation-technology company created by the merger of Asea of Sweden and Brown, Boveri of Switzerland. He flattened the organization and fragmented its businesses into small, local operating companies that reported to both a country manager and a business-area manager—a matrix, or dual basis of aggregation. This approach helped ABB digest acquisitions and reorganize and refocus operating units on new opportunities. The business–country matrix itself wasn't new, but ABB was one of the few companies that seemed to be able to make it work, through groundbreaking management information systems and many other linking mechanisms, both formal and informal.

Yet, as ABB was to demonstrate, complex aggregation schemes are hugely expensive and hard to manage. The challenge is magnified by the fact that there aren't just two potential dimensions for aggregation, countries and product lines, but many others as well: function, competence, client industry, key accounts, and on and on. Indeed, in 1993, Barnevik himself added a regional overlay to the matrix by grouping countries into three regions. Five years later, his successor as CEO, Göran Lindahl, removed this overlay because it was too costly.

Under Lindahl, ABB moved toward a more traditional global structure, organized by products, and also developed a global account-management structure to serve key accounts across borders. But pressures on the company continued to mount as a result of a slowdown in demand in the wake of the Asian financial crisis, which caused prices to plunge and efficiency requirements to escalate.

These conditions complicated ABB's already intricate efforts to market systems that integrated products from different business areas or for which the key customers were global or regional, not local. There were also other problems intertwined with the autonomy of the local companies.

In 2001, new CEO Jörgen Centerman replaced the matrix with a structure that combined front-end operations in a different way than it grouped its back-end functions. Specifically, ABB created four main customer-oriented units, defined by the industries (rather than the countries) that the customers were in, which were supposed to enhance the company's ability to create value for its global and regional customers in particular. Then it also created two back-end technological units, Power Technologies and Automation Technologies, which (assuming that appropriate linking mechanisms could be created) were supposed to aggregate technology development across the businesses in each of ABB's two main areas of technological competence.

Centerman, however, was forced out in 2002, amid pressures associated with the sluggishness of this new organization and asbestos-related liabilities picked up in the acquisition (under Barnevik) of the U.S. company Combustion Engineering. His successor, Jürgen Dormann, dismantled the front-end/back-end organization, which was deemed unworkable, sold off portions of the front end, and regrouped the remaining businesses into two divisions—Power Systems and Automation—thereby returning the company to just one primary basis of aggregation, products. But losses grew from $691 million in 2001 to $787 million in 2002, and questions persisted in mid-2003 about whether a turnaround was really at hand.

Perhaps the broader moral from the ABB story is that attempting to organize a global business without first understanding what one is hoping to achieve through cross-border activities—in particular whether one is trying to exploit similarities or differences—is a bit like putting the proverbial cart before the horse. Indeed, to limit the strategic discussion to structure and process is to presuppose that there is only one best global strategy. The discussion in this article should convince you that this is not the case.

manufacturer pointed out, "always Dubai" (a major entrepôt and smuggling hub). Clearly, legislation and law enforcement face a huge challenge.

Most forms of administrative arbitrage involve working with or around given rules. In some cases, though, companies can leverage political power to try to change the rules. In 1994, for example, four big Swedish corporations—ABB, Volvo, Ericsson, and Stora—threatened to send overseas as much as $6.6 billion in investments to pressure the Swedish government into limiting corporate tax rates. Similarly, companies can use powerful home governments to pressure foreign governments into granting favorable treatment. Enron, for example, enlisted the help of the Clinton State Department, which obligingly threatened to cut off development assistance to Mozambique, one of the poorest countries in the world, if it granted a gas deal to a South African competitor instead of to an Enron-led consortium. Unattractive though they are, stories like this suggest that the potential for using government influence to create administrative arbitrage opportunities remains high.

Geographic Arbitrage   Considering all that has been written about the alleged death of distance, it is hardly surprising that few strategy gurus take geographic arbitrage very seriously. It is true that transportation and communication costs have dropped sharply in the last few decades. But the drop does not necessarily translate into a decrease in the scope of geographic arbitrage strategies. Consider the case of air transportation, the cost of which has declined more than 90% in real terms since 1930, more sharply than older modes of transportation. In the process, new opportunities for geographic arbitrage have been created. For example, in the Netherlands' Aalsmeer international flower market, more than 20 million flowers and 2 million plants are auctioned off every day; blooms flown in from India are sold to customers in the United States or Europe on the day they arrive.

Although communication costs have dropped more sharply than transportation costs, there are cases in the telecom sector where returns earned by focusing on residual distance have been higher than those gained by building or exploiting global connectivity. Cable & Wireless, a far-flung and once high-flying telecom company headquartered in London, has two main areas of business, organized into a regional unit and a global one. Analysts assess the market value of the global unit, in which $10 billion has been invested since 1999, at about zero because competitors also invested in much the same kind of long-haul overcapacity and global connectivity. The valuable part of the company is its regional unit, which consists of subsidiaries providing a full range of telecommunication services to consumer and business customers in 33 small countries around the world—mainly islands, whose communication links with the outside world C&W still dominates.

The geographic arbitrageurs that *have* lost some ground in recent decades are the great general trading companies of the past, which traditionally took advantage of large international variations in prices for a broad array of products by getting them from market A to market B (and in the process somewhat eroding those price differentials). Lower transportation costs and greater connectivity have made it much easier for manufacturers and retailers to exploit these opportunities themselves. Yet the savviest trading companies have found ways to stay in business. For instance, instead of simply engaging in trading, Hong Kong-based Li & Fung derives most of its revenue from a more sophisticated kind of geographic arbitrage, setting up and managing multinational supply chains for clients through its offices in more than 30 countries.

Economic Arbitrage   In a sense, all arbitrage strategies that add value are economic. But I use the term here to refer to exploitation of specific economic factors that don't derive directly from a country's culture, geography, or administrative context. These factors include differences in the costs of labor and capital, as well as variations in more industry-specific inputs such as knowledge or the availability of complementary products, technologies, or infrastructures.

The best-known type of economic arbitrage is the exploitation of cheap labor, which is common in labor-intensive, capital-light industries like clothing. But high-tech, capital-intensive companies can use the strategy just as well. Consider the case of Embraer, the Brazilian firm that, among other types of aircraft, designs and assembles regional jets. Many factors contribute to Embraer's success, including managerial and technical excellence, but labor arbitrage has clearly played a critical role. Witness Embraer's employment costs, which came to $26,000 per employee in 2002, versus an estimated $63,000 in the regional jet business of its chief rival, Montreal-based Bombardier. If Embraer had had Bombardier's employment cost structure, its operating margin would have fallen from 21% of revenues to 7%, and its net income would have turned negative. Unsurprisingly, Embraer has focused its operations on final assembly, which is the most labor-intensive part of the production process, and has outsourced other operating activities to its supplier partners.

Labor arbitrage can be applied to R&D as well as to ongoing operations, as Embraer also demonstrates. The company is currently preparing for the certification and initial delivery of a 70-seater, the first model in a new, larger family of regional jets. When it was announced in 1999, the plane was projected to cost $850 million to develop. It would have cost $100 million more, the company estimated, had the 10 million engineering man-hours involved in developing the new family come from Canada.

One might argue that labor arbitrage is an unsustainable strategy in knowledge industries because labor costs quickly rise to match demand. But the experience of East Asian economies suggests that even if one assumes labor costs will converge in the long run (or that costs will eventually reflect productivity levels), the period between now and then can extend into decades. Indeed, the top Indian software services firms have consistently posted returns on capital employed in the range of 50% to 75% and have grown at 30% to 40% a year over the past decade. And the prospects are for continued profitable growth, in part because the reduction in

large companies' technology budgets makes labor cost advantages more important.

At first sight, capital cost differentials would seem to offer slimmer pickings than labor cost differences; they are measured in single percentage points rather than multiples of ten or 20. But considering that most companies (at least in the United States) earn returns within two to three percentage points of their cost of capital, such differences *are* consequential, especially in capital-intensive industries. Thus, CEMEX, the international cement company headquartered in Mexico, has striven to reduce the effects of "Mexico risk" on its finances not just by listing the company on the New York Stock Exchange. More uniquely among Mexican companies, CEMEX has also folded the ownership of all its non-Mexican assets into its operations in Spain (where interest costs are lower and are tax deductible) and has formed investment partnerships with entities such as the insurer AIG and the private equity arm of the Government of Singapore Investment Corporation. These moves have reportedly helped reduce CEMEX's capital costs by several hundred basis points and has solidified its position as the world's most profitable international cement manufacturer (as well as the largest trader).

The subtlest forms of economic arbitrage involve the exploitation of knowledge differentials.[2] Forget, for a moment, the tangible aspects of CEMEX's international operations and focus on its internationally recruited knowledge workers. The company seeks out graduates of leading business and other professional schools around the world and creates career paths for them that involve sending them abroad and immersing them in foreign cultures. (CEO Lorenzo Zambrano himself has an MBA from Stanford.) The company also makes heavy use of foreign (mostly U.S.) management and technical consultants and benchmarks its performance against best-in-class foreign

---

[2]Arbitrage aficionados are also fond of talking about "dynamic arbitrage," in which a broader global presence can enable companies to exploit exchange rate changes and other volatile financial fluctuations more quickly and efficiently. But the general benefits from such efforts, beyond pure portfolio insurance effects, remain in doubt.

companies (like Federal Express in logistics). Some analysts see these international influences as key ingredients in CEMEX's heavy emphasis on information technology, as well as in its decision to remain focused on the cement industry and expand geographically rather than diversify into other industries—the model followed by most other Mexican conglomerates. Whatever the truth of the claim, there is no doubt that the diverse experiences of CEMEX's international workforce has broadened the company's horizons.

Reconciling Difference and Similarity

One would think companies that try to exploit differences would not find it easy to exploit similarities as well. And indeed, a large body of research on the horizontal versus the vertical multinational enterprise has shown that there are fundamental tensions between pursuing scale economies and

playing the spreads. (See the table "Conflicting Challenges.") The data indicate that there is some merit to classifying companies according to the primary way they add value through their international operations over long periods of time. But that either/or characterization of globalization strategies is very broad. Finer-grained analysis of case studies—particularly of companies that have in various ways been global innovators—suggests that it is possible to combine the two approaches to some extent.

For a start, it's possible to apply different strategies to different elements of a business. CEMEX pursued a financial strategy of arbitraging capital cost differences even as it implemented a standardized operational strategy. It set up complete, uniform production-to-distribution chains in most of its major markets, reinforced by cross-border scale economies in such areas as trading, logistics, information technology, and innovation (in the broadest sense of

---

Conflicting Challenges

The challenges facing companies pursuing economies of scale through adaptation or aggregation are fundamentally different from those that companies face when pursing absolute economies through arbitrage.

	Adaptation or Aggregation	Arbitrage
Competitive Advantage Why globalize at all?	To achieve scale and scope economies through standardization	To reap absolute economies through specialization
Configuration Why locate in foreign countries?	To minimize the effects of distance by concentrating on foreign countries that are similar to one's home base	To exploit distance by operating in a more diverse set of countries
Coordination How should international operations be organized?	By business; to achieve economies of scale across borders by placing a greater emphasis on horizontal relationships	By function; to achieve absolute economies by placing a greater emphasis on vertical relationships (efficiently matching supply and demand across borders, for instance)
Control Systems What are the strategic dangers?	Excessive standardization, on the one hand; variety, complexity, or both, on the other	Narrowing differences between countries
Corporate Diplomacy What public issues need to be addressed?	The appearance of, and backlash against, cultural or other forms of domination (especially by U.S. companies)	The exploitation or bypassing of suppliers, channels, or intermediaries

the term). Mixing and matching was possible in this case because, to a large extent, CEMEX can choose how to raise capital independently from the way it chooses to compete in product markets.

Some companies have gone further. Consider the case of GE Medical Systems (GEMS), the division that Jeffrey Immelt built up between 1997 and 2000 before he was tapped to take over from Jack Welch as CEO. Immelt pushed for acquisitions to build up scale because, for the leading global competitors, an R&D-to-sales ratio of at least 8% represented a significant source of scale economies. But he also implemented a production strategy that was intended to arbitrage cost differences by concentrating manufacturing operations—and, ultimately, other activities—wherever in the world they could be carried out most cost effectively. By 2001, GEMS obtained 15% of its direct material purchases from, and had located 40% of its own manufacturing activities in, low-cost countries.

Like CEMEX, GEMS was able to pursue both approaches because it could organize its operations into relatively autonomous bundles of activities (like product development) in which economies of scale and standardization were essential and those (like procurement and manufacturing) where arbitrage economies were being pursued. What's more, it was able to coordinate its widely dispersed operations by applying centrally developed learning templates. In particular, Immelt applied the "pitcher–catcher concept," developed elsewhere in GE, in which for each move, a pitching team at a high-cost existing plant works with a catching team at a low-cost new location, and the move is not considered complete until the performance of the catching team meets or exceeds that of the pitching team. As a result, GEMS (and GE) seems to have managed to move production to low-cost countries faster than European competitors such as Philips and Siemens while also benefiting from greater scale economies.

A Brief History of Globalization and Arbitrage

Probably the single most overlooked fact in the history of globalization and strategy is that, for a number of centuries, firms' international economic activities were motivated entirely by considerations of arbitrage. The great trading companies of the seventeenth and eighteenth centuries arbitraged across extreme differences in cost and availability created by geography. Spices, to take just one example, could be grown in the East Indies but not in Northern Europe, where they originally cost several hundred times as much.

Arbitrage was also the strategy of the global whaling fleets of the late eighteenth century (which, with their floating factory ships, can be said to have originated offshore manufacturing). It was also behind the vertically integrated agricultural and mining companies that arose relatively early in the nineteenth century. The freestanding enterprises that dominated British foreign direct investment through the latter part of the nineteenth century attempted to arbitrage across differences in administrative structure (and power) by pursuing foreign investment opportunities under British law. Exports of labor-intensive, capital-light manufactured goods—textiles and clothing, for instance—by countries with relatively low labor costs involved arbitrage as well, but of economic rather than geographic or administrative differences.

The pursuit of scale, rather than of absolute, economies is quite new. Replicating successful business models in new locations didn't begin until the end of the nineteenth century. Since then, however, it has become the dominant strategy, which is why the net effect of most types of distance between countries is to reduce the economic activity between them.

But even the best management can get only so far in melding the two strategies. Acer, one of the world's largest computer manufacturers, supplies a cautionary tale of what can happen when companies go too far. Acer entered early into the contract manufacturing of personal computers, operating in low-wage Taiwan, and made good money with that arbitrage play. But in the early 1990s, it began to push Acer as a global brand, particularly in developed markets. This two-track approach turned out to be problematic. The branded business grew to significant volumes but continued to generate losses because the competitive environment was particularly tough for a late mover. Meanwhile, customers for Acer's contract-manufacturing arm worried that their business secrets would spill over to its competing line of business. They also feared that Acer could cross-subsidize its own brand with profits from its contract-manufacturing operations and so undercut their prices. In 2000, the strategy blew up when IBM canceled a major order, reducing its share of Acer's total contract-manufacturing revenues from 53% in the first quarter of 2000 to only 26% in the second quarter of 2001.

Acer responded by making some hard choices. Contract manufacturing has remained focused on customers in developed countries—and will gradually be spun off into a separate company. Meanwhile, sales of its own branded products have been focused on the East Asia region, particularly Greater China, where the contract customers cannot sell at a low enough price to compete. With this move, the company has acknowledged that the logic of exploiting similarities often calls for targeting countries similar to a company's home base, whereas the logic of arbitrage involves exploiting one or more of the differences inherent in distance.

The future of the globalization process is by no means obvious. Markets may integrate further once economic conditions improve. But some argue that the process could actually shift into reverse, toward even greater economic isolation, if the experience between the two World Wars is any precedent. Whatever the ultimate direction, though, the differences that make arbitrage valuable as well as the similarities that create scale economies will remain with us for the foreseeable future. That spells opportunity for those companies that have the imagination to see the full range of possibilities.

Reading 3-2   Global Strategy . . . in a World of Nations?

George S. Yip

Whether to globalize, and how to globalize, have become two of the most burning strategy issues for managers around the world. Many forces are

▌ At the time this article was originally prepared, George S. Yip was a visiting associate professor at the School of Business Administration, Georgetown University, and director of the PIMS Global Strategy Program. This contribution was updated by the author in 2006.
▌ Reprinted from "Global Strategy . . . In a World of Nations?" by George S. Yip, *MIT Sloan Management Review*, Vol. 31, 1989, pp. 29–41, by permission of the publisher. Copyright © 1989 by Massachusetts Institute of Technology. All rights reserved.

driving companies around the world to globalize by expanding their participation in foreign markets. Almost every product market in the major world economies—computers, fast food, nuts and bolts—has foreign competitors. Trade barriers are also falling; the North American Free Trade Agreement and the 1992 harmonization in the European Union are the two most dramatic examples. Japan is gradually opening up its long barricaded markets. Maturity in domestic markets is also driving companies to seek international expansion. This is particularly true of U.S. companies that, nourished by

Figure 1   Total Global Strategy

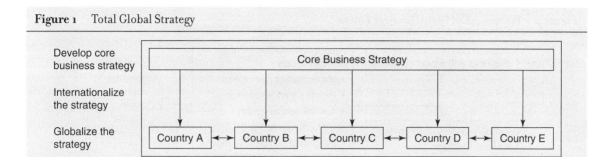

Develop core business strategy	Core Business Strategy
Internationalize the strategy	
Globalize the strategy	Country A ↔ Country B ↔ Country C ↔ Country D ↔ Country E

the huge domestic market, have typically lagged behind their European and Japanese rivals in internationalization.

Companies are also seeking to globalize by integrating their worldwide strategy. Such global integration contrasts with the multinational approach whereby companies set up country subsidiaries that design, produce, and market products or services tailored to local needs. This multinational model (also described as a "multidomestic strategy") is now in question.[1] Several changes seem to increase the likelihood that, in some industries, a global strategy will be more successful than a multidomestic one. One of these changes, as argued forcefully and controversially by Levitt, is the growing similarity of what citizens of different countries want to buy.[2] Other changes include the reduction of tariff and nontariff barriers, technology investments that are becoming too expensive to amortize in one market only, and competitors that are globalizing the rules of the game.

Companies want to know how to globalize—in other words, expand market participation—and how to develop an integrated worldwide strategy. As depicted in Figure 1, three steps are essential in developing a total worldwide strategy:

- Developing the core strategy—the basis of sustainable competitive advantage. It is usually developed for the home country first.
- Internationalizing the core strategy through international expansion of activities and through adaptation.
- Globalizing the international strategy by integrating the strategy across countries.

Multinational companies know the first two steps well. They know the third step less well since globalization runs counter to the accepted wisdom of tailoring for national markets.[3]

This article makes a case for how a global strategy might work and directs managers toward opportunities to exploit globalization. It also presents the drawbacks and costs of globalization. Figure 2 lays out a framework for thinking through globalization issues.[4]

[1] See T. Hout, M. E. Porter, and E. Rudden, "How Global Companies Win Out," *Harvard Business Review,* September–October 1982, pp. 98–108. My framework, developed in this article, is based in part on M.E. Porter's pioneering work on global strategy. His ideas are further developed in M.E. Porter, "Competition in Global Industries: A Conceptual Framework," in *Competition in Global Industries,* ed. M.E. Porter (Boston: Harvard Business School Press, 1986). Bartlett and Ghoshal define a "transnational industry" that is somewhat similar to Porter's "global industry." See: C.A. Bartlett and S. Ghoshal, "Managing across Borders: New Strategic Requirements," *Sloan Management Review,* Summer 1987, pp. 7–17.

[2] T. Levitt. "The Globalization of Markets," *Harvard Business Review,* May–June 1983, pp. 92–102.

[3] These obstacles are laid out in one of the rejoinders provoked by Levitt's article. See S.P. Douglas and Y. Wind, "The Myth of Globalization," *Columbia Journal of World Business,* Winter 1987, pp. 19–29.

[4] For a more theoretical exposition of this framework see: G.S. Yip, "An Integrated Approach to Global Competitive Strategy," in *Frontiers of Management,* ed. R. Mansfield (London: Routledge, 1989), pp. 180–194).

Figure 2   Framework of Global Strategy Forces

Table 1   Globalization Dimensions/Global Strategy Levers

Dimension	Setting for Pure Multidomestic Strategy	Setting for Pure Global Strategy
Market participation	No particular pattern	Significant share in major markets
Product offering	Fully customized in each country	Fully standardized worldwide
Location of value-added activities	All activities in each country	Concentrated—one activity in each (different) country
Marketing approach	Local	Uniform worldwide
Competitive moves	Stand-alone by country	Integrated across countries

Industry globalization drivers (underlying market, cost, and other industry conditions) are externally determined, while global strategy levers are choices available to the worldwide business. Drivers create the potential for a multinational business to achieve the benefits of global strategy. To achieve these benefits, a multinational business needs to set its global strategy levers (e.g., use of product standardization) appropriately to industry drivers, and to the position and resources of the business and its parent company.[5] The organization's ability to implement the strategy affects how well the benefits can be achieved.

What Is Global Strategy?

Setting strategy for a worldwide business requires making choices along a number of strategic dimensions. Table 1 lists five such dimensions or "global strategy levers" and their respective positions under a pure multidomestic strategy and a pure global strategy. Intermediate positions are, of course, feasible. For each dimension, a multidomestic strategy seeks to maximize worldwide performance by maximizing local competitive advantage, revenues, or profits; a global strategy seeks to maximize worldwide performance through sharing and integration.

Market Participation   In a multidomestic strategy, countries are selected on the basis of their stand-alone potential for revenues and profits. In a global strategy, countries need to be selected for their potential contribution to globalization

[5]The concept of the global strategy lever was first presented in: G. S. Yip, P. M. Loewe, and M. Y. Yoshino, "How to Take Your Company to the Global Market," *Columbia Journal of World Business,* Winter 1988, pp. 37–48.

benefits. This may mean entering a market that is unattractive in its own right, but has global strategic significance, such as the home market of a global competitor. Or it may mean building share in a limited number of key markets rather than undertaking more widespread coverage. A pattern of major share in major markets is advocated in Ohmae's USA–Europe–Japan "triad" concept.[6] In contrast, under a multidomestic strategy, no particular pattern of participation is required—rather, the pattern accrues from the pursuit of local advantage. The Electrolux Group, the Swedish appliance giant, is pursuing a strategy of building significant share in major world markets. The company aims to be the first global appliance maker. In 1986, Electrolux took over Zanussi Industries to become the top producer of appliances in Western Europe. Later that year, Electrolux acquired White Consolidated Industries, the third largest American appliance manufacturer.

Product Offering   In a multidomestic strategy, the products offered in each country are tailored to local needs. In a global strategy, the ideal is a standardized core product that requires minimal local adaptation. Cost reduction is usually the most important benefit of product standardization. Levitt has made the most extreme case for product standardization. Others stress the need for flexibility, or the need for a broad product portfolio, with many product varieties in order to share technologies and distribution channels.[7] In practice, some multinationals have pursued product standardization to a greater or lesser extent.[8] Differing worldwide needs can be met by adapting a standardized core product. In the early 1970s, sales of the Boeing 737 began to level off. Boeing turned to developing countries as

[6]K. Ohmae, *Triad Power: The Coming Shape of Global Competition* (New York: Free Press, 1985).

[7]G. Hamel and C.K Prahalad, "Do You Really Have a Global Strategy?" *Harvard Business Review,* July–August 1985, pp. 139–148; B. Kogut, "Designing Global Strategies: Profiting from Operational Flexibility," *Sloan Management Review,* Fall 1985, pp. 27–38.

[8]P.G.P. Walters, "International Marketing Policy: A Discussion of the Standardization Construct and Its Relevance for Corporate Policy," *Journal of International Business Studies,* Summer 1986, pp. 55–69.

an attractive new market, but found initially that its product did not fit the new environments. Because of the shortness of runways, their greater softness, and the lower technical expertise of their pilots, the planes tended to bounce a great deal. When the planes bounced on landing, the brakes failed. To fix this problem, Boeing modified the design by adding thrust to the engines, redesigning the wings and landing gear, and installing tires with lower pressure. These adaptations to a standardized core product enabled the 737 to become the best selling plane in history.

Location of Value-Added Activities   In a multidomestic strategy, all or most of the value chain is reproduced in every country. In another type of international strategy—exporting—most of the value chain is kept in one country. In a global strategy, costs are reduced by breaking up the value chain so each activity may be conducted in a different country. One value chain strategy is partial concentration and partial duplication. The key feature of a global position on this dimension is the strategic placement of the value chain around the globe.

Many electronics companies now locate part or all of their manufacturing operations in Southeast Asia because of that region's low-cost, skilled labor. In addition, a key component (the semiconductor chip) is very cheap there. Under the United States–Japan Semiconductor Agreement, the Japanese agreed not to sell chips in the United States below cost. But in an industry plagued by overcapacity, the chips had to go somewhere. The agreement resulted in Japanese chips being sold below cost in Southeast Asia. The lower cost of chips combined with the lower labor cost has attracted many manufacturers of computers and other electronic equipment to Southeast Asia.

Marketing Approach   In a multidomestic strategy, marketing is fully tailored for each country, being developed locally. In a global strategy, a uniform marketing approach is applied around the world although not all elements of the marketing mix need be uniform.[9] Unilever achieved great success with a fabric softener that used a globally common positioning, advertising theme, and symbol (a teddy bear), but a brand name that varied by country. Similarly, a product that serves a common need can be geographically expanded with a uniform marketing program, despite differences in marketing environments.

Competitive Moves   In a multidomestic strategy, the managers in each country make competitive moves without regard for what happens in other countries. In a global strategy, competitive moves are integrated across countries. The same type of move is made in different countries at the same time or in a systematic sequence: a competitor is attacked in one country in order to drain its resources for another country, or a competitive attack in one country is countered in a different country. Perhaps the best example is the counterattack in a competitor's home market as a parry to an attack on one's own home market. Integration of competitive strategy is rarely practised, except perhaps by some Japanese companies.[10]

Bridgestone Corporation, the Japanese tire manufacturer, tried to integrate its competitive moves in response to global consolidation by its major competitors—Continental AG's acquisition of Gencorp's General Tire and Rubber Company, General Tire's joint venture with two Japanese tire makers, and Sumitomo's acquisition of an interest in Dunlop Tire. These competitive actions forced Bridgestone to establish a presence in the major U.S. market in order to maintain its position in the world tire market. To this end, Bridgestone formed a joint venture to own and manage Firestone Corporation's worldwide tire business. This joint venture also allowed Bridgestone to gain access to Firestone's European plants.

[9]For a discussion of the possibilities and merits of uniform marketing see: R.D. Buzzell, "Can You Standardize Multinational Marketing?" *Harvard Business Review,* November–December 1968, pp. 102–113; and J.A. Quelch and E.J. Hoff, "Customizing Global Marketing," *Harvard Business Review,* May–June 1986, pp. 59–68.
[10]P. Kotler et al., *The New Competition* (Englewood Cliffs, NJ: Prentice-Hall, 1985), p. 174.

Benefits of a Global Strategy

Companies that use global strategy levers can achieve one or more of these benefits (see Figure 3):[11]

- cost reductions;
- improved quality of products and programs;
- enhanced customer preference; and
- increased competitive leverage.

Cost Reductions   An integrated global strategy can reduce worldwide costs in several ways. A company can increase the benefits from economies of scale by pooling production or other activities for two or more countries. Understanding the potential benefit of these economies of scale, Sony Corporation has concentrated its compact disc production in Terre Haute, Indiana, and Salzburg, Austria.

A second way to cut costs is by exploiting lower factor costs by moving manufacturing or other activities to low-cost countries. This approach has, of course, motivated the recent surge of offshore manufacturing, particularly by U.S. firms. For example, the Mexican side of the U.S.–Mexico border is now crowded with "maquiladoras"—manufacturing plants set up and run by U.S. companies using Mexican labor.

Global strategy can also cut costs by exploiting flexibility. A company with manufacturing locations in several countries can move production from location to location on short notice to take advantage of the lowest costs at a given time. Dow Chemical takes this approach to minimize the cost of producing chemicals. Dow uses a linear programming model that takes account of international differences in exchange rates, tax rates, and transportation and labor costs. The model comes up with the best mix of production volume by location for each planning period.

An integrated global strategy can also reduce costs by enhancing bargaining power. A company whose strategy allows for switching production among different countries greatly increases its

[11]Figure 3 is also presented in Yip (1989).

Figure 3 How Global Strategy Levers Achieve Globalization Benefits

Global Strategy Levers	Benefits				Major Drawbacks
	Cost Reduction	Improved Quality of Products and Programs	Enhanced Customer Preference	Increased Competitive Leverage	All Levers Incur Coordination Costs, Plus
Major market participation	Increases volume for economies of scale		Via global availability, global serviceability, and global recognition	Advantage of earlier entry Provides more sites for attack and counterattack, hostage for good behavior	Earlier or greater commitment to a market than warranted on own merits
Product standardization	Reduces duplication of development efforts Allows concentration of production to exploit economies of scale	Focuses development and management resources	Allows consumers to use familiar product while abroad Allows organizations to use same product across country units	Basis for low-cost invasion of markets	Less responsive to local needs
Activity concentration	Reduces duplication of activities Helps exploit economies of scale Exploits differences in country factor costs Partial concentration allows flexibility versus currency charges and bargaining parties	Focuses effort Allows more consistent quality control		Allows maintenance of cost advantage independent of local conditions	Distances activities from the customer Increases currency risk
Uniform marketing	Reduces design and production costs of marketing programs	Focuses talent and resources Leverages scarce, good ideas	Reinforces marketing messages by exposing customers to same mix in different countries		Reduces adaptation to local customer behavior and marketing environment
Integrated competitive moves				Provides more options and leverage in attack and defense	Local competitiveness may be sacrificed

bargaining power with suppliers, workers, and host governments. Labor unions in European countries are very concerned that the creation of the single European market after 1992 allows companies to switch production from country to country at will. This integrated production strategy would greatly enhance companies' bargaining power at the expense of unions.

Improved Quality of Products and Programs Under a global strategy, companies focus on a smaller number of products and programs than under a multidomestic strategy. This concentration can improve both product and program quality. Global focus is one reason for Japanese success in automobiles. Toyota markets a far smaller number of models around the world than does General Motors, even allowing for its unit sales being half that of General Motors's. Toyota has concentrated on improving its few models while General Motors has fragmented its development funds. For example, the Toyota Camry is the U.S. version of a basic worldwide model and is the successor to a long line of development efforts. The Camry is consistently rated as the best in its class of medium-sized cars. In contrast, General Motors's Pontiac Fiero started out as one of the most successful small sports cars, but was recently withdrawn. Industry observers blamed this on a failure to invest development money to overcome minor problems.

Enhanced Customer Preference Global availability, serviceability, and recognition can enhance customer preference through reinforcement. Soft drink and fast food companies are, of course, leading exponents of this strategy. Many suppliers of financial services, such as credit cards, must have a global presence because their service is travel-related. Manufacturers of industrial products can also exploit this benefit. A supplier that can provide a multinational customer with a standard product around the world gains from worldwide familiarity. Computer manufacturers have long pursued this strategy.

Increased Competitive Leverage A global strategy provides more points from which to attack and

counterattack competitors. In an effort to prevent the Japanese from becoming a competitive nuisance in disposable syringes, Becton Dickinson, a major U.S. medical products company, decided to enter three markets in Japan's backyard. Becton entered the Hong Kong, Singapore, and Philippine markets to prevent further Japanese expansion.[12]

Drawbacks of Global Strategy

Globalization can incur significant management costs through increased coordination, reporting requirements, and even added staff. It can also reduce the firm's effectiveness in individual countries if overcentralization hurts local motivation and morale. In addition, each global strategy lever has particular drawbacks.

A global strategy approach to market participation can incur an earlier or greater commitment to a market than is warranted on its own merits. Many American companies, such as Motorola, are struggling to penetrate Japanese markets, more in order to enhance their global competitive position than to make money in Japan for its own sake.

Product standardization can result in a product that does not entirely satisfy *any* customers. When companies first internationalize, they often offer their standard domestic product without adapting it for other countries, and suffer the consequences. For example, Procter & Gamble stumbled when it introduced Cheer laundry detergent in Japan without changing the U.S. product or marketing message (that the detergent was effective in all temperatures). After experiencing serious losses, P&G discovered two instances of insufficient adaptation. First, the detergent did not suds up as it should because the Japanese use a great deal of fabric softener. Second, the Japanese usually wash clothes in either cold tap water or bath water, so the claim of working in all temperatures was irrelevant. Cheer became successful in Japan only after the product was reformulated and the marketing message was changed.

A globally standardized product is designed for the global market but can seldom satisfy all needs

---

[12]M.R. Cvar, "Case Studies in Global Competition," in Porter (1986).

in all countries. For instance, Canon, a Japanese company, sacrificed the ability to copy certain Japanese paper sizes when it first designed a photocopier for the global market.

Activity concentration distances customers and can result in lower responsiveness and flexibility. It also increases currency risk by incurring costs and revenues in different countries. Recently volatile exchange rates have required companies that concentrate their production to hedge their currency exposure.

Uniform marketing can reduce adaptation to local customer behavior. For example, the head office of British Airways mandated that every country use the "Manhattan Landing" television commercial developed by advertising agency Saatchi and Saatchi. While the commercial did win many awards, it has been criticized for using a visual image (New York City) that was not widely recognized in many countries.

Integrated competitive moves can mean sacrificing revenues, profits, or competitive position in individual countries, particularly when the subsidiary in one country is asked to attack a global competitor in order to send a signal or to divert that competitor's resources from another country.

Finding the Balance

The most successful worldwide strategies find a balance between overglobalizing and underglobalizing. The ideal strategy matches the level of strategy globalization to the globalization potential of the industry. In Figure 4 both Business A and Business C achieve balanced global and national strategic advantage. Business A does so with a low level of strategy globalization to match the low globalization potential of its industry (e.g., frozen food products). Business C uses a high level of strategy globalization to match the high globalization potential of its industry (e.g., computer

Figure 4   Globalization Potential of Industry versus Globalization Strategy

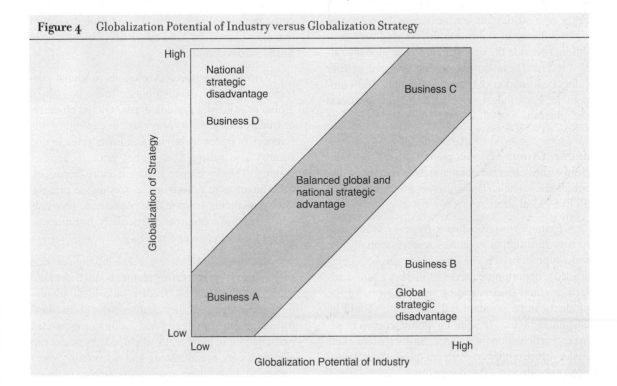

equipment). Business B is at a global disadvantage because it uses a strategy that is less globalized than the potential offered by its industry. The business is failing to exploit potential global benefits such as cost savings via product standardization. Business D is at a national disadvantage because it is too globalized relative to the potential offered by its industry. The business is not tailoring its products and programs as much as it should. While there is no systematic evidence, executives' comments suggest that far more businesses suffer from insufficient globalization than from excessive globalization. Figure 4 is oversimplified in that it shows only one overall dimension for both strategy and industry potential. As argued earlier, a global strategy has five major dimensions and many subdimensions. Similarly, the potential of industry globalization is multidimensional.

Industry Globalization Drivers

To achieve the benefits of globalization, the managers of a worldwide business need to recognize when industry globalization drivers (industry conditions) provide the opportunity to use global strategy levers. These drivers can be grouped in four categories: market, cost, governmental, and competitive. Each industry globalization driver affects the potential use of global strategy levers (see Figure 5).

Market Drivers Market globalization drivers depend on customer behavior and the structure of distribution channels. These drivers affect the use of all five global strategy levers.

• *Homogeneous Customer Needs.* When customers in different countries want essentially the same type of product or service (or can be so persuaded), opportunities arise to market a standardized product. Understanding which aspects of the product can be standardized and which should be customized is key. In addition, homogeneous needs make participation in a large number of markets easier because fewer different product offerings need to be developed and supported.

• *Global Customers.* Global customers buy on a centralized or coordinated basis for decentralized use. The existence of global customers both allows and requires a uniform marketing program. There are two types of global customers: national and multinational. A national global customer searches the world for suppliers but uses the purchased product or service in one country. National defense agencies are a good example. A multinational global customer also searches the world for suppliers, but uses the purchased product or service in many countries. The World Health Organization's purchase of medical products is an example. Multinational global customers are particularly challenging to serve and often require a global account management program. Companies that implement such programs have to beware of global customers using the unified account management to extract lower global prices. Having a single global account manager makes it easier for a global customer to negotiate a single global price. Typically, the global customer pushes for the lowest country price to become the global price. But a good global account manager should be able to justify differences in prices across countries.

• *Global Channels.* Analogous to global customers, channels of distribution may buy on a global or at least a regional basis. Global channels or middlemen are also important in exploiting differences in prices by buying at a lower price in one country and selling at a higher price in another country. Their presence makes it more necessary for a business to rationalize its worldwide pricing. Global channels are rare, but regionwide channels are increasing in number, particularly in European grocery distribution and retailing.

• *Transferable Marketing.* The buying decision may be such that marketing elements, such as brand names and advertising, require little local adaptation. Such transferability enables firms to use uniform marketing strategies and facilitates expanded participation in markets. A worldwide business can also adapt its brand names and advertising campaigns to make them more transferable, or, even better, design global ones to start with. Offsetting risks include the blandness of uniformly acceptable brand names or advertising, and the vulnerability of relying on a single brand franchise.

Cost Drivers   Cost drivers depend on the economics of the business; they particularly affect activity concentration.

• *Economies of Scale and Scope.*   A single-country market may not be large enough for the local business to achieve all possible economies of scale or scope. Scale at a given location can be increased through participation in multiple markets combined with product standardization or concentration of selected value activities. Corresponding risks include rigidity and vulnerability to disruption.

In the past few years, the economics of the electronics industry have shifted. As the cost of circuits has decreased, the economic advantage has gone to companies that can produce the lowest-cost components. Size has become a major asset. Thomson, the French electronics firm, understands the need to have a worldwide presence in an industry characterized by economies of scale. In 1987, Thomson greatly increased both its operating scale and its global coverage by acquiring the RCA television business from General Electric.

• *Learning and Experience.*   Even if economies of scope and scale are exhausted, expanded market participation and activity concentration can accelerate the accumulation of learning and experience. The steeper the learning and experience curves, the greater the potential benefit will be. Managers should beware, though, of the usual danger in pursuing experience curve strategies—overaggressive pricing that destroys not just the competition but the market as well. Prices get so low that profit is insufficient to sustain any competitor.

• *Sourcing Efficiencies.*   Centralized purchasing of new materials can significantly lower costs. Himont began as a joint venture between Hercules Inc. of the United States and Montedison Petrolchimica SpA of Italy, and is the leader in the global polypropylene market. Central to Himont's strategy is global coordination among manufacturing facilities in the purchase of raw materials, particularly monomer, the key ingredient in polypropylene production. Rationalization of raw material orders significantly strengthens the venture's low-cost production advantage.

• *Favorable Logistics.*   A favorable ratio of sales value to transportation cost enhances the company's ability to concentrate production. Other logistical factors include non perishability, the absence of time urgency, and little need for location close to customer facilities. Even the shape of the product can make a crucial difference. Cardboard tubes, such as those used as cores for textiles, cannot be shipped economically because they are mostly air. In contrast, cardboard cones are transportable because many units can be stacked in the same space.

• *Differences in Country Costs and Skills.* Factor costs generally vary across countries; this is particularly true in certain industries. The availability of particular skills also varies. Concentration of activities in low-cost or high-skill countries can increase productivity and reduce costs, but managers need to anticipate the danger of training future offshore competitors.[13]

Under attack from lower-priced cars, Volkswagen has needed to reduce its costs. It is doing so by concentrating its production to take advantage of the differences in various country costs. In Spain, hourly labor costs are below DM 20 per hour, while those in West Germany are over DM 40 per hour. To take advantage of this cost differential, the company moved production of Polos from Wolfsburg to Spain, freeing up the high-wage German labor to produce the higher-priced Golf cars. Another example of this concentration occurred when Volkswagen shut down its New Stanton, Pennsylvania, plant that manufactured Golfs and Jettas. The lower end of the U.S. market would be served by its low-wage Brazilian facility that produced the Fox.

[13]See: C.C. Markides and N. Berg, "Manufacturing Offshore Is Bad Business," *Harvard Business Review,* September–October 1988, pp. 113–120.

Figure 5 Effects of Industry Globalization Drivers on the Potential Use of Global Strategy Levers

Strategy Levers

Industry Drivers	Major Market Participation	Product Standardization	Activity Concentration	Uniform Marketing	Integrated Competitive Moves
Market					
Homogeneous needs	Fewer varieties needed to serve many markets	Standardized product is more acceptable			
Global customers			Marketing process has to be coordinated	Marketing content needs to be uniform	Allows sequenced invasion of markets
Global channels			Marketing process has to be coordinated	Marketing content needs to be uniform	
Transferable marketing	Easier to expand internationally			Allows use of global brands, advertising, etc.	
Cost					
Economies of scale and scope	Multiple markets needed to reach economic scale	Standardization needed to reach economic scale	Concentration helps reach economic scale	Uniform marketing cuts program development and production costs	Country interdependence affects overall scale economies
Learning and experience	Multiple markets accelerate learning	Standardization accelerates learning	Concentration accelerates learning		
Sourcing efficiencies			Centralized purchasing exploits efficiencies		
Favorable logistics	Easier to expand internationally		Allows concentrated production		Allows export competition

(continued)

Cost (*cont.*)					
Differences in country costs and skills			Exploited by activity concentration		Increase vulnerability of high-cost countries
Product development costs	Multiple markets needed to pay back investment	Standardization reduces development needs	Concentration cuts cost of development		
Government					
Favorable trade policies	Affects nature and extent of participation	May require or prevent product features	Local content rules affect extent of concentration possible		Integration needed to deal with competitive effects of tariffs/subsidies
Compatible technical standards	Affects markets that can be entered	Affects standardization possible			
Common marketing regulations				Affects approaches possible	
Competitive					
Interdependence of countries	More participation leverages benefits	Accept trade-offs to get best global product	Locate key activities in lead countries	Use lead country to develop programs	Integration needed to exploit benefits
Competitors globalized or might globalize	Expand to match or preempt	Match or preempt	Match or preempt	Match or preempt	Integration needed to exploit benefits

The higher end of the product line (Jetta and Golf) would be exported from Europe. This concentration and coordination of production has enabled the company to lower costs substantially.

• *Product Development Costs.*   Product development costs can be reduced by developing a few global or regional products rather than many national products. The automobile industry is characterized by long product development periods and high product development costs. One reason for the high costs is duplication of effort across countries. The Ford Motor Company's "Centers of Excellence" program aims to reduce these duplicating efforts and to exploit the differing expertise of Ford specialists worldwide. As part of the concentrated effort, Ford of Europe is designing a common platform for all compacts, while Ford of North America is developing platforms for the replacement of the midsized Taurus and Sable. This concentration of design is estimated to save "hundreds of millions of dollars per model by eliminating duplicative efforts and saving on retooling factories."[14]

Governmental Drivers   Government globalization drivers depend on the rules set by national governments and affect the use of all global strategy levers.

• *Favorable Trade Policies.*   Host governments affect globalization potential through import tariffs and quotas, nontariff barriers, export subsidies, local content requirements, currency and capital flow restrictions, and requirements on technology transfer.[15] Host government policies can make it difficult to use the global levers of major market participation, product standardization, activity concentration, and uniform marketing; they also affect the integrated-competitive-moves lever.

National trade policies constrain companies' concentration of manufacturing activities. Aggressive

U.S. government actions including threats on tariffs, quotas, and protectionist measures have helped convince Japanese automakers and other manufacturers to give up their concentration of manufacturing in Japan. Reluctantly, Japanese companies are opening plants in the United States. Honda has even made a public relations virtue out of necessity. It recently gave great publicity to the first shipment of a U.S.-made Honda car to Japan.

The easing of government restrictions can set off a rush for expanded market participation. European Union regulations for banking and financial services are among those harmonized in 1992. The European Union decision to permit the free flow of capital among member countries has led European financial institutions to jockey for position. Until recently, the Deutsche Bank had only fifteen offices outside of Germany, but it has recently established a major presence in the French market. In 1987, Deutsche Bank also moved into the Italian market by acquiring Bank of America's one hundred branches there. Other financial organizations, such as J.P. Morgan of the United States, Swiss Bank Corporation, and the S.P. Warburg Group in Britain have increased their participation in major European markets through acquisitions.

• *Compatible Technical Standards.*   Differences in technical standards, especially government-imposed standards, limit the extent to which products can be standardized. Often, standards are set with protectionism in mind. Motorola found that many of their electronics products were excluded from the Japanese market because these products operated at a higher frequency than was permitted in Japan.

• *Common Marketing Regulations.*   The marketing environment of individual countries affects the extent to which uniform global marketing approaches can be used. Certain types of media may be prohibited or restricted. For example, the United States is far more liberal than Europe about the kinds of advertising claims that can be made on television. The British authorities even veto the depiction of socially undesirable behavior. For example, British television authorities do not allow

---

[14]"Can Ford Stay on Top?" *BusinessWeek,* September 28, 1987, pp. 78–86.

[15]Three public sector activities that can protect domestic competitors are blocking access to the domestic market, providing subsidies, and creating spillovers in research and development. See: M.A. Spence, "Industrial Organization and Competitive Advantage in Multinational Industries," *American Economic Review,* 74 (May 1984), pp. 356–60.

scenes of children pestering their parents to buy a product. And, of course, the use of sex is different. As one extreme, France is far more liberal than the United States about sex in advertising. Various promotional devices, such as lotteries, may also be restricted.

Competitive Drivers   Market, cost, and governmental globalization drivers are essentially fixed for an industry at any given time. Competitors can play only a limited role in affecting these factors (although a sustained effort can bring about change, particularly in the case of consumer preferences). In contrast, competitive drivers are entirely in the realm of competitor choice. Competitors can raise the globalization potential of their industry and spur the need for a response on the global strategy levers.

• *Interdependence of Countries.*   A competitor may create competitive interdependence among countries by pursuing a global strategy. The basic mechanism is through sharing of activities. When activities such as production are shared among countries, a competitor's market share in one country affects its scale and overall cost position in the shared activities. Changes in that scale and cost will affect its competitive position in all countries dependent on the shared activities. Less directly, customers may view market position in a lead country as an indicator of overall quality. Companies frequently promote a product as, for example, "the leading brand in the United States." Other competitors then need to respond via increased market participation, uniform marketing, or integrated competitive strategy to avoid a downward spiral of sequentially weakened positions in individual countries.

In the automobile industry, where economies of scale are significant and where sharing activities can lower costs, markets have significant competitive interdependence. As companies like Ford and Volkswagen concentrate production and become more cost competitive with the Japanese manufacturers, the Japanese are pressured to enter more markets so that increased production volume will lower costs. Whether conscious of this or not,

Toyota made a concerted effort to penetrate the German market: between 1984 and 1987, Toyota doubled the number of cars produced for the German market.

• *Globalized Competitors.* More specifically, matching or preempting individual competitor moves may be necessary. These moves include expanding into or within major markets, being the first to introduce a standardized product, or being the first to use a uniform marketing program.

The need to preempt a global competitor can spur increased market participation. In 1986, Unilever, the European consumer products company, sought to increase its participation in the U.S. market by launching a hostile takeover bid for Richardson-Vicks Inc. Unilever's global arch rival, Procter & Gamble, saw the threat to its home turf and outbid Unilever to capture Richardson-Vicks. With Richardson-Vicks's European system, P&G was able to greatly strengthen its European positioning. So Unilever's attempt to expand participation in a rival's home market backfired to allow the rival to expand participation in Unilever's home markets.

In summary, industry globalization drivers provide opportunities to use global strategy levers in many ways. Some industries, such as civil aircraft, can score high on most dimensions of globalization.[16] Others, such as the cement industry, seem to be inherently local. But more and more industries are developing globalization potential. Even the food industry in Europe, renowned for its diversity of taste, is now a globalization target for major food multinationals.

Changes over Time   Finally, industry evolution plays a role. As each of the industry globalization drivers changes over time, so too will the appropriate global strategy change. For example, in the European major appliance industry, globalization forces seem to have reversed. In the late 1960s and early 1970s, a regional standardization strategy was successful for some key competitors.[17] But in the 1980s the

[16]M.Y. Yoshino, "Global Competition in a Salient Industry: The Case of Civil Aircraft," in Porter (1986).

[17]Levitt (May-June 1983).

situation appeared to have turned around, and the most successful strategies seemed to be national.[18]

In some cases, the actions of individual competitors can affect the direction and pace of change; competitors positioned to take advantage of globalization forces will want to hasten them. For example, a competitor with strong central manufacturing capabilities may want to accelerate the worldwide acceptance of a standardized product.

More than One Strategy Is Viable

Although they are powerful, industry globalization drivers do not dictate one formula for success. More than one type of international strategy can be viable in a given industry.

Industries Vary across Drivers   No industry is high on every one of the many globalization drivers. A particular competitor may be in a strong position to exploit a driver that scores low on globalization. For example, the dominance of national government customers offsets the globalization potential from other industry drivers, because government customers typically prefer to do business with their own nationals. In such an industry a competitor with a global strategy can use its other advantages, such as low cost from centralization of global production, to offset this drawback. At the same time, another multinational competitor with good government contacts can pursue a multidomestic strategy and succeed without globalization advantages, and single-country local competitors can succeed on the basis of their very particular local assets. The hotel industry provides examples both of successful global and of successful local competitors.

Global Effects Are Incremental   Globalization drivers are not deterministic for a second reason: the appropriate use of strategy levers adds competitive advantage to existing sources. These other sources may allow individual competitors to thrive with international strategies that are mismatched

with industry globalization drivers. For example, superior technology is a major source of competitive advantage in most industries, but can be quite independent of globalization drivers. A competitor with sufficiently superior technology can use it to offset globalization disadvantages.

Business and Parent Company Position and Resources Are Crucial   The third reason that drivers are not deterministic is related to resources. A worldwide business may face industry drivers that strongly favor a global strategy. But global strategies are typically expensive to implement initially even though great cost savings and revenue gains should follow. High initial investments may be needed to expand within or into major markets, to develop standardized products, to relocate value activities, to create global brands, to create new organization units or coordination processes, and to implement other aspects of a global strategy.

The strategic position of the business is also relevant. Even though a global strategy may improve the business's long-term strategic position, its immediate position may be so weak that resources should be devoted to short-term, country-by-country improvements. Despite the automobile industry's very strong globalization drivers, Chrysler Corporation had to deglobalize by selling off most of its international automotive businesses to avoid bankruptcy. Lastly, investing in nonglobal sources of competitive advantage, such as superior technology, may yield greater returns than global ones, such as centralized manufacturing.

Organizations Have Limitations   Finally, factors such as organization structure, management processes, people, and culture affect how well a desired global strategy can be implemented. Organizational differences among companies in the same industry can, or should, constrain the companies' pursuit of the same global strategy. Organization issues in globalization are a major topic, and cannot be covered in the space here.[19]

---

[18]C. Baden Fuller et al., "National or Global? The Study of Company Strategies and the European Market for Major Appliances," (London Business School Centre for Business Strategy, working paper series, No. 28, June 1987).

[19]See: Yip et al (1988); and C.K. Prahalad and Y.L. Doz, *The Multinational Mission: Balancing Local Demands and Global Vision* (New York: Free Press, 1987).

Reading 3-3 Competition in Global Industries: A Conceptual Framework

Michael E. Porter

International competition ranks high on the list of issues confronting firms today. The growing importance of international competition is well recognized in both the business and academic communities, for reasons that are clear when one examines just about any data set that exists on international trade or investment. Figure 1, for example, compares world trade and world gross national product (GNP). Something interesting started happening around the mid-1950s, when the growth in world trade began to exceed significantly the growth in world GNP.[1] A few years later, by 1963, foreign direct investment by firms in developing countries began to grow rapidly.[2] The 1950s marked the beginning of a fundamental change in the international competitive environment. The change has been accelerated by the emergence across a wide range of industries of potent new international competitors, from countries such as Japan, Korea, and Taiwan, calling into question theories of international competition that placed advanced nations in the driver's seat. It is a trend that continues to cause sleepless nights for many business managers.

The subject of international competition is far from new. A large body of literature rooted in the principle of comparative advantage has investigated the many implications of the various theoretical models of international trade.[3] Considerable research on the multinational firm exists, reflecting the growing importance of the multinational since the turn of the century. I think it is fair to characterize this work as resting heavily on the multinational's ability to exploit know-how and expertise gained in one country's market in other countries at low costs, thereby offsetting the unavoidable extra costs of doing business in a foreign country.[4] A related body of knowledge also exists in companies and in writing on the problems of entry into foreign markets and the life cycle of how a firm should compete abroad, beginning with export of licensing and ultimately moving to the establishment of foreign subsidiaries.[5] Finally, many of the functional fields in management have their branch of thinking about international issues, for example, international marketing or international finance. Most attention is concentrated, by and large, on the problems of doing business in a foreign country.

As rich as it is, however, our knowledge of international competition does not address some pressing questions facing today's international firms. Though research and practice have provided some guidance for considering incremental investment

---

This reading has benefited from comments by Richard A. Rawlinson, M. Therese Flaherty, and Louis T. Wells, Jr.

Reprinted from *Competition in Global Industries,* M. E. Porter (ed.), with permission from Harvard Business School Publishing.

[1]Intra-industry trade, where a country both exports and imports goods in the same industry, has grown markedly as well. The reasons will be made clear by the framework below.

[2]United Nations Center on Transnational Corporations (1884).

[3]For a survey, see Caves and Jones (1985).

[4]See, particularly, the work of Hymer, Kindleberger, and Caves. There are many books on the theory and management of the multinational, which are too numerous to cite here. For an excellent survey of the literature, see Caves (1982). A more recent stream of literature emphasizes how the multinational firm internalizes transactions to circumvent imperfections in various intermediate markets, most importantly the market for knowledge. Prominent examples of this work are Buckley and Casson (1976) and Teece (1981). For a survey and extension, see Teece (1985).

[5]Knickerbocker's (1973) work on oligopolistic reaction adds an important dimension to the process of entering foreign markets through illuminating bunching in the timing of entry into a country by firms in an industry and relating this to defensive considerations. Vernon's product cycle of international trade combines a view of how products mature with the evolution in a firm's international activities to predict the patterns of trade and investment in developed and developing countries (Vernon 1966). Vernon himself, among others, has raised questions about how general the product cycle pattern is today.

Figure 1   Growth of World Trade

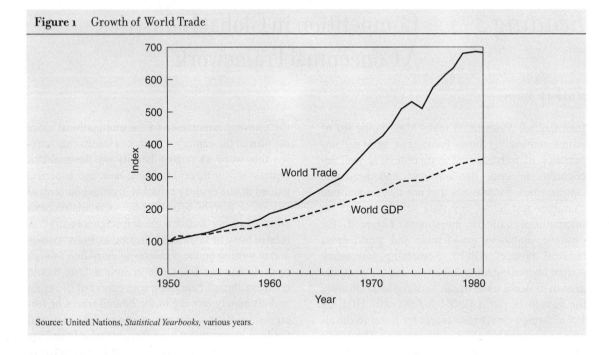

Source: United Nations, *Statistical Yearbooks,* various years.

decisions to enter new countries, at best we have an incomplete view of how to conceive of a firm's overall international strategy and how such a strategy should be selected. Put another way, we know more about the problems of becoming a multinational than about strategies for managing an established multinational.[6]

This article seeks to explore the implications of international competition for competitive strategy. In particular, what are the distinctive questions for competitive strategy that are raised by international, as opposed to domestic, competition? Many of the strategy issues for a company competing internationally are very much the same as for one competing domestically: a firm must still analyze its industry structure and competitors, understand its buyer and the sources of buyer value, diagnose its relative cost position, and seek to establish a sustainable competitive advantage within some

competitive scope, whether it be across the board or in an industry segment. These are subjects I have written about extensively.[7] But there are some questions for strategy that are peculiar to international competition and that add to rather than replace those examined by other authors. These questions all revolve, in one way or another, around how what a firm does in one country affects or is affected by what is going on in other countries—the degree of connection among country competition.

Patterns of International Competition

The appropriate unit of analysis in setting international strategy is the industry, because the industry is the arena in which competitive advantage is won or lost. The pattern of international competition differs markedly from industry to industry. Industries vary along a spectrum from *multidomestic* to *global* in their competitive scope.

---

[6]There are some notable exceptions to the general paucity of thinking on the strategy of established multinationals. See, for example, Stopford and Wells (1972), Franko (1976), Stobaugh et al. (1976).

[7]Porter (1980, 1985*a*).

In multidomestic industries, competition in each country (or small group of countries) is essentially independent of competition in other countries. A multidomestic industry is one that is present in many countries (e.g., there is a consumer banking industry in Sri Lanka, one in France, and one in the United States), but one in which competition occurs on a country-by-country basis. In a multidomestic industry, a multinational firm may enjoy a competitive advantage from the one-time transfer of know-how from its home base to foreign countries. However, the firm modifies and adapts its intangible assets in order to employ them in each country, and the competitive outcome over time is then determined by conditions in each country. The competitive advantages of the firm, then, are largely specific to the country. The international industry becomes a collection of essentially domestic industries—hence the term multidomestic. Industries where competition has traditionally exhibited this pattern include retailing, consumer packaged goods, distribution, insurance, consumer finance, and caustic chemicals.

At the other end of the spectrum are what I term global industries. The term global—like the word "strategy"—has become overused and perhaps misunderstood. The definition of a global industry employed here is an industry in which a firm's competitive position in one country is significantly affected by its position in other countries or vice versa.[8] Therefore, the international industry is not merely a collection of domestic industries but a series of linked domestic industries in which the rivals compete against each other on a truly worldwide basis. Industries exhibiting or evolving toward the global pattern today include commercial aircraft, TV sets, semiconductors, copiers, automobiles, and watches.

The implications for international strategy of this distinction between multidomestic and global are quite profound. In a multidomestic industry, a firm can and should manage its international activities like a portfolio. Its subsidiaries or other operations around the world should each control all the important activities necessary to do business in the industry and should enjoy a high degree of autonomy. The firm's strategy in a country should be determined largely by the competitive conditions in that country; the firm's international strategy should be what I term a country-centered strategy.

In a multidomestic industry, competing internationally is discretionary. A firm can choose to remain domestic or can expand internationally, if it has some advantage that allows it to overcome the extra costs of entering and competing in foreign markets. The important competitors in multidomestic industries will either be domestic companies or multinationals with stand-alone operations abroad. Such is the situation in each of the multidomestic industries listed earlier. In a multidomestic industry, then, international strategy collapses to a series of domestic strategies. The issues that are uniquely international revolve around how to do business abroad, how to select good countries in which to compete (or assess country risk), and how to achieve the one-time transfer of know-how or expertise. These are questions that are relatively well developed in the literature.

In a global industry, managing international activities like a portfolio will undermine the possibility of achieving competitive advantage. In a global industry, a firm must in some way integrate its activities on a worldwide basis to capture the linkages among countries. This integration will require more than transferring intangible assets among countries, though it will include such transfer. A firm may choose to compete with a country-centered strategy, focusing on specific market segments or countries where it can carve out a niche by responding to whatever local country differences are present. However, it does so at some considerable peril from competitors with global strategies. All the important competitors in the global industries listed above compete worldwide with increasingly coordinated strategies.

In international competition, a firm has to perform some functions in each of the countries in which it competes. Even though a global competitor must view its international activities as an

[8]The distinction between multidomestic and global competition and some of its strategic implications were first described in Hout, Porter, and Rudden (1982).

overall system, it still has to maintain some country perspective. It is the balancing of these two perspectives that becomes one of the essential questions in global strategy.[9]

Causes of Globalization

If we accept the distinction between multidomestic and global industries as an important taxonomy of patterns of international competition, a number of questions arise. When does an industry globalize? What exactly do we mean by a global strategy, and is there more than one kind? What determines the type of international strategy best suited to a particular industry?

An industry can be defined as global if there is some competitive advantage to integrating activities on a worldwide basis. To make this statement operational, however, we must be very precise about what we mean by activities and also what we mean by integrating. To diagnose the sources of competitive advantage in any context, whether it be domestic or international, it is necessary to adopt a disaggregated view of the firm, which I call the value chain.[10] Every firm is a collection of discrete activities performed to do business in its industry—I call them value activities. The activities performed by a firm

include such things as salespeople selling the product, service technicians performing repairs, scientists in the laboratory designing products or processes, and accountants keeping the books. Such activities are technologically and, in most cases, physically distinct. It is only at the level of these discrete activities, rather than the firm as a whole, that competitive advantage can be truly understood.

A firm may possess two types of competitive advantage: (1) *low cost* or (2) *differentiation*. These grow out of the firm's ability to perform the activities in the value chain either more cheaply or in a unique way relative to its competitors. The ultimate value a firm creates is what buyers are willing to pay for what the firm provides, which includes its physical product in addition to any ancillary services or benefits, such as design assistance, repair, or more timely delivery than competitors. Profit results if the value created through performing the required activities exceeds the collective cost of performing them. Competitive advantage is a function of either providing comparable buyer value more efficiently than competitors (low cost) or performing activities at comparable cost but in unique ways that create more buyer value than competitors and, hence, command a premium price (differentiation).

The value chain, shown in Figure 2, provides a systematic means of displaying and categorizing activities. The activities performed by a firm in any industry can be grouped into the nine generic categories shown. The labels may differ based on industry convention, but every firm performs these basic categories of activities in some way or another. Within each category, a firm typically performs a number of discrete activities that are particular to the industry and to the firm's strategy. In service, for example, firms typically perform such discrete activities as installation, repair, parts distribution, and upgrading.

The generic categories of activities can be grouped into two broad types. Along the bottom are what I call *primary* activities, which are those involved in the physical creation of the product or service, its delivery and marketing to the buyer, and its support after sale. Across the top are what I call

[9]Perlmutter's (1969) concept of ethnocentric, polycentric, and geocentric multinationals is an interesting but different one. It takes the firm, not the industry, as the unit of analysis and is decoupled from industry structure. It focuses on management attitudes, the nationality of executives, and other aspects of organization. Perlmutter presents ethnocentric, polycentric, and geocentric as stages of an organization's development as a multinational, with geocentric as the goal. A later paper (Wind, Douglas, and Perlmutter 1973) tempers this conclusion based on the fact that some companies may not have the required sophistication in marketing to attempt a geocentric strategy. Products embedded in the lifestyle or culture of a country are also identified as less susceptible to geocentrism. The Perlmutter et al. view does not attempt to link management orientation to industry structure and strategy. International strategy should grow out of the net competitive advantage in a global industry of different types of worldwide coordination. In some industries, a country-centered strategy, roughly analogous to Perlmutter's polycentric idea, may be the best strategy irrespective of company size and international experience. Conversely, a global strategy may be imperative given the competitive advantage that accrues from it. Industry and strategy should define the organization approach, not vice versa.

[10]Porter (1985a) describes value chain theory and its use in analyzing competitive advantage.

Figure 2   The Value Chain

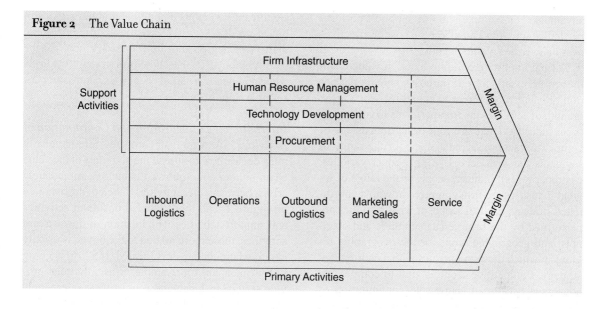

support activities, which provide inputs or infrastructure that allow the primary activities to take place on an ongoing basis.

Procurement is the obtaining of purchased inputs, such as raw materials, purchased services, machinery, and so on. Procurement stretches across the entire value chain because it supports every activity; that is, every activity uses purchased inputs of some kind. There are typically many different discrete procurement activities within a firm, often performed by different people. Technology development encompasses the activities involved in designing the product as well as in creating and improving the way the various activities in the value chain are performed. We tend to think of technology in terms of the product or manufacturing process. In fact, every activity involves a technology or technologies, which may be simple or sophisticated, and a firm has a stock of know-how about how to perform each activity. Technology development typically involves a variety of different discrete activities, some performed outside the R&D department.

Human resource management is the recruiting, training, and development of personnel. Every activity involves human resources, and thus human resource management activities span the entire chain. Finally, firm infrastructure includes activities such as general management, accounting, legal, finance, strategic planning, and all the other activities outside of specific primary or support activities but essential to enable the entire chain's operation. Each category of activities is of differing relative importance to competitive advantage in different industries, although they are present in all industries.

Activities in a firm's value chain are not independent, but are connected through what I call linkages. The way one activity is performed frequently affects the cost or effectiveness of other activities. If more is spent on the purchase of a raw material, for example, a firm may lower its cost of fabrication or assembly. There are many linkages that connect activities, not only within the firm but also with the activities of its suppliers, channels, and ultimately its buyers. The firm's value chain resides in a larger stream of activities that I term the value system. Suppliers have value chains that provide the purchased inputs to the firm's chain; channels have value chains through which the firm's product or service passes; buyers have value chains in which the firm's product or service is employed. The connections among activities in this system also become essential to competitive advantage. For example, the way suppliers perform particular activities can affect the cost or effectiveness of activities within the firm.

A final important building block in value chain theory, necessary for our purposes here, is the notion of *competitive scope*. Competitive scope is the breadth of activities the firm performs in competing in an industry. There are four basic dimensions of competitive scope: segment scope, or the range of segments the firm serves (e.g., product varieties, customer types); industry scope, or the range of related industries the firm competes in with a coordinated strategy; vertical scope, or what activities are performed by the firm versus suppliers and channels; and geographic scope, or the geographic regions in which the firm operates with a coordinated strategy. Competitive scope is vital to competitive advantage because it shapes the configuration of the value chain, how activities are performed, and whether activities are shared among units.

International strategy is an issue of geographic scope. Its analysis is quite similar to that of whether and how a firm should compete locally, regionally, or nationally within a country. In the international context, government tends to have a greater involvement in competition and there are more significant variations among geographic regions in buyer needs. Nevertheless, these differences are matters of degree and the framework here can be readily applied to the choice of strategy by firms who compete in large countries consisting of several regions or cities.

International Configuration and Coordination of Activities   A firm that competes internationally must decide how to spread the activities in the value chain among countries. A distinction immediately arises between the activities labeled downstream on Figure 3, and those labeled upstream activities and support activities. The location of downstream activities, those more related to the buyer, is usually tied to where the buyer is located. If a firm is going to sell in Japan, for example, it usually must provide service in Japan and it must have salespeople stationed in Japan. In some industries it is possible to have a single sales force that travels to the buyer's country and back again; some other specific downstream activities such as the production of advertising copy can sometimes also be performed centrally. More typically, however, the firm must locate the capability to perform downstream activities in each of the countries in which it operates.

Figure 3   Upstream and Downstream Activities

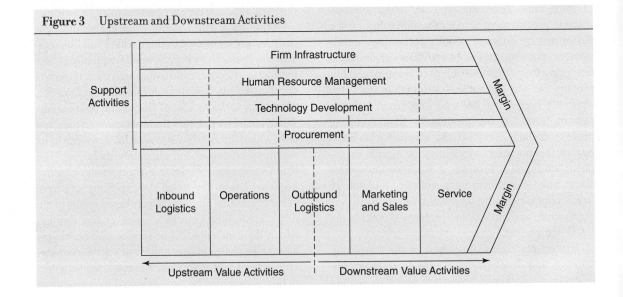

Upstream activities and support activities, conversely, could conceptually be decoupled from where the buyer is located in most industries.

This distinction carries some interesting implications. First, downstream activities create competitive advantages that are largely country specific: a firm's reputation, brand name, and service network in a country grow largely out of a firm's activities in that country and create entry/mobility barriers largely in that country alone. Competitive advantage in upstream and support activities often grows more out of the entire system of countries in which a firm competes than from its position in any one country.

Second, in industries where downstream activities or other buyer-tied activities are vital to competitive advantage, there tends to be a more multidomestic pattern of international competition. In many service industries, for example, not only downstream activities but frequently upstream activities are tied to buyer location, and global strategies are comparatively less common.[11] In industries where upstream and support activities such as technology development and operations are crucial to competitive advantage, global competition is more common. In global competition, the location and scale of these potentially footloose activities is optimized from a worldwide perspective.[12]

The distinctive issues in international, as contrasted to domestic, strategy can be summarized in two key dimensions of how a firm competes internationally. The first I call the *configuration* of a firm's activities worldwide or the location in the world where each activity in the value chain is performed, including in how many places. The second dimension I call *coordination,* which refers to how like or linked activities performed in different countries are coordinated with each other. If, for example, there are three plants—one in Germany, one in Japan, and one in the United States—how do the activities in those plants relate to each other?

A firm faces an array of options in both configuration and coordination for each activity in the value chain. Configuration options range from *concentrated*—performing an activity in one location and serving the world from it, for example, one R&D lab, one large plant—to *dispersed,* that is, performing the activity in every country. In the extreme case, each country would have a complete value chain. Table 1 illustrates an example of configuration of worldwide activities in an industry.[13] A firm need not concentrate all its activities in the same country. Today, in fact, it has become common to concentrate activities in many different countries.

Coordination options range from none to many. For example, a firm producing in three plants could at one extreme allow each plant to operate with full autonomy, including different production steps and different part numbers. At the other extreme, the plants could be tightly coordinated by employing the same information system, the same production process, the same parts, specifications, and so forth. Options for coordination in an activity are typically more numerous than the configuration options, because there are many possible types of coordination and many different facets of an activity on which to coordinate.

Table 2 lists some of the configuration issues and coordination issues for several categories of value activities. In technology development, for example, the configuration issue is where R&D is performed: at one location or two or more locations and in what countries? The coordination issues have to do with such things as the allocation of tasks among R&D centers, the extent of interchange among them, and the location and sequence of product introduction around the world. There are

---

[11]There is a growing globalization of service firm strategies, however, as service firms serve multinational buyers. Developments in information technology raise the importance of R&D, and automation pervades the primary activities of service firms. Service firms tend to draw advantages from a global strategy largely in the support activities in the value chain.

[12]Buzzell (1968), Pryor (1965), and Wind, Douglas, and Perlmutter (1973) point out that national differences are in most cases more critical with respect to marketing than with production and finance. This generalization reflects the fact that marketing activities are often inherently country based. However, this generalization is not reliable because in many countries, production and other activities are widely dispersed.

[13]In practice, a diagram such as Table 1 would involve each important discrete activity (not broad categories) and include all the countries in which a firm operates.

Table 1   Illustrative Configuration of Activities Globally for a U.S. Company

Activities	U.S.	Canada	U.K.	France	Germany	Japan
Inbound logistics	X		X		X	X
Operations						
Components	X		X			
Assembly	X				X	X
Testing	X				X	X
Outbound logistics						
Order processing	X					
Physical distribution	X	X	X	X	X	X
Marketing and sales						
Advertising	X	X	X	X	X	X
Sales force	X	X	X	X	X	X
Promotional materials	X					
Service	X	X	X	X	X	X
Procurement	X					X
Technology development	X					X
Human resource management	X	X	X	X	X	X
Firm infrastructure	X					

configuration issues and coordination issues for every activity.[14]

Figure 4 is a way of summarizing these basic choices in international strategy geographically on a single diagram, with coordination of activities on the vertical axis and configuration of activities on the horizontal axis. The firm has to make a set of choices for each activity. If a firm employs a very dispersed configuration, placing an entire value chain in every country (or small group of contiguous countries) in which it operates and coordinating little or not at all among them, then the firm is competing with a country-centered strategy.[15] The domestic firm, operating in only one country, is the extreme case of a firm with a country-centered strategy. As we move from the lower left-hand corner of the diagram up or to the right, we have strategies that are increasingly global. Figure 4 can be

employed to map strategic groups in an international industry because its axes capture the most important sources of competitive advantage from an international strategy.[16]

Figure 5 illustrates some of the possible variations in international strategy. The simplest global strategy is to concentrate as many activities as possible in one country, serve the world from this home base, and tightly coordinate through standarization those activities that must inherently be performed near the buyer. This is the pattern adopted by many Japanese firms in the 1960s and 1970s, such as Toyota. The position of Toyota is plotted on Figure 4 along with key competitors. However, the options apparent in Figures 5 and 6 make it clear that there is no such thing as one global strategy.

There are many different kinds of global strategies, depending on a firm's choices about configuration and coordination throughout the value chain. In copiers, for example, Xerox has until recently concentrated R&D in the United States, but dispersed other activities, in some cases using joint-venture

[14]M. Therese Flaherty provided helpful comments that clarified the configuration/coordination distinction.

[15]Here, the firm makes only a one-time transfer of knowledge in establishing each subsidiary, which gives it an advantage over local firms. Transaction costs dictate the multinational form rather than market transactions.

[16]Strategic groups are described in Porter (1980), chapter 7.

Table 2   Configuration and Coordination Issues by Category of Activity

Value Activity	Configuration Issues	Coordination Issues
Operations	Location of production facilities for components and end products	Allocation of production tasks among dispersed facilities Networking of international plants Transferring process technology and production know-how among plants
Marketing and sales	Product line selection Country (market) selection Location of preparation of advertising and promotional materials	Commonality of brand name worldwide Coordination of sales to multinational accounts Similarity of channels and product positioning worldwide Coordination of pricing in different countries
Service	Location of the service organization	Similarity of service standards and procedures worldwide
Technology development	Number and location of R&D centers	Allocation of research tasks among dispersed R&D centers Interchange among R&D centers Developing products responsive to market needs in many countries Sequence of product introductions around the world
Procurement	Location of the purchasing function	Locating and managing suppliers in different countries Transferring knowledge about input markets Coordinating purchases of common items

Figure 4   The Dimensions of International Strategy

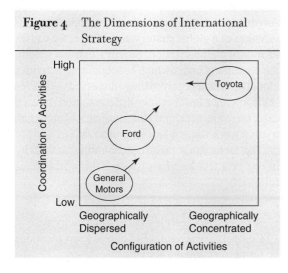

partners to perform them. On dispersed activities, however, coordination has been quite high. The Xerox brand, marketing approach, and servicing procedures have been quite standardized worldwide. Canon, on the other hand, has had a much more concentrated configuration of activities through somewhat less coordination of the dispersed activities. The vast majority of Canon's support activities plus most manufacturing have been performed in Japan. Aside from the requirement to use the Canon brand, however, local marketing subsidiaries have been given quite a bit of latitude in each region of the world.

Competitors with country-centered and global strategies can co-exist in an industry, but global strategies by some competitors frequently force

Figure 5   Types of International Strategy

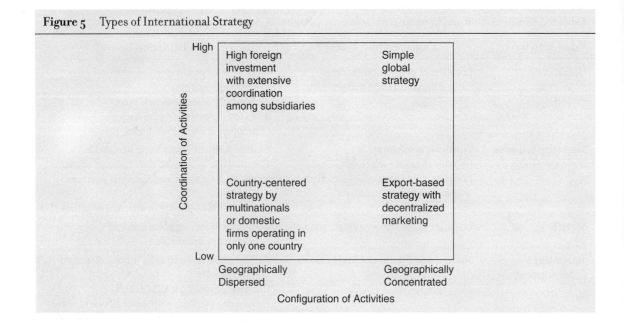

other firms to follow suit. In automobiles, for example, Toyota has employed a relatively simple global strategy to achieve the position of low-cost producer. General Motors has historically competed with a country-centered international strategy, with separate manufacturing facilities and even separate brand names in different regions, while Ford has practiced only regional coordination. As the arrows indicate, all three companies are modifying their international strategies today—the U.S. firms toward more global strategies and Toyota toward becoming more dispersed as its international position grows.

A global strategy can now be defined more precisely as one in which a firm seeks to *gain competitive advantage from its international presence through either a concentrated configuration, coordinating among dispersed activities, or both.* The one-time transfer of intangible assets, emphasized in the literature, is just one of many ways. Measuring the presence of a global industry empirically must reflect both dimensions and not just one. Market presence of firms in many countries and some export and import of components and end products are characteristic of most global industries. Hence, intraindustry trade is

a good sign of the presence of global competition, and its growth is one indication that the incidence of global industries has increased. High levels of foreign investment or the mere presence of multinational firms are not reliable measures, however, because firms may be managing foreign units like a portfolio.

Configuration/Coordination and Competitive Advantage   Understanding the competitive advantages of a global strategy and, in turn, the causes of industry globalization, requires that we specify the conditions under which concentrating activities globally and/or coordinating dispersed activities leads to either lower cost or differentiation. In each case, there are structural characteristics of an industry that work for and against globalization.

The factors that favor concentrating an activity in one or a few locations to serve the world are as follows:

- Economies of scale in the activity;
- A proprietary learning curve in the activity;
- Comparative advantage of one or a few locations for performing the activity;

- Coordination advantages of co-locating linked activities such as R&D and production.

The first two factors relate to *how many* sites an activity is performed at, while the last two relate to *where* these sites are. Comparative advantage can apply to any activity, not just production. There may be some locations in the world that are better places than others to perform other activities such as research or creation of advertising materials. India has become a center for software writing, for example. Government can promote the concentration of activities by providing subsidies or other incentives to employ a particular country as an export base—in effect altering comparative advantage—a role many governments are attempting to play today.

There are also structural characteristics that favor dispersion of an activity to many countries, because they create concentration costs. Local product needs may differ, nullifying the advantages of scale or learning from one-site operation of an activity. Dispersing a range of activities in a country may facilitate marketing in that country by signaling commitment to local buyers and/or providing greater local responsiveness. Dispersing an activity may facilitate learning or gaining know-how in the activity, as a number of sites increases information flow and managers get closer to more markets. Transport, communication, and storage costs can make it inefficient to concentrate the activity in one location.

Government is also frequently a powerful force for dispersing activities, through tariffs, nontariff barriers, and nationalistic purchasing (nationalistic purchasing can exist without a direct government role as well). Governments typically want firms to locate the entire value chain in their country, because this creates benefits and spillovers to the country that often go beyond local content.[17] Dispersing some activities may sometimes allow the concentration of others, through placating governments or through linkages among activities that will be described below. Dispersion is also encouraged by the risks of performing an activity at one place: exchange rate risk, political risk, risk of interruption, and so on. The balance between the advantages of concentrating and dispersing an activity normally differ for each activity (and industry). The best configuration for R&D is different from that for component fabrication, and this is different from that for assembly, installation, advertising, and procurement.[18]

The desirability of coordinating like or linked activities that are dispersed involves a similar balance of structural factors. Coordination potentially allows the sharing and accumulation of know-how and expertise among dispersed activities. If a firm learns how to operate the production process better in Germany, transferring that learning may make the process run better in U.S. and Japanese plants. Differing countries, with their inevitably differing conditions, provide a fertile basis for comparison as well as opportunities for arbitrating knowledge, obtained in different places about different aspects of the business. Knowledge may accumulate not only in product or process technology but also about buyer needs and marketing techniques. A firm coordinating internationally may also receive early warning of industry changes by spotting them in one or two leading countries before they become broadly apparent and transferring the knowledge to guide other activities elsewhere. The initial transfer of knowledge in establishing a foreign subsidiary is recognizable as one case of coordination among dispersed activities. However, it is clear that knowledge is continually created and can flow among all subsidiaries. The ability to accumulate and transfer this knowledge among units is a potent advantage of the global competitor over domestic or country-centered competitors.[19]

---

[17]For example, governments may desire national autonomy in decision making and the spillovers from domestic R&D and training of skilled workers.

[18]A number of authors have framed the globalization of industries in terms of the balance between imperatives for global integration and imperatives for national responsiveness, a useful distinction. See Prahalad (1975), Doz (1976), and Bartlett (1979). I relate that distinction here to more basic issues of where and how a firm performs the activities in the value chain internationally.

[19]Transactional failures make coordination between independent firms or coalition partners even more difficult than the initial transfer of knowledge in establishing a foreign subsidiary, not to mention ongoing coordination among subsidiaries.

Coordination among dispersed activities also potentially improves the ability to reap economies of scale in activities if subtasks are allocated among locations to allow some specialization, for example, each R&D center has a different area of focus. This illustrates how the way a network of foreign locations is managed can have a great influence on the ability to reap the benefits of any given configuration of activities. Viewed another way, close coordination is frequently a partial offset to dispersing an activity.

Closely related to this is the relationship between international coordination in one activity and the configuration of another. For example, coordination in the marketing activity involving information exchange about buyer needs in many countries may allow a central R&D facility to design a standard or easy-to-modify product for sale worldwide, unlocking the scale economies of a concentrated configuration in R&D and production. Such a linkage among separate activities has been exploited by Canon in the design of its personal copier. Similarly, dispersing procurement may allow concentrating manufacturing, since sourcing from many countries can open up the opportunity to export to them.

Coordination may also allow a firm to respond to *shifting* comparative advantage, where movements in exchange rates and factor costs are significant and hard to forecast. For example, incrementally increasing production at the location currently enjoying favorable exchange rates can lower costs. Coordination can also reinforce a firm's brand reputation with buyers through ensuring a consistent image and approach to doing business on a worldwide basis. This is particularly valuable if buyers are mobile or information about the industry flows freely around the world. Coordination may also differentiate the firm with multinational buyers if it allows the firm to serve them anywhere and in a consistent way. Coordination (and a global approach to configuration) enhances leverage with local governments if the firm is able to grow or shrink activities in one country at the expense of others. Finally, coordination yields flexibility in responding to competitors, by allowing the firm to

respond to them differently in different countries and to retaliate in one country to a challenge in another. A firm may choose, for example, to compete aggressively in the country from which a challenger draws its most important volume or cash flow in order to reduce the competitors' strength in other countries. IBM and Caterpillar have practiced this sort of defensive behavior in their Japanese operations.

Coordination of dispersed activities usually involves costs that differ by form of coordination and by industry. Local conditions in countries may vary in ways that may make a common approach across countries suboptimal. For example, if every plant in the world is required to use the same raw material, the firm pays a penalty in countries where that raw material is expensive relative to satisfactory substitutes. Business practices, marketing systems, raw material sources, local infrastructures, and a variety of other factors may differ across countries as well, in ways that may mitigate the advantages of a common approach or of the sharing of learning. Governments may restrain the flow of information required for coordination or impose other barriers to it. Transaction costs of coordination among countries can also be high. International coordination involves long distances, language problems, and cultural barriers to communication. Such problems may mean in some industries that coordination is not optimal. They also suggest that forms of coordination that involve relatively infrequent decisions, such as adopting common service standards or employing the same raw materials, will enjoy advantages over forms of coordination involving ongoing interchange, such as transshipping components and end products among facilities.

There are also substantial organizational challenges involved in achieving cooperation among subsidiaries, because of difficulties in aligning subsidiary managers' interests with those of the firm as a whole. The German branch does not necessarily want to tell the U.S. branch about their latest breakthroughs on the production line because it may make it harder for them to outdo the Americans in the annual comparison of operating efficiency among plants. These vexing organizational problems mean that country subsidiaries often view each other more as competitors than collaborators.[20] As with configuration, a firm must make an activity-by-activity choice about where there is net competitive advantage to coordinating in various ways.

Some factors favoring dispersion of activities also impede coordination, while others do not. Transport costs raise few barriers to coordination, for example, while product heterogeneity creates substantial ones. Product heterogeneity and the actions of government often have the special characteristics of impeding *both* concentration and coordination, giving them a particularly strategic role in affecting the pattern of international competition.

Coordination in some activities may be necessary to reap the advantages of configuration in others, as noted earlier. The use of common raw materials in each plant, for example, allows worldwide purchasing. Moreover, tailoring some activities to countries (not coordinating) may allow concentration and standardization of others. For example, tailored marketing in each country may allow the same product to be positioned differently and hence sold successfully in many countries, unlocking possibilities for reaping economies of scale in production and R&D. Thus, coordination and configuration interact.

Diversification into related industries can also shape the best global configuration/coordination in a single industry. For example, a diversified firm may be able to produce a number of related products in dispersed plants, instead of concentrating production of one product in a single plant, and still achieve economies of scale. This reflects the fact that sharing activities among units competing in related industries may serve the same strategic purpose as sharing them in competing in many countries—namely, scale or learning economies.[21]

Diversification can also create new options for bargaining with governments. For example, exports in one business unit can be traded for the ability to import in another. IBM follows this approach, seeking a balance of trade in each country in which it operates. Diversification in a variety of industries may also facilitate bartering. Conversely, diversification may raise a firm's overall commitment to a country, increasing the host government's leverage. For all these reasons, the extent of a firm's diversification should be a consideration in its choice of international strategy.

Configuration/Coordination and the Pattern of International Competition   Industries globalize when the benefits of configuring and/or coordinating globally exceed the costs of doing so. The way in which an industry globalizes reflects the specific benefits and costs of global configuration and/or coordination of each value activity. The activities in which global competitors gain competitive advantage will differ correspondingly. Configuration/coordination determines the ongoing competitive advantages of a global strategy, growing out of a firm's overall international position. These are additive to competitive advantages a firm derives/possesses from its domestic market positions. An initial transfer of knowledge from the home base to subsidiaries is thus one, but by no means the most important, advantage of a global competitor.[22]

In some industries, the competitive advantage from a global strategy comes in technology development, and firms gain little advantage from concentrating primary activities, which means that

---

[20] The difficulties in coordinating across business units competing in different industries within the diversified firm is described in Porter (1985*a*), chapter 11.

[21] For a discussion, see Porter (1985*a*), chapter 9.

[22] Empirical research has found a strong correlation between R&D and advertising intensity and the extent of foreign direct investment (for a survey, see Caves 1982). Both these factors have a place in our model of the determinants of globalization, but for quite different reasons. R&D intensity suggests scale advantages for the global competitor in developing products or processes that are manufactured abroad either due to low production scale economies or government pressures, or that require investments in service infrastructure. Advertising intensity, however, is much closer to proxying the possibilities for the classic transfer of marketing knowledge to foreign subsidiaries. High advertising industries are also frequently those where local tastes differ and manufacturing scale economies are modest, both reasons to disperse many activities.

they are dispersed around the world. A good example is the manufacture of glass and plastic containers, where transport cost leads to a dispersion of plants, but opportunities to perform R&D centrally and to transfer production know-how among plants yield significant advantages to global firms. In other industries, such as cameras or videocassette recorders, firms gain advantages from concentrating production to achieve economies of scale and learning but give subsidiaries much more autonomy in sales and marketing. Finally, in some industries there is no net advantage to a global strategy and country-centered strategies dominate; the industry is multidomestic.

An industry such as commercial aircraft represents an extreme case of a global industry (e.g., placement in the upper right-hand corner of Figure 4). Three competitors, Boeing, McDonnell Douglas, and Airbus, all have global strategies. In value activities important to cost and differentiation in the industry, there are compelling net advantages to concentrating most activities to serve worldwide markets and coordinating the dispersed activities extensively. Yet, host governments have a particular interest in the commercial aircraft industry because of its large trade potential, defense implications, and R&D spillovers. The competitive advantages of a global strategy are so great that all the successful aircraft producers have sought to achieve and preserve them. In addition, the power of government to intervene has been mitigated by the paucity of viable worldwide competitors and the enormous barriers to entry created, in part, by the advantages of a global strategy. The result has been that firms have been able to assuage government through procurement. Boeing, for example, is very careful about where it buys components. Boeing seeks to develop suppliers in countries that are large potential customers. This requires a great deal of extra effort by Boeing to transfer technology and to work with suppliers to ensure that they meet its standards. Boeing realizes that this is preferable to compromising the competitive advantage of its strongly integrated worldwide strategy. It is willing to employ one value activity (procurement), where the advantages

of concentration are modest, to help preserve the benefits of concentration in other activities. Recently, commercial aircraft competitors have entered into joint ventures and other coalition arrangements with foreign suppliers to achieve the same affect, as well as to spread the risk of huge development costs.

Segments and vertical stages of an industry frequently vary in their pattern of globalization. In aluminum, the upstream (alumina and ingot) stages are global industries. The downstream stage, semi-fabrication, is a group of multidomestic businesses, because product needs vary by country, transport costs are high, and intensive local customer service is required. Scale economies in the value chain are modest. In lubricants, automotive motor oil tends to be a multidomestic industry, while marine engine lubricants is a global industry. In automotive oil, countries have varying driving standards, weather conditions, and local laws. Production involves blending various kinds of base oils and additives and is subject to few economies of scale but high shipping costs. Distribution channels are important to competitive success and vary markedly from country to country. Country-centered competitors, such as Castrol and Quaker State, are leaders in most countries. In the marine segment, conversely, ships move freely around the world and require the same oil everywhere. Successful competitors are global. A third and different industry is lodging, where most segments are multidomestic because the majority of activities in the value chain are tied to buyer location and country differences lead to few benefits from coordination. In high-priced business-oriented hotels, however, competition is more global. Global competitors such as Hilton, Marriott, and Sheraton have dispersed value chains but employ common brand names, common service standards, and worldwide reservation systems to gain advantages in serving highly mobile business travelers.[23]

Just as the pattern of globalization may differ by segment or industry stage, so may the pattern

---

[23]This description draws on a study of the incidence of multinationals in the hotel industry by Dunning and McQueen (1981).

differ by groups of countries. There are often *sub-systems* of countries within which the advantages of configuration/coordination are greater than with other countries. For example, configuration/coordination possibilities may be high in competing in countries with similar climatic conditions (such as the Nordic countries) because they have similar product needs. Subsystems can be based on geographic regions, climatic conditions, language, state of economic development, extent of government intervention in competition, and historical or current political ties. In the record industry, for example, possibilities for coordination are great among the Spanish-speaking countries and countries with a large Spanish-speaking population such as the United States. Where there is extreme government intervention, geographic isolation, or very unusual product needs, countries can be effectively outside the global system or any subsystem.

International strategy has often been characterized as a choice between worldwide standardization and local tailoring, or as the tension between the economic imperative (large-scale efficient facilities) and the political imperative (local content, local production). It should be clear from the discussion so far that neither characterization captures the complexity of a firm's international strategy choices. A firm's choice of international strategy involves the search for competitive advantage from global configuration/coordination throughout the value chain. A firm may standardize (concentrate) some activities and tailor (disperse) others. It may also be able to standardize and tailor at the same time through the coordination of dispersed activities or use local tailoring of some activities (e.g., different product positioning in each country) to allow standardization of others (e.g., production). Similarly, the economic imperative is not always for a global strategy—in some industries, a country-centered strategy is the economic imperative. Conversely, the political imperative in some industries may be to concentrate activities where governments provide strong export incentives and locational subsidies.

The essence of international strategy is not to resolve tradeoffs between concentration and dispersion but to eliminate or mitigate them. This implies concentrating and dispersing different value activities depending on industry structure, dispersing some activities to allow concentration of others, and minimizing the tradeoff between concentration and dispersion by coordinating dispersed activities.[24]

The Process of Industry Globalization   Industries globalize because the net competitive advantage of a global approach to configuration/coordination becomes significant. Sometimes this is due to exogenous environmental changes, such as shifts in technology, buyer needs, government policy, or country infrastructure. In automotive supply, for example, the industry is globalizing as buyers (the auto producers) become increasingly global competitors. In other industries, strategic innovations by a competitor can unlock the potential for globalization. For example, a firm may perceive a means of providing local content without dispersing scale-sensitive value activities, such as local installation and testing. Other tools to unlock globalization include: reducing the cost of modifying a centrally designed and produced product to meet local needs, such as modularizing the power supply in an otherwise standard product; increasing product homogeneity by designing a product that incorporates the features demanded by every significant country; or homogenizing worldwide demand through product repositioning. In electronic products such as communications switching equipment, for example, Northern Telecom, NEC Corporation, and Ericsson have benefited from product architectures which permit modularization of software and relatively low-cost modification to fit different country needs. Environmental changes and strategic insights frequently go hand in hand in changing the pattern of international competition.

---

[24]There is an analogy here between the Lawrence and Lorsch (1967) idea that differentiation of functions within a firm along with providing effective integration improves performance, a point suggested by M. Therese Flaherty.

There may be problems in the transition from multidomestic to global competition in industries where domestic or country-centered competitors have already established entry or mobility barriers that are market-specific. The possession by country-centered or domestic competitors of strong brand names, strong distribution channel relationships, or long-standing buyer relationships, will retard the penetration of global firms. Firms also face difficulties in shifting from country-centered to global strategies if they have a legacy of dispersed worldwide activities and organizational norms that place great authority at the country level. Domestic firms can sometimes be more successful than established multinationals in becoming global competitors, because they start with a cleaner slate than do firms who must rationalize and reorient their international activities.

The ultimate leaders in global industries are often first movers: the first firms to perceive the possibilities for a global strategy and move to implement one. For example, Boeing was the first global competitor in aircraft, as was Honda in motorcycles, IBM in computers, Kodak in film, and Becton Dickinson in disposable syringes. First movers gain scale and learning advantages that make competing with them difficult. First-mover effects are particularly important in global industries, because of the association between globalization and economies of scale, learning, and flexibility achieved through worldwide configuration/coordination. Global leadership can shift if industry structural change provides the opportunity for leapfrogging to new products or new technologies that nullify past leaders' scale and learning; again, the first mover to the new generation/technology often wins.

Global leaders often begin with some advantage at home, whether it be low labor cost or a product design or marketing advantage. They use this as a lever to enter foreign markets. Once there, however, the global competitor converts the initial home advantage into competitive advantages that grow out of its overall worldwide system, such as production scale economies or the ability to amortize R&D costs. While the initial advantage may have been hard to sustain, the global strategy creates *new* advantages that can be much more durable.

A good example is automobiles, where Toyota and Nissan initially competed in simple, small cars on the basis of low labor costs. As these companies achieved worldwide penetration, however, they gained economies of scale and accelerated down the learning curve. World scale allowed aggressive investments in new equipment and R&D. Today, the Korean competitor Hyundai competes in small, simple cars based on low labor costs. Toyota and Nissan have long since graduated to broad lines of increasingly differentiated cars, drawing on the advantages of their worldwide positions.

Global Strategy and Comparative Advantage   It is useful to pause and reflect on the relationship between the framework I have presented and the notion of comparative advantage. Is there a difference? The traditional concept of comparative advantage is that factor-cost or factor-quality differences among countries lead to production in countries with advantages in a particular industry, which export the product elsewhere in the world. Competitive advantage, in this view, grows out of *where* firms perform activities.

The location of activities is clearly one source of potential advantage in a global firm. The global competitor can locate activities wherever comparative advantage lies, decoupling comparative advantage from the firm's home base or country of ownership. Indeed, the framework presented here suggests that the comparative advantage story is richer than typically told, because it not only involves production activities (the usual focus of discussions) but also applies to other activities in the value chain, such as R&D, processing orders, or designing advertisements. Comparative advantage is specific to the *activity* and not the location of the value chain as a whole.[25] One of the potent advantages of the

[25]It has been recognized that comparative advantage in different stages in a vertically integrated industry sector such as aluminum can reside in different countries. Bauxite mining will take place in resource-rich countries, for example, while smelting will take place in countries with low electrical power cost (see Caves and Jones 1985, p. 142). The argument here extends this thinking *within* the value chain of any stage, and suggests that the optimal location for performing individual activities may vary as well.

global firm is that it can spread activities to reflect different preferred locations, something a domestic or country-centered competitor does not do. Thus, components can be made in Taiwan, software written in India, and basic R&D performed in Silicon Valley, for example. This international specialization and arbitrage of activities within the firm is made possible by the growing ability to coordinate and configure globally and can be difficult to accomplish through arm's-length or quasi-arm's-length transactions because of risks of contracting with independent parties as well as high transaction costs.

While my framework suggests a more complex view of comparative advantage, it also suggests, however, that many forms of competitive advantage for the global firm derive less from *where* it performs activities than from *how* it performs them on a worldwide basis; economies of scale, proprietary learning, and differentiation with multinational buyers are not tied to countries but to the configuration and coordination of the firm's worldwide system. While these advantages are frequently quite sustainable, traditional sources of comparative advantage can be very elusive sources of competitive advantage for an international competitor today, because comparative advantage frequently shifts. A country with the lowest labor cost is overtaken within a few years by some other country, as has happened repeatedly in shipbuilding as Japan has replaced Europe only to be replaced by Korea. Moreover, falling direct labor cost as a percentage of total costs, increasingly global markets for raw materials and other inputs, and freer flowing technology have diminished the role of traditional sources of comparative advantage.

My research on a broad cross-section of industries suggests that the achievement of sustainable world leadership follows a more complex pattern than the exploitation of comparative advantage per se. A competitor may start with a comparative advantage-related edge that provides the basis for penetrating foreign markets, but this edge is rapidly translated into a broader array of advantages that arise from the global approach to configuration and coordination described earlier. Japanese firms, for

example, have done a masterful job in many industries of converting fleeting labor-cost advantages into durable systemwide advantages because of scale and proprietary know-how. Over time, these systemwide advantages are further reinforced with country-specific advantages such as brand identity in many countries as well as distribution channel access.

Many Japanese firms were fortunate enough to make their transitions from country-based comparative advantage to global competitive advantage in a buoyant world economy while nobody paid much attention to them. European and U.S. competitors were willing to cede market share in "less desirable" segments such as the low end of the product line, or so they thought. The Japanese translated these beachheads into world leadership by broadening their lines and reaping advantages in scale and proprietary learning. The Koreans and Taiwanese, the latest entrants in consumer electronics and other industries with low-price strategies, may have a hard time replicating Japan's success. Products have standardized and growth is slow, while Japanese and U.S. competitors are alert to the threat. Japanese firms enjoyed first-mover advantages in pursuing their strategies that the Koreans and Taiwanese do not.

Global Platforms

The interaction of the home country conditions and competitive advantages from a global strategy that transcend the country suggest a more complex role of the country in firm success than implied by the theory of comparative advantage. To understand this more complex role of the country, I define the concept of a "global platform." A country is a desirable global platform in an industry if it provides an environment yielding firms domiciled in that country an advantage in competing globally in that particular industry. The firm need not necessarily be owned by investors in the country, but the country is its home base for competing in a particular industry. An essential element of this definition is that it hinges on success *outside* the country, and not merely country conditions that allow firms to successfully master domestic competition. In global competition, a country must be viewed as a platform and not as the place where all a firm's activities are performed.

There are two broad determinants of a good global platform in an industry, which I have explored in more detail elsewhere.[26] The first is comparative advantage, or the factor endowment of the country as a site to perform particular important activities in the industry. Today, *simple factors* such as low-cost unskilled labor and natural resources are increasingly less important to global competition than *complex factors* such as skilled scientific and technical personnel as well as advanced infrastructure. Direct labor is a minor proportion of cost in many manufactured goods, and automation of nonproduction activities is shrinking it further, while markets for resources are increasingly global and technology has widened the number of sources of many resources. A country's factor endowment is partly exogenous but partly endogenous, the result of attention and investment in the country.

The second determinant of the attractiveness of a country as a global platform in an industry are the characteristics of a country's demand and local operating environment. A country's demand conditions include the size and timing of its demand in an industry, factors recognized as important by authors such as Linder and Vernon.[27] They also include, however, the sophistication and power of local buyers and channels and the particular product features and attributes demanded. These latter factors are frequently more important today than size and timing of demand, because income differences among many developed countries are relatively small and industries develop simultaneously in many countries. Local operating conditions relevant to investment success include the customs and conditions for doing business in a particular

industry as well as the intensity of local competition. Strong local competition frequently benefits a country's success in international competition rather than impedes it, a view sometimes used to advocate the creation of "national champions." Japanese machine tool and electronic firms, Italian ski boot manufacturers, German high performance automakers, and American minicomputer companies all illustrate the spur of local competition to success abroad.

Local demand and operating conditions provide a number of potentially powerful sources of competitive advantage to a global competitor based in that country. The first is first-mover advantages in perceiving and implementing the appropriate global strategy. Pressing local needs, particularly peculiar ones, lead firms to embark early to solve local problems and gain proprietary know-how. This is then translated into scale and learning advantages as firms move early to compete globally. The second benefit is motivation. Sophisticated, powerful customers, tough operating problems, and a formidable local rival or two promote rapid progress down the learning curve and conceiving of new ways of competing. The final potential benefit of local demand conditions is a baseload of demand for product varieties that will be sought after in international markets. The role of the country in the success of a firm internationally, then, is in the interaction among conditions of local supply, the composition and timing of country demand, and the nature of the local operating environment with economies of scale and learning.

The two determinants of country competitiveness in an industry interact in important and sometimes counterintuitive ways. Local demand and needs frequently influence private and social investment in endogenous factors of production. A nation with oceans as borders and dependence on sea trade, for example, is more prone to have universities and scientific centers dedicated to oceanographic education and research. Similarly, factor endowment seems to influence local demand. The per capita consumption of wine is highest in wine-growing regions, for example.

[26]See Porter (1985*b*). The issues in this section are the subject of a major current research project involving nine countries.

[27]See Linder (1961), Vernon (1966), and Gruber, Mehta, and Vernon (1967).

The competitive advant[...]
wide from concentrated[...]
while concentration costs[...]
rise in scale economies i[...]
of advancing technology[...]
scale of an auto assembl[...]
between 1960 and 1975,[...]
erage real cost of develop[...]
quadrupled. The pace of[...]
increased, creating mor[...]
R&D costs over worldwi[...]

Product needs have [...]
among countries, as inco[...]
rowed, information and c[...]
more freely around the[...]
increased.[29] Growing sim[...]
tices and marketing syste[...]
different countries have a[...]
tor in homogenizing need[...]
has been a parallel trend t[...]
mentation, which some o[...]
tory to the view that pr[...]
countries are becoming m[...]
ments today seem based l[...]
and more on buyer differe[...]
try boundaries, difference[...]
user-industry, or income [...]
cessfully employ global s[...]
which they serve a narrow[...]
worldwide, as do Daimler[...]

Another driver of post[...]
tion has been a sharp redu[...]
transportation. This has [...]
tions in transportation t[...]
creasingly large bulk carr[...]
and larger, more efficient a[...]
government impediments[...]
have been falling in the po[...]
ers have gone down, in[...]
patent-sharing agreements[...]
regional economic pacts[...]
Community have emerged[...]
vestment, albeit imperfectl[...]

"Comparative disadvantage" in some factors of production can be an advantage in global competition when combined with pressing local demand. Poor growing conditions have led Israeli farmers to innovate in irrigation and cultivation techniques, for example. The shrinking role of simple factors of production relative to complex factors such as technical personnel seem to be enhancing the frequency and importance of such circumstances. What is important today in international success is unleashing innovation in the proper direction, instead of passive exploitation of a country's static cost advantages, which shift rapidly and can be overcome. International success today is a dynamic process resulting from continued development of products and processes. The forces that guide firms to undertake such activity are central to the success of a country's firms in international competition.

A good example of the interplay among these factors is the television set industry. In the United States, early demand was in large screen console sets because TV sets were initially luxury items kept in the living room. As buyers began to purchase second and third sets, sets became smaller and more portable. They were used increasingly in the bedroom, the kitchen, the car, and elsewhere. As the TV set industry matured, table model and portable sets became the universal product variety. Japanese firms, because of the small size of Japanese homes, gained early experience in small sets. They dedicated most of their R&D to developing small picture tubes and compact sets. The Japanese also faced a compelling need to reduce power consumption of sets because of the existing energy crisis, which led them to rapid introduction of solid-state technology. This, in turn, facilitated reducing the number of components and automating manufacturing. The whole process was accelerated by the more rapid saturation of the Japanese home market than the American market and a large number of Japanese competitors who were competing fiercely for the same pie.

In the process of naturally serving the needs of their home market and dealing with local problems, then, Japanese firms gained early experience and

scale in segments of the industry that came to dominate world demand. U.S. firms, conversely, pioneered large-screen console sets with fine furniture cabinets. As the industry matured, the experience base of U.S. firms centered on a segment that was small and isolated to a few countries, notably the United States. Aided by intense competitive pressure, Japanese firms were able to penetrate world markets in a segment that was not only uninteresting to foreign firms but also one in which the Japanese had initial-scale learning- and labor-cost advantages. Ultimately the low-cost advantage disappeared as production was automated, but global scale and learning economies rapidly took over as the Japanese advanced product and process technology at a rapid pace. This example illustrates how early demand for TV sets in the United States proved to be a disadvantage rather than the advantage that some views of international competition paint it to be. Moreover, Japan's comparative disadvantage in energy proved to be an advantage in TV sets (and a number of other industries).

The two broad determinants of a good global platform rest on the interaction between country characteristics and firms' strategies. The literature on comparative advantage, through focusing on country factor endowments, minimizing the demand side, and suppressing the individual firm, is most appropriate in industries where there are few economies of scale, little proprietary technology or technological change, or few possibilities for product differentiation.[28] While these industry characteristics are those of many traditionally traded goods, they describe few of today's important global industries.

The Historical Evolution of International Competition

Having established a framework for understanding the globalization of industries, I am now in a position to view the phenomenon in historical perspective. This discussion provides a way of validating the

---

[29]Levitt's (1983) article provides a s[...]

[28]Where it does recognize scale economies, trade theory views them narrowly as arising from production in one country.

framework and isolati
competitors today. If c
atively few industries
most industries were l
reasons are rather se
my framework. Ther
scale in production t
and assembly-line tec
heterogeneous produc
countries, much less ;
few if any national r
Post was the first imj
the United States and
twenties. Communica
ficult before the teleg
systems became well c

These structural cc
tus for the widesprea
Those industries that
comparative-advantag
simply unavailable in ;
them from others, or i
of land resources, or s
tries desirable supplie
produced locally wa
global strategy adapte
widespread governm
trade during this per
were quite high in
commodities.

Developments arc
marked the beginnings
into the globalization
wave of modern globa
late 1800s and early
from local (or region
some began globalizin
Gillette, National Cas
Electric had comman
the teens and operate
strategies. Early globa
U.S. and European cor

Driving this first w
were rising productior
the advancements in t

Japanese multinationals had the advantage of embarking on international strategies in the 1950s and 1960s when the imperatives for a global approach to strategy were beginning to accelerate, but without the legacy of past international investments and modes of behavior.[30] Japanese firms also had an orientation toward highly concentrated activities that fit the strategic imperative of the time. Most European and many U.S. multinationals, conversely, were well established internationally before the war. They had legacies of local subsidiary autonomy that reflected the interwar environment. As Japanese firms spread internationally, they dispersed activities only grudgingly and engaged in extensive global coordination. European and country-centered U.S. companies struggled to rationalize overly dispersed configurations of activities and to boost the level of global coordination among foreign units. They found the decentralized organization structures so fashionable in the 1960s and 1970s to be a hindrance.

Strategic Implications of Globalization

When the pattern of international competition shifts from multidomestic to global in an industry, there are many implications for the strategy of an international firm. At the broadest level, globalization casts new light on many issues that have long been of interest to students of international business. In areas such as international finance, marketing, and business–government relations, the emphasis in the literature has been on the unique problems of adapting to local conditions and ways of doing business in a foreign country.

In a global industry these concerns must be supplemented with an overriding focus on the ways and means of international configuration and coordination. In government relations, for example, the focus must shift from stand-alone negotiations with host countries (appropriate in multidomestic

competition) to a recognition that negotiations in one country will both affect other countries and be shaped by possibilities for performing activities in other countries. In finance, measuring the performance of subsidiaries must be modified to reflect the contribution of one subsidiary to another's cost position or differentiation in a global strategy, instead of viewing each subsidiary as a stand-alone unit. In battling with global competitors, it may be appropriate in some countries to accept low profits indefinitely—in multidomestic competition this would be unjustified.[31] In global industries, the overall system matters as much or more than the country.

Overall International Strategy The most basic question raised by the globalization of an industry is what overall international strategy a firm should adopt. In a global industry, a global strategy that captures the particular advantages of configuration/coordination present in that industry is necessary to attain a leading position. The firm must examine each activity in the value chain to see if there is a competitive advantage to concentrating and/or to coordinating the activity globally in various ways. However, many firms may not have the resources or initial position to pursue a global strategy, particularly domestic competitors. It is important, as a result, to explore strategic options short of a full-blown global strategy that may be present in global industries.

Abstracting from the particular configuration/coordination a firm adopts for competing internationally, there are four broad types of possible strategies in a global industry, illustrated schematically in Figure 6. Any strategy involves a choice of the type of competitive advantage sought (low cost or differentiation) and the competitive scope within which the advantage is to be achieved.[32] In global industries, competitive scope involves both the industry segments in which a firm competes and whether it seeks the benefits of configuration/coordination across countries or chooses instead a country-centered

---

[30]Japan's limited prewar international sales were handled largely through trading companies. Trading companies still handled a good portion of Japanese exports in the 1970s but have become less important in newer and high-technology industries.

[31]For a discussion, see Hout, Porter, and Rudden (1982). For a recent treatment, see Hamel and Prahalad (1985).

[32]For a discussion, see Porter (1985*a*), chapters 1 and 2.

Figure 6   Strategic Alternatives in a Global Industry

Geographic Scope

	Global Strategy	Country-Centered Strategy
Many Segments	Global cost leadership or differentiation	Protected markets
Few Segments	Global segmentation	National responsiveness

(Segment Scope)

approach to competing. These dimensions lead to four broad strategies, illustrated in Figure 6:

Global Cost Leadership or Differentiation   seeking the cost or differentiation advantages of global configuration/coordination through selling a wide line of products to buyers in all or most significant country markets. Global cost leaders (e.g., Toyota, Komatsu) tend to sell standardized products and reap scale advantages in technology development, procurement, and production. Global differentiators (e.g., IBM, Caterpillar) often use their scale and learning advantages to lower the cost of differentiating (e.g., offering many models and frequent model changes) and exploit their worldwide position to reinforce their brand reputation and/or product differentiation with multinational buyers.

Global Segmentation   serving a particular industry segment worldwide, such as Toyota in lift trucks and Mercedes in automobiles. A variant of this strategy is competing in a subset of countries where the advantages of concentration/coordination are particularly great. In some industries, global segmentation is the only feasible global strategy because the advantages of a global configuration/coordination exist only in particular segments (e.g., high-priced business hotels). A global strategy can

make entirely new segmentations of an industry possible, because serving a segment worldwide overcomes scale thresholds that make serving the segment in one country impractical.

Global segmentation, which captures the advantages of a global strategy but marshals resources by focusing on a narrow segment, is frequently a viable option for a smaller multinational or domestic competitor. The strategy has been quite common among multinationals from smaller countries such as Finland and Switzerland. It is also frequently the first step in a sequenced strategy to move from a domestic to a global strategy. In industries such as motorcycles, farm tractors, and TV sets, for example, initial beachheads were established by Japanese firms following global segmentation strategies focused on the smaller-sized end of the product line, later expanded into full-line positions.

Protected Markets   seeking out countries where market positions are protected by host governments. The protected markets strategy rests on government impediments to global competition such as high tariffs, stringent import quotas, and high local content requirements, which effectively isolate a country from the global industry. Protected markets strategies usually imply the need for *early* foreign direct investment in a country and can encompass only a subset of countries, because if government impediments were pervasive the industry would be multidomestic. They are generally most feasible in developing countries with protectionist industrial policies such as India, Mexico, and Argentina, though developed countries such as France and Canada offer havens for protected markets strategies in selected industries.

National Responsiveness   focus on those industry segments most affected by local country differences though the industry as a whole is global. The firm aims to meet unusual local needs in products, channels, and marketing practices in each country, foregoing the competitive advantages of a global strategy. The national responsiveness strategy may imply that a firm competes only in those countries where segments with unusual needs are significant in size. The national responsiveness strategy is based on *economic* impediments to global configuration/coordination, while the protected markets strategy rests on government impediments. National responsiveness and protected markets can be pursued simultaneously if government protection only covers certain segments.

Protected markets or national responsiveness strategies rest on the costs of global configuration/coordination that remain even in industries that globalize. They rely on careful focus on certain segments/countries to hold off global competitors, and represent natural options for domestic firms without the resources to become international as well as multinationals who lack the resources or skills to concentrate/coordinate their activities worldwide. The sustainability of a national responsiveness strategy depends on continued national differences in some segments as well as the price differential between locally tailored and global varieties. If the extra cost to buy a better performing global variety is small or the price premium to buy a tailored local variety is too great, global competitors may overtake country-centered ones. Moreover, there is a tendency for global competitors to widen their product lines over time as they

overcome market-specific barriers to entry in a country, even into segments that appear subject to local differences. In motorcycles, for example, global Japanese competitors eventually entered the large bike segment even though it is insignificant in size in Japan and many other countries. They employed shared dealer networks, brand names, and production facilities built up through competing in the global small bike segment.[33]

The sustainability of the protected markets strategy rests on continued government impediments to global competitors as well as the sanctity of a firm's favored status. Governments often invite additional competitors into their markets as the markets grow, however, and also escalate their demands on a firm once it has sunk investments in a country. Because protected markets strategies lack a competitive advantage in economic terms, their choice depends on a sophisticated prediction about future government behavior.

In many industries, two or more of the strategies can co-exist.[34] Segments with strong national differences and/or countries with high levels of protection lead to situations where there are global competitors, country-centered multinationals, and domestic firms all competing in the industry. Timing plays an important role in the industry structures observed. Early entry by a global competitor often retards the development of country-centered multinationals and domestic firms. Conversely, first-mover advantages garnered by country-centered or domestic firms can erect country-specific entry/mobility barriers that offset the advantages of a global competitor. The importance of timing suggests that multiple outcomes may be possible.

---

[33]A key consideration in the sustainability of national responsiveness strategies is the ability of broad-line competitors to share activities among segments. See Porter (1985a), chapter 7, for a generic treatment.

[34]Mixed strategies are also observed in which a firm employs a global strategy in one group of countries and country-centered strategies in others. In the sewing machine industry, for example, otherwise global competitions produce pedal-powered sewing machines that meet local needs in developing countries with high levels of protection.

The Future of International Competition

Since the late 1970s, there have been some gradual but significant changes in the pattern of international competition that carry important implications for international strategy. Foreign direct investment has been growing more rapidly and flowing in new directions, while growth in trade has slowed. This article's framework provides a template with which I can examine these changes and probe their significance. The factors shaping the global configuration of activities by firms are developing in ways that contrast with the trends of the previous thirty years.

Homogenization of product needs among countries appears to be continuing, though segmentation within countries is as well. As a result, consumer packaged goods are becoming increasingly prone toward globalization, though they have long been characterized by multidomestic competition. There are also signs of globalization in some service industries as the introduction of information technology creates scale economies in support activities and facilitates coordination in primary activities. Global service firms are reaping advantages in hardware and software development as well as in procurement.

In many industries, however, limits have been reached in the scale economies that have been driving the concentration of activities. These limits grow out of classic diseconomies of scale that arise in very large facilities, as well as new, more flexible technology in manufacturing and other activities that are often not as scale sensitive as previous methods. At the same time, though, flexible manufacturing allows the production of multiple varieties (to serve different countries) in a single plant. This may encourage new movement toward globalization in industries in which product differences among countries have remained significant and have blocked globalization in the past. Another important change is the declining labor content in many industries due to automation of the value chain, which is reducing the incentive to locate activities in low-wage countries such as South Korea and Singapore.

There also appear to be some limits to further declines in transport costs, as innovations such as containerization, bulk ships, and larger aircraft have largely run their course. However, a parallel trend toward smaller, lighter products and components may keep some downward pressure on transport costs. The biggest change in the benefits and costs of concentrated configuration has been the sharp rise in protectionism in recent years and the resulting rise in nontariff barriers akin to the 1920s. As a group, these factors point to less need and less opportunity for highly concentrated configurations of activities and explain why growth in direct investment has been outpacing growth in trade. Falling labor content also suggests that more foreign investment will flow to developed countries (to secure market access) instead of low-wage countries.

When the coordination dimension is examined, the picture looks quite different. Communication and coordination costs are dropping sharply, driven by breathtaking advances in information systems and telecommunication technology. We have just seen the beginning of developments in this area, which are spreading throughout the value chain.[35] Boeing, for example, is employing computer-aided design technology to jointly design components on-line with foreign suppliers. Engineers in different countries are communicating via computer screens. Marketing systems and business practices continue to homogenize, facilitating the coordination of activities in different countries. The mobility of buyers and information is also growing rapidly, greasing the international spread of brand reputations and enhancing the importance of consistency in the way activities are performed worldwide. Increasing numbers of multinational and global firms are begetting globalization by their suppliers. There is also a sharp rise in the computerization of

---

[35]For a discussion, see Porter and Millar (1985).

manufacturing as well as other activities throughout the value chain, which greatly facilitates coordination among dispersed sites.

The imperative of global strategy is shifting, then, in ways that will require a rebalancing of configuration and coordination. Concentrating activities is less necessary in economic terms, and less possible as governments force more dispersion. These forces are pushing firms to intermediate positions on the configuration axis as shown in Figure 7. At the same time, the ability to coordinate globally throughout the value chain is increasing dramatically through modern technology. The need to coordinate is also rising to offset greater dispersion and to respond to buyer needs. Moreover, intermediate configurations often require greater coordination, and coordination can neutralize some of the costs of dispersion forced on firms by governments. These considerations imply an upward movement in Figure 7. Thus, simpler first-generation global strategies (e.g., concentration and export) seem to be giving way to more complex global strategies involving multiple though coordinated R&D activities, sophisticated networking of overseas plants, worldwide procurement, and so on.

Thus, today's game of global strategy seems increasingly to be a game of coordination— getting dispersed production facilities, R&D laboratories, and marketing activities to truly work together. Widespread coordination remains the exception rather than the rule today in many multinationals. Successful international competitors in the future will be those who can seek out competitive advantages from global configuration/coordination anywhere in the value chain and overcome the organizational barriers to exploiting them.

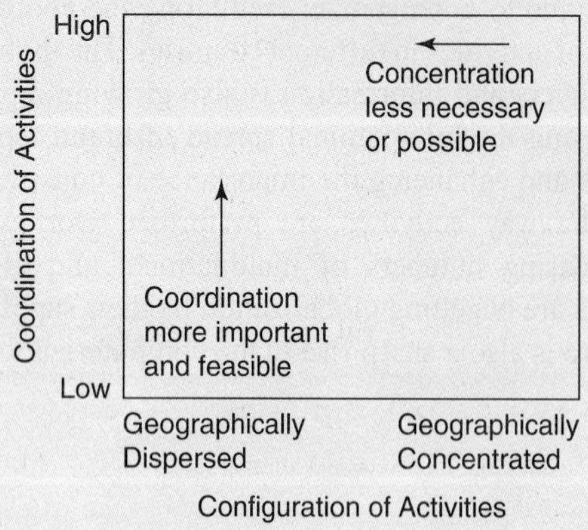

References

Bartlett, C. A. "Multinational Structural Evolution: The Changing Decision Environment in the International Division." D.B.A. diss., Harvard Graduate School of Business Administration, 1979.

Buckley, P. J., and M. C. Casson. *The Future of the Multinational Enterprise*. London: Holms and Meier, 1976.

Buzzell, R. D. "Can You Standardize Multinational Marketing?" *Harvard Business Review* (November/December 1968): 102–13.

Casson, M. C. "Transaction Costs and the Theory of the Multinational Enterprise," in A. Rugman, ed., *New Theories of the Multinational Enterprise.* London: Croom Helm, 1982.

Caves, R. E. *Multinational Enterprise and Economic Analysis.* Cambridge, England: Cambridge University Press, 1982.

Caves, R. E., and R. W. Jones. *World Trade and Payments,* fourth edition. Boston: Little, Brown, 1985.

Doz, Y. "National Policies and Multinational Management." D.B.A. diss., Harvard Graduate School of Business Administration, 1976.

Dunning, J., and M. McQueen. "The Eclectic Theory of International Production: A Case Study of the International Hotel Industry." *Managerial and Decision Economics* 2 (December 1981): 197–210.

Figure 7   Future Trends in International Competition

Franko, L. G. *The European Multinationals: A Renewed Challenge to American and British Big Business.* Stanford, Conn.: Greylock, 1976.

Gruber, W., D. Mehta, and R. Vernon. "The R&D Factor in International Trade and Investment of United States Industries." *Journal of Political Economy* (February 1967): 20–37.

Hamel, G., and C. K. Prahalad. "Do You Really Have a Global Strategy?" *Harvard Business Review* (July/August 1985): 139–48.

Hirsch, S. "Technological Factors in the Composition and Direction of Israel's Industrial Exports," in Vernon, R., ed., *Technological Factors in International Trade.* New York: National Bureau of Economic Research, 1970, 365–408.

Hladik, K. "International Joint Ventures: An Empirical Investigation into the Characteristics of Recent U.S.-Foreign Joint Venture Partnerships." Ph.D. diss., Business Economics Program, Harvard University, 1984.

Hout, T., M. E. Porter, and E. Rudden. "How Global Companies Win Out." *Harvard Business Review* (September/October 1982): 98–108.

Knickerbocker, F. *Oligopolistic Reaction and Multinational Enterprise.* Cambridge, Mass.: Harvard University Press, 1973.

Lawrence, P. R., and J. W. Lorsch. *Organization and Environment.* Boston: Division of Research, Harvard Graduate School of Business Administration, 1967.

Levitt, T. "The Globalization of Markets." *Harvard Business Review* (May/June 1983): 92–102.

Linder, S. *An Essay on Trade and Transformation.* New York: John Wiley, 1961.

Perlmutter, H. V. "The Tortuous Evolution of the Multinational Corporation." *Columbia Journal of World Business* (January/February 1969): 9–18.

Porter, M. E. *Competitive Strategy: Techniques for Analyzing Industries and Competitors.* New York: Free Press, 1980.

———. *Competitive Advantage: Creating and Sustaining Superior Performance.* New York: Free Press, 1985*a*.

———. "Beyond Comparative Advantage." Working Paper, Harvard Graduate School of Business Administration, August 1985*b*.

Porter, M. E., and V. Millar. "How Information Gives You Competitive Advantage." *Harvard Business Review* (July/August 1985): 149–60.

Prahalad, C. K. "The Strategic Process in a Multinational Corporation." D.B.A. diss., Harvard Graduate School of Business Administration, 1975.

Pryor, M. H. "Planning in a World-Wide Business." *Harvard Business Review* 43 (January/February 1965): 130–9.

Ronstadt, R. C. "International R&D: The Establishment and Evolution of Research and Development Abroad by Seven U.S. Multinationals. *Journal of International Business Studies* (Spring/Summer 1978): 7–23.

Stobaugh, R. B., et al. "Nine Investments Abroad and Their Impact at Home: Case Studies on Multinational Enterprise and the U.S. Economy." Boston: Division of Research, Harvard Business School, 1976.

Stopford, J. J., and L. T. Wells, Jr. *Managing the Multinational Enterprise: Organization of the Firm and Overlap of Subsidiaries.* New York: Basic Books, 1972.

Teece, D. J. "Multinational Enterprise: Market Failure and Market Power Considerations." *Sloan Management Review* 22, no. 3 (September 1981): 3–17.

———. "Transaction Cost Economics and the Multinational Enterprise: An Assessment." Working Paper IB-3, Business School, University of California at Berkeley, January 1985.

United Nations Center on Transnational Corporations, *Salient Features and Trends in Foreign Direct Investment*. United Nations, New York, 1984.

Vernon, R. "International Investment and International Trade in the Product Cycle." *Quarterly Journal of Economics* 80 (May 1966): 190–207.

Williamson, O. *Markets and Hierarchies*. New York: Free Press, 1975.

Wind, Y., S. P. Douglas, and H. B. Perlmutter. "Guidelines for Developing International Marketing Strategies." *Journal of Marketing* 37 (April 1973): 14–23.

CHAPTER 4

Developing a Transnational Organization:
Managing Integration, Responsiveness, and Flexibility

Having discussed how MNEs are responding to the forces requiring them to develop strategies that optimize the balance among global efficiency, national responsiveness, and worldwide innovation and learning, we now focus our attention on the kind of organizations they must build to manage these often conflicting strategic tasks. In this chapter, we begin by suggesting that this balance involves more than a search for an ideal structural solution; it requires that MNEs not only understand their present and future strategic task demands but also their historic organizational capabilities—something we call a company's "administrative heritage." As they respond to the need to develop transnational strategies, companies must build transnational organizations that reflect their need for multidimensional and flexible capabilities. In the final section of the chapter, we explore the attributes of such organizations, which we describe using a biological analogy, in that we detail the transnational's structure (anatomy), its processes, (physiology), and its culture (psychology). Finally, we examine the processes necessary to build such organizational capabilities.

In the preceding chapters, we described how changes in the international operating environment have forced MNEs to optimize global efficiency, national responsiveness, and worldwide learning simultaneously. Implementing such a complex, three-pronged strategic objective would be difficult under any circumstances, but the very act of "going international" multiplies a company's organizational complexity.

Most companies find it difficult enough to balance product divisions or business units with corporate staff functions. The thought of adding geographically oriented management and maintaining a three-way balance of organizational perspectives and capabilities among products, functions, and regions is intimidating. The difficulty is further increased because the resolution of tensions among the three different management groups must be accomplished by an organization whose operating units are divided by distance and time and whose key members are separated by barriers of culture and language.

Beyond Structural Fit

Because the choice of a basic organizational structure has such a powerful influence on the management process in an MNE, historically much of the attention of managers and researchers alike was focused on trying to find which formal structure provided the right "fit" in various conditions. The most widely recognized study on this issue was

Figure 4-1   Stopford and Wells's International Structural Stages Model

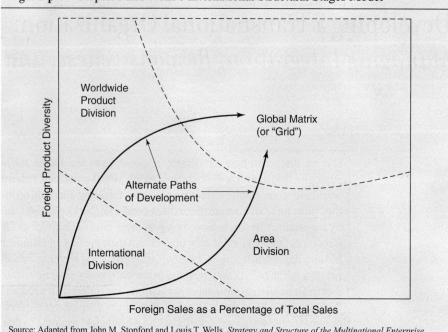

Source: Adapted from John M. Stopford and Louis T. Wells, *Strategy and Structure of the Multinational Enterprise* (New York: Basic Books, 1972).

John Stopford's research on the 187 largest U.S.-based MNEs.[1] His work resulted in a "stages model" of international organization structure that defined two variables to capture the strategic and administrative complexity most companies faced as they expanded abroad: the number of products sold internationally ("foreign product diversity" in Figure 4–1) and the importance of international sales to the company ("foreign sales as a percentage of total sales"). Plotting the structural changes in his sample of 187 companies, he found that worldwide corporations typically adopt different organizational structures at different stages of international expansion.

According to this model, worldwide companies typically managed their international operations through an international division at the early stage of foreign expansion. Subsequently, those companies that expanded their sales abroad without significantly increasing their foreign product diversity typically adopted an area structure (e.g., European region, Asia–Pacific region). Other companies that expanded by increasing their foreign product diversity tended to adopt a worldwide product division structure (e.g., chemicals division, plastics division). Finally, when both foreign sales and foreign product diversity were high, companies resorted to a global matrix in which a French chemicals manager might report to both the European regional head and the global chemicals division president at corporate headquarters.

---

[1]Stopford's research is described in John M. Stopford and Louis T. Wells, *Managing the Multinational Enterprise* (New York: Basic Books, 1972).

Although these ideas were presented as a descriptive model, consultants and managers soon began to apply them prescriptively. For many companies, it seemed that structure followed fashion more than strategy. And in the process, the debate was often reduced to generalized discussions of the comparative value of product- versus geography-based structures on the one hand or to simplistic choices between "centralization" and "decentralization" on the other.

Confronted with increasing complexity, diversity, and change in the 1980s, managers in many worldwide companies looked for ways to restructure. Conventional wisdom provided a ready solution: the global matrix. But for most companies, the results were disappointing. The promised land of the global matrix turned out to be an organizational quagmire from which they were forced to retreat.

Failure of the Matrix

In theory, the solution should have worked. Having frontline managers report simultaneously to different organizational groups (e.g., the French chemicals manager in the preceding example) should have enabled companies to maintain a balance among centralized efficiency, local responsiveness, and worldwide knowledge transfer. The multiple channels of communication and control promised the ability to nurture diverse management perspectives, and the ability to shift the balance of power within the matrix theoretically gave it great flexibility. The reality turned out to be otherwise however, and the history of companies that built formal global matrix structures was an unhappy one.

Dow Chemical, a pioneer of the global matrix organization, eventually returned to a more conventional structure with clear lines of responsibility given to geographic managers. Citibank, once a textbook example of the global matrix, also discarded this mode of dual reporting relationships after a few years of highly publicized experimentation. So too did scores of other companies that tried to manage their worldwide activities through this complex and rather bureaucratic structure.

Most encountered the same problems. The matrix amplified the differences in perspectives and interests by forcing all issues through the dual chains of command so that even a minor difference could become the subject of heated disagreement and debate.

Dual reporting led to conflict and confusion on many levels: The proliferation of channels created informational logjams, conflicts could be resolved only by escalating the problem, and overlapping responsibilities resulted in turf battles and a loss of accountability. Separated by barriers of distance, time, language, and culture, managers found it virtually impossible to clarify the confusion and resolve the conflicts. As a result, in company after company, the initial appeal of the global matrix structure quickly faded into a recognition that a different solution was required.

Building Organizational Capability

The basic problem underlying a company's search for a structural fit was that it focused on only one organizational variable—formal structure—and this single tool proved unequal to the job of capturing the complexity of the strategic tasks facing most MNEs.

First, as we indicated previously, this focus often forced managers to ignore the multidimensionality of the environmental forces when they made choices between product- versus geographically based structures. Second, structure defined a static set of roles, responsibilities, and relationships in a task environment that was dynamic and rapidly evolving. And third, restructuring efforts often proved harmful, as organizations were bludgeoned into a major realignment of roles, responsibilities, and relationships by overnight changes in structure. In an increasing number of companies, managers now recognize that formal structure is a powerful but blunt instrument of strategic change. Structural fit is becoming both less relevant and harder to achieve. To develop its vital multidimensional and flexible capabilities, a company must reorient managers' thinking and reshape the core decision-making systems. In doing so, the company's entire management process—including its administrative systems, communication channels, decision-making forums, and interpersonal relationships—becomes the means for managing such change.

As a first step in exploring some of the more subtle and sophisticated tools, we examine how administrative heritage—a company's history and its embedded management culture—influences its organization and its ability and willingness to change. It is a concept to which we have already alluded in previous chapters when we acknowledged how an MNE's management mentality and strategic posture may have been shaped by different motivations for international expansion, different historical and cultural factors, and different external industry forces.

Administrative Heritage

Whereas industry analysis can reveal a company's strategic challenges and market opportunities, its ability to fulfill that promise will be greatly influenced—and often constrained—by its existing internal world: its asset configuration and resource distribution, its historical definition of management responsibilities, and its ingrained organizational norms, for example. Clearly, a company's organization is shaped not only by current external task demands but also by past internal management biases. In particular, each company is influenced by the path by which it developed—its organizational history—and the values, norms, and practices of its management—its management culture. Collectively, these factors constitute what we call a company's administrative heritage.

Administrative heritage can be, at the same time, one of the company's greatest assets—the underlying source of its core competencies—and a significant liability, because it resists change and thereby prevents realignment. As managers in many companies have learned, whereas strategic plans can be scrapped and redrawn overnight, there is no such thing as a zero-based organization. Companies are, to a significant extent, captives of their past, and any organizational transformation has to focus at least as much on where the company is coming from—its administrative heritage—as on where it wants to go.

The importance of a company's administrative heritage can be illustrated by contrasting the development of a typical European MNE whose major international expansion occurred in the decades of the 1920s and 1930s, a typical American MNE that expanded abroad in the 1950s and 1960s, and a typical Japanese company that made its main overseas thrust in the 1970s and 1980s. Even if these companies were in the same industry, their different heritages would lead them to adopt some very different strategic and organizational models.

Decentralized Federation

Expanding abroad in a period of rising tariffs and discriminatory legislation, the typical European company was forced to build local production facilities to compete effectively with local competitors. With their own plants, national subsidiaries were able to modify products and marketing approaches to meet widely differing local market needs. The increasing independence of these self-sufficient national units was reinforced by the transportation and communication barriers that existed in that era, limiting headquarters' ability to intervene in the management of the company's spreading worldwide operations.

The emerging configuration of distributed assets and delegated responsibility fit well with the ingrained management norms and practices in many European companies. European companies, particularly those from the United Kingdom, the Netherlands, and France, developed an internal culture that emphasized personal relationships (an "old boys' network") rather than formal structures, as well as financial controls more than coordination of technical or operational detail. This management style tended to reinforce companies' willingness to delegate more operating independence and strategic freedom to their foreign subsidiaries. Highly autonomous national companies were often managed more as a portfolio of offshore investments rather than a single international business.

The resulting organization pattern was a loose federation of independent national subsidiaries, each focused primarily on its local market. As a result, many of these companies adopted what we have described in previous chapters as the multinational strategy and managed it through a decentralized federation organization model, as represented in Figure 4–2(a).

Coordinated Federation

American companies, many of which enjoyed their fastest international expansion in the 1950s and 1960s, developed in very different circumstances. Their main strength lay in the new technologies and management processes they had developed as a consequence of being located in the world's largest, richest, and most technologically advanced market. After World War II, their foreign expansion focused primarily on leveraging this strength, giving rise to the international product cycle theory referred to in Chapter 1.

Reinforcing this strategy was a professional managerial culture in most U.S.-based companies that contrasted with the "old boys' network" that typified the European companies' processes. The management approach in most U.S.-based companies was built on a willingness to delegate responsibility while retaining overall control through sophisticated management systems and specialist corporate staffs. The systems provided channels for a regular flow of information to be interpreted by the central staff and used by top management for coordination and control.

The main handicap such companies faced was that parent-company management often adopted a parochial and even superior attitude toward international operations, perhaps because of the assumption that new ideas and developments all came from the parent. Despite corporate management's increased understanding of its overseas markets, it often seemed to view foreign operations as appendages whose principal purpose was to leverage the capabilities and resources developed in the home market.

Nonetheless, the approach was highly successful in the postwar decades, and many U.S.-based companies adopted what we have described as the international strategy and

Figure 4-2   Organizational Configuration Models

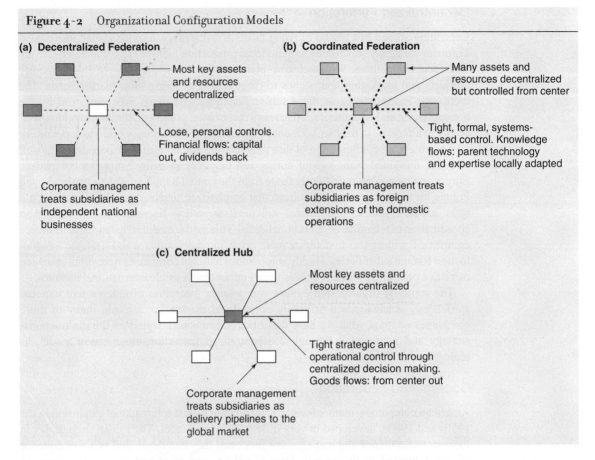

(a) **Decentralized Federation**

Most key assets and resources decentralized

Loose, personal controls. Financial flows: capital out, dividends back

Corporate management treats subsidiaries as independent national businesses

(b) **Coordinated Federation**

Many assets and resources decentralized but controlled from center

Tight, formal, systems-based control. Knowledge flows: parent technology and expertise locally adapted

Corporate management treats subsidiaries as foreign extensions of the domestic operations

(c) **Centralized Hub**

Most key assets and resources centralized

Tight strategic and operational control through centralized decision making. Goods flows: from center out

Corporate management treats subsidiaries as delivery pipelines to the global market

a coordinated federation organizational model shown in Figure 4–2(b). Their foreign subsidiaries were often free to adapt products or strategies to reflect market differences, but their dependence on the parent company for new products, processes, and ideas dictated a great deal more coordination and control by headquarters than did the decentralized federation organization. This relationship was facilitated by the existence of formal systems and controls in the headquarters–subsidiary link.

Centralized Hub

In contrast, the typical Japanese company, making its main international thrust in the 1970s and 1980s, faced a greatly altered external environment and operated with very different internal norms and values. With limited prior overseas exposure, it chose not to match the well-established local marketing capabilities and facilities of its European and U.S. competitors. (Indeed, well-established Japanese trading companies often provided it an easier means of entering foreign markets.) However, the rapid postwar growth of the Japanese economy gave it new, efficient, scale-intensive plants, and it was expanding into a global environment of declining trade barriers.

Together, these factors gave it th[e]
upstream end of the value-added ch[ain]
tages and quality assurance, dema[nd]
curement, and manufacturing. A c[entral]
strategy represented a perfect fit w[ith]
itive capabilities.

Such an approach also fit the
emerging Japanese MNE. At the f[oundation?]
tional cultural norms that emphas[ized]
reflected in management practic[es]
(shared decision making). By ke[eping]
ter, the Japanese company could
was so communications intens[ive]
growth through exporting made
lifetime employment. As a result, these comp[anies]
global strategy and developed a centralized hub organizational model, as
Figure 4–2(c), to support this strategic orientation.

The Transnational Challenge

In Chapters 2 and 3, we advanced the hypothesis that many worldwide industries were
transformed in the 1980s and 1990s from traditional multinational, international, and
global forms into transnational forms. Instead of demanding efficiency or responsiveness or learning as the key capability for success, these businesses now require participating firms to achieve all three capabilities simultaneously to remain competitive.

Table 4–1 summarizes the key characteristics of the decentralized federation, coordinated federation, and centralized hub organizations we have described in this chapter as
the supporting forms for companies pursuing multinational, international, and global

Table 4–1   Organizational Characteristics of Decentralized Federation, Coordinated Federation, and Centralized Hub Organizations

	Decentralized Federation	**Coordinated Federation**	**Centralized Hub**
Strategic approach	Multinational	International	Global
Key strategic capability	National responsiveness	Worldwide transfer of home-country innovations	Global-scale efficiency
Configuration of assets and capabilities	Decentralized and nationally self-sufficient	Sources of core competencies centralized, others decentralized	Centralized and globally scaled
Role of overseas operations	Sensing and exploiting local opportunities	Adapting and leveraging parent-company competencies	Implementing parent-company strategies
Development and diffusion of knowledge	Knowledge developed and retained within each unit	Knowledge developed at the center and transferred to overseas units	Knowledge developed and retained at the center

review of these characteristics immediately reveals the problems each archetypal company models might face in responding to the transnational ge.

ith its resources and capabilities consolidated at the center, the global company chieves efficiency primarily by exploiting potential scale economies in all its activities. In such an organization, however, national subsidiaries' lack of resources and responsibilities may undermine their motivation and ability to respond to local market needs, whereas the central groups often lack adequate understanding of market needs and production realities outside their home market. These are problems that a global organization cannot overcome without jeopardizing its trump card of global efficiency.

The classic multinational company suffers from other limitations. Although their dispersed resources and decentralized decision making allow national subsidiaries to respond to local needs, the fragmentation of activities leads to inefficiency. Learning also suffers, because knowledge is not consolidated and does not flow among the various parts of the company. As a result, local innovations often represent little more than the efforts of subsidiary management to protect its turf and autonomy or reinventions of the wheel caused by blocked communication or the not-invented-here (NIH) syndrome.

In contrast, the international company is better able to leverage the knowledge and capabilities of the parent company (but is still not very good at learning from its foreign operations). However, its resource configuration and operating systems make it less efficient than the global company and less responsive than the multinational company.

The Transnational Organization

There are three important organizational characteristics that distinguish the transnational organization from its multinational, international, or global counterparts: It develops and legitimizes multiple diverse internal perspectives, its physical assets and management capabilities are distributed internationally but are interdependent, and it has a robust and flexible internal integrative process. In this section, we describe and illustrate each of these characteristics.

Multidimensional Perspectives

Managing in an environment in which strategic forces are both diverse and changeable, the transnational company must create the ability to sense and analyze the numerous and often conflicting opportunities, pressures, and demands it faces worldwide. Strong *national subsidiary management* is needed to sense and represent the changing needs of local consumers and the increasing pressures from host governments; capable *global business management* is required to track the strategy of global competitors and provide the coordination necessary to respond appropriately; and influential *worldwide functional management* is needed to concentrate corporate knowledge, information, and expertise and facilitate their transfer among organizational units.

Unfortunately, in many companies, power is concentrated with the management group that has historically represented the company's most critical strategic tasks—often with the cost that other groups representing other needs are allowed to atrophy. For example, in *multinational* companies, key decisions were usually dominated by the country management group because it made the most critical contribution to achieving national responsiveness. In *global* companies, by contrast, managers in worldwide product divisions were typically the most influential, because strong business management played the key role in the company's efforts to seek global efficiency. And in *international* companies, functional management groups often came to assume this position of dominance because of their roles in building, accumulating, and transferring the company's skills, knowledge, and capabilities.

In *transnational* companies, however, biases in the decision-making process are consciously reduced by building up the capability, credibility, and influence of the less powerful management groups while protecting the morale and expertise of the dominant group. The objective is to build a multidimensional organization in which the influence of each of the three management groups is balanced. Some of the cases in this book focus explicitly on this issue of developing and maintaining such a balanced and multidimensional organization.

Distributed, Interdependent Capabilities

Having developed multidimensional management perspectives to sense the diverse opportunities and demands it faces, the transnational organization must be able to make choices among them and respond in a timely and effective manner to those that are deemed strategically important. When a company's decision-making process and organizational capabilities are concentrated at the center—as they are in the global organization's centralized hub configuration—it is often difficult to respond appropriately to diverse worldwide demands. Being distant from frontline opportunities and threats, the central group's ability to act in an effective and timely manner is constrained by its reliance on complex and intensive international communications.

In contrast, multinational organizations, with their response capabilities spread throughout the decentralized federation of independent operations, suffer from duplication of effort, inefficiency of operations, and barriers to international learning. In transnational organizations, management breaks away from the restricted view that assumes it must centralize the activities for which a global scale or specialized knowledge is important. Instead, management ensures that viable national units achieve global scale by specializing their activities and giving them the responsibility of becoming the company's world source for a given product or expertise. And by securing the cooperation and involvement of the individuals in the relevant national units, they tap into important technological advances and market developments wherever they are occurring around the globe.

One major consequence of such a distribution of specialized assets and responsibilities is that the interdependence of worldwide units automatically increases. Simple structural configurations like the decentralized federation, the coordinated federation, and the centralized hub are inadequate for the task facing the transnational corporation; what is needed is a structure we term the "integrated network" (see Figure 4–3).

In the integrated network configuration, management regards each of the worldwide units as a source of ideas, skills, capabilities, and knowledge that can be harnessed for the benefit of the total organization. Efficient local plants may be converted into international production centers; innovative national or regional development labs may be designated the company's "centers of excellence" for a particular product or process

Figure 4-3   Integrated Network Model

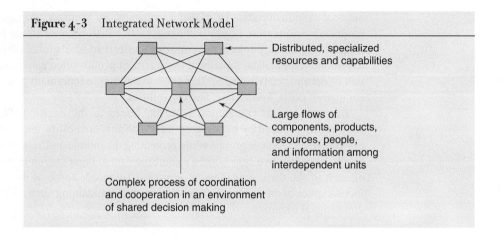

development; and creative subsidiary marketing groups may be given a lead role in developing worldwide marketing strategies for certain products or businesses.

Flexible Integrative Process

Finally, the transnational organization requires a management process that can resolve the diversity of interests and perspectives and integrate the dispersed assets and resources. In doing so, it cannot be bound by a symmetrical organizational process that defines the task in simplistic or static terms, such as, "Should responsibilities be centralized or decentralized?" It is clear that the benefits to be gained from central control of worldwide research or manufacturing activities may be much more important than those related to the global coordination of the sales and service functions. We have also seen how the pattern of functional coordination varies by business and by geographic area (e.g., aircraft engine companies need central control of more decisions than multinational food packagers; operations in developing countries may need more support from the center than those in advanced countries). Furthermore, all coordination needs to be able to change over time.

Thus, management must be able to differentiate its operating relationships and change its decision-making roles by function, across businesses, among geographic units, and over time. In turn, the management process must be able to change from product to product, from country to country, and even from decision to decision. Elaborating on the integration–responsiveness framework we developed in Chapter 3, we illustrate such a distribution of roles and responsibilities in Figure 4–4.

This distribution requires the development of rather sophisticated and subtle decision-making machinery based on three different but interdependent management processes. The first is a focused and constrained escalation process that allows top management to intervene directly in key decision content (e.g., major resource allocation commitments)—a subtle and carefully managed form of *centralization*. The second is a process in which management structures individual roles and administrative systems to influence specific decisions (typically, repetitive or routine activities like setting transfer

Figure 4-4 Integration and Differentiation Needs at Unilever

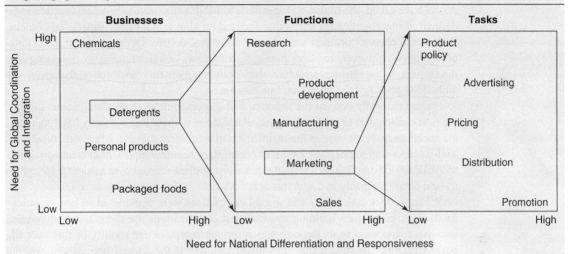

prices) through *formalization*. The third is a self-regulatory capability in which top management's role is to establish a broad culture and set of relationships that provide a supportive organizational context for delegated decisions—a sophisticated management process driven by *socialization*.

Anatomy, Physiology, and Psychology of the Transnational

The kind of organization we have described as a transnational clearly represents something quite different from its predecessors—the multinational, international, and global organizations. Building such an organization requires much more than choosing between a product or a geographic organization structure; managing it implies much more than centralizing or decentralizing decisions. By viewing the organizational challenge as one of creating and managing a decision process that responds to the company's critical task demands, the MNE manager is forced to adopt a very different approach from someone who defines the problem as one of discovering and installing the ideal structure.

If the classic structural stages model no longer provides a helpful description of international organization development, we need a different way to conceptualize the more complex array of tools and processes discussed in our previous descriptions of transnational organizations. The simple but useful framework adopted here describes the organization in terms of a physiological model. To be effective, change in an organization's anatomy (the formal structure of its assets, resources, and responsibilities) must be complemented by adaptations to its physiology (the organization's systems and decision processes) and its psychology (the organization's culture and management mentality).

We will now describe the different tools and processes used to build and manage the transnational using this physiological model.

Structuring the Organizational Anatomy

As we have noted, the traditional approach to MNE organization problems tended to be defined in macrostructural terms that focused on simple but rather superficial choices, such as the classic "product versus area" structural debate. Developing a transnational organization, however, requires management to pay equal attention to designing and developing a supporting structure that both supplements and counterbalances the embedded power of the dominant line managers.

Having carefully defined the structure and responsibilities of all management groups, the next challenge is to ensure that particularly those without line authority have appropriate access to and influence in the mainstream management process. Microstructural tools such as cross-unit teams, task forces, or committees become important in creating supplemental decision-making forums that often allow nonline managers to assume responsibility and obtain authority in a way that is not possible in the formal line organization.

Whereas once task forces and special committees were considered ad hoc, or quick-fix devices, companies building transnational organizations use them as legitimate and important structural tools through which top management can modify or fine-tune the basic structure. To stretch our anatomical analogy, if the formal line structure is the organization's backbone, the nonline structure is its rib cage, and these microstructural tools are the muscle and cartilage that give the organizational skeleton its flexibility.

Building the Organizational Physiology

One of the key roles of management is to influence the structure of the communication channels through which the organization's decision-making process operates. By adapting the various administrative systems, communication channels, and informal relationships, management can exert a powerful influence—and even control—over the volume, content, and direction of information flows. It is this flow of information—the lifeblood of all management processes—that defines the organizational physiology.

Many researchers have shown the link between the need for information and the complexity and uncertainty of the tasks to be performed. In the integrated network configuration, task complexity and uncertainty are very high. Operating an interdependent system in such a setting requires large volumes of complex information to be gathered, exchanged, and processed. In the complex integrated network that frames a transnational organization, formal systems alone cannot support the huge information processing needs, and companies are forced to look beyond their traditional tools and conventional systems.

For years, managers have recognized that a great deal of information exchange and even decision making—perhaps the majority—occurs through the organization's innumerable informal channels and relationships. Yet this part of the management process has often been dismissed as either unimportant ("office gossip" or "rumor mill") or unmanageable ("disruptive cliques" or "unholy alliances"). In the management of transnational organizations, such biases need to be reexamined. Because organizational units are widely separated and information is scarce, not only is it more important for managers of international operations to exert some control and influence over informal systems, it is also more feasible for them to do so.

Getting started is often remarkably easy, requiring managers to do little more than use their daily involvement in the ongoing management processes to shape the nature and quality of communications patterns and relationships. Because of their nature and intensity, informal relationships respond remarkably quickly to changes in the frequency and agenda of management trips and corporate meetings, the pattern of committee assignments, and the track of people's career development. Furthermore, management can recognize, legitimize, and reinforce existing informal relationships that contribute to the corporate objective.

Developing the Organizational Psychology

In addition to an anatomy and a physiology, each organization also has a psychology (that is, a set of explicit or implicit corporate values and shared beliefs) that greatly influences the way it operates. For companies operating in an international environment, it is a particularly important organizational attribute. When employees come from a variety of different national backgrounds, management cannot assume that all will share common values and relate to common norms. Furthermore, in an operating environment in which managers are separated by distance and time barriers, shared management understanding is often a much more powerful tool than formal structures and systems for coordinating diverse activities.

Of the numerous tools and techniques that can affect an organization's psychology, our review of transnational organizations has highlighted three that are particularly important. The first is the need for a clear, shared understanding of the company's mission and objectives. Matsushita's 250-year vision of its role of promoting general welfare in a world society, Nokia's commitment to "Connecting People," and Bill Gates's aspiration to create a world with "a computer on every desk and in every home running on Microsoft software" represent variants of this approach applied at different strategic and operational levels.

The second important tool is the visible behavior and public actions of senior management. Particularly in a transnational organization in which other signals may be diluted or distorted, top management's actions speak louder than words and tend to have a powerful influence on the company's culture. They represent the clearest role model of behavior and a signal of the company's strategic and organizational priorities. When Sony Corporation founder and CEO Akio Morita relocated to New York for several years to build the company's U.S. operations personally, he sent a message about Sony's commitment to its overseas businesses that could not have been conveyed as strongly by any other means.

The third and most commonly used set of tools for modifying organizational psychology in the transnational organization is nested in the company's personnel policies, practices, and systems. A company can develop a multidimensional and flexible organization process only if its personnel systems develop and reinforce the appropriate kinds of people. At Eli Lilly, we saw a good example of such an approach. Its recruiting and promotion policies emphasized the importance of good interpersonal skills and flexible, nonparochial personalities; its career path management was used not only to develop skills and knowledge but also to broaden individual perspectives and interpersonal relationships; and its measurement and reward systems were designed to reinforce the thrust of other organization-building efforts.

Although the process of adapting an organization's culture, values, or beliefs is slow and the techniques are subtle, this tool plays a particularly important role in the development of a transnational organization, because change in the organizational anatomy and physiology without complementary modifications to its psychology can lead to severe organizational problems.

Managing the Process of Change

Particularly in the United States, many managers have assumed that organizational change is driven and dominated by changes in the formal structure. One of the most dramatic examples was Westinghouse's reorganization of its operations. Dissatisfied with its worldwide product organization, top management assigned a team of executives to study the company's international organization problems for 90 days. Its proposal that Westinghouse adopt a global matrix was accepted, and the team was then given three months to "install the new structure."

The example is far from unusual—literally hundreds of other companies have done something similar. The managers involved seemed to assume that changes in formal roles and reporting relationships would force changes in the organizational relationships and decision processes, which in turn would reshape the way individual managers think and act. This model of the process of organizational change is illustrated in Figure 4–5.

But such an approach loses sight of the real organization behind the boxes and lines on the chart. The boxes that are casually shifted around represent people with abilities, motivations, and interests, not just formal positions with specified roles. The lines that are redrawn are not just formal reporting channels but interpersonal relationships that may have taken years to develop. As a result, forcing changes in the organizational process and management mentality by altering the formal structure can have a high cost. The new relationships defined in the reorganized structure will often take months to establish at the most basic level and a year or more to become truly effective. Developing new individual attitudes and behaviors will take even longer, because many employees will be frustrated, alienated, or simply unequal to the new job requirements.

Figure 4-5   Model I: The Traditional Change Process

Change in formal structure and responsibilities
(Anatomy)
↓
Change in interpersonal relationships and processes
(Physiology)
↓
Change in individual attitudes and mentalities
(Psychology)

Most European and Japanese companies tend to adopt a very different approach in managing organizational change. Top management in these companies consciously uses personnel assignments as an important mechanism of organizational change. Building on the informal relationships that dominated their earlier management processes, European companies often use assignments and transfers to forge interpersonal links, build organizational cohesion, and develop policy consistency. And Japanese companies typically place enormous emphasis on socializing the individual into the organization and shaping his or her attitudes to conform with overall corporate values. Organizational change in these companies is often driven more by intensive education programs than by reconfigurations of the structure or systems.

Although the specific change process and sequence must vary from one company to the next, the overall process adopted in these companies to manage change is very different from the process driven by structural realignment. Indeed, the sequence is often the reverse. The first objective for many European and Japanese companies seeking major change is to influence the understanding and perceptions of key individuals. Then follows a series of changes aimed to modify the communication flows and decision-making processes. Only in a final stage are the changes consolidated and confirmed by structural realignment. This process is represented by the model in Figure 4–6. Of course, these two models of organizational change in worldwide companies are both oversimplifications of the process and overgeneralizations of national difference.

All change processes inevitably involve substantial overlap and interaction in the alterations to organizational autonomy, physiology, and psychology; the two sequences merely reflect differences in the relative emphasis on each set of tools during the process. Furthermore, though the two models reflect historical national biases, those differences seem to be eroding. American, European, and Japanese companies appear to be learning from one another.

Although the more gradual change process is much less organizationally traumatic, in times of crisis—chronic poor performance, a badly misaligned structure, or a major structural change in the environment, for example—radical restructuring may be necessary to achieve rapid and sweeping change. For most organizations, however, dramatic structural change is highly traumatic and can distract managers from their external tasks as they focus on the internal realignment. Fortunately, most change processes can be managed in a more evolutionary manner, focusing first on the modification of individual perspectives and interpersonal relationships before tackling the formal redistribution of responsibilities and power.

Figure 4-6   Model II: The Emerging Change Process

Change in individual attitudes and mentalities
↓
Change in interpersonal relationships and processes
↓
Change in formal structure and responsibilities

The Transnational Organization in Transition

During the past decade or so, political, competitive, and social pressures have reinforced the need for MNEs to create organizations that can sense and respond to complex yet often conflicting demands. Yet, as more and more companies confront the need to build worldwide organizations that are both multidimensional and flexible, the form of the transnational organization they are creating continues to adapt. Among the most widespread transnational organizational trends we have observed in recent years are a disenchantment with formal matrix structures, the redefinition of primary organizational dimensions, and the changing role of functional management in transnationals.

Disenchantment with Formal Matrix Structures

As an increasing number of managers recognized the need to develop the multidimensional organizational capabilities that characterize a transnational organization, the initial reaction of many was to impose the new model through a global matrix structure.

Widespread press coverage of ABB's decade-long global expansion through such an organization encouraged some to believe that this structure was the key to exploiting global scale efficiencies while responding to local market needs. But as many soon discovered, the strategic benefits provided by such a complex organization came at an organizational cost.

Although some companies were able to create the culture and process vital to the success of the matrix structure—in ABB's case, they supported the company's ambitious global expansion for more than a decade—others were much less successful. One such failure was Proctor and Gamble's (P&G) much publicized Organization 2005, which boldly imposed a global product structure over the company's historically successful geographic organization. The global matrix so installed created problems that eventually cost CEO Durk Jager his job.

But despite continuing nervousness about the global matrix structure, most MNEs still recognize the need to create multidimensional and flexible organizations. The big lesson of the 1990s was that such organizations are best built by developing overlaid processes and supportive cultures, not just by formalizing multiple reporting relationships. A.G. Lafley, P&G's new CEO, put it well when he said, "We built this new house, then moved in before the plumbing and wiring were connected. You cannot change organization with structure alone."

Redefinition of Key Organization Dimensions

Historically, the dominant organization dimensions around which most MNEs built their worldwide operations were business or product management on one side and country or regional management on the other. But in the past decade or so, the primary organizational characteristics that defined the transnational corporation began to change, with the global customer dimension becoming increasingly important in many worldwide organizations.

The pressure to create such customer-driven organizations grew gradually during the 1990s. First, as global customers began demanding uniform prices and service levels from their suppliers, MNEs were forced to respond by creating dedicated global account managers who would take responsibility for all sales to customers around the world.

Second, as customers expected increasing levels of value-added services, companies began to shift from "selling products" to "providing solutions." These and similar forces led to the creation of transnational organizations in which front-end, customer-facing units bundled products from back-end, product-driven units. A good example of this was IBM's Global Services Organization, one of the most successful customer-facing organizations, which grew rapidly because of its ability to supply customers with a combination of IBM's products, consulting services, and often an additional package of related, outsourced products and services.

Changing the Functional Management Role

In transnational organizations built around business, geography, and, more recently, the customer, the functional managers responsible for finance, human resources, logistics, and other cross-business and cross-organizational specialties were often relegated to secondary staff roles. However, with the expansion of the information-based, knowledge-intensive service economy, the resources and expertise that resided in these specialized functions became increasingly important sources of competitive advantage. As a result, recent years have seen their roles become increasingly important in many transnational organizations.

Managers of finance, HR, and IT functions gained importance because of their control of the scarce strategic resources that were so critical to capture and leverage on a worldwide basis. With the globalization of financial markets, for example, the finance function was often able to play a critically important role in lowering the cost of capital for the MNE. Even more dramatic has been the role of the HR experts as MNEs tapped into scarce knowledge and expertise outside the home country and leveraged it for global competitive advantage. Similarly, the recent rise of chief knowledge officers reflects the importance that many companies are placing on the organization's ability to capture and leverage valuable information, best practices, or scarce knowledge wherever it exists in the company.

Again, this trend is creating a need for transnational companies to create organizational overlays supplemented by new channels of communication and forums of decision making that enable the MNE to develop and leverage its competitive advantage through its sophisticated organizational capabilities. The form and function of the transnational organization continues to adapt as MNE managers seek new ways to develop and deliver layers of competitive advantage.

Concluding Comments

In this chapter, we have looked at the organizational capabilities that the MNE must build to operate effectively in today's fast changing global business environment. The strategic challenge, as we have described it, requires the MNE to optimize global efficiency, national responsiveness, and worldwide learning simultaneously. To deliver on this complex and conflicting set of demands, a new form of organization is required, which we call the transnational. The transnational is characterized by its legitimization of multidimensional perspectives, its distributed and interdependent capabilities, and its flexible integrative processes.

Case 4-1   Philips versus Matsushita: A New Century, a New Round

Throughout their long histories, N.V. Philips (Netherlands) and Matsushita Electric (Japan) had followed very different strategies and emerged with very different organizational capabilities. Philips built its success on a worldwide portfolio of responsive national organizations while Matsushita based its global competitiveness on its centralized, highly efficient operations in Japan.

During the 1990s, both companies experienced major challenges to their historic competitive positions and organizational models, and at the end of the decade, both companies were struggling to reestablish their competitiveness. At the start of the new millennium, new CEOs at both companies were implementing yet another round of strategic initiatives and organizational restructurings. Observers wondered how the changes would affect their long-running competitive battle.

▊ Philips: Background

In 1892, Gerard Philips and his father opened a small light-bulb factory in Eindhoven, Holland. When their venture almost failed, they recruited Gerard's brother, Anton, an excellent salesman and manager. By 1900, Philips was the third largest light-bulb producer in Europe.

▊ This case derives from an earlier case, "Philips versus Matsushita: Preparing for a New Round," HBS No. 399-102, prepared by Professor Christopher A. Bartlett, which was an updated version of an earlier case by Professor Bartlett and Research Associate Robert W. Lightfoot, "Philips and Matsushita: A Portrait of Two Evolving Companies," HBS Case No. 392-156. The section on Matsushita summarizes "Matsushita Electric Industrial (MEI) in 1987," HBS Case No. 388-144, by Sumantra Ghoshal (INSEAD) and Christopher A. Bartlett. Some early history on Philips draws from "Philips Group-1987," HBS Case No. 388-050, by Professors Frank Aguilar and Michael Y. Yoshino. This version was also prepared by Professor Bartlett. HBS cases are developed solely as the basis for class discussion. Cases are not intended to serve as endorsements, sources of primary data, or illustrations of effective or ineffective management.

▊ Copyright © 2001 President and Fellows of Harvard College. All rights reserved. Harvard Business School case 302-049.

From its founding, Philips developed a tradition of caring for workers. In Eindhoven it built company houses, bolstered education, and paid its employees so well that other local employers complained. When Philips incorporated in 1912, it set aside 10% of profits for employees.

Technological Competence and Geographic Expansion   While larger electrical products companies were racing to diversify, Philips made only light-bulbs. This one-product focus and Gerard's technological prowess enabled the company to create significant innovations. Company policy was to scrap old plants and use new machines or factories whenever advances were made in new production technology. Anton wrote down assets rapidly and set aside substantial reserves for replacing outdated equipment. Philips also became a leader in industrial research, creating physics and chemistry labs to address production problems as well as more abstract scientific ones. The labs developed a tungsten metal filament bulb that was a great commercial success and gave Philips the financial strength to compete against its giant rivals.

Holland's small size soon forced Philips to look beyond its Dutch borders for enough volume to mass produce. In 1899, Anton hired the company's first export manager, and soon the company was selling into such diverse markets as Japan, Australia, Canada, Brazil, and Russia. In 1912, as the electric lamp industry began to show signs of overcapacity, Philips started building sales organizations in the United States, Canada, and France. All other functions remained highly centralized in Eindhoven. In many foreign countries Philips created local joint ventures to gain market acceptance.

In 1919, Philips entered into the Principal Agreement with General Electric, giving each company the use of the other's patents. The agreement also divided the world into "three spheres of influence":

General Electric would control North America; Philips would control Holland; but both companies agreed to compete freely in the rest of the world. (General Electric also took a 20% stake in Philips.) After this time, Philips began evolving from a highly centralized company, whose sales were conducted through third parties, to a decentralized sales organization with autonomous marketing companies in 14 European countries, China, Brazil, and Australia.

During this period, the company also broadened its product line significantly. In 1918, it began producing electronic vacuum tubes; eight years later its first radios appeared, capturing a 20% world market share within a decade; and during the 1930s, Philips began producing X-ray tubes. The Great Depression brought with it trade barriers and high tariffs, and Philips was forced to build local production facilities to protect its foreign sales of these products.

Philips: Organizational Development   One of the earliest traditions at Philips was a shared but competitive leadership by the commercial and technical functions. Gerard, an engineer, and Anton, a businessman, began a subtle competition where Gerard would try to produce more than Anton could sell and vice versa. Nevertheless, the two agreed that strong research was vital to Philips' survival.

During the late 1930s, in anticipation of the impending war, Philips transferred its overseas assets to two trusts, British Philips and the North American Philips Corporation; it also moved most of its vital research laboratories to Redhill in Surrey, England, and its top management to the United States. Supported by the assets and resources transferred abroad, and isolated from their parent, the individual country organizations became more independent during the war.

Because waves of Allied and German bombing had pummeled most of Philips' industrial plant in the Netherlands, the management board decided to build the postwar organization on the strengths of the national organizations (NOs). Their greatly increased self-sufficiency during the war had allowed most to become adept at responding to country-specific market conditions—a capability that became a valuable asset in the postwar era. For example, when international wrangling precluded any agreement on three competing television transmission standards (PAL, SECAM, and NTSC), each nation decided which to adopt. Furthermore, consumer preferences and economic conditions varied: in some countries, rich, furniture-encased TV sets were the norm; in others, sleek, contemporary models dominated the market. In the United Kingdom, the only way to penetrate the market was to establish a rental business; in richer countries, a major marketing challenge was overcoming elitist prejudice against television. In this environment, the independent NOs had a great advantage in being able to sense and respond to the differences.

Eventually, responsiveness extended beyond adaptive marketing. As NOs built their own technical capabilities, product development often became a function of local market conditions. For example, Philips of Canada created the company's first color TV; Philips of Australia created the first stereo TV; and Philips of the United Kingdom created the first TVs with teletext.

While NOs took major responsibility for financial, legal, and administrative matters, fourteen product divisions (PDs), located in Eindhoven, were formally responsible for development, production, and global distribution. (In reality, the NOs' control of assets and the PDs' distance from the operations often undercut this formal role.) The research function remained independent and, with continued strong funding, set up eight separate laboratories in Europe and the United States.

While the formal corporate-level structure was represented as a type of geographic/product matrix, it was clear that NOs had the real power. NOs reported directly to the management board, which Philips enlarged from 4 members to 10 to ensure that top management remained in contact with and control of the highly autonomous NOs. Each NO also regularly sent envoys to Eindhoven to represent its interests. Top management, most of whom had careers that included multiple foreign tours of duty, made frequent overseas visits to the NOs. In 1954, the board established the International

Concern Council to formalize regular meetings with the heads of all major NOs.

Within the NOs, the management structure mimicked the legendary joint technical and commercial leadership of the two Philips brothers. Most were led by a technical manager and a commercial manager. In some locations, a finance manager filled out the top management triad that typically reached key decisions collectively. This cross-functional coordination capability was reflected down through the NOs in front-line product teams, product-group–level management teams, and at the senior management committee of the NOs' top commercial, technical, and financial managers.

The overwhelming importance of foreign operations to Philips, the commensurate status of the NOs within the corporate hierarchy, and even the cosmopolitan appeal of many of the offshore subsidiaries' locations encouraged many Philips managers to take extended foreign tours of duty, working in a series of two- or three-year posts. This elite group of expatriate managers identified strongly with each other and with the NOs as a group and had no difficulty representing their strong, country-oriented views to corporate management.

Philips: Attempts at Reorganization   In the late 1960s, the creation of the Common Market eroded trade barriers within Europe and diluted the rationale for maintaining independent, country-level subsidiaries. New transistor- and printed circuit-based technologies demanded larger production runs than most national plants could justify, and many of Philips' competitors were moving production of electronics to new facilities in low-wage areas in East Asia and Central and South America. Despite its many technological innovations, Philips' ability to bring products to market began to falter. In the 1960s, the company invented the audiocassette but let its Japanese competitors capture the mass market. A decade later, its R&D group developed the V2000 videocassette format—superior technically to Sony's Beta or Matsushita's VHS—but was forced to abandon it when North American Philips decided to outsource, brand, and sell a VHS product which it manufactured under license from Matsushita.

Over three decades, seven chairmen experimented with reorganizing the company to deal with its growing problems. Yet, entering the new millennium, Philips' financial performance remained poor and its global competitiveness was still in question. (See **Exhibits 1** and **2.**)

Van Reimsdijk and Rodenburg Reorganizations, 1970s   Concerned about what one magazine described as "continued profitless progress," newly appointed CEO Hendrick van Riemsdijk created an organization committee to prepare a policy paper on the division of responsibilities between the PDs and the NOs. Their report, dubbed the "Yellow Booklet," outlined the disadvantages of Philips' matrix organization in 1971:

> Without an agreement [defining the relationship between national organizations and product divisions], it is impossible to determine in any given situation which of the two parties is responsible. . . . As operations become increasingly complex, an organizational form of this type will only lower the speed of reaction of an enterprise.

On the basis of this report, van Reimsdijk proposed rebalancing the managerial relationships between PDs and NOs—"tilting the matrix" in his words—to allow Philips to decrease the number of products marketed, build scale by concentrating production, and increase the flow of goods among national organizations. He proposed closing the least efficient local plants and converting the best into International Production Centers (IPCs), each supplying many NOs. In so doing, van Reimsdijk hoped that PD managers would gain control over manufacturing operations. Due to the political and organizational difficulty of closing local plants, however, implementation was slow.

In the late 1970s, his successor CEO, Dr. Rodenburg, continued this thrust. Several IPCs were established, but the NOs seemed as powerful and independent as ever. He furthered matrix simplification by replacing the dual commercial and technical leadership with single management at both the corporate and national organizational levels. Yet the power struggles continued.

Exhibit 1 Philips Group Summary Financial Data, 1970–2000 (millions of guilders unless otherwise stated)

	2000	1995	1990	1985	1980	1975	1970
Net sales	F83,437	F64,462	F55,764	F60,045	F36,536	F27,115	F15,070
Income from operations (excluding restructuring)	NA	4,090	2,260	3,075	1,577	1,201	1,280
Income from operations (including restructuring)	9,434	4,044	−2,389	N/A	N/A	N/A	N/A
As a percentage of net sales	11.3%	6.3%	−4.3%	5.1%	4.3%	4.5%	8.5%
Income after taxes	12,559	2,889	F−4,447	F1,025	F532	F341	F446
Net income from normal business operations	NA	2,684	−4,526	n/a	328	347	435
Stockholders' equity (common)	49,473	14,055	11,165	16,151	12,996	10,047	6,324
Return on stockholders' equity	42.8%	20.2%	−30.2%	5.6%	2.7%	3.6%	7.3%
Distribution per common share, per value F10 (in guilders)	F2.64	F1.60	F0.0	F2.00	F1.80	F1.40	F1.70
Total assets	86,114	54,683	51,595	52,883	39,647	30,040	19,088
Inventories as a percentage of net sales	13.9%	18.2%	20.7%	23.2%	32.8%	32.9%	35.2%
Outstanding trade receivables in month's sales	1.5	1.6	1.6	2.0	3.0	3.0	2.8
Current ratio	1.2	1.6	1.4	1.6	1.7	1.8	1.7
Employees at year-end (in thousands)	219	265	273	346	373	397	359
Wages, salaries and other related costs	NA	NA	F17,582	F21,491	F15,339	F11,212	F5,890
Exchange rate (period end; guilder/$)	2.34	1.60	1.69	2.75	2.15	2.69	3.62
Selected data in millions of dollars:							
Sales	$35,253	$40,039	$33,018	$21,802	$16,993	$10,098	$4,163
Operating profit	3,986	2,512	1,247	988	734	464	NA
Pretax income	5,837	2,083	−2,380	658	364	256	NA
Net income	5,306	1,667	−2,510	334	153	95	120
Total assets	35,885	32,651	30,549	19,202	18,440	11,186	5,273
Shareholders' equity (common)	20,238	8,784	6,611	5,864	6,044	3,741	1,747

Source: Annual reports; Standard & Poors' *Compustat*; Moody's Industrial and International Manuals.

Note: Exchange rate 12/31/00 was Euro/US$: 1.074

Exhibit 2 Philips Group, Sales by Product and Geographic Segment, 1985–2000 (millions of guilders)

	2000		1995		1990		1985	
Net Sales by Product Segment								
Lighting	F11,133	13%	F8,353	13%	F7,026	13%	F7,976	12%
Consumer electronics	32,357	39	22,027	34	25,400	46	16,906	26
Domestic appliances	4,643	6	—	—	—	—	6,644	10
Professional products/Systems	—	—	11,562	18	13,059	23	17,850	28
Components/Semiconductors	23,009	28	10,714	17	8,161	15	11,620	18
Software/Services	—	—	9,425	15	—	—	—	—
Medical systems	6,679	8	—	—	—	—	—	—
Origin	1,580	2	—	—	—	—	—	—
Miscellaneous	4,035	5	2,381	4	2,118	4	3,272	5
Total	83,437	100%	64,462	100%	F55,764	100%	F 64,266	100%
Operating Income by Sector								
Lighting	1,472	16%	983	24%	419	18%	F 910	30%
Consumer electronics	824	9	167	4	1,499	66	34	1
Domestic appliances	632	7	157	4	—	—	397	13
Professional products/Systems	—	—	—	—	189	8	1,484	48
Components/Semiconductors	4,220	45	2,233	55	−43	−2	44	1
Software/Services	372	4	886	22	—	—	—	—
Medical systems	2,343	25	—	—	—	—	—	—
Origin	−249	−3	—	—	—	—	—	—
Miscellaneous	−181	−2	423	10	218	10	200	7
Increase not attributable to a sector			(805)	(20)	−22	−1	6	0
Total	9,434	100%	4,044	100%	2,260	100%	F 3,075	100%

Source: Annual reports.

Notes: Conversion rate (12/31/00); 1 Euro: 2.20371 Dutch Guilders. Totals may not add due to rounding. Product sector sales after 1988 are external sales only; therefore, no eliminations are made; sector sales before 1988 include sales to other sectors; therefore, eliminations are made. Data are not comparable to consolidated financial summary due to restating.

Wisse Dekker Reorganization, 1982 Unsatisfied with the company's slow response and concerned by its slumping financial performance, upon becoming CEO in 1982, Wisse Dekker outlined a new initiative. Aware of the cost advantage of Philips' Japanese counterparts, he closed inefficient operations—particularly in Europe where 40 of the company's more than 200 plants were shut. He focused on core operations by selling some businesses (for example, welding, energy cables, and furniture) while acquiring an interest in Grundig and Westinghouse's North American lamp activities. Dekker also supported technology-sharing agreements and entered alliances in offshore manufacturing.

To deal with the slow-moving bureaucracy, he continued his predecessor's initiative to replace dual leadership with single general managers. He also continued to "tilt the matrix" by giving PDs formal product management responsibility, but leaving NOs responsible for local profits. And, he energized the management board by reducing its size, bringing on directors with strong operating experience, and creating subcommittees to deal with difficult issues. Finally, Dekker redefined the product planning process, incorporating input from the NOs, but giving global PDs the final decision on long-range direction. Still sales declined and profits stagnated.

Van der Klugt Reorganization, 1987 When Cor van der Klugt succeeded Dekker as chairman in 1987, Philips had lost its long-held consumer electronics leadership position to Matsushita, and was one of only two non-Japanese companies in the world's top ten. Its net profit margins of 1% to 2% not only lagged behind General Electric's 9%, but even its highly aggressive Japanese competitors' slim 4%. Van der Klugt set a profit objective of 3% to 4% and made beating the Japanese companies a top priority.

As van der Klugt reviewed Philips' strategy, he designated various businesses as core (those that shared related technologies, had strategic importance, or were technical leaders) and non-core (stand-alone businesses that were not targets for world

leadership and could eventually be sold if required). Of the four businesses defined as core, three were strategically linked: components, consumer electronics, and telecommunications and data systems. The fourth, lighting, was regarded as strategically vital because its cash flow funded development. The non-core businesses included domestic appliances and medical systems which van der Klugt spun off into joint ventures with Whirlpool and GE, respectively.

In continuing efforts to strengthen the PDs relative to the NOs, van der Klugt restructured Philips around the four core global divisions rather than the former 14 PDs. This allowed him to trim the management board, appointing the displaced board members to a new policy-making Group Management Committee. Consisting primarily of PD heads and functional chiefs, this body replaced the old NO-dominated International Concern Council. Finally, he sharply reduced the 3,000-strong headquarters staff, reallocating many of them to the PDs.

To link PDs more directly to markets, van der Klugt dispatched many experienced product-line managers to Philips' most competitive markets. For example, management of the digital audio tape and electric-shaver product lines were relocated to Japan, while the medical technology and domestic appliances lines were moved to the United States.

Such moves, along with continued efforts at globalizing product development and production efforts, required that the parent company gain firmer control over NOs, especially the giant North American Philips Corp. (NAPC). Although Philips had obtained a majority equity interest after World War II, it was not always able to make the U.S. company respond to directives from the center, as the V2000 VCR incident showed. To prevent replays of such experiences, in 1987 van der Klugt repurchased publicly owned NAPC shares for $700 million.

Reflecting the growing sentiment among some managers that R&D was not market oriented enough, van der Klugt halved spending on basic research to about 10% of total R&D. To manage what he described as "R&D's tendency to ponder the fundamental laws of nature," he made R&D the

Exhibit 3   Philips Research Labs by Location and Specialty, 1987

Location	Size (staff)	Specialty
Eindhoven, The Netherlands	2,000	Basic research, electronics, manufacturing technology
Redhill, Surrey, England	450	Microelectronics, television, defense
Hamburg, Germany	350	Communications, office equipment, medical imaging
Aachen, W. Germany	250	Fiber optics, X-ray systems
Paris, France	350	Microprocessors, chip materials, design
Brussels	50	Artificial intelligence
Briarcliff Manor, New York	35	Optical systems, television, superconductivity, defense
Sunnyvale, California	150	Integrated circuits

Source: Philips, in *BusinessWeek,* March 21, 1988, p. 156.

direct responsibility of the businesses being supported by the research. This required that each research lab become focused on specific business areas (see **Exhibit 3**).

Finally, van der Klugt continued the effort to build efficient, specialized, multi-market production facilities by closing 75 of the company's 420 remaining plants worldwide. He also eliminated 38,000 of its 344,000 employees—21,000 through divesting businesses, shaking up the myth of lifetime employment at the company. He anticipated that all these restructurings would lead to a financial recovery by 1990. Unanticipated losses for that year, however—more than 4.5 billion Dutch guilders ($2.5 billion)—provoked a class-action law suit by angry American investors, who alleged that positive projections by the company had been misleading. In a surprise move, on May 14, 1990, van der Klugt and half of the management board were replaced.

Timmer Reorganization, 1990   The new president, Jan Timmer, had spent most of his 35-year Philips career turning around unprofitable businesses. With rumors of a takeover or a government bailout swirling, he met with his top 100 managers and distributed a hypothetical—but fact-based—press release announcing that Philips was bankrupt. "So what action can you take this weekend?" he challenged them.

Under "Operation Centurion," headcount was reduced by 68,000 or 22% over the next 18 months, earning Timmer the nickname "The Butcher of Eindhoven." Because European laws required substantial compensation for layoffs—Eindhoven workers received 15 months' pay, for example—the first round of 10,000 layoffs alone cost Philips $700 million. To spread the burden around the globe and to speed the process, Timmer asked his PD managers to negotiate cuts with NO managers. According to one report, however, country managers were "digging in their heels to save local jobs." But the cuts came—many from overseas operations. In addition to the job cuts, Timmer vowed to "change the way we work." He established new performance rules and asked hundreds of top managers to sign contracts that committed them to specific financial goals. Those who broke those contracts were replaced—often with outsiders.

To focus resources further, Timmer sold off various businesses including integrated circuits to Matsushita, minicomputers to Digital, defense electronics to Thomson and the remaining 53% of appliances to Whirlpool. Yet profitability was still well below the modest 4% on sales he promised. In particular, consumer electronics lagged with slow growth in a price-competitive market. The core problem was identified by a 1994 McKinsey study that estimated that value added per hour in Japanese consumer electronic factories was still 68% above that of European plants. In this environment, most NO managers kept their heads down, using their distance from Eindhoven as their defense against the ongoing rationalization.

After three years of cost-cutting, in early 1994 Timmer finally presented a new growth strategy to the board. His plan was to expand software, services, and multimedia to become 40% of revenues by 2000. He was betting on Philips' legendary innovative capability to restart the growth engines. Earlier, he had recruited Frank Carrubba, Hewlett-Packard's director of research, and encouraged him to focus on developing 15 core technologies. The list, which included interactive compact disc (CD-i), digital compact cassettes (DCC), high definition television (HDTV), and multimedia software, was soon dubbed "the president's projects." Over the next few years, Philips invested over $2.5 billion in these technologies. But Timmer's earlier divestment of some of the company's truly high-tech businesses and a 37% cut in R&D personnel left it with few who understood the technology of the new priority businesses.

By 1996, it was clear that Philips' analog HDTV technology would not become industry standard, that its DCC gamble had lost out to Sony's Minidisc, and that CD-i was a marketing failure. And while costs in Philips were lower, so too was morale, particularly among middle management. Critics claimed that the company's drive for cost-cutting and standardization had led it to ignore new worldwide market demands for more segmented products and higher consumer service.

Boonstra Reorganization, 1996   When Timmer stepped down in October 1996, the board replaced him with a radical choice for Philips—an outsider whose expertise was in marketing and Asia rather than technology and Europe. Cor Boonstra was a 58-year-old Dutchman whose years as CEO of Sara Lee, the U.S. consumer products firm, had earned him a reputation as a hard-driving marketing genius. Joining Philips in 1994, he headed the Asia

Pacific region and the lighting division before being tapped as CEO.

Unencumbered by tradition, he immediately announced strategic sweeping changes designed to reach his target of increasing return on net assets from 17% to 24% by 1999. "There are no taboos, no sacred cows," he said. "The bleeders must be turned around, sold, or closed." Within three years, he had sold off 40 of Philips' 120 major businesses—including such well known units as Polygram and Grundig. He also initiated a major worldwide restructuring, promising to transform a structure he described as "a plate of spaghetti" into "a neat row of asparagus." He said:

> How can we compete with the Koreans? They don't have 350 companies all over the world. Their factory in Ireland covers Europe and their manufacturing facility in Mexico serves North America. We need a more structured and simpler manufacturing and marketing organization to achieve a cost pattern in line with those who do not have our heritage. This is still one of the biggest issues facing Philips.

Within a year, 3,100 jobs were eliminated in North America and 3,000 employees were added in Asia Pacific, emphasizing Boonstra's determination to shift production to low-wage countries and his broader commitment to Asia. And after three years, he had closed 100 of the company's 356 factories worldwide. At the same time, he replaced the company's 21 PDs with 7 divisions, but shifted day-to-day operating responsibility to 100 business units, each responsible for its profits worldwide. It was a move designed to finally eliminate the old PD/NO matrix. Finally, in a move that shocked most employees, he announced that the 100-year-old Eindhoven headquarters would be relocated to Amsterdam with only 400 of the 3000 corporate positions remaining.

By early 1998, he was ready to announce his new strategy. Despite early speculation that he might abandon consumer electronics, he proclaimed it as the center of Philips' future. Betting on the "digital revolution," he planned to focus on established technologies such as cellular phones (through a joint venture with Lucent), digital TV, digital videodisc, and web TV. Furthermore, he committed major resources to marketing, including a 40% increase in advertising to raise awareness and image of the Philips brand and de-emphasize most of the 150 other brands it supported worldwide—from Magnavox TVs to Norelco shavers to Marantz stereos.

While not everything succeeded (the Lucent cell phone JV collapsed after nine months, for example), overall performance improved significantly in the late 1990s. By 2000, Boonstra was able to announce that he had achieved his objective of a 24% return on net assets.

Kleisterlee Reorganization, 2001   In May 2001, Boonstra passed the CEO's mantle to Gerard Kleisterlee, a 54-year-old engineer (and career Philips man) whose turnaround of the components business had earned him a board seat only a year earlier. Believing that Philips had finally turned around, the board challenged Kleisterlee to grow sales by 10% annually and earnings 15%, while increasing return on assets to 30%.

Despite its stock trading at a steep discount to its breakup value, Philips' governance structure and Dutch legislation made a hostile raid all but impossible. Nonetheless, Kleisterlee described the difference as "a management discount" and vowed to eliminate it. "Our fragmented organization makes us carry costs that are too high," he said. "In some production activities where we cannot add value, we will outsource and let others do it for us."

The first sign of restructuring came within weeks, when mobile phone production was outsourced to CEC of China. Then, in August, Kleisterlee announced an agreement with Japan's Funai Electric to take over production of its VCRs, resulting in the immediate closure of the European production center in Austria and the loss of 1,000 jobs. The CEO acknowledged that he was seeking partners to take over the manufacturing of some of its other mass-produced items such as television sets.

But by 2001, a slowing economy resulted in the company's first quarterly loss since 1996, and by year's end the loss had grown to 2.6 billion euros compared to the previous year's 9.6 billion profit. Many felt that these growing financial pressures—and shareholders' growing impatience—were finally leading Philips to recognize that its best hope of survival was to outsource even more of its basic manufacturing and become a technology developer and global marketer. They believed it was time to recognize that its 30-year quest to build efficiency into its global operations had failed.

Matsushita: Background

In 1918, Konosuke Matsushita (or "KM" as he was affectionately known), a 23-year-old inspector with the Osaka Electric Light Company, invested ¥100 to start production of double-ended sockets in his modest home. The company grew rapidly, expanding into battery-powered lamps, electric irons, and radios. On May 5, 1932, Matsushita's 14th anniversary, KM announced to his 162 employees a 250-year corporate plan broken into 25-year sections, each to be carried out by successive generations. His plan was codified in a company creed and in the "Seven Spirits of Matsushita" (see **Exhibit 4**), which, along with the company song, continued to be woven into morning assemblies worldwide and provided the basis of the "cultural and spiritual training" all new employees received during their first seven months with the company.

In the post-war boom, Matsushita introduced a flood of new products: TV sets in 1952; transistor radios in 1958; color TVs, dishwashers, and electric ovens in 1960. Capitalizing on its broad line of 5,000 products (Sony produced 80), the company opened 25,000 domestic retail outlets. With more than six times the outlets of rival Sony, the ubiquitous "National Shops" represented 40% of appliance stores in Japan in the late 1960s. These not only provided assured sales volume, but also gave the company direct access to market trends and consumer reaction. When post-war growth slowed,

Exhibit 4	Matsushita Creed and Philosophy (Excerpts)

Creed

Through our industrial activities, we strive to foster progress, to promote the general welfare of society, and to devote ourselves to furthering the development of world culture.

Seven Spirits of Matsushita

Service through Industry
Fairness
Harmony and Cooperation
Struggle for Progress
Courtesy and Humility
Adjustment and Assimilation
Gratitude

KM's Business Philosophy (Selected Quotations)

"The purpose of an enterprise is to contribute to society by supplying goods of high quality at low prices in ample quantity."

"Profit comes in compensation for contribution to society. . . . [It] is a result rather than a goal."

"The responsibility of the manufacturer cannot be relieved until its product is disposed of by the end user."

"Unsuccessful business employs a wrong management. You should not find its causes in bad fortune, unfavorable surroundings, or wrong timing."

"Business appetite has no self-restraining mechanism. . . . When you notice you have gone too far, you must have the courage to come back."

Source: "Matsushita Electric Industrial (MEI) in 1987," Harvard Business School Case No. 388-144.

however, Matsushita had to look beyond its expanding product line and excellent distribution system for growth. After trying many tactics to boost sales—even sending assembly line workers out as door-to-door salesmen—the company eventually focused on export markets.

The Organization's Foundation: Divisional Structure   Plagued by ill health, KM wished to delegate more authority than was typical in Japanese companies. In 1933, Matsushita became the first Japanese company to adopt the divisional structure, giving each division clearly defined profit responsibility for its product. In addition to creating a "small business" environment, the product division structure generated internal competition that spurred each business to drive growth by leveraging its technology to develop new products. After the innovating division had earned substantial profits on its new product, however, company policy was to spin it off as a new division to maintain the "hungry spirit."

Under the "one-product-one-division" system, corporate management provided each largely self-sufficient division with initial funds to establish its own development, production, and marketing capabilities. Corporate treasury operated like a commercial bank, reviewing divisions' loan requests for which it charged slightly higher-than-market interest, and accepting deposits on their excess funds. Divisional profitability was determined after deductions for central services such as corporate R&D and interest on internal borrowings. Each division paid 60% of earnings to headquarters and financed all additional working capital and fixed asset requirements from the retained 40%. Transfer prices were based on the market and settled through the treasury on normal commercial terms. KM expected uniform performance across the company's 36 divisions, and division managers whose operating profits fell below 4% of sales for two successive years were replaced.

While basic technology was developed in a central research laboratory (CRL), product development and engineering occurred in each of the product divisions. Matsushita intentionally under-funded the CRL, forcing it to compete for additional funding from the divisions. Annually, the CRL publicized its major research projects to the product divisions, which then provided funding in exchange for technology for marketable applications. While it was rarely the innovator, Matsushita was usually very fast to market—earning it the nickname "Manishita," or copycat.

Matsushita: Internationalization   Although the establishment of overseas markets was a major thrust of the second 25 years in the 250-year plan, in an overseas trip in 1951 KM had been unable to find any American company willing to collaborate with Matsushita. The best he could do was a technology exchange and licensing agreement with Philips. Nonetheless, the push to internationalize continued.

Expanding Through Color TV   In the 1950s and 1960s, trade liberalization and lower shipping rates made possible a healthy export business built on black and white TV sets. In 1953, the company opened its first overseas branch office—the Matsushita Electric Corporation of America (MECA). With neither a distribution network nor a strong brand, the company could not access traditional retailers, and had to resort to selling its products under their private brands through mass merchandisers and discounters.

During the 1960s, pressure from national governments in developing countries led Matsushita to open plants in several countries in Southeast Asia and Central and South America. As manufacturing costs in Japan rose, Matsushita shifted more basic production to these low-wage countries, but almost all high-value components and subassemblies were still made in its scale-intensive Japanese plants. By the 1970s, projectionist sentiments in the West forced the company to establish assembly operations in the Americas and Europe. In 1972, it opened a plant in Canada; in 1974, it bought Motorola's TV business and started manufacturing its Quasar brand in the United States; and in 1976, it built a plant in Cardiff, Wales, to supply the Common Market.

Building Global Leadership Through VCRs
The birth of the videocassette recorder (VCR) propelled Matsushita into first place in the consumer electronics industry during the 1980s. Recognizing the potential mass-market appeal of the VCR—developed by Californian broadcasting company, Ampex, in 1956—engineers at Matsushita began developing VCR technology. After six years of development work, Matsushita launched its commercial broadcast video recorder in 1964, and introduced a consumer version two years later.

In 1975, Sony introduced the technically superior "Betamax" format, and the next year JVC launched a competing "VHS" format. Under pressure from MITI, the government's industrial planning ministry, Matsushita agreed to give up its own format and adopt the established VHS standard. During Matsushita's 20 years of VCR product development, various members of the VCR research team spent most of their careers working together, moving from central labs to the product divisions' development labs and eventually to the plant.

The company quickly built production to meet its own needs as well as those of OEM customers like GE, RCA, and Zenith, who decided to forego self-manufacture and outsource to the low-cost Japanese. Between 1977 and 1985, capacity increased 33-fold to 6.8 million units. (In parallel, the company aggressively licensed the VHS format to other manufacturers, including Hitachi, Sharp, Mitsubishi and, eventually, Philips.) Increased volume enabled Matsushita to slash prices 50% within five years of product launch, while simultaneously improving quality. By the mid-1980s, VCRs accounted for 30% of total sales—over 40% of overseas revenues—and provided 45% of profits.

Changing Systems and Controls   In the mid-1980s, Matsushita's growing number of overseas companies reported to the parent in one of two ways: wholly owned, single-product global plants reported directly to the appropriate product division, while overseas sales and marketing subsidiaries and overseas companies producing a broad product line for local markets reported to Matsushita Electric Trading Company (METC), a separate legal entity. (See **Exhibit 5** for METC's organization.)

Exhibit 5   Organization of METC, 1985

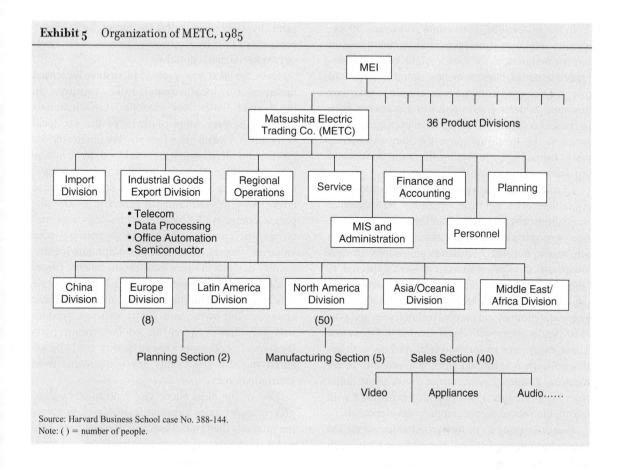

Source: Harvard Business School case No. 388-144.
Note: ( ) = number of people.

Throughout the 1970s, the central product divisions maintained strong operating control over their offshore production units. Overseas operations used plant and equipment designed by the parent company, followed manufacturing procedures dictated by the center, and used materials from Matsushita's domestic plants. Growing trends toward local sourcing, however, gradually weakened the divisions' direct control. By the 1980s, instead of controlling inputs, they began to monitor measures of output (for example, quality, productivity, inventory levels).

About the same time, product divisions began receiving the globally consolidated return on sales reports that had previously been consolidated in METC statements. By the mid-1980s, as worldwide planning was introduced for the first time, corporate management required all its product divisions to prepare global product strategies.

Headquarters–Subsidiary Relations   Although METC and the product divisions set detailed sales and profits targets for their overseas subsidiaries, local managers were told they had autonomy on how to achieve the targets. "Mike" Matsuoko, president of the company's largest European production subsidiary in Cardiff, Wales, however, emphasized that failure to meet targets forfeited freedom: "Losses show bad health and invite many doctors from Japan, who provide advice and support."

In the mid-1980s, Matsushita had over 700 expatriate Japanese managers and technicians on foreign assignment for four to eight years, but defended that high number by describing their pivotal role. "This vital communication role," said one manager, "almost always requires a manager from the parent company. Even if a local manager speaks Japanese, he would not have the long experience that is needed to build relationships and understand our management processes."

Expatriate managers were located throughout foreign subsidiaries, but there were a few positions that were almost always reserved for them. The most visible were subsidiary general managers whose main role was to translate Matsushita philosophy abroad. Expatriate accounting managers were expected to "mercilessly expose the truth" to corporate headquarters; and Japanese technical managers were sent to transfer product and process technologies and provide headquarters with local market information. These expatriates maintained relationships with senior colleagues at headquarters, who acted as career mentors, evaluated performance (with some input from local managers), and provided expatriates with information about parent company developments.

General managers of foreign subsidiaries visited Osaka headquarters at least two or three times each year—some as often as every month. Corporate managers reciprocated these visits, and on average, major operations hosted at least one headquarters manager each day of the year. Face-to-face meetings were considered vital: "Figures are important," said one manager, "but the meetings are necessary to develop judgment." Daily faxes and nightly phone calls between headquarters and expatriate colleagues were a vital management link.

Yamashita's Operation Localization   Although international sales kept rising, as early as 1982 growing host country pressures caused concern about the company's highly centralized operations. In that year, newly appointed company President Toshihiko Yamashita launched "Operation Localization" to boost offshore production from less than 10% of value-added to 25%, or half of overseas sales, by 1990. To support the target, he set out a program of four localizations—personnel, technology, material, and capital.

Over the next few years, Matsushita increased the number of local nationals in key positions. In the United States, for example, U.S. nationals became the presidents of three of the six local companies, while in Taiwan the majority of production divisions were replaced by Chinese managers. In each case, however, local national managers were still supported by senior Japanese advisors, who maintained a direct link with the parent company. To localize technology and materials, the company developed its national subsidiaries' expertise to source equipment locally, modify designs to meet local requirements, incorporate local components, and adapt corporate processes and technologies to accommodate these changes. And by the mid-1980s, offshore production subsidiaries were free to buy minor parts from local vendors as long as quality could be assured, but still had to buy key components from internal sources.

One of the most successful innovations was to give overseas sales subsidiaries more choice over the products they sold. Each year the company held a two-week internal merchandising show and product planning meeting where product divisions exhibited the new lines. Here, overseas sales subsidiary managers described their local market needs and negotiated for change in features, quantities, and even prices of the products they wanted to buy. Product division managers, however, could overrule the sales subsidiary if they thought introduction of a particular product was of strategic importance.

President Yamashita's hope was that Operation Localization would help Matsushita's overseas companies develop the innovative capability and entrepreneurial initiatives that he had long admired in the national organizations of rival Philips. (Past efforts to develop such capabilities abroad had failed. For example, when Matsushita acquired Motorola's TV business in the United States, its highly innovative technology group atrophied as

American engineers resigned in response to what they felt to be excessive control from Japan's highly centralized R&D operations.) Yet despite his four localizations, overseas companies continued to act primarily as the implementation arms of central product divisions. In an unusual act for a Japanese CEO, Yamashita publicly expressed his unhappiness with the lack of initiative at the TV plant in Cardiff. Despite the transfer of substantial resources and the delegation of many responsibilities, he felt that the plant remained too dependent on the center.

Tanii's Integration and Expansion   Yamashita's successor, Akio Tanii, expanded on his predecessor's initiatives. In 1986, feeling that Matsushita's product divisions were not giving sufficient attention to international development—in part because they received only 3% royalties for foreign production against at least 10% return on sales for exports from Japan—he brought all foreign subsidiaries under the control of METC. Tanii then merged METC into the parent company in an effort to fully integrate domestic and overseas operations. Then, to shift operational control nearer to local markets, he relocated major regional headquarters functions from Japan to North America, Europe, and Southeast Asia. Yet still he was frustrated that the overseas subsidiary companies acted as little more than the implementing agents of the Osaka-based product divisions.

Through all these changes, however, Matsushita's worldwide growth continued generating huge reserves. With $17.5 billion in liquid financial assets at the end of 1989, the company was referred to as the "Matsushita Bank," and several top executives began proposing that if they could not develop innovative overseas companies, they should buy them. Flush with cash and international success, in early 1991 the company acquired MCA, the U.S. entertainment giant, for $6.1 billion with the objective of obtaining a media software source for its hardware. Within a year, however, Japan's bubble economy had burst, plunging the economy into recession. Almost overnight, Tanii had to shift the company's focus from expansion to cost containment. Despite his best efforts to cut costs, the problems ran too deep. With 1992 profits less than half their 1991 level, the board took the unusual move of forcing Tanii to resign in February 1993.

Morishita's Challenge and Response   At 56, Yoichi Morishita was the most junior of the company's executive vice presidents when he was tapped as the new president. Under the slogan "simple, small, speedy and strategic," he committed to cutting headquarters staff and decentralizing responsibility. Over the next 18 months, he moved 6,000 staff to operating jobs. In a major strategic reversal, he also sold 80% of MCI to Seagram, booking a $1.2 billion loss on the transaction.

Yet the company continued to struggle. Japan's domestic market for consumer electronics collapsed—from $42 billion in 1989 to $21 billion in 1999. Excess capacity drove down prices and profits evaporated. And although offshore markets were growing, the rise of new competition—first from Korea, then China—created a global glut of consumer electronics, and prices collapsed.

With a strong yen making exports from Japan uncompetitive, Matsushita's product divisions rapidly shifted production offshore during the 1990s, mostly to low-cost Asian countries like China and Malaysia. By the end of the decade, its 160 factories outside Japan employed 140,000 people—about the same number of employees as in its 133 plants in Japan. Yet, despite the excess capacity and strong yen, management seemed unwilling to radically restructure its increasingly inefficient portfolio of production facilities or even lay off staff due to strongly-held commitments to lifetime employment. Despite Morishita's promises, resistance within the organization prevented his implementation of much of the promised radical change.

In the closing years of the decade, Morishita began emphasizing the need to develop more of its technology and innovation offshore. Concerned that only 250 of the company's 3,000 R&D scientists and engineers were located outside Japan, he began investing in R&D partnerships and technical exchanges, particularly in fast emerging fields. For example, in 1998 he signed a joint R&D agreement with the Chinese Academy of Sciences, China's leading research organization. Later that year, he announced the establishment of the Panasonic Digital Concepts Center in California. Its mission was to act as a venture fund and an incubation center for the new ideas and technologies emerging in Silicon Valley. To some it was an indication that Matsushita had given up trying to generate new technology and business initiatives from its own overseas companies.

Nakamura's Initiatives   In April 2000, Morishita became chairman and Kunio Nakamura replaced him as president. Profitability was at 2.2% of sales, with consumer electronics at only 0.4%, including losses generated by one-time cash cows, the TV and VCR divisions. (**Exhibits 6 and 7** provide the financial history for Matsushita and key product lines.) The new CEO vowed to raise this to 5% by 2004. Key to his plan was to move Matsushita beyond its

Exhibit 6   Matsushita, Summary Financial Data, 1970–2000[a]

	2000	1995	1990	1985	1980	1975	1970
In billions of yen and percent:							
Sales	¥7,299	¥6,948	¥6,003	¥5,291	¥2,916	¥1,385	¥932
Income before tax	219	232	572	723	324	83	147
As % of sales	3.0%	3.3%	9.5%	13.7%	11.1%	6.0%	15.8%
Net income	¥100	¥90	¥236	¥216	¥125	¥32	¥70
As % of sales	1.4%	1.3%	3.9%	4.1%	4.3%	2.3%	7.6%
Cash dividends (per share)	¥14.00	¥13.50	¥10.00	¥ 9.52	¥7.51	¥6.82	¥6.21
Total assets	7,955	8,202	7,851	5,076	2,479	1,274	735
Stockholders' equity	3,684	3,255	3,201	2,084	1,092	573	324
Capital investment	355	316	355	288	NA	NA	NA
Depreciation	343	296	238	227	65	28	23
R&D	526	378	346	248	102	51	NA
Employees (units)	290,448	265,397	198,299	175,828	107,057	82,869	78,924
Overseas employees	143,773	112,314	59,216	38,380	NA	NA	NA
As % of total employees	50%	42%	30%	22%	NA	NA	NA
Exchange rate (fiscal period end; ¥/$)	103	89	159	213	213	303	360
In millions of dollars:							
Sales	$68,862	$78,069	$37,753	$24,890	$13,690	$4,572	$2,588
Operating income before depreciation	4,944	6,250	4,343	3,682	1,606	317	NA
Operating income after depreciation	1,501	2,609	2,847	2,764	1,301	224	NA
Pretax income	2,224	2,678	3,667	3,396	1,520	273	408
Net income	941	1,017	1,482	1,214	584	105	195
Total assets	77,233	92,159	49,379	21,499	11,636	4,206	2,042
Total equity	35,767	36,575	20,131	10,153	5,129	1,890	900

Source: Annual reports; Standard & Poors' *Compustat;* Moody's Industrial and International Manuals.
[a] Data prior to 1987 are for the fiscal year ending November 20; data 1988 and after are for the fiscal year ending March 31.

Exhibit 7   Matsushita, Sales by Product and Geographic Segment, 1985–2000 (billion yen)

	2000		1995		FY 1990		FY 1985	
By Product Segment:								
Video and audio equipment	¥1,706	23%	¥1,827	26%	¥2,159	36%	¥2,517	48%
Home appliances and household equipment	1,306	18	—	—	—	—	—	—
Home appliances	—	—	916	13	802	13	763	14
Communication and industrial equipment	—	—	1,797	26	1,375	23	849	16
Electronic components	—	—	893	13	781	13	573	11
Batteries and kitchen-related equipment	—	—	374	4	312	5	217	4
Information and communications equipment	2,175	28	—	—	—	—	—	—
Industrial equipment	817	11	—	—	—	—	—	—
Components	1,618	21	—	—	—	—	—	—
Others	—	—	530	8	573	10	372	7
Total	¥7,682	100%	¥6,948	100%	¥6,003	100%	¥5,291	100%
By Geographic Segment:								
Domestic	¥3,698	51%	¥3,455	50%	¥3,382	56%	¥2,659	50%
Overseas	3,601	49	3,493	50	2,621	44	2,632	50

Source: Annual reports.
Notes: Total may not add due to rounding.

roots as a "super manufacturer of products" and begin "to meet customer needs through systems and services." He planned to flatten the hierarchy and empower employees to respond to customer needs, and as part of the implementation, all key headquarters functions relating to international operations were transferred to overseas regional offices.

But the biggest shock came in November, when Nakamura announced a program of "destruction and creation," in which he disbanded the product division structure that KM had created as Matsushita's basic organizational building block 67 years earlier. Plants, previously controlled by individual product divisions, would now be integrated into multi-product production centers. In Japan alone 30 of the 133 factories were to be consolidated or closed. And marketing would shift to two corporate marketing entities, one for Panasonic brands (consumer electronics, information and communications products) and one for national branded products (mostly home appliances).

In February, 2001, just three months after raising his earnings estimate for the financial year ending March 2001, Nakamuta was embarrassed to readjust his estimate sharply downward. As Matsushita's first losses in 30 years accelerated, the new CEO announced a round of emergency measures designed to cut costs. When coupled with the earlier structural changes, these were radical moves, but in a company that even in Japan was being talked about as a takeover target, observers wondered if they were sufficient to restore Matsushita's tattered global competitiveness.

Case 4-2   Rudi Gassner and the Executive Committee of BMG International (A)

Rudi Gassner, CEO of BMG International, paused and glanced around the hotel suite at the members of his executive committee. They were not coming to any consensus on the issue at hand. It was May 1993 and the BMG International executive committee was gathered for one of its quarterly meetings, this time in Boca Raton, Florida, during the annual Managing Directors Convention.

Gassner had just congratulated Arnold Bahlmann, a regional director and executive committee member, on his recent negotiation of a reduced manufacturing transfer price for the upcoming year's production of CDs, records, and cassettes. Because business plans for the year had been established in March based on the assumption of a higher manufacturing cost, the new price would realize an unanticipated savings of roughly $20 million.

As a result of these savings, the executive committee now faced some tough decisions. First, they had to decide whether or not to change the business targets for each country to reflect the new manufacturing price. If they chose to alter the targets, they had to address the even more delicate matter of whether managing directors' bonuses, which were based principally on the achievement of these targets, should be based on the old or new figures.

Gassner had already discussed this issue with Bahlmann and CFO Joe Gorman, who had run calculations on the impact of the new price for each operating company. These had been distributed to the executive committee before the meeting. Through previous discussions and evaluation of the financial impact, Gassner had formulated his opinion about what should be done.

▌ Research Associate Katherine Seger Weber prepared this case under the supervision of Professor Linda A. Hill as the basis for class discussion rather than to illustrate either effective or ineffective handling of an administrative situation.

In his mind, the issues were clear. BMG International had achieved tremendous success and growth in its short lifetime of six years, and the regional directors (RDs) and managing directors (MDs)[1] had every right to feel good about their exceptional performance. (See **Exhibits 1** and **2** for company organization charts.) But now Gassner wanted to guard against the company becoming a victim of its own success. He knew that they would have to carefully monitor the economics of the business and maintain their agility in order to meet the challenges of the future. In light of these concerns, Gassner felt that the MDs should be held accountable for the savings from the reduced manufacturing price. The executive committee needed seriously to consider not only adjusting the targets, but also the bonus basis. As he explained, "It seemed fair to me. These were windfall profits coming to the managing directors, and they didn't even have to lift a finger to get them. I didn't want them to become complacent during the year."

The executive committee, however, seemed unwilling even to entertain this possibility. Gassner suspected that some of the RDs were taking the "path of least resistance" because they did not want to return to their MDs and announce that the bonus targets had been changed. His frustration mounting, Gassner wondered if he should drop the issue for now or provoke them by saying what was on his mind: "Listen guys, you're thinking too much like MDs. You should be thinking about what is good for the whole company."

▌ Company Background

BMG International was a subsidiary of Bertelsmann AG, a German media conglomerate with over 200 companies and 50,000 employees operating in

▌ [1]Managing Directors managed local operations in a particular country; each MD reported to one of five Regional Directors.

Exhibit 1   Bertelsmann Music Group Organization Chart

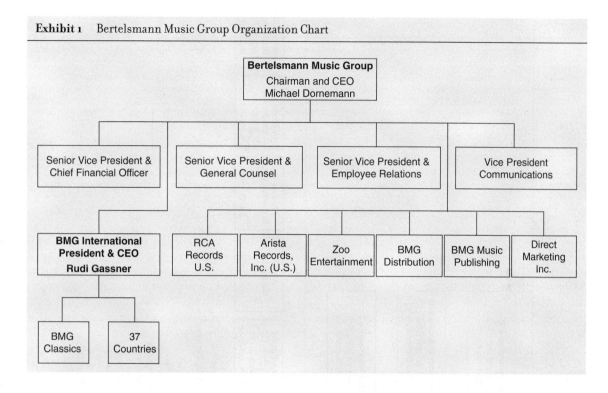

37 countries. Founded in 1835 as a lithographic printing company in Guetersloh, Germany, Bertelsmann's interests had grown to include businesses in music, film, television, radio, book, magazine, and newspaper publishing and distribution, as well as printing and manufacturing operations. Still headquartered in the small rural town, Bertelsmann had become the second-largest media enterprise in the world, with 1992 sales of $9.7 billion.

Bertelsmann's corporate charter mandated autonomous business divisions and entrepreneurial operating management, and emphasized respect for the cultural traditions of each country in which it operated. Each business unit had its own, usually local, entrepreneurial management with operating control over its business plan, the development of its assets, its human resources, and its contribution to overall profitability. Delegation of responsibility and authority was supported by performance-linked compensation for managers and profit-sharing by all employees.

In 1986, Bertelsmann entered the U.S. market with its purchases of Doubleday and Dell, two large publishing houses, and RCA Records, which had made music history with Elvis Presley in the 1950s. On acquiring RCA, Bertelsmann organized its worldwide music holdings—which also included the American record label Arista, the German label Ariola, and various smaller labels and music publishing and marketing operations—into the Bertelsmann Music Group (BMG). With RCA, BMG entered the ranks of the "Big Six" record companies—CBS, Warner, BMG, Capitol-EMI, PolyGram, and MCA—which supplied 80% of worldwide music sales.[2]

BMG was headquartered in New York under German Chairman and CEO Michael Dornemann, who split the company's operations into two divisions: the United States and the rest of the world. In

[2]Purkiss, Alan, "Let's Hear It for the Unsung Hero," *Accountancy*, June 1992, pp. 70–73.

Exhibit 2 BMG International Organization Chart, 1993

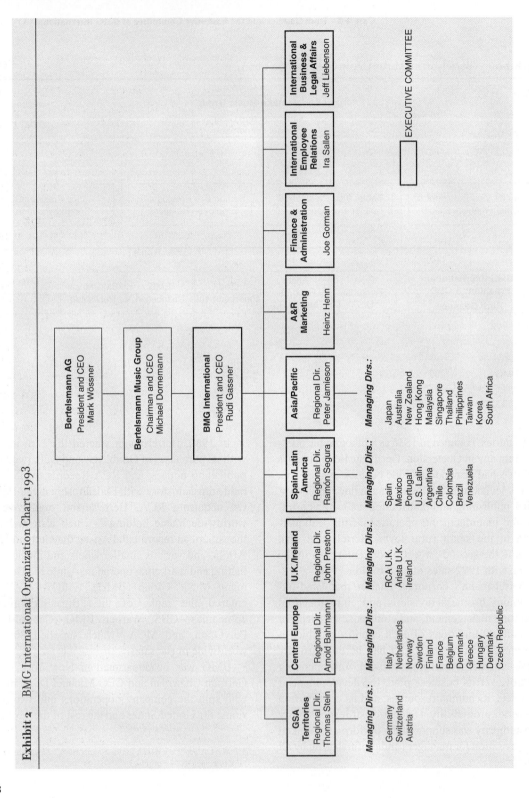

Bertelsmann AG
President and CEO
Mark Wössner

Bertelsmann Music Group
Chairman and CEO
Michael Dornemann

BMG International
President and CEO
Rudi Gassner

GSA Territories	Central Europe	U.K./Ireland	Spain/Latin America	Asia/Pacific	A&R Marketing	Finance & Administration	International Employee Relations	International Business & Legal Affairs
Regional Dir. Thomas Stein	Regional Dir. Arnold Bahlmann	Regional Dir. John Preston	Regional Dir. Ramón Segura	Regional Dir. Peter Jamieson	Heinz Henn	Joe Gorman	Ira Sallen	Jeff Liebenson

Managing Dirs.:

Germany
Switzerland
Austria

Managing Dirs.:

Italy
Netherlands
Norway
Sweden
Finland
France
Belgium
Denmark
Greece
Hungary
Denmark
Czech Republic

Managing Dirs.:

RCA U.K.
Arista U.K.
Ireland

Managing Dirs.:

Spain
Mexico
Portugal
U.S. Latin
Argentina
Chile
Colombia
Brazil
Venezuela

Managing Dirs.:

Japan
Australia
New Zealand
Hong Kong
Malaysia
Singapore
Thailand
Philippines
Taiwan
Korea
South Africa

☐ EXECUTIVE COMMITTEE

Exhibit 3   Rudi Gassner Career Highlights

Rudi Gassner

President and CEO, BMG International

German, 51 years old

- 1984–1987:   Executive VP, PolyGram International, London
- 1983–1984:   President, Polydor International (PolyGram), Hamburg
- 1980–1983:   President, Deutsche Grammophon (PolyGram), Hamburg
- Fall 1979:   Harvard Business School Program for Management Development (PMD)
- 1977–1980:   Managing Director, Metronome (PolyGram), Hamburg
- 1969–1977:   Sales Manager, Deutsche Grammophon (PolyGram), Munich
- 1964–1969:   Music Wholesaling, Munich

the United States, BMG's priority was to stem the losses from RCA (which posted a $35 million deficit in 1987) and build market share for the flagging U.S. labels.[3]

With BMG's overseas holdings, Dornemann formed an international division and hired German-born Rudi Gassner, then executive vice president of PolyGram International, as president and CEO (see **Exhibit 3**). According to Dornemann, Gassner "had the right background in the music business and the right international experience. He best fit the leadership qualities we were looking for."[4] At its inception in 1987, the international division, also headquartered in New York, comprised operations in 17 countries across the globe. Gassner described the fledgling organization as "a patchwork of companies around the world. It had no mission, no goals, and in total, it didn't make any money. . . . The only way from there was up."[5]

[3]Dannen, Frederick, *Hit Men: Power Brokers and Fast Money Inside the Music Business* (New York: Vintage Books, 1991), pp. 246–261.
[4]"BMG's Five Year Man," *Music Business International*, Vol. 3, No. 1 (January 1993), p. 18.
[5]Ibid.

In his first six years, Gassner led the company, which he named BMG International, through a tremendous period of growth. By launching new satellite companies, purchasing small labels, and forming joint ventures, BMG International's presence had expanded by 1993 to include 37 countries. Sales had increased an average of 20% annually, reaching $2 billion in 1993 (two-thirds of BMG's overall revenue that year). International market share, which was near 11% in 1987, was a healthy 17%, and as high as 25% in some territories.[6]

BMG International was responsible for marketing and distributing top-selling U.S. artists such as Whitney Houston and Kenny G across the globe.[7] In addition, the company developed such artists as Annie Lennox and Lisa Stansfield (Britain) and Eros Ramazzotti (Italy) in their local territories to be marketed worldwide. On a local level, groups such as B'z (Japan) and Bronco (Mexico) were extremely successful, selling in excess of 1 million units in their respective countries. The company also had extensive classics and jazz catalogues, with artists such as James Galway and Antonio Hart. (See **Exhibit 4** for roster of top-selling artists.)[8]

Rudi Gassner and BMG International

In 1987, at the age of 45, Gassner became the CEO of the newly-formed BMG International. "It was a once-in-a-lifetime opportunity," he reflected, "to build what I think a global company should look

[6]According to Gassner, a 1% worldwide market share gain was worth around $250 million in revenue. ("Charting the Future" speech, May 1993, Boca Raton, Florida.)
[7]The "prestige market" of the U.S. was the most important supplier of recorded music around the world, and BMG's Arista, led by long-time music executive Clive Davis, had launched two global superstars, Whitney Houston and Kenny G, who reached No. 1 and 2 on the *Billboard* album chart. In 1993, Houston's soundtrack for *The Bodyguard* sold 20 million copies and became one of the top-selling albums of all time, fueling a significant portion of BMG's revenue in the U.S. and abroad. (Lander, Mark, "An Overnight Success—After Six Years," *Business Week*, April 19, 1993, pp. 52–54.)
[8]In addition, BMG International had an agreement with MCA/Geffen to market and distribute that company's products outside the U.S. The MCA/Geffen deal gave BMG International access to such stars as Guns 'N' Roses, Nirvana, Aerosmith, Bobby Brown, and Cher.

Exhibit 4   Selected BMG International
Top-Selling Artists, 1993

Artist	Country of Origin	Units Sold 1992/1993 (in thousands)
Global Superstars:		
Whitney Houston	United States	11,800
Kenny G	United States	2,200
Annie Lennox	United Kingdom	1,200
David Bowie	United Kingdom	700
SNAP	Germany	700
Dr. Alban	Germany	600
Regional Superstars:		
Vaya Con Dios	Belgium	1,300
Juan Luis Guerra	Spain	1,100
Eros Ramazzotti	Italy	1,100
Die Prinzen	Germany	900
Take That	United Kingdom	700
Bonnie Tyler	Germany	500
Local Superstars:		
B'z	Japan	5,700
Bronco	Mexico	1,300
Joaquin Sabina	Spain	500
Jos Jos	Mexico	400
Lucio Dalla	Italy	250

like." When he arrived at BMG, Gassner adapted quickly to the Bertelsmann culture. "My 17 years at PolyGram gave me the experience to run a global business; that was my know-how," he explained. "But on the other hand, I very much liked the Bertelsmann style. It was very close to my personal style." One of his colleagues at BMG described Gassner's transition:

> Rudi came from PolyGram, which had a very different culture. The Philips PolyGram culture is highly politically charged; it is much more "stand by your beds when the senior management comes in." Rudi changed a lot when he came to BMG. He saw the value in the Bertelsmann managing style; he saw the freedom to do things, and he took it. He passed it on as well.

Building BMG International   One of Gassner's first priorities was to instill this culture in the newly acquired companies. He reflected on what he inherited when he joined BMG:

> My first step was basically to get to know the companies and the problems hands-on myself. RCA had been centrally managed out of New York, and the managers in the companies had the attitude that "I'm not doing anything unless somebody tells me what to do." I would find them hiding under tables. I spent the first two years preaching my gospel and saying to the managers, "You are responsible. I can give you advice, but don't send me a memo asking me to sign off here. You are in charge: you are Mr. Italy; you are Mr. France; you are Mr. Belgium."

At the same time, Gassner also began to communicate his vision for BMG International. "There were basically two strategic targets in my mind," he explained:

> One was globalization. Globalization allows you to serve a bigger world market. Every time we added a new country, we would increase our revenue accordingly. The other strategic target was domestic repertoire. I had a great fear of being too dependent on English-speaking repertoire. I made it clear to the managers that their foremost responsibility was developing domestic talent. Joint ventures and acquisitions were another way to add local repertoire.

Gassner also instituted yearly business plans with each of his managing directors. He described the process:

> We [Gassner and each MD] do a budget once a year. The budget is between you and me. I want to know where you are going and how much investment you will need. We talk about revenues and profits. I make a very aggressive bonus plan for them to be able to make a lot of money; if they exceed their targets significantly, they can make up to half their salary as a bonus. In America, this might not have been so sensational, but for those countries who were not used to that, it was pretty new.

According to Gassner, "the majority of the guys came through with flying colors." For those who did not fit with the new program, Gassner held "career counseling sessions," as one colleague referred to them: "When Rudi conducts a career counseling session, it's pretty much over. But he's so smooth and so good at it, that it takes them about a week to figure out that they may have just been fired."

Gassner also turned his attention inward, focusing on his corporate management structure. "One advantage, obviously, was that nothing existed. I could do it any way I wanted. That was fantastic." He made Joe Gorman, who had been the senior finance executive for RCA's international arm, the chief financial officer of BMG International. During Gassner's first two years, Gorman accompanied him as he travelled around the world assessing each operating company.

Gassner's next corporate hire was Heinz Henn to coordinate global A&R marketing.[9] Henn had spent 17 years at EMI in international positions. He described his job interview with Gassner:

Rudi and I met for the first time on February 17, 1987, at the Park Lane Hotel and had breakfast together. What got me the job was that I ate two breakfasts—I was really hungry that day. He was impressed that somebody could eat two full breakfasts on a job interview.

Seriously, Rudi asked me what I would do if he gave me the job, and I told him that I would do things differently than they had been done so far in the industry, particularly [the companies] where we had both come from. I wanted to cultivate local talent in individual markets to build hot acts which we could launch globally. He totally agreed with me. Ever since, he's let me do what I wanted to do.

Gassner described the need for Henn's role:

Heinz has a dual role: he not only has to break local artists worldwide, he also has to sell Whitney Houston to all the local companies. We need Heinz because the interests of the countries and the regions stop at the borders, and we need a global view on artists. This will give us the competitive advantage; there's more money to be made outside the borders if you do it right.

[9]"A&R" was a record industry term that stood for "artist and repertoire," record company products. In record companies, investing in A&R to develop talent was analogous to a manufacturing concern investing in R&D. "A&R marketing" was essentially product marketing.

Henn added:

You have to have coordination between the regions as far as marketing and promotion activities are concerned because recording and marketing expenses are far too great these days for any one [local] company to be able to earn back its investment in one country only. It requires coordination between regions and also globally.

To round out his corporate staff, Gassner added a human resource executive, Ira Sallen, and legal counsel, Jeff Liebenson. Sallen would be responsible for negotiating and maintaining the managing directors' contracts, as well as for worldwide personnel and organizational policies. Liebenson would serve as in-house counsel, assisting in the intricate contracts that were part of operating a complex global enterprise.

Gassner also instituted an annual Managing Directors' Convention in which Dornemann, Gassner, the corporate staff, and all of the MDs and joint-venture partners (JVs) would converge from around the world. A major objective of the annual MD Convention was to provide a forum for the MDs and JVs to give repertoire presentations to each other in an attempt to sell their local repertoire to the other countries.

Creating a Regional Structure   As BMG International's number of operating companies continued to grow, it became impossible for Gassner directly to oversee them all. By 1989, he concluded it was time to aggregate the countries into five regions and hire a regional director for each, a plan he had had in mind from the beginning. (See **Exhibit 2** for organization chart and **Exhibit 5** for revenue and profit distribution by region.) The role of the RD would be "to provide leadership for the region; to oversee the strategic development of the region, in conjunction with the whole company; and to manage the managing directors." He explained:

I divided Europe into three different categories: the United Kingdom, German-speaking territories, and the rest of Europe. At that time, the German-speaking territories contributed about 50% of our profit, so they were a very important group unto themselves. I promoted

Exhibit 5   BMG International Revenue and Operating Result Distribution by Region

Net Revenue by Region:

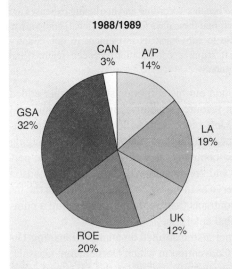

1988/1989

CAN 3%
A/P 14%
GSA 32%
LA 19%
UK 12%
ROE 20%

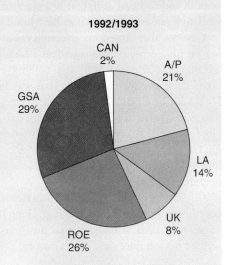

1992/1993

CAN 2%
A/P 21%
GSA 29%
LA 14%
UK 8%
ROE 26%

Operating Result (Betriebsergebnis) by Region:

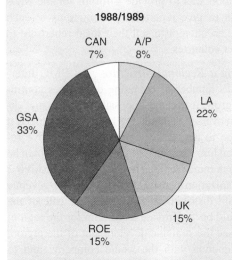

1988/1989

CAN 7%
A/P 8%
GSA 33%
LA 22%
UK 15%
ROE 15%

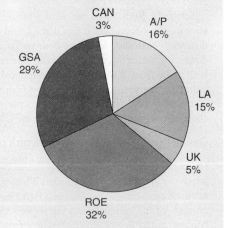

1992/1993

CAN 3%
A/P 16%
GSA 29%
LA 15%
UK 5%
ROE 32%

Legend:
A/P = Asia/Pacific; Can = Canada; LA = Latin America;
GSA = Germany/ Switzerland/Austria; ROE = Rest of Europe;
UK = United Kingdom.

Thomas Stein, who was the managing director of the German company, to regional director.

The United Kingdom, despite its relatively small profits, was our largest source of repertoire, a major supplier. I promoted John Preston, who was the MD of RCA Records U.K., to be the regional director of that region.

The MD for Ariola Spain, Ramón Segura, was an outstanding executive who also had, at that time, regional responsibilities for Ariola's Latin American companies. So I kept Spain/Latin America together as a region and made Segura the RD.

Now I needed someone for the rest of Europe. I hired Arnold Bahlmann, who was working in strategic analysis for Michael Dornemann. He was not one of the music managers coming through the ranks. He had never had a line job in his life. Still, I thought, you don't necessarily need the detailed day-to-day experience of running a company to manage a regional territory. It was an organizational task, and I thought Arnold had very good people skills. I thought he was ideal, though it was a hell of a risk to put him in.

At the same time as I promoted John Preston to RD in the United Kingdom, I asked the chairman of the RCA U.K. label, Peter Jamieson, to go out and establish our Asia/Pacific market. I remember a British competitor in the industry joking with me that "wasn't I worried about sending one of my best men out to the colonies?" I thought Jamieson was just the right person for the job. He accepted, and he's done a brilliant job building companies and repertoire in that region.

Gassner maintained the annual business planning system he had established with the MDs, but he now worked through the RDs. As Segura described it, "We are involved throughout the process, but Rudi has final approval." BMG International's fiscal year started July 1 and ran through June 30. In January, the MDs began to prepare their business plans, developing targets for critical measures such as revenue, *betriebsergebnis*[10], return on sales, market share, revenue per employee, days inventory, and days sales outstanding. Gassner was as

much interested in the assumptions used to arrive at the targets as the figures themselves; MDs were expected to include an in-depth analysis of the risks and opportunities they faced based on the current economic climate and market, new A&R releases, and their priority artists.

In February, the MDs met with the RDs to review their plans; the RDs then met with Gassner to discuss regional as well as local goals. Gorman described Gassner's stance in these meetings: "Rudi has a reputation for being tough—fair, but tough. One of the reasons he has that reputation is that he makes you do things which you know you should do, but which you don't want to do." One RD described these sessions as "the famous February meetings. Rudi and I dislike each other a lot in February. But by March we usually agree."

In March, the RDs returned to the MDs with a final plan and targets; Gassner and Gorman joined many of these sessions (see **Exhibit 6**). At this point, the MDs would have a final opportunity to discuss their plans and the targets would be agreed upon. Gorman described these meetings:

March is the critical planning month for us. We tell everybody, look, when the meeting is over, we all walk out of here with the same goals. Period. We can sit in the room an hour, or we can sit there for two days, but in the end nobody is going to leave this room disagreeing on what the goals are. In these meetings, MD bonus criteria are also defined, since *betriebsergebnis* is the primary criterion for bonuses.

One RD described Gassner's approach:

Rudi plays a different role with each MD, depending on their personality and where he wants the country to go. Sometimes he plays the good cop, and other times he plays the bad cop. He's very versatile, and very results-oriented. When necessary, he knows how to hit people's hot buttons and make them squirm.

According to one MD:

Rudi knows the business inside and out, and he has an amazing grasp of the details. When he is going through these plans, he will go into particular line items if he wants to. These business plans are like contracts between Rudi and me. Face-to-face with

---

[10] *Betriebsergebnis* was a German accounting term roughly translated to mean profit plus interest costs. The official language at BMG International was English (German was never spoken if a non-speaker was present); *betriebsergebnis* was the only German word the company used.

Exhibit 6   March 1992 Business Planning Meetings Attended by Rudi Gassner and Joe Gorman

Location:	Date:	Review:	
Munich	March 1	10:00 AM	Belgium
		11:30 AM	Netherlands
		2:00 PM	Italy
	March 2	10:00 AM	UK-RCA
		2:00 PM	UK-Arista
		4:00 PM	UK-Distrib.
	March 3	10:00 AM	GSA Overview
		11:30 AM	Munich Ariola
		2:00 PM	Germany Ariola
		3:45 PM	Hamburg Ariola
	March 4	10:00 AM	Germany Ariola
		11:30 AM	Austria
		2:00 PM	Switzerland
	March 5	10:00 AM	France Ariola
		11:30 AM	France Vogue
		1:30 PM	France RCA
		4:00 PM	European Regional Overview
New York	March 10	10:00 AM	Canada
		2:00 PM	Home Office
Hong Kong	March 16	10:00 AM	Australia
		3:00 PM	Hong Kong
	March 17	10:00 AM	Japan
		3:00 PM	Taiwan
	March 18	10:00 AM	South Africa
		3:00 PM	Malaysia
	March 19	10:00 AM	Asia/Pacific Regional Overview
New York	March 24	10:00 AM	Mexico
		2:00 PM	U.S. Latin
		4:00 PM	Portugal
	March 25	10:00 AM	Brazil
		2:00 PM	Spain
	March 26	10:00 AM	Latin America Regional Overview

him, I am committing to try to make this target. It's like a moral imperative to get it done.

According to Bahlmann, "The business plans serve their purpose well. If you ask me if I enjoy them—no. It's not enjoyable. I hate the process. But it works." Stein concurred: "The business plans help me explain what I think should be done in my region. It's a fair process because it's based on an objective financial measure." Another RD, however,

commented on the danger inherent in the system:

> The business plan process is a necessary and effective tool. But the danger is that it becomes too inflexible. Instead of a jacket which guides, a sort of loose piece of clothing which shapes the way we operate, it becomes a straightjacket and restricts the way we operate.

Even with the addition of the regional directors, Gassner maintained close contact with the local companies around the world. "I emphasize what I call a very flat hierarchical structure," he explained. "I'm never too far removed from what's really happening." While he was primarily in contact with the RDs, Gassner always reserved the right to call the MDs directly, and they "feel absolutely free to call me about anything," according to Gassner. "But they all know that it is a two-way information system. Whatever they tell me, they know I will pass on to their regional director. And whatever they tell the RD, they know he passes on to me." When possible, Gassner made it a point to reach further into the organization by talking informally with local employees "just to double-check that my messages come through."

Gassner's style of running a global business was extremely demanding. Travel was a way of life: he and his corporate staff spent 50% or more of their time away from New York headquarters, and the regional directors traveled constantly throughout their regions. According to Gorman,

Rudi believes that you are not managing an international company unless you travel extensively, because it's all about people. The financial statements are fine, the statistics are fine. But in the end, you have to sit down with somebody in a room and talk to them to get a real sense for the people and for what's going on. There are things that always come out "by the way . . . ." When you go out to dinner or you're at a concert until 4:00 in the morning, a lot of this comes out.

The Executive Committee and the ECMs

In 1989, after he had established his corporate staff and the regional structure, Gassner formally created an Executive Committee consisting of the five regional directors, the four senior staff members, and himself as the leader (see **Exhibit 7**). He recalled:

I had always intended to have an executive committee. I always wanted to run a business on the basis of a European board system, like a *vorstand*:[11] although it

[11] A *vorstand* was a German managing board consisting of full-time executive members who carried out the day-to-day operation of the company. It was distinguished from the supervisory board (*aufsichtsrat*), which consisted of shareholders and employee representatives. (Parkyn, Brian, *Democracy, Accountability, and Participation in Industry* (Bradford, West Yorkshire, England: MCB General Management Ltd., 1979), p. 105; and Kennedy, Thomas, *European Labor Relations* (Lexington, MA: Lexington Books, 1980), p. 185.

is chaired by one person and members have their own portfolios [regions], the committee decides business issues jointly.

The way I see it, the board should decide about important issues strategically or from an investment point of view. And I wanted everybody to be involved in the process, despite the fact that some issues may not have a direct consequence for their region.

You cannot run a global organization without breaking it down into regions—it just becomes impossible. On the other hand, you have to have a global strategy. In our business, the regions are interlinked by artist agreements and by the exchange of repertoire. So it needs both a regional organization and a global vision.

Bahlmann recalled Gassner introducing the concept of an executive committee by describing it as "the group which will lead BMG International." Gassner decided that the committee would meet four times per year at the New York headquarters to discuss current operating issues, and once a year outside of New York to examine long-term strategy. Before each executive committee meeting (ECM), members were polled for agenda items; Gassner then, as he described it, "edited" the suggestions to create the agenda, which was circulated to the group.

Gassner described the first ECM:

We needed to define the limitations and boundaries of authority among ourselves and the MDs. What should we allow our MDs to do without our approval? What should they have to bring to your level? What should you then bring to my level? We needed certain regulations; it makes our lives easier. It was interesting because of the history of the group coming together— they had not been organized before in a way that had these limitations, and they didn't like it.

I also had to explain the role of the New York staff. There was a lot of theoretical discussion about, for example, Heinz's responsibility. What can Heinz say about my repertoire and my country? How can Heinz say I have to spend a certain amount of money on an artist that is not valid for my region? My answer to that was always that Heinz cannot say. He can only sit down with you and try to convince you that this is the right thing for you. You've got to see the staff as somebody helping you; it is not some governing body who tells you what to do. They have a dotted-line relationship with your people.

Exhibit 7   BMG International Executive Committee

From left to right: Arnold Bahlmann, Thomas Stein, John Preston, Rudi Gassner, Heinz Henn, Peter Jamieson, Ramón Segura, Joe Gorman (*not pictured*: Ira Sallen, Jeff Liebenson).

Regional Directors

Arnold Bahlmann
Senior VP, Central Europe

- German, 41 years old.
- Promoted from: Senior VP Operations, BMG.
- 3 years strategic planning, Bertelsmann.
- Doctorate in Political Science.
- Master of Business Administration.

Thomas Stein
President, GSA Territories

- German, 44 years old.
- Promoted from: Managing Director, BMG Ariola, Munich.
- 14 years sales, marketing, and management in record business.

John Preston
Chairman, BMG Records (UK) Ltd.

- Scottish, 43 years old.

New York Corporate Staff

Heinz Henn
Senior VP, A&R/Marketing

- German, 38 years old.
- Promoted from: Director of International Division, Capitol/EMI America Records.
- 17 years A&R/marketing, promotion, and management in record business.

Joe Gorman
Senior VP, Finance and Administration

- American, 50 years old.
- Promoted from: Director, Operations Planning, RCA Records (U.S.).
- 10 years finance at RCA Records.
- 5 years Arthur Young & Company.
- Master of Business Administration.
- Military service, Captain, U.S. Army.

(*continued*)

Exhibit 7   *(concluded)*

Regional Directors	New York Corporate Staff
• Promoted from: Managing Director, RCA Records, U.K. • 19 years retail, marketing, and management in record business.	Ira Sallen VP, International Human Resources, BMG • American, 39 years old. • Promoted from: VP, Human Resources, Clean Harbors, Inc. • 4 years corporate human resources. • 2 years Consultant, Arthur Young & Company. • 5 years research and clinical psychology. • Master of Business Administration.
Ramón Segura President, Spain and Sr. VP, Latin America • Spanish, 52 years old. • Promoted from: MD, Spain, and VP Latin American Region, Ariola Eurodisc. • 31 years sales, A&R, marketing, and management in record business.	
Peter Jamieson Senior VP, Asia/Pacific • English, 48 years old. • Promoted from: Chairman, BMG Records U.K. • 26 years marketing, sales, and management in record business.	Jeff Liebenson VP, Int'l. Legal and Business Affairs, BMG • American, 40 years old. • Promoted from: Director, Legal and Business Affairs, SportsChannel America. • 15 years legal experience, including 12 in entertainment industry. • J.D and LL.M. law degrees.

Preston described his perspective on the early meetings:

> At first, there was no role for the RDs. Rudi had things he wanted to do; the agenda was laid out, and we would discuss ways of implementing the agenda. The staff people went into the meetings very well prepared and tried to establish a couple of policies with the help of Rudi in order to structure the business. It took us a certain amount of time to find a way of really working together.

Bahlmann echoed the same point:

> Rudi needed to establish himself and the regional structure; it was like him telling us, via the agenda, what we're going to do. It was our "educational process." Although I think we sometimes found it frustrating, we were so busy with our own companies [regions], there was not a lot of resistance.

Gassner found this lack of "resistance" somewhat disconcerting. According to Gorman,

> I remember after the first two ECMs, Rudi saying to me, "Everybody's too nice." He expects strong dissenting

opinions. He doesn't want a bunch of people just sitting there mildly accepting anything. To him, a heated argument over an opinion is part of the fun of the job, I suppose. But if you're not used to this, and when I first started with him I wasn't, it jars you a little.

In time, however, the RDs became more vocal. According to Henn, "It took quite some time until the group felt comfortable enough with each other that they dared to say what they really wanted to say." According to the RDs, the shift in the ECMs was due to their growing confidence and success in running their regions. As Bahlmann noted:

> About two years ago it turned around. The regional directors and the managing directors make the decisions about the operating businesses and acquisitions. Today in the ECMs, we go more into other issues. More and more, we are finally making decisions together and running the business as a team.

Preston also commented on this shift in emphasis: "In the beginning, the staff and Rudi were more dominant. But now, it's more balanced between Rudi and the RDs, and then the staff."

Working Together   By 1993, the executive committee and the ECMs had been in place for four years, and the meetings had fallen into a fairly regular pattern. Each agenda would include a presentation by Gorman on current financial results relative to targets; a discussion by Henn about A&R developments, new releases, and priority artists; a briefing by Sallen on significant worldwide human resource issues; and an update on each region by the RDs. Gassner described the importance of these regional reviews: "I want to give them room to explain to their colleagues what they're up to. Even though it's not relevant to somebody running South America, for example, he should listen, in my opinion, to what happened in Korea and how we do business in Korea. Here is where I try to get them involved in the global strategy."

Outside the ECMs there was frequent contact between Gassner and each RD. Contact among the RDs varied, and was most frequent among three of the European directors: Bahlmann, Stein, and Preston. Because they shared so many of the same circumstances and concerns, Gassner established a European subcommittee in 1991. As he explained,

> I created a European board because I didn't want to be in the middle of those discussions all the time. It seemed natural to make Arnold the chairman, since he is also the head of European-wide manufacturing and distribution. I told them: "You guys deal with European issues. Europe is your baby. If you cannot agree, I get the minutes and then I will make a ruling."

Since its inception, the European board had been very effective in achieving the purpose he had intended, according to Gassner:

> They deal with issues that are really not relevant to anybody else before they get to the ECM. They even discuss the ECM agenda before the meetings, and they sometimes come over with what I call a "prefabricated opinion." So now sometimes I have to work to break this group up a little bit.

Depending on their regional circumstances, the roles of the RDs varied significantly. Bahlmann, Preston, and Stein, for example, focused on continuing to carve out market share and bring costs down

in their increasingly mature markets. Because of his region's importance as a repertoire supplier, Preston was seen as the "repertoire expert"; Bahlmann, on the other hand, was the "strategy expert." Segura and Jamieson were most concerned with establishing new companies and developing talent in the relatively undeveloped markets of Asia and Latin America. Jamieson commented on the satisfaction of being a "pioneer," as he called it: "Asia/Pacific is a huge, multicultural, diverse, economically varied region which is on exactly the opposite side of the world from America. It has the most growth potential and the most musical excitement, really. It's a very, very exciting place to be." Segura described the unique challenges in his region: "I am constantly battling against the terrible political and economic instability that affects some of the countries in my region. These situations cannot be solved with easy solutions or off-the-shelf business recipes."

Over time, the executive committee members developed a strong sense of mutual respect for one another. According to Henn:

> Everybody in that room is the *best* at what he does. The absolute best, and we all know it. It's pretty amazing. We're also total egomaniacs, the whole group of us. But in this company we still work as a team because we give each other the space to be the fool that everyone can be sometimes. Nobody's perfect.

Another RD commented, "I wouldn't necessarily choose these guys as my friends, but when we get together it's pretty awesome."

The group maintained a balanced mix of camaraderie and competition. Gassner, who himself used to play professional soccer, described the committee as "more like a soccer team than [an American] football team"; they frequently played heated games of golf or soccer when they were together. Stein remarked with a laugh, "It's all healthy competition—it's very healthy as long as I'm on top of the others. But seriously, it's a good sort of competitiveness. We are all ambitious people, but we respect each other; there is no jealousy."

Another executive committee member mentioned a different aspect of competition: "Rudi is only

51 [years old], far from the required retirement age of 60; but chances are good that he could move on to other things at Bertelsmann. As a result, there is a certain amount of jockeying for position within the executive committee, and people wonder if a non-German could ever be tapped to run this company."

As for Gassner's role in the ECMs, committee members had varying perspectives. Stein commented that "Rudi has a good relationship with the team. He knows when to be part of the team, and when to say yes or no. But he's always open-minded, and you can discuss things with him; it's like a partnership with him." According to Sallen, "Rudi does a lot of consensus-taking. He floats ideas by people, testing them on the group. He does impose his will, but not often. While he does not hand down many edicts, it is generally clear to all what his feelings are on most issues."

Jamieson, however, observed: "Debates in the ECMs are very rare. Rudi's not a man who needs or wants too many debates. I have never had an informal brainstorming session with him, a relaxed, almost agenda-less discussion. Rudi's management style is essentially autocratic." Henn commented:

> Rudi's brilliant. He's a tyrant; no, not a tyrant, a dictator. He has to be. You don't have a leader if you don't have a dictator. If you don't have a dictator, you won't be successful. Show me a company run by democracy, and I'll show you a loser. There's always got to be one chief and plenty of Indians.
>
> He's very smooth. If he thinks we're coming to a conclusion that is not what his opinion is, he will make sure the whole thing will turn his way. He has the ability to make you feel it was your idea, and if that doesn't work, he'll tell you to go and do it anyway.

Many committee members agreed that it could be difficult to change Gassner's mind. According to Stein, "To influence Rudi, you have to convince him. You have to be prepared properly with logical arguments." Preston added: "You have to be prepared to stand up for your argument. A lot of what he is testing is how much you really believe in what you are saying."

One RD noted that "Rudi usually does not allow himself in any way to be influenced by people who are not speaking directly about the areas for which they are responsible. In other words, he'll be very receptive to me for everything within my area, but when I stray into areas of the general good, I find him very unreceptive. I also find that I can influence him more one-on-one than I can in the ECMs."

Stein commented that he used the ECMs "as a tool to influence things in a way that I think they should go and to make the other RDs aware of things. Whether or not the committee agrees with me is another question." Preston agreed, explaining that he viewed participation in the ECMs as an important responsibility, even if it was sometimes hard to have much influence: "I believe that I have a job in the context of the group to say the things that I believe in order to get the group to behave in ways that I think are the right ones."

Bahlmann described the ECM as "an opinion-building exercise," explaining that:

> Real decisions about who gets money for what acquisitions occur outside of the meetings. The other thing is that there has always been money there to do what we wanted. So for me, the group has never been tested to see whether we can really work as a team under pressure when it comes to a fight over who will get funds for what investment.

Jamieson commented:

> Sometimes I feel that the main benefit of my coming all the way from Hong Kong to New York for the ECM is the ability (a) to meet my colleagues and chat with them from time to time, and (b) to have my separate meeting with Rudi, which is my best opportunity to influence him.
>
> We have had some good meetings, and we have had some terrible meetings. Rudi occasionally runs them in an open way in which debate is invited and variations to policy are considered. In reality, there is not a team "working together" at the top; there are executives implementing predetermined policies in different areas. The enormous geography makes it difficult to manage by consensus. With Rudi, you know what you have to do, and you have the freedom to execute the policies in your own region with your own style. Nevertheless, you have to realize that Rudi's style works for him; the proof is his incredible success over the past six years.

Gassner suspected these feelings and opinions in the group. "Many of them probably think I am influencing them more than I should," he commented.

> Sometimes I hear grumblings and they say that they can't always express their long-term ideas at the meetings because the meetings are so focused. I think they feel a lot of things are a bit too prepared or precooked. It's true—they have a difficult time convincing me. I am a person who likes to win an argument.
>
> But my opinions are not just invented on the spot. I usually discuss issues one-to-one with certain people beforehand. If I have a subject on the agenda, I almost always have an opinion of what I think the outcome should be. And then in the ECM, I see if my belief is confirmed. Occasionally, I may not go ahead with my original idea because I see that the entire group is going in another direction. In that case, I will take a step back and try to analyze it one more time, and I may change my mind. But if I see that they agree, or if it's just very important to me, then I obviously try to push it along.

Reflecting on his original hopes for the role of the executive committee, Gassner commented:

> It turned out to be a little bit different than I thought. I thought there would be more interface on strategic issues. I had hoped that they would contribute to problems which went beyond their ultimate responsibility.
>
> In part, I guess it's because it's such a diverse group of people. Segura, for example, is an outstanding executive, but because he thinks his English is limited, he would rather discuss issues separately with me than in an open meeting. Bahlmann, on the other hand, is very interested in global strategy though sometimes he doesn't have as much impact as he would like to have. Stein and Jamieson are somewhere in the middle, and they are driven primarily by the success of their own regions. Preston is highly intellectual; he is also the biggest repertoire supplier, and sometimes he thinks we're not paying enough attention to his repertoire. It's a combination of very diverse people. That's probably why the results are still so much influenced by me.
>
> And it may very well have to do with me and the way I run things. I think I know what is good for us. Therefore, when I'm convinced that that's the right way to go, it takes a great effort to get me off that route. However, because it has been successful, it has been hard to say that I should change my style.

The May 1993 ECM

Gassner opened the 1993 Managing Director's Convention in Boca Raton with a speech in which he stressed that the company's key success factor for the future was creating repertoire. "It's local artist development, it's joint ventures, it's acquisitions. That is the way we are going to grow. That is how we will reach our goal of becoming Number 1," he told the audience. He also congratulated them on another year of success in surpassing their business targets, but joked that "I am so naive; you must be lowballing your plans every time, because you have never missed them."

The week-long convention also included a session by Henn on developing A&R; a financial presentation from Gorman in which he emphasized the need to reduce costs and improve efficiency as markets matured and growth in the record business leveled off; a presentation about new recording and media technologies; and a speech by Dornemann about the future of the emerging Entertainment Group at BMG.[12] While the RDs attended, they played no formal role in the convention.

Whereas the focus in past conventions had been primarily on growth, the topics which formed the agenda for the 1993 MD Convention—global artist development, new technologies, BMG's expansion into new entertainment arenas, and cost control—emphasized disciplined management to position BMG International for the next phase. The MDs were excited about the important new role that BMG International could take on in the future. As Gassner told them, "We're the only company in Bertelsmann that is really global; we're the only ones in Japan, and we have over 300 people there.

---

[12]In response to trends toward multimedia entertainment technology, Dornemann had begun to look toward expanding BMG's reach in the entertainment industry to include television and even film. Industry analysts speculated that Dornemann was interested in purchasing an independent film studio, but such a deal had not yet materialized. In September 1993, BMG announced a joint venture with Tele-Communications, Inc., the largest cable system operator in the U.S., to launch a hybrid music video/home shopping cable channel that would rival MTV and VH-1. (Robichaux, Mark and Johnnie L. Roberts, "TCI, Bertelsmann Join to Launch Music, Shopping Cable Channel," *The Wall Street Journal*, September 17, 1993.)

If Bertelsmann wants to sell film or video games globally, we are there. We have something Bertelsmann can build on."

On the other hand, many of the MDs expressed skepticism about Gassner's "conflicting messages." As one stated, "You can't grow market share unless you're willing to spend money, and you can't cut back on investing in new acts, because you never know who might be the next Rolling Stones." Gassner, however, did not see his goals in conflict: "Yes—it's inconvenient on the one hand to grow and on the other hand to control your costs. It's a difficult task, but I expect both. I cannot allow anyone to just charge ahead regardless of cost. I expect a balance; and I know they can do it."

These issues also figured heavily into Gassner's agenda at the May ECM, which took place during the convention. He knew that the future challenges would demand more cooperation and global strategic thinking on the part of the executive committee. They had all been extremely successful so far in their own regions, but a regional focus alone would no longer be enough to guide BMG International through the uncertain and ever-changing terrain of the next five years.

The Reduced Manufacturing Price   The reduced manufacturing price was a result of negotiations undertaken by Bahlmann with Sonopress, Bertelsmann's central manufacturing operation in Europe, which supplied product to the European countries. These countries were required to purchase a certain percentage of their CDs, records, and cassettes from Sonopress, and as part of his responsibilities as the head of central manufacturing, Bahlmann negotiated the transfer prices annually by comparing Sonopress's bid to those of outside vendors. Because the non-European countries did not source through Sonopress, they would not be affected by the new price.

As Gassner might have predicted, when he brought up the issue at the ECM by congratulating Bahlmann, Preston shot Stein a knowing glance. Preston was required to source his manufacturing through Sonopress even though he could get a better price by using a U.K. vendor. As he explained:

> Because the United Kingdom is such a large repertoire supplier, I have volume benefits which I offer Arnold. He takes my volume, combines it with the other European countries, and negotiates a manufacturing rate with Sonopress in Munich, and then I buy the product back with the exchange rate working against me. Austria pays the same price as I do, getting the benefit of my volume scale.

Gassner then raised the question of what to do in response to the new prices. There was a long pause at the table. Bahlmann responded first by suggesting that the "extra" profit from the regions be placed in investment funds for each territory. Stein argued that this was not necessary "since the money's always there if the investment is good anyway." The group agreed that the money did not need to be placed in a separate fund, but be left to each company to decide how to use.

"OK, so what about the targets?" Gassner asked. Looking down at his copy of the calculations that Gorman had distributed before the meeting, he continued, "There are significant variances here. An MD's *betriebsergebnis* in some cases could be increased by as much as 50% due solely to the price reduction."

Segura then spoke up: "This doesn't affect me in my region, so I can be objective.[13] We have never before changed targets once they have been set. Not for any reason. So I don't see why we should change them this time." Preston added: "I agree. Some years, I'm hurt by the transfer pricing and exchange rate, but our targets have never been eased to reflect this. So why would we change them now that it's working the other way? It doesn't seem fair."

Indeed, many of the executive committee members found the issue an unusual one for the ECM agenda. As Gorman explained,

> To tell you the truth, I was a little surprised when Rudi asked me to calculate adjusted business targets to reflect the new manufacturing price. I know I'm the one who has been pushing reexamination of our cost

---

[13]Since the Latin American region included Spain and Portugal, Segura was affected minimally by the reduced price.

structure. But we've never changed the targets. Whether you acquired a company, lost a company, lost a customer, had a major bankruptcy, an artist didn't release—we've had everything you can imagine happen, and I do not remember ever adjusting the targets for anybody, for any reason.

Gassner said, however, that he was concerned that some of the MDs might become "complacent" because their *betriebsergebnis* target would be substantially easier to meet if it were not adjusted.

"I want to maintain the challenge of an aggressive bonus target, I want the MDs to be held accountable for the savings. I want them to realize that it isn't just a Christmas gift," he explained to the group.

No one at the table responded or looked in Gassner's direction. Gassner then wondered how he could get them to address the question of changing the targets, a possibility they seemed unwilling even to consider.

Case 4-3   Bombardier Transportation and the Adtranz Acquisition

On January 10, 2001, it had been one month only since Pierre Lortie was appointed president and chief operating officer of St. Bruno, Quebec-based Bombardier Transportation (BT).[1] BT was one of three major operating groups of Montreal, Canada-based Bombardier Inc. (BBD) and, with 2000 revenues amounting to Cdn$3.45 billion, it was one of the world's largest manufacturers of passenger rail cars. In an effort to expand BT's presence in the

IVEY

Richard Ivey School of Business
The University of Western Ontario

[1]St. Bruno was located on the south shore of the St. Lawrence River, in the suburbs of Montreal.

global rail equipment industry, executives at BBD had recently completed a successful negotiation for the acquisition of Adtranz from DaimlerChrysler for US$725 million. At approximately twice the size of BT, Adtranz (headquartered in Berlin, Germany) would not only expand BT's revenues and geographic scope but would significantly increase its competencies in propulsion systems and train controls and would complete its product portfolio. However, before the deal could close, BT required, among others, the regulatory approval of the European Commission (EC). Lortie was well aware that the EC process could be long and protracted.

Although Lortie had not been directly involved in the acquisition decision or negotiations, he was a supporter of the merger efforts. As he assumed his new responsibilities, Lortie began a thorough review of the work accomplished and the planning efforts undertaken to ensure an efficient integration of the two entities. As part of this process, he undertook a series of one-to-one meetings with members of his senior management team. The meetings were designed to measure the strengths and weaknesses of his key managers, but also to discuss the strategic and operational priorities.

BT was structured into five geographically-based operating units—North America, Atlantic Europe,

Continental Europe, Mexico and China—and one market/functional unit, Total Transit Systems—which focused on turnkey projects. In contrast, Adtranz was organized around product segments (i.e. high speed trains, cars, subway trams) and functions (i.e. bogies, drives, car bodies) making its structure and allocation of responsibilities quite foreign to Bombardier. Although each business complemented the other nicely and constituted a good strategic fit, the organizational structures were incompatible. Even though, BT's management team in Europe had not been involved in the discussions and reviews with Adtranz that had preceded and immediately followed the deal, they were keenly aware of the organizational issues and eager to establish their position as soon as the nod could be given to proceed with the takeover.

On January 10, 2001, Lortie had just finished his first in-depth meeting with Rick Dobbelaere, vice-president of operations of Bombardier Transportation, Atlantic Europe. Dobbelaere had come prepared with questions about how BT and the senior management team would set priorities during the interim period while awaiting EC approval. He presented these to Lortie in question form:

> Do we sit and await approval from the EC before taking steps towards the potential integration of Adtranz? Should we focus our planning on ways to improve the product quality and reliability of Adtranz equipment with existing customers? Should we start to institute personnel changes within BT in anticipation of the merger, and if so, at what pace? Do we focus on top-line revenue growth or start to immediately focus on bottom-line cost cutting?

Dobbelaere was highly respected, not only within the Atlantic Europe division but throughout Bombardier, and Lortie was aware that his concerns and questions were shared by others, particularly in Continental Europe.[2] But Lortie realized that he faced additional issues, including concerns over BT's ongoing operating performance. As Bombardier expected EC approval of the acquisition

[2] BT Continental Europe was based in Berlin and included six manufacturing facilities in Germany and one each in Austria and the Czech Republic.

within a matter of weeks, Lortie and his team had little time to waste.

Bombardier Company History

The Early Years   In 1921, at the age of 19, Joseph-Armand Bombardier opened a garage in Valcourt, Quebec, where he earned his living as a mechanic. Early in his life he looked for a solution to the problem of traveling the snow-covered roads near his village, which kept many people isolated during the long winter months. Over a 10-year period, Bombardier used his garage to develop multiple prototypes of a vehicle that would make winter travel easier. In 1936, he submitted his B7 prototype, the precursor to today's snowmobile, for patent approval. This seven-seat passenger model sported a revolutionary rear-wheel drive and suspension system, both major innovations at that time.

After receiving an initial 20 orders, Bombardier assembled a work crew of friends and family to manufacture the B7s. Customers included country doctors, veterinarians, telephone companies and foresters. By 1940, Bombardier had built a modern factory in his village that had an annual capacity of 200 units. In 1942, Bombardier incorporated his business as L'Auto-Neige Bombardier Limitee (ANB). Shortly thereafter the company began to receive orders from the Canadian government for specialized all-track vehicles for use by the armed forces efforts during the Second World War. Between 1942 and 1946, ANB produced over 1,900 tracked vehicles for the Canadian armed forces. Although not a profitable venture, the war-time manufacturing experience allowed Bombardier to refine his manufacturing process and develop competence in government relations.

The 1950s saw technological advances in lighter engines, improved tracking and high-performance synthetic rubber. In 1959, Bombardier achieved his lifelong dream when ANB introduced a one-passenger snowmobile. At an original price of Cdn$900, the Ski-Doo sported five-foot wooden skis, a coil spring suspension system and could travel at speeds of up to 25 miles per hour (mph). Sales increased from 225 units in 1959 to 2,500 units in 1962 and 8,000 units in 1964. Joseph-Armand Bombardier died in 1964, leaving a Cdn$10 million company to his son, Germain.

In 1966, Germain Bombardier passed on the presidency to his 27-year-old brother-in-law, Laurent Beaudoin, and in 1967, the company name was changed to Bombardier Limited. In 1969, the company went public with the intention of utilizing the funds to vertically integrate and increase its manufacturing capability. BBD grew as the market for snowmobiles rapidly expanded in the late 1960s and early 1970s. The North American snowmobile market grew from 60,000 units to 495,000 units in the period between 1966 and 1972, and BBD captured one-third of this market. Between 1966 and 1972, BBD's sales soared from Cdn$20 million to Cdn$180 million while profits rose from Cdn$2 million to Cdn$12 million. Under Beaudoin's leadership, the company pushed into the lucrative U.S. market, unveiled new products and utilized aggressive marketing initiatives to drive the business. In 1970, the company completed the acquisition of Austrian-based Lohnerwerke GmbH. Lohnerwerke's subsidiary, Rotax, was a key supplier of engines for Bombardier Ski-Doo snowmobiles and also a tramway manufacturer. This provided BBD with its first entry, albeit involuntarily, into the rail business. The energy crisis of the mid-1970s put the brakes on the snowmobile industry, and when the dust settled, the largest of the six remaining manufacturers was BBD.

Bombardier Begins to Diversify   Laurent Beaudoin, the chief executive of Bombardier, realized that in order to reduce cyclical risks and ensure its long-term survival, the company needed to diversify into other products beyond snowmobiles. To bolster sagging snowmobile sales, Beaudoin began to seek out opportunities for BBD within a more broadly defined transportation industry. In the late 1960s and early 1970s, BBD made several strategic acquisitions.

Transportation   In 1974, snowmobiles represented 90 per cent of BBD revenues. By securing a Cdn$118 million contract (US$99.14 million) with the city of Montreal to supply the local transit authority with 423 subway cars, BBD had made its first major move to diversify its revenues away from its predominant snowmobile business. Using rubber-wheeled cars licensed from the supplier to the Paris subway system, BBD's work won positive reviews from Montreal commuters. Further contracts followed, including supplying 36 self-propelled commuter rail cars to Chicago in 1977, 21 locomotives and 50 rail cars to Via Rail Canada in 1978, 117 commuter cars to New Jersey Transit Corporation in 1980, 180 subway cars to Mexico City in 1982, and 825 subway cars to the City of New York, also in 1982.

The mid-1980s was a turbulent time in the rail transportation industry, and BT looked to capitalize on industry uncertainty by purchasing companies at low prices and growing its market share through these acquisitions. Pullman Technology was acquired in 1987, Transit America in 1988, and controlling interests in rail equipment companies in France and Belgium in 1988. In the early 1990s, BT also acquired Concarril (Mexico's top rail manufacturer) as well as UTDC in Canada. These acquisitions and investments established BT as one of the leading supplier of rail cars and cemented its international reputation.

Aerospace   In 1973, BBD commenced diversification into the aerospace business with the acquisition of a controlling interest in Heroux Limited of Longueuil, Quebec. Heroux designed, manufactured and repaired aeronautical and industrial components at its two Canadian plants. In 1986, following an international bidding contest, BBD acquired struggling Canadair from the Canadian government at a total cash and share price of Cdn$293 million. By applying aggressive marketing tactics, cost-cutting measures and tight controls, BBD was quickly able to turn operations around. Subsequent acquisitions of Short Brother PLC (an aircraft producer in Northern Ireland) in 1990, Learjet Corporation in 1990 and a controlling stake in de Havilland in 1992 and the remaining interest in 1997 firmly entrenched BBD in the civil aircraft industry. During the 1990s, BBD introduced a series of new planes including the Lear 60, the Challenger 600-3A, the Challenger 604 and the Lear 45. BBD delivered its first Canadair Regional Jet in 1992 and its first Global Express business jet in 1999, the CRJ 700 (75 seat jet) in 2001.

Corporate Balance   By the early 1990s, BBD had diversified to the point where snowmobile sales represented less than 15 per cent of the company's revenues. BBD still controlled 50 per cent of the Canadian market and 25 per cent of the U.S. market for snowmobiles, but BBD had clearly established itself as a diversified company. By 1992, sales had increased to US$3.43 billion and profits to US$104 million. While, in many cases, the companies acquired by Bombardier were in poor shape, observers noted that the majority of Beaudoin's deals and acquisitions had been turned around and were making money.

Different operating groups at BBD took centre stage at different times during the 1990s (see Exhibit 1). In 1994, the recreational products group seemed to surge forward, fuelled by increased snowmobile sales and sales of Sea-Doo watercraft, first introduced in 1968. Profits from this group represented 37 per cent of the company's profits and made the recreational products group central to the company's success. The mid-1990s saw a boom in the aerospace group as both regional and business jet sales took off with the expanding economy. Many observers credited Bombardier with creating an entirely new commuter jet segment as the result of product innovation. Aerospace group sales grew from 1996 levels of US$3.16 billion to 2000 levels of US$7.79 billion. In 2000, the aerospace group represented 66 per cent of the company's revenues and 85 per cent of its profits.

BT continued to grow during this period as well. BT was awarded a prestigious contract to produce specialized rail cars for the huge Eurotunnel engineering project. In early 1995, Waggonfabrik Talbot KG of Germany was acquired for $130 million cash. In late 1997, BT acquired DWA Deutsche Waggonbau GmbH of Berlin for Cdn$518 million (approximately US$359.52 million) and thus doubled its train and subway car manufacturing capacity in Europe. In December of that year, BT secured a US$1.18 billion contract with Virgin Rail Group of Great Britain to supply 78 diesel/electric multiple units and rail cars. In November 1999, the company entered into a joint venture to construct a manufacturing facility in China and to subsequently build 300 inter-city mass transit railcars for the Chinese Ministry of Railways (see Exhibit 2).

Bombardier Growth Philosophy   BBD sought acquisition opportunities that allowed it to add value to the business through the application of its existing competencies. Acquisitions were typically not viewed solely as financial plays but as a way for BBD to complement or strengthen its existing businesses. BBD prided itself on thoroughly evaluating target companies so that pay-back was not reliant on the divestiture of some aspect of the acquired business. In negotiations, BBD had also shown that it was not afraid to walk away from a deal if it meant overpaying for a business. But once a deal was completed, BBD had a reputation for being patient in the integration of the acquired company.

In addition to a strong track record of integrating acquisitions, BBD had strengths in product costing and tendering. It also had extensive experience in product assembly. Whether aircraft, recreational products or rail cars, most products made by BBD were assembled as opposed to manufactured. Utilizing external suppliers and adopting just-in-time delivery methods resulted in substantially reduced inventory levels, throughput time and assets. BBD sought ways to control product technology and design, assembly and distribution while outsourcing other non-core functions.

When taking over a business, BBD tried to eliminate waste and turn around underperforming assets by applying tried and tested management approaches over time as opposed to rushing to replace existing methods. This approach to acquisitions had garnered strong employee support over the years as

Exhibit 1   Bombardier Revenue and Profit History, 1992–2001 (Cdn$ million)

Fiscal Year*	Overall	Transportation	Aerospace	Recreational Products	Capital	Other
2001e	16,101	3,043	10,562	1,687	1,033	(224)
2000	13,619	3,446	8,126	1,473	739	(165)
1999	11,500	2,966	6,444	1,628	571	(109)
1998	8,509	1,679	4,621	1,633	245	332
1997	7,976	1,597	4,011	1,866	162	341
1996	7,123	1,575	3,309	1,641	140	459
1995	5,943	1,310	2,981	1,111	112	430
1994	4,769	1,312	2,243	791	97	323
1993	4,448	1,238	2,228	556	58	367
1992	3,059	726	1,519	391	56	366

Profits Before Taxes, Segmented by Division

Fiscal Year*	Overall	Transportation	Aerospace	Recreational Products	Capital	Other
2001e	1,428	121	1,237	86	(15)	—
2000	1,124	174	904	18	28	—
1999	827	148	682	(46)	43	—
1998	627	85	462	1	64	16
1997	606	63	270	212	47	14
1996	461	100	150	174	42	(6)
1995	346	66	141	117	22	(1)
1994	207	(24)	137	76	14	4
1993	151	(73)	181	29	7	7
1992	121	4	137	(9)	(12)	2

Revenue, Segmented by Region

Fiscal Year*	Overall	Canada	Europe	United States	Asia	Other
2001e	16,101	1,241	4,757	8,592	471	1,040
2000	13,619	1,013	4,362	7,139	327	779
1999	11,500	900	4,049	5,497	259	796
1998	8,509	962	2,260	3,964	760	563
1997	7,976	949	2,342	3,712	605	367
1996	7,123	4,504	1,779	841	—	—
1995	5,943	3,619	1,536	789	—	—
1994	4,769	2,696	1,431	642	—	—
1993	4,448	2,335	1,675	438	—	—
1992	3,059	1,331	1,373	355	—	—

e - estimate
* fiscal year end January 31. As a result, 2001 data essentially covers results from 2000.
Source: Company files.

Exhibit 2   Overview of Bombardier Businesses in 2000

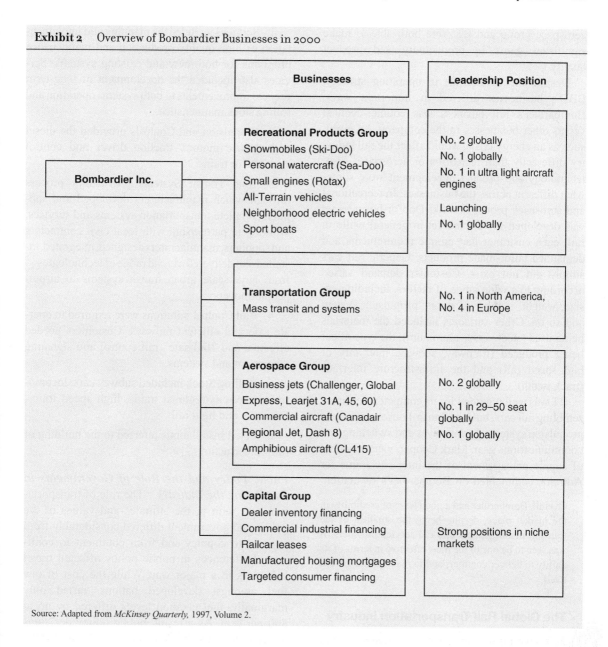

workers realized that BBD would invest in new products and thus protect jobs. When BBD entered the aerospace industry through acquisitions, it did not replace existing staff. Instead, it used personnel from BT to teach successful approaches and manu-facturing methods developed elsewhere in the organization. Transfers were not all one way; aerospace also shared its best practices in engineering management. With a commitment to excellence in assembly, inventory and management control, the aerospace group and BT were both able to make significant gains in productivity and product quality.

Despite the similarities in operating strategy, BBD's businesses differed in important ways. Bombardier's rail business was counter-cyclical versus other businesses in the company. An event, such as an energy crisis, would affect the rail industry differently than recreation or aerospace. Also, technology and product development were somewhat different across the businesses. In recreational and aerospace products, a Ski-Doo or business jet was developed for the market in general while in rail, each customer had unique requirements and demanded tailor-made products. Generic rail cars simply did not exist. Customer demand varied according to a wide range of factors, including car size, weight, number of doors, propulsion system and so on. Other variables included the materials being used (steel versus aluminum), the type of car being produced (tramway, subway, inter city or high-speed rail) and the infrastructure interface (track width).

BT was well regarded for its competencies in assembling rail cars, but it had no in-house expertise in propulsion systems, locomotives and switching and communications gear. Mark Cooper, vice-president of supply management of the inter-city trains for Adtranz, commented on Bombardier's reputation:

> Overall, Bombardier had a good level of credibility in the market place, despite being the smallest of the four rail manufacturers and rail service providers. It was seen to be one of the most effective in terms of its ability to deliver contracts and to manage and govern itself.

▮ The Global Rail Transportation Industry

In 2001, the railway transportation industry could be divided into six distinct segments: services, propulsion and controls, total transit systems, rail control solutions, rolling stock and fixed installations. Bombardier was absent from the last segment which it considered as non-strategic and quite distinct in nature from the others.

1. Services included the planning and implementation of high quality production and maintenance programs for both new and existing systems. Services also included the development of long-term process improvements to both systems operation and rolling stock maintenance.

2. Propulsion and Controls provided the diesel and electric motors, traction drives and control systems for trains.

3. Total Transit Systems provided a process through which manufacturers developed and supplied complete transportation systems and services. Working in partnership with local civil contractors and suppliers, manufacturers designed, integrated, installed and delivered a broad range of technologies— from large-scale urban transit systems to airport people-movers.

4. Rail Control Solutions were required to operate safe and efficient railways. Customers needed effective and "fail-safe" rail control and signaling equipment and systems.

5. Rolling Stock included subway cars, locomotives, inter-city/regional trains, high speed trains, tram cars and light rail.

6. Fixed Installations referred to the building of rail infrastructure.

Public Policy and the Role of Governments in Regulating the Industry   The role of transportation and, with it, the attitudes and values of the public and government differed considerably from country to country and from continent to continent. Differences in public policy affected travel behaviors in a major way. While the cost of raw fuel amongst developed nations varied only marginally, fuel taxation levels differed by up to 800 per cent. As a result, public policy decisions affected not only the demand for fuel but also the demand for public transportation as an alternative to the automobile. Because of lower gasoline taxes and the promotion of automobile travel in the United States, public transport ridership was three to nine times lower there than in European countries.

Most industry analysts believed that European policies promoting reductions in congestion, pollution abatement, urban development, traffic safety and energy conservation would continue and that support for public transportation systems would continue for the foreseeable future. The question was whether the United States would embrace European norms as congestion increased in that country. The combination of greater geographic distances, car-friendly culture, efficient and large air travel system and aversion to government subsidies convinced many that U.S. rail policy would take a great many years to significantly change in a direction that supported an increase in rail transportation usage and investment.

Government regulations significantly affected industry structure in one other important way. Because U.S. passenger trains frequently shared tracks with freight trains, the government mandated that U.S. passenger rail cars be reinforced and strengthened in order to sustain collisions without collapsing with the ensuring high casualties that would result. As a result, U.S. trains were substantially heavier than European trains and were uncompetitive and poorly adapted to markets outside North America. European Union standards were widely embraced by governments and customers throughout the world, particularly in emerging economies such as China and India.

Infrastructure Model   A common perception in both Europe and the United States was that the rail industry, as a whole, was best designed to operate as a monopoly. High sunk costs, low marginal costs and demands for managerial co-ordination perpetuated this opinion. However, the emerging approach in the European Union (EU) was to separate the high-speed train industry and subject its component parts to competition. Although the potential technical, economic and social gains associated with this approach were perceived as exceptional, the process was often complicated by different national visions of how the industry should be divided between public and private ownership. Most countries opted to retain state ownership of infrastructure

with the creation of a state agency to manage it. However, rolling stock companies were slowly becoming privatized. In 1998, the United Kingdom became the first country in the EU to totally privatize its rail system, including both infrastructure and rolling stock (see Exhibit 3).

The U.K. model of privately owned infrastructure and rolling stock had its troubles. The government was forced to operate the infrastructure element of the system when Railtrack, the private company it selected to manage the vast U.K. rail infrastructure (nearly 23,000 miles of track and 2,500 stations), went bankrupt in October 2001. Also, some in the United Kingdom worried about safety risks associated with spreading accountability across multiple for-profit companies. Conversely, the French model of public-owned, train operator had been a tremendous success. As one industry observer remarked,

> France was operating state-of-the-art 300 km/h trains on a new network of rail lines dedicated to fast passenger service, and making money doing it. Britain was operating 1960s technology, 200 km/h trains on the nation's undependable and failing 19th century freight/passenger network, and losing money.[3]

Despite the success of the publicly operated French system, the EU was not designed to promote monopolistic, country-centred railroad companies. As a result, the U.K. model of privatized rolling stock and state-operated infrastructure more closely fit the cultural and social paradigm emerging in the EU and was thus being adopted cautiously and to differing degrees throughout the EU. During the latter half of the 1990s, public sector funding gradually shifted from supporting nationally subsidized rail systems to include more significant involvement from local municipal governments and the private sector. The belief was that by shifting to private ownership of rolling stock, the railway industry would eventually emulate the automobile or air transport models. Airlines worked with governments to secure terminals and immediate air space

[3]Andersen, Svein and Eliassen, Kjell (2001), *Making Policy in Europe*, London, Sage, p. 72.

Exhibit 3 Growing Privatization of the European Union Rail Industry

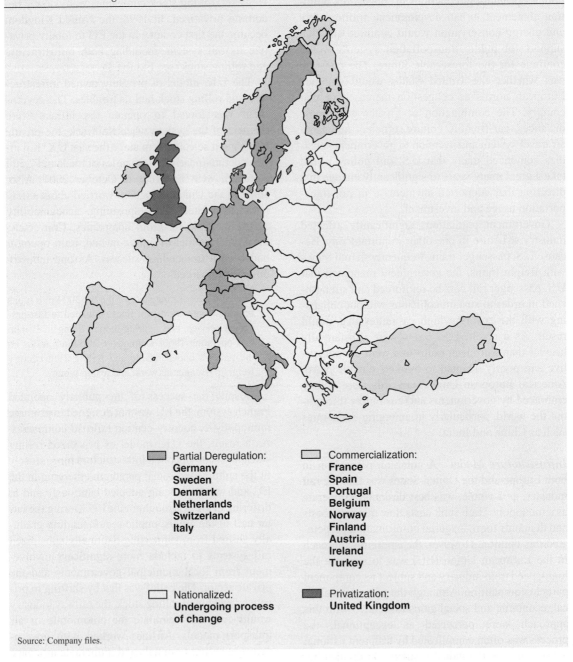

Partial Deregulation: **Germany** **Sweden** **Denmark** **Netherlands** **Switzerland** **Italy**		Commercialization: **France** **Spain** **Portugal** **Belgium** **Norway** **Finland** **Austria** **Ireland** **Turkey**	
Nationalized: **Undergoing process of change**		Privatization: **United Kingdom**	

Source: Company files.

and runways, while operating and maintaining their own or leased airplanes. In effect, the airlines rented the infrastructure. Many believed that rail companies should operate in a similar fashion.

High-Speed Trains   By the early 2000s, the European Commission continued to rank the development of a European-wide high-speed train infrastructure as its highest investment priority in transportation infrastructure. The Community of European Railways (COER), a continent-wide association of railway companies, asserted that high-speed rail services were especially appropriate for the 200 kilometre to 300 kilometre distances between heavily populated urban centres. Most of Europe fit this profile with mobility increasing as the prospects of a single European market progressed. But for Europe to fully benefit from the one market model, decisions in infrastructure policy required a European, and not a nationalistic, approach. However, many predicted that the tendency for governments to protect national producers would be detrimental to the continent-wide objectives for many years to come.

Customers   The privatization of many national railways had changed the financing arrangements and customer base within the European rail car industry. In the past, manufacturers like BT sold directly to government operated railroads. However, with the privatization of rolling stock operations increasing in Europe, leasing arrangements were now available to operators. In the United Kingdom, equipment manufacturers sold to one of three large rail equipment leasing companies (ROSCO) owned by one of three large British banks (Bank of Scotland, HSBC or Abbey National Bank) which then leased the new rolling stock to the train operators. This lease-versus-purchase option reduced up-front costs for rolling stock operators and significantly decreased their overall capital requirements. It also put a premium on standardized trains—necessary to protect residual values. This, in turn, significantly reduced the incentives to purchase rolling stock from within a rail operators' home country.

In countries with private rail operators, revenues were generated through ticket sales and government subsidies while expenses were incurred through infrastructure franchise fees, day-to-day train maintenance, fuel and labor costs and leasing expenses. Since leasing costs on old, existing stock were much cheaper than on new equipment, operators preferred to delay purchases for as long as possible. When equipment was ordered, rail operators would sometimes seek additional delays by complaining that delivered equipment suffered from low reliability, which prevented it from meeting defined service standards the operators had committed to achieve in order to gain the concession from the government to operate the train service. This, in turn, caused manufacturers to incur late delivery charges and inventory costs as rail cars piled up in shipping yards awaiting minor repairs or adjustments. Many observers believed that these dysfunctional practices would be repeated in other European nations as they evolved to private operating models.

DaimlerChrysler and Adtranz History

Although the roots of Chrysler go back to 1920 in the United States, the history of Daimler-Benz dates to the 1880s in Germany and to the efforts of two inventive engineers—Gottlieb Daimler and Carl Benz. After a series of initiatives, Daimler-Benz was officially incorporated in 1926 and began producing cars under the Mercedes Benz brand.

By the 1980s, competition in the global automobile market had increased dramatically, and Daimler-Benz was looking to diversify its business. Between February 1985 and February 1986, the company acquired three conglomerates[4] for a combined US$ 1.11 billion. The cash expenditures of these 1985/86 acquisitions put a strain on its

---

[4]Daimler owned 50 per cent of Motoren-und-Turbinen-Union (a manufacturer of aircraft engines and diesel motors for tanks and ships) and bought the remaining 50 per cent for $160 million. Daimler purchased 65.6 per cent of Dornier (a privately held manufacturer of spacecraft systems, commuter planes and medical equipment) for $130 million. Daimler additionally purchased control of AEG (a high-technology manufacturer of electronic equipment, such as turbines, robotics, data processing and household products) for $820 million.

balance sheet, and by mid-1993, Daimler-Benz reported its first loss since the Second World War. In 1994, operations recovered somewhat with the company showing US$750 million in profits. But in 1995, the company's fortunes sagged again as it reported a loss of US$4 billion—the largest in German industrial history.

In 1995, Daimler-Benz's chief executive officer (CEO), Edvard Reuter, was forced to resign and was replaced by the aerospace division head, Jurgen Schrempp. One of Schrempp's first moves as CEO was the acquisition of 50 per cent of the rail division of Swedish–Swiss ABB Asea Brown Boveri Ltd. in exchange for US$900 million cash from Daimler-Benz. This joint venture formed the new ABB Daimler-Benz Transportation (Adtranz). Adtranz would become the largest rail service provider in the world with annual sales of US$4.5 billion.

By the mid-1990s, Robert Eaton had assumed the position of CEO at Chrysler at a time when the economic conditions in the automobile industry included an excess manufacturing capacity and an Asian economic crisis. Industry analysts were projecting an annualized global overcapacity of 18.2 million vehicles by the early 2000s. It came as no surprise that both Eaton and Schrempp were seeking partners due to the inevitable consolidation within the industry.

DaimlerChrysler AG was formed in November of 1998 when Daimler-Benz and Chrysler merged in a US$37 billion deal. In 1998, the newly formed company had revenues of US$130 billion, factories in 34 countries and sales of 4.4 million vehicles making it the fifth largest automobile manufacturer in the world. In 1999, DaimlerChrysler acquired the remaining 50 per cent of Adtranz from ABB for US$472 million.

Adtranz

Although the name Adtranz dates back only as far as 1995, the multiple production facilities that comprised the company date back to the 19th century. By the time of the DaimlerChrysler merger, the rail business in Europe had narrowed to four primary players: Alstom (France), Siemens (Germany), Adtranz and Bombardier. Unlike Altsom and Siemens, which had strong single country affiliations, Adtranz facilities and staff were a collection of multiple companies in multiple countries across the continent. Many of these companies also had a history of unstable ownership. For example, since 1989, the Adtranz facility in Derby, England, had experienced the following ownership changes: 100 per cent British Rail Engineering, then 40 per cent ABB, 40 per cent Trafalgar Rail and 20 per cent employee ownership, then 100 per cent ABB, then 50 per cent Daimler Chrysler and 50 per cent ABB and finally 100 per cent DaimlerChrysler. Each new ownership group brought its own philosophies to manufacturing, sales, contract tendering, personnel, etc. Mark Cooper commented on the cultural challenges in Adtranz:

> I don't think that Adtranz has had enough time to fully develop its own culture. Every two years there seems to have been a change of ownership, a change in structure, a change in values, and a change in processes. So under those circumstances you don't get a good sense of who you are.

In the late 1990s, Adtranz represented less than three per cent of DaimlerChrysler's revenues. Revenues of US$3.3 billion were recorded at Adtranz in 1999, and in 2000, after years of continual losses, Adtranz reported its first year of break-even results. Although Adtranz revenues were up over 15 per cent in 2000, the annual revenue growth over the previous four years averaged only 4.5 per cent. Given the complexity of the business and its peripheral role in DaimlerChrysler's overall strategy, many observers believed DaimlerChrysler would eventually divest its rail business.

Production Challenges Although Daimler-Chrysler's assembly process and knock-down capabilities had been introduced, Adtranz's reputation for producing high quality products was poor. In particular, Adtranz was having quality, reliability and certification problems with its core Electrostar and Turbostar model trains designed for the U.K. market (see Exhibit 4). In 2000, the Electrostar model had only eight trains in service as customers

Exhibit 4   Bombardier's Electrostar

Intercity Transport

Electrostar* Electric Multiple Unit, Class 375/377
United Kingdom

Bombardier Transportation is responsible for supplying 182 Class 375/377 Electrostar* trains to the UK Govia owned rail operator, South Central Ltd. These state of the art, air-conditioned electric trains are either three or four cars in length. Each vehicle has two wide sliding powered doors per side capable of handling the passenger densities and flows required by busy urban and sub-urban services.

The trains operate at speeds up to 160 km/h on suburban services south of London. 15 of the 4-car trainsets are dual voltage capable of both 25 kV AC 50 Hz overhead and 750 V DC third rail operation. The remaining 167 electric trainsets in 3 and 4-car formations are single DC voltage only.

Particular attention has been paid to the provision of a high degree of reliability, safety and maintainability whilst ensuring low whole life costs.

The Class 375/377 Electrostar trains have a high level of passenger comfort with a very quiet interior environment and are fully compliant with the requirements of the Disability Discrimination Act. A modern passenger information system linked to the Global Positioning System relays messages in both visual and audible form. Each car will be fitted with a closed-circuit television surveillance system for enhanced internal security, allowing the driver to view car interiors whilst the train is stationary.

BOMBARDIER
TRANSPORTATION

Source: Company files.

were refusing to accept this train. Reliability was achieved under the terms of the contract.[5] The Turbostar had 279 trains in service, but only 86.5 per cent were available for operation. Reliability was also not achieved under the terms of the contract. Deciphering the causes of these reliability problems was a challenge for BT managers. Neil Harvey, director of public affairs at BT, provided one common interpretation:

> In terms of the reputation of Adtranz's products and its overall reputation as a company, many believed there was a certain amount of mismanagement. In particular, some felt that too many contracts were being bought, and there was often very poor follow-through on products, production and subsequent support.

In addition, Adtranz's customer support function and its initial contract bidding processes were viewed by some as inadequate. Many at BBD believed that Bombardier's structured governance system, manufacturing controls and proven bidding systems would be excellent complements to Adtranz.

A Strategic Acquisition for Bombardier

Despite awareness that certain management practices needed adjustment, BBD viewed the acquisition of Adtranz as a smart strategic move for several reasons. Europe is the nexus of technological advances in the industry. Asia and South America primarily utilized European engineering concepts and had a history of failing to develop new technologies on their own. North American trains were too heavy and, hence, more expensive and costly to operate compared to the refinements in other world markets and therefore not competitive. Also, the green movement and strong government support signaled long-term growth in the demand for rail transportation in Europe.

[5]Reliability is measured as the total distance travelled by the rail car between breakdowns. The total performance of all rail cars is then averaged together to get the mean reliability number as a factor of distance travelled by each train model. This is then measured in subsequent periods to evaluate performance and reliability levels going forward.

Not only did BBD find the European rail market attractive, but it was increasingly interested in balancing the revenue streams produced by its various groups. Strengthening the company's rail business was viewed as an important move to counter-balance Bombardier's growing, but cyclical, aerospace group. Dr. Yvan Allaire, executive vice-president at BBD, explained this strategic perspective: "Bombardier's value for shareholders is as a premium diversified company, not as an aerospace company."

Although margins were often lower in rail (in 2000, margins for the aerospace group were 11 percent—more than twice that of the transportation group), the industry benefited from the traditional business practice of advance and progress payments from customers. These payments translated to a low level of net utilized assets and very positive cash flow, contingent on a growing backlog of orders. These cash flows provided BBD with capital that was utilized throughout the company. Allaire explained this possibility:

> Transportation is a huge cash generator. While the margins are low, cash is large in this business. In fact, we have traditionally financed a large part of the investment in the aerospace sector from cash coming from transportation. A lot of people don't understand this.

Although low-margin businesses traditionally had profit levels driven by cost control, in the rail transportation industry, variability and project management performance were additional key drivers. For example, penalty charges for late delivery of each car generally amounted to 10 per cent of the value of such car. In comparison, period costs in sales, general and administration (SG&A) accounted for six per cent of expenses. Preliminary investigation by BT managers indicated that repair and late delivery charges amounted to nearly 20 per cent of Adtranz's expenses. By applying BT's production and cost control systems, it was thought that acquiring Adtranz would provide substantial upside potential to raise profits.

Finally, BT had a strong reputation for its expertise in subway, trams and light rail cars. Adtranz had expertise in propulsion systems, high-speed and inter-city cars and signaling systems. While the acquisition would clearly strengthen Bombardier's global reach, it would also bring needed technology and product expertise to the electrical locomotive, high-speed train, propulsion, and train control/communications. Closing this gap was becoming an imperative in Europe. For instance, in 2000, Bombardier was precluded to bid on the largest order ever awarded in the United Kingdom because Siemens, Alstom and Adtranz had refused to sell the propulsion system to them. In addition, Adtranz—at over twice the size of BT—would add $2.7 billion in backlog to maintenance and services while providing more service facilities for customers in the European marketplace.

The Acquisition

Financial analysts had anticipated that Daimler-Chrysler would seek a sales price of 25 per cent to 30 per cent of 1999 revenues of US$3.3 billion. However, ongoing problems in DaimlerChrysler's automobile business may have hastened their unloading of the non-core asset. Although Alstom and Siemens were BBD's main competitors in the rail industry, neither competed to acquire Adtranz in part because of the beliefs that the European Commission would probably not approve of the merger due to their current strong positions in several market segments.

On August 4, 2000, BBD announced its intention to buy Adtranz for US$715 million. In its negotiations with DaimlerChrysler, BBD agreed to pay the purchase price in two installments of cash—one at closing and one six months later. Under the deal, Bombardier also agreed to the assumption of certain debt. For the deal to proceed, regulatory approval was notably required in both the EU and the United States. Given the complimentary operations of both companies in the United States (mechanical versus propulsion), U.S. approval was never a significant issue. However, matters were different in Europe where it was initially estimated that the approval process would take between four and six months.

In negotiating the deal, DaimlerChrysler insisted on a limited due diligence process. In response, it was determined that any disagreement between the asset valuation done by BBD and the value given by DaimlerChrysler would lead to adjustments in a manner agreed upon; however, if adjustments exceeded a given amount, BBD could claim that there had been a material adverse change. This disagreement would then be submitted to an independent arbitrator for adjustment. Allaire commented on the limited due diligence process:

> It was certainly the first time that Bombardier agreed to go into an acquisition without first doing full due diligence. DaimlerChrysler basically said, "Look, have your people do an initial review and don't worry about the rest—we'll give you an equity guarantee. Adjustments will have to be made to the price if the provisions already taken in our books are not sufficient."

DaimlerChrysler had good reasons for wanting to limit the due diligence process. A new management team had just been put in place and was supposedly making progress streamlining Adtranz's operations. It was a natural concern that the management team would be seriously demoralized if Bombardier was invited in, only to later walk away from the transaction. And, secondly, Adtranz had serious worries about opening their books to a direct competitor. For Bombardier to come in and examine their pricing, cost structure, contracts and so on would have been off-limits under EU competition rules governing mergers and acquisitions.

Negotiations with the European Commission

With the negotiations complete, BBD then applied to the EC for regulatory approval. Since 1990, the system for monitoring merger transactions in Europe has been governed by the Merger Regulation Committee of the European Commission. The Merger Regulation Committee eliminated the need for companies to seek approval for certain large-scale mergers in all European countries separately and ensured that all such merger requests received equal treatment. The control of mergers and acquisitions was one of the pillars of the EU's competition policy. When companies combined through a merger, acquisition, or creation of a joint venture, this generally had a positive impact on markets: firms became more efficient, competition intensified and the final consumer benefited from higher quality goods at lower prices. However, mergers that created or strengthened a dominant market position were prohibited in order to prevent abuses. A firm was in a dominant position when it was able to act on the market without having to account for the reactions of its competitors, suppliers or customers. A firm in a dominant position could, for example, increase its prices above those of its competitors without fearing any significant loss of sales.

In order to merge competing companies in Europe, the approval of the EC's merger task force was required. A review was comprised of two phases. Phase 1 involved a preliminary review, although full approval could be granted at this stage. Should Phase 1 identify potential competitive issues or conflicts associated with the proposed merger, a deeper investigation proceeded to Phase 2. This second phase could take months or years to complete as the depth and breadth of the investigation increased.

While many mergers were ultimately approved by the EC merger task force, this was in no way guaranteed. During the prior year, Alcan's proposed purchase of Pechiney was turned down by the task force. And GE's proposed acquisition of Honeywell was facing growing opposition. With this track record, some feared that the EC might have a bias against North American companies buying European businesses.

BBD utilized a negotiation strategy that it hoped would prove successful in gaining regulatory approval. It identified potentially contentious issues in advance and developed tactics to minimize disagreement. In order to comply with the likely EC demands, BBD volunteered to divest non-strategic transportation assets in Germany and, to extend for several years a series of supply contracts with smaller companies based in Austria and Germany. BBD was the main customer for these small suppliers and, with the acquisition of Adtranz, technologies previously purchased from these companies could now be manufactured within the newly assembled Bombardier/Adtranz. The few years of continued sales to BBD allowed these small companies to transition into new industries or to find new customers.

On a separate matter, BBD realized that the market share of the combined companies might be an issue for certain product segments in certain countries and so tried to shape the focus of the merger task force to the European market in total and not to any specific country. Primary geographical areas of concern were Germany, Austria and the United Kingdom. The German market was a key area with annual sales over US$1.8 billion; in Germany, Bombardier/Adtranz would have had a 50 per cent share. Concessions were made to ensure that a third competitor (Stadler) was allowed to strengthen its position in the German regional train market. Allaire, who led the negotiating team at the EC, commented on the efforts to win regulatory approval.

> You always have to make concessions—that's part of the deal over there. You don't get through the EC review process without some concessions unless you are buying something totally unrelated. But if there is any relatedness, the acquiring party must come up with concessions that will make the transaction acceptable.

For BBD, the preliminary result of the negotiation was not a Phase 1 approval, but a shortened Phase 2 process because issues were identified in Phase 1 and solutions were already designed. BBD believed, in March 2001, that Phase 2 would conclude within a month or so of further negotiations. While BBD was pleased with the results of its efforts to this point, the company had no firm guarantees that the transaction would be approved, or if approved, under what final conditions and timelines.

Pierre Lortie

A graduate of Université Laval (Canada) and Université de Louvain (Belgium), Pierre Lortie was both an engineer and an economist by training. He also received an MBA with honors from the University of Chicago. Prior to taking over BT, Lortie had been president and chief operating officer of Bombardier Capital (2000–2001). He had also been president and chief operating officer of Bombardier International (1998–2000), president of Bombardier Aerospace, Regional Aircraft (1993–1998), and president of Bombardier Capital Group (1990–1993). Before joining Bombardier in 1990, Lortie had been chairman, chief executive officer and president of Provigo Inc.—a major, Quebec-based retailer (1985–1989)—and president and chief executive officer of the Montreal Stock Exchange (1981–1985).

Over the years, Lortie had developed a reputation within BBD as a turnaround expert. His movements throughout BBD corresponded with the transformation of under-performing businesses into market leaders within a few years of his taking the helm. His philosophy included a combination of approaches: strong and decisive leadership, hands-on management, good relationships with existing personnel and the development of pride within those on the team. He also believed in the importance of rapidly achieving small, visible wins in order to build the support necessary to make subsequent larger changes. Lortie summarized his approach:

> You have to figure out the business model and focus everything on the key factors. You also have to work with the people . . . making sure they are focusing on what has to be done . . . helping them, coaching them and removing roadblocks. You should never forget that people like successes and being on the winning team.

Lortie recognized that his style and methods of change management were in some ways different than approaches taken by others in turnaround situations. Although aware of the need to streamline costs, he did not follow the traditional approach of implementing massive, short-term, cost-cutting tactics as an initial step in the turnaround plan. Instead, he focused first on creating a healthy operating environment through the implementation of reporting and governance systems aimed at monitoring key metrics and assessing current and potential success. His main objective was to ensure a balance between cost reduction or restructuring initiatives and revenue growth. He strongly held the view that balance was necessary because halting growth would hurt the market performance of a company far more than would a failure to rapidly reduce costs.

In promoting change, he not only engaged and empowered people at all levels, he also sought to create the trust and credibility necessary for a leader to implement further, more difficult changes that may be required based on assessment of the metrics. Lortie commented on the rationale behind his move to BT:

> My job at Bombardier has been to turn around operations that were not doing well. This is what I did at Bombardier Capital and Regional Aircraft. When Bob Brown [CEO of BBD] asked me to take over the job at transportation, he was concerned that there were difficulties in the current transportation group and high expectations involving the Adtranz merger. He felt that the magnitude of the task of stitching together the two organizations and rapidly delivering acceptable performance required someone who had a track record. There was some concern that I had not been at Bombardier Capital long enough to complete the restructuring process I had set in motion. But Adtranz was going to be Bombardier's biggest acquisition ever and getting it right seemed to be more important than keeping me at Capital.

Determining a Course of Action   While Lortie was a veteran of Bombardier and had participated in the strategic plan and budget reviews of the group over the years, he admitted knowing relatively little about Bombardier Transportation operations, per se. But he was convinced that the process for building and operating trains was not dissimilar to commercial aircraft. Many of the key success factors were thought to be the same. Beyond this core belief, Lortie faced an overwhelming number of decisions. He summarized the long list.

> What was the best way for us to leverage the potentially increased size of Bombardier Transportation?

Should we take a top line approach to results or a bottom line approach? How can we tailor the integration to balance revenue and cost initiatives? How do we reconcile the fundamentally incompatible organizational structures, particularly in Europe? How do we go about designing the "best" organizational structure under the circumstances? How should we proceed to approve new bids [those arising in the first few weeks and longer term] and ensure they are profit-making propositions? How should we develop and instill a project management culture in an organization that has no such tradition (or lost it)? How do we get management focused on the operations, on "getting it right," avoid finger pointing at former Adtranz management, create a climate conducive to teamwork while conducting a thorough due diligence of all Adtranz contracts and operations? How and when should Bombardier integrate its manufacturing philosophies into the existing Adtranz operations?

What should Bombardier do to minimize tensions and maximize teamwork with personnel changes imminently on the horizon? How should those personnel changes be made? Who, in the management ranks of Adtranz and BT, should I keep and who should I replace and how should I go about the process of making these decisions? Should the headquarters of the merged companies be located in St. Bruno, Quebec, Berlin or a more neutral city like Brussels, Paris or London? And finally, what kind of style should I use in leading the organization forward? How directive should I be versus participative in making decisions?

The Richard Ivey School of Business gratefully acknowledges the generous support of The J. Armand Bombardier Foundation in the development of these learning materials.

Case 4-4   World Vision International's AIDS Initiative: Challenging a Global Partnership

On January 19, 2002, Ken Casey, director of World Vision International's HIV/AIDS Hope Initiative, walked into a safari lodge in South Africa to present the final session of a conference attended by 40 senior staff from 17 countries with the highest prevalence of HIV and AIDS in Africa and nearly 20 senior executives from worldwide support offices. As he stretched his back, he felt a sharp pain from wounds he had received during a vicious attack by a baboon on the hotel's patio the day before the conference began. Badly cut and bruised, Casey had staggered to the conference center where he had

been wrapped in towels and rushed to a hospital. It had required 135 stitches and 27 staples to close the wounds.

Determined to proceed with the conference, which he saw as a potential turning point in his year-long struggle to get the Hope Initiative off the ground, Casey had returned the next day. Largely driven by the senior leaders of World Vision International, the initiative was an ambitious attempt to implement common goals and strategies in fundraising, programming, and advocacy across the 48 independent members of the World Vision Partnership. But its future was unclear. Not only did its focus on HIV/AIDS represent a major shift in World Vision's programming, but in many ways, the initiative's top-down implementation challenged the federated organization model the partnership had pursued throughout the 1990s. As he addressed the

▌ Professor Christopher A. Bartlett and Daniel F. Curran, Director—Humanitarian Leadership Program, prepared this case. HBS cases are developed solely as the basis for class discussion. Cases are not intended to serve as endorsements, sources of primary data, or illustrations of effective or ineffective management.

conference, Casey worried that if it did not go well, the Hope Initiative might well be dead in the water.

Birth of World Vision International

World Vision International was a $1 billion Christian relief and development partnership linking 48 national members in a global federation. In 2002, the partnership raised over $732 million in cash and nearly $300 million in commodities. (See **Exhibit 1** for representative World Vision Partnership financial data.) Almost 50% of World Vision's funding flowed from private sources, mostly through child sponsorship. Governments and multilateral agencies provided the other 50%.

A Visionary Founder: "Faith in Action" Founded in the United States in August 1950 by Bob Pierce, a Christian evangelist who was moved by the suffering he witnessed in Korea, World Vision was funded by North American Christians whom Pierce connected to individual Korean orphans through photographs and personal correspondence. This innovative sponsorship program—later widely imitated—helped Pierce translate the massive needs he saw in Asia into personal terms in America. In 1952, the organization's first statement of purpose read: "World Vision is a missionary service organization meeting emergency needs in crisis areas of the world through existing evangelical agencies."

Although Pierce cultivated a small, dedicated staff, he called the shots in his young organization. He challenged his team by telling them, "Cut through the reasons why things can't be done. Don't fail to do something just because you can't do everything."[1] With this entrepreneurial attitude, Pierce soon extended World Vision's work into Hong Kong, Indonesia, Taiwan, India, and Japan.

By the 1960s, World Vision was opening offices in other countries. In 1961, an affiliate office opened in Canada as a separate national entity, and in 1966 a national entity was established in Australia. During this period, it also refined its "child sponsorship" model and, by the mid-1960s,

[1]Graeme Irvine, *Best Things in the Worst Times: An Insider's View of World Vision* (Wilsonville, OR: World Vision International, 1996), p. 18.

was supporting 15,000 children in Southeast Asia. Responding to church film screenings, radio advertising, and direct-mail appeals, Christians in the United States, Canada, and Australia were promised a loving connection to a poor child in the developing world for a monthly contribution of around $10. Full-time staff and hundreds of volunteers coordinated the delivery of photos and letters between children and sponsors, while more than a dozen marketers created appeals to attract more donors. It was a successful process requiring a great deal of administrative support.

By 1969, World Vision managed $5.1 million in funding of which 80% was delivered to 32,600 children in 388 projects. The remaining 20% supported fund-raising and administrative costs. All funding and most support services flowed through the headquarters offices in Monrovia, California. As the war in Vietnam began absorbing the organization's energy, significant changes in approach occurred. Instead of working through existing orphanages and ministries, World Vision staff opened refugee schools, recruited and trained local teachers, and built houses for the displaced.

A New Leader, A New Approach:
The Evolving Mission
Toward the end of the 1960s, however, World Vision began experiencing difficulties. A senior executive described the emerging problems: "Anyone looking at World Vision would see an organization that reflected Bob Pierce himself: action oriented, strongly evangelical, innovative, and progressive. But we had no long-range planning or adequate mechanisms for administration." But Pierce strongly resisted changes that many felt were needed. As money became short, tensions grew between him and his board. Finally, in 1967, Pierce resigned.

Pierce's successor, Stan Mooneyham, was another action-oriented risk taker. With the fall of South Vietnam and Laos and the rise of the Khmer Rouge in Cambodia, World Vision lost contact with much of its program staff in those countries. More importantly, nearly 30,000 sponsors lost contact with their sponsored children. But the four core

Exhibit 1   World Vision International FY2002 Financial Data

PARTNERSHIP INCOME FY2002
(Offices receiving $200,000 or more in thousands of U.S. dollars)[a]

National Offices	Contributions	Gifts-in-Kind	Total
Armenia	$ 360		$ 360
Australia	78,543	$ 14,844	93,387
Austria	2,121	543	2,664
Brazil	2,786		2,786
Burundi	205		205
Canada	105,656	38,924	144,580
Chad	339		339
Chile	265		265
Colombia	1,041		1,041
Costa Rica	274		274
Finland	1,407	—	1,407
Germany	34,370	2,987	37,357
Haiti	331		331
Hong Kong	25,885	1,237	27,122
India	1,214		1,214
Indonesia	219		219
Ireland	4,538		4,538
Japan	12,055	2,294	14,349
Korea	20,802	1,282	22,084
Malaysia	918		918
Mexico	1,410		1,410
Myanmar	213		213
Netherlands	3,973	372	4,345
New Zealand	13,459	21	13,480
Philippines	505		505
Sierra Leone	1,287		1,287
Singapore	2,615	—	2,615
South Africa	507		507
Switzerland	12,599	704	13,303
Taiwan	31,221	75	31,296
Tanzania	722		722
Thailand	3,707		3,707
United Kingdom	46,529	1,199	47,728
United States	317,744	235,086	552,830
Zambia	1,030		1,030
Other Offices	1,185		1,185
Total Partnership Income	**$732,035**	**$299,568**	**$1,031,603**

[a] In approximate U.S. dollars. Exact amounts depend on time currency exchange is calculated.

(continued)

Exhibit 1   (*concluded*)

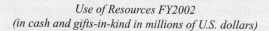

Use of Resources FY2002
(in cash and gifts-in-kind in millions of U.S. dollars)

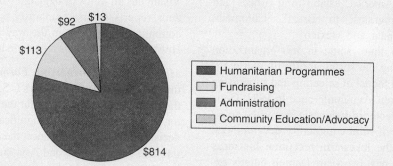

What World Vision's resources accomplish:

Humanitarian Programmes provide for emergency relief in natural and man-made disasters and for development work in food, education, health care, sanitation, income generation and other community needs. Also included are the costs of supporting such programmes in the field.

Fundraising supports humanitarian programmes by soliciting contributions through media and direct marketing appeals. Included are costs of marketing, creative services and publishing materials.

Administration includes donor relations, computer technology, finance, accounting, human resources and managerial oversight.

Community Education/Advocacy promotes awareness of poverty and justice issues through media campaigns, forums, speaking engagements, and public advocacy.

Ministry Support & Programmes by Region FY2002
(in case and gifts-in-kind in millions of U.S. dollars)

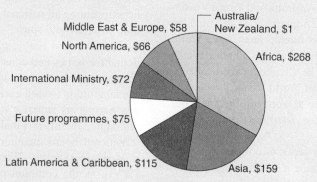

Source: World Vision International 2002 Annual Report.

fund-raising offices—in the United States, Canada, Australia, and New Zealand—found that most of their donors were willing to transfer their assistance to children elsewhere. The organization shifted its focus to Latin America, establishing offices and sponsorship programs in Brazil, Colombia, Ecuador, Guatemala, and Mexico.

At the same time, some in the organization began questioning the sustainability of World Vision's traditional model of selecting and supporting individual children. At a conference in 1971, Gene Daniels, WV director in Indonesia, proposed an alternative model of rural community development. Undeterred by the lukewarm reception his ideas received, for the next two years Daniels quietly experimented with this community development–based approach. As he began to succeed, others voiced an interest. Graeme Irvine, president of World Vision-Australia, supported a shift to longer-term commitments rather than "dump and run" emergency relief. He stated, "Development is not something you do for people. Those who wish to help may walk alongside, but not take over."[2]

Influenced by these voices, in 1972, Mooneyham promised that World Vision would build a Christian Children's Hospital in Phnom Penh. He presented a proposal to the international board but was disappointed to be turned down. Then the presidents of World Vision-Australia and World Vision-New Zealand offered to organize staff and fund the program themselves. Six months later, when World Vision opened the hospital in Phnom Penh, Mooneyham wrote, "The Cambodia medical program was an example of World Vision's emerging international partnership at work. It illustrated our principle of looking for alternative solutions to major problems."[3]

In 1973, following a series of consultations, the World Vision Board made a commitment to both relief and development in World Vision's mission. But the consensus over becoming a "transform" rather than a "transfer" organization meant significant changes to the structure and governance. "What you are doing in development is according people the dignity of voice and self-determination," stated Irvine. "But a big organization like World Vision has all kinds of baggage—bureaucracy, systems, reports, layers of authority, policies and many committees—that got in the way of development. How would we work as a partnership?"[4]

Moving Toward Partnership: Forming WVI   Until the early 1970s, World Vision's U.S. organization, as the founding country and by far the largest contributor, had made most of the significant programming decisions. Under its guidance, the overall organization had expanded beyond Asia and Latin America into Africa and the Middle East. Typically, each initiative had arisen from special circumstances or through initiatives led by interested groups, churches, or individuals.

Increasingly, however, the presidents of Canada, Australia, and New Zealand—the other key fund-raising (support) offices—wanted to move beyond just providing funds to program-delivery (field) offices. They wanted to participate in policy and strategy decisions. "This was not so much a desire for control as it was a need for accountability to donors," explained a World Vision-NZ executive. In 1973, Mooneyham responded by forming a study committee to recommend a basis for "a true partnership among all national entities: a partnership of both structure and spirit."

Over the next few years, the committee met to define the issues and consider the options. "At the core we saw it not as structure or even as process, but an attitude toward each other that did not view one partner as superior to any other," stated one committee member.[5] Finally, in April 1976, the international board unanimously decided to form a new distinct entity, World Vision International (WVI), as the common program-delivery arm of World Vision's four main fund-raising support offices—the United States, Canada, New Zealand, and Australia. The directors of each sat on the

---

[2]Irvine, p. 71.
[3]Irvine, p. 45.

[4]Irvine, p. 72.
[5]Irvine, p. 136.

international board. (World Vision-U.S. maintained the World Vision name and trademark but gave its WVI partners the right to use them.) World Vision national entities in developing countries (the field offices delivering the programs) became members of WVI's council but did not have equal-partner status with the four board members. The council agreed to WVI's mission and, in May 1978, adopted a formal declaration of internationalization.

Building the World Vision Partnership: Defining a Federation

To provide coordinated management of the global field operations funded by the core support offices, WVI's council created a central international office, colocated with the World Vision-U.S. office in Los Angeles. However, rather than functioning as a servant to the four council member organizations, it soon became a separate power base. A WVI manager at the time recalled:

> Mooneyham brought all of the bright and creative folks with him to the international office, and this had two unintended consequences. First, as the program-delivery mechanism became the dominant force in the organization, the value and importance of the fund-raising team left in the WV-U.S. was eroded. Second, because this organization separated its "marketing" and "production" functions, each group developed its own culture.

The separation lasted for almost a decade during which time the national directors of the largest support offices, again feeling frustrated at just delivering the funds they raised to the international office, started to demand more of a say in strategy. Said one senior WVI manager, "Our core competitive advantage—what we did particularly well—was our child sponsorship mechanism. It was the most sustainable form of fund-raising, and we had become one of the best in the world at doing it. But, at that time, we did not recognize it. No wonder they were frustrated."

Challenging Central Control   When Tom Houston became the new president of WVI in 1984, his attention was drawn to the devastating drought in Ethiopia. The global response from donors was staggering. Under agreements with the U.S.

government and U.N. agencies, WVI's Ethiopia response budget grew from $2.3 million in 1984 to $43.4 million in 1986. To manage the funding, World Vision's staff in Ethiopia grew from 100 to 3,650. In the following year, WVI launched 11 large development projects in six other African nations. Because of the need for coordination, all logistics and program functions were managed from the international office, giving even more power to this fast-growing group.

By 1987, World Vision had survived and grown through a decade of expansion. But there was discontent within the organization, and Houston discovered that the unhappy support-office directors were meeting together informally to share their frustrations. "Tom was abrupt and frank and did not like the notion of a dominant person pushing the little guys around," said one executive. "So he turned our culture upside down." To bring the support-office directors into the inner circle, he asked several of them to sit on the international planning committee, the president's primary consultative group on partnership decisions. In addition, he shook up the management of the international office by requiring that all regional vice presidents come from their regions.

But frustration reached a boiling point in August 1987 when national directors responsible for the work in over 60 countries gathered at a director's conference in Sierra Madre, California. When, as was the norm at these events, executives from the international office began to deliver presentations on strategy and operations, three new regional VPs from Brazil, Nigeria, and Egypt stood together. "If this is a director's conference, why are we working on your agenda?" they asked. The directors of the main support offices joined the "revolt." Recognizing the legitimacy of the challenge, Houston surrendered the agenda. Following the conference, 30 senior executives spent a year studying how to redefine the relationship between field and support offices and the international office.

Creating Area Development Programs   Meanwhile, the 11 large-scale development programs World Vision had launched in 1985 were struggling. Each had a budget of more than $1 million, a time span of more than three years, and a geographic scope greater than a single community. The causes of the problems were diagnosed as unrealistic initial expectations, lack of local management and technical expertise, and a top-down planning and control system.

A study commissioned to propose solutions to these problems recommended a new approach that sought to retain the benefits of scale while engaging more local involvement in community-level transformational development. Through the 1990s a new way to work, referred to as the Area Development Program (ADP), became the dominant means of program delivery for World Vision. In Africa, for example, over 300 ADPs were defined, each aiding 50,000 to 200,000 people. Wilfred Mlay, African regional vice president, explained their operation:

> Each ADP is managed by a coordinator from that country who understands the local language and customs. He or she negotiates an agreement with the community for a 10- to 15-year multisectoral engagement, then they sign a contract promising to work together. . . . Before, communities tended to consider the local projects—a bore hole, a school, a health center—as World Vision projects. If something went wrong, they said, "Come and fix your pump. Come and fix your vehicle." There was no ownership. . . . Now we don't just dig wells and provide clean water; we partner with each ADP area to identify root causes of their problems, then we work with them to provide a long-term program that will address the needs they identify. The strength of the approach is in finding local solutions to local problems.

Engaging Federalism   When Houston resigned as WVI's president in 1988, Irvine, former head of World Vision-Australia, took his place. Upon his appointment, Irvine made a commitment to make WVI "a professional, enlightened, efficient and humane organization [that] will nurture a climate of creativity in which people feel free to contribute."[6] He then launched a process to reexamine the organization's values, mission, and structure,

all of which were to be open to challenge and change.

A working group developed a set of core values (see **Exhibit 2**) that was adopted by the board of World Vision International in 1990. Next, after 24 drafts, in 1992 the board adopted a new mission. Finally, Irvine led the creation of a Covenant of Partnership (see **Exhibit 3**) that was signed by all members of the newly defined World Vision Partnership. "We want to be held together by shared agreements, values, and commitments rather than legal contracts or a controlling center," said Irvine. "The covenant is a statement of accountability to each other, setting out the privileges and responsibilities of national member-entities of the World Vision family."

By 1995, with over a million sponsored children in its care—up from 70,000 children 15 years earlier—the World Vision Partnership decided to build its formal organizational architecture on a "federal" model. (See **Exhibit 4**.) Recognizing that that simple decentralization would mean losing economies of scale, the partnership made the goal of the new structure to try to make all partners as self-sufficient as possible but to maintain a strong core of common language, systems, and operations. Bryant Myers, senior vice president of operations, explained the philosophy:

> We wanted to combine the strength of the central organization with centers of expertise and action that existed around the partnership, balancing the contributions and needs of each. That should result in centralizing the things that can be done better and cheaper that way and decentralizing other things that can be managed more effectively on the front lines. . . . We learned that the biggest misreading of federalism is to call it decentralization. The key to federalism is to ensure the right of intervention held by the leader at the center.

Designing the Structure and Governance   Under the resulting federal structure, membership in the WVI Partnership required a commitment to its core documents (mission statement, statement of faith, core values, and Covenant of Partnership), to WVI

---

[6]Irvine, p. 134.

Exhibit 2   Extracts from World Vision International's Statement of Core values

WE ARE CHRISTIAN   We acknowledge one God; Father, Son and Holy Spirit. In Jesus Christ the love, mercy and grace of God are made known to us and all people. . . . We seek to follow him—in his identification with the poor, the powerless, the afflicted, the oppressed, the marginalized; in his special concern for children; in his respect for the dignity bestowed by God on women equally with men; in his challenge to unjust attitudes and systems; in his call to share resources with each other; in his love for all people without discrimination or conditions; in his offer of new life through faith in him . . .

WE ARE COMMITTED TO THE POOR   We are called to serve the neediest people of the earth; to relieve their suffering and to promote the transformation of their condition of life. . . . We respect the poor as active participants, not passive recipients, in this relationship . . .

WE VALUE PEOPLE   We regard all people as created and loved by God. We give priority to people before money, structure, systems and other institutional machinery. . . . We celebrate the richness of diversity in human personality, culture and contribution. . . . We practice a participative, open, enabling style in working relationships. We encourage the professional, personal and spiritual development of our staff.

WE ARE STEWARDS   The resources at our disposal are not our own. They are a sacred trust from God through donors on behalf of the poor. We are faithful to the purpose for which those resources are given and manage them in a manner that brings maximum benefit to the poor. . . . We demand of ourselves high standards of professional competence and accept the need to be accountable through appropriate structures for achieving these standards. We share our experience and knowledge with others where it can assist them.

WE ARE PARTNERS   We are members of an international World Vision Partnership that transcends legal, structural and cultural boundaries. We accept the obligations of joint participation, shared goals and mutual accountability that true partnership requires. We affirm our inter-dependence and our willingness to yield autonomy as necessary for the common good. We commit ourselves to know, understand and love each other. . . . We maintain a co-operative stance and a spirit of openness towards other humanitarian organizations. We are willing to receive and consider honest opinions from others about our work.

WE ARE RESPONSIVE   We are responsive to life-threatening emergencies where our involvement is needed and appropriate. We are willing to take intelligent risks and act quickly. We do this from a foundation of experience and sensitivity to what the situation requires. We also recognize that even in the midst of crisis, the destitute have a contribution to make from their experience. . . . We are responsive to new and unusual opportunities. We encourage innovation, creativity and flexibility. We maintain an attitude of learning, reflection and discovery in order to grow in understanding and skill.

OUR COMMITMENT   We recognize that values cannot be legislated; they must be lived. No document can substitute for the attitudes, decisions and actions that make up the fabric of our life and work. Therefore, we covenant with each other, before God, to do our utmost individually and as corporate entities within the World Vision Partnership to uphold these Core Values, to honor them in our decisions, to express them in our relationships and to act consistently with them wherever World Vision is at work.

Source: World Vision International internal documents.

ministry policies, and to the WVI trademark agreement. Organizationally, the partnership was governed through a set of linked structures (see **Exhibit 5**).

By 2002, there were 48 national partners, each with one vote on the **international council,** the partnership's highest authority. Held once every three years, council meetings were attended by the international board members, the chairs of the national boards or advisory councils, national office directors, and elected delegates from all partner offices. The council reviewed the objectives of World Vision International, assessed the accomplishment of previous goals, and made recommendations to

Exhibit 3   Extracts from World Vision's Covenant of Partnership

THE COVENANT (EXTRACTS)

Regarding World Vision as a partnership of interdependent national entities, we, as a properly constituted national World Vision Board (or Advisory Council), do covenant with other World Vision Boards (or Advisory Councils) to:

A. UPHOLD THE FOLLOWING STATEMENTS OF WORLD VISION IDENTITY AND PURPOSE:
   The Statement of Faith
   The Mission Statement
   The Core Values.

B. CONTRIBUTE TO THE ENRICHMENT OF PARTNERSHIP LIFE AND UNITY BY:
   Sharing in strategic decision-making and policy formulation through consultation and mechanisms that offer all members an appropriate voice in Partnership affairs . . .
   Accepting the leadership and organizational structures established by the WVI Council and Board for the operation of the Partnership . . .
   Fostering an open spirit of exchange for ideas, proposals, vision and concern within the Partnership . . .

C. WORK WITHIN THE ACCOUNTABILITY STRUCTURES BY WHICH THE PARTNERSHIP FUNCTIONS, by:
   Affirming the principle of mutual accountability and transparency among all entities . . .
   Accepting Partnership policies and decisions established by WVI Board consultative processes.
   Honoring commitments to adopted budgets to the utmost extent possible . . .
   Executing an agreement with World Vision International to protect the trademark, name and symbols of World Vision worldwide . . .

D. OBSERVE AGREED FINANCIAL PRINCIPLES AND PROCEDURES, especially:
   Using funds raised under the auspices of World Vision exclusively in World Vision approved ministries.
   Keeping overhead and fund-raising expenses to a minimum to ensure a substantial majority of the funds raised are responsibly utilized in ministry among the poor.
   Accepting Financial Planning and Budgeting Principles adopted by the WVI Board.
   Ensuring that funds or commodities accepted from governments or multi-lateral agencies do not compromise World Vision's mission or core values, and that such resources do not become the major ongoing source of support.

E. PRESENT CONSISTENT COMMUNICATIONS MESSAGES, that:
   Reflect our Christian identity in appropriate ways.
   Include words, images, and statistics that are consistent with ministry realities.
   Avoid paternalism and cultural insensitivity.
   Are free from demeaning and degrading images.
   Build openness, confidence, knowledge and trust within the Partnership.
   In signing the Covenant, we are mindful of the rich heritage of Christian service represented by World Vision and of the privilege which is ours to join with others of like mind in the work of the Kingdom of God throughout the world. We therefore recognize that consistent failure to honour this Covenant of Partnership may provide cause for review of our status as a member of the Partnership by the Board of World Vision International.

Signed in behalf of (NAME OF NATIONAL ENTITY)
by resolution carried at a meeting of the [Board] (or Advisory Council) on

---

Chair of [Board] (or Advisory Council)

Source: World Vision International internal documents.

Exhibit 4	Key Elements of the WVI Partnership

The World Vision Partnership refers to the entire World Vision family throughout the world. Any expression of the World Vision ministry is in some way connected to the Partnership. The word "Partnership" is used in this document in a broad, informal sense, rather than a legal sense.

World Vision National Entities comprise the membership of the Partnership. The conditions and categories of membership are described in the By-Laws of World Vision International. All function with the guidance and advice of a National Board or Advisory Council.

World Vision International (WVI) is the registered legal entity which, through its Council and Board of Directors, provides the formal international structure for the Partnership.

The WVI Council provides the membership structure for the Partnership. It meets every three years to review the purpose and objectives of World Vision, assess the extent to which they have been accomplished and make recommendations to the WVI Board in relation to policy. All member-entities are represented on the Council.

The WVI Board of Directors is the governing body of World Vision International as outlined in the By-Laws. The membership of the Board is broadly representative of the Partnership and is appointed by a process determined by the Partnership.

The International Office is the functional unit of World Vision International, housing most of the central elements of WVI. It operates under the authority of the WVI Board of Directors.

Source: World Vision International internal documents.

the board in relation to global strategies and policies.

World Vision's **international board** was composed of the international president and 23 directors selected from the governing bodies of WVI's national offices. It oversaw the partnership, meeting twice a year to appoint WVI's senior officers, approve strategic plans and budgets, and set international policy.

Seven **regional forums** were composed of representatives from the national boards or advisory councils of each national office in each region. They shared experiences on regional programs and strategies and nominated representatives to the WVI Board.

The **partnership office** (previously the international office), located in Monrovia, California, was WVI's executive group. Headed by an international president and four regional and six functional vice presidents, its staff of around 160 supported the day-to-day operations of the partnership. Several other partnership support offices in cities such as Geneva, Los Angeles, and Vienna represented WVI in the international arena through lobbying and advocacy work.

Each of the four **regional offices**—in Costa Rica, Cyprus, Nairobi, and Bangkok—oversaw the program operations of the national offices in its region. These regional offices reported directly to the partnership office.

Most of WVI's 48 **national offices** were either primarily support (fund-raising) offices or field (program-delivery) offices, but a few did both. Each national office had equal direct representation on the international council and also took part in the election of regional representatives to the international board through its regional forum. Local governance and independence from the international office was determined by the national office's stage of development category:

• WVI's 22 branch offices were governed by national advisory committees, but WVI maintained legal responsibility and strong management control over their budgetary and personnel decisions through its regional offices.

• The 12 intermediate-stage offices were governed by local boards composed of business, church, and social service leaders. They voluntarily agreed to seek approval from WVI for critical management decisions such as appointment or termination of a national director or national board member, budget development, and off-budget expenditures.

Exhibit 5   World Vision International Organizational Structure

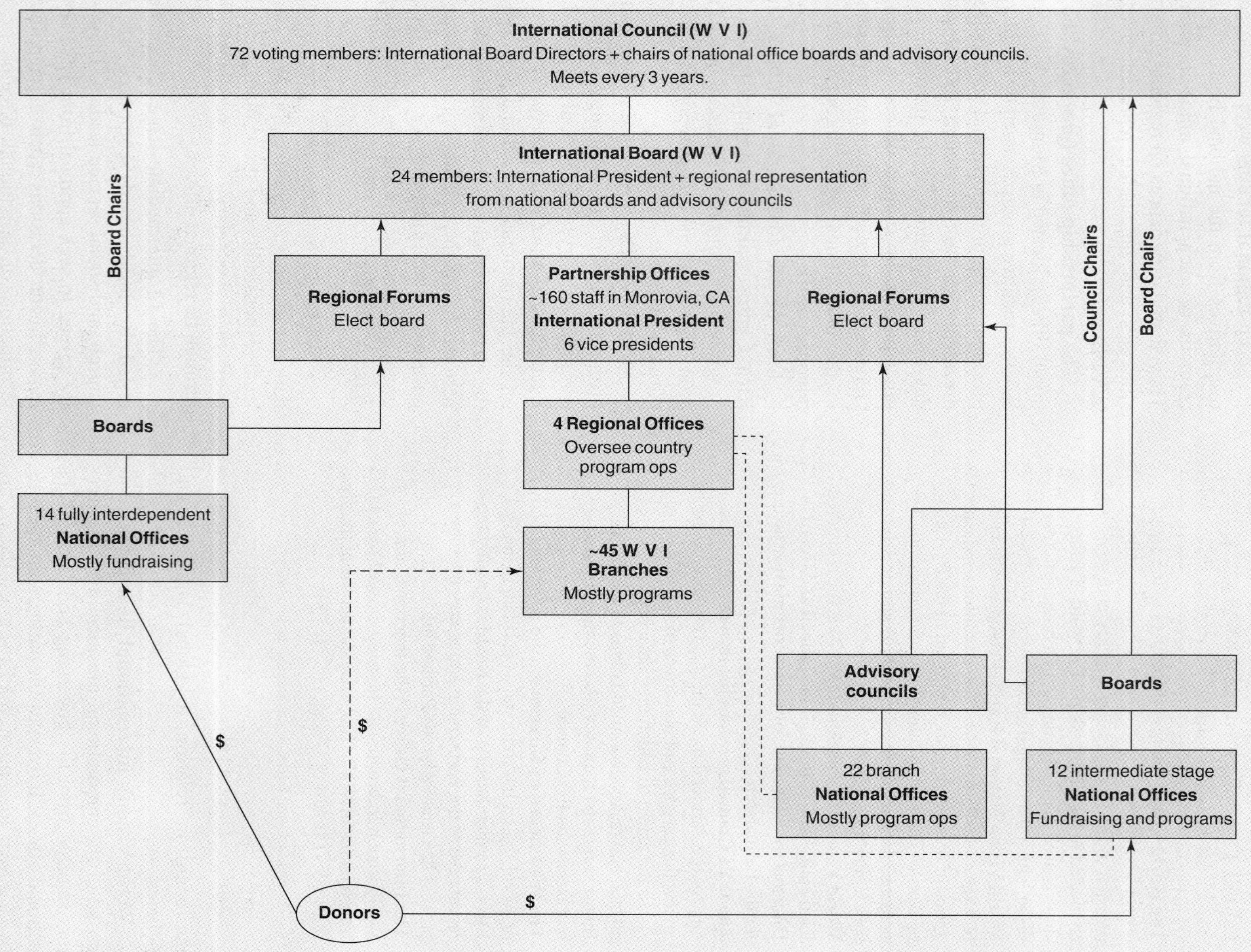

Source: Casewriter representation.

• The 14 fully interdependent offices were nationally registered nonprofit organizations with their own local boards of directors. Except for certain items specified in the Covenant of Partnership, they did not need WVI approval for decisions. Nonetheless, they were expected voluntarily to coordinate with the partnership office. (Branch and intermediate offices were considered to be in transition toward full interdependence. The process involved peer reviews, WVI consultation, and interaction with the international board.)

By 1996, when Dean Hirsch became the sixth president of WVI, the partnership-based governance model was in place. Hirsch had risen to the top job in WVI following two decades in which he had helped establish World Vision national programs in Rwanda, Zaire, Tanzania, Mali, Ghana, and Malawi then managed major donor marketing for WV-U.S. He described his role in the emerging federated partnership:

> My job is to cast a vision, to make sure that we have alignment between our mission and operations, and to ensure we stay strategic. Because of our dispersed governance, we must operate with trust. The best thing I can do is help to build relationships. So I am the biggest cheerleader in the world . . . but as president of WVI, I also hold a seat on every World Vision board in the world. Either one of my representatives or I attend all meetings. It provides an immediate means of keeping alignment. And I can intervene at any time if one of the partners drifts from our mission or core values.

Fund-Raising in the Partnership: World Vision-U.S.

Within the evolving World Vision global partnership, most national entities were adjusting to the more complex structure within which they had to operate. In the United States, for example, the WV-U.S. Board began to look for a new president to strengthen its fund-raising activity. In June 1998, it offered the job to Richard Stearns, an experienced manager who had spent 23 years in strategic and marketing roles in Gillette Company and Parker

Brothers Games and as CEO of Lenox, the well-known tableware and gift company. As WV-U.S. president, Stearns was responsible for all WV-U.S. operations, which included fund-raising, advocacy, and international program development, each run by one of the five senior VPs reporting to him.

Revitalizing WV-U.S.: Marketing, Metrics, and Money   Over the years, WV-U.S. had remained the largest financial contributor to the partnership, providing almost 50% of global revenues by 1998. "But the organization was missing opportunities and faltering in its operations," said Stearns. "In particular, our appeals had become costly, and we were inefficient. I was given two key goals: increase revenues and lower overhead ratios." (This ratio was the cash income raised divided by the cost of fund-raising. In 1998, it stood at around 3 to 1.)

In 2000, Stearns hired Atul Tandon as senior VP of marketing. Like Stearns, he had come from the corporate sector, serving for over 20 years with Citibank in marketing. In WV-U.S., Tandon saw his primary objectives to be to build the brand and improve customer satisfaction. "I soon realized that I was in a fundamentally different world," he said. "When I asked, 'What is our bottom line? To whom are we accountable?' no one could answer." Furthermore, staff members were unable to describe their outputs and measures. "There were no profit and loss statements, and people were unaware of our spending and the returns we were getting."

Tandon and Stearns reorganized the WV-U.S. office, laying off a number of staff and elevating innovators to senior positions. They replaced the traditional Direct Response Marketing Department with integrated product and channel marketing teams that worked with new communications and creative teams to focus on the key drivers of marketing effectiveness: cost of donor acquisition, costs and methods of donor retention, and long-term donor value. These new teams focused on growth through partnering, brand building, and new channels of recruiting and retaining donors. While the message to donors had to be altered to incorporate the more community development–based model that the ADP concept supported, they were able to do so under the umbrella of a modified $26 monthly child sponsorship program that was still the most effective means of raising funds for WV-U.S. The marketing team also found that while donors were difficult to recruit, if properly cultivated, they were relatively easy to keep.

Tandon expected marketing teams to be research driven in defining what appealed to donors. They were then required to work with three new channel-specific sales teams to design products specifically for church groups, major donors, and Internet sales. Believing strongly in "learning to listen to the customer," Tandon allocated nearly 75% of the $50 million marketing budget to donor recruitment, retention, and communications. With no increases in marketing and communications allocations over a four-year period, Tandon and his team devoted themselves to increasing revenues while holding expenses flat. "We call it widening the jaws," said Tandon.

The results came quickly: double-digit growth every year for four years with an unchanged marketing budget. "Over those four years, we increased our cash income to fund-raising cost ratio from 3 to 1, first, to 3.4 to 1, then to 4.1 to 1, and finally to 5.5 to 1," Tandon reported. Additionally, donor satisfaction increased, as did name awareness in the core target markets—from 49% to 76% over three years. To evaluate WV-U.S.'s efforts more effectively, Stearns introduced a balanced scorecard measurement system. (See **Exhibit 6** for copy of scorecard.) Tandon volunteered to make his marketing group the guinea pig for the new system, explaining:

> We identified specific numbers-driven goals and a few subjective goals. Most revolved around measuring brand strength, brand awareness, and customer satisfaction. Of these, I believe the most important driver is the customer satisfaction number. Ours is measured twice a year by survey, and we have increased satisfaction levels from 84% to 92% over the last three years. We don't have a good benchmark in the nonprofit world, but in the corporate sector, Amazon's customer satisfaction is the highest at 88%. So we are in the right ballpark.

Managing in the Partnership: All in the Family

In addition to running the operations at WV-U.S., Stearns sat on the Strategy Working Group (SWG), the key executive decision-making body of the World Vision Partnership. Chaired by WVI's president, Hirsch, the SWG included 16 senior executives from throughout the partnership. Coming from the corporate world, Stearns at first found working at WVI difficult. "I was bewildered by the lack of any real authority structure in the partnership," he said. "I kept wondering who was in charge." He also reflected on the governance structure: "The international board is truly representative. The U.S. appoints two of its 24 members and has a founder's chair. The other 21 are from other nations. Representing 50% of overall revenues, we clearly have financial influence, yet we hold only 12% of the formal political control. This would be unthinkable in the corporate world."

Over time, Stearns recognized that the partnership traded control and efficiency for richness of perspective and strength in local programming and fund-raising: "We are able to make our own decisions and set our own priorities. President Hirsch has no line authority over me. He does not participate in my performance review, and he issues no directives to me or any other CEO. But, through the SWG, we make joint decisions that benefit the global organization and our mission better than if any one of us acted alone."

Program Delivery in the Partnership: The AIDS Hope Initiative

By the late 1990s, the World Vision Partnership was beginning to feel more stable. The ADP concept had made program delivery more effective, the child sponsorship fund-raising model had been refined, and the federal organization framework was helping to integrate the global network of World Vision entities. Yet while World Vision had been struggling to refine its internal operations, the impact of HIV/AIDS was changing the needs of those it served externally. The global pandemic had reached crisis levels in many parts of the world, but nowhere more than in sub-Saharan Africa.

Exhibit 6 Balanced Scorecard for WV-U.S. Marketing Department

Marketing & Communications
Level 1 Scorecard

Atul Tandon
Reporting Period: Q4 of FYo3 (Jul, Aug, Sep)

Measure	Actual	Target	Variance (%)	Variance Flag	FYo3-Q1 FYo3 Actuals	FYo3-Q1 FYo2 Actuals	FYo3-Q2 FYo3 Actuals	FYo3-Q2 FYo2 Actuals	FYo3-Q3 FYo3 Actual	FYo3-Q3 FYo2 Actuals	FYo3-Q4 FYo3 Actual	FYo3-Q4 FYo2 Actuals
CHANGE HEARTS												
1 Media Impressions (in millions)	4,515	2,280	98%	●	625	570	2,717	1,880	3,230	2,815	4,515	3,445
INCREASE INVOLVEMENT												
2 Gross Sponsorship Assignments	144,613	182,941	−21%	■	43,139	44,751	82,473	89,921	116,700	129,514	144,613	169,028
3 Matrix Income ($1,000s)*	$8,797	$6,950	27%	●	$2,923	$3,514	$4,157	$4,507	$6,612	$6,070	$8,797	$6,795
4 Income ($1,000s)*	$229,007	$230,103	0%	◆	$60,054	$56,487	$114,404	$104,455	$171,997	$155,705	$229,161	$208,553
5 Sponsorship File Size	612,815	625,381	−2%	◆	594,216	555,325	601,842	564,575	610,636	574,131	612,815	581,874
6 Donor Involvement—Avg. Annual Giving	$296	$296	0%	●	$278	$271	$285	$276	$277		$296	$280
INCREASE EFFECTIVENESS												
7 Expenses ($1,000s)*	$52,304	$53,975	3%	●●	$14,920	$13,460	$28,912	$25,801	$40,453	$37,477	$52,304	$49,431
8 Sponsor Attrition Rate	16.2%	16.5%	2%	●	17.4%	19.5%	17.0%	18.5%	16.4%	17.7%	16.2%	17.4%
9 Donor Satisfaction	90.8%	N/A	N/A		N/A	N/A	90.3%	88.7%	N/A	N/A	90.8%	89.4%

Variance Thresholds   ● Meets Goal   ◆ <5% Adverse   ■ >5% Adverse

* MAC Yield to Ministry (Revenues less Expenses) was better than previous year by $19.5 million (11.7%) and better than budget by $2.4 million

Metric: Definition:

CHANGE HEARTS

1 Media Impressions (in millions)   Number of Christian & Secular Media impressions through publication or broadcast story

INCREASE INVOLVEMENT

2 Gross Sponsorship Assignments   Cum total gross sponsorship acquisitions (all channels except RM)

3 Matrix Income ($1,000s)   Income motivated by Marketing & Communications, but booked to other areas—Major Donor + Ethnic Mktg + Corp Partnership

4 Income ($1,000s)   Income generated by Marketing & Communications from all sources

5 Sponsorship File Size   # of Money Sponsorships Ending last period + Acquisitions—Cancels

6a Donor Involvement—Avg. Annual Giving   Rolling 12 mos giving / # donors (cash only for now; GIK to be added later)

INCREASE EFFECTIVENESS

7 Expenses ($1,000s)   YTD Total Marketing & Communications Expenses

8 Sponsor Attrition Rate   # of money sponsorships that have not made a payment in the last 6 months/total money sponsorships 6 months prior

9 Donor Satisfaction   Donor Satisfaction Rating (Sponsorship Only)

Source: World Vision International internal documents.

Recognizing the Need: Lessons for a Latecomer

Two months after joining World Vision, Stearns went on a field trip to Uganda. Visiting a household of three boys, aged 11 to 13, who lived alone after being orphaned by AIDS, Stearns learned that an estimated 10 million African children were living in similar circumstances. When he asked what World Vision was doing about it, the answer was, "Very little." Although he was new to the agency, he felt he had to speak out:

> When I was at Parker Brothers, we failed to realize that games were moving from the parlor table to the video screen. When new competitors came out with fast and interesting computer games, they stole 90% of the market from under our noses. This was what was happening to us with HIV/AIDS. We had developed top-notch skills at rural community organization, water systems, health, childcare, and economic regeneration and responded well to hurricanes, disasters, wars, and other emergencies. But while all of this was exemplary, we were not prepared to face the unprecedented scale of devastation wrought by the AIDS pandemic.

With 58,000 people in Africa dying from AIDS each week—equal to the entire loss of American lives in Vietnam—Stearns felt there was a real chance that decades of progress by the development community would be rolled back. He began to speak more forcefully, telling his colleagues that they were building beautiful sand castles on the beach while an 80-foot-high tidal wave was just offshore. "I kept saying it for over two years, fully mindful that I did not know what specifically I was proposing to do about it," he recounted. He was supported by Bruce Wilkinson, senior vice president of his International Programs Group. But while other members of the partnership listened, Stearns felt that, on their overloaded agenda, it was "just another woe to add to the list."

Then, in July 2000, Wilfred Mlay, African regional vice president, gave a powerful presentation to the SWG. "AIDS is killing our people," he said. "It is devastating our work, our families, our staff. I really need your help." A few months later, when *Time* ran a cover story on the 10 million to 12 million children in Africa estimated to be orphaned by AIDS, Stearns circulated a memo to senior executives of the partnership asking, "Why, as a child-focused organization, are we not addressing the AIDS crisis?"

Mlay's appeal and Stearns's prodding prompted the SWG to appoint Myers, vice president for International Programs Strategy, to study WVI's commitment to the crisis. After speaking with a number of people throughout the partnership, he wrote a draft document suggesting that HIV/AIDS needed to be a priority for World Vision for five reasons: it cared about children, including the 40 million projected to lose one or both parents to HIV/AIDS by 2010; it had over 900,000 sponsored children in the 30 worst-hit countries and nearly 2 million sponsored children at risk worldwide; it was investing almost $200 million a year in the 30 worst-hit countries; its worldwide staff was at risk, and many were personally affected by HIV/AIDS in their own extended families; and as a Christian organization, it had an opportunity to bring its mission to those affected by HIV/AIDS.

Launching the AIDS Hope Initiative

On World AIDS Day in December 2000, Hirsch preempted any formal decision on an HIV/AIDS strategy by announcing that World Vision would launch a $30 million initiative to address the crisis. Believing that the moment was right and that some members were already moving forward, Hirsch pushed the partnership into action. Over the following months, Myers prepared a plan entitled "The HIV/AIDS Hope Initiative," outlining the need and identifying the scope of the problem. The plan also categorized a series of programming approaches for high-prevalence countries, medium-prevalence countries, and the rest of World Vision's country programs.

Just before presenting the plan to the SWG at a meeting in Costa Rica in February 2001, Hirsch approached Casey and asked him if he would lead the AIDS initiative. "I was surprised by the request," recalled Casey. "It was an entirely new and different task for me. I had spent six years as a senior line manager in operations for the U.S. organization. Now I would be taking on a key strategic role within WVI's partnership office." For most of his eight years with WV-U.S., Casey had served as senior vice president for fund-raising and programs. But, in 1999, Stearns's reorganization had left him a senior executive without a portfolio. "For about a year, I worked on special projects within the senior management team. They were rewarding, but I was considering moving on," Casey said.

As he thought about it, Casey decided that this new project represented an interesting and worthwhile challenge. In March 2001, he assumed his new role as director of the HIV/AIDS Hope Initiative. He would report directly to Hirsch but continue to work out of the WV-U.S. office in Seattle.

Assessing the Challenge   Casey returned to Seattle with an approved operating budget of approximately $750,000 but no staff. As he reviewed the existing document, he recognized the difficulty of his task:

> I began working off of the document that Bryant [Myers] had prepared. Although it was good work, it had been devised almost entirely at the headquarters office. Essentially, I was being asked to implement an unprecedented worldwide program effort on perhaps the most controversial issue imaginable that would require new levels of coordination that we had never previously achieved. Yet there was no ownership or buy-in from the regional VPs.

Casey understood that, within the partnership, the four regional VPs (for Africa, Asia, Pacific, and Middle East/Eastern Europe) held a great deal of power over programs and operations due to the fact that all the national directors reported to them. In recent years, however, the national offices had been pushed by the international board to become more independent in their strategies and programs. Casey stated: "In our efforts to devolve autonomy to the national offices, we had worked for 10 years to develop viable governing boards for each one. But we also wanted them to be responsive to WVI's global priorities through their link to the regional VPs. Because national directors were answerable to two masters, this could cause problems."

To build support for the Hope Initiative, Casey began a six-month process of travel and discussion with the regional VPs and national directors. He wanted to make sure that the initiative would remain true to its ideal while also ensuring that the ambitious fund-raising and programmatic objectives were realistic from the field's perspective.

Resistance from Donors   Casey knew that funding such a big initiative would be a challenge and hoped to implement a joint marketing effort across the partnership offices, hopefully reaching out to new donors in the process. He also wanted the marketing effort to be well connected to the programs in the field. But almost from the outset, he encountered resistance from the marketing departments in the major partnership support offices. Stearns remembered:

> Our WV-U.S. marketing people were very skeptical. They told us that any work with HIV/AIDS would never sell with our donors. Our top people in brand building told us that we have a very wholesome child-focused image. People equate us helping children and families in need. They said that if we start talking about AIDS, prostitutes, drug users, long-haul truckers, and sexuality, it would hurt our image.

WV-U.S. commissioned a market survey among evangelical Christians and loyal donors in the United States. "It was devastating news," stated Casey. "We asked them if they would be willing to give to a respectable Christian organization to help children who lost both parents to AIDS. Only 7% said that they would definitely help, while over 50% said probably not or definitely not. Surveys in Canada and Australia found the same thing. It was stark and clear that our donors felt that AIDS sufferers somehow deserved their fate."

Beyond donor reaction, Casey dug deeper to understand the marketing organization's challenge. "Their incentives and targets for the year were based on the efficiency of their appeals," he said. "But by its very nature, this was going to be a costly appeal." Instead of returning a usual 4 or 5:1 ratio of revenues to expenses, the marketers felt that, in the beginning at least, any AIDS appeal would return something closer to 1:1. So when Casey asked the heads of the partnership offices to adjust the targets for HIV/AIDS programs for their marketing teams, the response was mixed. While Stearns convinced his board to remove the HIV/AIDS appeals from the normal cost-ratio calculations for U.S. appeal, Canada, the United Kingdom, and several other key fund-raising countries were less willing to do so.

Resistance from the Field   As he focused on program implications, Casey had Mlay as a natural ally. As regional vice president for Africa, Mlay reported to Hirsch at WVI and was responsible for 25 national country offices with over 8,000 staff (mostly field and program officers, but also technical specialists in areas such as microenterprise, health, child protection, and Christian ministry) and a budget of $500 million. To manage his domain, Mlay had divided Africa into three subregions, each headed by a director (based in Johannesburg, Dakar, and Nairobi) responsible for eight or nine countries. "I have structured the African region differently from any of the other regions," he said. "For example, in Asia, all the senior leaders share one office in Bangkok. But because it is difficult to travel and communicate, my senior leadership and technical teams are dispersed. And I want them to be where the action is happening."

Although he managed the African region as he saw fit, Mlay could also use services in the partnership: "I am in charge but have access to resources when needed. For example, we have some sophisticated protocols for emergency operations. If I put out the call for help, we will have a conference call within five hours. And I have access to a global rapid-response team that can allocate $1 million within 72 hours, so I can promise that WV will be present at a crisis within 24 hours."

Mlay worked with the boards and advisory councils in his 26 national offices to implement WVI priorities. But while he held regular meetings with national directors and hosted conferences and forums to determine how to allocate his technical resources, he had only limited ability to determine the strategy of national programs. "The advisory councils and boards help us to connect to the local community and society," he said. "But I have a reserved seat on every board in Africa, so World Vision management and local boards share the governance of our work." Managing the boards was a time-consuming task for Mlay, who sometimes had to act if a board went in a direction that WVI disapproved of: "For example, we discovered that the head of one of our boards had a set of values that conflicted with those of the organization. We intervened and asked him to step down. Most of the board was against us, but we prevailed. There is a fine line between granting autonomy and maintaining standards."

Despite his ability to intervene when necessary, Mlay had long encouraged his national directors to determine their own goals and strategies through the ADP system. Indeed, under the federated partnership structure, they could even have direct contact with any of the support offices to fund their ADP projects. But now that he wanted to push HIV/AIDS programs, he faced resistance. "There is a culture of silence around the issue," he said. "In Tanzania, entire families and villages are being wiped out by AIDS. We have grandmothers caring for 10 and 12 children. The ADPs are strong, but people are ashamed to speak about it. This is especially true of church leaders, who refuse to see this as their problem. Many even talk about AIDS as God's punishment of sinners."

Casey also reflected on the "phenomenon of denial" he encountered. On an early trip to Capetown, he spoke to a taxi driver who told him that his awareness of HIV/AIDS had not changed his lifestyle because it would not get him. "A few minutes later, he was describing how the trucking company for whom his sister worked had just adopted a new HR policy stating that employees could not attend more than three funerals per month," recalled Casey. "It was uncanny how he could hold both thoughts in his head and not make a connection. In the face of such clear evidence, even intelligent people did not want to recognize the crisis."

Exhibit 7 Hope Initiative 2001 Organizational Structure

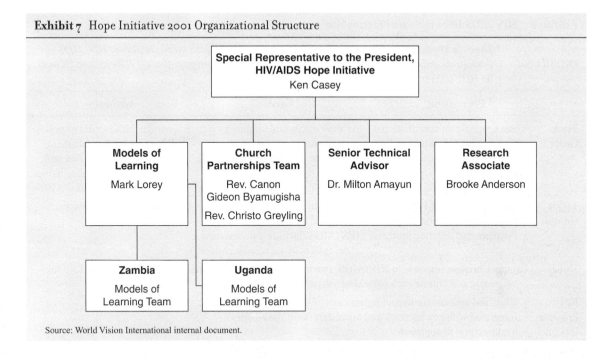

Source: World Vision International internal document.

Casey described the response to his first six months in the field: "Program officers were working flat out on existing projects and we came in telling them that, while those are important, we want you to change your whole focus. In addition, most program officers were skilled in technical sectors such as water, education, and economic development. Few knew about HIV/AIDS work. Their practical response was, 'It's not our expertise. What can we really do about AIDS?'"

Casey hired two teams of HIV/AIDS specialists, one in Uganda and one in Zambia, to create a "Models of Learning" program. He also hired a research associate to work out of the international office (see **Exhibit 7**). Hoping to build an active learning tool for the rest of the field, they prepared models of programming that they hoped to make available to others. But early response from a number of national offices was muted. "In the face of the overwhelming need and workload, many felt that this was just the emphasis of the day. Wait it out and it would go away," Casey explained. After all, it

was not the first time that field offices had been asked to implement cross-organizational strategies, as Myers recalled:

In the mid-1990s, we embarked on a long and expensive process of rebranding. Many national offices plunged time and resources into the effort but got little value out of it. And a subsequent initiative to move relief activities from the center out into the national offices ran into difficulty trying to mix the cowboy culture of the relief teams with the slower culture of the development teams on the front lines. Not surprisingly, some national offices are wary of any new top-down initiative—particularly now that they have so much independence.

The South African Conference

In December of 2001, Casey released a first draft of the Hope Initiative matrix (see **Exhibit 8** for a later version), which had been developed over months of dialogue and meetings with key personnel from across the partnership. It laid out the goals, beneficiaries, values, and key design principles for each of the three HIV/AIDS program areas: prevention,

Exhibit 8   HIV/AIDS Hope Initiative Program Matrix

Overall Goal	*The overall goal of the HIV/AIDS Hope Initiative is to reduce the global impact of HIV/AIDS through the enhancement and expansion of the World Vision programs and collaborations focused on HIV/AIDS prevention, care and advocacy.*		
	Prevention	**Care**	**Advocacy**
Track Goals	Make a significant contribution to the reduction of national HIV/AIDS prevalence rates	Achieve measurable improvements in the quality of life of children affected by HIV/AIDS	Encourage the adoption of policy and programs that minimize the spread of HIV/AIDS and maximize care for those living with or affected by HIV/AIDS
Target Groups	• Children, aged 5–15 years old • High-risk population groups • Pregnant and lactating mothers	Vulnerable Children (living with, affected by and orphaned by HIV/AIDS, including parents and caregivers of vulnerable children)	Policymakers (local, national, and international)
Values	Bring a Christian response to HIV/AIDS, one that reflects God's unconditional, compassionate love for all people and affirms each individual's dignity and worth.		
Key Program Design Principles	• Clear and measurable impact indicators • Integrated with key agencies and organizations in the country • Multisectoral in approach • Scalable—the ability to impact a large number of people • Empower, engage, and equip the local church as a primary partner, as well as other faith-based organizations • Integrated with WV national office program strategies		

Source: World Vision International internal documents.

care, and advocacy. An accompanying document outlined actions that would seek to meet several goals. First, it would aim to prevent new cases of HIV/AIDS by contributing to the reduction of national incidence rates, especially among children, high-risk groups, and pregnant and lactating mothers. Second, it would aim to provide measurable improvements in the quality of care for children affected by HIV/AIDS, including those orphaned by AIDS, living with HIV-positive parents, and in households fostering AIDS orphans. Finally, it would advocate the adoption of public policy and programs that would minimize the spread of the disease and provide care for those living with or affected by HIV/AIDS.

On January 12, 2002, the real rollout for the Hope Initiative was about to begin at a weeklong high-prevalence country workshop held at a safari lodge in South Africa. Casey's goal was to bring together the national directors, senior program officers, and area development managers from the 17 African countries hardest hit by the crisis. He planned to ask them to tackle the HIV/AIDS problem with the same energy with which they worked to bring communities clean water, education, health care, food security, and economic development. "It was a make-or-break time for the initiative," said Casey. "Without their energy and buy-in, the initiative would only exist on paper."

Reading 4-1   Making Global Strategies Work

W. Chan Kim
Renée A. Mauborgne

It is hardly a novel insight that global competitive forces compel multinationals to fully leverage the distinctive resources, knowledge, and expertise residing in their subsidiary operations. Questions of what are "winning" global strategic moves for the modern multinational have increasingly intoxicated international executives.[1] Yet for all the fanfare about global strategies and their increasingly undeniable link to multinational success, little has been said or written about how to make global strategies work. The key question we address here is just that: What does it take for multinationals to successfully execute global strategies?

Our research results paint a striking picture of the importance of the strategy-making process itself for effective global strategy execution. Over the last four years, we have done extensive research to understand how multinationals can successfully implement global strategies. Because subsidiary top managers are the key catalysts for, or obstacles preventing, global strategy execution, we asked them directly just what it was that motivated them to execute or to defy their companies' global strategic decisions.

W. Chan Kim is associate professor of strategy and international management, INSEAD. Renée A. Mauborgne is research associate of management and international business, INSEAD.

Special thanks are due to Sumantra Ghoshal, Philippe Haspeslagh, and Michael Scott Morton. Their comments greatly improved this paper. Special thanks are also due to INSEAD, especially Associate Dean Yves Doz, for generous financial support of this research.

[1]For an excellent review of the literature on global strategy, see: S. Ghoshal, "Global Strategy: An Organizing Framework," *Strategic Management Journal* 8 (1987): 425–440.

Subsidiary top managers were quick to rattle off a series of well-established implementation mechanisms: incentive compensation, monitoring systems, and rewards and punishments. They were equally quick to add that they did not believe these control mechanisms alone to be either sufficient or that effective. The general consensus was that these mechanisms were not particularly motivating and were easy to dodge and cheat. Even more recurrent in our discussions, however, were the dynamics of the global strategic decision-making process itself. When deciding whether or to what extent to carry out global strategies, subsidiary top managers accorded great importance to the way in which those strategies were generated. Their overriding concern involved a deceptively simple though evidently profound principle: due process should be exercised in the global strategic decision-making process.

In practical terms, due process means: (1) that the head office is familiar with subsidiaries' local situations; (2) that two-way communication exists in the global strategy-making process; (3) that the head office is relatively consistent in making decisions across subsidiary units; (4) that subsidiary units can legitimately challenge the head office's strategic views and decisions; and (5) that subsidiary units receive an explanation for final strategic decisions.

In short, we observed that, in the absence of these factors, subsidiary top managers were often upset and negatively disposed toward resulting strategic decisions. However, in the presence of these factors, the reaction was just the reverse. Subsidiary top managers were favorably disposed toward resulting decisions, thought them wise, and were motivated to implement them even if, and here is the biggest benefit of all, these decisions were not in line with their individual subsidiary units' interests.

We begin this paper by probing in depth just what subsidiary top managers mean by due process and why they judge its exercise important in the

Figure 1   What Is Due Process in Global Strategic Decision Making?

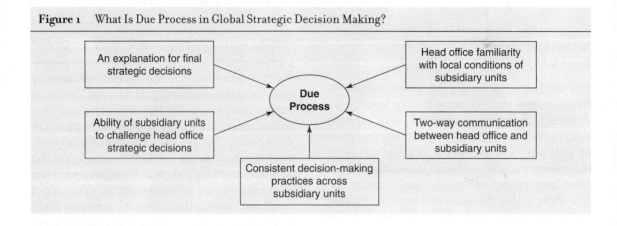

global strategy-making process. Next we examine what leads subsidiary top managers to view traditional implementation mechanisms as increasingly insufficient for global strategies. Finally, we trace the real effects of due process in global strategy making on global strategy execution and explore why they are so profound.

The Meaning of Due Process

To get to the heart of how multinationals can make global strategies work, we held extensive interviews with sixty-three subsidiary presidents.[2] Our initial objective was to get subsidiary presidents' honest evaluation of the factors that drove them to carry out or resist their organizations' global strategic decisions. As the interviews progressed, the one tendency that stood out was the subsidiary presidents' natural inclination to discuss how global strategies were generated. Time and

again, the dynamics of the global strategy-making process itself were the centerpiece of their discussions. Their principal concern was whether due process was exercised. That is, was the strategy-making process fair from the subsidiary unit perspective?

Through these interviews, we identified the five characteristics above that, taken together, defined due process in global strategic decision making (see Figure 1).[3] What is interesting is that these five characteristics were important regardless of the industry or the subsidiary's strategic importance. Appendix A profiles our sixty-three subsidiary presidents and discusses how they were selected. Here we discuss each of the characteristics and examine through the eyes of subsidiary top managers what makes each of them vital.

Head Office's Familiarity with Local Conditions

> The head office does not know a damn thing about what's going on down here. They tell me to further push their global "core" products even at the expense of our existing product lines. And you know what I

[2]For an extensive discussion on our field study, see: W.C. Kim and R.A. Mauborgne, "Implementing Global Strategies: The Role of Procedural Justice," *Strategic Management Journal* 12 (1991): 125–143; and W.C. Kim and R.A. Mauborgne, "Procedural Justice Theory and the Multinational Organization," in *Organization Theory and the Multinational Corporation,* eds. S. Ghoshal and E. Westney (London: MacMillan, 1993).

[3]The Q-sort technique was used to define the meaning of due process in global strategic decision making. For a detailed explanation of this process, see: Kim and Mauborgne (1991 and 1993a).

tell them? I tell them they're crazy. They don't realize that not only don't these "core" products sell in our local market but that we are already losing sales on our existing product lines from tough local competitors due to our lack of push on them.

This statement indicates subsidiary top managers' attitudes when the head office lacks knowledge of the local market. One manager explains why local familiarity is important:

The head office needs to invest in understanding the local market. How can I respect their decisions and follow them if I don't believe that they are made with an understanding of the local market?

When subsidiary managers believe the head office has a reasonable grasp of the local situation, they are apt to make statements like this one:

I have tremendous faith and trust in the head office's strategic decisions. They know the local market. When they make a decision, they understand the ramifications of that decision, be those ramifications good or bad. Whether I like their decisions or not, there's at least a method to their madness.

What it comes down to is that in the absence of local familiarity, subsidiary top managers do not judge the head office to be competent and sincere. They tend to think of the head office instead as incapable and apathetic toward their foreign operation. As a consequence, these managers have little respect for the decisions coming down. They quickly become skeptical of the soundness and quality of the resulting global strategies. This provides an excellent excuse for not only why they do not implement global strategies but why they should not. As one executive put it, "To not follow the global strategic decisions handed down to a subsidiary unit is not a curse but a blessing in disguise. Those decisions aren't based on reality; they are based on air." At the most, local familiarity gives confidence that global strategies are based on thoughtful analyses; at the least, it prevents subsidiary managers from using this seemingly reasonable justification for not executing global strategic decisions.

Two-Way Communication   When global strategic decisions are being made that affect a subsidiary unit, subsidiary top managers value the ability to voice their opinion and work back and forth with the head office in decision formulation. This communication symbolizes the respect the head office has for subsidiary units as well as the confidence it places in subsidiary managers' opinions and insights.

Our observation is that this respect and confidence is quickly reciprocated by subsidiary top managers as well. Although two-way communication often results in heated debates, it also builds a profound spirit of comradeship, unity, and mutual trust among the head office and subsidiary top management teams. Moreover, when subsidiary managers participate in global strategic decision making, they come to view the decisions as their own. As a result, they often defend and uphold these decisions. As one executive commented:

The open exchange of information and ideas is critical in global strategy making. It opens the ears of managers in both the head office and subsidiary units and typically results in better value judgments. When we [subsidiary managers] feel that our views are given sufficient attention, we are less likely to be dissatisfied with global strategic decisions or to feel antagonistic toward the head office and are better motivated to act rigorously to carry out the agreed-upon plan of action.

Consistent Decision-Making Practices   Consider two opposing comments made by different executives. One says:

Our global strategic decision making is a very political process. If you are on the "inside track," the head office treats you as a relatively important element of global strategic decision making. But if not, you and your unit are likely to be completely overlooked and just slapped with a set of strategic decisions that are supposed to be implemented. At times, I think the whole process is just a scam, a politicians' arena where strategic decisions reflect not competitive and economic dynamics but the dynamics of political interplay.

The other says:

Admittedly subsidiary units don't walk away with symmetric decision outcomes—one subsidiary unit may get what seems to be a windfall allocation of resources while another may take a cut. But all subsidiary units are treated relatively consistently when it comes to how these decisions are reached. It's a fair process. There doesn't seem to be much favoritism or political jockeying in this decision-making process.

These two comments shed light on why consistent decision-making practices across subsidiary units are a prized aspect of due process. Basically, they are thought to minimize the degree of politics and favoritism in the strategy generation process. Subsidiary managers are confident that there is a level playing field across subsidiary units. And this is important. Subsidiary managers do not expect the strategic decisions made across subsidiary units to be identical, as they understand that units are not equally important for the organization. But they do view the consistent application of decision-making rules as an essential element of due process.

In the absence of consistency, subsidiary managers are quick to judge the decision-making process as arbitrary, politically rigged, and hence not to be trusted. They find the confusion and uncertainty extremely frustrating, and they are inclined to attribute unfavorable strategic decisions to unfair decision rules as opposed to competitive and economic dynamics. Consequently, they become bitter and resentful and more apt to want to undermine resulting decisions.

Ability to Refute Decisions   Having the ability to refute the head office's strategic views and decisions also makes subsidiary managers feel that due process is being exercised. Admittedly this can be traced in part to managers' perceived increase in influence over strategic decisions, but our discussions suggest another reason why the ability to refute is important. It makes managers feel that the process is fair simply because they can clearly point out possible misperceptions or wrong assumptions made by head office managers concerning local conditions or subsidiary operations. But more than

this, the ability to challenge head office decisions inspires subsidiary managers to more willingly follow these decisions because they know that if the decisions should prove unreasonable or wrongheaded, the possibility always exists to correct them. As one executive explained:

When I know I have the right to openly challenge the head office's decisions, that automatically tells me that the head office is confident in their decisions, that they have faith that their underlying logic and analyses can stand the test of open scrutiny. But it also tells me that, despite the head office's confidence, they also recognize that being removed from the local market opens up the possibility that they will judge the local situation incorrectly. Not only do I respect the head office for this, but it in turn gives me confidence that the intentions and global strategic decisions of the head office are truly made in the interests of the overall organization and not based on politics.

An Explanation for Final Decisions   Subsidiary top managers think it only fair that the head office give them an explanation for final global strategic decisions. And they consider it an important aspect of due process. In short, subsidiary managers need an intellectual understanding of the rationale driving ultimate decisions. They want to know why they should carry out the decisions. This is especially true if those decisions override their expressed views or seem unfavorable to their own unit. To quote one executive:

When the head office provides an explanation for why decisions are made as they are, they provide evidence that they acted in a fair and impartial manner. This signals to me that the head office has at least considered the subsidiary point of view before they may have rejected it. When I understand why final strategic decisions are made as they are, I'm more inclined to implement those decisions even if I don't particularly view them as favorable.

What Makes Due Process Important for Global Strategy Execution

As our interviews with subsidiary presidents progressed and the meaning of due process became clear, a second equally important trend became visible: those managers who believed that due process was exercised in the firms' global strategy-making process were the same executives who trusted their head offices significantly, who were highly committed to their organizations, who felt a sense of comradeship or unity with the corporate center, and who were motivated to execute not only the letter but also the spirit of the decisions. That is, not only did subsidiary presidents articulate the importance of due process in global strategy making, but their attitudes and behavior were significantly affected by its perceived presence or absence. And not just any attitudes or behavior, but attitudes and behavior that determine the success or failure of global strategy execution.

A review of some of the most popular global strategic prescriptions makes this point clear. They are as follows: locate each value-added activity in the country that has the least cost for the factor that activity uses most intensely;[4] dexterously shift capital and resources across national markets, cross-subsidizing global units, to knock out global competitors;[5] institutionalize fully standardized product offerings, marketing approaches, and commonly used distribution systems worldwide to allow for maximum global efficiencies;[6] and, as argued recently, consciously consolidate worldwide knowledge, technology, marketing, and production skills to build reservoirs of distinctive core competencies that can act as engines for continuous new business development, innovation, and enhanced customer value.[7]

[4]B. Kogut, "Designing Global Strategies: Comparative and Competitive Value-Added Chains," *Sloan Management Review,* Summer 1985, pp. 15–28; and M.E. Porter, "Competition in Global Industries: A Conceptual Framework," in *Competition in Global Industries,* ed. M.E. Porter (Boston: Harvard Business School Press, 1986).
[5]G. Hamel and C.K. Prahalad, "Do You Really Have a Global Strategy?" *Harvard Business Review,* July–August 1985, pp. 139–148; and W.C. Kim and R.A. Mauborgne, "Becoming an Effective Global Competitor," *The Journal of Business Strategy,* January–February 1988, pp. 33–37.
[6]T. Levitt, "The Globalization of Markets," *Harvard Business Review,* May–June 1983, pp. 92–102; and G.S. Yip, "Global Strategy . . . In a World of Nations?" *Sloan Management Review,* Fall 1989, pp. 29–41.
[7]C.K. Prahalad and G. Hamel, "The Core Competence of the Corporation," *Harvard Business Review,* May–June 1990, pp. 79–91.

Each of these global strategic prescriptions is different. There is no one formula for success. Different global competitive and economic dynamics will always dictate different and multiple routes to success. Yet a fundamental thread runs through and unites each of these prescriptions, and that is the underlying condition necessary for the effective execution of each strategy.

Ask about any of these purported global strategies: What does it take to successfully execute it? Time and again the answer involves three underlying requirements: (1) the increasing sacrifice of subsystem for system priorities and considerations; (2) swift actions in a globally coordinated manner; and (3) effective and efficient exchange relations among the nodes of the multinational's global network. Which is to say that to implement global strategies, multinationals need subsidiary managers with a sense of commitment, trust, and social harmony. Organizational commitment inspires these managers to identify with the multinational's global objectives and to exert effort, accept responsibility, and exercise initiative on behalf of the overall organization—despite potential "costs" at the subsidiary unit level. Trust is essential to work out mutual wills in the multinational. It inspires subsidiary managers to more readily accept in good faith the intentions, actions, and decisions of the head office instead of second guessing, procrastinating, and opportunistically haggling over each directive. Which is to say that trust is necessary for quick and coordinated global actions. Lastly, social harmony is essential to strengthen the social fabric among members of global units. It encourages efficient and effective exchange relations, which have fast become indispensable to effective global strategy execution.

These salutary attitudes, however, are not in and of themselves sufficient to make global strategies work. Beyond this, multinationals need to ensure that subsidiary managers actually engage in not only compulsory but also voluntary execution of strategic decisions. By compulsory execution, we mean carrying out the directives of global strategic decisions in accordance with the multinational's formally required standards—satisfying, to the letter, the stipulated responsibilities. In contrast, by voluntary execution, we mean exerting effort beyond that which is formally required to execute decisions to the best of one's abilities. Put differently, it is the effort subsidiary top managers exert beyond the call of duty to implement global strategic decisions.[8]

What all this suggests is that the exercise of due process in global strategic decision making represents a potentially powerful though unexplored route to the implementation of global strategies. Not only do subsidiary top managers emphasize the importance of fairness and impartiality in global strategic decision making, they are so obsessed by the existence or nonexistence of due process that it profoundly affects their attitudes and behavior— attitudes and behavior that are virtually indispensable to making global strategies work. We are talking about commitment, trust, social harmony, and the motivation to execute not only the letter but also the spirit of decisions—that is, to engage in compulsory and voluntary execution of strategic decisions.

But what about other implementation mechanisms? Are traditional implementation mechanisms alone not sufficient for the effective execution of global strategies? If not, how does due process support these traditional mechanisms to make global strategies work?

Traditional Implementation Mechanisms

As mentioned earlier, when we asked subsidiary presidents what motivated them to implement or to defy global strategic decisions, they typically began with a list of well-established administrative mechanisms. Most of them mentioned incentive compensation, monitoring systems, the fist of the head

office, and the magnitude and precision of rewards and punishments. But as our discussions progressed, we found subsidiary presidents eager to add that they did not believe these implementation tools alone to be either sufficient or effective. For one thing, they were not particularly motivating. For another, the tools were increasingly easy to dodge and cheat.

Not Motivating?

I am not saying that rewards and punishments and auditing systems are useless in the implementation process. They certainly are useful. If the head office could assess exactly to what extent I followed global strategic decisions and rewarded me based precisely on that behavior, it would be a lie to say that this would not act as an incentive to execute global strategies. It would. It's just that this would not motivate me to do more than is absolutely necessary to satisfy the minimum requirements of global strategic decisions. It wouldn't inspire me to exert energy, exercise initiative, or to take on tasks that I am not directly compensated for in the execution of global strategies.

This comment, made by one executive, is representative of the general opinion of most of the subsidiary presidents we interviewed. Save for a few specific cases, we discovered that a reliance on instrumental approaches produced a utilitarian, contractual attitude toward compliance.[9] Stated succinctly: to the extent that subsidiary top managers judge that the head office can carefully monitor their behavior and will accurately allocate rewards and punishments, managers have an incentive to satisfy the minimum requirements of global strategic decisions. No more, no less. Instrumental approaches have the power to encourage only compulsory execution—execution to the letter, not to the spirit, of the decisions. The trouble, as we have already argued, is that to make global strategies work, subsidiary managers cannot simply "execute

---

[8]For an extensive discussion of these two forms of compliance, both the conceptual distinction between them and their theoretical root, see: C. O'Reilly and J. Chatman, "Organizational Commitment and Psychological Attachment: The Effects of Compliance, Identification, and Internalization on Prosocial Behavior," *Journal of Applied Psychology* 71 (1986): 492–499; and P.M. Blau and W.R. Scott, *Formal Organizations* (San Francisco, California: Chandler Publishing Company, 1962), pp. 140–141.

[9]That a reliance on instrumental approaches to compliance leads to utilitarian contractual attitude toward involvement relations finds strong support in the award-winning article: J. Kerr and J.W. Slocum, "Managing Corporate Culture through Reward Systems," *Academy of Management Executive* 1 (1987), 99–108.

this" or "undertake that" in some highly prescribed manner. Their actions must be secured less by rational calculations of individual gain than by kinship obligations. What we are talking about is voluntary execution. An example will bring this to life.

The Case of Global Learning   Global learning—the ability of a multinational to transfer the knowledge and expertise developed in each part of its global network to all other parts worldwide—has fast become an essential strategic asset.[10] For global learning to be actualized, we argue that nothing less than an affirmative attitude toward cooperation will suffice—that is, voluntary execution. One reason for this is that knowledge and expertise are often viewed as power and as such are not easily shared. Another reason is that the major benefits of internal diffusion of know-how accrue to recipients, not transmitters. Of course, were it possible for subsidiary units to "sell" their knowledge and expertise to other subsidiary units, these problems might be overcome. However, this is often and perhaps usually infeasible. As know-how is largely an intangible asset, its value to a "purchasing" unit cannot be known until the purchaser has it, but once the knowledge is disclosed, the purchaser has acquired it without cost.[11] In the absence of economic incentives and with the presence of perceived power disincentives to diffuse knowledge and expertise, it follows that full-blown global learning will not transpire as long as quid pro quo attitudes toward strategy execution prevail. Rather, the hoarding and withholding of knowledge and expertise are far more likely.

Easy to Dodge and Cheat?   Beyond the fact that subsidiary managers do not consider these instrumental approaches to be that motivating is the reality that managers increasingly find these tools easy to

dodge and cheat. And if they are easy to dodge and cheat, they are truly ineffective. Basically, the decline in their effectiveness can be explained by the collapse of the three distinctive features of hierarchy in the modern multinational. These three features are: (1) appraisal and control capability; (2) the power of the head office; and (3) common values and expectations.[12] Traditional implementation tools are increasingly easy to dodge as these hierarchical features collapse.[13] Let us take a quick look at the forces leading to the demise of these features.

Collapse of Appraisal and Control Capability International executives are witnessing a collapse in the multinationals' appraisal and control capability. Although, in theory, information systems can be designed to meet the complexity of any organization or situation, in reality, they are having a tough time meeting the modern multinational's demands. The predominant reason for this is the rapid increase in horizontal linkages and interdependencies across subsidiary units. As subsidiary units increasingly share resources and work together on single projects to realize global economies of scale and scope, the unique performance and contribution of each subsidiary unit is increasingly difficult to decipher.[14] Distinctions between faulty and meritorious performance are becoming tenuous. Confusion opens the door for shirking, opportunistic behavior and conflict. Moreover, this problem is made even more severe by the escalating size of most multinationals. The corporate center is limited in its ability to make accurate evaluations of each subsidiary unit.

Eroding Power of the Head Office   No longer do centrally directed orders elicit easy obedience from

[10]C.A. Bartlett and S. Ghoshal, "Managing across Borders: New Strategic Requirements," *Sloan Management Review,* Summer 1987, pp. 7–16; and S. Ghoshal and C.A. Bartlett, "Creation, Adoption, and Diffusion of Innovations by Subsidiaries of Multinational Corporations," *Journal of International Business Studies,* Fall 1988, pp. 365–388.

[11]K.J. Arrow, "The Organization of Economic Activity," *The Analysis and Evaluation of Public Expenditure: The PPB System* (Joint Economic Committee, Ninety-first Congress, First Session, 1969), pp. 59–73.

[12]For a brilliant discussion on the distinctive powers of hierarchy and internal organization, see: O.E. Williamson, *Markets and Hierarchies: Analysis and Antitrust Implications* (New York: Free Press, 1975).

[13]See the perspicacious article by Hedlund for further support for this argument: G. Hedlund, "The Hypermodern MNC-A Heterarchy?" *Human Resource Management* 25 (1986), pp. 9–25.

[14]For an extensive discussion on the ways in which interdependencies and joint efforts confound accountability and create monitoring difficulties, see: G.R. Jones and C.W.L. Hill, "Transaction Cost Analysis of Strategy-Structure Choice," *Strategic Management Journal* 9 (1988), pp. 159–172.

Figure 2   The Collapse of Hierarchy in the Modern Multinational Corporation

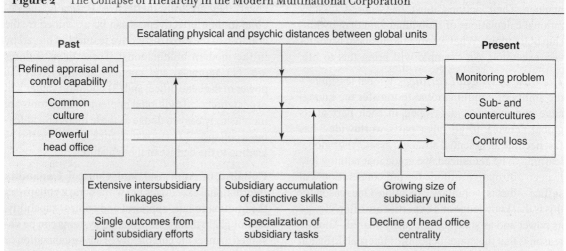

subsidiary units. One reason for the erosion in the head office's hierarchical power is subsidiary units' increasing size and resource parity. Subsidiaries are less reliant on the head office, and the head office is more dependent on subsidiary units. To the extent that dependence decreases power, the corporate center and overseas units are converging in power.[15] This situation is aggravated further by the mounting intensity of direct subsidiary-to-subsidiary linkages, which lessens the head office's centrality.[16]

Decline in Common Values and Expectations
As subsidiary units have increasingly accumulated distinct resources and capabilities in response to their different task environments, they have developed values and behavioral norms distinct from those in the home office.[17] On top of this, the non-trivial physical and psychic distances increasingly

separating overseas units from corporate centers fuel even further the emergence of subcultures and countercultures within the modern multinational. The result is more antagonistic relations between head office and subsidiary top management teams and a natural inclination on the part of subsidiary managers to pursue subsidiary-level objectives.[18]

The upshot of all this is that the distinctive features of hierarchy in the multinational used to support traditional implementation mechanisms are increasingly collapsing. As shown in Figure 2, the emergence of a monitoring problem, the intensification of sub- and countercultures, and mounting control loss increasingly plague the multinational, making its traditional implementation tools less and less effective.

How Does Due Process Support Traditional Implementation Mechanisms?   Although traditional implementation tools have become on the whole less effective, the extent to which this is true appears to be contingent in part on whether due process is exercised. Recall for a moment the due process characteristics. Two-way communication, the ability to refute the head office's viewpoints, and

[15]For an excellent discussion on the inverse relationship between power and dependence, see, for example: R.M. Emerson, "Power-Dependence Relations," *American Sociological Review* 27 (1962), pp. 31–41.

[16]For a discussion on the ways in which centrality affects power relations, see: L.C. Freeman, "Centrality in Social Networks: Conceptual Clarification," *Social Networks* 2 (1979), pp. 215–239.

[17]That business units or divisions accumulation of distinct capabilities and tasks reinforces distinct values and behavioral norms was empirically validated. See: P.R. Lawrence and J.W. Lorsch, *Organization and Environment* (Boston: Harvard University Press, 1967).

[18]See Hedlund (1986) for further elaboration of this point.

an accounting for final strategic decisions all foster open interaction and intensive information exchange between head office and subsidiary top managers. This open interaction almost forces the head office to keep rewards, punishments, and appraisal and control systems aligned with strategic decisions. An example will make this point clear.

One subsidiary president we interviewed had been requested to institute an aggressive price-reductions policy in his local market. The strategic aim was to counter an assertive price attack launched by global competitor in his company's home market. The subsidiary president understood that the execution of such a policy would benefit the overall organization—it would drain the resources of the global competitor's profit sanctuary, its home market. He also knew, however, that the policy would likely result in negative financial performance by his local operation.

The open interaction between him and the head office allowed him to address his concern directly. He stated that he understood why it was necessary for his unit to institute such a policy and that he would accept such a global strategic mission. But he argued that the execution of this mission would invalidate a sole reliance on "stand-alone" financial criteria for assessing his subsidiary unit's performance. He proposed having his unit's performance evaluated also by the strategic contribution it made to the overall organization. The head office managers and subsidiary president were able to develop a mutually acceptable set of performance evaluation criteria for his unit. In this way, the exercise of due process spurs the head office to keep traditional implementation tools aligned with strategic decisions.

Lessons from Our Field Observations

We can draw two overriding lessons from our field observations. The first is that the multinational increasingly faces a dilemma in executing its global strategies. On the one hand, the effective implementation of global strategies requires a sense of community and cooperation among all the nodes of the multinational's global network. On the other hand, multinationals are experiencing a loss in

hierarchical control and an increasing independence of subsidiary units, which creates an environment of calculative, utilitarian, and frictional interunit relations. This is not particularly conducive to efficient and effective exchange. In the face of this *multinational dilemma,* we need more than traditional implementation mechanisms to make global strategies work.

The second lesson is that the exercise of due process in global strategy making seems to be a powerful, yet unexplored, way to overcome the multinational dilemma and make global strategies work. This is traceable to two sources. The first is that due process helps to overcome the exchange difficulties in the multinational by inspiring a sense of commitment, trust, and social harmony among subsidiary top managers. The second is that, beyond these salutary attitudes, the exercise of due process inspires subsidiary top managers to more readily execute strategic decisions to not only the letter but also the spirit with which they were set forth.

The Tangible Effect of Due Process

At the end of our interviews, we presented our findings to the subsidiary presidents' head office managers. These head office managers found our results fascinating and provocative. They were intrigued by our proposition that instrumental calculations of gains and losses were not the dominant driver behind subsidiary managers' actions and found it particularly interesting that subsidiary managers had placed so much emphasis on the importance of due process in global strategy making. According to these executives, it was a challenging proposition that the presence or absence of due process had the power to influence not only the important attitudes of commitment, trust, and social harmony but also subsidiary managers' actual execution of resulting decisions.

Nonetheless, despite the executives' overall excitement with our findings, underneath this ran a current of hesitation. To quote one executive:

> Your findings are provocative. But to institute due process in global strategy making is a time-consuming,

difficult task. Before I start to embark on such an attempt, I would like to have more evidence of the tangible benefits of due process than just the observations made and insights gained from your field research.

This hesitation was valid. It challenged us to go beyond our field work and empirically test our propositions. This meant conducting an extensive mail survey to develop a bigger database that could test the validity of our field observations. In short, we set out to examine whether due process exercised a positive overall effect not only on the commitment, trust, and social harmony of subsidiary top managers but also on compulsory and voluntary execution. We also set out to test whether these effects were significantly stronger or particularly potent in those subsidiary managers who received unfavorable strategic decision outcomes vis-à-vis those who received favorable outcomes. Appendix B presents a profile of our sample population, the measurements used to estimate each variable, and the type of analyses we employed.

The Results   The results of our regression analyses confirmed our observation that due process in global strategy making is indeed positively related to subsidiary managers' sense of organizational commitment, trust in head office management, and social harmony between them and the head office. All slope coefficients proved to be statistically significantly $(p < .01)$,[19] which is to say that the more subsidiary managers believe that due process is exercised in the global strategy-making process, the more positive attitudes they have toward head office management and the organization as a whole.

Beyond this, we also found a positive relationship between due process and compulsory and voluntary execution. All slope coefficients again proved to be statistically significant $(p < .01)$. This provides evidence that the exercise of due process does more than inspire positive attitudes. It also triggers subsidiary managers to "go the extra mile" and carry out the spirit of global strategic decisions.

More interesting from an implementation perspective, however, are the results of another analysis. We wanted to see the effect of due process when subsidiary managers judged strategic decisions to be favorable or unfavorable for their unit. By strategic decisions we mean the strategic roles, resources, and responsibilities received by subsidiary units as a result of the last annual global strategy-making process.

During the course of our interviews, one of the most fascinating things we observed was that the effect of due process on subsidiary managers' attitudes and behavior was particularly strong precisely in those individuals who received decision outcomes viewed as unfavorable. Put differently, due process provided an especially strong "cushion of support" that mitigated the negative ramifications of unfavorable decisions by significantly inflating positive attitudes and behavior within recipients of unfavorable outcomes.[20] Figures 3a through 3c show the average commitment, trust, and social harmony scores for subsidiary top managers receiving favorable versus unfavorable strategic decision outcomes. As the figures consistently reveal, when decision outcomes were viewed as unfavorable, the exercise of due process did much to check discontent and to give "loser" subsidiary managers powerful reasons to stay committed to their organization (in Figure 3a, the mean commitment score increases from 3.2 to 5.9; $p < .01$), to have trust in head office

---

[19]That the exercise of due process or, as it is often referred to, procedural justice, has the power to effectuate the higher-order attitudes of commitment, trust, and social harmony finds theoretical and empirical support in other settings. See, for example: S. Alexander and M. Ruderman, "The Role of Procedural and Distributive Justice in Organizational Behavior," *Social Psychology Research* 1 (1987), pp. 177–198; and R. Folger and M. Konovsky, "Effects of Procedural and Distributive Justice on Reactions to Pay Raise Decision," *Academy of Management Journal* 32 (1989), pp. 115–130; and E.A. Lind and T.R. Tyler, *The Psychology of Procedural Justice* (New York: Plenum, 1988).

[20]This "cushion of support" effect not only finds support in the existing procedural justice literature but is recognized to be one of the most important effects of procedural justice or due process. See, for example: Lind and Tyler (1988); and T.R. Tyler, *Why People Obey the Law: Procedural Justice, Legitimacy, and Compliance* (New Haven, CT: Yale University Press, 1990).

Figure 3a   Due Process and Organizational Commitment

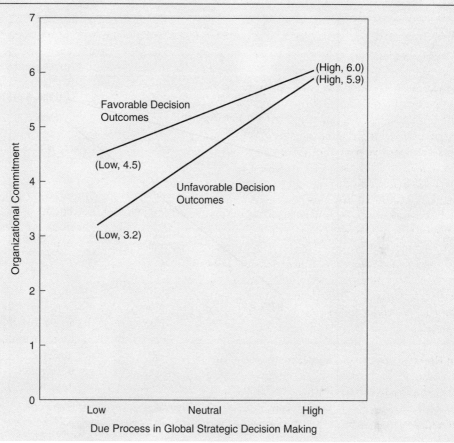

management (in Figure 3b, the mean trust score increases from 2.0 to 5.3; $p < .01$), and to cultivate an atmosphere of social harmony between them and the head office (in Figure 3c, the mean social harmony score increases from 2.3 to 4.7; $p < .01$). On the other hand, when outcomes were viewed as favorable, the due process effect, although undeniably present, was not as potent as with unfavorable outcomes. In particular, as due process heightened, the mean score for commitment increased from 4.5 to 6.0 ($p < .01$), that for trust from 4.4 to 5.6 ($p < .05$), and that for social harmony from 3.5 to 4.8 ($p < .05$). For all three salutary attitudes, the slope

coefficient differential between the favorable outcome and the unfavorable outcome group also proved to be statistically significant ($p < .01$).[21]

[21] We examined and confirmed the statistical difference in the due process effect between the favorable outcome and the unfavorable outcome group for organizational commitment, trust in head office management, and social harmony. This was done using what econometricians call the Chow test, which is able to examine the statistical significance in slope differentials between the groups. In our case, test statistics of F values for all three salutary attitudes were significant at the 1 percent level and hence indicated to reject the null hypotheses that no slope coefficient difference exists between the favorable outcome and the unfavorable outcome group. For a detailed discussion on the Chow test, see: G.C. Chow, "Tests of Equality between Subsets of Coefficients in Two Linear Regression," *Econometrica* (1960), pp. 591–605.

Figure 3b Due Process and Trust in Head Office Management

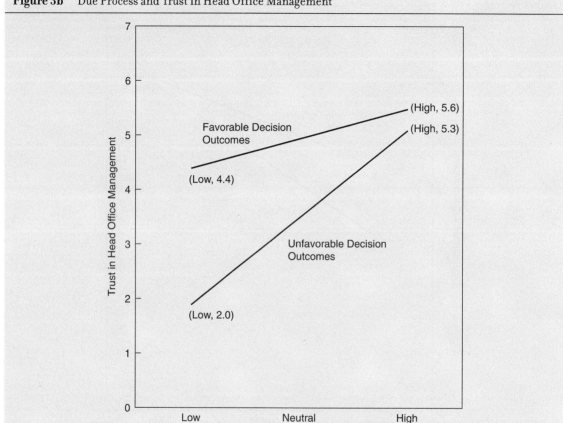

Figures 4a and 4b present the average compulsory and voluntary execution scores for subsidiary top managers receiving favorable versus unfavorable strategic decision outcomes. As Figure 4a reveals, the use of due process in global strategic decision making indeed appears to boost compulsory execution in managers who receive unfavorable decision outcomes to a greater extent than in those who receive favorable outcomes. Specifically, when decision outcomes were judged unfavorable, the exercise of due process did much to motivate subsidiary managers to perform the strategic roles and responsibilities assigned to their unit in accordance with the organization's formal requirements (mean compulsory execution score increased from 3.8 to 5.7; $p < .01$). On the other hand, when outcomes were viewed as favorable, the due process effect on compulsory execution, although undeniably present, was not as potent (mean score increased from 5.2 to 6.2; $p < .05$). The slope coefficient differential between the favorable outcome and the unfavorable outcome group proved to be statistically significant ($p < .05$).[22]

---

[22] The F value for compulsory execution was significant at the 5 percent level and hence indicated to reject the null hypothesis that no slope coefficient difference exists between the favorable outcome and the unfavorable outcome group. Ibid.

Figure 3c   Due Process and Social Harmony

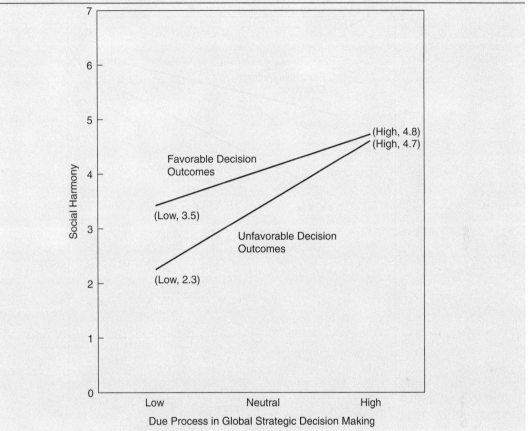

The same cannot be said, however, for voluntary execution. On the one hand, the voluntary execution of all subsidiary top managers significantly escalates as due process increases (in Figure 4b, mean voluntary execution score increases from 2.4 to 5.2 for recipients of unfavorable outcomes and from 2.9 to 5.5 for recipients of favorable outcomes; both significant at $p < .01$). On the other hand, the effect of due process on voluntary execution does not vary whether the decision outcomes are favorable or not. For voluntary execution, the slope coefficient differential between the favorable outcome and the unfavorable outcome group proved to be statistically not significant

$(p > .10)$.[23] These findings indicate that although decision outcomes do not seem to affect subsidiary managers' voluntary execution, the exercise of due process does inspire these managers to go beyond the call of duty to implement strategic decisions. This is further supported by our regression result that decision outcomes had no relationship with voluntary execution; the regression coefficient for this relationship was not statistically significant $(p > .10)$.

[23] The F value for voluntary execution was not significant $(p > .10)$ and hence indicated not to reject the null hypothesis that no slope coefficient difference exists between the favorable outcome and the unfavorable outcome group. Ibid.

Figure 4.a   Due Process and Compulsory Execution

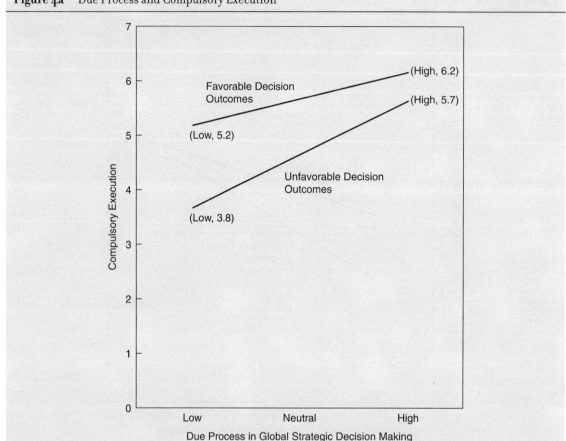

In summary, except in the case of voluntary execution, with a low level of due process, there is a big gap between the attitudes and behavior of subsidiary top managers with favorable and unfavorable decision outcomes.[24] As expected, with a low level of due process, subsidiary managers with unfavorable decision outcomes were generally dissatisfied with the head office and the overall organization and consequently felt a low level of commitment, trust, and social harmony. Not surprisingly, these same managers were not highly

motivated to execute global strategic decisions to the letter or spirit with which they were set forth.

However, with a high level of due process, the picture was different. There was little gap between those managers who had received favorable and unfavorable decision outcomes in their reported scores of commitment, trust, and social harmony and compulsory and voluntary execution; all these gaps proved to be statistically not significant ($p > .10$). Hence, the gap was significantly reduced as due process heightened. Which is to say that the power of due process is strong enough to overcome the negative ramifications of unfavorable outcomes and even inspires in those subsidiary top managers

[24]Variance analysis was employed to assess the statistical significance in the mean difference between the groups.

Figure 4.b   Due Process and Voluntary Execution

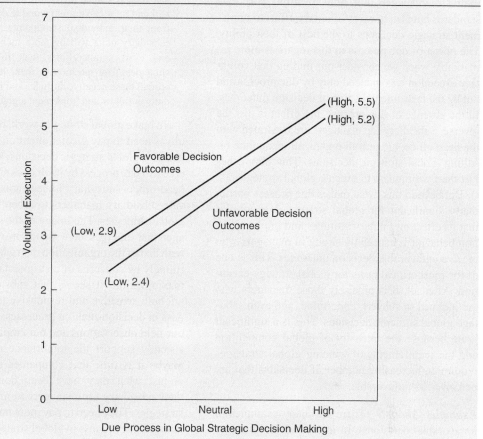

the positive disposition necessary for global strategy execution. Moreover, whether managers received favorable or unfavorable outcomes, their degree of commitment, trust, and social harmony and compulsory and voluntary execution was much higher when due process was exercised in global strategy making than when it was not. Hence, our empirical tests strongly support our field observations.

Conclusion

How can multinationals make global strategies work? The results of this research suggest that the answer resides in the quality of the global strategy-making process itself. When deciding whether or

not or to what extent to carry out global strategic decisions, subsidiary top managers accord great importance to the way in which global strategies are generated. Their overriding concern: Is due process exercised in the global strategy-making process?

In the presence of due process, subsidiary managers are motivated to implement global strategies. They feel a strong sense of organizational commitment, trust in head office management, and social harmony with their head office counterparts. These attitudes are not only important, they are the fundamental requirements for making global strategies work. Further, the exercise of due process translates directly into a high level of compulsory and voluntary execution, which is to say that due process motivates managers not only to fulfill corporate standards but also to exert voluntary effort to implement strategic decisions to the best of their ability. The power of due process in this regard is more remarkable when we consider our finding that voluntary execution was induced only by due process and not by the instrumental value of decision outcomes. In the absence of due process, the effect is just the reverse. Subsidiary top managers are frustrated with the head office, the overall organization, and the resulting global strategic decisions. This diminishes fast their willingness to execute global strategies.

But beyond this, what makes due process particularly significant for global strategy execution is that its effect on salutary attitudes and implementation behavior is especially strong in managers who receive unfavorable decision outcomes. This is one of the most critical tasks for global strategy execution. After all, it is precisely those managers who are inclined to subvert, undermine, and even sabotage global strategic decisions. This is a significant issue because the intensity of global competition and the requirements of winning global strategies require an increasing number of decisions that are perceived as unfavorable.

Examples Abound   There are many examples of unfavorable decisions. In one multinational we studied, subsidiary units were recently asked to forgo their national products in favor of global core products that many units considered to be either overstandardized or overpriced for their national markets. In another multinational, the U.S. subsidiary was required to transfer a large portion of its export sales to its sister European subsidiaries. Although this substitution substantially increased capacity utilization rates in Europe and decreased the losses suffered from overcapacity there, as one U.S. executive put it, "The transfer was nothing but a loss for us." And so the list goes, endlessly on. To cite one executive:

> Our modern enterprises live in a world of global competition. The key to win here is to think globally and fully leverage our globally dispersed resources, skills, and knowledge. It is important to maximize our

efficiency at the global level. To achieve this, it is unavoidable that an increasing number of subsidiaries will end up receiving unfavorable decision outcomes from their individual standpoints. No doubt, these subsidiary units will be more inclined to foot-drag and exert counterefforts than to execute global strategies. The question is then, how can we turn around these negative attitudes and inspire subsidiary units to follow and implement a global approach?

To make global strategies work, head office executives need to pay greater attention to the way they generate global strategic decisions. Although the exercise of due process by itself does not make difficult head office–subsidiary issues vanish, it does motivate subsidiary managers to accept and implement global strategies. The image of the subsidiary manager that emerges here stands in marked contrast with that of the organization man who is driven overridingly by concerns of instrumental and economic maximization. It seems that subsidiary managers are both sensitive and responsive to issues of fairness in decision-making processes. Given that both our field observations and our empirical study consistently support the importance of due process, maybe it is time that companies seriously reflect on just what they have been doing to motivate their subsidiary top managers to implement global strategies. They need to pay more heed to the importance of due process in global strategy making.

Appendix A

How did we conduct our field research? We solicited the participation of twenty-five multinationals by means of direct and indirect personal contacts with head office senior executives. Nineteen of these multinationals agreed to support this research, and they gave us the names of the subsidiary presidents heading their ten largest subsidiary operations in terms of annual sales. The dominant industries of these nineteen multinationals were: computers (five firms), packaged foods (four), electrical products (four), pharmaceuticals (three), automobiles (one), paper and wood products (one), and textiles (one).

We were able to successfully contact, via telephone, 141 of the subsidiary presidents. We guaranteed that all comments would be held strictly confidential and used solely for scientific research and that their head office managers would not be informed as to which subsidiary presidents ultimately participated in our study. Sixty-three of these subsidiary presidents were willing to participate. The remaining subsidiary presidents declined, most frequently because of a lack of time. We then held extensive interviews.

Appendix B

Sample Population We distributed the mail questionnaire to 195 subsidiary top managers. This pool comprised the 63 subsidiary presidents who participated in our field research and 132 other subsidiary top managers who directly participated in the last annual global strategic decision-making process between the head office and their national unit. The latter were also members of our nineteen original participation multinationals; their names were supplied by the 63 subsidiary presidents.[25] The titles of the subsidiary top managers ranged from president to executive vice president to director. These executives were considered to represent the key catalysts for global strategy execution in their national units.

We distributed the questionnaire within six weeks of the completion of the last annual global strategic decision-making process of our nineteen participating multinationals. Of the 195 questionnaires distributed, 142 were returned to the researchers. The questionnaire assessed the extent of due process in the last strategy-making process, subsidiary top managers' attitudes of organizational commitment, trust, and social harmony, and the perceived favorability of strategic decision outcomes.

Ten months later, just before the start of another annual global strategic decision-making process, we distributed a second questionnaire to the 142 managers who responded to our first-round questionnaire. In this one, we assessed subsidiary top managers' compulsory and voluntary execution of the global strategic decisions resulting from the preceding annual strategy-making process. Of these, 119 questionnaires were returned to the researchers and used in our analysis of the relationship between due process and compulsory and voluntary execution.[26]

Measurements

Due Process To assess whether or to what extent due process was exercised in global strategic decision making, we used a five-item measure in our survey questionnaire.[27] This involved having subsidiary top managers evaluate on a seven-point Likert-type scale each of the five identified aspects of due process, in short: (1) the extent to which the head office is knowledgeable of the subsidiary unit's local situation; (2) the extent to which two-way communication exists in the process; (3) the extent to which the head office is fairly consistent in making global strategic decisions across subsidiary units; (4) the extent to which subsidiary top managers can legitimately challenge the strategic views and decisions of the head office; and (5) the extent to which subsidiary top managers receive a full explanation for global strategic decisions.[28] The Cronbach's coefficient alpha for this five-item scale was .86.[29]

---

[25]For an extensive discussion on the design and administration of our mail questionnaire, see: Kim and Mauborgne (1991 and 1993a).

[26]For an extensive discussion on the design and administration of the second-wave questionnaire of our longitudinal study on subsidiary top managers' strategy execution, see: W.C. Kim and R.A. Mauborgne, "Procedural Justice, Attitudes, and Subsidiary Top Management Compliance with Multinationals' Corporate Strategic Decisions," *Academy of Management Journal,* forthcoming, June 1993b.

[27]Kim and Mauborgne (1991 and 1993a).

[28]We averaged the scores for these multiple items to estimate our due process measure. The same procedure was used for all of our other multi-item measures: organizational commitment, trust, social harmony, and strategic decision outcome favorability. For a detailed discussion on why this simple averaging approach yields an unbiased estimate, see: H.M. Blalock, "Multiple Indicators and the Causal Approach to Measurement Error," *American Journal of Sociology* 75 (1969), pp. 264–272.

[29]The Cronbach's coefficient alpha indicates the internal consistency reliability of a scale. Generally, a multi-item scale can be judged to be reliable when the value of its Cronbach alpha exceeds 0.70. Notice here that besides our due process measure, all of our other multi-item scales can be said to be reliable. For a detailed discussion on a measure's reliability, see: J. Nunnally, *Psychometric Methods* (New York: McGraw-Hill, 1978).

Organizational Commitment   Nine items were used to assess the top managers' organizational commitment.[30] Sample items include, "I am willing to put in a great deal of effort beyond that normally expected in order to help this organization be successful," and "This organization really inspires the very best in me in the way of job performance." All items were assessed on a seven-point scale with anchors labeled (1) strongly disagree and (7) strongly agree. The Cronbach's coefficient alpha for this nine-item scale was .91.

Trust in Head Office Management   To measure the trust subsidiary top managers have in the head office, we used four questions.[31] These are:

1. How much confidence and trust do you have in head office management?

2. Head office management at times must make decisions that seem to be against the interests of your unit. When this happens, how much trust do you have that your unit's current sacrifice will be justified by the head office's future support for your unit?

3. How willing are you to accept and follow those strategic decisions made by head office management?

4. How free do you feel to discuss with head office management the problems and difficulties faced by your unit without fear of jeopardizing your position or having your comment "held against" you later on?

Again, all four items were measured on seven-point scales. The Cronbach's coefficient alpha for this four-item scale was 94.

Social Harmony   A four-item measure assessed the perceived social harmony between head office

and subsidiary top managers.[32] The managers were asked to think of their relations with head office management when answering the following items: (1) how well they help each other out; (2) how well they get along with one another; (3) how well they stick together; and (4) the extent to which conflict characterizes their relations. These items were measured on seven-point scales with the fourth item reversely scored. The Cronbach's coefficient alpha for this four-item scale was .87.

Strategic Decision Outcome Favorability   Four items assessed the perceived favorability of global strategic decisions received by subsidiary units as a result of the last annual global strategic decision-making process.[33] Subsidiary top managers were asked to assess the extent to which the global strategic roles, responsibilities, and resources allocated to their unit: (1) reflected their unit's individual performance achieved; (2) mirrored their unit's relative contribution to the overall organization; (3) exceeded their unit's expectations; and (4) were absolutely favorable. All four items were measured on seven-point scales. The Cronbach's coefficient alpha for this four-item scale was .83.

Compulsory Execution   To assess the extent to which each subsidiary top manager carried out global strategic decisions in accordance with their formally required corporate standards, two questions were posed. First, for each of eight major activities (marketing and sales, research and development, manufacturing, purchasing, cost-reduction programs, general cash-flow utilization, human resource management, and other administrative activities), subsidiary top managers were asked to respond on a seven-point (1 = not at all, 7 = completely) scale to the following question: "Please try to recall as accurately as possible your overall

[30] The nine-item measure used to assess organizational commitment was developed by: R.T. Mowday, R.M. Steers, and L.W. Porter, "The Measurement of Organizational Commitment," *Journal of Vocational Behavior* 14 (1979), pp. 224–247.

[31] The items used to measure trust were drawn from the interpersonal trust measures of: W.H. Read, "Upward Communication in Industrial Hierarchies," *Human Relations* 15 (1962): 3–15; and R. Likert, *The Human Organization* (New York: McGraw-Hill, 1967).

[32] The indicators used to measure social harmony were drawn from the cohesiveness index developed by: S.E. Seashore, *Group Cohesiveness in the Industrial Work Group* (Ann Arbor: University of Michigan Press, 1954); and C. Cammann, M. Fichman, G. Douglas, and J.R. Klesh, "Assessing Attitudes and Perceptions of Organizational Members," in *Assessing Organizational Change,* eds. S.E. Seashore, E.E. Lawler, P.H. Mirvis, and C. Cammann (New York: John Wiley & Sons, 1983).

[33] The four-item measure used to assess strategic decision outcome favorability was originally developed by: Kim and Mauborgne (1991).

behavior and actions taken since the preceding annual global strategic-decision process between the head office and your national unit. Then for each of the eight outlined activities indicate the extent to which you executed these decisions in accordance with your organization's required standards. Note that you should not include in this assessment any efforts that may have been extended beyond your organization's required standards in order to achieve optimum performance in these activities." Organization was defined here as the multinational.

For each of these eight activities, we then had subsidiary top management rate on a five-point scale, ranging from "1 = not important" to "5 = extremely important," the degree of importance of each of these activities to the successful fulfillment of their overall job requirements. This assessment is important because although each of our respondents was a top manager with overarching responsibilities for and involvement in overall subsidiary unit operations across these activities, many reported having full responsibility for some activities but having only limited responsibility in the sense of giving final approval in other activities. Accordingly, to assess the extent of each manager's compulsory execution, these importance ratings were used as weights to reflect each activity's relative contribution or importance to the fulfillment of each manager's overall job requirements. Using these weights, we then obtained each manager's weighted-average compulsory execution score. Specifically, for each manager, we first multiplied the manager's compulsory execution score on each of the eight activities by his or her corresponding importance ratings and then added these weighted execution scores. Finally, we divided this added figure back by the sum of these importance ratings to arrive at each manager's weighted-average compulsory execution score.[34]

Voluntary Execution   To assess the extent to which subsidiary top managers exerted voluntary effort to carry out global strategic decisions to the best of their abilities, we used a similar approach to that used in our assessment of compulsory execution. First, for each of the eight major activities, the managers were asked to respond on a seven-point scale (1 = not at all, 7 = greatly) to the following question: "Please try to recall as accurately as possible your overall behavior and actions taken since the preceding annual global strategic decision process between the head office and your national unit. Then for each of the eight outlined activities indicate the extent to which you voluntarily exerted effort beyond the formally required standards of your organization to execute global strategic decisions to the best of your abilities. Rephrased, to what extent did you willingly exert energy, exercise initiative, and devote your effort beyond that which is formally required to achieve optimum performance in your execution of global strategic decisions in each of these activities?"

Using the same question on dimensional importance described above for compulsory execution to obtain weights, we derived a weighted-average measure of each manager's voluntary execution of global strategic decisions. The process used to derive this weighted-average measure of voluntary execution mirrors that used to arrive at our weighted-average measure of compulsory execution.[35]

Analyses   We used two tests to establish the effect of due process on the managers' attitudes and behavior. First, we performed regression analyses to see whether due process positively correlated with the managers' attitudes of organizational commitment, trust in head office management, and social harmony between them and head office management and whether due process was also related to the managers' compulsory and voluntary execution of the resulting decisions.

---

[34]The use of a multidimensional approach with criterion weights to measure both compulsory and voluntary execution is in line with Steers's advice and seemed particularly appropriate for taking into account subsidiary top managers' different levels of involvement in carrying out these activities and hence their different levels of contribution to the execution of these activities in accordance with their formal job requirements. See: R.M. Steers, "Problems in the Measurement of Organizational Effectiveness," *Administrative Science Quarterly* 20 (1975), pp. 546–558.

[35]Ibid.

Second, we tested whether due process produces a "cushion of support" that enhances salutary attitudes and execution to a greater extent in those managers who received unfavorable decision outcomes than those who received favorable outcomes. To perform this test, we first divided respondents into two groups based on the perceived favorability or unfavorability of strategic decision outcomes received in the last annual strategy-making process. Those managers with outcome favorability scores above the sample mean were classified as recipients of favorable strategic-decision outcomes; those below the sample mean were classified as recipients of unfavorable outcomes. We then further split our respondents based on the perceived degree of due process exercised. Respondents with due process scores above the sample mean were treated as experiencing a high level of due process, whereas those having due process scores below the sample mean were treated as experiencing a low level of due process. Finally, we calculated and compared the mean levels of reported organizational commitment, trust in head office management, social harmony, and compulsory and voluntary execution for each of our four groups: the high outcome favorability–high due process group; the high outcome favorability–low due process group; the low outcome favorability–high due process group; and the low outcome favorability–low due process group. As is described in the article, we used variance analysis and the slope coefficient differential test to test differences between these four groups. We observed no evidence for systematic differences in contextual variables such as industry type and subsidiary size across these four groups.

Reading 4-2   Building Ambidexterity into an Organization

Julian Birkinshaw and Cristina Gibson

The technological downturn, political turmoil and economic uncertainty of the last five years have reaffirmed to managers the importance of *adaptability*—the ability to move quickly toward new opportunities, to adjust to volatile markets and

▌ Julian Birkinshaw is an associate professor of strategic and international management at London Business School and a Fellow of the Advanced Institute of Management Research. Cristina Gibson is an assistant professor or organization and strategy at the Graduate School of Management, University of California, Irvine. Contact them at jbirkinshaw@london.edu and cgibson@uci.edu

▌ We acknowledge the contributions of James O'Toole, Tom Williams and others at Booz Allen Hamilton Inc., the World Economic Forum and the Center for Effective Organizations.

to avoid complacency. But while adaptability is important, it is not enough. Successful companies are not just nimble, innovative and proactive; they are also good at exploiting the value of their proprietary assets, rolling out existing business models quickly and taking the costs out of existing operations. They have, in other words, an equally important capability we call *alignment*—a clear sense of how value is being created in the short term and how activities should be coordinated and streamlined to deliver that value.

For a company to succeed over the long term, it needs to master both adaptability and alignment—an attribute that is sometimes referred to as *ambidexterity*.[1] For example, Finland's Nokia Corp. is trying out a vast array of new mobile technology

About the Research

Ambidexterity has been seen as a desirable organizational trait for decades, but the concept has typically been associated only with the structural separation of activities. We offer a complementary way of thinking about ambidexterity that sees it emerging through a company's organizational context as well as through its structure.

Our research was conducted over a three-year period in cooperation with researchers from the Center for Effective Organizations (Marshall School of Business, University of Southern California) and Booz Allen Hamilton Inc., and with the collaboration of the World Economic Forum. We adopted a systematic, multiphase research design, consisting of (1) interviews with top executives in 10 multinational companies; (2) interviews in two to seven business units in each corporation; (3) development of a detailed survey to measure organization context, ambidexterity and performance; (4) administration of the survey to a stratified, random sample of 50–500 employees at four hierarchical levels in each business unit; (5) identification and understanding of the key context characteristics through qualitative analysis of interview notes and quantitative analysis of survey data; and (6) feedback sessions in each company. The total number of survey respondents was 4,195 individuals across 41 business units in the 10 multinational companies.

Ambidexterity and Performance

To examine the link between ambidexterity and performance, we surveyed two separate groups of individuals. In each business, we interviewed midlevel managers about their company's alignment and adaptability, asking them to rate a variety of factors. We then multiplied the overall alignment and adaptability ratings to arrive at a measure of the company's ambidexterity. Similarly, we then asked a set of senior managers to rate business performance. We examined the correlation between ambidexterity and performance across the 41 business units and found it to be highly significant ($r = 0.76, p < 0.01$), as shown below.

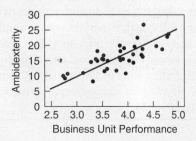

Note: Business unit performance is measured on a scale from 1 (very low) to 7 (very high). Ambidexterity is the product of alignment and adaptability, each one measured on a scale from 1 (very low) to 7 (very high).

Organizational Context and Ambidexterity

The second stage of statistical analysis sought to test two hypotheses. The first argued that a supportive organizational context—characterized by a combination of performance management and social support—would be associated with a higher level of ambidexterity. To test this, we asked respondents questions about a range of contextual factors, out of which we created two indexes—one for performance management, the other for social support. We multiplied these two to create an overall index for organizational context. The correlation between organizational context and ambidexterity across the 41 business units was highly significant ($r = 0.55, p < 0.01$), as shown on next page.

The second hypothesis argued that ambidexterity would mediate the relationship between organizational context and performance. To test this, we undertook a series of regression analyses, which showed that (a) ambidexterity is correlated with performance, (b) organizational context is correlated with ambidexterity, (c) organizational context is correlated with performance and, the critical step, (d) when ambidexterity and organizational context *together* are analyzed as predictors of performance, only ambidexterity has a significant influence. This is known as *full mediation,* and it demonstrates that the influence of organizational context on performance only occurs through the creation of ambidexterity.

For a full description of the research and statistical analyses, please refer to C.B. Gibson and J. Birkinshaw, "The Antecedents, Consequences and Mediating Role of Organizational Ambidexterity," *Academy of Management Journal* 47, no. 2 (2004): 209–226.

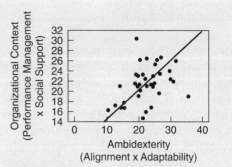

Note: Ambidexterity is the product of alignment and adaptability, each one measured on a scale from 1 (very low) to 7 (very high). Organizational context is the product of performance management and social support, each one measured on a scale from 1 (very low) to 7 (very high).

offerings, while continuing to invest in its dominant handsets franchise. GlaxoSmithKline Plc is experimenting with alternative organization models, alliance partners and technologies in its search for new blockbuster drugs, and it is also pushing hard to maximize the return from its existing drug portfolio.

The trouble is, it's difficult to find the right balance between adaptability and alignment. Focus too much on alignment and the short-term results will look good, but changes in the industry will blindside you sooner or later. Lloyds TSB Bank Plc, based in the United Kingdom, delivered spectacular shareholder returns throughout the 1980s and 1990s, in large part through CEO Brian Pitman's single-minded focus on return on equity. But little attention was paid to understanding changing customer needs or to the morale of the workforce, which ultimately undermined the company's performance. From 1998 to 2003, Lloyds TSB lost 60% of its market value.

Similarly, too much attention to the adaptability side of the equation means building tomorrow's business at the expense of today's. Consider the case of Sweden's Ericsson, which has led the technological development of the mobile telephony industry. Ericsson developed one of the first analog mobile systems; it led the industrywide development of the global system for mobile communica-

tion; and it has pioneered general packet radio system and third-generation mobile technology standards. But the impressive growth in sales in Ericsson's systems business masked a high-cost and bloated organizational structure. At its peak, the R&D organization employed 30,000 people in approximately 100 technology centers with considerable duplication of effort. Adaptability, in other words, had taken precedent over alignment, and the subsequent crash in the telecom industry meant that Ericsson was hit harder than most. Since its peak in 2000, Ericsson has laid off around 60,000 employees and closed most of its technology centers in a bid to restore the profitability of its current businesses.

Two Forms of Ambidexterity

The concept of organizational ambidexterity has been around for years, but the evidence suggests that many companies have struggled to apply it. The standard approach is to create *structural ambidexterity,* that is, to create separate structures for different types of activities.[2] For example, the core business units are given responsibility for creating alignment with the existing products and markets; and the R&D department and business development group are given the job of prospecting for new markets, developing new technologies and keeping track of emerging industry trends. Structural separation is necessary, the argument goes, because the two sets of activities are so dramatically different that they cannot effectively coexist.

But separation also can lead to isolation, and many R&D and business-development groups have failed to get their ideas accepted because of their lack of linkages to the core businesses. Many companies have experimented with variants of the structural ambidexterity model. Some pull individuals out of their current jobs to work in a dedicated cross-functional team for a limited period of time. Others separate the different types of activities within a single business unit—for example, they create a small business-development team attached to a business unit. These approaches avoid the extreme form of separation that is typical of dual structures. But they nonetheless remain top-down in nature in that they rely on business-unit managers to judge how best to divide employees' time between one set of activities and another.

In an attempt to shed new light on the phenomenon, we have developed and explored the concept of *contextual ambidexterity*,[3] which calls for individual employees to make choices between alignment-oriented and adaptation-oriented activities in the context of their day-to-day work. (See "About the Research.") In business units that are either solely aligned *or* solely adaptive, employees have clear mandates and are rewarded accordingly. But in a business unit that is ambidextrous, the systems and structures are more flexible, allowing employees to use their own judgment as to how they divide their time between adaptation-oriented and alignment-oriented activities. For example, should they focus on current customer accounts to meet quota, or should they nurture new customers with slightly different needs? To foster this sort of ambidexterity on the individual level, a much greater level of attention has to be paid to the human side of the organization.

Contextual ambidexterity differs from structural ambidexterity in many important ways (see "Structural Ambidexterity vs. Contextual Ambidexterity," p. 425), but the two approaches are best viewed as complementary. Indeed, many successful companies, including Hewlett-Packard, 3M and Intel, use a combination of both approaches to deliver simultaneously on the needs for alignment and adaptability.

Contextual Ambidexterity   Our research, which included interviews with a wide variety of employees, ranging from senior executives to front-line workers, identified four ambidextrous behaviors in individuals:

Ambidextrous Individuals Take the Initiative and Are Alert to Opportunities Beyond the Confines of Their Own Jobs   For example, a regional sales manager for a large computer company, in discussions with one large client, became aware of the need for a new software module that no company currently offered. Rather than try to sell the client something else or just pass the lead on to the business development team, he took it upon himself to work up a business case for the new module; once he received the goahead, he moved full time into the development of the product.

Ambidextrous Individuals Are Cooperative and Seek Out Opportunities to Combine Their Efforts with Others   A large beverage company's marketing manager for Italy was primarily involved in supporting a newly acquired subsidiary, and she was frustrated with the lack of contact she had with her peers in other countries. Rather than wait for someone at headquarters to act, she began discussions with peers in other countries that led to the creation of a European marketing forum. This group met quarterly to discuss issues, share best practices and collaborate on marketing plans.

Ambidextrous Individuals Are Brokers, Always Looking to Build Internal Linkages   On a routine visit to the head office in St. Louis, a Canadian plant manager for a large consumer products company heard discussions about plans for a $10 million investment in a new tape manufacturing plant. He inquired further into these plans, and on his return to Canada, he called a regional manager in Manitoba, who he knew was looking for ways of building his business. With some generous support from the Manitoba government, the regional manager bid for, and ultimately won, the $10 million investment.

Ambidextrous Individuals Are Multitaskers Who Are Comfortable Wearing More than One Hat

For example, the operations manager in France for a major coffee and tea distributor was initially charged with making that plant run as efficiently as possible, but he took it upon himself to identify new value-added services for his clients. He developed a dual role for himself, managing operations four days a week and on the fifth developing a promising electronic module that automatically reported impending problems inside a coffee vending machine. He arranged corporate funding, found a subcontractor to develop the software and then piloted the module in his own operations. The module worked so well that operations managers in several other countries subsequently adopted it.

These four attributes—which collectively describe an ambidextrous employee—have several important commonalities. First, they constitute acting outside the narrow confines of one's job and taking actions in the broader interests of the organization. Second, they describe individuals who are sufficiently motivated and informed to act sponta-

neously, without seeking permission or support from their superiors. Third, they encourage action that involves adaptation to new opportunities but is clearly aligned with the overall strategy of the business. Such behaviors are the essence of ambidexterity—and they illustrate how a dual capacity for alignment and adaptability can be woven into the fabric of an organization on the individual level.

Still, an individual's ability to exhibit ambidexterity is facilitated (or constrained) by the organizational context in which he or she operates, so contextual ambidexterity can also be diagnosed and understood as a higher-order organizational capability. At the *organizational level,* contextual ambidexterity can be defined as the collective orientation of the employees toward the simultaneous pursuit of alignment and adaptability. It is manifested in the behaviors of hundreds of individuals in the ways described above and in the unwritten routines that develop in organizations. In this respect it is analogous to the well-established concept of *market orientation,* which is a collective orientation of people throughout a business toward the gathering, interpretation and dissemination of market knowledge.[4] And just as with market orientation, ambidexterity is a potentially important capability for contributing to long-term performance.

	Structural Ambidexterity	**Contextual Ambidexterity**
Structural Ambidexterity vs. Contextual Ambidexterity		
How is ambidexterity achieved?	Alignment-focused and adaptability-focused activities are done in separate units or teams	Individual employees divide their time between alignment-focused and adaptability-focused activities
Where are decisions made about the split between alignment and adaptability?	At the top of the organization	On the front line—by salespeople, plant supervisors, office workers
Role of top management	To define the structure, to make trade-offs between alignment and adaptability	To develop the organizational context in which individuals act
Nature of roles	Relatively clearly defined	Relatively flexible
Skills of employees	More specialists	More generalists

The traditional view of organizational ambidexterity revolves around a structural separation of initiatives and activities. The notion of contextual ambidexterity, which manifests on an individual level, represents a complementary process.

So what does an ambidextrous organization look like? There are numerous paths to ambidexterity, but consider two examples from companies whose units rated very high in our research on both contextual ambidexterity and performance.

Renault, the French automobile company, went through a radical transformation during the 1990s. When Louis Schweitzer became CEO in 1992, the state-owned company was languishing. Schweitzer cut costs through a number of well-publicized plant closures, but he also invested in new-product development (leading to such models as the Espace and Megane) and began the search for a strategic partner to take Renault into the top tier of the industry. After an abortive merger with Volvo in 1993, Renault gained control of a struggling Nissan in 1998 and, to the surprise of many observers, quickly turned around its performance. By 2001, the Renault-Nissan Alliance had joined the ranks of industry leaders and was one of the most profitable auto companies in the world.

How did the transformation take place? Schweitzer developed a simple and consistent strategy built around what he called the "seven strategic goals." The strategic planning and budgeting processes, and the bonuses and stock option plans, were all aligned with these goals. The communication of the message was, in the words of one executive, "doggedly consistent."

At the same time, the company developed what one executive called a "deep desire to adapt." The seven strategic goals were updated every two or three years, the organization had an informal style of management in which expressing alternative views was encouraged and managers developed a self-critical approach, always looking to improve. The result was an organization that became proficient at continually making small adaptations to its strategy without losing alignment.

As a second example, Oracle Corp. is the leading enterprise software company in the world with more than $10 billion in revenues. Oracle's rapid growth, and the continuing presence of its founder, Larry Ellison, created an entrepreneurial style of management that eschewed formal structures and processes wherever possible. And perhaps because of this, the concept of ambidexterity sits easily with its senior executives. As one of them put it, "We align around adaptability."

The company has shown a "remarkable ability to turn on a dime." Consider Oracle's shift into e-business in 1999 and its current shift into services. Oracle achieved this adaptability by hiring very smart people, setting aggressive but not unrealistic targets and avoiding too much formalization. As one executive explained, "Moving at this high rate of speed makes it impossible to maintain formal processes. Instead, a lot of people are making unilateral decisions." At the same time, though, the objectives, goal setting programs and incentive systems are carefully aligned. "Employees in all lines of business have a clear idea of the company's objectives," observed one manager.

Renault and Oracle are not alone. Tesco Plc, the leading grocery chain in the United Kingdom, delivers industry-leading profit margins through a well-aligned operational strategy while continuing to push the development of new store concepts and new product lines. 3M Co. is famous for its highly innovative work practices, also delivering impressive margins through its systematic financial control and continuous improvement systems. An ambidextrous organizational context can be achieved through a variety of means, but they all share one thing in common: They enable individuals in the organization to exhibit initiative, cooperation, brokering skills and multitasking abilities.

Building Contextual Ambidexterity

How can managers begin to think about building contextual ambidexterity into their organizations? Sumantra Ghoshal and Chris Bartlett define context as the often invisible set of stimuli and pressures that motivate people to act in a certain way.[5] Along that line of thinking, top managers shape organizational context through the systems, incentives and controls they put in place and through the actions they take on a day-to-day basis. It is then reinforced through the behaviors and attitudes of people throughout the organization.

Ghoshal and Bartlett argue that four sets of attributes—stretch, discipline, support and trust—interact to define an organization's context. In combination, these attributes create two dimensions of organizational context: The first, *performance management* (a combination of stretch and discipline), is concerned with stimulating people to deliver high-quality results and making them accountable for their actions; the second, *social support* (a combination of support and trust), is concerned with providing people with the security and latitude they need to perform.

Performance management and social support are equally important and mutually reinforcing. The strong presence of each will create a *high-performance organizational context* that gives rise to a truly ambidextrous organization. However, if there is an imbalance in these organizational characteristics, or a lack of both, a less than optimal organizational context will exist. (See "Four Types of Organizational Context.")

For example, a demanding, results-driven orientation that lacks social support will create a *burnout context*. Many people will perform well for a limited time in such a scenario, but its depersonalized, individualistic and authority-driven nature typically results in a high level of employee turnover, making ambidexterity difficult to achieve. Conversely, strong social support without high-performance expectations will engender a *country-club context*[6] in which employees benefit from and enjoy a collegial environment but rarely produce up to their potential. Companies in this position also have low ambidexterity and produce satisfactory but lackluster results. An absence of both a high-performance ethic and social support will, of course, produce a *low-performance organizational context*. Employees are unlikely to be either aligned or adaptive, let alone ambidextrous.

Creating a High-Performance Organizational Context

While performance management and social support factors do not directly create high performance, they do shape the individual and collective behaviors that over time enable ambidexterity, which does lead to superior performance. The challenges of building such a high-performance context are illustrated by the cases of Renault and Oracle.

Renault's transformation during the 1990s involved a shift from the country-club to the high-performance context. Until 1990, employees had viewed the company as a comfortable and secure place to work, with an informal atmosphere. Over the following 10 years, a number of changes were brought about, primarily through top-down initiatives revolving around cost reduction and quality and through greater focus on, and commitment to, key strategic objectives. One executive commented that his business unit was run as a "commando-type organization—appraisal and evaluation interviews are run in a pyramidal form and compensation is [now] geared toward short-term objectives."Most of these changes were instituted through a new executive team that gave people more structure, which led to a focus on new products and new opportunities as a means of delivering on the more ambitious goals. Stated slightly differently, the emphasis during the transition was placed on performance management but building on the social support that had existed in the early 1990s. Indeed, two of

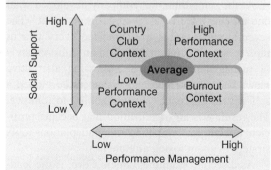

Four Types of Organizational Context

The more a company emphasizes performance management and social support, the more likely are its employees to behave ambidextrously—aligned and adaptive—and the more likely the organization is to achieve high performance. A deficiency of either performance management or social support will create less than optimal contests for ambidexterity.

Schweitzer's seven goals were concerned with the internal organizational context (develop a coherent and open group; work more effectively together).

Compare this to Oracle, which was positioned on the cusp between the high-performance and burnout contexts. Performance expectations were very high, people were well rewarded and the style of working was competitive and aggressive. One executive, for example, compared the business to "the engine of a Ferrari, which revs at very high rpm but can burn out at any minute." But at the same time, employees rated the company moderately high on social support, citing the development of a balanced-scorecard system and the leadership forums at which the top 275 managers gather to share ideas.

The contrast between these two companies raises three critical points:

First, there is no single pathway to ambidexterity: Renault achieved it by building a performance context around its existing social support; Oracle built a performance context first, then looked for ways of building support and trust across the organization.

Second, there is no single leadership model for an ambidextrous organization. Larry Ellison is charismatic and directive; Louis Schweitzer is no less powerful, but he works in a more collegial manner.

Third, despite all their differences, Renault and Oracle both exhibit a clear and simple set of priorities. In our survey analysis, Oracle employees emphasized goal setting, individual performance appraisal and risk management; Renault employees highlighted capital allocation, recruiting and vision. Obviously, the choice of focal elements is important, but even more important, our evidence suggests, is the consistency with which they are applied and the number of employees they affect.

Escaping From Suboptimal Contexts

Many companies find themselves mired in contexts that do not effectively support ambidexterity and high performance. Those companies have to look for ways to engineer dramatic shifts in the behaviors they encourage.

The burnout context, for example, puts so much emphasis on performance management that social support systems are either neglected or never put in place. Eventually, performance suffers as exhausted and disenchanted employees have neither the capacity nor the incentive to execute or innovate. Clifford Chance Llp, the world's largest law firm, had clearly reached this stage in October 2002 when an internal memo was leaked to the press revealing that staff in the New York office were expected to bill 2,420 hours per year—or roughly 10 hours per day. The memo explicitly stated that "the stress of billable hours is dehumanizing and verging on an abdication of our professional responsibilities."

Scotch Inc. (not its real name), one of the largest consumer products companies in the world, provides another example of burnout. Scotch had grown quickly during the late 1990s through a strategy of focusing on a small number of core brands and rolling them out quickly on a global basis. By 2000, however, growth was slowing, and the foreign subsidiary managers were starting to voice some concerns. The managers had limited influence over the positioning of the global brands in their local markets; they were short of resources; and they felt the strategic planning process was too top-down. At the same time, the growth goals were demanding, and there was little or no tolerance for failure. The emphasis on performance management had led to solid growth, but executives were concerned about where the next phase of growth would come from. Scotch senior management recognized the potential for burnout and introduced several initiatives to increase the quality social support offered by the organizational context, including changes to the strategic planning process, introduction of systems for sharing best practices among subsidiaries and refinement of programs for professional development.

The country-club context—in which there is a strong sense of support and trust, but no one works too hard and mediocre performance is tolerated—can be as dysfunctional as the burnout context. Many government agencies, universities and state-owned companies fall naturally into this category

Diagnosing Your Organizational Context

How does your company rate in terms of organizational context? To get a quick indication, answer the questions below, calculate your average scores, and plot your answers on the graph.

EVALUATE PERFORMANCE MANAGEMENT CONTEXT

Managers in my organization . . .	*Not at all*		*Neutral*			*To a very great extent*
Set challenging/aggressive goals	1	2	3	4	5	6	7
Issue creative challenges to their people instead of narrowly defining tasks	1	2	3	4	5	6	7
Make a point of stretching their people	1	2	3	4	5	6	7
Use business goals and performance measures to run their businesses	1	2	3	4	5	6	7
Hold people accountable for their performances	1	2	3	4	5	6	7
Encourage and reward hard work through incentive compensation	1	2	3	4	5	6	7

Average score for performance management context _____

EVALUATE SOCIAL SUPPORT CONTEXT

Managers in my organization . . .	*Not at all*		*Neutral*			*To a very great extent*
Devote considerable effort to developing subordinates	1	2	3	4	5	6	7
Push decisions down to the lowest appropriate level	1	2	3	4	5	6	7
Have access to the information they need to make good decisions	1	2	3	4	5	6	7
Quickly replicate best practices across organizational boundaries	1	2	3	4	5	6	7
Treat failure in a good effort as a learning opportunity, not as something to be ashamed of	1	2	3	4	5	6	7
Are willing and able to take prudent risks	1	2	3	4	5	6	7

Average score for social support context _____

PLOT SCORES ON THE GRAPH

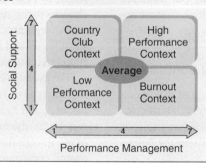

as do a fair number of commercial organizations. For example, Lufthansa AG had such a culture during the late 1980s in large part because, as *the* state-owned airline, it was too important to fail. When Jurgen Weber took over as CEO in 1991, however, he clearly demonstrated that the company was very close to bankruptcy. He put a performance management dimension in place, and the context began to shift toward high performance.[7]

Similarly, Cowes Ltd. (not its real name), a formerly stateowned European dairy-products company, sold farm produce to consumer goods companies, typically within a strict set of regulations and quotas. Faced with impending deregulation, however, Cowes' country-club culture put the company in a noncompetitive position. Senior executives realized this and made two significant changes: They broke the company down into distinct profit and loss units and instituted a pay-for-performance scheme for unit managers, and they introduced innovation processes to seek out new sources of top-line growth.

Although the strategies employed by Scotch, Lufthansa and Cowes were initiated in a top-down fashion, each sought—by emphasizing performance management alongside social support—to create a high-performance context in which ambidextrous behavior on the *individual* level would be encouraged and rewarded.

At some companies, there is not only little concern for performance, but also no sense of trust or support among the employees. That is the worst of both the country-club and burnout syndromes and constitutes a *low-performance context* in which ambidexterity is impossible. For example in one company we studied, there was evidence of inconsistent messages from top management (making it hard to create trust) and a sense that the business lacked the ambition or focus needed to generate stretch. As one manager said, "There is no overarching vision, each division devises its own vision and objectives." In another company, there was evidence of a lack of follow-through when using management systems (making it hard to create discipline). For example, there had been a number of new initiatives, which according to one manager "had lost accountability and steam" within less than a year. Support systems, in terms of providing training, feedback sessions and information across the functions, could be identified in both companies, but were insufficient on their own to develop an effective organizational context.

Companies that find themselves in a low-performance context must place an immediate priority on developing improved performance management. Social support mechanisms can follow well before the risk of burnout becomes an issue.

Pathways to Ambidexterity

For executives who are seeking to build an ambidextrous organization, there are five key lessons that emerge from our work.

Diagnose Your Organizational Context   Before an organization can take steps toward a high-performance context, it must discover where it currently stands in terms of performance management, social support and the balance between the two. A simple diagnostic tool (see "Diagnosing Your Organizational Context") that involves responses from a large cross-section of people throughout the company will produce a basic, helpful quantitative analysis. It can be supplemented with a more qualitative discussion of the context in the organization. To the extent that the two analyses reinforce each other, a reliable picture emerges of what changes need to be made along what lines to move the organization toward high performance.

Focus on a Few Levers, and Employ Them Consistently   We found no evidence that specific organizational levers, such as incentive compensation or risk management, were consistently linked to success. There are many ways to build an organizational context that enables ambidexterity. The higher-performing companies, however, are those that focus consistently on just a few levers. For example, Scotch decided to focus on levers intended to bolster its social support side of the equation: professional development, knowledge transfer and a more participative strategic-planning process. The more consistently those are applied, the easier it will be for employees across the organization to make sense of the changes that are under way. Consistency is crucial since organizational context does not, on its own, create high performance but enables the individual-level ambidexterity that, over time, leads to high performance.

Build Understanding at all Levels of the Company
In our survey research, we found that the lower the respondent was in the corporate hierarchy, the lower he or she rated the organization's ambidextrous characteristics—a pattern we call the erosion effect. Intriguingly, the magnitude of the erosion effect varied with the performance of the company. In lower-performing companies, front-line employees rated elements of organizational context an average of 1.5 points lower on a 7-point scale than did their top-management counterparts. In the more ambidextrous and higher-performing companies, the rating disparity was typically 0.5 points or less.

The interview component of the study revealed that the erosion effect is a measure of the consistency and quality of communication in the organization. That is, for organizational context to be effective in creating ambidexterity, its message has to be disseminated clearly and consistently throughout the organization.Unless lower-level employees genuinely understand the initiatives of top management, the initiatives will have a minimal impact on individuals' capacity for ambidexterity.

View Contextual Ambidexterity and Structural Ambidexterity as Complements   Almost all the previous research on ambidexterity has focused on structural separation between alignment-oriented and adaptability-oriented activities. There is evidence that this approach can be highly effective, but there is also evidence that it can create as many problems as it solves. For example, many large companies, including British American Tobacco, Royal & SunAlliance and British Airways, established corporate venture units during the dot-com boom to nurture new business ideas, but as those units lacked sufficient connective tissue with the

core business, most eventually became isolated and irrelevant to the company's strategy.[8]

Contextual ambidexterity isn't an alternative to structural ambidexterity but rather a complement. Structural separation may at times be essential, but it should also be temporary, a means to give a new initiative the space and resources to get started. The eventual goal should be reintegration with the mainstream organization as quickly as possible. Contextual ambidexterity can enhance both the separation and reintegration processes.

View Contextual Ambidexterity Initiatives as "Driving Leadership," Not as Being "Leadership-Driven"   Ambidexterity arises not just through formal structure or through the vision statements of a charismatic leader. Rather, it is achieved in large part through the creation of a supportive context in which individuals make their own choices about how and where to focus their energies. Leadership, in other words, becomes a characteristic displayed by everyone in the organization.[9] The impetus toward ambidexterity may sometimes be driven by top-down initiatives, but the goal is to allow leadership to emerge from the organization at all levels and for that ubiquitous, emergent leadership to be inherently ambidextrous.

---

[1]A number of business writers have used the term "ambidexterity" over the years. See R.B. Duncan, "The Ambidextrous Organization: Designing Dual Structures for Innovation," in "The Management of Organization Design: Strategies and Implementation. Volume 1," eds. R.H. Kilmann, L.R. Pondy and D. Slevin (New York: North-Holland, 1976), 167-188; E. McDonough III and R. Leifer, "Using Simultaneous Structures To Cope With Uncertainty," Academy of Management Journal 26, no. 4 (1983): 727-735; M.L. Tushman and C.A. O'Reilly III, "The Ambidextrous Organization: Managing Evolutionary and Revolutionary Change," California Management Review 38, no. 4 (1996): 8-30; and C.A. O'Reilly III and M.L. Tushman, "The Ambidextrous Organization," Harvard Business Review 82 (April 2004): 74-82. For a full description of the research and statistical analyses, please refer to C.B. Gibson and J. Birkinshaw, "The Antecedents, Consequences and Mediating Role of Organizational Ambidexterity," Academy of Management Journal 47, no. 2 (2004): 209-226.

[2]Duncan argued that ambidexterity should be managed through "dual structures." The concept of structural separation between different types of activities is also evident in much of the organization literature. See P.R. Lawrence and J.W. Lorsch, "Organization and Environment: Managing Differentiation and Integration" (Boston: Harvard University Press, 1967); P.F. Drucker, "Innovation and Entrepreneurship: Practice

and Principles" (New York: Harper & Row, 1985); and J.R. Galbraith, "Designing the Innovating Organization," Organizational Dynamics 10 (winter 1982): 5-25.

[3] The term "contextual ambidexterity" is new, but a number of similar ideas can be found in the literature. See P.S. Adler, B. Goldoftas and D.I. Levine, "Flexibility Versus Efficiency? A Case Study of Model Changeovers in the Toyota Production System," Organization Science 10 (January 1999): 43-68; and S. Ghoshal and C.A. Bartlett, "Linking Organizational Context and Managerial Action: The Dimensions of Quality of Management," Strategic Management Journal 15 (summer 1994): 91-112.

[4] The concept of market orientation emerged in the early 1990s. See B.J. Jaworski and A.K. Kohli, "Market Orientation: Antecedents and Consequences," Journal of Marketing 57 (July 1993): 53-70; and J.C. Narver & S.F. Slater, "The Effect of a Market Orientation on Business Profitability," Journal of Marketing 54 (October 1990): 20-35.

[5] See S. Ghoshal and C.A. Bartlett, "The Individualized Corporation: A Fundamentally New Approach to Management" (New York: Harper Business, 1997).

[6] The term "country-club context" was first used by Robert Blake and Jane Mouton to describe a particular type of individual in their managerial grid. While their work focused on the individual level of analysis, there are strong parallels with our work on contextual ambidexterity. See R.R. Blake and J.S. Mouton, "Corporate Excellence Through Grid Organization Development: A Systems Approach" (Houston: Gulf Publishing Co., 1968).

[7] This example is taken from H. Bruch and S. Ghoshal, "Lufthansa: The Challenge of Globalization," London Business School teaching case, ECCH no. 396-142-1 (Bedfordshire, United Kingdom: European Case Clearing House, 2000).

[8] See A. Campbell, J. Birkinshaw, A. Morrison and R. van Basten Batenburg, "The Future of Corporate Venturing," MIT Sloan Management Review 45 (fall 2003): 30-37.

[9] For additional insights on this approach to leadership, see J. O'Toole, "When Leadership Is an Organizational Trait" in "The Future of Leadership: Today's Top Leadership Thinkers Speak to Tomorrow's Leaders," eds. W. Bennis, G.M. Spreitzer and T.G. Cummings (San Francisco: Jossey-Bass, 2001); B.A. Pasternack and J. O'Toole, "Yellow-Light Leadership: How the World's Best Companies Manage Uncertainty," Strategy+Business 28 (second quarter 2002); and B.A. Pasternack, P.F. Anderson and T.D. Williams, "Leadership as an Institutional Trait," Strategy+Business 26 (second quarter 2000): 11.

Reading 4-3   Matrix Management: Not a Structure, a Frame of Mind

Christopher A. Bartlett and Sumantra Ghoshal

Top-level managers in many of today's leading corporations are losing control of their companies. The problem is not that they have misjudged the demands created by an increasingly complex environment and an accelerating rate of environmental change, nor even that they have failed to develop strategies appropriate to the new challenges. The problem is that their companies are organizationally incapable of

[*] Christopher A. Bartlett is a professor of general management at the Harvard Business School, where he is also chairman of the International Senior Management program. Sumantra Ghoshal is an associate professor who teaches business policy at the European Institute of Business Administration (INSEAD) in Fontainebleau, France. This article is based on their book, *Managing Across Borders: The Transnational Solution* (Harvard Business School Press, 1989).

carrying out the sophisticated strategies they have developed. Over the past 20 years, strategic thinking has far outdistanced organizational capabilities.

All through the 1980s, companies everywhere were redefining their strategies and reconfiguring their operations in response to such developments as the globalization of markets, the intensification of competition, the acceleration of product life cycles, and the growing complexity of relationships with suppliers, customers, employees, governments, even competitors. But as companies struggled with these changing environmental realities, many fell into one of two traps—one strategic, one structural.

The strategic trap was to implement simple, static solutions to complex and dynamic problems. The bait was often a consultant's siren song promising to simplify or at least minimize complexity and discontinuity. Despite the new demands of overlapping industry boundaries and greatly altered value-added chains, managers were promised success if they would "stick to their knitting." In a swiftly changing international political economy, they were urged to rein in dispersed overseas operations and focus on the triad markets, and in an increasingly intricate and sophisticated competitive environment, they were encouraged to choose between alternative generic strategies—low cost or differentiation.

Yet the strategic reality for most companies was that both their business and their environment really *were* more complex, while the proposed solutions were often simple, even simplistic. The traditional telephone company that stuck to its knitting was trampled by competitors who redefined their strategies in response to new technologies linking telecommunications, computers, and office equipment into a single integrated system. The packaged-goods company that concentrated on the triad markets quickly discovered that Europe, Japan, and the United States were the epicenters of global competitive activity, with higher risks and slimmer profits than more protected and less competitive markets such as Australia, Turkey, and Brazil. The consumer electronics company that adopted an either-or generic strategy found itself facing competitors able to develop cost and differentiation capabilities at the same time.

In recent years, as more and more managers recognized oversimplification as a strategic trap, they began to accept the need to manage complexity rather than seek to minimize it. This realization, however, led many into an equally threatening organizational trap when they concluded that the best response to increasingly complex strategic requirements was increasingly complex organizational structures.

The obvious organizational solution to strategies that required multiple, simultaneous management capabilities was the matrix structure that became so fashionable in the late 1970s and the early 1980s. Its parallel reporting relationships acknowledged the diverse, conflicting needs of functional, product, and geographic management groups and provided a formal mechanism for resolving them. Its

multiple information channels allowed the organization to capture and analyze external complexity. And its overlapping responsibilities were designed to combat parochialism and build flexibility into the company's response to change.

In practice, however, the matrix proved all but unmanageable—especially in an international context. Dual reporting led to conflict and confusion; the proliferation of channels created informational logjams as a proliferation of committees and reports bogged down the organization; and overlapping responsibilities produced turf battles and a loss of accountability. Separated by barriers of distance, language, time, and culture, managers found it virtually impossible to clarify the confusion and resolve the conflicts.

In hindsight, the strategic and structural traps seem simple enough to avoid, so one has to wonder why so many experienced general managers have fallen into them. Much of the answer lies in the way we have traditionally thought about the general manager's role. For decades, we have seen the general manager as chief strategic guru and principal organizational architect. But as the competitive climate grows less stable and less predictable, it is harder for one person alone to succeed in that great visionary role. Similarly, as formal, hierarchical structure gives way to networks of personal relationships that work through informal, horizontal communication channels, the image of top management in an isolated corner office moving boxes and lines on an organization chart becomes increasingly anachronistic.

Paradoxically, as strategies and organizations become more complex and sophisticated, top-level general managers are beginning to replace their historical concentration on the grand issues of strategy and structure with a focus on the details of managing people and processes. The critical strategic requirement is not to devise the most ingenious and well-coordinated plan but to build the most viable and flexible strategic process; the key organizational task is not to design the most elegant structure but to capture individual capabilities and motivate the entire organization to respond cooperatively to a complicated and dynamic environment.

Building an Organization

Although business thinkers have written a great deal about strategic innovation, they have paid far less attention to the accompanying organizational challenges. Yet many companies remain caught in the structural-complexity trap that paralyzes their ability to respond quickly or flexibly to the new strategic imperatives.

For those companies that adopted matrix structures, the problem was not in the way they defined the goal. They correctly recognized the need for a multi-dimensional organization to respond to growing external complexity. The problem was that they defined their organizational objectives in purely structural terms. Yet the term *formal structure* describes only the organization's basic anatomy. Companies must also concern themselves with organizational physiology—the systems and relationships that allow the lifeblood of information to flow through the organization. They also need to develop a healthy organizational psychology—the shared norms, values, and beliefs that shape the way individual managers think and act.

The companies that fell into the organizational trap assumed that changing their formal structure (anatomy) would force changes in interpersonal relationships and decision processes (physiology), which in turn would reshape the individual attitudes and actions of managers (psychology).

But as many companies have discovered, reconfiguring the formal structure is a blunt and sometimes brutal instrument of change. A new structure creates new and presumably more useful managerial ties, but these can take months and often years to evolve into effective knowledge-generating and decision-making relationships. And because the new job requirements will frustrate, alienate, or simply overwhelm so many managers, changes in individual attitudes and behavior will likely take even longer.

As companies struggle to create organizational capabilities that reflect rather than diminish environmental complexity, good managers gradually stop searching for the ideal structural template to impose on the company from the top down. Instead, they focus on the challenge of building up an appropriate set of employee attitudes and skills and linking them together with carefully developed processes and relationships. In other words, they begin to focus on building the organization rather than simply on installing a new structure.

Indeed, the companies that are most successful at developing multi-dimensional organizations begin at the far end of the anatomy–physiology–psychology sequence. Their first objective is to alter the organizational psychology—the broad corporate beliefs and norms that shape managers' perceptions and actions. Then, by enriching and clarifying communication and decision processes, companies reinforce these psychological changes with improvements in organizational physiology. Only later do they consolidate and confirm their progress by realigning organizational anatomy through changes in the formal structure.

No company we know of has discovered a quick or easy way to change its organizational psychology to reshape the understanding, identification, and commitment of its employees. But we found three principal characteristics common to those that managed the task most effectively:

1. They developed and communicated a clear and consistent corporate vision.
2. They effectively managed human resource tools to broaden individual perspectives and to develop identification with corporate goals.
3. They integrated individual thinking and activities into the broad corporate agenda by a process we call co-option.

Building a Shared Vision

Perhaps the main reason managers in large, complex companies cling to parochial attitudes is that their frame of reference is bounded by their specific responsibilities. The surest way to break down such insularity is to develop and communicate a clear sense of corporate purpose that extends into every corner of the company and gives context and meaning to each manager's particular roles and responsibilities. We are not talking about a slogan, however catchy and pointed. We are talking about a company vision, which must be crafted and articulated with clarity, continuity, and consistency. We are talking about clarity of expression that makes company objectives understandable and meaningful; continuity of purpose that underscores their enduring importance; and consistency of application across business units and geographical boundaries that ensures uniformity throughout the organization.

Clarity   There are three keys to clarity in a corporate vision: simplicity, relevance, and reinforcement. NEC's integration of computers and communications—C&C—is probably the best single example of how simplicity can make a vision more powerful. Top management has applied the C&C concept so effectively that it describes the company's business focus, defines its distinctive source of competitive advantage over large companies like IBM and AT&T, and summarizes its strategic and organizational imperatives.

The second key, relevance, means linking broad objectives to concrete agendas. When Wisse Dekker became CEO at Philips, his principal strategic concern was the problem of competing with Japan. He stated this challenge in martial terms—the U.S. had abandoned the battlefield; Philips was now Europe's last defense against insurgent Japanese electronics companies. By focusing the company's attention not only on Philips's corporate survival but also on the protection of national and regional interests, Dekker heightened the sense of urgency and commitment in a way that legitimized cost-cutting efforts, drove an extensive rationalization of plant operations, and inspired a new level of sales achievements.

The third key to clarity is top management's continual reinforcement, elaboration, and interpretation of the core vision to keep it from becoming obsolete or abstract. Founder Konosuke Matsushita developed a grand, 250-year vision for his company, but he also managed to give it immediate relevance. He summed up its overall message in the "Seven Spirits of Matsushita," to which he referred constantly in his policy statements. Each January he wove the company's one-year operational objectives into his overarching concept to produce an an-

nual theme that he then captured in a slogan. For all the loftiness of his concept of corporate purpose, he gave his managers immediate, concrete guidance in implementing Matsushita's goals.

Continuity   Despite shifts in leadership and continual adjustments in short-term business priorities, companies must remain committed to the same core set of strategic objectives and organizational values. Without such continuity, unifying vision might as well be expressed in terms of quarterly goals.

It was General Electric's lack of this kind of continuity that led to the erosion of its once formidable position in electrical appliances in many countries. Over a period of 20 years and under successive CEOs, the company's international consumer-product strategy never stayed the same for long. From building locally responsive and self-sufficient "mini-GEs" in each market, the company turned to a policy of developing low-cost offshore sources, which eventually evolved into a de facto strategy of international outsourcing. Finally, following its acquisition of RCA, GE's consumer electronics strategy made another about-face and focused on building centralized scale to defend domestic share. Meanwhile, the product strategy within this shifting business emphasis was itself unstable. The Brazilian subsidiary, for example, built its TV business in the 1960s until it was told to stop; in the early 1970s, it emphasized large appliances until it was denied funding, then it focused on housewares until the parent company sold off that business. In two decades, GE utterly dissipated its dominant franchise in Brazil's electrical products market.

Unilever, by contrast, made an enduring commitment to its Brazilian subsidiary, despite volatile swings in Brazil's business climate. Company chairman Floris Maljers emphasized the importance of looking past the latest political crisis or economic downturn to the long-term business potential. "In those parts of the world," he remarked, "you take your management cues from the way they dance. The samba method of management is two steps forward then one step back." Unilever built—two steps forward and one step back—a profitable $300 million business in a rapidly growing economy with 130 million consumers, while its wallflower competitors never ventured out onto the floor.

Consistency   The third task for top management in communicating strategic purpose is to ensure that everyone in the company shares the same vision. The cost of inconsistency can be horrendous. It always produces confusion and, in extreme cases, can lead to total chaos, with different units of the organization pursuing agendas that are mutually debilitating.

Philips is a good example of a company that, for a time, lost its consistency of corporate purpose. As a legacy of its wartime decision to give some overseas units legal autonomy, management had long experienced difficulty persuading North American Philips (NAP) to play a supportive role in the parent company's global strategies. The problem came to a head with the introduction of Philips's technologically first-rate videocassette recording system, the V2000. Despite considerable pressure from world headquarters in the Netherlands, NAP refused to launch the system, arguing that Sony's Beta system and Matsushita's VHS format were too well established and had cost, feature, and system-support advantages Philips couldn't match. Relying on its legal independence and managerial autonomy, NAP management decided instead to source products from its Japanese competitors and market them under its Magnavox brand name. As a result, Philips was unable to build the efficiency and credibility it needed to challenge Japanese dominance of the VCR business.

Most inconsistencies involve differences between what managers of different operating units see as the company's key objectives. Sometimes, however, different corporate leaders transmit different views of overall priorities and purpose. When this stems from poor communication, it can be fixed. When it's a result of fundamental disagreement, the problem is serious indeed, as illustrated by ITT's problems in developing its strategically vital System 12 switching equipment. Continuing differences between the head of the European organization and the company's chief technology officer over the location and philosophy of the develop-

ment effort led to confusion and conflict throughout the company. The result was disastrous. ITT had difficulty transferring vital technology across its own unit boundaries and so was irreparably late introducing this key product to a rapidly changing global market. These problems eventually led the company to sell off its core telecommunications business to a competitor.

But formulating and communicating a vision—no matter how clear, enduring, and consistent—cannot succeed unless individual employees understand and accept the company's stated goals and objectives. Problems at this level are more often related to receptivity than to communication. The development of individual understanding and acceptance is a challenge for a company's human resource practices.

Developing Human Resources

While top managers universally recognize their responsibility for developing and allocating a company's scarce assets and resources, their focus on finance and technology often overshadows the task of developing the scarcest resource of all—capable managers. But if there is one key to regaining control of companies that operate in fast-changing environments, it is the ability of top management to turn the perceptions, capabilities, and relationships of individual managers into the building blocks of the organization.

One pervasive problem in companies whose leaders lack this ability—or fail to exercise it—is getting managers to see how their specific responsibilities relate to the broad corporate vision. Growing external complexity and strategic sophistication have accelerated the growth of a cadre of specialists who are physically and organizationally isolated from each other, and the task of dealing with their consequent parochialism should not be delegated to the clerical staff that administers salary structures and benefit programs. Top managers inside and outside the human resource function must be leaders in the recruitment, development, and assignment of the company's vital human talent.

Recruitment and Selection   The first step in successfully managing complexity is to tap the full range of available talent. It is a serious mistake to permit historical imbalances in the nationality or functional background of the management group to constrain hiring or subsequent promotion. In today's global marketplace, domestically oriented recruiting limits a company's ability to capitalize on its worldwide pool of management skill and biases its decision-making processes.

After decades of routinely appointing managers from its domestic operations to key positions in overseas subsidiaries, Procter & Gamble realized that the practice not only worked against sensitivity to local cultures—a lesson driven home by several marketing failures in Japan—but also greatly underutilized its pool of high-potential non-American managers. (Fortunately, our studies turned up few companies as shortsighted as one that made overseas assignments on the basis of *poor* performance, because foreign markets were assumed to be "not as tough as the domestic environment.")

Not only must companies enlarge the pool of people available for key positions, they must also develop new criteria for choosing those most likely to succeed. Because past success is no longer a sufficient qualification for increasingly subtle, sensitive, and unpredictable senior-level tasks, top management must become involved in a more discriminating selection process. At Matsushita, top management selects candidates for international assignments on the basis of a comprehensive set of personal characteristics, expressed for simplicity in the acronym SMILE: specialty (the needed skill, capability, or knowledge); management ability (particularly motivational ability); international flexibility (willingness to learn and ability to adapt); language facility; and endeavor (vitality, perseverance in the face of difficulty). These attributes are remarkably similar to those targeted by NEC and Philips, where top executives also are involved in the senior-level selection process.

Training and Development   Once the appropriate top-level candidates have been identified, the next

challenge is to develop their potential. The most successful development efforts have three aims that take them well beyond the skill-building objectives of classic training programs: to inculcate a common vision and shared values; to broaden management perspectives and capabilities; and to develop contacts and shape management relationships.

To build common vision and values, white-collar employees at Matsushita spend a good part of their first six months in what the company calls "cultural and spiritual training." They study the company credo, the "Seven Spirits of Matsushita," and the philosophy of Konosuke Matsushita. Then they learn how to translate these internalized lessons into daily behavior and even operational decisions. Culture-building exercises as intensive as Matsushita's are sometimes dismissed as innate Japanese practices that would not work in other societies, but in fact, Philips has a similar entry-level training practice (called "organization cohesion training"), as does Unilever (called, straight-forwardly, "indoctrination").

The second objective—broadening management perspectives—is essentially a matter of teaching people how to manage complexity instead of merely to make room for it. To reverse a long and unwieldy tradition of running its operations with two- and three-headed management teams of separate technical, commercial, and sometimes administrative specialists, Philips asked its training and development group to de-specialize top management trainees. By supplementing its traditional menu of specialist courses and functional programs with more intensive general management training, Philips was able to begin replacing the ubiquitous teams with single business heads who also appreciated and respected specialist points of view.

The final aim—developing contacts and relationships—is much more than an incidental byproduct of good management development, as the comments of a senior personnel manager at Unilever suggest: "By bringing managers from different countries and businesses together at Four Acres [Unilever's international management-training college], we build contacts and create bonds that we could never achieve by other means. The company spends as much on training as it does on R&D not only because of the direct effect it has on upgrading skills and knowledge but also because it plays a central role in indoctrinating managers into a Unilever club where personal relationships and informal contacts are much more powerful than the formal systems and structures."

Career-Path Management   Although recruitment and training are critically important, the most effective companies recognize that the best way to develop new perspectives and thwart parochialism in their managers is through personal experience. By moving selected managers across functions, businesses, and geographic units, a company encourages cross-fertilization of ideas as well as the flexibility and breadth of experience that enable managers to grapple with complexity and come out on top.

Unilever has long been committed to the development of its human resources as a means of attaining durable competitive advantage. As early as the 1930s, the company was recruiting and developing local employees to replace the parent-company managers who had been running most of its overseas subsidiaries. In a practice that came to be known as "-ization," the company committed itself to the Indianization of its Indian company, the Australization of its Australian company, and so on.

Although delighted with the new talent that began working its way up through the organization, management soon realized that by reducing the transfer of parent-company managers abroad, it had diluted the powerful glue that bound diverse organizational groups together and linked dispersed operations. The answer lay in formalizing a second phase of the -ization process. While continuing with Indianization, for example, Unilever added programs aimed at the "Unileverization" of its Indian managers.

In addition to bringing 300 to 400 managers to Four Acres each year, Unilever typically has 100 to 150 of its most promising overseas managers on short- and long-term job assignments at corporate headquarters. This policy not only brings fresh, close-to-the-market perspectives into corporate decision making but also gives the visiting managers a strong sense of Unilever's strategic vision and organizational values. In the words of one of the expatriates in the corporate offices, "The experience initiates you into the Unilever Club and the clear norms, values, and behaviors that distinguish our people—so much so that we really believe we can spot another Unilever manager anywhere in the world."

Furthermore, the company carefully transfers most of these high-potential individuals through a variety of different functional, product, and geographic positions, often rotating every two or three years. Most important, top management tracks about 1,000 of these people—some 5% of Unilever's total management group—who, as they move through the company, forge an informal network of contacts and relationships that is central to Unilever's decision-making and information-exchange processes.

Widening the perspectives and relationships of key managers as Unilever has done is a good way of developing identification with the broader corporate mission. But a broad sense of identity is not enough. To maintain control of its global strategies, Unilever must secure a strong and lasting individual commitment to corporate visions and objectives. In effect, it must co-opt individual energies and ambitions into the service of corporate goals.

Co-Opting Management Efforts

As organizational complexity grows, managers and management groups tend to become so specialized and isolated and to focus so intently on their own immediate operating responsibilities that they are apt to respond parochially to intrusions on their organizational turf, even when the overall corporate interest is at stake. A classic example, described earlier, was the decision by North American Philips's consumer electronics group to reject the parent company's VCR system.

At about the same time, Philips, like many other companies, began experimenting with ways to convert managers' intellectual understanding of the corporate vision—in Philips's case, an almost evangelical determination to defend Western electronics against the Japanese—into a binding personal commitment. Philips concluded that it could co-opt individuals and organizational groups into the broader vision by inviting them to contribute to the corporate agenda and then giving them direct responsibility for implementation.

In the face of intensifying Japanese competition, Philips knew it had to improve coordination in its consumer electronics among its fiercely independent national organizations. In strengthening the central product divisions, however, Philips did not want to deplete the enterprise or commitment of its capable national management teams.

The company met these conflicting needs with two cross-border initiatives. First, it created a top-level World Policy Council for its video business that included key managers from strategic markets—Germany, France, the United Kingdom, the United States, and Japan. Philips knew that its national companies' long history of independence made local managers reluctant to take orders from Dutch headquarters in Eindhoven—often for good reason, because much of the company's best market knowledge and technological expertise resided in its offshore units. Through the council, Philips co-opted their support for company decisions about product policy and manufacturing location.

Second, in a more powerful move, Philips allocated global responsibilities to units that previously had been purely national in focus. Eindhoven gave NAP the leading role in the development of Philips's projection television and asked it to coordinate development and manufacture of all Philips television sets for North America and Asia. The change in the attitude of NAP managers was dramatic.

A senior manager in NAP's consumer electronics business summed up the feelings of U.S. managers: "At last, we are moving out of the dependency relationship with Eindhoven that was so frustrating to us." Co-option had transformed the defensive, territorial attitude of NAP managers into a more collaborative mind-set. They were making important contributions to global corporate strategy instead of looking for ways to subvert it.

In 1987, with much of its TV set production established in Mexico, the president of NAP's consumer electronics group told the press, "It is the commonality of design that makes it possible for us to move production globally. We have splendid cooperation with Philips in Eindhoven." It was a statement no NAP manager would have made a few years earlier, and it perfectly captured how effectively Philips had co-opted previously isolated, even adversarial, managers into the corporate agenda.

The Matrix in the Manager's Mind

Since the end of World War II, corporate strategy has survived several generations of painful transformation and has grown appropriately agile and athletic. Unfortunately, organizational development has not kept pace, and managerial attitudes lag even farther behind. As a result, corporations now commonly design strategies that seem impossible to implement, for the simple reason that no one can effectively implement third-generation strategies through second-generation organizations run by first-generation managers.

Today the most successful companies are those where top executives recognize the need to manage the new environmental and competitive demands by focusing less on the quest for an ideal structure and more on developing the abilities, behavior, and performance of individual managers. Change succeeds only when those assigned to the new transnational and interdependent tasks understand the overall goals and are dedicated to achieving them.

One senior executive put it this way: "The challenge is not so much to build a matrix structure as it is to create a matrix in the minds of our managers." The inbuilt conflict in a matrix structure pulls managers in several directions at once. Developing a matrix of flexible perspectives and relationships within each manager's mind, however, achieves an entirely different result. It lets individuals make the judgments and negotiate the trade-offs that drive the organization toward a shared strategic objective.

CHAPTER 5

Creating Worldwide Innovation and Learning:
Exploiting Cross-Border Knowledge Management

> In the information-based, knowledge-intensive economy of the 21st century, entities are not competing only in terms of their traditional ability to access new markets and arbitrage factor costs. Today the challenge is to build transnational organizations that can sense an emerging consumer trend in one country, link it through a new technology in another, develop a creative new product or service in a third, then diffuse that innovation rapidly around the world. In this chapter, we contrast this transnational innovation process with more traditional "center-for-global" and "local-to-local" approaches. We then describe the nature of the organizational capabilities that must be developed to make these central, local, and transnational innovations more effective.

In Chapter 3, we described how companies competing in today's global competitive environment are being required to build layers of competitive advantage—in particular, the ability to capture global scale efficiencies, local market responsiveness, and worldwide learning capability. As MNEs have found ways to match one another in the more familiar attributes of global scale efficiency and local responsiveness, the leading-edge competitive battles have shifted to companies' ability to link and leverage their resources to capture advantage through worldwide learning.

The very largest MNEs often need to manage an enormous volume of innovations. A company such as Sony owns more than 30,000 patents. With this sort of breadth of proprietary intellectual property, the challenge is somehow to maximize the return from accumulated learning. The most profitable department in a major MNE, on a per employee basis, often is the one responsible for licensing intellectual property. Many technology-intensive MNEs now generate more profit from licensing than they do from their own manufacturing operations.

In a competitive environment in which the ability to develop and rapidly diffuse innovations around the world is vital, offshore subsidiaries are being asked to take on important new roles. They must act as the sensors of new market trends or technological developments; they must be able to attract scarce talent and expertise; and they must be able to act collectively with other subsidiaries to exploit the resulting new products and initiatives worldwide, regardless of where they originated. Yet developing this capability to create, leverage, and apply knowledge worldwide is not a simple task for most large MNEs. Although people are innately curious and naturally motivated to learn from one another, most modern corporations are constructed in a way that constrains and sometimes kills this natural human instinct. In this chapter, we focus on one of the most important current challenges facing MNE management: how to develop and diffuse knowledge to support effective worldwide innovation and learning.

Central, Local, and Transnational Innovation

Traditionally, MNEs' innovative capabilities were dominated by one of two classic processes. In what we describe as the *center-for-global* innovation model, the new opportunity was usually sensed in the home country; the centralized resources and capabilities of the parent company were brought in to create the new product or process, usually in the main R&D center; and implementation involved driving the innovation through subsidiaries whose role it was to introduce that innovation to their local market. Pfizer's development of Viagra or Intel's creation of Pentium processors are two classic examples of this model. In contrast, what we call *local-for-local* innovation relies on subsidiary-based knowledge development. Responding to perceived local opportunities, subsidiaries use their own resources and capabilities to create innovative responses that are then implemented in the local market. Unilever's development of a detergent bar in response to the Indian market's need for a product suitable for stream washing is a good illustration of the process, as is Philippines-based Jollibee's strategy of adapting its fast-food products to the local market preferences of each country it entered.

Most MNEs have tried to develop elements of both models of innovation, but the tension that exists between the knowledge management processes supporting each usually means that one dominates. Not surprisingly, the center-for-global innovation tends to dominate in companies we describe as global or international, whereas local-for-local processes fit more easily into the multinational strategic model. However, in recent years, traditional strategic mentalities have evolved into two new transnational innovation processes. *Locally leveraged* innovation involves ensuring that the special resources and capabilities of each national subsidiary are available not only to that local entity but also to other MNE units worldwide. For example, two of Sara Lee Corporation's biggest new brands in the household and body care division in the 1990s—Sanex and Ambi Pur—were first developed in Spain and subsequently rolled out on a worldwide basis. *Globally linked* innovation pools the resources and capabilities of many different units—typically at both the parent company and the subsidiary level—to create and manage an activity jointly. For example, the idea for Volkswagen's New Beetle came originally out of the U.S. head office in Detroit; the design was led by the company's design studios in California; the development and engineering work was conducted at corporate headquarters in Wolfsburg, Germany; and the final production was implemented by numerous VW plants around the world.

Both these transnational innovation models rely on the sophisticated ability to take market intelligence developed in one part of the organization, perhaps link it to specialized expertise located in a second entity and a scarce resource in a third, and then eventually diffuse the new product or proposal worldwide. This innovative process was the kind Procter and Gamble first developed through the creation of "Eurobrand" development teams that resulted in the creation of the heavy-duty liquid detergent, Vizir. Recognizing the power of this cross-unit innovation and learning capability, the company gradually built it into a core competence that it now regards as the centerpiece of its global competitive strategy.

Although these processes are becoming more widespread, they have supplemented rather than replaced the traditional center-for-global and local-for-local innovation processes. In a competitive environment, most companies recognize the need to engage their resources and capabilities in as many ways as they can. The challenge is to build an organization that can simultaneously facilitate all four processes of innovation and learning, which requires that they understand not only the power of each but also their limitations:

• The greatest risk of center-for-global innovation is market insensitivity and the accompanying resistance of local subsidiary management to what they may view as inappropriate new products and processes.

• Local-for-local innovations often suffer from needless differentiation and "reinvention of the wheel" caused by resource-rich subsidiaries trying to protect their independence and autonomy.

• Locally leveraged innovations can be threatened by the "not-invented-here" syndrome that often blocks the successful transfer of products and processes from the innovative subsidiary to others in the company.

• The major impediment to globally linked innovation tends to be the high coordination cost required to link widely dispersed assets, resources, and capabilities into an effective, integrated network of free-flowing ideas and innovations.

Building a portfolio of innovative processes to drive worldwide learning requires that the companies overcome two related but different problems. Not only must they avoid the various pitfalls associated with each process, they must also find ways to overcome the organizational contradictions among them as they try to manage all the sources of innovation simultaneously. The well-known NUMMI partnership between General Motors (GM) and Toyota illustrates this challenge. Located in Fremont, California, NUMMI quickly became one of the highest productivity auto plants in North America. Yet despite the active involvement of hundreds of GM managers in running the plant, and GM's stated intention of learning from Toyota, the American partner was slow to create an effective mechanism for transferring the knowledge gained through NUMMI to other GM plants. Although learning ultimately occurred, as Table 5–1 indicates, subsequent analysis revealed that a lengthy set of learning obstacles had to be overcome.

Making Central Innovations Effective

The key strength on which many Japanese companies built their global leadership positions in a diverse range of businesses, from zippers to automobiles, lay in the effectiveness of their center-for-global innovations. This is not to say that many did not use some other operative modes, but in general, the Japanese became the champion managers of centralized innovation in the 1980s and have remained so. Three factors stand out as the most important explanations of Japanese success in managing the center-for-global process: (1) gaining the input of subsidiaries into centralized activities;

Table 5-1   Overcoming Learning Obstacles

Learning Obstacle	GM Actions that Helped Overcome the Obstacles
Causal ambiguity (i.e., managers do not understand the relationship between organizational actions and outcomes)	Training; visits to NUMMI by GM and supplier employees; sharing of information facilitated by the Technical Liaison Office (TLO); creation of a network of NUMMI-experienced managers; direct involvement of GM leadership; time (about eight years before real learning began).
Lack of leadership commitment to learning	Jack Smith appointed CEO in 1992; former NUMMI advisors promoted within GM; GM leaders developed an understanding of lean production.
Unwillingness to invest in learning	Expansion of the scope of the TLO's mandate to encompass a broad set of learning activities; replication of the TLO for several GM plants.
Failure to build a system that captures the learning of individual managers	Development of advisor system (personal development requirements, GM mentors, planned reentry assignments); learning network of NUMMI alumni; NUMMI assignments recognized within GM as important and desirable developmental experiences.
Not-invented-here syndrome	Learning network; experience with lean manufacturing in NUMMI; establishing new facility in Germany with the objective "to build a plant like NUMMI"; superior performance within NUMMI relative to other GM plants.

Source: Andrew C. Inkpen, "Learning Through Alliances: General Motors and NUMMI," *California Management Review* 47, no. 4 (2005), p. 131.

(2) ensuring that all functional tasks are linked to market needs; and (3) integrating value chain functions such as development, production, and marketing by managing the transfer of responsibilities among them.

Gaining Subsidiary Input: Multiple Linkages

The two most important problems facing a company with highly centralized operations are that those at the center may not understand market needs, and those in the subsidiaries required to implement the central innovation may not be committed to it. These problems are best addressed by building multiple linkages between headquarters and overseas subsidiaries to give not only headquarters managers a better understanding of country-level needs and opportunities but also subsidiary managers greater access to and involvement in centralized decisions and tasks.

Matsushita, for example, does not try to limit the number of linkages between headquarters and subsidiaries or focus them through a single point, as many companies do for the sake of efficiency. Rather, it tries to preserve the different perspectives, priorities, and even prejudices of its diverse groups worldwide and ensure that they have linkages to those in the headquarters who can represent and defend their views.

Responding to National Needs: Market Mechanisms

Like many other companies, Matsushita has created an integrative process to ensure that headquarters managers responsible for R&D, manufacturing, marketing, and so on are not sheltered from the constraints and demands felt by managers on the front lines of the operations. One of the key elements in achieving this difficult organizational task is the company's willingness to use internal "market mechanisms" to direct and regulate central activities.

For example, approximately half of Matsushita's total research budget is allocated not to research laboratories but to the product divisions. The purpose of the split budget is to create a context in which technologically driven and market-led ideas can compete for attention. Each year, the product divisions suggest a set of research projects that they would like to sponsor. At the same time, the various research laboratories hold annual exhibitions and write specific proposals to highlight research projects they want to undertake. The engineering and development groups of the product divisions mediate the subsequent contracting and negotiation process. Specific projects are sponsored by the divisions and allocated to the laboratories or research groups of their choice, along with requisite funds and other resources.

Managing Responsibility Transfer: Personnel Flow

In local-for-local innovation processes, cross-functional integration across research, manufacturing, and marketing is facilitated by the smaller size and closer proximity of the units responsible for each stage of activity. Because this is not true when parent company units take the lead role in the development and manufacture of new products and processes, more centralized organizations must build alternative means to integrate different tasks.

At Matsushita, for example, the integrative systems rely heavily on the transfer of people. The career paths of research engineers are structured to ensure that a majority of them spend about five to eight years in the central research laboratories engaged in pure research, then another five years in the product divisions in applied research and development, and finally in a direct operational function, such as production or marketing, wherein they take line management positions for the rest of their working lives. More important—and in stark contrast to the approach in most Western companies—each engineer usually makes the transition from one department to the next coincident with the transfer of the major project on which he or she has been working. This parallel advance ensures that specific knowledge about the project moves with the individual.

Another mechanism for cross-functional integration in Matsushita works in the opposite direction. Wherever possible, the company tries to identify the manager who will head the production task for a new product under development and makes him or her a full-time member of the research team from the initial stage of the development process. This system not only injects direct production expertise into the development team but also facilitates the transfer of the project after the design is completed. Matsushita also uses this mechanism as a way to transmit product expertise from headquarters to its worldwide sales subsidiaries.

Making Local Innovations Efficient

If the classic global companies in Japan are the champion managers of central innovation, the archetypal multinational companies from Europe are often masters at managing local innovations. Of the many factors that facilitate local-for-local innovations in European companies, three abilities are the most significant: to empower local management in national subsidiaries, to establish effective mechanisms for linking these local managers to corporate decision-making processes, and to force tight cross-functional integration within each subsidiary.

Empowering Local Management

Perhaps the most important factor supporting local innovations is the dispersal of the organizational assets and resources and the delegation of authority that occur so easily in decentralized federation companies. Why would companies such as Nestlé or Philips establish a structure in which the country manager is king? Consider the example of Philips. Since it was founded in 1891, Philips has recognized the need to expand its operations beyond its small domestic market, but the successive barriers—poor transport and communication linkages in the early decades of the century, protectionist pressures in the 1930s, and the disruption of World War II—encouraged the company to build national organizations with substantial degrees of autonomy and self-sufficiency. Such dispersed managerial and technological resources, coupled with local autonomy and decentralized control over resources, enabled subsidiary managers to be more effective in managing local development, manufacturing, and other functional tasks.

Linking Local Managers to Corporate Decision-Making Processes

Whereas local resources and autonomy make it feasible for subsidiary managers to be creative and entrepreneurial, linkages to corporate decision-making processes are necessary to make these local-for-local tasks effective for the company as a whole. In many European companies, a cadre of entrepreneurial expatriates plays a key role in developing and maintaining such linkages.

At Philips, many of the best managers spend most of their careers in national operations, working for three to four years in a series of subsidiaries—jobs that are often much larger and have higher status than those available in the small home country market of the Netherlands.

Not surprisingly, such a career assignment pattern has an important influence on managerial attitudes and organizational relationships. The expatriate managers tend to identify strongly with the national organization's point of view, and this shared identity creates a strong bond and distinct subculture within the company. In contrast to Philips, Matsushita has been able to generate very little interaction among its expatriate managers, who tend to regard themselves as parent-company executives temporarily on assignment in a foreign company.

Integrating Subsidiary Functions

Finally, the local innovativeness of decentralized federation organizations is enhanced because of the strong cross-functional integration that typically exists within each national operation. Most Philips subsidiaries use integration mechanisms at three organizational levels. For each project, there is what Philips calls an "article team" consisting of relatively junior managers from the commercial and technical functions. It is the responsibility of this team to evolve product policies and prepare annual sales plans and budgets.

At the product level, cross-functional coordination is accomplished through a product group management team of technical and commercial representatives, which meets once a month to review results, suggest corrective actions, and resolve any interfunctional differences. Restraining control and conflict resolution to this level facilitates sensitive and rapid responses to initiatives and ideas generated at the local level.

The highest subsidiary-level coordination forum is the senior management committee (SMC), which consists of the top commercial, technical, and financial managers in the subsidiary. Acting essentially as a local board, the SMC coordinates efforts among the functional groups and ensures that the national operation retains primary responsibility for its own strategies and priorities. Each of these three forums facilitates local initiative by encouraging that issues be resolved without escalation for approval or arbitration.

Making Transnational Processes Feasible

The complexity of the innovation and learning processes in a multinational corporation is significantly exacerbated by the fact that new opportunities can emerge from anywhere—and often a long way from either complementary capabilities or the key decision makers. For example, in 2001, when GM's global product head saw the new sports coupe that GM's Australian subsidiary had launched as the Holden Monaro, he decided it was the ideal car to introduce in the United States as a resurrection of the Pontiac GTO. With a domestic demand of only 5,000 Monaros, the GM Holden had to expand its capacity significantly to the expected export volume of 18,000 Pontiacs after the 2003 U.S. launch of the GTO.

In a case such as this, the transnational company needs to embrace a mindset in which subsidiary managers are encouraged to take the initiative and headquarters managers are more accepting of the capabilities and potential of their overseas operations. And it needs to build linkages among different units of the company (e.g., between the Australian design and production operations and GM's Detroit-based global marketing and sales operation) to leverage existing resources and capabilities, regardless of their locations, and exploit opportunities that arise in any part of the company's dispersed operations.

In many MNEs, three simplifying assumptions traditionally have blocked the organizational capabilities necessary for managing such transnational operations. The need to reduce organizational and strategic complexity made these assumptions extremely widespread among large MNEs:

• An often implicit assumption that roles of different organizational units are uniform and symmetrical. This assumption leads companies to manage very different businesses, functions, and national operations in essentially the same way.

• An assumption, conscious or unconscious, that headquarters–subsidiary relationships should be based on clear and unambiguous patterns of dependence or independence.

• The assumption that corporate management has a responsibility to exercise decision making and control uniformly.

Companies that are most successful in developing transnational innovations challenge these assumptions. Instead of treating all businesses, functions, and subsidiaries the same way, they systematically differentiate tasks and responsibilities. Instead of seeking organizational clarity by basing relationships on dependence or independence, they build and manage interdependence among the different units of the companies. And instead of considering control their key task, corporate managers search for complex mechanisms to coordinate and coopt the differentiated and interdependent organizational units into sharing a vision of the company's strategic tasks.

From Symmetry to Differentiation

Like many other companies, Unilever built its international operations with an implicit assumption of organizational symmetry. Managers of diverse local businesses, with products ranging from packaged foods to chemicals and detergents, all reported to strongly independent national subsidiary managers, who in turn reported through regional directors to the board. In the post–World War II era, as management began to recognize the need to capture potential economies across national boundaries and transfer learning worldwide, product coordination groups were formed at the corporate center. Under the assumption of organizational symmetry, the number of coordination groups grew from three in 1962 to six in 1969 and to ten by 1977.

By the early 1980s, however, there was a growing recognition that different businesses faced different demands for integration and responsiveness. Whereas standardization, coordination, and integration paid high dividends in the chemical and detergent businesses, for example, important differences in local tastes and national cultures impeded the same degree of coordination in foods.

As Unilever tackled the challenge of managing some businesses in a more globally coordinated manner, it was also confronted with the question of what to coordinate. Historically, most national subsidiaries chose to develop, manufacture, and market products they thought appropriate. Over time, however, decentralization of all functional responsibilities became increasingly difficult to support. For the sake of cost control and competitive effectiveness, Unilever needed to break with tradition and begin centralizing European product development and purchasing, but it was less compelled to pull local sales and promotional responsibilities to the center.

In addition to differentiating the way they managed their various businesses and functions, most companies eventually recognized the importance of differentiating the management of diverse geographic operations. Although various national subsidiaries operated with very different external environments and internal constraints, operations in Sydney, Singapore, and Shanghai often reported through the same channels, were managed by standardized planning and control systems, and worked under a set of common and generalized subsidiary mandates.

Recognizing that such symmetrical treatment could constrain strategic capabilities, many companies made changes. At Unilever, for example, Europe's highly competitive markets and closely linked economies led management gradually to increase the role of European product coordinators until they eventually had direct line responsibility for all operating companies in their businesses. In Latin America, however, national management maintained its historic line management role, and product coordinators acted only as advisers. Unilever has thus moved in sequence from a symmetrical organization managed through a uniformly decentralized federation to a much more differentiated one: differentiating first by product, then by function, and finally by geography.

From Dependence or Independence to Interdependence

As we described in Chapter 4, national subsidiaries in decentralized federation organizations enjoyed considerable independence from the headquarters, whereas those in centralized hub organizations remained strongly dependent on the parent company for resources and capabilities. But the emerging strategic demands make organizational models based on such simple interunit dependence or independence inappropriate.

Independent units risk being picked off one by one by competitors whose coordinated global approach gives them two important strategic advantages: the ability to integrate scale-efficient operations and the opportunity to cross-subsidize the losses from battles in one market with funds generated by profitable operations in others. However, foreign operations that depend totally on a central unit run the risk of being unable to respond effectively to strong national competitors or to sense potentially important local market or technical intelligence.

But it is not easy to change relationships of dependence or independence that have been built over a long history. Most companies found that attempts to improve interunit collaboration by adding layer upon layer of administrative mechanisms to foster greater cooperation were disappointing. Independent units feigned compliance while fiercely protecting their independence, and dependent units discovered that the new cooperative spirit bestowed little more than the right to agree with those on whom they depended.

To create an effective interdependent organization, two requirements must be met. First, the company must develop a configuration of resources that is neither centralized nor decentralized but is both dispersed and specialized. Such a configuration lies at the heart of the transnational company's integrated network mode of operations, as we already discussed in Chapter 4.

Second, it must build interunit integration mechanisms to ensure that task interdependencies lead to the benefits of synergy rather than the paralysis of conflict. Above all else, interunit cooperation requires good interpersonal relations among managers in different units. The experiences of Ericsson, the Swedish telecommunications company, suggest that the movement of people is one of the strongest mechanisms for breaking down local dogmas. Ericsson achieved this with a long-standing policy of transferring large numbers of people back and forth between headquarters and subsidiaries. Whereas its Japanese competitor NEC may transfer a new technology through a few key managers sent on temporary assignment, Ericsson will send a team of 50 or 100 engineers and managers for a year or two; whereas NEC's flow is primarily from headquarters to subsidiary, Ericsson's is a balanced two-way flow in which people come to the parent company to both learn and provide their expertise; and whereas NEC's transfers are predominantly Japanese, Ericsson's multidirectional process involves all nationalities.

However, any organization in which there are shared tasks and joint responsibilities requires additional decision-making and conflict-resolution forums. In Ericsson, the often divergent objectives and interests of the parent company and the local subsidiary are exchanged in the national company's board meetings. Unlike many companies whose local boards are designed solely to satisfy national legal requirements, Ericsson uses its local boards as legitimate forums for communicating objectives, resolving differences, and making decisions.

From Unidimensional Control to Differentiated Coordination

The simplifying assumptions of organizational symmetry and dependence (or independence) allowed the management processes in many companies to be dominated by simple controls—tight operational controls in subsidiaries that depend on the center, or a looser system of administrative or financial controls in decentralized units. When companies began to challenge the assumptions underlying organizational relationships, however, they found they also needed to adapt their management processes. The growing interdependence of organizational units strained the simple control-dominated systems and underlined the need to supplement existing processes with more sophisticated ones.

As organizations simultaneously became more diverse and more interdependent, there was an explosion in the number of issues that had to be linked, reconciled, or integrated. But the costs of coordination are high, in both financial and human terms, and coordinating capabilities are always limited. Most companies, though, tended to concentrate on a primary means of coordination and control—"the company's way of doing things."

In analyzing how managers might develop a coordination system that best fits the needs of various functions and tasks, it is helpful to think about the various flows among the organizational units involved in the execution of each task. Three flows are the lifeblood of any organization but are of particular importance in a transnational company. The first is the flow of goods: the complex interconnections through which companies source their raw materials and other supplies, link the flows of components and subassemblies, and distribute finished goods. The second is the flow of resources, which encompasses not only the allocation of capital and repatriation of dividends but also the transfer of technology and the movement of personnel throughout the system. The third is the flow of valuable information and knowledge—from raw data and analyzed information to accumulated knowledge and embedded expertise—that companies must diffuse throughout the worldwide network of national units.

It can be very difficult to coordinate the flows of *goods* in a complex integrated network of interdependent operations. But in most companies, this coordination process can be managed effectively at lower levels of the organization through clear procedures and strong systems—or in other words, through a *formalized* management process. For example, within its network of manufacturing plants in different countries, Ericsson learned to coordinate product and material flows by standardizing as many procedures as possible and formalizing the logistics control.

It is more difficult to coordinate flows of financial, human, and technological *resources*. Allocation of these scarce resources represents the major strategic choices the company makes and must therefore be controlled at the corporate level. We have described the transnational company as an organization of diverse needs and perspectives, many of which conflict and all of which are changing. In such an organization, only managers with an overview of the total situation can make critical decisions about the funding of projects, the sharing of scarce technological resources, and the allocation of organizational skills and capabilities. Managing the flow of resources is a classic example of the need for coordination by *centralization*.

Perhaps the most difficult task is to coordinate the huge flow of strategic information and proprietary *knowledge* required to operate a transnational organization. The diversity and changeability of the flow make it impossible to coordinate through formal systems, and the sheer volume and complexity of the information would overload headquarters if coordination were centralized. The most effective way to ensure that worldwide organizational units analyze their diverse environments appropriately is to sensitize local managers to broader corporate objectives and priorities. That goal is best reached by transferring personnel with the relevant knowledge or creating organizational forums that allow for the free exchange of information and foster interunit learning. In short, the *socialization* process is the classic solution for the coordination of information flows.

Naturally, none of these broad characterizations of the fit between flows and processes is absolute, and companies use a variety of coordinative mechanisms to manage all three flows. Goods flows may be centrally coordinated, for example, for products under allocation, when several plants operate at less than capacity, or if the cost structures or host government demand change. And as information flows become routine, they can be coordinated through formalization if appropriate management information systems have been installed.

Realistically, a one-size-fits-all approach to capturing the benefits of innovation will not work in a large MNE. As Figure 5–1 suggests, the most effective way to exploit the

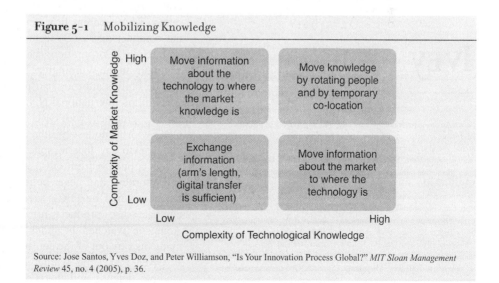

Figure 5-1   Mobilizing Knowledge

Complexity of Market Knowledge — High / Low

Complexity of Technological Knowledge — Low / High

High / Low:
Move information about the technology to where the market knowledge is

High / High:
Move knowledge by rotating people and by temporary co-location

Low / Low:
Exchange information (arm's length, digital transfer is sufficient)

Low / High:
Move information about the market to where the technology is

Source: Jose Santos, Yves Doz, and Peter Williamson, "Is Your Innovation Process Global?" *MIT Sloan Management Review* 45, no. 4 (2005), p. 36.

knowledge within an organization depends on the complexity of the technology itself and the understanding of the focal market. In practice, the best way to capture innovation will sometimes be to move people and sometimes to move or exchange the information.

Concluding Comments

The approaches to innovation in MNEs have changed considerably. Whereas once MNEs relied on simple models of centralized or localized innovation, the vast majority now find it necessary to build their innovation processes around multiple operating units and geographically disparate sources of knowledge. In this chapter, we identify three generic approaches to innovation, and for each, we identify its typical limitations and the approaches MNEs can use to overcome them. To be clear, there is no one right way of managing the innovation process in an MNE, because each company has its own unique administrative heritage that it cannot and should not disavow. Nonetheless, it is possible to identify certain principles—around the differentiation of roles, interdependence of units, and modes of control—that underpin the development of an effective transnational organization.

Case 5-1   Time Warner Inc. and the ORC Patents

In early July 1992, John Adamson, president of Optical Recording Corporation (ORC), sat depressed

Richard Ivey School of Business
The University of Western Ontario

John Adamson prepared this case under the supervision of Professor Paul Beamish solely to provide material for class discussion. The authors do not intend to illustrate either effective or ineffective handling of a managerial situation. The authors may have disguised certain names and other identifying information to protect confidentiality. Ivey Management Services prohibits any form of reproduction, storage or transmittal without its written permission. This material is not covered under authorization from CanCopy or any reproduction rights organization. To order copies or request permission to reproduce materials, contact Ivey Publishing, Ivey Management Services, c/o Richard Ivey School of Business, The University of Western Ontario, London, Ontario, Canada, N6A 3K7; phone (519) 661-3208; fax (519) 661-3882; e-mail cases@ivey.uwo.ca.

and second-guessed his company's decision to sue Time Warner Inc. for patent infringement. An in-house patent counsel from the U.S. Philips Corporation, whose parent firm developed and licensed the compact disc (CD) technology in partnership with Sony Corporation, had just finished his testimony in the Wilmington, Delaware, courtroom.

The Philips attorney had just advised the court that Philips International N.V. had indeed signed a license agreement with ORC but only to "get rid of ORC with a modest nuisance payment." He had gone on to say that in spite of their decision to accept a license from ORC, the Philips engineers and attorneys had never believed that the Russell patents owned by ORC were valid nor that any compact disc products infringed these patents. Adamson watched in shock as the Philips man made his way out of the courtroom.

Given that Time Warner had mounted a very credible defense and that ORC's entire licensing program might be at risk, Adamson needed to decide whether he should make a modest settlement with Time Warner, just to save the licensing program.

Background

Optical Recording Corporation (ORC) was incorporated in 1984 to exploit a technology invented by James T. Russell, an American inventor, then working in laboratories in Salt Lake City, Utah. Due to the desperate financial straits of SLC[1], his employer, Russell had made little progress in the previous two years and both he and SLC were anxious to secure a buyer for the technology.

Through Wayne White, a fellow MBA 1972 graduate from the University of Western Ontario, then working with Dominion Securities in Toronto, John Adamson was put in contact with Dr. R. Moses and Dr. A. Stein. These two Toronto businessmen had been working for close to a year to buy Russell's technology. By happenstance, Adamson had contacted White looking for business opportunities to start his next business, preferably in electronics or software, just days after Moses and Stein had advised White that they were going to throw in the towel on their Russell project. In spite of the considerable time that they had spent, it appeared unlikely that they would be successful in securing the necessary finances to proceed.

Adamson negotiated an option with these gentlemen to assume their "interests" in the Russell project, on the condition that he secure the necessary funding for a technology transfer by April 1, 1985, a propitious date as it would turn out. In return, Adamson agreed to reimburse their expenses to date and to give to each, a five per cent equity interest in the incorporation formed to exploit the Russell project in Toronto.

After completing a "due diligence" investigation of the Russell technology, with the assistance of Warner Sharkey, an alumnus and friend from the

---

[1]Due to a series of commercial lawsuits lasting 10 years with Russell's former employer, the author prefers to omit any real name reference to this company that had been a party to the technology transfer agreements with ORC. It is referred to here as "SLC." In all other references herein to persons, places or businesses, the actual names are used.

Royal Military College of Canada and a senior technology consultant, who operated from offices in New York and Toronto, Adamson began planning in earnest. He wanted to transfer the Russell technology to Toronto, where he expected a well qualified team of scientists and engineers could be assembled to pursue a cost-effective development of a pocket-portable digital storage device.

For the next nine excruciating months, he worked to find investors for an issue of special debentures from his Toronto start-up. These debentures also offered a very attractive cash-back feature under a research tax credit program of the Canadian government. Funding was secured and the technology transfer agreements were signed on March 28, 1985, only three days before the option agreement with Moses and Stein would have expired. Adamson had resisted the temptation to request an extension of time on his option agreement with Moses and Stein. He feared that, better informed, they might rekindle their interest in the Russell technology and work to obstruct what little chance he still had to find funding prior to the option expiry on the first of April.

With the debenture funding and the transfer agreements signed, the new Toronto company, soon to be called Optical Recording Corporation (ORC), was now ready to hire Russell and transfer SLC's technology to Toronto.

Jim Russell

By 1984, Jim Russell had worked for close to 20 years toward an improvement in recorded music beyond what was possible with the analog magnetic tape technology. This quest was motivated in part by his love of opera and a desire to listen to more accurate playbacks of recorded performances. When Adamson first visited Russell's lab in Salt Lake City, he was treated to the playback of a recording of Richard Wagner's "Ride of the Valkyries" (or *Die Walkure*" in the original German). It was a most rousing introduction to a technology!

Russell had accomplished this playback by shining an argon ion laser beam onto a pre-recorded glass plate, the size of an index card. This was the latest of his laboratory prototypes designed to demonstrate his patented techniques. These techniques were claimed in his extensive portfolio of 26 U.S. patents with corresponding foreign issues in seven other countries.

In Russell's way of recording music, the acoustic signal of the music was first preprocessed into a single *digital* bit stream from a series of time-coincident frequency samples. A laser, an *optical* device, was then used as the energy source to mark the music, as digital bits, onto a glass plate in the recording step and then used to read the music, as digital bits, in the playback step. This technology was known as *digital optical* audio recording.

Adamson was not the first to visit Russell's lab, far from it. Over the course of the previous 10 years, both at SLC in Salt Lake City, and at Battelle Northwest Laboratories in Richland, Washington, electronics manufacturers around the world beat a path to Russell's laboratory door and at his invitation. SLC had been trying to sell technology licenses to the Russell technology but with virtually no success. Prominent among the visitors to SLC's labs were representatives from Philips International N.V., the multinational electric/electronics giant headquartered in Eindhoven, the Netherlands. They had made three separate visits over that 10-year period.

Prior to the commercial availability of the diode laser in the early 1980s, Russell's recording and playback devices were operated with the use of a gas ion laser and as such could be made no smaller than the dimensions of an office desk. Gas ion lasers were too bulky, complicated and expensive to be used in consumer products. This may explain SLC's lack of success in licensing and their resultant financial distress. With the advent of the diode laser, essentially a powerful light source on a silicon chip, a light, compact and economical consumer product such as the compact disc was possible. Although never well funded, SLC's money troubles really began in 1981, just as the mass commercialization of a

digital optical audio recording device became feasible.

From Adamson's viewpoint, Russell's greatest achievement was not any one of his inventions, but his success in demonstrating the technical feasibility of recording a digital audio signal optically. Before Russell had successfully demonstrated this technical feat in 1975, no one else had even attempted it. By early 1984, however, the electronics trade papers were reporting that Sony and Philips were developing a so-called compact disc player. SLC and Russell must have felt that they were being left on the sidelines in Salt Lake City, a bitter fate for the inventor and his investors who had all contributed so much.

In bringing Russell and his technology to Toronto, Adamson had decided that there was little point in continuing audio research toward a digital optical tape recorder. The opportunity to develop a massive random access data storage device using credit card-sized media was seen a less ambitious technical challenge and possibly of greater commercial value than a music device like the CD. With the insight of Russell, Adamson envisioned books, medical records, equipment schematics, maintenance instructions and records on this type of device—and all pocket-portable.

In order to determine what protection the existing Russell patents would provide to the new research focus, Adamson employed the services of John Orange, a patent agent, then with the Toronto law firm of McCarthy & McCarthy. (Orange was recommended by Daniel Cooper, a corporate attorney with the same law firm, who earlier had prepared all of the financing and technology transfer agreements for ORC.)

After working with Russell for several months, Orange advised Adamson in early 1986 that the Russell patents may not provide much protection to the new company's research focus, as the most relevant patents appeared to be limited in their claims to audio applications. Adamson had already understood that it was the precise language of the claims within a patent that determined the patent's intellectual property rights.

Discovering a Treasure

In completing his study of ORC's patents with the assistance of Russell, Orange also concluded that the newly released compact disc players and discs might infringe one or more of the claims in the Russell patents. What a finding!

Russell had mentioned this possibility to Adamson during their first meeting in the Salt Lake City lab; however, Adamson had put little faith in Russell's remark at the time, as no consumer electronics firm had bothered to license the technology, in spite of SLC's efforts. Furthermore there were no CD products on the market then and its commercial success could not be anticipated.

Encouraged by the report from Orange and the early market success of the compact disc by the spring of 1986, Adamson retained the services of Adrian Horne, an established patent licensing professional of Dolby acoustic research fame. With Horne's assistance, ORC set out to advise every electronics firm likely to market a compact disc player anywhere in the world that "they may infringe the Russell patents" by doing so. Horne was most clear on the point that ORC must not appear to threaten legal action in their notice, as it may give grounds to the recipients to file a preemptive request for Declaratory Judgment and thereby force ORC into premature legal proceedings that ORC could ill afford.

In conjunction with the initial contact of alleged infringers, Adamson prepared cost estimates for the licensing effort and started to gain some early information on what it would cost to sue for patent infringement. He knew that once launched, any investment in the licensing program was certain to be incurred, whereas the return by way of royalty revenues would be anything but certain. He also made early estimates of the royalty potential for the licensing program, but these royalty estimates carried an enormous emotional impact.

Simple arithmetic established that if 100 million CD players were sold in ORC's patent-protected territories at an average manufacturer's selling price of US$100 and if ORC licensed their patent rights for this product at two per cent of revenues, ORC's projected royalties would total US$200 million. And this figure ignored the royalties to be earned on the manufacture and sale of the compact disc media itself! It was clear that a successful licensing program could be mounted given these simple estimates. Adamson chose not to dwell on these figures, however, as his typical reaction oscillated between a measured excitement and a raw fear of the business of licensing beyond what little he knew.

ORC's first meeting with a suspected infringer took place in the early summer of 1986 in Tarrytown, New York, in the offices of N.A. Philips Corporation. Legal representatives for both N.A. Philips and their Philips parent in Eindhoven, the Netherlands, and for the DuPont Corporation of Wilmington, Delaware, were in attendance. For ORC there were Cooper, Orange, and Adamson and a lawyer from Battelle Laboratories of Columbus, Ohio, Jim Russell's first employer, and the original owner and assignor of the Russell patents, first to SLC and then to ORC.

This first meeting with the Philips and DuPont people ended three and one-half hours later, after a full exchange of views and some acrimony, but no progress toward a licensing agreement. The attorneys representing both Philips and DuPont were of the view that no patents were infringed and further that there was some question about the validity of the Russell patents in the first place. There seemed little point in a further meeting and it seemed very likely that ORC might get no further without filing a patent infringement suit.

In August 1986, Adamson made a first trip to Tokyo on behalf of ORC, with Horne and Russell. A week-long series of company presentations had been arranged by Horne, with the assistance of Far East Associates, a technology licensing agency based in Tokyo, with whom Mr. Horne had collaborated in his Dolby days. Only one prominent manufacturer was invited to each meeting.

On Horne's advice, ORC had booked conference room space at the prestigious Okura Hotel, located directly across from the American Embassy in

Minato-ku, a district of central Tokyo. Adamson choked on the daily expense of US$2,000 per day for a meeting room that comfortably held only six people. Horne, however, had stressed the importance of the location to ensure that the status-sensitive Japanese gained the best initial impression of ORC and its business offering.

The ORC team was overwhelmed by the turnout to their presentations. Each firm sent at least four executives and engineers; and in two instances, a group of over 10 people arrived, forcing the ORC team to scramble for a larger meeting room. Many guests recognized Horne from his previous Dolby research licensing days and more than a few appeared quite knowledgeable of Russell's research and patents. In fact, three firms clearly had comprehensive files on Russell's work and appeared very familiar with the technology.

The ORC presentations were made in English. Horne had advised that the executives in the international departments of all Japanese companies were invariably fluent in English. The younger members, however, tended to be more at ease in English, while some of the more experienced guests appeared to be there simply to witness the process and tone of the meeting and to gage the visitors as adversaries. Adamson concluded that some of the groups had arrived en masse, ready to take notes, in order to do a team translation, once they returned to their corporate offices. This would explain the large numbers of guests from some companies.

Nonetheless, this initial series of meetings convinced the ORC team that their patent infringement claims were being taken seriously by the Japanese firms. Apart from Philips, only the Japanese had announced CD player products by the fall of 1986.

During this initial trip by the ORC team to Tokyo, Yoshihide (Josh) Nakamura, then senior general manager, Intellectual Property, Sony Corporation invited the ORC team to Sony's headquarters for another meeting on their next visit to Japan.

Adamson returned to Tokyo with Orange and Horne in November 1986, for another series of presentations and meetings, but this time at each

company's offices as prearranged again by Far East Associates. The most important of these meetings was with Sony Corporation, as the ORC team felt certain that Sony's decision on whether to license the Russell patents, would predetermine ORC's success with all other firms in Japan. (It was a Philips–Sony partnership that had launched the compact disc and taught an industry how to make them.)

On a schedule of two and even three meetings each day, including shuttles between companies located around Tokyo and Osaka, the ORC team made 12 more presentations. All discussions were held in English, again with only a perfunctory objection from the Japanese hosts. Everyone appreciated that the United States represented the largest domestic market for the compact disc industry and as Jim Russell had first filed his patents in the United States, it was also likely to be the site of ORC's most comprehensive patent protection.

In fact, ORC's patents were most comprehensive in the United States, Britain and Canada, but appeared to provide a weaker protection in Germany, France and the Netherlands. The prosecution of ORC's patents before the Japanese Patent Office had been stalled for many years, partly due to SLC's lack of funds. As such, while virtually all of the CD players were being manufactured in Japan, apart from those made by Philips, the greatest exposure of these Japanese manufacturers to ORC's claims of infringement lay in their export shipments to North America and Europe. Their shipments within Japan and to the rest of the world would only be exposed if ORC succeeded in getting the Japanese Patent Office to issue a key patent. (ORC never succeeded at having their Japanese patent issued.)

Some firms, including Sony, had gone to the expense of having an U.S. patent attorney present at all meetings with ORC, but Sony appeared the most ready to enter into substantive discussions. In this second round of discussions, Sony's team of six or seven engineers and executives presented ORC with a package of over 25 U.S. patents, all cited as Prior Art against the Russell patents.

Publishing the "Blue Book"

Adamson had been warned by both Horne and Orange to expect such a patent defense from Sony. He understood that if the techniques that Russell had claimed in his patents as inventions could be found in any reference that had been published or made public prior to the filing of his patents (i.e. Prior Art), Russell's patents would be found "invalid" and unenforceable. In spite of the warnings, Adamson was highly alarmed and wondered whether ORC was in for a challenge.

On returning to Toronto and on the suggestion of Orange, Adamson tasked him to collaborate with Russell in a review of documents that Sony had provided. Orange prepared a technical response for each reference and compiled these results in a bound booklet for distribution to each prospective licensee. Thus, the so-called "Blue Book" was born. It was thought that by making a general distribution of the "Blue Book," any duplication of effort from one set of technical discussions to another could be minimized, while hopefully speeding all talks toward the signing of licenses.

Adamson had no sense whether one or other of the Prior Art references might hold a "golden arrow" that would pierce the assumed validity for the Russell patents. He knew that a patent was generally assumed to be valid as issued, and therefore enforceable before the courts, but any unanswered Prior Art reference could quickly dispose of ORC's credibility and their licensing prospects.

Distractions Along the Way

Adamson had another more urgent reason to wish the licensing talks to progress quickly. As a research firm, ORC was funding its operations from its initial financing, gained through a tax credit program of the Canadian government. With an initial net investment of just Cdn$6.5 million and a monthly "burn-rate" approaching Cdn$250,000 for the research program, Adamson knew that ORC would likely run out of cash by the end of 1987, at the latest. (Luckily for ORC, the mid-1980s were a period of rampant inflation and ORC was earning 10 per cent, and 12 per cent per annum on its cash hoard.)

To add to the general instability of the situation, the Canadian government, SLC (the firm that had transferred the Russell technology to ORC) and the inventor himself, Russell, were now all objecting to the terms of the agreements that had brought the technology to Toronto. The Canadian government wished to rescind their tax credits and were demanding an immediate cash reimbursement while SLC and Jim Russell were both interpreting their respective agreements in their favor, to secure some respective right to ORC's potential licensing windfall from the compact disc industry.

Adamson remained of the view that all claimants were incorrect in their positions and vowed privately to resist their claims even into bankruptcy. Despite all of these distractions, he also knew that ORC had to maintain the appearance of complete stability, control and competence, in order to avoid "losing face" before their Japanese prospective licensees. Many hours of sleep were lost during this desperate period.

The Sony Protocol

By their second meeting with ORC, the Sony team were stating that they wished to deal directly with ORC and not through Far East Associates, as Sony reportedly had for their patent license with the Dolby firm. They also indicated that if Sony agreed to a license, they would want the right to act as ORC's exclusive agent to license all other manufacturers based in Japan, for their CD player production. As only Japanese manufacturers were then making CD players, apart from Philips in the Netherlands, this was difficult to agree to, given that ORC had resisted a similar proposal from Far East Associates.

Both the services of Horne and Far East Associates had been contracted on a fee-for-service basis, with ORC retaining all licensing rights to the Russell patents. Both could be terminated without cause in the normal course of business. As consultants, their services were required only as long as the client thought they were adding value. Far East Associates had indicated a desire to assume a full agency role on behalf of ORC with the full authority to license ORC's patents on behalf of ORC, but Adamson had resisted this overture, convinced that ORC would be better served by dealing with each manufacturer directly.

Now Sony was asking ORC to terminate Far East Associates and to make presentations directly to Japanese manufacturers, in anticipation of Sony agreeing to a patent license. This license, however, would only apply to CD players, with Sony assuming the role of exclusive agent, possibly for all of Asia. Adamson accepted this protocol with Sony, but he had to trust that Sony was in earnest in their desire to be the exclusive agent and not just leading ORC toward a dead end.

Further, as with Far East Associates, he had no idea how ORC was to monitor the work and licensing progress of an exclusive agent based in the Far East, directly licensing Asian manufacturers. How was one to know when a license was signed and royalties collected, if not by the exclusive agent? In any case, as co-licenser with Philips of the CD technology, Sony's support was clearly paramount to ORC.

So a pattern developed. Every four to eight weeks, Adamson and Orange traveled to Tokyo, Osaka and other cities in Japan to hold patent infringement and licensing discussions with the major Japanese consumer electronics firms such as Matsushita (Panasonic), Toshiba, Hitachi, Sanyo, Pioneer, Sharp and particularly Sony.

With each visit, new Prior Art references were put forward by one or other of the manufacturers, and ORC, in the person of Orange, would respond "on the fly" if an obvious separation from the art could be discerned. If not, ORC would fax a response to all participants upon returning to Toronto.

As the months passed, it was becoming increasingly clear to all that the Russell patents as presented by the ORC team, could withstand the invalidity challenges from the Prior Art. Equally important, the compact disc technical standard that ensured manufactured compatibility across all compliant CD products included techniques claimed in the Russell patents. To comply with this CD standard was to infringe the Russell patents! In short it appeared that the Russell patents were valid and infringed by all CD products!

To balance this rosy picture, however, it was equally clear that, month by month, ORC's cash was disappearing into its research program. The company had lost any of the financial strength with which to mount a credible court challenge against even one of the established manufacturers: Sony, Philips or any of the twenty other firms of similar bulk.

The End Game?

Finally in the fall of 1987, Adamson realized that neither Sony nor any other firm was likely to accept a license without more pressure being applied and more pressure than ORC could bring to the negotiating table. With nothing left to lose, Adamson flew to Tokyo in mid-January 1988, for a final meeting with Sony Corporation. No other firm was as advanced in discussions with ORC as Sony and Adamson reasoned that Sony had become fairly certain of the profit potential as ORC's master licensee for Japan. Sony would also have something to lose if the talks with ORC failed.

To add to this pressure, he could advise Sony that ORC was close to bankruptcy and, if ORC went into bankruptcy, the Russell patents would revert to their former owner, SLC, a firm that, in his direct experience, proved to be very litigious. The Sony team requested a lunch break.

Over lunch Josh Nakamura asked Adamson whether he would continue to be involved with the Russell patent licensing if ORC went bankrupt. Adamson replied that while his ownership of the patents would be lost, he could no doubt strike a deal with SLC such that the licensing program would not "skip a beat." However the program would then be well financed by a very litigious American backer and, under the circumstances, Adamson would have little interest in favoring Sony in any way. Given his rocky relations with SLC, Adamson painted a most optimistic view of his future.

Returning to the Sony offices after lunch, the Sony team requested a further break and Adamson and Cooper sat quietly for an hour and a half in the meeting room at the Sony corporate head offices in Kita-Shinagawa; Adamson pondering his fate.

ORC's First License

Back in the meeting, Nakamura advised that Sony would be ready to sign a license with ORC. The license, however, would only cover CD players, not compact disc media. Further, ORC had to significantly reduce their royalty demands, accept Sony as the exclusive agent with full authority to license all CD player manufacturers based in Asia and pay Sony an administrative fee for their exclusive agency representation out of the royalties to be received. The proposal also required that ORC transfer the right to sue Asian CD player manufacturers for patent infringement to Sony as their exclusive agent. Adamson felt he had no choice but to accept this proposal if he wished to maintain his control of the Russell patents.

It was then agreed that the outline of the license and agency agreements be developed that very afternoon with a final negotiation of royalty rates to occur by telephone in the following week. Cooper took on the task of drafting the required changes to ORC's standard patent license agreement. Negotiations were then completed by telephone the following week and the Sony CD player agreement was signed in early February 1988.

From this shaky last-minute effort, Adamson had managed to retain his full ownership of the Russell patents through ORC. By licensing Sony, ORC now had a royalty cash flow with which to maintain the research program underway in Toronto, as well as the resources to fend off the law suits from the Government of Canada and SLC. For the first time in its existence, ORC was cash flow positive and in that sense, time was now on ORC's side; however, when measured against industry norms, the license with Sony cost ORC plenty. Nakamura and the Sony team had done their job well.

Apart from Sony's hard bargain, they were always gracious but now as business partners, Nakamura and Sony's negotiating team seemed to relish this role even more.

Adamson came to look forward to an invitation to dine at one restaurant in particular. High above Akasaka in central Tokyo, directly overlooking the Diet, Japan's national parliament, there was a restaurant laid out in a series of private dining rooms, each in a unique Western décor of a particular color and at least one Monet or similar Old Master painting dominating the room. Their chefs were trained at the Paul Bocuse culinary school in France and the wine list read like a vintners' award booklet.

Adamson also came to realize that the superb ambiance and staff service of the Hotel Okura was very habit-forming and in spite of the expense, he opted to stay there whenever he was in Tokyo. Horne had been right. Being invited to lunch or dinner at the Hotel Okura, was also a great treat for ORC's licensing prospects and other business associates in Tokyo.

Onward

Among the more difficult challenges that ORC faced in mounting the licensing program was the determination of the size of the infringing production unit volumes and sales revenues. A prospective licensee is not about to divulge this data, as it would impair their negotiating position and possibly increase their chances of being sued before one of their competitors. Nevertheless in the case of CD media, it was pretty obvious that the five sisters of sound; Philips (Deutsche Grammophon), Sony (Columbia), Time Warner (Warner), EMI (London and Angel) and Bertelsmann (RCA) were the largest manufacturers of CD media. After Philips and Sony, Time Warner was likely to be the largest compact disc maker in the United States.

Government agencies and industry trade associations publish trade statistics, but this data is usually on an industry-wide basis (not by company) and for broad product categories, not for individual products, such as a CD player. Beyond these sources, there are industry consultants of varying usefulness and reliability. Nevertheless the licenser must develop estimates of the production and sales volumes for the infringing product by manufacturer and for each year from the start of the infringement to the expiry of the patent or the end of the infringement, whichever comes first.

Without such numbers it is not possible to decide which companies are the more lucrative licensing prospects and more importantly whether a licensing program is even feasible. Without this data the licenser cannot know which infringer to sue or in which jurisdiction to bring the suit, to ensure the most favorable cost–benefit ratio for such an action.

In the ensuing 12 months, Sony sub-licensed over 50 per cent of the remaining Japanese production for CD players and ORC began to develop a substantial "war-chest." Still unresolved were ORC's equivalent infringement claims against the manufacturers of the discs, the compact disc media. Sony had refused to include this item in the initial license as they advised that they needed more time to study the matter. They also stated the view that the Russell patents were less likely to be infringed by the discs.

In the summer of 1988, however, ORC succeeded in licensing the Philips Corporation for both CD players and media and with this success, somewhat confirming Sony's earlier license commitment, Sony agreed to sign a license for CD media in November 1988. By the end of 1988, ORC had a cash position well in excess of US$10 million and the licensing program was on a roll.

The next largest manufacturer of CD media in the United States, by production volume, after American subsidiaries of Sony and Philips-Dupont, was known to be WEA Manufacturing, a subsidiary of Time Warner Inc. Commencing in 1987, Adamson held several discussions, by mail, telephone and face-to-face meetings, with Time Warner's in-house counsel. These discussions lead nowhere however as Time Warner's often-repeated view was the standard "non-infringement and invalid patents" position of an alleged infringer.

Enforcing ORC's Patent Rights

In early 1990, ORC had retained Davis Hoxie Faithfull & Hapgood, a patent law firm, just next door to Time Warner's corporate head office in the Rockefeller Center in New York City. Charles

Bradley, a senior patent litigating attorney with Davis Hoxie had been recommended to Adamson on a chance encounter, while in Tokyo, with an American attorney who had the misfortune of opposing Bradley in a previous patent case. Bradley and Lawrence Goodwin, his partner, were engaged to pursue ORC's interests with the respect to the alleged infringement by WEA Manufacturing, a subsidiary of Time Warner Inc. Goodwin became the "lead" attorney on the ORC file with Bradley providing oversight, senior counsel and strategic advice to Goodwin.

On ORC's behalf, the Davis Hoxie firm filed a patent infringement complaint against WEA Manufacturing in the Federal District Court in Wilmington, Delaware, in June 1990. Like many other major American corporations, Time Warner and its subsidiary, WEA Manufacturing, were incorporated in the State of Delaware.

Not the least of Adamson's concerns in deciding to sue Time Warner in early 1991 was a looming patent expiry date in July 1992 for a U.S. patent, the key to ORC's infringement claims against CD media manufacturers.

The greatest threat that a patent-holder has against a recalcitrant infringer is a court injunction to stop the infringer's production lines. By 1991, this threat was all but lost to ORC as the July 1992 expiry date of ORC's key U.S. patent was likely to pass before any court could rule on the matter.

Without the threat of a court order to stop an infringing production, the patent-holder's leverage is reduced to the probability of a favorable court award being considerably more arduous for the infringer than the royalty payable if a license had been accepted. Even this leverage is diminished by the reality that, at any time prior to an appeal court ruling on a lower court award, the infringer is free to negotiate a settlement with the licenser, even well past a court decision which declares them to be infringing. The infringer can also hope that the patent-holder will capitulate before the end of a full trial, for lack of sufficient funds.

These considerations were very much on Adamson's mind in March 1992 as he drafted a letter (see Exhibit 1) to be sent directly to Time

Exhibit 1   Draft Letter to Time Warner's In-House Counsel

CONFIRMATION ONLY

FACSIMILE MESSAGE OF TWO PAGES TO: 1 (212) 522-1252

March 4, 1992

<u>WITHOUT PREJUDICE</u>

Dear

<u>RE:</u>   <u>ORC vs Time Warner Inc.</u>

Over the past week, we have prepared estimates on the costs and probable outcome of this case. We share this information with you now, in the hope of developing a common understanding from which a mutually satisfactory settlement might result. Our New York counsel is aware of this communication but, the views expressed here may not necessarily coincide with theirs.

Assuming that your costs to date equal ours, Time Warner has spent US$1,000,000 in out-of-pocket expenses alone,. Assuming that we will each spend another US$1,000,000 to the end of trial and then another US$200,000 on an appeal, we will each have spent another US$1,200,000 for a total of US$2,200,000 on this case. Give or take a few $100,000, these costs have a 100% probability of being incurred, if we proceed.

As to the outcome, it is our view that ORC has a significantly stronger case, as Justice Farnan's recent rulings might suggest. Further, we have substantial confidence in our representation. Nevertheless, we accept that the trial process is highly unpredictable. Therefore, we would attach a conservative estimate of perhaps 50% to the probability of ORC winning at both, trial and appeal.

Our licensing program had been based on the royalty rate of US$0.015 per disk and against the estimated and actual production totals for WEA and Allied of 400 million disks, a royalty amount of US$6,000,000 can be estimated. The size of award by the court could vary up or down from this royalty estimate but, it is our view that US$6,000,000 is a good average to assume of all possible court awards. If we assume a 50% probability that ORC will win, then it follows that there is a 50% probability that Time Warner will be required to pay the average award of US$6,000,000.

(continued)

Exhibit 1   (*concluded*)

-2-

To summarize, at this point in time, Time Warner has a 50% probability of paying out $6,000,000 in award and a 100% probability of paying $1,200,000 in continuing litigation costs, if we proceed.

We believe that a final attempt at settlement is in the interest of both companies at this time. Therefore, we now propose a patent license to Time Warner for their manufacture of Compact Disc in the United States, for $3,000,000; that is, for 50% of the $6,000,000, which we contend that Time Warner has at least a 50% probability of incurring as a court award.

This offer will remain open until 5:00 pm, Friday, March 6, 1992, after which, this and all previous offers will be withdrawn.

We would appreciate your comments on the logic presented here, particularly if you have a significantly divergent view on any point. Please feel free to call me directly if you wish to discuss any point in this letter.

Yours very truly,

G. John Adamson
President

GJA/gj

OPTICAL RECORDING CORPORATION

141 JOHN STREET, TORONTO, CANADA M5V 2E4 • TELEPHONE (416) 596-6862 • FAX (416) 596-0452

Source: Company files.

Warner's in-house counsel with a copy to Goodwin. Goodwin had advised against sending the letter, given that ORC had filed their patent infringement suit against Time Warner almost two years earlier, however, Adamson felt certain that Time Warner should be willing to settle for the modest sum of US$3 million, just to avoid the patent infringement trial now scheduled for June 1992, with all of its costs and disruption. Of no surprise to Goodwin, Time Warner politely declined ORC's settlement proposal, perhaps thinking that the letter was a clear indication that ORC was about to capitulate, if they had not already, with their modest US$3 million settlement offer.

Will They Like Us in Wilmington?

Now faced with the certainty of a trial in the United States, Adamson had to deal with a personal overriding concern. Could an American jury be prejudiced against a Canadian company such as ORC? Goodwin had told him not to worry about it, but Adamson was concerned that Goodwin simply did not know.

Too embarrassed to advise Goodwin of his continuing concern with a potential American prejudice toward a Canadian company, Adamson hired the New York office of Goldfarb Consultants, a Canadian market survey firm. Their assignment was to conduct an opinion survey on attitudes, toward Canadian companies, of people drawn from the "jury-pool" population around Wilmington, Delaware. The Goldfarb team suggested that they conduct this survey with focus group interviews based on a set of questions pre-cleared by ORC.

In April 1992, Adamson traveled to Wilmington to witness the interviews firsthand by watching the proceedings on a video monitor in an adjacent room. There were three sessions comprising a total of 35 participants, who gave up a part of their evening for the survey in return for dinner and a modest stipend.

The interviews were conducted in two parts. The first part was designed to solicit an unprompted reference to Canada, in its role as a trading partner of the United States. The second part was designed to solicit directly any opinions that they may hold toward Canadian companies and then specifically a Canadian company's right to protect their American rights by suing an American company in Delaware.

The survey was of great benefit to Adamson as it quickly became clear that he should not be concerned about an American prejudice toward Canadian companies. If a prejudice did exist, it could only be positive because the survey, in every focus group, turned into a love-fest for Canada and Canadians.

Each focus group became frustrated with the first part of the survey. In trying to find the trading partner that they might be concerned about, Canada was never mentioned, even in their desperate attempts to finally yell out the "correct answer." This desperation was then followed by groans when Canada was finally noted by the session moderator at the beginning of the second part of the survey. Very few of those surveyed knew that Canada was indeed the largest trading partner of the United States.

With Canada now on the table and not hiding as in a trick question, many positive views were openly expressed. In fact more than a few had vacationed in Canada, some had close Canadian relatives and one woman was so effusive as to simply say, "I love Canadians," quickly adding that she and her husband vacationed regularly in the Montreal area.

A little sheepishly, Adamson returned to Toronto and phoned Goodwin to advise him that "the ball was now in his court" and that ORC would see the Time Warner case through to appeal, if necessary. He did not mention the survey.

The Rubber Meets the Road

Led by Goodwin, the Davis Hoxie team was comprised of one other full-time attorney, Robert Cote, and a support staff of three, all of whom stayed in Wilmington for the duration of the trial (with some weekends at home in New York). This Delaware team worked from the offices of a Wilmington law firm. This law firm in turn provided its own legal and support staff to ORC's team on an as-required basis. At Davis Hoxie in New York, at least one additional full-time attorney, Peter Bucci, and various other support staff were employed in research and document preparation for the duration of the trial. This entire trial effort was monitored and when appropriate, coached by Charles Bradley.

The trial began in the last days of May 1992, and it was to run for five and one-half weeks. Throughout the trial period, the Davis Hoxie team worked a daily double shift, one in courtroom and then a second in their law offices and hotel rooms, debriefing the day's events and preparing for the next day's court sessions. This preparation included a review of salient facts, prior affidavits, deposition testimony and then general court procedures with each individual witness, in preparation for the court appearance.

It also included a daily review of defendant witness testimony for discrepancies. The review of the court plan for the following day might include witness questioning, preparing motions that pulled together now-important facts and revising presentation materials imperiled by the day's events.

Adamson had decided to remain in Wilmington and attend every court session, given the importance of its outcome for ORC. Having watched the jury selection a few days before, he was highly stressed on the morning of the first day of the trial. He took some comfort in the size and evident competence of the Davis Hoxie team until the Time Warner team appeared.

Either by chance or design, 20 minutes prior to the official court start-time, opposing attorneys began to file into the courtroom. First they filled to overflowing the small defendant's bench in front of the commons rail, and then gradually they occupied the entire commons observer section on the defendant side of the courtroom, spacing themselves comfortably. Adamson sat as a lone observer for ORC directly behind the Davis Hoxie team of five on the plaintiff's side until three more groups of attorneys whom he had never met, filed in to sit behind him, also on the plaintiff's side.

Possibly the entire recording industry, including a few Japanese firms with still unlicensed CD plants in the United States, had sent attorneys, some 30 in all, to observe the start of the trial. The contrast between the sizes of the defendant and plaintiff legal teams was so evident that, prior to the jury entrance, lead counsel for Time Warner told the attorneys behind him to scatter into the plaintiff's observer benches.

Apparently unfazed by the obvious imbalance, a few minutes later, Goodwin stood up to address judge, jury and courtroom on behalf of ORC in a calm, humble but masterful tone. He was to continue as he had started through five and one-half weeks of trial, through surprise, setback, equipment failure, client panic and one or two staff confusions.

ORC's case was further strengthened by the skill of a superb expert witness, Leonard Laub. Laub was responsible for explaining ORC's highly technical infringement case, to a jury with no technical training except for one retired man with an engineering degree dating back to the 1930s. This was accomplished with Laub's testimony guided by questioning from Goodwin and with the use of circuit diagram blow-ups and point summaries on white three feet by five feet storyboards. Adamson was satisfied that if there were a chance that the jury could come to understand ORC's case, it would be solely through the ample teaching skills of Goodwin and Laub.

ORC asked the court and jury for an award in lieu of royalty of six cents per disc against Time Warner and their American subsidiaries and a tripling of that award in punitive damages for willful infringement. The decision to ask for six cents per disc was partly based on ORC's initial licensing request of three cents per disc. Legally, licensers are able to change their royalty demands at any point in a negotiation, before or after the filing of a suit, just as infringers are free to agree to previously unacceptable terms.

(In normal licensing practice, it is simply wise to give active infringers some substantial incentive to sign a license prior to the filing of a suit. This is usually accomplished by increasing the royalty rate by some multiple of the original, say two, three, five or even 10 times. The practical upper limit of a royalty rate is, of course, at that point where the manufacturer can make little profit after paying the royalty, as it is unlikely that any judge or jury would endorse a more onerous royalty request.)

Hearing Goodwin make this request for six cents per disc in open court was a thrilling moment early in the trial. Weeks later the Time Warner attorney was obliged to produce for the court, the unit volumes of their subsidiary's infringing production of compact discs. Their infringement for the period covering the start of production in 1986 through July 1992, the month of the expiry of ORC's patent, totalled over 450 million discs and, at six cents per disc, represented a potential court award for ORC of over US$27 million. The addition of pre-judgment interest and a possible tripling of those damages were more than Adamson could fathom or entertain.

In spite of the good efforts of the Davis Hoxie team with Laub and several other strong witnesses, including Russell, the inventor, and the prospect of an enormous court award, all was not well. After the court appearance by the Philips attorney, Adamson believed that ORC's decision to sue Time Warner might have been taken too lightly.

Goodwin had warned that corporate litigation in the United States was a very expensive enterprise. It was also very demanding of management time, given the need to find, assemble and organize relevant business records, to educate the attorneys in the minutiae of events that usually had happened long ago and to attend court hearings as observers and witnesses. He had also noted that, in the normal course of a robust cross-examination, the combatants and their witnesses could expect personal insults and general verbal abuse. Adamson observed somewhat ruefully that Goodwin had been correct on all counts.

Preliminary motions, production and review of plaintiff and defendant business records and correspondence files, witness depositions, private investigators and trial preparations for the attorneys, company personnel and expert witnesses had already consumed close to US$750,000 of ORC's hard won royalties all before the actual trial had begun. Adamson had budgeted an additional US$1.5 million for fees and expenses to be incurred from the trial itself; however, after the first three weeks of the trial, Adamson saw no end in sight to the trial or its expense.

As was its right as the plaintiff, ORC had chosen to have its case against Time Warner heard before a jury. Even this decision seemed to backfire as it was clear that the jury was putting a good deal of attention and apparent credence into what the defendant's attorneys had to say. The Time Warner litigating team had mounted a very credible defense. They seemed to cloud the technical issues of patent validity and product infringement as these related to the Russell patent claims and the compact disc technology, so that even Adamson found himself confused with ORC's claims from time to time. He had little hope left that the jury would be able to sort through the haze.

With this technical complexity and possible jury confusion, Adamson worried that the direct and damning statements of the Philips attorney toward the Russell patents and ORC's infringement claims could be disastrous for ORC, as these arguments gave the jury, a reasonable and easy "out," from all the confusing technical jargon. Perhaps he was simply someone who knew better about these matters than they could ever hope to know.

Adamson also reflected on the fact that he had been forced to curtail the on-going licensing program for the other CD manufacturers. He had been concerned that some event within ORC's licensing program, such as an agreement with a royalty rate for CD discs below the six cents per

disc demanded in the court case, might affect the outcome of the case; however, this concern was made moot by the simple fact that the other CD manufacturers had displayed little interest in signing a license with ORC as long as a major record company such as Time Warner was challenging ORC's infringement claims in court.

Should the court case result in anything less than a complete endorsement of ORC's infringement claims, ORC's entire licensing program could collapse including the all important quarterly payments from Sony. The CD player license with Sony may have been a "done deal." As a matter of practicality, Adamson wondered whether ORC would be prudent to take Sony to court, should Sony simply stop paying royalties to ORC after a jury verdict had cleared Time Warner of ORC's patent infringement claims.

Over the course of the six years from 1986 to 1992, Adamson had been drawn away from ORC's research effort and future prospects and ever deeper into patent licensing and then this litigation struggle. As he had testified in the Time Warner trial, "there seems little point in investing in the creation and development of new intellectual property rights if major industrial firms are prepared to ignore and infringe existing patent rights that you already own." Playing somewhat to the jury, he knew that he had purposefully overstated his predicament but the basic truth of his simple observation resonated in the momentary silence of the court that day.

Adamson had made the very difficult decision early in 1991 to temporarily shelve ORC's research program and to reduce the Company's technology development team to a skeleton staff of five team leaders. This move had been made for reasons other than the need to focus the Company's resources on the Time Warner litigation. Nonetheless as he sat in that Delaware courtroom, watching the door close after the hasty exit of the Philips attorney, Adamson felt that he had bet ORC's entire future on the outcome of the court case against Time Warner.

The Richard Ivey School of Business gratefully acknowledges the generous support of John Adamson (MBA '72) in the development of this case as part of THE JOHN ADAMSON JAPAN CASE SERIES.

Case 5-2   P&G Japan: The SK-II Globalization Project

In November 1999, Paolo de Cesare was preparing for a meeting with the Global Leadership Team (GLT) of P&G's Beauty Care Global Business Unit (GBU) to present his analysis of whether SK-II, a prestige skin care line from Japan, should become a global P&G brand. As president of Max Factor Japan, the hub of P&G's fast-growing cosmetics business in Asia, and previous head of its European skin care business, de Cesare had considerable credibility with the GLT. Yet, as he readily acknowledged, there were significant risks in his proposal to expand SK-II into China and Europe.

Chairing the GLT meeting was Alan ("A. G.") Lafley, head of P&G's Beauty Care GBU, to which de Cesare reported. In the end, it was his organization—and his budget—that would support such a global expansion. Although he had been an early champion of SK-II in Japan, Lafley would need strong evidence to support P&G's first-ever proposal to expand a Japanese brand worldwide. After all, SK-II's success had been achieved in a culture where the consumers, distribution channels, and competitors were vastly different from those in most other countries.

Another constraint facing de Cesare was that P&G's global organization was in the midst of the bold but disruptive Organization 2005 restructuring program. As GBUs took over profit responsibility historically held by P&G's country-based organizations, management was still trying to negotiate their new working relationships. In this context, de Cesare, Lafley, and other GLT members struggled to answer some key questions: Did SK-II have the potential to develop into a major global brand? If so, which markets were the most important to enter now? And how should this be implemented in P&G's newly reorganized global operations?

▌ Professor Christopher A. Bartlett prepared this case. HBS cases are developed solely as the basis for class discussion. Cases are not intended to serve as endorsements, sources of primary data, or illustrations of effective or ineffective management. Certain data have been disguised, but key relationships have been retained.

P&G's Internationalization: Engine of Growth

De Cesare's expansion plans for a Japanese product was just the latest step in a process of internationalization that had begun three-quarters of a century earlier. But it was the creation of the Overseas Division in 1948 that drove three decades of rapid expansion. Growing first in Europe, then Latin America and Asia, by 1980 P&G's operations in 27 overseas countries accounted for over 25% of its $11 billion worldwide sales. (**Exhibit 1** summarizes P&G's international expansion.)

Exhibit 1	P&G's Internationalization Timetable
Year	**Markets Entered**
1837–1930	United States and Canada
1930–1940	United Kingdom, Philippines
1940–1950	Puerto Rico, Venezuela, Mexico
1950–1960	Switzerland, France, Belgium, Italy, Peru, Saudi Arabia, Morocco
1960–1970	Germany, Greece, Spain, Netherlands, Sweden, Austria, Indonesia, Malaysia, Hong Kong, Singapore, Japan
1970–1980	Ireland
1980–1990	Colombia, Chile, Caribbean, Guatemala, Kenya, Egypt, Thailand, Australia, New Zealand, India, Taiwan, South Korea, Pakistan, Turkey, Brazil, El Salvador
1990–2000	Russia, China, Czech Republic, Hungary, Poland, Slovak Republic, Bulgaria, Belarus, Latvia, Estonia, Romania, Lithuania, Kazakhstan, Yugoslavia, Croatia, Uzbekistan, Ukraine, Slovenia, Nigeria, South Africa, Denmark, Portugal, Norway, Argentina, Yemen, Sri Lanka, Vietnam, Bangladesh, Costa Rica, Turkmenistan

Source: Company records.

Local   Adaptiveness   Meets   Cross-Market Integration   Throughout its early expansion, the company adhered to a set of principles set down by Walter Lingle, the first vice president of overseas operations. "We must tailor our products to meet consumer demands in each nation," he said. "But we must create local country subsidiaries whose structure, policies, and practices are as exact a replica of the U.S. Procter & Gamble organization as it is possible to create." Under the Lingle principles, the company soon built a portfolio of self-sufficient subsidiaries run by country general managers (GMs) who grew their companies by adapting P&G technology and marketing expertise to their knowledge of their local markets.

Yet, by the 1980s, two problems emerged. First, the cost of running all the local product development labs and manufacturing plants was limiting profits. And second, the ferocious autonomy of national subsidiaries was preventing the global roll-out of new products and technology improvements. Local GMs often resisted such initiatives due to the negative impact they had on local profits, for which the country subsidiaries were held accountable. As a result, new products could take a decade or more to be introduced worldwide.

Consequently, during the 1980s, P&G's historically "hands-off" regional headquarters became more active. In Europe, for example, Euro Technical Teams were formed to eliminate needless country-by-country product differences, reduce duplicated development efforts, and gain consensus on new-technology diffusion. Subsequently, regionwide coordination spread to purchasing, finance, and even marketing. In particular, the formation of Euro Brand Teams became an effective forum for marketing managers to coordinate regionwide product strategy and new product rollouts.

By the mid-1980s, these overlaid coordinating processes were formalized when each of the three European regional vice presidents was also given coordinative responsibility for a product category. While these individuals clearly had organizational influence, profit responsibility remained with the country subsidiary GMs. (See **Exhibit 2** for the 1986 European organization.)

Birth of Global Management   In 1986, P&G's seven divisions in the U.S. organization were broken into 26 product categories, each with its own product development, product supply, and sales and marketing capabilities. Given the parallel development of a European category management structure, it was not a big leap to appoint the first global category executives in 1989. These new roles were given significant responsibility for developing global strategy, managing the technology program, and qualifying expansion markets—but not profit responsibility, which still rested with the country subsidiary GMs.

Then, building on the success of the strong regional organization in Europe, P&G replaced its International Division with four regional entities—for North America, Europe, Latin America, and Asia—each assuming primary responsibility for profitability. (See **Exhibit 3** for P&G's structure in 1990.) A significant boost in the company's overseas growth followed, particularly in opening the untapped markets of Eastern Europe and China.

By the mid-1990s, with operations in over 75 countries, major new expansion opportunities were shrinking and growth was slowing. Furthermore, while global category management had improved cross-market coordination, innovative new products such as two-in-one shampoo and compact detergent were still being developed very slowly—particularly if they originated overseas. And even when they did, they were taking years to roll out worldwide. To many in the organization, the matrix structure seemed an impediment to entrepreneurship and flexibility.

P&G Japan: Difficult Childhood, Struggling Adolescence

Up to the mid-1980s, P&G Japan had been a minor contributor to P&G's international growth. Indeed, the start-up had been so difficult that, in 1984, 12 years after entering the Japan market, P&G's board reviewed the accumulated losses of $200 million, the ongoing negative operating margins of 75%, and the eroding sales base—decreasing from 44 billion yen (¥) in 1979 to ¥26 billion in 1984—

Exhibit 2 P&G European Organization, 1986

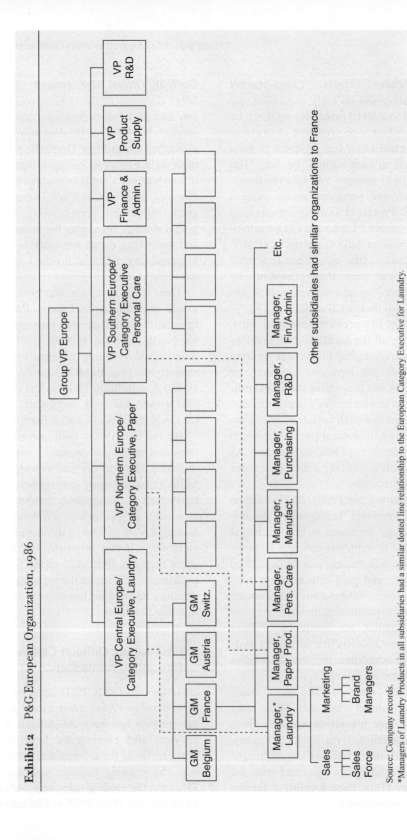

Source: Company records.

*Managers of Laundry Products in all subsidiaries had a similar dotted line relationship to the European Category Executive for Laundry.

Other subsidiaries had similar organizations to France

Exhibit 3 P&G's Worldwide Organization Structure, 1990

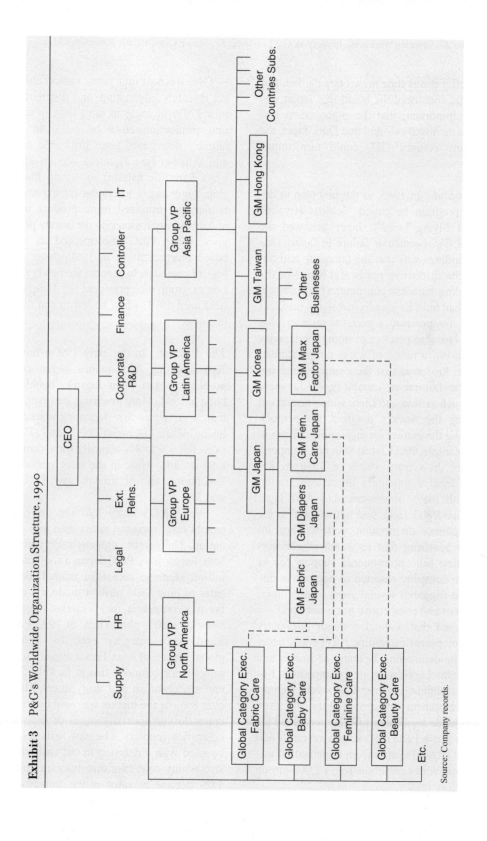

Source: Company records.

and wondered if it was time to exit this market. But CEO Ed Artzt convinced the board that Japan was strategically important, that the organization had learned from its mistakes—and that Durk Jager, the energetic new country GM, could turn things around.

The Turnaround   In 1985, as the first step in developing a program he called "Ichidai Hiyaku" ("The Great Flying Leap"), Jager analyzed the causes of P&G's spectacular failure in Japan. One of his key findings was that the company had not recognized the distinctive needs and habits of the very demanding Japanese consumer. (For instance, P&G Japan had built its laundry-detergent business around All Temperature Cheer, a product that ignored the Japanese practice of doing the laundry in tap water, not a range of water temperatures.) Furthermore, he found that the company had not respected the innovative capability of Japanese companies such as Kao and Lion, which turned out to be among the world's toughest competitors. (After creating the market for disposable diapers in Japan, for example, P&G Japan watched Pampers' market share drop from 100% in 1979 to 8% in 1985 as local competitors introduced similar products with major improvements.) And Jager concluded that P&G Japan had not adapted to the complex Japanese distribution system. (For instance, after realizing that its 3,000 wholesalers were providing little promotional support for its products, the company resorted to aggressive discounting that triggered several years of distributor disengagement and competitive price wars.)

Jager argued that without a major in-country product development capability, P&G could never respond to the demanding Japanese consumer and the tough, technology-driven local competitors. Envisioning a technology center that would support product development throughout Asia and even take a worldwide leadership role, he persuaded his superiors to grow P&G's 60-person research and development (R&D) team into an organization that could compete with competitor Kao's 2,000-strong R&D operation.

Over the next four years, radical change in market research, advertising, and distribution resulted in a 270% increase in sales that, in turn, reduced unit production costs by 62%. In 1988, with laundry detergents again profitable and Pampers and Whisper (the Japanese version of P&G's Always feminine napkin) achieving market leadership, Jager began to emphasize expansion. In particular, he promoted more product introductions and a bold expansion into the beauty products category. When P&G implemented its new region-based reorganization in 1990, Jager became the logical candidate to assume the newly created position of group vice president for Asia, a position he held until 1991, when he left to run the huge U.S. business.

The Relapse   In the early 1990s, however, P&G Japan's strong performance began eroding. The problems began when Japan's "bubble economy" burst in 1991. More troubling, however, was the fact that, even within this stagnating market, P&G was losing share. Between 1992 and 1996 its yen sales fell 3% to 4% annually for a cumulative 20% total decline, while in the same period competitor Unicharm's annual growth was 13% and Kao's was 3%.

Even P&G's entry into the new category of beauty care worsened rather than improved the situation. The parent company's 1991 acquisition of Max Factor gave P&G Japan a foothold in the $10 billion Japanese cosmetics market. But in Japan, sales of only $300 million made it a distant number-five competitor, its 3% market share dwarfed by Shiseido's 20% plus. Then, in 1992 P&G's global beauty care category executive announced the global launch of Max Factor Blue, a top-end, self-select color cosmetic line to be sold through general merchandise and drug stores. But in Japan, over 80% of the market was sold by trained beauty counselors in specialty stores or department store cosmetics counters. The new self-select strategy, coupled with a decision to cut costs in the expensive beauty-counselor distribution channel, led to a 15% decline in sales in the Japanese cosmetics business. The previous break-even performance became a negative operating margin of 10% in 1993. Things became even worse the following year, with losses running at $1 million per week.

In 1994, the Japanese beauty care business lost $50 million on sales of less than $300 million. Among the scores of businesses in the 15 countries reporting to him, A. G. Lafley, the newly arrived vice president of the Asian region, quickly zeroed in on Max Factor Japan as a priority problem area. "We first had to clean up the Max Factor Blue mass-market mess then review our basic strategy," he said. Over the next three years, the local organization worked hard to make Max Factor Japan profitable. Its product line was rationalized from 1,400 SKUs (or stock-keeping units) to 500, distribution support was focused on 4,000 sales outlets as opposed to the previous 10,000, and sales and marketing staff was cut from 600 to 150. It was a trying time for Max Factor Japan.

Organization 2005: Blueprint for Global Growth

In 1996 Jager, now promoted to chief operating officer under CEO John Pepper, signaled that he saw the development of new products as the key to P&G's future growth. While supporting Pepper's emphasis on expanding into emerging markets, he voiced concern that the company would "start running out of white space towards the end of the decade." To emphasize the importance of creating new businesses, he became the champion of a Leadership Innovation Team to identify and support major companywide innovations.

When he succeeded Pepper as CEO in January 1999, Jager continued his mission. Citing P&G breakthroughs such as the first synthetic detergent in the 1930s, the introduction of fluoride toothpaste in the 1950s, and the development of the first disposable diaper in the 1960s, he said, "Almost without exception, we've won biggest on the strength of superior product technology. . . . But frankly, we've come nowhere near exploiting its full potential." Backing this belief, in 1999 he increased the budget

for R&D by 12% while cutting marketing expenditures by 9%.

If P&G's growth would now depend on its ability to develop new products and roll them out rapidly worldwide, Jager believed his new strategic thrust had to be implemented through a radically different organization. Since early 1998 he and Pepper had been planning Organization 2005, an initiative he felt represented "the most dramatic change to P&G's structure, processes, and culture in the company's history." Implementing O2005, as it came to be called, he promised would bring 13% to 15% annual earnings growth and would result in $900 million in annual savings starting in 2004. Implementation would be painful, he warned; in the first five years, it called for the closing of 10 plants and the loss of 15,000 jobs—13% of the worldwide workforce. The cost of the restructuring was estimated at $1.9 billion, with $1 billion of that total forecast for 1999 and 2000.

Changing the Culture   During the three months prior to assuming the CEO role, Jager toured company facilities worldwide. He concluded that P&G's sluggish 2% annual volume growth and its loss of global market share was due to a culture he saw as slow, conformist, and risk averse. (See **Exhibit 4** for P&G's financial performance.) In his view, employees were wasting half their time on "non–value-added work" such as memo writing, form filling, or chart preparation, slowing down decisions and making the company vulnerable to more nimble competition. (One observer described P&G's product development model as "ready, aim, aim, aim, aim, fire.") He concluded that any organizational change would have to be built on a cultural revolution.

With "stretch, innovation, and speed" as his watchwords, Jager signaled his intent to shake up norms and practices that had shaped generations of highly disciplined, intensely loyal managers often referred to within the industry as "Proctoids." "Great ideas come from conflict and dissatisfaction with the status quo," he said. "I'd like an organization where there are rebels." To signal the importance of risk taking and speed, Jager gave a green

Exhibit 4   P&G Select Financial Performance Data, 1980–1999

Annual Income Statement ($ millions)	June 1999	June 1998	June 1997	June 1996	June 1995	June 1990	June 1985	June 1980
Sales	38,125	37,154	35,764	35,284	33,434	24,081	13,552	10,772
Cost of Goods Sold	18,615	19,466	18,829	19,404	18,370	14,658	9,099	7,471
Gross Profit	19,510	17,688	16,935	15,880	15,064	9,423	4,453	3,301
Selling, General, and Administrative Expense	10,628	10,035	9,960	9,707	9,632	6,262	3,099	1,977
of which:								
Research and Development Expense	1,726	1,546	1,469	1,399	1,148	693	400	228
Advertising Expense	3,538	3,704	3,466	3,254	3,284	2,059	1,105	621
Depreciation, Depletion, and Amortization	2,148	1,598	1,487	1,358	1,253	859	378	196
Operating Profit	6,734	6,055	5,488	4,815	4,179	2,302	976	1,128
Interest Expense	650	548	457	493	511	395	165	97
Non-Operating Income/Expense	235	201	218	272	409	561	193	51
Special Items	−481	0	0	75	−77	0	0	0
Total Income Taxes	2,075	1,928	1,834	1,623	1,355	914	369	440
Net Income	3,763	3,780	3,415	3,046	2,645	1,554	635	642
Geographic Breakdown: Net Sales								
Americas	58.4%	54.7%	53.8%	52.9%	55.1%			
United States						62.5%	75.4%	80.9%
Europe, Middle East, and Africa	31.9%	35.1%	35.3%	35.2%	32.9%			
International						39.9%	22.3%	22.4%
Asia	9.7%	10.2%	10.9%	11.9%	10.8%			
Corporate					1.2%	−2.1%	2.3%	−3.3%
Number of Employees	110,000	110,000	106,000	103,000	99,200	94,000	62,000	59,000

Abbreviated Balance Sheet ($ millions)	June 1999	June 1998	June 1997	June 1996	June 1995	June 1990	June 1985	June 1980
ASSETS								
Total Current Assets	11,358	10,577	10,786	10,807	10,842	7,644	3,816	3,007
Plant, Property & Equipment, net	12,626	12,180	11,376	11,118	11,026	7,436	5,292	3,237
Other Assets	8,129	8,209	5,382	5,805	6,257	3,407	575	309
TOTAL ASSETS	32,113	30,966	27,544	27,730	28,125	18,487	9,683	6,553
LIABILITIES								
Total Current Liabilities	10,761	9,250	7,798	7,825	8,648	5,417	2,589	1,670
Long-Term Debt	6,231	5,765	4,143	4,670	5,161	3,588	877	835
Deferred Taxes	362	428	559	638	531	1,258	945	445
Other Liabilities	2,701	3,287	2,998	2,875	3,196	706	0	0
TOTAL LIABILITIES	20,055	18,730	15,498	16,008	17,536	10,969	4,411	2,950
TOTAL EQUITY	12,058	12,236	12,046	11,722	10,589	7,518	5,272	3,603
TOTAL LIABILITIES & EQUITY	32,113	30,966	27,544	27,730	28,125	18,487	9,683	6,553

Source: SEC filings, Standard & Poor's Research Insight.

light to the Leadership Innovation Team to implement a global rollout of two radically new products: Dryel, a home dry-cleaning kit; and Swiffer, an electrostatically charged dust mop. Just 18 months after entering their first test market, they were on sale in the United States, Europe, Latin America, and Asia. Jager promised 20 more new products over the next 18 months. "And if you are worried about oversight," he said, "I am the portfolio manager."

Changing the Processes Reinforcing the new culture were some major changes to P&G's traditional systems and processes. To emphasize the need for greater risk taking, Jager leveraged the performance-based component of compensation so that, for example, the variability of a vice president's annual pay package increased from a traditional range of 20% (10% up or down) to 80% (40% up or down). And to motivate people and align them with the overall success of the company, he extended the reach of the stock option plan from senior management to virtually all employees. Even outsiders were involved, and P&G's advertising agencies soon found their compensation linked to sales increases per dollar spent.

Another major systems shift occurred in the area of budgets. Jager felt that the annual ritual of preparing, negotiating, and revising line item sales and expenses by product and country was enormously time wasting and energy sapping. In future, they would be encouraged to propose ambitious stretch objectives. And going forward, Jager also argued to replace the episodic nature of separate marketing, payroll, and initiative budgets with an integrated business planning process where all budget elements of the operating plan could be reviewed and approved together.

Changing the Structure In perhaps the most drastic change introduced in O2005, primary profit responsibility shifted from P&G's four regional organizations to seven global business units (GBUs) that would now manage product development, manufacturing, and marketing of their respective categories worldwide. The old regional organizations were reconstituted into seven market development organizations (MDOs) that assumed responsibility for local implementation of the GBUs' global

strategies.[1] And transactional activities such as accounting, human resources, payroll, and much of IT were coordinated through a global business service unit (GBS). (See **Exhibit 5** for a representation of the new structure.)

Beyond their clear responsibility for developing and rolling out new products, the GBUs were also charged with the task of increasing efficiency by standardizing manufacturing processes, simplifying brand portfolios, and coordinating marketing activities. For example, by reducing the company's 12 different diaper-manufacturing processes to one standard production model, Jager believed that P&G could not only reap economies but might also remove a major barrier to rapid new-product rollouts. And by axing some of its 300 brands and evaluating the core group with global potential, he felt the company could exploit its resources more efficiently.

The restructuring also aimed to eliminate bureaucracy and increase accountability. Overall, six management layers were stripped out, reducing the levels between the chairman and the front line from 13 to 7. Furthermore, numerous committee responsibilities were transferred to individuals. For example, the final sign-off on new advertising copy was given to individual executives, not approval boards, cutting the time it took to get out ads from months to days.

New Corporate Priorities Meet Old Japanese Problems

The seeds of Jager's strategic and organizational initiatives began sprouting long before he assumed the CEO role in January 1999. For years, he had been pushing his belief in growth through innovation, urging businesses to invest in new products and technologies. Even the organizational review that resulted in the O2005 blueprint had begun a year before he took over. These winds of change blew through all parts of the company, including the long-suffering Japanese company's beauty care business, which was finally emerging from years of problems.

---

[1] In an exception to the shift of profit responsibility to the GBUs, the MDOs responsible for developing countries were treated as profit centers.

Exhibit 5   P&G Organization, 1999 (Post O2005 Implementation)

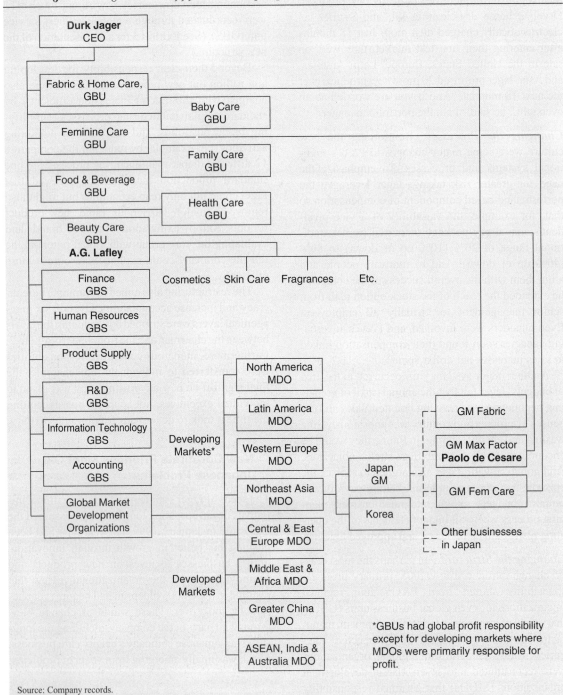

*GBUs had global profit responsibility except for developing markets where MDOs were primarily responsible for profit.

Source: Company records.

Exhibit 6   Beauty Counselor Work Flow

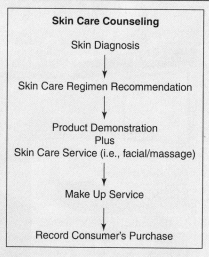

Skin Care Counseling

Skin Diagnosis

↓

Skin Care Regimen Recommendation

↓

Product Demonstration
Plus
Skin Care Service (i.e., facial/massage)

↓

Make Up Service

↓

Record Consumer's Purchase

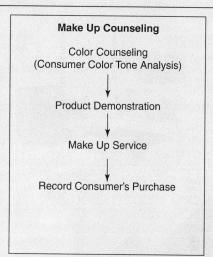

Make Up Counseling

Color Counseling
(Consumer Color Tone Analysis)

↓

Product Demonstration

↓

Make Up Service

↓

Record Consumer's Purchase

Source: Company documents.

Building the Base: From Mass to Class By 1997 the Japanese cosmetics business had broken even. With guidance and support from Lafley, the vice president for the Asian region, the Japanese team had focused its advertising investment on just two brands—Max Factor Color, and a prestige skin care brand called SK-II.[2] "Poring through the Japanese business, we found this little jewel called SK-II," recalled Lafley. "To those of us familiar with rich Western facial creams and lotions, this clear, unperfumed liquid with a distinctive odor seemed very different. But the discriminating Japanese consumer loved it, and it became the cornerstone of our new focus on the prestige beauty-counselor segment."

Max Factor Japan began rebuilding its beauty-counselor channels, which involved significant investments in training as well as counter design and installation (see **Exhibits 6** and **7**). And because SK-II was such a high margin item, management launched a bold experiment in TV advertising featuring a well-respected Japanese actress in her late 30s. In three years SK-II's awareness ratings rose from around 20% to over 70%, while sales in the same period more than doubled.

Building on this success, management adapted the ad campaign for Hong Kong and Taiwan, where SK-II had quietly built a loyal following among the many women who took their fashion cues from Tokyo. In both markets, sales rocketed, and by 1997, export sales of $68 million represented about 30% of the brand's total sales. More important, SK-II was now generating significant operating profits. Yet within P&G, this high-end product had little visibility outside Japan. Paolo de Cesare, general manager of P&G's European skin care business in the mid-1990s, felt that, because the company's skin care experience came from the highly successful mass-market Olay brand, few outside Japan understood SK-II. "I remember some people saying that SK-II was like Olay for Japan," he recalled. "People outside Japan just didn't know what to make of it."

[2] SK-II was an obscure skin care product that had not even been recognized, much less evaluated, in the Max Factor acquisition. Containing Pitera, a secret yeast-based ingredient supposedly developed by a Japanese monk who noticed how the hands of workers in sake breweries kept young looking, SK-II had a small but extremely loyal following. Priced at ¥15,000 ($120) or more per bottle, it clearly was at the top of the skin care range.

Exhibit 7   In-Store SK-II Counter Space

Source: Company documents.

Responding to the Innovation Push   Meanwhile, Jager had begun his push for more innovation. Given his firmly held belief that Japan's demanding consumers and tough competitors made it an important source of leading-edge ideas, it was not surprising that more innovative ideas and initiatives from Japan began finding their way through the company. For example, an electrostatically charged cleaning cloth developed by a Japanese competitor became the genesis of P&G's global rollout of Swiffer dry mops; rising Japanese sensitivity to hygiene and sanitation spawned worldwide application in products such as Ariel Pure Clean ("beyond whiteness, it washes away germs"); and dozens of other ideas from Japan—from a waterless car-washing cloth to a disposable stain-removing pad to a washing machine–based dry-cleaning product—

were all put into P&G's product development pipeline.

Because Japanese women had by far the highest use of beauty care products in the world, it was natural that the global beauty care category management started to regard Max Factor Japan as a potential source of innovation. One of the first worldwide development projects on which Japan played a key role was Lipfinity, a long-lasting lipstick that was felt to have global potential.

In the mid-1990s, the impressive but short-lived success of long-lasting lipsticks introduced in Japan by Shiseido and Kenebo reinforced P&G's own consumer research, which had long indicated the potential for such a product. Working with R&D labs in Cincinnati and the United Kingdom, several Japanese technologists participated on a global team that developed a new product involving a durable color base and a renewable moisturizing second coat. Recognizing that this two-stage application would result in a more expensive product that involved basic habit changes, the global cosmetics category executive asked Max Factor Japan to be the new brand's global lead market.

Viewing their task as "translating the breakthrough technology invention into a market-sensitive product innovation," the Japanese product management team developed the marketing approach—concept, packaging, positioning, communications strategy, and so on—that led to the new brand, Lipfinity, becoming Japan's best-selling lipstick. The Japanese innovations were then transferred worldwide, as Lipfinity rolled out in Europe and the United States within six months of the Japanese launch.

O2005 Rolls Out   Soon after O2005 was first announced in September 1998, massive management changes began. By the time of its formal implementation in July 1999, half the top 30 managers and a third of the top 300 were new to their jobs. For example, Lafley, who had just returned from Asia to head the North American region, was asked to prepare to hand off that role and take over as head of the Beauty Care GBU. "It was a crazy year," recalled Lafley. "There was so much to build, but beyond the grand design, we were not clear about how it should operate."

In another of the hundreds of O2005 senior management changes, de Cesare, head of P&G's European skin care business, was promoted to vice president and asked to move to Osaka and head up Max Factor Japan. Under the new structure he would report directly to Lafley's Beauty Care GBU and on a dotted-line basis to the head of the MDO for Northeast Asia.

In addition to adjusting to this new complexity where responsibilities and relationships were still being defined, de Cesare found himself in a new global role. As president of Max Factor Japan he became a member of the Beauty Care Global Leadership Team (GLT), a group comprised of the business GMs from three key MDOs, representatives

from key functions such as R&D, consumer research, product supply, HR, and finance, and chaired by Lafley as GBU head. These meetings became vital forums for implementing Lafley's charge "to review P&G's huge beauty care portfolio and focus investment on the top brands with the potential to become global assets." The question took on new importance for de Cesare when he was named global franchise leader for SK-II and asked to explore its potential as a global brand.

A New Global Product Development Process
Soon after arriving in Japan, de Cesare discovered that the Japanese Max Factor organization was increasingly involved in new global product development activities following its successful Lipfinity role. This process began under the leadership of the Beauty Care GLT when consumer research identified an unmet consumer need worldwide. A lead research center then developed a technical model of how P&G could respond to the need. Next, the GLT process brought in marketing expertise from lead markets to expand that technology "chassis" to a holistic new-product concept. Finally, contributing technologists and marketers were designated to work on the variations in ingredients or aesthetics necessary to adapt the core technology or product concept to local markets.

This global product development process was set in motion when consumer researchers found that, despite regional differences, there was a worldwide opportunity in facial cleansing. The research showed that, although U.S. women were satisfied with the clean feeling they got using bar soaps, it left their skin tight and dry; in Europe, women applied a cleansing milk with a cotton pad that left their skin moisturized and conditioned but not as clean as they wanted; and in Japan, the habit of using foaming facial cleansers left women satisfied with skin conditioning but not with moisturizing. Globally, however, the unmet need was to achieve soft, moisturized, clean-feeling skin, and herein the GBU saw the product opportunity—and the technological challenge.

A technology team was assembled at an R&D facility in Cincinnati, drawing on the most qualified technologists from its P&G's labs worldwide. For example, because the average Japanese woman spent 4.5 minutes on her face-cleansing regime compared with 1.7 minutes for the typical American woman, Japanese technologists were sought for their refined expertise in the cleansing processes and their particular understanding of how to develop a product with the rich, creamy lather.

Working with a woven substrate technology developed by P&G's paper business, the core technology team found that a 10-micron fiber, when woven into a mesh, was effective in trapping and absorbing dirt and impurities. By impregnating this substrate with a dry-sprayed formula of cleansers and moisturizers activated at different times in the cleansing process, team members felt they could develop a disposable cleansing cloth that would respond to the identified consumer need. After this

technology "chassis" had been developed, a technology team in Japan adapted it to allow the cloth to be impregnated with a different cleanser formulation that included the SK-II ingredient, Pitera. (See **Exhibit 8** for an overview of the development process.)

A U.S.-based marketing team took on the task of developing the Olay version. Identifying its consumers' view of a multistep salon facial as the ultimate cleansing experience, this team came up with the concept of a one-step routine that offered the benefits of cleansing, conditioning, and toning—"just like a daily facial." Meanwhile, another team had the same assignment in Japan, which became the lead market for the SK-II version. Because women already had a five- or six-step cleansing routine, the SK-II version was positioned not as a "daily facial" but as a "foaming massage cloth" that built on the ritual experience of increasing skin circulation through a massage while boosting skin clarity due to

Exhibit 8   Representation of Global Cleansing Cloth Development Program

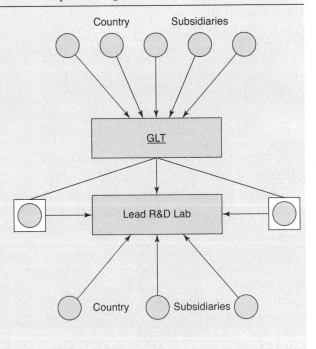

1. Consumer research on facial cleansing needs by country.

2. Identification of an unmet worldwide consumer need for cleansing that resulted in "soft, moisturized clean-feeling skin."

3. Technologists and marketers from key labs and markets are assembled in a lead R&D lab to develop a technology "chassis" and a core product concept.

4. Local technologists and marketers adapt the core technology and product concept to fit local needs and opportunities.

Source: Case writer's interpretation.

the microfibers' ability to clean pores and trap dirt. (See **Exhibit 9** for illustration of the Foaming Massage Cloth with other core SK-II products.)

Because of its premium pricing strategy, the SK-II Foaming Massage Cloth was packaged in a much more elegant dispensing box and was priced at ¥6,000 ($50), compared to $7 for the Olay Facial Cloth in the United States. And Japan assigned several technologists to the task of developing detailed product performance data that Japanese beauty magazines required for the much more scientific product reviews they published compared to their

---

Exhibit 9   SK-II Product Line Illustration

pitera soak

FACIAL TREATMENT ESSENCE
Skin Balancing Essence

The heart of the SK-II range, the revolutionary **Facial Treatment Essence** is the second point in your Ritual. This unique Pitera-rich product helps boost moisture levels to improve texture and clarity for a more beautiful, glowing complexion.

Women are so passionate about **Facial Treatment Essence** that they describe it as their 'holy' water. It contains the most concentrated amount of Pitera of all our skincare products—around 90% pure SK-II Pitera. It absorbs easily and leaves your skin looking radiant, with a supple, smooth feel.

FOAMING MASSAGE CLOTH
Purifying Cleansing Cloth

These innovative **Foaming Massage Cloths** leave your skin feeling smooth and velvety. A single sheet offers the outstanding effects of a cleanser, facial wash and massage. It gently washes away impurities, excess oil and non-waterproof eye make-up, leaving your skin clean, pure and refreshed.

FACIAL TREATMENT CLEAR LOTION
Clear Purifying Lotion

For a perfectly conditioned and ultra-fresh skin, use the **Facial Treatment Clear Lotion** morning and evening after cleansing your face and neck. The final part of your cleansing process, this Lotion helps remove residual impurities and dead skin cells.

Source: Company brochure.

Western counterparts. In the end, each market ended up with a distinct product built on a common technology platform. Marketing expertise was also shared—some Japanese performance analysis and data were also relevant for the Olay version and were used in Europe, for example—allowing the organization to leverage its local learning.

The SK-II Decision: A Global Brand?

After barely six months in Japan, de Cesare recognized that he now had three different roles in the new organization. As president of Max Factor Japan, he was impressed by the turnaround this local company had pulled off and was optimistic about its ability to grow significantly in the large Japanese beauty market. As GLT member on the Beauty Care GBU, he was proud of his organization's contribution to the GBU-sponsored global new-product innovation process and was convinced that Japan could continue to contribute to and learn from P&G's impressive technology base. And now as global franchise leader for SK-II, he was excited by the opportunity to explore whether the brand could break into the $9 billion worldwide prestige skin care market. (See **Exhibit 10** for prestige market data.)

Exhibit 10   Global Prestige Market: Size and Geographic Split

Global Prestige Market: 1999
(Fragrances, Cosmetics, Skin) = $15 billion at retail
level (of which approximately 60% is skin care)

United States	26%
Canada	2
Asia/Pacific[a]	25
United Kingdom	5
France	5
Germany	5
Rest of Europe	16
Rest of World	16

Source: Company data.
[a]Japan represented over 80% of the Asia/Pacific total.

Exhibit 11   Global Skin Care Market Size: 1999

Skin Care (Main market and prestige)

Region/Country	Retail Sales ($ million)	Two-Year Growth Rate
Western Europe	8,736	7%
France	2,019	7
Germany	1,839	14
United Kingdom	1,052	17
North America	6,059	18
United States	5,603	18
Asia/Pacific	11,220	2
China	1,022	28
Japan	6,869	6
South Korea	1,895	9
Taiwan	532	18
Hong Kong	266	6

Source: Company data.

When he arrived in Japan, de Cesare found that SK-II's success in Taiwan and Hong Kong (by 1999, 45% of total SK-II sales) had already encouraged management to begin expansion into three other regional markets—Singapore, Malaysia, and South Korea. But these were relatively small markets, and as he reviewed data on the global skin care and prestige beauty markets, he wondered if the time was right to make a bold entry into one or more major markets. (See **Exhibits 11** and **12** for global skin-care market and consumer data.)

As he reviewed the opportunities, three alternatives presented themselves. First, the beauty care management team for Greater China was interested in expanding on SK-II's success in Taiwan and Hong Kong by introducing the brand into mainland China. Next, at GLT meetings de Cesare had discussed with the head of beauty care in Europe the possibilities of bringing SK-II into that large Western market. His third possibility—really his first option, he realized—was to build on the brand's success in SK-II's rich and proven home Japanese market.

Exhibit 12   Skin Care and Cosmetics Habits and Practices: Selected Countries

Product Usage (% Past 7 Days)	United States[a]	Japan[a]	China[b]	United Kingdom[a]
Facial Moisturizer—Lotion	45%	95%	26%	37%
Facial Moisturizer—Cream	25	28	52	45
Facial Cleansers (excluding Family Bar Soap)	51	90	57	41
Foundation	70	85	35	57
Lipstick	84	97	75	85
Mascara	76	27	13	75

Source: Company data.
[a] Based on broad, representative sample of consumers.
[b] Based on upper-income consumers in Beijing City.

The Japanese Opportunity Japanese women were among the most sophisticated users of beauty products in the world, and per capita they were the world's leading consumers of these products. Despite its improved performance in recent years, Max Factor Japan claimed less than a 3% share of this $10 billion beauty product market. "It's huge," boasted one local manager. "Larger than the U.S. laundry market."

Although SK-II had sales of more than $150 million in Japan in 1999, de Cesare was also aware that in recent years its home market growth had slowed. This was something the new manager felt he could change by tapping into P&G's extensive technological resources. The successful experience of the foaming massage cloth convinced him that there was a significant opportunity to expand sales by extending the SK-II line beyond its traditional product offerings. For example, he could see an immediate opportunity to move into new segments by adding anti-aging and skin-whitening products to the SK-II range. Although this would take a considerable amount of time and effort, it would exploit internal capabilities and external brand image. Compared to the new-market entry options, investment would be quite low.

An exciting development that would support this home market thrust emerged when he discovered that his SK-II technology and marketing teams had come together to develop an innovative

beauty imaging system (BIS). Using the Japanese technicians' skills in miniaturization and software development, they were working to create a simplified version of scientific equipment used by P&G lab technicians to qualify new skin care products by measuring improvements in skin condition. The plan was to install the modified BIS at SK-II counters and have beauty consultants use it to boost the accuracy and credibility of their skin diagnosis. The project fit perfectly with de Cesare's vision for SK-II to become the brand that solved individual skin care problems. He felt it could build significant loyalty in the analytically inclined Japanese consumer.

With the company having such a small share of such a rich market, de Cesare felt that a strategy of product innovation and superior in-store service had the potential to accelerate a growth rate that had slowed to 5% per annum over the past three years. Although Shiseido could be expected to put up a good fight, he felt SK-II should double sales in Japan over the next six or seven years. In short, de Cesare was extremely excited about SK-II's potential for growth in its home market. He said: "It's a fabulous opportunity. One loyal SK-II customer in Japan already spends about $1,000 a year on the brand. Even a regular consumer of all P&G's other products—from toothpaste and deodorant to shampoo and detergent—all together spends nowhere near that amount annually."

The Chinese Puzzle   A very different opportunity existed in China, where P&G had been operating only since 1988. Because of the extraordinarily low prices of Chinese laundry products, the company had uncharacteristically led with beauty products when it entered this huge market. Olay was launched in 1989 and, after early problems, eventually became highly successful by adopting a nontraditional marketing strategy. To justify its price premium—its price was 20 to 30 times the price of local skin care products—Shivesh Ram, the entrepreneurial beauty care manager in China, decided to add a service component to Olay's superior product formulation. Borrowing from the Max Factor Japan model, he began selling through counters in the state-owned department stores staffed by beauty counselors. By 1999, Olay had almost 1,000 such counters in China and was a huge success.

As the Chinese market opened to international retailers, department stores from Taiwan, Hong Kong, and Singapore began opening in Beijing and Shanghai. Familiar with Olay as a mass-market brand, they questioned allocating it scarce beauty counter space alongside Estee Lauder, Lancôme, Shiseido, and other premium brands that had already claimed the prime locations critical to success in this business. It was at this point that Ram began exploring the possibility of introducing SK-II, allowing Olay to move more deeply into second-tier department stores, stores in smaller cities, and to "second-floor" cosmetics locations in large stores. "China is widely predicted to become the second-largest market in the world," said Ram. "The prestige beauty segment is growing at 30 to 40% a year, and virtually every major competitor in that space is already here."

Counterbalancing Ram's enthusiastic proposals, de Cesare also heard voices of concern. Beyond the potential impact on a successful Olay market position, some were worried that SK-II would be a distraction to P&G's strategy of becoming a mainstream Chinese company and to its competitive goal of entering 600 Chinese cities ahead of Unilever, Kao, and other global players. They argued that targeting an elite consumer group with a niche product

was not in keeping with the objective of reaching the 1.2 billion population with laundry, hair care, oral care, diapers, and other basics. After all, even with SK-II's basic four-step regimen, a three-month supply could cost more than one month's salary for the average woman working in a major Chinese city.

Furthermore, the skeptics wondered if the Chinese consumer was ready for SK-II. Olay had succeeded only by the company's educating its customers to move from a one-step skin care process—washing with bar soap and water—to a three-step cleansing and moisturizing process. SK-II relied on women developing at least a four- to six-step regimen, something the doubters felt was unrealistic. But as Ram and others argued, within the target market, skin care practices were quite developed, and penetration of skin care products was higher than in many developed markets.

Finally, the Chinese market presented numerous other risks, from the widespread existence of counterfeit prestige products to the bureaucracy attached to a one-year import-registration process. But the biggest concern was the likelihood that SK-II would attract import duties of 35% to 40%. This meant that even if P&G squeezed its margin in China, SK-II would have to be priced significantly above the retail level in other markets. Still, the China team calculated that because of the lower cost of beauty consultants, the product could still be profitable. (See **Exhibit 13** for cost estimates.)

Despite the critics, Ram was eager to try, and he responded to their concerns: "There are three Chinas—rural China, low-income urban China, and sophisticated, wealthy China concentrated in Shanghai, Beijing, and Guangzhou. The third group is as big a target consumer group as in many developed markets. If we don't move soon, the battle for that elite will be lost to the global beauty care powerhouses that have been here for three years or more."

Ram was strongly supported by his regional beauty care manager and by the Greater China MDO president. Together, they were willing to experiment with a few counters in Shanghai, and if successful, to expand to more counters in other

Exhibit 13 Global SK-II Cost Structure (% of net sales)[a]

FY1999/2000	Japan	Taiwan/ Hong Kong	PR China Expected	United Kingdom Expected
Net sales	100%	100%	100%	100%
Cost of products sold	22	26	45	29
Marketing, research, and selling/ administrative expense	67	58	44	63
Operating income	11	16	11	8

Source: Company estimates.
[a] Data disguised.

major cities. Over the first three years, they expected to generate $10 million to $15 million in sales, by which time they expected the brand to break even. They estimated the initial investment to build counters, train beauty consultants, and support the introduction would probably mean losses of about 10% of sales over that three-year period.

The European Question As he explored global opportunities for SK-II, de Cesare's mind kept returning to the European market he knew so well. Unlike China, Europe had a relatively large and sophisticated group of beauty-conscious consumers who already practiced a multistep regimen using various specialized skin care products. What he was unsure of was whether there was a significant group willing to adopt the disciplined six- to eight-step ritual that the most devoted Japanese SK-II users followed.

The bigger challenge, in his view, would be introducing a totally new brand into an already crowded field of high-profile, well-respected competitors including Estee Lauder, Clinique, Lancôme, Chanel, and Dior. While TV advertising had proven highly effective in raising SK-II's awareness and sales in Japan, Taiwan, and Hong Kong, the cost of television—or even print—ads in Europe made such an approach there prohibitive. And without any real brand awareness or heritage, he wondered if SK-II's mystique would transfer to a Western market.

As he thought through these issues, de Cesare spoke with his old boss, Mike Thompson, the head of P&G's beauty business in Europe. Because the Max Factor sales force sold primarily to mass-distribution outlets, Thompson did not think it provided SK-II the appropriate access to the European market. However, he explained that the fine-fragrance business was beginning to do quite well. In the United Kingdom, for example, its 25-person sales force was on track in 1999 to book $1 million in after-tax profit on sales of $12 million. Because it sold brands such as Hugo Boss, Giorgio, and Beverly Hills to department stores and Boots, the major pharmacy chain, its sales approach and trade relationship was different from the SK-II model in Japan. Nevertheless, Thompson felt it was a major asset that could be exploited.

Furthermore, Thompson told de Cesare that his wife was a loyal SK-II user and reasoned that since she was a critical judge of products, other women would discover the same benefits in the product she did. He believed that SK-II provided the fine-fragrance business a way to extend its line in the few department stores that dominated U.K. distribution in the prestige business. He thought they would be willing to give SK-II a try. (He was less optimistic about countries such as France and Germany, however, where prestige products were sold through thousands of perfumeries, making it impossible to justify the SK-II consultants who would be vital to the sales model.)

Initial consumer research in the United Kingdom had provided mixed results. But de Cesare felt that while this kind of blind testing could provide useful data on detergents, it was less helpful in this case. The consumers tested the product blind for one week, then were interviewed about their impressions. But because they lacked the beauty counselors' analysis and advice and had not practiced the full skin care regimen, he felt the results did not adequately predict SK-II's potential.

In discussions with Thompson, de Cesare concluded that he could hope to achieve sales of $10 million by the fourth year in the U.K. market. Given the intense competition, he recognized that he would have to absorb losses of $1 million to $2 million annually over that period as the start-up investment.

The Organizational Constraint   While the strategic opportunities were clear, de Cesare also recognized that his decision needed to comply with the organizational reality in which it would be implemented. While GBU head Lafley was an early champion and continuing supporter of SK-II, his boss, Jager, was less committed. Jager was among those in P&G who openly questioned how well some of the products in the beauty care business—particularly some of the acquired brands—fit in the P&G portfolio. While he was comfortable with high-volume products like shampoo, he was more skeptical of the upper end of the line, particularly fine fragrances. In his view, the fashion-linked and promotion-driven sales models of luxury products neither played well to P&G's "stack it high, sell it cheap" marketing skills nor leveraged its superior technologies.

The other organizational reality was that the implementation of O2005 was causing a good deal of organizational disruption and management distraction. This was particularly true in Europe, as Thompson explained:

> We swung the pendulum 180 degrees, from a local to a global focus. Marketing plans and budgets had previously been developed locally, strongly debated with European managers, then rolled up. Now they were developed globally—or at least regionally—by new people who often did not understand the competitive and trade differences across markets. We began to standardize and centralize our policies and practices out of Geneva. Not surprisingly, a lot of our best local managers left the company.

One result of the O2005 change was that country subsidiary GMs now focused more on maximizing sales volume than profits, and this had put the beauty care business under significant budget pressure. Thompson explained the situation in Europe in 1999:

> One thing became clear very quickly: It was a lot easier to sell cases of Ariel [detergent] or Pampers [diapers] than cases of cosmetics, so guess where the sales force effort went? At the same time, the new-product pipeline was resulting in almost a "launch of the month," and with the introduction of new products like Swiffer and Febreze, it was hard for the MDOs to manage all of these corporate priorities. . . . Finally, because cosmetics sales required more time and effort from local sales forces, more local costs were assigned to that business, and that has added to profit pressures.

Framing the Proposal   It was in this context that de Cesare was framing his proposal based on the global potential of SK-II as a brand and his plans to exploit the opportunities he saw. But he knew Lafley's long ties and positive feelings towards SK-II would not be sufficient to convince him. The GBU head was committed to focusing beauty care on the core brands that could be developed as a global franchise, and his questions would likely zero in on whether de Cesare could build SK-II into such a brand.

Case 5-3   McKinsey & Company: Managing Knowledge and Learning

In April 1996, halfway through his first three-year term as managing director of McKinsey & Company, Rajat Gupta was feeling quite proud as he flew out of Bermuda, site of the firm's second annual Practice Olympics. He had just listened to twenty teams outlining innovative new ideas they had developed out of recent project work, and, like his fellow senior partner judges, Gupta had come away impressed by the intelligence and creativity of the firm's next generation of consultants.

But there was another thought that kept coming back to the 47 year old leader of this highly successful $1.8 billion consulting firm (see **Exhibit 1** for a twenty year growth history). If this represented the tip of McKinsey's knowledge and expertise iceberg, how well was the firm doing in developing, capturing, and leveraging this asset in service of its clients worldwide? Although the Practice Olympics was only one of several initiatives he had championed, Gupta wondered if it was enough, particularly in light of his often stated belief that "knowledge is the lifeblood of McKinsey."

The Founders' Legacy[1]

Founded in 1926 by University of Chicago professor, James ("Mac") McKinsey, the firm of "accounting and engineering advisors" that bore his name grew rapidly. Soon Mac began recruiting experienced executives, and training them in the integrated approach he called his General Survey outline. In Saturday morning sessions he would lead consul-

tants through an "undeviating sequence" of analysis—goals, strategy, policies, organization, facilities, procedures, and personnel—while still encouraging them to synthesize data and think for themselves.

In 1932, Mac recruited Marvin Bower, a bright young lawyer with a Harvard MBA, and within two years asked him to become manager of the recently opened New York office. Convinced that he had to upgrade the firm's image in an industry typically regarded as "efficiency experts" or "business doctors," Bower undertook to imbue in his associates the sense of professionalism he had experienced in his time in a law partnership. In a 1937 memo, he outlined his vision for the firm as one focused on issues of importance to top-level management, adhering to the highest standards of integrity, professional ethics, and technical excellence, able to attract and develop young men of outstanding qualifications, and committed to continually raising its stature and influence. Above all, it was to be a firm dedicated to the mission of serving its clients superbly well.

Over the next decade, Bower worked tirelessly to influence his partners and associates to share his vision. As new offices opened, he became a strong advocate of the One Firm policy that required all consultants to be recruited and advanced on a firm-wide basis, clients to be treated as McKinsey & Company responsibilities, and profits to be shared from a firm pool, not an office pool. And through dinner seminars, he began upgrading the size and quality of McKinsey's clients. In the 1945 New Engagement Guide, he articulated a policy that every assignment should bring the firm something more than revenue—experience or prestige, for example.

Elected Managing Partner in 1950, Bower led his ten partners and 74 associates to initiate a series of major changes that turned McKinsey into an elite consulting firm unable to meet the demand for its services. Each client's problems were seen as

[1]The Founders' Legacy section draws on Amar V. Bhide, "Building the Professional Firm: McKinsey & Co., 1939–1968," HBS Working Paper 95-010.

Exhibit 1   McKinsey & Company: 20 Year Growth Indicators

Year	# Office Locations	# Active Engagements	Number of CSS[a]	Number of MGMs[b]
1975	24	661	529	NA
1980	31	771	744	NA
1985	36	1823	1248	NA
1990	47	2789	2465	348
1991	51	2875	2653	395
1992	55	2917	2875	399
1993	60	3142	3122	422
1994	64	3398	3334	440
1995	69	3559	3817	472

Source: Internal McKinsey & Company documents.
[a] CSS = Client Service Staff (All professional consulting staff).
[b] MGM = Management Group Members (Partners and directors).

unique, but Bower and his colleagues firmly believed that well trained, highly intelligent generalists could quickly grasp the issue, and through disciplined analysis find its solution. The firm's extraordinary domestic growth through the 1950s provided a basis for international expansion that accelerated the rate of growth in the 1960s. Following the opening of the London Office in 1959, offices in Geneva, Amsterdam, Düsseldorf, and Paris followed quickly. By the time Bower stepped down as Managing Director in 1967, McKinsey was a well established and highly respected presence in Europe and North America.

A Decade of Doubt

Although leadership succession was well planned and executed, within a few years, McKinsey's growth engine seemed to stall. The economic turmoil of the oil crisis, the slowing of the divisionalization process that had fueled the European expansion, the growing sophistication of client management, and the appearance of new focused competitors like Boston Consulting Group (BCG) all contributed to the problem. Almost overnight, McKinsey's enormous reservoir of internal self-confidence and even self-satisfaction began to turn to self-doubt and self-criticism.

Commission on Firm Aims and Goals   Concerned that the slowing growth in Europe and the U.S. was more than just a cyclical market downturn, the firm's partners assigned a committee of their most respected peers to study the problem and make recommendations. In April 1971, the Commission on Firm Aims and Goals concluded that the firm had been growing too fast. The authors bluntly reported, "Our preoccupation with the geographic expansion and new practice possibilities has caused us to neglect the development of our technical and professional skills." The report concluded that McKinsey had been too willing to accept routine assignments from marginal clients, that the quality of work done was uneven, and that while its consultants were excellent generalist problem solvers, they often lacked the deep industry knowledge or the substantive specialized expertise that clients were demanding.

One of the Commission's central proposals was that the firm had to recommit itself to the continuous development of its members. This meant that growth would have to be slowed and that the associate to MGM ratio be reduced from 7 to 1 back to 5 or 6 to 1. It further proposed that emphasis be placed on the development of what it termed "T-Shaped" consultants—those who supplemented a broad generalist perspective with an in-depth industry or functional specialty.

Practice Development Initiative When Ron Daniel was elected Managing Director (MD) in 1976—the fourth to hold the position since Bower had stepped down nine years earlier—McKinsey was still struggling to meet the challenges laid out in the Commission's report. As the head of the New York office since 1970, Daniel had experienced first hand the rising expectations of increasingly sophisticated clients and the aggressive challenges of new competitors like BCG. In contrast to McKinsey's local office-based model of "client relationship" consulting, BCG began competing on the basis of "thought leadership" from a highly concentrated resource base in Boston. Using some simple but powerful tools, such as the experience curve and the growth-share matrix, BCG began to make strong inroads into the strategy consulting market. As McKinsey began losing both clients and recruits to BCG, Daniel became convinced that his firm could no longer succeed pursuing its generalist model.

One of his first moves was to appoint one of the firm's most respected and productive senior partners as McKinsey's first full-time director of training. As an expanded commitment to developing consultants' skills and expertise became the norm, the executive committee began debating the need to formally update the firm's long-standing mission to reflect the firm's core commitment not only to serving its clients but also to developing its consultants. (**Exhibit 2.**)

But Daniel also believed some structural changes were necessary. Building on an initiative he and his colleagues had already implemented in the New York office, he created industry-based Clientele Sectors in consumer products, banking, industrial goods, insurance, and so on, cutting across the geographic offices that remained the primary organizational entity. He also encouraged more formal development of the firm's functional expertise in areas like strategy, organization and operations where knowledge and experience were widely diffused and minimally codified. However, many—including Marvin Bower—expressed concern that any move towards a

Exhibit 2   McKinsey's Mission and Guiding Principles (1996)
McKinsey Mission
To help our clients make positive, lasting, and substantial improvements in their performance and to build a great Firm that is able to attract, develop, excite, and retain exceptional people.
Guiding Principles
Serving Clients
Adhere to professional standards
Follow the top management approach
Assist the client in implementation and capability building
Perform consulting in a cost-effective manner
Building the Firm
Operate as one Firm
Maintain a meritocracy
Show a genuine concern for our people
Foster an open and nonhierarchical working atmosphere
Manage the Firm's resources responsibly
Being a Member of the Professional Staff
Demonstrate commitment to client service
Strive continuously for superior quality
Advance the state-of-the-art management
Contribute a spirit of partnership through teamwork and collaboration
Profit from the freedom and assume the responsibility associated with self-governance
Uphold the obligation to dissent

product driven approach could damage McKinsey's distinctive advantage of its local office presence which gave partners strong connections with the business community, allowed teams to work on site with clients and facilitated implementation. It was an approach that they felt contrasted sharply with the "fly in, fly out" model of expert-based consulting that BCG ran from its Boston hub.

Nonetheless, Daniel pressed ahead. Having established industry sectors, the MD next turned his attention to leveraging the firm's functional expertise. He assembled working groups to develop knowledge in two areas that were at the heart of McKinsey's practice—strategy and organization. To head up the first group, he named Fred Gluck, a director in the New York office who had been outspoken in urging the firm to modify its traditional generalist approach. In June 1977, Gluck invited a "Super Group" of younger partners with strategy expertise to a three day meeting to share ideas and develop an agenda for the strategy practice. One described the meeting:

> We had three days of unmitigated chaos. Someone from New York would stand up and present a four-box matrix. A partner from London would present a nine-box matrix. A German would present a 47 box matrix. It was chaos . . . but at the end of the third day some strands of thought were coming together.

At the same time, Daniel asked Bob Waterman who had been working on a Siemens-sponsored study of "excellent companies" and Jim Bennett, a respected senior partner to assemble a group that could articulate the firm's existing knowledge in the organization arena. One of their first recruits was an innovative young Ph.D. in organizational theory named Tom Peters.

Revival and Renewal

By the early 1980s, with growth resuming, a cautious optimism returned to McKinsey for the first time in almost a decade.

Centers of Competence   Recognizing that the activities of the two practice development projects could not just be a one-time effort, in 1980 Daniel asked Gluck to join the central small group that comprised the Firm Office and focus on the knowledge building agenda that had become his passion. Ever since his arrival at the firm from Bell Labs in 1967, Gluck had wanted to bring an equally stimulating intellectual environment to McKinsey. Against some strong internal resistance, he set out to convert his partners to his strongly held beliefs— that knowledge development had to be a core, not a peripheral firm activity; that it needed to be ongoing and institutionalized, not temporary and project based; and that it had to be the responsibility of everyone, not just a few.

To complement the growing number of Clientele Industry Sectors, he created 15 Centers of Competence (virtual centers, not locations) built around existing areas of management expertise like strategy, organization, marketing, change management, and systems. In a 1982 memo to all partners, he described the role of these centers as two-fold: to help develop consultants and to ensure the continued renewal of the firm's intellectual resources. For each Center, Gluck identified one or two highly motivated, recognized experts in the particular field and named them practice leaders. The expectation was that these leaders would assemble from around the firm, a core group of partners who were active in the practice area and interested in contributing to its development. (See **Exhibit 3** for the 15 Centers and 11 Sectors in 1983.)

Exhibit 3   McKinsey's Emerging Practice Areas: Centers of Competence and Industry Sectors, 1983

Centers of Competence	Clientele Sectors
Building Institutional Skills	Automotive
Business Management Unit	Banking
Change Management	Chemicals
Corporate Leadership	Communications and Information
Corporate Finance	Consumer Products
Diagnostic Scan	Electronics
International Management	Energy
Integrated Logistics	Health Care
Manufacturing	Industrial Goods
Marketing	Insurance
Microeconomics	Steel
Sourcing	
Strategic Management	
Systems	
Technology	

To help build a shared body of knowledge, the leadership of each of the 15 Centers of Competence began to initiate activities primarily involving the core group and, less frequently, the members of the practice network. A partner commented on Gluck's commitment to the centers:

> Unlike industry sectors, the centers of competence did not have a natural, stable client base, and Fred had to work hard to get them going. . . . He basically told the practice leaders, "Spend whatever you can—the cost is almost irrelevant compared to the payoff." There was no attempt to filter or manage the process, and the effect was "to let a thousand flowers bloom."

Gluck also spent a huge amount of time trying to change an internal status hierarchy based largely on the size and importance of one's client base. Arguing that practice development ("snowball making" as it became known internally) was not less "macho" than client development ("snowball throwing"), he tried to convince his colleagues that everyone had to become snowball makers *and* snowball throwers. In endless discussions, he would provoke his colleagues with barbed pronouncements and personal challenges: "Knowing what you're talking about is not necessarily a client service handicap" or "Would you want your brain surgery done by a general practitioner?"

Building a Knowledge Infrastructure   As the firm's new emphasis on individual consultant training took hold and the Clientele Sectors and Centers of Competence began to generate new insights, many began to feel the need to capture and leverage the learning. Although big ideas had occasionally been written up as articles for publication in newspapers, magazines or journals like *Harvard Business Review*, there was still a deep-seated suspicion of anything that smacked of packaging ideas or creating proprietary concepts or standard solutions. Such reluctance to document concepts had long constrained the internal transfer of ideas and the vast majority of internally developed knowledge was never captured.

This began to change with the launching of the McKinsey Staff Paper series in 1978, and by the early 1980s the firm was actively encouraging its consultants to publish their key findings. The initiative got a major boost with the publication in 1982 of two major bestsellers, Peters and Waterman's *In Search of Excellence* and Kenichi Ohmae's *The Mind of the Strategist*. But books, articles, and staff papers required major time investments, and only a small minority of consultants made the effort to write them. Believing that the firm had to lower the barrier to internal knowledge communication, Gluck introduced the idea of Practice Bulletins, two page summaries of important new ideas that identified the experts who could provide more detail. A partner elaborated:

> The Bulletins were essentially internal advertisements for ideas and the people who had developed them. We tried to convince people that they would help build their personal networks and internal reputations. . . . Fred was not at all concerned that the quality was mixed, and had a strong philosophy of letting the internal market sort out what were the really big ideas.

Believing that the firm's organizational infrastructure needed major overhaul, in 1987 Gluck launched a Knowledge Management Project. After five months of study, the team made three recommendations. First, the firm had to make a major commitment to build a common database of knowledge accumulated from client work and developed in the practice areas. Second, to ensure that the databases were maintained and used, they proposed that each practice area (Clientele Sector and Competence Center) hire a full time practice coordinator who could act as an "intelligent switch" responsible for monitoring the quality of the data and for helping consultants access the relevant information. And finally, they suggested that the firm expand its hiring practices and promotion policies to create a career path for deep functional specialists whose narrow expertise would make them more I-shaped than the normal profile of a T-shaped consultant.

The task of implementing these recommendations fell to a team led by Bill Matassoni, the firm's director of communications and Brook Manville, a newly recruited Yale Ph.D. with experience with electronic publishing. Focusing first on the Firm Practice Information System (FPIS), a computerized database of client engagements, they installed new systems and procedures to make the data more complete, accurate, and timely so that it could be accessed as a reliable information resource, not just an archival record. More difficult was the task of capturing the knowledge that had accumulated in the practice areas since much of it had not been formalized and none of it had been prioritized or integrated. To create a computer based Practice Development Network (PDNet), Matassoni and Manville put huge energy into begging, cajoling and challenging each practice to develop and submit documents that represented their core knowledge. After months of work, they had collected the 2,000 documents that they believed provided the critical mass to launch PDNet.

At the last minute, Matassoni and his team also developed another information resource that had not been part of the study team's recommendations. They assembled a listing of all firm experts and key document titles by practice area and published it in a small book, compact enough to fit in any consultant's briefcase. The Knowledge Resource Directory (KRD) became the McKinsey Yellow Pages and found immediate and widespread use firmwide. Although the computerized databases were slow to be widely adopted, the KRD found almost immediate enthusiastic acceptance.

Making the new practice coordinator's position effective proved more challenging. Initially, these roles were seen as little more than glorified librarians. It took several years before the new roles were filled by individuals (often ex-consultants) who were sufficiently respected that they could not only act as consultants to those seeking information about their area of expertise, but also were able to impose the discipline necessary to maintain and build the practice's databases.

Perhaps the most difficult task was to legitimize the role of a new class of I-shaped consultants—the specialist. The basic concept was that a professional could make a career in McKinsey by emphasizing specialized knowledge development rather than the broad based problem solving skills and client development orientation that were deeply embedded in the firm's value system. While several consultants with deep technical expertise in specialties like market research, finance or steel making were recruited, most found it hard to assimilate into the mainstream. The firm seemed uncomfortable about how to evaluate, compensate or promote these individuals, and many either became isolated or disaffected. Nonetheless, the partnership continued to support the notion of a specialist promotion track and continued to struggle with how to make it work.

Matassoni reflected on the changes:

> The objective of the infrastructure changes was not so much to create a new McKinsey as to keep the old "one firm" concept functioning as we grew . . . Despite all the talk of computerized data bases, the knowledge management process still relied heavily on personal networks, old practices like cross-office transfers, and strong "One Firm" norms like helping other consultants when they called. And at promotion time, nobody reviewed your PD documents. They looked at how you used your internal networks to have your ideas make an impact on clients.

Managing Success

By the late 1980s, the firm was expanding rapidly again. In 1988, the same year Fred Gluck was elected managing director, new offices were opened in Rome, Helsinki, Sao Paulo, and Minneapolis bringing the total to 41. The growing view amongst the partners, however, was that enhancing McKinsey's reputation as a thought leader was at least as important as attracting new business.

Refining Knowledge Management   After being elected MD, Gluck delegated the practice development role he had played since 1980 to a newly constituted Clientele and Professional

Development Committee (CPDC). When Ted Hall took over leadership of this committee in late 1991, he felt there was a need to adjust the firm's knowledge development focus. He commented:

> By the early 1990s, too many people were seeing practice development as the creation of experts and the generation of documents in order to build our reputation. But knowledge is only valuable when it is between the ears of consultants and applied to clients' problems. Because it is less effectively developed through the disciplined work of a few than through the spontaneous interaction of many, we had to change the more structured "discover-codify-disseminate" model to a looser and more inclusive "engage-explore-apply-share" approach. In other words, we shifted our focus from developing knowledge to building individual and team capability.

Over the years, Gluck's philosophy "to let 1,000 flowers bloom" had resulted in the original group of 11 sectors and 15 centers expanding to become what Hall called "72 islands of activity," (Sectors, Centers, Working Groups, and Special Projects) many of which were perceived as fiefdoms dominated by one or two established experts. In Hall's view, the garden of 1,000 flowers needed weeding, a task requiring a larger group of mostly different gardeners. The CPDC began integrating the diverse groups into seven sectors and seven functional capability groups (see **Exhibit 4**). These sectors and groups were led by teams of five to seven partners (typically younger directors and principals) with the objective of replacing the leader-driven knowledge creation and dissemination process with a "stewardship model" of self-governing practices focused on competence building.

Client Impact   With responsibility for knowledge management delegated to the CPDC, Gluck began to focus on a new theme—client impact. On being elected managing director, he made this a central theme in his early speeches, memos, and his first All Partners Conference. He also created a Client Impact Committee, and asked it to explore the ways in which the firm could ensure that the expertise it was developing created positive measurable results in each client engagement.

One of the most important initiatives of the new committee was to persuade the partners to redefine the firm's key consulting unit from the engagement team (ET) to the client service team (CST). The traditional ET, assembled to deliver a three or four month assignment for a client was a highly efficient and flexible unit, but it tended to focus on the immediate task rather than on the client's long-term need. The CST concept was that the firm could add long-term value and increase the effectiveness of individual engagements if it could unite a core of individuals (particularly at the partner level) who were linked across multiple ETs, and commit them to working with the client over an extended period. The impact was to broaden the classic model of a single partner "owning" a client to a group of partners with shared commitment to each client.

In response to concerns within the partnership about a gradual decline in associates' involvement in intellectual capital development, the CPDC began to emphasize the need for CSTs to play a central role in the intellectual life of McKinsey. (See **Exhibit 5** for a CPDC conceptualization.) Believing that the CSTs (by 1993 about 200 firm-wide) represented the real learning laboratories, the CPDC sent memos to the new industry sector and capability group leaders advising them that their practices would be evaluated by their coverage of the firm's CSTs. They also wrote to all consultants emphasizing the importance of the firm's intellectual development and their own professional development, for which they had primary responsibility. Finally, they assembled data on the amount of time consultants were spending on practice and professional development by office, distributing the widely divergent results to partners in offices worldwide.

Developing Multiple Career Paths   Despite (or perhaps because of) all these changes, the specialist consultant model continued to struggle. Over the

Exhibit 4   Group Framework for Sectors and Centers

Functional Capability Groups	Clientele Industry Sectors
Corporate Governance and Leadership • Corporate organization • Corporate management processes • Corporate strategy development • Corporate relationship design and management • Corporate finance • Post-merger management	Financial Institutions • Banking • Insurance • Health care payor/provider
Organization (OPP/MOVE) • Corporate transformation design and leadership • Energizing approaches • Organization design and development • Leadership and teams • Engaging teams	Consumer • Retailing • Consumer industries • Media • Pharmaceuticals
Information Technology/Systems • To be determined	Energy • Electrical utilities • Petroleum • Natural gas • Other energy
Marketing • Market research • Sales force management • Channel management • Global marketing • Pricing • Process and sector support	Basic Materials • Steel • Pulp and paper • Chemicals • Other basic materials
Operations Effectiveness • Integrated logistics • Manufacturing • Purchasing and supply management	Aerospace, Electronics, and Telecom • Telecom • Electronics • Aerospace
Strategy • Strategy • Microeconomics • Business dynamics • Business planning processes	Transportation Automotive, Assembly, and Machinery • Automotive • Assembly
Cross Functional Management • Innovation • Customer satisfaction • Product/technology development and commercialization • Core process redesign	

Source: Internal McKinsey & Company document.

Exhibit 5   CPDC Proposed Organizational Relationships

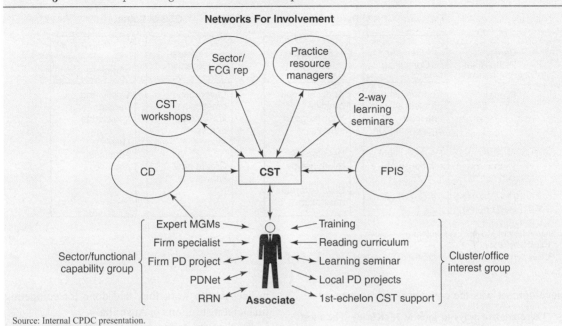

Source: Internal CPDC presentation.

years, the evaluation criteria for the specialist career path had gradually converged with the mainstream generalist promotion criteria. For example, the specialist's old promotion standard of "world-class expertise" in a particular field had given way to a more pragmatic emphasis on client impact; the notion of a legitimate role as a consultant to teams had evolved to a need for specialists to be "engagement director capable"; and the less pressured evaluation standard of "grow or go" was replaced by the normal associate's more demanding "up or out" requirement, albeit within a slightly more flexible time frame.

Although these changes had reduced the earlier role dissonance—specialists became more T shaped—it also diluted the original objective. While legitimizing the two client service staff tracks, in late 1992 the Professional Personnel Committee decided to create two career paths for client service support and administrative staff. The

first reaffirmed a path to partnership for practice-dedicated specialists who built credibility with clients and CSTs through their specialized knowledge and its expert application. Their skills would have them in high demand as consultants to teams (CDs) rather than as engagement directors (EDs). The second new option was the practice management track designed to provide a career progression for practice coordinators, who had a key role in transferring knowledge and in helping practice leaders manage increasingly complex networks. Valuable administrators could also be promoted on this track. (See **Exhibit 6** for an overview.)

Yet despite the announcement of the new criteria and promotion processes, amongst associates and specialists alike there was still some residual confusion and even skepticism about the viability of the specialist track to partnership. As he dealt with this issue, Gluck kept returning to his long-term theme that, "it's all about people," even suggesting people

Exhibit 6   Alternative Career Path Focus and Criteria

	CSS[1] Paths		CSSA[2] Paths	
Career Paths/Roles	General Consulting	Specialized Consulting	Practice Expertise	Practice Management Administration
Focus	Perform general problem solving and lead implementation Develop client relationships	Apply in-depth practice knowledge to studies Develop client relationships Build external reputation	Leverage practice knowledge across studies Create new knowledge	Codify and transfer knowledge Help administer practice

Source: Internal McKinsey & Company presentation.
[1] Client Service Staff
[2] Client Service Support and Administration

development was the company's primary purpose:

> There are two ways to look at McKinsey. The most common way is that we are a client service firm whose primary purpose is to serve the companies seeking our help. That is legitimate. But I believe there is an even more powerful way for us to see ourselves. We should begin to view our primary purpose as building a great institution that becomes an engine for producing highly motivated world class people who in turn will serve our clients extraordinarily well.

Knowledge Management on the Front

To see how McKinsey's evolving knowledge management processes were being felt by those on the firm's front lines, we will follow the activities of three consultants working in three diverse locations and focused on three different agendas.

Jeff Peters and the Sydney Office Assignment John Stuckey, a director in McKinsey's Sydney office felt great satisfaction at being invited to bid for a financial services growth strategy study for one of Australia's most respected companies. Yet the opportunity also created some challenges. As in most small or medium sized offices, most consultants in Sydney were generalists. Almost all with financial industry expertise had been "conflicted out" of the

project due to work they had done for competing financial institutions in Australia.

Stuckey immediately began using his personal network to find how he might tap into McKinsey's worldwide resources for someone who could lead this first engagement for an important new client. After numerous phone calls and some lobbying at a directors' conference he identified Jeff Peters, a Boston-based senior engagement manager and veteran of more than 20 studies for financial institutions. The only problem was that Peters had two ongoing commitments that would make him unavailable for at least the first six weeks of the Australian assignment.

Meanwhile, Stuckey and Ken Gibson, his engagement director on the project, were working with the Sydney office staffing coordinator to identify qualified, available and nonconflicted associates to complete the team. Balancing assignments of over 80 consultants to 25 ongoing teams was a complex process that involved matching the needs of the engagement and the individual consultants' development requirements. A constant flow of consultants across offices helped buffer constraints, and also contributed to the transfer of knowledge. At any one time 15 to 25 Australian consultants were on short- or long-term assignments abroad, while another 10 to 15 consultants from other offices were working in Australia. (Firm-wide, nearly 20% of work was performed by consultants on inter-office loans.)

They identified a three-person team to work with Peters. John Peacocke was a New Zealand army engineer with an MBA in finance from Wharton and two years of experience in McKinsey. Although he had served on a four-month study for a retail bank client in Cleveland, since returning to Australia he had worked mostly for oil and gas clients. Patty Akopiantz was a one-year associate who had worked in investment banking before earning an MBA at Harvard. Her primary interest and her developing expertise was in consumer marketing. The business analyst was Jonathan Liew, previously an actuary who was embarking on his first McKinsey assignment.

With Peters' help, Stuckey and Gibson also began assembling a group of internal specialists and experts who could act as consulting directors (CDs) to the team. James Gorman, a personal financial services expert in New York agreed to visit Sydney for a week and to be available for weekly conference calls; Majid Arab, an insurance industry specialist committed to a two-week visit and a similar "on-call" availability; Andrew Doman, a London-based financial industry expert also signed on as a CD. Within the Sydney office, Charles Conn, a leader in the firm's growth strategies practice, agreed to lend his expertise, as did Clem Doherty, a firm leader in the impact of technology.

With Gibson acting more as an engagement manager than an engagement director, the team began scanning the Knowledge Resource Directory, the FPIS and the PDNet for leads. (Firm-wide, the use of PDNet documents had boomed in the eight years since its introduction. By early 1996, there were almost 12,000 documents on PDNet, with over 2,000 being requested each month.) In all, they tracked down 179 relevant PD documents and tapped into the advice and experience of over 60 firm members worldwide. Team member Patty Akopiantz explained:

> Ken was acting as engagement manager, but he was not really an expert in financial services, so we were even more reliant than usual on the internal network. Some of the ideas we got off PDNet were helpful, but the trail of contacts was much more valuable. . . . Being on a completely different time zone had great advantages. If you hit a wall at the end of the day, you could drop messages in a dozen voicemail boxes in Europe and the United States. Because the firm norm is that you respond to requests by colleagues, by morning you would have seven or eight new suggestions, data sources, or leads.

At the end of the first phase, the team convened an internal workshop designed to keep client management informed, involved, and committed to the emerging conclusions. Out of this meeting, the team was focused on seven core beliefs and four viable options that provided its agenda for the next phase of the project. It was at this point that Peters was able to join the team:

> By the time I arrived, most of the hard analysis had been done and they had been able to narrow the focus from the universe to four core options in just over a month. It was very impressive how they had been able to do that with limited team-based expertise and a demanding client. . . . With things going so well, my main priority was to focus the team on the end product. Once we got a clear logical outline, I assigned tasks and got out of the way. Most of my time I spent working on the client relationship. . . . It was great learning for John and Patty, and both of them were ready to take on a management role in their next engagements.

In November, the team presented its conclusions to the board, and after some tough questioning and challenging, they accepted the recommendations and began an implementation process. The client's managing director reflected on the outcome:

> We're a tough client, but I would rate their work as very good. Their value added was in their access to knowledge, the intellectual rigor they bring, and their ability to build understanding and consensus among a diverse management group. . . . If things don't go ahead now, it's our own fault.

John Stuckey had a little different post-engagement view of the result:

> Overall, I think we did pretty good work, but I was a bit disappointed we didn't come up with a radical

breakthrough. . . . We leveraged the firm's knowledge base effectively, but I worry that we rely so much on our internal expertise. We have to beware of the trap that many large successful companies have fallen into by becoming too introverted, too satisfied with their own view of the world.

Warwick Bray and European Telecoms   After earning his MBA at Melbourne University, Warwick Bray joined McKinsey's Melbourne office in 1989. A computer science major, he had worked as a systems engineer at Hewlett-Packard and wanted to leverage his technological experience. For two of his first three years, he worked on engagements related to the impact of deregulation on the Asia-Pacific telecommunications industry. In early 1992, Bray advised his group development leader (his assigned mentor and adviser) that he would be interested in spending a year in London. After several phone discussions the transfer was arranged, and in March the young Australian found himself on his first European team.

From his experience on the Australian telecom projects, Bray had written a PD document, "Negotiating Interconnect" which he presented at the firm's annual worldwide telecom conference. Recognizing this developing "knowledge spike," Michael Patsalos-Fox, telecom practice leader in London, invited Bray to work with him on a study. Soon he was being called in as a deregulation expert to make presentations to various client executives. "In McKinsey you have to earn that right," said Bray. "For me it was immensely satisfying to be recognized as an expert."

Under the leadership of Patsalos-Fox, the telecom practice had grown rapidly in the United Kingdom. With deregulation spreading across the continent in the 1990s, however, he was becoming overwhelmed by the demands for his help. Beginning in the late 1980s, Patsalos-Fox decided to stop acting as the sole repository for and exporter of European telecom information and expertise, and start developing a more interdependent network. To help in this task, he appointed Sulu Soderstrom, a Stanford MBA with a strong technology background, as full-time practice coordinator. Over the next few years she played a key role in creating the administrative glue that bonded together telecom practice groups in offices throughout Europe. Said Patsalos-Fox:

> She wrote proposals, became the expert on information sources, organized European conferences, helped with cross-office staffing, located expertise and supported and participated in our practice development work. Gradually she helped us move from an "export"-based hub and spokes model of information sharing to a true federalist-based network.

In this growth environment and supported by the stronger infrastructure, the practice opportunities exploded during the 1990s. To move the knowledge creation beyond what he described as "incremental synthesis of past experience," Patsalos-Fox launched a series of practice-sponsored studies. Staffed by some of the practice's best consultants, they focused on big topics like "The Industry Structure in 2005," or "The Telephone Company of the Future." But most of the practice's knowledge base was built by the informal initiatives of individual associates who would step back after several engagements and write a paper on their new insights. For example, Bray wrote several well-received PD documents and was enhancing his internal reputation as an expert in deregulation and multimedia. Increasingly he was invited to consult to or even join teams in other parts of Europe. Said Patsalos-Fox:

> He was flying around making presentations and helping teams. Although the internal audience is the toughest, he was getting invited back. When it came time for him to come up for election, the London office nominated him but the strength of his support came from his colleagues in the European telecom network.

In 1996, Patsalos-Fox felt it was time for a new generation of practice leadership. He asked his young Australian protégé and two other partners— one in Brussels, one in Paris—if they would take on a co-leadership role. Bray reflected on two challenges he and his co-leaders faced. The first was to make telecom a really exciting and interesting practice so it could attract the best associates. "That meant taking on the most interesting work, and running our engagements so that people felt they were developing and having fun," he said.

The second key challenge was how to develop the largely informal links among the fast-growing European telecom practices. Despite the excellent job that Soderstrom had done as the practice's repository of knowledge and channel of communication, it was clear that there were limits to her ability to act as the sole "intelligent switch." As a result, the group had initiated a practice-specific intranet link designed to allow members direct access to the practice's knowledge base (PD documents, conference proceedings, CVs, etc.), its members' capabilities (via home pages for each practice member), client base (CST home pages, links to client web sites), and external knowledge resources (MIT's Multimedia Lab, Theseus Institute, etc.). More open yet more focused than existing firm-wide systems like PDNet, the Telecom Intranet was expected to accelerate the "engage-explore-apply-share" knowledge cycle.

There were some, however, who worried that this would be another step away from "one firm" towards compartmentalization, and from focus on building idea-driven personal networks towards creating data-based electronic transactions. In particular, the concern was that functional capability groups would be less able to transfer their knowledge into increasingly strong and self-contained industry-based practices. Warwick Bray recognized the problem, acknowledging that linkages between European telecom and most functional practices "could be better":

> The problem is we rarely feel the need to draw on those groups. For example, I know the firm's pricing practice has world-class expertise in industrial pricing, but we haven't yet learned how to apply it to telecom. We mostly call on the pricing experts within our practice. We probably should reach out more.

Stephen Dull and the Business Marketing Competence Center
After completing his MBA at the University of Michigan in 1983, Stephen Dull spent the next five years in various consumer marketing jobs at Pillsbury. In 1988, he was contacted by an executive search firm that had been retained by McKinsey to recruit potential consultants in consumer marketing. Joining the Atlanta office, Dull soon discovered that there was no structured development program. Like the eight experienced consumer marketing recruits in other offices, he was expected to create his own agenda.

Working on various studies, Dull found his interests shifting from consumer to industrial marketing issues. As he focused on building his own expertise, however, Dull acknowledged that he did not pay enough attention to developing strong client relations. "And around here, serving clients is what really counts," he said. So, in late 1994—a time when he might be discussing his election to principal—he had a long counseling session with his group development leader about his career. The GDL confirmed that he was not well positioned for election, but proposed another option. He suggested that Dull talk to Rob Rosiello, a principal in the New York office who had just launched a business-to-business marketing initiative within the marketing practice. Said Dull:

> Like most new initiatives, "B to B" was struggling to get established without full-time resources, so Rob was pleased to see me. I was enjoying my business marketing work, so the initiative sounded like a great opportunity. . . . Together, we wrote a proposal to make me the firm's first business marketing specialist.

The decision to pursue this strategy was not an easy one for Dull. Like most of his colleagues, he felt that specialists were regarded as second-class citizens—"overhead being supported by real consultants who serve clients," Dull suggested. But his GDL told him that recent directors meetings had reaffirmed the importance of building functional expertise, and some had even suggested that 15%–20% of the firm's partners should be functional experts within the next five to seven years. (As of 1995, over 300 associates were specialists, but only 15 of the 500 partners.) In April 1995, Dull and Rosiello took their proposal to Andrew Parsons and David Court, two leaders of the Marketing practice. The directors suggested a mutual trial of the concept until the end of the year and offered to provide Dull the support to commit full time to developing the B to B initiative.

Dull's first priority was to collect the various concepts, frameworks and case studies that existed within the firm, consolidating and synthesizing them in several PD documents. In the process, he and Rosiello began assembling a core team of interested contributors. Together, they developed an agenda of half a dozen cutting-edge issues in business marketing—segmentation, multi-buyer decision making and marketing partnerships, for example—and launched a number of study initiatives around them. Beyond an expanded series of PD documents, the outcome was an emerging set of core beliefs, and a new framework for business marketing.

The activity also attracted the interest of Mark Leiter, a specialist in the Marketing Science Center of Competence. This center, which had developed largely around a group of a dozen or so specialists, was in many ways a model of what Dull hoped the B to B initiative could become, and having a second committed specialist certainly helped.

In November, another major step to that goal occurred when the B to B initiative was declared a Center of Competence. At that time, the core group decided they would test their colleagues' interest and their own credibility by arranging an internal conference at which they would present their ideas. When over 50 people showed up including partners and directors from four continents, Dull felt that prospects for the center looked good.

Through the cumulative impact of the PD documents, the conference and word of mouth recommendations, by early 1996 Dull and his colleagues were getting more calls than the small center could handle. They were proud when the March listing of PDNet "Best Sellers" listed B to B documents at

numbers 2, 4 and 9 (see **Exhibit 7**). For Dull, the resulting process was enlightening:

> We decided that when we got calls we would swarm all over them and show our colleagues we could really add value for their clients. . . . This may sound strange—even corny—but I now really understand why this is a profession and not a business. If I help a partner serve his client better, he will call me back. It's all about relationships, forming personal bonds, helping each other.

While Dull was pleased with the way the new center was gaining credibility and having impact, he was still very uncertain about his promotion prospects. As he considered his future, he began to give serious thought to writing a book on business to business marketing to enhance his internal credibility and external visibility.

A New MD, A New Focus

In 1994, after six years of leadership in which firm revenue had doubled to an estimated $1.5 billion annually, Fred Gluck stepped down as MD. His successor was 45 year old Rajat Gupta, a 20 year McKinsey veteran committed to continuing the emphasis on knowledge development. After listening to the continuing debates about which knowledge development approach was most effective, Gupta came to the conclusion that the discussions were consuming energy that should have been directed towards the activity itself. "The firm did not have to make a choice," he said. "We had to pursue *all* the options." With that conclusion, Gupta launched a four-pronged attack.

First, he wanted to capitalize on the firm's long-term investment in practice development driven by Clientele Industry Sectors and Functional Capability Groups and supported by the knowledge infrastructure of PDNet and FPIS. But he also wanted to create some new channels, forums, and mechanisms for knowledge development and organizational learning.

Then, building on an experiment begun by the German office, Gupta embraced a grass-roots knowledge-development approach called Practice

Exhibit 7   PDNet "Best-Sellers": March and Year-to-Date, 1996

Number Requested	Title, Author(s), Date, PDNet #	Functional Capability Group/Sector
	March 1996	
21	**Developing a Distinctive Consumer Marketing Organization** *Nora Aufreiter, Theresa Austerberry, Steve Carlotti, Mike George, Liz Lempres (1/96, #13240)*	Consumer Industries/ Packaged Goods; Marketing
19	**VIP: Value Improvement Program to Enhance Customer Value in Business to Business Marketing** *Dirk Berensmann, Marc Fischer, Heiner Frankemölle, Lutz-Peter Pape, Wolf-Dieter Voss (10/95, #13340)*	Marketing; Steel
16	**Handbook For Sales Force Effectiveness—1991 Edition** *(5/91, #6670)*	Marketing
15	**Understanding and Influencing Customer Purchase Decisions in Business to Business Markets** *Mark Leiter (3/95, #12525)*	Marketing
15	**Channel Management Handbook** *Christine Bucklin, Stephen DeFalco, John DeVincentis, John Levis (1/95, #11876)*	Marketing
15	**Platforms for Growth in Personal Financial Services (PFS201)** *Christopher Leech, Ronald O'Hanley, Eric Lambrecht, Kristin Morse (11/95, #12995)*	Personal Financial Services
14	**Developing Successful Acquisition Programs to Support Long-Term Growth Strategies** *Steve Coley, Dan Goodwin (11/92, #9150)*	Corporate Finance
14	**Understanding Value-Based Segmentation** *John Forsyth, Linda Middleton (11/95, #11730)*	Consumer Industries/ Packaged Goods; Marketing
14	**The Dual Perspective Customer Map for Business to Business Marketing** *(3/95, #12526)*	Marketing
13	**Growth Strategy—Platforms, Staircases and Franchises** *Charles Conn, Rob McLean, David White (8/94, #11400)*	Strategy
	Cumulative Index (January–March)	
54	**Introduction to CRM (Continuous Relationship Marketing)—Leveraging CRM to Build PFS Franchise Value (PFS221)** *Margo Geogiadis, Milt Gillespie, Tim Gokey, Mike Sherman, Marc Singer (11/95, #12999)*	Personal Financial Services
45	**Platforms for Growth in Personal Financial Services (PFS201)** *Christopher Leech, Ronald O'Hanley, Eric Lambrecht, Kristin Morse (11/95, #12995)*	Personal Financial Services
40	**Launching a CRM Effort (PFS222)** *Nick Brown, Margo Georgiadis (10/95, #12940)*	Marketing
38	**Building Value Through Continuous Relationship Marketing (CRM)** *Nich Brown, Mike Wright (10/95, #13126)*	Banking and Securities
36	**Combining Art and Science to Optimize Brand Portfolios** *Richard Benson-Armer, David Court, John Forsyth (10/95, #12916)*	Marketing; Consumer Industries/Packaged Goods
35	**Consumer Payments and the Future of Retail Banks (PA202)** *John Stephenson, Peter Sands (11/95, #13008)*	Payments and Operating Products
34	**CRM (Continuous Relationship Marketing) Case Examples Overview** *Howie Hayes, David Putts (9/95, #12931)*	Marketing
32	**Straightforward Approaches to Building Management Talent** *Parke Boneysteele, Bill Meehan, Kristin Morse, Pete Sidebottom (9/95, #12843)*	Organization
32	**Reconfiguring and Reenergizing Personal Selling Channels (PFS213)** *Patrick Wetzel, Amy Zinsser (11/95, #12997)*	Personal Financial Services
31	**From Traditional Home Banking to On-Line PFS (PFS211)** *Gaurang Desai, Brian Johnson, Kai Lahmann, Gottfried Leibbrandt, Paal Weberg (11/95, #12998)*	Personal Financial Services

Source: *Month By Month* (McKinsey's internal staff magazine).

Olympics. Two- to six-person teams from offices around the world were encouraged to develop ideas that grew out of recent client engagements and formalize them for presentation at a regional competition with senior partners and clients as judges. The twenty best regional teams then competed at a firm-wide event. Gupta was proud that in its second year, the event had attracted over 150 teams and involved 15% of the associate body.

Next, in late 1995 the new MD initiated six special initiatives—multi-year internal assignments led by senior partners that focused on emerging issues that were of importance to CEOs. The initiatives tapped both internal and external expertise to develop "state-of-the-art" formulations of each key issue. For example, one focused on the shape and function of the corporation of the future, another on creating and managing strategic growth, and a third on capturing global opportunities. Gupta saw these initiatives as reasserting the importance of the firm's functional knowledge yet providing a means to do longer term, bigger commitment, cross-functional development.

Finally, he planned to expand on the model of the McKinsey Global Institute, a firm-sponsored research center established in 1991 to study implications of changes in the global economy on business. The proposal was to create other pools of dedicated resources protected from daily pressures and client demands, and focused on long term research agendas. A Change Center was established in 1995 and an Operations Center was being planned. Gupta saw these institutes as a way in which McKinsey could recruit more research-oriented people and link more effectively into the academic arena.

Most of these initiatives were new and their impact had not yet been felt within the firm. Yet Gupta was convinced the direction was right:

> We have easily doubled our investment in knowledge over these past couple of years. There are lots more people involved in many more initiatives. If that means we do 5–10% less client work today, we are willing to pay that price to invest in the future. Since Marvin Bower,

every leadership group has had a commitment to leave the firm stronger than it found it. It's a fundamental value of McKinsey to invest for the future of the firm.

Future Directions   Against this background, the McKinsey partnership was engaged in spirited debate about the firm's future directions and priorities. The following is a sampling of their opinions:

> I am concerned that our growth may stretch the fabric of the place. We can't keep on disaggregating our units to create niches for everyone because we have exhausted the capability of our integrating mechanisms. I believe our future is in developing around CSTs and integrating across them around common knowledge agendas.
>
> Historically, I was a supporter of slower growth, but now I'm convinced we must grow faster. That is the key to creating opportunity and excitement for people, and that generates innovation and drives knowledge development. . . . Technology is vital not only in supporting knowledge transfer, but also in allowing partners to mentor more young associates. We have to be much more aggressive in using it.
>
> There is a dark side to technology—what I call technopoly. It can drive out communication and people start believing that e-mailing someone is the same thing as talking to them. If teams stop meeting as often or if practice conferences evolve into discussion forums on Lotus Notes, the technology that has supported our growth may begin to erode our culture based on personal networks.
>
> I worry that we are losing our sense of village as we compartmentalize our activities and divide into specialties. And the power of IT has sometimes led to information overload. The risks is that the more we spend searching out the right PD document, the ideal framework, or the best expert, the less time we spend thinking creatively about the problem. I worry that as we increase the science, we might lose the craft of what we do.

These were among the scores of opinions that Rajat Gupta heard since becoming MD. His job was to sort through them and set a direction that would "leave the firm stronger than he found it."

Case 5-4 The Transformation of BP

The Transformation of BP

On June 25th 1992 the Board of BP, the UK's largest industrial enterprise, cut its dividend and removed its Chief Executive Robert Horton. The move came as the company sought to overcome a series of interlinked challenges—the transition to private sector ownership which had coincided with the stock market collapse in 1987; the fall in oil prices after the Gulf War; rising debts and increasing unit costs.

Within a decade the company was leading the restructuring of the sector, had reduced costs and debt and was earning after-tax income of over $1 billion a month. By 2001 BP was generating annual revenues of $120 billion, employing 100,000 people in over 100 countries, and had taken its place as one of the three supermajors in the oil industry (see financials in Exhibit 1).

Within the oil industry and beyond, BP had become a model of both financial performance and corporate social responsibility, breaking ranks by accepting that the risks of climate change were too dangerous to ignore and by refusing to accept the long entrenched trade off between environmental protection and increased energy consumption which many had come to take for granted.

This study looks at how that transformation was achieved, and in particular at the way in which

This case was written by Michelle Rogan, PhD student, together with Lynda Gratton and Sumantra Ghoshal, both members of the faculty, at the London Business School.

London Business School

© London Business School, March 03.

Sussex Place, Regent's Park, London NW1 4SA, United Kingdom.

changes in the management of the company influenced both performance and reputation.

Building the Platform for Superior Performance
In retrospect it is possible to see that a number of the changes necessary to achieve the transformation of BP had begun before 1992.

As Chairman and Chief Executive, Horton had begun a process of "cultural change" shaking up BP's entrenched bureaucracies and reducing staff numbers. John Browne, Chief Executive of BP Exploration from 1989 to 1995 and subsequently Chief Executive of BP as a whole had initiated radical steps in 1989 to focus exploration spending on a limited number of the best prospects around and to reduce costs.

The real impact of such developments only became apparent however after 1992 under the leadership of Horton's successor David Simon (later to become a Minister in Tony Blair's first Government as Lord Simon of Highbury). Simon stabilized the company increasing revenues and reducing costs and laid the foundation for the process of transformation which can be dated from 1995 when Browne, backed by his deputy Rodney Chase, took over the reins of the business.

Nick Butler, policy advisor to Browne and his top team throughout the period, described what followed as "Act 1, taking the steps to create a high-grade business portfolio and human capital. Creating the base for something interesting."

Ralph Alexander one of BP's Group Vice Presidents recalled:

When Browne stepped in as CEO in 1995, we knew we had to create something different. We looked at the

Exhibit 1   Balance Sheet and Income Statement

BP Amoco Statement of Financial Position (1991 to 1999)

	Dec91	Dec92	Dec93	Dec94	Dec95	Dec96	Dec97	Dec98	Dec99
Assets									
Cash & equivalents	1,340.79	377.50	310.28	293.28	616.20	258.57	275.56	875.00	1,551.00
Receivables—total (net)	7,954.98	6,979.22	5,245.13	6,639.36	7,141.68	8,740.68	7,005.20	6,835.00	10,488.00
Inventories—total	5,596.91	5,102.29	3,941.97	4,302.48	4,389.84	5,085.21	4,284.46	3,642.00	5,124.00
Prepaid expenses	2,141.15	1,901.09	1,613.43	1,703.52	2,031.12	2,540.07	2,704.14	3,508.00	4,230.00
Current assets—other	1,568.93	1,550.77	1,168.70	940.68	1,020.24	1,546.35	1,822.68	2,366.00	2,084.00
Current assets—total	18,602.76	15,910.87	12,279.50	13,879.32	15,199.08	18,170.88	16,092.04	17,226.00	23,477.00
Plant, property & equip (gross)	64,571.10	61,390.56	59,623.04	63,034.92	66,856.92	69,587.44	71,811.60	120,820.00	121,925.00
Accumulated depreciation	27,642.34	28,320.05	29,149.60	31,749.12	35,160.84	36,343.45	37,482.80	63,469.00	66,242.00
Plant, property & equip (net)	36,928.76	33,070.51	30,473.44	31,285.80	31,696.08	33,243.99	34,328.80	57,351.00	55,683.00
Investments at equity	2,131.80	2,429.59	2,433.44	2,669.16	3,263.52	3,302.26	3,570.66	4,162.00	4,334.00
Investments and advances—other	1,335.18	747.45	484.62	525.72	157.56	157.17	117.86	5,121.00	5,319.00
Intangibles	452.54	374.48	156.62	137.28	152.88	157.17	147.74	151.00	292.00
Deferred charges	0.00	0.00	0.00	0.00	0.00	0.00	0.00	0.00	0.00
Assets—other	0.00	0.00	0.00	0.00	0.00	15.21	318.72	489.00	456.00
Total assets	**59,451.04**	**52,532.90**	**45,827.62**	**48,497.28**	**50,469.12**	**55,046.68**	**54,575.82**	**84,500.00**	**89,561.00**
Liabilities									
Accounts payable	5,873.67	5,278.96	4,476.83	5,959.20	6,809.40	7,843.29	6,407.60	5,450.00	8,680.00
Notes payable	2,008.38	2,450.73	1,009.13	787.80	965.64	1,235.39	1,093.94	1,659.00	3,809.00
Accrued expenses	3,857.81	3,405.05	2,309.33	2,375.88	2,717.52	2,638.09	2,631.10	2,897.00	4,041.00
Taxes payable	1,277.21	1,254.81	1,155.41	1,054.56	1,725.36	2,055.04	2,353.88	2,395.00	2,558.00
Debt (long-term) Due in one year	1,071.51	1,221.59	817.06	837.72	185.64	552.63	793.48	1,178.00	1,091.00
Other current liabilities	3,683.90	3,178.55	2,579.72	2,383.68	2,730.00	3,618.29	3,514.22	4,587.00	3,096.00
Total current liabilities	17,772.48	16,789.69	12,347.47	13,398.84	15,133.56	17,942.73	16,794.22	18,166.00	23,275.00
Long-term debt	12,168.09	11,667.77	10,555.26	8,899.80	7,425.60	5,871.06	5,330.26	10,918.00	9,644.00
Deferred taxes (balance sheet)	755.48	619.10	366.42	444.60	586.56	684.45	647.40	1,632.00	1,783.00
Investment tax credit	0.00	0.00	0.00	0.00	0.00	0.00	0.00	0.00	0.00
Minority interest	561.00	385.05	147.75	170.04	168.48	184.21	92.96	1,072.00	1,061.00
Liabilities—other	8,271.01	8,003.00	8,008.05	8,335.08	8,725.08	8,740.68	8,285.06	10,926.00	10,517.00
Total liabilities	**39,528.06**	**37,464.61**	**31,424.95**	**31,248.36**	**32,039.28**	**33,423.13**	**31,149.90**	**42,714.00**	**46,280.00**

Shareholders' Equity

Preferred stock	21.00	21.00	19.92	20.28	18.72	18.72	17.73	18.12	22.44
Common stock	4,871.00	4,842.00	2,392.06	2,387.97	2,174.64	2,146.56	2,013.83	2,046.05	2,520.76
Capital surplus	3,684.00	3,056.00	3,776.50	3,733.21	3,347.76	3,244.80	2,968.30	3,251.03	3,925.13
Retained earnings (net other)	34,705.00	33,867.00	17,237.44	15,482.09	12,888.72	11,838.84	9,402.81	9,753.09	13,454.65
Less: treasury stock	0.00	0.00	0.00	0.00	0.00	0.00	0.00	0.00	0.00
Total shareholders' equity	**43,281.00**	**41,786.00**	**23,425.92**	**21,623.55**	**18,429.84**	**17,248.92**	**14,402.67**	**15,068.29**	**19,922.98**
Total liabilities & equity	89,561.00	84,500.00	54,575.82	55,046.68	50,469.12	48,497.28	45,827.62	52,532.90	59,451.04

BP Amoco Income Statement (1991 to 1999)

Sales (net)	83,566.00	68,304.00	71,274.40	69,780.36	57,047.48	50,667.48	51,638.63	58,852.50	57,725.01
Cost of goods sold	65,995.00	53,059.00	56,424.20	55,305.12	43,950.86	39,076.20	39,116.81	45,612.90	43,140.21
Gross profit	17,571.00	15,245.00	14,850.20	14,475.24	13,096.62	11,591.28	12,521.81	13,239.60	14,584.80
Selling, general, & admin expenses	5,541.00	5,609.00	5,546.48	5,277.48	5,389.38	4,680.27	5,664.74	6,984.42	6,637.50
Operating income before depreciation	12,030.00	9,636.00	9,303.72	9,197.76	7,707.24	6,911.01	6,857.08	6,255.18	7,947.30
Depreciation, depletion, & amortiz	4,708.00	5,255.00	3,047.12	3,463.20	3,220.04	3,333.87	3,856.28	3,927.63	4,403.76
Operating income after depreciation	7,322.00	4,381.00	6,256.60	5,734.56	4,487.20	3,577.14	3,000.80	2,327.55	3,543.54
Interest expense	1,359.00	1,172.00	577.28	700.44	837.40	872.10	1,085.96	1,355.82	1,407.15
Non-operating income/expense	3,343.00	784.00	401.80	1,491.36	954.32	729.81	363.47	985.89	(7.08)
Special items	(2,280.00)	850.00	(101.68)	(804.96)	(1,529.44)	55.08	(354.60)	(1,759.38)	0.00
Pretax income	7,026.00	4,843.00	5,979.44	5,720.52	3,074.68	3,489.93	1,923.71	198.24	2,129.31
Income taxes—total	1,880.00	1,520.00	1,915.52	1,726.92	1,309.82	1,058.76	1,012.09	1,000.05	1,451.40
Minority interest	138.00	63.00	13.12	12.48	(7.90)	18.36	2.96	8.85	(56.64)
Income before extraordinary items & discontinued operations (EI&DO)	5,006.00	3,258.35	4,049.16	3,979.56	1,771.18	2,411.28	907.19	(812.43)	732.78
Extraordinary items	0.00	0.00	0.00	0.00	0.00	0.00	0.00	0.00	0.00
Discontinued operations	0.00	0.00	0.00	0.00	0.00	0.00	0.00	0.00	0.00

(Continued)

Exhibit 1 *(concluded)*

	Dec91	Dec92	Dec93	Dec94	Dec95	Dec96	Dec97	Dec98	Dec99
				BP Amoco Statement of Financial Position (1991 to 1999)					
Net income (loss)	734.55	(810.66)	908.66	2,412.81	1,772.76	3,981.12	4,050.80	3,260.00	5,008.00
Income before EI&DO	732.78	(812.43)	907.19	2,411.28	1,771.18	3,979.56	4,049.16	3,258.35	5,006.00
Preferred dividends	1.77	1.77	1.48	1.53	1.58	1.56	1.64	1.65	2.00
Available for common before EI&DO	732.78	(812.43)	907.19	2,411.28	1,771.18	3,979.56	4,049.16	3,258.35	5,006.00
Common stk equivalents—savings	0.00	0.00	0.00	0.00	0.00	0.00	0.00	0.00	0.00
Adjusted available for common	732.78	(812.43)	907.19	2,411.28	1,771.18	3,979.56	4,049.16	3,258.35	5,006.00
Earnings per Share									
Primary—excluding EI&DO	1.68	(1.80)	2.00	5.29	3.83	8.52	4.26	2.04	1.55
Primary—including EI&DO	1.68	(1.80)	2.00	5.29	3.83	8.52	4.26	2.04	1.55
Fully diluted—excluding EI&DO	1.68	(1.80)	2.00	5.29	3.83	8.52	4.26	2.04	1.54
Fully diluted—including EI&DO	1.68	(1.80)	2.00	5.29	3.83	8.52	4.26	2.04	1.54
Common Shares									
For primary EPS calculation	448.25	450.42	452.92	456.17	461.50	467.75	950.30	1,606.33	3,231.00
For fully diluted EPS calculation	—	—	—	—	—	—	—	1,606.33	3,249.50
Outstanding at fiscal year end	449.41	451.55	454.26	458.55	464.61	470.85	960.43	1,613.84	3,247.34

Source: Compustat, accessed February 14, 2001.

ROACE; we were all operating within a limited space. We realised that to break out we had to redefine ourselves. It was not about beating Exxon, but how to beat the ROACE of Microsoft. We wanted to create a company with sufficient scale to take regional shocks and with enough reach to thrive in almost any circumstances.

Thus began a series of mergers and acquisitions that would put BP in the superweight category. Browne led BP through two critical and successful mergers totalling $120 billion, first with Amoco in 1998 and then with ARCO in 1999. BP had become the third largest company in the oil industry, trailing behind only Royal Dutch Shell and Exxon-Mobil. With its acquisition of Burmah Castrol in July 2000, BP had become a combined group with a market value of more than $200 billion. BP's goals moving forward from the three mergers were to lop $4 billion off its annual costs worldwide, to sell assets of $10 billion and to boost capital spending to a total of $26 billion over the three years to the end of 2001.

While achieving scale, these mergers also created a large, fragmented company. By 2000, the company consisted of three camps, divided by their very different heritages: approximately 60,000 from BP, 40,000 from Amoco and 20,000 from ARCO. BP's management had to decide how to bring together the diverse strengths of the three different heritage companies into a single new business. Though unifying the company would be a challenge, management believed a single global brand supported by an integrated global organization was the best way forward.

Sir John Browne explained the core premises on which the management of BP based its responses to this challenge:

The organization that we evolved from 1995 onwards was founded on several simple concepts. Number one was our observation that people work better in smaller units, because the closer you can identify people to objectives and targets, the better things happen. So we started off with what we came to call the "Atomic Structure," so that the big, long-term targets of the company could be divided up and deployed into smaller units that could take full ownership of these targets . . .

. . . The second premise was contradictory to that, and that was our observation that any organization of scale could create proprietary knowledge through learning . . . so the question was how could you get independent atomic units to work together to share information, to learn and to retain that learning . . .

. . . The third theme we observed was the very different interaction between people of equal standing, if you will, when they reviewed each other's work, than there was when a superior reviewed the work of a subordinate. We concluded that the way to get the best answers would be to get peers to challenge and support each other, than to have a hierarchical challenge process.

. . . The fourth organizational element was very much oriented towards the strategic and operating foundation of the company, in a pure business sense. You could have strategic aims for each business segment, and it could all be translated into targets, but there had to be more to it. That more had to do with the company, as a whole, so we focused on something called reputation.

Creating Performance Leaders: The Atomic Organization   A cornerstone of Act I was an increasing emphasis on leadership development and deployment. To quote Nick Butler:

10 or 12 years ago, BP was a collection of fiefdoms. These fiefdoms were extremely separate: they lived in separate buildings, had separate management systems and different philosophies. The fiefdoms did not mix and the people barely came together at the top. John's fundamental philosophy was that to succeed, these disparate parts had to be brought together as one company with a coherent overall strategic direction, one share price and one set of metrics. That was the only way to extract the benefits of the synergies and to make the whole something more than the parts.

At the centre of this integration were the 400 men and women who collectively led the enterprise. Leading this group were the six Managing Directors, who had total, collective responsibility for the policy of the enterprise. This group formally met in weekly meetings to review and gather experiences. They also used these meetings as an opportunity to discuss the movement of people within the top 300. A separate committee met as needed to allocate capital. The team met in away days twice a year—once with the full main board, including the non-exec's—to consider longer-term strategy. Informal dialogue within the team was high. As Nick Butler explained,

> Initially the different businesses were located in separate buildings and only met at formal meetings, The first step was to move into the same building. At first they were on separate floors in the same building, but they were still not really meeting. So the process took another step forward. The whole management team was integrated; they were located on the same floor in the same building. That produced real change—real cooperation and a close association across the boundary lines.

This close association was further bonded through their respective chiefs of staff who met to discuss agendas and schedules, and make sure that all the links were working.

Browne and his team believed the primary task of the top management was to focus on strategic issues: about reputation, economic shifts, societal shifts, and strategic issue based governance. To achieve this, the board rarely used any operational reports. As Chase commented, "If you preoccupy your management with operational not strategic issues, you never get to this position. We have chosen a form of organisation that has given almost the entirety of operational delivery to some very young men and women of fantastic talent around the world. We preoccupy ourselves strategically."

Next came the 40 Group Vice Presidents, who oversaw large pieces of the business. Until the reorganization of 2001, this group did not have individual accountability for specific business areas, but shared collective responsibility for the total operation. Their primary roles were to coach the Business Unit leaders, to manage the succession process and to make sure that each BU head had a performance contract which was both achievable and a stretch.

This group of Vice Presidents was also the primary feed for top management succession. In Browne's words: "this is the group from which the top 6 (the Managing Directors of the future) will be identified. It means that at any one time there are about 15 who could be my successor, and that in turn means that we have a sufficient pool of talent both to manage a company of this size and to ensure that there is no complacency."

At the base, and core, of BP's organization, below the level of the Group VPs, lay a relatively simple architecture of 150 Business Units, each led by its own Business Unit leader. While the top team managed the external relations of the firm, particularly with the governments, and engaged in debate regarding long-term strategic meaning and purpose, the Business Unit leaders focused on the delivery of operating performance.

Chase described the Business Unit structure of BP as "an extraordinarily flat, dispersed, decentralised process of delivery." A Business Unit could be an oil field, a gas field, a refinery, a chemical plant, or a regional marketing area. As Chase explained, "The reason we selected 150 was that each had to be potentially material to the rest of the group. If there wasn't potential to build a billion-dollar business, we would not make it a business unit." The dismantling of the hierarchical, functionally based company had begun in 1990 when CEO Robert Horton launched Project 1990 which included a large scale restructuring of BP and the removal of many management layers. David Simon, who assumed the role of CEO in 1992, continued this decomposition by further breaking down the functional walls and restructuring the company into 90 different Business Units. Browne and his team continued this process and by 2000 the company consisted of 150 separate Business Units held together by strong performance management processes.

Horizontally, the 150 Business Units were further organised into 15 Peer Groups. The Peer Groups consisted of a network of related Business Units within a particular business stream—essentially those in a similar business, facing similar challenges.

Setting the Targets: The Performance Contract
Driving down vertically through the business was the Performance Contract process designed to

create a clear "line of sight" for individual Business Unit leaders and the collective corporate business goals (see Exhibit 2). As Chase described, "We run our businesses with very tightly defined key performance indicators. Some are financial. Others relate to our commitment to be a force for good. We use exactly the same process—define the goal, define the input to achieve the goal and then start monitoring."

David Watson, Group Vice President, Business Information, described the performance management process as a "structure for having conversations." The Performance Contract was the product of a series of such conversations—within the

Exhibit 2   Performance Management Process

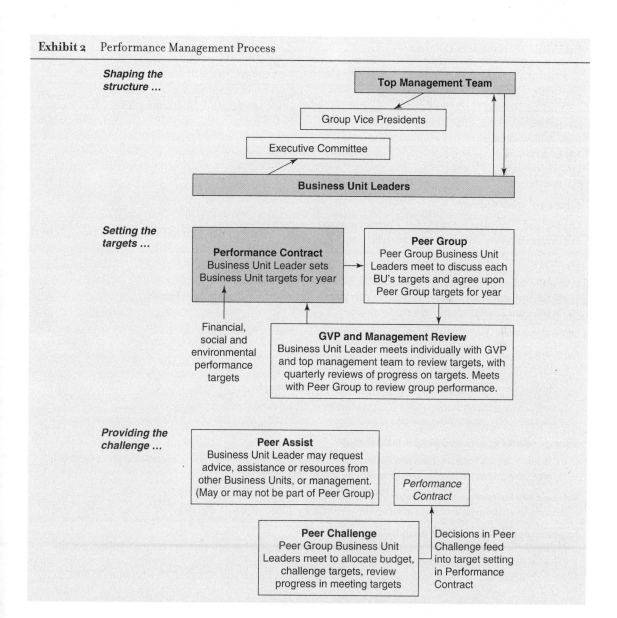

Business Unit, within the Peer Group and with the top management team. In an annual process, Business Unit leaders worked with their teams to identify their unit's goals for the year—financial, social and environmental—and documented them in the Performance Contract. Next they met with their Business Unit peer group to align each unit's targets with those of the collective peer group. The final conversation was with the top management team (see Exhibit 3 for an example of a performance contract).

"The actual contract is relatively simple," said Chase. "A few financial goals—profit before tax, cash flow, investment, return on invested capital—I have never seen more than four. Then there are two or three high-level non-financial targets. Once the

Exhibit 3   Performance Contract

1999 BU Performance Contract				
Financial	**1998 Baseline**	**1998 Actual**	**1999 Contract**	**1999 Stretch**
Net income				
Income improvement[1]				
Net cash flow				
Prize delivery[2]				
Net investment				

Creating a Safety Culture

Develop and implement Poland Safety Contract to Employees and Contractors.
Implement employee near-miss program achieving 300 near miss reports in 1999.

People Basics

100% BP Staff employees receive appraisals for their 1998 performance.
100% BP Staff employees engage in a career development discussion with their Team Leader.
100% BP Team Leaders receive upward feedback.

Other

Establish Poland as a business unit
   Establish comprehensive safety programme—2Q.

   • Institute assurance programme—3Q (planned for September 15th).

   Establish Management information processes to ensure reliable and timely reporting—3Q.
      Manage lobby plan with values tied to each category and 100% deliverables with 1999 key contacts plan.

Manage volume growth and protect market share
   • Balance growth, market share and profitability. Considering this balance, ensure operational processes are in place to achieve 1999 volume increases of xx in LPG and xx in retail.

Rebase costs for current environment
   Identify levers to re-base costs to achieve 10% ROACE by 2002—1Q.

Improve capital efficiency and decapitalise as suitable
   Deliver 30% capital efficiency improvement in new builds and complete **full cost** builds for xx million per site.
   Develop decapitalisation options & landbank strategy—2Q.
   Develop Retail strategy to support consideration for further investment with Financial Memorandum to CAC in 2Q.

(continued)

Exhibit 3   *(concluded)*

	Leading Indicators of Progress				
Prize/Key Activity Set	**1Q**	**2Q**	**3Q**	**4Q**	**Yr**
New build start-ups					
Specific divestments ($6 million)					
Additional divestments ($4 million)					
LPG Slawkow terminal on-line					
Management Information improved processes and streamline transaction accounting					

KPI's	**1998 Actual**	**1999 Plan**	**1999 Latest Estim.**	**1999 Stretch**	**PG5 Range**	**PG3 CoCo Avg.**
Fuel margin (cpl)						
Retail volume growth						
Retail MSC like-for-like growth						
MSC/onsite costs (incl. depr)						
CoCo onsite costs ($k/site)						
Offsite costs ($million)						
Onsite costs/GP						
Offsite costs/SOC						
SOC/$ invested (CoCo)						

	1998 Actual	**1999 Plan**	**1999 Latest Estim.**	**1999 Stretch**	**PG5 BM**	**LPG PG Avg.**
LPG volume						
LPG bulk installations (#)						
LPG unit margin ($/tonne)						
LPG debtor days (end-year)						
LPG fixed cost cover						
S&D retail added value (cpl)						
Supply LPG added value ($/tonne)						
Filling plants ($million)						
Transport cylinder ($/tonne)						
Transport bulk ($/tonne)						

[1] 99 Income (including prize) less delta margin less delta forex less delta tax rate less 98 income.
[2] No prize delivery until income improvement = target improvement − prize.

contract is decided, people are free to achieve them in whatever way they find appropriate."

Quarterly, the top team met with the Business Unit leaders to review progress towards the goals. Failure to meet the terms of the contract was a seri-ous matter and at times meant reassignment of the Business Unit leader. "There is an understanding here . . . that this is a performance culture and either you deliver or you don't," explained Richard New-ton, Group Vice President. Chase commented, "You deliver what you promise—that is our performance mantra. If you do not believe you can deliver, do not make the promise." What if someone does not deliver? "We start from the assumption that if you can't cut it in a particular job you might be able to somewhere else. You are given one or two options to perform somewhere else."

Providing the Stretch: The Peer Challenge   Performance Contracts set the unit's targets, but Peer Groups provided the challenge and stretch to each unit. The peer group played three roles in the challenge. First, business goals were discussed within the Peer Groups prior to the finalisation of the Performance Contract. Second, Peer Groups were a key mechanism for determining resource allocation. Finally, they were the primary means of knowledge sharing. One executive described Peer Groups as "the forum in which Business Units must fight their corner, justify their promises to their closest colleagues and prove they deserve the resources they seek in competition with other Business Units."

"The Peer Challenge," Polly Flinn, Business Unit Head and Vice President Retail Marketing, explained, "was about convincing people in similar positions to support your investment proposal knowing they could invest that same capital [elsewhere] and going eyeball to eyeball with them—and then having to reaffirm whether you have made it or not over the coming months or quarters."

The key for the Peer Group process to reach its full potential was an obligation for every high performing Business Unit to assist and improve the under-performing units. Chase summarized the reasons why the peer group structure worked for BP:

> One of the things we find when we talk to other companies is that they disbelieve us when we say that our performance units have a high capacity and bias to improve one another. The point is they have to do that or they can't meet their goals, because they have performance outputs for the whole peer group. Today the top three Business Units in the Peer Group are responsible for the improvement of the bottom three. That's how they work in a structural sense. They are measured for it.

The performance measurement associated with the peer group processes forced the Business Unit leaders to "grab good ideas from one another and to impose their good ideas on one another," added Chase. This motivation was built into the bonus structure. 50% of a Business Unit leader's bonus was based on peer group performance and 50% on Business Unit performance.

Integration through Collective Learning   If performance management was the foundation of Act I then relentless collective learning was the leverage point.

"In order to generate extraordinary value for shareholders, a company has to learn better than its competitors and apply that knowledge throughout its business faster and more widely than they do," said Sir John Browne. "Any organisation that thinks it does everything the best and that it need not learn from others is incredibly arrogant and foolish." This commitment to knowledge and insight was deeply ingrained in BP. John Manzoni, Head of BP's Gas, Renewables and Power business, explained,

> I always say to people, your seat at the table inside BP depends on your level of insight, it does not depend on the position where you sit in the organisation. And you find all over the place that people get to sit at important tables and have important conversations and the reason that they are there is because they bring insight.

Four factors converged to help BP become a learning organisation: the intellectual curiosity of the top management team, the firm-wide attention to relentlessly building human capital, the Peer Assist processes and the depth and quality of conversations. Together they ensured that insights were leveraged across the company.

Intellectual Curiosity at the Top   Balancing the competitive nature of the performance-driven side of BP's culture was the intellectual curiosity and openness to knowledge sharing of the people in the company, especially evident in the top team. Browne and his colleagues were described by a *Financial Times* journalist as "an unusually active and well-financed university faculty—earnest, morally engaged and careful of other's sensibilities."[1] Strategic thinking and deep questioning of business purpose were the normal way of operating. In Sir John Browne's words,

> This company is founded on a deep belief in intellectual rigour. In my experience, unless you can lay out rational arguments as the foundation of what you do, nothing happens. Rigour implies that you understand the assumptions you have made . . . assumptions about the state of the world, of what you can do, and how your competitors will interact with it, and how the policy of the world will or will not allow you to do something.

While Browne's appetite for knowledge was insatiable, he himself was a creator of knowledge—a sort of theory builder. As theory builder he relentlessly engaged his top team in discussions around ideas. The resulting intellectual, strategic focus of the team was extraordinary. Asked about the genesis of the strategic nature of the senior team, Chase had this to say,

> We are a deeply questioning team; we constantly inspect what we do to find out whether it is in fact the exercise of laziness or prejudice. We do it in every area; we do it behaviourally, in business process terms, and in operational delivery. . . . It helps if your CEO is a very strategic thinker. John is not only a strategic thinker by predisposition but by intellectual learning and a constant search for strategic improvement. He is a continuous researcher for new ideas. He is an unusual CEO; he constantly surrounds himself with strategic stimuli.

Asked to describe some of the strategic issues discussed in the top management team, John Browne elaborated,

> . . . We look at economic history, the rate of change in capital intensive industries and we ask ourselves how we think the oil industry will change as a result of transportation changes . . . based on what happened, for instance, when canals were put in the UK in the late 18th century. We think about these long-term trends, and what are the consequences of doing

the business we are doing, and how we can manage these consequences. Those consequences matter. Environmental questions related to burning oil and gas influence supply and demand parameters of oil and gas because if people worry about that, then they inevitably change their attitude about how they get their energy. . . . We test our assumptions. . . . What is really going to happen. Could the price of oil drop below $10 a barrel over the medium term? Unlikely, but what happens if it does? We think about how technological substitution in the short term will work . . . the main point is that all these things we keep interrogating and asking ourselves how dependent are we on one or the other of these factors.

This openness to questioning and learning extended beyond the boundaries of the enterprise. The members of the top team had also established networks of talking partners across industry. Sir John Browne's membership of the boards of Intel and Goldman Sachs provided added insights into industry models. As Nick Butler explained,

> Membership of the board of Intel has been critical to him. About 18 months ago people thought that established businesses like BP would be destroyed by IT, there would be no need for intermediaries. What he had seen at Intel convinced him that this was not the case, there was some potential in B2B, but very little in B2C. The insights from Intel averted risks of over investment even though we looked old fashioned at the time.

The team were also involved with Cambridge University, having set up a multidisciplinary institute on fluid flow analysis which brought together chemists, engineers, physicists, and academic staff. Members of the top team visited the institute four or five times per year and maintained contacts with numerous faculties not just in Cambridge but also at Stanford, Yale, and a wide range of other very high quality academic institutions around the world. As Nick Butler, who held many of these links on behalf of Browne explained, "the process keeps us in touch with people who know more than we do. It is a daily reminder that we are only one relatively small part of a complex world. It is a reminder of all things we do not know."

[1]Lloyd, John, "Company Law," *The Business Financial Times Weekend Magazine,* September 9, 2000.

Relentlessly Building Human Capital   The intellectual curiosity of the top team provided a model for the company. Seeking those within the company who had the insight necessary to run the business was an obsession. The focus on the development of individual talent began from the top with the profound obligation the top team felt to the long-term intellectual health of BP. Much of their time on a day-to-day basis was spent coaching the talented men and women in the organisation. Each member typically coached and mentored cohorts of seven to ten Group Vice Presidents. Chase described how he saw this role,

> I gossip with them about what is really going on within the inner cabinet, I share confidences, I tell them about my discussions with John Browne. I build trust with them. I agree with them what their weaknesses are, and agree to work with them. You have to take the time to engage them with examples that will make them broader and wiser. To develop their sense of responsibility for the firm; who are they developing. The greatest pleasure I get is from this development of talent.

In turn, the Group Vice Presidents coached the Business Unit Heads. A subgroup also sat on the Learning and Development Committee. The committee met monthly to discuss the long-term development of key talent. As David Watson, a member of the committee explained, "We are experimenting with a new learning model based on reflection. Each committee meeting is two days of deep, meaningful dialogue." Watson continued, "The whole way we are thinking about learning and development is starting with the brand values: the possibility that actually what we should be developing for future leadership is people with the brand values deeply embedded, not just people who know how to run a part of the business."

BP's management also created forums for the development and expression of its collective intellect through university based education programs for executives. In a special programme developed at Cambridge University, BP executives debated issues such as the social impact of business, the future of international society, valuing nature and ethics. At Stanford and Harvard they used case studies to hone their knowledge of globalisation and sources of competitive advantage, and their skills in country risk analysis. The themes of all the programs had a common thread summed up in the name of the Cambridge program, "Thinking into the Future—Learning from the Past." The programs represented a new orientation of the company towards society, its customers and its employees.

Through formal processes, high potential individuals had the option to enter the Group Development Program (GDP). This program was a combination of skill assessment, training and development and career progression. A subset of those individuals in the GDP was selected to serve as "turtles" or personal assistant.[2] As a turtle, the executive would become a shadow to Chase, Browne, or another top team member and be involved in all conversations, all meetings, and all discussions of the top management. "They come with us around the world. They sit in all our executive meetings," explained Chase, "It is a 15 hour a day job and they do it for about 12 months. But in return they see everything."

Turtles and the GDP were examples of the "stretch" that was part of a career at BP. Manzoni, who was the first personal assistant to Browne even before the word "turtle" was used, explained, "I have had tremendous opportunities for learning because I have had no bloody idea how to do the job that I have been put into almost every single time." Those that succeeded were rewarded with rapid advancement in their careers at BP.

But this relentless building of human capital was not simply limited to those on the Group Development Program or the "turtles." From the end of 1999 onwards the company had put substantial resources behind stitching together the 275 human resource Intranet systems it had developed and inherited. As Dave Latin, who managed the project commented, "Following the mergers we saw this as

---

[2]Derived from Teenage Mutant Ninja Turtles, adventure cartoon characters popular in the 1980s, the term "turtle" was used to describe a person who is able to do "high-energy, surprising things and appear to be normal," explained Lee Edwards, former turtle to CEO Sir John Browne.

an opportunity to simplify. What got the board excited was the aspiration that e-hr could touch each of the 100,000 employees and cause a shift in behaviour." Over the following two years an ever increasing portfolio of Intranet based developmental tools was rolled out across the world.

"Competencies Online" enabled individuals to assess their current skills and development needs by seeking e-enabled feedback from their peers and colleagues; individuals profiled and communicated their competencies and job aspirations on my-Profile, whilst myAgent continuously scouted and reported back job and project vacancies with similar competency needs. Managers who posted the competency profiles of the job and project vacancies in their team using myJobMarket automatically received matched information from the many thousands of on-line resumes. Within a year BP had created a vibrant and transparent internal labour market, with over 17,000 logging in every week to the myCareer portal. The goal was to get to a situation, by the end of 2001, when all BP employees would use the portal to profile their skills, find job matches, identify their development needs and access learning and development opportunities.

Leveraging through Peer Assist Performance Contracts and Peer Challenge were the backbone of the performance management process. However the heart of the collective intellectual and social capital of the organization was most evident in Peer Assists. Business Unit leaders regularly provided help to one another—to help identify the best strategy, to learn more about a new area of work, or to give validation to a decision—in the form of advice or actual resources through a Peer Assist. Peer Assists spanned peer group boundaries, often requiring the involvement of people in multiple divisions of the company.

Polly Flinn, former Amoco employee and Vice President of Retail Marketing, learned quickly at BP that federal behaviour was the norm. While serving as the retail Business Unit lead in Poland in 1999, Flinn asked for assistance from four leaders at BP who came together in a Peer Assist team to look at the Poland strategy and give Flinn their advice. After Flinn implemented the advice from the Peer Assist, the retail marketing business in Poland became profitable for the first time. In 1998, the Business Unit lost $20 million; in 2000 it earned $6 million. "This was BP at its best," recalled Flinn. When Flinn was faced with the near impossible task of masterminding the development and rollout of BP's new retail offering, BP Connect, she called on the Peer Assist process once again, but this time on a much grander scale. "The BP Connect Peer Assist was Poland times 30," recalled Flinn. "Of the 300 people involved, only 10% actually had Performance Contract goals related to BP Connect, yet because of their desire to share their skills and their expectations of federal behaviour, people contributed."

Leaders at BP viewed participation in a Peer Assist as having mutual benefits for both parties. "First, the team that has asked for the Peer Assist obtains strategic and operational insight from the most respected experts in BP," explained Flinn. "Secondly it is a development opportunity for the people who participate. People want to do it." Top management also participated in Peer Assists, especially regarding strategic issues. Chase, deputy CEO, visited the prototype BP Connect in Atlanta and "became in effect the brand champion for this offer in terms of explaining it to other businesses in BP. He helped to build support for the retail network" said Flinn.

Creating Purposeful Conversations People learn and share learning through conversations. At BP, management explicitly focused on enhancing the depth, breadth and quality of conversations at all levels, as a means to supporting organization-wide learning. As Rodney Chase described,

> One of the most pressing reasons to create a dialogue . . . has been the rise of connectivity within the space in which BP operates. There are people who by dint of communications, flexibility and immediacy have the capacity to find things out and transmit the information instantaneously. . . . It is palpable, it is very real and it is expressed with great frequency. It is on my screen now everyday.

"There's no point in just changing a process," explained Watson. "It has to start with changing the fabric—the information. If it is the same information, we'll get the same conversations, so we have to provide different information for different conversations." The source of the information that fuelled the conversations had shifted—no longer were communications primarily a top down process. There was a growing recognition that the information for dialogue and conversation came from many sources including families and young employees.

"This organisation does not work as a series of instructions—it works by conversations and consensus. It takes longer to get there but once you do, the whole organisation moves," Manzoni explained.

Beyond enhancing the richness and diversity of information, the company made an effort to improve and sharpen the quality of conversations through two means: linking conversations to purpose, and legitimizing dissent and challenge.

According to John Browne, "people do not learn, at least in a corporate environment, without a target. You can implore people to learn, and they will to some extent. But if you say 'look the learning is necessary in order to cut the cost of drilling a well by 10%', then they will learn with a purpose." This philosophy was built into BP by linking as many conversation processes as possible to tangible and concrete goals. Peer assists and peer reviews, performance contracts—they were all primarily aimed at developing intense, purposeful conversations, driven by concrete goals and targets.

The other basis of enhancing the learning value of conversations was to legitimize dissent and challenge. Again in the words of John Browne,

> People are challenged the whole time. "Just run that by me one more time" is the mildish challenge. "I don't understand it" to "surely you've got this wrong" to "no, that is far too conventional and we have to think of a different way"—the discussions, debates and challenges happen everywhere. I participate in it; everyone participates in it. If you were sitting in the management committee, sometimes it gets very hot indeed. "No it doesn't make sense"—"well make it make sense!" The questions are continuously

around . . . for example Rodney and I have worked together since 1984, and we have worked close up through the ranks and it is a very close relationship. You would think we would be so familiar with each other that we would know the way each other thinks, but it is actually the reverse. We challenge each other very hard, in a very appropriate way, but it is the purpose of the relationship to get a better result, and we do that. And that, in turn, encourages others to do that.

Deep inside the organization, conversations and dialogue occurred in forums such as Performance Contract discussions or message boards on the intranet. Use of the intranet was not limited to young hires. Rodney Chase, a thirty year veteran of BP, checked the message boards daily and was actively engaged in the communication. Chase saw dialogue with employees and stakeholders as essential to operating as a business in society.

> For a global institution we are very nimble. When we want something to happen around the world, we can get all the swallows in our worldwide organization to flip like that. They can go in this direction, they can go in that direction. How does it happen? I have no idea. It is some combination of informal word of mouth, networks, which are encouraged, informal networks based on career friendships or based on professional groupings, or based on clubs on the Intranet. If you've got an important message that needs to get out in the firm it will happen in 24 hours. And you can be certain that every thinker in the organization will have heard about it and will be thinking about it. It means that the forces for inertia have been largely swept away.

Aligning Organizational and Individual Values

When John Browne and Rodney Chase joined what was then British Petroleum as young graduates, they were joining one of the United Kingdom's most prestigious branded companies. But over time the relationship between the oil industry and society had become increasingly tense. While society demanded the products of energy—heat, light and mobility—it also demanded that the production of these things be done harmlessly. When accidents occurred, public outrage was the result. In 1989, the Exxon Valdez oil spill in Alaska was one such accident. Later in 1995, the Shell Brentspar incident was another.[3] The two major points of tension were the societal impact of the extraction of oil and the environmental impact of emissions during refining and consumption of fuel.

This tension came to a head for BP in 1997 when an NGO, Amnesty International, accused BP of funding private armies in Colombia. A team of BP engineers had discovered what they soon realised to be the largest oil reservoir in the western hemisphere. The oil find had attracted merchants and investors, labourers and contractors, the army, and the guerrillas who wanted to extract their own political rent from the process. The team was in the middle of a region of underdeveloped infrastructure, complex social problems, and a government fighting a 35-year civil war. Upon setting up exploration operations, BP was accused by Amnesty International of providing lethal training to the Colombian security forces through the services of a British-owned private security firm. The Amnesty International news release asserted that these "Colombian security forces have been responsible for widespread extrajudicial executions, torture and 'disappearances' of civilians." BP's reputation was badly tarnished. Though BP denied the accusation, the management realized that a change in the way that BP worked with local communities needed to occur.

Awakening of a Force for Good — The question "What is your personal Colombia?" echoed in the minds of all BP's executives. Memories of the incident affected every decision made by an executive and shaped a new outlook regarding BP's role as a business. Edwards explained, "When we talked to the outside world, the oil industry was seen as big, powerful, dirty, secretive, grey—and we didn't want that. We didn't want to be an unknown player in a big sector not known for goodness or as a force

[3] Shell in 1995 planned to dispose of an offshore loading buoy by scuttling it in deep water off the northwestern coast of Britain. Environmentalists were outraged and a consumer boycott ensued. Shell stations were vandalised, some of them firebombed, or shot upon with automatic weapons. Finally Shell brought the buoy to a Norwegian port and eventually dismantled it.

for goodness." Chase described the formation of the concept of force for good,

> We now have a century of dealing with nations with the fundamental task of the search for and extraction of energy raw materials. It is very much out of that history that the commitment to becoming a force for good was born. . . . It's not enough for us simply to find the resources and create for the host nations the wealth extraction from the release of those resources. It is not seen either by them or us as a sufficient force for good. We have to recognise and plan more specifically other goals which are not so obviously the role of the commercial enterprise.

John Browne personally saw the company's efforts at being a force of good more in terms of building reputation—the last of the core premises of organizational design he had enumerated. "There is, I believe, no conflict between investing in reputation and creating long-term shareholder value," he said. The primary benefit of reputation, however, lay in building the emotional strength of the organization. As he described,

> The interesting thing about the behaviour of this firm is that we always start with the foundation of rationality but we recognize that that in itself will not take you far. What you have to apply on top of it is an emotional state. . . .
>
> It is easy to detach the employees from a company. A company is pretty impersonal and artificial, and it produces continuous contradictions which have to be resolved. We have the contradiction that we produce oil and gas, and we want to reduce the impact of that on the environment. The question to us is how do you genuinely allow people to transform all their individuality into the company because if they can do that then people will begin to think and behave in a way that is aligned to the goals of the company.
>
> To build the reputation, we picked four areas. First, safety: when you invite someone to come and work, you should send them home in the same shape as when they arrived—that is a minimum requirement for respect of a person, and you have to take that terribly seriously. Second, you have to take care of the natural environment. It is important because people do not want companies to make a mess and leave them behind. Third, everyone wants a place in the ideal which

is free of all discrimination; it doesn't matter what you stand for in terms of your race, gender, sexual orientation or religious beliefs. All that matters is merit. Fourth, the company has to invest in the community from which the people have come, so as to narrow the gap between life within the company and life outside the company.

In a show of commitment to these goals, Browne took an unusual and risky stand in a speech regarding climate change at Stanford University. He admitted that global climate change was a problem that BP could no longer ignore and outlined BP's plans for addressing the problem.

> The time to consider the policy dimensions of climate change is not when the link between greenhouse gases and climate change is conclusively proven but when the possibility cannot be discounted and is taken seriously by the society of which we are part. We in BP have reached that point. . . . To be absolutely clear— we must now focus on what can and what should be done, not because we can be certain climate change is happening, but because the possibility can't be ignored. If we are all to take responsibility for the future of our planet, then it falls to us to begin to take precautionary action now.[4]

The steps Browne outlined were to control BP's emissions, to fund continuing scientific research, to take initiatives for joint implementation, to develop alternative fuels for the long term, and to contribute to the public policy debate in search of the wider global answers to the problem. In an industry characterized by an old boys network spanning the major oil companies, this move was met with surprise and hostility. "Some of the sceptics and the press said, 'He has left the church. He is no longer with the industry,'" recalled Edwards, "But as soon as [Browne] made this speech, the internal feedback was unbelievable—from children of employees, spouses." BP officially removed itself from the Global Climate Coalition, a lobbying and public relations organisation based in Washington, D.C. which opposed government intervention with

regard to the climate. Browne was, in fact, responding to internal pressures to leave the coalition. BP's employees felt that what the coalition was arguing for was "intellectually unjustifiable" because credible scientists were finding the opposite—that gas emissions were contributing to global warming.

A year later, in April 1998, BP began to receive recognition for its bold moves. *Oil & Gas Journal* highlighted BP in a review of financial strategies of the top oil and gas companies.

> Within the top 10, there is one striking example of a company being driven by a different vision. BP has designated corporate citizenship and being "forward-thinking about the environment, human rights, and dealing with people and ethics" as "the new fulcrum of competition between oil companies in the late 1990s." Several of the other leading companies have adopted parts of this approach, with Shell probably going the furthest. But none has been as explicit or committed as BP.[5]

The stand that Browne took placed BP in a distinctive position in its industry. As an example, following the Stanford speech, BP struck up an agreement with the Environmental Defense Fund to design a system for trading greenhouse gas emissions within BP. In this system, revenues and costs of carbon trades were treated like actual cash flows, which allowed BP to measure environmental performance as financial performance. These actions were part of the company's increasing concern with being progressive and green—in other words being a force for good. Being a force for good was about having "goals that are worth pursuing for everyone; that have to do with making society better as a result of our participation than if we had not been there," remarked Chase.

From Act I to Act II: The Challenges and Questions   In July 2000, after a wide ranging exercise involving staff throughout the company as well as external specialists, BP launched a new corporate branding designed to project both the

---

[4]Sir John Browne in a speech at Stanford University, California, May 19, 1997.

[5]Common financial strategies found among top 10 oil and gas firms. *Oil & Gas Journal,* Tulsa, April 20, 1998, Anonymous.

Exhibit 4   BP, Royal Dutch Shell (RD), Exxon Mobil (XOM), and S&P 500 Index Share Price Comparison

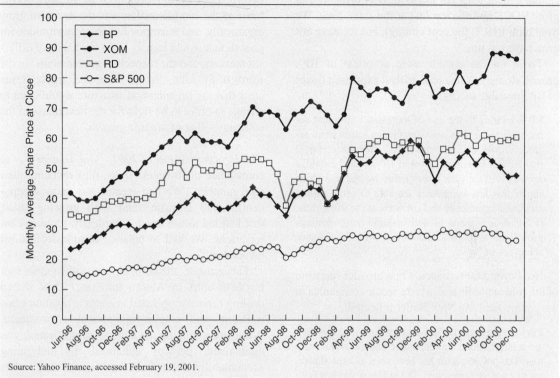

Source: Yahoo Finance, accessed February 19, 2001.

changes which had taken place and the company's aspirations for the future.

The company would be known simply as "bp," with the familiar BP shield and Amoco torch replaced by a fresh, new symbol depicting a vibrant sunburst of green, white and yellow. Named the Helios mark after the sun god of ancient Greece, the new logo was intended to exemplify dynamic energy—in all its forms, from oil and gas to solar—that the company delivered to its ten million daily customers around the world. The attributes of the brand—progressive, green, innovative and performance-driven—were the values that would shape BP's future.

At a press conference, the launch of the new brand, under the provocative slogan "beyond petroleum" was described by one analyst as "a sun rise brand for a sun set company." Though the company had made great progress on many fronts, BP clearly

needed to produce a final proof point, that it could achieve long term growth with short-term returns.

BP's financial situation, relative to that of the other super majors, Exxon Mobil and Royal Dutch Shell, added to the challenge of achieving long term growth. Over 90% of BP's 500,000 shareholders were individual investors. As of the end of the third quarter of 2000, its net debt-to-capital ratio was 25%, increased from 19% in the previous quarter and well above Exxon Mobil's 9.5% and Royal Dutch's 1.7%.[6] Although BP's ROCE, at 19.7%, was the highest of the international majors in 2000,[7] its stock was trading at a discount to Exxon Mobil (see Exhibit 4 for comparison).[8] Alexander, as the voice of concern of BP's management,

[6]Salomon Smith Barney Equity Research Report, November 13, 2000.
[7]Ibid.
[8]UBS Warburg Global Equity Research Report, November 9, 2000.

explained the challenge the company faced, "We cannot deliver what our brand means unless we can grow ROCE and the top line at the same time. We have built ROCE [by cost cutting], but we have not grown the top line."

Those on the outside were sceptical of BP's growth strategy. A financial analyst expressed doubt of BP's possible success.

> BP is coming to the end of its restructuring and acquisition phase. It is now signalling a return to an organic growth oriented strategy. . . . We are sceptical that BP can sustain its target of 10% annual earnings growth. . . . Our view is supported by history, which shows that few companies are able to grow capital employed organically and cut costs at the same time. If BP does manage to deliver underlying earnings growth of over 10% annually it will be a major achievement.[9]

But beyond these issues was a broader question of the role of public and private sector companies in the energy field. As Nick Butler reflected:

> I believe that over the last century the world has been artificially divided into the public and the private sectors. The private sector has been seen as exploitative, narrow and self-interested. The public world has been seen as representing the interests of the whole community. This dichotomy has been established and underpins the political debate. This was not always the case in economic history . . . the two used to run together and to work for common purpose. It is interesting now to see if the moment is coming when the two sectors can once again work in harmony. The possibility is very interesting for a company such as BP.

Sir John Browne echoed the same issue:

> However big Shell, Exxon-Mobil and BP are, together they control only 9% of the world's oil production. This is not exactly market dominance. The rest is controlled by different versions of state-owned organizations. We are looking at how the interface is changing, and as you see what is happening in China and in Saudi Arabia, you recognize that that interface is changing. Who will get to do what? Will states do things themselves or will there be some new partnership?

[9]Commerzbank Securities Research Report, September 22, 2000.

To respond to these questions and challenges, Browne once again reorganized BP in 2001. At the heart of the reorganization was the desire to grow organically, and to respond to the opportunities for growth that would largely lie in the hands of different markets, and the respective governments. In the words of Sir John, "As we set up the targets, it was clear that the organization structure would need to change in order to be right for the next phase of the company—that of organic growth."

The Reorganization of 2001   One change was to consolidate the business units, thus reducing their total number. "We had created too many components," said Browne "and with growing scale, that had led to too much complexity, too many interactions. We had to balance complexity against ownership."

For example, the company consolidated its four business units in Alaska into one. They shared drilling capacity, operated in a single taxation environment, and single reputational environment. While consolidating the units, decentralization was maintained, perhaps enhanced, by delegating accountability down from the business unit leaders to the next level of managers.

The role and deployment of the Group Vice Presidents were also changed. Instead of being jointly and severely responsible for performance, they were made personally accountable for the performance of the sum of their business units. Previously, in order to integrate the leadership cadre, they had all been located in London. "That worked," said Sir John, "but actually in a decentralized model, the senior managers of the company should be out there with the business units to build relationships." So, he distributed the Group VP's around the world—as Presidents or Regional Directors in the U.S., in Asia, in Latin America, and so on. "Now they have both business and regional accountability," he said. "They have a specific remit, and they are the face of the company."

At the heart of this change was an acknowledgement of the regional role as an enabler of organic growth. "It is not completely clear to me," said Sir

John, in a marvelous example of British understatement, "that the business goals of the corporate and the goals of the government are automatically aligned without a lot of effort. . . . You can say to them you want them to work five times harder and they will say why? So that you can bring in imported equipment and take out the money?"

"Take the case of Trinidad," he said. "I have heard this time and again from Prime Ministers and Presidents there. They used to be a big producer of sugar, and they couldn't afford to buy the boiled sweets that were made in the U.K. . . . We have a gigantic amount of gas in Trinidad, and we have to think and we have to do several things. We have to work with the government to build capacity. Our role is very much recruitment and training of people—we are less good at doing what governments should be doing such as building roads. Number two, we need to work with them to expand the number of small and medium enterprises in the country . . . build things with other people who will use some of that gas. . . . We are going to be a part of all that investment, not exclusively, but our reputation and the fact that we will be there and making sure the project works will allow other people to come in and invest. This is good news for us, because they will use the gas, and it is good news for the government. We have to build this mutuality."

To build this mutuality, BP needed strong local relationships. "It would be extraordinarily unwise to continuously go to a government, flying in from London, saying I need the following things. You need someone who can set it in the context and say the company is doing this, and this is where the mutual advantage is." This was the enhanced role for the Group VP's—thereby opening doors for the business units so that they could effectively do their work to grow the business.

The third element of the 2001 reorganization was a consolidation and strengthening of the functional competencies of BP. "We believed that greater emphasis was needed for enhancing our marketing skills, and understanding the differences between marketing and sales. That difference is now put in real organizational terms, so for the first

time in the company's history, we have a marketing director and she is in charge of the strategic side." Similarly, the technology group was given full accountability for the strategic goals and targets in the areas of technology development, and for deployment of people. "We have to focus heavily not only on how we retain and deploy people in this area, but how we continuously renew the quality of people because this is a very fundamental part of our functional capability," said Sir John.

Similarly, the highly fragmented internal supply and trading organization was consolidated into one entity, with the goal of stopping internal transactions and to leverage scale. In the words of Sir John, "It is certainly true that returns to supply and trading increase with scale—they just do, and you can prove it—and we have reached such a scale that we had to consider that benefit. But, equally, your reputation is highly dependent on how you use that scale, especially in unregulated markets, and that worries us a lot. In unregulated markets, these decisions of judgment are critical to the reputation of the firm, and that is something that has to be done in one place."

While describing these organizational changes, John Browne emphasized BP's fundamental philosophy about organizing:

> The thing about organization is nothing is ever fixed, at least in BP, and we renew ourselves by learning what is good about the past and changing all things that are not so good. They are behaviour dependent. Grouping the Group Vice Presidents in London to make them into a team so that they knew each other, and could interact among themselves in a way that made the peer groups effective—that worked. I believe that investment will endure, and now we can send them outside London. In three or five years time, we may have to change again because it might become silo-like, and we might think that the best way would be to bring them all back to London or New York, or try something completely different.

Was this reorganization enough, or even right, as a response to the challenges and questions? Sir John was slightly philosophical in his reply:

> Some of our competitors do not have a good reputation. Yet they trade at a higher multiple than BP. Does

reputation matter? If you are from Mars, would you not say that those with worse reputations are valued more highly? . . . This debate which still goes on is about deep-seated values. Recruitment, motivation, great place to work . . . these should all in theory be

expressed in market value at the end, but in practice may take more than one period to do so. But, in the end, I firmly believe that the more a company reflects the values of the society from which its people are drawn, the better the company is.

Reading 5-1   Unleash Innovation in Foreign Subsidiaries

Julian Birkinshaw and Neil Hood

The challenge of going global is not simply to sell products wherever customers are but to take advantage of bright ideas wherever they spring up. Indeed, growth-triggering innovation often emerges in foreign subsidiaries—from employees closest to customers and least attached to the procedures and politesse of the home office. NCR's automatic teller business, for instance, took off only when the development team shifted activities from corporate headquarters in Dayton, Ohio, to Dundee, Scotland. Under the guidance of a charismatic leader with scrappy persistence, NCR's Scottish operation became the largest manufacturer of ATMs in the world and brought the moribund Dundee manufacturing center back from the brink of extinction.

But as every multinational manager knows, making the most of foreign subsidiaries is tricky. Too often, heavy-handed responses from headquarters squelch local enthusiasm and drive out good ideas—and good people. Even when headquarters tries to do the right thing by democratizing the innovation process and ceding more power to

▌ Julian Birkinshaw is an associate professor of strategy and international management at London Business School. Neil Hood is a professor of business policy and codirector of the Strathclyde International Business Unit at the University of Strathclyde in Glasgow, Scotland.
▌ Reprinted by permission of *Harvard Business Review.* "Unleash Innovation in Foreign Subsidiaries" by Julian Birkinshaw and Neil Hood (March 2001).
▌ Copyright © 2001 by Harvard Business School Publishing Corporation. All rights reserved.

subsidiaries, the results are not always stellar. (See the box "A Worst-Case Scenario.")

For the last eight years, we have studied more than 50 multinational corporations to understand what companies can do differently to encourage innovation in foreign subsidiaries—what we call "innovation at the edges." Our observations suggest that when companies start to think of foreign subsidiaries as peninsulas rather than as islands—as extensions of the company's strategic domain rather than as isolated outposts—innovative ideas flow more freely from the periphery to the corporate center. (We first heard the peninsula concept articulated by managers at Monsanto Canada as they grappled with the challenge of redefining their role after the 1989 Free Trade Agreement with the United States.) But even more than a change in mind-set, corporate executives require a new set of practices, with two aims: to improve the formal and informal channels of communication between headquarters and subsidiaries and to give foreign subsidiaries more authority to see their ideas through. Only then can companies ensure that bright ideas—and the smart people who dream them up—don't end up marooned on desert islands.

▌ Peninsulas, Not Islands

Fostering innovation in foreign subsidiaries is a familiar goal, but it is extremely difficult to achieve in real life. In the past, multinationals recognized the

A Worst-Case Scenario

To illustrate the challenges that entrepreneurs in subsidiaries typically face, consider the story of Scott McTaggart, a 29-year-old business development manager in the Canadian subsidiary of a diversified industrial company.

He couldn't have seen it coming, but when McTaggart joined the subsidiary in the mid-1990s, he was in for a rocky ride. With a reputation for decentralization and programs that encouraged individual initiative, the U.S.-based business was one of the most reliably profitable companies in the world. Not only were employees encouraged to practice an informal style of management, but the company had also established several initiatives that encouraged frontline employees to play active roles in improving business processes. These programs resulted in large cost savings, and, perhaps even more important, they spawned a new creativity and enthusiasm among employees—an atmosphere, you would think, in which entrepreneurs could thrive.

At the Canadian subsidiary where McTaggart worked, however, the glory days were largely a thing of the past. As the oldest of 30 international subsidiaries, the Canadian group had once operated as a miniature replica of its parent company with a CEO who was fully responsible for the profits of the Canadian operating divisions. But in the 1980s, the parent company had moved to a more integrated model for North American operations. It created a dozen strategic business units, all headquartered in the United States. Thus the role of the Canadian CEO was reduced to that of mere figurehead, and the Canadian subsidiary was left to deal with mundane issues such as new legislation and tax accounting. It was only through a small business-development group that entrepreneurial activities were formally encouraged.

Soon after his arrival, McTaggart identified an opportunity to bid for a massive, government-sponsored energy management project that entailed the installation and financing of energy-efficient lightbulbs, motors, and other electrical equipment in 150 federal buildings throughout Canada. With potential revenues in the billions, energy management was a great opportunity, in McTaggart's view, not just for the Canadian subsidiary but for the entire company. Lacking a budget of his own, McTaggart convinced one division president to provide $1 million in seed money to test the market. Elated, McTaggart quickly put together a small project team and started to go after business.

That's when the problems began. A few months after McTaggart's initiative got under way, the business unit went through a dramatic reorganization. Following the abrupt resignation of the unit's president, the new president withdrew support for the energy management project. Suddenly orphaned, McTaggart found a new sponsor in another business unit after a series of emphatic presentations and 11th-hour phone calls.

Even as McTaggart scrambled for funds, the fledgling business was becoming a player in the energy management business—several pilot projects were completed and four new contracts were secured. But again problems emerged. McTaggart and his new sponsor came to realize at virtually the same painful moment that even though energy management fit well with the existing business's product lines, the energy management business's life cycle was wildly out of sync with the rest of the division's product portfolio.

Clearly, McTaggart needed to make a number of up-front investments and take several calculated risks to grow his business. But his new sponsor, obsessed with controlling costs and intent on being involved in day-to-day decisions (or so it seemed to McTaggart), kept urging McTaggart to curb his growth expectations. Finally, matters came to a head: faced with yet another demand to scale back his projections, McTaggart decided to resign. The energy management business limped along for another 18 months but never regained its previous pace. A disillusioned McTaggart started his own company, this time better equipped, he hoped, to control its destiny.

McTaggart's experience is all too common. His idea was consonant with the company's entrepreneurial spirit and was aligned with corporate growth targets, but McTaggart faced obstacle after obstacle: lack of fit with existing businesses, changing agendas at the top, risk-averse managers, culture clashes, and time lost fighting internal resistance. He lost a great opportunity to take his ideas to the limit, and the company wasted time, money, and that precious commodity, initiative.

---

need to tap into a few select subsidiaries, but today successful corporate executives recognize that good ideas can come from any foreign subsidiary. (See the box "Three Eras of the Multinational.") The challenge is to find ways to liberalize, not tighten, internal systems and to delegate more authority to local subsidiaries. It isn't enough to ask subsidiary managers to be innovative; corporate managers need to give them incentives and support systems to facilitate their efforts. That's more easily said than done, of course, but our observations suggest four approaches:

- Give seed money to subsidiaries.
- Use formal requests for proposals.
- Encourage subsidiaries to be incubators.
- Build international networks.

When these practices are set in motion, we can expect far more creative and genuinely innovative ideas to emerge from the edges of the corporation. Let's take a look at each approach.

Give Seed Money to Subsidiaries   It's easy to argue that subsidiary companies need access to seed money, but corporate executives must strike a balance between demanding that subsidiaries meet short-term results and granting them sufficient freedom to pursue new ideas. Put too much focus on the former, and you know that subsidiaries will hide profits—not to pursue their new ideas but to protect themselves in case of a rainy day. Put too much emphasis on the latter, and there will be a proliferation of so-called strategic projects whose returns will fall below target levels. One way to achieve the necessary balance is to give subsidiaries discretionary budgets to test ideas

within limits imposed by corporate headquarters. But it's also a matter of who holds the purse strings for which types of investments. Major investments can and should be made at a corporate level. But seed money can be handled on a more decentralized basis by giving local subsidiaries discretionary budgets to test ideas.

For example, in the late 1980s, Hilary Smith, a market development manager at 3M Canada, identified a market for systems that would allow library visitors to check out books without assistance. Her proposal fell on deaf ears at corporate headquarters, partly because the market for traditional library security machines in the United States was still growing rapidly. She pursued it anyway, using seed funding from the Canadian R&D budget to put together a prototype. At the American Library Association meeting where the prototype debuted, she discovered that 3M Australia had been working on a similar product. Hearing enthusiastic comments from potential customers, she and her Australian counterpart agreed to work together to bring out a single 3M product. Additional funding was supplied by the U.S.-based library systems business unit, and Smith was given worldwide responsibility for the product's launch. Manufacturing was transferred to St. Paul, Minnesota, where the U.S. business unit was based. The Australian subsidiary retained product and business development rights in Australia and New Zealand. Self-Check is now one of the main products in 3M Library Systems' portfolio—thanks in no small part to the initial funding from the Canadian and Australian divisions.

It often happens, of course, that an idea seeded by a business unit, having developed into a viable

Three Eras of the Multinational

Multinationals have evolved through three phases over the past 50 years, both in terms of their geographic scope and the roles played by their foreign subsidiaries:

Paternalism

In the first half of the twentieth century, the dominant model for multinationals was to innovate in the home country and then roll out new products across the corporate empire. U.S. companies like Caterpillar, IBM, and Procter & Gamble became masters of this model. But as foreign markets for the established multinationals became more sophisticated and as the foreign subsidiaries in those countries grew stronger, it gradually became apparent that the home country did not have a monopoly on innovation and leading-edge thinking.

Expansionism

In the 1970s and 1980s, many multinational corporations set up "scanning units" to tap into the ideas coming out of key foreign markets, and they built R&D sites abroad to gain access to scientific communities. But welcome as they were, corporate investments of this type represented but a halfhearted attempt to tap into the ideas and opportunities in foreign markets. There were two major problems. First, scanning units and foreign R&D labs were attractive in principle but difficult to manage effectively. For example, many European multinationals, including Volkswagen, Volvo, and Ericsson, established development centers in California, but in most cases the units struggled to successfully transfer and integrate their ideas with those of their parent companies. Second, by defining certain units as responsible for picking up new ideas, corporate managers were implicitly signaling to all other foreign units that they did not have to bother. Such an approach limited growth opportunities to a few select markets or technologies and dampened the initiative of subsidiary managers in other foreign units.

Liberalism

A third model, now emerging, takes a more democratic approach to the pursuit of new opportunities. It builds on two basic arguments: first, useful new business ideas can emerge from anywhere in the world, particularly those parts of the organization that are in direct contact with customers, suppliers, and other external parties. Second, the greater the distance from the center, the less constrained individuals are by the traditions, norms, and belief structures of the corporation. This is the argument that subsidiaries should be viewed as peninsulas rather than islands. As multinationals take such an approach, we can expect far more creative and genuinely innovative ideas to emerge from the edge of the corporation than from the center. The challenge becomes one of tapping into the ideas and leveraging them effectively.

---

business, is eventually abandoned because it doesn't fit well with the rest of the unit. Corporate-sponsored development projects therefore are an important alternative to business-unit–level investments. ABB, the global engineering and technology firm with headquarters in Zurich, provides both seed money at the subsidiary level and corporate funding for new ideas that cross the boundaries of existing business units. In ABB's 12 corporate research centers, located around the world, employees are encouraged to propose "high impact" projects—those with broad, cross-business-unit applications—which are then funded from a corporate budget. One such project led to the creation of a state-of-the-art electrical transformer factory in Athens, Georgia. Dubbed the "factory of the future," the test factory is fully automated, from ordering through production to the delivery of the finished product. The results have been truly spectacular: labor costs have been cut by half, cycle times have been cut by 90%, and time from order entry to shipping has been reduced from 30 days to one day.

Use Formal Requests for Proposals   Providing seed money to subsidiaries is a start, but funds alone won't generate valuable innovations from a passive subsidiary manager. Executives must also find ways to increase the demand for seed money. To that end, it helps to think of subsidiaries as freelance contractors that are granted licenses to manufacture or develop certain products. When you want to make a new investment, you send out a request for proposal (RFP), which may yield three or four competing bids. Volkswagen's decision to manufacture the New Beetle in Puebla, Mexico, for example, was the result of a lengthy review in which the Puebla site was compared with sites in Germany and Eastern Europe. It also required heavy-duty championing from executives in Mexico and the United States, who saw a local production base as essential to their plans for reviving the VW brand in North America.

An RFP approach can also stimulate subsidiaries to develop creative solutions to corporate challenges. Monsanto's Canadian management team picked up on a tentative corporate plan to build a dry-formulation plant for its Roundup herbicide and pushed hard for that investment to be made in Canada. In preparing their proposal, they were able to shape the product's specifications—as any contracting company knows, that's the only way to win competitive tenders. But the members of the Canadian group knew they wouldn't get the nod based on cost alone, so they developed their proposal around such innovative practices as self-directed work teams, empowerment, and outsourcing. Their proposal focused on the competencies of the Canadian operation and demonstrated how the investment could help forestall a threat from another company rumored to be developing a competing product in central Canada. Consequently, the Canadian proposal won the contract, beating out a Monsanto site in Louisiana and an independent manufacturer in Iowa.

We have seen this approach to new investments work well in a variety of multinational companies. But we have also seen companies shy away from it

because the costs of reviewing and evaluating multiple bids can be prohibitive. The best approach is to limit the list of competing proposals to three or four—as long as the narrowing process is designed to increase, rather than suppress, variance. It is best to avoid formal reviews in which two mediocre options are set up alongside the preferred candidate for the sake of appearances. This happens all too often, and it is a splendid way of killing the initiative of subsidiary managers.

Encourage Subsidiaries to Be Incubators   Subsidiary managers often comment that their distance from headquarters makes it hard for them to attract attention. But distance can become an advantage. It allows foreign subsidiaries to experiment with unconventional or unpopular projects that would be closed down if they were more visible to headquarters. It allows them to become incubators that can provide shelter and resources for businesses that are not yet strong enough to stand on their own.

Consider the actions of Ulf Borgström, manager of the Swedish subsidiary of a U.S. minicomputer manufacturer. The company was struggling in the early 1990s because of a weak product line, and the Swedish subsidiary was on the verge of bankruptcy. Borgström was able to turn around the operation by disregarding orders from headquarters and pursuing whatever business he could find in the Swedish market. Unable to sell his own company's products, he decided to offer service contracts on competitors' products. Needless to say, his superiors in the home office immediately discredited his strategy, but Borgström persevered, and the service contracts proved to be a significant factor in the subsidiary's revival. By 1997, headquarters had come around to his way of thinking, and the Swedish subsidiary was hailed as a success story.

Or take Ericsson as another example. Outsiders know that Ericsson has successfully caught two of the biggest waves in the telecommunications business in recent years: the emergence of second-generation digital radio technology and the subsequent boom in the handsets business. Insiders admit, however, that both businesses struggled to gain acceptance while they were being developed and would have been killed if their sponsors had not been persistent. In fact, in the latter case, Åke Lundqvist, the president of the nascent handsets unit, moved himself and his team to southern Sweden, which gave him the time and space to get the business going without interference from corporate executives. More recently, Ericsson has created a new unit called Ericsson Business Innovation, whose mandate, in the words of its director, Jöran Hoff, "is to create the next core business" for the corporation. It acts as a venture fund by providing seed money and management expertise to promising new projects—not just Stockholm-based projects, but those in places as diverse as southern California, North Carolina, and Finland.

The subsidiary-as-incubator model is promising, but as with all corporate venturing, there is a risk that a new business idea won't find a home within the corporate portfolio. The critical success factor is typically how well the project champion is connected with other parts of the corporation. Hence the importance of international networks.

Build International Networks As every corporate executive—and entrepreneur, for that matter—knows, it's essential to give would-be innovators access to professional and informal networks. But such networks are not easily manufactured. Some companies have tried to build international networks by creating employee rotation programs, but too often these personnel moves have been ineffective because they've been artificial—they haven't been linked to practical business initiatives. If employees don't do real work during their overseas assignments, they never become part of local teams or become integrated into networks. A number of corporations, however, now deploy talented employees on short-term overseas assignments that are tied to tangible business goals. In the short term, these assignments furnish useful resources for current projects; in the long term, they increase the number and variety of professional networks from which the next ideas are likely to emerge.

For example, when ABB acquired Taylor Instruments, a Rochester, New York–based automation and controls company, the entire management team of ABB's automation and controls business was temporarily moved from Sweden to ABB's U.S. headquarters in Stamford, Connecticut, to oversee the integration process and help develop a new identity for the business. After three years, the management team, which by then included a couple of Americans, was moved back to Sweden.

Similarly, Hewlett-Packard often brings in an experienced management team from corporate headquarters to get new subsidiary operations started. The team's job is to get performance on track, bring a local management team up to speed, and move on to another project. At both companies, the creation of strong international networks is the by-product of real work rather than an end in itself.

Multinationals also need to create roles for what we have come to think of as idea brokers. In a crowded marketplace, brokers add value through their ability to bring buyers and sellers together. For innovation at the edges to thrive, entrepreneurs in foreign subsidiaries need to be linked with sources of funding, complementary assets, and sponsors in other parts of the company. That's where idea brokers come into the picture. With their wealth of contacts and experiences, they play three important roles.

First, they link seed money with new ideas. Consider the story of Mats Leijon, an electrical engineer in one of ABB's corporate research labs who came up with a disruptive technology called the Powerformer—a high-voltage generator that allows power to go directly from the generator to overhead cables without a step-up transformer. Without the assistance of Harry Frank, the head of one of ABB's corporate research labs, Leijon's invention might never have seen the light of day, especially given that the Powerformer promised to wipe out more than one of ABB's core businesses. Frank brokered the idea by translating it into business terms, and Leijon's project received funding from the Swedish country manager, Bert-Olof Svanholm. It was launched in 1998. Today, several leading ABB customers are adopting the Powerformer, and the story of Mats Leijon's innovation has become a touchstone for other entrepreneurs at ABB.

Second, idea brokers help find the right organizational home for new ideas. In one product development group in Hewlett-Packard's Canadian subsidiary, initial funding for a new software product came from HP Canada, which was enough to get the product to market. But for the business to grow, the development group's general manager realized he needed to find a home for his product in one of HP's major divisions. He began to sound out his contacts, including several group vice presidents who were able to use their broad knowledge of the HP businesses to put him in touch with various parent divisions. After one false start, he found the right home in a small, Seattle-based division that was selling to the same customer sectors as his group. In HP, the group vice presidents are the idea brokers, and a significant part of their time is spent balancing the portfolio of businesses—splitting up large divisions, merging small divisions, shifting emerging businesses between divisions to create better opportunities for growth, and so on.

The third role idea brokers play is in cross-selling products and services among businesses. Skandia AFS, the financial services group, provides a good example. It is organized as a federation of national businesses, each of which is free to develop its own product lines for the local marketplace (they share a common business model and information system). Recognizing that a country-centered approach could restrict the transfer of new ideas across borders, Skandia created an internal brokering unit called the International Support Unit (ISU). Its role is to take new products developed in one country and cross-sell them into other countries; managed as a profit center, Skandia ISU earns its revenues through commissions on cross-border product sales.

In an era in which new business ideas are as likely to come from Stockholm as from Silicon Valley, multinational companies cannot afford to limit their creative gene pools to corporate R&D labs or a few select outposts. They must find ways to tap into the diverse and multifaceted opportunities that exist in foreign operations. Taken together, the four practices we've outlined can help corporate executives unleash innovation at the edges and fulfill, at last, the promise of going global.

Reading 5-2   Connect and Develop: Inside Procter & Gamble's New Model for Innovation

Larry Huston and Nabil Sakkab

Procter & Gamble launched a new line of Pringles potato crisps in 2004 with pictures and words—trivia questions, animal facts, jokes—printed on each crisp. They were an immediate hit. In the old days, it might have taken us two years to bring this product to market, and we would have shouldered all of the investment and risk internally. But by applying a fundamentally new approach to innovation, we were able to accelerate Pringles Prints from concept to launch in less than a year and at a fraction of what it would have otherwise cost. Here's how we did it.

Back in 2002, as we were brainstorming about ways to make snacks more novel and fun, someone suggested that we print pop culture images on Pringles. It was a great idea, but how would we do it? One of our researchers thought we should try ink-jetting pictures onto the potato dough, and she used the printer in her office for a test run. (You can imagine her call to our computer help desk.) We

▌ Larry Huston (huston.la@pg.com) is the vice president for innovation and knowledge and Nabil Sakkab (sakkab.ny@pg.com) is the senior vice president for corporate research and development at Procter & Gamble in Cincinnati.

quickly realized that every crisp would have to be printed as it came out of frying, when it was still at a high humidity and temperature. And somehow, we'd have to produce sharp images, in multiple colors, even as we printed thousands upon thousands of crisps each minute. Moreover, creating edible dyes that could meet these needs would require tremendous development.

Traditionally, we would have spent the bulk of our investment just on developing a workable process. An internal team would have hooked up with an ink-jet printer company that could devise the process, and then we would have entered into complex negotiations over the rights to use it.

Instead, we created a technology brief that defined the problems we needed to solve, and we circulated it throughout our global networks of individuals and institutions to discover if anyone in the world had a ready-made solution. It was through our European network that we discovered a small bakery in Bologna, Italy, run by a university professor who also manufactured baking equipment. He had invented an ink-jet method for printing edible images on cakes and cookies that we rapidly adapted to solve our problem. This innovation has helped the North America Pringles business achieve double-digit growth over the past two years.

From R&D to C&D

Most companies are still clinging to what we call the invention model, centered on a bricks-and-mortar R&D infrastructure and the idea that their innovation must principally reside within their own four walls. To be sure, these companies are increasingly trying to buttress their laboring R&D departments with acquisitions, alliances, licensing, and selective innovation outsourcing. And they're launching Skunk Works, improving collaboration between marketing and R&D, tightening go-to-market criteria, and strengthening product portfolio management.

But these are incremental changes, bandages on a broken model. Strong words, perhaps, but consider the facts: Most mature companies have to create organic growth of 4% to 6% year in, year out.

How are they going to do it? For P&G, that's the equivalent of building a $4 billion business this year alone. Not long ago, when companies were smaller and the world was less competitive, firms could rely on internal R&D to drive that kind of growth. For generations, in fact, P&G created most of its phenomenal growth by innovating from within—building global research facilities and hiring and holding on to the best talent in the world. That worked well when we were a $25 billion company; today, we're an almost $70 billion company.

By 2000, it was clear to us that our invent-it-ourselves model was not capable of sustaining high levels of top-line growth. The explosion of new technologies was putting ever more pressure on our innovation budgets. Our R&D productivity had leveled off, and our innovation success rate—the percentage of new products that met financial objectives—had stagnated at about 35%. Squeezed by nimble competitors, flattening sales, lackluster new launches, and a quarterly earnings miss, we lost more than half our market cap when our stock slid from $118 to $52 a share. Talk about a wake-up call.

The world's innovation landscape had changed, yet we hadn't changed our own innovation model since the late 1980s, when we moved from a centralized approach to a globally networked internal model—what Christopher Bartlett and Sumantra Ghoshal call the transnational model in *Managing Across Borders*.

We discovered that important innovation was increasingly being done at small and midsize entrepreneurial companies. Even individuals were eager to license and sell their intellectual property. University and government labs had become more interested in forming industry partnerships, and they were hungry for ways to monetize their research. The Internet had opened up access to talent markets throughout the world. And a few forward-looking companies like IBM and Eli Lilly were beginning to experiment with the new concept of open innovation, leveraging one another's (even competitors') innovation assets—products, intellectual property, and people.

As was the case for P&G in 2000, R&D productivity at most mature, innovation-based companies today is flat while innovation costs are climbing faster than top-line growth. (Not many CEOs are going to their CTOs and saying, "Here, have some more money for innovation.") Meanwhile, these companies are facing a growth mandate that their existing innovation models can't possibly support. In 2000, realizing that P&G couldn't meet its growth objectives by spending more and more on R&D for less and less payoff, our newly appointed CEO, A.G. Lafley, challenged us to reinvent the company's innovation business model.

We knew that most of P&G's best innovations had come from connecting ideas across internal businesses. And after studying the performance of a small number of products we'd acquired beyond our own labs, we knew that external connections could produce highly profitable innovations, too. Betting that these connections were the key to future growth, Lafley made it our goal to acquire 50% of our innovations outside the company. The strategy wasn't to replace the capabilities of our 7,500 researchers and support staff, but to better leverage them. Half of our new products, Lafley said, would come *from* our own labs, and half would come *through* them.

It was, and still is, a radical idea. As we studied outside sources of innovation, we estimated that for every P&G researcher there were 200 scientists or engineers elsewhere in the world who were just as good—a total of perhaps 1.5 million people whose talents we could potentially use. But tapping into the creative thinking of inventors and others on the outside would require massive operational changes. We needed to move the company's attitude from resistance to innovations "not invented here" to enthusiasm for those "proudly found elsewhere." And we needed to change how we defined, and perceived, our R&D organization—from 7,500 people inside to 7,500 *plus* 1.5 million outside, with a permeable boundary between them.

It was against this backdrop that we created our *connect and develop* innovation model. With a clear sense of consumers' needs, we could identify promising ideas throughout the world and apply our own R&D, manufacturing, marketing, and purchasing capabilities to them to create better and cheaper products, faster.

The model works. Today, more than 35% of our new products in market have elements that originated from outside P&G, up from about 15% in 2000. And 45% of the initiatives in our product development portfolio have key elements that were discovered externally. Through connect and develop—along with improvements in other aspects of innovation related to product cost, design, and marketing—our R&D productivity has increased by nearly 60%. Our innovation success rate has more than doubled, while the cost of innovation has fallen. R&D investment as a percentage of sales is down from 4.8% in 2000 to 3.4% today. And, in the last two years, we've launched more than 100 new products for which some aspect of execution came from outside the company. Five years after the company's stock collapse in 2000, we have doubled our share price and have a portfolio of 22 billion-dollar brands.

According to a recent Conference Board survey of CEOs and board chairs, executives' number one concern is "sustained and steady top-line growth." CEOs understand the importance of innovation to growth, yet how many have overhauled their basic approach to innovation? Until companies realize that the innovation landscape has changed and acknowledge that their current model is unsustainable, most will find that the top-line growth they require will elude them.

Where to Play

When people first hear about connect and develop, they often think it's the same as outsourcing innovation—contracting with outsiders to develop innovations for P&G. But it's not. Outsourcing strategies typically just transfer work to lower-cost providers. Connect and develop, by contrast, is about finding good ideas and bringing them in to enhance and capitalize on internal capabilities.

To do this, we collaborate with organizations and individuals around the world, systematically searching for proven technologies, packages, and products that we can improve, scale up, and market, either on our own or in partnership with other companies. Among the most successful products we've brought to market through connect and develop are Olay Regenerist, Swiffer Dusters, and the Crest SpinBrush.

For connect and develop to work, we realized, it was crucial to know exactly what we were looking for, or where to play. If we'd set out without carefully defined targets, we'd have found loads of ideas but perhaps none that were useful to us. So we established from the start that we would seek ideas that had some degree of success already; we needed to see, at least, working products, prototypes, or technologies, and (for products) evidence of consumer interest. And we would focus on ideas and products that would benefit specifically from the application of P&G technology, marketing, distribution, or other capabilities.

Then we determined the areas in which we would look for these proven ideas. P&G is perhaps best known for its personal hygiene and household-cleaning products—brands like Crest, Charmin, Pampers, Tide, and Downy. Yet we produce more than 300 brands that span, in addition to hygiene and cleaning, snacks and beverages, pet nutrition, prescription drugs, fragrances, cosmetics, and many other categories. And we spend almost $2 billion a year on R&D across 150 science areas, including materials, biotechnology, imaging, nutrition, veterinary medicine, and even robotics.

To focus our idea search, we directed our surveillance to three environments:

Top Ten Consumer Needs   Once a year, we ask our businesses what consumer needs, when addressed, will drive the growth of their brands. This may seem like an obvious question, but in most companies, researchers are working on the problems that they find interesting rather than those that might contribute to brand growth. This inquiry produces a top-ten-needs list for each business and one for the company overall. The company list, for example, includes needs such as "reduce wrinkles, improve skin texture and tone," "improve soil repellency and restoration of hard surfaces," "create softer paper products with lower lint and higher wet strength," and "prevent or minimize the severity and duration of cold symptoms."

These needs lists are then developed into science problems to be solved. The problems are often spelled out in technology briefs, like the one we sent out to find an ink-jet process for Pringles Prints. To take another example, a major laundry need is for products that clean effectively using cold water. So, in our search for relevant innovations, we're looking for chemistry and biotechnology solutions that allow products to work well at low temperatures. Maybe the answer to our cold-water-cleaning problem is in a lab that's studying enzymatic reactions in microbes that thrive under polar ice caps, and we need only to find the lab.

Adjacencies   We also identify adjacencies—that is, new products or concepts that can help us take advantage of existing brand equity. We might, for instance, ask which baby care items—such as wipes and changing pads—are adjacent to our Pampers disposable diapers, and then seek out innovative emerging products or relevant technologies in those categories. By targeting adjacencies in oral care, we've expanded the Crest brand beyond toothpaste to include whitening strips, power toothbrushes, and flosses.

Technology Game Boards   Finally, in some areas, we use what we call technology game boards to evaluate how technology acquisition moves in one area might affect products in other categories. Conceptually, working with these planning tools is like playing a multilevel game of chess. They help us explore questions such as "Which of our key technologies do we want to strengthen?" "Which technologies do we want to acquire to help us better compete with rivals?" and "Of those that we already own, which do we want to license, sell, or codevelop further?" The answers provide an array of broad targets for our innovation searches and, as important, tell us where we shouldn't be looking.

How to Network

Our global networks are the platform for the activities that, together, constitute the connect-and-develop strategy. But networks themselves don't provide competitive advantage any more than the phone system does. It's how you build and use them that matters.

Within the boundaries defined by our needs lists, adjacency maps, and technology game boards, no source of ideas is off-limits. We tap closed proprietary networks and open networks of individuals and organizations available to any company. Using these networks, we look for ideas in government and private labs, as well as academic and other research institutions; we tap suppliers, retailers, competitors, development and trade partners, VC firms, and individual entrepreneurs.

Here are several core networks that we use to seek out new ideas. This is not an exhaustive list; rather, it is a snapshot of the networking capabilities that we've found most useful.

Proprietary Networks   We rely on several proprietary networks developed specifically to facilitate connect-and-develop activities. Here are two of the largest ones.

Technology Entrepreneurs   Much of the operation and momentum of connect and develop depends on our network of 70 technology entrepreneurs based around the world. These senior P&G people lead the development of our needs lists, create adjacency maps and technology game boards, and write the technology briefs that define the problems we are trying to solve. They create external connections by, for example, meeting with university and industry researchers and forming supplier networks, and they actively promote these connections to decision makers in P&G's business units.

The technology entrepreneurs combine aggressive mining of the scientific literature, patent databases, and other data sources with physical prospecting for ideas—say, surveying the shelves of a store in Rome or combing product and technology fairs. Although it's effective and necessary to scout for ideas electronically, it's not sufficient. It was a technology entrepreneur who, exploring a local market in Japan, discovered what ultimately became the Mr. Clean Magic Eraser. We surely wouldn't have found it otherwise. (See the exhibit "The Osaka Connection.")

The technology entrepreneurs work out of six connect-and-develop hubs, in China, India, Japan, Western Europe, Latin America, and the United States. Each hub focuses on finding products and technologies that, in a sense, are specialties of its region: The China hub, for example, looks in particular for new high-quality materials and cost innovations (products that exploit China's unique ability to make things at low cost). The India hub seeks out local talent in the sciences to solve problems—in our manufacturing processes, for instance—using tools like computer modeling.

Thus far, our technology entrepreneurs have identified more than 10,000 products, product ideas, and promising technologies. Each of these discoveries has undergone a formal evaluation, as we'll describe further on.

Suppliers   Our top 15 suppliers have an estimated combined R&D staff of 50,000. As we built connect and develop, it didn't take us long to realize that they represented a huge potential source of innovation. So we created a secure IT platform that would allow us to share technology briefs with our suppliers. If we're trying to find ways to make detergent perfume last longer after clothes come out of the dryer, for instance, one of our chemical suppliers may well have the solution. (Suppliers can't see others' responses, of course.) Since creating our supplier network, we've seen a 30% increase in innovation projects jointly staffed with P&G's and suppliers' researchers. In some cases, suppliers' researchers come to work in our labs, and in others, we work in theirs—an example of what we call "cocreation," a type of collaboration that goes well beyond typical joint development.

We also hold top-to-top meetings with suppliers so our senior leaders can interact with theirs. These meetings, along with our shared-staff arrangements, improve relationships, increase the flow of ideas, and strengthen each company's understanding of the other's capabilities—all of which helps us innovate.

Open Networks   A complement to our proprietary networks are open networks. The following four are particularly fruitful connect-and-develop resources.

The Osaka Connection

In the connect-and-develop world, chance favors the prepared mind. When one of P&G's technology entrepreneurs discovered a stain-removing sponge in a market in Osaka, Japan, he sent it to the company for evaluation. The resulting product, the Mr. Clean Magic Eraser, is now in third-generation development and has achieved double its projected revenues.

German chemical company BASF manufactures a melamine resin foam called Basotect for soundproofing and insulation in the construction and automotive industries.

LEC, a Tokyo-based consumer-products company, markets Basotect foam in Japan as a household sponge called Cleenpro.

2001

Discover Japan-based technology entrepreneur with P&G discovers the product in an Osaka grocery store, evaluates its market performance in Japan, and establishes its fit with the P&G homecare product development and marketing criteria.

2002

Evaluate The technology entrepreneur sends samples to R&D product researchers in Cincinnati for performance evaluation and posts a product description and evaluation of market potential on P&G's internal "eureka catalog" network.

Market research confirms enthusiasm for the product. Product is moved into portfolio for development; P&G negotiates purchase of Basotect from BASF and terms for further collaboration.

2003

Launch Basotect is packaged as-is and launched nationally as Mr. Clean Magic Eraser.

Mr. Clean Magic Eraser is launched in Europe.

BASF and P&G researchers collaborate in shared labs to improve Basotect's cleaning properties, durability, and versatility.

2004

Cocreate The first cocreated Basotect product, the Magic Eraser Duo, is launched nationally in the United States.

The cocreated Magic Eraser Wheel & Tire is launched nationally in the United States.

BASF and P&G collaborate on next-generation Magic Eraser products.

NineSigma P&G helped create NineSigma, one of several firms connecting companies that have science and technology problems with companies, universities, government and private labs, and consultants that can develop solutions. Say you have a technical problem you want to crack—for P&G, as you'll recall, one such problem is cold-temperature washing. NineSigma creates a technology brief that describes the problem, and sends this to its network of thousands of possible solution providers worldwide. Any solver can submit a nonconfidential proposal back to NineSigma, which is transmitted to the contracting company. If the company likes the proposal, NineSigma connects the company and solver, and the project proceeds from there. We've

distributed technology briefs to more than 700,000 people through NineSigma and have as a result completed over 100 projects, with 45% of them leading to agreements for further collaboration.

InnoCentive Founded by Eli Lilly, InnoCentive is similar to NineSigma—but rather than connect companies with contract partners to solve broad problems across many disciplines, InnoCentive brokers solutions to more narrowly defined scientific problems. For example, we might have an industrial chemical reaction that takes five steps to accomplish and want to know if it can be done in three. We'll put the question to InnoCentive's 75,000 contract scientists and see what we get back. We've had

Leading Connect and Develop

The connect-and-develop strategy requires that a senior executive have day-to-day accountability for its vision, operations, and performance. At P&G, the vice president for innovation and knowledge has this responsibility. Connect-and-develop leaders from each of the business units at P&G have dotted-line reporting relationships with the VP. The managers for our virtual R&D networks (such as NineSigma and our supplier network), the technology entrepreneur and hub network, our connect-and-develop legal resources, and our training resources report directly.

The VP oversees the development of networks and new programs, manages a corporate budget, and monitors the productivity of networks and activities. This includes tracking the performance of talent markets like NineSigma and InnoCentive as well as measuring connect-and-develop productivity by region—evaluating, for example, the costs and output (as measured by products in market) of foreign hubs. Productivity measurements for the entire program are reported annually.

problems solved by a graduate student in Spain, a chemist in India, a freelance chemistry consultant in the United States, and an agricultural chemist in Italy. About a third of the problems we've posted through InnoCentive have been solved.

YourEncore   In 2003, we laid the groundwork for a business called YourEncore. Now operated independently, it connects about 800 high-performing retired scientists and engineers from 150 companies with client businesses. By using YourEncore, companies can bring people with deep experience and new ways of thinking from other organizations and industries into their own.

Through YourEncore, you can contract with a retiree who has relevant experience for a specific, short-term assignment (compensation is based on the person's preretirement salary, adjusted for inflation). For example, we might tap a former Boeing engineer with expertise in virtual aircraft design to apply his or her skills in virtual product prototyping and manufacturing design at P&G, even though our projects have nothing to do with aviation. What makes this model so powerful is that client companies can experiment at low cost and with little risk on cross-disciplinary approaches to problem solving. At any point, we might have 20 retirees from YourEncore working on P&G problems.

Yet2.com   Six years ago, P&G joined a group of *Fortune* 100 companies as an initial investor in Yet2.com, an online marketplace for intellectual property exchange. Unlike NineSigma and InnoCentive, which focus on helping companies find solutions to technology problems, Yet2.com brokers technology transfer both into and out of companies, universities, and government labs. Yet2.com works with clients to write briefs describing the technology that they're seeking or making available for license or purchase, and distributes these briefs throughout a global network of businesses, labs, and institutions. Network members interested in posted briefs contact Yet2.com and request an introduction to the relevant client. Once introduced, the parties negotiate directly with each other. Through Yet2.com, P&G was able to license its low-cost microneedle technology to a company specializing in drug delivery. As a result of this relationship, we have ourselves licensed technology that has applications in some of our core businesses.

When to Engage

Once products and ideas are identified by our networks around the world, we need to screen them internally. All the screening methods are driven by a core understanding, pushed down through the entire organization, of what we're looking for. It's beyond the scope of this article to describe all of the processes we use to evaluate ideas from outside. But a look at how we might screen a new product found by a technology entrepreneur illustrates one common approach.

When our technology entrepreneurs are meeting with lab heads, scanning patents, or selecting

Words of Warning

Procter & Gamble's development and implementation of connect and develop has unfolded over many years. There have been some hiccups along the way, but largely it has been a methodical process of learning by doing, abandoning what doesn't work and expanding what does. Over five years in, we've identified three core requirements for a successful connect-and-develop strategy.

• Never assume that "ready to go" ideas found outside are truly ready to go. There will always be development work to do, including risky scale-up.

• Don't underestimate the internal resources required. You'll need a full-time, senior executive to run any connect-and-develop initiative.

• Never launch without a mandate from the CEO. Connect and develop cannot succeed if it's cordoned off in R&D. It must be a top-down, companywide strategy.

products off store shelves, they're conducting an initial screening in real time: Which products, technologies, or ideas meet P&G's where-to-play criteria? Let's assume a technology entrepreneur finds a promising product on a store shelf that passes this initial screening. His or her next step will be to log the product into our online "eureka catalog," using a template that helps organize certain facts about the product: What is it? How does it meet our business needs? Are its patents available? What are its current sales? The catalog's descriptions and pictures (which have a kind of Sharper Image feel) are distributed to general managers, brand managers, R&D teams, and others throughout the company worldwide, according to their interests, for evaluation.

Meanwhile, the technology entrepreneur may actively promote the product to specific managers in relevant lines of business. If an item captures the attention of, say, the director of the baby care business, she will assess its alignment with the goals of the business and subject it to a battery of practical questions—such as whether P&G has the technical infrastructure needed to develop the product—meant to identify any showstopping impediments to development. The director will also gauge the product's business potential. If the item continues to look promising, it may be tested in consumer panels and, if the response is positive, moved into our product development portfolio. Then we'll engage our external business development (EBD) group to contact the product's manufacturer and begin negotiating licensing, collaboration, or other

deal structures. (The EBD group is also responsible for licensing P&G's intellectual property to third parties. Often, we find that the most profitable arrangements are ones where we both license to and license from the same company.) At this point, the product found on the outside has entered a development pipeline similar in many ways to that for any product developed in-house.

The process, of course, is more complex and rigorous than this thumbnail sketch suggests. In the end, for every 100 ideas found on the outside, only one ends up in the market.

Push the Culture

No amount of idea hunting on the outside will pay off if, internally, the organization isn't behind the program. Once an idea gets into the development pipeline, it needs R&D, manufacturing, market research, marketing, and other functions pulling for it. But, as you know, until very recently, P&G was deeply centralized and internally focused. For connect and develop to work, we've had to nurture an internal culture change while developing systems for making connections. And that has involved not only opening the company's floodgates to ideas from the outside but actively promoting internal idea exchanges as well.

For any product development program, we tell R&D staff that they should start by finding out whether related work is being done elsewhere in the company; then they should see if an external source—a partner or supplier, for instance—has a solution. Only if those two avenues yield nothing should we consider inventing a solution from scratch. Wherever the solution comes from (inside or out), if the end product succeeds in the marketplace, the rewards for employees involved in its development are the same. In fact, to the extent that employees get recognition for the speed of product development, our reward systems actually favor innovations developed from outside ideas since, like Pringles Prints, these often move more quickly from concept to market.

We have two broad goals for this reward structure. One is to make sure that the best ideas, wherever they come from, rise to the surface. The other is to exert steady pressure on the culture, to continue to shift mind-sets away from resistance to "not invented here." Early on, employees were anxious that connect and develop might eliminate jobs or that P&G would lose capabilities. That stands to reason, since as you increase the ideas coming in from the outside you might expect an equivalent decrease in the need for internal ideas. But with our growth objectives, there is no limit to our need for solid business-building ideas. Connect and develop has not eliminated R&D jobs, and it has actually required the company to develop new skills.

There are still pockets within P&G that have not embraced connect and develop, but the trend has been toward accepting the approach, even championing it, as its benefits have accrued and people have seen that it reinforces their own work.

Adapt or Die

We believe that connect and develop will become the dominant innovation model in the twenty-first century. For most companies, as we've argued, the alternative invent-it-ourselves model is a sure path to diminishing returns.

To succeed, connect and develop must be driven by the top leaders in the organization. It is destined to fail if it is seen as solely an R&D strategy or isolated as an experiment in some other corner of the company. As Lafley did at P&G, the CEO of any organization must make it an explicit company strategy and priority to capture a certain amount of innovation externally. In our case, the target is a demanding—even radical—50%, but we're well on our way to achieving it.

Don't postpone crafting a connect-and-develop strategy, and don't approach the process incrementally. Companies that fail to adapt to this model won't survive the competition.

Reading 5-3   Building Effective R&D Capabilities Abroad

Walter Kuemmerle

An increasing number of companies in technologically intensive industries such as pharmaceuticals and electronics have abandoned the traditional

Walter Kuemmerle is an assistant professor at the Harvard Business School in Boston, Massachusetts, where he teaches technology and operations management, as well as entrepreneurial finance. His research focuses on the technology strategies of multinational companies, patterns of strategic interaction between small and large companies, and foreign direct investment.

approach to managing research and development and are establishing global R&D networks in a noteworthy new way. For example, Canon is now carrying out R&D activities in 8 dedicated facilities in 5 countries, Motorola in 14 facilities in 7 countries, and Bristol-Myers Squibb in 12 facilities in 6 countries. In the past, most companies—even those with a considerable international presence in terms of sales and manufacturing—carried out the majority of their R&D activity in their home countries.

Laboratory Sites Abroad in 1995

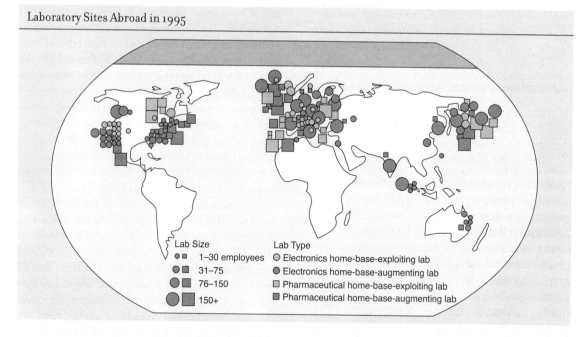

Conventional wisdom held that strategy development and R&D had to be kept in close geographical proximity. Because strategic decisions were made primarily at corporate headquarters, the thinking went, R&D facilities should be close to home.

But such a centralized approach to R&D will no longer suffice for two reasons. First, as more and more sources of potentially relevant knowledge emerge across the globe, companies must establish a presence at an increasing number of locations to access new knowledge and to absorb new research results from foreign universities and competitors into their own organizations. Second, companies competing around the world must move new products from development to market at an ever more rapid pace. Consequently, companies must build R&D networks that excel at tapping new centers of knowledge and at commercializing products in foreign markets with the speed required to remain competitive. And more and more, superior manufacturers are doing just that. (See the exhibit "Laboratory Sites Abroad in 1995.")

In an ongoing study on corporate strategy and the geographical dispersion of R&D sites, I have been examining the creation of global research networks by 32 U.S., Japanese, and European multinational companies.[1] The most successful companies in my study brought each new site's research productivity up to full speed within a few years and quickly transformed knowledge created there into innovative products. I found that establishing networks of such sites poses a number of new, complex managerial challenges. According to my research, managers of the most successful R&D networks understand the new dynamics of global R&D, link corporate strategy to R&D strategy, pick the appropriate sites, staff them with the right

[1]In a systematic effort to analyze the relationship of global strategy and R&D investments in technologically intensive industries, I have been collecting detailed data on all dedicated laboratory sites operated by 32 leading multinational companies. The sample consists of 10 U.S., 12 Japanese, and 10 European companies. Thirteen of the companies are in the pharmaceutical industry, and 19 are in the electronics industry. Data collection includes archival research, a detailed questionnaire, and in-depth interviews with several senior R&D managers in each company. Overall, these companies operate 238 dedicated R&D sites, 156 of them abroad. About 60% of the laboratory sites abroad were established after 1984. I have used this sample, which is the most complete of its kind, as a basis for a number of quantitative and qualitative investigations into global strategy, competitive interaction, and R&D management.

people, supervise the sites during start-up, and integrate the activities of the different foreign sites so that the entire network is a coordinated whole.

Adopting a Global Approach to R&D

Adopting a global approach to R&D requires linking R&D strategy to a company's overall business strategy. And that requires the involvement of managers at the highest levels of a company.

Creating a Technology Steering Committee   The first step in creating a global R&D network is to build a team that will lead the initiative. To establish a global R&D network, the CEOs and top-level managers of a number of successful companies that I studied assembled a small team of senior managers who had both technical expertise and in-depth organizational knowledge. The technology steering committees reported directly to the CEOs of their respective companies. They were generally small—five to eight members—and included managers with outstanding managerial and scientific records and a range of educational backgrounds and managerial responsibilities. The committees I studied included as members a former bench scientist who had transferred into manufacturing and had eventually become the head of manufacturing for the company's most important category of therapeutic drugs; a head of marketing for memory chips who had worked before in product development in the same electronics company; and an engineer who had started out in product development, had moved to research, and eventually had become the vice president of R&D. Members of these committees were sufficiently senior to be able to mobilize resources at short notice, and they were actively involved in the management and supervision of R&D programs. In many cases, members included the heads of major existing R&D sites.

Categorizing New R&D Sites   In selecting new sites, companies find it helpful first to articulate each site's primary objective. (See the exhibit "Establishing New R&D Sites.") R&D sites have one of two missions. The first type of site—what I

call a *home-base–augmenting site*—is established in order to tap knowledge from competitors and universities around the globe; in that type of site, information flows *from* the foreign laboratory *to* the central lab at home. The second type of site—what I call a *home-base–exploiting site*—is established to support manufacturing facilities in foreign countries or to adapt standard products to the demand there; in that type of site, information flows *to* the foreign laboratory *from* the central lab at home. (See the exhibit "How Information Flows Between Home-Base and Foreign R&D Sites.")

The overwhelming majority of the 238 foreign R&D sites I studied fell clearly into one of the two categories. Approximately 45% of all laboratory sites were home-base–augmenting sites, and 55% were home-base–exploiting sites. The two types of sites were of the same average size: about 100 employees. But they differed distinctly in their strategic purpose and leadership style.[2] (See the insert "Home-Base–Augmenting and Home-Base–Exploiting Sites: Xerox and Eli Lilly.")

Choosing a Location for the Site   Home-base–augmenting sites should be located in regional clusters of scientific excellence in order to tap new sources of knowledge. Central to the success of corporate R&D strategy is the ability of senior researchers to recognize and combine scientific advancements from different areas of science and technology. Absorbing the new knowledge can happen in a number of ways: through participation in formal or informal meeting circles that exist within a geographic area containing useful knowledge (a knowledge cluster), through hiring employees from competitors, or through sourcing laboratory equipment and research services from the same suppliers that competitors use.

---

[2]My research on global R&D strategies builds on earlier research on the competitiveness of nations and on research on foreign direct investment, including Michael E. Porter, *The Competitive Advantage of Nations* (New York: The Free Press, 1990), and Thomas J. Wesson, "An Alternative Motivation for Foreign Direct Investment" (Ph.D. dissertation, Harvard University, 1993). My research also builds on an existing body of knowledge about the management of multinational companies. See, for example, Christopher A. Bartlett and Sumantra Ghoshal, *Managing Across Borders* (New York: The Free Press, 1989).

Establishing New R&D Sites

Types of R&D Sites	Phase 1 Location Decision	Phase 2 Ramp-Up Period	Phase 3 Maximizing Lab Impact
Home-Base–Augmenting Laboratory Site Objective of establishment: absorbing knowledge from the local scientific community, creating new knowledge, and transferring it *to* the company's central R&D site	–Select a location for its scientific excellence –Promote cooperation between the company's senior scientists and managers	–Choose as first laboratory leader a renowned local scientist with international experience—one who understands the dynamics of R&D at the new location –Ensure enough critical mass	–Ensure the laboratory's active participation in the local scientific community –Exchange researchers with local university laboratories and with the home-base lab
Home-Base–Exploiting Laboratory Site Objective of establishment: commercializing knowledge by transferring it *from* the company's home base to the laboratory site abroad and from there to local manufacturing and marketing	–Select a location for its proximity to the company's existing manufacturing and marketing locations –Involve middle managers from other functional areas in startup decisions	–Choose as first laboratory leader an experienced product-development engineer with a strong companywide reputation, international experience, and knowledge of marketing and manufacturing	–Emphasize smooth relations with the home-base lab –Encourage employees to seek interaction with other corporate units beyond the manufacturing and marketing units that originally sponsored the lab

How Information Flows Between Home-Base and Foreign R&D Sites

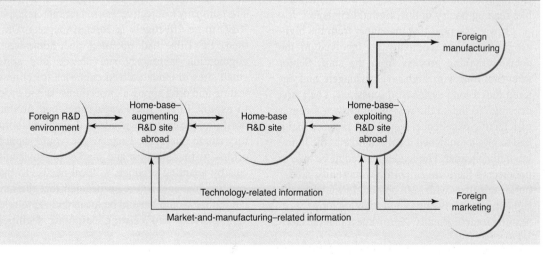

Home-Base–Augmenting and Home-Base–Exploiting Sites: Xerox and Eli Lilly

The particular type of foreign R&D site determines the specific challenges managers will face. Setting up a *home base–augmenting site*—one designed to gather new knowledge for a company—involves certain skills. And launching a *home-base–exploiting site*—one established to help a company efficiently commercialize its R&D in foreign markets—involves others. The cases of Xerox and Eli Lilly present an instructive contrast.

Xerox established a home-base–augmenting laboratory in Grenoble, France. Its objective: to tap new knowledge from the local scientific community and to transfer it back to its home base. Having already established, in 1986, a home-base–augmenting site in Cambridge, England, Xerox realized in 1992 that the research culture in continental Western Europe was sufficiently different and complementary to Great Britain's to justify another site. Moreover, understanding the most advanced research in France or Germany was very difficult from a base in Great Britain because of language and cultural barriers. One senior R&D manager in the United States notes, "We wanted to learn firsthand what was going on in centers of scientific excellence in Europe. Being present at a center of scientific excellence is like reading poetry in the original language."

It was essential that managers from the highest levels of the company be involved in the decision-making process from the start. Senior scientists met with high-level managers and entered into a long series of discussions. Their first decision: to locate the new laboratory at a center of scientific excellence. Xerox also realized that it had to hire a renowned local scientist as the initial laboratory leader. The leader needed to be able to understand the local scientific community, attract junior scientists with high potential, and target the right university institutes and scholars for joint research projects. Finally, Xerox knew that the laboratory would have an impact on the company's economic performance only if it had the critical mass to become an accepted member of the local scientific community. At the same time, it could not become isolated from the larger Xerox culture.

Xerox considered a number of locations and carefully evaluated such aspects as their scientific excellence and relevance, university liaison programs, licensing programs, and university recruiting programs. The company came up with four potential locations: Paris, Grenoble, Barcelona, and Munich. At that point, Xerox also identified potential laboratory leaders. The company chose Grenoble on the basis of its demonstrated scientific excellence and hired as the initial laboratory leader a highly regarded French scientist with good connections to local universities. Xerox designed a facility for 40 researchers and made plans for further expansion. In order to integrate the new laboratory's scientists into the Xerox community, senior R&D management in Palo Alto, California, allocated a considerable part of the initial laboratory budget to travel to other Xerox sites and started a program for the temporary transfer of newly hired researchers from Grenoble to other R&D sites. At the same time, the Grenoble site set out to integrate itself within the local research community.

In 1989, Eli Lilly considered establishing a home-base–exploiting laboratory in East Asia. The company's objective was to commercialize its R&D more effectively in foreign markets. Until then, Eli Lilly had operated one home-base–augmenting laboratory site abroad and some small sites in industrialized countries for clinical testing and drug approval procedures. But in order to exploit Lilly's R&D capabilities and product portfolio, the company needed a dedicated laboratory site in East Asia. The new site would support efforts to manufacture and market pharmaceuticals by adapting products to local needs. To that end, the management team decided that the new laboratory would have to be located close to relevant markets and existing corporate facilities.

able to overcome formal barriers wh
access to new ideas in local universiti
tific communities.

Appointing an outstanding scientis
who has no management experience
trous. In one case, a leading U.S. elec
pany decided to establish a home-base
site in the United Kingdom. The engi
appointed as the first site leader was a
researcher but had little managemer
outside the company's central labora
ment. The leader had difficulties marsh
essary resources to expand the laborato
starting size of 14 researchers. Further
a tough time mediating between the res
tory and the company's product devel
Eleven of the 14 researchers had been
and therefore lacked deep ties to the co
needed a savvy corporate advocate w
derstand company politics and could
research results within the company.
they didn't have such an advocate was t
three managers at the company's l
people who had promoted the establis
new R&D lab—had quit about six mo
lab had opened because they disa
the company's overall R&D strateg
manager had moved to a different depa

In an effort to improve the situati
pany appointed a U.S. engineer as l
U.K. site. He realized that few ideas
from the site to the home base, but he
problem to an inherently slow scienti
process rather than to organizational ba
the company. After about two years, se
ment finally replaced the initial labor
and the U.S. liaison engineer with two
one from the United Kingdom and
United States. The managers had exp
seeing one of the company's U.S. join
technology, and they also had good tra
researchers. Finally, under their leader
dramatically increased its impact on th
product portfolio. In conjunction with
in scientific output, the site grew to
size of 225 employees and is now highl

It also determined that the initial laboratory leader would have to be an experienced manager from Lilly's home base—a manager with a deep understanding of both the company's local operations and its overall R&D network.

The team considered Singapore as a potential location because of its proximity to a planned Lilly manufacturing site in Malaysia. But ultimately it decided that the new home-base–exploiting laboratory would have the strongest impact on Lilly's sales if it was located in Kōbe, Japan. By establishing a site in the Kōbe-Osaka region—the second-largest regional market in Japan and one that offered educational institutions with high-quality scientists—Lilly would send a signal to the medical community there that the company was committed to the needs of the Japanese market. Kōbe had another advantage. Lilly's corporate headquarters for Japan were located there, and the company was already running some of its drug approval operations for the Japanese market out of Kōbe. The city therefore was the logical choice.

The team assigned an experienced Lilly researcher and manager to be the initial leader of the new site. Because he knew the company inside and out—from central research and development to international marketing—the team reasoned that he would be able to bring the new laboratory up to speed quickly by drawing on resources from various divisions within Lilly. In order to integrate the new site into the overall company, some researchers from other Lilly R&D sites received temprory transfers of up to two years to Kōbe, and some locally hired researchers were temporarily transferred to other Lilly sites. It took about 30 months to activate fully the Kōbe operation—a relatively short period. Today the site is very productive in transferring knowledge from Lilly's home base to Kōbe and in commercializing that knowledge throughout Japan and Asia.

For example, the Silicon Valley knowledge cluster boasts a large number of informal gatherings of experts as well as more formal ways for high-tech companies to exchange information with adjacent universities, such as industrial liaison programs with Stanford University and the University of California at Berkeley. In the field of communication technology, Siemens, NEC, Matsushita, and Toshiba all operate laboratory sites near Princeton University and Bell Labs (now a part of Lucent Technologies) to take advantage of the expertise located there. For similar reasons, a number of companies in the same industry have established sites in the Kanto area surrounding Tokyo. Texas Instruments operates a facility in Tsukuba Science City, and Hewlett-Packard operates one in Tokyo.

After a company has picked and established its major R&D sites, it might want to branch out. It might selectively set up secondary sites when a leading competitor or a university succeeds in building a critical mass of research expertise in a more narrowly defined area of science and technol-ogy outside the primary cluster. In order to benefit from the resulting miniclusters of expertise, companies sometimes establish additional facilities. For that reason, NEC operates a small telecommunications-oriented R&D facility close to a university laboratory in London, and Canon operates an R&D facility in Rennes, France, close to one of France Telecom's major sites.

Home-base–exploiting sites, in contrast, should be located close to large markets and manufacturing facilities in order to commercialize new products rapidly in foreign markets. In the past, companies from industrialized countries located manufacturing facilities abroad primarily to benefit from lower wages or to overcome trade barriers. Over time, however, many of those plants have taken on increasingly complex manufacturing tasks that require having an R&D facility nearby in order to ensure the speedy transfer of technology from research to manufacturing. A silicon-wafer plant, for example, has to interact closely with product development engineers during trial runs of a new

generation of microchips. The sam
manufacture of disk drives and othe
ware. For that reason, Hewlett-Pac
Instruments both operate laboratori
close to manufacturing facilities.

The more complex and varied
process is, the more often manufac
will have to interact with product de
neers. For example, in the case of
laptop-computer–manufacturing
model is introduced to the manufac
two weeks. The introduction has t
lessly, without disturbing the produ
models on the same line. In orde
remedy bugs during initial produc
opment engineers and manufact
meet several times a week. Th
Toshiba's laptop-development labor
ufacturing plant greatly facilitates

Establishing a New R&D Fa

Whether establishing a home-base–
home-base–exploiting facility, con
the same three-stage process: select
ratory leader, determining the opti
new laboratory site, and keeping clo
lab during its start-up period in orde
is merged into the company's exist
network and contributes sufficiently
product portfolio and its economic p

Selecting the Best Site Leader

best leader for a new R&D site is
important decisions a company fa
to establish a successful global R&
research shows that the initial lea
site has a powerful impact not only
the site but also on its long-term
and performance. The two types of
ferent types of leaders, and each ty
fronts a particular set of challenges

The initial leaders of home-b
sites should be prominent local scie
will be able to fulfill their primary
nurture ties between the new site a
entific community. If the site doe

indeed absorb local knowledge and transfer it to their home base—particularly in the case of home-base–augmenting sites—they also create important positive economic effects for the host nation. The laboratory leader of a new R&D site needs to communicate that fact locally in order to reduce existing barriers and prevent the formation of new ones.

Determining the Optimal Size of the New R&D Site

My research indicates that the optimal size for a new foreign R&D facility during the start-up phase is usually 30 to 40 employees, and the best size for a site after the ramp-up period is about 235 employees, including support staff. The optimal size of a site depends mainly on a company's track record in international management. Companies that already operate several sites abroad tend to be more successful at establishing larger new sites.

Companies can run into problems if their foreign sites are either too small or too large. If the site is too small, the resulting lack of critical mass produces an environment in which there is little cross-fertilization of ideas among researchers. And a small R&D site generally does not command a sufficient level of respect in the scientific community surrounding the laboratory. As a result, its researchers have a harder time gaining access to informal networks and to scientific meetings that provide opportunities for an exchange of knowledge. In contrast, if the laboratory site is too large, its culture quickly becomes anonymous, researchers become isolated, and the benefits of spreading fixed costs over a larger number of researchers are outweighed by the lack of cross-fertilization of ideas. According to one manager at such a lab, "Once people stopped getting to know one another on an informal basis in the lunchroom of our site, they became afraid of deliberately walking into one another's laboratory rooms to talk about research and to ask questions. Researchers who do not know each other on an informal basis are often hesitant to ask their colleagues for advice: they are afraid to reveal any of their own knowledge gaps. We realized that we had crossed a critical threshold in size. We subsequently scaled back somewhat and made an increased effort to reduce the isolation of individual

researchers within the site through communication tools and through rotating researchers among different lab units at the site."

Supervising the Start-Up Period

During the initial growth period of an R&D site, which typically lasts anywhere from one to three years, the culture is formed and the groundwork for the site's future productivity is laid. During that period, senior management in the home country has to be in particularly close contact with the new site. Although it is important that the new laboratory develop its own identity and stake out its fields of expertise, it also has to be closely connected to the company's existing R&D structure. Newly hired scientists must be aware of the resources that exist within the company as a whole, and scientists at home and at other locations must be aware of the opportunities the new site creates for the company as a whole. Particularly during the start-up period, senior R&D managers at the corporate level have to walk a fine line and decide whether to devote the most resources to connecting the new site to the company or to supporting ties between the new site and its local environment.

To integrate a new site into the company as a whole, managers must pay close attention to the site's research agenda and create mechanisms to integrate it into the company's overall strategic goals. Because of the high degree of uncertainty of R&D outcomes, continuous adjustments to research agendas are the rule. What matters most is speed, both in terms of terminating research projects that go nowhere and in terms of pushing projects that bring unexpectedly good results.

The rapid exchange of information is essential to integrating a site into the overall company during the start-up phase. Companies use a number of mechanisms to create a cohesive research community in spite of geographic distance. Hewlett-Packard regularly organizes an in-house science fair at which teams of researchers can present projects and prototypes to one another. Canon has a program that lets researchers from home-base–augmenting sites request a temporary transfer to home-base–exploiting sites. At Xerox, most sites are linked by a sophisticated information system that allows senior R&D managers to determine within minutes the current state of research projects and the number of researchers working on those projects. But nothing can replace face-to-face contact between active researchers. Maintaining a global R&D network requires personal meetings, and therefore many researchers and R&D managers have to spend time visiting not only other R&D sites but also specialized suppliers and local universities affiliated with those sites.

Failing to establish sufficient ties with the company's existing R&D structure during the start-up phase can hamper the success of a new foreign R&D site. For example, in 1986, a large foreign pharmaceutical company established a biotechnology research site in Boston, Massachusetts. In order to recruit outstanding scientists and maintain a high level of creative output, the company's R&D management decided to give the new laboratory considerable leeway in its research agenda and in determining what to do with the results—although the company did reserve the right of first refusal for the commercialization of the lab's inventions. The new site was staffed exclusively with scientists handpicked by a newly hired laboratory leader. A renowned local biochemist, he had been employed for many years by a major U.S. university, where he had carried out contract research for the company. During the start-up phase, few of the company's veteran scientists were involved in joint research projects with the site's scientists—an arrangement that hindered the transfer of ideas between the new lab and the company's other R&D sites. Although the academic community now recognizes the lab as an important contributor to the field, few of its inventions have been patented by the company, fewer have been targeted for commercialization, and none have reached the commercial stage yet. One senior scientist working in the lab commented that ten years after its creation, the lab had become so much of an "independent animal" that it would take a lot of carefully balanced guidance from the company to instill a stronger sense of commercial orientation without a risk of losing the most creative scientists.

There is no magic formula that senior managers can follow to ensure the success of a foreign R&D site during its start-up phase. Managing an R&D network, particularly in its early stages, is delicate and complex. It requires constant tinkering—evaluation and reevaluation. Senior R&D managers have to decide how much of the research should be initiated by the company and how much by the scientist, determine the appropriate incentive structures and employment contracts, establish policies for the temporary transfer of researchers to the company's other R&D or manufacturing sites, and choose universities from which to hire scientists and engineers.

Flexibility and experimentation during a site's start-up phase can ensure its future productivity. For example, Fujitsu established a software-research laboratory site in San Jose, California, in 1992. The company was seriously thinking of establishing a second site in Boston but eventually reconsidered. Fujitsu realized that the effort that had gone into establishing the San Jose site had been greater than expected. Once the site was up and running, however, its productive output also had been higher than expected. Furthermore, Fujitsu found that its R&D managers had gained an excellent understanding of the R&D community that created advanced software-development tools. Although initially leaning toward establishing a second site, the managers were flexible. They decided to enlarge the existing site because of its better-than-expected performance as well as the limited potential benefits of a second site. The San Jose site has had a major impact on Fujitsu's software development and sales—particularly in Japan but in the United States, too. Similarly, at Alcatel's first foreign R&D site in Germany, senior managers were flexible. After several months, they realized that the travel-and-communications budget would have to be increased substantially beyond initial projections in order to improve the flow of knowledge from the French home base. For instance, in the case of a telephone switchboard project, the actual number of business trips between the two sites was nearly twice as high as originally projected.

Integrating the Global R&D Network

As the number of companies' R&D sites at home and abroad grows, R&D managers will increasingly face the challenging task of coordinating the network. That will require a fundamental shift in the role of senior managers at the central lab. Managers of R&D networks must be global coordinators, not local administrators. More than being managers of people and processes, they must be managers of knowledge. And not all managers that a company has in place will be up to the task.

Consider Matsushita's R&D management. A number of technically competent managers became obsolete at the company once it launched a global approach to R&D. Today managers at Matsushita's central R&D site in Hirakata, Japan, continue to play an important role in the research and development of core processes for manufacturing. But the responsibility of an increasing number of senior managers at the central site is overseeing Matsushita's network of 15 dedicated R&D sites. That responsibility includes setting research agendas, monitoring results, and creating direct ties between sites.

How does the new breed of R&D manager coordinate global knowledge? Look again to Matsushita's central R&D site. First, high-level corporate managers in close cooperation with senior R&D managers develop an overall research agenda and assign different parts of it to individual sites. The process is quite tricky. It requires that the managers in charge have a good understanding of not only the technological capabilities that Matsushita will need to develop in the future but also the stock of technological capabilities already available to it.

Matsushita's central lab organizes two or three yearly off-site meetings devoted to informing R&D scientists and engineers about the entire company's current state of technical knowledge and capabilities. At the same meetings, engineers who have moved from R&D to take over manufacturing and marketing responsibilities inform R&D members about trends in Matsushita's current and potential future markets. Under the guidance of senior project managers, members from R&D, manufacturing, and marketing determine timelines and resource requirements for specific home-base–augmenting and home-base–exploiting projects. One R&D manager notes, "We discuss not only why a specific scientific insight might be interesting for Matsushita but also how we can turn this insight into a product quickly. We usually seek to develop a prototype early. Prototypes are a good basis for a discussion with marketing and manufacturing. Most of our efforts are targeted at delivering the prototype of a slightly better mousetrap early rather than delivering the blueprint of a much better mousetrap late."

To stimulate the exchange of information, R&D managers at Matsushita's central lab create direct links among researchers across different sites. They promote the use of videoconferencing and frequent face-to-face contact to forge those ties. Reducing the instances in which the central lab must act as mediator means that existing knowledge travels more quickly through the company and new ideas percolate more easily. For example, a researcher at a home-base–exploiting site in Singapore can communicate with another researcher at a home-base–exploiting site in Franklin Park, Illinois, about potential new research projects much more readily now that central R&D fosters informal and formal direct links.

Finally, managers at Matsushita's central lab constantly monitor new regional pockets of knowledge as well as the company's expanding network of manufacturing sites to determine whether the company will need additional R&D locations. With 15 major sites around the world, Matsushita has decided that the number of sites is sufficient at this point. But the company is ever vigilant about surveying the landscape and knows that as the landscape changes, its decision could, too.

As more pockets of knowledge emerge worldwide and competition in foreign markets mounts, the imperative to create global R&D networks will grow all the more pressing. Only those companies that embrace a global approach to R&D will meet the competitive challenges of the new dynamic. And only those managers who embrace their fundamentally new role as global coordinators and managers of knowledge will be able to tap the full potential of their R&D networks.

CHAPTER 6

Engaging in Cross-Border Collaboration:
Managing across Corporate Boundaries

In this chapter, we acknowledge that in the international business environment of the twenty-first century, few companies have all the resources and capabilities they need to develop the kind of multidimensional strategies and adaptive organizational capabilities we have described. Increasingly, they must collaborate with their suppliers, distributors, customers, agents, licensors, joint venture partners, and others to meet the needs of the increasingly complex global environment. This requirement implies that today's MNEs must develop the skills to not only manage assets and resources under their own direct control but also span their corporate boundaries and capture vital capabilities in the partnerships and alliances that are becoming central to the strategic response capability of so many companies. After exploring the motivation for entering into such partnerships, we examine some of the costs and risks of collaboration before discussing the organizational and managerial skills required to build and manage these boundary-spanning relationships effectively.

Historically, the strategic challenge for a company has been viewed primarily as one of protecting potential profits from erosion through either competition or bargaining. Such erosion of profits could be caused not only by the actions of competitors but also by the bargaining powers of customers, suppliers, and governments. The key challenge facing a company was assumed to be its ability to maintain its independence by maintaining strong control over its activities. Furthermore, this strategic approach emphasized the defensive value of making other entities depend on it by capturing critical resources, building switching costs, and exploiting other vulnerabilities.[1]

This view of strategy subsequently underwent a sea change. The need to pursue multiple sources of competitive advantage simultaneously (see Chapter 3) led to the need for building not only an interdependent and integrated network organization within the company (Chapter 5) but also collaborative relationships externally with other firms, be they competitors, customers, suppliers, or a variety of other institutions.

This important shift in strategic perspective was triggered by a variety of factors, including rising R&D costs, shortened product life cycles, growing barriers to market entry, increasing needs for global-scale economies, and the expanding importance of global standards. Such dramatic changes led managers to recognize that many of the

---

[1]For the most influential exposition of this view, see Michael E. Porter, *Competitive Strategy* (New York: Free Press, 1980).

human, financial, and technological resources they required to compete effectively lay beyond their boundaries, and were often—for political or regulatory reasons—not for sale. In response, many shifted their strategic focus away from an all-encompassing obsession with preempting competition to a broader view of building competitive advantage through selective, often simultaneous reliance on both collaboration and competition.

The previously dominant focus on value appropriation that characterized all dealings across a company's organizational boundary changed to the simultaneous consideration of both value creation and value appropriation. Instead of trying to enhance their bargaining power over customers, companies began to build partnerships with them, thereby bolstering the customer's competitive position and, at the same time, leveraging their own competitiveness and innovative capabilities.

However, perhaps the most visible manifestation of this growing role of collaborative strategies appears in the phenomenon often described as strategic alliances: the increasing propensity of MNEs to form cooperative relationships with their global competitors (see Case 6.2 about Renault/Nissan for an illustration). As described by Carlo de Benedetti, the ex-chairman of Olivetti and the key instigator of the variety of partnerships that Olivetti developed with companies such as AT&T and Toshiba, "We have entered the age of alliances. . . . In the high-tech markets of the 1990s, we will see a shaking out of the isolated and a shaking in of the allied." It was a prediction that proved quite accurate, and by the turn of the century, strategic alliances had become central components of most MNE strategies.

Although our analysis of the causes and consequences of such collaborative strategies in this chapter focuses on the phenomenon of strategic alliances among global companies, some of our arguments can be applied to a broader range of cooperative relations, including those with customers, suppliers, and governments. We begin with a discussion of the key motivations for forming strategic alliances.

Why Strategic Alliances?

The term strategic alliance currently is widely used to describe a variety of interfirm cooperation agreements, ranging from shared research to formal joint ventures and minority equity participation (see Figure 6-1).

The key challenges surrounding the management of the various types of alliances detailed in Figure 6-1 will vary. In some it may relate to the "fairness" of management or technology payments; in others, it may be related to where the organizational problems typically will arise. Every form of alliance has predictable strengths and weaknesses, because each form is intended for particular circumstances.

Large numbers of firms worldwide, including many industry leaders, are increasingly involved in strategic alliances. Furthermore, several surveys suggest that such partnerships may be distinguished from traditional foreign investment joint ventures in several important ways.

Classically, traditional joint ventures were formed between a senior multinational headquartered in an industrialized country and a junior local partner in a less-developed or less-industrialized country. The primary goal that dominated their formation was to

Figure 6-1   Range of Strategic Alliances

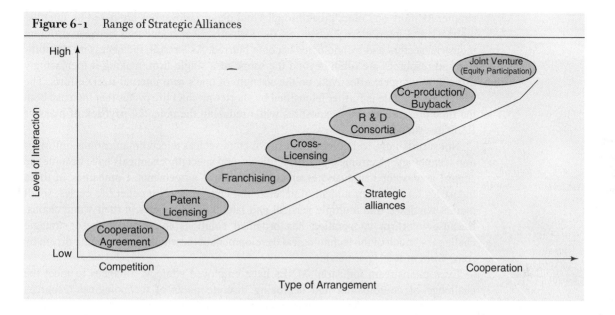

gain new market access for existing products. In this classic contractual agreement, the senior partner provided existing products while the junior partner provided the local marketing expertise, the means to overcome any protectionist barriers, and the governmental contacts to deal with national regulations. Both partners benefited: The multinational achieved increased sales volume, and the local firm gained access to new products and often learned important new skills from its partner.

In contrast, the scope and motivations for the modern form of strategic alliances are clearly broadening. There are three trends that are particularly noteworthy. First, present-day strategic alliances are frequently between firms in industrialized countries. Second, the focus is often on the creation of new products and technologies rather than the distribution of existing ones. And third, present-day strategic alliances are often forged for only short durations.

All of these characteristics mean the new forms of strategic alliances considerably expand the strategic importance of cooperation beyond that which existed for classic joint ventures, and today the opportunity for competitive gain and loss through partnering is substantial. In the following sections, we discuss in more detail why this rapidly developing form of business relationship has become so important by focusing on five key motivations that are driving the formation of strategic alliances: technology exchange, global competition, industry convergence, economies of scale, and alliances as an alternative to merger.

Technology Exchange

Technology transfer or R&D collaboration is a major objective of many strategic alliances. The reason that technological exchange is such a strong driver of alliances is simple: As more and more breakthroughs and major innovations are based on interdisciplinary and interindustry advances, the formerly clear boundaries between different industrial sectors and technologies become blurred. As a result, the necessary capabilities and resources are often beyond the scope of a single firm, making it increasingly difficult to compete effectively on the strength of one's own internal R&D efforts. The need to collaborate is further intensified by shorter product life cycles that increase both the time pressure and risk exposures while reducing the potential payback of massive R&D investments.

Not surprisingly, technology-intensive sectors such as telecommunications, information technology, electronics, pharmaceuticals, and specialty chemicals have become the central arenas for major and extensive cooperative agreements. Companies in these industries face an environment of accelerating change, short product life cycles, small market windows, and multiple vertical and lateral dependencies in their value chains. Because interfirm cooperation has provided solutions to many of these strategic challenges, much of the technological development in these industries is being driven by some form of R&D partnership.

Even mainstream industrial MNEs have employed strategic alliances to meet the challenge of coordinating and deploying discrete pools of technological resources without sacrificing R&D and commercialization scale advantages. For example, several advanced material suppliers have teamed up with global automotive companies to transfer their specialized technology across geographic borders, as exemplified by the key role GEC played in transferring the Ford Xenoy bumper technology from Europe and adapting it to the U.S. market.

Global Competition

A widespread perception has emerged that global competitive battles will increasingly be fought between teams of players aligned in strategic partnerships. Robert P. Collin, former head of the U.S. subsidiary of a joint venture between General Electric and Fanuc, the Japanese robot maker, was blunt in his evaluation of the importance of using alliances as a key tool in competitive positioning. "To level out the global playing field," he said, "American companies will have to find partners." In the new game of global networks, successful MNEs from any country of origin may well be those that have chosen the best set of corporate allies.

Particularly in industries in which there is a dominant worldwide market leader, strategic alliances and networks allow coalitions of smaller partners to compete more effectively against a global "common enemy" rather than one another. For example, the Symbian alliance among Psion, Ericsson, Nokia, Matsushita, and Motorola was created as a response to Microsoft's entry into the personal digital assistant (PDA) market. The partners recognized that their only hope of challenging Microsoft's new PDA operating system, Windows CE, was to develop a common standard in mobile phone and PDA operating systems.

Industry Convergence

Many high-technology industries are converging and overlapping in a way that seems destined to create a huge competitive traffic jam. Producers of computers, telecommunications, and components are merging; biological and chip technologies are intersecting; and advanced materials applications are creating greater overlaps in diverse applications from the aerospace to the automotive industry. Again, the preferred solution has been to create cross-industry alliances.

Furthermore, strategic alliances are sometimes the only way to develop the complex and interdisciplinary skills necessary in the time frame required. Alliances become a way of shaping competition by reducing competitive intensity, excluding potential entrants and isolating particular players, and building complex integrated value chains that can act as barriers to those who choose to go it alone.

Nowhere are the implications of this cross-industry convergence and broad-based collaboration clearer than in the case of high-definition television (HDTV). As with many other strategically critical technologies of the future—biotechnology, superconductivity, advanced ceramics, artificial intelligence—HDTV not only dwarfs previous investment requirements but extends beyond the technological capabilities of even the largest and most diversified MNEs. As a result, the development of this important new industry segment has been undertaken almost exclusively by country-based, cross-industry alliances of large powerful companies. In Japan, companies allied to develop the range of products necessary for a system offering. At the same time, a European HDTV consortium banded together to develop a competitive system. But in the United States, the legal and cultural barriers that prevented companies from working together in such partnerships threatened to compromise U.S. competitiveness in this major new industry.

Economies of Scale and Reduction of Risk

There are several ways strategic alliances and networks allow participating firms to reap the benefits of scale economies or learning—advantages that are particularly interesting to smaller companies trying to match the economic benefits that accrue to the largest MNEs. First, partners can pool their resources and concentrate their activities to raise the scale of activity or the rate of learning within the alliance significantly over those of each firm were it to operate separately. Second, alliances enable partners to share and leverage the specific strengths and capabilities of each of the other participating firms. Third, trading different or complementary resources among companies can result in mutual gains and save each partner the high cost of duplication.

One company activity that is particularly motivated by the risk-sharing opportunities of such partnerships is R&D, where product life cycles are shortening and technological complexity is increasing. At the same time, R&D expenses are being driven sharply higher by personnel and capital costs. Because none of the participating firms bears the full risk and cost of the joint activity, alliances are often seen as an attractive risk-hedging mechanism.

One alliance driven by these motivations is the Renault–Nissan partnership. These two companies came together in 1999, with Renault taking a 36 percent share in Nissan and installing Carlos Ghosn as its chief operating officer. Although Nissan's perilous financial position was evidently a key factor in the decision to bring in a foreign partner, the underlying driver of the alliance was the need—on both sides—for greater economies of scale and scope to achieve competitive parity with General Motors (GM),

Ford, and Toyota. The alliance led to a surprisingly fast turnaround of Nissan's fortunes, largely through Ghosn's decisive leadership, and subsequently to a broad set of projects to deliver synergies in product development, manufacturing, and distribution. Although still much smaller than GM or Ford, Renault–Nissan is now believed likely to be one of the long-term surviving players in the global automobile industry. In fiscal 2004, Nissan had a record year.

Alliance as an Alternative to Merger

Finally, there remain industry sectors in which political, regulatory, and legal constraints limit the extent of cross-border mergers and acquisitions. In such cases, companies often create alliances not because they are inherently the most attractive organizational form but because they represent the best available alternative to a merger.

The classic examples of this phenomenon occur in the airline and telecommunications industries. Many countries still preclude foreign ownership in these industries. But a simple analysis of the economics of the industry—in terms of potential economies of scale, concentration of suppliers, opportunities for standardization of services, and competitive dynamics—would highlight the availability of substantial benefits from global integration. So as a means of generating at least some of the benefits of global integration but not breaking the rules against foreign ownership, most major airlines have formed themselves into marketing and code-sharing partnerships, including Star Alliance and OneWorld, and many telecom companies have formed telecommunications alliances.

Alliances of this type often lead to full-scale global integration if restrictions on foreign ownership are lifted. For example, as the telecommunications industry was gradually deregulated during the 1990s, alliances such as Concert and Unisource gave way to the emergence of true multinational players such as Worldcom, France Telecom, and Deutsche Telekom.

The Risks and Costs of Collaboration

Because of these different motivations, there was an initial period of euphoria during which partnerships were seen as the panacea for most of MNEs' global strategic problems and opportunities. The euphoria of the 1980s to form relationships was fueled by two fashionable management concepts of the period: triad power[2] and stick to your knitting.[3]

The triad power concept emphasized the need to develop significant positions in the three key markets of the United States, western Europe, and Japan as a prerequisite for competing in global industries. Given the enormous costs and difficulties of accessing any one of these developed and highly competitive markets independently, many companies with unequal legs on their geographic stool regarded alliances as the only feasible way to develop this triadic position.

[2]See Kenichi Ohmae, *Triad Power* (New York: Free Press, 1985).
[3]This idea is one of the lessons developed in the highly influential book by Thomas Peters and Robert Waterman, *In Search of Excellence* (New York: Harper & Row, 1982).

The stick-to-your-knitting prescription in essence urged managers to disaggregate the value chain and focus their investments, efforts, and attention on only those tasks in which the company had a significant competitive advantage. Other operations were to be externalized through outsourcing or alliances. The seductive logic of both arguments, coupled with rapidly evolving environmental demands, led to an explosion in the formation of such alliances.

Since then, the experience companies have gathered through such collaborative ventures highlighted some of the costs and risks of such partnerships. Some risks arise from the simultaneous presence of both collaborative and competitive aspects in the relationships. Others arise from the higher levels of strategic and organizational complexity involved in managing cooperative relationships outside the company's own boundaries.

The Risks of Competitive Collaboration

Some strategic alliances—including some of the most visible—involve partners who are fierce competitors outside the specific scope of the cooperative venture. Such relationships create the possibility that the collaborative venture might be used by one or both partners to develop a competitive edge over the other, or at least that the benefits from the partnership will be asymmetrical for the two parties, which might change their relative competitive positions. There are several factors that might cause such asymmetry.

A partnership is often motivated by the desire to join and leverage complementary skills and resources. For example, the two partners may have access to different technologies that could be combined to create new businesses or products. For example, SonyEricsson was created to bring together Sony's world-leading capabilities in consumer electronics and design with Ericsson's advanced technological know-how in mobile phones and strong relationships with mobile operators. Such an arrangement for competency pooling inevitably entails the possibility that, in the course of the partnership, one of the partners will learn and internalize the other's skills while carefully protecting its own, thereby creating the option of discarding the partner and appropriating all the benefits created by the partnership. This possibility becomes particularly salient when the skills and competencies of one partner are tacit and deeply embedded in complex organizational processes (and thereby difficult to learn or emulate), whereas those of the other partner are explicit and embodied in specific individual machines or drawings (and thereby liable to relatively easy observation and emulation).

When General Foods entered into a partnership with Ajinimoto, the Japanese food giant, it agreed to make available its advanced processing technology for products such as freeze-dried coffee. In return, its Japanese partner would contribute its marketing expertise to launch the new products on the Japanese market. After several years, however, the collaboration deteriorated and was eventually dissolved when Ajinomoto had absorbed the technology transfer and management felt it was no longer learning from its American partner. Unfortunately, General Foods had not done such a good job learning about the Japanese market and left the alliance with some bitterness.

Another predatory tactic might involve capturing investment initiative to use the partnership to erode the other's competitive position. In this scenario, the company ensures that it, rather than the partner, makes and keeps control over the critical investments. Such investments can be in the domain of product development, manufacturing, marketing, or wherever the most strategically vital part of the business value chain is located. Through these tactics, the aggressive company can strip its partner of the necessary infrastructure for competing independently and create one-way dependence in the collaboration that can be exploited at will.

Although they provide lively copy for magazine articles, such Machiavellian intentions and actions remain the exception, and the vast majority of cross-company collaborations are founded and maintained on a basis of mutual trust and shared commitment. Yet even the most carefully constructed strategic alliances can become problematic. Although many provide short-term solutions to some strategic problems, they also serve to hide the deeper and more fundamental deficiencies that cause those problems. The short-term solution takes the pressure off the problem without solving it and makes the company highly vulnerable when the problem finally resurfaces, usually in a more extreme and immediate form.

Furthermore, because such alliances typically involve task sharing, each company almost inevitably trades off some of the benefits of "learning by doing" the tasks that it externalizes to its partner. Thus, even in the best-case scenario of a partnership that fully meets all expectations, the very success of the partnership leads to some benefits for each partner and therefore to some strengthening of a competitor. Behind the success of the alliance, therefore, lies the ever-present possibility that a competitor's newly acquired strength will be used against its alliance partner in some future competitive battle.[4] Consider the example of Shanghai Automotive Industry Corp., one of China's larger state-owned enterprises. In April 2006, it announced that it was going to start producing a car under its own name. Shanghai Automotive had been operating large joint ventures with both Volkswagen and GM for the Chinese market for many years; under Chinese law, foreign companies wishing to produce automobiles in China must have a local partner who owns at least 50 percent of the business. Henceforth, the Volkswagen and GM joint ventures with Shanghai Automotive would be competing with Shanghai Automotive's wholly owned subsidiary.

Finally, there is the risk that collaborating with a competitor might be a precursor to a takeover by one of the firms. In early 2000, General Motors Defense was assessing whether to bid on a multibillion dollar contract alone or in partnership with a firm that was much larger in this sector, General Dynamics. The company was concerned first with the short-term issue of building firewalls around information flows so that only contract-specific proprietary knowledge would be shared. More fundamentally though, it confronted the question of whether this partnership might lead to eventually being acquired. Although this question legitimately arises in many alliances and joint ventures, it is worth reiterating that in most instances, MNEs are able to resolve the risks and costs of collaboration.

The Cost of Strategic and Organizational Complexity

Cooperation is difficult to attain even in the best of circumstances. One of the strongest forces facilitating such behavior within a single company's internal operations is the

---

[4]These potential risks of competitive collaboration are the focus of Reading 6–2 by Gary Hamel, Yves L. Doz, and C. K. Prahalad, "Collaborate with Your Competitor—and Win," *Harvard Business Review,* January/February 1989.

understanding that the risks and rewards ultimately accrue to the company's own accounts and therefore, either directly or indirectly, to the participants. This basic motivation is diluted in strategic alliances. Furthermore, the scope of most alliances and the environmental uncertainties they inevitably face often prevent a clear understanding of the risks that might be incurred or rewards that might accrue in the course of the partnership's evolution. As a result, cooperation in the context of allocated risks and rewards and divided loyalties inevitably creates additional strategic and organizational complexity that in turn involves additional costs to manage.

International partnerships bring together companies that are often products of different economic, political, social, and cultural systems. Such differences in the administrative heritages of the partner companies, each of which brings its own strategic mentality and managerial practices to the venture, further exacerbate the organizational challenge. For example, tensions between Xerox and Fuji Xerox—a successful but often troubled relationship—were as much an outgrowth of the differences in the business systems in which each was located as of the differences in the corporate culture between the U.S. company and its Japanese joint venture.

Organizational complexity, due to the very broad scope of operations typical of many strategic alliances, also contributes to added difficulties. As we have described, one of the distinguishing characteristics of present-day alliances is that they often cover a broad range of activities. This expansion of scope requires partners not only to manage the many areas of contact within the alliance but also to coordinate the different alliance-related tasks within their own organizations. And the goals, tasks, and management processes for the alliance must be constantly monitored and adapted to changing conditions.

Building and Managing Collaborative Ventures

As we have described in the preceding sections, alliances are neither conventional organizations with fully internalized activities nor well-specified transaction relationships through which externalized activities may be linked by market-based contracts. Instead, they combine elements of both. The participating companies retain their own competitive strategies and performance expectations, as well as their national, ideological, and administrative identities. Yet to obtain the required benefits of a partnership, diverse organizational units in different companies and different countries must effectively and flexibly coordinate their activities.

There are numerous reasons such collaborative ventures inevitably present some significant management challenges: strategic and environmental disparities among the partners, lack of a common experience and perception base, difficulties in interfirm communication, conflicts of interest and priorities, and inevitable personal differences among the individuals who manage the interface. As a result, though it is manifest to most managers that strategic alliances can provide great benefits, they also realize that there is a big difference between making alliances and making them work.

The challenge can be considered in two parts, reflecting the pre-alliance tasks of analysis, negotiation, and decision making and the post-alliance tasks of coordination, integration, and adaptation.

Building Cooperative Ventures

The quality of the pre-alliance processes of partner selection and negotiation influence the clarity and reciprocity of mutual expectations from the alliance. There are three aspects of the pre-alliance process to which managers must pay close attention if the alliance is to have the best possible chance of success: partner selection, escalating commitment, and alliance scope.[5]

Partner Selection: Strategic and Organizational Analysis

The process of analyzing a potential partner's strategic and organizational capabilities is an important yet difficult pre-alliance task. Several factors impede the quality of the choice-making process.

The most important constraint lies in the availability of information required for an effective evaluation of the potential partner. Effective pre-alliance analysis needs data about the partner's relevant physical assets (e.g., the condition and productivity of plants and equipment), as well as less tangible assets (e.g., strength of brands, quality of customer relationships, level of technological expertise) and organizational capabilities (e.g., managerial competence, employee loyalty, shared values). The difficulty of obtaining such information in the short time limits in which most alliances are finalized is further complicated by the barriers of cultural and physical distance that MNEs must also overcome.

The pressures of time and distance sometimes result in suboptimal partner selection. As Figure 6-2 suggests, there is no real upside to selecting a partner who is competent but with whom you may not be comfortable working. Nor, however, should partners be selected on the basis of comfort rather than competence.

A key lesson emerging from the experience of most strategic alliances is that changes in each partner's competitive positions and strategic priorities have crucial impacts on the viability of the alliance over time. Even if the strategic trajectories of two companies cross at a particular point of time, creating complementarities and the potential for a partnership, their paths may be so divergent as to make such complementarities too transient for the alliance to have any lasting value. Case 6-3, about Eli Lilly in India, explores whether the Eli Lilly–Ranbaxy joint venture still meets each partner's strategic objectives, 15 years after it was established.

Although it is difficult enough to make a static assessment of a potential partner's strategic and organizational capabilities, it is almost impossible to make an effective pre-alliance analysis of how those capabilities are likely to evolve over time.

There probably is no solution to this problem, but companies that recognize alliances as a permanent and important part of their future organization have made monitoring their partners an ongoing rather than an ad hoc process. Some have linked such activities to their integrated business intelligence system, which was set up to monitor competitors. By having this group not only analyze competitors'

---

[5]The pre-alliance process is in many ways similar to a preacquisition process and shares the same needs. See David B. Jemison and Sim B. Sitkin, "Acquisitions: The Process Can Be a Problem," *Harvard Business Review*, no. 2 (1986), pp. 107–14.

Figure 6-2   Partner Selection: Comfort vs. Competence

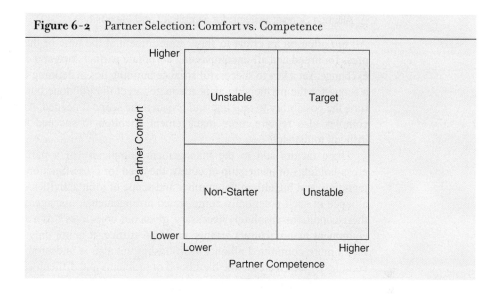

potential strategies but also assess their value as acquisition or alliance candidates, these companies find themselves much better prepared when a specific alliance opportunity arises.

Escalating Commitment: Thrill of the Chase

The very process of alliance planning and negotiations can cause unrealistic expectations and wrong choices. In particular, some managers involved in the process can build up a great deal of personal enthusiasm and expectations in trying to sell the idea of the alliance within their own organization. This escalation process is similar to a process observed in many acquisition decisions where, in one manager's words, "The thrill of the chase blinds pursuers to the consequences of the catch." Because the champions of the idea—those most often caught in a spiral of escalating commitment—may not be the operational managers who are later given responsibility for making the alliance work, major problems arise when the latter are confronted with inevitable pitfalls and less visible problems.

The most effective way to control this escalation process is to ensure that at least the key operating managers likely to be involved in the implementation stage of the alliance are involved in the pre-decision negotiation process. Their involvement not only ensures greater commitment but also creates continuity between pre- and post-alliance actions. But the greatest benefit accrues to the long-term understanding that must develop between the partners. By ensuring that the broader strategic goals that motivate the alliance are related to specific operational details in the negotiation stage, the companies can enhance the clarity and consistency of both the definition and the understanding of the alliance's goals and tasks. The Nora Sakari example in Case 6-1 considers in detail the challenges of negotiating such a venture.

Alliance Scope: Striving for Simplicity and Flexibility

All too often, in an effort to show commitment at the time of the agreement, partners press for broad and all-encompassing corporate partnerships and equity participation or exchange. Yet a key to successful alliance building lies in defining as simple and focused a scope for the partnership as is adequate to get the job done but to retain at the same time the possibility to redefine and broaden the scope if needed. Alliances that are more complex also require more management attention to succeed and tend to be more difficult to manage.

Three factors add to the management complexity of a partnership: complicated cross-holdings of ownership or equity, the need for cross-functional coordination or integration, and breadth in the number and scope of joint activities. Before involving any alliance in such potentially complicated arrangements, management should ask: "Are these conditions absolutely necessary, given our objectives?" If a simple OEM (original equipment manufacturer) arrangement can suffice, it is not only unnecessary to enter into a more committed alliance relationship but also is undesirable because the added complexity will increase the likelihood of problems and difficulties in achieving the objectives of the partnership.

At the same time, it might be useful to provide some flexibility in the terms of the alliance for renegotiating and changing the scope, if and when necessary. Even when a broad-based and multifaceted alliance represents the ultimate goal, many companies have found it preferable to start with a relatively simple and limited partnership whose scope is expanded gradually as both partners develop a better understanding of and greater trust in each other's motives, capabilities, and expectations.

Managing Cooperative Ventures

Although the pre-alliance analysis and negotiation processes are important, a company's ability to manage an ongoing relationship also tends to be a key determining factor for the success or failure of an alliance. Among the numerous issues that influence a company's ability to manage a cooperative venture, there are three that appear to present the greatest challenges: managing the boundary, managing knowledge flows, and providing strategic directions.

Managing the Boundary: Structuring the Interface

There are many different ways in which the partners can structure the boundary of an alliance and manage the interface between this boundary and their own organizations. At one extreme, an independent legal organization can be created and given complete freedom to manage the alliance tasks. Alternatively, the alliance's operations can be managed by one or both parents with more substantial strategic, operational, or administrative controls. In many cases, however, the creation of such a distinct entity is not necessary, and simpler, less bureaucratic governance mechanisms such as joint committees may be enough to guide and supervise shared tasks. Also, given the potentially enormous breadth in the scope of activities (see Figure 6-3), it may be more practical to start with a limited agreement. It is always easier to gain a partner's agreement to expand than to contract an alliance's terms of reference.

Figure 6-3   Scope of Activity

Narrow	vs.	Wide
Single, geographic market	vs.	Multi-country
Single function	vs.	Complete value chain
Single industry/customer group	vs.	Multi-industry
Modest investment	vs.	Large scale
Existing business	vs.	New business
Limited term	vs.	Forever

The choice among alternative boundary structures depends largely on the scope of the alliance. When the alliance's tasks are characterized by extensive functional interdependencies, there is a need for a high level of integration in the decision-making process related to those shared tasks. In such circumstances, the creation of a separate entity is often the only effective way to manage such dense interlinkages. In contrast, an alliance between two companies with the objective of marketing each other's existing products in noncompetitive markets may need only a few simple rules that govern marketing parameters and financial arrangements and a single joint committee to review the outcomes periodically.

Managing Knowledge Flows: Integrating the Interface

Irrespective of the specific objectives of any alliance, the very process of collaboration creates flows of information across the boundaries of the participating companies and creates the potential for learning from each other. Managing these knowledge flows involves two kinds of tasks for the participating companies. First, they must ensure full exploitation of the created learning potential. Second, they must prevent the outflow of any information or knowledge they do not wish to share with their alliance partners.

In terms of the first point, the key problem is that the individuals managing the interface may not be the best users of such knowledge. To maximize its learning from a partnership, a company must effectively integrate its interface managers into the rest of its organization. The gatekeepers must have knowledge of and access to the different individuals and management groups within the company that are likely to benefit most from the diverse kinds of information that flow through an alliance boundary. Managers familiar with the difficulties of managing information flows within the company's boundaries will readily realize that such cross-boundary learning is unlikely to occur unless specific mechanisms are in place to make it happen.

The selection of appropriate interface managers is perhaps the single most important factor for facilitating such learning. Interface managers should have at least three key attributes: They must be well versed in the company's internal organizational process; they must have the personal credibility and status necessary to access key managers in different parts of the organization; and they must have a sufficiently broad understanding of the company's business and strategies to be able to recognize useful information and knowledge that might cross their path.

Merely placing the right managers at the interface is not sufficient to ensure effective learning, however. Supportive administrative processes also must be developed to facilitate the systematic transfer of information and monitor the effectiveness of those transfers. Such support is often achieved most effectively through simple systems and mechanisms, such as task forces or periodic review meetings.

While exploiting the alliance's learning potential, however, each company must also manage the interface to prevent unintended flows of information to its partner. It is a delicate balancing task for the gatekeepers to ensure the free flow of information across the organizational boundaries while effectively regulating the flow of people and data to ensure that sensitive or proprietary knowledge is appropriately protected.

Providing Strategic Direction: The Governance Structure

The key to providing leadership and direction, ensuring strategic control, and resolving interorganizational conflicts is an effective governance structure. Unlike acquisitions, alliances are often premised on the equality of both partners, but an obsession to protect such equality can prevent companies from creating an effective governance structure for the partnership. Committees consisting of an equal number of participants from both companies and operating under strict norms of equality are often incapable of providing clear directions or forcing conflict resolution at lower levels. Indeed, many otherwise well-conceived alliances have floundered because of their dependence on such committees for their leadership and control.

To find their way around such problems, partners must negotiate on the basis of "integrative" rather than "distributive" equality. With such an agreement, each committee is structured with clear, single-handed leadership, but each company takes the responsibility for different tasks. However, such delicately balanced arrangements can work only if the partners can agree on specific individuals, delegate the overall responsibility for the alliance to these individuals, and protect their ability to work in the best interests of the alliance itself rather than those of the parents.

Concluding Comments

Perspectives on strategic alliances have oscillated between the extremes of euphoria and disillusionment. Finally, however, there seems to be some recognition that though such partnerships may not represent perfect solutions, they are often the best solution available to a particular company at a particular point in time.

Easy—but Sometimes Not the Best Solution

Perhaps the biggest danger for many companies is to pretend that the "quick and easy" option of a strategic alliance is also the best or only option available. Cooperative arrangements are perhaps too tempting in catch-up situations in which the partnership might provide a façade of recovery that masks serious problems.

Yet, though going it alone may well be the most desirable option for a specific objective or task in the long term, almost no company can afford to meet all of its objectives in this way. When complete independence and self-sufficiency are not possible because of resource scarcity, lack of expertise, or time—or any other such constraint—strategic alliances often become the most realistic option.

Alliances Need Not Be Permanent

Another important factor commonly misunderstood is that the dissolution of a partnership is not synonymous with failure. Many companies appear to have suffered because of their unwillingness or inability to terminate partnership arrangements when changing circumstances made those arrangements inappropriate or because they failed to discuss upfront with their partner whether the alliance should have a sunset clause. All organizations create internal pressures for their own perpetuation, and an alliance is no exception to this enduring reality. One important task for senior managers of the participating companies is to ask periodically why the alliance should not be terminated and then continue with the arrangement only if they find compelling reasons to do so.

Flexibility Is Key

The original agreement for a partnership typically is based on limited information and unrealistic expectations. Experience gained from the actual process of working together provides the opportunity for fine-tuning and often finding better ways to achieve higher levels of joint value creation. In such circumstances, the flexibility to adapt the goals, scope, and management of the alliance to changing conditions is essential. In addition, changing environmental conditions may make original intentions and plans obsolete. Effective partnering requires the ability to monitor such changes and allow the partnership to evolve in response.

An Internal Knowledge Network: Basis for Learning

Finally, learning is one of the main benefits that a company can derive from a partnership, irrespective of whether it represents one of the formal goals. For such learning to occur, however, a company must be receptive to the knowledge and skills available from the partner and have an organization able to diffuse and leverage such learning. In the absence of an internal knowledge network, information obtained from the partner cannot be transferred and applied, regardless of its potential value. Thus, building and managing an integrated network organization, as described in Chapter 4, is an essential prerequisite for not only effective internal processes but also effective management across organizational boundaries.

Case 6-1   Nora-Sakari: A Proposed JV in Malaysia (Revised)

On Monday, July 15, 2003, Zainal Hashim, vice-chairman of Nora Holdings Sdn Bhd[1] (Nora), arrived at his office about an hour earlier than usual. As he looked out the window at the city spreading below, he thought about the Friday evening reception which he had hosted at his home in Kuala Lumpur (KL), Malaysia, for a team of negotiators from Sakari Oy[2] (Sakari) of Finland. Nora was a leading supplier of telecommunications (telecom) equipment in Malaysia while Sakari, a Finnish conglomerate, was a leader in the manufacture of cellular phone sets and switching systems. The seven-member team from Sakari was in KL to negotiate with Nora the formation of a joint venture (JV) between the two telecom companies.

This was the final negotiation which would determine whether a JV agreement would materialize. The negotiation had ended late Friday afternoon, having lasted for five consecutive days. The JV company, if established, would be set up in Malaysia to manufacture and commission digital switching exchanges to meet the needs of the telecom industry in Malaysia and in neighbouring countries, particularly Indonesia and Thailand. While Nora would benefit from the JV in terms of technology transfer, the venture would pave the way for Sakari to acquire knowledge and gain access to the markets of South-east Asia.

The Nora management was impressed by the Finnish capability in using high technology to enable Finland, a small country of only five million people, to have a fast-growing economy. Most successful Finnish companies were in the high-tech industries. For example, Kone was one of the world's three largest manufacturers of lifts, Vaisala was the world's major supplier of meteorological equipment, and Sakari was one of the leading telecom companies in Europe. It would be an invaluable opportunity for Nora to learn from the Finnish experience and emulate their success for Malaysia.

The opportunity emerged two and half years earlier when Peter Mattsson, president of Sakari's Asian regional office in Singapore, approached Zainal[3] to explore the possibility of forming a cooperative venture between Nora and Sakari. Mattsson said:

> While growth in the mobile telecommunications network is expected to be about 40 per cent a year in Asia in the next five years, growth in fixed networks would not be as fast, but the projects are much larger. A typical mobile network project amounts to a maximum of €50 million, but fixed network projects can be estimated in hundreds of millions. In Malaysia and Thailand, such latter projects are currently approaching contract stage. Thus it is imperative that Sakari establish its presence in this region to capture a share in the fixed network market.

[1]Sdn Bhd is an abbreviation for Sendirian Berhad, which means private limited company in Malaysia.
[2]Oy is an abbreviation for Osakeyhtiot, which means private limited company in Finland.

[3]The first name is used because the Malay name does not carry a family name. The first and/or middle names belong to the individual and the last name is his/her father's name.

The large potential for telecom facilities was also evidenced in the low telephone penetration rates for most South-east Asian countries. For example, in 1999, telephone penetration rates (measured by the number of telephone lines per 100 people) for Indonesia, Thailand, Malaysia and the Philippines ranged from three to 20 lines per 100 people compared to the rates in developed countries such as Canada, Finland, Germany, United States and Sweden where the rates exceeded 55 telephone lines per 100 people.

The Telecom Industry in Malaysia

Telekom Malaysia Bhd (TMB), the national telecom company, was given the authority by the Malaysian government to develop the country's telecom infrastructure. With a paid-up capital of RM2.4 billion,[4] it was also given the mandate to provide telecom services that were on par with those available in developed countries.

TMB announced that it would be investing in the digitalization of its networks to pave the way for offering services based on the ISDN (integrated services digitalized network) standard, and investing in international fibre optic cable networks to meet the needs of increased telecom traffic between Malaysia and the rest of the world. TMB would also facilitate the installation of more cellular telephone networks in view of the increased demand for the use of mobile phones among the business community in KL and in major towns.

As the nation's largest telecom company, TMB's operations were regulated through a 20-year license issued by the Ministry of Energy, Telecommunications and Posts. In line with the government's Vision 2020 program which targeted Malaysia to become a developed nation by the year 2020, there was a strong need for the upgrading of the telecom infrastructure in the rural areas. TMB estimated that it would spend more than RM1 billion each year on the installation of fixed networks, of which 25 per cent would be allocated for the expansion of rural telecom. The objective was to increase the telephone penetration rate to over 50 per cent by the year 2005.

Although TMB had become a large national telecom company, it lacked the expertise and technology to undertake massive infrastructure projects. In most cases, the local telecom companies would be invited to submit their bids for a particular contract. It was also common for these local companies to form partnerships with large multinational corporations (MNCs), mainly for technological support. For example, Pernas–NEC, a JV company between Pernas Holdings and NEC, was one of the companies that had been successful in securing large telecom contracts from the Malaysian authorities.

Nora's Search for a JV Partner

In October 2002, TMB called for tenders to bid on a five-year project worth RM2 billion for installing digital switching exchanges in various parts of the country. The project also involved replacing analog circuit switches with digital switches. Digital switches enhanced transmission capabilities of telephone lines, increasing capacity to approximately two million bits per second compared to the 9,600 bits per second on analog circuits.

Nora was interested in securing a share of the RM2 billion contract from TMB and more importantly, in acquiring the knowledge in switching technology from its partnership with a telecom MNC. During the initial stages, when Nora first began to consider potential partners in the bid for this contract, telecom MNCs such as Siemens, Alcatel, and Fujitsu seemed appropriate candidates. Nora had previously entered into a five-year technical assistance agreement with Siemens to manufacture telephone handsets.

Nora also had the experience of a long-term working relationship with Japanese partners which would prove valuable should a JV be formed with Fujitsu. Alcatel was another potential partner, but the main concern at Nora was that the technical standards used in the French technology were not compatible with the British standards already

[4]RM is Ringgit Malaysia, the Malaysian currency. As at December 31, 2002, US$1 = RM3.80.

adopted in Malaysia. NEC and Ericsson were not considered, as they were already involved with other local competitors and were the current suppliers of digital switching exchanges to TMB. Their five-year contracts were due to expire soon.

Subsequent to Zainal's meeting with Mattsson, he decided to consider Sakari as a serious potential partner. He was briefed about Sakari's SK33, a digital switching system that was based on an open architecture, which enabled the use of standard components, standard software development tools, and standard software languages. Unlike the switching exchanges developed by NEC and Ericsson which required the purchase of components developed by the parent companies, the SK33 used components that were freely available in the open market. The system was also modular, and its software could be upgraded to provide new services and could interface easily with new equipment in the network. This was the most attractive feature of the SK33 as it would lead to the development of new switching systems.

Mattsson had also convinced Zainal and other Nora managers that although Sakari was a relatively small player in fixed networks, these networks were easily adaptable, and could cater to large exchanges in the urban areas as well as small ones for rural needs. Apparently Sakari's smaller size, compared to that of some of the other MNCs, was an added strength because Sakari was prepared to work out customized products according to Nora's needs. Large telecom companies were alleged to be less willing to provide custom-made products. Instead, they tended to offer standard products that, in some aspects, were not consistent with the needs of the customer.

Prior to the July meeting, at least 20 meetings had been held either in KL or in Helsinki to establish relationships between the two companies. It was estimated that each side had invested not less than RM3 million in promoting the relationship. Mattsson and Ilkka Junttila, Sakari's representative in KL, were the key people in bringing the two companies together. (See Exhibits 1 and 2 for brief background information on Malaysia and Finland respectively.)

Nora Holdings Sdn Bhd

The Company   Nora was one of the leading companies in the telecom industry in Malaysia. It was established in 1975 with a paid-up capital of RM2 million. Last year, the company recorded a turnover of RM320 million. Nora Holdings consisted of 30 subsidiaries, including two public-listed companies: Multiphone Bhd, and Nora Telecommunications Bhd. Nora had 3,081 employees, of which 513 were categorized as managerial (including 244 engineers) and 2,568 as non-managerial (including 269 engineers and technicians).

The Cable Business   Since the inception of the company, Nora had secured two cable-laying projects. For the latter project worth RM500 million, Nora formed a JV with two Japanese companies, Sumitomo Electric Industries Ltd (held 10 per cent equity share) and Marubeni Corporation (held five per cent equity share). Japanese partners were chosen in view of the availability of a financial package that came together with the technological assistance needed by Nora. Nora also acquired a 63 per cent stake in a local cable-laying company, Selangor Cables Sdn Bhd.

The Telephone Business   Nora had become a household name in Malaysia as a telephone manufacturer. It started in 1980 when the company obtained a contract to supply telephone sets to the government-owned Telecom authority, TMB, which would distribute the sets to telephone subscribers on a rental basis. The contract, estimated at RM130 million, lasted for 15 years. In 1985 Nora secured licenses from Siemens and Nortel to manufacture telephone handsets and had subsequently developed Nora's own telephone sets—the N300S (single line), N300M (micro-computer controlled), and N300V (hands-free, voice-activated) models.

Upon expiry of the 15-year contract as a supplier of telephone sets to the TMB, Nora suffered a major setback when it lost a RM32 million contract to supply 600,000 N300S single-line telephones. The contract was instead given to a Taiwanese manufacturer, Formula Electronics, which quoted a lower

---

Exhibit 1   Malaysia: Background Information

Malaysia is centrally located in South-east Asia. It consists of Peninsular Malaysia, bordered by Thailand in the north and Singapore in the south, and the states of Sabah and Sarawak on the island of Borneo. Malaysia has a total land area of about 330,000 square kilometres, of which 80 per cent is covered with tropical rainforest. Malaysia has an equatorial climate with high humidity and high daily temperatures of about 26 degrees Celsius throughout the year.

In 2000, Malaysia's population was 22 million, of which approximately nine million made up the country's labour force. The population is relatively young, with 42 per cent between the ages of 15 and 39 and only 7 per cent above the age of 55. A Malaysian family has an average of four children and extended families are common. Kuala Lumpur, the capital city of Malaysia, has approximately 1.5 million inhabitants.

The population is multiracial; the largest ethnic group is the Bumiputeras (the Malays and other indigenous groups such as the Ibans in Sarawak and Kadazans in Sabah), followed by the Chinese and Indians. Bahasa Malaysia is the national language but English is widely used in business circles. Other major languages spoken included various Chinese dialects and Tamil.

Islam is the official religion but other religions (mainly Christianity, Buddhism and Hinduism) are widely practised. Official holidays are allocated for the celebration of Eid, Christmas, Chinese New Year and Deepavali. All Malays are Muslims, followers of the Islamic faith.

During the period of British rule, secularism was introduced to the country, which led to the separation of the Islamic religion from daily life. In the late 1970s and 1980s, realizing the negative impact of secularism on the life of the Muslims, several groups of devout Muslims undertook efforts to reverse the process, emphasizing a dynamic and progressive approach to Islam. As a result, changes were introduced to meet the daily needs of Muslims. Islamic banking and insurance facilities were introduced and prayer rooms were provided in government offices, private companies, factories, and even in shopping complexes.

Malaysia is a parliamentary democracy under a constitutional monarchy. The Yang DiPertuan Agung (the king) is the supreme head, and appoints the head of the ruling political party to be the prime minister. In 2000 the Barisan Nasional, a coalition of several political parties representing various ethnic groups, was the ruling political party in Malaysia. Its predominance had contributed not only to the political stability and economic progress of the country in the last two decades, but also to the fast recovery from the 1997 Asian economic crisis.

The recession of the mid 1980s led to structural changes in the Malaysian economy which had been too dependent on primary commodities (rubber, tin, palm oil and timber) and had a very narrow export base. To promote the establishment of export-oriented industries, the government directed resources to the manufacturing sector, introduced generous incentives and relaxed foreign equity restrictions. In the meantime, heavy investments were made to modernize the country's infrastructure. These moves led to rapid economic growth in the late 1980s and early 1990s. The growth had been mostly driven by exports, particularly of electronics.

The Malaysian economy was hard hit by the 1997 Asian economic crisis. However, Malaysia was the fastest country to recover from the crisis after declining IMF assistance. It achieved this by pegging its currency to the USD, restricting outflow of money from the country, banning illegal overseas derivative trading of Malaysian securities and setting up asset management companies to facilitate the orderly recovery of bad loans. The real GDP growth rate in 1999 and 2000 were 5.4% and 8.6%, respectively (Table 1).

Malaysia was heavily affected by the global economic downturn and the slump in the IT sector in 2001 and 2002 due to its export-based economy. GDP in 2001 grew only 0.4% due to an 11% decrease in exports. A US $1.9 billion fiscal stimulus package helped the country ward off the worst of the recession and the GDP growth rate rebounded to 4.2% in 2002 (Table 1). A relatively small foreign debt and adequate foreign exchange reserves make a crisis similar to the 1997 one unlikely. Nevertheless, the economy remains vulnerable to a more protracted slowdown in the U.S. and Japan, top export destinations and key sources of foreign investment.

(continued)

Exhibit 1 *(concluded)*

Table 1 Malaysian Economic Performance 1999 to 2002

Economic Indicator	1999	2000	2001	2002
GDP per capita (US$)	3,596	3,680	3,678	3,814
Real GDP growth rate	5.4%	8.6%	0.4%	4.2%
Consumer price inflation	2.8%	1.6%	1.4%	1.8%
Unemployment rate	3.0%	3.0%	3.7%	3.5%

Source: IMD, various years, "The World Competitiveness Report."

In 2002, the manufacturing sector was the leading contributor to the economy, accounting for about 30 per cent of gross national product (GDP). Malaysia's major trading partners are United States, Singapore, Japan, China, Taiwan, Hong Kong and Korea.

Sources: Ernst & Young International, 1993, "Doing Business in Malaysia"; other online sources.

Exhibit 2 Finland: Background Information

Finland is situated in the north-east of Europe, sharing borders with Sweden, Norway and the former Soviet Union. About 65 per cent of its area of 338,000 square kilometres is covered with forest, about 15 per cent lakes and about 10 per cent arable land. Finland has a temperate climate with four distinct seasons. In Helsinki, the capital city, July is the warmest month with average mid-day temperature of 21 degrees Celsius and January is the coldest month with average mid-day temperature of –3 degrees Celsius.

Finland is one of the most sparsely populated countries in Europe with a 2002 population of 5.2 million, 60 per cent of whom lived in the urban areas. Helsinki had a population of about 560,000 in 2002. Finland has a well-educated work force of about 2.3 million. About half of the work force are engaged in providing services, 30 per cent in manufacturing and construction, and eight per cent in agricultural production. The small size of the population has led to scarce and expensive labour. Thus Finland had to compete by exploiting its lead in high-tech industries.

Finland's official languages are Finnish and Swedish, although only 6 per cent of the population speaks Swedish. English is the most widely spoken foreign language. About 87 per cent of the Finns are Lutherans and about one per cent Finnish Orthodox.

Finland has been an independent republic since 1917, having previously been ruled by Sweden and Russia. A president is elected to a six-year term, and a 200-member, single-chamber parliament is elected every four years.

In 1991, the country experienced a bad recession triggered by a sudden drop in exports due to the collapse of the Soviet Union. During 1991–1993, the total output suffered a 10% contraction and unemployment rate reached almost 20%. Finnish Markka experienced a steep devaluation in 1991–1992, which gave Finland cost competitiveness in the international market.

With this cost competitiveness and the recovery of Western export markets the Finnish economy underwent a rapid revival in 1993, followed by a new period of healthy growth. Since the mid 1990s the Finnish growth has mainly been bolstered by intense growth in telecommunications equipment manufacturing. The Finnish economy peaked in the year 2000 with a real GDP growth rate of 5.6% (Table 2).

Finland was one of the 11 countries that joined the Economic and Monetary Union (EMU) on January 1, 1999. Finland has been experiencing a rapidly increasing integration with Western Europe. Membership in the EMU

(continued)

Exhibit 2   *(concluded)*

Table 2   Finnish Economic Performance 1999 to 2002

Economic Indicator	1999	2000	2001	2002
GDP per capita (US$)	24,430	23,430	23,295	25,303
Real GDP growth rate	3.7%	5.6%	0.4%	1.6%
Consumer price inflation	1.2%	3.3%	2.6%	1.6%
Unemployment	10.3%	9.6%	9.1%	9.1%

Source: IMD, various years, "The World Competitiveness Report."

provides the Finnish economy with an array of benefits, such as lower and stable interest rates, elimination of foreign currency risk within the Euro area, reduction of transaction costs of business and travel, and so forth. This provided Finland with a credibility that it lacked before accession and the Finnish economy has become more predictable. This will have a long-term positive effect on many facets of the economy.

Finland's economic structure is based on private ownership and free enterprise. However, the production of alcoholic beverages and spirits is retained as a government monopoly. Finland's major trading partners are Sweden, Germany, the former Soviet Union and United Kingdom.

Finland's standard of living is among the highest in the world. The Finns have small families with one or two children per family. They have comfortable homes in the cities and one in every three families has countryside cottages near a lake where they retreat on weekends. Taxes are high, the social security system is efficient and poverty is virtually non-existent.

Until recently, the stable trading relationship with the former Soviet Union and other Scandinavian countries led to few interactions between the Finns and people in other parts of the world. The Finns are described as rather reserved, obstinate, and serious people. A Finn commented, "We do not engage easily in small talk with strangers. Furthermore, we have a strong love for nature and we have the tendency to be silent as we observe our surroundings. Unfortunately, others tend to view such behaviour as cold and serious." Visitors to Finland are often impressed by the efficient public transport system, the clean and beautiful city of Helsinki with orderly road networks, scenic parks and lakefronts, museums, cathedrals, and churches.

Sources: Ernst & Young International, 1993, "Doing Business in Finland"; other online sources.

price of RM37 per handset compared to Nora's RM54. Subsequently, Nora was motivated to move towards the high end feature phone domestic market. The company sold about 3,000 sets of feature phones per month, capturing the high-end segment of the Malaysian market.

Nora had ventured into the export market with its feature phones, but industry observers predicted that Nora still had a long way to go as an exporter. The foreign markets were very competitive and many manufacturers already had well-established brands.

The Payphone Business   Nora's start-up in the payphone business had turned out to be one of the company's most profitable lines of business. Other than the cable-laying contract secured in 1980, Nora had a 15-year contract to install, operate and maintain payphones in the cities and major towns in Malaysia. In 1997, Nora started to manufacture card payphones under a license from GEC Plessey Telecommunications (GPT) of the United Kingdom. The agreement had also permitted Nora to sell the products to the neighbouring countries in South-east Asia as well as to eight other markets approved by GPT.

While the payphone revenues were estimated to be as high as RM60 million a year, a long-term and stable income stream for Nora, profit margins were only about 10 per cent because of the high investment and maintenance costs.

Other Businesses   Nora was also the sole Malaysian distributor for Nortel's private automatic branch exchange (PABX) and NEC's mobile telephone sets. It was also an Apple computer distributor in Malaysia and Singapore. In addition, Nora was involved in: distributing radio-related equipment; supplying equipment to the broadcasting, meteorological, civil aviation, postal and power authorities; and manufacturing automotive parts (such as the suspension coil, springs, and piston) for the local automobile companies.

The Management   When Nora was established, Osman Jaafar, founder and chairman of Nora Holdings, managed the company with his wife, Nora Asyikin Yusof, and seven employees. Osman was known as a conservative businessman who did not like to dabble in acquisitions and mergers to make quick capital gains. He was formerly an electrical engineer who was trained in the United Kingdom and had held several senior positions at the national Telecom Department in Malaysia.

Osman subsequently recruited Zainal Hashim to fill in the position of deputy managing director at Nora. Zainal held a master's degree in microwave communications from a British university and had several years of working experience as a production engineer at Pernas–NEC Sdn Bhd, a manufacturer of transmission equipment. Zainal was later promoted to the position of managing director and six years later, the vice-chairman.

Industry analysts observed that Nora's success was attributed to the complementary roles, trust, and mutual understanding between Osman and Zainal. While Osman "likes to fight for new business opportunities," Zainal preferred a low profile and concentrated on managing Nora's operations.

Industry observers also speculated that Osman, a former civil servant and an entrepreneur, was close to Malaysian politicians, notably the Prime Minister, while Zainal had been a close friend of the Finance Minister. Zainal disagreed with allegations

that Nora had succeeded due to its close relationships with Malaysian politicians. However, he acknowledged that such perceptions in the industry had been beneficial to the company.

Osman and Zainal had an obsession for high-tech and made the development of research and development (R&D) skills and resources a priority in the company. About one per cent of Nora's earnings was ploughed back into R&D activities. Although this amount was considered small by international standards, Nora planned to increase it gradually to five to six per cent over the next two to three years. Zainal said:

> We believe in making improvements in small steps, similar to the Japanese *kaizen* principle. Over time, each small improvement could lead to a major creation. To be able to make improvements, we must learn from others. Thus we would borrow a technology from others, but eventually, we must be able to develop our own to sustain our competitiveness in the industry. As a matter of fact, Sakari's SK33 system was developed based on a technology it obtained from Alcatel.

To further enhance R&D activities at Nora, Nora Research Sdn Bhd (NRSB), a wholly-owned subsidiary, was formed, and its R&D department was absorbed into this new company. NRSB operated as an independent research company undertaking R&D activities for Nora as well as private clients in related fields. The company facilitated R&D activities with other companies as well as government organizations, research institutions, and universities. NRSB, with its staff of 40 technicians/engineers, would charge a fixed fee for basic research and a royalty for its products sold by clients.

Zainal was also active in instilling and promoting Islamic values among the Malay employees at Nora. He explained:

> Islam is a way of life and there is no such thing as Islamic management. The Islamic values, which must be reflected in the daily life of Muslims, would influence their behaviours as employers and employees. Our Malay managers, however, were often influenced by their western counterparts, who tend to stress knowledge and mental capability and often forget the effectiveness of the softer side of management which emphasizes relationships, sincerity and consistency.

I believe that one must always be sincere to be able to develop good working relationships.

Sakari Oy

Sakari was established in 1865 as a pulp and paper mill located about 200 kilometres northwest of Helsinki, the capital city of Finland. In the 1960s, Sakari started to expand into the rubber and cable industries when it merged with the Finnish Rubber Works and Finnish Cable Works. In 1973 Sakari's performance was badly affected by the oil crisis, as its businesses were largely energy-intensive.

However, in 1975, the company recovered when Aatos Olkkola took over as Sakari's president. He led Sakari into competitive businesses such as computers, consumer electronics, and cellular phones via a series of acquisitions, mergers and alliances. Companies involved in the acquisitions included: the consumer electronics division of Standard Elektrik Lorenz AG; the data systems division of L.M. Ericsson; Vantala, a Finnish manufacturer of colour televisions; and Luxury, a Swedish state-owned electronics and computer concern.

In 1979, a JV between Sakari and Vantala, Sakari–Vantala, was set up to develop and manufacture mobile telephones. Sakari–Vantala had captured about 14 per cent of the world's market share for mobile phones and held a 20 per cent market share in Europe for its mobile phone handsets. Outside Europe, a 50–50 JV was formed with Tandy Corporation which, to date, had made significant sales in the United States, Malaysia and Thailand.

Sakari first edged into the telecom market by selling switching systems licensed from France's Alcatel and by developing the software and systems to suit the needs of small Finnish phone companies. Sakari had avoided head-on competition with Siemens and Ericsson by not trying to enter the market for large telephone networks. Instead, Sakari had concentrated on developing dedicated telecom networks for large private users such as utility and railway companies. In Finland, Sakari held 40 per cent of the market for digital exchanges. Other competitors included Ericsson (34 per cent), Siemens (25 per cent), and Alcatel (one per cent).

Sakari was also a niche player in the global switching market. Its SK33 switches had sold well in countries such as Sri Lanka, United Arab Emirates, China and the Soviet Union. A derivative of the SK33 main exchange switch called the SK33XT was subsequently developed to be used in base stations for cellular networks and personal paging systems.

Sakari attributed its emphasis on R&D as its key success factor in the telecom industry. Strong in-house R&D in core competence areas enabled the company to develop technology platforms such as its SK33 system that were reliable, flexible, widely compatible and economical. About 17 per cent of its annual sales revenue was invested into R&D and product development units in Finland, United Kingdom and France. Sakari's current strategy was to emphasize global operations in production and R&D. It planned to set up R&D centres in leading markets, including South-east Asia.

Sakari was still a small company by international standards (see Exhibit 3 for a list of the world's major telecom equipment suppliers). It lacked a strong marketing capability and had to rely on JVs such as the one with Tandy Corporation to enter the world market, particularly the United States. In its efforts to develop market position quickly, Sakari had to accept lower margins for its products, and often the Sakari name was not revealed on the product. In recent years, Sakari decided to emerge from its hiding place as a manufacturer's manufacturer and began marketing under the Sakari name.

In 1989 Mikko Koskinen took over as president of Sakari. Koskinen announced that telecommunications, computers, and consumer electronics would be maintained as Sakari's core business, and that he would continue Olkkola's efforts in expanding the company overseas. He believed that every European company needed global horizons to be able to meet global competition for future survival. To do so, he envisaged the setting up of alliances of varying duration, each designed for specific purposes. He said, "Sakari has become an interesting partner with which to cooperate on an equal footing in the areas of R&D, manufacturing and marketing."

Exhibit 3   Ten Major Telecommunication Equipment Vendors

Rank	Company	Country	1998 Telecom Equipment Sales (US$ billions)
1	Lucent	USA	26.8
2	Ericsson	Sweden	21.5
3	Alcatel	France	20.9
4	Motorola	USA	20.5
5	Nortel	Canada	17.3
6	Siemens	Germany	16.8
7	Nokia	Finland	14.7
8	NEC	Japan	12.6
9	Cisco	USA	8.4
10	Hughes	USA	5.7

Source: International Telecommunication Union, 1999, Top 20 Telecommunication Equipment Vendors 1998. http://www.itu.int/ITU-D/ict/statistics/at_glance/Top2098.html.

The recession in Finland which began in 1990 led Sakari's group sales to decline substantially from FIM22 billion[5] in 1990 to FIM15 billion in 1991. The losses were attributed to two main factors: weak demand for Sakari's consumer electronic products, and trade with the Soviet Union which had come to almost a complete standstill. Consequently Sakari began divesting its less profitable companies within the basic industries (metal, rubber, and paper), as well as leaving the troubled European computer market with the sale of its computer subsidiary, Sakari Macro. The company's new strategy was to focus on three main areas: telecom systems and mobile phones in a global framework, consumer electronic products in Europe, and deliveries of cables and related technology. The company's divestment strategy led to a reduction of Sakari's employees from about 41,000 in 1989 to 29,000 in 1991. This series of major strategic moves was accompanied by major leadership succession. In June 1992, Koskinen retired as Sakari's President and was replaced by Visa Ketonen,

formerly the President of Sakari Mobile Phones. Ketonen appointed Ossi Kuusisto as Sakari's vice-president.

After Ketonen took over control, the Finnish economy went through a rapid revival in 1993, followed by a new period of intense growth. Since the mid 1990s the Finnish growth had been bolstered by intense growth in telecommunications equipment manufacturing as a result of an exploding global telecommunications market. Sakari capitalized on this opportunity and played a major role in the Finnish telecommunications equipment manufacturing sector.

In 2001, Sakari was Finland's largest publicly-traded industrial company and derived the majority of its total sales from exports and overseas operations. Traditionally, the company's export sales were confined to other Scandinavian countries, Western Europe and the former Soviet Union. However, in recent years, the company made efforts and succeeded in globalizing and diversifying its operations to make the most of its high-tech capabilities. As a result, Sakari emerged as a more influential player in the international market and had gained international brand recognition. One of Sakari's strategies was to form JVs to enter new foreign markets.

[5]FIM is Finnish Markka, the Finnish currency until January 1, 1999. Markka coins and notes were not withdrawn from circulation until January 1, 2002, when Finland fully converted to the Euro. As at December 31, 2000, US$1 = FIM6.31, and €1 = FIM5.95.

The Nora–Sakari Negotiation

Nora and Sakari had discussed the potential of forming a JV company in Malaysia for more than two years. Nora engineers were sent to Helsinki to assess the SK33 technology in terms of its compatibility with the Malaysian requirements, while Sakari managers travelled to KL mainly to assess both Nora's capability in manufacturing switching exchanges and the feasibility of gaining access to the Malaysian market.

In January 2003, Nora submitted its bid for TMB's RM2 billion contract to supply digital switching exchanges supporting four million telephone lines. Assuming the Nora–Sakari JV would materialize, Nora based its bid on supplying Sakari's digital switching technology. Nora competed with seven other companies short listed by TMB, all offering their partners' technology—Alcatel, Lucent, Fujitsu, Siemens, Ericsson, NEC, and Samsung. In early May, TMB announced five successful companies in the bid. They were companies using technology from Alcatel, Fujitsu, Ericsson, NEC, and Sakari. Each company was awarded one-fifth share of the RM2 billion contract and would be responsible for delivering 800,000 telephone lines over a period of five years. Industry observers were critical of TMB's decision to select Sakari and Alcatel. Sakari was perceived to be the least capable of supplying the necessary lines to meet TMB's requirements, as it was alleged to be a small company with little international exposure. Alcatel was criticized for having the potential of supplying an obsolete technology.

The May 21 Meeting   Following the successful bid and ignoring the criticisms against Sakari, Nora and Sakari held a major meeting in Helsinki on May 21 to finalize the formation of the JV. Zainal led Nora's five-member negotiation team which comprised Nora's general manager for corporate planning division, an accountant, two engineers, and Marina Mohamed, a lawyer. One of the engineers was Salleh Lindstrom who was of Swedish origin, a Muslim and had worked for Nora for almost 10 years.

Sakari's eight-member team was led by Kuusisto, Sakari's vice-president. His team comprised Junttila, Hussein Ghazi, Aziz Majid, three engineers, and Julia Ruola (a lawyer). Ghazi was Sakari's senior manager who was of Egyptian origin and also a Muslim who had worked for Sakari for more than 20 years while Aziz, a Malay, had been Sakari's manager for more than 12 years.

The meeting went on for several days. The main issue raised at the meeting was Nora's capability in penetrating the South-east Asian market. Other issues included Sakari's concerns over the efficiency of Malaysian workers in the JV in manufacturing the product, maintaining product quality and ensuring prompt deliveries.

Commenting on the series of negotiations with Sakari, Zainal said that this was the most difficult negotiation he had ever experienced. Zainal was Nora's most experienced negotiator and had single-handedly represented Nora in several major negotiations for the past 10 years. In the negotiation with Sakari, Zainal admitted making the mistake of approaching the negotiation applying the approach he often used when negotiating with his counterparts from companies based in North America or the United Kingdom. He said:

> Negotiators from the United States tend to be very open and often state their positions early and definitively. They are highly verbal and usually prepare well-planned presentations. They also often engage in small talk and "joke around" with us at the end of a negotiation. In contrast, the Sakari negotiators tend to be very serious, reserved and "cold." They are also relatively less verbal and do not convey much through their facial expressions. As a result, it was difficult for us to determine whether they are really interested in the deal or not.

Zainal said that the negotiation on May 21 turned out to be particularly difficult when Sakari became interested in bidding a recently-announced tender for a major telecom contract in the United Kingdom. Internal politics within Sakari led to the formation of two opposing "camps." One "camp" held a strong belief that there would be very high growth in the Asia-Pacific region and that the JV company in

Malaysia was seen as a hub to enter these markets. Although the Malaysian government had liberalized its equity ownership restrictions and allowed the formation of wholly-owned subsidiaries, JVs were still an efficient way to enter the Malaysian market for a company that lacked local knowledge. This group was represented mostly by Sakari's managers positioned in Asia and engineers who had made several trips to Malaysia, which usually included visits to Nora's facilities. They also had the support of Sakari's vice-president, Kuusisto, who was involved in most of the meetings with Nora, particularly when Zainal was present. Kuusisto had also made efforts to be present at meetings held in KL. This group also argued that Nora had already obtained the contract in Malaysia whereas the chance of getting the U.K. contract was quite low in view of the intense competition prevailing in that market.

The "camp" not in favour of the Nora–Sakari JV believed that Sakari should focus its resources on entering the United Kingdom, which could be used as a hub to penetrate the European Union (EU) market. There was also the belief that Europe was closer to home, making management easier, and that problems arising from cultural differences would be minimized. This group was also particularly concerned that Nora had the potential of copying Sakari's technology and eventually becoming a strong regional competitor. Also, because the U.K. market was relatively "familiar" and Sakari had local knowledge, Sakari could set up a wholly-owned subsidiary instead of a JV company and consequently, avoid JV-related problems such as joint control, joint profits, and leakage of technology.

Zainal felt that the lack of full support from Sakari's management led to a difficult negotiation when new misgivings arose concerning Nora's capability to deliver its part of the deal. It was apparent that the group in favour of the Nora–Sakari JV was under pressure to further justify its proposal and provide counterarguments against the U.K. proposal. A Sakari manager explained, "We are tempted to pursue both proposals since each has its own strengths, but our current resources are very limited. Thus a choice has to made, and soon."

The July 8 Meeting   Another meeting to negotiate the JV agreement was scheduled for July 8. Sakari's eight-member team arrived in KL on Sunday afternoon of July 7, and was met at the airport by the key Nora managers involved in the negotiation. Kuusisto did not accompany the Sakari team at this meeting.

The negotiation started early Monday morning at Nora's headquarters and continued for the next five days, with each day's meeting ending late in the evening. Members of the Nora team were the same members who had attended the May 21 meeting in Finland, except Zainal, who did not participate. The Sakari team was also represented by the same members in attendance at the previous meeting plus a new member, Solail Pekkarinen, Sakari's senior accountant. Unfortunately, on the third day of the negotiation, the Nora team requested that Sakari ask Pekkarinen to leave the negotiation. He was perceived as extremely arrogant and insensitive to the local culture, which tended to value modesty and diplomacy. Pekkarinen left for Helsinki the following morning.

Although Zainal had decided not to participate actively in the negotiations, he followed the process closely and was briefed by his negotiators regularly. Some of the issues which they complained were difficult to resolve had often led to heated arguments between the two negotiating teams. These included:

1. Equity Ownership   In previous meetings both companies agreed to form the JV company with a paid-up capital of RM5 million. However, they disagreed on the equity share proposed by each side. Sakari proposed an equity split in the JV company of 49 per cent for Sakari and 51 per cent for Nora. Nora, on the other hand, proposed a 30 per cent Sakari and 70 per cent Nora split. Nora's proposal was based on the common practice in Malaysia as a result of historical foreign equity regulations set by the Malaysian government that allowed a maximum of 30 per cent foreign equity ownership unless the company would export a certain percentage of its products. Though these regulations were liberalized by the Malaysian government effective from July 1998 and new regulations had replaced the old ones, the 30–70 foreign–Malaysian ownership divide was still commonly observed.

Equity ownership became a major issue as it was associated with control over the JV company. Sakari was concerned about its ability to control the accessibility of its technology to Nora and about decisions concerning the activities of the JV as a whole. The lack of control was perceived by Sakari as an obstacle to protecting its interests. Nora also had similar concerns about its ability to exert control over the JV because it was intended as a key part of Nora's long-term strategy to develop its own digital switching exchanges and related high-tech products.

2. Technology Transfer   Sakari proposed to provide the JV company with the basic structure of the digital switch. The JV company would assemble the switching exchanges at the JV plant and subsequently install the exchanges in designated locations identified by TMB. By offering Nora only the basic structure of the switch, the core of Sakari's switching technology would still be well-protected.

On the other hand, Nora proposed that the basic structure of the switch be developed at the JV company in order to access the root of the switching technology. Based on Sakari's proposal, Nora felt that only the technical aspects in assembling and installing the exchanges would be obtained. This was perceived as another "screw-driver" form of technology transfer while the core of the technology associated with making the switches would still be unknown.

3. Royalty Payment   Closely related to the issue of technology transfer was the payment of a royalty for the technology used in building the switches. Sakari proposed a royalty payment of five per cent of the JV gross sales while Nora proposed a payment of two per cent of net sales.

Nora considered the royalty rate of five per cent too high because it would affect Nora's financial situation as a whole. Financial simulations prepared by Nora's managers indicated that Nora's return on investment would be less than the desired 10 per cent if royalty rates exceeded three per cent of net sales. This

was because Nora had already agreed to make large additional investments in support of the JV. Nora would invest in a building which would be rented to the JV company to accommodate an office and the switching plant. Nora would also invest in another plant which would supply the JV with surface mounted devices (SMD), one of the major components needed to build the switching exchanges.

An added argument raised by the Nora negotiators in support of a two per cent royalty was that Sakari would receive side benefits from the JV's access to Japanese technology used in the manufacture of the SMD components. Apparently the Japanese technology was more advanced than Sakari's present technology.

4. Expatriates' Salaries and Perks   To allay Sakari's concerns over Nora's level of efficiency, Nora suggested that Sakari provide the necessary training for the JV technical employees. Subsequently, Sakari had agreed to provide eight engineering experts for the JV company on two types of contracts, short-term and long-term. Experts employed on a short-term basis would be paid a daily rate of US$1260 plus travel/accommodation. The permanent experts would be paid a monthly salary of US$20,000. Three permanent experts would be attached to the JV company once it was established and the number would gradually be reduced to only one, after two years. Five experts would be available on a short-term basis to provide specific training needs for durations of not more than three months each year.

The Nora negotiation team was appalled at the exorbitant amount proposed by the Sakari negotiators. They were surprised that the Sakari team had not surveyed the industry rates, as the Japanese and other western negotiators would normally have done. Apparently Sakari had not taken into consideration the relatively low cost of living in Malaysia compared to Finland. In 2000, though the average monthly rent for a comfortable, unfurnished three-bedroom apartment was about the same (US$660) in Helsinki and Kuala Lumpur, the cost of living was considerably lower in KL. The cost of living index (New York = 100) of a basket of goods in major cities, excluding housing, for Malaysia was only 83.75, compared to 109.84 for Finland.[6]

In response to Sakari's proposal, Nora negotiators adopted an unusual "take-it or leave-it" stance. They deemed the following proposal reasonable in view of the comparisons made with other JVs which Nora had entered into with other foreign parties:

Permanent experts' monthly salary ranges to be paid by the JV company were as follows:

1. Senior expert (seven to 10 years experience) RM24,300–RM27,900.
2. Expert (four to six years experience) RM22,500–RM25,200.
3. Junior expert (two to three years experience) RM20,700–RM23,400.
4. Any Malaysian income taxes payable would be added to the salaries.
5. A car for personal use.
6. Annual paid vacation of five weeks.
7. Return flight tickets to home country once a year for the whole family of married persons and twice a year for singles according to Sakari's general scheme.
8. Any expenses incurred during official travelling.

Temporary experts are persons invited by the JV company for various technical assistance tasks and would not be granted residence status. They would be paid the following fees:

1. Senior expert RM1,350 per working day.
2. Expert RM1,170 per working day.
3. The JV company would not reimburse the following:
   • Flight tickets between Finland (or any other country) and Malaysia.
   • Hotel or any other form of accommodation.
   • Local transportation.

In defense of their proposed rates, Sakari's negotiators argued that the rates presented by Nora were too low. Sakari suggested that Nora's negotiators take into consideration the fact that Sakari would have to subsidize the difference between the experts' present salaries and the amount paid by the JV company. A large difference would require that large amounts of subsidy payments be made to the affected employees.

5. Arbitration   Another major issue discussed in the negotiation was related to arbitration. While both parties agreed to an arbitration process in the event of future disputes, they disagreed on the location for dispute resolution. Because Nora would be the majority stakeholder in the JV company, Nora insisted that any arbitration should take place in KL. Sakari, however, insisted on Helsinki, following the norm commonly practised by the company.

At the end of the five-day negotiation, many issues could not be resolved. While Nora could agree on certain matters after consulting Zainal, the Sakari team, representing a large private company, had to refer contentious items to the company board before it could make any decision that went beyond the limits authorized by the board.

The Decision

Zainal sat down at his desk, read through the minutes of the negotiation thoroughly, and was disappointed that an agreement had not yet been reached. He was concerned about the commitment Nora had made to TMB when Nora was awarded the switching contract. Nora would be expected to fulfill the contract soon but had yet to find a partner to provide the switching technology. It was foreseeable that companies such as Siemens, Samsung and Lucent, which had failed in the bid, could still be potential partners. However, Zainal had also not rejected the possibility of a reconciliation with Sakari. He could start by contacting Kuusisto in Helsinki. But should he?

[6]IMD & World Economic Forum, 2001, "The World Competitiveness Report."

Case 6-2   Renault/Nissan: The Making of a Global Alliance

Renault's Point of View

Geneva, March 3, 1999. International Motor Show   As a traditional get-together for the leading automobile manufacturers, the Geneva International Motor Show provides an opportunity to unveil new prototypes and gauge market trends. This year, however, conversations in the main hall of the exhibition focused as much on the strategic movements of international companies as on products. For since the start of the year, major manœuvres had been under way to form an alliance with Nissan, Japan's second-biggest manufacturer, and they had to be finalised before March 30, which marks the end of the tax year in Japan.

Two candidates were in the ring. In one corner, the French group Renault, the world's ninth-largest manufacturer with 4.3% of the market, which had been negotiating with Nissan for more than 10 months; in the other, German-American giant DaimlerChrysler, the fifth-largest manufacturer with 8.4% of the world market, which began taking an interest in December 1998.

The cases were written by:

EM LYON

Renault's point of view: Olivier Masclef, Doctoral Students; EM Lyon.

Nissan's point of view: LBS MBA students Naoko Hida and Ashok Krishnan (FT-2000), under the joint supervision of Professor Asakawa of Keio Business School, Professor Gomez of Lyon Business School and Professor Korine of London Business School. The financial support of the Strategic Leadership Research Programme at LBS, the *"Rodolphe Mérieux"* Foundation for Research in Venturing at EM Lyon, and overseas case development fund at Keio Business School are gratefully acknowledged.

The cases are based on interviews conducted in Paris and Tokyo during the Spring of 2000 with the following executives:

Renault's point of view: MM. Dassas *VP, finance* De Andria *VP, corporate planning,* Douin *EVP, Alliance coordinator* Husson *VP, legal* Levy *EVP, finance* Schweitzer *Chairman and CEO.*

Nissan's point of view: MM. Anraku, *managing director in charge of finance and accounting* Shiga, Sugino, Suzuki, *Nissan Corporate Planning,* Hanawa *Chairman and CEO.*

For Renault, it was a difficult bout. For a start, DaimlerChrysler's financial clout made it the favourite. Second, Renault's previous attempt to form such an alliance, with Swedish manufacturer Volvo six years earlier, had ended in a resounding defeat after years of negotiations. Daimler and Chrysler, on the other hand, had just rocked the automobile sector by pulling off a spectacular merger less than a year earlier. And an alliance with an Asian partner seemed a vital part of DaimlerChrysler's international strategy to complete the consolidation of a company with a strong presence in all three of the world's major economic centres.

Tension mounted with the arrival in Geneva of Jürgen Schremp, Co-Chairman of DaimlerChrysler, and Louis Schweitzer, Chairman and C.E.O. of the Renault Group. Everyone was certain that the future of Nissan would be decided in the days to come. Most economic observers were expecting to see a new giant formed: DaimlerChrysler-Nissan.

But Renault's bosses were convinced that the struggle was not yet over. Looking beyond superficial reasoning, they felt that the potential synergies between Renault and Nissan were greater than those between DaimlerChrysler and Nissan because they did not simply concern commercial and technological issues. Despite the size difference between the two rivals, Renault did have some noteworthy advantages. Was it a question of personal conviction or objective reasons? While only a few days were left to convince the Nissan executives, the force of Renault's arguments and the ability to communicate them had already been established by the relationship built up by the company's teams of negotiators over several months.

Renault's Strategic Alternative   In the spring of 1997, Georges Douin, Executive Vice President in charge of corporate strategy, had submitted an international development plan to Renault's

Management Committee, at the request of Louis Schweitzer. Major changes were taking place on the world automobile stage. A round of large-scale mergers had begun, with Volkswagen AG taking the initiative in Europe, but now the Asian slow-down called the Japanese car companies' potential into question, particularly regarding finance. New opportunities for international cooperation began to take shape. The shift towards the globalisation of the industry looked irreversible.

Against this background, the plan referred to the strengths and weaknesses of the Renault group, as well as its prospects for expansion. The company could choose between remaining a significant but restricted player in the European market, with a share of around 5% of the world market, or become a major player helping to define the rules of the game, which would mean winning 10% of market share worldwide and extending its product range. The second choice would mean a strategy of alliances with partners in the other main economic regions.

The collapse of a recently attempted merger with the Swedish group Volvo in 1993 had left its mark on the company. The operation, which had been the subject of extremely careful negotiations between February 1990 and December 1993, had been based on shared synergies between the two companies. It formed part of European industrial policy, and was encouraged by the authorities because Renault was owned by the French state. The industry minister had played a part in the negotiations and brought the country's political influence into the balance. Both partners were Europeans, with relatively close national cultures. After a long period of rapprochement, it was expected that Renault and Volvo would merge. The matter appeared to have been finalised when, in December 1993, Volvo shareholders voted against the agreement.

> "Our partner did not appreciate the strong involvement of the French state. For our part, there was also a lack of diplomacy and an over-eagerness to take control." (Mr Dassas, VP, Financial Operations)

So the merger never took place. Renault found itself thrown back five years in the race to gain international stature. As time went by, the need to come up with an alliance policy became more pressing. The plan put forward by Georges Douin stressed the need for the firm to position itself chiefly in the Asian market. One scenario introduced some potential partners, including Subaru, Mitsubishi, Suzuki and Nissan. Apart from Nissan, they were all smaller than Renault and therefore appeared to be within its reach, especially as the company had been privatised in 1996 and the French state now had only a 46% stake. Attitudes in France had changed significantly and the separation of political and economic influences was the order of the day. Renault could therefore count on its shareholders to give the management a totally free hand to implement its chosen strategy.

Louis Schweitzer weighed up the dangers and difficulties of the strategic choice that had to be made. Staying European meant condemning the company to obey the market rules imposed by the biggest firms, with perhaps a loss of independence in the long term due to inadequate resources. But failing once more to form an international alliance would be disastrous for Renault's credibility, not to mention the wasted effort and strategic and financial losses involved. Time was running out because opportunities for alliances were bound to become increasingly infrequent and hard to negotiate. The chairman made a decision: Renault's expansion would be international and would include an alliance in Asia. The plan was approved. But how should Renault set about finding the right partner?

Patient Prospecting   Renault had been keeping a close watch on the Asian market since the mid-1980s. Although it had not yet worked out an alliance policy, the group was monitoring opportunities and familiarising itself both with the Asian motor industry and with Asian negotiating methods. One man embodies that policy: Georges Douin, first as technical director, then as the person in charge of orchestrating Renault Group projects from 1992 to 1997. He is currently EVP, Product & Strategic Planning and International Operations.

"We must be constantly on the alert (. . .). It's true that the Renault-Nissan negotiations were brought to a conclusion in nine months—they took place between June 1998 and April 1999—but in fact they were based on a great deal of work behind the scenes by Renault, which was a pioneer in the field, as well as on a solid foundation of relations with the Japanese." (Georges Douin, EVP)

Between 1985 and 1995, therefore, contacts were occasional but continual. In 1987 Renault planned a research programme on diesel engines with Honda which never came to fruition. New relations were established in 1995 on other joint research projects. Around the same time talks were held with the Korean companies Daewoo and Samsung. Like the Japanese, the Korean companies were looking for ways to penetrate the European market, which was protected by quotas restricting imports of Asian vehicles, by forming alliances with local manufacturers. One particularly clear opportunity presented itself in 1993. One of the issues on the table during the ongoing talks between Volvo and Renault was what would happen to Volvo's partner Mitsubishi. The Renault teams, led by Georges Douin, went to Japan to evaluate potential synergies with the Japanese company, in what was a fresh opportunity to understand how the country's businesses worked and to make contacts with their executives.

"In the proposed alliance with Volvo, part of the Volvo 'package,' was Mitsubishi (. . .) I went to see them several times. They quickly took the decision to buy some Renault engines—that made our relations easier too—we sold diesel engines to Mitsubishi, we sold them gearboxes (. . .). So I was 'very Mitsubishi'" (Georges Douin, EVP)

However, relations with Mitsubishi were interrupted by the failure of the Renault–Volvo merger. Further contacts were made in 1996, with the Korean company Daewoo. All the possible synergies were discussed as well, but the talks ended abruptly after four months.

So Asia and Japan were not totally unknown territory to Renault when its international development plan was introduced. It was already familiar with the industry, and personal ties had been forged with its leaders. But restricted projects and continual failures showed that Asia was still a difficult market for European manufacturers to enter. Had Renault's strategic monitoring allowed it to build up sufficient experience for it to grasp the opportunity of an alliance when the time was right?

An Unexpected Hunt   After the international strategic plan was approved, a Renault delegation began to canvass Japanese companies in April 1998.

"I had been on an assignment to meet Japanese banks, and even Japanese motor industry analysts, to see how things were going for the country's manufacturers. I had seen four or five big international banks and met with automobile specialists (. . .). It was an exploratory mission, to see how many problems the Japanese motor industry had . . . and which Japanese manufacturers were most likely to be interested in alliances." (Mr Dassas, VP, Financial Operations)

Some Japanese manufacturers could be eliminated as potential partners very quickly. General Motors had a large stake in Suzuki, and Subaru offered few opportunities for synergies because of its technological originality. After the assignment, two companies stood out as the most likely candidates for an alliance: Mitsubishi and Nissan. Georges Douin went to Japan to look further into the opportunities for working with the two manufacturers. Mitsubishi looked like the favourite because of its size and its previous cooperation with Renault during the Volvo episode. Nissan seemed too big to be a potential partner. Nonetheless, the Renault delegation members were struck by the attentiveness of the Japanese representatives and the interest they showed for cooperating with the French.

"It was Renault that took the initiative of contacting them, which produced the very positive reaction that in a way surprised us at first (. . .). The surprise was to see that Nissan was perfectly willing to start talks with us." (Mr De Andria, VP, Strategic Planning)

So the names of the two potential partners were put to Mr Schweitzer. At around the same time, a major piece of news broke in the automobile industry: the merger between Daimler-Benz and Chrysler.

"Obviously, we were surprised by the Daimler-Chrysler merger in April–May 1998. Mr Schweitzer learned it from the press" (Georges Douin, EVP). "Daimler-Chrysler was a major shake-up. And it was against that background that the alliance was formed" (Mr De Andria, VP, Strategic Planning).

"Daimler-Chrysler was a shock in the automobile world, especially in France. We were aware that things were moving very quickly and that there were no taboos any more." (Mr Husson, VP, General Counsel)

The deal meant that globalisation suddenly speeded up, and therefore the need to make or grasp the best opportunities very quickly. In June 1998 DaimlerChrysler started negotiating with Nissan with a view to taking over the group's truck division, Nissan Diesel. Meanwhile, Louis Schweitzer wrote to the chairmen of Mitsubishi and Nissan outlining the terms of a possible partnership between Renault and each company.

"In June I wrote a letter saying *'I believe we should be thinking strategically. Can we do that together?'* Obviously, before writing that I had decided to take action should the opportunity present itself. I was ready to reach agreement on a system along the lines of the one we ended up with, in other words acquisition of a stake in the other company, and possibly a reciprocal one, which would not lead to a complete merger." (Louis Schweitzer, Chairman)

While Mitsubishi took a long time to get back to Renault, Nissan reacted quickly.

"Bankers came to see us saying: 'We know someone who can talk to someone who can talk to someone who can talk to Nissan, so we might be able to establish a relationship between you and Nissan in a few months. But of course if you write to them, that's the best way to make sure of failure because it's unthinkable, it simply isn't done.' Well, I wrote to Hanawa in June and he answered in July." (Louis Schweitzer, Chairman)

Straight away, a French delegation was sent to Japan to draw up a shopping list. At the end of July, Louis Schweitzer met Nissan's chairman, Yoshikazu Hanawa, in Tokyo. A relationship of trust was quickly established between the two men.

"Mr Schweitzer and Mr Hanawa learned to trust each other very quickly. I think that this trust between the chairmen has lasted all the way through, with no stumbling blocks, deviations or betrayals" (Georges Douin, EVP).

"There was a sort of mutual respect and complementarity between Hanawa and Schweitzer. Those are very important factors. The first handshake decides everything." (Mr Husson, VP, General Counsel).

"I think they [the Japanese] greatly appreciated Mr Schweitzer's style. An article published in the Japanese press commented: *'But it's incredible! We've found a boss in the automobile sector who isn't a brute!'*" (Mr Dassas, Finance Director)

In July and August the two companies pinpointed about 20 potential opportunities for joint synergies: geographical distribution of their markets, complementarity of their product ranges and the possibility of sharing common platforms. Matters moved quickly enough for the chairmen to sign a memorandum on September 10 concerning the financial evaluation and joint costing of those synergies with a view to a possible strategic alliance. At the same time, Louis Schweitzer decided to make no further approaches to the Mitsubishi group.

"I described that once in an interview by saying that we went hunting for rabbits and we found a deer." (Mr De Andria, VP, Strategic Planning)

The planned alliance concerned only Nissan Motors, Nissan's automobile division, and an exclusive negotiation clause until the end of December 1998 was included in the memorandum. Amid the greatest secrecy, the two companies started a campaign to pinpoint cost cooperation opportunities. At Renault, the campaign was given the code name *Operation Pacific*.

But could the French company ensure rapid success with its new partner after failing with a better known and culturally closer potential partner like Volvo?

Operation Pacific   Twenty Franco-Japanese teams were given the task of evaluating the main issues that would shape an alliance between Renault and Nissan. The process, which lasted until November

1998, took the form of a series of joint studies. The team leaders were chosen from the company that had the most experience of the subject being studied. In all, about 100 people from each company were involved. The joint studies played a fundamental role in creating a climate of confidence at the grass roots between the two manufacturers. Two main types of issue emerged rapidly.

The first was the question of synergies. In this respect, Renault gradually discovered that the situation was exceptionally promising, surpassing its expectations. First of all the companies' product ranges were extremely complementary. Renault was ahead of the field in mid-range cars and light commercial vehicles, while Nissan Motors specialised in mid-range vehicles and the four-wheel-drive vehicles and pickups typical of the American light commercial vehicles market, in which Renault was not represented. The outlook was equally good on a geographical level. Renault was firmly established in Western Europe and South America, while Nissan had the strongest foothold in North and Central America, Asia, Japan and Africa. In terms of expertise, Renault had achieved excellent cost control, formalised a global strategy for platforms and purchasing, and was known for designing vehicles of innovative style and appearance. Nissan stood out more through its quality control, R&D programmes and technology.

Between September and December the two companies evaluated synergies, assessed their financial value and the technical feasibility of working together more closely. The French and Japanese teams exchanged information about their know-how, expertise and projects. Their work showed that the potential synergies should yield, on paper, savings of 51.5 million euros in 2000, 1 billion euros in 2001 and 1.5 billion euros in 2002 through the rationalisation of platforms and a joint purchasing and distribution policy.

"It was extraordinary in terms of synergies. We really believed in it, or at least those taking part in the negotiations did. . . . Quite frankly, we were so complementary in terms of geography, products, personality (. . .). So we had great confidence. The maps of where

we were established were completely different (. . .). Their products are of extraordinarily high quality. Two of the best factories in the world belong to Nissan, one in England and one in the United States (. . .). Our engineers were full of admiration for Nissan's manufacturing processes." (Mr Dassas, VP, Financial Operations)

Nonetheless, although the industrial outlook was promising, the same could not be said of organisational matters. In 1998 Nissan Motors was a company with major financial problems. A succession of years showing losses had left the company with total debts of 23 billion euros and a list of annual repayments that was becoming increasingly difficult to respect. The reason was a complex combination of internal management problems: Nissan headed a Keiretsu which had been built up gradually over the years. The company had never established a rational purchasing policy or system of relations with suppliers. Manufacturing costs were high and its product range was too diverse. Quality came at a high price. Moreover, Nissan's global market share had slumped from 6.4% in 1990 to 4.9% in 1998.

Engineering culture took precedence over managerial culture, while the quest for performance and quality won out over costing. Promotion was based entirely on length of service. Apparently, Mr Hanawa was acutely aware that the company was heading towards bankruptcy. He set a symbolic date, March 30, 1999, as a deadline. It was the end of the Japanese financial year, when short-term credit lines were to be renegotiated.

"That seemed to me both highly artificial and extremely useful. Artificial because it was tied in with the end of the fiscal year, and the end of the fiscal year only exists on the day accounts are published. So it seemed to me a completely artificial deadline (. . .). But it was useful because, in any negotiations, failure to set a deadline has many disadvantages because the talks may drag on and on (. . .). Nissan's rating was a subject that Mr Hanawa brought up frequently." (Louis Schweitzer, Chairman)

"They were afraid that their Japanese rating would fall too. Now that would have been a disaster because they could not have coped with the resulting increase in their expenses." (Mr Dassas, VP, Financial Operations)

Such a decline would have meant official recognition of the company's ailing finances. So Nissan found itself in the paradoxical situation of being justly proud of its products and technological capacity while sustaining financial losses that could lead to its collapse or to it falling into the hands of a competitor. The need to "save face," a basic requirement in the balance of Japanese company relations, was one of the keys to understanding the negotiations.

Nissan had to join forces with a partner which would bail it out financially in the short term, on condition that this went along with sufficient restructuring to reorganise the production system, purchasing policy and its Keiretsu generally so that the company would remain competitive on a world scale.

> "The Japanese executives had understood that, looking more closely, Renault's expertise included a number of complementary factors that would be easier to implement than those with Daimler. In other words, the restructuring processes that we introduced, Renault's expertise in cost reduction, purchasing, production sites, engineering, services . . . And probably Renault's expertise in marketing and product innovation too. . . . Those factors counterbalanced the fact that the DaimlerChrysler group may have looked stronger financially on the surface but . . . Renault could really help Nissan to find the way out of its difficulties. . . . When the Japanese said that it was better to learn to catch fish than to be given them, I think that was what they meant. Without a doubt, Daimler was in a position to be able to give them fish, but there was no guarantee that they would teach them to catch their own. Renault was more likely to teach them the art of fishing." (Mr Lévy, EVP)

Japanese-style corporate governance tends to water down the responsibility of individual managers into a system of collective responsibility. It is difficult in such circumstances to define strategies through which the managers would have to call themselves into question.

> "There were no decision-makers outside Nissan. Identifying the person who made a decision was extremely difficult. Because we've all read the literature

that says a Japanese company is managed collectively, that the Board of Directors has 37 members (. . .). But, when you come down to it, why would an independent company bigger than Renault enter an agreement under which it became equal to Renault, at most? In a way, it meant acknowledging a need that is not natural for any kind of management." (Louis Schweitzer, Chairman)

Did Renault have sufficient credibility to face not just the industrial challenge but also the financial and managerial challenge at Nissan?

The Big Picture: Pass or Fail   While the French negotiators were surprised by the quality of the relationship that was being built with their opposite numbers at Nissan and by the speed with which talks on manufacturing issues were progressing, the French were also perfectly aware of their handicaps. They pinpointed three main ones: Renault's lack of a strong image in Japan, its low capital compared to Nissan and its history as a public-sector company with large financial deficits.

As a mainly European company, Renault was little known on the Japanese market. This meant that the acquisition of Japan's second-biggest company by an unknown French firm would not give Nissan's partners the impression of a prestigious alliance, which might have made up for the humiliation of being bought by a foreigner. Moreover, Renault's financial position would not enable it to wipe out the Japanese manufacturer's debts. Its participation could only be partial and would have to be accompanied by firm guarantees about Nissan's ability to rebalance its books. The danger was that Nissan's deficit might also drag Renault into the red after the spectacular economic recovery of the previous ten years. Breaking with its past as a public company, Renault had modernised production, rationalised its purchasing network and become one of the world's most efficient manufacturers. Its ultra-modern research centre just outside Paris was a potent symbol of its capacity for innovation. Going further, one man was a symbol of that economic rationalisation policy: Carlos Ghosn, who was EVP at the time of the negotiations. His reputation as a "cost killer" highlighted both the radical financial modernisation of Renault and the attention the company paid to staying on a sound footing. In those circumstances, an alliance with a partner whose Keiretsu-style organisation and cost management was the opposite of Renault's did not look promising.

Very early on, in October 1998, Mr Schweitzer had a clear view of the feasibility of the alliance between Renault and Nissan. He felt it had to be based on two principles over which there could be no compromise: equal status and participation in management.

"We had to move closer strategically, but it could not be a simple acquisition or a merger, because a Franco-Japanese merger is no easy matter." (. . .)

"I suggested to him [Mr Hanawa] that three people from Renault should become members of the Nissan Board of Directors: the COO, the VP Product Planning and the Deputy Chief Financial Officer. (. . .) I told Ghosn: *"I won't do this deal if you don't go to Japan!"* Before proposing the COO position, I had to have someone (. . .). In my opinion, I didn't have anyone else who could do the job." (Louis Schweitzer, Chairman)

Mr Schweitzer waited for the right moment to talk about his idea to Mr Hanawa. At the end of October, the two men discussed a draft for what might become Renault's letter of intent at the end of the negotiating period.

"Well, they don't really understand what a COO is because there's no such thing in Japan. There's no word in Japanese to describe a COO. But there were no talks about that. I only asked for those three, I didn't ask for any other jobs except those three and he [Mr Hanawa] didn't try to argue about any of them." (Louis Schweitzer, Chairman)

However, the entire Nissan management still had to be convinced that only an alliance offering a global solution to its problems was feasible and that this could only be concluded on the basis of the principles put forward by Renault. So far the joint studies had done a considerable amount of work in the field to establish trust between the teams. But the strategic negotiations had only involved a few people at Nissan: Mr Hanawa and the three

corporate planning executives, Mr Shiga, Mr Suzuki and Mr Sugino.

"Mr Hanawa talked to me, but I don't know how he managed to achieve a consensus at Nissan (. . .). Throughout my negotiations with Nissan, I never knew who was 'for' and who was 'against,' and I never knew who made the decisions." (Louis Schweitzer, Chairman)

It was agreed that the French would submit the outlines of a proposed capital alliance to the Nissan Management Committee. This was Operation Big Picture. In Tokyo, on November 11, 1998, Louis Schweitzer, Georges Douin and Carlos Ghosn spent three hours explaining their strategic outlook, Nissan's need for an alliance and the conditions for it to succeed, and describing at length the stages of Renault's recovery in earlier years. They felt that it was a decisive moment because they were revealing the situation quite openly, and it was not favourable to the Japanese.

"It shook them up quite a bit, obviously, because we were showing them that they had rather too many factories, rather too many employees and rather too many business activities in rather too many difficult areas (. . .). They were shocked that anyone outside the company should be speaking to them so frankly. At the time we were afraid that our approach might cause a breakdown in the talks because they seemed so affected" (Mr De Andria, VP, Strategic Planning).

"By that point, I was perspiring heavily! I really felt that we had plunged headlong into an attitude of arrogance" (Louis Schweitzer, Chairman).

"We knew we were playing with fire. We had the growing impression of being on slippery ground, not to say enemy territory (. . .). We weren't at all sure we could pull it off—that was certain." (Mr Douin, Vice-Chairman)

As agreed earlier, no discussion followed the case put forward by the French, and the two sides took their leave in silence. The Japanese had until the end of December before the exclusive negotiating period ran out to reach a conclusion about the strategic viewpoint defended by Renault.

Tokyo, December 23, 1998 Renault's official letter of intent defining the general conditions of the alliance was due to be discussed when a sudden new development occurred. Behind the scenes, Mr Hanawa warned his French counterpart that Renault's proposal had to cover all Nissan's business activities—not just Nissan Motors but also Nissan Diesel. Until then only the automobile division had been mentioned and Renault knew nothing about the trucks division. And for the final round of negotiations aimed at reaching agreement on an alliance in March 1999, Renault's exclusivity clause was not renewed.

A new player had come on the scene: Daimler-Chrysler. Had the Japanese understood only too well the lesson they had been given by the French?

Competition for an Alliance   DaimlerChrysler had been negotiating the acquisition of Nissan Diesel since June. The loss-making Japanese trucks subsidiary was in a critical condition which is why, after months of evaluation, the German-American group suggested taking over the entire Nissan group, acquiring a majority stake in the company. The financial soundness and prestige of Daimler-Chrysler could solve Nissan's problems and ensure that its absorption by an international company controlled by the German Daimler-Benz was accepted by the Japanese.

The French did not change their stand in any respect. They maintained their proposal for an equal alliance that would guarantee Nissan's independence and give Renault a 36% stake in the group. They stressed their proposed involvement in restructuring Nissan's management, and their experience in that area, and agreed without hesitation that Nissan Diesel would be included in the deal.

> "Keeping 40% of Nissan Diesel raised a number of problems for us so what we did was this: we told them [Nissan Motors]: *'We're going to buy from you part of your share of Nissan Diesel so that we own 22.5% each.'* This had the advantage of being a simple financial holding for Renault (. . .), and secondly it also prevented us from having to consolidate a larger stake in our accounts. It was a shrewd piece of accounting." (Mr Lévy, EVP)

The due diligence period began in January 1999. It was difficult because the French did not know what was being negotiated with DaimlerChrysler, so their hopes fluctuated. The Renault teams continued to apply the negotiating rules laid down by top management since the start of negotiations: treating the people at Nissan as equals, avoiding all forms of arrogance, remaining attentive while maintaining the two principles put forward by Mr Schweitzer as conditions for a win-win situation for both sides of the alliance.

> "And that was where our retrospective assessment of all our previous experiences was very useful to us (. . .). Above all we tried—even if we didn't manage it 100%—to avoid putting ourselves forward as the company making an acquisition, the side that comes out on top. We always wanted to have due regard for form, to have due consideration for the Japanese (. . .). We kept in view the lessons that could be learned from our previous experiences." (Mr De Andria, VP, Strategic Planning).

Urged on by the rivalry with DaimlerChrysler, Renault found itself in the role of outsider which encouraged the French to underline their strengths and show their willingness to adapt further to Japanese sensitivities. They felt that they were putting forward the more appropriate answer to Nissan's situation compared to the German-American steamroller twice their size. Even so, while the technical teams continued to make progress in evaluating future cooperation, the strategic teams had the impression that they were working mainly for form's sake. Nissan had to choose between a merger and a partnership, and its choice would depend on what clauses to preserve its identity were being negotiated at DaimlerChrysler headquarters in Stuttgart.

No details leaked out of the discussions between the Japanese and the Germans, but international motor industry experts gave DaimlerChrysler a decisive advantage. Only the Germans had the financial capacity to absorb Nissan's deficits and take charge of an industrial restructuring that seemed bound to be long, difficult and expensive against the notoriously opaque background of Japanese finances and labour relations.

In Geneva, everyone was waiting for the statement that would start a new chapter in the story of the globalisation of the motor industry. It was early March, and the French had absolutely no idea what the outcome would be.

> "The situation was very tense. . . . We felt that they were tempted by the German proposal (. . .). The impression we had had during the negotiations, when apparently they were no longer interested by what we were saying, when we thought their minds were elsewhere . . . now we said: 'That was it. It was the Germans.' It was mainly with regard to the Germans that our hopes waxed and waned" (Mr Dassas, VP, Financial Operations).

> "There was a week when we just lost all faith (. . .). It was at the start of March, I believe (. . .). We gave up hope. It was all over. The negotiations were awful. Nothing happened, nothing at all . . . it was distressing." (Mr Husson, VP, General Counsel)

The Outcome   Geneva, March 10, 1999. Jürgen Shremp, CEO of DaimlerChrysler called a press conference.

> "This is the result of a three-month period where both parties assess the strengths and financial options of a global cooperation. We had to accept that the opportunities a close relationship with Nissan offer are not achievable as quickly and smoothly as initially expected." (Jürgen Schremp, Co-Chairman of Daimler-Chrysler)

The news came as a surprise to most observers. DaimlerChrysler had proved unable to grasp the opportunity to form an alliance with Nissan and had left the door open for Renault. Now there was nothing to stand in the way of Renault signing the alliance on the terms put forward by Louis Schweitzer, who insisted that none of the company's original proposals be changed.

> "The decision we made during the final negotiations was not to change our position. It was an important choice on our part to say: *'It's not because Daimler is no longer around that we are changing our proposal.'* In other words, it wasn't because there was no-one else to up the stakes that we were planning to change the conditions of the deal, because we knew that they would have to make a deal with someone and there was nobody against me. I decided not to do that because I felt it would destroy the relationship of trust which was

> indispensable for us to work together (. . .). It seemed more important to show that we were loyal, stable and reliable partners." (Louis Schweitzer, Chairman)

News of the breakdown of the Daimler talks surprised the team of French negotiators as they got off the plane in Tokyo, where they were due to continue talks on the legal aspects of the alliance. In the big meeting hall, the atmosphere was solemn.

> "We went to Ginza and met our Japanese friends. We said to them: 'We have learned of the event that has changed the circumstances of our negotiations. We note the withdrawal of Daimler-Chrysler. From now on, we want you to know that it isn't Renault's style and culture to take advantage of its partner's problems.' Mr Shiga got up, he did this [mime of the Japanese salute] and sat down again." (Mr Husson, VP, General Counsel)

The alliance between Renault and Nissan was concluded on March 27, 1999. Both companies retained their independence. Three French representatives left Renault to become members of the Nissan Board: Carlos Ghosn, COO, Patrick Pélata, who is responsible for strategy, and Thierry Moulonguet, who is in charge of finance. A Global Alliance Committee was set up to meet monthly to manage the alliance. Eleven global teams were formed to start work in the field on the various aspects. The world's fourth-biggest automobile manufacturer was born, with 9.4% of the international market and strong prospects for growth. In the autumn of 1999, Carlos Ghosn submitted the Nissan Revival Plan.

Nissan's Point of View

Ginza, June 1998   On a hot June morning in 1998, Nissan President Yoshikazu Hanawa arrived for work at the company headquarters in the Ginza district of downtown Tokyo. He was greeted by the uniformed employees at the reception desk and walked past a 1957 Datsun convertible to the elevator that exclusively served the executive offices on the 15th floor.

Entering his office, he was informed by an executive vice president of Renault's interest in a potential partnership with Nissan.

Problems Facing Nissan (1996–1998)   Hanawa had come to power in the middle of the recession in Japan. As of 1996, Nissan had accumulated a debt to sales ratio of 62%. Nissan had sustained continued losses since 1992. This also was having profound effects on the approximately 1400 holding suppliers, dealerships and other subsidiaries of Nissan, throwing them into financial disarray.

Over the first two years of Hanawa's tenure, the situation continued to deteriorate. For the fiscal year ending in March 1998, Nissan reported losses of 14 billion yen, with the debt to sales ratio rising to 66%.

Nissan's problems need to be understood in the context of the changes taking place in the automotive industry. One major factor was the world-wide over-capacity in the car market. It was estimated that automakers had a capacity to produce 70 million vehicles, while demand amounted to only 52 million units.[1] The second factor affecting the automotive industry was the stricter environmental and safety regulations that increased R&D costs per car.

Global over-capacity within the automotive industry and rising costs per vehicle made it increasingly important for industry players to seek size through strategic partnerships or mergers. Ford's acquisition of Volvo in 1998 and the merger of Daimler and Chrysler in the same year sent signals to the industry that served to accelerate the trend.

History   Nissan Motor Co. Ltd. was established in 1933 by Yoshisuke Aikawa to manufacture and sell small Datsun passenger cars and auto parts.

(i) Prewar   The first small-size Datsun passenger car rolled off the assembly line at the Yokohama Plant in April 1935, and vehicle exports to Australia were also launched that same year. The slogan "The Rising Sun as the flag and Datsun as the car of choice"[2] was originated at that time, symbolising Japan's rapid industrialisation.

In 1936, as the signs of the war grew stronger, production emphasis shifted from small-size Datsun passenger cars to military trucks.

(ii) Postwar   Nissan suffered from a major loss of sales force in the early postwar period. This was due to the fact that many leading auto dealerships, previously affiliated with the old Nissan network, switched to Toyota after the dissolution of Japan Motor Vehicle Distribution Co. Ltd., which had monopolised vehicle distribution during the war.

Nissan resumed production of Nissan trucks in 1945 and Datsun passenger cars in 1947. Post-war progress was swift. By 1958, the Datsun 210 could be entered in the grueling Australian Rally, and, by 1960, the company received the Deming Prize for engineering excellence.

(iii) 1960s   The 1959 Bluebird and the 1960 Cedric captivated the imagination of Japanese car buyers and quickened the pace of motorization in Japan. The Sunny was introduced in 1966 during the "my car" era in Japan. Nissan's model lines during the 1960s were indicative of the company's competition with Toyota: the Bluebird lined up against Toyota's Corona, and the Cedric against Toyota's Crown.[3]

This was a period of growth for Nissan. In 1961, the company established Nissan Mexicana, S.A. de C.V., its first overseas manufacturing operation. Nissan also set up two state-of-the-art manufacturing facilities in Japan, the Oppama Plant in 1962 and the Zama Plant in 1965. In the mid-60s, the Japanese government suggested a merger of Nissan and Prince Motor Co. Ltd. to create a larger company that would be better equipped to handle any hostile takeover attempts by foreign companies, leading to the 1966 merger between Nissan Motor and Prince Motor. Nissan maintains a strong link with the Japanese government and to this day provides a large percentage of government limousines.

(iv) 1970s   The two energy crises of the 1970s increased the demand for small Japanese cars worldwide and led to a surge in exports. In 1973, the Sunny ranked first in the fuel and economy tests conducted by the U.S. Environmental Protection Agency and thus gained instant popularity in the U.S. market under the advertising slogan of

---

[1] Nissan estimates.
[2] Nissan corporate web-site.

[3] Nissan Fact File 1999.

"Datsun saves." The sporty Z car also built a large following in the U.S. during the 1970s.

In 1975, Nissan opened the Kyushu Plant, a leading edge facility that today can still boast of the most advanced automation technology in the world.

(v) 1980s   During the 1980s, Nissan was the second Japanese car company, following Honda, to establish a manufacturing base in the U.S. (1980; Nissan Motor Manufacturing Corp., U.S.A) and Datsun Truck and Sentra production began in the U.S. Nissan then moved to establish a manufacturing base in Europe, the first among the Japanese car companies to do so (1984; Nissan Motor Manufacturing Corp. UK).

Rapid overseas expansion was initiated by the 11th Nissan President, Takashi Ishihara (1977–1985). During the 1980s, Nissan's domestic sales began to fall. In order to stem declining sales, Ishihara sought out opportunities in overseas markets and started establishing new plant facilities in the U.S. and the UK. But declining sales in the domestic market remained unsolved, leading Nissan into a vicious cycle of over-capacity, falling sales, and domestic price cuts. This caused conflicts between the Japanese unions and the management. Nissan employees protested against the idea of increasing production capacity overseas when their domestic plants itself were under utilised. However, Ishihara did not stop to hear these voices and continued with his plan for global expansion. This was an example of Ishihara's so called "impulsive management strategy" and unilateral approach.

The continuous conflict with the union badly affected the image of Nissan. The 12th Nissan President, Yutaka Kume (1985–1992) realised the need to stimulate the Nissan brand image and focused on new model introductions. The up-market Cima for the executive class and the sporty Silvia for the younger generation were introduced in the late 1980s as part of a brand enhancement scheme. With the help of a booming economy, the cars became extremely popular.

In addition, Kume realised that the internal health of the company was also a reflection of the Nissan brand. By the time of his designation as President, employees had become tired of the continuous conflict between the management and the unions during the previous Ishihara era. Kume emphasized improving the environment of the workers, up to the point of creating an organisation in which people would not feel hesitant to call him by his name, Kume-san, rather than by his title.

(vi) 1990s   Kume, who focused on creating a better image for Nissan, had once said, "I want to make the cars more attractive for the younger generation. Therefore, I believe when a concept for a new model is being developed, the voices have to come from the bottom up." However, the bottom-up approach seemed to lead to a loss of direction in the overall policy for model developments. Moreover, since 50% of Nissan dealerships were owned by Nissan (Toyota owned only 10% of its dealerships), dealers had no autonomy in selecting car models, and market feedback was poor. This prompted Kume to worry that "Nissan cars are becoming further and further away from the true voice of our customers."[4]

With the burst of Japan's bubble economy, Nissan's profits plummeted from 101.3 billion in March 1992 to a loss of 166 billion yen by March 1995. The 13th Nissan President, Yoshifumi Tsuji (1992–1996), who had spent most of his career on the production side, focused on improving domestic sales. He made frequent visits to all of the domestic dealerships, meeting with dealer representatives, sales board members and sales regional managers. The meetings with the dealer representatives had little effect. Domestic sales appeared to be declining not because Nissan lacked in sales capability, but because there was a fundamental flaw in the concept and the style of the product per se. Without combating the fundamental problem of product improvement, Tsuji presented a drastic down-sizing plan in February 1993 with a target to reduce costs by 200 billion yen by year 1995 in order to obtain profitability even at a low 2 million unit production level.

The Hanawa Era   In 1996, Yoshikazu Hanawa became the 14th President of Nissan. After obtaining

---

[4]"Toyota's Ambition and Nissan's Commitment" by Yoshio Tsukuda.

an economics degree at the University of Tokyo in 1957, he joined Nissan to start his first assignment in the Human Resource Department. He later became involved in Nissan's overseas operations and was designated as head of the committee responsible to establish Nissan's Tennessee plant in the US. By 1985, he was promoted as the first and youngest director in the Corporate Planning Department. He was also involved in numerous restructuring plans such as the closure of the Zama plant in 1995. Many of the Nissan top managers were Tokyo University graduates, and Hanawa had the ideal profile to become the President of Nissan.

(i) Hanawa's Mission   In one of his first interviews upon becoming President, Hanawa said,

> Nissan must cooperate and integrate all efforts towards one vector in order to show better results. We must change the "Nissan Bureaucracy" which has long been our image. . . .[5]

When Hanawa took over as President, Nissan's domestic market share had dropped to 15.9%,[6] only half of that of Toyota. Hanawa's initial plans focused on new car development, with the aim of recovering domestic market share and an objective of 25%[7] by the year 2000. When announcing this target, he said, "It is not a healthy situation both for the companies as well as for the customers for one car company to dominate sales. I would like to establish an era for two mutual companies so that both Toyota and Nissan can stimulate one another and grow together."[8]

(ii) Internal Organisation   From the early stages of Hanawa's time as President, his main concern was to change the culture of the organisation. Hanawa was deeply concerned that Nissan had become complacent and lacked a sense of "urgency," despite the economic distress experienced in Japan after the burst of the bubble economy and the poor market and financial performance of the company.

When Hanawa joined Nissan in 1957, Nissan was still a small operating company, fresh with new ideas and innovation. Recalling his early days at Nissan, Hanawa said, "As Nissan grew larger in scale, a new culture took over. Most employees became more concerned with their own line of business or function and did not know where value was being added for Nissan as a whole. The company lacked both in cross-functional and cross-regional communication. The passive internal culture was reflected in our cars, making them unattractive and far away from customers' taste. Nissan had always thought that as long as there is quality, our cars will sell at a high price. But that logic is no longer true in today's market. It is more about designing, and it is more about customer orientation. But there is a bureaucratic culture rooted into our organisation, which makes it very difficult to implement change . . . but we needed a change, and one solution was to bring in a new wind."

(iii) Global Business Reform Plan   Shortly after the end of the 1998 Japanese fiscal year, Nissan's Corporate Planning Department presented a "Global Business Reform Plan" to Hanawa and the board. 1998 had resulted in net losses of 14 billion yen on a consolidated basis, tracable to a fall in domestic vehicle demand, the write-down in the carrying value of vehicles in the U.S. lease portfolio, and evaluation losses on marketable securities.[9]

It was evident to the employees that Nissan's future was not very bright. Nissan had been showing consecutive losses since 1992. Everyone knew that something had to be done about it, but nobody seemed to know what or who should take the initiative to unwind the bad cycle the company had become trapped in.

The "Global Business Reform Plan" presentation proposed to achieve a consolidated operating profit to sales ratio of 5% in the fiscal year ending March 2001 and 6% in the fiscal year ending March 2003. There were two options presented in this plan in order to realise these targets. One approach was

---

[5]"Will Nissan Revive?" by Nikkei Shinbunsha.
[6]The figure includes mini-cars.
[7]The figure excludes mini-cars.
[8]"Will Nissan Revive?" by Nikkei Shinbunsha.

[9]Nissan Press Release (27 May 1998).

to implement an independent survival plan by drastic down-sizing: through reduced development costs, integration of platforms, streamlining sales channels, divesting non-core business assets and other cost cutting strategies. The second approach was to form a global alliance and to survive through increased scale.

It was in this context that a global strategic alliance was proposed.

Another Joint Cooperation with Renault?

Hanawa contacted Yutaka Suzuki, Director & General Manager at Corporate Planning Department, to respond to the proposal from Renault. Suzuki and Toshiyuki Shiga, Senior Manager at the Corporate Planning Department, were specifically told by Hanawa to proceed with an immediate investigation on Renault. Shiga was responsible for dealing with all external proposals such as technology alliances and joint cooperation. In fact, when Shiga was contacted by Hanawa regarding the proposal from Renault, he first thought of previous talks for a possible joint development with Renault. Shiga had met André Douin, head of Renault's Planning Department, in Paris in September 1997 concerning a possibility for Renault to produce pickup trucks under a Nissan license in the Mercosur area. Therefore, not only did Shiga already know something of Renault, but also thought that this was merely an extension of the possible joint cooperation Renault was seeking with Nissan since the previous year.

However, Renault was not merely asking for another joint cooperation this time. Renault wanted to know if Nissan might be interested in pursuing a global alliance at the corporate level. Nevertheless, when Shiga received orders to study this proposal from Hanawa, he was not surprised. Nissan had received cooperation proposals in the past from various car companies and it was his task to investigate the potential of each proposal.

The Alliance Process

(i) Phase I: Preliminary Study (July–September 1998) Nissan's Corporate Planning Department was the right place to start off the investigation for a global alliance possibility. It was the only department that included representatives from each of the main functional departments within Nissan: production, purchasing, development, overseas sales, domestic sales, financial affairs, legal and HR. The Corporate Planning Department rolled out the investigation plan in the following manner.

The Research Group within the Corporate Planning Department conducted a thorough internal study of Renault. It was the first time they had conducted such an in-depth analysis on a European car company.

Taiji Sugino, manager at the Corporate Planning Department with a background in international law and corporate governance, had been involved in the research and commented:

> My task was to get to know more about Renault as a company. Renault was not very well known in Japan and we knew very little to start with. Before considering an alliance, we needed to gain an understanding of how it might be possible to integrate with Renault from a business cooporation perspective. We also needed to see the economic benefits of forming an alliance. I conducted a competitor intelligence gathering exercise, a SWOT analysis and further strategic studies to understand the potential synergy effects on a daily basis.

On the strength of this research, Nissan saw considerable potential in the alliance. There were three main reasons for optimism: first, the two companies showed strength in different regions of the world (Nissan in Asia and the US, Renault in Europe), and collaboration between the two companies would give increased geographical coverage. Second, Renault was better at making smaller cars, while Nissan was better at making larger cars. However, despite the fact that the two companies' cars were not in direct competition with one another, there was strong potential for platform integration, indicating a possibility of reduced costs and increased efficiency for both companies. Third, the size of the two companies in terms of market capitalization and number of units produced was very similar as of 1998, lessening threats of future dominance or possible take over from either side.

Sugino said,

> "We marvelled at the success of Renault, because light and small vehicles generate much smaller margins compared to Nissan's large size vehicles. Nevertheless, Renault had managed to turn around its performance in a very short span of time [on the basis of small cars]." (Sugino, manager at the Corporate Planning)

At the time the alliance formation process was begun (1998), Renault had an earnings before tax margin (EBT) of 4.6%. Since the loss-making year of 1996 (EBT: 3.6%), Renault had managed to become profitable and grow total sales from 184,078 million FF to 243,934 million FF (1998).

However, Renault faced limitations for future growth. With over 80% of their sales coming from Europe, Renault wanted to broaden coverage, gain scale, and solidify its market position.

When the potential for a global alliance became clearer, the investigation was forwarded to the Strategic Group within the Corporate Planning Department at Nissan. There, the people got together to develop a shopping list of potential joint projects which could possibly take place between Nissan and Renault.

The Planning Department at Renault had developed a similar shopping list. In July 1998, Suzuki, Shiga and Keiichi Maekawa, an engineering manager from the Corporate Planning Department, left for Paris to exchange the two shopping lists. Initially, the combined shopping lists had approximately 100 possible joint projects, of which ultimately 21 projects were prioritised after numerous negotiations between the two Planning Departments during the months of July and August. With this list in hand, the three Nissan representatives went back to Japan and reported to Hanawa on the progress of their investigation.

(ii) Phase II: Joint Study Teams (September–December 1998)   In September 1998, Suzuki was asked by Hanawa to proceed with the 21 joint projects by forming "Joint Study Teams" between Nissan and Renault.

Now, for the first time, the operational level became involved in joint studies. However, the Corporate Planning Department was given strict orders of confidentiality by Hanawa. They were told not to reveal the purpose of the studies to the engineers involved and that the teams should not know of each other or of the bigger picture that their work fit into. They were to think that this was just like other joint study projects previously undertaken. There had been joint study projects in the past, for example the Volkswagen Santana project. Under this proposal, Nissan would have assembled VW cars at the Zama Plant. The cooperation with VW fell through because engineers at VW and Nissan did not work well together. It was therefore very important to assess the soft elements, such as operational fit at the engineering level, in the joint study teams.

The Corporate Planning Department was also not informed of the purpose nor the direction with which Hanawa was planning to proceed with the joint studies. They only received repeated emphasis by Hanawa that from this stage onwards, the engineers should take complete control in order to allow room for in-depth studies.

Faced with many uncertainties and a very short deadline for results (December 1998), the Corporate Planning Department of Nissan in cooperation with Renault quickly formed the following teams:

Group A:	Regional Operation Group
	A-1) European Team
	A-2) Asian Team
	A-3) Mexico Team
	A-4) South African Team
	A-5) Mercosur Team
Group B:	Product Group
Group C:	Platform Integration Group
Group D:	Powertrain Group
Total:	21 Joint Study Teams

The 21 joint study teams worked under team leaders, and 10 operational people from each company participated in the typical team.

Within teams, questions did arise about the level of cooperation. For example, the Nissan A-3 team members asked why Nissan should allow

Renault into their Mexico Plant. Suzuki responded to them:

> "If we allow Renault into our Mexico Plant, then perhaps we can gain access to Renault's Brazil/Argentina Plant. We need to take a give and take perspective."

Suzuki, Shiga and Sugino were responsible for answering all questions raised by the teams from the Nissan side.

Synergy meant two things for Nissan; complementarity and mutual efficiency. It made no sense for Nissan if two companies having the same capability got together. It only made sense if the companies complemented one another bringing overall efficiency and benefits for both companies.

There was a great amount of secrecy between the two companies initially. However, in order to see the synergy effect and the actual benefits for both companies, the facts had to be revealed as Renault and Nissan progressed with their joint studies. Shiga recalled, "The kind of information that we were sharing with each other prior to the alliance agreement was a very rare case."

For example, one joint study was made on the development of a 1 liter gasoline engine. Based on the joint study conducted by the joint study teams, Nissan calculated the NPV of this investment. In addition to this, Nissan had projected a reference case on this development if it had been conducted separately with the different research capabilities that Nissan and Renault individually had. If the combined NPV of Renault and Nissan had exceeded the NPV resulted by the joint study teams, it made no sense to proceed with the joint project. The difference of the two resulting NPVs was what Nissan called the "synergy effect."

There were a few "win-lose" projects but most of the projects resulted in a "win-win" projection. The aim was to achieve benefits for both sides.

(iii) Phase III: Reporting The 21 Joint Study Teams produced a progress report each month between October and December. Shiga reported the results to Hanawa and Suzuki.

As Renault and Nissan progressed with their joint studies, the two Planning Departments had come down to a common strategy,

> "The two Planning Departments of Renault and Nissan agreed that after identifying a strategic link through the joint studies, we must form a common strategy in order to achieve profitable growth for both companies. The basic policy for the alliance strategy would be to distinguish the brand identity from any kind of synergy. We saw the possibility of manufacturing integration but not brand integration, just as we saw possibilities of back office integration but not front office integration. In other words, Renault and Nissan felt that we should integrate only the processes that were far away from customers." (Shiga, manager at the Corporate Planning)

On 15 December 1998, a final report produced by the 21 Joint Study Teams was submitted to Hanawa.

(iv) Alliance Formation Process (January–March) In the beginning of 1999, the negotiation became more aggressive and rapid, focusing on the restructuring of the organisation as well as financial and legal affairs. Due diligence commenced on 15 January 1999 for the purpose of validating mutual claims. Shiga commented on the alliance formation process,

> Since both sides had strong individual needs to make themselves stronger, the joint study took place "sincerely." It was not just a handshake between the top managers.

Sugino added his perspective on the alliance formation process,

> For Nissan, the negotiations and the execution of the alliance contract were a process and not an objective. The objective was not to finalise the contract wording but to examine how to share best practices. For example, it was evident that Renault had strengths in two things: cost management and customer satisfaction. Nissan had strengths in technology, productivity, quality control, and global-level operations. Nissan wanted to know how Renault managed to maintain such a low cost structure, but Renault would not reveal this information unless an alliance was formed. Therefore, forming an alliance was a means of obtaining this know-how, and not an objective per se. Agreement finalisation was only the starting point of the alliance.

(v) Employee Involvement   Sugino explained the relationship between Renault and Nissan at the operational level to be the following:

> Nissan employees thought of Renault as a company that placed emphasis on communication improvement rather than negotiation.

Because of Renault's emphasis on communication, it was easy for Nissan to understand Renault. However, Sugino thought that the situation was quite the opposite for Renault.

> "The only point of contact on the Nissan side, who really knew the entire picture, was Mr. Hanawa, and hence I think that it must have been difficult for Renault to understand Nissan. (. . .) All of us were not really well aware of what was happening apart from what could be found in the papers. I knew in January 1999 because I had to prepare for due diligence. But I think most directors did not know about it until the day of announcement in March 1999. Only board members, Mr. Shiga and Mr. Sugino were informed by Mr. Hanawa." (Anraku, managing director in charge of finance and accounting)

Hanawa, always at the center of control, was very quick to respond to his lieutenants: Suzuki, Shiga and Sugino.

> "He would normally respond within the day. His decision making was very quick. That's when I sensed that Mr. Hanawa and Mr. Schweitzer were talking to each other very frequently, otherwise Mr. Hanawa could not have responded to me so quickly." (Sugino, manager at the Corporate Planning)

Although the word "global alliance" was never spelled out to his lieutenants by Hanawa, they gradually grew convinced that Nissan would really form an alliance with Renault in the near future. Unusual actions such as Hanawa's frequent calls to the Corporate Planning Department for feedback on the joint projects, or getting the managers there actively involved instead of confiding to his board members, or even the rapid response from Hanawa concerning queries during the process, made Suzuki, Shiga and Sugino gain confidence that soon a big decision would be made by Hanawa.

There was also a sense of confidence building at the planning level. Although the decision would ultimately be made by Hanawa, the actions leading up to the alliance were taken by the Corporate Planning Department. As Suzuki said, "We made the alliance happen. We did it."

However, some people at Nissan wished that there were more key persons within the company involved during the discussions with Renault. This would have helped avoid the shock that followed and allowed Human Resources to have considered issues relating to post-alliance integration.

Hanawa and Schweitzer

(i) Letter (June 1998)   Hanawa explained that initially, he did not think that a global alliance was really necessary. But rather, he felt the need to strengthen Nissan's overseas operation through their central office in Japan. Hanawa commented, "At first I did not think of forming an alliance with Renault, but I did consider possible joint cooperation. After all, everybody was doing that."

> "I think Mr. Hanawa initially wanted to take the independent survival approach when the options were opened to him after the Global Business Reform Plan presentation in May 1998. During the months between July and December I think he tried to do both, but ultimately, came down to the global alliance approach." (Shiga, manager at the Corporate Planning)

(ii) Negotiation with Schweitzer (July–December 1998)   In July 1998, Hanawa decided to meet Louis Schweitzer, the Chairman of Renault. This was the first of many meetings to follow.

Between July and December, 1998, the two men met more than ten times in addition to numerous private telephone calls, to discuss the alliance. All of the meetings were one-on-one affairs, with Hanawa's long-time translator the only outsider present.

> "The relationship I had with Mr. Schweitzer was one of honesty. In fact, the first thing I said to Mr. Schweitzer when I met him in July was, 'I am going to be frank with you, whatever the negotiation

results may be. So let's be frank with each other.' But with many people around, it is difficult to tell each other the truth, that is why I decided to negotiate alone. This also avoids insider risk. I think Mr. Schweitzer, on the other hand, was more careful about opening up to me because of the previous experience with Volvo. I believe the process leading up to an alliance is all about telling the truth; dishonesty only makes the process longer." (Hanawa, President)

(iii) Proposal of Potential Synergies   During the course of their discussions, Hanawa and Schweitzer both agreed on the need to conduct joint studies prior to the alliance, in order to assess the organisational fit at the operational level. Both CEOs indicated to their Planning Departments to form a shopping list of possible joint projects and to perform these projects specifically in the form of "joint study teams." The CEOs wanted the potential synergies to be proposed by the operational level of both sides and set a year-end deadline for the results.

> "In a car company, when there's a problem, the problem normally rises from the engineering department. So engineers were selected from both sides to work on research topics for 3 months. Similar projects were performed for other departments as well. As a result, there seemed to be a good chemistry between Renault and Nissan." (Hanawa, President)

As the joint study progressed between Renault and Nissan, Schweitzer and Hanawa started to see an organisational fit between the two companies.

> "I was impressed with two things about Renault. Firstly, I was impressed with Mr. Schweitzer's courageous decision to embrace a new business opportunity, and secondly, the fact that we had agreed on the terms of equal position. This was important for me, as dominance destroys motivation. Once Nissan picks up, we will buy a share in Renault's equity. These are the terms that we both agreed on." (Hanawa, President)

Hanawa emphasised that the assessment from the joint study teams was the determining factor for the alliance.

"Take for example, platform integration between Renault and Nissan. Nissan currently has 26 ranges of platforms and Renault has 8. If after the alliance, we can produce a common range of 10 platforms, it would reduce cost and increase efficiency. We all know that the concept is good, but we will never know if it is the right decision to make unless we do it. So I decided on the alliance to let actions take over. . . . Mr. Schweitzer told me about Carlos Ghosn's key role in the turn around of Renault three years back . . . I let him know that I wanted that man [to help Nissan]." (Hanawa, President)

(iv) Renault's "Big Picture" Presentation (10 November 1998)   In October 1998, Schweitzer met Hanawa and articulated his perspective on the potential alliance between the two companies. Hanawa commented, "I did not agree with it from the start of course. But I was not surprised. Through our discussions, I felt that Mr. Schweitzer always had a more comprehensive view of the partnership than I did. I took it as one opinion."

At this time, Schweitzer expressed an interest in sharing his views with a larger set of people at Nissan. Hanawa agreed to let Schweitzer and his team fly over to Japan and make a presentation about Renault's cost reduction experience, as well as the potential synergies to be gained from an alliance between the two companies. The presentation to Hanawa and some of Nissan's top executives was held on 10 November at Nissan headquarters. Schweitzer, Douin and Ghosn explained Renault's cost reduction capabilities and presented a comprehensive turn-around plan.

> "At the presentation, the participants were informed for the first time of the overall direction which the joint studies might be leading towards. But to be frank, I myself was amazed at the details of their study concerning the potential synergies. I was surprised at the level of research as well as the level of involvement with which Renault had progressed with the alliance plans. Because at Nissan, the negotiation was strictly kept between Mr. Schweitzer and I. This was the difference between Renault and Nissan. Renault knew exactly what they wanted from the beginning. I think our board only understood it as one possibility." (Hanawa, President)

(v) Final Meeting (21–23 December 1998)   On 15 December, the final reports from the joint study teams were submitted, and the "synergy effect" figures were presented. Based on these figures, Schweitzer and Hanawa met on 21–23 December to hold a final meeting on the alliance plans. On 23 December, Hanawa let Schweitzer know that the alliance talks would not be exclusive, and that Renault would be asked to bid for both Nissan Motor and Nissan Diesel.

In effect, DaimlerChrysler had been in negotiations with Nissan Diesel, Nissan's affiliate truck company, since May 1998. Juergen Hubbert, DaimlerChrysler board member for passenger cars remarked that, "Nissan Motor would help Daimler-Chrysler to achieve its aim of 20–25% of group sales being in Asia within 10 years. In the short-term we can do without a foothold in passenger cars in Asia, but we cannot do without one in trucks. Entering the Asian truck business is most urgent for DaimlerChrysler, but Nissan Diesel and Nissan Motor are interwoven in such a way that we are forced to talk about both."[10]

Hanawa later commented upon the interest of DaimlerChrysler,

> When Daimler and Chrysler merged in May 1998, Mr. Schremp talked about his interest in Nissan Diesel. This caused problems as it was supposed to be internal information, but by then, the Japanese press took it up as a great scoop.

Just a rumor?

> "Determining an alliance partner actually involves a lot of work, joint study teams, bottom-up reporting, etc. . . . In view of all the work that was put into the study process with Renault, I imagine that evaluating another alliance deal at the same time would really be a major undertaking." (Shiga, Corporate Planning)

(vi) Final Run   After December 23 and until March 13, when Renault and Nissan finalized the

[10]*Financial Times,* March 8, 1999.

basic alliance agreement, Hanawa and Schweitzer met only twice more. The core of the negotiations ended in December 1998.

> "Alliances are not a money-game, especially for car companies. We have responsibility for people at all levels. We all believed and trusted in Mr. Hanawa's decision. We believe he did the right thing." (Shiga, Corporate Planning).

On 15 January, due diligence commenced and the legal and finance departments took over. Hanawa had set a deadline of March because he felt that prolonging the process only created conflict and turmoil.

DaimlerChrysler ended all talks with Nissan on March 11, 1999. The Renault/Nissan alliance agreement was officially signed on 27 March 1999. This agreement aimed at strengthening Nissan's financial position and achieving profitable growth for both companies. On 28 May 1999, Renault invested 643 billion yen and acquired 36.8% of the equity of Nissan Motor and 22.5% of Nissan Diesel.

Appendices

Appendix 1	Global Ranking of Major Automakers (1998)	
	Volume Mil. Units	**Market Share**
Global Ranking		
General Motors	8.90	15%
Ford Motors	8.50	15%
Toyota Motors	6.40	10%
Renault/Nissan	4.80	9%
Volkswagen	4.30	9%
Daimler/Chrysler	4.00	8%

Source: Warburg Dillion Reed Global Auto Analyser (September 1999).

Appendix 2 Comparison: DaimlerChrysler, Nissan and Renault

	DaimlerChrysler	Nissan	Renault
Annual Revenue ($ mio)	147.745.000	50.212.000	41.349.000
Net income ($ mio)	5.404.000	−213.000	1.500.000
Work force	441.500	135.800	140.900
World market share (value)	8.4%	4.9%	4.3%
Vehicle production	3.9	2.6	2.1
(in millions—1998)	Daimler: 1.1		
	Chrysler: 2.8		

Appendix 3 Renault and Nissan around the World

Vehicles Sold (1998)	Renault		Nissan	
	Volume	Market Share (value)	Volume	Market Share (value)
Western Europe	1.798.160	11%	505.768	3.1%
North America	—	—	656.704	4%
South America	110.656	5.1%	—	—
Japan	—	—	902.968	15.3%
ASEAN	—	—	129.172	10.8%
Turkey, Middle East, North Africa	117.040	7.9%	116.512	9.1%
Rest of world	102.144		336.296	

Number of Plants (1998)	Full-fledged Plants	Local Assembly Sites	Full-fledged Plants	Local Assembly Sites
Europe	18	—	3	—
Japan	—	—	12	—
Asia	1 (China)	2	2	3
North America	1 (Mexico)	—	4	—
South America	3	2	—	—
Africa	—	1 (Morocco)	1 (South Africa)	—

Appendix 4 Model Categories of Renault and Nissan

Renault		Model Categories	Nissan	
Names	Volume Sold (approx, 1998)		Volume Sold (approx, 1998)	Names
Twingo	250.000	Entry level	—	—
Clio	600.000	Sub-compact	350.000	March, Micra, Cube
Mégane, Scénic, R19	800.000	Compact	550.000	Almera, Sunny
Laguna	250.000	Mid-size	350.000	Bluebird, Primera
Safrane, Spider	50.000	Luxury	500.000	Altima, Maxima, Infiniti, Q45, Cedric
Espace	100.000	Minivan	150.000	Quest, Elgrand, Prairie
—	—	4*4	250.000	Safari, Patrol, Terrano
—	—	Pick-up	250.000	Pick-up
Express, Kangoo, Trafic, Master	350.000	Utility	150.000	Atlas Civilian

Appendix 5   Competences of Renault and Nissan (recognized at alliance signing)

Renault	Nissan
Cost management	Engineering competence
Global platform and purchase strategies	Technology
Innovative products	Plant productivity
Marketing and design	Product and process quality management

Appendix 6   Platform Integration

Example: Common platform (Clio/Micra)

	Common Range of Platforms		
	Renault	Nissan	Alliance
Number of platforms	8	26	10
Volume per platform (000 units)	280	105	500

Example: Components (joint development of a small diesel engine)

	Common Range of Engines and Transmission Families		
	Renault	Nissan	Alliance
Number of engine platforms	7	20	8
Volume per platform (000 units)	320	140	630

Source: Schroders; Renault-Nissan Strategic Alliance Report (April 1999).

Appendix 7   History of Renault

1898:	Renault Frères founded in Boulogne, at Billancourt (production: 1 vehicle).
1903:	Death of Marcel Renault. Louis Renault takes over (production: 778 vehicles).
1941:	Occupation and collaboration with Axis.
1944:	Arrest of Louis Renault by Allies (he dies September 24); factories are requisitioned.
1945:	Nationalization decreed because of collaboration. Creation of Régie Nationale des Usines Renault. President: Pierre Lefaucheux (production: 12.031 vehicles).
1969:	Creation of Renault-Finance to support international evolution (production: 1.047.986 vehicles).
1979:	22,8% participation taken in AMC (US). 10% participation in Volvo (Su) with an option for 20% (production: 1.872.526 vehicles).
1980:	Increased participation in AMC to 46,4% (production: 2.053.677 vehicles).
1981:	RVI (Renault Véhicules Industriels) buys Dodge Trucks (US) (production: 1.764.701 vehicles).

(continued)

Appendix 7 *(concluded)*

1983:   Agreement with Matra. Renault takes control of Mack (US) (production: 2.035.133 vehicles).

1984:   With debts of 57 billion francs (half annual revenue) and annual losses of 12,5 billion, Renault is virtually bankrupt (production: 1.740.737 vehicles).

1985:   Resignation of Bernard Hanon. Georges Besse becomes president, puts in place a restructuring policy: recapitalisation of 8 billion by the French state, financial restructuring with RVI by 500 million francs, policy of disengagement and refocusing, 2.550 redundancies at RVI, plan to reduce headcount by 21.000 people in 2 years (production: 1.637.634 vehicles).

1986:   Georges Besse is assassinated by Action Directe on 17 November. RVI announces 2.624 lay-offs, the Mexican factory of Sahagun is closed, 13.5 ha of factory space at Billancourt are put up for sale (production: 1.754.332 vehicles).

1987:   Raymond Lévy president of Renault. Further lightening: AMC is sold to Chrysler. Renault becomes a for-profit firm again and prepares to follow a logic of profit after a second phase of recapitalization (10 billion francs) by the French state and shareholder (production: 1.831.390 vehicles).

1990:   Renault becomes an SA (Société Anonyme) and Volvo now owns 20% of the capital (production: 1.848.078 vehicles).

1992:   Raymond Lévy reaches age limit and cedes his place to Louis Schweitzer on 27 May (production: 2.094.774 vehicles).

1993:   6 September: the merger Renault-Volvo is announced. December: Volvo abandons merger (production: 1.761.496 vehicles).

1994:   Renault goes public: the French state holds only 52,97% of the capital (production: 1.914.662 vehicles).

1996:   Privatization. First losses since the 1980s 80 (production: 1.804.910 vehicles).

1997:   Vilvorde factory (B) is closed (2.700 jobs). Return to profitability. French state: 46% of capital.

Appendix 8   Recovery of Renault (in FF mio)

	1983	1984	1985	1986
Revenue	104.145.000	110.274.000	117.584.000	122.138.000
Net income	−1.420.000	−1.576.000	−12.555.000	−10.897.000
CAF (MBA)	1.446.000	1.938.000	−6.481.000	−6.003.000
Equity	10.119.000	11.164.000	1.851.000	−7.365.000
Work force	215.000	219.805	213.725	196.414

	1988	1989	1990	1995
Revenue	147.510.000	161.438.000	174.477.000	178.537.000
Net income	3.256.000	8.834.000	9.289.000	3.636.000
CAF (MBA)	10.010.000	15.260.000	15.050.000	12.145.000
Equity	−5.726.000	14.012.000	22.466.000	42.784.000
Work force	188.900	181.715	174.573	138.279

Appendix 9   Renault S.A. (France)—Financial Snapshot

				Renault S.A. (France) (mil. FF)			
	12/31/1992	12/31/1993	12/31/1994	12/31/1995	12/31/1996	12/31/1997	12/31/1998
Sales	184,252	169,789	178,537	184,065	184,078	207,912	243,934
R&D expenses	6,190	6,902	7,707	7,904	9,125	9,038	10,189
Income before taxes	6,481	1,094	3,485	1,976	−5,645	4,095	11,145
EBT margin	3.52%	0.64%	1.95%	1.07%	−3.07%	1.97%	4.57%
No of shares (mil)	224	227	238	239	240	240	240
Earnings per share	28.93	4.09	15.65	9.02	−22.07	22.78	36.97
Total shareholders'	33,965	33,877	42,784	43,796	37,770	43,917	51,562
Total debt	8,727	7,851	−1,458	3,368	9,385	2,097	−12,650
Debt/equity ratio	26%	23%	−3%	8%	25%	5%	−25%
Debt/sales ratio	5%	5%	−1%	2%	5%	1%	−5%
R&D costs/sales	3.36%	4.07%	4.32%	4.29%	4.96%	4.35%	4.18%

Source: Renault Annual Report

Appendix 10   Japanese Automakers Profitability (1998)

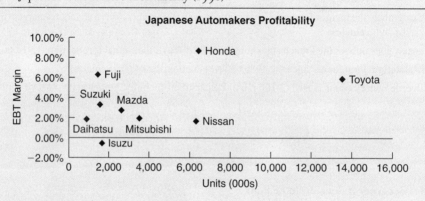

Source: Schroders; Renault-Nissan Strategic Alliance Report (April 1999).

Appendix 11   Structural Excess Capacity at Nissan (1998)

Region	No of Plants	Capacity	Production	Excess Capacity	%
Japan	4	2000000	1600000	400000	20%
Rest of Asia	3	260000	106000	154000	59%
N. America	3	720000	500000	220000	31%
Europe	2	430000	280000	150000	35%
Total		3410000	2486000	924000	27%

Source: *Automobile News.*

Appendix 12 Nissan Motor Co.—Financial Snapshot

				Nissan Motor Co. (Mil. Yen)			
	03/31/1992	03/31/1993	03/31/1994	03/31/1995	03/31/1996	03/31/1997	03/31/1998
Sales	6,417,931	6,197,599	5,800,857	5,834,123	6,039,107	6,658,875	6,564,637
Operating income (loss)	154,279	−5,417	−142,319	−102,717	43,235	199,880	84,346
Income (loss) before tax	166,371	−56,545	−101,331	−179,745	−81,454	101,073	−24,458
EBT margin	2.59%	−0.91%	−1.75%	−3.08%	−1.35%	1.52%	−0.37%
Total income taxes	67,859	7,842	−1,357	2,901	12,504	31,619	−6,842
Net income (loss)	101,295	−55,998	−86,915	−166,054	−88,418	77,743	−14,007
Number of shares (mil)	2,512	2,512	2,512	2,513	2,513	2,513	2,437
Net income (loss) per share	40.32	−22.28	−34.59	−66.09	−35.18	30.94	−5.57
Sales ('000 units)		2,813	2,691	2,700	2,671	2,710	2,568
Total long-term debt	2,045,135	2,331,172	2,680,736	2,209,000	3,728,000	3,839,000	4,342,000
Total shareholders' equity		1,580,000	1,429,000	1,429,000	1,356,000	1,356,000	1,282,000
Debt/Equity ratio		148%	188%	155%	275%	283%	339%
Debt/Sales ratio	32%	38%	46%	38%	62%	58%	66%

Source: *Nissan Annual Report.*

Appendix 13   Global Demand by Country

	Global Automobile Demand (000 units)						
	1995	1996	1997	1998	1999(exp)	2000(exp)	2001(exp)
United States	14800	15097	15115	15697	16900	16300	16300
% change		2.01%	0.12%	3.85%	7.66%	−3.55%	0.00%
Europe							
– Germany	3314	3508	3528	3740	3880	3980	3950
% change		5.85%	0.57%	6.01%	3.74%	2.58%	−0.75%
– France	1930	2132	1713	1944	2130	2160	2080
% change		10.47%	−19.65%	13.49%	9.57%	1.41%	−3.70%
– Italy	1720	1719	2412	2364	2350	2400	2420
% change		−0.06%	40.31%	−1.99%	−0.59%	2.13%	0.83%
– U. K.	1945	2026	2171	2247	2180	1950	1880
% change		4.16%	7.16%	3.50%	−2.98%	−10.55%	−3.59%
– Spain	833	909	1012	1191	1450	1450	1400
% change		9.12%	11.33%	17.69%	21.75%	0.00%	−3.45%
Total Europe	9742	10294	10836	11486	11990	11940	11730
% change		5.67%	5.27%	6.00%	4.39%	−0.42%	−1.76%
Asia							
– Japan	6865	6896	6726	5880	5886	6000	6200
% change		0.45%	−2.47%	−12.58%	0.10%	1.94%	3.33%
– China	912	976	1085	1027	1120	1305	1493
% change		7.02%	11.17%	−5.35%	9.06%	16.52%	14.41%
– Korea	1556	1644	1513	780	1092	1190	1273
% change		5.66%	−7.97%	−48.45%	40.00%	8.97%	6.97%
Total Asia	9333	9516	9324	7687	8098	8495	8966
% change		1.96%	−2.02%	−17.56%	5.35%	4.90%	5.54%
Latin America							
– Brazil	1579	1632	1827	1415	1100	1250	1450
% change		3.36%	11.95%	−22.55%	−22.26%	13.64%	16.00%
– Argentina	319	362	396	437	445	493	510
% change		13.48%	9.39%	10.35%	1.83%	10.79%	3.45%
Total Latin America	1898	1994	2223	1852	1545	1743	1960
% change		5.06%	11.48%	−16.69%	−16.58%	12.82%	12.45%
Rest of the World	5910	5446	6019	6000	6314	6765	6957
% change		−7.85%	10.52%	−0.32%	5.23%	7.14%	2.84%
World Total	41683	42347	43517	42722	44847	45243	45913
% change		1.59%	2.76%	−1.83%	4.97%	0.88%	1.48%

Source: Warburg Dillion Reed Global Auto Analyser (September 1999).

Appendix 14   Market Shares by Region

	1995	1996	1997	1998	1999(exp)
European Market Shares					
VW	18.30%	17.20%	17.20%	18.10%	18.90%
PSA	12.70%	12.00%	11.30%	11.40%	11.50%
Japanese	11.40%	11.10%	11.50%	11.70%	11.50%
GM	13.30%	12.50%	12.10%	1.50%	11.60%
Ford	12.40%	11.60%	11.30%	10.20%	11.50%
Renault	10.70%	10.10%	9.90%	10.70%	10.60%
Fiat	12.00%	11.10%	11.90%	10.90%	10.40%
BMW	6.40%	6.30%	6.10%	5.70%	5.20%
DaimlerChrysler	3.80%	3.60%	4.40%	5.00%	5.40%
US Market Shares					
GM	33.10%	31.70%	31.50%	29.40%	29.60%
Ford	36.20%	25.90%	25.70%	25.00%	24.70%
DaimlerChrysler	15.60%	17.30%	16.50%	17.70%	16.90%
Toyota	7.30%	7.70%	8.10%	8.70%	8.60%
Honda	5.40%	5.60%	6.20%	6.40%	6.30%
Nissan	5.20%	5.00%	4.80%	4.00%	3.90%
VW	0.90%	1.10%	1.10%	1.70%	2.20%
Mazda	1.90%	1.60%	1.50%	1.50%	1.50%
Koreans	90.00%	1.00%	1.10%	1.10%	1.90%
Japanese Market Shares					
Toyota	29.60%	30.50%	29.60%	28.90%	28.20%
Nissan	16.00%	15.90%	15.40%	15.30%	13.60%
Mitsubishi	11.90%	10.90%	10.10%	10.10%	10.20%
Honda	8.30%	10.20%	11.50%	11.60%	11.10%
Suzuki	9.00%	9.00%	8.90%	9.40%	10.50%
Daihatsu	6.00%	6.80%	6.70%	7.40%	9.10%
Mazda	5.30%	4.80%	5.00%	5.40%	5.40%
Fuji Heavy	5.00%	5.10%	4.50%	4.70%	5.10%
Imports	5.70%	6.20%	5.40%	4.70%	4.70%

Source: Warburg Dillion Reed Global Auto Analyser (September 1999).

Appendix 15   Global Automakers Profitability (EBIT Margin)

	1996	1997	1998	1999(exp)
GM	2.50%	−0.30%	3.50%	6.80%
Ford	3.40%	6.60%	6.70%	7.70%
DaimlerChrysler	5.20%	4.70%	5.60%	8.70%
VW	3.00%	3.00%	4.90%	5.00%
Renault	−3.30%	1.00%	4.40%	4.10%
Fiat	2.30%	3.90%	1.60%	1.40%
BMW	4.50%	5.50%	4.70%	5.20%
Toyota	4.90%	6.60%	6.30%	5.90%
Nissan	2.40%	1.70%	1.60%	1.60%
Honda	6.70%	9.80%	9.30%	8.70%
Suzuki	4.10%	3.50%	3.30%	3.30%

Source: Warburg Dillion Reed Global Auto Analyser (September 1999).

Case 6-3   Eli Lilly in India: Rethinking the Joint Venture Strategy

In August 2001, Dr. Lorenzo Tallarigo, president of Intercontinental Operations, Eli Lilly and Company (Lilly), a leading pharmaceutical firm based in the United States, was getting ready for a meeting in New York, with D. S. Brar, chairman and chief executive officer (CEO) of Ranbaxy Laboratories Limited (Ranbaxy), India. Lilly and Ranbaxy had started a joint venture (JV) in India, Eli Lilly–Ranbaxy Private Limited (ELR) that was incorporated in March 1993. The JV had steadily grown to a full-fledged organization employing more than 500 people in 2001. However, in recent months Lilly was re-evaluating the directions for the JV, with Ranbaxy signaling an intention to sell its stake. Tallarigo was scheduled to meet with Brar to decide on the next steps.

The Global Pharmaceutical Industry in the 1990s

The pharmaceutical industry had come about through both forward integration from the manufacture of organic chemicals and a backward inte-

Ivey

Richard Ivey School of Business
The University of Western Ontario

Nikhil Celly prepared this case under the supervision of Professors Charles Dhanaraj and Paul W. Beamish solely to provide material for class discussion. The authors do not intend to illustrate either effective or ineffective handling of a managerial situation. The authors may have disguised certain names and other identifying information to protect confidentiality. Ivey Management Services prohibits any form of reproduction, storage, or transmittal without its written permission. This material is not covered under authorization from CanCopy or any reproduction rights organization. To order copies or request permission to reproduce materials, contact Ivey Publishing, Ivey Management Services, c/o Richard Ivey School of Business, The University of Western Ontario, London, Ontario, Canada, N6A 3K7; phone (519) 661-3208; fax (519) 661-3882; e-mail cases@ivey.uwo.ca.
Copyright © 2004, Ivey Management Services. Version: (A) 2005-12-02. One-time permission to reproduce Ivey cases granted by Ivey Management Services April 4, 2006.

gration from druggist-supply houses. The industry's rapid growth was aided by increasing worldwide incomes and a universal demand for better health care; however, most of the world market for pharmaceuticals was concentrated in North America, Europe and Japan. Typically, the largest four firms claimed 20 per cent of sales, the top 20 firms 50 per cent to 60 per cent and the 50 largest companies accounted for 65 per cent to 75 per cent of sales (see Exhibit 1). Drug discovery was an expensive process, with leading firms spending more than 20 per cent of their sales on research and development (R&D). Developing a drug, from discovery to launch in a major market, took 10 to 12 years and typically cost US$500 million to US$800 million (in 1992). Bulk production of active ingredients was the norm, along with the ability to decentralize manufacturing and packaging to adapt to particular market needs. Marketing was usually equally targeted to physicians and the paying customers. Increasingly, government agencies, such as Medicare, and health management organizations (HMOs) in the United States were gaining influence in the buying processes. In most countries, all activities related to drug research and manufacturing were strictly controlled by government agencies, such as the Food and Drug Administration (FDA) in the United States, the Committee on Proprietary Medicinal Products (CPMP) in Europe, and the Ministry of Health and Welfare (MHW) in Japan.

Patents were the essential means by which a firm protected its proprietary knowledge. The safety provided by the patents allowed firms to price their products appropriately in order to accumulate funds for future research. The basic reason to patent a new drug was to guarantee the exclusive legal right to profit from its innovation for a certain number of years, typically 20 years for a product patent. There was usually a time lag of about eight to 10 years

Exhibit 1   World Pharmaceutical Suppliers 1992 and 2001 (US$ millions)

Company	Origin	1992 Sales*	Company	Origin	2001 Sales**
Glaxo	US	8,704	Pfizer	USA	25,500
Merck	UK	8,214	GlaxoSmithKline	UK	24,800
Bristol-Myers Squibb	US	6,313	Merck & Co	USA	21,350
Hoechst	GER	6,042	AstraZeneca	UK	16,480
Ciba-Geigy	SWI	5,192	Bristol-Myers Squibb	USA	15,600
SmithKline Beecham	US	5,100	Aventis	FRA	15,350
Roche	SWI	4,897	Johnson & Johnson	USA	14,900
Sandoz	SWI	4,886	Novartis	SWI	14,500
Bayer	GER	4,670	Pharmacia Corp	USA	11,970
American Home	US	4,589	Eli Lilly	USA	11,540
Pfizer	US	4,558	Wyeth	USA	11,710
Eli Lilly	US	4,537	Roche	SWI	8,530
Johnson & Johnson	US	4,340	Schering-Plough	USA	8,360
Rhone Poulenc Rorer	US	4,096	Abbott Laboratories	USA	8,170
Abbott	US	4,025	Takeda	JAP	7,770
			Sanofi-Synthélabo	FRA	5,700
			Boehringer Ingelheim	GER	5,600
			Bayer	GER	5,040
			Schering AG	GER	3,900
			Akzo Nobel	NTH	3,550

* Market Share Reporter, 1993.
** Pharmaceutical Executive, May 2002.

from the time the patent was obtained and the time of regulatory approval to first launch in the United States or Europe. Time lags for emerging markets and in Japan were longer. The "product patent" covered the chemical substance itself, while a "process patent" covered the method of processing or manufacture. Both patents guaranteed the inventor a 20-year monopoly on the innovation, but the process patent offered much less protection, since it was fairly easy to modify a chemical process. It was also very difficult to legally prove that a process patent had been created to manufacture a product identical to that of a competitor. Most countries relied solely on process patents until the mid-1950s, although many countries had since recognized the product patent in law. While companies used the global market to amortize the huge investments required to produce a new drug, they were hesitant to invest in countries where the intellectual property regime was weak.

As health-care costs soared in the 1990s, the pharmaceutical industry in developed countries began coming under increased scrutiny. Although patent protection was strong in developed countries, there were various types of price controls. Prices for the same drugs varied between the United States and Canada by a factor of 1.2 to 2.5.[1] Parallel trade or trade by independent firms taking advantage of such differentials represented a serious threat to pharmaceutical suppliers, especially in Europe.

[1]Estimates of industry average wholesale price levels in Europe (with Spanish levels indexed at 100 in 1989) were: Spain 100; Portugal 107; France 113; Italy 118; Belgium 131; United Kingdom 201; The Netherlands 229; West Germany 251. Source: T. Malnight, "Globalization of an Ethnocentric Firm: An Evolutionary Perspective," *Strategic Management Journal,* 1995, Vol. 16, p.128.

Also, the rise of generics, unbranded drugs of comparable efficacy in treating the disease but available at a fraction of the cost of the branded drugs, were challenging the pricing power of the pharmaceutical companies. Manufacturers of generic drugs had no expense for drug research and development of new compounds and only had limited budgets for popularizing the compound with the medical community. The generic companies made their money by copying what other pharmaceutical companies discovered, developed and created a market for. Health management organizations (HMOs) were growing and consolidating their drug purchases. In the United States, the administration under President Clinton, which took office in 1992, investigated the possibility of a comprehensive health plan, which, among other things, would have allowed an increased use of generics and laid down some form of regulatory pressure on pharmaceutical profits.

The Indian Pharmaceutical Industry in the 1990s

Developing countries, such as India, although large by population, were characterized by low per capita gross domestic product (GDP). Typically, healthcare expenditures accounted for a very small share of GDP, and health insurance was not commonly available. The 1990 figures for per capita annual expenditure on drugs in India were estimated at US$3, compared to US$412 in Japan, US$222 in Germany and US$191 in the United Kingdom.[2] Governments and large corporations extended health coverage, including prescription drug coverage, to their workers.

In the years before and following India's independence in 1947, the country had no indigenous capability to produce pharmaceuticals, and was dependent on imports. The Patent and Designs Act of 1911, an extension of the British colonial rule, enforced adherence to the international patent law, and gave rise to a number of multinational firms' subsidiaries in India, that wanted to import drugs from their respective countries of origin. Post-independence, the first public sector drug company, Hindustan Antibiotics Limited (HAL), was established in 1954, with the help of the World Health Organization, and Indian Drugs and Pharmaceutical Limited (IDPL) was established in 1961 with the help of the then Soviet Union.

The 1970s saw several changes that would dramatically change the intellectual property regime and give rise to the emergence of local manufacturing companies. Two such key changes were the passage of the Patents Act 1970 (effective April 1972) and the Drug Price Control Order (DPCO). The Patents Act in essence abolished the product patents for all pharmaceutical and agricultural products, and permitted process patents for five to seven years. The DPCO instituted price controls, by which a government body stipulated prices for all drugs. Subsequently, this list was revised in 1987 to 142 drugs (which accounted for 72 per cent of the turnover of the industry). Indian drug prices were estimated to be five per cent to 20 per cent of the U.S. prices and among the lowest in the world.[3] The DPCO also limited profits pharmaceutical companies could earn to approximately six per cent of sales turnover. Also, the post-manufacturing expenses were limited to 100 per cent of the production costs. At the World Health Assembly in 1982 Indira Gandhi, then Prime Minister of India, aptly captured the national sentiment on the issue in an often-quoted statement:

> The idea of a better-ordered world is one in which medical discoveries will be free of patents and there will be no profiteering from life and death.

With the institution of both the DPCO and the 1970 Patent Act, drugs became available more cheaply, and local firms were encouraged to make copies of drugs by developing their own processes, leading to bulk drug production. The profitability

---

[2]Organization of Pharmaceutical Producers of India Report.

[3]According to a study from Yale University, Ranitidine (300 tabs/10 pack) was priced at Rs18.53, whereas the U.S. price was 57 times more, and Ciprofloxacin (500 mg/4 pack) was at Rs28.40 in India, whereas the U.S. price was about 15 times more.

was sharply reduced for multinational companies, many of which began opting out of the Indian market due to the disadvantages they faced from the local competition. Market share of multinational companies dropped from 80 per cent in 1970 to 35 per cent in the mid-1990s as those companies exited the market due to the lack of patent protection in India.

In November 1984, there were changes in the government leadership following Gandhi's assassination. The dawn of the 1990s saw India initiating economic reform and embracing globalization. Under the leadership of Dr. Manmohan Singh, then finance minister, the government began the process of liberalization and moving the economy away from import substitution to an export-driven economy. Foreign direct investment was encouraged by increasing the maximum limit of foreign ownership to 51 per cent (from 40 per cent) in the drugs and pharmaceutical industry (see Exhibit 2). It was in this environment that Eli Lilly was considering getting involved.

Eli Lilly and Company

Colonel Eli Lilly founded Eli Lilly and Company in 1876. The company would become one of the largest pharmaceutical companies in the United States from the early 1940s until 1985 but it began with just $1,400 and four employees, including Lilly's 14-year-old son. This was accomplished with a company philosophy grounded in a commitment to scientific and managerial excellence. Over the years, Eli Lilly discovered, developed, manufactured and sold a broad line of human health and agricultural products. Research and development was crucial to Lilly's long-term success.

Before 1950, most OUS (a company term for "Outside the United States") activities were export focused. Beginning in the 1950s, Lilly undertook systematic expansion of its OUS activities, setting up several affiliates overseas. In the mid-1980s, under the leadership of then chairman, Dick Wood,

Exhibit 2   India Economy at a Glance

	1992	1994	1996	1998	2000
Gross domestic product (GDP) at current market prices in US$	244	323	386	414	481
Consumer price index (June 1982 = 100) in local currency, period average	77.4	90.7	108.9	132.2	149.3
Recorded official unemployment as a percentage of total labor force	9.7	9.3	9.1	9.2	9.2
Stock of foreign reserves plus gold (national valuation), end-period	8,665	23,054	23,784	29,833	48,200
Foreign direct investment inflow (in US$ millions)[1]	252	974	2,525	2,633	2,319
Total exports	19,563	25,075	33,055	33,052	43,085
Total imports	23,580	26,846	37,376	42,318	49,907

Year	Population*
1991	846
2001	1,027

Source: The Economist Intelligence Unit.
[1] United Nations Commission on Trade and Development.
[2] 1991, 2001 Census of India.
* In millions.

Lilly began a significant move toward global markets. A separate division within the company, Eli Lilly International Corporation, with responsibility for worldwide marketing of all its products, took an active role in expanding the OUS operations. By 1992, Lilly's products were manufactured and distributed through 25 countries and sold in more than 130 countries. The company had emerged as a world leader in oral and injectable antibiotics and in supplying insulin and related diabetic care products. In 1992, Lilly International was headed by Sidney Taurel, an MBA from Columbia University, with work experience in South America and Europe, and Gerhard Mayr, an MBA from Stanford, with extensive experience in Europe. Mayr wanted to expand Lilly's operations in Asia, where several countries including India were opening up their markets for foreign investment. Lilly also saw opportunities to use the world for clinical testing, which would enable it to move forward faster, as well as shape opinion with leaders in the medical field around the world; something that would help in Lilly's marketing stage.

Ranbaxy Laboratories

Ranbaxy began in the 1960s as a family business, but with a visionary management grew rapidly to emerge as the leading domestic pharmaceutical firm in India. Under the leadership of Dr. Parvinder Singh, who held a doctoral degree from the University of Michigan, the firm evolved into a serious research-oriented firm. Singh, who joined Ranbaxy to assist his father in 1967, rose to become the joint managing director in 1977, managing director in 1982, and vice-chairman and managing director in 1987. Singh's visionary management, along with the operational leadership provided by Brar, who joined the firm in 1977, was instrumental in turning the family business into a global corporation. In the early 1990s, when almost the entire domestic pharmaceutical industry was opposing a tough patent regime, Ranbaxy was accepting it as given. Singh's argument was unique within the industry in India:

The global marketplace calls for a single set of rules; you cannot have one for the Indian market and the

other for the export market. Tomorrow's global battles will be won by product leaders, not operationally excellent companies. Tomorrow's leaders must be visionaries, whether they belong to the family or not. Our mission at Ranbaxy is to become a research based international pharmaceutical company.[4]

By the early 1990s, Ranbaxy grew to become India's largest manufacturer of bulk drugs[5] and generic drugs, with a domestic market share of 15 per cent (see Exhibit 3).

One of Ranbaxy's core competencies was its chemical synthesis capability, but the company had begun to outsource some bulk drugs in limited quantities. The company produced pharmaceuticals in four locations in India. The company's capital costs were typically 50 per cent to 75 per cent lower than those of comparable U.S. plants and were meant to serve foreign markets in addition to the Indian market. Foreign markets, especially those in more developed countries, often had stricter quality control requirements, and such a difference meant that the manufacturing practices required to compete in those markets appeared to be costlier from the perspective of less developed markets. Higher prices in other countries provided the impetus for Ranbaxy to pursue international markets; the company had a presence in 47 markets outside India, mainly through exports handled through an international division. Ranbaxy's R&D efforts began at the end of the 1970s; in 1979, the company still had only 12 scientists. As Ranbaxy entered the international market in the 1980s, R&D was responsible for registering its products in foreign markets, most of which was directed to process R&D; R&D expenditures ranged from two per cent to five per cent of the annual sales with future targets of seven per cent to eight per cent.

The Lilly Ranbaxy JV

Ranbaxy approached Lilly in 1992 to investigate the possibility of supplying certain active ingredients or sourcing of intermediate products to Lilly in

---

[4]Quoted in *Times of India,* June 9, 1999.
[5]A bulk drug is an intermediate product that goes into manufacturing of pharmaceutical products.

Exhibit 3   Top 20 Pharmaceutical Companies in India by Sales 1996 to 2000 (Rs billions)

Company	1996*	Company	2000
Glaxo-Wellcome	4.97	Ranbaxy	20.00
Cipla	2.98	Cipla	12.00
Ranbaxy	2.67	Dr. Reddy's Labs	11.30
Hoechts-Roussel	2.60	Glaxo (India)	7.90
Knoll Pharmaceutical	1.76	Lupin Labs	7.80
Pfizer	1.73	Aurobindo Pharma	7.60
Alembic	1.68	Novartis	7.20
Torrent Pharma	1.60	Wockhardt Ltd.	6.80
Lupin Labs	1.56	Sun Pharma	6.70
Zydus-Cadila	1.51	Cadilla Healthcare	5.80
Ambalal Sarabhai	1.38	Nicholas Piramal	5.70
Smithkline Beecham	1.20	Aventis Pharma	5.30
Aristo Pharma	1.17	Alembic Ltd.	4.80
Parke Davis	1.15	Morepen Labs	4.70
Cadila Pharma	1.12	Torrent Pharma	4.40
E. Merck	1.11	IPCA Labs	4.20
Wockhardt	1.08	Knoll Pharma	3.70
John Wyeth	1.04	Orchid Chemicals	3.60
Alkem Laboratories	1.04	E Merck	3.50
Hindustan Ciba Geigy	1.03	Pfizer	3.40

Source: "Report on Pharmaceutical Sector in India," *Scope Magazine,* September 2001, p.14.
*1996 figures are from ORG, Bombay as reported in Lanjouw, J.O., www.oiprc.ox.ac.uk/EJWP0799.html, NBER working paper No. 6366.

order to provide low-cost sources of intermediate pharmaceutical ingredients. Lilly had had earlier relationships with manufacturers in India to produce human or animal insulin and then export the products to the Soviet Union using the Russia/India trade route, but those had never developed into on-the-ground relationships within the Indian market. Ranbaxy was the second largest exporter of all products in India and the second largest pharmaceutical company in India after Glaxo (a subsidiary of the U.K.-based firm).

Rajiv Gulati, at that time a general manager of business development and marketing controller at Ranbaxy, who was instrumental in developing the strategy for Ranbaxy, recalled:

In the 1980s, many multinational pharmaceutical companies had a presence in India. Lilly did not. As a result of both the sourcing of intermediate products as well as the fact that Lilly was one of the only players not yet in India, we felt that we could use Ranbaxy's knowledge of the market to get our feet on the ground in India. Ranbaxy would supply certain products to the joint venture from its own portfolio that were currently being manufactured in India and then formulate and finish some of Lilly's products locally. The joint venture would buy the active ingredients and Lilly would have Ranbaxy finish the package and allow the joint venture to sell and distribute those products.

The first meeting was held at Lilly's corporate center in Indianapolis in late 1990. Present were Ranbaxy's senior executives, Dr. Singh, vice-chairman, and D.S. Brar, chief operating officer (COO), and Lilly's senior executives including Gene Step and Richard Wood, the CEO of Lilly.

Rickey Pate, a corporate attorney at Eli Lilly who was present at the meeting, recalled:

> It was a very smooth meeting. We had a lot in common. We both believed in high ethical standards, in technology and innovation, as well as in the future of patented products in India. Ranbaxy executives emphasized their desire to be a responsible corporate citizen and expressed their concerns for their employees. It was quite obvious Ranbaxy would be a compatible partner in India.

Lilly decided to form the joint venture in India to focus on marketing Lilly's drugs there, and a formal JV agreement was signed in November 1992. The newly created JV was to have an authorized capital of Rs200 million (equivalent of US$7.1 million), and an initial subscribed equity capital of Rs84 million (US$3 million), with equal contribution from Lilly and Ranbaxy, leading to an equity ownership of 50 per cent each. The board of directors for the JV would comprise six directors, three from each company. A management committee was also created comprising two directors, one from each company, and Lilly retained the right to appoint the CEO who would be responsible for the day-to-day operations. The agreement also provided for transfer of shares, in the event any one of the partners desired to dispose some or its entire share in the company.

In the mid-1990s, Lilly was investigating the possibility of extending its operations to include generics. Following the launch of the Indian JV, Lilly and Ranbaxy, entered into two other agreements related to generics, one in India to focus on manufacturing generics, and the other in the United States to focus on the marketing of generics. However, within less than a year, Lilly made a strategic decision not to enter the generics market and the two parties agreed to terminate the JV agreements related to the generics. Mayr recalled:

> At that time we were looking at the Indian market although we did not have any particular time frame for entry. We particularly liked Ranbaxy, as we saw an alignment of the broad values. Dr. Singh had a clear vision of leading Ranbaxy to become an innovation driven company. And we liked what we saw in them.

> Of course, for a time we were looking at the generic business and wondering if this was something we should be engaged in. Other companies had separate division for generics and we were evaluating such an idea. However, we had a pilot program in Holland and that taught us what it took to be competitive in generics and decided that business wasn't for us, and so we decided to get out of generics.

The Start-Up   By March 1993, Andrew Mascarenhas, an American citizen of Indian origin, who at the time was the general manager for Lilly's Caribbean basin, based in San Juan, Puerto Rico, was selected to become the managing director of the joint venture. Rajiv Gulati, who at the time spearheaded the business development and marketing efforts at Ranbaxy, was chosen as the director of marketing and sales at the JV. Mascarenhas recalled:

> Lilly saw the joint venture as an investment the company needed to make. At the time India was a country of 800 million people: 200 million to 300 million of them were considered to be within the country's middle class that represented the future of India. The concept of globalization was just taking hold at Lilly. India, along with China and Russia were seen as markets where Lilly needed to build a greater presence. Some resistance was met due to the recognition that a lot of Lilly's products were already being sold by Indian manufacturers due to the lack of patent protection and intellectual property rights so the question was what products should we put in there that could be competitive. The products that were already being manufactured had sufficient capacity; so it was an issue of trying to leverage the markets in which those products were sold into.

> Lilly was a name that most physicians in India did not recognize despite its leadership position in the United States, it did not have any recognition in India. Ranbaxy was the leader within India. When I was informed that the name of the joint venture was to be Lilly Ranbaxy, first thing I did was to make sure that the name of the joint venture was Eli Lilly Ranbaxy and not just Lilly Ranbaxy. The reason for this was based on my earlier experience in India, where "good quality" rightly or wrongly, was associated with foreign imported goods. Eli Lilly Ranbaxy sounded foreign enough!

Early on, Mascarenhas and Gulati worked on getting the venture up and running with office space and an employee base. Mascarenhas recalled:

I got a small space within Ranbaxy's set-up. We had two tables, one for Rajiv and the other for me. We had to start from that infrastructure and move towards building up the organization from scratch. Rajiv was great to work with and we both were able to see eye-to-eye on most issues. Dr. Singh was a strong supporter and the whole of Ranbaxy senior management tried to assist us whenever we asked for help.

The duo immediately hired a financial analyst, and the team grew from there. Early on, they hired a medical director, a sales manager and a human resources manager. The initial team was a good one, but there was enormous pressure and the group worked seven days a week. Ranbaxy's help was used for getting government approvals, licenses, distribution and supplies. Recalled Gulati:

We used Ranbaxy's name for everything. We were new and it was very difficult for us. We used their distribution network as we did not have one and Lilly did not want to invest heavily in setting up a distribution network. We paid Ranbaxy for the service. Ranbaxy was very helpful.

By the end of 1993, the venture moved to an independent place, began launching products and employed more than 200 people. Within another year, Mascarenhas had hired a significant sales force and had recruited medical doctors and financial people for the regulatory group with assistance from Lilly's Geneva office. Mascarenhas recalled:

Our recruiting theme was "Opportunity of a Lifetime" i.e., joining a new company, and to be part of its very foundation. Many who joined us, especially at senior level, were experienced executives. By entering this new and untested company, they were really taking a huge risk with their careers and the lives of their families.

However, the employee turnover in the Indian pharmaceutical industry was very high. Sandeep Gupta, director of marketing, recalled:

Our biggest problem was our high turnover rate. A sales job in the pharmaceutical industry was not the most sought-after position. Any university graduate could be employed. The pharmaceutical industry in India is very unionized. Ranbaxy's HR practices were designed to work with unionized employees. From the very beginning, we did not want our recruits to join unions. Instead, we chose to show recruits that they had a career in ELR. When they joined us as sales graduates they did not just remain at that level. We took a conscious decision to promote from within the company. The venture began investing in training and used Lilly's training programs. The programs were customized for Indian conditions, but retained Lilly's values [see Exhibit 4].

Within a year, the venture team began gaining the trust and respect of doctors, due to the strong values adhered to by Lilly. Mascarenhas described how the venture fought the Indian stigma:

Lilly has a code of ethical conduct called the Red Book, and the company did not want to go down the path where it might be associated with unethical behavior. But Lilly felt Ranbaxy knew how to do things the right way and that they respected their employees, which was a very important attribute. So following Lilly's Red Book values, the group told doctors the truth; both the positive and negative aspects of their drugs. If a salesperson didn't know the answer to something, they didn't lie or make up something; they told the doctor they didn't know. No bribes were given or taken, and it was found that honesty and integrity could actually be a competitive advantage. Sales people were trained to offer product information to doctors. The group gradually became distinguished by this "strange" behavior.

Recalled Sudhanshu Kamat, controller of finance at ELR:

Lilly from the start treated us as its employees, like all its other affiliates worldwide. We followed the same systems and processes that any Lilly affiliate would worldwide.

Much of the success of the joint venture is attributed to the strong and cohesive working relationship of Mascarenhas and Gulati. Mascarenhas recalled:

We both wanted the venture to be successful. We both had our identities to the JV, and there was no Ranbaxy versus Lilly politics. From the very start when we had

---

Exhibit 4   Values at Eli Lilly Ranbaxy Limited

People

"The people who make up this company are its most valuable assets."

- Respect for the individual
  - o Courtesy and politeness at all times
  - o Sensitivity to other people's views
  - o Respect for ALL people regardless of caste, religion, sex or age
- Careers NOT jobs
  - o Emphasis on individual's growth, personal and professional
  - o Broaden experience via cross-functional moves

"The first responsibility of our supervisors is **to build men, then medicines**."

Attitude

"There is very little difference between people. But that difference makes a BIG difference. The little difference is attitude. The BIG difference is … whether it is POSITIVE or NEGATIVE."
"Are we part of the PROBLEM or part of the SOLUTION?"

Team

"None of us is as smart as all of us."

Integrity

- Integrity outside the company
  a. "We should not do anything or be expected to take any action that we would be ashamed to explain to our family or close friends"
  b. "The red-faced test"
  c. "Integrity can be our biggest competitive advantage"
- Integrity inside the company
  o With one another: openness, honesty

Excellence

- Serving our customers

"In whatever we do, we must ask ourselves: how does this serve my customer better?"

- Continuous improvement

"Nothing is being done today that cannot be done better tomorrow."

- Become the Industry Standard

"In whatever we do, we will do it so well that we become the Industry Standard."

---

our office at Ranbaxy premises, I was invited to dine with their senior management. Even after moving to our own office, I continued the practice of having lunch at Ranbaxy HQ on a weekly basis. I think it helped a lot to be accessible at all times and to build on the personal relationship.

The two companies had very different business focuses. Ranbaxy was a company driven by the generics business. Lilly, on the other hand, was driven by innovation and discovery.

Mascarenhas focused his effort on communicating Eli Lilly's values to the new joint venture:

I spent a lot of time communicating Lilly's values to newly hired employees. In the early days, I interviewed our senior applicants personally. I was present in the two-day training sessions that we offered for the new employees, where I shared the values of the company. That was a critical task for me to make sure that the right foundations were laid down for growth.

The first products that came out of the joint venture were human insulin from Lilly and several Ranbaxy products; but the team faced constant challenges in dealing with government regulations on the one hand and financing the affiliate on the other. There were also cash flow constraints.

The ministry of health provided limitations on Lilly's pricing, and even with the margin the Indian government allowed, most of it went to the wholesalers and the pharmacies, pursuant to formulas in the Indian ministry of health. Once those were factored out of the gross margin, achieving profitability was a real challenge, as some of the biggest obstacles faced were duties imposed by the Indian government on imports and other regulatory issues. Considering the weak intellectual property rights regime, Lilly did not want to launch some of its products, such as its top-seller, Prozac.[6] Gulati recalled:

> We focused only on those therapeutic areas where Lilly had a niche. We did not adopt a localization strategy such as the ones adopted by Pfizer and Glaxo[7] that manufactured locally and sold at local prices. India is a high-volume, low price, low profit market, but it was a conscious decision by us to operate the way we did. We wanted to be in the global price band. So, we did not launch several patented products because generics were selling at 1/60th the price.

Product and marketing strategies had to be adopted to suit the market conditions. ELR's strategy evolved over the years to focus on two groups of products: one was off-patent drugs, where Lilly could add substantial value (e.g. Ceclor), and two, patented drugs, where there existed a significant barrier to entry (e.g. Reopro and Gemzar). ELR marketed Ceclor, a Ranbaxy manufactured product, but attempted to add significant value by providing medical information to the physicians and other

unique marketing activities. By the end of 1996, the venture had reached the break-even and was becoming profitable.

The Mid-Term Organizational Changes Mascarenhas was promoted in 1996 to managing director of Eli Lilly Italy, and Chris Shaw, a British national, who was then managing the operations in Taiwan, was assigned to the JV as the new managing director. Also, Gulati, who was formally a Ranbaxy employee, decided to join Eli Lilly as its employee, and was assigned to Lilly's corporate office in Indianapolis in the Business Development–Infectious Diseases therapeutic division. Chris Shaw recalled:

> When I went to India as a British national, I was not sure what sort of reception I would get, knowing its history. But my family and I were received very warmly. I found a dynamic team with a strong sense of values.

Shaw focused on building systems and processes to bring stability to the fast-growing organization; his own expertise in operations made a significant contribution during this phase. He hired a senior level manager and created a team to develop standard operating procedures (SOPs) for ensuring smooth operations. The product line also expanded. The JV continued to maintain a 50–50 distribution of products from Lilly and Ranbaxy, although there was no stipulation to maintain such a ratio. The clinical organization in India received top-ratings in internal audits by Lilly, making it suitable for a wider range of clinical trials. Shaw also streamlined the sales and marketing activities around therapeutic areas to emphasize and enrich the knowledge capabilities of the company's sales force. Seeing the rapid change in the environment in India, ELR, with the support of Mayr, hired the management-consulting firm, McKinsey, to recommend growth options in India. ELR continued its steady performance with an annualized growth rate of about eight per cent during the late 1990s.

In 1999, Chris Shaw was assigned to Eli Lilly's Polish subsidiary, and Gulati returned to the ELR as

---

[6]Used as an antidepressant medication.

[7]An industry study by McKinsey found that Glaxo sold 50 per cent of its volume, received three per cent of revenues and one per cent of profit in India.

its managing director, following his three-year tenure at Lilly's U.S. operations. Recalled Gulati:

> When I joined as MD in 1999, we were growing at eight per cent and had not added any new employees. I hired 150 people over the next two years and went about putting systems and processes in place. When we started in 1993 and during Andrew's time, we were like a grocery shop. Now we needed to be a company. We had to be a large durable organization and prepare ourselves to go from sales of US$10 million to sales of US$100 million.

ELR created a medical and regulatory unit, which handled the product approval processes with government. Suman Das, the chief financial officer (CFO), commented:

> We worked together with the government on the regulatory part. Actually, we did not take shelter under the Ranbaxy name but built a strong regulatory [medical and corporate affairs] foundation.

By early 2001, the venture was recording an excellent growth rate (see Exhibit 5), surpassing the average growth rate in the Indian pharmaceutical industry. ELR had already become the 46th largest pharmaceutical company in India out of 10,000 companies. Several of the multinational subsidiaries, which were started at the same time as ELR, had either closed down or were in serious trouble. Das summarized the achievements:

The JV did add some prestige to Ranbaxy's efforts as a global player as the Lilly name had enormous credibility while Lilly gained the toehold in India. In 10 years we did not have any cannibalization of each other's employees, quite a rare event if you compare with the other JVs. This helped us build a unique culture in India.

The New World, 2001

The pharmaceutical industry continued to grow through the 1990s. In 2001, worldwide retail sales were expected to increase 10 per cent to about US$350 billion. The United States was expected to remain the largest and fastest growing country among the world's major drug markets over the next three years. There was a consolidation trend in the industry with ongoing mergers and acquisitions reshaping the industry. In 1990, the world's top 10 players accounted for just 28 per cent of the market, while in 2000, the number had risen to 45 per cent and continued to grow. There was also a trend among leading global pharmaceutical companies to get back to basics and concentrate on core high-margined prescription preparations and divest non-core businesses. In addition, the partnerships between pharmaceutical and biotechnology companies were growing rapidly. There were a number of challenges, such as escalating R&D costs, lengthening development and approval times for new products, growing competition

Exhibit 5   Eli Lilly-Ranbaxy India Financials 1998 to 2001 (Rs'000s)

	1998-1999	1999-2000	2000-2001
Sales	559,766	632,188	876,266
Marketing Expenses	37,302	61,366	96,854
Other Expenses	157,907	180,364	254,822
Profit after Tax	5,898	12,301	11,999
Current Assets	272,635	353,077	466,738
Current Liabilities	239,664	297,140	471,635
Total Assets	303,254	386,832	516,241
No. of Employees	358	419	460
Exchange Rate (Rupees/US$)	42.6	43.5	46.8

Source: Company reports.
Note: Financial year runs from April 1 to March 31.

from generics and follow-on products, and rising cost-containment pressures, particularly with the growing clout of managed care organizations.

By 1995, Lilly had moved up to become the 12th leading pharmaceutical supplier in the world, sixth in the U.S. market, 17th in Europe and 77th in Japan. Much of Lilly's sales success through the mid-1990s came from its antidepressant drug, Prozac. But with the wonder drug due to go off patent in 2001, Lilly was aggressively working on a number of high-potential products. By the beginning of 2001, Lilly was doing business in 151 countries, with its international sales playing a significant role in the company's success (see Exhibits 6 and 7). Dr. Lorenzo Tallarigo recalled:

When I started as the president of the intercontinental operations, I realized that the world was very different in the 2000s from the world of 1990s. Particularly there were phenomenal changes in the markets in India and China. While I firmly believed that the partnership we had with Ranbaxy was really an excellent one, the fact that we were facing such a different market in the 21st century was reason enough to carefully evaluate our strategies in these markets.

Ranbaxy, too, had witnessed changes through the 1990s. Dr. Singh became the new CEO in 1993 and formulated a new mission for the company: to become a research-based international pharmaceutical company with $1 billion in sales by 2003. This vision saw Ranbaxy developing new drugs through basic research, earmarking 20 per cent of the R&D budget for such work. In addition to its joint venture with Lilly, Ranbaxy made three other manufacturing/marketing investments in developed markets: a joint venture with Genpharm in Canada ($1.1 million), and the acquisitions of Ohm Labs in the United States ($13.5 million) and Rima Pharmaceuticals ($8 million) in Ireland. With these deals, Ranbaxy had manufacturing facilities around the globe. While China and Russia were expected to remain key foreign markets, Ranbaxy was looking at the United States and the United Kingdom as its core international markets for the future. In 1999, Dr. Singh handed over the reins of the company to Brar, and later the same year, Ranbaxy lost this visionary leader due to an untimely death. Brar continued Singh's vision to keep Ranbaxy in a leadership position. However, the vast network of

Exhibit 6   Lilly Financials 1992 to 2000 (US$ millions)

	1992	1994	1996	1998	2000
Net sales	4,963	5,711	6,998	9,236	10,862
Foreign sales	2,207	2,710	3,587	3,401	3,858
Research and development expenses	731	839	1,190	1,739	2,019
Income from continuing operations before taxes and extraordinary items	1,194	1,699	2,131	2,665	3,859
Net income	709	1,286	1,524	2,097	3,058
Dividends per share*	1.128	1.260	0.694	0.830	1.060
Current assets	3,006	3,962	3,891	5,407	7,943
Current liabilities	2,399	5,670	4,222	4,607	4,961
Property and equipment	4,072	4,412	4,307	4,096	4,177
Total assets	8,673	14,507	14,307	12,596	14,691
Long-term debt	582	2,126	2,517	2,186	2,634
Shareholder equity	4,892	5,356	6,100	4,430	6,047
Number of employees*	24,500	24,900	27,400	29,800	35,700

Source: Company files.
*Actual value

Exhibit 7   Product Segment Information Lilly and Ranbaxy 1996 and 2000

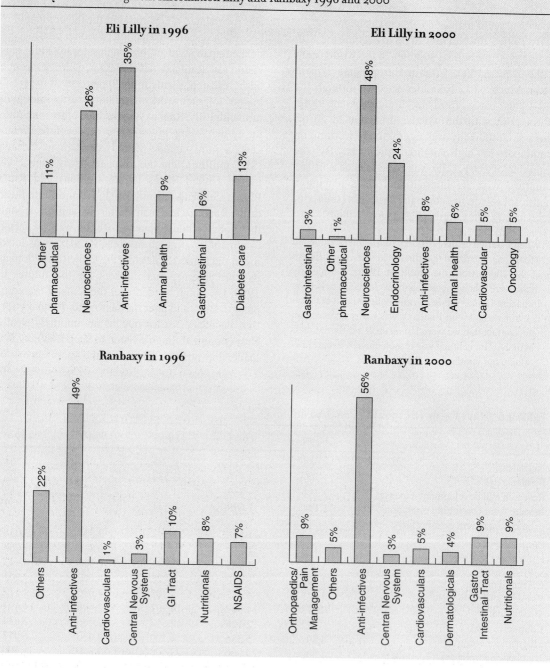

Exhibit 8   Ranbaxy Financials 1992 to 2000 (Rs millions)

	1992–93	1994–95	1996–97	1998*	2000
Sales	4,607	7,122	11,482	10,641	17,459
Foreign sales	1,408	3,019	5,224	4,414	8,112
Profit before tax	358	1,304	1,869	1,240	1,945
Profit after tax	353	1,104	1,604	1,170	1,824
Equity dividend	66.50	199.80	379.10	560.10	869.20
Earnings per share (Rs)	16.21	25.59	32.47	13.46	15.74
Net current assets	1,737	5,790	9,335	8,321	8,258
Share capital	217.90	430.50	494.00	1,159.00	1,159.00
Reserves and surplus	1,028	6,000	11,056	12,849	16,448
Book value per share (Rs)	57.16	149.08	233.70	120.90	136.60
No. of employees	4,575	4,703	6,131	5,469	5,784
Exchange rate (US$1 = Rs)	29.00	31.40	35.90	42.60	46.80

Source: Company files.

*The financial year for Ranbaxy changed from April 1 to March 31 to calendar year in 1998. Also, the company issued a 1:2 bonus issue (see the changes in share capital and book value per share). The 1998 figures are based on nine months April to December 1998.

international sales that Ranbaxy had developed created a large financial burden, depressing the company's 2000 results, and was expected to significantly affect its cash flow in 2001 (see Exhibit 8). Vinay Kaul, vice-chairman of Ranbaxy in 2001 and chairman of the board of ELR since 2000, noted:

We have come a long way from where we started. Our role in the present JV is very limited. We had a smooth relationship and we have been of significant help to Lilly to establish a foothold in the market here in India. Also, we have opened up a number of opportunities for them to expand their network. However, we have also grown, and we are a global company with presence in a number of international markets including the United States. We had to really think if this JV is central to our operations, given that we have closed down the other two JV agreements that we had with Lilly on the generics manufacturing. It is common knowledge that whether we continue as a JV or not, we have created a substantial value for Lilly.

There were also significant changes in the Indian business environment. India signed the General Agreement on Tariffs and Trade (GATT) in April 1994 and became a World Trade Organization (WTO) member in 1995. As per the WTO, from the year 2005, India would grant product patent recognition to all new chemical entities (NCEs), i.e., bulk drugs developed from then onward. Also, the Indian government had made the decision to allow 100 per cent foreign direct investment into the drugs and pharmaceutical industry in 2001.[8] The Indian pharmaceutical market had grown at an average of 15 per cent through the 1990s, but the trends indicated a slowdown in growth, partly due to intense price competition, a shift toward chronic therapies and the entry of large players into the generic market. India was seeing its own internal consolidation of major companies that were trying to bring in synergies through economies of scale. The industry would see more mergers and alliances. And with India's entry into the WTO and its agreement to begin patent protection in 2004–2005, competition on existing and new products was expected to intensify. Government guidelines were expected to include rationalization of price controls and the

[8]In order to regulate the parallel activities of a foreign company, which had an ongoing joint venture in India, the regulations stipulated that the foreign partner must get a "No objection letter" from its Indian partner, before setting up a wholly owned subsidiary.

encouragement of more research and development. Recalled Gulati:

> The change of institutional environment brought a great promise for Lilly. India was emerging into a market that had patent protection and with tremendous potential for adding value in the clinical trials, an important component in the pharmaceutical industry. In Ranbaxy, we had a partner with whom we could work very well, and one which greatly respected Lilly. However, there were considerable signals from both sides, which were forcing us to evaluate the strategy.

Dr. Vinod Mattoo, medical director of ELR, commented:

> We have been able to achieve penetration in key therapeutic areas of diabetes and oncology. We have created a high caliber, and non-unionized sales force with world-class sales processes. We have medical infrastructure and expertise to run clinical trials to international standards. We have been able to provide clinical trial data to support global registrations, and an organization in place to maximize returns post-2005.

Evaluating Strategic Options

Considering these several developments, Tallarigo suggested a joint task force comprising senior executives from both companies:

> Soon after assuming this role, I visited India in early 2000, and had the pleasure of meeting Dr. Brar and the senior executives. It was clear to me that both Brar and I were in agreement that we needed to think carefully how we approached the future. It was there that I suggested that we create a joint task force to come up with some options that would help us make a final decision.

A task force was set up with two senior executives from Lilly's Asia-Pacific regional office (based in Singapore) and two senior executives from Ranbaxy. The task force did not include senior executives of the ELR so as to not distract the running of the day-to-day operations. Das, the chief financial officer of ELR, was assigned to support the task force with the needed financial data. The task force developed several scenarios and presented different options for the board to consider.

There were rumors within the industry that Ranbaxy expected to divest the JV, and invest the cash in its growing portfolio of generics manufacturing business in international markets. There were also several other Indian companies that offered to buy Ranbaxy's stake in the JV. With India recognizing patent protection in 2005, several Indian pharmaceutical companies were keen to align with multinationals to ensure a pipeline of drugs. Although there were no formal offers from Ranbaxy, the company was expected to price its stakes as high as US$70 million. One of the industry observers in India commented:

> I think it is fair for Ranbaxy to expect a reasonable return for its investment in the JV, not only the initial capital, but also so much of its intangibles in the JV. Ranbaxy's stock has grown significantly. Given the critical losses that Ranbaxy has had in some of its investments abroad, the revenue from this sale may be a significant boost for Ranbaxy's cash flow this year.

Gerhard Mayr, who in 2001, was the executive vice-president and was responsible for Lilly's demand realization around the world, continued to emphasize the emerging markets in India, China and Eastern Europe. Mayr commented on Ranbaxy:

> India is an important market for us and especially after patent protection in 2005. Ranbaxy was a wonderful partner and our relationship with them was outstanding. The other two joint ventures we initiated with them in the generics did not make sense to us once we decided to get out of the generics business. We see India as a good market for Lilly. If a partner is what it takes to succeed, we should go with a partner. If it does not, we should have the flexibility to reconsider.

Tallarigo hoped that Brar would be able to provide a clear direction as to the venture's future. As he prepared for the meeting, he knew the decision was not an easy one, although he felt confident that the JV was in good shape. While the new regulations allowed Lilly to operate as a wholly-owned subsidiary in India, the partnership has been a very positive element in its strategy. Ranbaxy provided manufacturing and logistics support to the JV, and breaking up the partnership would require a significant amount of renegotiations. Also, it was not clear what the financial implications of such a move would be. Although Ranbaxy seemed to favor a sell-out, Tallarigo thought the price expectations might be beyond what Lilly was ready to accept. This meeting with Brar should provide clarity on all these issues.

Reading 6-1   The Design and Management of International Joint Ventures

Paul W. Beamish

An international joint venture is a company that is owned by two or more firms of different nationality. International joint ventures may be formed from a starting (or greenfield) basis or may be the result of several established companies deciding to merge existing divisions. However they are formed, the purpose of most international joint ventures is to allow partners to pool resources and coordinate their efforts to achieve results that neither could obtain acting alone.

A broad range of strategic alliances exists. They vary widely in terms of the level of interaction and type. Most of the comments in this reading focus on equity joint venture—the alliance form usually requiring the greatest level of interaction, cooperation, and investment. While the discussion which follows usually considers a two-party joint venture, it is worth noting that many joint ventures have three or more partners.

Joint ventures have moved from being a way to enter foreign markets of peripheral interest to become a part of the mainstream of corporate activity. Virtually all MNEs are using international joint ventures, many as a key element of their corporate strategies. Merck, for example, has joint ventures with Johnson & Johnson (2004 JV sales of $.3 billion), Pasteur Mérieux Connaught (now Sanofi Pasteur S.A., 2004 JV sales of $.8 billion), Rhône-Poulenc (now Sanofi-Aventis S.A., 2004 JV sales of $2.0 billion), and so forth. Even firms that have traditionally operated independently around the world are increasingly turning to joint ventures.

The popularity and use of international joint ventures and cooperative alliances remained strong through the 1990s. The rate of joint venture use does not change much from year to year. In general, joint ventures are the mode of choice 25–35 percent of the time by U.S. multinationals and in about 40 percent of foreign subsidiaries formed by Japanese multinationals.

The popularity of alliances has continued despite their reputation for being difficult to manage. Failures exist and are usually widely publicized. Dow Chemical, for example, reportedly lost more than $100 million after a dispute with its Korean joint venture partners caused the firm to sell its 50 percent interest in its Korean venture at a loss, and to sell below cost its nearby wholly owned chemical plant. Also, after Lucent's joint venture in wireless handsets with Philips Electronics ended, Lucent took a $100 million charge at the time on selling its consumer phone equipment business. Similarly, HealthMatics, a joint venture between Glaxo Smith Kline and Physician Computer Network Inc., shut down after losing more than $50 million.

While early surveys suggested that as many as half the companies with international joint ventures were dissatisfied with their ventures' performance, there is reason to believe that some of the earlier concern can now be ameliorated. This is primarily because there is far greater alliance experience and insight to draw from. There is now widespread appreciation that joint ventures are not necessarily transitional organization forms, shorter-lived, or less profitable. For many organizations they are the mode of choice.

There now also exists an Association of Strategic Alliance Professionals (ASAP). It was created to support the professional development of alliance managers and executives to advance the state-of-the-art of alliance formation and management and to provide a forum for sharing alliance best practices, resources and opportunities to help companies improve their alliance management capabilities.

Why do managers keep creating new joint ventures? The reasons are presented in the remainder of this reading, as are some guidelines for international joint venture success.

Why Companies Create International Joint Ventures

International joint ventures can be used to achieve one of four basic purposes. As shown in Exhibit 1, these are: to strengthen the firm's existing business, to take the firm's existing products into new markets, to obtain new products that can be sold in the firm's existing markets, and to diversify into a new business.

Companies using joint ventures for each of these purposes will have different concerns and will be looking for partners with different characteristics. Firms wanting to strengthen their existing business, for example, will most likely be looking for partners among their current competitors, while those wanting to enter new geographic markets will be looking for overseas firms in related businesses with good local market knowledge. Although often treated as a single category of business activity, international joint ventures are remarkably diverse, as the following descriptions indicate.

Strengthening the Existing Business International joint ventures are used in a variety of ways by firms wishing to strengthen or protect their existing businesses. Among the most important are joint ventures formed to achieve economies of scale, joint ventures that allow the firm to acquire needed technology and know-how, and ventures that reduce the financial risk of major projects. Joint ventures formed for the latter two reasons may have the added benefit of eliminating a potential competitor from a particular product or market area.

Achieving Economies of Scale Firms often use joint ventures to attempt to match the economies of scale achieved by their larger competitors. Joint ventures have been used to give their parents

---

Exhibit 1   Motives for International Joint Venture Formation

	Existing Products	New Products
New Markets	To take existing products to foreign markets	To diversify into a new business
Existing Markets	To strengthen the existing business	To bring foreign products to local markets

economies of scale in raw material and component supply, in research and development, and in marketing and distribution. Joint ventures have also been used as a vehicle for carrying out divisional mergers, which yield economies across the full spectrum of business activity.

Very small, entrepreneurial firms are more likely to participate in a network than an equity joint venture in order to strengthen their business through economies of scale. Small firms may form a network to reduce the costs, and increase the potential, of foreign market entry, or to meet some other focused objective. Most of these networks tend to have a relatively low ease of entry and exit and a loose structure and require a limited investment (primarily time, as they might be self-financing through fees). International equity joint ventures by very small firms are unusual because such firms must typically overcome some combination of liabilities of size, newness, foreignness, and relational orientation (often the small firms were initially successful because of their single-minded, do-it-themselves orientation).

Raw Material and Component Supply   In many industries the smaller firms create joint ventures to obtain raw materials or jointly manufacture components. Automakers, for instance, may develop a jointly owned engine plant to supply certain low-volume engines to each company. Producing engines for the parents provides economies of scale, with each company receiving engines at a lower cost than it could obtain if it were to produce them itself.

The managers involved in such ventures are quick to point out that these financial savings do not come without a cost. Design changes in jointly produced engines, for example, tend to be slow because all partners have to agree on them. In fact, one joint venture that produced computer printers fell seriously behind the state of the art in printer design because the parents could not agree on the features they wanted in the jointly designed printer. Because all of the venture's output was sold to the parents, the joint venture personnel had no direct contact with end customers and could not resolve the dispute.

Transfer pricing is another issue that arises in joint ventures that supply their parents. A low transfer price on products shipped from the venture to the parents, for instance, means that whichever parent buys the most product obtains the most benefit. Many higher-volume-taking parents claim that this is fair, as it is their volume that plays an important role in making the joint venture viable. On the other hand, some parents argue for a higher transfer price, which means that the economic benefits are captured in the venture and will flow, most likely via dividends, to the parents in proportion to their share holdings in the venture. As the share holdings generally reflect the original asset contributions to the venture and not the volumes taken out every year, this means that different parents will do well under this arrangement. Clearly, the potential for transfer price disputes is significant.

Research and Development   Shared research and development efforts are increasingly common. The rationale for such programs is that participating firms can save both time and money by collaborating and may, by combining the efforts of the participating companies' scientists, come up with results that would otherwise have been impossible.

The choice facing firms wishing to carry out collaborative research is whether to simply coordinate their efforts and share costs or to actually set up a jointly owned company. Hundreds of multi-company research programs are not joint ventures. Typically, scientists from the participating companies agree on the research objectives and the most likely avenues of exploration to achieve those objectives. If there are, say, four promising ways to attack a particular problem, each of four participating companies would be assigned one route and told to pursue it. Meetings would be held, perhaps quarterly, to share results and approaches taken and when (hopefully) one route proved to be successful, all firms would be fully informed on the new techniques and technology.

The alternative way to carry out collaborative research is to establish a jointly owned company and to provide it with staff, budget, and a physical location. Yet even here, problems may occur. In the United States, the president of a joint research company established by a dozen U.S. computer firms discovered that the participating companies were not sending their best people to the new company. He ended up hiring more than 200 of the firm's 330 scientists from the outside.

A sensitive issue for firms engaging in collaborative research, whether through joint ventures or not, is how far the collaboration should extend. Because the partners are usually competitors, the often expressed ideal is that the joint effort will focus only on "precompetitive" basic research and not, for example, on product development work. This is often a difficult line to draw.

Marketing and Distribution   Many international joint ventures involve shared research, development, and production but stop short of joint marketing. The vehicles coming out of the widely publicized NUMMI joint venture between Toyota and General Motors in California, for instance, are clearly branded as GM or Toyota products and are sold competitively through each parent's distribution network. Antitrust plays a role in the decision to keep marketing activities separate, but so does the partners' intrinsic desire to maintain separate brand identities and increase their own market share. These cooperating firms have not forgotten that they are competitors.

There are, nevertheless, some ventures formed for the express purpose of achieving economies in marketing and distribution. Here, each firm is hoping for wider market coverage at a lower cost. The trade-off is a loss of direct control over the sales force, potentially slower decision making, and a possible loss of direct contact with the customer.

Somewhat similar in intent are cooperative marketing agreements, which are not joint ventures but agreements by two firms with related product lines to sell one another's products. Here companies end up with a more complete line to sell, without the managerial complications of a joint venture. Sometimes the cooperative marketing agreement can in fact entail joint branding.

Divisional Mergers   Multinational companies with subsidiaries that they have concluded are too small to be economic have sometimes chosen to create a joint venture by combining their "too small" operations with those of a competitor. Fiat and Peugeot, for example, merged their automobile operations in Argentina, where both companies were doing poorly. The new joint venture started life with a market share of 35 percent and a chance for greatly improved economies in design, production, and marketing. Faced with similar pressures, Ford and Volkswagen have done the same thing in Brazil, creating a jointly owned company called Auto Latina.

A divisional merger can also allow a firm a graceful exit from a business in which it is no longer interested. Honeywell gave up trying to continue alone in the computer industry when it folded its business into a venture with Machines Bull of France and NEC of Japan. Honeywell held a 40 percent stake in the resulting joint venture.

Acquiring Technology in the Core Business
Firms that have wanted to acquire technology in their core business area have traditionally done so through license agreements or by developing the technology themselves. Increasingly, however, companies are turning to joint ventures for this purpose, because developing technology in-house is seen as taking too long, and license agreements, while giving the firm access to patent rights and engineers' ideas, may not provide much in the way of shop floor know-how. The power of a joint venture is that a firm may be able to have its employees working shoulder to shoulder with those of its partner, trying to solve the same problems. For example, the General Motors joint venture with Toyota provided an opportunity for GM to obtain a source of low-cost small cars and to watch firsthand how Toyota managers, who were in operational control of the venture, were able to produce high-quality automobiles

at low cost. Some observers even concluded that the opportunity for General Motors to learn new production techniques was more significant than the supply of cars coming from the venture.

Reducing Financial Risk   Some projects are too big or too risky for firms to tackle alone. This is why oil companies use joint ventures to split the costs of searching for new oil fields, and why the aircraft industry is increasingly using joint ventures and "risk-sharing subcontractors" to put up some of the funds required to develop new aircraft and engines.

Do such joint ventures make sense? For the oil companies the answer is a clear yes. In these ventures, one partner takes a lead role and manages the venture on a day-to-day basis. Management complexity, a major potential drawback of joint ventures, is kept to a minimum. If the venture finds oil, transfer prices are not a problem—the rewards of the venture are easy to divide between the partners. In situations like this, forming a joint venture is an efficient and sensible way of sharing risk.

It is not as obvious that some other industry ventures are a good idea, at least not for industry leaders. Their partners are not entering these ventures simply in the hopes of earning an attractive return on their investment. They are gearing up to produce, sooner or later, their own product. Why would a company be willing to train potential competitors? For many firms, it is the realization that their partner is going to hook up with someone anyway, so better to have a portion of a smaller future pie than none at all, even if it means you may be eventually competing against yourself.

Taking Products to Foreign Markets   Firms with domestic products that they believe will be successful in foreign markets face a choice. They can produce the product at home and export it, license the technology to local firms around the world, establish wholly owned subsidiaries in foreign countries, or form joint ventures with local partners. Many firms conclude that exporting is unlikely to lead to significant market penetration, building wholly owned subsidiaries is too slow and requires too

many resources, and licensing does not offer an adequate financial return. The result is that an international joint venture, while seldom seen as an ideal choice, is often the most attractive compromise.

Moving into foreign markets entails a degree of risk, and most firms that decide to form a joint venture with a local firm are doing so to reduce the risk associated with their new market entry. Very often, they look for a partner that deals with a related product line and, thus, has a good feel for the local market. As a further risk-reducing measure, the joint venture may begin life as simply a sales and marketing operation, until the product begins to sell well and volumes rise. Then a "screwdriver" assembly plant may be set up to assemble components shipped from the foreign parent. Eventually, the venture may modify or redesign the product to better suit the local market and may establish complete local manufacturing, sourcing raw material and components locally. The objective is to withhold major investment until the market uncertainty is reduced.

Following Customers to Foreign Markets   Another way to reduce the risk of a foreign market entry is to follow firms that are already customers at home. Thus, many Japanese automobile suppliers have followed Honda, Toyota, and Nissan as they set up new plants in North America and Europe. Very often these suppliers, uncertain of their ability to operate in a foreign environment, decide to form a joint venture with a local partner. There are, for example, a great many automobile supplier joint ventures in the United States originally formed between Japanese and American auto suppliers to supply the Japanese "transplant" automobile manufacturers. For the Americans, such ventures provide a way to learn Japanese manufacturing techniques and to tap into a growing market.

Investing in "Markets of the Future"   Some joint ventures are established by firms taking an early position in what they see as emerging markets. These areas offer very large untapped markets, as well as a possible source of low-cost raw materials and labor. The major problems faced by Western firms in penetrating such markets are their unfamiliarity with the local culture, establishing Western attitudes toward quality, and, in some areas, repatriating earnings in hard currency. The solution (sometimes imposed by local government) has often been the creation of joint ventures with local partners who "know the ropes" and can deal with the local bureaucracy.

Bringing Foreign Products to Local Markets

For every firm that uses an international joint venture to take its product to a foreign market, a local company sees the joint venture as an attractive way to bring a foreign product to its existing market. It is, of course, this complementarity of interest that makes the joint venture possible.

Local partners enter joint ventures to get better utilization of existing plants or distribution channels, to protect themselves against threatening new technology, or simply as an impetus for new growth. Typically, the financial rewards that the local partner receives from a venture are different from those accruing to the foreign partner. For example:

- Many foreign partners make a profit shipping finished products and components to their joint ventures. These profits are particularly attractive because they are in hard currency, which may not be true of the venture's profits, and because the foreign partner captures 100 percent of them, not just a share.

- Many foreign partners receive a technology fee, which is a fixed percentage of the sales volume of the joint venture. The local partner may or may not receive a management fee of like amount.

- Foreign partners typically pay a withholding tax on dividends remitted to them from the venture. Local firms do not.

As a result of these differences, the local partner is often far more concerned with the venture's bottom line earnings and dividend payout than the foreign partner. This means the foreign partner is likely to be happier to keep the venture as simply a marketing or assembly operation, as previously described, than to develop it to the point where it buys less imported material.

Although this logic is understandable, such thinking is shortsighted. The best example of the benefits that can come back to a parent from a powerful joint venture is Fuji Xerox, a venture begun in Japan in 1962 between Xerox and Fuji Photo. This is among the best known American–Japanese joint ventures in Japan.

For the first 10 years of its life, Fuji Xerox was strictly a marketing organization. It did its best to sell Xerox copiers in the Japanese market, even though the U.S. company had done nothing to adapt the machine to the Japanese market. For example, to reach the print button on one model, Japanese secretaries had to stand on a box. After 10 years of operation, Fuji Xerox began to manufacture its own machines, and by 1975 it was redesigning U.S. equipment for the Japanese market. Soon thereafter, with the encouragement of Fuji Photo, and in spite of the resistance of Xerox engineers in the United States, the firm began to design its own copier equipment. Its goal was to design and build a copier in half the time and at half the cost of previous machines. When this was accomplished, the firm set its sights on winning the Deming award, a highly coveted Japanese prize for excellence in total quality control. Fuji Xerox won the award in 1980.

It was also in 1980 that Xerox, reeling under the impact of intense competition from Japanese copier companies, finally began to pay attention to the lessons that it could learn from Fuji Xerox. Adopting the Japanese joint venture's manufacturing techniques and quality programs, the parent company fought its way back to health in the mid-1980s. By 1991, Xerox International Partners was established as a joint venture between Fuji Xerox and Xerox Corporation to sell low-end printers in North America and Europe. In 1998, exports to the United States grew substantially with digital color copiers and OEM printer engines. In 2000, Xerox Corporation transferred its China/Hong Kong Operations to Fuji Xerox and Fuji Photo raised its stake in the venture to 75 percent in 2001. By 2005, Fuji Xerox Co. Ltd. employed 36,000 people, had about $9.6 billion in revenues, was responsible for the design and manufacture of many digital color copiers and printers for Xerox worldwide, and was an active partner in research and development. Both the lessons learned from Fuji Xerox and the contributions they have made to Xerox have inevitably helped Xerox prosper as an independent company.

Using Joint Ventures for Diversification   As the previous examples illustrate, many joint ventures take products that one parent knows well into a market that the other knows well. However, some break new ground and move one or both parents into products and markets that are new to them.

Arrangements to acquire the skills necessary to compete in a new business is a long-term proposition, but one that some firms are willing to undertake. Given the fact that most acquisitions of unrelated businesses do not succeed, and that trying to enter a new business without help is extremely difficult, choosing partners who will help you learn the business may not be a bad strategy if you are already familiar with the partner. However, to enter a new market, with a new product, and a new partner—even when the probability of success for each is 80 percent—leaves one with an overall probability of success of ($.8 \times .8 \times .8$) about 50 percent!

Joint ventures can also be viewed as vehicles for learning. Here the modes of learning go beyond knowledge transfer (i.e., existing know-how) to include transformation and harvesting. In practice, most IJV partners engage in the transfer of existing knowledge, but stop short of knowledge transformation or harvesting. Although many multinational enterprises have very large numbers of international equity joint ventures and alliances, only a small percentage dedicate resources explicitly to learning about the alliance process. Few organizations go to the trouble of inventorying/cataloguing the corporate experience with joint ventures, let alone how the accumulated knowledge might be transferred within or between divisions. This oversight will be increasingly costly for firms, especially as some of the bilateral alliances become part of multilateral networks.

Requirements for International Joint Venture Success

The checklist in Exhibit 2 presents many of the items that a manager should consider when establishing an international joint venture. Each of these is discussed in the following sections.

Testing the Strategic Logic   The decision to enter a joint venture should not be taken lightly. As mentioned earlier, joint ventures require a great deal of

---

Exhibit 2   Joint Venture Checklist

1. Test the strategic logic.
   - Do you really need a partner? For how long? Does your partner?
   - How big is the payoff for both parties? How likely is success?
   - Is a joint venture the best option?
   - Do congruent performance measures exist?
2. Partnership and fit.
   - Does the partner share your objectives for the venture?
   - Does the partner have the necessary skills and resources? Will you get access to them?
   - Will you be compatible?
   - Can you arrange an "engagement period"?
   - Is there a comfort versus competence trade-off?
3. Shape and design.
   - Define the venture's scope of activity and its strategic freedom vis-à-vis its parents.
   - Lay out each parent's duties and payoffs to create a win-win situation. Ensure that there are comparable contributions over time.
   - Establish the managerial role of each partner.
4. Doing the deal.
   - How much paperwork is enough? Trust versus legal considerations?
   - Agree on an endgame.
5. Making the venture work.
   - Give the venture continuing top management attention.
   - Manage cultural differences.
   - Watch out for inequities.
   - Be flexible.

management attention, and, in spite of the care and attention they receive, many prove unsatisfactory to their parents.

Firms considering entering a joint venture should satisfy themselves that there is not a simpler way, such as a nonequity alliance, to get what they need. They should also carefully consider the time period for which they are likely to need help. Joint ventures have been labeled "permanent solutions to temporary problems" by firms that entered a venture to get help on some aspect of their business; then, when they no longer needed the help, they were still stuck with the joint venture.

The same tough questions a firm may ask itself before forming a joint venture need to be asked of its partner(s). How long will the partner(s) need it? Is the added potential payoff high enough to each partner to compensate for the increased coordination/communications costs which go with the formation of a joint venture?

A major issue in the discussion of strategic logic is to determine whether congruent measures of performance exist. As Exhibit 3 suggests, in many joint ventures, incongruity exists. In this example the foreign partner was looking for a joint venture that would generate 20 percent return on sales in a 1–2 year period and require a limited amount of senior management time. The local partner in turn was seeking a JV that would be quickly profitable and be able to justify some high-paying salaried positions (for the local partner and several family members/friends). While each partner's performance objectives seem defensible, this venture would need to resolve several major problem areas in order to succeed. First, each partner did not make explicit all their primary performance objectives. Implicit measures (those below the dotted line in Exhibit 3), are a source of latent disagreement/misunderstanding. Second, the explicit versus implicit measures of each partner were internally inconsistent. The foreign partner wanted high profitability while using little senior management time and old technology. The local partner wanted quick profits but high-paying local salaries.

Exhibit 3   Measuring JV Performance: The Search for Congruity

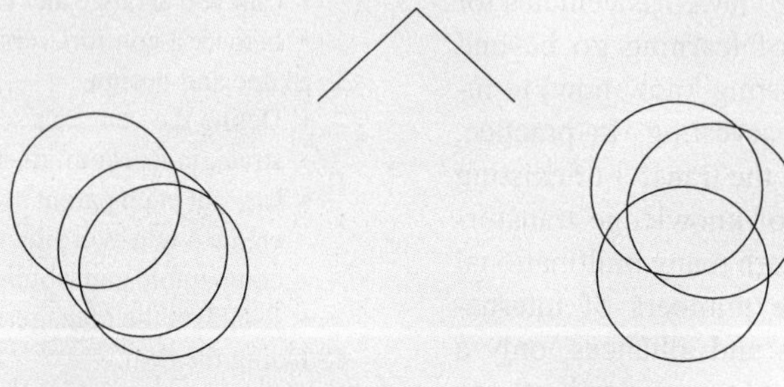

Foreign Partner

1. Profitability - 20% ROS
   (within 12–24 months)
2. Require limited senior
   management time
   ----
3. Maximize local sales
4. Exploit peripheral or
   mature technology

Local Partner

1. Profitability
   (within 9–12 months)
2. High paying salaried
   positions
   ----
3. Opportunity to export
4. Obtain newest
   technology

Partnership and Fit   Joint ventures are sometimes formed to satisfy complementary needs. But when one partner acquires (learns) another's capabilities, the joint venture becomes unstable. The acquisition of a partner's capabilities means that the partner is no longer needed. If capabilities are only accessed, the joint venture is more stable. It is not easy, before a venture begins, to determine many of the things a manager would most like to know about a potential partner, like the true extent of its capabilities, what its objectives are in forming the venture, and whether it will be easy to work with. A hasty answer to such questions may lead a firm into a bad relationship or cause it to pass up a good opportunity.

For these reasons, it is often best if companies begin a relationship in a small way, with a simple agreement that is important but not a matter of life and death to either parent. As confidence between the firms grows, the scope of the business activities can broaden.

A good example is provided by Corning Glass, which in 1970 made a major breakthrough in the development of optical fibers that could be used for telecommunication applications, replacing tradiitional copper wire or coaxial cable. The most likely customers of this fiber outside the United States were the European national telecoms, which were well known to be very nationalistic purchasers. To gain access to these customers, Corning set up development agreements with companies in England, France, Germany, and Italy that were already suppliers to the telecoms. These agreements called for the European firms to develop the technology necessary to combine the fibers into cables, while Corning itself continued to develop the optical fibers. Soon the partners began to import fiber from Corning and cable it locally. Then, when the partners were comfortable with each other and each market was ready, Corning and the partners set up joint ventures to produce optical fiber locally. These ventures worked well.

When assessing issues around partnership and fit, it is useful to consider whether the partner not only shares the same objectives for the venture but also has a similar appetite for risk. In practice this often results in joint ventures having parents of roughly comparable size. It is difficult for parent firms of very different size to establish sustainable joint ventures because of varying resource sets, payback period requirements, and corporate cultures.

Corporate culture similarity—or compatibility—can be a make-or-break issue in many joint ventures. It is not enough to find a partner with the necessary skills; you need to be able to get access to them and to be compatible. Managers are constantly told that they should choose a joint venture partner they trust. As these examples suggest, however, trust between partners is something that can only be developed over time as a result of shared experiences. You can't start with trust.

Shape and Design   In the excitement of setting up a new operation in a foreign country, or getting access to technology provided by an overseas partner, it is important not to lose sight of the basic strategic requirements that must be met if a joint venture is to be successful. The questions that must be addressed are the same when any new business is proposed: Is the market attractive? How strong is the competition? How will the new company compete? Will it have the required resources? And so on.

In addition to these concerns, three others are particularly relevant to joint venture design. One is the question of strategic freedom, which has to do with the relationship between the venture and its parents. How much freedom will the venture be given to do as it wishes with respect to choosing suppliers, a product line, and customers? In the Dow Chemical venture referred to earlier, the dispute between the partners centered on the requirement that the venture buy materials, at what the Koreans believed to be an inflated price, from Dow's new wholly owned Korean plant. Clearly the American and Korean vision of the amount of strategic freedom open to the venture was rather different.

The second issue of importance is that the joint venture be a win-win situation. This means that the payoff to each parent if the venture is successful should be a big one, because this will keep both parents working for the success of the venture when times are tough. If the strategic analysis suggests that the return to either parent over time will be marginal, the venture should be restructured or abandoned.

Finally, it is critical to decide on the management roles that each parent company will play. The venture will be easier to manage if one parent plays a dominant role and has a lot of influence over both the strategic and the day-to-day operations of the venture, or if one parent plays a lead role in the day-to-day operation of the joint venture. More difficult to manage are shared management ventures, in which both parents have a significant input into both strategic decisions and the everyday operations of the venture. A middle ground is split management decisions, where each partner has primary influence over those functional areas where it is most qualified. This is the most common and arguably most effective form.

In some ventures, the partners place too much emphasis on competing with each other about which one will have management control. They lose sight of the fact that the intent of the joint venture is to capture benefits from two partners that will allow the venture (not one of the partners) to compete in the market better than would have been possible by going it alone.

The objective of most joint ventures is superior performance. Thus the fact that dominant-parent ventures are easier to manage than shared-management ventures does not mean they are the appropriate type of venture to establish. Dominant-parent ventures are most likely to be effective when one partner has the knowledge and skill to make the venture a success and the other party is contributing simply money, a trademark, or perhaps a one-time transfer of technology. Such a venture, however, begs the question "What are the unique continuing contributions of the partner?" Shared-management ventures are necessary when the venture needs active consultation between members of each parent company, as when deciding how to modify a product supplied by one parent for the local market that is well known by the other, or to modify a production process designed by one parent to be suitable for a workforce and working conditions well known by the other.

A joint venture is headed for trouble when a parent tries to take a larger role in its management than makes sense. An American company with a joint venture in Japan, for instance, insisted that one of its people be the executive vice president of the venture. This was not reasonable, because the manager had nothing to bring to the management of the venture. He simply served as a constant reminder to the Japanese that the American partner did not trust them. The Americans were pushing for a shared-management venture when it was more logical to allow the Japanese, who certainly had all the necessary skills, to be the dominant or at least the leading firm. The major American contribution to the venture was to allow it to use its world-famous trademarks and brand names.

A second example, also in Japan, involved a French firm. This company was bringing complex technology to the venture that needed to be modified for the Japanese market. It was clear that the French firm required a significant say in the management of the venture. On the other hand, the French had no knowledge of the Japanese market and, thus, the Japanese also needed a significant role in the venture. The logical solution would have been a shared-management venture and equal influence in decisions made at the board level. Unfortunately, both companies wanted to play a dominant role, and the venture collapsed in a decision-making stalemate.

Finally, every joint venture must resolve how much of the JV will be owned by each of the partners. Some firms equate ownership with control, assuming more is always better. Such an assumption would be incorrect. Research has shown that once a foreign firm has about a 40 percent equity stake, there is little difference in the survivability of that subsidiary than if they had had, for example, an 80 percent stake (see Exhibit 4).

Exhibit 4   Effect of Foreign Equity Holding on Subsidiary Mortality Risk

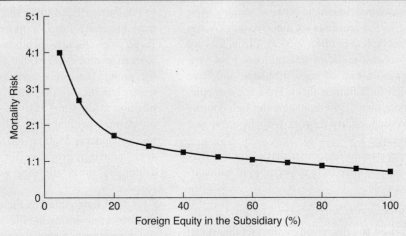

1:1 = equivalent to wholly owned subsidiary

Source: Dhanaraj, Charles and Paul W. Beamish, 2004. "Effect of Equity Ownership on the Survival of International Joint Ventures." *Strategic Management Journal,* 25(3): 295–305.

Doing the Deal   Experienced managers argue that it is the relationship between the partners that is of key importance in a joint venture, not the legal agreement that binds them together. Nevertheless, most are careful to ensure that they have a good agreement in place—one that they understand and are comfortable with.

Most of the principal elements of a joint venture agreement are straightforward. One item that often goes un-discussed is the termination of the venture.

Although some managers balk at discussing termination during the getting-acquainted period, it is important to work out a method of terminating the venture in the event of a serious disagreement, and to do this at a time when heads are cool and goodwill abounds. The usual technique is to use a shotgun clause, which allows either party to name a price at which it will buy the other's shares in the venture. However, once this provision is activated and the first company has named a price, the second firm has the option of selling at this price or buying

the first company's shares at the same price. This ensures that only fair offers are made, at least as long as both parents are large enough to be capable of buying each other out.

Making the Venture Work   Joint ventures need close and continuing attention, particularly in their early months. In addition to establishing a healthy working relationship between the parents and the venture general manager, managers should be on the lookout for the impact that cultural differences may be having on the venture and for the emergence of unforeseen inequities.

International joint ventures, like any type of international activity, require that managers of different national cultures work together. This requires the selection of capable people in key roles. Unless managers have been sensitized to the characteristics of the culture that they are dealing with, this can lead to misunderstandings and serious problems. Many Western managers, for instance, are frustrated by the slow, consensus-oriented decision-making style of the Japanese. Equally, the Japanese find American individualistic decision making to be surprising, as the decisions are made so quickly, but the implementation is often so slow. Firms that are sophisticated in the use of international joint ventures are well aware of such problems and have taken action to minimize them. Ford, for example, has put more than 1,500 managers through courses to improve their ability to work with Japanese and Korean managers.

It is important to remember that cultural differences do not just arise from differences in nationality. For example:

• Small firms working with large partners are often surprised and dismayed by the fact that it can take months, rather than days, to get approval of a new project. In some cases the cultural differences appear to be greater between small and large firms of the same nationality than, say, between multinationals of different nationality, particularly if the multinationals are in the same industry.

• Firms working with two partners from the same country have been surprised to find how different the companies are in cultural habits. A Japanese automobile firm headquartered in rural Japan may be a very different company from one run from Tokyo.

• Cultural differences between managers working in different functional areas may be greater than those between managers in the same function in different firms. European engineers, for example, discovered when discussing a potential joint venture with an American partner that they had more in common with the American engineers than with the marketing people in their own company.

A very common joint venture problem is that the objectives of the parents, which coincided when the venture was formed, diverge over time. Such divergences can be brought on by changes in the fortunes of the partners. This was the case in the breakup of the General Motors–Daewoo joint venture in Korea. Relations between the partners were already strained due to GM's unwillingness to put further equity into the venture, in spite of a debt to equity ratio of more than 8 to 1, when, faced with rapidly declining market share, the Korean parent decided that the venture should go for growth and maximize market share. In contrast General Motors, itself in a poor financial position at the time, insisted that the emphasis be on current profitability. When Daewoo, without telling General Motors, introduced a concessionary financing program for the joint venture's customers, the relationship was damaged, never to recover.

A final note concerns the unintended inequities that may arise during the life of a venture. Due to an unforeseen circumstance, one parent may be winning from the venture while the other is losing. A venture established in the late 1990s between Indonesian and American parents, for instance, was buying components from the American parent at prices based in dollars. As the rupiah declined in value, the Indonesian partner could afford fewer components in each shipment. The advice of many experienced venture managers is that, in such a situation, a change in the original agreement should be made, so the hardship is shared between the parents. That was done in this case, and the venture is surviving, although it is not as profitable as originally anticipated.

In reviewing any checklist of the things to be considered when forming a joint venture, it is important to recognize that such a list will vary somewhat depending on where the international joint venture is established. The characteristics of joint ventures will vary according to whether they are established in developed versus emerging markets.

Most of the descriptions of the characteristics considered are self-explanatory. Yet, more fine-grained analyses are always possible. For example, the discussion in this reading has generally assumed a traditional equity joint venture, one focused between two firms from two different countries. Yet other types of equity joint ventures exist, including those between firms from two different countries that set up in a third country (i.e., trinational), those formed between subsidiaries of the same MNE (i.e., intrafirm) and those formed with companies of the same nationality but located in a different country (i.e., cross-national domestic joint ventures). Further, many joint ventures have more than two partners. Interestingly, the traditional JVs (at least those formed by Japanese MNEs) tend to simultaneously be more profitable and to have a higher termination rate than the alternative structures available.

Summary

International joint ventures are an increasingly important part of the strategy of many firms. They are, however, sometime difficult to design and manage well, in part because some organizations do not treat them as "true" "joint" ventures (see Exhibit 5).

The fact that some ventures are performing below their management's expectations should not be an excuse for firms to avoid such ventures. In many industries, the winners are going to be the companies that most quickly learn to manage international ventures effectively. The losers will be the managers who throw up their hands and say that joint ventures are too difficult, so we had better go it alone.

In the future, will we see more or fewer international joint ventures? Certainly the reduction in investment regulations in many countries, coupled with increased international experience by many firms, suggests there may be fewer joint ventures. Yet other countervailing pressures exist. With shortening product life cycles, it is increasingly difficult to go it alone. And with the increase in the number of MNEs from emerging markets, both the supply and demand of potential partners will likely escalate.

Exhibit 5   The True Joint Venture versus the Pseudo Joint Venture

	The True Alliance	**The Pseudo Alliance**
Planned level of parent input and involvement	Continuing	One-time
Distribution of risks/rewards	Roughly even	Uneven
Parent attitude toward the JV	A unique organization with unique needs	One more subsidiary
The formal JV agreement	Flexible guidelines	Frequently referenced rulebook
Performance objectives	Clearly specified and congruent	Partially overlapping/ambiguous

Reading 6-2   Collaborate with Your Competitors—and Win

Gary Hamel, Yves L. Doz, and C. K. Prahalad

Collaboration between competitors is in fashion. General Motors and Toyota assemble automobiles, Siemens and Philips develop semiconductors, Canon supplies photocopiers to Kodak, France's Thomson and Japan's JVC manufacture videocassette recorders. But the spread of what we call "competitive collaboration"—joint ventures, outsourcing agreements, product licensings, cooperative research—has triggered unease about the long-term consequences. A strategic alliance can strengthen both companies against outsiders even as it weakens one partner vis-à-vis the other. In particular, alliances between Asian companies and Western rivals seem to work against the Western partner. Cooperation becomes a low-cost route for new competitors to gain technology and market access.[1]

Yet the case for collaboration is stronger than ever. It takes so much money to develop new products and to penetrate new markets that few companies can go it alone in every situation. ICL, the British computer company, could not have developed its current generation of mainframes without Fujitsu. Motorola needs Toshiba's distribution capacity to break into the Japanese semiconductor market. Time is another critical factor. Alliances can provide shortcuts for Western companies racing to improve their production efficiency and quality control.

We have spent more than five years studying the inner workings of 15 strategic alliances and

monitoring scores of others. Our research (see the box "About Our Research") involves cooperative ventures between competitors from the United States and Japan, Europe and Japan, and the United States and Europe. We did not judge the success or failure of each partnership by its longevity—a common

---

▌ [1]For a vigorous warning about the perils of collaboration, see Robert B. Reich and Eric D. Mankin, "Joint Ventures with Japan Give Away Our Future," *HBR,* March–April 1986, p. 78.

About Our Research

We spent more than five years studying the internal workings of 15 strategic alliances around the world. We sought answers to a series of interrelated questions. What role have strategic alliances and outsourcing agreements played in the global success of Japanese and Korean companies? How do alliances change the competitive balance between partners? Does winning at collaboration mean different things to different companies? What factors determine who gains most from collaboration?

To understand who won and who lost and why, we observed the interactions of the partners firsthand and at multiple levels in each organization. Our sample included four European–U.S. alliances, two intra-European alliances, two European–Japanese alliances, and seven U.S.–Japanese alliances. We gained access to both sides of the partnerships in about half the cases and studied each alliance for an average of three years.

Confidentiality was a paramount concern. Where we did have access to both sides, we often wound up knowing more about who was doing what to whom than either of the partners. To preserve confidentiality, our article disguises many of the alliances that were part of the study.

mistake when evaluating strategic alliances—but by the shifts in competitive strength on each side. We focused on how companies use competitive collaboration to enhance their internal skills and technologies while they guard against transferring competitive advantages to ambitious partners.

There is no immutable law that strategic alliances *must* be a windfall for Japanese or Korean partners. Many Western companies do give away more than they gain—but that's because they enter partnerships without knowing what it takes to win. Companies that benefit most from competitive collaboration adhere to a set of simple but powerful principles.

Collaboration is competition in a different form. Successful companies never forget that their new partners may be out to disarm them. They enter alliances with clear strategic objectives, and they also understand how their partners' objectives will affect their success.

Harmony is not the most important measure of success. Indeed, occasional conflict may be the best evidence of mutually beneficial collaboration. Few alliances remain win-win undertakings forever. A partner may be content even as it unknowingly surrenders core skills.

Cooperation has limits. Companies must defend against competitive compromise. A strategic alliance is a constantly evolving bargain whose real terms go beyond the legal agreement or the aims of top management. What information gets traded is determined day to day, often by engineers and operating managers. Successful companies inform employees at all levels about what skills and technologies are off-limits to the partner and monitor what the partner requests and receives.

Learning from partners is paramount. Successful companies view each alliance as a window on their partners' broad capabilities. They use the alliance to build skills in areas outside the formal agreement and systematically diffuse new knowledge throughout their organizations.

Why Collaborate?

Using an alliance with a competitor to acquire new technologies or skills is not devious. It reflects the commitment and capacity of each partner to absorb the skills of the other. We found that in every case in which a Japanese company emerged from an alliance stronger than its Western partner, the Japanese company had made a greater effort to learn.

Strategic intent is an essential ingredient in the commitment to learning. The willingness of Asian companies to enter alliances represents a change in competitive tactics, not competitive goals. NEC, for example, has used a series of collaborative ventures to enhance its technology and product competences. NEC is the only company in the world with a leading position in telecommunications, computers, and semiconductors—despite its investing less in R&D (as a percentage of revenues) than competitors like Texas Instruments, Northern Telecom, and L.M. Ericsson. Its string of partnerships, most notably with Honeywell, allowed NEC to leverage its in-house R&D over the last two decades.

Western companies, on the other hand, often enter alliances to avoid investments. They are more interested in reducing the costs and risks of entering new businesses or markets than in acquiring new skills. A senior U.S. manager offered this analysis of his company's venture with a Japanese rival: "We complement each other well—our distribution capability and their manufacturing skill. I see no reason to invest upstream if we can find a secure source of product. This is a comfortable relationship for us."

An executive from this company's Japanese partner offered a different perspective: "When it is necessary to collaborate, I go to my employees and say, 'This is bad, I wish we had these skills ourselves. Collaboration is second best. But I will feel worse if after four years we do not know how to do what our partner knows how to do.' We must digest their skills."

The problem here is not that the U.S. company wants to share investment risk (its Japanese partner does too) but that the U.S. company has no ambition *beyond* avoidance. When the commitment to learning is so one-sided, collaboration invariably leads to competitive compromise.

Many so-called alliances between Western companies and their Asian rivals are little more than

Competition for Competence

In the article "Do You Really Have a Global Strategy?" (*HBR,* July–August 1985), Gary Hamel and C. K. Prahalad examined one dimension of the global competitive battle: the race for brand dominance. This is the battle for control of distribution channels and global "share of mind." Another global battle has been much less visible and has received much less management attention. This is the battle for control over key technology-based competences that fuel new business development.

Honda has built a number of businesses, including marine engines, lawn mowers, generators, motorcycles, and cars, around its engine and power train competence. Casio draws on its expertise in semiconductors and digital display in producing calculators, small-screen televisions, musical instruments, and watches. Canon relies on its imaging and microprocessor competences in its camera, copier, and laser printer businesses.

In the short run, the quality and performance of a company's products determine its competitiveness. Over the longer term, however, what counts is the ability to build and enhance core competences—distinctive skills that spawn new generations of products. This is where many managers and commentators fear Western companies are losing. Our research helps explain why some companies may be more likely than others to surrender core skills.

Alliance or Outsourcing?

Enticing Western companies into outsourcing agreements provides several benefits to ambitious OEM partners. Serving as a manufacturing base for a Western partner is a quick route to increased manufacturing share without the risk or expense of building brand share. The Western partners' distribution capability allows Asian suppliers to focus all their resources on building absolute product advantage. Then OEMs can enter markets on their own and convert manufacturing share into brand share.

Serving as a sourcing platform yields more than just volume and process improvements. It also generates low-cost, low-risk market learning. The downstream (usually Western) partner typically provides information on how to tailor products to local markets. So every product design transferred to an OEM partner is also a research report on customer preferences and market needs. The OEM partner can use these insights to read the market accurately when it enters on its own.

A Ratchet Effect

Our research suggests that once a significant sourcing relationship has been established, the buyer becomes less willing and able to reemerge as a manufacturing competitor. Japanese and Korean companies are, with few exceptions, exemplary suppliers. If anything, the "soft option" of outsourcing becomes even softer as OEM suppliers routinely exceed delivery and quality expectations.

Outsourcing often begins a ratchetlike process. Relinquishing manufacturing control and paring back plant investment leads to sacrifices in product design, process technology, and, eventually, R&D budgets. Consequently, the OEM partner captures product-development as well as manufacturing initiative. Ambitious OEM partners are not content with the old formula of "You design it and we'll make it." The new reality is, "You design it, we'll learn from your designs, make them more manufacturable, and launch our products alongside yours."

Reversing the Verdict

This outcome is not inevitable. Western companies can retain control over their core competences by keeping a few simple principles in mind.

A Competitive Product Is Not the Same Thing as a Competitive Organization While an Asian OEM partner may provide the former, it seldom provides the latter. In essence, outsourcing is a way of renting someone else's competitiveness rather than developing a long-term solution to competitive decline.

Rethink the Make-Or-Buy Decision Companies often treat component manufacturing operations as cost centers and transfer their output to assembly units at an arbitrarily set price. This transfer price is an accounting fiction, and it is unlikely to yield as high a return as marketing or distribution investments, which require less research money and capital. But companies seldom consider the competitive consequences of surrendering control over a key value-creating activity.

Watch Out for Deepening Dependence Surrender results from a series of outsourcing decisions that individually make economic sense but collectively amount to a phased exit from the business. Different managers make outsourcing decisions at different times, unaware of the cumulative impact.

Replenish Core Competencies Western companies must outsource some activities; the economics are just too compelling. The real issue is whether a company is adding to its stock of technologies and competences as rapidly as it is surrendering them. The question of whether to outsource should always provoke a second question: Where can we outpace our partner and other rivals in building new sources of competitive advantage?

---

sophisticated outsourcing arrangements (see the box "Competition for Competence"). General Motors buys cars and components from Korea's Daewoo. Siemens buys computers from Fujitsu. Apple buys laser printer engines from Canon. The traffic is almost entirely one way. These OEM deals offer Asian partners a way to capture investment initiative from Western competitors and displace customer competitors from value-creating activities. In many cases this goal meshes with that of the Western partner: to regain competitiveness quickly and with minimum effort.

Consider the joint venture between Rover, the British automaker, and Honda. Some 25 years ago, Rover's forerunners were world leaders in small car design. Honda had not even entered the automobile business. But in the mid-1970s, after failing to penetrate foreign markets, Rover turned to Honda for technology and product-development support. Rover has used the alliance to avoid investments to design and build new cars. Honda has cultivated skills in European styling and marketing as well as multinational manufacturing. There is little doubt which company will emerge stronger over the long term.

Troubled laggards like Rover often strike alliances with surging latecomers like Honda. Having fallen behind in a key skills area (in this case, manufacturing small cars), the laggard attempts to compensate for past failures. The late-comer uses the alliance to close a specific skills gap (in this case, learning to build cars for a regional market). But a laggard that forges a partnership for short-term gain may find itself in a dependency spiral: as it contributes fewer and fewer distinctive skills, it must reveal more and more of its internal operations to keep the partner interested. For the weaker company, the issue shifts from "Should we collaborate?" to "With whom should we collaborate?" to "How do we keep our partner interested as we lose the advantages that made us attractive to them in the first place?"

There's a certain paradox here. When both partners are equally intent on internalizing the other's skills, distrust and conflict may spoil the alliance and threaten its very survival. That's one reason joint ventures between Korean and Japanese companies have been few and tempestuous. Neither side wants to "open the kimono." Alliances seem to run most smoothly when one partner is intent on learning and the other is intent on avoidance—in essence, when one partner is willing to grow dependent on the other. But running smoothly is not the point; the point is for a company to emerge from an alliance more competitive than when it entered it.

One partner does not always have to give up more than it gains to ensure the survival of an alliance. There are certain conditions under which mutual gain is possible, at least for a time.

The partners' strategic goals converge while their competitive goals diverge. That is, each partner allows for the other's continued prosperity in the shared business. Philips and Du Pont collaborate to develop and manufacture compact discs, but neither side invades the other's market. There is a clear upstream/downstream division of effort.

The size and market power of both partners is modest compared with industry leaders. This forces each side to accept that mutual dependence may have to continue for many years. Long-term collaboration may be so critical to both partners that neither will risk antagonizing the other by an overtly competitive bid to appropriate skills or competence. Fujitsu's 1 to 5 disadvantage with IBM means it will be a long time, if ever, before Fujitsu can break away from its foreign partners and go it alone.

Each partner believes it can learn from the other and at the same time limit access to proprietary skills. JVC and Thomson, both of whom make VCRs, know that they are trading skills. But the two companies are looking for very different things. Thomson needs product technology and manufacturing prowess; JVC needs to learn how to succeed in the fragmented European market. Both sides believe there is an equitable chance for gain.

How to Build Secure Defenses

For collaboration to succeed, each partner must contribute something distinctive: basic research, product development skills, manufacturing capacity, access to distribution. The challenge is to share enough skills to create advantage vis-à-vis companies outside the alliance while preventing a wholesale transfer of core skills to the partner. This is a very thin line to walk. Companies must carefully select what skills and technologies they pass to their partners. They must develop safeguards against unintended, informal transfers of information. The goal is to limit the transparency of their operations.

The type of skill a company contributes is an important factor in how easily its partner can internalize the skills. The potential for transfer is greater when a partner's contribution is easily transported (in engineering drawings, on computer tapes, or in the heads of a few technical experts); easily interpreted (it can be reduced to commonly understood equations or symbols); and easily absorbed (the skill or competence is independent of any particular cultural context).

Western companies face an inherent disadvantage because their skills are generally more vulnerable to transfer. The magnet that attracts so many companies to alliances with Asian competitors is their manufacturing excellence—a competence that is less transferable than most. Just-in-time inventory systems and quality circles can be imitated, but this is like pulling a few threads out of an oriental carpet. Manufacturing excellence is a complex web of employee training, integration with suppliers, statistical process controls, employee involvement, value engineering, and design for manufacture. It is difficult to extract such a subtle competence in any way but a piecemeal fashion.

There is an important distinction between technology and competence. A discrete, stand-alone technology (for example, the design of a semiconductor chip) is more easily transferred than a process competence, which is entwined in the social fabric of a company. Asian companies often learn more from their Western partners than vice versa because they contribute difficult-to-unravel strengths, while Western partners contribute easy-to-imitate technology.

So companies must take steps to limit transparency. One approach is to limit the scope of the formal agreement. It might cover a single technology rather than an entire range of technologies; part of a product line rather than the entire line; distribution in a limited number of markets or for a limited period of time. The objective is to circumscribe a partner's opportunities to learn.

Moreover, agreements should establish specific performance requirements. Motorola, for example, takes an incremental, incentive-based approach to technology transfer in its venture with Toshiba. The agreement calls for Motorola to release its microprocessor technology incrementally as Toshiba delivers on its promise to increase Motorola's penetration in the Japanese semiconductor market. The greater Motorola's market share, the greater Toshiba's access to Motorola's technology.

Many of the skills that migrate between companies are not covered in the formal terms of collaboration. Top management puts together strategic alliances and sets the legal parameters for exchange. But what actually gets traded is determined by day-to-day interactions of engineers, marketers, and product developers: who says what to whom, who gets access to what facilities, who sits on what joint committees. The most important deals ("I'll share this with you if you share that with me") may be struck four or five organizational levels below where the deal was signed. Here lurks the greatest risk of unintended transfers of important skills.

Consider one technology-sharing alliance between European and Japanese competitors. The European company valued the partnership as a way to acquire a specific technology. The Japanese company considered it a window on its partner's entire range of competences and interacted with a broad spectrum of its partner's marketing and product-development staff. The company mined each contact for as much information as possible.

For example, every time the European company requested a new feature on a product being sourced from its partner, the Japanese company asked for detailed customer and competitor analyses to justify the request. Over time, it developed a sophisticated picture of the European market that would assist its own entry strategy. The technology acquired by the European partner through the formal agreement had a useful life of three to five years. The competitive insights acquired informally by the Japanese company will probably endure longer.

Limiting unintended transfers at the operating level requires careful attention to the role of gatekeepers, the people who control what information flows to a partner. A gatekeeper can be effective only if there are a limited number of gateways through which a partner can access people and facilities. Fujitsu's many partners all go through a single office, the "collaboration section," to request information and assistance from different divisions. This way the company can monitor and control access to critical skills and technologies.

We studied one partnership between European and U.S competitors that involved several divisions of each company. While the U.S. company could only access its partner through a single gateway, its partner had unfettered access to all participating divisions. The European company took advantage of its free rein. If one division refused to provide certain information, the European partner made the same request of another division. No single manager in the U.S. company could tell how much information had been transferred or was in a position to piece together patterns in the requests.

Collegiality is a prerequisite for collaborative success. But *too much* collegiality should set off warning bells to senior managers. CEOs or division presidents should expect occasional complaints from their counterparts about the reluctance of lower level employees to share information. That's a sign that the gatekeepers are doing their jobs. And senior management should regularly debrief operating personnel to find out what information the partner is requesting and what requests are being granted.

Limiting unintended transfers ultimately depends on employee loyalty and self-discipline. This was a real issue for many of the Western companies we studied. In their excitement and pride over technical achievements, engineering staffs sometimes shared information that top management considered sensitive. Japanese engineers were less likely to share proprietary information.

There are a host of cultural and professional reasons for the relative openness of Western technicians. Japanese engineers and scientists are more loyal to their company than to their profession. They are less steeped in the open give-and-take of university research since they receive much of their training from employers. They consider themselves team members more than individual scientific contributors. As one Japanese manager noted, "We don't feel any need to reveal what we know. It is not an issue of pride for us. We're glad to sit and listen.

If we're patient we usually learn what we want to know."

Controlling unintended transfers may require restricting access to facilities as well as to people. Companies should declare sensitive laboratories and factories off-limits to their partners. Better yet, they might house the collaborative venture in an entirely new facility. IBM is building a special site in Japan where Fujitsu can review its forthcoming mainframe software before deciding whether to license it. IBM will be able to control exactly what Fujitsu sees and what information leaves the facility.

Finally, which country serves as "home" to the alliance affects transparency. If the collaborative team is located near one partner's major facilities, the other partner will have more opportunities to learn—but less control over what information gets traded. When the partner houses, feeds, and looks after engineers and operating managers, there is a danger they will "go native." Expatriate personnel need frequent visits from headquarters as well as regular furloughs home.

Enhance the Capacity to Learn

Whether collaboration leads to competitive surrender or revitalization depends foremost on what employees believe the purpose of the alliance to be. It is self-evident: to learn, one must *want* to learn. Western companies won't realize the full benefits of competitive collaboration until they overcome an arrogance born of decades of leadership. In short, Western companies must be more receptive.

We asked a senior executive in a Japanese electronics company about the perception that Japanese companies learn more from their foreign partners than vice versa. "Our Western partners approach us with the attitude of teachers," he told us. "We are quite happy with this, because we have the attitude of students."

Learning begins at the top. Senior management must be committed to enhancing their companies' skills as well as to avoiding financial risk. But most learning takes place at the lower levels of an alliance. Operating employees not only represent the front

lines in an effective defense but also play a vital role in acquiring knowledge. They must be well briefed on the partner's strengths and weaknesses and understand how acquiring particular skills will bolster their company's competitive position.

This is already standard practice among Asian companies. We accompanied a Japanese development engineer on a tour through a partner's factory. This engineer dutifully took notes on plant layout, the number of production stages, the rate at which the line was running, and the number of employees. He recorded all this despite the fact that he had no manufacturing responsibility in his own company, and that the alliance didn't encompass joint manufacturing. Such dedication greatly enhances learning.

Collaboration doesn't always provide an opportunity to fully internalize a partner's skills. Yet just acquiring new and more precise benchmarks of a partner's performance can be of great value. A new benchmark can provoke a thorough review of internal performance levels and may spur a round of competitive innovation. Asking questions like, "Why do their semiconductor logic designs have fewer errors than ours?" and "Why are they investing in this technology and we're not?" may provide the incentive for a vigorous catch-up program.

Competitive benchmarking is a tradition in most of the Japanese companies we studied. It requires many of the same skills associated with competitor analysis: systematically calibrating performance against external targets; learning to use rough estimates to determine where a competitor (or partner) is better, faster, or cheaper; translating those estimates into new internal targets; and recalibrating to establish the rate of improvement in a competitor's performance. The great advantage of competitive collaboration is that proximity makes benchmarking easier.

Indeed, some analysts argue that one of Toyota's motivations in collaborating with GM in the much-publicized NUMMI venture is to gauge the quality of GM's manufacturing technology. GM's top manufacturing people get a close look at Toyota, but the reverse is true as well. Toyota may be learning whether its giant U.S. competitor is capable of closing the productivity gap with Japan.

Competitive collaboration also provides a way of getting close enough to rivals to predict how they will behave when the alliance unravels or runs its course. How does the partner respond to price changes? How does it measure and reward executives? How does it prepare to launch a new product? By revealing a competitor's management orthodoxies, collaboration can increase the chances of success in future head-to-head battles.

Knowledge acquired from a competitor-partner is only valuable after it is diffused through the organization. Several companies we studied had established internal clearinghouses to collect and disseminate information. The collaborations manager at one Japanese company regularly made the rounds of all employees involved in alliances. He identified what information had been collected by whom and then passed it on to appropriate departments. Another company held regular meetings where employees shared new knowledge and determined who was best positioned to acquire additional information.

Proceed with Care—But Proceed

After World War II, Japanese and Korean companies entered alliances with Western rivals from weak positions. But they worked steadfastly toward independence. In the early 1960s, NEC's computer business was one-quarter the size of Honeywell's, its primary foreign partner. It took only two decades for NEC to grow larger than Honeywell, which eventually sold its computer operations to an alliance between NEC and Group Bull of France. The NEC experience demonstrates that dependence on a foreign partner doesn't automatically condemn a company to also-ran status. Collaboration may sometimes be unavoidable; surrender is not.

Managers are too often obsessed with the ownership structure of an alliance. Whether a company controls 51% or 49% of a joint venture may be much less important than the rate at which each partner learns from the other. Companies that are confident of their ability to learn may even prefer some ambiguity in the alliance's legal structure. Ambiguity creates more potential to acquire skills and technologies. The challenge for Western companies is not to write tighter legal agreements but to become better learners.

Running away from collaboration is no answer. Even the largest Western companies can no longer outspend their global rivals. With leadership in many industries shifting toward the East, companies in the United States and Europe must become good borrowers—much like Asian companies did in the 1960s and 1970s. Competitive renewal depends on building new process capabilities and winning new product and technology battles. Collaboration can be a low-cost strategy for doing both.

CHAPTER 7

Implementing the Strategy:
Building Multidimensional Capabilities

Just as the new transnational strategic imperatives put demands on MNEs' existing organizational capabilities, so have emerging transnational organization models defined new managerial tasks for those operating within them. In this chapter, we examine the changing roles and responsibilities of three typical management groups that find themselves at the table in today's transnational organizations: the global business manager, the worldwide functional manager, and the national subsidiary manager. Although different organizations may define the key roles differently (bringing global account managers or regional executives to the table, for example), the major challenge facing all MNEs is to allocate their many complex strategic tasks and organizational roles among key management groups, then give each of those groups the appropriate legitimacy and influence within the ongoing organization decision-making process. The chapter concludes with a review of the role of top management in integrating these diverse perspectives and engaging them around a common direction.

The MNE in the early 21st century is markedly different from its ancestors. It has been transformed by an environment in which multiple, often conflicting forces accelerate simultaneously. The globalization of markets, the acceleration of product and technology life cycles, the assertion of national governments' demands, and, above all, the intensification of global competition have created an environment of complexity, diversity, and change for most MNEs.

As we have seen, the ability to compete on the basis of a single dominant competitive advantage gave way to a need to develop multiple strategic assets: global-scale efficiency and competitiveness, national responsiveness and flexibility, and worldwide innovation and learning capabilities. In turn, these new strategic task demands put pressure on existing organization structures and management processes. Traditional hierarchical structures, with their emphasis on either/or choices, have evolved toward organizational forms we have described as transnational, characterized by integrated networks of assets and resources, multidimensional management perspectives and capabilities, and flexible coordinative processes.

The managerial implications of all this change are enormous. To succeed in the international operating environment of the present, managers must be able to sense and interpret complex and dynamic environmental changes; they must be able to develop and integrate multiple strategic capabilities; and they must be able to build and manage complicated yet subtle new organizations required to deliver coordinated action on a worldwide basis. Unless those in key management positions are highly skilled and knowledgeable, companies simply cannot respond well to the major new challenges they face.

Yet surprisingly little attention is devoted to the study of the implications of all these changes in the roles and responsibilities of those who manage today's MNEs. Academics, consultants, and even managers themselves focus an enormous amount of time and energy on analyzing the various international environmental forces, on refining the concepts of global strategy, and on understanding the characteristics of effective transnational organizations. But without effective managers in place, sophisticated strategies and organizations will fail. The great risk for most MNEs today is that they are trying to implement third-generation strategies through second-generation organizations with first-generation managers.

In this chapter, we examine the management roles and responsibilities implied by the new challenges facing MNEs—those that take the manager beyond the first-generation assumptions. The tasks differ considerably for those in different parts and different levels of the organization, so rather than generalizing, we focus on the core responsibilities of different key management groups. In this chapter, we examine the roles and tasks of three specific groups in the transnational company: the global business manager, the worldwide functional manager, and the country subsidiary manager. (Recall that in Chapter 4, we suggested that variations often occur in the nature of transnational structures. As a result, other key executives—global account managers, for example—may also have a seat at the table.) To close the chapter, we review the role of top management in integrating these often-competing perspectives and capabilities.

Global Business Management

The challenge of developing global efficiency and competitiveness requires that management capture the various scale and scope economies available to the MNE as well as capitalize on the potential competitive advantages inherent in its worldwide market positioning. These requirements demand a perspective that considers opportunities and risks across national boundaries and functional specialties and the skill to coordinate and integrate activities across these barriers to capture the potential benefits. This is the fundamental task of the global business manager.

In implementing this important responsibility, the global business manager will be involved in a variety of diverse activities, whose balance varies considerably depending on the nature of the business and the company's administrative heritage. Nonetheless, there are three core roles and responsibilities that almost always fall to this key manager: He or she will be the global product or business strategist, the architect of worldwide asset and resource configuration, and the coordinator and controller of cross-border transfers.

Global Business Strategist

Because competitive interaction increasingly takes place on a global chessboard, only a manager with a worldwide perspective and responsibility can assess the strategic position and capability in a given business. Therefore, companies must configure their information, planning, and control systems so that they can be consolidated into consistent, integrated global business reports. This recommendation does not imply that the global business manager alone has the perspective and capability to formulate strategic priorities, or that he or she should undertake that vital task unilaterally. Depending on the nature of the business, there will almost certainly be some need to incorporate the perspectives of geographic and functional managers who represent strategic interests that may run counter to the business manager's drive to maximize global efficiency. Equally important, the business strategy must fit within the broader corporate strategy, which should provide a clear vision of what the company wants to be and explicit values pertaining to how it will accomplish its mission. These are among the key issues requiring resolution in Case 7-2, "BRL Hardy: Globalizing an Australian Wine Company."

In the final analysis, however, the responsibility to reconcile different views falls to the global business manager, who needs to prepare an integrated strategy of how the company will compete in his or her particular business. In many companies, the manager's ability to do so is compromised because the position has been created by anointing domestic product division managers with the title of global business manager. Overseas subsidiary managers often feel that these managers are not only insensitive to nondomestic perspectives and interests but also biased toward the domestic organization in making key strategic decisions like product development and capacity plans. In many cases, their concerns are justified.

The preferred career path for the global business strategist is arguably via the country manager route. The challenges facing the manager of a major subsidiary are inevitably multidimensional and can serve as good training ground for future overall business strategists. Case 7-4, "Taming the Dragon: Cummins in China," provides a good example.

In the true transnational company, the global business manager need not be located in the home country, and in many cases, great benefits can accrue to relocating several such management groups abroad. Asea Brown Boveri (ABB), the Swiss-based electrical engineering company, has deliberately tried to leverage the capabilities of its strong operating companies worldwide and exploit their location in key strategic markets by locating its worldwide business area management wherever such organizational and strategic dimensions coincide. In its global power transmission business, for example, the business area manager for switchgears was located in Sweden, for power transformers in Germany, for distribution transformers in Norway, and for electric metering in the United States.

Even well-established MNEs with a tradition of close control of worldwide business strategy are changing. The head of IBM's $6 billion telecommunications business moved her division headquarters to London. She explained that the rationale was not only to move the command center closer to the booming European market for computer networking but also "[to] give us a different perspective on all our markets." And when General Electric acquired Amersham, the British-based life sciences and diagnostics leader, it not only tapped CEO Sir William Castell to head GE's $15 billion healthcare business, it relocated the business headquarters to the United Kingdom to better leverage the technology and entrepreneurial management it had acquired with Amersham.

Architect of Asset and Resource Configuration

Closely tied to the challenge of shaping an integrated business strategy is the global business manager's responsibility for overseeing the worldwide distribution of key assets and resources. Again, we do not mean to imply that he or she can make such decisions unilaterally. The input of interested geographic and functional managers must be weighed. It is the global business manager, however, who is normally best placed to initiate and lead the debate on asset configuration, perhaps through a global strategy committee or a world board with membership drawn from key geographic and functional management groups.

In deciding where to locate key plants or develop vital resources, the business manager can never assume a zero base. Indeed, such decisions must be rooted in the company's administrative heritage. In multinational companies like Philips, Unilever, ICI, or Nestlé, many of the key assets and resources that permitted them to expand internationally have long been located in national companies operating as part of a decentralized federation. Any business manager trying to shape such companies' future configurations must build on rather than ignore or destroy the important benefits that such assets and resources represent. And particularly in cases of plant closures, he or she has to demonstrate enormous political dexterity to overcome the inevitable resistance from local stakeholders.

The challenge to the business manager is to shape the future configuration by leveraging existing resources and capabilities and linking them in a configuration that resembles the integrated network form. GE Medical Systems' reconfiguration of its development centers and sourcing plants (described in Case 3-4) represents a classic model of the construction of such a distributed yet integrated transnational structure.

Cross-Border Coordinator

This discussion leads directly to the third key role played by most global business managers, that of a cross-border coordinator. Although less overtly strategic than the other two responsibilities, it is nonetheless a vital operating function, because it involves deciding on sourcing patterns and managing cross-border transfer policies and mechanisms.

The task of coordinating flows of materials, components, and finished products becomes extremely complex as companies build transnational structures and capabilities. Rather than producing and shipping all products from a fully integrated central plant (the centralized hub model) or allowing local subsidiaries to develop self-sufficient capabilities (the decentralized federation model), transnational companies specialize their operations worldwide, building on the most capable national operations and capitalizing on locations of strategic importance. The resulting integrated network of specialized operations is highly interdependent, perhaps linking high labor content component plants in Poland and Korea with highly skilled subassembly operations in Germany and Singapore, which in turn supply specialized finished-product plants in the United States, England, France, and Japan. To achieve such interdependence involves both corporate-owned and outsourced supply. Either form requires the resolution of issues ranging from how to divide the task of serving end-users to controlling the quality of the end product to managing the flow of design and production knowledge to subcontractors. And all of this must occur while trying to minimize the likelihood of technology loss if outsourcing is used.

The coordination mechanisms available to the global business manager vary from direct central control over quantities shipped and prices charged to the establishment of rules that essentially create an internal market mechanism to coordinate cross-border activities. The former means of control is more likely for products of high strategic importance (e.g., Pfizer's control over quantities and pricing of shipments of the active ingredients of Viagra, or Coca-Cola's coordination of the supply of Coke syrup worldwide).

As products become more commodity-like, however, global product managers recognize that internal transfers should reflect the competitive conditions set by the external environment. This recognition has led many to develop internal quasi-markets as the principal means of coordination.

For example, in the consumer electronics giant Matsushita, once the parent company develops prototypes of the following year's models of video cameras, CD players, and so on, global product managers offer them internally to buyers at merchandise meetings that are, in effect, huge internal trade fairs. At these meetings, national sales and marketing directors from Matsushita's sales subsidiaries worldwide enter into direct discussions with the global product managers, negotiating modifications in product design, price, and delivery schedule to meet their local market needs.

Worldwide Functional Management

Worldwide functional management refers to those individuals with the responsibility for primary activities like R&D, manufacturing, and marketing, as well as those responsible for support activities, such as the chief financial officer and the chief information officer. Their job, broadly speaking, is to diffuse innovations and transfer knowledge on a worldwide basis. This vital task is built on knowledge that is highly specialized by function—technological capability, marketing expertise, manufacturing know-how, and so on—and to do it effectively requires that functional managers evolve from the secondary staff roles they often have played and take active roles in transnational management.

The tasks facing functional managers vary widely by specific function (e.g., technology transfer may be more intensive than the transfer of marketing expertise) or by business (companies in transnational industries such as telecommunications demand more functional linkages and transfers than do those in multinational industries such as retailing). Nonetheless, we highlight three basic roles and responsibilities that most worldwide functional managers should play: worldwide scanner of specialized information and intelligence, cross-pollinator of "best practices," and champion of transnational innovation.

Worldwide Intelligence Scanner

Most innovations start with some stimulus driving the company to respond to a perceived opportunity or threat. It may be a revolutionary technological breakthrough, an emerging consumer trend, a new competitive challenge, or a pending government regulation. And it may occur anywhere in the world. A typical example occurred when the radical Green political party first began achieving important victories in gaining popular support for environmental protection in Germany in the late 1980s. Companies with good sensory mechanisms in Germany recognized the significance of this development and began adjusting their products, processes, and company policies. As these political forces and market demands spread worldwide during the 1990s, those companies without the benefit of advance warning systems found themselves trying to respond not only to the growing political and consumer pressures but also to more responsive competitors touting that they had several years' head start in developing more environmentally friendly products and strategies.

Although strategically important information often was sensed in the foreign subsidiaries of classic multinational or global companies, it was rarely transmitted to those who could act on it or was ignored when it did get through. The communication problem was due primarily to the fact that the intelligence was usually of a specialist nature, not always well understood by the generalists who controlled the line organization. To capture and transmit such information across national boundaries required the establishment of specialist information channels that linked local national technologists, marketers, and production specialists with others who understood their needs and shared their perspective.

In transnational companies, functional managers are linked through informal networks that are nurtured and maintained through frequent meetings, visits, and transfers. Through such linkages, these managers develop the contacts and relationships that enable them to transmit information rapidly around the globe. The functional managers at the corporate level become the linchpins in this effort and play a vital role as facilitators of communication and repositories of specialist information.

Cross-Pollinator of "Best Practices"

Overseas subsidiaries can be more than sources of strategic intelligence, however. In a truly transnational company, they can be the source of capabilities, expertise, and innovation that can be transferred to other parts of the organization. Caterpillar's leading-edge flexible manufacturing first emerged in its French and Belgian plants, for example, and much of P&G's liquid detergent technology was developed in its European Technology Center. In both cases, this expertise was transferred to other countries with important global strategic impact. Such an administrative ability to transfer new ideas and developments requires a considerable amount of management time and attention to break down the not-invented-here (NIH) syndrome that often thrives in international business. In this process, those with worldwide functional responsibilities are ideally placed to play a central cross-pollination role. Not only do they have the specialist knowledge required to identify and evaluate leading-edge practices, they also tend to have a well-developed informal communications network developed with others in their functional area.

Corporate functional managers in particular can play a vital role in this important task. Through informal contacts, formal evaluations, and frequent travel, they can identify where the best practices are being developed and implemented. They are also in a position to arrange cross-unit visits and transfers, host conferences, form task forces, or take other initiatives that will expose others to the new ideas.

Champion of Transnational Innovation

The two previously identified roles ideally position the functional manager to play a key role in developing what we call transnational innovations. As described in Chapter 5, these are different from the predominantly local activity that dominated the innovation process in multinational companies or the centrally driven innovation in international and global companies. The first (and simplest) form of transnational innovation is what we call locally leveraged. By scanning their companies' worldwide operations, corporate functional managers can identify local innovations that have applications elsewhere. In Unilever, for example, product and marketing innovation for many of its global brands occurred in national subsidiaries. Snuggle fabric softener was born in Unilever's German company, Timotei herbal shampoo originated in its Scandinavian operations, and Impulse body spray was first introduced by its South African unit. Recognizing the potential that these local innovations had for the wider company, the parent company's marketing and technical groups created the impetus to spread them to other subsidiaries.

The second type of transnational innovation, which we call globally linked, requires functional managers to play a more sophisticated role. This type of innovation fully exploits the company's access to worldwide information and expertise by linking and leveraging intelligence sources with internal centers of excellence, wherever they may be located. For example, P&G's global liquid detergent was developed by managing a complex network of relationships among technical and marketing managers worldwide. The product's desired performance responded to the Europeans' need for water-softening capability, the Americans' desire for improved cleaning capability, and the Japanese sensing of an opportunity for a liquid detergent with cold-water effectiveness. The product was developed by incorporating technological breakthroughs that had occurred in creating a bleach substitute and enzyme stabilizer from the European Technical Center, an improved surfactant developed in the corporate labs, and new low-temperature performance capabilities contributed by the International Technical Center. By linking and leveraging the company's intelligence and resources worldwide, P&G developed a product that was vastly superior to those being worked on locally and centrally. The new product was successfully introduced as Liquid Tide in the United States, Liquid Ariel in Europe, and Liquid Cheer in Japan.

Geographic Subsidiary Management

In many MNEs, a successful tour as a country subsidiary manager is often considered the acid test of general management potential. Indeed, it is often a necessary qualification on the résumé of any candidate for a top management position. Not only does it provide frontline exposure to the realities of today's international business environment, but it also puts the individual in a position where he or she must deal with enormous strategic complexity from an organizational position that is severely constrained. Moreover, the role of "country manager" is, if anything, becoming more difficult as more MNEs move toward structures dominated by global business units and global customers. In such situations, the manager of the country is often held accountable for results but has only limited formal authority over the people and assets within his or her jurisdiction. Such is the reality in Case 7-3, "Silvio Napoli at Schindler India."

We have described the strategic challenge facing the MNE as one that requires resolving the conflicting demands for global efficiency, multinational responsiveness, and worldwide learning. The country manager is at the center of this strategic tension—defending the company's market positions against global competitors, satisfying the demands of the host government, responding to the unique needs of local customers, serving as the "face" of the entire organization at the national level, and leveraging its local resources and capabilities to strengthen the company's competitive position worldwide.

There are many vital tasks the country manager must play. We identify three that capture the complexity of the task and highlight its important linkage role: acting as a bicultural interpreter, becoming the chief advocate and defender of national needs, and the vital frontline responsibility of being the implementer of the company's strategy.

Bicultural Interpreter

The requirement that the country manager become the local expert who understands the needs of the local market, the strategy of competitors, and the demands of the host government is clear. But his or her responsibilities are also much broader. Because managers at headquarters do not understand the environmental and cultural differences in the MNE's diverse foreign markets, the country manager must be able to analyze the information gathered, interpret its implications, and even predict the range of feasible outcomes. This role suggests an ability not only to act as an efficient sensor of the national environment but also to become a cultural interpreter able to communicate the importance of that information to those whose perceptions may be obscured by ethnocentric biases.

There is another aspect to the country manager's role as an information broker that is sometimes ignored. Not only must the individual have a sensitivity to and understanding of the national culture, he or she must also be comfortable in the corporate culture at the MNE. Again, this liaison-style bicultural role implies much more than being an information conduit communicating the corporation's goals, strategies, and values to a group of employees located thousands of miles from the parent company. The country subsidiary manager must also interpret those broad goals and strategies so they become meaningful objectives and priorities at the local level of operation and apply those corporate values and organizational processes in a way that respects local cultural norms.

National Defender and Advocate

As important as the communication role is, it is not sufficient for the country manager to act solely as an intelligent mailbox. Information and analysis conveyed to corporate headquarters must be not only well understood but also acted upon, particularly in MNEs where strong business managers are arguing for a more integrated global approach and corporate functional managers are focusing on cross-border linkages. The country manager's role is to counterbalance these centralizing tendencies and ensure that the needs and opportunities that exist in the local environment are well understood and incorporated into the decision-making process.

As the national organization evolves from its early independence to a more mature role as part of an integrated worldwide network, the country manager's normal drive for national self-sufficiency and personal autonomy must be replaced by a less parochial perspective and a more corporate-oriented identity. This shift does not imply, however, that he or she should stop presenting the local perspective to headquarters management or stop defending national interests. Indeed, the company's ability to become a true transnational depends on having strong advocates of the need to differentiate its operations locally and be responsive to national demands and pressures.

Two distinct but related tasks are implied by this important role. The first requires the country manager to ensure that the overall corporate strategies, policies, and organization processes are appropriate from the national organization's perspective. If the interests of local constituencies are violated or the subsidiary's position might be compromised by the global strategy, it is the country manager's responsibility to become the defender of national needs and perspectives.

In addition to defending national differentiation and responsiveness, the country manager must become an advocate for his or her national organization's role in the corporation's worldwide integrated system, of which it is a part. As MNEs develop a more transnational strategy, national organizations compete not only for corporate resources but also for roles in the global operations. To ensure that each unit's full potential is realized, country managers must be able to identify and represent their particular national organization's key assets and capabilities, as well as the ways in which they can contribute to the MNE as a whole.

It is the country manager's job to mentor local employees and support those individuals in their fight for corporate resources and recognition. In doing so, they build local capability that can be a major corporate asset. As the former head of the Scottish subsidiary of a U.S. computer company observed, "It is my *obligation* to seek out new investment. No one else is going to stand up for these workers at head office. They are doing a great job, and I owe it to them to build up this operation. I get very angry with some of my counterparts in other parts of the country, who just toe the party line. They have followed their orders to the letter, but when I visit their plants I see unfulfilled potential everywhere."

Frontline Implementer of Corporate Strategy

Although the implementation of corporate strategy may seem the most obvious of tasks for the manager of a frontline operating unit, it is by no means the easiest. The first challenge stems from the multiplicity and diversity of constituents whose demands and pressures compete for the country manager's attention. Being a subsidiary company of some distant MNE seems to bestow a special status on many national organizations and subject them to a different and a more intense type of pressure than that put on other local companies. Governments may be suspicious of their motives, unions may distrust their national commitment, and customers may misunderstand their way of operating. Compounding the problem, corporate management often underestimates, or appears to the subsidiary general manager to underestimate, the significance of these demands and pressures. Case 7-1, "Larson in Nigeria," illustrates such a tension.

In addition, the country manager's implementation task is complicated by the corporate expectation that he or she take the broad corporate goals and strategies and translate them into specific actions that are responsive to the needs of the national environment. As we have seen, these global strategies are usually complex and finely balanced, reflecting multiple conflicting demands. Having been developed through subtle internal negotiation, they often leave the country manager with very little room to maneuver.

Pressured from without and constrained from within, the country manager needs keen administrative sense to plot the negotiating range in which he or she can operate. The action decided on must be sensitive enough to respect the limits of the diverse local constituencies, pragmatic enough to achieve the expected corporate outcome, and creative enough to balance the diverse internal and external demands and constraints.

As if this were not enough, the task is made even more difficult by the fact that the country manager does not act solely as the implementer of corporate strategy. As we discussed previously, it is important that he or she also plays a key role in its formulation. Thus, the strategy the country manager is required to implement will often reflect some decisions against which he or she lobbied hard. Once the final decision is taken, however, the country manager must be able to convince his or her national organization to implement it with commitment and enthusiasm.

Top-Level Corporate Management

Nowhere are the challenges facing management more extreme than at the top of an organization that is evolving toward becoming a transnational corporation. Not only do these senior executives have to integrate and provide direction for the diverse management groups we have described, but in doing so, they also first have to break with many of the norms and traditions that historically defined their role.

Historically, as increasingly complex hierarchical structures forced them further and further from the frontlines of their businesses, top management's role became bureaucratized in a rising sea of systems and staff reports. As layers of management slowed decision making, and the corporate headquarters role of coordination and support evolved to one of control and interference, top management's attention was distracted from the external demands of customers and competitive pressures and began to focus internally on an increasingly bureaucratic process.

The transnational organization of today cannot afford to operate this way. Like executives at all levels of the organization, top management must add value, which means liberating rather than constraining the organization below them. For those at the top of a transnational, this means more than just creating a diverse set of business, functional, and geographic management groups and assigning them specific roles and responsibilities. It also means maintaining the organizational legitimacy of each group, balancing and integrating their often divergent influences in the ongoing management process, and maintaining a unifying sense of purpose and direction in the face of often conflicting needs and priorities. This tension is at the core of Case 7-2, "BRL Hardy."

This constant balancing and integrating role is perhaps the most vital aspect of top management's job. It is reflected in the constant tension managers feel between ensuring long-term viability and achieving short-term results, or between providing a clear overall corporate direction and leaving sufficient room for experimentation. This tension is reflected in the three core top management tasks we highlight here. The first, which focuses on the key role of providing long-term direction and purpose, is in some ways counterbalanced by the second, which highlights the need to achieve current results by leveraging performance. The third key task of ensuring continual renewal again focuses on long-term needs but at the same time may require the organization to challenge its current directions and priorities.

Providing Direction and Purpose

In an organization built around the need for multidimensional strategic capabilities and the legitimacy of different management perspectives, diversity and internal tension can create an exciting free market of competing ideas and generate an enormous amount of individual and group motivation. But there is always the risk that these same powerful centrifugal forces could pull the company apart. By creating a common vision of the future and a shared set of values that overarch and subsume managers' more parochial objectives, top management can, in effect, create a corporate lightning rod that captures this otherwise diffuse energy and channels it toward powering a single company engine.

We have identified three characteristics that distinguish an energizing and effective strategic vision from a catchy but ineffective public relations slogan. First, the vision must be clear; simplicity, relevance, and continuous reinforcement are the key to such clarity. NEC's integration of computers and communications—C&C—is a good example of how clarity can make a vision more powerful and effective. Top management in NEC has applied the C&C concept so effectively that it describes the company's business focus, defines its distinctive source of competitive advantage over large companies like IBM and AT&T, and summarizes its strategic and organizational initiatives. Throughout the company, the rich interpretations of C&C are understood and believed.

Second, continuity of a vision can provide direction and purpose. Despite shifts in leadership and continual adjustments in short-term business priorities, top management must remain committed to the company's core set of strategic objectives and organizational values. Without such continuity, the unifying vision takes on the transitory characteristics of the annual budget or quarterly targets—and engenders about as much organizational enthusiasm.

Third, in communicating the vision and strategic direction, it is critical to establish consistency across organizational units—in other words, to ensure that the vision is shared by all. The cost of inconsistency can be horrendous. At a minimum, it can result in confusion and inefficiency; at the extreme, it can lead individuals and organizational units to pursue agendas that are mutually debilitating.

Leveraging Corporate Performance

Although aligning the company's resources, capabilities, and commitments to achieve common long-term objectives is vital, top management must also achieve results in the short term to remain viable among competitors and credible with stakeholders. Top management's role is to provide the controls, support, and coordination to leverage resources and capabilities to their highest level of performance.

In doing so, top managers in transnational companies must abandon old notions of control that are based primarily on responding to below-budget financial results. Effective top managers rely much more on control mechanisms that are personal and proactive. In discussions with their key management groups, they ensure that their particular responsibilities are understood in relation to the overall goal and that strategic and operational priorities are clearly identified and agreed upon. They set demanding standards and use frequent informal visits to discuss operations and identify new problems or opportunities quickly.

When such issues are identified, the old model of top-down interference must be replaced by one driven by corporate-level support. Having created an organization staffed by experts and specialists, top management must resist the temptation to send in the headquarters "experts" to take charge at the first sign of difficulty. Far more effective is an approach of delegating clear responsibilities, backing them with rewards that align those responsibilities with the corporate goals, then supporting each of the management groups with resources, specialized expertise, and other forms of support available from the top levels of the company.

Perhaps the most challenging task for top management as it tries to leverage the overall performance of the corporation is the need to coordinate the activities of an organization deliberately designed around diverse perspectives and responsibilities. As we described in Chapter 4, there are three basic cross-organizational flows that must be carefully managed—goods, resources, and information—and each demands a different means of coordination. Goods flows can normally be routinized and managed through formal systems and procedures. Decisions involving the allocation of scarce resources (e.g., capital allocation, key personnel assignments) are usually centralized because top management wants to be involved directly and personally. And flows of information and knowledge are generated and diffused most effectively through personal contact.

These three flows are the lifeblood of any company, and any organization's ability to make them more efficient and effective depends on top management's ability to develop a rich portfolio of coordinative processes. By balancing the formalization, centralization, and socialization processes, they can exploit the company's synergistic potential and greatly leverage performance.

Ensuring Continual Renewal

Despite their enormous value, either of these first two roles, if pursued to the extreme, can result in a company's long-term demise. A fixation on an outmoded mission can be just as dangerous as a preoccupation with short-term performance. Even together, they can doom a company with its continuing success, especially if successful strategies become elevated to the status of unquestioned wisdom and effective organizational processes become institutionalized as routines. As strategies and processes ossify, management loses its flexibility, and eventually the organization sees its role as protecting its past heritage. Thus, when Jin Zhiguo became the president of China's massive Tsingtao Brewery Co. Ltd. in 2001, not only did he have competitive challenges, he needed to implement internal reforms. As he noted, "Tsingtao Brewery has been an arrogant company. We must have an open mind and learn from other companies. A strong learning ability will lead to powerful innovations."[1]

It is top management's role to prevent this ossification from occurring, and there are several important ways it can ensure that the organization continues to renew itself rather than just reinventing its past. First, by reducing the internal bureaucracy and constantly orienting the organization to its customers and benchmarking it against its best competitors, top management can ensure an external orientation.

Second, equally important is its role in constantly questioning, challenging, stirring up, and changing things in a way that forces adaptation and learning. By creating a "dynamic imbalance" among those with different objectives, top management can prevent a myopic strategic posture from developing. (Clearly, this delicate process requires a great deal of top management time if it is not to degenerate into anarchy or corporate politics.)

Third, top management can ensure renewal by defining the corporate mission and values statements so that they provide some stretch and maneuverability for management, and also legitimize new initiatives. More than this, those at the top levels must monitor closely the process of dynamic imbalance they create and strongly support some of the more entrepreneurial experimentation or imaginative challenges to the status quo that emerge from such a situation.

Concluding Comments

In this chapter, we shift the level of analysis down to the individual manager. Rather than think in terms of the changing nature of the business environment or the conflicting strategic imperatives facing the MNE, we examine the new roles of three groups of managers—those responsible for a global business unit, a worldwide function (e.g., finance, marketing), and a geographic territory (typically a country). We also look at the new role of top-level corporate management in integrating and providing direction for these three groups. Each role involves many familiar tasks as well as several new ones. Worldwide functional managers, for example, must become thought leaders in their discipline and active cross-pollinators of best practices across countries. And country managers need to develop the capacity to translate political and social trends in their local market into business imperatives for the MNE.

These new roles and responsibilities are hard to put in place because they require managers to rethink many of their traditional assumptions about the nature of their work. This is ultimately the biggest challenge facing the transnational organization—to create a generation of managers that have the requisite skills and the sense of perspective needed to operate in a multibusiness, multifunctional, multinational system.

---

[1] As quoted in the CEIBS-Ivey case by Shengjun Liu, "Tsingtao Brewery Co., Ltd. (B)," Case Number 9B05M070, p. 9.

Case 7-1 Larson in Nigeria (Revised)

David Larson, vice-president of international operations for Larson Inc., was mulling over the decisions he was required to make regarding the company's Nigerian operation. He was disturbed by the negative tone of the report sent to him on January 4, 2004, by the chief executive officer (CEO) of the Nigerian affiliate, George Ridley (see Exhibit 1). Larson believed the future prospects for Nigeria were excellent and was concerned about what action he should take.

Company Background

Larson Inc. was a New York–based multinational corporation in the wire and cable business. Wholly-owned subsidiaries were located in Canada and the United Kingdom, while Mexico, Venezuela, Australia, and Nigeria were the sites of joint ventures. Other countries around the world were serviced through exports from the parent or one of its subsidiaries.

The parent company was established in 1925 by David Larson's grandfather. Ownership and management of the company remained in the hands of

Ivey

Richard Ivey School of Business
The University of Western Ontario

Professor Paul W. Beamish and Harry Cheung revised this case (originally prepared by Professor I.A. Litvak) solely to provide material for class discussion. The authors do not intend to illustrate either effective or ineffective handling of a managerial situation. The authors may have disguised certain names and other identifying information to protect confidentiality. Ivey Management Services prohibits any form of reproduction, storage, or transmittal without its written permission. This material is not covered under authorization from CanCopy or any reproduction rights organization. To order copies or request permission to reproduce materials, contact Ivey Publishing, Ivey Management Services, c/o Richard Ivey School of Business, The University of Western Ontario, London, Ontario, Canada, N6A 3K7; phone (519) 661-3208; fax (519) 661-3882; e-mail cases@ivey.uwo.ca.

the Larson family and was highly centralized. The annual sales volume for the corporation worldwide approximated $936 million in 2003. Revenue was primarily generated from the sale of power, communication, construction and control cables.

Technical service was an important part of Larson Inc.'s product package; therefore, the company maintained a large force of engineers to consult with customers and occasionally supervise installation. As a consequence, licensing was really not a viable method of serving foreign markets.

Background on Nigeria

Nigeria is located in the west-central part of the African continent. With 134 million people in 2003, it was the most populous country in Africa and the ninth most populous nation in the world. Population growth was estimated at 2.5 per cent annually. About 44 per cent of the population was under 15 years of age. A majority of the labor force in Nigeria worked in agriculture but there was a trend of more people moving to urban centres.

The gross domestic product in 2003 was about $55 billion. While per capita GDP was only about $433, on a purchasing power parity basis it was substantially higher at $900. GDP had grown from 1998 to 2003 at about two per cent to three per cent annually. This increase was fuelled in part by growth in agriculture and the export sales of Nigeria's oil reserves.

During the 1998 to 2003 period, Nigeria's annual inflation rate had ranged between 10 and 11.7 per cent. This high level had contributed to the change in the value of the naira from 85.3 to the U.S. dollar in 1998 to 129.8 to the U.S. dollar in 2003.

The Nigerian Operation

Larson Inc. established a joint venture in Nigeria in 1994 with a local partner who held 25 per cent of the joint venture's equity. In 1999, Larson Inc.

Exhibit 1   The Ridley Report

In response to the request from head office for a detailed overview of the Nigerian situation and its implications for Larson Inc., Ridley prepared the following report in December 2003. It attempts to itemize the factors in the Nigerian environment that have contributed to the problems experienced by Larson's joint venture in Nigeria.

REPATRIATION OF CAPITAL

1. While the Nigerian Investment Promotions Commission (NIPC) has removed time constraints and ceilings on repatriation, the divesting firm still has to submit evidence of valuation. In most cases the valuation is unrealistically low. This has represented substantial real-capital asset losses to the overseas companies concerned.

REMITTANCE

2. A problem regarding remittances has arisen as a result of the Nigerian Insurance Decree No. 59, under which cargoes due for import to Nigeria have to be insured with a Nigerian-registered insurance company. For cargoes imported without confirmed letters of credit, claims related to cargo loss and damage are paid in Nigeria; however, foreign exchange for remittance to pay the overseas suppliers is not being granted on the grounds that the goods have not arrived.

PROBLEMS AFFECTING LIQUIDITY AND CASH FLOW

3. A number of problems have arisen during the last two years that are having a serious effect upon liquidity and cash flow, with the result that the local expenses can be met only by increasing bank borrowing, which is not only an additional cost but also becoming more difficult to obtain.
   a. Serious delays exist in obtaining payment from federal and state government departments for supplies and services provided, even in instances where payment terms are clearly written into the contract concerned. This is particularly true for state governments where payment of many accounts is 12 months or more in arrears. Even after payment, further delays and exchange-rate losses are experienced in obtaining foreign currency for the part that is remittable abroad. This deterioration in cash flow from government clients had, in turn, permeated through to the private clients.
   b. There is a requirement that a 100 per cent deposit be made on application for foreign currency to cover letters of credit.
   c. In order to clear the cargo as soon as possible and to avoid possible loss at the wharf, importers normally pay their customs duty before a ship arrives.
   d. Most company profits are taxed at a flat rate of 30 per cent. Firms operating in Nigeria must contend with a number of arbitrary levies and taxes, imposed mainly by state governments eager to augment their extremely thin revenue bases. The federal government attempted to put a halt to such practices by specifying which taxes all three (federal, state and local) tiers of government can collect, but it has not been entirely successful in enforcing compliance. Tax authorities are constantly trying to "trip up" companies in the course of inspections or audits, through their "interpretation" of the tax legislation. Consequently, net earnings after tax are insufficient to cover increased working capital requirements.

INCOMES AND PRICES POLICY GUIDELINES

4. Many of the guidelines issued by the Productivity, Prices and Incomes Board are of direct discouragement, as they make operations in Nigeria increasingly less attractive in comparison with other areas in the world. Although these guidelines were removed in 1987, increases for wage, salary, fees for professional services and auditing are still subject to final government approval.

OFFSHORE TECHNICAL AND MANAGEMENT SERVICES

5. Restrictions on the reimbursement of expenses to the parent company for offshore management and technical services are a cause of great concern, since such services are costly to provide.

(continued)

Exhibit 1   *(continued)*

PROFESSIONAL FEES

6. The whole position regarding fees for professional services provided from overseas is most unsatisfactory. Not only are the federal government scales substantially lower than those in most other countries, but also the basis of the project cost applied in Nigeria is out of keeping with normally accepted international practice. The arbitrary restriction on the percentage of fees that may be remitted is a further disincentive to attracting professional services. Moreover, payment of professional fees in themselves produces cash flow problems exacerbated by long delays in payments and remittance approvals.

ROYALTIES AND TRADEMARKS

7. The National Office of Technology Acquisition and Promotion (NOTAP) restricts the payment of royalties for the use of trademarks for a period of 10 years, which is out of keeping with the generally accepted international practice. This can be extended only under special cases. Limits for licensing and technical service fees are between one per cent to five per cent of net sales. Management fees are chargeable at two per cent to five per cent of a company's profit before tax (or one per cent to two per cent of net sales when no profits are anticipated during the early years). The maximum foreign share of consulting fees is five per cent. Such applications, however, are only granted for advanced technology projects for which indigenous technology is not available. Further, service agreements for such projects have to include a schedule of training for Nigerian personnel for eventual takeover and Nigerian professionals are required to be involved in the project from inception.

QUOTAS, WORK PERMITS, AND ENTRY VISAS

8. It must be recognized that expatriate expertise is a very important element for this business, but expatriate staff is very costly. Unfortunately, at the present time there are a number of difficulties and frustrations, such as the arbitrary cuts in expatriate quotas, the delays in approving quota renewal, and in some cases, the refusal of entry visas and work permits for individuals required for work in Nigeria. Expatriate quotas are usually granted for two to three years subject to renewal.

EXPATRIATE STAFF

9. In general, the conditions of employment and life in Nigeria are regarded as unattractive when compared with conditions in many other countries competing for the same expertise. These differences are due to: the general deterioration in law and order; the restrictions on salary increase and home remittance; the difficulties in buying air tickets; the poor standard of health care; the unsatisfactory state of public utilities such as electricity, water, and telecommunications; the harassment from the police, airport authorities and other government officials; the general frustrations related to visas and work permits mentioned above. The situation has now reached a stage where not only is recruitment of suitably qualified, skilled experts becoming increasingly difficult, but we are also faced with resignations and refusals to renew contracts even by individuals who have worked and lived here for some years. Furthermore, the uncertainty over the length of time for which employment in Nigeria will be available (due to doubts whether the necessary expatriate quotas will continue to be available to the employer) is most unsettling to existing staff. This and the restriction of contracts to as little as two years are important factors in deterring the more highly qualified applicants from considering posts in Nigeria. These factors are resulting in a decline in the quality of expatriate staff it is possible to recruit.

LOCAL STAFF

10. Nigeria has one of the strongest national unions in Africa—the National Labor Congress (NLC). It is almost impossible to discipline a worker without attracting confrontation with the union. On certain occasions, some union members can be very militant. The union is also continuously attacking the employment of expatriates and trying to replace them with Nigerian staff.

11. Inadequate local technical training leads to low quality workers who tend to be lazy and not quality conscious.

(continued)

Exhibit 1 *(concluded)*

---

12. The desirability of maintaining a tribal balance in the work force limits the options in recruiting the best workers.

13. Nigerian companies suffer heavily from pilferage, which normally accounts for two per cent of sales.

PUBLIC UTILITIES

14. The constant interruption in public utility services not only affects the morale of all employees but also has a very serious impact upon the operation of the business itself. Unless reasonable and continuing supplies of electricity, water, petroleum products and telecommunications can be assured, and the highway adequately maintained, the costs related to setting up and operating escalate.

CONTINUITY OF OPERATING CONDITIONS

15. The general and growing feeling of uncertainty about the continuity of operating conditions is a matter of considerable concern. It would seem that this uncertainty is engendered by a whole range of matters related to: short notice changes (sometimes even retrospective) in legislation and regulations; imprecise definition of legislation and regulations, which leads to long periods of negotiation and uncertainty; delays between public announcement of measures and promulgation of how they are to be implemented; and sometimes inconsistent interpretation of legislation and regulations by Nigerian officials.

GOVERNMENT OFFICIALS

16. Foreign partners have to rely on their Nigerian counterpart to handle the government officials. But it is impossible to measure its performance nor to control its expense in these activities. In addition, carefully cultivated relationships with officials could disappear, as they are transferred frequently.

BRIBERY

17. Surrounding many of the problems previously listed is the pervasive practice of bribery, known locally as the *dash*. Without such a payment it is very difficult to complete business or government transactions with native Nigerians.

---

promised Nigerian authorities that the share of local ownership would be increased to 51 per cent within the next five to seven years. Such indigenization requests from developing country governments were quite common.

Sales revenue for the Nigerian firm totalled $45 million in 2003. Of this revenue, $39.4 million was realized in Nigeria, while $5.6 million was from exports. About 40 per cent of the firm's Nigerian sales ($16 million) were made to various enterprises and departments of the government of Nigeria. The company was making a reasonable profit of 10 per cent of revenue, but with a little bit of luck and increased efficiency, it was believed it could make a profit of 20 per cent.

The Nigerian operation had become less attractive for Larson Inc. in recent months. Although it was widely believed that Nigeria would become one of the key economic players in Africa in the 2000s and that the demand for Larson's products would remain very strong there, doing business in Nigeria was becoming more costly. Furthermore, Larson Inc. had become increasingly unhappy with its local partner in Nigeria, a lawyer who was solely concerned with quick "paybacks" at the expense of reinvestment and long-term growth prospects.

David Larson recognized that having the right partner in a joint venture was of paramount importance. The company expected the partner or partners to be actively engaged in the business, "not business people interested in investing money alone." The partner was also expected to hold a substantial equity in the venture. In the early years of the joint venture, additional funding was often required and it was necessary for the foreign partner to be in a strong financial position.

The disillusionment of George Ridley, the Nigerian firm's chief executive officer (CEO), had been increasing since his early days in that position. He was an expatriate from the United Kingdom who, due to his background as a military officer, placed a high value upon order and control. The chaotic situation in Nigeria proved very trying for him. His problems were further complicated by his inability to attract good, local employees in Nigeria, while his best expatriate staff requested transfers to New York or Larson Inc.'s other foreign operations soon after their arrival in Nigeria. On a number of occasions, Ridley was prompted to suggest to head office that it reconsider its Nigerian commitment.

The Decision

David Larson reflected on the situation. He remained convinced that Larson Inc. should maintain its operations in Nigeria; however, he had to design a plan to increase local Nigerian equity in the venture to 51 per cent. Larson also wondered what should be done about Ridley. On the one hand, Ridley had been with the company for many years and knew the business intimately; on the other hand, Larson felt that Ridley's attitude was contributing to the poor morale in the Nigerian firm and wondered if Ridley had lost his sense of adaptability. Larson knew Ridley had to be replaced, but he was unsure about the timing and the method to use, since Ridley was only two years away from retirement.

Larson had to come to some conclusions fairly quickly. He had been requested to prepare an action plan for the Nigerian operation for consideration by the board of directors of Larson Inc. in a month's time. He thought he should start by identifying the key questions, whom he should contact, and how he should handle Ridley in the meantime.

Case 7-2   BRL Hardy: Globalizing an Australian Wine Company

In January 1998, Christopher Carson smiled as he reviewed the Nielsen market survey results that showed Hardy was the top-selling Australian wine brand in Great Britain and held the overall number two position (to Gallo) among all wine brands sold in Britain's off-trade (retailers, excluding hotels and restaurants). As managing director of BRL Hardy Europe, Carson felt proud of this achievement that reflected a 10-fold increase in volume since his first year with Hardy in 1991.

But his mental celebration was short-lived. In front of him were two files, each involving major decisions that would not only shape the future success of the company in Europe but also have major implications for BRL Hardy's overall international strategy:

- The first file contained details of the proposed launch of D'istinto, a new line of Italian wines developed in collaboration with a Sicilian winery. Carson and his U.K. team were deeply committed to this project, but several questions had been raised by Australian management. Not least was their concern about Mapocho, another joint-venture sourcing agreement Carson had initiated that was now struggling to correct a disappointing market launch and deteriorating relations with the Chilean sourcing partner.

- The second issue he had to decide concerned two competing proposals for a new entry-level

Exhibit 1   BRL Hardy Limited: Summary Group Financial Results—1992–1997 (Aus$millions)

	1992	1993	1994	1995	1996	1997
Sales revenue	151.5	238.3	256.4	287.0	309.0	375.6
Operating profit (before interest, tax)	16.7	26.6	30.2	34.0	39.3	49.2
Net after tax profit	8.8	13.3	15.8	17.4	21.2	28.4
Earnings per share	13.2¢	14.1¢	15.7¢	15.7¢	18.1¢	23.3¢
Total assets	216.8	234.6	280.7	329.0	380.6	455.5
Total liabilities	117.4	127.4	146.6	160.4	194.4	205.8
Shareholders' equity	99.4	107.2	134.1	168.6	186.2	249.7
Debt/equity ratio	70%	57%	57%	53%	58%	41%

Source: Company documents.

Australian wine. His U.K.-based management had developed considerable commitment to Kelly's Revenge, a brand they had created specifically in response to a U.K. market opportunity. But the parent company was promoting Banrock Station, a product it had launched successfully in Australia which it now wanted to roll out as a global brand at the same price point.

Watching over these developments was Steve Millar, managing director of the South Australia–based parent company that had experienced a period of extraordinary growth, due in large part to BRL Hardy's successful overseas expansion (**Exhibit 1**). A great believer in decentralized responsibility, he wanted Carson to be deeply involved in the decisions. But he also wanted to ensure that the European unit's actions fit with the company's bold new strategy to become one of the world's first truly global wine companies. Neither did he want to jeopardize BRL Hardy's position in the critically important U.K. market that accounted for two-thirds of its export sales. For both Millar and Carson, these were crucial decisions.

Industry Background[1]

Vines were first introduced into Australia in 1788 by Captain Arthur Phillip, leader of the group of

[1]For a full account, see Christopher A. Bartlett, *Global Wine Wars: New World Challenges Old (A)*, HBS No. 303-056 (Boston: Harvard Business School Publishing, 2002); and (*B*), HBS. No. 304-016 (Boston: Harvard Business School Publishing, 2003).

convicts and settlers who comprised the first fleet of migrants to inhabit the new British colony. A wave of European settlers attracted by the gold rush of the mid-nineteenth century provided a boost to the young industry, both in upgrading the availability of vintner skills and in increasing primary demand for its output. Still, the industry grew slowly, and as late as 1969 annual per capita wine consumption in this beer-drinking country was only 8.2 liters—mostly ports and fortified wines—compared with over 100 liters per person per annum in France and Italy.

In the following 25 years, the Australian wine industry underwent a huge transformation. First, demand for fortified wines declined and vineyards were replanted with table wine varieties. Then, as consumers became more sophisticated, generic bulk wine sales—often sold in the two-liter "bag in a box" developed in Australia—were replaced by bottled varietals such as cabernet sauvignon, chardonnay, and shiraz, the classic grape type increasingly associated with Australia. By the mid-1990s, domestic consumption stood at 18½ liters per capita, eighteenth in the world.

Over this two-century history, more than 1,000 wineries were established in Australia. By 1996, however, the 10 largest accounted for 84% of the grape crush and 4 controlled over 75% of domestic branded sales. Most of these were public corporations, the largest of which was Southcorp whose brands included Penfolds, Lindeman, and Seppelt. The number two company was BRL Hardy Ltd.

Exhibit 2   Australian Wine Export Forecasts—Selected Markets 1996–2025

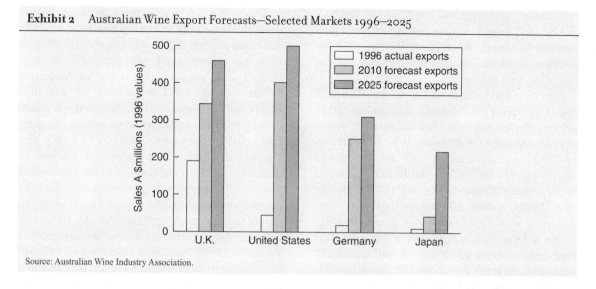

Source: Australian Wine Industry Association.

(BRLH), selling under the Hardy, Houghton, Leasingham, and other labels.

During the 1980s and 1990s changes in the global wine industry had a major impact on these emerging Australian companies. A rationalization and consolidation among wine wholesalers and retailers was increasing the power of historically fragmented distribution channels. At the same time, however, large-scale wine suppliers from New World countries such as United States, South America, South Africa, and Australia were exploiting modern viticulture and more scientific wine-making practices to produce more consistent high-quality wine. These developments were occurring in an environment of rapidly growing demand from new consumers in nontraditional markets.

During this period of change, Australian wines began to find large markets abroad, and by 1995 exports accounted for more than 27% of production. But despite its rapid growth, the Australian industry accounted for less than 2% of the world wine production by volume and 2.5% by value. However, because only A$13 billion of the total A$65 billion global wine sales was traded product (80% of wine was consumed in the country of production), the Australian companies' A$450 million in 1995 exports represented 3.5% of the world export market.

But in an industry that was becoming increasingly fashion-driven, Australian wine was becoming a "hot trend," and an ambitious industry association saw export potential growing to A$2.5 billion by 2025—a 16% share of the projected traded value.[2] Together with an increase in domestic consumption, this translated to A$4.5 billion in Australian wine sales and a doubling of production to 1.7 million tonnes by 2025.

The Australian industry association saw four export markets as key—the United Kingdom, the United States, Germany, and Japan. While the U.K. market would decrease in relative importance (in 1996 it was the world's largest non-producing wine importer and accounted for over 40% of Australian wine exports), over the next 25 years these four markets were expected to continue accounting for 60% of export sales. (See **Exhibit 2.**)

Company Background and History

BRLH's roots could be traced back to 1853 when Thomas Hardy, a 23-year-old English vineyard laborer, acquired land near Adelaide, South Australia, and planted it with vines. In 1857 he produced his

[2]All forecast values are in 1996 Australian dollars at wholesale prices. At 1996 year-end, the exchange rate was A$1 = US$0.8.

first vintage, exporting two hogsheads to England, and by 1882 he had won his first international gold medal at Bordeaux. When Hardy died in 1912, his company was Australia's largest winemaker, but also one of the most respected.

Shortly after Hardy's death, in the Riverland region northeast of Adelaide, 130 Italian grape growers formed Australia's first cooperative winery in 1916, naming it the Renmano Wine Cooperative. In 1982 Renmano merged with the Riverland's largest winery and distillery, the Berri Cooperative to form Berri Renmano Limited (BRL). By the early 1990s, almost 500 member growers were delivering over 50,000 tonnes of grapes to BRL, giving it the second-largest crush in Australia. This huge-volume grape crush and its bulk-packaging operations led some to refer to BRL disparagingly as "the oil refinery of the wine industry."

Throughout their respective histories, Thomas Hardy & Sons and BRL followed quite different strategies and developed very different organizations. Hardy became known for award-winning quality wines, while the combined cooperatives specialized in fortified, bulk, and value wines—some sold under private labels. And in contrast to Hardy's "polite and traditional" values, BRL's culture was more "aggressive and commercial," according to one observer of both companies.

International Roots   Although BRL experienced considerable success when it began selling abroad in the late 1980s (particularly in Scandinavia where it sold 6 million liters of bulk wines per annum), its efforts seemed quite modest when compared with Hardy's long history of exporting much higher-value-added bottled products and the huge additional commitments it was making in that same period. To expand on its U.K. sales base of 12,000 cases per annum, Hardy believed it needed to stop relying on importers, distributors, and agents who carried scores of brands from dozens of vineyards. After a long search, in 1989 it acquired Whiclar and Gordon, a respected U.K.-based wine importer–distributor, including its agency rights for a range of French, Chilean, and South African wines.

This move led management to begin talking about the possibility of buying European wineries that could provide their newly acquired distributors with the critical mass and credibility to give Hardy's wines greater access to Europe. Motivated by the looming 1992 target date for a unified European Community (EC) market, and stimulated by the notion that such alternative sources of supply could cushion the ever-present risk of a poor vintage in one region, Hardy's board felt this was an ideal time to invest. In contrast to the painstaking process of identifying acquisition targets for U.K. distribution, however, the vineyard purchasing decision seemed more opportunistic. In 1990, two Hardy directors visited the wine-growing regions in France and Italy, looking at properties on the market. Passing through southern France, they acquired the century-old Domaine de la Baume, a winery with extensive sources in the Languedoc region and several established domestic and export brands. Six months later, they took over Brolio de Ricasoli, a beautiful castle on a Tuscan hillside that made a well-known Chianti and was reputed to be Italy's oldest winery.

Almost immediately, however, problems surfaced in all three of the European acquisitions and soon they were bleeding the parent company of millions of dollars. Combined with a recession-driven market slowdown at home, these problems plunged Hardy into losses. Meanwhile, BRL was also struggling and was looking for ways to expand and upgrade its business. When one of Hardy's banks called in a loan and the company was forced to look for a financial partner, BRL was there. Despite its own marginal financial performance, BRL management decided to propose a merger. Said one ex-BRL manager, "We had access to fruit, funds, and disciplined management; they brought marketing expertise, brands, and winemaking know-how. It was a great fit if we could learn to work together." Others, however, were less sanguine. Despite the fact that together the companies accounted for 22% of the Australian wine market and 17% of national wine exports, the dismissive industry view was, "When you put two dogs together, all you get is louder barking." Nonetheless, the companies merged in June 1992 and three months later became a publicly listed company.[3]

New Management, New Strategies

Following the merger, ex-BRL executives assumed the majority of top jobs in BRLH: the newly merged company's deputy-chairman, CEO, operations and technical director, and the international trading director all came from BRL. From the other side, only Hardy's managing director (who became BRLH's business development director) and the Australian sales and marketing manager survived as members of the new top executive team. Steve Millar, formerly BRL's managing director and now CEO of the merged company, explained his early priorities:

> Our first task was to deal with the financial situation. Both companies had performed poorly the previous year, and although we thought our forecasts were conservative, the market was concerned we would not meet the promises made in our IPO [initial public offering]. . . . Then we had to integrate the two organizations. This meant selecting a management team that could both implement the necessary retrenchments and position us for growth. Since the Australian market accounted for the vast bulk of our profit, we initially concentrated our attention at home. . . . Only after getting these two priorities straight could we focus on our new strategy.

The Domestic Turnaround   The strategy that emerged was simple: the company would protect its share of the bulk cask business but concentrate on branded bottle sales for growth. This would require a commitment to quality that would support its brands. The initial management focus would be on the domestic market, first getting merger efficiencies, then implementing the new strategy.

As important as developing a clear strategy, in Millar's mind, was the need to change the company's culture and management style. His sense

was that, although there was great potential in the company's middle management, much of it—particularly in the ex-Hardy team—had been held back by being resource constrained and excluded from major decisions. Millar's objective was to create a more decentralized approach, but to hold management accountable. He explained:

> It took time to get the message understood because Hardy management had tended to take a few big swings on high-risk decisions while keeping tight control over the small decisions. I wanted to delegate the small risks—to create a "have a go" mentality. The objective was to have us trying 20 things and getting 80% right rather than doing one or two big things that had to be 100% right.

The prerequisite to delegation, however, was that managers had to be willing to challenge the status quo, accept responsibility for the outcome of decisions that were delegated, and admit when they had made a mistake. David Woods, previously Hardy's national sales manager and now appointed to the same position in the merged company, recalled that the new management style was not easy for everyone to adopt: "Many of us from Hardy felt like outsiders, unsure if we would be allowed into meetings. It became easier after the first year or so when you had shown you could perform. But you definitely had to earn your stripes."

Woods "earned his stripes" by integrating the two sales forces, capturing the economies from the combination, and repositioning the product portfolio in line with the new strategy emphasizing quality branded bottle sales. The results were impressive with both domestic bottle market share and profitability increasing significantly in the first two years of BRLH's operation.

Relaunching International   Meanwhile, Millar had appointed Stephen Davies, an ex-BRL colleague whom he regarded as a first-class strategic marketer, as group marketing and export manager for BRLH. A 12-year veteran of BRL, Davies had been responsible for establishing that company's export division in 1985 and had been credited with its successful expansion abroad. While the rest of

---

[3]The Italian Ricasoli operations were explicitly excluded from the merger due to their continued substantial losses and the likelihood they would continue.

top management's attention was focused on a major restructuring of the domestic operations, Davies began evaluating the company's international operations. What he found was a dispersed portfolio of marginal-to-weak market positions: a U.K. business selling a small volume of Hardy wines and just breaking even, a rapidly eroding BRL bulk business in Sweden, a weak Hardy-U.S. presence supported by a single representative, and a virtually nonexistent presence in Asia or the rest of Europe.

In Davies's mind, a few clear priorities began to emerge, many of which shadowed the domestic approach. The first priority had to be to clean up the operating problems that were the source of the financial problems. Only then would they focus on building on their strengths, starting with their position in the U.K. market. Making "Quality Wines for the World" the company's marketing slogan, Davies began to build the export strategy on the basis of a strong quality brand image. From the existing broad portfolio of exported products, he initiated a program to rationalize the line and reposition a few key brands in a stepstair hierarchy from simple entry level products to fine wines for connoisseurs. At the mass market price points, for example, he focused the line on Nottage Hill and Stamps as the Hardy's "fighting brands," while at the top end he targeted the Eileen Hardy brand. (See **Exhibit 3** for rationalized export portfolio of brands.)

BRL Hardy in Europe

In the large, developed U.K. market, Davies found a turnaround had already begun under the leadership of Christopher Carson, managing director of Hardy's U.K. company. Carson was an experienced marketing manager with over 20 years in the wine business and particular expertise in Italian wines. He had been hired by Hardy in October 1990 to head the U.K. company's sales and marketing function, including the recently acquired distributor. Within a week of his joining, however, Carson realized that the financial situation in these companies was disastrous. He flew to Australia to tell Hardy's management that they would own a bankrupt U.K.

organization unless drastic action was taken. He then proposed a series of cost-cutting steps.

In February 1991, Carson was appointed U.K. managing director and immediately began to implement his cost-cutting plan. Over the next 18 months, he pruned the product line from 870 items to 230 and reduced the headcount from 31 to 18 (including a separation with three of the six executive directors). He also installed strong systems, controls, and policies that put him firmly in charge of key decisions. As these actions were implemented, the 1990 losses became a breakeven operation in 1991, and by the time of the mid-1992 merger, it looked as if the European operations would be profitable again. (For BRLH Europe financials, see **Exhibit 4.**)

Developing the Headquarters Relationship In his discussions with Davies in late 1992, Carson highlighted the key problems and priorities as he saw them. First was the need to build quickly on the 178,000 cases of Hardy-brand products that had represented less than a quarter of his total volume in 1991 (500,000 of his 700,000 case sales in 1991 were accounted for by a variety of low-margin French wines handled under agency agreements that had come with the purchase of Whiclar and Gordon). At the same time, if the company was going to restore the financial health of its French winemaker, Domaine de la Baume, he felt he would have to build substantially on the 10,000 cases of its product which he had sold in 1991. (He reported 1992 sales were on track to double their previous year's volume.) And finally, he wanted to protect an unstable imported Chilean product that had come as a Whiclar and Gordon agency. Carson told Davies of his plans to grow the high potential brand from 20,000 cases in 1991 to a forecast 60,000 cases for 1992.

Davies agreed with Carson's plans, particularly endorsing the focus on the Hardy brands. Yet the relationship was an uneasy one in the post-merger management uncertainties. The BRL-dominated headquarters management supported delegation—but only to those who had "earned their stripes."

Exhibit 3   BRL Hardy Domestic versus Export Product Portfolio, 1993

Soft Pack (Cask) Wine

- 2 litre   Renmano and Stanley range
- 3 litre   Berri fortified range
- 4 and 5 litre   Stanley, Berri and Buronga Ridge range
- 10, 15, and 20 litre   Stanley and Berri range

Bottled Table Wine

- Less than $6.00

       Brentwood range
       Brown Bin 60
       Hardy Traditional range
    * Hardy Stamp Series
       Spring Gully range
    * Nottage Hill
       Leasingham Hutt Creek
       McLaren Vale hermitage

- $6.00 to $10.00

    * Houghton White Burgandy
       Hardy Siegersdorf range
    * Leasingham Domaine range
    * Houghton Wildflower Ridge range
       Hardy Bird Series range
       Hardy Tintara range
       Moondah Brook Estate range
       Renmano Chairman's Selection range
       Redman Claret and Cabernet Sanvignon
       Barossa Valley Estate range
       Chais Baumiere range

- $10.00 to $15.00

    * Hardy Collection range
    * Houghton Gold Reserve range
    * Chateau Reynella Stony Hill range

- Over $15.00

    * Eileen Hardy range
       Lauriston range
       E&E Black Pepper Shiraz

Sparkling Wine

- Less than $6.00

       Courier Brut
       Hardy Grand Reserve
       Chateau Reynella Brut

- $6.00 to $10.00   * Hardy's Sir James Cuvee Brut
- Over $10.00   Hardy's Classique Cuvee
       Lauriston Methode Champenoise

Fortified Wine

- Less than $6.00

       Brown Bin 60
       Cromwell
    * Tall Ships
       Stanley 2 litre port soft pack (cask)

- $6.00 to $10.00   Rumpole
    * Old Cave
- Over $10.00   Lauriston Port & Muscat
       Hardy Show Port
       Vintage Port
       Chateau Reynella Vintage Port

Brandy

    * Hardy Black Bottle
       Berri
       Renmano

All prices are based on the recommended retail price.
* Rationalized export line (13 of 48 brands)
Source: Company documents.

Exhibit 4   BRL Hardy Europe Ltd.: Key Historical Data (£'000)

		1990	1991	1992	1993	1994
Net sales turnover	In GB £	£10,788	£12,112	£12,434	£15,521	£18,813
	In Australian $	A$22,243	A$24,973	A$29,965	A$33,830	A$37,946
Gross profit (after distribution expense)		£1,173	£1,429	£1,438	£1,595	£1,924
GP %/sales		10.9%	11.8%	11.6%	10.3%	10.2%
Administrative cost		£1,104	£1,261	£1,164	£1,172	£1,308
Admin %/sales		10.2%	10.4%	9.4%	7.6%	7.0%
Profit after tax		−£26	£6	£157	£266	£395
PAT %/sales		−0.2%	0.0%	1.3%	1.7%	2.1%
Average no. of employees		31	27	19	20	22
£ Sales per employee		£348	£449	£654	£776	£855
Stock @ year end		£1,226	£1,043	£605	£897	£1,392
Stock turnover		7.8	10.2	18.2	15.5	12.1
Return on investment		−2.1%	0.5%	11.2%	17.9%	24.5%

Source: Company documents.

Within the Hardy-built European company, on the other hand, there were questions about whether their bulk-wine-oriented BRL colleagues understood international marketing. "There was a real tension," said one observer. "A real feeling of us versus them. I think Christopher and Stephen had some difficult conversations." The relationship was delicate enough that Steve Millar decided to have Carson report directly to him on the U.K. company's profit performance but through Davies for marketing and brand strategy. (For BRLH international organization, see **Exhibit 5.**) But Millar did not want the shared reporting relationship to pull him into a role of resolving disputes on operating issues. Instead, he hoped for negotiation:

> Christopher had a good reputation and knew the market well. I assumed he would be a key player and was willing to let him prove it. He and Stephen just clashed, but confrontation can be healthy as long as it is constructive. I just kept urging them to work with together—they could learn a lot from one another.

The biggest disputes seemed to emerge around marketing strategies, particularly branding and labeling issues. Although Hardy exported a dozen brands covering the full price range, its entry-level brands in the United Kingdom were Hardy's Stamps, blended red and white wines that then retailed for £2.99 and Hardy's Nottage Hill, a single varietal red and white at the £3.69 price point. Together, these two brands accounted for over 80% of Hardy brand sales by value and even more by volume. Carson was concerned that the image of these brands had eroded in the United Kingdom, and that he wanted to relabel, reposition, and relaunch them. But it was difficult to convince the home office, and he expressed his frustration:

> Australia controlled all aspects of the brand and they kept me on a pretty tight leash. When I took my message to Reynella [BRLH's corporate office near Adelaide], they didn't want to hear. They expect you to get runs on the board before they give you much freedom. . . . But we were in the U.K. market and they weren't. Finally they agreed, and in 1993 we relabeled and relaunched Nottage Hill and repositioned Stamps. By 1994 our volume of Hardy's brands quadrupled from 1992 and represented more than half our total sales. [See **Exhibit 6.**]

Davies acknowledged that he yielded on the Stamps and Nottage Hill decisions, believing "it

1995	1996	1997	Plan 1998	Plan 1999	Plan 2000	Plan 2001
				Forecast per BRLH Europe Strategic Plan		
£27,661	£32,271	£40,100	£53,848	£66,012	£78,814	£91,606
A$57,734	A$69,532	A$82,680	A$111,027	A$136,107	A$162,503	A$188,878
£2,592	£3,202	£4,212	£5,453	£6,488	£7,630	£8,787
9.4%	9.9%	10.5%	10.1%	9.8%	9.7%	9.67%
£1,896	£2,118	£2,717	£3,649	£4,473	£5,340	£6,207
6.9%	6.8%	6.8%	6.8%	6.8%	6.8%	6.8%
£426	£723	£948	£1,087	£1,286	£1,460	£1,644
1.5%	2.2%	2.4%	2.0%	1.9%	1.9%	1.8%
24	28	34	48	62	76	91
£1,153	£1,153	£1,179	£1,122	£1,065	£1,037	£1,007
£1,265	£1,504	£1,500	£2,100	£2,600	£3,300	£3,900
19.8	19.3	23.9	23.0	22.9	21.6	21.2
23.5%	35.7%	39.7%	38.0%	37.8%	36.1%	37.2%

Exhibit 5   BRL Hardy's International Organization, 1993

Steve Millar — Managing Director

David Woods — Australian Sales & Marketing Manager

Peter Beckwith — Finance Director

Angus Kennedy — Ops & Technical Director

Stephen Davies — Group Marketing and Export Manager

John Whelan — Company Secretary/ Group Counsel

Chris Day — Group Strategic Planning Manager

Christopher Carson — Managing Director BRL Hardy Europe

BRLH New Zealand

BRLH U.S.A.

BRLH Canada

Export Manager Asia/Pacific

Source: Company documents.

Exhibit 6   BRL Hardy Europe Ltd.: Case Summary History

In Std. 9 Liter Cases	1991	1992	1993	1994	1995	1996	1997
Hardy	178,500	194,303	411,084	856,876	1,031,071	1,383,772	1,763,698
Domaine de la Baume	10,000	19,564	49,698	63,540	89,256	155,608	158,587
Chile	20,000	58,848	24,855	76,775	112,954	120,540	50,537
French Agencies (AGW)	497,500	618,878	528,606	545,198	446,445	51,257	{186,180
French Projects					2,162	58,744	
Grand total	706,000	891,593	1,014,243	1,542,389	1,681,888	1,769,921	2,159,002

Source: Company documents.

was better to let people follow a course they believe in—then the implementation will be better." But he became increasingly concerned about the demand for local control over branding, labeling, and pricing decisions, especially as the company's long-term strategy began to evolve.

The Evolving Strategy   In Reynella, by the mid-1990s, Millar and Davies began to conceive of BRL Hardy not as just a "quality exporter" but as an "international wine company" with worldwide product access backed by the marketing capability and distribution muscle to create global brands. As Millar explained:

> It was an important strategic shift. Most packaged goods businesses are dominated by multinational companies with global brands—like Coke or Kraft. We realized that there were no really established global wine companies and, despite our newness at the game, we had a real chance to be one. . . . I began describing BRL Hardy to our shareholders as a company based on three core strengths: our world-class production facilities, our global brands, and our international distribution. Controlling those assets allows us to control our destiny in any major market in the world.

Within the industry, the notion of building global wine brands ran counter to the established wisdom. For example, Jean-Louis Duneu, the head of the Paris office of Lander, a branding consulting firm, recognized the potential of global branding, but was skeptical about its applicability to wine. "The promise of a brand is that it will be the same

quality every time," he said. "That means that branded wine probably has to be blended to ensure consistency. The result is never as satisfying." Jonathan Knowles, another corporate identity consultant warned of another potential problem. "Wine lovers look for something they haven't heard of," he claimed. "There's almost an anti-branding mentality. When people who are not in the know get to know the brand name, people in the know no longer want the product."

That view also seemed widespread among traditional wine producers. In the highly fragmented European industry—there were 12,000 producers in Bordeaux alone—only a few top-of-the-market names like Lafite, d'Yquem, and Veuve Clicquot had achieved global recognition, but these held minuscule market shares. Of those that had attempted to build mass market global brands over the years, only a handful—Mateus Rosé, Blue Nun, Mouton Cadet, and Hirondelle, for example—had succeeded. And of these, most had managed to capture only relatively small volumes and for brief periods of time. After years of trying, Gallo, the world's biggest wine brand, accounted for considerably less than 1% of global wine sales, mostly in its home market.

Nonetheless, Millar and Davies believed that changes in wine-making, the opening of global markets, and the changing consumer profile would all support their objective to become a truly international wine company built on a global branding capability. To implement this strategic shift, Davies felt the Reynella headquarters had to be the "global brand owners." He explained:

> Although we believe in decentralization and want to listen to and support overseas ideas and proposals, we also have to be clear about Reynella's role. Everyone has opinions on label design, but we'll lose control of the brand if we decentralize too much. Our role should be as brand owners deciding issues relating to labeling, pricing, and branding, and overseas should be responsible for sales, distribution, and promotion strategy.

Carson and his U.K. management team had some difficulty with this concept, and disagreements between the two executives continued through the mid-1990s. Carson tried to convince Davies that, unlike the Australian market where branded products accounted for 90% of sales mostly through hotels and bottle shops, the United Kingdom was not yet a branded wine market. Retailers' own labels dominated, particularly in the supermarkets that accounted for more than 50% of retail wine sales. (Indeed, both BRL and Hardy had previously been sources for private labels, but had since discontinued the practice.) Proximity to Continental sources meant that another big segment was claimed by a proliferation of tiny vineyard or village labels with little or no brand recognition, leaving only 12% of sales to recognized proprietary branded wines in 1995. In such a market, Carson argued, it would be hard to support a brand-driven strategy. He elaborated:

> We have to manage a progression from commodity to commodity brand to soft brand to hard brand. And at the early stage of that progression, distribution is key. It's more push than pull, and you need retailers' support to get your product on their shelves. That's why labeling is so important. Women represent 60% of the supermarket wine buyers and the label has to appeal to them.

As the decade rolled on, the debate between Carson and Davies continued. But, as Steve Millar put it, "With 70% growth, we could support the tension."

The 1997 Watershed Decisions

On the basis of the U.K. company's excellent performance, Carson was appointed chief executive of BRL Hardy Europe in 1995. He immediately began putting together some bold plans for the company's continued growth and, over the next couple of years, set in motion some initiatives that were to create a mixture of excitement and apprehension within the organization.

The Outsourcing Ventures For the first five years following the merger, Carson had focused most of his attention on building sales of the Hardy brand wines. However, he remained acutely aware of the importance of the other non-Australian product lines he had inherited through the Whiclar and Gordon acquisition. Not only did the added volume bring scale economies to his sales and distribution operation, they also provided BRLH Europe with some other important strategic benefits.

As an agricultural product, every region's grape harvest was vulnerable to weather, disease, and other factors affecting the quality and quantity of a vintage. Carson recognized that sourcing from multiple regions was one way to minimize that risk. Furthermore, he became increasingly aware that major retailers—particularly grocery chains like Sainsbury's—were trying to rationalize their suppliers. To simplify wine buying, they wanted to deal with only a few key suppliers who could provide them with a broad line of quality products. And finally, currency fluctuations exposed traded products like wine exports to currency-driven price variations that could substantially affect marketability, particularly for lower-priced products. (See **Exhibit 7**.)

Exhibit 7 Key Currency Fluctuations Affecting BRLH Europe

	$Aus/£	It Lira/£	Chilean Peso/£	$US/£
12/92	2.197	2239	NA	1.514
12/93	2.213	2516	NA	1.492
12/94	2.013	2546	NA	1.559
12/95	2.080	2455	630.8	1.541
12/96	2.088	2544	703.0	1.664
12/97	2.505	2892	727.1	1.659

Source: Company documents.

For all these reasons, in 1997 Carson began to devote more of his time and attention to two non-Australian wine sources—a move that seemed to fit with Reynella's new emphasis on becoming "an international wine company." This shift was triggered by the unpleasant revelation in late 1996 that Caliterra, a brand he and his sales organization had built into the leading Chilean import in the United Kingdom, would not be renewing its distribution agreement. The supplier, Caliterra Limitade, had signed a joint venture agreement with U.S. winemaker Robert Mondavi.

Determined never again to invest in a brand he did not control, Carson initiated action on two fronts. In early 1997, he negotiated a 50/50 joint venture agreement with Jose Canopa y CIA Limitada under which the Chileans would provide the fruit and the winemaking facility while BRL Hardy would send in one of its winemakers to make several wines that it would sell in Europe under the Mapocho brand, using its marketing and distribution capabilities. Despite several mishaps, difficulties, and delays during the negotiations (including a near derailing when Carson's main contact left Canepa), by late 1997 the supply arrangements were in place.

At the same time he was finalizing the Chilean deal, Carson was also exploring alternative European sources, particularly for red wine. In March 1997, he made initial contact with Casa Vinicola Calatrasi, a family-owned winery in Sicily with links to a major grape grower's cooperative. After explaining his interest in developing a line of branded products to be sold through BRLH's distribution channels, he began analyzing product availability, volume forecasts, and prices.

Over the following months, he returned to Sicily a couple more times, meeting with the co-op farmers to explain how branding could give them security of demand and eventually better prices for their fruit. He told them of BRL Hardy's expertise in viticulture, and offered the help of the company's highly regarded technical experts to further enhance the value of their harvest through more productive vineyard techniques and new winemaking methods. Having experienced difficult negotiations

with the Chilean joint venture, Carson wanted to avoid similar problems and emphasized that this would work only if it was a true partnership. He wanted the farmers' best fruit and their commitment to make the project work. At his first presentation, 60 farmers showed up. When the word spread, Carson found he had an audience of 135 receptive co-op members at his second presentation. "We all had a very good feeling about the relationship," said Carson. "It felt much more like a partnership than the Chilean JV where they were acting more like suppliers than part owners."

Returning to London, Carson engaged his organization in developing a strategy for the product code-named Mata Hardy. While detailed marketing plans were being developed internally, an external consultant began generating over 2,000 possible brand names. As Carson and his sales and marketing staff began narrowing the choices, they engaged a designer to develop labels and packaging that would capture the Mediterranean lifestyle they wanted the brand to reflect.

By July 1997, the marketing plans were developed to the point that Carson was ready to review his proposal with management in Reynella. He described how he wanted to offset projected Australian red wine shortages with alternative sources. Presenting his vision of sourcing from both the northern and southern hemispheres, he outlined his need for a full line to maximize his leverage as a distributor. He then described the broad objective of developing a brand that would respond to the average wine consumer who was interested in wine but not necessarily very knowledgeable about it. The new product was designed to give them the information they needed on appealing, easy-to-read labels with a pronounceable brand name. The objective was to give them a wine they would enjoy and a brand they would trust.

Carson then presented the portfolio of eight new Italian-sourced wines spread across the low and low-middle price points. At the baseline £3.49 price point would be wines made from less well known indigenous Sicilian grapes. At the next level would be blends of indigenous and premium varietals (a Catarrato-Chardonnay white and Nero d'Avola-Sangiovese red, for example) priced at £3.99. At £4.99 he planned to offer pure premium varietals such as Syrah and Sangiovese, while to top out the line he wanted to offer blends of super-varietals such as Cabernet-Merlot at £5.99.

The highlight of the presentation was when Carson unveiled his idea about creating a strong branded product, revealing both the final name choice—D'istinto, which translated as "instinctively"—and the boldly distinctive labels and other packaging designs. (See **Exhibit 8.**) (He swore all who saw the branding materials to secrecy since his intention was to reveal the new name and label with great fanfare just before its planned launch in early 1998.) The plan was to give D'istinto a unique image built around the Mediterranean lifestyle—passionate, warm, romantic, and relaxed—and to link it strongly to food. Each bottle would have a small booklet hung on its neck,

describing the wine and inviting the buyer to write for free recipes. The intention was to create a database of wine-and-food-loving consumers to whom future promotions could be mailed. "This line can help us build BRLH Europe in size, impact, and reputation," said Carson. "We need to become known as a first-class branding company—a company able to leverage great distribution and strong marketing into recognized consumer brands."

In the meanwhile, however, early signs were that the Mapocho project was not going well. For months, Canepa managers had been raising doubts and concerns about the JV. For example, they claimed their costs went up, and wanted to renegotiate the supply price. By the time things got back on track, the Chilean company had made other commitments and the new venture lost its opportunity to get early access to the pick of the 1997 grape harvest. As a result, first samples of Mapocho sent to London by BRL Hardy's winemaker were disappointing. The Chileans thought the problem was due to the winemaker sent from BRL Hardy being unfamiliar with Chilean wine, while he insisted they had not provided him with quality fruit. Early sales were disappointing and forecasts were that the first vintage would sell only 15,000 cases against the 80,000 originally planned. Unless there was a rapid turnaround, the company stood to lose up to £400,000. Despite this poor showing, however, the U.K. sales and marketing group was forecasting 1998 sales of 150,000 cases and the company was about to make a commitment to Canepa for this volume of their new vintage due in February. It was a forecast that made many in the Reynella headquarters very nervous.

As a consequence, while the Australians were impressed by Carson's ambitious ideas for D'istinto, many questions and doubts were raised and approval was slow in coming. Some senior management still had bad feelings about the Italian wine business left over from Hardy's earlier ill-fated Italian venture. Even those who had not lived through the Ricasoli losses had concerns about the troublesome ongoing experiment with the Chilean sourcing joint venture. And still others, including

---

Exhibit 8   *D'istinto* Proposed Packaging and Positioning

Capsule Product Position/Brand Image

- Value
- Quality
- Mass appeal

- Mediterranean lifestyle
- Food-friendly

- Relaxed
- Warm
- Romantic

Source: Company documents.

Stephen Davies, were concerned that the new Sicilian line could cannibalize Hardy's two fighting brands. D'istinto was initially proposed as a product to fill the price points that had been vacated as Stamps and Nottage Hill had become more expensive. But, as the Australian management pointed out, the extended Sicilian line now clearly overlapped with Hardy's core offerings—not only Stamps at £4.49 but even with Nottage Hill now selling for £5.49 (see **Exhibit 9**).

Finally, Steve Millar raised a more organizational concern. He was worried about the possibility of Carson losing his focus and about the strength of the European sales organization to carry another brand when it was already struggling with Mapocho. In the context of the U.K.'s over-commitment to the Mapocho launch, he was even more concerned when he saw D'istinto's projected sales of 160,000 cases in the first year rising to 500,000 by year four. "You will never do those numbers," said Millar. Carson's response was that he thought D'istinto had global potential and could eventually reach a million cases. "By the next century, we'll even be exporting Italian wine to Australia!" he said.

Yet despite the lighthearted exchange with his boss, the widely expressed doubts he confronted in the Australian review meeting caused Carson to reflect. The financial investment in the branding, packaging, and launch expenses was relatively small—probably less than £100,000. But in a situation of continued difficulty with Mapocho sales, Carson understood that the real financial risk could come later in the form of contract commitments and excess inventory. Furthermore, he knew that the questions Steve Millar had raised about organizational capacity and his own risk of distraction were real. Would D'istinto overload human resources already stretched thin by the rapid expansion of the previous five years? And would it prove to be too big a competitor for management time, corporate funding, and eventually consumer sales? The questions were complicated by another decision Carson faced—one relating to the development of a new Australian product to extend the company's existing range of fighting brands.

The Australian Opportunity As the Stamps and Nottage Hill brands gradually migrated upward to straddle the £4.49/£4.99/£5.49 price points, Carson believed there was an opening for a new low-end Australian brand to fill in the first rungs on the Hardy's price ladder. Because the price points below £4.49 represented more than 80% of the market, he felt it was an important gap to fill. Being fully occupied with the Chilean and Italian projects, however, he found himself unable to devote the time he wanted to developing a new Australian brand. To Steve Millar, this presented the ideal opportunity to push an agenda he had been urging on Carson for some time—the need to develop the senior levels of the U.K. organization, particularly on the marketing side. Said Millar:

> Christopher had done an amazing job of building the U.K. But he had driven much of it himself. . . . For a couple of years I'd been telling him, "Get people even better than you *below* you." We'd even sent a few Australians to support him in marketing and help the communication back home. But most of them got chewed up pretty quickly.

Finding himself stretched thin, and recognizing he had to stand back from controlling operations, Carson agreed to take on a new expat Australian marketing manager. The person he chose was Paul Browne, an eight-year company veteran whose career had taken him from public relations to brand management in Australia. Most recently, he had been responsible for export marketing for the United States and Oceania, reporting to the president of BRL Hardy USA. Carson explained his choice:

> I wanted a driver. Someone who could take charge and get things done. As an Australian with an understanding of group level activities, Paul fit our need to fill the weakness in marketing. He roared into the business with great enthusiasm and linked up with our sales director and national accounts manager to understand the local market's needs.

Browne concluded that there was an opportunity for a Hardy's brand positioned at the £3.99 price point, but able to be promoted at £3.49. He felt the market was ready for a fun brand—even slightly

Exhibit 9 U.K. Product Price Point Matrix

Recommended Retail Price Point (£)	Hardy	Leasingham Chateau Reynella	Houghton	Mapocho	D'istinto
27.99	Eileen Hardy Shiraz Thomas Hardy Cab Sauv		Jack Mann Red		
24.99		E&E Black Pepper Classic Clare Shiraz			
19.99					
12.99	Eileen Hardy Chardonnay	Ebenezer Shiraz Ebenezer Cab Merlot Ch Reynella Shiraz Ch Rey Cab Merlot	Crofters Cab Merlot		
11.99					
9.99	Coonawarra Cab Sauv	Leasingham Shiraz Leas Cab Malbec			
8.99		Ebenezer Chardonnay Ch Rey Chard Leas Chard	Crofters Chardonnay		
7.99	Pathway Chardonnay	Domain Grenache Leas Chardonnay Leas Semillon			
6.99	Bankside Shiraz		Wildflower Shiraz		
6.49	Nottage Hill Sparkling Bankside Chardonnay				
5.99	Nottage Hill Shiraz Stamps Sparkling		Wildflower Chardonnay Wildflower Chenin Blanc	Merlot	Cabernet Merlot
5.49	Nottage Hill Cab Shiraz				
4.99	Nottage Hill Chardonnay Nottage Hill Reisling Stamp Shiraz Cabernet Stamp Grenche Shiraz			Cab. Sauv. Chardonnay	Syrah Sangiovese
4.49	Stamp Chardonnay Sem Stamp ReislingG/Traminer			Sauv. Blanc	
3.99					Cataratto/Chardonnay Sangiovese/Merlot
3.49					Trebiano/Insolia Nero d' Aviola

Source: Company documents.

quirky—which would appeal to a younger consumer, perhaps a first-time wine drinker who would later trade up to Stamps and Nottage Hill. The brand he came up with was Kelly's Revenge, named for an important character in the history of the Australian wine industry, but also suggestive of Ned Kelly, the infamous Australian bushranger (outlaw) of the early nineteenth century. With backing and support of the U.K. sales management, they pursued the concept, designing a colorful label and preparing a detailed marketing plan. (See **Exhibit 10.**) As excitement and enthusiasm increased, Carson stood back and gave his new product team its head.

Meanwhile, in Reynella, BRLH in Australia was developing a major new product targeted at a similar price point. In 1995, the company had acquired Banrock Station, a 1,800-hectare cattle grazing property in South Australia's Riverland district, with the intention of converting a portion of it to

viticulture. During the planting and development phase, visitors' universally positive reaction to BRLH's ongoing conservation efforts—planting only 400 hectares while returning the remaining land to its native state including the restoration of natural wetlands—convinced management that the property had brand potential. (See **Exhibit 11.**)

Positioned as an environmentally responsible product with part of its profits allocated to conservation groups, the Banrock Station brand was launched in Australia in 1996. The brand's image was reflected in its earth-tone labels and its positioning as an unpretentious, down-to-earth wine was captured by the motto "Good Earth, Fine Wine." Blended Banrock Station wines started at A$4.95, but the line extended up to premium varietals at A$7.95. In the United Kingdom, it would be positioned at the same price points as the proposed Kelly's Revenge. The product was an immediate

---

Exhibit 10   *Kelly's Revenge:* Label and Product Concept

Proposed Promotion Material/Back Label

It has taken 130 years for Dr. Alexander Kelly to have his revenge. Kelly was the first to recognize the wine growing potential to Australia's McLaren Vale region. His vision, however, was ahead of its time, and his eventual bankruptcy enabled the acquisition of the original Tintara Winery by Thomas Hardy. Hardy's wines eventually established the reputation of the McLaren Vale, winning tremendous praise at the Colonial and Indian Wine Exhibition in 1885. Kelly's descendents have continued to forge Hardy's wine-making tradition, and to this day Tintara Cellars are the home of Hardy's Wines, one of Australia's finest and most highly awarded winemakers. This wine is dedicated to the spirit of our pioneers.

Source: Company documents.

Exhibit 11   *Banrock Station:* Environmentally Responsible Product Positioning

Proposed Product Promotion Material

Banrock Station's precious soil is treated with respect and in return it nurtures the premium grape varieties that create our value-for-money, easy drinking wines of great character. Situated in the heart of South Australia's Riverland region, directly opposite the historic Cobb & Co. stage coach station, Banrock Station is a 4,500 acre property featuring some of the world's most picturesque scenery. In its midst lie 400 acres of premium sun-soaked vineyard.

Because we understand that good earth is the starting point for most of nature's bounty, we are working with like minded organizations to ensure this natural haven which surrounds the vineyards of Banrock Station is preserved for future generations to appreciate and enjoy. Every sip of Banrock Station fine wine gives a little back to the good earth from whence it came.

Banrock Station: Good Earth, Fine Wine.

Source: Company documents.

success in Australia, and soon thereafter became the largest-selling imported brand in New Zealand.

Convinced of Banrock Station's potential as a global brand, Davies and Millar urged BRLH companies in Europe and North America to put their best efforts behind it. Canadian management agreed to launch immediately, while in the United

States, the decision was made to withdraw the Stamps product, which local management felt was devaluing the Hardy's image, and replace it with Banrock Station. But in Europe, where the Kelly's Revenge project was in its final development stages, the management team expressed grave doubts about Banrock Station. They argued that the label design was too dull and colorless to stand out on supermarket shelves, and that the product's environmental positioning would have limited appeal to U.K. consumers half a world away.

Steve Millar described the conflict that emerged around the competing concepts:

> I accept it as my mistake. I'd been pushing Christopher to delegate more and trying to get more Australians on his staff to help build links back to Australia. But Paul Browne became our biggest problem. He just didn't have the skills for the job but he wanted to control everything. Then on top of that he started playing politics to block Banrock Station. When we asked him to give the new concept a try, he kept insisting it would never work. We got the feeling he had even organized customers to tell us how bad the label was. Instead of helping communications between Australia and Europe he became a major barrier.

Meanwhile, Browne presented his new Kelly's Revenge concept to the Australian management to a very skeptical reception. Davies's reaction was immediate, strong, and negative, seeing it as "kitsch, downmarket, and gimmicky." He and his Reynella-based staff felt they knew more about marketing Australian wines than the European management. In Davies's words, "By decentralizing too much responsibility, we realized we risked losing control of brand issues. We wanted to take back more control as the brand owners."

Steve Millar recalled his reaction to the Kelly's Revenge proposal:

> I told them I thought it was terrible, but that it really didn't matter what I thought. I suggested we get the customers' reaction. When we took Kelly's Revenge to ASDA, the UK grocery chain, they were not enthralled. So I took that as an opportunity to suggest we give Banrock Station a try.

Although Christopher Carson had been backing his new marketing manager to this point, with Banrock Station succeeding elsewhere and senior management behind it as a global brand, the issue was becoming very complex. He knew the organization could not support both brands and felt the time had come when he would have to commit to one project or the other. For Steve Millar, the situation was equally complex. Given the U.K.'s strong performance, he wanted to give Carson as much freedom as possible, but also felt responsible for the implementation of the company's global strategy. Running through his mind was how he would respond if Carson and his U.K. organization remained firm in its commitment to Kelly's Revenge over Banrock Station.

Case 7-3   Silvio Napoli at Schindler India (A)

"Monsieur Napoli, si vous vous plantez ici vous êtes fini! Mais si vous réussissez, vous aurez une très bonne carrière." (Translation: "Mr. Napoli, if you fall on your face here you are finished! But if you succeed, you will have a very nice career.") The words echoed off the walls of Silvio Napoli's empty living room and disappeared down the darkened hallway like startled ghosts. The parquet was still wet from the five inches of water that had flooded the first floor of the Napoli home in suburban New Delhi several days before, during one of the sewer system's periodic backups. Standing in the empty room were Napoli and Luc Bonnard, vice chairman, board of directors of Schindler Holdings Ltd., the respected Swiss-based manufacturer of elevators and escalators. It was November 1998, and Bonnard was visiting New Delhi for the first time to review progress on the start-up of the company's Indian subsidiary, which Napoli had been dispatched to run eight months earlier. Things were not going according to plan.

Napoli, a 33-year-old Italian former semiprofessional rugby player, had arrived in March with his pregnant wife and two young children and had quickly set about creating an entirely new organization from scratch. Since March, he had established offices in New Delhi and Mumbai, hired five Indian top managers, and begun to implement the aggressive business plan he had written the previous year while head of corporate planning in Switzerland. The plan called for a $10 million investment and hinged on selling "core, standardized products," with no allowance for customization. To keep costs down and avoid India's high import tariffs, the plan also proposed that all manufacturing and logistics activities be outsourced to local suppliers.

Shortly before Bonnard's visit, however, Napoli was confronted with three challenges to his plan. First, he learned that for the second time in two months, his Indian managers had submitted an order for a nonstandard product—calling for a glass rear wall in one of the supposedly standard elevators. At the same time, his business plan had come under intense cost pressures, first from a large increase in customs duties on imported elevator components, then from an unanticipated rise in transfer prices for the "low-cost" product lines imported from Schindler's European factories. Finally, as Napoli began accelerating his strategy of developing local sources for elevator components, he found that his requests for parts lists, design specifications, and engineering support were not forthcoming from Schindler's European plants.

Senior Research Associate Perry L. Fagan and Professor Michael Y. Yoshino prepared the original version of this case, "Silvio Napoli at Schindler India (A)," HBS No. 302-053 (Boston: Harvard Business School Publishing, 2002). This version was prepared by Professor Christopher A. Bartlett. HBS cases are developed solely as the basis for class discussion. Cases are not intended to serve as endorsements, sources of primary data, or illustrations of effective or ineffective management.

As the implementation of his business plan stalled, Napoli wondered what he should do. Eight months in India and he still had not installed a single elevator, while his plan showed first-year sales of 50 units. And now Bonnard was visiting. Should he seek his help, propose a revised plan, or try to sort out the challenges himself? These were the thoughts running through Napoli's head as the vice chairman asked him, "So, how are things going so far, Mr. Napoli?"

Schindler's India Explorations

Schindler had a long and rather disjointed history with the Indian market. Although its first elevator in India was installed in 1925, the company did not have a local market presence until it appointed a local distributor in the late 1950s. Almost 40 years later, Schindler decided it was time to take an even bolder step and enter the market through its own wholly owned subsidiary.

The Growing Commitment   Established in 1874 in Switzerland by Robert Schindler, the company began manufacturing elevators in 1889. Almost a century later, the 37-year-old Alfred N. Schindler became the fourth generation of the family to lead the company, in 1987. Over the next decade, he sought to transform the company's culture from that of an engineering-based manufacturing company to one of a customer-oriented service company.

By 1998, Schindler had worldwide revenues of 6.6 billion Swiss francs (US$4 billion) and was widely perceived as the technology leader in elevators. It was also the number one producer of escalators in the world. The company employed over 38,000 people in 97 subsidiaries but did not yet have its own operations in India, a market Alfred Schindler felt had great potential.

Although the first Schindler elevator in India was installed in 1925, it was not until 1958 that the company entered into a long-term distribution agreement with ECE, an Indian company. In 1985, Schindler terminated that agreement and entered into a technical collaboration with Mumbai-based

Bharat Bijlee Ltd. (BBL) to manufacture, market, and sell its elevators. After acquiring a 12% equity stake in BBL, Schindler supported the local company as it became the number two player in the Indian elevator market, with a 10%–15% share a decade later.

On assuming the role of chairman in 1995, Alfred Schindler decided to take a six-month "sabbatical" during which he wanted to step back and review the long-term strategy of Schindler. As part of that process, he undertook to travel through several markets—China, Japan, and several other Far Eastern markets—that he felt were important to the company's growth. He spent several weeks in India, traveling over 3,000 kilometers in a small Ford rental car. "After his trip Mr. Schindler saw India as a second China," said a manager in Switzerland. "He saw huge growth potential. And once he targets something, he's like a hawk."

With the objective of raising its involvement, Schindler proposed to BBL that a separate joint venture be created for the elevator business, with Schindler taking management control. But negotiations proved difficult and eventually collapsed. In late 1996, collaboration with BBL ended, and Schindler began considering options to establish its own operation in India.

Silvio Napoli's Role   Meanwhile, after graduating from the MBA program at Harvard Business School, Silvio Napoli had joined Schindler in September 1994. He accepted a position at the company's headquarters in Ebikon, Switzerland, reporting directly to the CEO as head of corporate planning.

With its 120 years of history, Schindler was a formal Swiss company where the hierarchy was clear, politeness important, and first names rarely used. Napoli's office was on the top floor of the seven-story headquarters building, a floor reserved for the three members of the company's executive committee and the legal counsel. (For profiles of top management, see **Exhibit 1**.) "As soon as I arrived, I was aware that people were very responsive to my requests," said Napoli. "Just by my physical location, I generated fearful respect, and I

Exhibit 1 Schindler Top Management Profiles

Name:	Alfred N. Schindler	Luc Bonnard	Alfred Spöerri
Position:	Chairman and Chief Executive Officer	Vice Chairman of the Board and Member of the Executive Committee	Member of the Board of Directors Member of the Executive Committee
Date of Birth:	March 21, 1949	October 8, 1946	August 22, 1938
Education:	*1976–1978:* MBA, Wharton, USA *1974–1976:* Certified Public Accountant School, Bern *1969–1974:* University of Basel–Law School (lic. jur.), Abschluss:lic.iur.	*1971:* Diploma in Electrical Engineering at ETH (Technical University), Zurich	
Experience:	*Since 1995:* Chairman of the Board and Chief Executive Officer *1985–1995:* Chairman of the Corporate Executive (CEO) *1984–1985:* Member of Corporate Management *1982–1984:* Head of Corporate Planning *1978–1979:* Deputy Head of Corporate Planning	*1996:* Vice Chairman *1991–1996:* Member of the Executive Committee *1986–1990:* COO Elevators and Escalators, Member Corporate Executive Committee *1985–1986:* Member, Executive Committee *1983–1985:* Group Management Member, North Europe *1973:* Management, Schindler, in France	*1991–1998:* Member, Executive Committee *1997–1998:* Chief Financial Officer *1979–1988:* Corporate Controller—Treasurer *1975–1979:* COO of Mexico *1971–1974:* Area Controller, Latin America *1968–1974:* Financial Officer of Mexico *1968:* Joined Schindler Group

Source: Schindler India.

realized I would have to manage my situation very carefully." A 20-year Schindler veteran recalled his reaction to Napoli's arrival: "He was the assistant to Mr. Schindler, so I knew I'd better be nice to him."

As head of corporate planning, Napoli was responsible for coordinating the annual strategic review process and undertaking external benchmarking and competitor analysis. But his most visible role was as staff to the corporate executive committee, the Verwaltungsrat Ausschuss (VRA)—which was composed of Alfred Schindler, Luc Bonnard, and Alfred Spöerri, the chief financial officer. As the only nonmember to attend VRA meetings, Napoli was responsible for taking meeting minutes and for following up on action items and special projects defined by the VRA.

The Swatch Project   In 1995, Napoli took on the Swatch Project, a major assignment that grew out of a concern by VRA members that margins on new-product sales were eroding as each competitor strove to expand its installed base of elevators. Since such sales were a vital source of profitable long-term maintenance and service contracts, the project's goal was to develop a standardized elevator at a dramatically lower cost than the existing broad line of more customized products. It was an assignment that involved the young newcomer in sensitive discussions with Schindler's plants in Switzerland, France, and Spain to discuss design, determine costs, and explore sourcing alternatives. Napoli described the process and outcome of the Swatch Project:

> As you might imagine, I was viewed with some suspicion and concern. Here was this young MBA talking about getting costs down or outsourcing core tasks that the plants felt they owned. . . . In the end, we developed the S001, an elevator that could not be customized, used many parts obtained from outside suppliers, and incorporated processes never before seen in the group. All of this was unthinkable in the past. We redesigned the entire supply chain and halved the industry's standard 20- to 30-week cycle time.

The Indian Entry Project   Meanwhile, as negotiations with BBL broke down in India, the VRA engaged Boston Consulting Group (BCG) to identify and evaluate alternative local partners with whom Schindler might build its business in India. As the company's point man on the project, Napoli worked with the consultants to narrow the list of 34 potential partners to eight candidates for review by the VRA. As the team pursued the final choices, however, it concluded that there was no ideal partner. But it learned that it was now legally feasible to start up a 100% wholly owned company in India. The VRA then asked Napoli and the head of Schindler's mergers and acquisitions department to explore that option.

Napoli contacted experts in India who helped him expand his understanding of the situation. Through discussions with market experts and studies by local consultants, Napoli spent nine months developing a detailed analysis of the market size, legal environment, and competitive situation in the Indian elevator market. He integrated this into a business plan for Schindler's market entry and submitted it to the VRA. The plan was approved in October. Soon after, Napoli was offered the job of creating the Indian subsidiary. Napoli recalled his reaction:

> I realized that the future manager of the new company would be key to the success of the business plan I had been working on. Deep down, I knew I could do it and was conscious that my early involvement made me a candidate, so when the offer came, I was not surprised. More surprising was the reaction of my headquarters colleagues, who thought I was crazy to take such a high-risk career move that involved dragging my family to a developing country.

Bonnard explained the choice of Napoli:

> There are two possible profiles in a country like India. The first is a young guy who knows the company, people, and products; the second is someone who is 55 years old with grown kids looking for a new challenge. . . .
>
> Silvio knew lots of people. He was open to go new ways. We needed someone who could handle different cultures, who was young and flexible. We needed to trust the person we sent, and we trusted Mr. Napoli 100%. And we needed a generalist, not a pure specialist. We needed someone who had courage. Finally, I believe that the people who make the business plan

should have to realize it. Of course, we also needed to have someone who was willing to go.

In November Napoli and his wife Fabienne, a French-German dual national, made their first trip to India. "We went on a 'look and see' visit, starting in Mumbai," Napoli recounted. "When we arrived in Delhi my wife looked around and said she would be more comfortable living here. After reaching an agreement on the relocation package back in Switzerland, I accepted the job."

Over the next several months, Napoli made three more trips to India to lay the groundwork for the move. In one key move, he engaged the executive search firm Egon Zehnder to identify candidates for his top management team. Although he had to await government approval to start the new company, when he moved to India, he wanted to have key managers in place.

Forming Schindler India

As vice president for South Asia, Napoli was responsible for India and a few nearby export markets in Schindler's elevators and escalators division (see **Exhibit 2**). In March, Napoli relocated to India and began the task of building the company that would implement his business plan.

New Culture, New Challenges   On his first day in the Delhi office, Napoli got stuck in one of BBL's elevators. It proved to be an omen of things to come. He recalled:

> On our first morning in Delhi, six hours after the family had landed, my two-year-old daughter opened her forehead falling in the hotel room. The deep wound required hospitalization and stitching under total anesthesia. Two weeks later, Fabienne got infectious food poisoning, which required one-week hospitalization, threatening a miscarriage. The day she came back from hospital, my three-year-old son fell in the hotel bathroom and broke his front tooth. Rushing to an emergency dentist in a hotel car, I really wondered, for the only time in my life, whether I could stand this much longer.

Although Napoli and his family were in New Delhi, where he had opened a marketing and service office, he spent most of a typical week at the company's headquarters in Mumbai. "The first two months were really a hard-fought battle between family relocation and company start-up," he recalled. "Weeks were consumed shuttling between Delhi and Mumbai, hunting for office space, filing government registrations, and completing legal paperwork. On the family front, I had to get them started in a totally different system: housing, schools, doctors, grocery shopping . . . all things which are totally different in India."

In the process, Napoli found he had to adapt his management approach. "For example," he recalled, "all types of characters started to approach me offering their services. They had heard that I was representing a Swiss firm about to invest in India. I soon learned to be careful in deciding who I could trust."

Recruiting the Team   Meanwhile, Egon Zehnder had identified several promising candidates for top positions in the new company. Mehar Karan ("M.K.") Singh, 42, was tapped for the role of managing director, a position that reported to Napoli but was viewed as a stepping stone to heading the subsidiary (for profiles of key Indian managers, see **Exhibit 3**). "At some point in your career you will report to someone younger than yourself," said Singh. "I decided that Schindler was an exciting opportunity to test this scenario."

Napoli explained the choice of Singh: "Having led construction projects for some of India's largest hotels, M.K. had firsthand experience in building an organization from scratch. But most of all, he had been on our customers' side. He would know how to make a difference in service." In addition, being 10 years older and having grown up in India, Singh brought valuable experience and a different perspective. He was also more sensitive to organizational power and relationships, as Napoli soon recognized:

> The first question M.K. asked me after joining the company was, "Who are your friends inside the company? Who doesn't like you?" I never thought about it this way. And I said to him: "Listen, you will have to develop a sense of that yourself. As far as I know, probably people are a little bit cautious of me because

Exhibit 2   Schindler Organization Chart, Elevator and Escalator Division

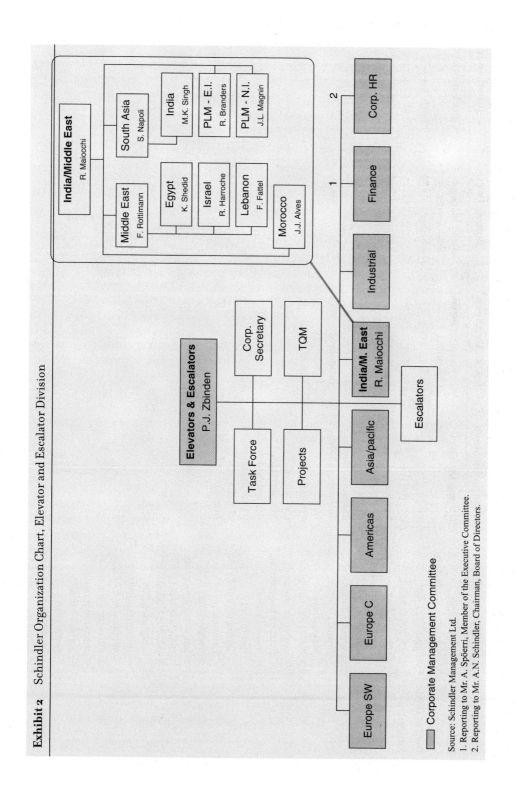

Source: Schindler Management Ltd.
1. Reporting to Mr. A. Spöerri, Member of the Executive Committee.
2. Reporting to Mr. A.N. Schindler, Chairman, Board of Directors.

Exhibit 3 Schindler India: Key Managers' Profiles

Name:	Silvio Napoli	Mehar Karan Singh	T.A.K. Matthews	Ronnie Dante	Jujudhan Jena
Position:	Vice President, Schindler South Asia	Managing Director	Vice President—Field Operations	General Manager—Engineering	Chief Financial Officer
Date of Birth:	August 23, 1965	April 12, 1955	March 12, 1964	November 3, 1959	March 3, 1967
Education:	*1992–1994:* MBA, Harvard University Graduate School of Business Administration, Boston, Massachusetts *1984–1989:* Graduate degree in Materials Science Engineering, Swiss Federal Institute of Technology (EPFL), Lausanne, Switzerland; Lausanne University rugby captain (1987) *1983–1984:* Ranked among top 20% foreign students admitted to EPFL, one-year compulsory selection program, Swiss Federal Institute of Technology (EPFL), Cours de Mathematiques Special, Lausanne, Switzerland	*1977:* B.E.—Mechanical Engineering; ranked top of his class in Indian Institute of Technology, Delhi, India *1979:* MBA, Indian Institute of Management, Ahmedabad, India (Awarded President of India's Gold Medal)	*1986:* B.Sc.—Civil Engineering, University of Dar-E-Salaam, Tanzania *1989:* MBA, Birla Institute of Technology, Ranchi, India	*1977:* HSC, D.G. Ruparel College, Mumbai, India	*1990:* Chartered Accountant, Institute of Chartered Accountancy, India

Experience:

Since 1998: Vice President, South Asia, Schindler Management Ltd.	*Since 1998:* Managing Director, Schindler India Pvt. Ltd., Mumbai, India	*Since 1998:* Vice President—Field Operations, Schindler India Pvt. Ltd., Mumbai	*Since 1998:* General Manager—Engineering, Schindler India Pvt. Ltd., Mumbai	*Since 1998:* Chief Financial Officer, Schindler India Pvt. Ltd., Mumbai
1994–1997: Vice President, Head of Corporate Planning, Schindler, Switzerland	*1979–1998:* Head of Projects and Development Group, Taj Group of Hotels, India (setting up hotels in India and abroad; joint ventures with state governments, local authorities, and international investors, including the Singapore Airlines, Gulf Co-operation Council Institutional investors. Responsible for financial restructuring of the international operations after the Gulf War, culminating with the successful 1995 GDR offering).	*1998:* Modernization Manager, Otis Elevator Company, Mumbai	*1995–1998:* National Field Engineering Manager, Otis Elevator, Mumbai	*1997–1998:* Financial Controller, Kellogg India Ltd., Mumbai
1991–1992: Technical Market Development Specialist, Dow Europe, Rheinmuenster, Germany		*1989–1998:* Otis Elevator Company, New Delhi • Service & Service Sales Manager • Construction Manager • Assistant Construction Manager • Management Trainee	*1991–1995:* National Field Auditor, Otis Elevator, Mumbai	*1996–1997:* Group Manager, Procter & Gamble India Ltd., Mumbai
1989–1991: Technical Service & Development Engineer, Dow Deutscheland, Rheinmuenster, Germany		*1986–1987:* Civil Engineer, Construction Companies, Tanzania	*1989–1991:* Supervisor, Otis Elevator	*1995–1996:* Treasury Manager, Procter & Gamble India Ltd.
1989–1992: French Semi-Pro Rugby League (Strasbourg)			*1984–1989:* Commissioning of New Products, Otis Elevator, Singapore, Malaysia, and Mumbai	*1990–1995:* Financial Analyst, Procter & Gamble India Ltd.
			1982–1984: Commissioning Engineer, Otis Elevator Company, Gujarat	
			1977–1982: Apprentice, Otis Elevator Company, Maharashtra	

Source: Schindler India.

they know I used to work for the big bosses at head-quarters. But we will have to wait and see."

To head field operations (sales, installation, and maintenance) Napoli hired T.A.K. Matthews, 35, who had worked for nine years at Otis India. Matthews recalled: "I had been approached before by elevator people, but after hearing a bit about Schindler's plans, I realized that you don't have a chance to get involved with a start-up every day." For Napoli, Matthews brought the business expertise he needed:"With M.K. and I as generalists, I absolutely needed someone with direct elevator experience to complement our management team. T.A.K. came across as a dynamic and ambitious hands-on manager waiting for the chance to exploit his potential."

Next, Napoli hired Ronnie Dante, 39, as his general manager for engineering. Dante had 24 years of experience at Otis. "Even with T.A.K., we missed a real hard-core elevator engineer capable of standing his ground in front of his European counterparts," said Napoli. "Such people are the authentic depositories of an unpublished science, and they are really very hard to find. Honestly, nobody in the group expected us to find and recruit someone like Ronnie. He is truly one of the best."

Hired to head the company's human resources department, Pankaj Sinha, 32, recalled his interview: "Mr. Napoli and Mr. Singh interviewed me together. There was a clarity in terms of what they were thinking that was very impressive." Napoli offered his assessment of Sinha: "Mr. Schindler had convinced me that the company really needed a front-line HR manager who was capable of developing a first-class organization. But I certainly did not want a traditional Indian ivory tower personnel director. Pankaj convinced us to hire him through his sheer determination to care about our employees."

Finally, he recruited Jujudhan Jena, 33, as his chief financial officer. (See **Exhibit 4** for an organization chart.) Napoli explained his approach to hiring: "You try to see whether the character of the person is compatible with yours, whether you have a common set of values, which in our case range from high ethical standards, integrity, assiduousness

to work, and drive. Mostly we were looking for people with the right attitude and energy, not just for elevator people."

Developing the Relationships   As soon as the senior managers were on board, Napoli began working to develop them into an effective team. He recalled the early meetings with his new hires:

> Because some of them were still finishing up their previous jobs, the first Schindler India staff meetings were held at night, in the Delhi Hotel lounge. I'll never forget working together on our first elevator project offer, late after holding a series of interviews for the first employees who would report to the top team. But most of those "undercover" sessions were dedicated to educating the new team about their new company and building consensus around our business plan. . . . The team was really forged through days of late work, fueled by the common motivation to see our project succeed.

In the team-forming process, the different management styles and personal characteristics of Schindler India's new leaders became clear. Even before he was assigned to India, Napoli was recognized as a "strong-headed and single-minded manager," as one manager at Swiss headquarters described him. "There couldn't have been a better environment to send Silvio than India," said another Swiss colleague. "He wants everything done yesterday. And in India, things don't get done yesterday."

Napoli acknowledged the personal challenge. "To survive in India you have to be half monk and half warrior," he said. "I was certainly more inclined to the warrior side, and when I left Switzerland, Mr. Bonnard told me, 'You will have to work on your monk part.'"

Napoli's Indian staff and colleagues described him as "driving very hard," "impulsive," "impatient," and at times "over-communicative." "Mr. Napoli gets angry when deadlines are not met," added a member of his New Delhi staff. "He's a pretty hard taskmaster." The HR director, Sinha, was more circumspect: "Silvio has a lot of energy. When he focuses on an issue he manages to get everybody else's focus in that direction."

Exhibit 4   Schindler India Organization Chart

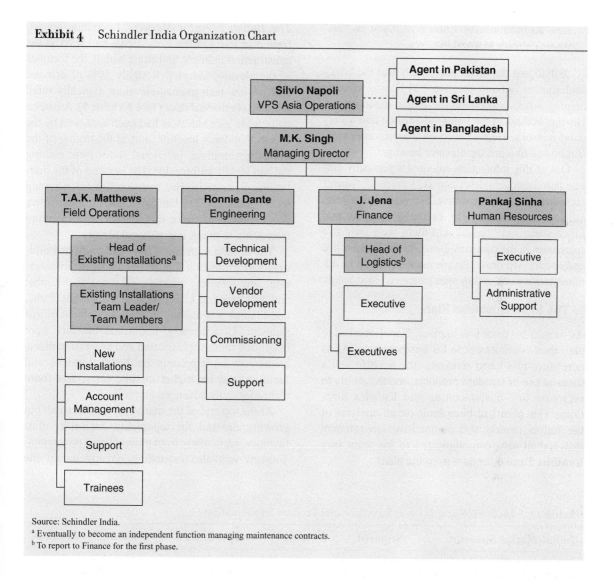

Source: Schindler India.

[a] Eventually to become an independent function managing maintenance contracts.

[b] To report to Finance for the first phase.

Descriptions of Napoli contrasted sharply with those of Singh, whom one manager saw as "friendly and easygoing." Another described him as "much more patient, but he can also be tough." Jena, the finance director, reflected on his first encounter with the two company leaders: "During the interview Silvio came across banging on the table, but I don't think that concerned me. Still, I remember wondering during the interview how two guys as different as M.K. and Silvio would fit

together in a start-up." Matthews, the field operations manager, added another perspective:

It's true that if you look at Silvio, M.K., and me we are all very different. At first we had sessions where the discussion would get pulled in every direction, but I think in the end, it did bring about a balance. . . . I would put it this way. Silvio came to India from Switzerland. But things here are very different: You can't set your watch by the Indian trains. M.K. came from the hotel industry where even if you say "no," it's always made to sound like "yes."

"Silvio was the driver and clearly was the boss," said another Indian executive. "M.K. was great in helping Silvio understand the Indian environment. Having worked in the hotel industry he had a very good network. He had been on the customer side. But he had to learn the elevator business."

Out of this interaction emerged a company culture that employees described as "informal," "open," "responsive," and "proactive." It was also a lean, efficient organization. For example, furniture and office space were rented, and there were only two secretaries in the company—one for the Delhi office and one for Mumbai. "People must do their own administrative work or they won't survive," said Singh.

The India Business Plan

As soon as his team was in place, Napoli worked to gain their commitment to his business plan. At its core were two basic elements: the need to sell a focused line of standard products, and the ability to outsource key manufacturing and logistics functions. This plan had been built on an analysis of the Indian market and competitive environment that Napoli also communicated to his team (see **Exhibits 5** and **6** for data from the plan).

The Indian Elevator Market Economic liberalization in India in the early 1990s had revived the construction industry, and along with it, the fortunes of the elevator industry. Roughly 50% of demand was for low-tech manual elevators, typically fitted with unsafe manual doors (see **Exhibit 5**). A ban on collapsible gate elevators had been approved by the Indian Standards Institute, and, at the urging of the Indian government, individual states were making the ban legally enforceable. The low end of the market was characterized by intense competition among local companies. The ban, when fully implemented, was expected to make this market segment more interesting to major international players.

The middle segment of low- and mid-rise buildings was promising due to India's rapid urbanization. The resulting shortage of space in Mumbai and fast-growing cities such as Bangalore, Pune, and Madras was leading to the development of this segment. Concurrently, traditional builders were becoming more sophisticated and professionalized, leading to an emphasis on better services and facilities and on higher quality, safer, and more technologically advanced elevators.

At the top end of the market, there was small but growing demand for top-quality, high-rise office facilities, particularly from multinational companies. Tourism was also expanding, greatly aiding the

---

Exhibit 5 Indian Elevator Market, Structure, and Product Segmentation

Indian Market Structure	Segment	Stops	Speeds MPS	Schindler Products
	Manual	2–8	0.5–0.7	NIL
	Low rise	2–15	0.6–1.5	S001
	Mid rise	16–25	1.5	S300P
	High rise	>25	>1.5	S300P

Manual 50%, Low Rise 35%, Mid Rise 14%, High Rise 1%

Source: Schindler India.

domestic hotel industry, a major buyer of top-line elevators. Although the top-end segment was very small, the average value per elevator was five to six times that of low-end installations.

At the end of 1997, the installed base of elevators in India was 40,000, with an estimated 5,600 units sold during the year. Although this installed base was small compared with those of China (140,000 units) and Japan (400,000 units), India's growth potential was significant. The rapidly expanding residential segment accounted for 70% of the Indian market, followed by the commercial segment (office buildings and shopping centers) with a 20% share. The balance was accounted for by hotels (4%) and others (6%). Total revenues for the industry were US$125 million, including service income. For the first half of the decade, the market grew at a compound annual rate of 17% in units and 27% by value, but in 1996, a slump in the real estate market slowed unit growth to 10%. The unit growth forecast for 1998 was 5% but was expected to rise to 8%–12% in subsequent years. Together, Mumbai and New Delhi represented 60% of the total Indian elevator market.

In India, most sales were of single-speed elevators (65%), followed by two-speed (20%), variable frequency (13%), and hydraulic (2%). Sales of single-speed elevators dominated the residential market, while variable frequency was most commonly used in higher-end commercial applications. Although the Indian market was biased toward the simplest products, it was expected to shift gradually toward two-speed or higher technology in the future.

Competition   Napoli's business plan also documented that four major players accounted for more than three-quarters of the Indian market value: Otis (50%), BBL (8.6%), Finland's Kone (8.8%), and ECE (8.4%). Mitsubishi had recently begun importing premium elevators for hotels and commercial developments, and Hyundai Elevators had entered into a joint venture to manufacture high-end elevators in India. At this stage, however, they accounted for only 1% of sales. With the exception of Mitsubishi, all multinational players relied on local manufacturing for the majority of their components.

The remaining 23% of the market—mostly the price-sensitive low end—was controlled by 25 regional players characterized by a lack of technical expertise and limited access to funds.

Otis India had an installed base of 26,000 elevators, 16,000 of which were under maintenance contracts. It manufactured its own components, spare parts, and fixtures at an aging plant in Mumbai and a new state-of-the art manufacturing plant near Bangalore. The company staffed 70 service centers, including a national service center in Mumbai, and held an estimated 85% of the high-end hotels and commercial segment. ("You couldn't name any building over 15 floors that did not have an Otis elevator," said ex-Otis employee Matthews. "Otis, Otis, Otis. Any special equipment, it goes Otis. Any fast elevator goes Otis.") Otis was reportedly one of the most profitable industrial companies in India, and its 3,500 employees had an average tenure of 20 years.

The Indian market was highly price sensitive, and most analysts agreed that elevators were becoming commodity products and that price pressures would increase. However, surveys indicated that service was also important in the buying decision, as were the financial terms (**Exhibit 6**).

The elevator life cycle had seven distinct phases: engineering, production, installation, service, repair, modernization, and replacement. Over the 30-year life cycle of an elevator, the first three stages accounted for about one-third of the labor content but only 20% of the profits. In contrast, the latter four accounted for two-thirds of labor content but 80% of profits. As a result, annual maintenance contracts covering routine maintenance and breakdown service were vital. (High-margin spare parts were billed separately.) Service response time varied across segments. Most five-star hotels with multiple installations had a technician on call or on-site; for important commercial buildings and hospitals, the response time was usually within two hours, but many residential and some commercial customers reported an average response time of between six and eight hours.

The Standard Product Strategy   Napoli felt that Schindler could not compete just by matching what others did. It had to find its own unique source of advantage. His analysis of the Indian environment coupled with his work on the Swatch Project led him to conclude that, although it was a radically different approach from that of his key competitors, the most effective way for Schindler to enter this market would be to focus on a narrow product line of simple, standardized elevators.

He proposed building the business around the Schindler 001 (S001)—the product developed in the Swatch Project—and the Schindler 300P (S300P), a more sophisticated model being manufactured in Southeast Asia. The plan was to use the S001 to win share in the low-rise segment as a primary target, then pick up whatever sales the company could in the mid-rise segment with the

Exhibit 6   Market Research on Indian Elevator Market, 1996

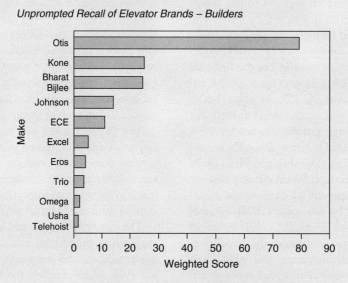

Unprompted Recall of Elevator Brands – Builders

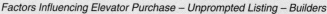

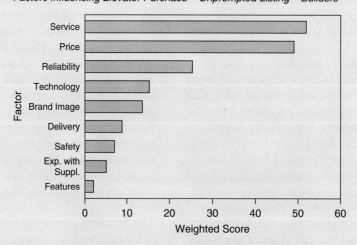

Factors Influencing Elevator Purchase – Unprompted Listing – Builders

Source: Schindler India.

S300P. Both products could be adapted to meet Indian requirements with only minor modifications (e.g., adding a ventilator, a fire rescue controller function, a stop button, and different guide rails). Equally important, as long as the company stuck to the principle of no customization, both products could be priced appropriately for the local market. The plan called for Schindler India to sell 50 units

in the first year and to win a 20% share of the target segments in five years. It also projected Schindler India would break even after four years and eventually would generate double-digit margins.

After communicating this strategy to his management team, Napoli was pleased when they came back with an innovative approach to selling the standard line. If the product was standardized, they

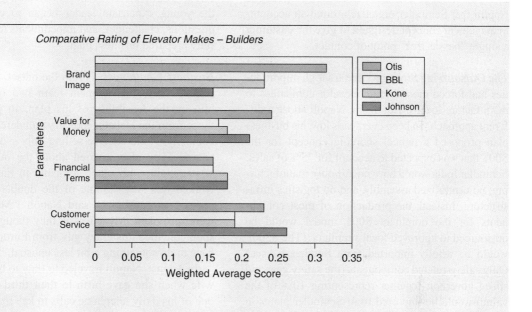

Comparative Rating of Elevator Makes – Builders

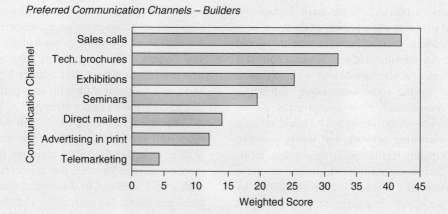

Preferred Communication Channels – Builders

argued, the sales and service should be differentiated. Singh's experience with hotel construction led him to conclude that projects were more effectively managed when one individual was responsible for designing, planning, contracting, and implementing. Yet, as Matthews knew, the traditional sales structure in the elevator industry had different specialists dedicated to sales, technical, and installation, each of whom handed the project off to the next person. Together, these managers proposed to Napoli that Schindler organize around an account-management concept designed to give the customer a single "hassle-free" point of contact.

The Outsourcing Strategy   India's high import duties had forced most foreign elevator companies to manufacture locally. But again, Napoli chose a different approach. To keep overheads low, his business plan proposed a radical sourcing concept for the S001 that was expected to account for 75% of sales: Schindler India would have no in-house manufacturing, no centralized assembly, and no logistics infrastructure. Instead, the production of most components for the dominant S001 model would be outsourced to approved local suppliers. (The S300P would be wholly imported from Southeast Asia.) Only safety-related components (the safety gear and speed governor, together representing 10% of the value) would be imported from Schindler plants in Europe. In addition, the entire logistics function would be outsourced to an internationally reputed logistics service provider. Some basic installation work—part of the on-site assembly of the drive, controller, car, doors, rails, and counterweight—would also be outsourced. However, maintenance contracts resulting from new sales would stay with Schindler.

Inspired by the local automotive industry—Mercedes outsourced most components of its Indian vehicles—Napoli believed he could set up a local manufacturing network that would preserve Schindler's quality reputation. To ensure this, localization of each component would follow the same "product-creation process" criteria used by Schindler worldwide. Furthermore, before the first pre-series batch could be released, it would face an additional hurdle of testing and approval by experts from Schindler's European factories and competence centers.

From Analysis to Action: Implementing the Plan

By June, Napoli's management team members had settled into their roles, and the newly hired sales force was in the field. Almost immediately, however, the young expatriate leader began to experience questions, challenges, and impediments to his carefully prepared business plan.

Business Challenges   From the outset, several of Napoli's new management team had questioned him on the feasibility of his plan. In particular, those from the elevator industry wondered how the company would survive selling only standard elevators. They also worried about the outsourcing strategy, since no other company in the industry worked this way. "Some of the doubts were expressed as questions," said Napoli. "Many more were unspoken. My guess is they thought, 'We'll soon convince this crazy guy from Europe that we have to do something a bit less unusual.'"

In August, Napoli traveled to Italy to be with his wife when she gave birth to their third child. On one of his daily telephone calls to key managers in India, he discovered that the company had accepted an order for an expensive glass pod elevator that was to be imported from Europe. "I was at first just surprised, and then pretty angry, since it clearly was a violation of the strategy we had all agreed on," said Napoli. "The project was committed, and it was too late to stop it. But I had a long talk with M.K. and followed it up with an e-mail reminding him and the others of our strategy."

After his return to India, Napoli was delighted when he heard that the company was ready to accept another order for four S001 elevators for a government building in Mumbai. But in later conversations with a field salesman he discovered that there was a good possibility that each of the elevators would be specified with a glass wall. Although the managers insisted that this was really a minor modification to the standard S001 product, Napoli believed that, especially for a new team, installing it would be much more difficult than they expected.

The next challenge to his plan came when the cost estimates for the first order enquiries was received to Schindler's plants in Europe. (Sources had not yet been qualified for local production.) Napoli was shocked when he saw the transfer prices on the basic S001 elevators at 30% above the costs he had used to prepare his plans. "When I called to complain, they told me that my calculations had been correct six months ago, but costs had increased, and a new transfer costing system had also been introduced," recalled Napoli.

The impact of the transfer price increase was made worse by the new budget the Indian government had passed during the summer. It included increased import duties on specific "noncore goods" including elevators, whose rates increased from 22% to 56%. Napoli recalled the impact:

> This was devastating to our planned break-even objectives. The first thing I did was to accelerate our plans to outsource the S001 to local suppliers as soon as possible. We immediately started working with the European plants to get design details and production specifications. Unfortunately, the plants were not quick to respond, and we were becoming frustrated at our inability to get their assistance in setting up alternative local sources.

Reflections of a Middle Manager

As darkness enveloped the neighborhood surrounding his townhouse, Napoli sat in his living room reflecting on his job. Outside, the night was filled with the sounds of barking dogs and the piercing whistles of the estate's security patrol. "Each family here has its own security guard," he explained. "But because guards fall asleep at their posts, our neighborhood association hired a man who patrols the neighborhood blowing his whistle at each guard post and waiting for a whistle in response. But now the whistling has gotten so bad that some families have begun paying this man not to whistle in front of their houses. Incredible, isn't it?"

Thinking back on his eight months in his new job, Napoli described the multiple demands. On one hand, he had to resolve the challenges he faced in India. On the other, he had to maintain contact with the European organization to ensure he received the support he needed. And on top of both these demands was an additional expectation that the company's top management had of this venture. Napoli explained:

> When we were discussing the business plan with Mr. Schindler, he said, "India will be our Formula One racing track." In the auto industry, 90% of all innovations are developed for and tested on Formula One cars and then reproduced on a much larger scale and adapted for the mass market. We are testing things in India—in isolation and on a fast track—that probably could not be done anywhere else in the company. The expectation is that what we prove can be adapted to the rest of the group.

While the viability of the Formula One concept was still unclear, Alfred Schindler commented on Napoli's experience:

> This job requires high energy and courage. It's a battlefield experience. This is the old economy, where you have to get involved in the nitty-gritty. We don't pay the big bucks or give stock options. We offer the pain, surprises, and challenges of implementation. The emotions start when you have to build what you have written. Mr. Napoli is feeling what it means to be in a hostile environment where nothing works as it should.

Napoli reflected, "You know the expression, 'It's lonely at the top?' Well, I'm not at the top, but I feel lonely in the middle. . . . I have to somehow swim my way through this ocean. Meanwhile, we have yet to install a single elevator and have no maintenance portfolio." At this point, Napoli's reflections were interrupted by the question of visiting vice chairman Luc Bonnard, "So, how are things going so far, Mr. Napoli?"

Case 7-4   Taming the Dragon: Cummins in China (Condensed)

January 21, 2000, was a busy day, as usual, for Steve Chapman, vice-president (VP) of East and Southeast Asia Area Business Organizations (ABOs) for Cummins Inc., a Columbus, Indiana-based American company that specialized in diesel engines. The telephone call from Tim Solso, chairman and chief executive officer (CEO) of the company, brought a welcome break from Chapman's hectic schedule: "Effective today, you will be taking over as the VP of international business, with responsibility for all our international operations." For Chapman, a Yale graduate just turning 46, with more than 15 years of work at Cummins, most of which was spent outside the United States, the change in responsibility was a significant move. He had spent six years in Singapore before moving to Beijing in 1996. Solso and the company's board were pushing for a major thrust on international markets, and China, with its possible entry into the World Trade Organization, was to play a big part in that plan. Despite the fact that China had been a

profitable market for Cummins since its entry in the late 1970s, the company had difficulty reaching its ambitious targets. There were pressing issues that needed immediate attention.

Cummins History

Cummins emerged from humble beginnings in February 1919 as a result of a partnership between William Glanton "W.G." Irwin, a successful Columbus banker-investor, and Clessie Lyle Cummins, a self-taught mechanic-inventor. To get started, Cummins secured manufacturing rights for a diesel engine from a Dutch inventor and marketed an improvised design. Within two decades, Cummins gained a commanding position supplying diesel engines for the truck market. However, the deregulation of the U.S. trucking industry in 1980 triggered consolidation as engine producers and truck-makers merged. Cummins, which had commanded a 62 per cent market share, saw its share slip to 23 per cent. Partly to offset its decline in market share in the heavy duty diesel segment, Cummins developed new businesses such as a filtration business that manufactured sophisticated filters for diesel engines under the brand names Fleetguard and Nelson. Cummins also acquired several new businesses related to the diesel engines. The acquisition of Newage, a British company, enabled the company's expansion to the power generation business. The acquisition of Holset, another British company that specialized in turbochargers, enabled Cummins to develop the quality and capacity of its engines.

Despite stiff competition from powerful players such as Caterpillar and Daimler, Cummins emerged as a global power leader, with a blend of complementary business units serving three broad market segments. The automotive segment focused on engines for trucks, buses and other commercial

IVEY

Professors Charles Dhanaraj, Maria Morgan, Jing Li and Paul W. Beamish prepared this case solely to provide material for class discussion. The authors do not intend to illustrate either effective or ineffective handling of a managerial situation. The authors may have disguised certain names and other identifying information to protect confidentiality. Ivey Management Services prohibits any form of reproduction, storage, or transmittal without its written permission. This material is not covered under authorization from CanCopy or any reproduction rights organization. To order copies or request permission to reproduce materials, contact Ivey Publishing, Ivey Management Services, c/o Richard Ivey School of Business, The University of Western Ontario, London, Ontario, Canada, N6A 3K7; phone (519) 661-3208; fax (519) 661-3882; e-mail cases@ivey.uwo.ca.

Copyright © 2005, Ivey Management Services. Version: (A) 2006-01-17. One-time permission to reproduce Ivey cases granted by Ivey Management Services April 4, 2006.

vehicles, most of which were diesel powered. This included some light duty trucks such as pickup trucks which were sometimes classified under passenger vehicles. The power segment included diesel engines used for power generation—a popular segment in developing countries where electric power supply was inadequate or unreliable. The industrial segment was an assortment of original equipment manufacturers (OEMs) in defence, construction, mining, agriculture, marine and rail applications. Common to all three segments was the need for aftermarket service, necessitating an extensive network of dealers for supplying parts and services.

Drive for expansion beyond North America began with Henry Schacht, who recognized that the company was too heavily dependent on the North American truck market. Cummins opened its first manufacturing facility outside the United States in Shotts, Scotland, in 1956. In 1962, the company began licensing in Japan and Mexico and started a joint venture (JV) in India. In the early 1990s, this international effort moved forward with major manufacturing ventures in Japan, China and India. As of early 2000, Cummins operated in 131 countries, with overseas revenue amounting to nearly 40 per cent of its total sales. With 28,500 employees worldwide, Cummins had sales of $6.6 billion in 1999 (see Exhibit 1).

The Cummins international organization was structured into nine area business organizations

Exhibit 1   Cummins Earnings 1995 to 2001 (US$ in millions, except per share data)

	Actual 1995	Actual 1996	Actual 1997	Actual 1998	Actual 1999	Est. 2000	Est. 2001
Heavy-duty engines	1,506	1,261	1,354	1,554	1,787	1,250	1,125
Mid-range engines	581	587	587	527	513	480	455
Power generation	1,130	1,213	1,205	1,230	1,356	1,490	1,640
Industrial engines	643	863	1,044	1,054	1,022	1,085	1,085
Bus and Light commercial	687	599	681	847	903	995	950
Governmental	37	—	—	—	—	—	—
Marine	93	—	—	—	—	—	—
Components (Filtration & others)	568	734	754	1,054	1,058	1,150	1,245
Total	5,245	5,257	5,625	6,266	6,639	6,450	6,500
Cost of Goods Sold	3,974	4,072	4,345	4,925	5,221	5,041	5,042
Gross profit	1,271	1,185	1,280	1,341	1,418	1,409	1,458
Gross margin (%)	24	23	23	21	21	22	22
SG&A	692	725	744	787	781	878	810
R&E	263	252	260	255	245	254	255
Interest expense	13	18	26	71	75	75	75
Gain from affiliates	—	—	10	30	28	—	—
Other expense	8	(24)	(20)	(13)	8	5	5
Pretax profit	295	214	286	211	281	288	313
Taxes	65	54	74	60	70	81	88
Minority interest	—	—	—	11	6	15	15
Net income	230	160	212	140	205	192	210
Earnings per share	$5.65	$4.01	$5.48	$3.62	$5.29	$5.00	$5.45

Source: Company documents and Credit Suisse Investment Reports (February 2000).

Exhibit 2 Organization Chart of Cummins East Asia Area Business Organization 2001

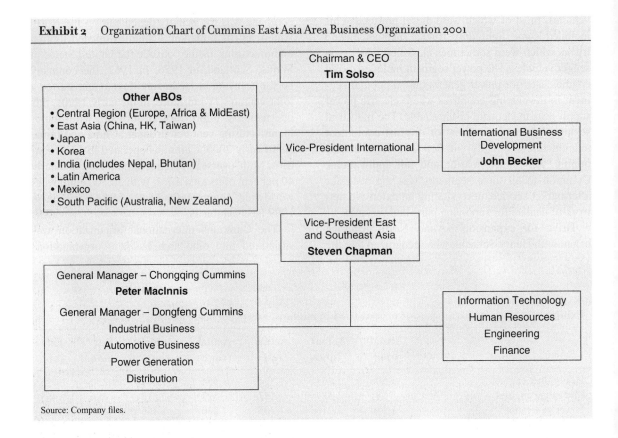

Source: Company files.

(ABOs) reporting to a VP of International Business at the headquarters, who in turn reported directly to the CEO (see Exhibit 2). The ABO was responsible for sales, service and support of all Cummins' products and for nurturing the business relationships within their respective areas. The ABO focused on deriving maximum value of its presence within a country and had enough autonomy as long as it remained within annual operating plans and ensured strong customer support. The ABOs worked in concert with the market business units (MBUs), which were based on product segments (e.g. power generation, automotive, industrial, etc.) and were responsible worldwide for all activities in their product segment.

China—An Emerging Power in the 1990s

When Deng Xiaoping assumed power in 1978, he called for the modernization of agriculture, industries, the military and science and technology. The primary means of achieving such objectives lay in the importation of foreign technology, the introduction of a two-tier price system that allowed market forces to partially set prices outside the plan, a household responsibility system in the country that provided incentives to peasants to increase productivity and production, and greater management autonomy to urban industrial enterprises. The government also created four special economic zones in the southern provinces of

Guangdong and Fujian, and then opened numerous coastal cities along similar lines to attract foreign investment and technology. The overall effect of liberalizing the Chinese economy lifted millions out of poverty and led to soaring demand for imported vehicles.

The Ministry of Machine-Building Industry (MOMI) and China National Automotive Industry Commission played a central role in overseeing technology transfer and approval of JVs and licensing agreements in the automotive sector in the 1980s. The government's objective at the time was to stop the drain on foreign exchange reserve. However, because JVs in the auto sector inevitably involved the import of auto parts, completely knocked down kits or semi-knocked down kits for the start-up foreign JVs, JVs hardly solved the immediate problem of foreign exchange drain. Hence the government came up with an additional requirement of 60 per cent localization of content for JV approval. The prospects of higher pay and more jobs from foreign JVs made provincial and local governments enthusiastic allies of foreign investors in promoting the auto industry. Local governments exerted far greater influence in the approval of JVs than did the central government.

The Diesel Engines Industry in China

Since the 1990s, China's auto diesel engine industry had experienced rapid growth. Over the previous decade, the output of diesel engine-powered vehicles had grown 850 per cent, and accounted for more than 73 per cent of the medium- and light-tonnage trucks, a major sector for diesel engines. The truck market was essentially a duopoly, with the top two manufacturers claiming over 90 per cent of the market share, split between First Auto Works (FAW) at 57 per cent and Dong Feng Motors (DFM) at 35 per cent. Originally started as a military factory, FAW had diversified into commercial vehicles. DFM was established in 1969 and had three automobile production bases in the Hubei province, manufacturing a variety of products including heavy-duty, medium-duty and light trucks and passenger cars. A division of DFM located in Xiangfan, Hubei specialized in light trucks, diesel engines, castings and related spare parts. About 90 per cent of the division's total profits in 2000 were contributed by the diesel engine business. China National Heavy Duty Truck Corporation (CNHTC) in Jinan was trailing the third largest firm, but was expected to grow by more than 100 per cent in 2000.

Agricultural equipment and power generation were the two major non-automotive applications for the diesel engines. Beiqi Futian Vehicle Corporation was leading the group that specialized in agricultural automobile products. In 1996, Beiqi Futian merged 100 state-owned enterprises (SOEs), establishing a shareholding company. The company was listed on the Shanghai Stock Exchange in June 1998. Plans were in place for Beiqi Futian and nine other SOEs to consolidate and establish Beijing Futian Engine Co. to assemble high-end clean engines.

Of the stand-alone diesel engine manufacturers, China Yuchai International and Shanghai Diesel Engine Works (SDEW) were the dominant players. Yuchai was the largest medium-duty diesel engine producer in China, primarily targeted for light-duty trucks. Yuchai was a major supplier of diesel engines to DFM for their medium-duty commercial vehicle. SDEW, the first independent diesel engine company in China, was ranked No. 4 in 1999 in the domestic market.

Foreign Direct Investment in the Trucking Industry

With the liberalization of the Chinese economy, several foreign players entered the auto industry in China in the 1980s and 1990s. Isuzu Motors Ltd., a Japanese automaker, entered in 1985 through a JV called Qingling Motors Ltd., which was established in Chongqing for the production and sale of Isuzu light-duty trucks, pickup trucks, multipurpose vehicles, etc. In 1993, Isuzu partnered with ITOCHU Corp and Jiangxi Automobile Factory to form its second JV to produce trucks in China. Jiangling-Isuzu Motors Co. Ltd. was owned 50 per cent by Jiangxi Automobile Factory and 25 per cent each by Isuzu and ITOCHU and produced Elf trucks and Rodeo pickup trucks. Despite the growing ties between Jiangling Motors Co. and Isuzu, market observers perceived them to have difficulty establishing their presence in China.

The Swedish firm, Volvo, established a bus manufacturing JV with Xi'an Aircraft Industry Co. in 1993. In 1998, Volvo initiated a 50-50 JV with CNHTC to produce trucks in Jinan. However, attempts to set up the JV were stalled in 2000 because CNHTC was experiencing a financial crisis. Volvo was seeking other opportunities as well for bus manufacturing, construction equipment and industrial engines. Hino Motors Ltd., the truck-and-bus making affiliate of Toyota Motor Corp., was considering plans to enter the Chinese bus market jointly with Toyota Tsusho Corp., a trading-house affiliate of Toyota. Ford paid about US$40 million to own 30 per cent of Jiangling Auto, which manufactured the Transit series, newly designed by Ford, including buses, vans and trucks. Caterpillar Inc., the U.S. heavy equipment manufacturer, signed a JV agreement in 1994 with SDEW to build advanced engines in China. It was the first JV for Caterpillar in China, and Caterpillar owned 55 per cent of the JV, called Caterpillar Shanghai Engine Co. Ltd. Engines were built in China with Caterpillar technology and marketed in China as Caterpillar engines. However, the JV ceased in 1997 due to cost and price issues.

Cummins' Early Efforts in China—Two Key Licensees

Cummins was one of the few American companies that explored the Chinese markets early on. John Becker, who was leading the international business development team during Cummins' internationalization efforts, recalled:

As Cummins expanded internationally to Europe in the 1950s and Mexico, India and Japan in the 1960s, we looked for major, developing market opportunities for expansion. Our chairman, Irwin Miller, visited China in 1975 and was one of the earliest American industrial leaders to seek business opportunities there. Subsequent visits by other senior executives, in the late 1970s, developed a technology licensing approach to market entry that fit the Chinese shortage of foreign exchange plus their requirements against foreign direct investment. This approach would allow Cummins to participate in China on a relatively low-risk basis, while learning from our many new experiences.

Cummins established its presence in China in 1979 while negotiating its first license agreements. In early 1981, Cummins signed a 10-year licence for some heavy-duty engines, and these in turn were assigned to the Chongqing Automotive Engine Plant (CQAEP) at Chongqing (see Exhibit 3). With Cummins' technical support, CQAEP won several Chinese government awards, including designation as the "Best Recipient of Western Technology." The early success at Chongqing gave Cummins broad recognition for its commitment to China.

In 1984, DFM, which was earlier called Second Automobile Works (SAW), based in Shiyan, Hubei, was negotiating with Nissan for new vehicle technology, including Nissan diesel engines. Henry Schacht, then-chairman of Cummins, along with a Beijing staff, intervened and convinced the Chinese authorities to use Cummins' B Series engines in the Nissan-licensed vehicles. Cummins offered a free trial of a Cummins engine in a Nissan truck. DFM signed up as a licensee for B engines for a factory in Xiangfan in late 1986. The B engines were used primarily for *Dongfeng* trucks, which were assembled in Shiyan, north of Xiangfan in Hubei province. These license agreements provided Cummins with substantial profit streams from technical fees, royalties and component sales at zero capital risk for the company and built a level of awareness and credibility in the marketplace that created opportunities for sale of other Cummins products not produced in China.

In 1985, Chapman joined Cummins and immediately became involved on the Cummins team negotiating the B engine license.

Exhibit 3   Map of China

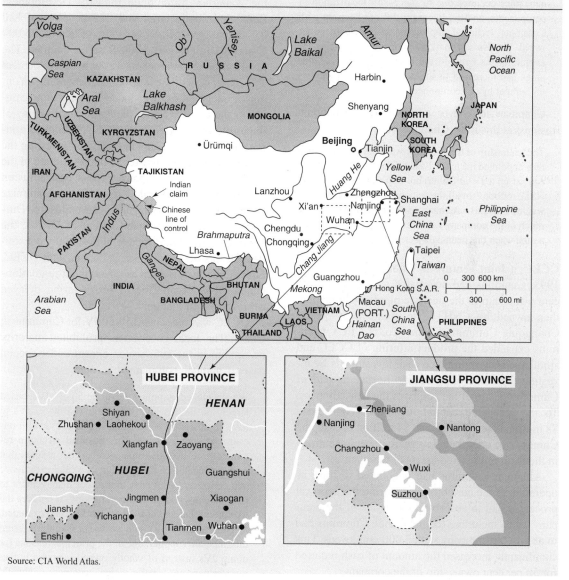

Source: CIA World Atlas.

From Licensing to Joint Ventures   The Chinese business environment began to move from a strictly centralized command economy toward a greater appreciation for the value that committed foreign investors could bring. Cummins took advantage of the changing environment. By the early 1990s,

Cummins had amassed many years of experience in China, working with licensees and developing a significant market presence with imported engines. John Becker recalled:

> We saw that continued significant participation in the business at our licensees required direct investment

and management as the stream of profits from component sales declined due to successful localization of components, and the licensees did not keep up with Cummins' technical improvements elsewhere in the world. We also saw market opportunities opening for engine ranges between the B and NH and that volumes had increased to the point that would support investment by our component companies.

Chapman took over as head of International Business at this time. Chapman recalled:

The leadership of the company was very specific when they appointed me to the East Asia area business: "You can set up a JV in China, but don't invest more than US$2 million." In all the initiatives we undertook, we wanted to make sure that we were not throwing in too much of the company's scarce resources, especially at a time when our financials were tight.

CCEC, a Joint Venture in Chongqing   By early 1993, Cummins had negotiated to acquire 50 per cent ownership in the licensee plant at Chongqing, then owned by CNHTC, to create a 50-50 JV, Chongqing Cummins Engine Co. (CCEC). Cummins expanded the product offering of CCEC and simultaneously minimized cash investments by investing the value of its engine licence as part of Cummins' share of the equity in the new company. To the registered capital, Cummins contributed $8 million in technology and $4 million in cash; the Chinese side contributed its share of capital entirely in the form of the fixed assets of the plant.

Although Cummins had negotiated to limit its operation to the core business, during the approval process it had to absorb all the assets of the company, as is, including the personnel. Cummins had to absorb the company with 3,000 employees. This significantly increased the amount of cash required for 50 per cent ownership of the company.

DCEC, a Joint Venture in Xiangfan   In May 1996, Cummins agreed to form a second JV with DFM to produce the C engines. These engines had higher horsepower than the B engines and had both automotive and non-automotive applications. Dongfeng Cummins Engine Company (DCEC) was thus established as a 50-50 JV between DFM

and Cummins. DCEC was a greenfield start-up in the Xiangfan Automobile Industry Development Zone. It initially employed 275 people and had an annual production capacity of about 25,000 C series engines and 6,000 B series engines. The localization of components was between 40 percent and 70 per cent of the input value, depending on engine models. DCEC was located on the same campus as the DFM B Series plant and shared many of the utility services. As with CCEC, Cummins minimized cash investments in DCEC by investing the value of its C Series licence as part of a share of the equity in the new company. Further cash infusion was spread over several years to further minimize Cummins and Dongfeng financial exposure. During negotiations for establishment of DCEC, the company agreed in principle to eventually consolidate DFM's licenced B Series factory with DCEC, but various factors such as government regulations and a DFM organizational restructuring delayed achievement of that goal.

DCEC was the second 50-50 JV for Cummins in China. The local government prohibited majority ownership in the auto sector, except under special cases. Chapman commented:

We developed a policy favoring 50-50 JVs based largely on the research which showed 50-50 JVs to have significantly better longevity than JVs with uneven ownership shares. This business structure requires more intensive management, but assures that each partner more fully brings its skills, experience and concerns to the table and forces management to achieve consensus in decision making. It reduces the likelihood that one of the partners will feel excluded, lose interest in the JV and leave. For Cummins, as an intermediate supplier, one of the principal reasons for doing JVs instead of wholly owned ventures is that our partners are usually major customers of the JV and keeping their energies focused on the success of the venture is critical. Over the years, we have developed a core competency in managing this form of joint venture. It has led to successes in China where many others have failed.

Cummins also depended a lot on the local management and typically operated with a much lower number of expatriates than most other foreign companies. John Becker articulated Cummins' philosophy:

> We believe that we are most successful when the management team is local. This not only saves the high costs of expatriate staffing but drives better integration of the company into the local business environment. It requires better forward planning to assure Cummins-experienced skills are available when needed. This has been critical to our success in Chinese business.

The JVs were structured to generate multiple streams of earnings for Cummins. While the focus was on the basic success of the JV company itself and the dividends it generated, Cummins also made money several other ways, including the licence fees, royalty fees and profits from component sales to the JV.

Cummins' Non-Automotive Business in China

During the early and mid-1990s, the prime power generation business in China, especially in southern China, was booming. The Chinese government mandated that all high-rises, hospitals and telecommunications have back-up generator sets. Cummins was serving the market with imported generator sets and saw an opportunity to leverage domestic engine manufacturing to compete with lower cost domestic products. In 1996, Newage invested in a majority-owned JV in Wuxi to manufacture Newage alternators for sale to the domestic market. In 1997, Cummins established a new brand for domestically produced generator sets, Dynasty, to participate in separate segments of the market while protecting margins on imported sets. Cummins invested in a wholly owned assembly plant called Cummins Gen Set Assembly Plant (Dynasty) in a greenfield site located in Beijing Economic Development Zone. The operation assembled Dynasty Gen Set, using engines produced at CCEC. It was a one-shift, low-volume operation with an annual production of about 400 Dynasty gen-sets. Cummins also established a 50-50 gen-set JV with CCEC in Shenzhen. Dynasty was competitive in price in the domestic market and

allowed Cummins to serve as the repair, maintenance and reconstruction centre for the Chinese market.

In 1996, Fleetguard established a 50-50 JV with Shenlong Automotive Accessories Ltd., a DFM affiliate, in Shanghai and pursued the multi-channel distribution system appropriate for their predominantly aftermarket product. Holset also established a majority-owned (55 per cent) JV with Wuxi Power Engineering Ltd. in Wuxi and sold products to numerous engine manufacturers, including the two Cummins engine JVs.

In order to facilitate the multiple investments in China, Cummins established a holding company in 1996, Cummins (China) Inc. (CCI), located in the World Trade Center in Beijing, which served as the Cummins headquarters in China. Apart from holding the equity shares in the Chinese JVs, the holding company also owned Cummins Beijing which served as Cummins' wholly owned distributor and gen-set manufacturer in China. As a holding company, it could share legal, finance, HR and other resources among the JVs and engage in currency transactions among the JVs. Such a holding company also offered the advantage of being able to engage in direct sale through the branches it set up and controlling the dealerships through these branches.

Challenges Facing Cummins China in 2000

As of early 2000, Cummins had a total corporate investment in China of more than $100 million. With its numerous subsidiaries and affiliates (see Exhibit 4), this was deemed the largest commitment to China of any foreign company in the diesel engine industry. The potential for Cummins in China seemed huge, with further expansion of the heavy-duty trucks market as roads continued being built and long-distance hauling in China projected to become increasingly dependent on trucks rather than railways. China's membership in the WTO was promising, not only in terms of increased economic activity within China, but it was also expected to

Exhibit 4 Overview of Cummins Organization in China (April 2000)

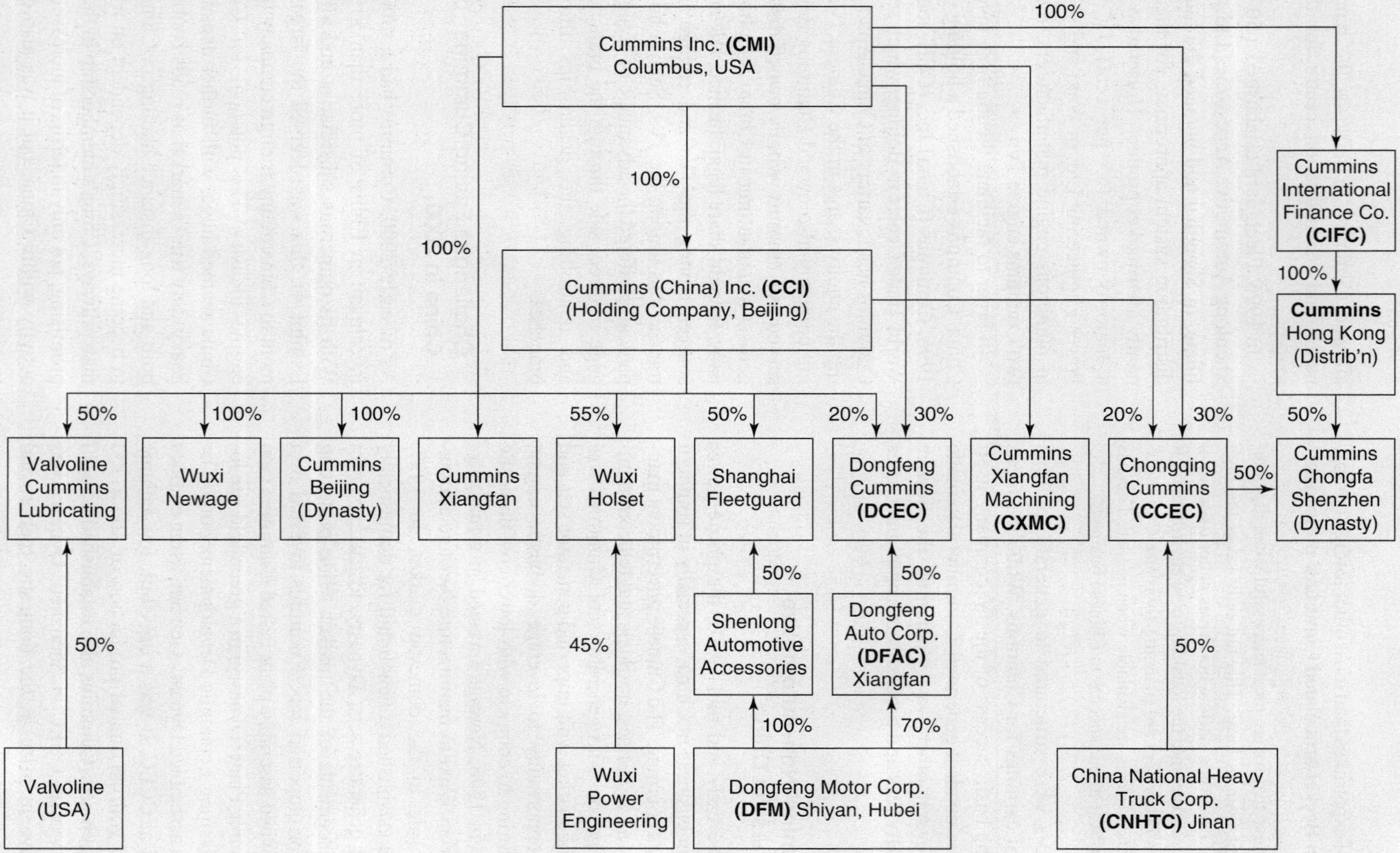

Source: Company files.

increase its openness to foreign firms. The average import tariff for diesel engines in China would be reduced to four per cent to five per cent from the existing levels of nine per cent to 10 per cent. It was imperative that strategic action be taken to exploit Cummins' first mover advantage in China. Major areas stood out in Chapman's mind: streamlining the JV in Chongqing, organizing the parts and service activity as an integral piece within Cummins' global strategy and staffing the China organization.

1. Streamlining Chongqing Cummins Joint Venture

When Cummins and CNHTC signed the CCEC JV agreement, engine sales were booming in the Chinese heavy-duty trucking market, a potential target for the newly invested M11 engine. However, by 1996, it was apparent that CNHTC would not follow through with its commitment to make M11 engines available in their vehicles. The economic downturn from 1995 to 1998 slowed demand for heavy-duty engines. Bad debts and account receivables mounted. Cummins also underestimated the difficulties of absorbing an SOE, which included trying to reduce a work force of 3,000 employees, and spin off much of the social welfare appendages such as workers' dormitory, primary school, technical school, medical clinic, cafeteria and guest house. Many of the agreements to retain employees and assets were made on the assumption that growth would absorb the costs over time. Volumes dropped and CCEC was struggling slightly above breakeven profitability, thereby deteriorating the relationship between the partners.

The first Cummins GM at CCEC, while being a proven manufacturing manager in the United States, did not speak Chinese, and the local party Secretary made life very difficult for him to run the factory. The top management team of the JV clashed repeatedly due to differences in expectations, management style, language, culture and a generation gap. In 1998, Cummins put in place a new general manager, Peter MacInnis, an American who had lived in China for several years but an outsider to Cummins and the heavy truck industry. He was assisted by Kirpal Singh, plant manager, from India. Chapman commented on the leadership team:

> It was very difficult to get senior executives with both technical competence and language and cultural skills. So we took the team approach to building the leadership at the JVs. Peter MacInnis was fluent in Chinese and knew China very well, and Kirpal Singh was very good technically. They formed an excellent team.

Peter MacInnis, then general manager of CCEC, recalled:

> When we collaborated with the state-owned company, there should have been an adjustment period and some corresponding methods to facilitate this process. We had been their technology licensor for 15 years. We were like a teacher, consultant, supplier of technology, supplier of training expertise. We were very close friends based on that relationship. Now there is the change of the management team. Many did not understand that. Nobody had the opportunity to explain to them. There is no such an adjustment period in the company. When you looked at the JV contract, nothing had changed in the Chinese side. People did not expect anything to change. No change of the number of people coming to work. When Cummins brought me to Chongqing, the local employees thought I had never been here before, and I barely knew anything about China. There were already people in place. Why did they need me to come here to be their boss?

Management had to face some difficult issues in collaborating with representatives from the Chinese party. Peimin Zhao was a party representative within the company. Although Cummins management treated him with respect as a labor representative, Zhao wanted to be treated as a partner in the JV. MacInnis recalled:

> In 1998, when I was sent to CCEC, Shangdong [CNHTC] sent Ruilin Han to CCEC. Both of us were told to strive for good performance. Both of us were new. This was a plus. When Han and I came, we decided to co-operate. Party secretary Zhao wanted to participate in the management. I said no. Zhao should not have anything to do with management. There was a big fight. Zhao and I did not talk for more than a year. That caused the difficulty. Forty per cent of the employees are party members. Key positions are all party members. Employees thought there were frictions between Zhao and me. It was hard for them to work. Our friction was awful for Han. Han is a party

member. Zhao gave Han a hard time during the party meetings. I might not be able to find the key successful factors to turn around the JV later. But I could tell this was one of the failure factors for CCEC.

Chapman recalled,

The party leadership wanted to keep the status quo and did not show an interest in taking up any of the growth challenges, including an opportunity to export engines to Cummins USA. We were also under pressure from Columbus, which treated CCEC almost as a nuisance, since the profit from it was very marginal. If we could not move up the growth curve, we were ready to pull the plug on this.

With the new management team at CCEC, the plant was manufacturing about 3,800 engines a year and was beginning to show profits (see Exhibit 5). It had managed to reduce its work force by half to 1,500 through attrition and early-retirement incentives. However, there was still a redundancy of workers in the plant. Management was attempting to introduce new incentives to raise productivity. MacInnis recalled:

The inventory level was very high. Even worse, nobody from the Chinese side thought keeping too much inventory was a bad thing. They thought the more the better since customers do not have to wait. We had to do something.

Complicating matters further, in August 1999, China abolished the ministry that controlled CNHTC,

the JV partner, and effectively abolished CNHTC as well. The intent was to transfer the CNHTC equity to the Chongqing municipal government, which was China's largest independent municipality with more than 30 million people—larger than the population of Beijing or Shanghai. The Chongqing government was particularly eager to see the industries under its charge prosper and was thus supportive of CCEC. But some complications related to CNHTC debt delayed the transfer, and Cummins was left with no effective Chinese partner.

When the CCEC's operating team was brought together during the first week of 2000 for a Six-Sigma–type performance evaluation, management recognized that CCEC had fallen short on every measurable criterion—operating environment, product quality, working capital, process capability, productivity, sales and finances. Chapman, however, did note one bright spot: through all the issues at CCEC, profits remained slightly positive.

2. Distribution and Service Organization in China   China prohibited distribution and service of the auto products in any plant except those produced at that plant. The establishment of CCI, the holding company for Cummins, partially was a resolution to this problem because a holding company such as CCI could engage in imports and exports. With the growth in engine population in China, Cummins had to develop a direct capability to service customers

Exhibit 5   Joint Venture Sales and Profits 1997 to 2000 (in US$000s)

	1997	1998	1999	2000E
Chongqing Cummins Engine Company (CCEC)				
Sales	37,623	37,174	38,470	41,075
Profit after tax	858	1,417	700	1,574
Net cashflow		4,350	(2,595)	1,744
Dongfeng Cummins Engine Company (DCEC)				
Sales	767	2,679	7,683	31,763
Profit after tax	(817)	(363)	(59)	(52)
Net cashflow	1,425	(2,769)	(1,793)	103

Source: Company files.

locally. Over the years, Cummins had developed a distribution system under CCI with branches in 10 major cities around China. As of 2000, Cummins also had about 100 dealer locations, making the company second only to Yulin Diesel, which had the best coverage in the Chinese market. In addition to these, DFM had its own distribution system to care for trucks (and the installed engines); however, DFM viewed the aftermarket as a cost of selling trucks and not as a profit centre. There were about 400 DFM dealers that serviced Cummins engines in DFM trucks. In a similar manner, CCEC also had its own network of about 40 dealers.

There were issues that needed to be resolved with regard to the parts distribution activities, both for the locally made and imported ones. The imported components were typically supplied to China from the United States or the United Kingdom through an intermediate warehouse, Parts Distribution Center, in Singapore. Mark-ups were applied at each broad step in the supply chain. Beyond increasing the price, lead times were long and unresponsive to the market needs. The localization drive created another problem. Component suppliers to DCEC and CCEC were selling the parts into the aftermarket at prices that left no margin for a distribution and service system. There were also intellectual property issues as parts suppliers were getting access to proprietary technologies of Cummins.

Given the proliferation of dealer networks and the inconsistency of quality and service of the aftermarket, Cummins was considering the option of initiating a stand-alone service division that would own and operate the service operations. Management argued that, apart from alleviating the service and quality problems, it would also provide a steady stream of cash flow to the company by providing valued-added services to the end customers.

3. Staffing the Organization Cummins East Asia ABO had been managed by Steve Chapman for several years and had grown dramatically during his tenure. With Chapman's appointment to head International for Cummins, the challenge was selecting the appropriate management to replace him. The

rapid growth of the EA ABO seemed to call for management that could instill more formal Cummins processes to manage the larger organization than had been required during the rapid growth phase under Chapman. Cummins leadership felt that there was not any candidate internally within China that was ready in 2000 to take this position. Cummins leadership at Columbus was seriously considering someone from the Korean ABO to move into this position. Chapman commented on the job:

> The role of country manager is changing in Cummins. However, in emerging markets, such as China, India and Russia, it is likely to remain the same. In other places, we are moving to product-oriented divisions that are run as a part of the global operations. As a country manager, your job is to maximize the profit stream for Cummins. You don't want to waste a lot of money creating an empire or create local capabilities that already exist elsewhere. Your job is to create local capabilities, have them linked with functional leaders around the world and focus them on where you are going. You set a long-term direction to the organization. Get them to understand where you are going, and actually get there.

There was also the broader challenge of finding senior executives in the power generation business and the distribution activities, given the potential for rapid growth in these sectors. Now that Chapman was responsible for the international office, he could leave behind a vibrant organizational unit that was adaptive and capable of exploiting the new opportunities and cross the billion-dollar revenue mark for China by 2005. As Chapman reviewed the progress of East Asia over the prior decade, he was pleased that, on average, the ABO had been able to accomplish a cumulative average growth rate of 25 per cent. The challenge was to devise an execution plan to reach US$1 billion in China by 2005. The China business had grown from US$300 million in 1996 to just over US$400 million. Chapman thought that although the target was a feasible one, much needed to be done to achieve these targets. For example, the automotive segment had only US$36 million sales in 1996, and Chapman felt strongly that this could easily grow tenfold by 2005, with half of these coming from the DCEC.

Reading 7-1   Local Memoirs of a Global Manager

Gurcharan Das

There was a time when I used to believe with Diogenes the Cynic that "I am a citizen of the world," and I used to strut about feeling that a "blade of grass is always a blade of grass, whether in one country or another." Now I feel that each blade of grass has its spot on earth from where it draws its life, its strength; and so is man rooted to the land from where he draws his faith, together with his life.

In India, I was privileged to help build one of the largest businesses in the world for Vicks Vaporub, a hundred-year-old brand sold in 147 countries and now owned by Procter & Gamble. In the process, I learned a number of difficult and valuable lessons about business and about myself. The most important lesson was this: to learn to tap into the roots of diversity in a world where global standardization plays an increasingly useful role.

"Think global and act local," goes the saying, but that's only half a truth. International managers must also think local and then apply their local insights on a global scale.

The fact is that truths in this world are unique, individual, and highly parochial. They say all politics is local. So is all business. But this doesn't keep either from being global. In committing to our work we commit to a here and now, to a particular place and time; but what we learn from acting locally is often universal in nature.

This is how globalization takes place. Globalization does not mean imposing homogeneous solutions in a pluralistic world. It means having a global vision and strategy, but it also means cultivating roots and individual identities. It means nourishing local insights, but it also means reemploying communicable ideas in new geographies around the world.

The more human beings belong to their own time and place, the more they belong to *all* times and places. Today's best global managers know this truth. They nourish each "blade of grass."

Managerial basics are the same everywhere, in the West and in the Third World. There is a popular misconception among managers that you need merely to push a powerful brand name with a standard product, package, and advertising in order to conquer global markets, but actually the key to success is a tremendous amount of local passion for the brand and a feeling of local pride and ownership.

I learned these lessons as a manager of international brands in the Third World and as a native of India struggling against the temptation to stay behind in the West.

▍ On Going Home

I was four years old when India became free. Before they left, the British divided us into two countries, India and Pakistan, and on a monsoon day in August 1947 I suddenly became a refugee. I had to flee east for my life because I was a Hindu in predominantly Muslim West Punjab. I survived, but a million others did not, and another 12 million were rendered homeless in one of the great tragedies of our times.

I grew up in a middle-class home in East Punjab as the eldest son of a civil engineer who built canals and dams for the government. Our family budget was always tight: after paying for milk and school fees, there was little left to run the house. My mother told us heroic stories from the *Mahabharata* and encouraged in us the virtues of honesty, thrift, and responsibility to country.

I grew up in the innocence of the Nehru age when we still had strong ideals. We believed in secularism, democracy, socialism, and the U.N.; and we were filled with the excitement of building a nation.

I came to the United States at the age of 12, when the Indian government sent my father to Washington, D.C., on temporary assignment. When my family returned to India a few years later, I won a scholarship to Harvard College and spent four happy years on the banks of the Charles River. My tutor taught me that the sons of Harvard had an obligation to serve, and I knew that I must one day use my education to serve India.

In 1964, in the towering confidence of my 21 years, I returned home. Some of my friends thought I had made a mistake. They said I should have gone on to graduate school and worked for a few years in the West. In fact, I missed the West in the beginning and told myself that I would go back before long; but I soon became absorbed in my new job with Richardson-Vicks in Bombay, and like the man who came to dinner, I stayed on.

From a trainee, I rose to become CEO of the company's Indian subsidiary, with interim assignments at Vicks headquarters in New York and in the Mexican subsidiary. When I became CEO, the Indian company was almost bankrupt, but with the help of a marvelous all-Indian organization, I turned it around in the early 1980s and made it one of the most profitable companies on the Bombay Stock Exchange. In 1985 we were acquired by Procter & Gamble, and so began another exciting chapter in my life. We successfully incorporated the company into P&G without losing a single employee, and we put ourselves on an aggressive growth path, with an entry first into sanitary napkins and then into one of the largest detergent markets in the world.

At three stages in my life, I was tempted to settle in the West. Each time I could have chosen to lead the cosmopolitan life of an expatriate. Each time I chose to return home. The first after college; the second when I was based in the New York office of Vicks, where I met my Nepali wife with her coveted Green Card (which we allowed to lapse); the third when I was in Mexico running our nutritional foods business, when once again I came home to earn a fraction of what I would have earned abroad.

Apart from a lurking wish to appear considerable in the eyes of those I grew up with, I ask myself why I keep returning to India. I have thrice opted for what appeared to be the less rational course in terms of career and money. The only remotely satisfying answer I have found comes from an enigmatic uncle of mine who once said, "You've come back, dear boy, because as a child you listened to the music of your mother's voice. They all say, 'I'll be back in a few years,' but the few years become many, until it is too late and you are lost in a lonely and homeless crowd."

Yet I think of myself as a global manager within the P&G world. I believe my curious life script has helped to create a mind-set that combines the particular with the universal, a mind-set rooted in the local and yet open and nonparochial, a mind-set I find useful in the global management of P&G brands.

On One-Pointed Success

I first arrived on the island of Bombay on a monsoon day after eight years of high school and college in America. That night, 15-foot waves shattered thunderously against the rocks below my window as the rain advanced from the Arabian Sea like the disciplined forward phalanx of an army.

The next morning I reported for duty at Richardson-Vicks' Indian headquarters, which turned out to be a rented hole-in-the-wall with a dozen employees. This was a change after the company's swank New York offices in midtown Manhattan, where I had been interviewed. That evening my cousin invited me for dinner. He worked in a big British company with many factories, thousands of employees, and plush multistoried marble offices. I felt ashamed to talk about my job.

"How many factories do you have?" he wanted to know.

"None," I said.

"How many salesmen do you have?" he asked.

"None," I said.

"How many employees?"

"Twelve."

"How big are your offices?"

"A little smaller than your house."

Years later I realized that what embarrassed me that night turned out to be our strength. All 12 of our employees were focused on building our brands without the distraction of factories, sales forces, industrial relations, finance, and other staff departments. Our products were made under contract by Boots, an English drug company; they were distributed under contract by an outside distribution house with 100 salesmen spread around the country; our external auditors had arranged for someone to do our accounting; and our lawyers took care of our government work. We were lean, nimble, focused, and very profitable.

All my cousin's talk that night revolved around office politics, and all his advice was about how to get around the office bureaucracy. It was not clear to me how his company made decisions. But he was a smart man, and I sensed that with all his pride in working for a giant organization, he had little respect for its bureaucratic style.

If marketing a consumer product is what gives a company its competitive advantage, then it seems to me it should spend all its time building marketing and product muscle and employ outside suppliers to do everything else. It should spin off as many services as someone else is willing to take on and leave everyone inside the company focused on one thing—creating, retaining, and satisfying consumers.

There is a concept in Yoga called one-pointedness (from the Sanskrit *Ekagrata*). All 12 of us were one-pointedly focused on making Vicks a household name in India, as if we were 12 brand managers. I now teach our younger managers the value of a one-pointed focus on consumer satisfaction, which P&G measures every six months for all of its major brands.

Concentrating on one's core competence thus was one of the first lessons I learned. I learned it because I was face-to-face with the consumer, focused on the particular. Somehow I feel it would have taken me longer to learn this lesson in a glass tower in Manhattan.

As so often in life, however, by the time I could apply the lesson I had learned, we had a thousand people, with factories, sales forces, and many departments that were having a lot of fun fighting over turf. I believe that tomorrow's big companies may well consist of hundreds of small decentralized units, each with a sharp focus on its particular customers and markets.

On the Kettle That Wrote My Paycheck

For months I believed that my salary came from the payroll clerk, so I was especially nice to her. (She was also the boss's secretary.) Then one day I discovered the most important truth of my career—I realized who really paid my salary.

Soon after I joined the company, my boss handed me a bag and a train ticket and sent me "upcountry." A man of the old school, he believed that you learned marketing only in the bazaar, so I spent 10 of my first 15 months on the road and saw lots of up-country bazaars.

On the road, I typically would meet our trade customers in the mornings and consumers in the evenings. In the afternoons everyone slept. One evening I knocked on the door of a middle-class home in Surat, a busy trading town 200 miles north of Bombay. The lady of the house reluctantly let me in. I asked her, "What do you use for your family's coughs and colds?" Her eyes lit up, her face became animated. She told me that she had discovered the most wonderful solution. She went into the kitchen and brought back a jar of Vicks Vaporub and a kettle. She then showed me how she poured a spoon of Vaporub into the boiling kettle and inhaled the medicated vapors from the spout.

"If you don't believe me, try it for yourself," she said. "Here, let me boil some water for you."

Before I could reply she had disappeared into the kitchen. Instead of drinking tea that evening we inhaled Vicks Vaporub. As I walked back to my hotel, I felt intoxicated: I had discovered it was she who paid my salary. My job also became clear to me: I must reciprocate her compliment by striving relentlessly to satisfy her needs.

The irony is that all the money a company makes is made *outside* the company (at the point of sale), yet the employees spend their time *inside* the company, usually arguing over turf. Unfortunately, we don't see customers around us when we show up for work in the mornings.

When I became the CEO of the company I made a rule that every employee in every department had to go out every year and meet 20 consumers and 20 retailers or wholesalers in order to qualify for their annual raise. This not only helps to remind us who pays our salaries, we also get a payoff in good ideas to improve our products and services.

The ideal of being close to the customer may be obvious in the commercial societies of the West, but it was not so obvious 20 years ago in the protected, bureaucratic Indian environment. As to the lady in Surat, we quickly put her ideas into our advertising. She was the first consumer to show me a global insight in my own backyard.

Of Chairs, Armchairs, and Monsoons

Two years after I joined, I was promoted. I was given Vicks Vaporub to manage, which made me the first brand manager in the company. I noticed we were building volume strongly in the South but having trouble in the North. I asked myself whether I should try to fix the North or capitalize on the momentum in the South. I chose the latter, and it was the right choice. We later discovered that North Indians don't like to rub things on their bodies, yet the more important lesson was that it is usually better to build on your strength than to try and correct a weakness. Listen to and respect the market. Resist the temptation to impose your will on it.

We were doing well in the South partially because South Indians were accustomed to rubbing on balms for headaches, colds, bodyaches, insect bites, and a host of other minor maladies. We had a big and successful balm competitor, Amrutanjan, who offered relief for all these symptoms. My first impulse was to try to expand the use of Vaporub to other symptoms in order to compete in this larger balm market.

My boss quickly and wisely put a stop to that. In an uncharacteristically loud voice, he explained that Vaporub's unique function was to relieve colds.

"Each object has a function," he said. "A chair's function is to seat a person. A desk is to write on. You don't want to use a chair for writing and a desk for sitting. You never want to mix up functions."

A great part of Vaporub's success in India has been its clear and sharp position in the consumer's mind. It is cold relief in a jar, which a mother rubs tenderly on her child's cold at bedtime. As I thought more about balms, I realized that they were quite the opposite. Adults rub balms on themselves for headaches during the day. Vaporub was succeeding precisely because it was not a balm; it was a rub for colds.

Every brand manager since has had to learn that same lesson. It is of the utmost importance to know who you are and not be led astray by others. Tap into your roots when you are unsure. You cannot be all things to all people.

This did not prevent us from building a successful business with adults, but as my boss used to say, "Adult colds, that is an armchair. But it is still a chair and not a desk."

When I took over the brand we were spending most of our advertising rupees in the winter, a strategy that worked in North America and other countries. However, my monthly volume data stubbornly suggested that we were shipping a lot of Vaporub between July and September, the hot monsoon season. "People must be catching lots of colds in the monsoon," I told my boss, and I got his agreement to bring forward a good chunk of our media to the warm monsoon months. Sure enough, we were rewarded with an immediate gain in sales.

I followed this up by getting our agency to make a cinema commercial (we had no television at that time) showing a child playing in the rain and catching cold. We coined a new ailment, "wet monsoon colds," and soon the summer monsoon season became as important as the winter in terms of sales.

Another factor in our success was the introduction of a small 5-gram tin, which still costs 10 cents and accounts for 40% of our volume. At first it was not successful, so we had to price it so that it was cheaper to buy four 5-gram tins than a 19-gram jar. The trade thought we were crazy. They said henceforth no one would buy the profitable jar; they would trade down to the tin. But that didn't happen. Why? Because we had positioned the tin for the working class. We were right in believing that middle-class consumers would stay loyal to the middle-class size.

Moves like these made us hugely successful and placed us first in the Indian market share by far. But instead of celebrating, my boss seemed depressed. He called me into his office, and he asked me how much the market was growing.

"Seven percent," I said.

"Is that good?"

"No," I replied, "But *we* are growing 20%, and that's why we're now number one in India."

"I don't give a damn that we are number one in a small pond. That pond has to become a lake, and then an ocean. We have to grow the market. Only then will we become number one in the world."

Thus I acquired another important mind-set: when you are number one, you must not grow complacent. Your job is to grow the market. You always must benchmark yourself against the best in the world, not just against the local competition. In the Third World this is an especially valuable idea, because markets there are so much less competitive.

Being receptive to regional variations, tapping the opportunity that the monsoon offered, introducing a size for the rural and urban poor, and learning to resist complacency and grow the market—all are variations on the theme of local thinking, of tapping into the roots of pluralism and diversity.

On Not Reinventing the Wheel

We could not have succeeded in building the Vicks business in India without the support of the native traders who took our products deep into the hinterland, to every nook and corner of a very large country. Many times we faced the temptation to set up an alternative Western-style distribution network. Fortunately, we never gave in to it. Instead, we chose each time to continue relying on the native system.

Following the practice of British companies in India, we appointed the largest wholesaler in each major town to become our exclusive stock point and

direct customer. We called this wholesaler our stockist. Once a month our salesman visited the stockist, and together they went from shop to shop redistributing our products to the retailers and wholesalers of the town. The largest stockist in each state also became our Carrying-and-Forwarding Agent (in other words, our depot) for reshipping our goods to stockists in smaller towns. Over time, our stockists expanded their functions. They now work exclusively on P&G business under the supervision of our salesmen; they hire local salesmen who provide interim coverage of the market between the visits of our salesmen; they run vans to cover satellite villages and help us penetrate the interior; they conduct local promotions and advertising campaigns; and they are P&G's ambassadors and lifeline in the local community. The stockists perform all these services for a 5% commission, and our receivables are down to six days outstanding.

In our own backyard, we found and adopted an efficient low-cost distribution system perfected by Indian traders over hundreds of years. Thank God we chose to build on it rather than reinvent the wheel.

On Taking Ancient Medicine

We learned our most important lesson about diversity and tapping into roots shortly after I became head of the company in the early 1980s. We found ourselves against a wall. The chemists and pharmacists had united nationwide and decided to target our company and boycott our products in their fight for higher margins from the entire industry. At the same time, productivity at our plant was falling, while wages kept rising. As a result, our profitability had plummeted to two percent of sales.

Beset by a hostile environment, we turned inward. The answer to our problems came as a flash of insight about our roots, for we suddenly realized that Vicks Vaporub and other Vicks products were all-natural, herbal formulas. All their ingredients were found in thousand-year-old Sanskrit texts. What was more, this ancient *Ayurvedic* system of medicine enjoyed the special patronage of the government. If we could change our government registration from Western medicine to Indian medicine, we could expand our distribution to food shops, general stores, and street kiosks and thus reduce dependence on the pharmacists. By making our products more accessible, we would enhance consumer satisfaction and build competitive advantage. What was more, a new registration would also allow us to set up a new plant for Vicks in a tax-advantaged "backward area," where we could raise productivity dramatically by means of improved technology, better work practices, and lower labor costs.

I first tested the waters with our lawyers, who thought our solution to the problem quite wonderful. We then went to the government in Delhi, which was deeply impressed to discover all the elements of Vaporub's formula in the ancient texts. They advised to check with the local FDA in Bombay. The regulators at the FDA couldn't find a single fault with our case and, to our surprise and delight, promptly gave us a new registration.

Lo and behold, all the obstacles were gone! Our sales force heroically and rapidly expanded the distribution of our products to the nondrug trade, tripling the outlets which carried Vicks to roughly 750,000 stores. Consumers were happy that they could buy our products at every street corner. At the same time we quickly built a new plant near Hyderabad, where productivity was four times what it was in our Bombay plant. Our after-tax profits rose from 2% to 12% of sales, and we became a blue chip on the Bombay Stock Exchange.

Finally, we decided to return the compliment to the Indian system of medicine. We persuaded our headquarters to let us establish an R&D Center to investigate additional all-natural, Ayurvedic therapies for coughs and colds. When I first mooted this idea, my bosses at the head office in the United States practically fell off their chairs. Slowly, however, the idea of all-natural, safe, and effective remedies for a self-limiting ailment sold around the world under the Vicks name grew on them.

We set up labs in Bombay under the leadership of a fine Indian scientist who had studied in the United States. They began by creating a computerized data bank of herbs and formulas from the ancient texts; they invented a "finger-printing" process to standardize herbal raw materials with the help of computers; and they organized clinical trials in Bombay hospitals to confirm the safety and efficacy of the new products. We now have two products being successfully sold in the Indian market—Vicks Vaposyrup, an all-natural cough liquid, and Vicks Hot-sip, a hot drink for coughs and colds. The lab today is part of P&G's global health-care research effort and has 40 scientists and technicians working with state-of-the-art equipment.

Of Local Passions and Golden Ghettos

The story of Vicks in India brings up a mistaken notion about how multinationals build global brands. The popular conception is that you start with a powerful brand name, add standardized product, packaging, and advertising, push a button, and bingo—you are on the way to capturing global markets. Marlboro, Coke, Sony Walkman, and Levis are cited as examples of this strategy.

But if it's all so easy, why have so many powerful brands floundered? Without going into the standardization versus adaptation debate, the Vicks story demonstrates at least one key ingredient for global market success: *the importance of local passion.* If local managers believe a product is theirs, then local consumers will believe it too. Indeed, a survey of Indian consumers a few years ago showed that 70% believed Vicks was an Indian brand.

What is the universal idea behind Vicks Vaporub's success in India? What is it that made it sell? Was it "rubbing it on the child with tender, loving care?" Could that idea be revived in the United States? Some people argue that the United States has become such a rushed society that mothers no longer have time to use a bedtime rub on their children when they've got a cold. Others feel that Vaporub could make its marketing more meaningful by striking a more contemporary note.

The Vicks story shows that a focus on the particular brings business rewards. But there are also psychic rewards for the manager who invests in the local. Going back to my roots reinvigorated me as a person and brought a certain fullness to my life.

Not only was it pleasant to see familiar brown faces on the street, it also was enormously satisfying to be a part of the intense social life of the neighborhood, to experience the joys and sorrows of politics, and to share in the common fate of the nation. But at another level I also began to think of my work as a part of nation building, especially training and developing the next generation of young managers who would run the company and the country. It discharged a debt to my tutor at Harvard and a responsibility that we all have to the future.

Equally, it seems to me, there are powerful though less obvious psychic rewards for an international manager on transfer overseas who chooses to get involved in the local community. When such people approach the new country with an open mind, learn the local language, and make friends with colleagues and neighbors, they gain access to the wealth of a new culture. Not only will they be more effective as managers, they also will live fuller, richer lives.

Unfortunately, my experience in Mexico indicates that many expatriate managers live in "golden ghettos" of ease with little genuine contact with locals other than servants. Is it any surprise that they become isolated and complain of rootlessness and alienation in their new environment? The lesson for global companies is to give each international manager a local "mentor" who will open doors to the community. Ultimately, however, it is the responsibility of individual managers to open their minds, plunge into their local communities, and try to make them their own.

On Global Thinking

It would be wrong to conclude from the Vicks story that managing a global brand is purely a local affair. On the contrary, the winners in the new borderless economy will be the brands and companies that make best use of the richness of experience they get from their geographical diversity. Multinational companies have a natural advantage over local companies because they have talented people solving similar problems for identical brands in different parts of the world, and these brand managers can learn from each other's successes and failures. If a good idea emerges in Egypt, a smart brand manager in Malaysia or Venezuela will at least give it a test.

The Surat lady's teakettle became the basis of a national campaign in India. "One-pointedness" emerged from a hole-in-the-wall in Bombay, but it became the fulcrum on which we built a world-class business over a generation. Advertising for colds during the hot monsoon months seems highly parochial, but it taught us the importance of advertising year round in other places. The stockist system found applicability in Indonesia and China. Even the strange Ayurvedic system of medicine might plausibly be reapplied in the form of efficacious herbal remedies for common ailments in Western countries.

Business truths are invariably local in origin, but they are often expressions of fundamental human needs that are the same worldwide. Local insights with a universal character thus can become quickly global—though only in the hands of flexible, open-minded managers who can translate such ideas into new circumstances with sensitivity and understanding. My admonition to think local is only half the answer. Managers also must remember to think global. The insights we glean from each microcosm are ultimately universal.

Organizational specialists often express a fear that companies will demotivate their local managers by asking them to execute standardized global marketing packages. If they impose these standardized marketing solutions too rigidly, then this fear may be justified. However, this does not happen in successful companies. In fact, the more common disease in a global company is the "not invented here" syndrome, which especially afflicts subsidiaries and managers whose local triumphs have left them arrogant and unwilling to learn from successes in other parts of the world.

We in India were no different. But slowly and painfully we learned that useful lessons can emerge anywhere. For all our efforts to tap into the roots of Indian pluralism, we were dealing with a global brand. The product itself, the positioning, and the packaging were basically the same everywhere. Global brands are not free-for-alls, with each subsidiary doing its own thing. It took us six months, for example, to persuade our marketing people to try a new advertising idea for Vaporub that came from Mexico. It asked the consumer to use Vaporub on three parts of the body to obtain three types of relief. When we finally tried "Three-by-Three" in our advertising, it worked brilliantly.

It is deeply wrong to believe that going global is a one-stop, packaged decision. Local managers can add enormous value as they tap into local roots for insights. But it is equally wrong to neglect the integrity of the brand's core elements. Smart global managers nourish each blade of grass without neglecting the garden as a whole.

On Karma

Although the principles of managing a business in the Third World are the same as in the West, there are still big differences between the two. For me, the greatest of these is the pervasive reality of poverty.

I have lost the towering confidence of my youth, when I believed that socialism could wipe away poverty. The problem of socialism is one of performance, not vision. If it worked, we would all be socialists. Ironically, the legacy of the collectivist bias in Indian thinking has been the perpetuation of poverty. We created an over-regulated private sector and an inefficient public sector. We did not allow the economy to grow and produce the surplus that might

have paid for direct poverty programs. We created an exploitative bureaucracy that fed on itself. Today, happily, we are righting the balance by liberalizing the economy, reducing state control, and restoring legitimacy to the market. I am confident that these changes will foster the entrepreneurialism and economic vitality India needs to create prosperity and eliminate the destitution of so many of its people.

Despite the problems, I find managers in India and other poor countries more optimistic than their counterparts in rich nations. The reason is that we believe our children will be better off than our parents were, and this idea is a great source of strength. We see our managerial work as nation building. We are the benign harbingers of technology and modernity. As we learn to manage complex enterprises, we empower people with the confidence they need to become responsible, innovative, and self-reliant.

It seems to come down to commitment. In committing to our work we commit to a here and now, to a particular place and time. The meaning in our lives comes from nourishing a particular blade of grass. It comes from absorbing ourselves so deeply in the microcosm of our work that we forget ourselves, especially our egos. The difference between subject and object disappears. The Sanskrit phrase *nishkama karma* describes this state of utter absorption, in which people act for the sake of the action, not for the sake of the reward from the action. This is also the meaning of happiness.

Reading 7-2   Tap Your Subsidiaries for Global Reach

Christopher A. Bartlett and Sumantra Ghoshal

In 1972, EMI developed the CAT scanner. This technological breakthrough seemed to be the

innovation that the U.K.–based company had long sought in order to relieve its heavy dependence on the cyclical music and entertainment business and to strengthen itself in international markets. The medical community hailed the product, and within four years EMI had established a medical electronics business that was generating 20% of the company's worldwide earnings. The scanner enjoyed a dominant market position, a fine reputation, and a strong technological leadership situation.

Nevertheless, by mid-1979 EMI had started losing money in this business, and the company's deteriorating performance eventually forced it to accept a takeover bid from Thorn Electric. Thorn immediately divested the ailing medical electronics business. Ironically, the takeover was announced the same month that Godfrey Hounsfield, the EMI scientist who developed the CAT scanner, was awarded a Nobel Prize for the invention.

How could such a fairy-tale success story turn so quickly into a nightmare? There were many contributing causes, but at the center were a structure and management process that impeded the company's ability to capitalize on its technological assets and its worldwide market position.

The concentration of EMI's technical, financial, and managerial resources in the United Kingdom made it unresponsive to the varied and changing needs of international markets. As worldwide demand built up, delivery lead times for the scanner stretched out more than 12 months. Despite the protests of EMI's U.S. managers that these delays were opening opportunities for competitive entry, headquarters continued to fill orders on the basis of when they were received rather than on how strategically important they were. Corporate management would not allow local sourcing or duplicate manufacturing of the components that were the bottlenecks causing delays.

The centralization of decision making in London also impaired the company's ability to guide strategy to meet the needs of the market. For example, medical practitioners in the United States, the key market for CAT scanners, considered reduction of scan time to be an important objective, while EMI's central research laboratory, influenced by feedback from the domestic market, concentrated on improving image resolution. When General Electric eventually brought out a competitive product with a shorter scan time, customers deserted EMI.

In the final analysis, it was EMI's limited organizational capability that prevented it from capitalizing on its large resource base and its strong global competitive position. The company lacked:

- The ability to sense changes in market needs and industry structure occurring away from home.

- The resources to analyze data and develop strategic responses to competitive challenges that were emerging worldwide.

- The managerial initiative, motivation, and capability in its overseas operations to respond imaginatively to diverse and fast-changing operating environments.

While the demise of its scanner business represents an extreme example, the problems EMI faced are common. With all the current attention being given to global strategy, companies risk underestimating the organizational challenge of managing their global operations. Indeed, the top management in almost every one of the MNCs we have studied has had an excellent idea of what it needed to do to become more globally competitive; it was less clear on how to organize to achieve its global strategic objectives.

United Nations Model and HQ Syndrome

Our study covered nine core companies in three industries and a dozen secondary companies from a more diverse industrial spectrum. They were selected from three areas of origin—the United States, Europe, and Japan. Despite this diversity, most of these companies had developed their international operations around two common assumptions on how to organize. We dubbed these well-ingrained beliefs the "U.N. model assumption" and the "headquarters hierarchy syndrome."

Although there are wide differences in importance of operations in major markets like Germany, Japan, or the United States, compared with subsidiaries in Argentina, Malaysia, or Nigeria, for example, most multinationals treat their foreign subsidiaries in a remarkably uniform manner. One executive we talked to termed this approach "the U.N. model of multinational management." Thus, it is common to see managers express subsidiary roles and responsibilities in the same general terms, apply their planning control systems uniformly system-wide, involve country managers to a like degree in planning, and evaluate them against standardized criteria. The uniform systems and procedures tend to paper over any differences in the informal treatment of subsidiaries.

When national units are operationally self-sufficient and strategically independent, uniform treatment may allow each to develop a plan for dealing with its local environment. As a company reaches for the benefits of global integration, however, there is little need for uniformity and symmetry among units. Yet the growing complexity of the corporate management task heightens the appeal of a simple system.

The second common assumption we observed, the headquarters hierarchy syndrome, grows out of and is reinforced by the U.N. model assumption. The symmetrical organization approach encourages management to envision two roles for the organization, one for headquarters and another for the national subsidiaries. As companies moved to build a consistent global strategy, we saw a strong tendency for headquarters managers to try to coordinate key decisions and control global resources and have the subsidiaries act as implementers and adapters of the global strategy in their localities.

As strategy implementation proceeded, we observed country managers struggling to retain their freedom, flexibility, and effectiveness, while their counterparts at the center worked to maintain their control and legitimacy as administrators of the global strategy. It's not surprising that relationships between the center and the periphery often became strained and even adversarial.

The combined effect of these two assumptions is to severely limit the organizational capability of a company's international operations in three important ways. First, the doctrine of symmetrical treatment results in an overcompensation for the needs of smaller or less crucial markets and a simultaneous underresponsiveness to the needs of strategically important countries. Moreover, by relegating the na-

tional subsidiaries to the role of local implementers and adapters of global directives, the head office risks grossly underutilizing the company's worldwide assets and organizational capabilities. And finally, ever-expanding control by headquarters deprives the country managers of outlets for their skills and creative energy. Naturally, they come to feel demotivated and even disenfranchised.

Dispersed Responsibility

The limitations of the symmetrical, hierarchical mode of operation have become increasingly clear to MNC executives, and in many of the companies we surveyed we found managers experimenting with alternative ways of managing their worldwide operations. And as we reviewed these various approaches, we saw a new pattern emerging that suggested a significantly different model of global organization based on some important new assumptions and beliefs. We saw companies experimenting with ways of selectively varying the roles and responsibilities of their national organizations to reflect explicitly the differences in external environments and internal capabilities. We also saw them modifying central administrative systems to legitimize the differences they encountered.

Such is the case with Procter & Gamble's European operations. More than a decade ago, P&G's European subsidiaries were free to adapt the parent company's technology, products, and marketing approaches to their local situation as they saw fit—while being held responsible, of course, for sales and earnings in their respective countries. Many of these subsidiaries had become large and powerful. By the mid-1970s, economic and competitive pressures were squeezing P&G's European profitability. The head office in Cincinnati decided that the loose organizational arrangement inhibited product development, curtailed the company's ability to capture Europewide scale economies, and afforded poor protection against competitors' attempts to pick off product lines country by country.

So the company launched what became known as the Pampers experiment—an approach firmly grounded in the classic U.N. and HQ assumptions. It created a position at European headquarters in Brussels to develop a Pampers strategy for the whole continent. By giving this manager responsibility for the Europewide product and marketing strategy, management hoped to be able to eliminate the diversity in brand strategy by coordinating activities across subsidiary boundaries. Within 12 months, the Pampers experiment had failed. It not only ignored local knowledge and underutilized subsidiary strengths but also demotivated the country managers to the point that they felt no responsibility for sales performance of the brand in their areas.

Obviously, a different approach was called for. Instead of assuming that the best solutions were to be found in headquarters, top management decided to find a way to exploit the expertise of the national units. For most products, P&G had one or two European subsidiaries that had been more creative, committed, and successful than the others. By extending the responsibilities and influence of these organizations, top management reasoned, the company could make the success infectious. All that was needed was a means for promoting intersubsidiary cooperation that could offset the problems caused by the company's dispersed and independent operations. For P&G the key was the creation of "Eurobrand" teams.

For each important brand the company formed a management team that carried the responsibility for development and coordination of marketing strategy for Europe. Each Eurobrand team was headed not by a manager from headquarters but by the general manager and the appropriate brand group from the "lead" subsidiary—a unit selected for its success and creativity with the brand. Supporting them were brand managers from other subsidiaries, functional managers from headquarters, and anyone else involved in strategy for the particular product. Team meetings became forums for the lead-country group to pass on ideas, propose action, and hammer out agreements.

The first Eurobrand team had charge of a new liquid detergent called Vizir. The brand group in the lead country, West Germany, had undertaken product and market testing, settled on the package design and advertising theme, and developed the marketing strategy. The Eurobrand team ratified all these elements, then launched Vizir in six new markets within a year. This was the first time the company had ever introduced a new product in that many markets in so brief a span. It was also the first time the company had gotten agreement in several subsidiaries on a single product formulation, a uniform advertising theme, a standard packaging line, and a sole manufacturing source. Thereafter, Eurobrand teams proliferated; P&G's way of organizing and directing subsidiary operations had changed fundamentally.

On reflection, company managers feel that there were two main reasons why Eurobrand teams succeeded where the Pampers experiment had failed. First, they captured the knowledge, the expertise, and most important, the commitment of managers closest to the market. Equally significant was the fact that relationships among managers on Eurobrand teams were built on interdependence rather than on independence, as in the old organization, or on dependence, as with the Pampers experiment. Different subsidiaries had the lead role for different brands, and the need for reciprocal cooperation was obvious to everyone.

Other companies have made similar discoveries about new ways to manage their international operations—at NEC and Philips, at L. M. Ericsson and Matsushita, at ITT and Unilever, we observed executives challenging the assumptions behind the traditional head office–subsidiary relationship. The various terms they used—lead-country concept, key-market subsidiary, global-market mandate, center of excellence—all suggested a new model based on a recognition that their organizational task was focused on a single problem: the need to resolve imbalances between market demands and constraints on the one hand and uneven subsidiary capabilities on the other. Top officers understand that the option of a zero-based organization is not open to an established multinational organization. But they seem to have hit on an approach that works.

Black Holes, etc. The actions these companies have taken suggest an organizational model of differentiated rather than homogeneous subsidiary roles and of dispersed rather than concentrated responsibilities. As we analyzed the nature of the emerging subsidiary roles and responsibilities, we were able to see a pattern in their distribution and identify the criteria used to assign them. Exhibit 1 represents a somewhat oversimplified conceptualization of the criteria and roles, but it is true enough for discussion purposes.

The strategic importance of a specific country unit is strongly influenced by the significance of its national environment to the company's global strategy. A large market is obviously important, and so is a competitor's home market or a market that is particularly sophisticated or technologically advanced. The organizational competence of a particular subsidiary can, of course, be in technology, production, marketing, or any other area.

Strategic Leader   This role can be played by a highly competent national subsidiary located in a strategically important market. In this role, the subsidiary serves as a partner of headquarters in developing and implementing strategy. It must not only be a sensor for detecting signals of change but also a help in analyzing the threats and opportunities and developing appropriate responses.

The part played by the U.K. subsidiary of Philips in building the company's strong leadership position in the teletext-TV business provides an illustration. In the early 1970s, the BBC and ITV (an independent British TV company) simultaneously launched projects to adapt existing transmission capacity to permit broadcast of text and simple diagrams. But teletext, as it was called, required a TV receiver that would accept and decode the modified transmissions. For TV set manufacturers, the market opportunity required a big investment in R&D and production facilities, but commercial possibilities of teletext were highly uncertain, and most producers decided against making the investment. They spurned teletext as a typical British toy—fancy and not very useful. Who would pay a heavy premium just to read text on a TV screen?

Philips' U.K. subsidiary, however, was convinced that the product had a future and decided to pursue its own plans. Its top officers persuaded Philips' component manufacturing unit to design and produce the integrated-circuit chip for receiving teletext and commissioned their Croydon plant to build the teletext decoder.

In the face of poor market acceptance (the company sold only 1,000 teletext sets in its first year), the U.K. subsidiary did not give up. It lent support to the British government's efforts to promote teletext and make it widely available. Meanwhile, management kept up pressure on the Croydon factory to find ways of reducing costs and improving reception quality—which it did.

In late 1979, teletext took off, and by 1982 half a million sets were being sold annually in the United Kingdom. Today almost three million teletext sets are in use in Britain, and the concept is spreading abroad. Philips has built up a dominant position in markets that have accepted the service. Corporate management has given the U.K. subsidiary formal responsibility to continue to exercise leadership in the development, manufacture, and marketing of teletext on a companywide basis. The Croydon plant

Exhibit 1   Roles for National Subsidiaries

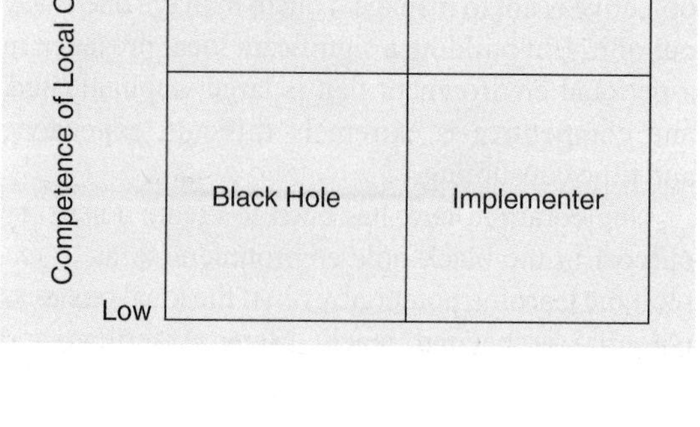

is recognized as Philips' center of competence and international sourcing plant for teletext-TV sets.

Contributor   Filling this role is a subsidiary operating in a small or strategically unimportant market but having a distinctive capability. A fine example is the Australian subsidiary of L. M. Ericsson, which played a crucial part in developing its successful AXE digital telecommunications switch. The down-under group gave impetus to the conversion of the system from its initial analog design to the digital form. Later its engineers helped construct several key components of the system.

This subsidiary had built up its superior technological capability when the Australian telephone authority became one of the first in the world to call for bids on electronic telephone switching equipment. The government in Canberra, however, had insisted on a strong local technical capability as a condition for access to the market. Moreover, heading this unit of the Swedish company was a willful, independent, and entrepreneurial country manager who strengthened the R&D team, even without full support from headquarters.

These various factors resulted in the local subsidiary having a technological capability and an R&D resource base that was much larger than subsidiaries in other markets of similar size or importance. Left to their own devices, management worried that such internal competencies would focus on local tasks and priorities that were unnecessary or even detrimental to the overall global strategy. But if the company inhibited the development activities of the local units, it risked losing these special skills. Under the circumstances, management saw the need to co-opt this valuable subsidiary expertise and channel it toward projects of corporate importance.

Implementer   In the third situation, a national organization in a less strategically important market has just enough competence to maintain its local operation. The market potential is limited, and the corporate resource commitment reflects it. Most national units of most companies are given this role. They might include subsidiaries in the devel-

oping countries, in Canada, and in the smaller European countries. Without access to critical information, and having to control scarce resources, these national organizations lack the potential to become contributors to the company's strategic planning. They are deliverers of the company's value added; they have the important task of generating the funds that keep the company going and underwrite its expansion.

The implementers' efficiency is as important as the creativity of the strategic leaders or contributors—and perhaps more so, for it is this group that provides the largest leverage that affords MNCs their competitive advantage. The implementers produce the opportunity to capture economies of scale and scope that are crucial to most companies' global strategies.

In Procter & Gamble's European introduction of Vizir, the French company played an important contributing role by undertaking a second market test and later modifying the advertising approach. In the other launches during the first year, Austria, Spain, Holland, and Belgium were implementers; they took the defined strategy and made it work in their markets. Resisting any temptation to push for change in the formula, alteration of the package, or adjustment of the advertising theme, these national subsidiaries enabled P&G to extract profitable efficiencies.

The Black Hole   Philips in Japan, Ericsson in the United States, and Matsushita in Germany are black holes. In each of these important markets, strong local presence is essential for maintaining the company's global position. And in each case, the local company hardly makes a dent.

The black hole is not an acceptable strategic position. Unlike the other roles we have described, the objective is not to manage it but to manage one's way out of it. But building a significant local presence in a national environment that is large, sophisticated, and competitive is extremely difficult, expensive, and time consuming.

One common tack has been to create a sensory outpost in the black hole environment so as to exploit the learning potential, even if the local business potential is beyond reach. Many American and

European companies have set up small establishments in Japan to monitor technologies, market trends, and competitors. Feedback to headquarters, so the thinking goes, will allow further analysis of the global implications of local developments and will at least help prevent erosion of the company's position in other markets. But this strategy has often been less fruitful than the company had hoped. Look at the case of Philips in Japan.

Although Philips had two manufacturing joint ventures with Matsushita, not until 1956 did it enter Japan by establishing a marketing organization. When Japan was emerging as a significant force in the consumer electronics market in the late 1960s, the company decided it had to get further into that market. After years of unsuccessfully trying to penetrate the captive distribution channels of the principal Japanese manufacturers, headquarters settled for a Japan "window" that would keep it informed of technical developments there. But results were disappointing. The reason, according to a senior manager of Philips in Japan, is that to sense effectively, eyes and ears are not enough. One must get "inside the bloodstream of the business," he said, with constant and direct access to distribution channels, component suppliers, and equipment manufacturers.

Detecting a new development after it has occurred is useless, for there is no time to play catch-up. One needs to know of developments as they emerge, and for that one must be a player, not a spectator. Moreover, being confined to window status, the local company is prevented from playing a strategic role. It is condemned to a permanent existence as a black hole.

So Philips is trying to get into the bloodstream of the Japanese market, moving away from the window concept and into the struggle for market share. The local organization now sees its task as winning market share rather than just monitoring local developments. But it is being very selective and focusing on areas where it has advantages over strong local competition. The Japanese unit started with coffee makers and electric shavers. Philips' acquisition of Marantz, a hi-fi equipment producer, gives it

a bid to expand on its strategic base and build the internal capabilities that will enable the Japanese subsidiary to climb out of the black hole.

Another way to manage one's way out of the black hole is to develop a strategic alliance. Such coalitions can involve different levels of cooperation. Ericsson's joint venture with Honeywell in the United States and AT&T's with Philips in Europe are examples of attempts to fill up a black hole by obtaining resources and competence from a strong local organization in exchange for capabilities available elsewhere.

Shaping, Building, Directing   Corporate management faces three big challenges in guiding the dispersion of responsibilities and differentiating subsidiaries' tasks. The first is in setting the strategic direction for the company by identifying its mission and its business objectives. The second is in building the differentiated organization, not only by designing the diverse roles and distributing the assignments but also by giving the managers responsible for filling them the legitimacy and power to do so. The final challenge is in directing the process to ensure that the several roles are coordinated and that the distributed responsibilities are controlled.

Setting the Course   Any company (or any organization, for that matter) needs a strong, unifying sense of direction. But that need is particularly strong in an organization in which tasks are differentiated and responsibilities dispersed. Without it, the decentralized management process will quickly degenerate into strategic anarchy. A visitor to any NEC establishment in the world will see everywhere the company motto "C&C," which stands for computers and communications. This simple pairing of words is much more than a definition of NEC's product markets; top managers have made it the touchstone of a common global strategy. They emphasize it to focus the attention of employees on the key strategy of linking two technologies. And they employ it to help managers think how NEC can compete with larger companies like IBM and AT&T, which are perceived as vulnerable insofar as they lack a balance in the two technologies and markets.

Top management at NEC headquarters in Tokyo strives to inculcate its worldwide organization with an understanding of the C&C strategy and philosophy. It is this strong, shared understanding that permits greater differentiation of managerial processes and the decentralization of tasks.

But in addition to their role of developing and communicating a vision of the corporate mission, the top officers at headquarters also retain overall responsibility for the company's specific business strategies. While not abandoning this role at the heart of the company's strategic process, executives of many multinational companies are co-opting other parts of the organization (and particularly its diverse national organizations) into important business strategy roles, as we have already described. When it gives up its lead role, however, headquarters management always tracks that delegated responsibility.

Building Differentiation   In determining which units should be given the lead, contributor, or follower roles, management must consider the motivational as well as the strategic impact of its decisions. If unfulfilled, the promise offered by the new organization model can be as demotivating as the symmetrical hierarchy, in which all foreign subsidiaries are assigned permanent secondary roles. For most national units, an organization in which lead and contributor roles are concentrated in a few favorite children represents little advance from old situations in which the parent dominated the decision making. In any units continually obliged to implement strategies developed elsewhere, skills atrophy, entrepreneurship dies, and any innovative spark that existed when it enjoyed more independence now sputters.

By dealing out lead or contributing roles to the smaller or less developed units, even if only for one or two strategically less important products, the headquarters group will give them a huge incentive. Although Philips N.V. had many other subsidiaries closer to large markets or with better access to corporate know-how and expertise, headquarters awarded the Taiwan unit the lead role in the small-screen monitor business. This vote of confidence gave the Taiwanese terrific motivation to do well and made them feel like a full contributing partner in the company's worldwide strategy.

But allocating roles isn't enough; the head office has to empower the units to exercise their voices in the organization by ensuring that those with lead positions particularly have access to and influence in the corporate decision-making process. This is not a trivial task, especially if strategic initiative and decision-making powers have long been concentrated at headquarters.

NEC discovered this truth about a decade ago when it was trying to transform itself into a global enterprise. Because NTT, the Japanese telephone authority, was dragging its feet in converting its exchanges to the new digital switching technology, NEC was forced to diverge from its custom of designing equipment mainly for its big domestic customer. The NEAC 61 digital switch was the first outgrowth of the policy shift; it was aimed primarily at the huge, newly deregulated U.S. telephone market.

Managers and engineers in Japan developed the product; the American subsidiary had little input. Although the hardware drew praise from customers, the switch had severe software deficiencies that hampered its penetration of the U.S. market.

Recognizing the need to change its administrative setup, top management committed publicly to becoming "a genuine world enterprise" rather than a Japanese company operating abroad. To permit the U.S. subsidiary a greater voice, headquarters helped it build a local software development capability. This plus the unit's growing knowledge about the Bell operating companies—NEC's target customers—gave the American managers legitimacy and power in Japan.

NEC's next-generation digital switch, the NEAC 61-E, evolved quite differently. Exercising their new influence at headquarters, U.S. subsidiary managers took the lead in establishing its features and specifications and played a big part in the design.

Another path to empowerment takes the form of dislodging the decision-making process from the home office. Ericsson combats the headquarters hierarchy syndrome by appointing product and functional managers from headquarters to subsidiary boards. The give-and-take in board meetings is helpful for both subsidiary and parent. Matsushita holds an annual review of each major worldwide function (like manufacturing and human resource management) in the offices of a national subsidiary it considers to be a leading exponent of the particular function. In addition to the symbolic value for employees of the units, the siting obliges officials from Tokyo headquarters to consider issues that the front lines are experiencing and gives local managers the home-court advantage in seeking a voice in decision making.

Often the most effective means of giving strategy access and influence to national units is to create entirely new channels and forums. This approach permits roles, responsibilities, and relationships to be defined and developed with far less constraint than through modification of existing communication patterns or through shifting of responsibility boundaries. Procter & Gamble's Eurobrand teams are a case in point.

Directing the Process   When the roles of operating units are differentiated and responsibility is more dispersed, corporate management must be prepared to deemphasize its direct control over the strategic content but develop an ability to manage the dispersed strategic process. Furthermore, headquarters must adopt a flexible administrative stance that allows it to differentiate the way it manages one subsidiary to the next and from business to business within a single unit, depending on the particular role it plays in each business.

In units with lead roles, headquarters plays an important role in ensuring that the business strategies developed fit the company's overall goals and priorities. But control in the classic sense is often quite loose. Corporate management's chief function is to support those with strategy leadership responsibility by giving them the resources and the freedom needed for the innovative and entrepreneurial role they have been asked to play.

With a unit placed in a contributor role, the head-office task is to redirect local resources to programs outside the unit's control. In so doing, it has to counter the natural hierarchy of loyalties that in most national organizations puts local interests above global ones. In such a situation, headquarters must be careful not to discourage the local managers and technicians so much that they stop contributing or leave in frustration. This has happened to many U.S. companies that have tried to manage their Canadian subsidiaries in a contributor role. Ericsson has solved the problem in its Australian subsidiary by attaching half the R&D team to headquarters, which farms out to these engineers projects that are part of the company's global development program.

The head office maintains tighter control over a subsidiary in an implementor role. Because such a group represents the company's opportunity to capture the benefits of scale and learning from which it gets and sustains its competitive advantage, headquarters stresses economy and efficiency in selling the products. Communication of strategies developed elsewhere and control of routine tasks can be carried out through systems, allowing headquarters to manage these units more efficiently than most others.

As for the black hole unit, the task for top executives is to develop its resources and capabilities to make it more responsive to its environment. Managers of these units depend heavily on headquarters for help and support, creating an urgent need for intensive training and transfer of skills and resources.

Firing the Spark Plugs

Multinational companies often build cumbersome and expensive infrastructures designed to control their widespread operations and to coordinate the diverse and often conflicting demands they make. As the coordination and control task expands, the typical headquarters organization becomes larger and more powerful, while the national subsidiaries are increasingly regarded as pipelines for centrally developed products and strategy.

But an international company enjoys a big advantage over a national one: it is exposed to a wider and more diverse range of environmental stimuli. The broader range of customer preferences, the wider spectrum of competitive behavior, the more serious array of government demands, and the more diverse sources of technological information represent potential triggers of innovation and thus a rich source of learning for the company. To capitalize on this advantage requires an organization that is sensitive to the environment and responsive in absorbing the information it gathers.

So national companies must not be regarded as just pipelines but recognized as sources of information and expertise that can build competitive advantage. The best way to exploit this resource is not through centralized direction and control but through a cooperative effort and co-option of dispersed capabilities. In such a relationship, the entrepreneurial spark plugs in the national units can flourish.

CHAPTER 8

The Future of the Transnational:
An Evolving Global Role

In this final chapter, we address the question of how the role and responsibility of the MNE might evolve in the global political economy in the twenty-first century. In the closing decades of the last century, the powerful forces of globalization unleashed a period of growth that drove the overseas development and expansion of many MNEs. The same was true for the vast majority of countries in which MNEs operated, as their economic and social infrastructure benefited from the value created through booming cross-border trade and investment.

However, there was another group of countries that remained in the backwash of the powerful development forces of globalization. While the richest nations argued that the rising tide of globalization would lift all boats, to those in the poorest countries, it appeared to be lifting mainly the luxury yachts. And developed country government-sponsored aid programs designed to narrow the growing gap between rich and poor nations had exhibited little positive impact despite half a century of effort. With almost half the world's population subsisting on less than two dollars a day, many began to feel that the MNEs that had benefited so greatly from global economic expansion now had a responsibility to help deal with the unequal distribution of their benefits. It was a point emphasized at demonstrations outside WTO and World Bank meetings in the early years of the new millennium.

In this chapter, after discussing this evolving situation, we describe four different postures that MNEs have adopted in recent decades, ranging from the exploitative and the transactional, to the responsive and the transformational. Although these are presented as descriptive rather than normative categories, in today's global environment there is a clear push to have companies move away from the exploitive end of the spectrum toward the responsive and even transformative end. In a variety of industries, voluntary norms and standards have been set to provide guidance to the way the MNEs might think about their responsibilities abroad; and the United Nations Global Compact also sets a standard of behavior to which companies can aspire as they expand their operations into the 21st century.

For most transnational companies, the dawning of the new millennium offered exciting prospects of continued growth and prosperity. Yet, in the poorest nations on earth, the reputation of large Western MNEs was shaky at best, and in some quarters, it was in complete tatters. Indeed, a series of widely publicized events in the closing years of the twentieth century led many to ask what additional constraints and controls needed to be placed on the largely unregulated activities of these companies:

- In Indonesia, Nike's employment of children and others in unhealthy work environments, paying them $1.80 a day to make athletic shoes being sold for a $150 a pair to affluent Western buyers.

- In Europe, Coca-Cola's refusal to take responsibility when consumers of soft drinks produced at its Belgian plant reported getting sick, then finally acknowledging the problem two weeks later, but only after 100 people had been hospitalized and five countries had banned the sale of its products.

- In India, Enron's high-profile dispute with a regional government that was trying to cancel a contract for the construction of the Dabhol power station and the supply of power, citing the company's "fraud and misrepresentation" during the original negotiations.

- In South Africa, 39 Western pharmaceutical companies' action in suing to prevent the government from importing cheap generic versions of patented AIDS drugs to treat the country's 4.5 million HIV-positive patients.

Each of these situations involved complex, multifaceted issues to which a group of intelligent managers apparently was trying to respond in what they saw as a logical, justifiable manner—conforming to local labor laws and practices at Nike, conducting quality tests and communicating the data at Coke, enforcing legal contract provisions at Enron, and protecting intellectual property rights by the drug companies. Yet in the court of public opinion, their rational, subtle, or legalistic arguments were swamped by an overarching view of Western multinational companies operating out of greed, arrogance, and self-interest. They were seen as the hammer driving home the widening wedge between the "haves" and the "have nots."

The Growing Discontent

Partly as a result of this growing distrust of MNEs, a popular groundswell against globalization began to gather strength during the closing years of the twentieth century. At that time, in most countries in the developed world—and certainly within the MNEs they had spawned—globalization was viewed as a powerful engine of economic development, spreading the benefits of free market capitalism around the world. Yet fewer developing countries had seen the benefits of this much discussed tidal wave of trade and investment. Indeed, to some living in these countries, the growing gap between the rich and the poor offered clear evidence that "globalization" was just the latest term for their continued exploitation by MNEs.

As a result, delegates from a number of developing nations agreed to block what they saw as unfair rules being imposed by richer nations at the World Trade Organization (WTO) meeting in Seattle in 1999. Supported by a large number of demonstrators, this conference represented the first high-profile protest against the increasing globalization of the world's economy, which many in the West had seen as being as beneficial as it was inevitable. And the prime targets of the protests were the trade ministers from the G7 countries (as they were then) and the multinational corporations that the demonstrators saw as the main drivers and beneficiaries of globalization.

Their protests were given even more public attention when Seattle police began using pepper spray and tear gas against demonstrators, mobilizing a great deal of public sympathy and support for their cause. Soon their arguments were being buttressed by some powerful allies, including the Nobel Laureate Joseph Stiglitz, a former chairman of the Council of Economic Advisors and chief economist at the World Bank. In his book *Globalization and Its Discontents*, Stiglitz suggests that previous actions of WTO, the International Monetary Fund (IMF), and the World Bank had often damaged developing countries' economies more than they had helped them.[1] Regarding the WTO, he points out that though the First World preaches the benefits of free trade, it still protects and subsidizes agricultural products, textiles, and apparel, precisely the goods exported by Third World countries. And rather than seeing MNEs as creating value in developing countries, he suggests that their effect is often to crowd out local enterprise, then use their monopoly power to raise prices.

But the most helpful support of the protesters' arguments was provided by the World Bank's ongoing annual reports of the number of people worldwide living below the poverty threshold.[2] Its data showed that 2.8 billion of the world's 6 billion people were living on less than $2 a day, with more than 40 percent of that number living on less than $1 a day. Despite the great progress made in reducing the number of people in this category in rapidly industrializing countries like India and China, the World Bank reported that the number had increased during the 1990s, the decade of globalization-driven growth for the economies of the developed world and of the profitable expansion of most large MNEs.

The Challenge Facing MNEs

Given the extent of global poverty and the lack of clear significant progress in reducing it, there is a growing view that because there has been such limited progress in dealing with the problem, perhaps it is time to radically rethink the basic approach. William Easterly, a former research economist at the World Bank, points out that after $2.3 trillion of aid has flowed from developed countries to developing countries over the past five decades, it is clear that the West's model of development has failed.[3] Like the old colonialists, a large portion of foreign aid takes a paternalistic view, in that it defines both the problems and the solutions and provides for neither accountability nor feedback. As a result, for example, over the past 25 years, $5 billion has been spent on a publicly owned steel mill in Nigeria that has yet to produce any steel.

Meanwhile, the outstanding success stories such as India and China have been achieved by unleashing the power of their market economies rather than through massive aid programs. In what the World Bank has called this "the greatest poverty

[1]Joseph E. Stiglitz, *Globalization and Its Discontents* (New York: WW Norton & Company, 2002).
[2]World Bank, *Poverty Reduction and the World Bank* (Washington DC: World Bank, 1999); World Bank, *Attacking Poverty* (New York, Oxford University Press, 2001).
[3]William Easterly, *White Man's Burden* (New York: Penguin Press, 2006).

reduction program in human history," hundreds of millions of people have moved out of poverty during the past 25 years. In large part, this amazing transformation has been due to the actions of the many MNEs that, following the announcement of China's open-door policy in 1979, invested hundreds of billions of dollars in that now rapidly developing country. Indeed, 90 percent of the world's top 500 firms now have projects in China. While helping China, the investments also had an overwhelming economic impact on these firms. According to Deloitte Consultancy, the same firms "sent about $250 billion in profits out of China in the period from 1990 to 2004." Such a win–win consequence is due to one undeniable reality: The faster the poor gain wealth, the faster they become customers.

In this environment, the eyes of many in the international community began to turn toward the MNEs to provide at least a part of the solution to the problems that remain in so many other countries. More than just a public relations exercise extolling the benefits of free trade and openness to foreign investment, it has meant understanding what role MNEs might play in dealing with some of the underlying causes of the widespread discontent in the developing world. Certainly they controlled much of the financial resources, technical and commercial expertise, and managerial talent that would be necessary to bring about lasting change to the lives of people living in the world's most underdeveloped economies. In financial power alone, the World Bank estimated that the flows of foreign direct investment into developing countries in 2000 was about $250 billion, more than four times the amount of foreign aid and development funding flowing into that same group of countries.

Entering the new millennium, there was an emerging sense in the global community that with the MNEs' large and growing power, new expectations of the role they could and should play had emerged. Their immediate challenge has been to decide how to respond to the growing resistance to the forces of globalization that drove their growth and expansion during the previous half century. The longer term issue facing them is determining whether they are willing to step up and take a leadership role in dealing with the problems that are the underlying causes of the anti-globalization movement.

Responding to Developing World Needs: Four MNE Postures

In this section, we describe four somewhat archetypical responses along a spectrum of possible action, ranging from an approach we label "exploitive" to one we describe as "transformative." It is our belief that most MNEs have clearly moved away from the former model; it is our hope that they are shifting toward the latter.

The Exploitive MNE: Taking Advantage of Disadvantage

As we saw in Chapter 1, because one of the strongest and most enduring motivations for a company to internationalize is its desire to access low-cost factors of production, the ability to locate low-cost labor has long encouraged many MNEs to locate in emerging markets. To anyone operating in these environments, it soon became clear that not only were the wages and hours worked vastly different than those in developed countries but so too were the health and safety of the working conditions, and even the human rights of the workers. The question facing management was how to respond to that situation.

For a subset of the companies that we describe as "exploitive MNEs," the lower the labor rate, the longer the work week, the fewer the restrictions on working conditions, and the less regulation on workers' rights, the better. These companies believe that cross-country differences in wages, working conditions, legal requirements, and living standards all represent unfettered opportunities to capture competitive advantage.

Such an attitude received its strongest support in the 1970s in the writings and speeches of University of Chicago economist Milton Friedman. Guided by the view that all companies had a responsibility to maximize profits and that shareholders were their only legitimate stakeholder, he argued that "[those who believe that] business has a 'social conscience' and takes seriously its responsibilities for providing employment, eliminating discrimination, avoiding pollution . . . are preaching pure and unadulterated socialism." [4] Such bold, clear absolutes from a Nobel Laureate in Economics provided those desirous of such an approach all the comfort they needed to embrace an exploitive stance. And particularly during that decade, many did.

One of the most commonly held negative images of MNEs relates to the use of what are often called "sweatshops"—work places characterized by some combination of hot, crowded, poorly ventilated, poorly lit, and unsafe environments, in which the labor force—often including children only 10 or 12 years old—receives less than a "living wage" despite their long hours of work.

Far from being examples of extreme situations from an era long past, sweatshops still exist in many countries today. For example, *The New York Times* recently reported that a large number of workers from Bangladesh each paid $1,000 to $3,000 in return for the promise of work in Jordanian factories producing garments for Target and Wal-Mart. After they arrived at their new place of work, their passports were confiscated to ensure they did not quit. Not only were they were paid less than promised and far less than the country's minimum wage, they were forced to work 20-hour days and were hit by supervisors if they complained.[5]

Some MNEs have tried to sidestep the sweatshop issue by outsourcing manufacturing to arm's-length suppliers, but as the Nike case illustrated in Chapter 2, such tactics are no longer effective in insulating the MNE from taking responsibility. As other experiences seem to confirm, the relentless attempt to exploit low-cost labor has great risks attached and often can backfire.[6]

Yet despite the risks, when the pressure from governments, nongovernmental organization (NGO) advocates, and supranational agencies becomes too great, MNEs committed to an exploitive approach will simply close down and move the factory to another city, state, or country. In doing so, they often find another opportunity to exploit the situation. Understanding that because most countries are actively working to develop employment, increase their tax base, and capture spin-off benefits from new investment,

---

[4]Milton Friedman. "The Social Responsibility of Business Is to Increase its Profits," *The New York Times Magazine,* September 13, 1970.

[5]Steven Greenhouse and Michael Barbaro, "An Ugly Side of Free Trade: Sweatshops in Jordan," *The New York Times,* May 3, 2006.

[6]See, for example, Paul Beamish, "The High Cost of Cheap Chinese Labor," *Harvard Business Review,* June 2006; Ivey Case # 9B04M033, "Jinjian Garment Factory: Motivating Go-Slow Workers."

the exploitive MNE will not hesitate to play countries against one another, demanding more and more concessions to guarantee their investment.

In countries where corruption and bribery are common, this push for concessions and subsidies from local government officials and regulators has led some exploitive MNEs to illegal activities. Justifying their actions with an attitude of "when in Rome . . . ," some firms are not above engaging in such practices in the name of maximizing profits. For example, in the mid-1970s, the president of United Brands was charged with bribing the president of Honduras to help maintain a banana monopoly. If local politicians did not cooperate, some exploitive MNEs even proved they were willing to help remove democratically elected governments. In the early 1970s, the American conglomerate ITT was accused of not only making political payoffs in the United States but also conspiring to work with the CIA to overthrow the democratically elected government of Chile.[7]

Global exploitation can move well beyond the relentless pursuit of low-cost labor and subsidized investment. It has led some companies to seek market expansion regardless of the likely resulting economic, social, or cultural damage. One classic example unfolded in the 1970s, when Nestlé and other infant formula manufacturers became concerned that birth rates in most industrialized countries were flattening and declining. Shifting their attention to what seemed like huge opportunities in the emerging country markets, they began a major marketing push in those countries, employing dozens of sales promoters dressed as nurses to hand out samples of their product.

The product was soon seen as "modern and Western," and as sales increased, the practice of breast feeding declined. But subsequent reports of increases in infant mortality and malnourishment soon had many concerned that the practice was having major negative health consequences. It was discovered that mothers who could not afford to use the formula at the recommended level diluted it to make it last longer. Not only was the baby not receiving the nutrients it needed, but the water being used to mix the formula often was unsanitary, leading to diarrhea, dehydration, and malnutrition. Equally concerning was the fact that the baby was not receiving all the immunities that normally would be transferred from the mother via breast feeding, again making the child less resistant to sickness. A great deal of public outrage followed, with consumers worldwide boycotting Nestlé products. What was immediately clear, not only to Nestlé but also to other MNEs selling into the developing world, was that products intended for developed country markets could have seriously harmful effects if sold into emerging markets without a full appreciation of and responsiveness to the particular country's different cultural, social, and economic situation.

Beyond the direct way it affects the lives of its employees and customers, the MNE also has an impact on the local communities in which it operates. In its single-minded focus on maximizing profit, however, an exploitive MNE accepts no responsibility for the social or environmental consequences of its actions, even when the impact is severe.

One of the most severe industrial tragedies in history involved a gas leak from a Union Carbide facility in Bhopal, India, in 1984. Thousands of people died, and many others suffered long-term disabilities. Union Carbide was accused of using unproven technology at the plant, conducting insufficient safety checks, and being unprepared for

---

[7]Anthony Sampson, *The Sovereign State of ITT* (:Stein and Day, 1973).

and slow to respond to problems, along with many other negligent acts. But the company claimed that the gas release was caused by employee sabotage and that it had responded as quickly and comprehensively as it could. What is not subject to debate is that Union Carbide paid $470 million to the Indian government in a legal settlement and, with the rest of the chemical industry, "worked to develop and implement its 'Responsible Case' program, designed to prevent any future events through improving community awareness, emergency preparedness and process safety standards."[8]

Particularly during the 1970s, when controversies were raging around the events pertaining to United Brands, ITT, and Nestlé, many felt that the MNE's ability to operate outside the legal framework of any single government had made it a force that needed to be better regulated and controlled. In short, there were concerns that too many companies were adopting the attitude of exploitive MNEs. Because most supranational organizations and agencies (e.g., ILO, UNCTAD, UNESCO) had been relatively ineffective in influencing or controlling MNE behavior, various global NGOs began to assume the role of monitors and controllers of the actions of exploitive MNEs. As the Nestlé example that we described clearly illustrates, these NGOs exercised their power through their ability to organize protests, boycotts, or political action, targeting the MNE's customers, stock owners, or regulators.

Not surprisingly, exploitive MNEs soon developed adversarial attitudes toward NGOs, and that relationship was reciprocated. Consider the example of the multinational tobacco companies that had been targeting developing country markets for decades as regulatory pressure and consumer education shrank their markets in the West. During the early 1990s, when the former Soviet Union split into several independent countries, the laws previously in place banning tobacco advertising, forbidding smoking in many public places, and requiring health warnings on cigarette packages were no longer binding in the newly created states. According to researchers, "posttransition, the (multinational) tobacco companies exploited confusion over the legality of this Soviet legislation by advertising heavily to establish their brands."[9] Subsequent surveys indicate there has been an increase in youth smoking, particularly among women in cities. All of this is occurring in a part of the world where tobacco is already responsible for twice the number of deaths among men as in the West and with a product that public health professionals view as the greatest single cause of preventable mortality in the developed world.

The response from public health researchers and anti-MNE and anti-smoking NGOs has been loud and sustained. They have lobbied various newly established governments to reestablish anti-smoking controls and worked actively to publicize the negative implications of MNE activities in the region. The tobacco MNEs have countered by emphasizing the job creation and increased taxes available to local governments from the investments they have made. The adversarial relationship between the groups continues.

Overall, the picture of the exploitive MNE is not a pretty one. It is an organization that is willing to ignore the welfare of its end consumers and employees, collude with

---

[8]See www.bhopal.com and www.responsiblecare.org.

[9]A.B. Gilmore and M. McKee, "Tobacco and Transition: An Overview of Industry Investment, Impact, and Influence in the Former Soviet Union,: *Tobacco Control* 13 (2004), pp. 136–42.

political elites, violate environmental norms, and expose emerging market communities to potential harm. Fortunately, it seems to be a species in rapid decline.

The Transactional MNE: Doing Deals, Respecting the Law

Few companies today operate in the extreme manner of profit maximization in the sole service of the shareholder, as Milton Friedman advocated. For example, whereas he opposed corporations making any charitable donations or acting in response to any social issue, most publicly owned corporations demonstrate at least a little charitable generosity and show at least some sensitivity toward their communities. Because there is little evidence that such actions have been frowned on by shareholders, it is hardly surprising that in the international environment, one finds fewer examples of truly exploitive MNEs today than previously. The minimum expectation of MNE behavior today tends to be based on what we describe as a transactional attitude.

The difference between a transactional attitude and an exploitive one is that the former implies an approach that is both legally compliant and nonoppressive in its emerging market dealings. Yet though the transactional MNE's relationships with its environment remain almost exclusively commercial, unlike its exploitive counterpart, it does not pursue the bottom line at all costs. Indeed, many companies that once were uncaring about or insensitive to the serious problems that their aggressive or indifferent attitudes created have evolved from their exploitive approach (often under pressure from NGOs or regulatory authorities) to adopt a more responsible transactional posture. It is a position that manifests itself in a somewhat different attitude toward each stakeholder.

The transactional MNE's relationship toward its emerging market customers avoids the egregious missteps that the Nestlé experience highlighted as being so inappropriate and dangerous. This shift implies having the sensitivity not to promote socially or economically unsuitable products originally developed for consumers with very different needs or markets with very different characteristics. Beyond this appropriate caution, these companies are often willing to make minor product or service adaptations to meet local needs or preferences, but only if there is a high degree of certainty that the change will expand market share, increase profits, or meet some other commercial need.

For example, global fast-food giants such as McDonald's and KFC are often willing to make minor changes to their product offering or service approach on a country-by-country basis, but they seldom stray very far from their standard menu. And though they are generally regarded as good, law-abiding, tax-paying corporate citizens in the countries in which they operate, they have also been accused of cultural insensitivity or worse. For example, many national health services have expressed concern about the increasing health risks for people in developing countries who are persuaded to change their eating habits from the high-fiber natural foods of their local diets to the high-fat refined foods that dominate fast-food menus.

With regard to employee relations, because the transactional MNE respects local labor laws and ILO guidelines, it usually relates to its employees in a much less brutal or oppressive way than the exploitive company. For example, the transactional MNE would not be willing to have its own employees, or those of its subcontractors, work in the sweatshop-like conditions we described in the previous section. Yet, though they conform to labor laws and workplace regulations, these companies would be more likely to maintain pressure on employees and suppliers to capture the value of the lower cost labor that attracted their original investment.

As the case in Chapter 2 illustrated, Nike was forced to move some way along this learning curve when it was confronted by well-organized boycotts to protest what several NGOs claimed were well-documented exploitive activities in developing countries. For many years, Nike had either ignored pressure from NGOs about labor practices employed in the manufacture if its shoes or denied that they were its responsibility, arguing that it was the subcontractors, not Nike, that employed the workers. But in the mid-1990s, following relentless NGO pressure in many countries, Nike changed its position. After *Life Magazine* ran a photo of a very young Pakistani boy stitching a Nike soccer ball, the company raised its minimum age for workers from 14 to 16 years for apparel and to 18 years for footwear, both above the ILO minimum of 15; after organized strikes by thousands of workers in Indonesia, Vietnam, and China protesting Nike's subminimum wages, it set a policy of paying the higher of the minimum wage or the industry standard; and after investigations found toxic fumes at 177 times the legal Vietnamese limit, the company agreed to set U.S. standards for occupational health and safety in plants worldwide.

In its attitude toward local communities and the broader society, the transactional MNE does not exhibit the same level of indifference and irresponsibility that characterizes the exploitive MNE. The experiences of Union Carbide in Bhopal, the multinational tobacco companies in the former Soviet Union, ITT in Chile, and United Fruit in Central America have all served as cautionary tales. One of the lessons that transactional-oriented MNEs appear to have learned is that it usually makes economic sense to obey both the letter and the spirit of local and international laws and regulations. Take the example of environmental standards. Historically, any MNE's announcement of plans to establish potentially environmentally sensitive facilities in emerging markets immediately raised the question as to whether it was doing so to take advantage of low environmental standards or lax enforcement. So when the Free Trade Agreement between Canada and the United States was extended to include Mexico, much discussion ensued as to whether that country would become a pollution haven for dirty industries. Twelve years later, careful research has concluded that "no discernable migration of dirty industry has occurred."[10] That the expected migration to Mexico of dirty chemical, metals, or paper plants has not occurred tends to suggest that most MNEs have established at least a law-abiding, nonexploitive attitude toward emerging markets.

At a minimum, the transactional-oriented MNE takes a Hippocratic Oath–style approach to communities. (The ancient Greek physician Hippocrates is credited with the expression "First, do no harm," which forms part of the oath taken by physicians.) Such an attitude, applied to MNEs, increases the likelihood that the worst potential corporate abuses will be avoided, but that does not mean that transactional MNEs are fully trusted or that their actions are not carefully monitored by regulators or NGOs. And in recent years, it has often been the global NGOs that have taken the more active role in pushing MNEs to take more responsibility for their social, economic, and environmental impact.

[10]Gustavo Alanis-Ortega, "Is Global Environmental Governance Working?" *The Environmental Forum,* May/June 2006, p. 23.

Take the case of Nike. Despite the major concessions it made to the NGOs' many demands in the late 1990s, it was clear NGOs would remain interested in the company's practices simply because it is a highly profitable, highly visible industry leader, dealing with 700 factories that collectively employ over half a million people, mostly in emerging markets. But Nike's relationship with the many NGOs with which it sparred in the mid-1990s has slowly changed. Although some remnants of the activist-driven boycotts and protests remain in place, the heat has been greatly reduced. As the company moved to comply with more of the NGOs' demands, their role evolved from active adversary to vigilant watchdog.

Although not enthusiastically embraced by Nike and other MNEs, this relationship between NGOs and transactional companies is based less on confrontation and accusation and more on monitoring and challenging. Yet though the NGOs might agree that "doing no harm" is certainly a positive characteristic, they also challenge companies to consider whether that is a sufficient role for the multinational enterprise of the 21st century.

The Responsive MNE: Making a Difference

In the past, a large number—perhaps a majority—of MNEs might have exhibited behavior that was significantly or even predominantly exploitive or transactional, as we have described those behaviors. In recent years, however, the concept of "sustainability" has gained far more attention within the corporate world. As it has, management's concept of a sustainable strategy has migrated from a passing acknowledgement of the need to develop a responsible corporate environmental policy to a recognition that companies must articulate a philosophy that reflects their long-term viability as key participants in the broader social and economic environment. This perspective requires managers to take a somewhat broader perspective of their constituencies and their roles and responsibilities in the societies in which they operate.

A recent McKinsey survey seems to support the notion that executives around the world are becoming more aware of their larger responsibilities and increasingly convinced that they have a broader role to play. In the survey of 4,238 executives from 116 countries, only 16 percent of respondents saw their own responsibility as being to focus on the maximization of shareholder returns, whereas 84 percent expressed the opinion that high returns to shareholders must be balanced with contributions to a broader good.[11]

The responsive MNE, as we have dubbed it, reflects this view and undertakes to be more than merely a law-abiding entity: It makes a conscious commitment to be a contributing corporate citizen in all the environments in which it operates. In contrast to its exploitive and transactional counterparts, the responsive MNC is more sensitive to the different needs of the stakeholders in developing countries and manifests this behavior more proactively in the way in which it deals with its customers, employees, and the community at large.

In his book *The Fortune at the Bottom of the Pyramid,* C. K. Prahalad argues that MNEs have not only a responsibility to contribute to development in the poorest nations

---

[11]"McKinsey Global Survey of Business Executives: Business and Society" *McKinsey Quarterly,* January 2006, available at http://www.mckinseyquarterly.com/article_page.aspx?ar=1741&L2=39&L3=29.

of the world (i.e., "Big corporations should solve big problems") but also a huge opportunity to access a largely untapped market of four billion people. By investing in developing markets, creating jobs and wealth, and catering to un- or underserved consumers, Prahalad argues that MNEs have an opportunity to bring millions of consumers into the marketplace from among the two-thirds of the global population that earns less than $2000 per annum.[12]

Some companies have understood this opportunity for decades, probably none more so than Hindustan Lever. As Unilever's operating company in India for more than a century, this company has long understood that the key to developing scale and driving growth in that densely populated country is to expand its target market well beyond the middle- and upper-class consumers that are the typical focus of most MNEs entering huge developing markets like India. For many decades, Hindustan Lever has aimed at expanding its operations to serve the rural poor by adapting the company's products and technologies to their very different needs and economic means. For example, it developed a way to incorporate Unilever's advanced detergent technology into simple laundry bars, thereby providing superior washing capabilities in the cold-water, hand-washing methods that characterize India's widespread practice of doing laundry in the local stream or village washhouse. At the same time, the company adapted to local economic realities by selling the product as affordable single bars.

Even in sophisticated product markets such as medical diagnostic equipment, there is opportunity for MNEs to adopt a more responsive approach that can bring advanced technology to developing countries. For example, GE Medical Systems has adapted its range of diagnostic products to the simpler needs and more cost-constrained budgets of developing country health care systems. Although the economy model of its CT scanner sells for about one-third of the price of the advanced models in the United States, the market potential for such a product in less developed markets is huge. Already, this low-end product range accounts for approximately 20 percent of the CT scanner market worldwide.

To meet the needs of this large, previously unserved market, GE has gone beyond the adaptation of its current line to create a business it calls its Gold Seal Program. Through this program, the company acquires used x-ray machines and CT scanners, refurbishes them to their original specifications, and then resells them to developing country markets. Although these may not be the latest models with the most up-to-date technological features, they are in high demand, and GE's initiative has earned it a 30 percent share of a $1 billion global market for refurbished diagnostic equipment. Better still, the market is growing at 15 percent per annum.

But the responsive MNE sees its role as more than being an open and receptive commercial participant in developing countries' economies. These companies also feel the responsibility to be good corporate citizens that have a positive impact on those whose lives they touch. For example, Starbucks has accepted the responsibility to help its farmer suppliers in the face of lower global commodity prices for coffee.

---

[12]C.K. Prahalad, *The Fortune at the Bottom of the Pyramid* (Upper Saddle River, NJ: Wharton School Publishing/ Pearson, 2005).

In 2004, it collaborated with Conservation International to create its Coffee and Farmer Equity (CAFE) practices, which set out Starbucks's expectations about its suppliers' labor and environmental practices. In return for their compliance, Starbucks promises those who meet CAFE standards "preferred supplier" status, which involves long-term contracts and a price premium—$1.20 per pound compared with the prevailing 2004 market price of 40–50 cents. By 2007, the company expects that 60 percent of its supply will come from farms that follow its CAFE guidelines for environmental and labor practices.

Heineken has gone even further in reaching out to its stakeholders. To help deal with the devastating impact of AIDS in Africa, it provides anti-retroviral drug coverage not only to its 6,000 African employees but also their dependents. It is a commitment that will cost the company $2 million a year, but it reflects a sense of responsibility that Heineken and a growing number of other employers in Africa feel toward their employees and their families.

Many of the actions of these and other responsive MNEs reflect the aspirational standards of behavior contained in the voluntary Global Compact, signed by almost 2,500 companies (including 105 of the world's largest 500) from 87 countries since it was introduced in 1999 at the World Economic Forum in Davos by Kofi Annan, the Secretary General of the United Nations. (See Exhibit 8-1 for a summary of the key principles of the Global Compact.) Although it is a voluntary and self-regulated set of aspirational norms, rather than a legislated and enforceable code, the Global Compact seems to represent a way forward that can encourage MNEs to embrace a more responsive and constructive role in the developing world.

Exhibit 8-1   The Global Compact's Ten Principles

Human Rights
1. Businesses should support and respect the protection of internationally proclaimed human rights; and
2. make sure that they are not complicit in human rights abuses.

Labour Standards
3. Businesses should uphold the freedom of association and the effective recognition of the right to collective bargaining;
4. the elimination of all forms of forced and compulsory labour;
5. the effective abolition of child labour; and
6. the elimination of discrimination in respect of employment and occupation.

Environment
7. Businesses should support a precautionary approach to environmental challenges;
8. undertake initiatives to promote greater environmental responsibility; and
9. encourage the development and diffusion of environmentally friendly technologies

Anti-Corruption
10. Businesses should work against all forms of corruption, including extortion and bribery.

Source: www.unglobalcompact.org/AboutTheGC/TheTenPrinciples/index.html.

The Transformative MNE: Leading Broad Change

In recent years, there have been a growing number of examples of private enterprises not only being sensitive and responsive to the problems and needs of the developing world but also taking the initiative to lead broad-scale efforts to deal with their root causes. Because of the cost and commitment required to take such action, it is hardly surprising that the boldest and most visible of such initiatives have been those taken by private individuals and/or their foundations. George Soros and Bill Gates are perhaps the most visible of these individual entrepreneurs who are using funds generated by their highly successful global companies to attack some of the biggest problems of health, education, and welfare among the world's neediest populations.

Yet despite the commitment required, a growing number of companies is also leading major initiatives to help deal with problems facing the developing world. We describe these as transformative MNEs. Beyond being good corporate citizens, these companies have come to the conclusion that they can and should take a larger role in the less advantaged countries in which they operate by bringing their resources to bear on the massive problems their populations and governments face.

One way they do so is to make significant investments in developing products or services to meet important unfilled needs in poorer nations. And they often do so even if the economics do not support such developments or when other investments offer greater returns. For example, Nokia recognized the need for a lower cost mobile cellular telephone in emerging markets, most of which lack the hard-wired infrastructure necessary to provide landline telephone service to remote communities. After extensive ethnographic research and numerous consumer interviews in China, India, and Nepal, they developed an understanding of how illiterate people manage in their lives without understanding letters and numbers. This understanding led to the development of a software program built around a menu that uses a list of images rather than numbers and letters. At the same time, Nokia's hardware developers were working on designing a phone that would be simple, durable, and appropriate for outdoor use in the tropics. Understanding that it would be one of the most expensive purchases ever made by their potential consumers, the company also specified that the phone should be able to last for many years. The result was a product designed specifically for the needs of the developing world, built with a durable, moisture-resistant casing and a screen that would be legible even in bright sunlight. Most important, Nokia made this product simple enough for anyone to use and available at an extremely low price. Although not a high-profit item, it responded to a social need of less educated, poor people living in remote communities.

Some truly transformative MNEs even go beyond a commercial relationship with consumers and offer their products and services to those who most desperately need them, regardless of their ability to pay. One of the largest and most sustained commitments was made by the pharmaceutical giant Merck in 1987 after it developed a drug to prevent river blindness. Recognizing that few of the more than 18 million sufferers of this debilitating disease—almost all of whom live in the developing world—could afford the treatment, the company decided to make the drug freely available for as long as it was needed to anyone suffering from or at risk of becoming exposed. Over the past 20 years, the program has delivered over 1 billion tablets in 350 million patient treatments. It currently reaches 45 million people and prevents an estimated 40,000 cases of blindness each year. (Case 8-2 describes a similar effort being undertaken by Genzyme, a biotech company specializing in finding treatments for so called "orphan diseases," on which little research is conducted due to the rarity of their occurrence. The company has committed to seeking out sufferers of Gaucher disease throughout the world. In poor countries, it provides, free of charge, treatments for the disease, which costs over $100,000 per annum in Western countries.)

Transformational MNEs' desire to bring about a positive change also extends to the workplace and the communities in which they operate. They reject the notion of passively complying with local labor laws that do not meet their own higher standard of fairness to employees, and they are willing to challenge established community norms that deny human rights. In doing so, these companies become agents of change, willing to use their influence to bring about improvements in exploitive or unfair situations. For example, where local employment practices are unsafe, unhealthy, or do not provide a living wage, the transformational MNE becomes the new standard that others must eventually match; where social or economic conditions are oppressive or unjust, they become advocates for the disadvantaged, often leading the action to bring about change.

Because they typically challenge deeply embedded practices, developing such transformational responses is often difficult, particularly in the very different social and economic environments governed by very different cultural norms and legal frameworks. As a result, it often requires a long process of learning and adaptation on the company's part. Case 8-1 charts IKEA's process of learning after it was confronted with the knowledge that some of its Indian and Pakistani rug suppliers were employing child labor. From a position of ignorance and naiveté, the company went through a painful, decade-long process of learning how to respond appropriately to the widespread and socially accepted practice of sending children to work. The challenge in dealing with this issue was that it occurred not only in the factories where it might be more easily monitored and controlled but also in the homes of those to whom most suppliers subcontracted much of their rug weaving.

Another characteristic of the transformational NME is that it moves beyond fulfilling its responsibility to its direct stakeholders and begins to contribute to the broader social and economic needs of the countries in which it operates. For example, Nokia, in partnership with Pearson Publishing, the International Youth Foundation (IYF), and the U.N. Development Program, created a program called BridgeIt that uses mobile technology to deliver digital education materials to schools in remote areas of developing countries. Nokia has also joined with IYF to run an initiative called Make a Connection that has delivered educational development programs aimed at young people, primarily in developing countries. Through training, mentoring, and other means, the program develops a range of life skills, from teamwork to conflict resolution and from self-confidence to active leadership. Since its launch in 2000, Make a Connection has reached almost 240,000 young people in 23 countries.

In many of these activities, the MNEs have found themselves working in partnership with NGOs or supragovernment agencies that can provide expertise in social program delivery that the companies typically lack. In doing so, they have developed a very different relationship with these groups than the adversarial or defensive exchanges that characterize exploitive or transactional MNEs' experiences with NGOs. It is a partnership that appears to leverage the resources and capabilities of both groups and may well prove the engine that can drive the changes that have been so elusive in attempts to accelerate economic and social development in the world's poorest nations.

Conclusion

Over time, there has been an evolution in the roles, responsibilities, and expectations of MNEs operating in host countries around the world. In his seminal books *Sovereignty at Bay* and *Storm over the Multinationals,* both published in the 1970s, Ray Vernon expressed concerns about the "economic hegemony and economic dependence" that often characterized the relationship between MNEs and host country governments in the developing world in that era.[13] And various corrupt or exploitive acts by those companies during this time period created what Vernon described as a sense of "tension and anxiety on the part of many nation-states."

As the anecdotes that open this chapter illustrate, MNEs are still susceptible to charges of insensitivity and irresponsibility. But in the three decades since Vernon's research was published, the widespread concerns once held about MNE domination of host governments have largely subsided. (Indeed, the careful reader will have noted that most of the examples in the "exploitive" section describe activities that occurred in the 1970s.) And though there has been little success in creating the effective supranational global agencies that once were thought vital to reining in the unfettered power of the MNE, the rise of numerous, highly effective, global NGOs has filled the role of the active "watchdog." As the several examples cited in this chapter show, NGOs have become very effective at using their clout with consumers, share owners, and other company stakeholders as a way to bring about change.

But the biggest change has occurred in the evolving attitudes of companies toward their sense of corporate social responsibility and their commitment to a strategy of sustainability.

Although a few firms have remained stuck in an exploitive mode with regard to the most vulnerable foreign environments in which they operate, most have adopted, at a minimum, a transactional approach. And with the growing shareholder and social expectations that MNEs should play a more active role, the trend is clearly moving toward responsive and even transformative models.

The social needs in emerging markets are great, and multinational enterprises and their managers have much to contribute. Increasingly, they are feeling both pressure and encouragement to ignore any uncertainty or timidity that could lead to inaction. In addition to transforming the lives of those in emerging markets, their commitment of resources, sensibly and sensitively provided to those at the "bottom of the pyramid," may very well represent one of the most important investments the MNE will ever make.

[13]Raymond Vernon, *Sovereignty at Bay* (New York: Basic Books, 1971); Raymond Vernon, *Storm Over the Multinationals: The Real Issues* (Cambridge: Harvard University Press, 1977).

MNE/Stakeholder Relationships in Emerging Markets: A Typology

	Stakeholders					
	Economic			Societal	Political/Regulatory	
MNE Responses and Attitudes	Shareholders	Customers	Employees/Suppliers	Local Communities	Government and Supranational Agencies/Regulators (e.g., U.N. Agencies)	NGOs
Exploitive *Views differences in wages, working conditions and living standards as exploitable opportunities.*	Adopts classic Milton Friedman view: Its only legitimate role is to maximize returns to shareholders.	Sells existing products and services, even if they have negative social or economic impact.	Exploits existing local wages, working conditions, and suppliers, driving them lower if possible.	Accepts no community responsibility for its social or environmental impact.	Seeks concessions and subsidies, using bargaining power to play national investment boards against each other. If bribery and corruption exist, engages in local practices to win benefits.	An adversary: NGOs actively work to force the MNE to change its behavior through protests, boycotts, political activism, etc.
Transactional *Engages in law-abiding, nonexploitive, commercial interactions.*	Focus on shareholder returns, but believes a pure Friedman approach is inconsistent with the long-term interests of its shareholders.	Treats it as any another market. Makes product adaptations if they are economically viable and can increase market share.	Complies with local labor laws and workplace regulations. Uses cost-efficient local sources, pressuring them on price.	Adopts a Hippocratic Oath approach toward communities: (i.e., "First, do no harm").	Obeys local laws and regulations but uses country differences to gain competitive advantage.	A watchdog: NGO monitors the MNE's actions, urging or pushing it to do more.

Responsive *Acts in a way that is sensitive and responsive to the needs of all its immediate stakeholders.*	Feels a responsibility to be a "good corporate citizen" in the environments in which it operates.	Invests in potentially significant product or service developments and/or adaptations to meet local needs.	Committed to caring for its employees and developing their skills. Actively engages local sources, using its buyer power to improve working conditions for employees.	Aims to affect positively those whose lives it touches in communities in which it operates.	Sets its standard of behavior above minimum local legal requirements. Conforms to higher international standards (e.g., set by ILO or UNESCO).	An observer: NGO may be neutral or partially engaged with MNE. Limited mutual trust.
Transformative *Commits to leading initiatives to bring life-enhancing changes to the broader society.*	Persuades investors of the need for companies to be part of the solution by bringing their resources to bear on the root causes of problems.	Believes that by helping move people out of poverty, it will create stability and goodwill and help grow the world's customer base. Develops products or services specifically to meet local needs.	Committed to upgrading the lives of its employees, inside and outside the workplace. Brings work standard–compliant local suppliers into global supply chain networks.	Leads in developing the quality of life in the broad community (e.g., upgrading health, education).	Actively raises local standards (e.g., transferring developed world workplace health and safety standards.) Supports change agenda of international agencies (e.g., WHO, UNESCO).	A partner: NGO works with and supports the MNE working toward the same objectives.

Case 8-1   IKEA's Global Sourcing Challenge: Indian Rugs and Child Labor (A)

In May 1995, Marianne Barner faced a tough decision. After just two years with IKEA, the world's largest furniture retailer, and just two months into her new job as business area manager for carpets, she was faced with a decision of cutting off one of the company's major suppliers of Indian rugs. While such a move would disrupt supply and affect sales, she found the reasons to do so quite compelling. A German TV station had just broadcast an investigative report naming the supplier as one that used child labor in the production of rugs made for IKEA. What frustrated Barner was that, like all other IKEA suppliers, this large, well-regarded company had recently signed an addendum to its supply contract explicitly forbidding the use of child labor on pain of termination.

Even more difficult than this short-term decision was the long-term action Barner knew IKEA must take on this issue. On one hand, she was being urged to sign up to an industry-wide response to growing concerns about the use of child labor in the Indian carpet industry. A recently formed partnership of manufacturers, importers, retailers, and Indian NGOs was proposing to issue and monitor the use of "Rugmark," a label to be put on carpets certifying that they were made without child labor. Simultaneously, Barner had been having conversations with people at the Swedish Save the Children organization who were urging IKEA to ensure that its response to the situation was "in the best interest of the child"—whatever that might imply. Finally,

there were some who wondered if IKEA should just leave this hornet's nest. Indian rugs accounted for a tiny part of IKEA's turnover, and to these observers, the time, cost, and reputation risk posed by continuing this product line seemed not to be worth the profit potential.

The Birth and Maturing of a Global Company[1]

To understand IKEA's operations, one had to understand the philosophy and beliefs of its 70-year-old founder, Ingvar Kamprad. Despite stepping down as CEO in 1986, almost a decade later, Kamprad retained the title of honorary chairman and was still very involved in the company's activities. Yet perhaps even more powerful than his ongoing presence were his strongly-held values and beliefs that long ago had been deeply embedded in IKEA's culture.

Kamprad was 17 years old when he started the mail-order company he called IKEA, a name that combined his initials with those of his family farm, Elmtaryd, and parish, Agunnaryd, located in the forests of southern Sweden. Working out of the family kitchen, he sold goods such as fountain pens, cigarette lighters and binders which he purchased from low priced sources and then advertised in a newsletter to local shopkeepers. When Kamprad matched his competitors by adding furniture to his newsletter in 1948, the immediate success of the new line led him to give up the small items.

In 1951, to reduce product returns, he opened a display store in nearby Älmhult village to allow customers to inspect products before buying. It was an immediate success, with customers traveling seven hours from the capital Stockholm by train to

Professor Christopher A. Bartlett, Executive Director of the HBS Europe Research Center Vincent Dessain and Research Associate Anders Sjöman prepared this case. Some supplier names and company information has been disguised for confidentiality. HBS cases are developed solely as the basis for class discussion. Cases are not intended to serve as endorsements, sources of primary data, or illustrations of effective or ineffective management.

[1]This section draws on company histories detailed in Bertil Torekull, *Leading by Design–The IKEA Story* (New York: Harper Business, 1998), and on the IKEA Web site, available at http://www.ikea.com/ms/en_GB/about_ikea/splash.html, accessed October 5, 2005.

visit. Based on the store's success, IKEA stopped accepting mail orders. Later Kamprad reflected, "The basis of the modern IKEA concept was created [at this time] and in principle it still applies. First and foremost, we use a catalog to tempt people to visit an exhibition, which today is our store. . . . Then, catalog in hand, customers can see simple interiors for themselves, touch the furniture they want to buy and then write out an order."[2]

As Kamprad developed and refined his furniture retailing business model he became increasingly frustrated with the way a tightly knit cartel of furniture manufacturers controlled the Swedish industry to keep prices high. He began to view the situation not just as a business opportunity but also as an unacceptable social problem that he wanted to correct. Foreshadowing a vision for IKEA that would later be articulated as "creating a better life for the many people," he wrote:

> A disproportionately large part of all resources is used to satisfy a small part of the population. . . . IKEA's aim is to change this situation. We shall offer a wide range of home furnishing items of good design and function at prices so low that the majority of people can afford to buy them. . . . We have great ambitions.[3]

The small newsletter soon expanded into a full catalog. The 1953 issue introduced what would become another key IKEA feature: self-assembled furniture. Instead of buying complete pieces of furniture, customers bought them in flat packages and put them together themselves at home. Soon, the "knockdown" concept was fully systemized, saving transport and storage costs. In typical fashion, Kamprad turned the savings into still lower prices for his customers, gaining an even larger following among young post-War householders looking for well designed but inexpensive furniture. Between 1953 and 1955, the company's sales doubled from SEK 3 million to SEK 6 million.[4]

Managing Suppliers: Developing Sourcing Principles

As its sales took off in the late 1950s, IKEA's radically new concepts began to encounter stiff opposition from Sweden's large furniture retailers. So threatened were they that when IKEA began exhibiting at trade fairs, they colluded to stop the company from taking orders at the fairs, and eventually even from showing its prices. The cartel also pressured manufacturers not to sell to IKEA, and the few that continued to do so often made their deliveries at night in unmarked vans.

Unable to meet demand with such constrained local supply, Kamprad was forced to look abroad for new sources. In 1961, he contracted with several furniture factories in Poland, a country still in the Communist eastern block. To assure quality output and reliable delivery, IKEA brought its know-how, taught its processes, and even provided machinery to the new suppliers, revitalizing Poland's furniture industry as it did so. Poland soon became IKEA's largest source and, to Kamprad's delight, at much lower costs—once again allowing him to reduce his prices.

Following its success in Poland, IKEA adopted a general procurement principle that it should not own its means of production but should seek to develop close ties by supporting its suppliers in a long-term relationship.[5] Beyond supply contracts and technology transfer, the relationship led IKEA to make loans to its suppliers at reasonable rates, repayable through future shipments. "Our objective is to develop long-term business partners," explained a senior purchasing manager. "We commit to doing all we can to keep them competitive—as long as they remain equally committed to us. We are in this for the long run."

---

[2]Ingvar Kamprad, as quoted in Bertil Torekull, *Leading by Design–The IKEA Story,* New York: Harper Business, 1998, page 25.

[3]Quoted in Christopher A. Bartlett and Ashish Nanda, "Ingvar Kamprad and IKEA," HBS No. 390-132 (Boston: Harvard Business School Publishing, 1990).

[4]Ibid.

[5]This policy was modified after a number of East European suppliers broke their contracts with IKEA after the fall of the Berlin Wall opened new markets for them. IKEA's subsequent supply chain problems and loss of substantial investments led management to develop an internal production company, Swedwood, to ensure delivery stability. However, it was decided that only a limited amount of IKEA's purchases (perhaps 10%) should be sourced from Swedwood.

Although the relationship between IKEA and its suppliers was often described as one of mutual dependency, suppliers also knew that they had to remain competitive to keep their contract. From the outset they understood that if a more cost-effective alternative appeared, IKEA would try to help them respond, but if they could not do so, it would move production.

In its constant quest to lower prices, the company developed an unusual way of identifying new sources. As a veteran IKEA manager explained: "We do not buy products from our suppliers. We buy unused production capacity." It was a philosophy that often led its purchasing managers to seek out seasonal manufacturers with spare off-season capacity. There were many classic examples of how IKEA matched products to supplier capabilities: they had sail makers make seat cushions, window factories produce table frames, and ski manufacturers build chairs in their off-season. "We've always worried more about finding the right management at our suppliers than finding hi-tech facilities. We will always help good management to develop their capacity."

Growing Retail: Expanding Abroad   Building on the success of his first store, Kamprad self-financed a store in Stockholm in 1965. Recognizing a growing use of automobiles in Sweden, he bucked the practice of having a downtown showroom and opted for a suburban location with ample parking space. When customers drove home with their furniture in flat packed boxes, they assumed two of the costliest part of traditional furniture retailing—home delivery and assembly.

In 1963, even before the Stockholm store had opened, IKEA had expanded into Oslo, Norway. A decade later, Switzerland became its first non-Scandinavian market, and in 1974 IKEA entered Germany which soon became its largest market. (See **Exhibit 1** for IKEA's worldwide expansion.) At each new store the same simple Scandinavian-design products were backed up with a catalog and off-beat advertising, presenting the company as "those impossible Swedes with strange ideas."

Exhibit 1   IKEA Stores, Fiscal Year Ending August 1994

a. Historical Store Growth

	1954	1964	1974	1984	1994
Number of Stores	0	2	9	52	114

b. Country's First Store

Year	Country	City
1958	Sweden	Älmhult
1963	Norway	Oslo
1969	Denmark	Copenhagen
1973	Switzerland	Zürich
1974	Germany	Munich
1975	Australia	Artamon
1976	Canada	Vancouver
1977	Austria	Vienna
1978	Netherlands	Rotterdam
1978	Singapore	Singapore
1980	Spain	Gran Canaria
1981	Iceland	Reykjavik
1981	France	Paris
1983	Saudi Arabia	Jeddah
1984	Belgium	Brussels
1984	Kuwait	Kuwait City
1985	United States	Philadelphia
1987	United Kingdom	Manchester
1988	Hong Kong	Hong Kong
1989	Italy	Milan
1990	Hungary	Budapest
1991	Poland	Platan
1991	Czech Republic	Prague
1991	United Arab Emirates	Dubai
1992	Slovakia	Bratislava
1994	Taiwan	Taipei

Source: IKEA Web site, http://franchisor.ikea.com/txtfacts.html, accessed 15 October 2004.

And reflecting the company's conservative values, each new entry was financed by previous successes.[6]

[6]By 2005, company lore had it that IKEA had only taken one bank loan in its corporate history—which it had paid back as soon as the cash flow allowed.

During this expansion, the IKEA concept evolved and became increasingly formalized. (**Exhibit 2** summarizes important events in IKEA's corporate history.) It still built large, suburban stores with knock-down furniture in flat packages which the customers brought home to assemble themselves. But as the concept was refined, the company required that each store followed a pre-determined design, set up to maximize customers' exposure to the product range. The concept mandated for instance that the living room interiors should follow immediately after the entrance. IKEA also serviced customers with features such as a play room for children, a low-priced restaurant, and a "Sweden Shop" for groceries that had made IKEA Sweden's leading food exporter. At the same time, the range gradually expanded beyond furniture to include a full line of home furnishing products such as textiles, kitchen utensils, flooring, rugs and carpets, lamps and plants.

The Emerging Culture and Values[7]   As Kamprad's evolving business philosophy was formalized into the IKEA vision statement, "to create a better everyday life for the many people," it became the foundation of the company's strategy of selling affordable, good quality furniture to mass market consumers around the world. The cultural norms and values that developed to support the strategy's implementation was also, in many ways, an extension of Kamprad's personal beliefs and style. "The true IKEA spirit," he remarked, "is founded on our enthusiasm, our constant will to renew, on our cost-consciousness, on our willingness to assume responsibility and to help, on our humbleness before the task, and on the simplicity of our behavior." As well as a summary of his aspiration for the company's behavioral norms, it was also a good statement of Kamprad's own personal management style.

---

[7]This section draws on Christopher A. Bartlett and Ashish Nanda, "Ingvar Kamprad and IKEA," HBS No. 390-132 (Boston: Harvard Business School Publishing, 1990).

Exhibit 2   IKEA History: Selected Events

Year	Event
1943	IKEA is founded. Ingvar Kamprad constructs the company name from his initials (**I**ngvar **K**amprad), his home farm (**E**lmtaryd), and its parish (**A**gunnaryd).
1945	The first IKEA ad appears in press, advertising mail order products.
1948	Furniture is introduced into the IKEA product range.
1951	The first IKEA catalogue is distributed.
1955	IKEA starts to design its own furniture.
1956	Self-assembly furniture in flat packs is introduced.
1958	The first IKEA store opens in Älmhult, Sweden.
1961	Contract with Polish sources, IKEA's first non-Scandinavian suppliers. First delivery is 20,000 chairs.
1963	The first IKEA store outside Sweden opens in Norway.
1965	IKEA opens in Stockholm, introducing the self-serve concept to furniture retailing.
1965	IKEA stores add a section called the "The Cook Shop," offering quality utensils at low prices.
1973	The first IKEA store outside Scandinavia opens in Spreitenbach, Switzerland.
1974	A plastic chair developed at a supplier that usually made buckets.
1978	The BILLY bookcase is introduced to the range, becoming an instant top seller.
1980	One of IKEA's best-sellers, the KLIPPAN sofa with removable, washable covers, is introduced.
1980	Introduction of LACK coffee table, made from a strong, light material by an interior door factory.
1985	The first IKEA Group store opens in the US
1985	MOMENT sofa with frame built by a supermarket trolley factory is introduced. Wins a design prize.
1991	IKEA establishes its own industrial group, Swedwood

Source: Adapted from IKEA Facts and Figures, 2003 and 2004 editions and IKEA internal documents.

Over the years a very distinct organization culture and management style emerged in IKEA reflecting these values. For example, the company operated very informally as evidenced by the open-plan office landscape, where even the CEO did not have a separate office, and the familiar and personal way all employees addressed each other. But that informality often masked an intensity that derived from the organization's high self-imposed standards. As one senior executive explained, "Because there is no security available behind status or closed doors, this environment actually puts pressure on people to perform."

The IKEA management process also stressed simplicity and attention to detail. "Complicated rules paralyze!" said Kamprad. The company organized "anti-bureaucrat week" every year, requiring all managers to spend time working in a store to re-establish contact with the front line and the consumer. The work pace was such that executives joked that IKEA believed in "management by running around."

Cost consciousness was another strong part of the management culture. "Waste of resources," said Kamprad, "is a mortal sin at IKEA. Expensive solutions are often signs of mediocrity, and an idea without a price tag is never acceptable." Although cost consciousness extended into all aspects of the operation, travel and entertainment expenses were particularly sensitive. "We do not set any price on time," remarked an executive, recalling that he had once phoned Kamprad to get approval to fly first class. He explained that economy class was full, and that he had an urgent appointment to keep. "There is no first class in IKEA," Kamprad had replied. "Perhaps you should go by car." The executive completed the 350-mile trip by taxi.

The search for creative solutions was also highly prized with IKEA. Kamprad had written, "Only while sleeping one makes no mistakes. The fear of making mistakes is the root of bureaucracy and the enemy of all evolution." Though planning for the future was encouraged, over-analysis was not. "Exaggerated planning can be fatal." Kamprad

advised his executives. "Let simplicity and common sense characterize your planning."

In 1976, Kamprad felt the need to commit to paper the values that had developed in IKEA during the previous decades. His thesis, *Testament of a Furniture Dealer,* became an important means for spreading the IKEA philosophy particularly during its period of rapid international expansion. (Extracts of the *Testament* are given in **Exhibit 3.**) Specially trained "IKEA ambassadors" were assigned to key positions in all units to spread the company's philosophy and values by educating their subordinates and by acting as role models.

In 1986, when Kamprad stepped down, Anders Moberg, a company veteran who had once been Kamprad's personal assistant, took over as President and CEO. But Kamprad remained intimately involved as chairman, and his influence extended well beyond the ongoing daily operations: he was the self-appointed guardian of IKEA's deeply embedded culture and values.

Waking Up to Environmental and Social Issues

By the mid 1990s, IKEA was the world's largest specialized furniture retailer. Sales for the IKEA Group for the financial year ending August 1994 totaled SEK 35 billion (about $4.5 billion). In the previous year, more than 116 million people had visited one of the 98 IKEA stores in 17 countries, most of them drawn there by the company's product catalog which was printed yearly in 72 million copies in 34 languages. The privately held company did not report profit levels, but one estimate put its net margin at 8.4% in 1994, yielding a net profit of SEK 2.9 billion (about $375 million).[8]

After decades of seeking new sources, in the mid-1990s IKEA worked with almost 2,300 suppliers in 70 countries, sourcing a range of around 11,200 products. Its relationship with its suppliers was dominated by commercial issues, and its 24 trading service offices in 19 countries primarily

[8]Estimation in Bo Pettersson, "Han släpper aldrig taget," *Veckans Affärer,* March 1, 2004, pp. 30–48.

Exhibit 3   "A Furniture Dealer's Testament"—A Summarized Overview

In 1976, Ingvar Kamprad listed nine aspects of IKEA that he believed formed the basis of the IKEA culture together with the vision statement "To create a better everyday life for the many people." These aspects are given to all new employees a pamphlet titled "A Furniture Dealer's Testament." The following table summarizes the major points:

Cornerstone	Summarized Description
1. The Product Range—Our Identity	IKEA sells well-designed, functional home furnishing products at prices so low that as many people as possible can afford them.
2. The IKEA Spirit—A Strong and Living Reality	IKEA is about enthusiasm, renewal, thrift, responsibility, humbleness toward the task and simplicity.
3. Profit Gives Us Resources	IKEA will achieve profit (which Kamprad describes as a "wonderful word") through the lowest prices, good quality, economical development of products, improved purchasing processes and cost savings.
4. Reaching Good Results with Small Means	"Waste is a deadly sin."
5. Simplicity is a Virtue	Complex regulations and exaggerated planning paralyze. IKEA people stay simple in style and habits as well as in their organizational approach.
6. Doing it a Different Way	IKEA is run from a small village in the woods. IKEA asks shirt factories to make seat cushions and window factories to make table frames. IKEA discounts its umbrellas when it rains. IKEA does things differently.
7. Concentration—Important to Our Success	"We can never do everything everywhere, all at the same time." At IKEA, you choose the most important thing to do and finish that before starting a new project.
8. Taking Responsibility—A Privilege	"The fear of making mistakes is the root of bureaucracy." Everyone has the right to make mistakes; in fact, everyone has obligation to make mistakes.
9. Most Things Still Remain to be Done. A Glorious Future!	IKEA is only at the beginning of what it might become. 200 stores is nothing. "We are still a small company at heart."

Source: Adapted by case writers from IKEA's "A Furniture Dealer's Testament"; Bertil Torekull, *Leading by Design: The IKEA Story,* New York: Harper Business, 1998, page 112; and own interviews.

monitored production, tested new product ideas, negotiated prices, and checked quality. (See **Exhibit 4** for selected IKEA figures in 1994.) That relationship began to change during the 1980s, however, when environmental problems emerged with some of its products. And it was even more severely challenged in the mid 1990s when accusations of IKEA suppliers using child labor surfaced.

The Environmental Wake-Up: Formaldehyde
In the early 1980s, Danish authorities passed regulations to define limits for formaldehyde emissions permissible in building products. The chemical compound was used as binding glue in materials such as plywood and particleboard, and often seeped out as gas. At concentrations above 0.1 mg/kg in the air, it could cause watery eyes, headaches, a burning sensation in the throat and difficulty breathing.[9] With IKEA's profile as a leading local furniture retailer using particleboard in many of its products, it became a prime target for regulators wanting to publicize the new standards. So when tests showed that some IKEA products emitted more formaldehyde than was allowed by legislation, the case was

---

[9]Description of formaldehyde based on "Formaldehyde" entry on public encyclopedia Wikipedia, available at http://en.wikipedia.org/wiki/Formaldehyde, accessed October 5, 2005.

Exhibit 4   IKEA in Figures 1993/94 (Fiscal Year Ending August 31, 1994)

a. Sales

Country/Region	SEK Billion	Percentage
Germany	10.4	29.70%
Sweden	3.9	11.20%
Austria, France, Italy, Switzerland	7.7	21.90%
Belgium, Netherlands, United Kingdom, Norway	7.3	20.80%
North America (USA and Canada)	4.9	13.90%
Czech Republic, Hungary, Poland, Slovakia	0.5	1.50%
Australia	0.4	1.00%
	35.0	

b. Purchasing

Country/Region	Percentage
Nordic Countries	33.4%
East and Central Europe	14.3%
Rest of Europe	29.6%
Rest of the World	22.7%

Source: IKEA Facts and Figures 1994.

widely publicized and the company was fined. More significantly—and the real lesson for IKEA—was that due to the publicity, its sales dropped 20% in Denmark.

In response to this situation, the company quickly established stringent requirements regarding formaldehyde emissions, but soon found that suppliers were failing to meet its standards. The problem was that most of its suppliers bought from sub-suppliers, who in turn bought the binding materials from glue manufacturers. Eventually, IKEA decided it would have to work directly with the glue producing chemical companies, and with the collaboration of companies such as ICI and BASF, soon found ways to reduce the formaldehyde off-gassing in its products.[10]

A decade later, however, the formaldehyde problem returned. In 1992, an investigative team from a large German newspaper and TV company found that IKEA's best-selling bookcase series, Billy, had emissions higher than German legislation allowed. This time however, the source of the problem was not the glue but the lacquer on the bookshelves. In the wake of headlines describing "deadly poisoned bookshelves," IKEA immediately stopped both the production and sales of Billy bookcases worldwide and corrected the problem before resuming distribution. Not counting the cost of lost sales and production or the damage to goodwill, the Billy incident was estimated to have cost IKEA $6 to $7 million.[11]

These events prompted IKEA to address broader environmental concerns more directly. Since wood was the principal material in about half of all IKEA products, forestry became a natural starting point. Following discussions with both Greenpeace and WWF (formerly World Wildlife Fund, now World Wide Fund for Nature), and using standards set by the Forest Stewardship Council, IKEA established a forestry policy stating that IKEA would not accept any timber, veneer, plywood or layer-glued wood from intact natural forests or from forests with a high conservation value. This meant that IKEA had to be willing to take on the task of tracing all wood used in IKEA products back to its source.[12] To monitor compliance, the company appointed forest managers to carry out random checks of wood suppliers and run projects on responsible forestry around the world.

[10]Based on case study by The Natural Step, "Organizational Case Summary: IKEA," available at http://www.naturalstep.org/learn/docs/cs/case_ikea.pdf, accessed October 5, 2005.

[11]Ibid.

[12]"IKEA—Social and Environmental Responsibility Report 2004", p. 33, available at http://www.ikea-group.ikea.com/corporate/PDF/IKEA_SaER.pdf, accessed October 5, 2005.

In addition to forestry, IKEA identified four other areas where environmental criteria were to be applied to its business operations: adapting the product range; working with suppliers; transport and distribution; and ensuring environmentally conscious stores. For instance, in 1992, the company began using chlorine-free recycled paper in its catalogs; it redesigned the best-selling OGLA chair—originally manufactured from beech—so it could be made using waste material from yogurt cup production; and it redefined its packaging principles to eliminate any use of PVC. The company also maintained its partnership with WWF, resulting in numerous projects on global conservation, and funded a Global Forest Watch program to map intact natural forests worldwide. In addition, it engaged in an ongoing dialogue with Greenpeace on forestry.[13]

The Social Wake-Up: Child Labor   In 1994, as IKEA was still working to resolve the formaldehyde problems, a Swedish television documentary showed children in Pakistan working at weaving looms. Among the several Swedish companies mentioned in the film as importers of carpets from Pakistan, IKEA was the only high profile name on the list. As IKEA's newly appointed business area manager for carpets, Marianne Barner recalled the shockwaves that the TV program sent through the company:

> The use of child labor was not a high profile public issue at the time. In fact, the UN Convention on the Rights of the Child had only been published in December, 1989. So, media attention like this TV program had an important role to play in raising awareness on a topic not well known and understood—including at IKEA. . . . We were caught completely unaware. It was not something we had been paying attention to. For example, I had spent a couple of months in India learning about trading, but got no exposure to child labor. Our buyers met suppliers in their city offices and rarely got out to where production took place. . . . Our immediate response to the

program was to apologize for our ignorance and acknowledge that we were not in full control of this problem. But we also committed to do something about it.

As part of its response, IKEA sent a legal team to Geneva to seek input and advice from the International Labor Organization (ILO) on how to deal with the problem. They learned that Convention 138, adopted by the ILO in 1973 and ratified by 120 countries, committed ratifying countries to working for the abolition of labor by children under 15 or the age of compulsory schooling in that country. India, Pakistan, and Nepal were not signatories to the convention.[14] Following these discussions with the ILO, IKEA added a clause to all supply contracts—a "black-and-white" clause as Barner put it—stating simply that if the supplier employed children under legal working age, the contract would be cancelled.

To take the load off field trading managers and to provide some independence to the monitoring process, the company appointed a third party agent to monitor child labor practices at its suppliers in India and Pakistan. Because this type of external monitoring was very unusual, IKEA had some difficulty locating a reputable and competent company to perform the task. Finally, they appointed a well-known Scandinavian company with extensive experience in providing external monitoring of companies' quality assurance programs, and gave them the mandate not only to investigate complaints but also to undertake random audits of child labor practices at supplies' factories.

Early Lessons: A Deeply Embedded Problem   With India being the biggest purchasing source for carpets and rugs, Barner contacted Swedish Save the Children, UNICEF and the ILO to expand her understanding and to get advice about

---

[13]Ibid, pp. 19–20.

[14]Ratification statistics available on ILO Web site, page titled "Convention No. C138 was ratified by 142 countries," available at http://www.ilo.org/ilolex/cgi-lex/ratifce.pl?C138, accessed December 4, 2005.

the issue of child labor, especially in South Asia. She soon found that hard data was often elusive. While estimates of child labor in India varied from the government's 1991 census figure of 11.3 million children under 15 working[15] to Human Rights Watch's estimate of between 60 and 115 million child laborers,[16] it was clear that a very large number of Indian children as young as 5 years old worked in agriculture, mining, quarrying, and manufacturing, as well as acting as household servants, street vendors, or beggars. Of this total, an estimated 200,000 were employed in the carpet industry, working on looms in large factories, small sub-contractors, and in homes where whole families worked on looms to earn extra income.[17]

Children could be bonded—essentially placed in servitude—in order to pay off debts incurred by their parents, typically in the range of 1000 to 10,000 rupees ($30 to $300). But due to the astronomical interest rates and the very low wages offered to children, it could take years to pay off such loans. Indeed, some indentured child laborers eventually passed on the debt to their own children. The Indian government stated that it was committed to the abolition of bonded labor which had been illegal since the Children (Pledging of Labour) Act passed under British rule in 1933. The practice continued to be widespread, however, and to reinforce the earlier law, the government passed the Bonded Labour System (Abolition) Act in 1976.[18]

But the government took a less absolute stand on unbonded child labor which it characterized as "a socio-economic phenomenon arising out of poverty and the lack of development." The Child Labour (Prohibition and Regulation) Act of 1986 prohibited the use of child labor (applying to those under 14) in certain defined "hazardous industries," and regulated children's hours and working conditions in others. But the government felt that the majority of child labor involved "children working alongside and under the supervision of their parents" in agriculture, cottage industries, and service roles. Indeed, the law specifically permitted children to work in craft industries "in order not to outlaw the passage of specialized handicraft skills from generation to generation."[19] Critics charged that even with these laws on the books, exploitive child labor—including bonded labor—was widespread because laws were poorly enforced and prosecution rarely severe.[20]

Action Required: New Issues, New Options

In the fall of 1994, after managing the initial response to the crisis, Barner and her direct manager traveled to India, Nepal and Pakistan to learn more. Barner recalled the trip: "We felt the need to educate ourselves, so we met with our suppliers. But we also met with unions, politicians, activists, NGOs, UN organizations and carpet export organizations. We even went out on unannounced carpet factory raids with local NGOs; we saw child labor and we were thrown out of some places."

On the trip, Barner also learned of the formation of the Rugmark Foundation, a recently initiated industry response to the child labor problem in the Indian carpet industry. Triggered by a consumer awareness program started by human rights organizations, consumer activists, and trade unions in Germany in the early 1990s, the Indo-German Export Promotion Council had joined up with key

[15]Indian Government Policy Statements, "Child Labor and India," available at http://www.indianembassy.org/policy/Child_Labor/childlabor_2000.htm, accessed October 1, 2005.

[16]Human Rights Watch figures, available at http://www.hrw.org/reports/1996/India3.htm, accessed October 1, 2005.

[17]Country Reports in Human Rights, U.S. State Department, February 2000, available at http://www.state.gov/g/drl/rls/hrrpt/2000/, accessed October 1, 2005.

[18]Indian Government Policy Statements, "Child Labor and India," available at http://www.indianembassy.org/policy/Child_Labor/childlabor_2000.htm, accessed October 1, 2005.

[19]Ibid.

[20]Human Rights Watch data, available at http://www.hrw.org/reports/1996/India3.htm, accessed October 1, 2005.

Indian carpet manufacturers and exporters and some Indian NGOs to develop a label certifying that the hand-knotted carpet to which it was attached was made without the use of child labor. To implement this idea, the Rugmark Foundation was organized to supervise the use of the label. It expected to begin exporting rugs carrying a unique identifying number in early 1995. As a major purchaser of Indian rugs, IKEA was invited to sign up to Rugmark as a way of dealing with the ongoing potential for child labor problems on products sourced from India.

On her return to Sweden, Barner again met frequently with Swedish Save the Children's expert on child labor. "The people there had a very forward looking view on the issue, and taught us a lot," said Barner. "Above all, they emphasized the need to ensure you always do what is in the best interests of the child." This was the principle set at the heart of the U.N. Convention on the Rights of the Child (1989), a document with which Barner was now quite familiar. (See **Exhibit 5** for Article 32 from the U.N. Conventions on the Right of the Child.)

The more Barner learned the more complex the situation became. As a business area manager with full P&L responsibility for carpets, she knew she had to protect not only her business, but also the IKEA brand and image. Yet she viewed her responsibility as broader than this: She felt the company should do something that would make a difference in the lives of the children she had seen. It was a view that was not universally held within IKEA where many were concerned that a very proactive stand could put the business at a significant cost disadvantage to its competitors.

A New Crisis   Then, in the spring of 1995, a year after IKEA began to address this issue, a well-known German documentary maker notified the company that a film he had made was about to be broadcast on German television showing children working at looms at Rangan Exports, one of IKEA's major suppliers. While refusing to let the company preview the video, the film maker produced still shots taken directly from the video. The producer then invited IKEA to send someone to take part in a live discussion during the airing of the program. Said Barner, "Compared to the Swedish program which documented the use of child labor in Pakistan as a serious report about an important issue, without targeting any single company, it was immediately clear that this German-produced program planned to take a confrontational and aggressive approach aimed directly at IKEA and one of its suppliers."

For Barner, the first question was whether to recommend that IKEA participate in the program, or decline the invitation. Beyond the immediate public relations issue, she also had to decide how to deal with Rangan Exports' apparent violation

---

Exhibit 5   The U.N. Convention on the Rights of the Child: Article 32

States Parties recognize the right of the child to be protected from economic exploitation and from performing any work that is likely to be hazardous or to interfere with the child's education, or to be harmful to the child's health or physical, mental, spiritual, moral, or social development.

States Parties shall take legislative, administrative, social, and educational measures to ensure the implementation of the present article. To this end, and having regard to the relevant provisions of other international instruments, States Parties shall in particular:

a.   Provide for a minimum age for admission to employment.
b.   Provide for appropriate regulation of hours and conditions of employment.
c.   Provide for appropriate or other sanctions to ensure the effective enforcement of the present article.

Source: Excerpt from "Conventions on the Right of the Child," from the Web site of the Office of the United Nations High Commissioner for Human Rights, available at http://www.unhchr.ch/html/menu3/b/k2crc.htm, accessed October 2005.

of the contractual commitment it had made not to use child labor. And finally, this crisis raised the issue of whether the overall approach IKEA had been taking to the issue of child labor was appropriate. Should the company continue to try to deal with the issue through its own relationships with its suppliers? Should it step back and allow Rugmark to monitor the use of child labor on its behalf? Or should it recognize that the problem was too deeply embedded in the culture of these countries for it to have any real impact, and simply withdraw?

Case 8-2   Genzyme's Gaucher Initiative: Global Risk and Responsibility

In May 2001, Tomye Tierney faced a big decision on an important initiative she had helped create almost three years earlier. Since 1998, Genzyme Corporation's Gaucher Initiative had been providing the company's life-saving drug Cerezyme®[1] to sufferers of Gaucher disease worldwide, regardless of their ability to pay. But now Tierney faced a decision that would determine the future of the bold experiment. Established as a partnership with the respected humanitarian organization Project HOPE, the Gaucher Initiative had been very effective in locating and treating Gaucher patients in many less developed countries and had built a particularly strong program in Egypt. However, Genzyme's sales organization was becoming increasingly concerned that the fast-growing free distribution program in Egypt represented a barrier to their commercial objectives.

Although the company had grown rapidly in recent years, the high-risk biotech business required that it manage its resources carefully. (**Exhibits 1** and **2** summarize Genzyme's financial history.) From the outset, therefore, Genzyme CEO Henri Termeer had told Tierney that the company's commitment to universal provision could not undermine its commercial viability. Specifically, he emphasized that the Gaucher Initiative was not to be viewed as a permanent solution to providing care in any country. Recognizing this, Tierney wondered if the time had come to transfer the care of these patients to the government of Egypt. What if it refused to accept the responsibility? What if Project HOPE was unwilling to scale back its activities? In short, how exactly could the company balance the strong humanitarian and commercial principles it had built into its culture and values?

Birth of a Company

In contrast to other biotechnology firms that burst on the scene with impressive science-based, discovery-driven business models, Genzyme began by focusing on supplying raw materials—enzymes, fine chemicals, and reagents—to large research labs and pharmaceutical companies. Company co-founder Henry Blair had worked at the New England Enzyme Center of Tufts University School of Medicine and had many contacts in the research community. He founded the company in 1981 on

▌ Professor Christopher A. Bartlett and Research Associate Andrew N. McLean prepared this case. HBS cases are developed solely as the basis for class discussion. Cases are not intended to serve as endorsements, sources of primary data, or illustrations of effective or ineffective management. Certain names and data have been disguised.

▌ [1]Genzyme®, Cerezyme®, and Ceredase® are registered trademarks of Genzyme Corporation. All rights reserved.

Exhibit 1 Genzyme Corp. Selected Consolidated Balance Sheets ($000s)

Year ending December 31	2000	1999	1998	1997	1996	1991	1986	1981[a]
Assets:								
Current assets								
Cash and equivalents	$ 236,213	$ 130,156	$ 118,612	$ 102,406	$ 93,132	$ 29,031	$ 2,309	$ 828
Short-term investments	104,586	255,846	175,453	51,259	56,608	78,147	19,496	—
Accounts receivable	205,094	166,803	163,042	118,277	116,833	31,838	2,728	—
Inventories	170,341	117,269	109,833	139,681	125,265	16,329	4,243	—
Prepaid expenses & other	37,681	18,918	31,467	17,361	100,287	3,688	299	—
Deferred tax assets—current	46,836	41,195	41,195	27,601	17,493	—	—	—
Non-current assets								
Net property, plant & equipment	504,412	383,181	382,619	385,348	393,839	32,057	4,020	—
Long-term investments	298,841	266,988	281,664	92,676	38,215	172,529	—	—
Notes receivable—related party	10,350	—	—	2,019	—	4,000	—	—
Net intangibles	1,539,782	253,153	279,516	271,275	247,745	13,362	—	—
Deferred tax assets—non-current	—	18,631	24,277	29,479	42,221	4,186	—	—
Investments in equity securities	121,251	97,859	51,977	30,047	—	—	—	—
Other non-current assets	42,713	37,283	30,669	28,024	38,870	5,371	—	2,098
TOTAL ASSETS	$3,318,100	$1,787,282	$1,690,324	$1,295,453	$1,270,508	$390,538	$33,095	$2,926
Liabilities and stockholders' equity:								
Current liabilities								
Accounts payable	$ 26,165	$ 27,853	$ 27,604	$ 19,787	$ 22,271	$ 4,584	$ 1,004	$ 382
Accrued expenses	139,683	73,359	72,370	72,103	70,124	10,964	548	476
Payable to joint venture	—	—	1,181	—	—	—	—	—
Income taxes payable	46,745	27,946	16,543	11,168	17,926	4,305	—	—
Deferred revenue	8,609	3,700	2,731	1,800	2,693	1,987	—	—
Current LT debt and lease obligations	19,897	5,080	100,568	905	999	1,484	225	—
Non-current liabilities								
Long-term debt and lease obligations	391,560	18,000	3,087	140,978	241,998	101,044	162	—
Convertible notes and debentures	273,680	272,622	284,138	29,298	—	—	—	—
Deferred tax liability	230,384	—	8,078	—	—	—	176	—
Other non-current liabilities	6,236	2,330	—	7,364	12,188	6,298	—	1,924
TOTAL LIABILITIES	$1,142,959	$ 430,890	$ 516,300	$ 283,403	$ 368,199	$130,666	$ 2,115	$2,782
Stockholders' equity	2,175,141	1,356,392	1,172,554	1,012,050	902,309	259,872	30,979	180
	$3,318,100	$1,787,282	$1,688,854	$1,295,453	$1,270,508	$390,538	$33,094	$2,962

Source: Adapted by casewriters from Genzyme Corp. Annual Reports.

[a] 1981 results cover the period from company inception on June 8, 1981. (Source: Genzyme 1986 IPO Prospectus.)

Exhibit 2 Genzyme Corp. Selected Consolidated Income Statement ($ooos)

Year ending December 31	2000	1999	1998	1997	1996	1991	1986	1981[a]
Revenues:								
Product sales	$811,897	$683,482	$613,685	$529,927	$424,483	$72,019	$9,770	$2,167
Service sales	84,482	79,448	74,791	67,158	68,950	21,503	—	—
Revenue from R&D contracts	6,941	9,358	20,859	11,756	25,321	28,394	2,366	—
TOTAL REVENUES	$903,320	$772,288	$709,335	$608,841	$518,754	$121,916	$12,136	$2,167
Expenses:								
Cost of products sold	$232,383	$182,337	$211,076	$206,028	$155,930	$33,164	$5,421	$936
Cost of services sold	50,177	49,444	48,586	47,289	54,082	14,169	—	—
Selling, admin. & general	264,551	242,797	215,203	200,476	162,264	39,118	5,084	838
Research and development	169,478	150,516	119,005	89,558	80,849	27,232	2,285	57
Purchase of in-process R&D	200,191	5,436	—	7,000	130,639	—	—	—
Charge for impaired asset	4,321	—	—	—	—	—	—	—
Amortization of intangibles	22,974	24,674	24,334	17,245	8,849	—	—	—
TOTAL EXPENSES	$944,075	$655,204	$618,204	$567,596	$592,613	$113,683	$12,790	$1,831
Income (loss) before unusual items	($40,755)	$117,084	$91,131	$41,245	($73,859)	$8,233	($654)	$336
Investment income	$45,593	$36,158	$25,055	$11,409	$15,341	$12,371	$889	—
Interest expense	(15,710)	(21,771)	(22,593)	(12,667)	(6,990)	(2,088)	(194)	(92)
Equity in net loss of unconsolidated affiliates	(44,965)	(42,696)	(29,006)	(12,258)	(5,373)	—	—	—
Affiliate sale of stock	22,689	6,683	2,369	—	1,013	—	—	—
Sale of equity securities	15,873	(3,749)	(6)	—	1,711	—	—	—
Minority interest	4,625	3,674	4,285	—	—	—	—	—
Sale of product line	—	—	—	—	—	4,065	—	—
Sale of Gene-Trak	—	—	—	—	—	8,387	—	—
Credit from operating loss carry forward	—	—	31,202	—	—	—	—	—
Other revenue (expense)	5,188	14,527	—	(2,000)	(1,465)	2,726	—	—
Income (loss) before income taxes	($7,462)	$117,928	$102,437	$25,729	($69,622)	$33,694	$41	$244
Provision for income taxes	(55,478)	(46,947)	(39,870)	(12,100)	(3,195)	(12,848)	0	(165)
NET INCOME (LOSS)	($62,940)	$70,981	$62,567	$13,629	($72,817)	$20,846	$41	$79

Source: Adapted by casewriters from Genzyme Corp. Annual Reports.
[a] 1981 results cover the period from company inception on June 8, 1981. (Source: Genzyme 1986 IPO Prospectus.)

the conservative belief that it should use revenues generated by selling reagents to generate cash flow and to create a track record that would allow it to fund further growth.

With a small pilot plant and office in a loft in Boston's Chinatown, Blair began searching for larger facilities to manufacture enzyme factors and reagents on a large scale. Within a year, he had located a company in the United Kingdom that was producing enzymes, substrates, and intermediates. Dissatisfied with the plant's efficiency and quality, Blair personally relocated to England to improve processes and increase yields. Within a few months the plant was profitable, and Genzyme was generating a positive cash flow. Sales in the first year were $2.2 million.

Laying the Foundation   Among all of Genzyme's early supply agreements, one had particular importance. Building on a long-term relationship he had with the National Institutes of Health (NIH), Blair obtained a contract to manufacture and supply the enzyme glucocerebrosidase (GCR) being used by Dr. Roscoe Brady in research on Gaucher (pronounced GO-shay) disease. Gaucher disease is an extremely rare and deadly condition caused by the body's inability to manufacture the GCR enzyme. Cells of the spleen, liver, lymph nodes, and bone marrow need GCR to break down and dispose of fatty residues from red blood cells' normal deterioration processes. Without this enzyme, fats collect and cause pain, fatigue, bone deterioration, fractures, and swelling of the affected organs.

Current estimates are that one in 400 of the general population carries the genetic mutations that cause Gaucher disease, but because both parents must pass on the mutation for a person to develop the disease, fewer than six of every one million people worldwide are predicted to have Gaucher disease. Of those 20,000 to 30,000 people, only about a quarter were thought to be ill enough to require treatment. (Populations with more intermarriage report a higher incidence of the disease. For example, among Jewish people of Eastern European ancestry, one in every 450 children is affected.) At the time of Brady's research, the treatment of choice was bone marrow transplantation, an extremely costly procedure with a 10% mortality rate.[2]

Throughout most of the 1970s, Brady's efforts to develop an enzyme replacement therapy had been unsuccessful, but in 1978, some members of his research team began suggesting that the large GCR molecule could better enter affected cells if the carbohydrate portion was modified, or "pruned." However, to put this idea into human trials involved expensive and risky protocols, and other team members expressed serious doubt that the modified molecule would work. After years of divisive internal debate, the NIH team put the "pruned molecule" hypothesis to the test in 1983. In its support role, Genzyme developed a production process for the enzyme required for the trials.

New Management, New Priorities   Meanwhile, Genzyme's top management was in transition. While Blair had been cleaning up the U.K. production processes, company co-founder Sheridan (Sherry) Snyder had been managing the financial and administrative side of the start-up. Although he had a background in the packaging business, Snyder was an entrepreneur and investor more than a professional manager, and the board decided the young company needed to engage a president to support him.

A search firm recommended Henri Termeer, a 36-year-old executive running a business making therapeutic products to treat hemophiliacs at medical products giant Baxter International. Termeer had joined Baxter in 1974 after completing his MBA and had built his reputation as an effective country manager of the company's German subsidiary. The search firm believed that his impressive management record, his broad industry knowledge, and his particular knowledge of blood-derived therapeutic treatment of genetic diseases made him an ideally qualified candidate.

[2]Estimates of prevalence were gathered from National Gaucher Foundation Web site, http://www.gaucherdisease.org/prev.htm, accessed July 18, 2002; and from "Genzyme Corp. Strategic Challenges with Ceredase," HBS Case No. 793–120 (Boston: Harvard Business School Publishing, 1994), pp. 7–8.

Immediately upon joining Genzyme in October 1983, Termeer initiated a series of weekend discussions involving top management, members of the company's scientific advisory board of MIT and Harvard faculty, key investors, and a few outside advisors. Over several months they developed a few broad strategic principles that would guide Genzyme's future activities. First, Genzyme would be committed to building a diversified portfolio of targeted products and well-defined markets, with a particular focus on niches where needs were largely unmet. Equally important was its determination to remain independent by generating revenues from the start, by integrating vertically across the whole value chain, and by funding new development with internally generated funds or nonequity financial mechanisms.

Termeer also confronted several operating problems. Although he was aware that internal controls were all but nonexistent, the new president was still surprised to discover that one of the U.K. plants listed as an asset a particularly unsuccessful racehorse named Genzyme Gene. At that point he realized he had quite a job ahead in building a professional team and a sound management structure.

While working on the strategic and operational issues, Termeer also began to articulate the values he hoped to build in Genzyme. Over and over, he emphasized the centrality of the patient and the need for everyone to link what they were doing to those whose lives they could affect. Setting the tone himself, Termeer preferred to visit patients rather than just studying their diseases or trying to master the science behind the therapies being developed. He explained that patient contact gave him the emotional energy to work towards finding a cure, a feeling and commitment he wanted to convey to his entire organization.

Betting the Ranch   Meanwhile, Brady's new "pruned molecule" NIH trials were progressing. The results were disappointing yet tantalizing: only one patient out of the seven in the trial showed any response to the therapy, but his symptoms were dramatically reversed. The blind trial protocols masked

the identity of the study participants, and critics of the modified enzyme in Brady's lab blocked the supporters' proposal to investigate the reason for the widely differing outcomes.

When the results of the trial became known, most within Genzyme were pessimistic about the prospects for this therapy. But Termeer was not ready to give up. After learning that the identity of the one patient who was in dramatic recovery was Ben Bryant, a 4-year-old boy from the Washington, D.C., area, he called the family.[3] Over the following months, he visited Ben and his family regularly and was very impressed that treatment resulted in a total reversal of symptoms, but when the injections stopped, Ben relapsed. Yet while Termeer became convinced the therapy could work, Genzyme's scientific advisory board was much less optimistic. For one whole day the scientists debated the issue with management, trying to answer three questions: Does it work? Is it safe? And could it be made profitable?

On the first question, the scientific advisors were doubtful, arguing that there was no strong indicator that this one case could have general implications. While agreeing with Termeer that Ben's recovery was impressive, they did not share his belief that this was no aberration. The debate about safety was equally troubling. The enzyme used in the trial was extracted from the rare proteins found in human placentas collected from maternity wards in four large Boston hospitals. Growing publicity about risks of HIV and hepatitis C had led to widespread public concern about products derived from human tissue, leading the advisory board to suggest it would be more prudent to wait until biotechnology could create a recombinant version. Finally, there were questions about whether a business could be created. Some raised concerns about accessing enough placentas, while others focused on the huge investment required to develop this product. Blair, conservative by nature, was worried it could bankrupt the company. Snyder also argued against the proposal.

Despite these many concerns, Termeer decided that it was unacceptable that product development

---

[3]Patient's name disguised.

should not proceed with a therapy potentially able to reverse this terrible disease. At this time, the company's best guess was that 2,000 patients worldwide could eventually use the product, with the potential of generating profits on a projected $100 million in annual sales—*if* further trials proved successful and *if* the product could qualify for "orphan drug" status, which would raise high entry barriers to any competing therapy for seven years. (Genzyme faced no patent barriers or licensing costs, since the government had decided not to patent the discovery of the modified GCR molecule to encourage further research.)

Throughout this process, Termeer and Blair had been talking to Scott Furbish, one member of the NIH team advocating the pruned molecule treatment. Frustrated by the infighting, Furbish was ready to quit NIH. They convinced him to join Genzyme and head up the research that would take his NIH work to fruition. But Termeer also took his scientific advisors' recommendation seriously and initiated parallel research on a recombinant form of the GCR enzyme.

Furbish and his team soon hypothesized that it was Ben Bryant's small size that allowed the therapy to succeed. By increasing the dosage to adult patients, they believed further clinical trials would show it was equally effective on them. Recalling all the uncertainties of 1985 as Genzyme made a new-drug application for a Ceredase® enzyme under the Orphan Drug Act, Furbish said, "I would like to ask Henri how he had the guts to make that decision."

Going Public   By 1985, Termeer had tightened Genzyme's operations, set its broad strategic direction, strengthened its ongoing businesses, and committed to several important new research initiatives, of which the Gaucher therapies were the boldest. With sales of 32 research reagents, diagnostic intermediaries, and fine chemicals generating almost $10 million in revenues, the company was approaching the financial break-even point. Termeer felt it was now time to take Genzyme public.

With the board's full support, he became CEO in late 1985 (Snyder had left the company) and soon after began planning an IPO for 1986. (See **Exhibit 3** for excerpts from the prospectus.) Recognizing that most of the $27.4 million IPO cash infusion would be needed to finance the growth of existing operations, Termeer began exploring other means of funding product development. Unlike most other biotech companies, which financed research and development (R&D) by raising equity or entering into partnerships with large pharmaceutical companies, Genzyme elected to do so by creating a limited research partnership. Sales of the partnership units in 1987 raised a crucial $10 million to continue Ceredase development, splitting the risk and rewards of R&D but leaving Genzyme the option to buy back successful developments at a preset price.

Genzyme in Liftoff

By 1989 Ceredase approval seemed only a few years away, but public concern about the transmission of HIV from human-derived factors was growing. Recognizing that Genzyme could not develop a genetically engineered version of GCR quickly enough in-house, Termeer jumped at the opportunity to merge with Integrated Genetics (IG), a Massachusetts-based biotech firm with expertise in recombinant genetic engineering but an empty development pipeline following a patent-suit loss to Amgen.

Pursuing its strategy of diversification, Genzyme continued product development on multiple fronts—researching enzyme replacement for Fabry disease, developing genetic-screening tests, and working on therapies for cystic fibrosis, for example. With a continuing need for funding, a second limited research partnership in 1989 raised $36.7 million, followed by a second public stock offering for $39.1 million. In 1990 a special-purpose publicly traded research company was created, raising an additional $47.3 million for targeted genetic research, including promising work on cystic fibrosis. But the real excitement at Genzyme focused on bringing Ceredase to market.

Building a Product Pipeline   As the Ceredase trials continued, the company worked to ensure product supply. First-stage processing was contracted to the French Institute Merieux in Lyon, where rare

---

Exhibit 3   Excerpts from Genzyme's 1986 IPO Prospectus

The Company

- Genzyme develops, manufactures, and markets a variety of biological products used in human health care applications.
- Genzyme has additional human health care products under development. . . . [It] believes its practical experience in the production and sale of biological products will enhance its ability to manufacture and commercialize new products.
- As of March 1980, the company had 169 employees, of whom 39 are engaged in R&D.

Risk Factors

- Short operating history and losses . . . during each of its last few years.
- Regulation by government agencies . . . no assurance that . . . approvals will be granted.
- Uncertainty of product development.
- Patents with proprietary technology.
- Engaged in a segment of health care which is extremely competitive.
- Product liability.

Genzyme's principal products and process development programs, 1986

Products and Processes	Applications	Status
Therapeutics		
Hyaluronic acid	Ophthalmic surgery	Development stage
	Soft-tissue implants	Development stage
	Surgical trauma	Research stage
	Joint disorders	Research stage
	Drug delivery	Research stage
Glycoprotein remodeling	Therapeutic glycoproteins	Research stage
Glucocerebrosidase	Treatment of Gaucher disease	NIH clinical trials
Ceramide trihexoside	Treatment of Fabry disease	NIH development stage
Bulk pharmaceuticals	Active ingredients in branded and generic pharmaceuticals	Product sales
Diagnostics and reagents		
Diagnostic enzymes and substrates	Manufacture of diagnostic kits	Product sales
Research reagents	Lymphokine and glycoprotein research	Product sales
Fine chemicals		
Chiral compounds	Production of single isomer drugs	Development stage
Organic chemicals	Bioprocess compounds	Product sales

Source: Adapted by casewriters from Genzyme Corp. 1986 IPO Prospectus.

---

proteins—among them GCR—were extracted from placentas shipped from the United States and all over Europe. (A year's supply of Ceredase for the average patient contained enzyme extracted and purified from 20,000 human placentas, or 27 tons of material.)

Back in Boston, Genzyme modified the GCR enzyme then processed it to ensure its safety, purity, and concentration.

The U.S. Food and Drug Administration (FDA) finally approved Ceredase for marketing in the

United States in 1991, giving Genzyme the momentum for another $143 million stock offering. As approved, Ceredase had the distinction of being the most expensive therapy on the market. The complex extraction process, the limited availability of raw material, and the small number of patients combined to make production extremely costly. (Even when it was collecting 35% of all the placentas in the United States and over 70% of those in Europe, Genzyme could effectively supply Ceredase to only 1,000 to 1,500 patients.) Over one-third of this cost was attributable to acquiring and processing raw material, compared with raw material costs of 5% to 10% in typical drug manufacturing processes. (See **Exhibit 4** for cost estimates.) Protocols called for patients with the severe form of the disease to initially receive 50 units of Ceredase per kilo of body weight every two weeks. At $3.70 per unit, the first year's treatment could cost over $300,000, and although maintenance therapy could drop to roughly two-thirds of the initial dosage, the

cost was high enough to attract the attention of regulators and politicians. (See **Exhibit 5** for dosage calculations and costs.)

Meanwhile, a team of biochemists from Genzyme and IG spliced the human gene responsible for producing GCR into cells cultured from Chinese hamster ovaries, producing recombinant GCR. Others worked on scaling up production from the two-and-a-half grams of product made in a one-liter container for the trials to a new proposed production facility with four bioreactors of 2,000 liters each. In 1992, well before the production process was fully developed and more than a year before Genzyme would be ready to file the new-drug application for the product to be called Cerezyme, construction began on the new plant. To help finance the $180 million investment, a dramatic structure on the Charles River that stamped Genzyme's presence on Boston's skyline, Genzyme raised $100 million in debt. When commissioned, the plant's round-the-clock, 365-day-a-year production capacity would be

Exhibit 4   Ceredase Cost and Profit Estimate, 1994

	$	$	%
Per patient annual price		$150,000	100%
Less Cost of Goods			
Material	$47,900		
Mfg. Labor, overhead	5,300	$ 53,200	35
Gross Profit		$ 96,800	65
Less Operating Expenses			
Selling/reimbursement expense	$12,200		
Distribution	10,500		
R&D amortization	4,500		
Mfg. development amortization	2,000		
Corporate/admin. expenses	12,600		
Bad-debt provision	4,900		
Medicaid allowance	2,800		
Free goods	1,500	$ 51,000	34
Pretax Operating Profit		$ 45,800	31
Less state/federal taxes		14,600	10
Net Income		$ 31,300	21

Source: Adapted by casewriters from Elyse Tanouye, "What Ails Us—What's Fair?" *The Wall Street Journal*, May 20, 1994, p. R11.
(Source of data in the article given as Genzyme figures.)
Note: Estimated average per patient revenue includes pediatric and adult patients on initial and maintenance treatments.

Exhibit 5   Dosage Annual Cost Calculations for Ceredase and Cerezyme

Regimen and Patient Weight	Annual Cost
Initial Treatment of 50 units /kg.	
165 lbs. (75 kg.)	$360,750
110 lbs. (50 kg.)	240,500
33 lbs. (15 kg.)	72,150
Maintenance Treatment of 35 units /kg.	
165 lbs. (75 kg.)	$252,525
110 lbs. (50 kg.)	168,350
33 lbs. (15 kg.)	50,505

Source: Prepared by casewriters with information supplied by Genzyme Corp.

Note: Assumes biweekly infusions at $3.70 per unit medicine cost. Annual cost = price × dosage × weight × annual number of infusions.

six kilos of medicine annually—an output that would fit in a six-pack cooler but still sufficient for the 2,000 patients Genzyme hoped to treat worldwide.

Responding to Regulatory Pressures   The political environment in which Ceredase was launched was a difficult one for pharmaceutical and biotech companies. The emphasis on health-care reform in President Clinton's first term turned the spotlight on high-priced therapies, and along with a few other products such as Burroughs Welcome's AZT treatment for AIDS, Ceredase was singled out as an example of a drug that was seeking protection by exploiting the Orphan Drug Act.[4] Termeer's response was immediate and strong. (See **Exhibit 6** for an editorial expressing his views.) He went to Washington and asked members of Congress and the regulatory authorities what they wanted to know. He recalled: "I invited them to visit our operations and offered to open our books so they could see what it cost to develop and produce the product. I asked them for their suggestions—to tell me if we had done anything wrong. We would listen. Our

approach was to be completely open and transparent. We were proud of what we had done and had nothing to hide."

In addition to showing his visitors the facilities and giving the Congressional Office of Technology Assessment (OTA) access to the books, Termeer also explained the company's philosophy: "Since the beginning, I have told this organization that our first responsibility is to treat patients with the disease, not to maximize financial returns. Regardless of where those people are or the financial circumstances they find themselves in, we take it as our responsibility to see they are treated."

To implement this "universal provision" philosophy, Genzyme created the Ceredase Assistance Program (CAP) even before Ceredase was approved to market. A CAP committee reviewed cases of extreme need—patients who had lost insurance coverage, for example—and where there was no alternative provided Ceredase free. But they always continued working with the patients to try to secure an ongoing supportive, paying party. In addition to Termeer, the CAP review committee consisted of medical, legal, and caseworker professionals.

After a detailed examination, the October 1992 OTA report concluded that, while the benefits of NIH research and the Orphan Drug Act did reduce its risk, Genzyme had also invested significantly in R&D and production facilities. It found Genzyme's pretax profit margin on the drug to be in line with industry norms. (OTA's calculation excluded any R&D unrelated to Ceredase, bad debt, and free goods expenses.) Furthermore, OTA found that insurers were reimbursing the cost of the therapy because it was less expensive than surgery or extensive hospitalization.[5]

Going to Market   Meanwhile, the company had been tackling the formidable task of bringing to market an extremely expensive therapy for a rare, poorly understood, and seldom-diagnosed disease. Termeer knew that once again he would have to

[4]Larry Thompson, "The high cost of rare diseases: When patients can't afford to buy lifesaving drugs," *The Washington Post,* June 25, 1991, p. Z10; David Stipp, "Genzyme counters criticism over high cost of drug," *The Wall Street Journal,* June 23, 1992, p. B4; John Carey, "How many times must a patient pay?" *BusinessWeek,* February 1, 1993, p. 30.

[5]"Federal and Private Roles in the Development and Provision of Alglucerase Therapy for Gaucher Disease," Office of Technology Assessment, Washington, D.C.: Government Printing Office (1992).

Exhibit 6   *The Wall Street Journal* Op Ed Page, November 16, 1993, p. A28

The Cost of Miracles

BY HENRI A. TERMEER

As part of his continuing attack on the pharmaceutical industry, President Clinton has proposed establishing a federal committee to review the prices of "breakthrough" drugs, including those developed by the biotechnology industry. The Senate's Special Committee on Aging is scheduled to hold hearings today on the subject. Its chairman, Sen. David Pryor (D., Ark.), says the purpose of the hearings is to determine whether market forces are adequate to restrain prices.

The real danger, however, is not that the prices of new drugs will be too high, but that government controls, whether direct or indirect, will discourage investors from taking risks on biotechnology companies that develop new drugs.

The truth is that breakthrough drugs already face an onerous review: It's called the marketplace. Today, companies such as mine that develop breakthrough drugs can expect to have meaningful market exclusivity for only a few years. While a company's patent, or the special protection it can claim for its so-called orphan drugs, may preclude competitors from selling an identical product, it does not preclude others from designing and selling substantially similar products.

My own company's product, Ceredase, is an example of how market forces work. In the early 1980s, Genzyme was the only company working on a treatment for Gaucher's disease, a rare, inherited enzyme deficiency that causes crippling, and sometimes fatal, bone and organ deterioration. The CEO of another major biotechnology company had considered and rejected the idea of developing a treatment for such a rare disease because he could not imagine how his company could get an adequate return on a product intended for a few thousand patients.

Success Breeds Competition

Since Genzyme developed Ceredase, however, other companies have jumped into Gaucher's disease research. We are now competing with a company working on a variation of our drug, and two others are competing with us to develop gene-therapy approaches. There could be as many as four or five treatments for Gaucher's disease on the market within the next four years. If we hadn't taken the first step, there would be no market and no additional research on the disease.

My point is this: When an innovator company proves that its product works, and that a sufficient market exists to earn a return, it encourages other companies to develop similar products that enable them to compete for a share of that market. Given the breathtaking pace of biotechnology progress, it takes a relatively short time for other companies to develop substantially similar drugs. These will succeed, of course, only if they offer either price or therapeutic advantages over the innovator product.

Market forces are thus already creating price competition among pharmaceutical companies. A number of companies are implementing such programs as customer rebates and money-back guarantees. No government regulatory mechanism was necessary to induce this result.

In this respect, it is ironic that the same commentators who complain about pharmaceutical companies developing "me too" drugs (new versions of existing drugs) often fail to recognize that, at the very least, the introduction of such drugs helps constrain the prices of similar products, especially under a managed competition system in which insurance companies provide physicians with a greater incentive to consider the cost-effectiveness of the products they prescribe.

Congress should be less concerned about the possibility that a company might someday charge a high price for its AIDS vaccine for the two or three years before a competing product is available than about that company's ability to obtain the research-and-development funds needed to develop the vaccine in the first place. It is imperative that Congress and the administration consider the following question: If we alter market mechanisms by imposing price controls on breakthrough drugs, will we continue to get breakthrough drugs?

(*continued*)

Exhibit 6   (*concluded*)

A breakthrough drug committee is not needed to ensure that drugs are priced reasonably. If a drug's benefit is not commensurate with its cost, physicians won't prescribe it, particularly under a managed competition system. From the patient's perspective, a committee's refusing to provide Medicare coverage for "excessively priced" drugs would substitute a bureaucrat's judgment for a physician's. It would also result in second-class medical care for aging Americans: Medicare patients would be denied access to drugs that are covered for the privately insured.

A breakthrough drug committee as proposed by Mr. Clinton is not only unnecessary, it is counterproductive. It will discourage investors from seeing the development of breakthrough drugs as an investment capable of reaping returns that are commensurate with the risks. Another Clinton proposal would allow the secretary of health and human services to negotiate prices for new drugs, under threat of excluding them from Medicare. Taken together, these proposals would constitute a price-control system that discriminates against biotechnology and other innovating pharmaceutical companies by threatening to blacklist their products unless government bureaucrats concur with company pricing decisions.

These Clinton proposals do little more than constrain our ability to develop breakthrough medicines. In the first eight months of this year, biotechnology stocks declined by 30%; and through initial public offerings and other investor appeals companies were able to raise only about 25% of the amount they spent during this period. Obviously, this is not sustainable for an industry that lost $3.6 billion last year.

My own company raised $100 million two years ago to fund its research and development of a treatment for cystic fibrosis, a common fatal genetic disease that kills the average patient at the age of 29. Even though we recently performed the first successful clinical trial of a gene-therapy treatment for cystic fibrosis, Genzyme would be hard-pressed to raise half that amount in today's investment environment. Yet we will need to make a total investment of more than $400 million to bring this product to market. If we succeed, we will be able to treat successfully 30,000 Americans who, in the severe phase of the disease, now receive annual medical care costing up to $50,000.

Proposals that discourage breakthrough drug development may be smart politics. But they are bad medicine and an ineffective means of cost control.

Japan, which has a single-payer system in which the government sets reimbursement rates for all health care products and services, uses government regulation of drug prices as a form of industrial policy to reward breakthrough drug development with a pricing premium. It is typical for the Japanese government to set prices for biotechnology drugs and other breakthrough pharmaceutical products at two to three times U.S. market prices, reflecting such a premium. On the other hand, the Japanese government cuts the prices of older pharmaceuticals annually according to a formula. The message to Japanese industry is clear: Innovate or die.

No Price Abuse

Sen. Pryor and the White House propose precisely the opposite—that breakthrough drugs be subject to government policies aimed at preventing "excessive" prices while old drugs continue to escalate in price at the general inflation rate.

In citing Japanese policy, I do not intend to suggest that the U.S. should adopt that system. To the contrary, I think that the relatively higher prices that the Japanese government willingly pays for breakthrough drugs are compelling evidence that American companies are not abusing the pricing freedom they enjoy in a system like ours.

Finally, let me note that the Japanese government has targeted biotechnology as an industry Japan wants to dominate by the year 2000. The U.S. will only forfeit its leadership position to Japan if its government encourages the development of breakthrough drugs and our own does not. The Japanese threat to our industry is not nearly as great as the threat from our own government.

Mr. Termeer is CEO of Genzyme Corp. in Cambridge, Mass.

attract different kinds of people to take on the challenge: "Recruiting the right people has been a key part of Genzyme's success. . . . I look for people with a passion to tackle things that seem impossible to solve. Practical dreamers who have a sense of compassion but believe they can change things. . . . And we attract people who see what we are doing as a worthwhile fight. There has to be a real personal involvement."

Drawing on the pool of biotech sales veterans in the Boston area, the company recruited an eight-person pioneering sales force with good industry knowledge whose members fit Termeer's "passionate practical dreamer" profile. In contrast to the traditional pharmaceutical model of making sales calls to doctors, pharmacies, and hospital purchasing agents, the Ceredase team focused on patients. After working to identify who they were, they educated them about the disease, organized them in support groups, and found treatment for them. They also educated physicians and reassured them about reimbursement.

Very quickly, the field sales force found the need for a support staff of caseworkers—typically, trained nurses and social workers—who advocated for patients with insurance companies. The caseworkers explained the therapy to the insurance representatives, provided supporting research materials, and handled the huge administrative demands for each submission. Said one of the early sales force members: "Because of insurance, it was a patient-oriented approach. Then, as the patient got better, the physician became motivated. We worked patient by patient, physician by physician. . . . This company is really about caring for our patients and doing the right thing for them. When a patient calls, you respond—it's the culture here."

Patient profiles were prominent in Genzyme's annual reports, photos of patients were pinned on cubicle walls in the offices, and company employees spoke passionately about how patients motivated them. Alison Lawton from regulatory affairs was typical: "Two months after I joined Genzyme, I went to a Gaucher patient meeting in Israel. . . . I cried my eyes out just seeing the patients and hearing them basically begging the Ministry to get them

the therapy. . . . I remember thinking, 'I'm really going to make a difference if I can get this product registered here.'"

Yet some in the R&D labs claimed to be unmoved by Termeer's regular attempts to link their work to real patients' stories, believing their scientific training forced a more disciplined attitude. "If you are immersed in the science, you become intrigued by trying to figure out the problems," said one. "You're not inspired by stories of human tragedies or a picture of a kid on the wall." But others were. Furbish felt that most Genzyme scientists were different from others in the industry:

> There are clear philosophical divides in the biotech world. Technology looks down on sales and marketing, and Ph.D.s are trained to sneer at profit. But that doesn't hold at Genzyme. The patient focus builds from Henri down. His commitment is real and it affects everyone—even the Ph.D.s. Yet he also sets very aggressive business goals, and we come to appreciate that this is paying the bills as well as helping patients.

The same attitude had spread to plant engineers and technicians. For Blair Okita, vice president of Therapeutics Manufacturing and Development, Genzyme was much different from earlier experiences at SmithKline Beecham and Merck: "Here we are motivated by a patient focus—right down to the technician level. For example, before doing their first run of the new Pompe product, our staff in the fill and finish area had a family with a child with Pompe's disease talk to them. . . . Each one of us is providing a life-saving therapy to a patient. That is a powerful motivating force."

As the network of educated patients and aware physicians expanded, sales of Ceredase grew rapidly. In 1993, after three years on the market, 1,000 patients were being treated, and cumulative sales were almost $250 million. Regulatory applications for Ceredase were pending in many international markets, and Cerezyme, the recombinant version of the therapy, was due for FDA approval in the United States in 1994. Genzyme's future looked promising indeed.

Opening Foreign Markets

Even before Ceredase was launched, Genzyme had been approached by companies wanting to cross-license or distribute the product abroad. True to his principle of controlling his business both upstream and downstream, Termeer refused. "International markets were an exciting opportunity," he said. "Besides, we were committed to seeking out and responding to Gaucher patients."

Pioneering Initiatives In late 1990, Termeer called Tomye Tierney, an ex-colleague at Baxter, and convinced her to lead Genzyme's thrust into Europe. With her experience marketing Baxter's hemophilia products in many markets around the globe, Tierney had strong skills in building relationships with patients, physicians, and government officials. Said Termeer, "Tomye is one of those unusual people you can send into an impossible country where there are all kinds of roadblocks, and she can find a way."

Joining at the same time Genzyme was recruiting its U.S. sales force, Tierney had no sales model to build on. "Henri told me I would have to develop the international strategy," she recalled. "And when I asked him how long I had, he told me, 'Two weeks.'" She headed straight to Europe and within two months she had contacted her old physician friends, been referred to the few specialists working on Gaucher disease, located known patients in the United Kingdom, France, and the Netherlands, and begun connecting the network. Winning "investigational new drug" use approval, she made the first sales by December 1990.

Having set up the basic network, in September 1991 Tierney called another old Baxter colleague, Jan van Heek, and told him about Genzyme's European plans. Van Heek had just been offered a promotion at Baxter so was not very interested. "But I went to a patient and physician meeting and was astonished how much Genzyme meant to those people," he recalled. "There was an enormous sense of optimism and hope in the company, and I decided on the spot to join." By year's end, he had established Genzyme's temporary European headquarters—a rented house with a phone and a fax—and had hired the five entrepreneurial individuals who would develop the European market.

As the company pursued the long, complicated process of registration and approval in each of Europe's national health care systems, the high cost of Ceredase inevitably led to equally long and complex negotiations over price. But Genzyme's response was always simple, straightforward, and unwavering. The company had a universal global pricing policy. Termeer explained:

> We have only two prices—the commercial price or free. By taking an absolutely transparent position, the discussion finishes quickly. We have not exploited our position by increasing prices—we have remained basically the same over that whole period. As our margin has gone up, we have taken on more responsibility to support patients around the world.

A Mobile Missionary With van Heek running Europe, Termeer asked Tierney to become vice president and general manager of emerging markets and develop opportunities in the rest of the world. Although she began initiatives in many markets, including Canada, Latin America, and Australia, it was the Middle East that captured much of her time and attention. Due to its high concentration of Gaucher patients, Israel was a priority and in 1993 became the first country outside the United States to approve Ceredase. Another market that seemed to offer potential was Egypt, and since 1990 Tierney had been in contact with Dr. Khalifa, a physician with an interest in Gaucher disease.

After four years, Tierney had built her widespread portfolio of markets into a $16 million business. In 1996, Termeer asked her to relocate to Asia, a market previously thought to have limited potential. Setting up her base in Singapore, she continued her missionary work. By that time, she had established a clear step-by-step approach to entering new markets. She explained:

> The key is to hire a smart local person to manage the process. For example, in Korea I found a pharmacist who had worked for the German drug company Boehringer. I connected him to a physician who we

felt could be a local thought leader. She was treating a Gaucher patient willing to pay for his own treatment. This gave us the base to create a forum for patients and help them channel their frustration at not having access to therapy toward the government. Our local manager then worked with the patients, physicians, and government to enact orphan drug legislation and approve Cerezyme for reimbursement. It's a lot of work, but the Genzyme credo is "you've got to find a way."

As she opened markets in Japan, South Korea, Taiwan, Hong Kong, and other developed Asian countries, Tierney was increasingly aware that there were other, less developed economies—China, India, and Vietnam, for example—that simply could not afford this therapy. It was an issue that had become a growing concern for Termeer as well. For several years, patients from countries without access to Cerezyme had been coming to Boston to request free product from the CAP committee. (See **Exhibit 7** for one well-publicized example.) This presented Termeer with a real dilemma: "We were having families moving to the United States asking to get free drug and treatment here forever. The real solution had to be to get treatment in their home country. It's less disruptive for the family and also educates the country about the therapy so more patients can be treated."

To the critics, however, the requirement to return home seemed to be a hard-hearted and even manipulative tactic designed to use patient needs to develop new market opportunities. It was a charge Termeer strongly refuted:

> What I will never tolerate is to create a blackmail situation where the patient is in the middle. There can be no circumstance where a patient on therapy is taken off therapy to create leverage. Or where a patient that needs therapy is denied it to create leverage. We have to make sure there is a critical need, then we must respond to the need. But we cannot take on the responsibility forever and we need to make people aware of the role they must play to help. . . . In the Peruvian family's case, we asked them to move back, then worked very hard with the government and got reimbursement in Peru. In the end we were able to help other Peruvian patients get the treatment also.

The Gaucher Initiative

As Termeer thought about how to address the question of providing treatment to Gaucher sufferers in less developed countries, he decided this would be an ideal next project for Tierney. But Tierney was not so sure. After nine months of persuasion and negotiation, she returned to Boston in June 1998 with a mandate to develop a humanitarian program for emerging markets—but without jeopardizing the company's existing or future commercial opportunities.

Setting Up the Program   As soon as Tierney returned, she scheduled a meeting with Termeer to review the parameters of her new assignment. She found he was deeply involved in the issues, and the meeting turned into the first of many brainstorming sessions she had with Termeer and Sandy Smith, the vice president of International, to whom she reported. The first issue Termeer addressed with Tierney was the charter of what they began calling the Gaucher Initiative. He recalled the guidelines clearly: "It was really just a continuation of the philosophy we had implemented through CAP. Where there is a critical need, we will respond. But we cannot take on the responsibility forever. Our goal must be to create a situation in which the country itself will eventually take responsibility for the treatment. That's where we need to get to."

Implementation of this philosophy was complicated by the conjunction of the company's humanitarian commitment to universal provision and its commercial objective of a universal price. Recognizing that the humanitarian provision needed to be insulated from the commercial operations, Tierney and Termeer concluded they would need to work with an independent agency that had the infrastructure to distribute Cerezyme around the world. To ensure Genzyme's efforts would be both direct and discrete yet would not involve the company in decisions about who would receive treatment, they would also need an independent, medically qualified committee of experts to make case-by-case diagnoses and decisions about the relative needs of candidates for treatment.

As she developed the program design, Tierney worked with a corporate philanthropy consultant and

Exhibit 7   *The Boston Sunday Globe* Article, April 11, 1993, p. 1

A Father, a Drug and an Ailing Son

BY PHILIP BENNETT
GLOBE STAFF

Justo Ascarza knows the logic of big business, of borders, of probable endings. But he lives by the logic of a parent whose child is dying, which is something else entirely.

"To struggle for the life of a child, for the life of a son, is to put yourself above rules, and even above laws," he said in a waiting room at Massachusetts General Hospital, impatient for his son to get better.

It was thinking like this that led Ascarza, without money, influence, or an understanding of English, across the globe to Boston to persuade doctors, hospitals, and Genzyme Corp. to save his son for free with one of the world's most costly drugs.

For a few months, Ascarza, a grade-school principal from Peru, made the system work for him. But, perhaps not surprisingly, it hasn't lasted. He says now that he is being made to work for the system, with the health of his son, Amaru, as leverage.

Ascarza and Genzyme are at odds over how long Amaru, 13, will receive free doses of Ceredase, the Cambridge biotechnology firm's premier drug, which the company says costs patients an average of $140,000 annually. Genzyme says the boy's next free dose, on Thursday, will be his last unless the Ascarzas return to Peru, where they would receive three more free months for introducing Ceredase to the country. The company then expects the government of Peru to pay for Amaru's treatment.

While the scheme might open a new South American market for Genzyme, Ascarza fears it may also result in suffering and death for his son. Peru is a country with shortages of medical resources and a surplus of tragedies. Ascarza, whose school salary is about $90 a month, asserts the government there will not pay for the drug, a claim supported even by the Lima physician Genzyme obtained for the family.

While the case is unusual, its issues are at the core of the health care debate, involving responsibility for care and its enormous expense and conflict over treatment that is costly to institutions but priceless for individuals and their families.

Because the Ascarzas are Peruvian, their case raises another, increasingly common question: should foreigners or unnaturalized immigrants living in the United States have the same rights to emergency care—some of it unavailable anywhere else—as U.S. citizens?

What nobody disputes is that Amaru Ascarza is very sick. He has Gaucher's disease, a rare genetic illness. Its symptoms include severe enlargement of the liver and spleen, excessive bleeding, and erosion of bones until they may start breaking. The disease can be fatal if untreated.

At 13, Amaru is 4 feet tall and weights 68 pounds. His abdomen is swollen grotesquely. His gums bleed. Struck with headaches, he presses his palms against his skull as if to hold the bone in place. His hands are delicate and tiny. He plays the flute and is a talented cartoonist.

He is a thoughtful and self-conscious teenager, usually quiet. His father says that prior to receiving Ceredase Amaru would often be prostrated by pain, wailing helplessly.

An effective treatment
Ceredase replaces an enzyme missing in Gaucher's victims, in many cases reversing the disease. Such has been the case with Amaru, who during three months of treatment has improved "miraculously," his father says, "inside and out."

"The medicine makes me feel better," Amaru said. "I go outside, do more things. When it wears off I feel sick again."

(continued)

Exhibit 7   (*continued*)

Since Ceredase was approved in the United States two years ago, it has been a bonanza for Genzyme. The company says that fewer than 6,000 of an estimated 20,000 Gaucher's patients worldwide can benefit from treatment with the drug, but its extraordinary cost has made it Genzyme's sales leader, generating $100 million last year.

The company currently has a monopoly on Ceredase under the Orphan Drug Law, which gives economic incentives to companies to develop drugs for rare diseases. And the drug attracts faithful customers: like insulin for diabetics, it is usually taken regularly for life.

Genzyme has been criticized for the cost of Ceredase, which can exceed $200,000 a year for patients. Executives say the drug is fairly priced. In addition, they say, no Gaucher's patient has been deprived of Ceredase for inability to pay, and they point by way of example to the day Justo Ascarza came to the door.

Ascarza, originally from a provincial town in the Andes, is an elementary school principal in a poor urban neighborhood in Lima. He speaks no English. He and his wife, Gladys, who joined him here recently, worry about their two other children, who remain in Peru. Yet with a relentlessness that can be breathtaking, he has made his case to any physician, attorney, government official, executive, or journalist who will listen.

His efforts have probably saved his son. In Peru, where no cases of Gaucher's had been previously noted, Amaru's condition went undiagnosed for five years. The Ascarzas were told their son might have leukemia until physicians correctly identified the illness and put the Ascarzas in touch with the National Institutes of Health, near Washington.

Company could benefit

Physicians studying Gaucher's disease invited the family to NIH last November. The Ascarzas persuaded American Airlines to donate airfare. A doctor there who examined Amaru found him seriously ill. But because he was not affected neurologically, he did not qualify for an NIH study that would have resulted in free treatment and was discharged.

It was then, with airfare donated by an NIH physician, that the Ascarzas with the help of a distant relative living in Cambridge, turned to Genzyme. They were accepted into a program of free treatment, "conditioned on the full cooperation of the parents and the patient," said Henri Termeer, Genzyme's chairman and chief executive.

In the Ascarzas' case, those conditions require them to return to Peru by the end of April in order to receive three more months of the drug for free. After that, the family must find financing, presumably from the government of Peru, to pay Genzyme an estimated $82,000 a year.

If the Ascarzas were to succeed in Peru, the benefits for Genzyme would be clear. Ceredase would presumably receive expedited approval for use. Publicity about the case would bring forward patients with Gaucher's disease who are currently undiagnosed. And, as in countries such as Brazil and Argentina, where Ceredase is now subsidized, the company would have a government guarantee of payment.

But Ascarza said he appealed to the wife of Peru's president, Alberto Fujimori, for aid and was turned down. Ceredase would be a great expense in a country where nurses at public hospitals earn less than $100 a month and tens of thousands of children die each year of dehydration caused by diarrhea because the government cannot afford to provide even the most basic care.

Question of responsibility

Genzyme executives, for their part, point out that they cannot solve the problems of health care in Peru and that the company is not a charity.

"We never give up on attempts to make the patient part of a safety net," said Termeer. But, he said, "We cannot do this in a way that we lose total leverage on the system. We cannot allow ourselves to be used in a way that takes everybody off the hook."

(continued)

Exhibit 7   (concluded)

Genzyme has assured the Ascarzas that the company has arranged care from a respected Lima hematologist, Dr. Jose Galvez, and is ready to ship the Ceredase. Yet, in a telephone interview last week, Galvez was hardly reassuring.

"I don't know anything really," Galvez said. "His physician called me last week and told me about the patient and that they'd send me something in the mail. I'm just waiting. I just don't know anything else."

Asked whether he believed the Peruvian government would pay for the treatment, Galvez said: "I don't think so. I have to be honest with you. We have a lot of problems here and this is not a priority. Things are not good here."

Meanwhile, Ascarza said that he has been rebuffed only once for seeking free care for his son in the United States. Ironically, he said it came from a Peruvian doctor practicing here.

But the issue is more widespread.

"It's a horrible problem," said Dr. Norman Barton, who examined Amaru at the NIH. "To what extent do we as a society have the responsibility to provide advanced technologies to countries that have no means to pay for them?"

"I don't know," Ascarza said. "Maybe what I am doing is wrong. But it is my responsibility to guarantee that Amaru doesn't die because he didn't have the luck to be born in a developed country."

shared development ideas with the program director for the Mectizan Donation Program, Merck's initiative to combat river blindness.[6] In October, after carefully screening several partner candidates suggested by the outside consultant, Tierney selected Project HOPE for its worldwide distribution network, long track record, emphasis on health education, and sterling reputation. Additionally, the organization had a strong presence in China and Egypt, markets which Tierney knew had a recognized need for this therapy. Project HOPE's emphasis on health-care development within a country, rather than ongoing charitable health-care provision, was also consistent with Genzyme's long-term commercial goals.

For its part, however, Project HOPE took some convincing. It wanted assurances that it would not be mixing a commercial agenda with its humanitarian mission and that the program would be run independently of Genzyme. Finally, an agreement was reached, and Tierney worked feverishly to get the program up and running by January 1, 1999. (See **Exhibit 8** for contract highlights.)

Implementing the Program   Tierney's first task was to work to establish a secretariat with a full-time program manager and an independent case review board. She then won Termeer's agreement to supplement the in-kind donation of Cerezyme with a yearly budget to support the program manager and secretariat and provide training, travel, and office peripherals for local treatment centers. Eager to begin shipment of the drug to Egypt and China, Tierney appealed to the quality control personnel at Genzyme to inspect and approve Project HOPE's delivery system immediately. With excitement about the new program running high at Genzyme (Termeer and Tierney had widely communicated the company's commitment to the Gaucher Initiative), plant personnel helped to bypass a two-month backlog, and the first product was shipped ahead of Tierney's year-end target date.

Working with Project HOPE, Tierney convened the independent six-member medical review board that would meet three times a year to establish patient-intake procedures, qualify new cases, and decide to terminate treatment for patients who did not respond to the therapy. The board consisted of three leading experts in Gaucher disease, Genzyme's chief medical officer, a Project HOPE staff

---

[6]Peter Wehrwein, "Pharmaco-Philanthropy," *Harvard Public Health Review,* Summer 1999, pp. 32–39.

Exhibit 8   Highlights of Gaucher Initiative Agreement

Program Objectives

- "To establish Expert Committee to provide technical, ethical and programmatic guidance."
- "To coordinate and facilitate training of eight physicians on the treatments of Gaucher disease."
- "To organize and carry out the timely shipment and delivery of Ceredase/Cerezyme to identified locations in the People's Republic of China and Egypt."
- "To provide treatment to approximately 60 patients" annually.

Project HOPE Responsibilities

- "Establish a Secretariat . . . to direct and manage the day-to-day activities and administration."
- Identify Project HOPE field staff to assist with implementation from the local level.
- "Establish an Expert Committee, which will meet bi-annually . . . to provide technical, ethical and programmatic guidance to the Gaucher Initiative. Provide a voting member to the Expert Committee."
- Coordinate and facilitate the training of four physicians from China, two from Egypt, and two from Project HOPE.
- "Arrange for the timely shipment and delivery of appropriate quantities of Ceredase/Cerezyme."
- "Provide liaison with participating hospitals and medical institutions, physicians and medical personnel, and the patients selected for participation in the Gaucher Initiative."
- "Collaborate with appointed Genzyme representatives to . . . publicize the Gaucher Initiative."
- "Submit to Genzyme quarterly financial and narrative reports on progress."

Genzyme Responsibilities

- "Identify patients . . . for selection by the Expert Committee for inclusion in the program."
- "Assist in the creation of the Expert Committee. Provide a voting member."
- "Donate to Project HOPE appropriate quantities of Ceredase/Cerezyme."
- "Facilitate the training of eight physicians . . . at the Gaucher workshop held at Genzyme."
- "Provide Project HOPE with technical assistance in the training aspects and treatment of Gaucher disease."
- "Collaborate with Project HOPE . . . to publicize the Gaucher Initiative."
- "Genzyme shall be responsible for funding the Gaucher Initiative."

Resolution of Disputes

- In the event of a dispute, "the parties shall first attempt to resolve the dispute through friendly discussions." After 14 days "the parties may mutually select a third party" for "non-binding mediation." After another 14 days "either party may refer the dispute to arbitration and withdraw from the Program" with 30 days' written notice.

Liability

- "Project HOPE will be responsible for obtaining liability insurance to protect the Expert Committee from any suits resulting from decisions concerning patient selection and program guidance."
- "Any liability associated with the products Ceredase/Cerezyme will be the responsibility of Genzyme."
- "Local liability concerning the treatment of patients will be the responsibility of the local physician."

Duration, Extension, and Termination

- Duration: five years.
- Extended by "mutual agreement and the signing of a letter defining the length of the extension."
- The agreement may be terminated "without cause upon giving 90 days' written notice."

Source: Adapted by casewriters from memorandum of understanding between Project HOPE and Genzyme Corp., effective January 1, 1999.

member, and a medical ethicist, who quickly tested the board's independence.

As Project HOPE spread the word in Egypt and China, local doctors made case-by-case requests to the local Project HOPE office. Applications were forwarded to Genzyme, which coordinated a case docket for the medical advisory board. After medical advisory board approval, Genzyme prepared patient and dosage lists for distribution to Project HOPE, which then shipped the drug overseas in coolers. At its destination it was carried by truck—or sometimes by hand—to local hospitals, where it was reconstituted and prepared for infusion. Project HOPE qualified local doctors to administer the therapy and participate in the program. In its first year, the Gaucher Initiative treated 60 patients worldwide (37 in Egypt and 23 in China); by 2001 the number was 140.

The Humanitarian/Commercial Tension   To the employees at Genzyme, the commitment to the Gaucher Initiative was another confirmation of the values they had heard Termeer espouse since the company's earliest days. Yet within the commercial organization, some voices of concern were emerging, particularly from those responsible for less developed markets. "We have a person who covers most of our Eastern European markets who was really concerned that if people began to understand we would give product away, it would be impossible to sell," Tierney recalled.

Christi van Heek, president of Genzyme's therapeutics division, reinforced the view that reimbursement could easily be lost if health-care providers felt they could obtain free product. She described how she had visited a physician in the Czech Republic who explained that his hospital lacked the money to buy Tylenol. Yet he eventually had six children on Cerezyme therapy. "He got reimbursement through the system," she said. "He had to fight for it, but this drug really works."

However, as the product penetration in developed nations approached saturation—sales growth increased only 6% between 2000 and 2001—the opportunities in markets outside the most developed economies begun to attract more attention. (See

Exhibit 9 for sales and patient growth.) Furthermore, Ceredase had come off orphan drug protection in 1998, and Cerezyme's would expire in 2001. Already competitors had applied for marketing approval for different therapies. Although Genzyme analysis cast doubts on their safety and effectiveness, it was a clear signal that this larger-than-expected market was attractive to competitors. "The interesting question will be what the entry of competitors will do to this responsibility we have taken on," said Termeer. "Will it be a burden for us alone, or will it be a joint responsibility? We have not begun to sort that one out."

The Egyptian Dilemma

Even after she moved to Singapore, Tierney had kept her eye on the nascent opportunity in Egypt. It was a responsibility that would absorb much time and energy in coming years.

Building a Presence, Having an Impact   In late 1996, Khalifa had informed her that he had obtained funding to treat a child with Gaucher disease. On a "named-patient basis," he also had obtained permission to import Cerezyme on humanitarian grounds even though it was not registered for sale in Egypt. However, several months later, when Tierney was visiting Egypt, she found that the funding was insufficient to cover the required treatment, and the patient was not responding to the low dosage provided. She immediately offered to request Genzyme's CAP program to sponsor a matching dose. Under this partial reimbursement arrangement, over the next two years Khalifa and Dr. Khaled, another physician now involved, expanded treatment to a dozen patients, mostly children who were reimbursed under the government's Student Fund.

But now, with Tierney leading the Gaucher Initiative, responsibility for the Egyptian market was transferred to the general manager of Genzyme's Israel subsidiary, Zev Zelig. As a way of handing off her commercial responsibilities, Tierney introduced the Jordanian sales associate hired to cover Arab markets to her key physician and health insurance contacts. She also introduced him to the Project HOPE staff in Egypt. "The HOPE people were

Exhibit 9   Ceredase and Cerezyme Revenues and Patient Growth, 1991–2001

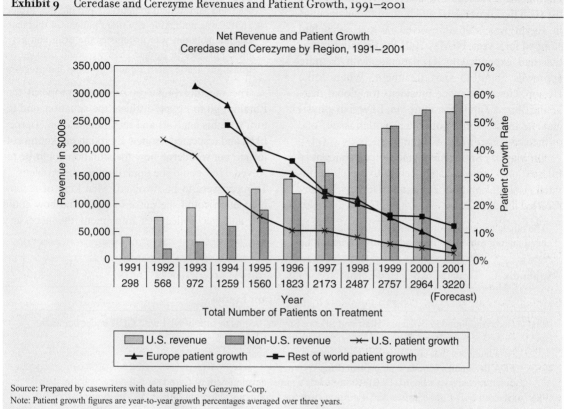

Net Revenue and Patient Growth
Ceredase and Cerezyme by Region, 1991–2001

Source: Prepared by casewriters with data supplied by Genzyme Corp.
Note: Patient growth figures are year-to-year growth percentages averaged over three years.

a little uncomfortable that we were actually making money on some of these patients," she explained. "They wanted a clear separation."

New Demands, New Expectations   In Project HOPE's first year in Egypt, the number of patients grew from 12 to 37, many of them infants, since children under five were not covered by the government-financed Student Fund. Sales through the partial reimbursement program were also up, increasing from $82,200 in 1998 to $146,500 in 1999. But the growing number of "named patients" attracted the attention of regulatory authorities, and in early 2000 Zelig was told that Genzyme would have to register Cerezyme. Zelig asked one of the company's regulatory staff to help him assess the task, but after talking to the Egyptian authorities, they concluded that registration would be too expensive to be justified.

After the first quarter of 2000, sales stopped. Almost immediately, Tierney began to feel pressure from Zelig to scale back her program in Egypt. She recalled: "At our strategic planning meeting, Zev kept saying, 'I can't do it because she's giving away free drug.' And I'd come back, 'You need to hire an Egyptian sales associate and register in Egypt.' We went back and forth for almost a year."

Meanwhile, Project HOPE had just appointed Dr. John Howe as its new CEO. A well-respected cardiologist from Texas, Howe joined the organization with much energy and an ambition to expand its operations. "He told me he wanted to grow Project HOPE at least 50%," said Tierney. "And he was particularly interested in expanding the relationship with Genzyme."

Facing the Problem   In early 2001, the tension between the commercial and humanitarian agendas in Egypt was still unresolved. While sales had stopped for a year, by May 2001 the Gaucher Initiative had expanded to 41 patients, with 5 more approvals about to start treatment. When Mike Heslop, Genzyme's vice president for global marketing, hired Tarek Ebrahim, an Egyptian physician, he made "sorting out the Egyptian issue" one of the newcomer's first assignments.

On May 25, Smith, Genzyme's vice president of International, convened a meeting to which he invited Heslop, Ebrahim, Zelig, and Tierney. Tierney recalled the discussion:

> The others were all from the commercial side and had been talking to Zev. So they were sitting there telling

me to put a lid on the free drug program. Zev took the lead and said we had to get the word out that Project HOPE was not taking any more patients. I told them that the solution was to register the drug and get a local presence in Egypt. Then we could manage the transition. I told them I could not stop the program.

The meeting broke up with the proposal that Ebrahim go to Egypt, evaluate the situation, and return with his analysis and recommendation. Tierney liked and respected her new Egyptian marketing colleague but wondered how the situation could be resolved. How could she think through the problem? If Termeer were to be involved, what kind of recommendation could she make to him? And how could she and her colleagues implement the necessary changes?

Appendix A   Timeline of Selected Corporate Events, Genzyme Corp.

Year	Significant Events
1981	Genzyme founded by Henry Blair and Sherry Snyder, begins to supply NIH with GCR under contract.
1983	Genzyme hires Henri Termeer as president; becomes CEO, 1985.
	NIH launches first GCR enzyme-replacement trial.
1985	FDA designates Ceredase an orphan drug.
	Scientific advisory board (BIA) recommends against development of Ceredase.
1986	Genzyme IPO, June, raises $27.4 million cash for a company valuation of over $83 million.
1987	Forms R&D limited partnership, raising $10 million to develop Ceredase.
1989	Ceredase approved for seriously ill patients prior to marketing approval.
	Raises $39.1 million through public stock offering and $36.7 million through Genzyme Development Partners.
	Acquires Integrated Genetics (founded in 1981).
1990	Ceredase available outside United States on a named-patient basis.
	Forms Neozyme I, raises $47.3 million to fund R&D.
1991	Ceredase approved and receives orphan drug status.
	Raises $100 million in 10-year 6% debt, and raises $143 million in public stock offering.
1992	Begins work on gene therapy to treat cystic fibrosis.
	Congressional OTA report issued on the development of Ceredase.
	Forms Neozyme II, raises $85 million; purchases four research programs from Neozyme I for $49 million.
1993	New-drug application to FDA for Cerezyme.
1994	Cerezyme approved in United States, Germany, France, Holland, Australia, United Kingdom.
	Break-even on Ceredase.
1995	Ceredase sales approved in Portugal, Italy, New Zealand, Sweden, Spain.
	Genzyme General public offering raises $141 million.
1996	Japan approves Cerezyme.
1998	Genzyme General places $250 million 5.25% seven-year debt.
1999	Launches Gaucher Initiative.

Source: Adapted by casewriters from Genzyme Corp. sources.

Reading 8-1   The Myth of the Generic Manager: New Personal Competencies for New Management Roles

Christopher A. Bartlett
Sumantra Ghoshal

Over the years, the Boston Celtics have won more National Basketball Association championships than any other team in the league. They have achieved that record through the effectiveness of their organization—the exceptional leadership ability of their general managers, as epitomized by the legendary Red Auerbach, the strong team development skills of coaches such as Tom Heinson, and the outstanding on-court talent of players like Larry Bird. But it is clear to everyone in the Celtics organization that the capable general manager, the savvy coach, and the star player all add value in very different ways. While Auerbach's career demonstrates that a good player can occasionally evolve into a great coach, and even go on to become an exceptional general manager, the instances of such a progression are extremely rare. Success in one role is not a good predictor of performance in another. Heinson made the transition from player to coach with ease, yet was not seen to have general management potential; and despite the fact he was one of the game's greatest players ever, few expect Larry Bird to become as successful a coach as Heinson, let alone a general manager of Auerbach's standing.

When it comes to management of companies, both our theory and our practice are very different. In theory, we believe in a generic role called "the manager," who is expected to add value to the company in a generic way, carrying out a generic set of tasks and possessing some generic capabilities. This assumption is manifest in the scores of books and articles on "the manager's job"[1] and in generic distinctions such as those between management and leadership.[2] It is also embedded in the currently burgeoning literature on management competencies.[3] With some important exceptions,[4] our theory of management is that at each organizational level, managers play similar roles and have similar responsibilities, only for a different size and scope of activities. The metaphor is that of the Russian doll: at each level of the hierarchy, the manager is similar but bigger than the manager a level below.

[1]Henry Mintzberg's book *The Nature of Managerial Work* (New York, NY: Harper and Row, 1973) is one of the most celebrated pieces of work on this topic. In his analysis, Mintzberg compares the work patterns of managers in very different kinds of managerial jobs in some very different kinds of organizations (such as companies, schools, and public hospitals), treating them as a sample from a population of "managers." The concept of a generic management role is inherent in the study design. The same assumption is also manifest in Peter Drucker's *The Practice of Management* (London: Heinemann, 1955) and John Kotter's *The General Managers* (New York, NY: The Free Press, 1982), although the focus of these authors is clearly on the role of corporate top management. There are some exceptions to this rule, however (see Note 4).

[2]See John Kotter, *A Force of Change: How Leadership Differs from Management* (New York, NY: The Free Press, 1990).

[3]For a recent and comprehensive review of this literature, see Elena P. Antonacopoulou and Louise FitzGerald, "Reframing Competency in Management Development," *Human Resource Management Journal,* 6/1 (1996): 27–48.

[4]Joseph L. Bower's book *Managing the Resource Allocation Process: A Study of Corporate Planning and Investment* (Boston, MA: Division of Research, Graduate School of Business Administration, Harvard University, 1970) is a good example of such exceptions. Based on this study of the resource allocation process, Bower develops a model in which front-line, middle, and top-level managers play clearly differentiated roles. Rosabeth Kanter's article "The Middle Manager as Innovator" [*Harvard Business Review,* 60/4 (1982): 95–105] also highlights such differences in management roles by suggesting the special role that middle managers can play in facilitating innovations.

Practice, however, has always been very different from this theory. The Russian doll model of management is firmly rooted in a hierarchical model of organizations. But, in reality, a hierarchy sharply differentiates roles vertically. In hierarchical organizations, top-level managers set direction by formulating strategy and controlling resources; middle-level managers mediate the vertical information processing and resource allocation processes by assuming the role of administrative controllers; and, swamped by direction and control from above, front-line managers find themselves in the role of operational implementers. Despite their differences, however, theory and practice have actually reinforced each other: the theory has made the hierarchy legitimate while the practice has made it operational.

Over the last decade, top-level managers around the world have recognized the limitations of the classic hierarchy. Alarmed by the loss of efficiency, speed, and flexibility, they have delayered and destaffed their organizations, reengineered their operations, and invested significant amounts of money and management time to spread the message of "empowerment" throughout their companies.[5] However, in most cases all they have bought is a little breathing time. How their companies function has not changed because the behaviors and relationships of their people have not changed.

The reason for this failure is simple. The problems of the hierarchy cannot be overcome without explicitly challenging both the Russian doll theory and the pecking-order practice of management. The reality is that large, diversified companies have and need a CEO or a leadership team, just as much as they have and need managers to run individual units and others to provide intermediate-level coordination and integration. Unless their activities and expected contributions are explicitly defined, these managers will tend to slip into the comfortable and familiar role structure of grand strategists, administrative controllers, and operational implementers. The only way to prevent this hierarchical relationship is to define the distinct value added of each of the management groups in terms of the different roles they need to play.

This is a key lesson from our recent research in twenty large European, American, and Asian companies.[6] Based on our analysis of the experiences of these companies, we have developed a model of the roles that front-line, senior, and top-level managers need to play for companies to achieve the organizational capabilities they are seeking.[7] These changes in management roles and personal capabilities are part of a fundamental change in organizational philosophy that is redefining the modern corporation.

---

[5]While these trends are well-known and have been widely documented in the business press, Nitin Nohria's research on the changes in strategy, organization, culture, and governance of the 100 largest U.S.-based companies over the 1978–1994 period provides clear and systematic evidence of these developments. A brief report of this study is available in Nitin Nohria, "From the M-form to the N-form: Taking Stock of Changes in the Large Industrial Corporation," Working Paper no. 16/1996, the Strategic Leadership Research Programme, London Business School, 1996.

[6]The twenty companies we studied were: Intel, 3M, AT&T, Corning, Beckton Dickensen, and Andersen Consulting in the United States; Asea Brown Boveri (ABB), IKEA, International Service Systems (ISS), Richardson Sheifield, Cartier, Royal Dutch Shell, Lufthansa, and Philips in Europe; and the LG Group (erstwhile Lucky Goldstar), Canon, Kao Corporation, Komatsu, Toyota, and Reliance Industries in Asia. In each of these companies, we conducted extensive interviews with managers (over 400, in total) at different levels, both in their corporate headquarters and in their different divisions and national subsidiaries. We also collected additional data from a variety of internal and external documents. Except for Toyota, we have written and published detailed case studies on all these companies, which are available either through the Harvard case clearing system or from the International Case Clearing House (ICCH). Our overall findings and conclusions from this study are available in Sumantra Ghoshal and Christopher A. Bartlett, *The Individualized Corporation* (New York, NY: HarperCollins, 1997).

[7]We have described these managerial roles in Christopher A. Bartlett and Sumantra Ghoshal, "Beyond the M-form: Toward a Managerial Theory of the Firm," *Strategic Management Journal,* 14 (Special Issue, Winter 1993): 23–46. In that article, written primarily for our academic colleagues, we have compared and contrasted our descriptions of these roles vis-à-vis those that are implied in some of the key strands of the related literature. In the present article, written primarily for a practitioner audience, we do not refer to this academic literature, but those interested in such references can find them in the 1993 article.

New Organization Model: New Management Roles

To understand the new management roles, one must first recognize the major elements of the emerging organizational framework that is shaping them. Despite the considerable differences in businesses, national origin, and corporate history in companies as diverse as GE, Komatsu, ABB, and Corning, we found that they were converging on a similar post-transformational organization model that represented a major change from their traditional authority-based hierarchies. Other companies we studied—such as 3M, ISS, and Kao—already shared many of these emerging organizational characteristics and therefore had avoided the worst aspects of the classic authority-based hierarchy. In many ways, this latter group provided both the inspiration and the example for other companies undergoing major organizational transformations.

The clearest and most widespread trend we observed was that companies were rethinking their old approach of dividing the organization from the top down into groups, sectors, and divisions. Instead, they were building from the bottom up on a foundation of small front-line operating units. For example, the $35 billion Swiss-based electro-technical giant, ABB, divided its operations into 1,300 local operating companies, each of which operates as a separate legal entity with its own balance sheet and P&L responsibilities. In 3M, the company's $15 billion dollars of sales generated by a portfolio of over 60,000 products are managed by 3,900 profit centers that are at the heart of the company's entrepreneurial process. ISS, the Denmark-based cleaning services organization, attributes its growth into a $2 billion multinational corporation to its policy of forming not one national subsidiary, but four or five small autonomous businesses in each of the 17 countries it has expanded into, allowing each of them to grow by serving a particular client group.

The second common characteristic in the emerging organizational model is the portfolio of cross-unit integrative processes. These processes are designed to break down the insulated vertically oriented relationships that have dominated the classic authority-based hierarchy. In ABB, the tensions embodied in the company's global matrix were resolved through a proliferation of business boards, functional councils, and project teams designed to play a primary role in ABB's management process at every level of the organization. At 3M, the R&D community's carefully developed network of communication channels and decision-making forums became the model for similar relationships to link the company's marketing and manufacturing resources across its portfolio of innovative front-line units. ISS made extensive use both of training and development and of cross-unit meetings and committees to ensure that knowledge and expertise developed in one part of the company were rapidly transferred system-wide.

Finally, in the emerging organization, these changes to the old structure and processes were supported by a strong commitment to genuine empowerment, a philosophy that represented a formidable challenge to the authority-based culture in most classic hierarchies. In ABB, CEO Percy Barnevik based the company's management practice on the twin principles of radically decentralized responsibility and tightly held individual accountability. 3M was known for its core principles that espoused a commitment to entrepreneurship and a belief in the individual. The company had long worked to translate those beliefs into a culture that "stimulates ordinary people to produce extraordinary performance." In his 30 years as the CEO of ISS, Poul Andreassen had developed a set of guiding principles, central to which was a genuine respect for his workers and a delegation of responsibility as close to the individual cleaning contract as possible.

This radically decentralized yet horizontally linked organizational model with a strong culture of empowerment required companies to break with the old hierarchy of nested roles that was implicit in the Russian doll model of management. In these and other companies we studied, operating-level managers had to evolve from their traditional role as front-line implementers to become innovative entrepreneurs; senior-level managers had to redefine their primary role from administrative controllers to developmental coaches; and top-level executives were forced to see themselves less as their company's strategic architects and more as their organizational leaders. The implications of such role changes on the distribution of key tasks and responsibilities are profound.

The Operating-Level Entrepreneurial Role   In identifying the new roles and responsibilities of those running business units, national subsidiaries, or other such front-line units, we studied the activities of scores of operating-level managers as they struggled to adjust to the demands of the new corporate model. We focus here on a select group of managers at ABB, 3M, and ISS not as definitive role models, but as illustrations of the framework of management tasks we have developed.

Don Jans headed the relays business unit that was part of Westinghouse's troubled power transmission and distribution business that was sold to ABB in 1989. Westinghouse had long regarded relays as a mature business, and Jans and his team had been encouraged to milk their slowly declining, modestly profitable operation. Yet, when exposed to ABB's decentralized entrepreneurial environment, the same management group turned their mature business into one with the performance profile of a young growth company. Within three years of the ownership change, export sales skyrocketed, new products were introduced, and operating profits doubled. Equally important, the revitalized U.S. relays unit began developing an electronic capability to supplement its traditional electro-mechanical expertise, thus laying the foundation for long-term expansion into a major new growth area.

At 3M, we saw a similar example of front-line entrepreneurship. In 1989, Andy Wong became the leader of a project team that had been struggling for over a decade to commercialize a portfolio of the company's optical technologies that had never found market applications. Over the next four years, Wong redeployed the unit's resources, refocused its energy and attention, protected the operations from several threats to shut them down, and remotivated the discouraged team. By 1994, Wong's unit had become a showcase within 3M by introducing two new products, both of which proved to be highly successful in the marketplace.

At ISS, we observed Theo Buitendijk take over the firm's small Dutch commercial cleaning business and double revenues within two years. He took the company into the specialized higher margin segment of slaughterhouse cleaning, eventually becoming the company's center of expertise in this sector and supporting its expansion throughout Europe. Like Jans, Buitendijk had previously been a traditional line manager in a classic authoritarian hierarchy (in his case, Exxon), but found that the different organizational context in ISS not only allowed, but encouraged him to redefine his role and change his behavior.

In each of these companies, a similar framework of organizational structure, processes, and culture supported the entrepreneurial activities of front-line managers like Jans, Wong, and Buitendijk as they took the initiative to drive the performance and enhance the capabilities of their units. Among their many tasks and responsibilities, we identified three that were central to their role as entrepreneurs rather than just implementers (see Table 1).

The most striking set of activities and achievements common to the operating-level entrepreneurs we studied were those related to their taking the initiative to create and pursue new business opportunities. In contrast to the role they played in their previous situations (as implementers of programs and priorities pushed down from above), managers such as Jans and Buitendijk found that they were not only free to initiate new activities, they were expected to do so. Jans rose to the challenge by expanding into export markets in Mexico, Canada, and the Far East and by committing to the development of microprocessor-based relays (despite the substantial up-front investment involved). Buitendijk's move into abattoir cleaning initially caused a sharp drop in his company's profitability but then proved to be a much more attractive segment than the company's highly competitive core business of office cleaning.

Table 1   Transformation of Management Roles and Tasks

	Operating-Level Managers	Senior-Level Manager	Top-Level Managers
Changing role	• From operational implementers to aggressive entrepreneurs	• From administrative controllers to supportive coaches	• From resource allocators to institutional leaders
Primary value added	• Driving business performance by focusing on productivity, innovation and growth within front-line units	• Providing the support and coordination to bring large company advantage to the independent front-line units	• Creating and embedding a sense of direction, commitment, and challenge to people throughout the organization
Key activities and tasks	• Creating and pursuing new growth opportunities for the business	• Developing individuals and supporting their activities	• Challenging embedded assumptions while establishing a stretching opportunity horizon and performance standards
	• Attracting and developing resources and competencies	• Linking dispersed knowledge, skills, and best practices across units	• Institutionalizing a set of norms and values to support cooperation and trust
	• Managing continuous performance improvement within the unit	• Managing the tension between short-term performance and long-term ambition	• Creating an overarching corporate purpose and ambition

Beyond developing new products and markets, these front-line entrepreneurs had all expanded the assets, resources, and capabilities of their operating units. Rather than playing the more traditional passive-dependent role defined by corporate processes such as head count authorization, capital budget allocation, and management development procedures, these individuals saw it as their responsibility to develop the limited resources they had and, as one of them described it, "do more with less." Andy Wong's actions in upgrading his unit's existing technological and manufacturing resources were impressive enough, but his creation of an entirely new marketing capability in a resource-constrained operation was truly entrepreneurial. Through persistent negotiations with senior management, creative internal resource reallocations,

and persuasive recruiting within the company, he was able to reinforce his small struggling unit with an experienced marketing manager. He then backed this manager with the distribution support of two other 3M divisions that agreed to help bring his unproven product to market. Don Jans' ability to develop a microprocessor-based product line exhibited the same commitment to build on and leverage existing capabilities. He became recognized as a "giver" rather than a "receiver," as ABB terminology referred to managers who became net developers rather than consumers of the organization's scarce resources.

The third basic responsibility of front-line managers was the one with which they were most familiar: to ensure continuous performance improvement in their operating units. In the new organizational context, however, they were given considerably more freedom, incentive, and support to find ways to do so. Although Don Jans had long been working to maximize operating performance in Westinghouse, within the ABB organization he was able to achieve substantial additional expense cuts, inventory and receivables reductions, and operating efficiency improvements largely because he was given what Barnevik described as "maximum degrees of freedom to execute."

Andy Wong knew that by leveraging his unit's existing assets and resources he could build the credibility and confidence he would need to obtain additional investment and support. It was for this reason that Wong initially invested a large part of his energy in focusing development attention on only two technologies and reducing manufacturing costs by 50%. It was only after gaining organizational confidence in his operating effectiveness that he won both the freedom to engage in the resource development and the time to implement his unit's entrepreneurial new product launch.

These three cases show the untapped potential for performance improvement available to most companies. The dramatically changed management behavior of Jans and Buitendijk along with Wong's rapid transition from engineer to project team leader suggests that inside every hierarchy, even the most authoritarian, there are entrepreneurial hostages waiting to be unleashed. But the new entrepreneurial tasks can only be accomplished after the historical structures, processes, and cultural norms are replaced by a new organizational framework that requires front-line managers to abandon their old implementation role.

The Senior-Level Developmental Role   The risk of redefining the role of operating-level managers as entrepreneurs rather than implementers is that it will fragment the company's resources and capabilities and lead to the kind of undisciplined, localized expansion that conglomerates experienced in the 1960s. To prevent this, the senior-level managers—those between the front-line units and the corporate-level management—must redefine their role from

the historic preoccupation with authority-based control to a focus on support-based management and organization development.

Traditionally, senior managers' power came from their pivotal position in large and complex hierarchies (where they typically were responsible for the organization's divisions, regions, or key functions). They played a vital intermediary role, disaggregating corporate objectives into business unit targets and aggregating business unit plans for corporate review. They were the linchpins in the resource allocation process due to corporate management's reliance on their input in capital budgeting and personnel appointment decisions. They stood at the crossroads of internal communication, interpreting and broadcasting management's priorities, then channeling and translating front-line feedback.

These classic senior management tasks have been challenged by the creation of small independent front-line units, the radical decentralization of assets and resources to support them, and the empowerment of the operating managers in charge. They have been further undermined by the delayering of middle levels of the organization and the impact of new information technologies on internal communication. Left to fulfill their traditional role, senior managers find themselves increasingly frustrated by the irrelevance and powerlessness of their position. Unless there is a radical realignment of their role, this group can become the silent subverters of change whose invisible, yet persistent resistance can derail even the most carefully planned transformation program.

Some companies have successfully redesigned the senior management role by making it a key part of supporting the front-line units, both by coordinating their activities and by coaching their operating-level entrepreneurs. Ulf Gundemark, Don Jans' boss and the head of ABB's worldwide relays business area, played a central role in managing the tension inherent in the company's ambition "to be global and local, big and small, radically decentralized with central reporting and control." Similarly, Paul Guehler, vice president of 3M's Safety and Security Systems Division to which Andy Wong's unit belonged, challenged Wong to define the focus and priorities in his business, while simultaneously helping him build the support and obtain the resources necessary to make it succeed. At ISS, Waldemar Schmidt, head of the European region, supported Theo Buitendijk's new business initiative despite its short-term profit impact, and he led the effort to leverage the expertise his unit developed into a European business capability.

In none of these cases did these managers see their roles in the traditional terms of administrative controllers and information relays. Instead of dominating their front-line managers, usurping their authority, or compromising their sense of responsibility for their operations, this new generation of senior managers added value to that activity through three core tasks. First, they become a vital source of support and guidance for the front-line entrepreneurs; second, they took primary responsibility for linking and leveraging the resources and competencies developed in the front-line units; and third, they played a key role in ensuring resolution of the numerous tensions and conflicts built into the management process (see Table 1).

When a company decides to change its dominant management model from one driven by authority to one built on empowerment, the basic orientation of the senior manager's task is changed from direction and control to development and support. ABB not only reflected this change in its cultural norms, it institutionalized it in the way key senior-level jobs were structured. For example, although Ulf Gundemark was the relays business area head, he had a staff of only four to help him run the $250 million worldwide business. As a result, he routinely asked managers in operating units to take on broader responsibilities, stretching their abilities and developing their contacts and support as they did so. To develop the worldwide relays strategy, he assembled a nine-person team of managers drawn from the front lines of his operating companies. To guide the ongoing business operations, he created a business area board that included his staff members and four key company presidents, including Don Jans. As Jans put it, "I'm

a much broader manager today than I was at Westinghouse. . . . We feel we are rediscovering management."

Paul Guehler described his primary job as "to help develop the people to develop the business." He worked intensively with Wong and his team, challenging them to refine their plans, forcing them to commit them to paper, and, most important, encouraging them to communicate and defend them in multiple forums in order to build up their struggling unit's thin support within 3M. At ISS, Waldemar Schmidt had a similar philosophy about his role, stating that "the most important thing I can do is to show an interest, to show that I care about them and their performance." He backed his words with actions, developing a strongly supportive relationship with his front-line managers that manifested itself in frequent telephone calls to say "Well done!" or "How can I help?"

The second element of this role focuses more on the level of organization development, as senior-level managers take on the task of linking the knowledge and expertise developed in their frontline units and embedding them as organizational capabilities to be leveraged company-wide. Gundemark's actions in forcing his front-line relays companies to rationalize and specialize in overlapping structures and responsibilities was a first step in integrating the portfolio of independent relays operations. He then appointed key specialists in each of the companies to functional councils whose primary purpose was to identify best practice and capture other benefits of coordination in R&D, quality, and purchasing. Waldemar Schmidt achieved similar cross-unit linkages through his regular meetings specifically devoted to leveraging the expertise of particular country units. When Theo Buitendijk's unit in Holland was shown to have superior performance in customer retention, for example, Schmidt gave him a day at his next European presidents conference to discuss his approach.

Beyond these important developmental tasks, however, those in senior management positions still must accept responsibility for the performance of the front-line units they supervise. The common bottom-line contribution of the three managers we described is that they all played the pivotal role in ensuring that those reporting to them kept the strategic objectives and operating priorities in balance. In ABB, this task was framed by a global matrix that was designed to legitimize rather than minimize the tensions and paradoxes inherent in most management decisions. To manage the conflict resolution vital to the organization's smooth operation, senior-level managers such as Ulf Gundemark developed and managed a portfolio of supplemental communications' channels and decision forums such as the worldwide business board and the functional councils we described. These and other forums (such as the steering committees that act as local boards for each of the front-line companies) not only serve a development and integration role, but they also become the place where differences are aired and resolution obtained on the conflicting perspectives and interests created by the matrix.

In 3M, this critical balancing role is so ingrained in the culture that senior-level managers such as Paul Guehler have integrated it into their ongoing management approach. For example, in what he terms his "give-and-take management style," Guehler tightened the screws on Wong's operations by requiring them to make the cuts necessary to meet their financial objectives, while behind the scenes he was defending against attempts to close the unit down and was lining up resources and support to back their proposed development initiatives.

Senior-level managers are often the forgotten and forsaken group in the organizational transformation process. Amid rounds of delayering, destaffing, and downsizing, many corporate executives have overlooked the fact that the success of small, empowered front-line units depends on a company's ability to bring large company benefits to those units. Organizations that dismantle their vertical integration mechanisms without simultaneously creating the horizontal coordination processes quickly lose potential scale economies. Even more important, they lose the benefits that come from leveraging each unit's assets, knowledge, and capabilities company-wide. At the same time, such intense horizontal

flows can also paralyze the organization by distracting or overburdening front-line managers. It is the managers in the middle who can make "inverting the pyramid" operational, not only by developing and supporting the front-line entrepreneurs, but also by absorbing most of the demands of the cross-business, cross-functional, and cross-geographic integration needs. In this way, they can prevent those at the operating level from becoming overwhelmed by the ambiguity, complexity, and potential conflicts that often accompany such horizontal networked organizations and allow them instead to focus on their vital entrepreneurial tasks.

The Top Management Leadership Role   Those at the apex of many of today's large, complex organizations find themselves playing out a role that they have inherited from their corporate forbears: to be the formulators of strategy, the builders of structure, and the controllers of systems. As these three tools became increasingly sophisticated, there was a growing assumption that they could allow organizations to drive purposefully towards their clearly defined goals, largely free from the idiosyncrasies of individual employees and the occasional eccentricities and pathologies of their behavior. To some extent, the objective was achieved. Under the strategy, structure, and systems doctrine of management, most large companies eventually became highly standardized and efficient operations, with individual employees being managed as inputs in the predicable but depersonalized system.

To free these entrepreneurial hostages requires a rollback of this dehumanizing management paradigm and thus a rethinking of top management's role. The role has to change from one grounded in the old doctrine of strategy, structure, and systems to one based on a new philosophy focusing on purpose, process, and people. Those at the top of most of the entrepreneurial companies in our study had evolved from being the formulators of corporate strategy to becoming the shapers of a broader corporate purpose with which individual employees could identify and feel a sense of personal commitment. Instead of focusing on formal structures that gave them control over the firm's financial resources, they devoted much of their efforts to building processes that added value by having the organization work more effectively together. Rather than becoming overly dependent on the management systems that isolated them from the organization and treated employees as factors of production, they created a challenging organizational context that put them back in touch with people and focused them on affecting individual inputs rather than just monitoring collective outputs.

In this radically redefined view of their role, those at the top first had to create a work environment that fostered entrepreneurial initiative rather than compliant implementation. Poul Andreassen was not someone who readily accepted the status quo. Like many of the CEOs we observed, he was constantly questioning the past and challenging his organization to achieve more. To overcome the constrained potential of continuing to operate ISS as a Danish office cleaning business, Andreassen began to conceive of the company as a more broadly defined professional service organization. His explicit objective was to create a world-class company, "to make ISS and service as synonymous as Xerox and photocopying." By broadening the opportunity horizon, he legitimized the entrepreneurial initiatives of his management team as they expanded into new markets and unexplored business segments. The challenging environment that he developed continued to support the entrepreneurial initiatives of operating-level managers such as Theo Buitendijk (as he developed the abattoirs cleaning business in Holland) and the ISS manager in Germany who saw an opportunity to expand into the former East Germany to start a business in the removal of building rubble.

The second key task common to the top managers we studied was to shape the organizational context necessary to support the radically decentralized structure and the management philosophy of empowerment. To ensure that the organization did not fragment its efforts or dissipate its scarce resources in this more decentralized form, traditional control-based values had to be replaced with norms

of trust and support. Over the years, 3M's top managers have created an organization with such values, allowing resources and expertise to move freely across its 3,900 profit centers located in 47 divisions and 57 country operations. From the earliest days, they developed clear integrating norms such as the recognition that while products belong to the division, technologies belong to the company. They reinforced such beliefs by carefully developing a framework for collaboration and support. For example, the strong mutually supportive relationships within 3M's scientific community were formed and reinforced through institutionalized grassroots forums, internal technology fairs, and cross-unit transfer practices. Overarching all of this was a sense of trust embedded in the respect those at the top had for individuals and their ideas. As current CEO Livio "Desi" DeSimone reminds his managers, they must listen carefully to subordinates and continually ask, "What do you see that I am missing?" It was this respectful, supportive, and trusting environment that allowed entrepreneurs like Andy Wong to take risks and that encouraged senior managers like Paul Guehler to back them.

Finally, the top-level managers we observed also played the vital role of providing the organization with a stabilizing and motivating sense of purpose. As chief executive of ABB, Percy Barnevik believed that he had to develop more than just a clear strategy for his newly merged worldwide entity. He felt that he had to create an organizational environment that made people proud to belong and motivated to work for the company. He articulated ABB's overall mission not in terms of its market share, competitive position, or profit objectives, but in terms of the ways in which ABB could contribute to sustainable economic growth and world development. He emphasized a sensitivity to environmental protection and a commitment to improving living standards worldwide, reflecting those beliefs not only in the company's formal mission statement, but also in the major strategic decisions he took. The company's pioneering investments in Eastern Europe, its transfer of technology to China and India, and its innovations in environmentally sensitive processes gave substance to its articulated purpose. These efforts also made ABB's employees feel that they were contributing to changing the world for the better. As corporate executive VP Goran Lindahl explained, "In the end, managers are loyal not to a particular boss or even to a company, but to a set of values they believe in and find satisfying."

The approach taken by Barnevik and Lindahl (and their counterparts in companies such as 3M and ISS) reflected the simple belief that their job as the top-level leaders was not simply to manage an economic entity whose activities could be directed through strategic plans, resource allocation processes, and management control systems. Equally important was their role as the principal architects of a social institution able to capture the energy, commitment, and creativity of those within it by treating them as valued organizational members, not just contracted company employees. In addition to managing the strategy and structure, they took the time to develop a corporate purpose and shape the integrating organizational processes. Rather than simply monitoring the performance of divisions or subsidiaries through abstract systems, they focused their attention on the people within the organizations—those whose motivations and actions would drive the company's performance.

New Management Roles, New Personal Competencies

Over the past few years, companies as diverse as AT&T, British Airways, BP, Siemens, and The World Bank have invested enormous amounts of management time and effort to define the ideal profile of their future corporate leaders. Siemens, for example, has defined 22 desirable management characteristics under five basic competencies of understanding, drive, trust, social competence, and what they call a "sixth sense." The World Bank's ideal profile identifies 20 attributes and groups them into seven quite different categories of intellectual leadership, team leadership, staff development, work program management, communication, interpersonal impact, and client orientation. Pepsico's desired competency profile for its executives of the

future has 18 key dimensions defining how individuals see the world, how they think, and the way they act.

This focus on personal characteristics is understandable given the widespread problems that so many individuals have had adjusting to the transformed organizational environment and performing the redefined management tasks. Indeed, this emerging interest in individual competencies has created a cottage industry among consultants eager to promote their expertise in identifying, measuring, and developing the desired personal capabilities to lead in the new corporate environment. Yet, despite prodigious efforts in designing questionnaires, conducting interviews, and running seminars to define the profile of leadership competencies, few of these programs have won the kind of credibility and support necessary for widespread adoption and application.

One problem is that the profiles that have been generated often include an inventory of personality traits, individual beliefs, acquired skills, and other personal attributes and behaviors assembled on the basis of unclear selection criteria and with little logical linkage to bind them. Furthermore, these profiles are often developed based on surveys of current managers or analysis of the most successful individual performers in the existing context. As such, they risk defining future leadership needs in terms of the historical organizational roles and capabilities that were required to succeed in the old organizational forms.

The most important limitation of these management competency exercises is that they are almost always defined as a single ideal profile. While such an assumption may not have been entirely irrational in the more symmetrical roles typical of the traditional authority-based hierarchy, this extension of the Russian doll model is not viable in the emerging delayered organization with its differentiated set of management roles and tasks.

As part of our research into post-transformation organizations, we studied the adaptation of managers to their redefined responsibilities. Instead of asking managers to describe the personal characteristics they felt were most important, we observed those who had demonstrated their effectiveness in performing the key tasks of the redefined management roles. Rather than trying to develop a list of generic competencies with universal application, we were able to differentiate the profiles of managers who succeeded in adding value in very different ways at each level of the organization.

Despite the fact that we were developing more differentiated profiles based on performance rather than opinion, the notion of individual competencies still seemed too vague and unfocused to be of great practical value. To be more useful to managers, the concept had to be more sharply defined and more clearly applicable to human resource discussions and activities. This led us to develop a simple classification model that helped us allocate the broadly defined competencies into three categories. In the first, we listed deeply embedded personal characteristics like attitudes, traits, and values that were intrinsic parts of the individual's character and personality. The second category included attributes such as knowledge, experience, and understanding that generally could be acquired through training and career path development. The third category was composed of specialized skills and abilities that were directly linked to the job's specific task requirements and were built on the individual's intrinsic capabilities and acquired knowledge (see Table 2).

By categorizing management competencies in this way, we not only gave the concept a sharper definition, but were also able to identify much more clearly how managers could focus attention on different attributes of the profile in various important human resource decisions. In particular, our observations led us to develop some propositions about the role different attributes play in the vital management responsibilities for selecting, developing, and supporting people in their particular job responsibilities.

Selecting for Embedded Traits   There is a high rate of failure among managers attempting to adapt from their historic roles in traditional companies to their newly defined tasks in transformed and reengineered organizations. This underscores the importance of identifying selection criteria that can help product success in radically redefined roles. For example, when ABB was created in 1988 through merger, 300 top and senior management positions were filled. Despite the careful selection of those appointed to these positions, over 40% of them were no longer with the company six years later. As the company's leadership recognized at the time, the central problem was to identify the candidates who had already developed the personal traits that were needed to succeed in the radically different organizational and managerial context that Percy Barnevik had defined for ABB.

When faced with such a situation, most companies we observed tended to select primarily on the basis of an individual's accumulated knowledge and job experience. These were, after all, the most visible and stable qualifications in an otherwise tumultuous situation. Furthermore, selecting on this basis was a decision that could be made by default, simply by requiring existing managers to take on totally redefined job responsibilities.

In such situations, however, past experience did not prove to be a good predictor of future success. The most obvious problem was that much of the acquired organizational expertise was likely to reflect old management models and behavioral norms. Equally problematic were the personal characteristics of those who had succeeded in the old organizational environment. As many companies discovered, the highly task-oriented senior managers who were both comfortable and successful in the well-structured work environment of their traditional company often found great personal difficulty in adjusting to the coaching and integrating roles that became an important part of their redefined responsibilities.

As a result, many companies are coming to believe that it is much more difficult to convince an authoritarian industry expert to adopt a more people-sensitive style than to develop industry expertise in a strong people manager. It is a recognition that is leading them to conclude that innate personal characteristics should dominate acquired

Table 2   Management Competencies for New Roles

Role/Task	Attitude/Traits	Knowledge/Experience	Skills/Abilities
Operating-Level Entrepreneurs	**Results-Oriented Competitor**	**Detailed Operating Knowledge**	**Focuses Energy on Opportunities**
• Creating and pursuing opportunities	• Creative, intuitive	• Knowledge of the business's technical, competitive, and customer characteristics	• Ability to recognize potential and make commitments
• Attracting and utilizing scarce skills and resources	• Persuasive, engaging	• Knowledge of internal and external resources	• Ability to motivate and drive people
• Managing continuous performance improvement	• Competitive, persistent	• Detailed understanding of the business operations	• Ability to sustain organizational energy around demanding objectives
Senior-Management Developers	**People-Oriented Integrator**	**Broad Organizational Experience**	**Develops People and Relationships**
• Reviewing, developing, supporting individuals and their initiates	• Supportive, patient	• Knowledge of people as individuals and understanding of how to influence them	• Ability to delegate, develop, empower
• Linking dispersed knowledge, skills, and practices	• Integrative, flexible	• Understanding of the interpersonal dynamics among diverse groups	• Ability to develop relationships and build teams.
• Managing the short-term and long-term pressures	• Perceptive, demanding	• Understanding the means-ends relationships linking short-term priorities and long-term goals	• Ability to reconcile differences while maintaining tension
Top-Level Leaders	**Institution-Minded Visionary**	**Understanding Company in Its Context**	**Balances Alignment and Challenge**
• Challenging embedded assumptions while setting stretching opportunity horizons and performance standards	• Challenging, stretching	• Grounded understanding of the company, its businesses and operations	• Ability to create an exciting, demanding work environment
• Building a context of cooperation and trust	• Open-minded, fair	• Understanding of the organization as a system of structures, processes, and cultures	• Ability to inspire confidence and belief in the institution and its management
• Creating an overarching sense of corporate purpose and ambition	• Insightful, inspiring	• Broad knowledge of different companies, industries and societies	• Ability to combine conceptual insight with motivational challenges

experience as the key selection criteria. Equally importantly, they are recognizing that because the management roles and tasks differ widely at each level of the organization, so too will the attitudes, traits, and values of those most likely to succeed in each position. Recruitment and succession planning in such an environment becomes a much more sophisticated exercise of identifying the very different kinds of individuals who can succeed as operating-level entrepreneurs, senior-level developers, and top management leaders.

In ISS, for example, the company had long recognized the vital importance of recruiting individuals who were result-oriented competitors to run their front-line operating units. Although the front-line manager's job at ISS could be regarded as a low-status position managing supervisors in the mature and menial office cleaning business, ISS knew that by structuring the role to give managers status and autonomy, they could attract the kind of energetic, independent, and creative individuals they wanted. Like many of ISS's operating-level entrepreneurs, Theo Buitendijk had spent his early career in a traditional hierarchical company, but he had been frustrated by the constraints, controls, and lack of independence he felt. Status elements like the "managing director" title and the prestige company car signaled the importance ISS attached to this position, but entrepreneurial individuals like Buitendijk were even more attracted by the independence offered by operating their own business behind what ISS managers called "Chinese walls" to prevent unwanted interference. By creating an environment that motivated self-starters would find stimulating, ISS had little difficulty in training them in industry knowledge and helping them develop the specific job skills they required to succeed.

The personal profile required to move to the next level of management was quite different, however, and few of the operating-level entrepreneurs were expected or indeed had an ambition to move up to the divisional management level. One who did was Waldemar Schmidt, an operating-level entrepreneur who had turned around the company's Brazilian business before being appointed head of the European division. Despite his relatively limited knowledge of the European market, Schmidt impressed Poul Andreassen as a people-oriented individual who had a genuine interest in developing and supporting others. Indeed, the company's Five Star training program had originated in Brazil as part of Schmidt's commitment to continually upgrade his employees. Furthermore, he was recognized as being a very balanced individual who tended to operate by influence more than authority, yet was demanding of himself and others. These were qualities that Andreassen regarded as vital in his senior managers and felt they far outweighed Schmidt's more limited European knowledge or experience.

At the top level of the organization, another set of personal qualities was felt to be important. When Poul Andreassen became the president of ISS in 1962, he too was selected primarily on the basis of his personal traits rather than his experience in the company or his proven leadership skills. As a young engineer in his mid-30s, he was frustrated in his job with a traditional large company and was looking for the opportunity to build a very different kind of organization. Despite his lack of industry background of ISS-specific management skills, he was attractive because he was much less interested in running an ongoing company than he was in building a more ambitious organization. His most appealing characteristic was his willingness to question and challenge everything, and even after thirty years in the job, he still felt that his best days were when he could go into the field and confront his division or business unit managers so as to help "stir up new things."

Like Red Auerbach of the Boston Celtics, there will be a few individuals who have the breadth of personal traits and the temperamental range to adapt to the very different roles and tasks demanded of them at different organizational levels. At ISS, Waldemar Schmidt progressed from successful operating-level entrepreneur to effective senior management developer, and, after Poul Andreassen's retirement, was asked to succeed him as top-level corporate leader. One of management's most important challenges is to identify the personal characteristics that will allow an individual to succeed in a new and often quite different role and, equally important, to recognize when someone who is successful at one level lacks the individual traits to succeed at the next. For those with the perceived potential, however, the next key challenge is to develop the knowledge and expertise that can support and leverage their embedded personal traits.

Developing for Knowledge Acquisition   While training and development activities are rarely very effective in changing the deeply embedded personal traits, attitudes, and values, they are extremely appropriate means of developing the kind of knowledge and experience that allows an individual to build on and apply those embedded individual attributes. For example, as a person who is naturally creative, engaging, and competitive learns more about a particular business, its customers, and technologies, he or she becomes a much more effective and focused operating-level entrepreneur. Poul Andreassen understood this well and made training and development one of the few functions that he controlled directly from ISS's small corporate office. Under the ISS philosophy of ensuring that all employees had the opportunity to use their abilities to the fullest, the Five Star development program defined five levels of training that allowed front-line supervisors with the appropriate profile to gain the knowledge and experience they would need in a broader management job.

Because of its strong promote-from-within culture, 3M also had a long-standing commitment to develop its people to their potential. Soon after a new employee enters the company (within six months for a clerical employee or three years for a laboratory scientist) a formal Early Career Assessment process is initiated both to ensure that the individual is a proper fit with the company and to define a program to prepare them for their next career opportunity. For example, a promising accounting clerk might be set the personal education goal of becoming a Certified Public Accountant within three years, while at the same time being given an internal development assignment to provide experience in preparing financial statements and participating in audits. This process continues (albeit in a somewhat less structured format) throughout an individual's career in 3M, with the company providing internal business courses and technical seminars as well as supporting participation in external education programs.

On-the-job training is still the primary emphasis, and those with the will and the perceived personal potential are given every opportunity to develop that promise. For example, Andy Wong, who turned the struggling Optical Systems (OS) project into a showcase of entrepreneurial success, was carefully prepared for that role over five years. This quiet engineer first caught the eye of Ron Mitsch, a senior R&D executive who was impressed by the young man's tenacious, self-motivated competitiveness—personal qualities that 3M looked for in its front-line entrepreneurs. Wanting to give him the opportunity to prove that potential, the mentor told Wong about an opportunity to lead a small technical development team in the OS unit. While demonstrating his energy and persuasive persistence, Wong began to expand his knowledge about the unit's optical technologies, as he struggled to develop the understanding he needed to focus his team's rather fragmented efforts. After a couple of years in the OS laboratory, Wong was asked to take on the additional responsibility for the unit's inefficient manufacturing operations. Although he had no prior production or logistics experience, his initiatives in rationalizing the complex sourcing arrangements, simplifying the manufacturing process, and consolidating production in a single plant resulted in a 50% cost reduction and simultaneous improvement in product quality. It was through these experiences that Wong was able to broaden his knowledge of the business beyond his focused understanding of the technology and expand his familiarity with the organization's resources beyond his scientific contacts. Through careful career path development, he developed the kind of knowledge and experience he needed to allow him to use his naturally competitive traits effectively as the newly appointed project team leader for optical systems.

While the developmental path for operating-level entrepreneurs focused on enhancing knowledge and expertise in a particular business, market, or function, the track to the next level of management usually required a much richer understanding of the organization and how it operated. Wong's boss Paul Guehler also began his 3M career in the R&D laboratory and was also identified as someone who looked beyond the technologies he was developing to the businesses they represented. It was this budding entrepreneurial attitude that led to his transfer to 3M's New Business Ventures Division. In this position, his natural curiosity and intuitiveness were leveraged by focusing him on the task of exploring market opportunities and business applications for high potential ideas and innovations. After a decade in this division, Guehler was transferred to the Occupational Health and Safety Products Division. In this position, his experience as an R&D manager gave him the opportunity to broaden his understanding of the mainstream organizational processes and how to manage them. A subsequent move to the Disposable Products Division helped him build on that experience, particularly when he was appointed Business Director for disposable products in Europe. This responsibility for a highly competitive product in a fast-changing market greatly expanded his experience in assessing the capabilities and limitations of a diverse group of individuals and organizational units and further expanded his understanding of the organizational dynamics and strategic tensions of having them work together. By the time he was appointed as general manager and later vice president of the Safety and Security Systems Division of which Wong's OS unit was a part, he brought not only hard-headed business knowledge, but some sensitive organizational insights into his new role. As his diagnosis of the OS unit's situation indicates:

> You have to have people in these positions who recognize other people's talents and support their ideals for building a business. My job is to create an environment where people come forward with ideas and are supported to succeed. . . . So while the OS group probably thought I was being too tough, my objective

was to get them to recognize their opportunities, to hold them accountable for their actions, to help them build their credibility, and ultimately to support them so they could succeed. . . . One of my most important roles is not only to develop business, but to develop the people who can develop the business.

At the top level of 3M management, the need for a breadth of knowledge and experience was even greater. In 1991, when the company was planning the transition to a new chief executive, board member and ex-CEO Lou Lehr said that the successful candidate was likely to be a career 3M executive five to ten years from retirement (for no other reason than it usually took 30 to 35 years to accumulate the breadth of experience to be effective in the top job in this diversified company).

Desi DeSimone, the CEO elected in 1991, was described in one news account as "a textbook example of the quintessential 3M CEO." He had moved up through technical, engineering, and manufacturing management positions to assume general management roles as managing director of the Brazilian subsidiary and eventually area vice president of 3M's Latin American operations. He was recognized as a senior manager with top management potential. "There were always people taking an interest in my development," DeSimone said on assuming the CEO job. In classic 3M fashion, he was brought back to corporate headquarters where he could be given experiences that would provide him with the background and knowledge to help him succeed in top-level positions.

Through the 1980s, he was assigned to head up each of 3M's three business sectors in succession, to broaden his knowledge of their markets and technologies as well as to refine the skills necessary to have an impact on their performance. After spending most of his career focused on the company's far-flung units in Canada, Australia, and Latin America, it was important for him to get a better sense of the organization's core structure, processes, and culture. By immersing him in corporate-level activities for more than a decade, 3M's top management and the board's appraisal committee wanted to ensure that he had the organizational understanding that was vital for any leader. Finally, DeSimone's promotion to the board in 1986 was important not only in bringing his expertise to board-level decisions, but also in broadening him as an executive by exposing him to the perspectives and experiences of top-level executives from other companies in different industries.

In companies like 3M where an understanding of the strongly held organizational values and cultural norms are central to the source of competitive advantage, the importance of a career-long development process must not be underestimated. Sometimes, however, a manager's strong links to the company's existing policies and practices become disadvantageous, particularly when the embedded beliefs have deteriorated into blind assumptions or outmoded conventional wisdom. In such cases, selection of an outsider with the desired personal characteristics can break the pathological cycle of inwardly focused indoctrination. But it does so at the risk of stranding the new leader without the relevant knowledge required to develop the appropriate top management skills for the company. The risks are particularly high were knowledge and experience accumulated in prior work is of limited relevance in the new situation. So while Larry Bossidy was able to make a relatively smooth transition from his top management job at GE to the leadership of Allied, another traditionally structured diversified industrial goods company, John Sculley's move from Pepsico to Apple became problematic due to his lack of computer industry background and his inexperience in managing the more informal network culture of Silicon Valley. Such problems underscore the important linkage between personal traits and acquired knowledge, on the one hand, and the development of the skills and abilities required to perform a job effectively, on the other.

Coaching for Skills Mastery Of all the elements in the competencies profile, the particular skills and abilities an individual develops are probably the best indicators of job success, since they are the most directly linked to a position's key roles and tasks. Not everyone becomes effective in these highly specific yet critical personal skills, and the challenge for management is to identify those who can succeed and to help them develop these skills. The reason is that most of these skills rely heavily on tacit knowledge and capabilities that often grow out of the interaction between an individual's embedded traits and accumulated experience. So, for example, the critical entrepreneurial ability to recognize potential in people and situations is not an easily trainable skill, but one that often develops naturally in individuals who are curious and intuitive by nature and who have developed a richly textured understanding of their particular business and organizational environment.

Thus while some broader skills can be selected for and other simpler ones can be trained for, most of the critical skills are largely self-developed through on-the-job experience as individuals apply their natural talents and accumulated experience to the particular challenges of the job. In this process, the most effective role management can play is to coach and support those they have selected and prepared for the job by providing the resources, reinforcement, and guidance to encourage the self-development process.

ABB executive vice president Goran Lindahl clearly articulated the notion that an individual's natural characteristics should be the dominant factor in selection: "I will always pick a person with tenacity over one with just experience." Lindahl also spent a substantial amount of his time planning developmental job experiences for the individuals he selected. However, he considered his principal and most difficult management role to be acting as a teacher and a coach to help those in the organization leverage their experiences and fulfill their natural potential. It was this commitment "to help engineers become managers, and managers grow into leaders" that was vital to the development of the skills required to meet the demanding new job requirements.

Don Jans was surprised when he was asked to continue to head the relays company that ABB took over as part of the acquired Westinghouse power transmission and distribution business. "The prevailing view was that we had lost the war," he said, "and that the occupying troops would just move in." Yet Lindahl and Ulf Gundemark (his worldwide relays business manager) were impressed that Jans, like most of the Westinghouse managers, was a very capable individual with long industry experience. They felt that, with proper coaching, his natural energy, persistence, and competitiveness could be channeled towards the new skills he would need to manage in a very different way within ABB.

Jans met their expectations and—with his bosses' encouragement, support, and coaching—was able to develop a whole range of new skills that helped him turn around his relays company. By redefining Jans's company as part of an interdependent global network, ABB's senior-level management was able to refocus his attention on export markets, thereby helping him reignite his latent ability to identify and exploit opportunities. Through their own highly motivating and inspiring management approach, Barnevik, Lindhal, Gundemark, and others provided Jans with role models that encouraged him to tap into his own engaging personality and develop a more motivating approach to drive his people to higher levels of performance. ABB's cultural norm of high interest and involvement in the operations (what Lindahl called the "fingers in the pie" approach) led Jans to expand on his natural results-orientated competitiveness and develop a skill for creating and sustaining energy around the demanding objectives he set for his organization.

Meanwhile, Lindahl was helping support a very different set of new skills in the select few operating-level entrepreneurs that had been identified to take on senior-level business or regional responsibilities. One such individual was Ulf Gundemark, the young manager who was running the Swedish relays company and who had twelve years of experience in various parts of the organization. Lindahl promoted him to worldwide relays manager because he demonstrated the vital personality characteristics that Lindahl described as "generous, flexible, and

statesmanlike." Driven by his boss's urging to become a "giver" rather than a "receiver" of management resources and constrained by his lack of division-level staff, Gundemark leveraged his naturally supportive disposition into a sophisticated skill of developing the operating-level managers reporting to him by delegating responsibilities and empowering them to make decisions. Lindahl also encouraged Gundemark to establish formal and informal management forums at all levels of his organization. By applying his flexible and integrative personality to his growing understanding of the organizational dynamics, Gundemark gradually acquired a strong ability to develop interpersonal relationships and team behavior. Finally, largely by following the example of his boss, Gundemark developed the vital senior management skill of maintaining the pressure for both long- and short-term objectives while helping the organization to deal with the conflicts that were implied. Although many were unwilling or unable to manage the very different task requirements of a senior manager's job (indeed, Lindahl estimated that even after careful selection, half the candidates for these positions either stepped aside or were moved out of the role), managers like Gundemark—who were able to develop their people skills and relationship-building skills—usually succeeded in these roles.

At the top levels of management, an even more subtle and sophisticated set of skills and abilities was necessary. More than just driving the company's ongoing operations or developing its resources and capabilities, these individuals had to be able to lead the company to becoming what Lindahl described as "a self-driven, self-renewing organization." The most fundamental skill was one that CEO Percy Barnevik had encouraged in all his top team—to create an exciting and demanding work environment. Harnessing his own innate restlessness, Lindahl focused his naturally striving and questioning personal style on his broad knowledge of the company and its businesses to develop a finely honed ability to challenge managers' assumptions while stretching them to reach for new objectives. His bi-monthly business meetings were far from traditional review sessions. Lindahl led his senior managers through scenario exercises that forced them to think beyond straight-line projections and consider how they could respond to new trade barriers, political realignments, or environmental legislation. He also recognized that it was top management's role to develop the organization's values. "In the end," he said "managers are not really loyal to a particular boss or even to a company, but to the values they represent." One of the most vital was to create an environment of mutual cooperation and trust. By consistently applying his own natural forthright and open personal approach to a sophisticated understanding of the organization, he was able to create a belief in the institution and in the fairness of its management processes that was a prior condition for both entrepreneurial risk taking and shared organizational learning.

Finally, Lindahl's sharp mind and inspiring personal manner were able to articulate messages that provided the organization with conceptual insight about the business while simultaneously providing them with concrete motivational challenges. He routinely demonstrated this ability in his far-sighted views about ABB's role in helping develop the industrial infrastructure in a realigned global political economy. Furthermore, he translated those insights into challenges for his management. As a result of his skills and abilities, the company was able to radically rebalance its own value chain from the developed world to the emerging giants such as China, India, and Eastern Europe.

The reason this set of top management skills is so difficult to develop is that it both reflects and reinforces the conflicts, dilemmas, and paradoxes framed by the post-transformational organization. Unlike the classic top management task that focused on managing "alignment" and ensuring "fit," the role we have described involves at least as much energy being devoted to questioning, challenging and even defying the company's traditional strategic assumptions and embedded organizational practices. The required competencies involve an even greater level of subtlety and sophistication to maintain a balance between challenging embedded

beliefs and creating a unifying sense of purpose and ambition. Not surprisingly, only a handful of people have the potential to develop these scarce leadership skills, and perhaps the most critical task of top management is to identify these individuals and provide them with the necessary development opportunities and coaching support to allow them to fulfill that potential.

From Organization Man to Individualized Corporation

The dramatic changes in management roles and the individual competencies required to implement them are part of a broader redefinition of the relationship between the corporation and its employees in the post-transformational organization. In earlier decades, when capital was the scarce resource, top management's primary role was to use its control over investments to determine strategy as well as to create structures and systems to shape employee behavior in ways that would support those capital allocation decisions. The strategy-structure-systems doctrine of management led to the development of what William Whyte termed "the organization man"—the employee whose behavior was molded to suit the needs of the corporation and to support its strategic investments.

As the industrial era evolves into the information age, however, the scarce resource is shifting from capital to knowledge. But because the organization's vital knowledge, expertise, and strategic information exist at the operating levels rather than at the top, the whole authoritarian hierarchy has had to be dismantled and the roles and tasks of each management level radically redefined. Far from wanting to subjugate individual differences by requiring conformity to a standardized organizational model, companies are recognizing that in a knowledge-based environment, diversity of employee perspectives, experience, and capabilities can be an important organizational asset.

This realization implies a fundamental reconceptualization of the underlying management philosophy. Instead of forcing the individual to conform to the company's policies and practices, the overall objective is to capture and leverage the knowledge and expertise that each organizational member brings to the company. Thus the notion of "the organization man" and the Russian Doll model of nested roles that it reflected and supported are giving way to a concept we call "the individualized corporation"— one that capitalizes on the idiosyncrasies and even the eccentricities of exceptional people by recognizing, developing, and applying their unique capabilities.

This change in organizational philosophy has important implications for management practice. One of the most basic needs is to change the multitude of personnel practices aimed at recruiting, developing, and promoting people on the basis of a single corporate model—an approach most recently exemplified by the unrealistic competency lists of personal characteristics, many of which seem to resemble the idealized profile of the Boy Scout Law (trustworthy, loyal, helpful, friendly, and so on). Equally important, however, is the need for employees to accept that their career paths may not lead inexorably up the hierarchy, but will more likely take them where they best fit and therefore where they can add the most value for the organization. Together these changes are exposing the myth of the generic manager and are redefining the basic relationship between companies and their employees in a way that recognizes and capitalizes on diversity rather than trying to minimize and suppress it.

Reading 8-2   Serving the World's Poor, Profitably

C.K. Prahalad and Allen Hammond

Consider this bleak vision of the world 15 years from now: The global economy recovers from its current stagnation but growth remains anemic. Deflation continues to threaten, the gap between rich and poor keeps widening, and incidents of economic chaos, governmental collapse, and civil war plague developing regions. Terrorism remains a constant threat, diverting significant public and private resources to security concerns. Opposition to the global market system intensifies. Multinational companies find it difficult to expand, and many become risk averse, slowing investment and pulling back from emerging markets.

Now consider this much brighter scenario: Driven by private investment and widespread entrepreneurial activity, the economies of developing regions grow vigorously, creating jobs and wealth and bringing hundreds of millions of new consumers into the global marketplace every year. China, India, Brazil, and, gradually, South Africa become new engines of global economic growth, promoting prosperity around the world. The resulting decrease in poverty produces a range of social benefits, helping to stabilize many developing regions and reduce civil and cross-border conflicts. The threat of terrorism and war recedes. Multinational companies expand rapidly in an era of intense innovation and competition.

Both of these scenarios are possible. Which one comes to pass will be determined primarily by one factor: the willingness of big, multinational companies to enter and invest in the world's poorest markets. By stimulating commerce and development at the bottom of the economic pyramid, MNCs could radically improve the lives of billions of people and help bring into being a more stable, less dangerous world. Achieving this goal does not require multinationals to spearhead global social development initiatives for

C.K. Prahalad is the Harvey C. Fruehauf Professor of Business Administration at the University of Michigan Business School in Ann Arbor and the chairman of Praja, a software company in San Diego. Allen Hammond is the CIO, senior scientist, and director of the Digital Dividend project at the World Resources Institute in Washington, DC.

charitable purposes. They need only act in their own self-interest, for there are enormous business benefits to be gained by entering developing markets. In fact, many innovative companies—entrepreneurial outfits and large, established enterprises alike—are already serving the world's poor in ways that generate strong revenues, lead to greater operating efficiencies, and uncover new sources of innovation. For these companies—and those that follow their lead—building businesses aimed at the bottom of the pyramid promises to provide important competitive advantages as the twenty-first century unfolds.

Big companies are not going to solve the economic ills of developing countries by themselves, of course. It will also take targeted financial aid from the developed world and improvements in the governance of the developing nations themselves. But it's clear to us that prosperity can come to the poorest regions only through the direct and sustained involvement of multinational companies. And it's equally clear that the multinationals can enhance their own prosperity in the process.

Untapped Potential

Everyone knows that the world's poor are distressingly plentiful. Fully 65% of the world's population earns less than $2,000 each per year—that's 4 billion people. But despite the vastness of this market, it remains largely untapped by multinational companies. The reluctance to invest is easy to understand. Companies assume that people with such low incomes have little to spend on goods and services and that what they do spend goes to basic needs like food and shelter. They also assume that various barriers to commerce—corruption, illiteracy, inadequate infrastructure, currency fluctuations, bureaucratic red tape—make it impossible to do business profitably in these regions.

But such assumptions reflect a narrow and largely outdated view of the developing world. The fact is, many multinationals already successfully do business in developing countries (although most currently focus on selling to the small upper-middle-class segments of these markets), and their experience shows that the barriers to commerce—

although real—are much lower than is typically thought. Moreover, several positive trends in developing countries—from political reform, to a growing openness to investment, to the development of low-cost wireless communication networks—are reducing the barriers further while also providing businesses with greater access to even the poorest city slums and rural areas. Indeed, once the misperceptions are wiped away, the enormous economic potential that lies at the bottom of the pyramid becomes clear.

Take the assumption that the poor have no money. It sounds obvious on the surface, but it's wrong. While individual incomes may be low, the aggregate buying power of poor communities is actually quite large. The average per capita income of villagers in rural Bangladesh, for instance, is less than $200 per year, but as a group they are avid consumers of telecommunications services. Grameen Telecom's village phones, which are owned by a single entrepreneur but used by the entire community, generate an average revenue of roughly $90 a month—and as much as $1,000 a month in some large villages. Customers of these village phones, who pay cash for each use, spend an average of 7% of their income on phone services—a far higher percentage than consumers in traditional markets do.

It's also incorrect to assume that the poor are too concerned with fulfilling their basic needs to "waste" money on nonessential goods. In fact, the poor often do buy "luxury" items. In the Mumbai shantytown of Dharavi, for example, 85% of households own a television set, 75% own a pressure cooker and a mixer, 56% own a gas stove, and 21% have telephones. That's because buying a house in Mumbai, for most people at the bottom of the pyramid, is not a realistic option. Neither is getting access to running water. They accept that reality, and rather than saving for a rainy day, they spend their income on things they can get now that improve the quality of their lives.

Another big misperception about developing markets is that the goods sold there are incredibly cheap and, hence, there's no room for a new competitor to come in and turn a profit. In reality, consumers at the bottom of the pyramid pay much higher prices for most things than middle-class consumers do, which means that there's a real opportunity for companies, particularly big corporations with economies of scale and efficient supply chains, to capture market share by offering higher quality goods at lower prices while maintaining attractive margins. In fact, throughout the developing world, urban slum dwellers pay, for instance, between four and 100 times as much for drinking water as middle- and upper-class families. Food also costs 20% to 30% more in the poorest communities since there is no access to bulk discount stores. On the service side of the economy, local moneylenders charge interest of 10% to 15% *per day,* with annual rates running as high as 2,000%. Even the lucky small-scale entrepreneurs who get loans from nonprofit microfinance institutions pay between 40% and 70% interest per year—rates that are illegal in most developed countries. (For a closer look at how the prices of goods compare in rich and poor areas, see the exhibit "The High-Cost Economy of the Poor.")

It can also be surprisingly cheap to market and deliver products and services to the world's poor. That's because many of them live in cities that are densely populated today and will be even more so in the years to come. Figures from the UN and the World Resources Institute indicate that by 2015, in Africa, 225 cities will each have populations of more than 1 million; in Latin America, another 225; and in Asia, 903. The population of at least 27 cities will reach or exceed 8 million. Collectively, the 1,300 largest cities will account for some 1.5 billion to 2 billion people, roughly half of whom will be bottom-of-the-pyramid (BOP) consumers now served primarily by informal economies. Companies that operate in these areas will have access to millions of potential new customers, who together have billions of dollars to spend. The poor in Rio de Janeiro, for instance, have a total purchasing power of $1.2 billion ($600 per person). Shantytowns in Johannesburg or Mumbai are no different.

The slums of these cities already have distinct ecosystems, with retail shops, small businesses, schools, clinics, and moneylenders. Although there are few reliable estimates of the value of commercial transactions in slums, business activity appears to be thriving. Dharavi—covering an area of just 435 acres—boasts scores of businesses ranging from leather, textiles, plastic recycling, and surgical sutures to gold jewelry, illicit liquor, detergents, and groceries. The scale of the businesses varies from one-person operations to bigger, well-recognized producers of brand-name products. Dharavi generates an estimated $450 million in manufacturing revenues, or about $1 million per acre of land. Established shantytowns in São Paulo, Rio, and Mexico City are equally productive. The seeds of a vibrant commercial sector have been sown.

While the rural poor are naturally harder to reach than the urban poor, they also represent a large untapped opportunity for companies. Indeed, 60% of India's GDP is generated in rural areas. The critical barrier to doing business in rural regions is distribution access, not a lack of buying power. But new information technology and communications infrastructures—especially wireless—promise to become an inexpensive way to establish marketing and distribution channels in these communities.

Conventional wisdom says that people in BOP markets cannot use such advanced technologies, but that's just another misconception. Poor rural women in Bangladesh have had no difficulty using GSM cell phones, despite never before using phones of any type. In Kenya, teenagers from slums are being successfully trained as Web page designers. Poor farmers in El Salvador use telecenters to negotiate the sale of their crops over the Internet. And women in Indian coastal villages have in less than a week learned to use PCs to interpret real-time satellite images showing concentrations of schools of fish in the Arabian Sea so they can direct their husbands to the best fishing areas. Clearly, poor communities are ready to adopt new technologies that improve their economic opportunities or their quality of life. The lesson for multinationals: Don't hesitate to deploy advanced technologies at the bottom of the pyramid while, or even before, deploying them in advanced countries.

A final misperception concerns the highly charged issue of exploitation of the poor by MNCs. The informal economies that now serve poor communities are full of inefficiencies and exploitive intermediaries. So if a microfinance institution charges 50% annual interest when the alternative is either 1,000% interest or no loan at all, is that exploiting or helping the poor? If a large financial company such as Citigroup were to use its scale to offer microloans at 20%, is that exploiting or helping the poor? The issue is not just cost but also quality—quality in the range and fairness of financial services, quality of food, quality of water. We argue that when MNCs provide basic goods and services that reduce costs to the poor and help improve their standard of living—while generating an acceptable return on investment—the results benefit everyone.

The Business Case

The business opportunities at the bottom of the pyramid have not gone unnoticed. Over the last five years, we have seen nongovernmental organizations (NGOs), entrepreneurial start-ups, and a handful of forward-thinking multinationals conduct vigorous commercial experiments in poor communities. Their experience is a proof of concept: Businesses can gain three important advantages by serving the poor—a new source of revenue growth, greater efficiency, and access to innovation. Let's look at examples of each.

Top-Line Growth   Growth is an important challenge for every company, but today it is especially critical for very large companies, many of which appear to have nearly saturated their existing markets. That's why BOP markets represent such an opportunity for MNCs: They are fundamentally new sources of growth. And because these markets are in the earliest stages of economic development, growth can be extremely rapid.

Latent demand for low-priced, high-quality goods is enormous. Consider the reaction when Hindustan Lever, the Indian subsidiary of Unilever,

recently introduced what was for it a new product category—candy—aimed at the bottom of the pyramid. A high-quality confection made with real sugar and fruit, the candy sells for only about a penny a serving. At such a price, it may seem like a marginal business opportunity, but in just six months it became the fastest-growing category in the company's portfolio. Not only is it profitable, but the company estimates it has the potential to generate revenues of $200 million per year in India and comparable markets in five years. Hindustan Lever has had similar successes in India with low-priced detergent and iodized salt. Beyond generating new sales, the company is establishing its business and its brand in a vast new market.

There is equally strong demand for affordable services. TARAhaat, a start-up focused on rural India, has introduced a range of computer-enabled education services ranging from basic IT training to English proficiency to vocational skills. The products are expected to be the largest single revenue generator for the company and its franchisees over the next several years.[1] Credit and financial services are also in high demand among the poor. Citibank's ATM-based banking experiment in India, called Suvidha, for instance, which requires a minimum deposit of just $25, enlisted 150,000 customers in one year in the city of Bangalore alone.

Small-business services are also popular in BOP markets. Centers run in Uganda by the Women's Information Resource Electronic Service (WIRES) provide female entrepreneurs with information on markets and prices, as well as credit and trade support services, packaged in simple, ready-to-use formats in local languages. The centers are planning to offer other small-business services such as printing, faxing, and copying, along with access to accounting, spreadsheet, and other software. In Bolivia, a start-up has partnered with the Bolivian Association of Ecological Producers Organizations to offer business information and communications services to more than 25,000 small producers of ecoagricultural products.

[1] Andrew Lawlor, Caitlin Peterson, and Vivek Sandell, "Catalyzing Rural Development: TARAhaat.com" (World Resources Institute, July 2001).

It's true that some services simply cannot be offered at a low-enough cost to be profitable, at least not with traditional technologies or business models. Most mobile telecommunications providers, for example, cannot yet profitably operate their networks at affordable prices in the developing world. One answer is to find alternative technology. A microfinance organization in Bolivia named PRO-DEM, for example, uses multilingual smart-card ATMs to substantially reduce its marginal cost per customer. Smart cards store a customer's personal details, account numbers, transaction records, and a fingerprint, allowing cash dispensers to operate without permanent network connections—which is key in remote areas. What's more, the machines offer voice commands in Spanish and several local dialects and are equipped with touch screens so that PRODEM's customer base can be extended to illiterate and semiliterate people.

Another answer is to aggregate demand, making the community—not the individual—the network customer. Gyandoot, a start-up in the Dhar district of central India, where 60% of the population falls below the poverty level, illustrates the benefits of a shared access model. The company has a network of 39 Internet-enabled kiosks that provide local entrepreneurs with Internet and telecommunications access, as well as with governmental, educational, and other services. Each kiosk serves 25 to 30 surrounding villages; the entire network reaches more than 600 villages and over half a million people.

Networks like these can be useful channels for marketing and distributing many kinds of low-cost products and services. Aptech's Computer Education division, for example, has built its own network of 1,000 learning centers in India to market and distribute Vidya, a computer-training course specially designed for BOP consumers and available in seven Indian languages. Pioneer Hi-Bred, a DuPont company, uses Internet kiosks in Latin America to deliver agricultural information and to interact with customers. Farmers can report different crop diseases or weather conditions, receive advice over the wire, and order seeds, fertilizers, and pesticides. This network strategy increases both sales and customer loyalty.

Reduced Costs   No less important than top-line growth are cost-saving opportunities. Outsourcing operations to low-cost labor markets has, of course, long been a popular way to contain costs, and it has led to the increasing prominence of China in manufacturing and India in software. Now, thanks to the rapid expansion of high-speed digital networks, companies are realizing even greater savings by locating such labor-intensive service functions as call centers, marketing services, and back-office transaction processing in developing areas. For example, the nearly 20 companies that use OrphanIT.com's affiliate-marketing services, provided via its telecenters in India and the Philippines, pay one-tenth the going rate for similar services in the United States or Australia. Venture capitalist Vinod Khosla describes the remote-services opportunity this way: "I suspect that by 2010, we will be talking about [remote services] as the fastest-growing part of the world economy, with many trillions of dollars of new markets created." Besides keeping costs down, outsourcing jobs to BOP markets can enhance growth, since job creation ultimately increases local consumers' purchasing power.

But tapping into cheap labor pools is not the only way MNCs can enhance their efficiency by operating in developing regions. The competitive necessity of maintaining a low cost structure in these areas can push companies to discover creative ways to configure their products, finances, and supply chains to enhance productivity. And these discoveries can often be incorporated back into their existing operations in developed markets.

For instance, companies targeting the BOP market are finding that the shared access model, which disaggregates access from ownership, not only widens their customer base but increases asset productivity as well. Poor people, rather than buying their own computers, Internet connections, cell phones, refrigerators, and even cars, can use such equipment on a pay-per-use basis. Typically, the providers of such services get considerably more revenue per dollar of investment in the underlying assets. One shared Internet line, for example, can serve as many as 50 people, generating more revenue per day than if it were dedicated to a single customer at a flat fee. Shared access creates the opportunity to gain far greater returns from all sorts of infrastructure investments.

In terms of finances, to operate successfully in BOP markets, managers must also rethink their business metrics—specifically, the traditional focus on high gross margins. In developing markets, the profit margin on individual units will always be low. What really counts is capital efficiency—getting the highest possible returns on capital employed (ROCE). Hindustan Lever, for instance, operates a $2.6 billion business portfolio with zero working capital. The key is constant efforts to reduce capital investments by extensively outsourcing manufacturing, streamlining supply chains, actively managing receivables, and paying close attention to distributors' performance. Very low capital needs, focused distribution and technology investments, and very large volumes at low margins lead to very high ROCE businesses, creating great economic value for shareholders. It's a model that can be equally attractive in developed and developing markets.

Streamlining supply chains often involves replacing assets with information. Consider, for example, the experience of ITC, one of India's largest companies. Its agribusiness division has deployed a total of 970 kiosks serving 600,000 farmers who supply it with soy, coffee, shrimp, and wheat from 5,000 villages spread across India. This kiosk program, called e-Choupal, helps increase the farmers' productivity by disseminating the latest information on weather and best practices in farming, and by supporting other services like soil and water testing, thus facilitating the supply of quality inputs to both the farmers and ITC. The kiosks also serve as an e-procurement system, helping farmers earn higher prices by minimizing transaction costs involved in marketing farm produce. The head of ITC's agribusiness reports that the company's procurement costs have fallen since e-Choupal was implemented. And that's despite paying higher prices

to its farmers: The program has enabled the company to eliminate multiple transportation, bagging, and handling steps—from farm to local market, from market to broker, from broker to processor—that did not add value in the chain.

Innovation BOP markets are hotbeds of commercial and technological experimentation. The Swedish wireless company Ericsson, for instance, has developed a small cellular telephone system, called a MiniGSM, that local operators in BOP markets can use to offer cell phone service to a small area at a radically lower cost than conventional equipment entails. Packaged for easy shipment and deployment, it provides stand-alone or networked voice and data communications for up to 5,000 users within a 35-kilometer radius. Capital costs to the operator can be as low as $4 per user, assuming a shared-use model with individual phones operated by local entrepreneurs. The MIT Media Lab, in collaboration with the Indian government, is developing low-cost devices that allow people to use voice commands to communicate—without keyboards—with various Internet sites in multiple languages. These new access devices promise to be far less complex than traditional computers but would perform many of the same basic functions.[2]

As we have seen, connectivity is a big issue for BOP consumers. Companies that can find ways to dramatically lower connection costs, therefore, will have a very strong market position. And that is exactly what the Indian company n-Logue is trying to do. It connects hundreds of franchised village kiosks containing both a computer and a phone with centralized nodes that are, in turn, connected to the national phone network and the Internet. Each node, also a franchise, can serve between 30,000 and 50,000 customers, providing phone, e-mail, Internet services, and relevant local information at affordable

[2]Michael Best and Colin M. Maclay, "Community Internet Access in Rural Areas: Solving the Economic Sustainability Puzzle," *The Global Information Technology Report 2001–2002: Readiness for the Networked World,* ed. Geoffrey Kirkman (Oxford University Press, 2002), available online at http://www.cid.harvard.edu/cr/gitrr_030202.html.

The High-Cost Economy of the Poor

When we compare the costs of essentials in Dharavi, a shantytown of more than 1 million people in the heart of Mumbai, India, with those of Warden Road, an upper-class community in a nice Mumbai suburb, a disturbing picture emerges. Clearly, costs could be dramatically reduced if the poor could benefit from the scope, scale, and supply-chain efficiencies of large enterprises, as their middle-class counterparts do. This pattern is common around the world, even in developed countries. For instance, a similar, if less exaggerated, disparity exists between the inner-city poor and the suburban rich in the United States.

Cost	Dharavi	Warden Road	Poverty Premium
Credit (annual interest)	600%–1,000%	12%–18%	53X
Municipal-grade water (per cubic meter)	$1.12	$0.03	37X
Phone call (per minute)	$0.04–$0.05	$0.025	1.8X
Diarrhea medication	$20	$2	10X
Rice (per kilogram)	$0.28	$0.24	1.2X

prices to villagers in rural India. Capital costs for the n-Logue system are now about $400 per wireless "line" and are projected to decline to $100—at least ten times lower than conventional telecom costs. On a per-customer basis, the cost may amount to as little as $1.[3] This appears to be a powerful model for ending rural isolation and linking untapped rural markets to the global economy.

New wireless technologies are likely to spur further business model innovations and lower costs even more. Ultrawideband, for example, is currently licensed in the United States only for limited, very low-power applications, in part because it spreads a signal across already-crowded portions of the broadcast spectrum. In many developing countries, however, the spectrum is less congested. In fact, the U.S.-based Dandin Group is already building an ultrawideband communications system for the Kingdom of Tonga, whose population of about 100,000 is spread over dozens of islands, making it a test bed for a next-generation technology that could transform the economics of Internet access.

E-commerce systems that run over the phone or the Internet are enormously important in BOP

[3]Joy Howard, Erik Simanis, and Charis Simms, "Sustainable Deployment for Rural Connectivity: The n-Logue Model" (World Resources Institute, July 2001).

markets because they eliminate the need for layers of intermediaries. Consider how the U.S. start-up Voxiva has changed the way information is shared and business is transacted in Peru. The company partners with Telefónica, the dominant local carrier, to offer automated business applications over the phone. The inexpensive services include voice mail, data entry, and order placement; customers can check account balances, monitor delivery status, and access prerecorded information directories. According to the Boston Consulting Group, the Peruvian Ministry of Health uses Voxiva to disseminate information, take pharmaceutical orders, and link health care workers spread across 6,000 offices and clinics. Microfinance institutions use Voxiva to process loan applications and communicate with borrowers. Voxiva offers Web-based services, too, but far more of its potential customers in Latin America have access to a phone.

E-commerce companies are not the only ones turning the limitations of BOP markets to strategic advantage. A lack of dependable electric power stimulated the U.K.-based start-up Freeplay Group to introduce hand-cranked radios in South Africa that subsequently became popular with hikers in the United States. Similar breakthroughs are being pioneered in the use of solar-powered devices such as battery chargers and water pumps. In China, where pesticide costs have often limited the use of modern agricultural techniques, there are now 13,000 small farmers—more than in the rest of the world combined—growing cotton that has been genetically engineered to be pest resistant.

Strategies for Serving BOP Markets

Certainly, succeeding in BOP markets requires multinationals to think creatively. The biggest change, though, has to come in the attitudes and practices of executives. Unless CEOs and other business leaders confront their own preconceptions, companies are unlikely to master the challenges of BOP markets. The traditional workforce is so rigidly conditioned to operate in higher-margin markets that, without formal training, it is unlikely to see the vast potential of the BOP market. The most pressing need, then, is education. Perhaps MNCs should create the equivalent of the Peace Corps: Having young managers spend a couple of formative years in BOP markets would open their eyes to the promise and the realities of doing business there.

To date, few multinationals have developed a cadre of people who are comfortable with these markets. Hindustan Lever is one of the exceptions. The company expects executive recruits to spend at least eight weeks in the villages of India to get a gut-level experience of Indian BOP markets. The new executives must become involved in some community project—building a road, cleaning up a water catchment area, teaching in a school, improving a health clinic. The goal is to engage with the local population. To buttress this effort, Hindustan Lever is initiating a massive program for managers at all levels—from the CEO down—to reconnect with their poorest customers. They'll talk with the poor in both rural and urban areas, visit the shops these customers frequent, and ask them about their experience with the company's products and those of its competitors.

In addition to expanding managers' understanding of BOP markets, companies will need to make structural changes. To capitalize on the innovation potential of these markets, for example, they might set up R&D units in developing countries that are specifically focused on local opportunities. When Hewlett-Packard launched its e-Inclusion division, which concentrates on rural markets, it established a branch of its famed HP Labs in India charged with developing products and services explicitly for this market. Hindustan Lever maintains a significant R&D effort in India, as well.

Companies might also create venture groups and internal investment funds aimed at seeding entrepreneurial efforts in BOP markets. Such investments reap direct benefits in terms of business experience and market development. They can also play an indirect but vital role in growing the overall BOP market in sectors that will ultimately benefit the multinational. At least one major U.S. corporation is planning to launch such a fund, and the G8's Digital Opportunity Task Force is proposing a similar one focused on digital ventures.

MNCs should also consider creating a business development task force aimed at these markets. Assembling a diverse group of people from across the corporation and empowering it to function as a skunk works team that ignores conventional dogma will likely lead to greater innovation. Companies that have tried this approach have been surprised by the amount of interest such a task force generates. Many employees want to work on projects that have the potential to make a real difference in improving the lives of the poor. When Hewlett-Packard announced its e-Inclusion division, for example, it was overwhelmed by far more volunteers than it could accommodate.

Making internal changes is important, but so is reaching out to external partners. Joining with businesses that are already established in these markets can be an effective entry strategy, since these companies will naturally understand the market dynamics better. In addition to limiting the risks for each player, partnerships also maximize the existing infrastructure—both physical and social. MNCs seeking partners should look beyond businesses to NGOs and community groups. They are key sources of knowledge about customers' behavior, and they often experiment the most with new services and new delivery models. In fact, of the social enterprises experimenting with creative uses of digital technology that the Digital Dividend Project Clearinghouse tracked, nearly 80% are NGOs. In Namibia, for instance, an organization called SchoolNet is providing low-cost, alternative technology solutions—such as solar power and wireless approaches—to schools and community-based groups throughout the country. SchoolNet is currently linking as many as 35 new schools every month.

Entrepreneurs also will be critical partners. According to an analysis by McKinsey & Company, the rapid growth of cable TV in India—there are 50 million connections a decade after introduction—is largely due to small entrepreneurs. These individuals have been building the last mile of the network, typically by putting a satellite dish on their own houses and laying cable to connect their neighbors. A note of caution, however. Entrepreneurs in BOP markets lack access to the advice, technical help, seed funding, and business support services available in the industrial world. So MNCs may need to take on mentoring roles or partner with local business development organizations that can help entrepreneurs create investment and partnering opportunities.

It's worth noting that, contrary to popular opinion, women play a significant role in the economic development of these regions. MNCs, therefore, should pay particular attention to women entrepreneurs. Women are also likely to play the most critical role in product acceptance not only because of their childcare and household management activities but also because of the social capital that they have built up in their communities. Listening to and educating such customers is essential for success.

Regardless of the opportunities, many companies will consider the bottom of the pyramid to be too risky. We've shown how partnerships can limit risk; another option is to enter into consortia. Imagine sharing the costs of building a rural network with the communications company that would operate it, a consumer goods company seeking channels to expand its sales, and a bank that is financing the construction and wants to make loans to and collect deposits from rural customers.

Investing where powerful synergies exist will also mitigate risk. The Global Digital Opportunity Initiative, a partnership of the Markle Foundation and the UN Development Programme, will help a small number of countries implement a strategy to harness the power of information and communications technologies to increase development. The countries will be chosen in part based on their interest and their willingness to make supportive regulatory and market reforms. To concentrate resources and create reinforcing effects, the initiative will encourage international aid agencies and global companies to assist with implementation.

Sharing Intelligence

What creative new approaches to serving the bottom-of-the-pyramid markets have digital technologies made possible? Which sectors or countries show the most economic activity or the fastest growth? What new business models show promise? What kinds of partnerships—for funding, distribution, public relations—have been most successful?

The Digital Dividend Project Clearinghouse (digitaldividend.org) helps answer those types of questions. The Web site tracks the activities of organizations that use digital tools to provide connectivity and deliver services to underserved populations in developing countries. Currently, it contains information on 700 active projects around the world. Maintained under the auspices of the nonprofit World Resources Institute, the site lets participants in different projects share experiences and swap knowledge with one another. Moreover, the site provides data for trend analyses and other specialized studies that facilitate market analyses, local partnerships, and rapid, low-cost learning.

All of the strategies we've outlined here will be of little use, however, unless the external barriers we've touched on—poor infrastructure, inadequate connectivity, corrupt intermediaries, and the like—are removed. Here's where technology holds the most promise. Information and communications technologies can grant access to otherwise isolated communities, provide marketing and distribution channels, bypass intermediaries, drive down transaction costs, and help aggregate demand and buying power. Smart cards and other emerging technologies are inexpensive ways to give poor customers a secure identity, a transaction or credit history, and even a virtual address—prerequisites for interacting with the formal economy. That's why high-tech companies aren't the only ones that should be interested in closing the global digital divide; encouraging the spread of low-cost digital networks at the bottom of the pyramid is a priority for virtually all companies that want to enter and engage with these markets. Improved connectivity is an important catalyst for more effective markets, which are critical to boosting income levels and accelerating economic growth.

Moreover, global companies stand to gain from the effects of network expansion in these markets. According to Metcalfe's Law, the usefulness of a network equals the square of the number of users. By the same logic, the value and vigor of the economic activity that will be generated when hundreds of thousands of previously isolated rural communities can buy and sell from one another and from urban markets will increase dramatically—to the benefit of all participants.

Since BOP markets require significant rethinking of managerial practices, it is legitimate for managers to ask: Is it worth the effort?

We think the answer is yes. For one thing, big corporations should solve big problems—and what is a more pressing concern than alleviating the poverty that 4 billion people are currently mired in? It is hard to argue that the wealth of technology and talent within leading multinationals is better allocated to producing incremental variations of existing products than to addressing the real needs—and real opportunities—at the bottom of the pyramid. Moreover, through competition, multinationals are likely to bring to BOP markets a level of accountability for performance and resources that neither international development agencies nor national governments have demonstrated during the last 50 years. Participation by MNCs could set a new standard, as well as a new market-driven paradigm, for addressing poverty.

But ethical concerns aside, we've shown that the potential for expanding the bottom of the market is just too great to ignore. Big companies need to focus on big market opportunities if they want to generate real growth. It is simply good business strategy to be involved in large, untapped markets that offer new customers, cost-saving opportunities, and access to radical innovation. The business opportunities at the bottom of the pyramid are real, and they are open to any MNC willing to engage and learn.

Index

Page numbers followed by n indicate notes.